Index to Scientific Names of Organisms Cited in the Linnaean Dissertations

together with a

Synoptic Bibliography of the Dissertations

and a

Concordance for Selected Editions

Robert W. Kiger
Charlotte A. Tancin
Gavin D. R. Bridson

Hunt Institute for Botanical Documentation
Carnegie Mellon University
Pittsburgh
1999

Linné

Carl Linnaeus (1707—1778). Line engraving by G. F. L. Jaquemot. Karlsruhe, Kunstverlag W.
Creuzbauer, n.d.

Preface

This work has grown from an initial effort by RWK, who set out to index all instances of scientific names of organisms in the 186 Linnaean dissertations. To that index CAT has added a synoptic bibliography of the dissertations as they originally appeared, along with an account of subsequent collected editions and a concordance for the most important of the latter. The synoptic bibliography is based on a handlist prepared by GDRB, who has also provided much advice and other assistance, and the account of collected editions is based on information, assembled by numerous Hunt Institute staff, from the draft catalogue of the Strandell Collection of Linnaeana. The concordance was constructed to help researchers locate citations from the original dissertations in later collected editions. The compilers take responsibility for any errors that may appear in this volume; corrections and additions are most welcome.

Contents

Index to Scientific Names

Introduction

This Index accounts for over 30,700 occurrences of more than 13,900 different formal names of plant and animal taxa that appear in the original editions of the 186 dissertations defended by students of Carolus Linnaeus (Carl von Linné, 1707–1778), during the period 1743–1776. It is intended to serve as a finding aid, not a nomenclator, and for the sake of organizational simplicity the entries are not always exact transcriptions of the names as they appear in the dissertations (see below under Rendition). Especially for nomenclatural matters, which may hinge on precise details of format and context, the dissertations themselves should be consulted.

The dissertations were reprinted a number of times in collected editions, two of them edited by Linnaeus himself (*Amoenitates academicae*). Besides being entirely reset, and paged differently, these reprinted versions often differ from the originals in actual content. Since this Index was compiled from copies of the original editions (specifically, the two complete sets in the Strandell Collection at the Hunt Institute), it does not reflect any of the additions, corrections and deletions that Linnaeus made in the *Amoenitates* versions, and of course the page numbers cited here are not those of the *Amoenitates* or other collected editions. Still, the Index, together with the following Concordance, should prove generally useful for finding corresponding citations in the later editions.

Coverage

The Index cites each occurrence of each formal (thus "scientific") Latin (or Latinized) designation of a plant or animal taxon at the generic level or below — whether uninomial, binomial or polynomial, whether in a taxonomic citation, prose or a note, and whether newly described, accepted, synonymized or noted in passing. Exceptions are: occurrences of such names in dedications, invocations or epigrams that are not part of the dissertation content proper; occurrences when the taxa are mentioned comparatively for only descriptive (not differential) purposes (e.g., to indicate size or habit); and occurrences as part of a title.

Common names, including Latin renderings, are not included, except when they are identical to formal ("scientific") names and the two usages could not be discriminated (usually in prose contexts and involving uninomials). Also not covered are purely pharmaceutical (pharmacopoeic) denotations, when the name is used to designate a pharmaceutical entity, not a plant or animal qua taxon (even if the name is identical to the corresponding taxonomic one).

1

Organization

The Index entries are in alphabetical sequence by taxon name, and word division is significant in the ordering.

Within each entry the citations are arranged by dissertation sequence number (Lidén number, shown in parentheses following the abbreviated dissertation title), thus providing a roughly chronological record of appearance, and then in page order for each dissertation. Imputed page numbers are indicated with square brackets.

Notes appear within square brackets, either following the entry names themselves or following the individual page-number citations, as pertinent.

Rendition

The names are transcribed literally from the dissertations, as to typography, orthography and word separation, *except that:*

ABBREVIATED WORDS are silently expanded to their full forms, when those are clearly discernable.

ALCHEMICAL AND ASTROLOGICAL SYMBOLS representing words or parts of words are silently translated to the equivalent Latin orthographies.

ALTERNATIVE NAMES contained within a single citation (i.e., when generic names or sets of epithets are separated by "sive" or "vel" or "seu," or when a trivial epithet is marked off parenthetically or typographically within a polynomial) are indexed separately, each silently expanded to full form — e.g., "Mus seu Cuniculus indicus" is indexed as both "Mus indicus" and "Cuniculus indicus," and "Ispida (viridis) supra ferruginiaea" as both "Ispida viridis" and "Ispida supra ferruginiaea";

AMPERSANDS are transcribed as "et";

AUTOCHTHONOUS (LINNAEAN) TYPOGRAPHIC ERRORS AND ORTHOGRAPHIC LAPSES OR VARIANTS are changed to conform with present general taxonomic usage, and the erroneous or variant dissertation usages are noted within brackets;

CAPITAL LETTERS (initial or internal) in any words that follow the generic name are silently changed to lower case — this includes words that are themselves generic names in other contexts;

GREEK-LETTER VARIETAL DESIGNATIONS that follow binomials or polynomials are transcribed as "alpha, "beta" etc. — those that precede names cited in synonymy are silently deleted;

HYPHENS are silently deleted or inserted to accord with prevailing contemporary usage, or with modern nomenclatural usage when pertinent, in order to achieve consistency in the rendition of names that are otherwise the same;

INFLECTED FORMS are silently transposed to the nominative case;

LIGATURED VOWELS (in diphthongs) are silently dissociated;

LOWER-CASE INITIALS in words used as generic names are silently changed to capitals;

PUNCTUATION (commas, semicolons, colons and periods) within names is sometimes silently added or deleted to make substantively parallel citations sort in parallel;

ROMAN NUMERALS are transcribed as arabic numerals;

VARIANT TYPOGRAPHY is silently changed to conform with present general taxonomic usage; e.g., 'i' versus 'j' and 'y', 'u' versus 'v'.

I have made no systematic attempt to uncover the apparently numerous inaccuracies in Linnaeus' renderings of names that he was citing from other sources. In the time available it would have been impossible to track down the original source of every such name (often Linnaeus did not indicate the source), discover the disparities (changes in word order, elisions of words, differing orthographies and Latin constructions), and reconcile them. However, when I have happened to notice such variant renditions, the differences are noted in square brackets.

Authorities and sources that are cited in the dissertations along with the names proper are not transcribed, except when they are integral parts of the names.

Question marks associated with (indicating taxonomic uncertainty about) generic names or epithets are not transcribed.

Notes

Pan Svecicus (Lidén no. 26) presents peculiar difficulties. The list of species therein follows the scheme of Linnaeus' *Flora Svecica* (Stockholm, 1745), and the *Flora* numbers are cited first, followed by names that mostly are just ad-hoc short-hand references to the full names that appear in the *Flora*. Linnaeus indicated that he had done this deliberately, as a matter of convenience, and so the shortened names themselves cannot be regarded as "formal" usages. However, it seemed less than satisfactory to include in the Index only the generic names involved, and on the other hand it seemed equally unsatisfactory to translate to the full names from the *Flora*. So I have cited these shortened versions as they appeared, even though they are informal in nature, and even when they are literally ungrammatical.

3

No thorough bibliographic comparison and analysis of multiple copies of the individual Linnaean dissertations has been reported, and it is not certain that textual variations do not occur within the original editions. If users of the Index encounter any such variations that conflict with the entries herein, it will be helpful and much appreciated if they will bring them to our attention.

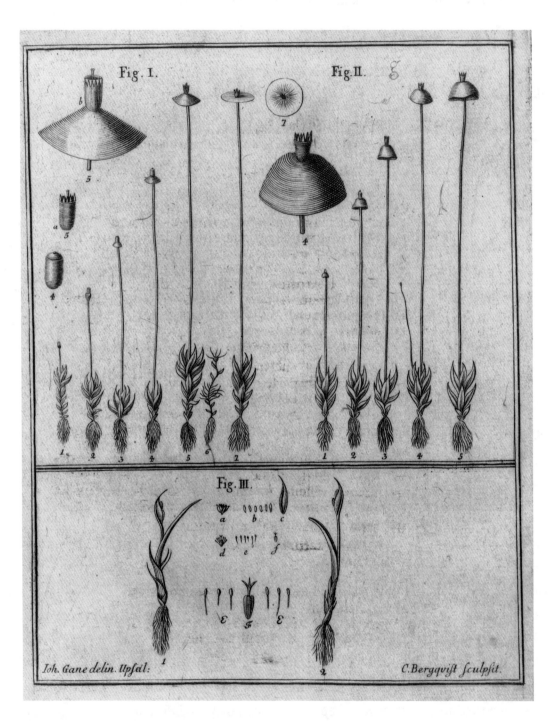

Plate from Dissertatio botanica sistens Splachnum ... *(1750), a dissertation defended by L. J. Montin with Linnaeus as praeses.*

Scientific Names

Abcdaria — Herb. Amboin. (57) 28

Abelmoschus — Ambros. (100) 14

Abies — Hort. Upsal. (7) 21; Spons. pl. (12) [2], 39; Vir. pl. (13) 24; Fl. oecon. (17) 25; Oecon. nat. (20) 15, 18, 29; Gem. arb. (24) 11; Sapor. med. (31) 15; Pl. escul. (35) 25, 27, 28; Morb. hyeme (38) 12; Mirac. insect. (45) 15; Mus ind. (62) 14; Hort. acad. (63) 16; Metam. pl. (67) 24; Calend. fl. (72) [11]; Migr. avium (79) 36; Pane diaet. (83) 17; Transm. frum. (87) 3; Pand. insect. (93) 21; Arb. Svec. (101) 15, 30; Nom. bot. (107) 18; Polit. nat. (109) 8, 10; Usum musc. (148) 6, 7

Abies larix — Gem. arb. (24) 31

Abies picea — Hosp. insect. fl. (43) 36

Abies rubra — Gem. arb. (24) 31; Pan Svec. (26) 36

Abrotanum — Vir. pl. (13) 23; Nom. bot. (107) 17

Abrotanum africanum, foliis argenteis angustis, floribus spicatis — Pl. rar. Afr. (115) 26[as Abrothanum]

Abrus — Hort. Upsal. (7) 36; Somn. pl. (68) 9

Abrus frutex — Herb. Amboin. (57) 19

Absinthium — Anandria (9) 4; Vir. pl. (13) 7, 23, 33; Generat. calc. (22) 17; Sapor. med. (31) 18; Pl. escul. (35) 23; Oves (61) 16; Nom. bot. (107) 17

Absus — Somn. pl. (68) 9

Abutilon folio profunde dissecto, pedunculis multifloris — Nova pl. gen. 1751 (32) 31

Abutilon hirsutum — Herb. Amboin. (57) 15

Abutilon indicum — Cent. II. pl. (66) 26

Abutilon indicum, flore luteo minore — Cent. II. pl. (66) 26

Abutilon laeve — Herb. Amboin. (57) 15

Abutilon vesicarium, flore fructuque majore non crispo — Cent. II. pl. (66) 26

Acacia — Vir. pl. (13) 33; Sapor. med. (31) 15; Somn. pl. (68) 9

Acacia aegyptiaca — Hort. Upsal. (7) 36[as Acasia]

Acacia sylvestris — Pot. theae (142) 8

Acalypha — Hort. Upsal. (7) 36; Vir. pl. (13) 27

Acalypha virgata — Pl. Jam. (102) 28; Fl. Jam. (105) 21

Acalypha virginica — Demonstr. pl. (49) 25; Pl. Jam. (102) 28; Fl. Jam. (105) 21

Acanthus — Hort. Upsal. (7) 35; Pl. hybr. (33) 7

Acanthus dioscoridis — Cent. II. pl. (66) 23; Fl. Palaest. (70) 23

Acanthus dioscoridis verus sativus — Cent. II. pl. (66) 23

Acanthus foliis ciliatis inermibus — Pl. hybr. (33) 25

Acanthus foliis lanceolatis integerrimis margine spinosis — Cent. II. pl. (66) 23

Acanthus foliis pinnatifidis spinosis — Pl. hybr. (33) 25

Acanthus ilicifolius — Herb. Amboin. (57) 28

Acanthus medius rarioribus et brevioribus aculeis notatus — Pl. hybr. (33) 26

Acanthus mollis — Demonstr. pl. (49) 17; Pl. officin. (52) 6; Fl. Monsp. (74) 20; Pl. tinct. (97) 20

Acanthus spinosus — Demonstr. pl. (49) 17

Acarus — Spons. pl. (12) 27; Oecon. nat. (20) 31; Hosp. insect. fl. (43) 18; Noxa insect. (46) 9, 12, 28, 29, 30; Cynogr. (54) 21; Oves (61) 22; Exanth. viva (86) 6ff.[as Acharus]; Pand. insect. (93) 2, [17, as 38]; Lepra (140) 7, 9; Mund. invis. (149) 10; Fund. entom. (154) 5, 19

Acarus alceae — Hosp. insect. fl. (43) 28

Acarus aphidioides — Pand. insect. (93) 21

Acarus batatas — Pand. insect. (93) 12

Acarus fagi — Hosp. insect. fl. (43) 35; Pand. insect. (93) 20

Acarus farinae — Mirac. insect. (45) 20

Acarus fungorum — Pand. insect. (93) [23, as 31]

Acarus holosericeus — Pand. fl. Ryb. (165) 16

Acarus humanus subcutaneus — Mirac. insect. (45) 20

Acarus ricinus — Pand. fl. Ryb. (165) 16

Acarus ruber — Hosp. insect. fl. (43) 36

Acarus salicinae rosae — Hosp. insect. fl. (43) 37

Acarus salicinus — Pand. insect. (93) 22

Acarus siro — Pand. fl. Ryb. (165) 16

Acarus telarius — Pand. insect. (93) 16

Acarus tiliae — Hosp. insect. fl. (43) 26; Noxa insect. (46) 26

Accipiter — Noxa insect. (46) 31; Cynogr. (54) 9

Accipiter cauda furcata — Migr. avium (79) 14

Acer — Spons. pl. (12) 33, 34; Vir. pl. (13) 25; Fl. oecon. (17) 9; Pl. escul. (35) 13, 29; Vern. arb. (47) 10, table; Calend. fl. (72) [20]; Fl. Monsp. (74) 7; Fr. Svec. (91) [ii]; Pand. insect. (93) 22; Arb. Svec. (101) 30; Nom. bot. (107) 19; Mund. invis. (149) 16

Acer campestre — Fl. Angl. (56) 25; Fl. Monsp. (74) 29; Prodr. fl. Dan. (82) 25; Fr. Svec. (91) 3, 7, 23, 24; Arb. Svec. (101) 8; Fl. Belg. (112) 23; Colon. pl. (158) 8

Acer candidum — Gem. arb. (24) 19

Acer folio subtus incano — Gem. arb. (24) 19

Acer frutescens folio argenteo — Fl. Palaest. (70) 32

Acer monspessulanum — Fl. Palaest. (70) 32; Fl. Monsp. (74) 29

Acer negundo — Demonstr. pl. (49) 27

Acer platanoides — Gem. arb. (24) 19; Pan Svec. (26) 21[as patanoides]; Hosp. insect. fl. (43) 20; Stat. pl. (55) 17; Fl. Angl. (56) 6; Calend. fl. (72) [10]; Fl. Monsp. (74) 5, 28; Arb. Svec. (101) 8, 17; Fl. Åker. (162) 20; Pand. fl. Ryb. (165) 22

Acer pseudoplatanus — Demonstr. pl. (49) 27; Fl. Angl. (56) 25; Fl. Monsp. (74) 28; Prodr. fl. Dan.

(82) 25; Arb. Svec. (101) 8, 9[as pseudoplantanus], 28, 29; Fl. Belg. (112) 23

Acetabulum — Corallia Balt. (4) 10

Acetosa — Peloria (3) 10; Vir. pl. (13) 33, 36; Sapor. med. (31) 14; Rhabarbarum (41) 23; Cul. mut. (88) 2; Nom. bot. (107) 12; Scorb. (180) 16

Acetosa canapon. — Fl. Palaest. (70) 18[under Rumex]

Acetosa montana, folio cubulati oblongatiore crispo, floribus in subviridi luteolis — Rhabarbarum (41) 6

Achantus — Pl. hybr. (33) 3

Achillea — Vir. pl. (13) 23; Nom. bot. (107) 17

Achillea aegyptiaca — Fl. Palaest. (70) 28

Achillea ageratum — Pl. officin. (52) 4; Fl. Monsp. (74) 26

Achillea alpina — Fl. alp. (71) 22; Fl. Monsp. (74) 26; Hist. nat. Rossia (144) 33

Achillea atrata — Fl. alp. (71) 22

Achillea bipinnata — Fl. Palaest. (70) 28

Achillea clavennae — Fl. alp. (71) 22

Achillea foliis linearibus pinnatifidis pubescentibus, foliolis tripartitis transversalibus media longiore — Pl. Mart.-Burs. (6) 10

Achillea foliis pinnatis, lanugine totis obductis, floribus albis umbellatis — Pl. Mart.-Burs. (6) 10

Achillea foliis pinnatis, pinnis longis acutis subhirsutis raro dentatis — Pl. Mart.-Burs. (6) 10

Achillea impatiens — Hist. nat. Rossia (144) 33

Achillea inodora — Fl. Cap. (99) 18

Achillea macrophylla — Fl. alp. (71) 22

Achillea millefolium — Pan Svec. (26) 33; Herbat. Upsal. (50) 13; Pl. officin. (52) 13; Fl. Angl. (56) 22; Calend. fl. (72) [15]; Fl. Monsp. (74) 26; Prodr. fl. Dan. (82) 23; Fl. Belg. (112) 21; Rar. Norv. (157) 16; Fl. Åker. (162) 18; Pand. fl. Ryb. (165) 22

Achillea nana — Fl. alp. (71) 22

Achillea nobilis — Fl. Monsp. (74) 26

Achillea ptarmica — Pan Svec. (26) 33; Pl. officin. (52) 16; Fl. Angl. (56) 22; Calend. fl. (72) [14]; Fl. Monsp. (74) 26; Prodr. fl. Dan. (82) 23; Fl. Belg. (112) 21; Pl. rar. Afr. (115) 6; Hort. cul. (132) 24; Hist. nat. Rossia (144) 33

Achillea santolina — Fl. Palaest. (70) 28

Achimenes — Fl. Jam. (105) 27

Achras zapota — Fl. Jam. (105) 15; Obs. mat. med. (171) 3[as sapota]; Pl. Surin. (177) 7[as sapota]

Achyranthes — Herb. Amboin. (57) 21

Achyranthes aspera — Demonstr. pl. (49) 7[as Achyrantes]; Herb. Amboin. (57) 26; Somn. pl. (68) 16[as Achyrantes]; Fl. Palaest. (70) 15; Fl. Jam. (105) 14

Achyranthes lappacea — Herb. Amboin. (57) 26

Acidoton — Fl. Jam. (105) 26

Acipenser — Cul. mut. (88) 9

Acipenser huso — Hist. nat. Rossia (144) 17

Acipenser ruthenus — Hist. nat. Rossia (144) 17

Acipenser tuberculis carens — Mat. med. anim. (29) 13

Acisanthera — Fl. Jam. (105) 27[as Alisanthera]

Acmella — Vir. pl. (13) 23

Acnida — Nova pl. gen. 1751 (32) 10, [13, as 15], 32, 33, 48

Acnide — Nova pl. gen. 1751 (32) 10, [13, as 15], 32

Aconitum — Hort. Upsal. (7) 33; Vir. pl. (13) 12, 21, 24, 31, 37; Fl. oecon. (17) 15; Oecon. nat. (20) 36; Pan Svec. (26) 3, 7; Pl. rar. Camsch. (30) 22; Odor. med. (40) 16; Cui bono? (42) 20; Nom. bot. (107) 14; Nect. fl. (122) 5, 13; Fund. fr. (123) 16, 23; Pot. theae (142) 10; Usum hist. nat. (145) 18, 20, 22, 23; Mund. invis. (149) 4; Cimicifuga (173) 8, 9

Aconitum anthora — Demonstr. pl. (49) 15; Pl. officin. (52) 4; Fl. alp. (71) 18; Calend. fl. (72) [17]

Aconitum coeruleum seu napellus — Pl. Mart.-Burs. (6) 14

Aconitum lapponicum — Pan Svec. (26) 25

Aconitum lycoctonum — Demonstr. pl. (49) 15; Stat. pl. (55) 16; Cervus (60) 8; Fl. alp. (71) 18; Calend. fl. (72) [12]; Fl. Monsp. (74) 18

Aconitum lycoctonum luteum — Pl. Mart.-Burs. (6) 14

Aconitum napellus — Pl. Mart.-Burs. (6) 14; Pan Svec. (26) 25; Pl. hybr. (33) 10; Demonstr. pl. (49) 15; Stat. pl. (55) 14; Calend. fl. (72) [17]; Prodr. fl. Dan. (82) 19; Hort. cul. (132) 24; Colon. pl. (158) 9; Obs. mat. med. (171) 4; Cimicifuga (173) 9

Aconitum pyrenaicum — Demonstr. pl. (49) 15; Fl. alp. (71) 18; Calend. fl. (72) [14]; Hist. nat. Rossia (144) 23, 30

Aconitum pyrenaicum, ampliore folio tenui laciniato — Pl. Mart.-Burs. (6) 14

Aconitum variegatum — Demonstr. pl. (49) 15; Calend. fl. (72) [18]

Acorus — Hort. Upsal. (7) 41; Vir. pl. (13) 25; Fl. oecon. (17) 9; Sapor. med. (31) 19; Pl. escul. (35) 13, 29; Odor. med. (40) 15; Nom. bot. (107) 12; Usum hist. nat. (145) 27

Acorus calamus — Demonstr. pl. (49) 10; Stat. pl. (55) 13; Fl. Angl. (56) 14; Prodr. fl. Dan. (82) 16; Fl. Belg. (112) 15; Hist. nat. Rossia (144) 29; Fl. Åker. (162) 10

Acorus calamus verus — Pl. officin. (52) 3; Herb. Amboin. (57) 20

Acorus calamus vulgaris — Pl. officin. (52) 6

Acorus palustris — Pan Svec. (26) 20

Acridium — Fund. entom. (154) 30

Acrostichum — Acrostichum (10) 3, 8

Acrostichum aculeatum — Fl. Jam. (105) 23[as Acrosticum]

Acrostichum aureum — Fl. Jam. (105) 22[as Acrosticum]

Acrostichum barbarum — Fl. Cap. (99) 19

Acrostichum calomelanos — Fl. Jam. (105) 23[as Acrosticum]

Acrostichum caulibus triquetris, fronde brevi digitata lineari integerrima aequali — Acrostichum (10) 10

Acrostichum ebenum — Fl. Jam. (105) 23[as Acrosticum]

Acrostichum fronde duplicato-pinnata, foliolis alternis: pinnis lanceolatis pinnatifidis — Acrostichum (10) 16

Acrostichum fronde duplicato-pinnata, foliolis alternis, pinnis lanceolatis sessilibus; inferioribus serrato incisis — Acrostichum (10) 13

Acrostichum fronde duplicato-pinnata: foliolis oppositis lanceolatis: infimis cruciatim appendiculatis — Acrostichum (10) 16

Acrostichum fronde duplicato-pinnata: foliolis oppositis: pinnulis lanceolatis, obtusis serratis sessilibus alternis — Acrostichum (10) 16

Acrostichum fronde lineari-lacinata — Acrostichum (10) 10

Acrostichum fronde pinnata, foliolis ternatis lanceolatis — Acrostichum (10) 15

Acrostichum fronde pinnata, pinnis alternis linearibus apice serratis — Acrostichum (10) 15

Acrostichum fronde pinnata, pinnis alternis linguiformibus integerrimis glabris — Acrostichum (10) 14

Acrostichum fronde pinnata, pinnis alternis sursum pinnulatis linearibus, inferioribus bipartitis — Acrostichum (10) 12

Acrostichum fronde pinnata, pinnis linearibus integerrimis patentibus connatis — Acrostichum (10) 12

Acrostichum fronde pinnata, pinnis oblongo-ovatis subcordatis hirsutis subserratis — Acrostichum (10) 17[as Acrosticum]

Acrostichum fronde pinnata, pinnis sessilibus oblongis sinuatis: summis brevissimis integerrimis — Acrostichum (10) 13

Acrostichum frondibus integerrimis glabris petiolatis, sterilibus subrotundis, fertilibus linearibus — Acrostichum (10) 9

Acrostichum frondibus lanceolato-ovatis integerrimis, caule scandente — Acrostichum (10) 10

Acrostichum frondibus lineari-lanceolatis acutis, caule scandente — Acrostichum (10) 9

Acrostichum frondibus pinnatis, pinnis alternis ovatis crenatis sessilibus sursum arcuatis — Acrostichum (10) 13

Acrostichum furcatum — Fl. Jam. (105) 23[as Acrosticum]; Iter Chin. (161) 7

Acrostichum ilvense — Herbat. Upsal. (50) 9; Stat. pl. (55) 23; Fl. Angl. (56) 25[as Acrosticum]; Fl. Åker. (162) 20[as Acrosticum]

Acrostichum maderaspatanum, foliis laciniatis — Acrostichum (10) 12[as madraspatanum]

Acrostichum marginatum — Fl. Jam. (105) 22[as Acrosticum]

Acrostichum nudum, spica secunda adscendente reflexa compressa — Acrostichum (10) 11

Acrostichum parvum septentrionale — Acrostichum (10) 10

Acrostichum pectinatum — Fl. Cap. (99) 8, 19

Acrostichum polypodioides — Fl. Jam. (105) 23[as Acrosticum]

Acrostichum pulchrum — Fl. Monsp. (74) 29[as Acrosticum]

Acrostichum rufum — Fl. Jam. (105) 23[as Acrosticum]

Acrostichum rupestre — Pan Svec. (26) 38

Acrostichum sanctum — Fl. Jam. (105) 22[as Acrosticum]

Acrostichum septentrionale — Herbat. Upsal. (50) 8; Stat. pl. (55) 23; Fl. Angl. (56) 25[as Acrosticum]; Fl. Monsp. (74) 29[as Acrosticum]; Fl. Åker. (162) 20[as Acrosticum]; Pand. fl. Ryb. (165) 23[as Acrosticum]

Acrostichum siliquosum — Herb. Amboin. (57) 28

Acrostichum sorbifolium — Fl. Jam. (105) 23[as Acrosticum]

Acrostichum thelypteris — Fl. Angl. (56) 25[as Acrosticum]; Fl. Monsp. (74) 29[as Acrosticum]

Acrostichum trifoliatum — Fl. Jam. (105) 22[as Acrosticum]

Actaea — Mus. Ad.-Frid. (11) 21; Vir. pl. (13) 21, 31, 35, 37; Fl. oecon. (17) 14; Pl. rar. Camsch. (30) 22; Pl. hybr. (33) 7[as Actea], 16; Odor. med. (40) 13; Inebr. (117) 12[as Actea]; Fund. fr. (123) 18; Cimicifuga (173) 2, 9

Actaea cimicifuga — Hist. nat. Rossia (144) 30; Usum hist. nat. (145) 27[as Actea], plate [1]

Actaea fructibus siccis plurimis — Cimicifuga (173) 6[as sicis]

Actaea nigra — Pan Svec. (26) 25

Actaea racemis longissimis — Nova pl. gen. 1747 (14) [33][as Acteae]; Rad. senega (23) 11; Pl. rar. Camsch. (30) 22

Actaea racemis paniculatis, fructibus quadricapsularibus — Cimicifuga (173) 3, 6

Actaea racemo ovato — Pl. rar. Camsch. (30) 22

Actaea racemosa — Demonstr. pl. (49) 14; Pl. officin. (52) 4; Calend. fl. (72) [16]; Specif. Canad. (76) 15, 28; Cimicifuga (173) 2

Actaea spicata — Herbat. Upsal. (50) 8; Stat. pl. (55) 8, 17; Fl. Angl. (56) 17; Cervus (60) 8; Fl. Monsp. (74) 18; Specif. Canad. (76) 28; Prodr. fl. Dan. (82) 19; Pl. tinct. (97) 19; Fl. Åker. (162) 13; Pand. fl. Ryb. (165) 19

Adansonia — Demonstr. pl. (49) 27

Adansonia digitata — Demonstr. pl. (49) 27; Fl. Palaest. (70) 25

Adelia — Fl. Jam. (105) 26, 27

Adelia acidoton — Pl. Jam. (102) 29; Fl. Jam. (105) 22

Adelia bernardia — Fl. Jam. (105) 22

Adelia ricinella — Pl. Jam. (102) 29; Fl. Jam. (105) 22

Adenanthera — Nect. fl. (122) 9

Adenanthera falcata — Cent. I. pl. (65) 2

Adenanthera falcata, foliis subtus tomentosis — Herb. Amboin. (57) 14

Adenanthera pavonina, foliis utrinque glabris — Herb. Amboin. (57) 14

Adhatoda — Hort. Upsal. (7) 36

Adiantum — Acrostichum (10) 3, 6, 7, 8; Herb. Amboin. (57) 26

Adiantum acrosticon — Acrostichum (10) 10

Adiantum aculeatum — Fl. Jam. (105) 23

Adiantum aureum — Usum musc. (148) 13

Adiantum aureum minimum facie planta marina — Corallia Balt. (4) 10

Adiantum calomelanos americanum — Acrostichum (10) 13

Adiantum capillus veneris — Pl. officin. (52) 6; Fl. Angl. (56) 25; Fl. Palaest. (70) 32; Fl. Monsp. (74) 29

Adiantum cristatum — Fl. Jam. (105) 23

Adiantum nigro simile, albissimo pulvere conspersum — Acrostichum (10) 13

Adiantum nigrum — Acrostichum (10) 8

Adiantum nigrum foliis prona parte candidissimis — Acrostichum (10) 13

Adiantum radicans — Fl. Jam. (105) 23

Adiantum trapeziforme — Fl. Jam. (105) 23[as trapoziforme]

Adiantum villosum — Fl. Jam. (105) 23

Adiantum volubile — Herb. Amboin. (57) 26

Admirabilis jasmini rosa — Cent. I. pl. (65) 34[as rossa]

Adonis — Hort. Upsal. (7) 33; Cui bono? (42) 20; Nom. bot. (107) 14; Fund. fr. (123) 23

Adonis aestivalis — Hort. cul. (132) 23

Adonis annua — Demonstr. pl. (49) 15; Fl. Belg. (112) 18

Adonis annua atropurpurea [error for atrorubens?] — Fl. Monsp. (74) 18[as Adorus]

Adonis annua atrorubens — Fl. Angl. (56) 18; see also A. a. atropurpurea

Adonis annua phoenicea — Fl. Monsp. (74) 18[as Adorus]

Adonis annua rubra — Calend. fl. (72) [12]

Adonis annua serotina — Calend. fl. (72) [19], [22]

Adonis annua vernalis — Fl. Monsp. (74) 18[as Adorus]

Adonis apennina — Demonstr. pl. (49) 15; Calend. fl. (72) [10]; Pl. Alstr. (121) 6; Hist. nat. Rossia (144) 23[as apenina], 30

Adonis autumnalis — Hort. cul. (132) 23

Adonis capensis — Fl. Cap. (99) 15

Adonis helleborus foeniculaceus — Betula (1) 12

Adonis perennis — Pan Svec. (26) 26

Adonis sibirica — Calend. fl. (72) [16]

Adonis vernalis — Demonstr. pl. (49) 15; Stat. pl. (55) 22; Calend. fl. (72) [10], [11]; Colon. pl. (158) 6

Adoxa moschata — Pan Svec. (26) 22

Adoxa moschatellina — Herbat. Upsal. (50) 11[as moscatellina]; Stat. pl. (55) 17; Fl. Angl. (56) 15[as moschatella]; Calend. fl. (72) [9][as moscatellina]; Fl. Monsp. (74) 15; Prodr. fl. Dan. (82) 17; Fl. Åker. (162) 11

Adpendix arborum — Herb. Amboin. (57) 25

Adpendix cuscuaria — Herb. Amboin. (57) 25

Adpendix duplofolio — Herb. Amboin. (57) 25

Adpendix erecta — Herb. Amboin. (57) 25

Adpendix laciniata — Herb. Amboin. (57) 25

Adpendix procellanica — Herb. Amboin. (57) 25

Aedes — Aer habit. (106) 22

Aegilops — Pl. Mart.-Burs. (6) 5; Fund. agrost. (152) 16, 25, 35

Aegilops bromoides juba purpurascente — Cent. II. pl. (66) 33

Aegilops incurva — Fund. agrost. (152) 32

Aegilops ovata — Fl. Palaest. (70) 32; Fl. Monsp. (74) 28

Aegilops spartea villosa — Cent. II. pl. (66) 33

Aegopodium — Fl. oecon. (17) 8

Aegopodium podagraria — Herbat. Upsal. (50) 15[as podagria]; Stat. pl. (55) 20; Fl. Angl. (56) 13; Fl. Monsp. (74) 13; Prodr. fl. Dan. (82) 16; Fl. Belg. (112) 15; Fl. Åker. (162) 9

Aegopodium repens — Pan Svec. (26) 19

Aegopricum — Pl. Surin. (177) 4[as Aegoprcum], 15

Aepala — Nova pl. gen. 1747 (14) 17

Aerucago apula — Pl. hybr. (33) 25

Aeschynomene — Spons. pl. (12) 12[as Aeschynemone]

Aeschynomene americana — Fl. Jam. (105) 19[as Aeschymene]

Aeschynomene foliis acaciae latioribus, frondibus longissimos aculeos habentibus — Cent. I. pl. (65) 13

Aeschynomene indica — Herb. Amboin. (57) 16

Aeschynomene sesban — Fl. Palaest. (70) 25

Aeschynomene spinosa quinta — Cent. I. pl. (65) 13

Aesculus — Sapor. med. (31) 15; Pand. insect. (93) 13; Arb. Svec. (101) 30; Nom. bot. (107) 12

Aesculus hippocastanum — Gem. arb. (24) 20[as Esculus]; Hosp. insect. fl. (43) 20[as Esculus]; Arb. Svec. (101) 7, 9, 28; Fl. Belg. (112) 16; Hort. cul. (132) 25; Febr. interm. (167) 41

Aethusa — Fl. oecon. (17) 7[as Ethusa]; Cent. I. pl. (65) 9; Mors. serp. (119) 2

Aethusa artedii — Pan Svec. (26) 19[as Ethusa]

Aethusa cynapium — Herbat. Upsal. (50) 15[as Ethusa]; Stat. pl. (55) 19; Fl. Angl. (56) 13; Calend. fl. (72) [22]; Fl. Monsp. (74) 13; Prodr. fl. Dan. (82) 16; Fl. Belg. (112) 15; Fl. Åker. (162) 9; Pand. fl. Ryb. (165) 18

Agallochum — Herb. Amboin. (57) 8

Agallochum secundarium — Herb. Amboin. (57) 8

Agallochum spurium — Herb. Amboin. (57) 8

Agaricus — Spons. pl. (12) 19; Vir. pl. (13) 25; Fl. oecon. (17) 29; Fl. alp. (71) 25; Mac. olit. (113) 16; Mund. invis. (149) 12, 15, 22; Med. purg. (181) 24

Agaricus chantarellus — Prodr. fl. Dan. (82) 26

Agaricus georgii — Prodr. fl. Dan. (82) 26

Agaricus muscarius — Prodr. fl. Dan. (82) 26

Agave — Nova pl. gen. 1751 (32) 40, 48

Agave americana — Demonstr. pl. (49) 10; Usum hist. nat. (145) 16

Agave foliis dentato-spinosis, scapo ramoso — Nova pl. gen. 1751 (32) 40

Agave foliis dentato-spinosis, scapo simplicissimo — Nova pl. gen. 1751 (32) 40

Agave foliis spinoso-dentatis mucronatisque — Nova pl. gen. 1751 (32) 40

Ageratum — Hort. Upsal. (7) 36

Ageratum altissimum — Calend. fl. (72) [21]

Ageratum conyzoides — Fl. Jam. (105) 19; Pl. rar. Afr. (115) 6

Agrimonia — Vir. pl. (13) 27; Oecon. nat. (20) 17; Nom. bot. (107) 13; Fund. fr. (123) 23; Erica (163) 2; Fraga (170) [1], 2, 3

Agrimonia eupatoria — Herbat. Upsal. (50) 8; Pl. officin. (52) 4; Stat. pl. (55) 20; Fl. Angl. (56) 16; Calend. fl. (72) [15]; Fl. Monsp. (74) 17; Specif. Canad. (76) 26; Prodr. fl. Dan. (82) 18; Fl. Belg. (112) 17; Fl. Åker. (162) 12; Pand. fl. Ryb. (165) 19

Agrimonia eupatoria odorata — Demonstr. pl. (49) 13

Agrimonia molucca — Herb. Amboin. (57) 26

Agrimonia officinarum — Vir. pl. (13) 30; Pan Svec. (26) 24; Pl. hybr. (33) 10

Agrostemma — Fl. oecon. (17) 11; Nom. bot. (107) 13[as Agrostema]

Agrostemma agrestis — Pan Svec. (26) 23

Agrostemma coronaria — Calend. fl. (72) [22]; Hort. cul. (132) 24, 25

Agrostemma flos jovis — Fl. alp. (71) 17

Agrostemma githago — Herbat. Upsal. (50) 13[as Agrostema]; Stat. pl. (55) 19[as Agrostema]; Fl. Angl. (56) 16[as Agrostema]; Fl. Monsp. (74) 16; Prodr. fl. Dan. (82) 18[as Agrostema]; Fl. Belg. (112) 17; Fl. Åker. (162) 12; Pand. fl. Ryb. (165) 19[as Agrostema]; Esca avium (174) 12

Agrostarium — Fund. agrost. (152) 16

Agrostis — Fl. oecon. (17) 3; Fund. agrost. (152) 27, 31, 37

Agrostis arundinacea — Herbat. Upsal. (50) 11; Stat. pl. (55) 18; Usum hist. nat. (145) 19; Fund. agrost. (152) 7, 11; Fl. Åker. (162) 6; Erica (163) 15

Agrostis canina — Prodr. fl. Dan. (82) 13; Fl. Åker. (162) 6; Esca avium (174) 10

Agrostis capillaris — Fl. Monsp. (74) 9

Agrostis cruciata — Pl. Jam. (102) 7; Fl. Jam. (105) 13

Agrostis enodis — Pan Svec. (26) 13

Agrostis indica — Fl. Jam. (105) 13

Agrostis minima — Fl. Monsp. (74) 9

Agrostis pyramidalis — Pan Svec. (26) 13

Agrostis radiata — Pl. Jam. (102) 7; Fl. Jam. (105) 13

Agrostis rubra — Demonstr. pl. (49) 3; Herbat. Upsal. (50) 14; Fl. Angl. (56) 10; Prodr. fl. Dan. (82) 13; Fl. Åker. (162) 6

Agrostis spica venti — Pan Svec. (26) 13; Herbat. Upsal. (50) 12; Stat. pl. (55) 19; Fl. Angl. (56) 10; Fl. Palaest. (70) 12; Prodr. fl. Dan. (82) 13; Fl. Belg. (112) 13; Usum hist. nat. (145) 10; Fund. agrost. (152) 5, 7; Fl. Åker. (162) 6; Esca avium (174) 10

Agrostis spicata — Fund. agrost. (152) 7

Agrostis stolonifera — Pan Svec. (26) 13; Demonstr. pl. (49) 3; Herbat. Upsal. (50) 14; Fl. Angl. (56) 10; Fl. Belg. (112) 13; Fund. agrost. (152) 7; Fl. Åker. (162) 6

Agrostis supina — Pan Svec. (26) 14

Agrostis tenuissima — Pan Svec. (26) 13

Ahaetulla — Surin. Grill. (16) 17; Curios. nat. (18) 17[as Aëtulla]

Ahaetulla ceylanensis — Hort. Upsal. (7) 43[as zeilonensis]; Surin. Grill. (16) 15[as ceylonensis]

Ai — Surin. Grill. (16) 7

Aira — Vir. pl. (13) 31; Fl. oecon. (17) 3; Splachnum (27) 2; Cui bono? (42) 17; Pand. insect. (93) 11; Anim. comp. (98) 6; Fund. agrost. (152) 28, 31, 37

Aira alpina — Pan Svec. (26) 14; Stat. pl. (55) 16; Fl. alp. (71) 12; Fund. agrost. (152) 7

Aira aquatica — Stat. pl. (55) 13; Fl. Angl. (56) 10; Prodr. fl. Dan. (82) 13; Fl. Belg. (112) 13; Fund. agrost. (152) 7, 31

Aira avenacea alpina — Pan Svec. (26) 14

Aira caerulea — Herbat. Upsal. (50) 8; Stat. pl. (55) 14; Fl. Angl. (56) 10; Prodr. fl. Dan. (82) 13[as coerulea]; Fl. Åker. (162) 6

Aira canescens — Stat. pl. (55) 22; Fl. Angl. (56) 10; Prodr. fl. Dan. (82) 13; Fl. Belg. (112) 13; Colon. pl. (158) 8

Aira caryophyllea — Fl. Angl. (56) 10; Fl. Monsp. (74) 9

Aira cespitosa — Herbat. Upsal. (50) 6; Fl. Angl. (56) 10; Fl. Monsp. (74) 9[as caespitosa]; Prodr. fl. Dan. (82) 13[as caespitosa]; Fl. Belg. (112) 13[as caespitosa]; Fund. agrost. (152) 6[as caespitosa], 7[as caespitosa], 9[as caespitosa]; Fl. Åker. (162)

6[as caespitosa]; Pand. fl. Ryb. (165) 16[as caespitosa]

Aira cristata — Fl. Angl. (56) 10; Fl. Monsp. (74) 9

Aira dalekarlica — Pan Svec. (26) 14

Aira flexuosa — Pan Svec. (26) 14; Herbat. Upsal. (50) 13; Stat. pl. (55) 23; Fl. Angl. (56) 10; Fl. Åker. (162) 6; Erica (163) 12; Pand. fl. Ryb. (165) 16

Aira foliis planis, panicula coarctata, floribus pedunculatis muticis convoluto subulatis — Pl. Mart.-Burs. (6) [1]

Aira foliis planis, panicula patente, floribus muticis laevibus calyce longioribus — Pl. Mart.-Burs. (6) 4

Aira foliis setaceis, culmis subnudis, panicula divaricata, pedunculis flexuosis — Pl. Mart.-Burs. (6) 2

Aira lanata — Pan Svec. (26) 14

Aira mariae borussorum — Pan Svec. (26) 14

Aira miliacea — Pan Svec. (26) 14

Aira montana — Fl. alp. (71) 12; Fl. Belg. (112) 13; Fund. agrost. (152) 7

Aira praecox — Stat. pl. (55) 22; Fl. Angl. (56) 10[as precox]; Prodr. fl. Dan. (82) 13; Colon. pl. (158) 8

Aira radice jubata — Pan Svec. (26) 14

Aira spica lavendulae — Pan Svec. (26) 14

Aira spicata — Fl. alp. (71) 12

Aira trivialis — Fund. agrost. (152) 7

Aira xerampelina — Pan Svec. (26) 14

Aizoon — Pl. rar. Afr. (115) 4

Aizoon canariense — Demonstr. pl. (49) 14

Aizoon foliis obverse ovatis — Hort. Upsal. (7) 40

Aizoon hispanicum — Fl. Jam. (105) 17

Aizoon paniculatum — Fl. Cap. (99) 15

Ajax — Vir. pl. (13) 14

Ajuga — Nom. bot. (107) 14

Ajuga pyramidalis — Herbat. Upsal. (50) 8; Pl. officin. (52) 8; Stat. pl. (55) 18; Fl. Angl. (56) 18; Fl. Monsp. (74) 19; Prodr. fl. Dan. (82) 20; Rar. Norv. (157) 11; Fl. Åker. (162) 14; Pand. fl. Ryb. (165) 20; Esca avium (174) 13

Ajuga reptans — Fl. Angl. (56) 18; Fl. Monsp. (74) 19; Prodr. fl. Dan. (82) 20; Fl. Belg. (112) 18

Ajuga verna — Pan Svec. (26) 26

Alaternus — Hort. Upsal. (7) 35; Gem. arb. (24) 6; Fl. Monsp. (74) 7

Alauda — Morb. hyeme (38) 3, 13; Cui bono? (42) 24; Migr. avium (79) 31; Instr. peregr. (96) 11; Polit. nat. (109) 13; Fund. ornith. (137) 25

Alauda alpestris — Migr. avium (79) 15

Alauda arborea — Migr. avium (79) 31

Alauda arvensis — Migr. avium (79) 31; Fund. ornith. (137) 27

Alauda campestris — Migr. avium (79) 31

Alauda pratensis — Migr. avium (79) 31

Alauda tungusica — Hist. nat. Rossia (144) 16

Albuca — Nect. fl. (122) 14

Alca — Polit. nat. (109) 13; Fund. ornith. (137) 19

Alca arctica — Nat. pelagi (84) 13[as artica]

Alca grylle — Nat. pelagi (84) 13[as gryllus]

Alca impennis — Nat. pelagi (84) 13; Fund. ornith. (137) 10, 16

Alca lomvia — Nat. pelagi (84) 13

Alca torda — Migr. avium (79) 25; Nat. pelagi (84) 13

Alcea — Vir. pl. (13) 32; Sapor. med. (31) 12

Alcea ficifolia — Demonstr. pl. (49) 18

Alcea filicifolia — Fl. Palaest. (70) 24

Alcea floridana quinquecapsularis, laurinis, foliis leviter crenatis, seminibus coniferarum instar alatis — Nova pl. gen. 1747 (14) 24

Alcea folio rotundo, laciniato — Vir. pl. (13) 34

Alcea indica floribus rosaceis parvis, fructibus parvis quinquepartitis hispidis lappaceis — Nova pl. gen. 1747 (14) 17

Alcea maritima galloprovincialis, geranii folio — Cent. I. pl. (65) 22

Alcea minor maritima tenuifolia procumbens — Cent. I. pl. (65) 22

Alcea rosea — Demonstr. pl. (49) 18; Pl. officin. (52) 12; Calend. fl. (72) [22][as Alceae]; Cul. mut. (88) 3; Hort. cul. (132) 24, 25

Alcea tenuifolia humilis maritima galloprovincialis, foliis inferioribus nonnihil ad geranium accedentibus — Cent. I. pl. (65) 22

Alceae affinis indica abutilon dicta, flore parvo, foliis mollibus profunde venosis, siliculis lanuginosis — Cent. II. pl. (66) 26

Alces — Mat. med. anim. (29) 6

Alchemilla — Vir. pl. (13) 12[as Alchimilla], 27[as Alchimilla]; Fl. oecon. (17) 5; Pl. hybr. (33) 7; Fl. Angl. (56) 5; Pand. insect. (93) 11[as Alchimilla]; Nom. bot. (107) 10; Fund. fr. (123) 23; Fraga (170) [1][as Alchimilla], 2, 3

Alchemilla alpina — Pan Svec. (26) 16; Demonstr. pl. (49) 4; Fl. Angl. (56) 11; Fl. alp. (71) 13; Fl. Monsp. (74) 10

Alchemilla alpina pubescens minor — Pl. hybr. (33) 23[as Alchimilla]

Alchemilla foliis digitatis — Pl. hybr. (33) 23[as Alchimilla]

Alchemilla foliis lobatis — Pl. hybr. (33) 23[as Alchimilla]

Alchemilla pentaphylla — Fl. alp. (71) 13

Alchemilla vulgaris — Pan Svec. (26) 16; Hosp. insect. fl. (43) 16; Herbat. Upsal. (50) 7; Pl. officin. (52) 4[as Alchimilla]; Stat. pl. (55) 22; Fl. Angl. (56) 11; Fl. Monsp. (74) 10; Prodr. fl. Dan. (82) 14; Fl. Belg. (112) 13; Raphania (126) 18; Fl. Åker. (162) 7; Pand. fl. Ryb. (165) 17; Esca avium (174) 11

Alcorum — Herb. Amboin. (57) 20

Alcyonium arboreum — Mund. invis. (149) 8

Alcyonium ramoso-digitatum molle, astericis undique ornatum — Corallia Balt. (4) 10

Aldrovanda — Nova pl. gen. 1751 (32) 39, 40[as Androvanda], 48; Nect. fl. (122) 5

Aldrovanda vasculosa — Colon. pl. (158) 6

Aletris — Nova pl. gen. 1751 (32) 9, [13, as 15], 15, 16, 48; Fung. melit. (69) 2

Aletris capensis — Fl. Cap. (99) 13[as Alethris]

Aletris farinosa — Specif. Canad. (76) 10; Mors. serp. (119) 17

Alga — Fl. Cap. (99) 3

Alga angustifolia vitriariorum — Nova pl. gen. 1747 (14) 27, 28

Alga marina graminea angustifolia seminifera ramosior — Nova pl. gen. 1747 (14) 27

Alisma — Hort. Upsal. (7) 41

Alisma cordifolia — Fl. Jam. (105) 15

Alisma damasonium — Fl. Angl. (56) 15; Fl. Monsp. (74) 15

Alisma erecta — Pan Svec. (26) 21

Alisma natans — Pan Svec. (26) 21; Stat. pl. (55) 13; Prodr. fl. Dan. (82) 17

Alisma plantago — Herbat. Upsal. (50) 10; Fl. Belg. (112) 16; Pand. fl. Ryb. (165) 18

Alisma plantago aquatica — Stat. pl. (55) 13; Fl. Angl. (56) 15; Fl. Palaest. (70) 18; Fl. Monsp. (74) 15; Prodr. fl. Dan. (82) 17; Fl. Åker. (162) 10

Alisma ranunculoides — Demonstr. pl. (49) 11; Stat. pl. (55) 13; Fl. Angl. (56) 15; Fl. Monsp. (74) 15; Prodr. fl. Dan. (82) 17; Fl. Belg. (112) 16; Colon. pl. (158) 7[as rarunculoides]

Allamanda cathartica — Pl. Surin. (177) 6

Alliaria — Odor. med. (40) 12; Herb. Amboin. (57) 9

Allium — Vir. pl. (13) 7, 8, 20; Fl. oecon. (17) 8; Gem. arb. (24) 5; Sem. musc. (28) 6; Sapor. med. (31) 19; Pl. hybr. (33) 29; Pl. escul. (35) 12; Odor. med. (40) 12, 14, 15; Cui bono? (42) 20; Cul. mut. (88) 2, 8; Spigelia (89) 6; Nom. bot. (107) 12; Esca avium (174) 4

Allium ampeloprasum — Fl. Angl. (56) 14[as ampelohrasum]

Allium amphicarpon — Fl. Angl. (56) 28

Allium angulosum — Demonstr. pl. (49) 9; Fl. Monsp. (74) 14; Hist. nat. Rossia (144) 28

Allium arenarium — Demonstr. pl. (49) 9; Colon. pl. (158) 7

Allium ascalonicum — Fl. Palaest. (70) 17

Allium bicorne proliferum — Fl. Angl. (56) 28

Allium canadense — Demonstr. pl. (49) 9

Allium carinatum — Prodr. fl. Dan. (82) 16; Fl. Belg. (112) 15

Allium cepa — Demonstr. pl. (49) 9; Pl. officin. (52) 7; Fl. Palaest. (70) 17; Fl. Jam. (105) 24; Hort. cul. (132) 13

Allium descendens — Demonstr. pl. (49) 9; Calend. fl. (72) [17]

Allium fistulosum — Demonstr. pl. (49) 9; Hort. cul. (132) 18

Allium flavum — Fl. Monsp. (74) 14

Allium flore obsoletiore — Fl. Monsp. (74) 29

Allium lineare — Hist. nat. Rossia (144) 28

Allium moly — Demonstr. pl. (49) 9; Calend. fl. (72) [12]; Fl. Monsp. (74) 14

Allium monspessulanum — Fl. Monsp. (74) 29

Allium montanum 3 — Fl. Monsp. (74) 29

Allium montanum bicorne latifolium, flore dilute purpurascente — Pl. Mart.-Burs. (6) 6

Allium montanum pumilum, gramineo folio, floribus purpureis — Pl. Mart.-Burs. (6) 6

Allium moschatum — Odor. med. (40) 12; Demonstr. pl. (49) 9; Fl. Palaest. (70) 17; Fl. Monsp. (74) 14; Ambros. (100) 14; Hort. cul. (132) 19

Allium nutans — Demonstr. pl. (49) 9; Hist. nat. Rossia (144) 28

Allium obliquum — Demonstr. pl. (49) 9; Hist. nat. Rossia (144) 28

Allium oleraceum — Demonstr. pl. (49) 9; Herbat. Upsal. (50) 10; Stat. pl. (55) 22; Fl. Angl. (56) 14; Prodr. fl. Dan. (82) 16; Fl. Åker. (162) 10; Pand. fl. Ryb. (165) 18

Allium paniculatum — Fl. Palaest. (70) 17

Allium porrum — Demonstr. pl. (49) 9; Pl. officin. (52) 15; Fl. Palaest. (70) 17; Calend. fl. (72) [17]; Fl. Jam. (105) 24; Hort. cul. (132) 13

Allium pyrenaeum — Fl. alp. (71) 15

Allium ramosum — Demonstr. pl. (49) 9; Hist. nat. Rossia (144) 28

Allium roseum — Fl. Monsp. (74) 14

Allium sativum — Demonstr. pl. (49) 9; Pl. officin. (52) 4; Fl. Palaest. (70) 17; Fl. Cap. (99) 2; Fl. Jam. (105) 24; Hort. cul. (132) 13

Allium scapo nudo tereti, foliis subulatis, umbella globosa, staminibus tricuspidatis — Fl. Palaest. (70) 17

Allium schoenoprasum — Demonstr. pl. (49) 9[as schoenoprosum, corr. p. 27]; Hort. cul. (132) 18; Hist. nat. Rossia (144) 28

Allium scorodoprasum — Demonstr. pl. (49) 9; Prodr. fl. Dan. (82) 16; Hort. cul. (132) 13

Allium senescens — Demonstr. pl. (49) 9; Fl. Monsp. (74) 14; Hist. nat. Rossia (144) 28

Allium sphaerocephalum — Fl. Monsp. (74) 14; Prodr. fl. Dan. (82) 16; Hist. nat. Rossia (144) 28[as spaerocephalum]

Allium sphaerocephalum bifolium — Pl. Mart.-Burs. (6) 5

Allium subhirsutum — Fl. Palaest. (70) 17; Fl. Cap. (99) 13

Allium tenuissimum — Hist. nat. Rossia (144) 28

Allium ursinum — Pan Svec. (26) 20; Demonstr. pl. (49) 9; Stat. pl. (55) 17; Fl. Angl. (56) 14; Fl. Monsp. (74) 14; Prodr. fl. Dan. (82) 16; Polit. nat. (109) 5; Fl. Belg. (112) 15; Fl. Åker. (162) 10

Allium vcronense — Fl. Palaest. (70) 17

Allium victorialis — Pl. officin. (52) 20; Fl. alp. (71) 15

Allium vineale — Fl. Angl. (56) 14; Fl. Monsp. (74) 14; Prodr. fl. Dan. (82) 16; Fl. Belg. (112) 15

Allophylus — Nova pl. gen. 1747 (14) [vi], 14, 15

Alnus — Spons. pl. (12) 32, 41; Fl. oecon. (17) 22; Oecon. nat. (20) 17; Gem. arb. (24) 5, 11; Pan Svec. (26) 6; Cui bono? (42) 20; Hosp. insect. fl. (43) 40; Noxa insect. (46) 26; Vern. arb. (47) 10, table; Oves (61) 18; Migr. avium (79) 34; Fr. Svec. (91) 24; Pand. insect. (93) 19; Arb. Svec. (101) 21, 27, 30; Nom. bot. (107) 18; Fl. Belg. (112) 8

Alnus folio incano — Arb. Svec. (101) 24

Alnus folio oblongo — Fl. Palaest. (70) 30[under Betula]

Alnus glutinosa — Gem. arb. (24) 31; Pan Svec. (26) 35; Hosp. insect. fl. (43) 32

Alnus incana — Oves (61) 18

Alnus rotundifolia glutinosa viridis — Arb. Svec. (101) 24

Aloe — Vir. pl. (13) 20, 31, 33; Oecon. nat. (20) 19; Sapor. med. (31) 18; Pl. hybr. (33) 29; Fl. Cap. (99) 7, 9; Fl. Jam. (105) 8; Pl. rar. Afr. (115) 4; Pl. Alstr. (121) 5; Fund. fr. (123) 18; Aphyteia (185) 6

Aloe africana arborescens, floribus albicantibus fragrantissimis — Nova pl. gen. 1751 (32) 40

Aloe americana — Herb. Amboin. (57) 21

Aloe disticha — Demonstr. pl. (49) 10; Fl. Cap. (99) 13

Aloe floribus pedunculatis cernuis corymbosis subcylindricis — Med. purg. (181) 8

Aloe foliis canaliculatis trifariam imbricatis, caulinis apice retroflexo patulis — Hort. Upsal. (7) 39

Aloe foliis canaliculatis trifariam imbricatis radicatis erectis, angulis ternis cartilagineis — Hort. Upsal. (7) 39

Aloe foliis caulinis dentatis amplexicaulibus vaginantibus — Hort. Upsal. (7) 39

Aloe foliis integerrimis — Nova pl. gen. 1751 (32) 40

Aloe foliis integerrimis patentiusculis, aculeo terminatis, radice caulescente — Nova pl. gen. 1751 (32) 40

Aloe foliis lanceolatis dentatis spina cartilaginea terminatis radicalibus — Hort. Upsal. (7) 40

Aloe foliis lanceolatis planis erectis radicatis — Hort. Upsal. (7) 39

Aloe foliis lanceolatis spina cartilaginea terminali, floribus alternis sessilibus — Nova pl. gen. 1751 (32) 40

Aloe foliis linguiformibus patulis distichis — Hort. Upsal. (7) 39

Aloe foliis ovatis acuminatis: caulinis quinquefariam imbricatis — Hort. Upsal. (7) 39

Aloe foliis ovato-lanceolatis carnosis apice triquetris, angulis inermibus dentatis — Hort. Upsal. (7) 39

Aloe foliis ovato-subulatis acuminatis, tuberculis cartilagineis undique adspersis — Hort. Upsal. (7) 39

Aloe foliis rhomboidalibus crassis quinquefariam imbricatis apice triquetris plano exstantibus — Hort. Upsal. (7) 39

Aloe foliis spinosis confertis dentatis vaginantibus maculatis — Med. purg. (181) 8

Aloe foliis spinosis confertis dentatis vaginantibus planis maculatis — Hort. Upsal. (7) 40

Aloe humilis — Fl. Cap. (99) 13

Aloe hyacinthoides — Demonstr. pl. (49) 10; Fl. Cap. (99) 13

Aloe perfoliata — Demonstr. pl. (49) 10; Pl. officin. (52) 4; Stat. pl. (55) 11; Fl. Cap. (99) 13; Pl. Surin. (177) 7; Med. purg. (181) 8

Aloe perfoliata humilis — Demonstr. pl. (49) 10

Aloe perfoliata vera — Demonstr. pl. (49) 10; Fl. Jam. (105) 15

Aloe plicatilis — Fl. Cap. (99) 13

Aloe pumila — Fl. Cap. (99) 13

Aloe pumila arachnoidea — Demonstr. pl. (49) 10

Aloe retusa — Demonstr. pl. (49) 10; Fl. Cap. (99) 13

Aloe spiralis — Demonstr. pl. (49) 10; Fl. Cap. (99) 13

Aloe uvaria — Fl. Cap. (99) 4, 9, 13

Aloe variegata — Demonstr. pl. (49) 10; Fl. Cap. (99) 13

Aloe vera — Fl. Cap. (99) 13

Aloe viscosa — Demonstr. pl. (49) 10; Fl. Cap. (99) 13

Aloe vivipara — Herb. Amboin. (57) 21; Fl. Jam. (105) 15

Alopecuro-Veronica — Herb. Amboin. (57) 26

Alopecurus — Fl. oecon. (17) 2; Cui bono? (42) 17; Fl. Monsp. (74) 7; Fund. agrost. (152) 21, 26, 30, 36

Alopecurus erectus — Pan Svec. (26) 13

Alopecurus geniculatus — Herbat. Upsal. (50) 7; Stat. pl. (55) 14[as Alopecorus]; Fl. Angl. (56) 10; Fl. Monsp. (74) 9; Prodr. fl. Dan. (82) 13; Fl. Belg. (112) 13; Fund. agrost. (152) 7; Fl. Åker. (162) 6; Pand. fl. Ryb. (165) 16

Alopecurus infractus — Pan Svec. (26) 13

Alopecurus monspeliensis — Fl. Palaest. (70) 12; Fl. Monsp. (74) 9

Alopecurus paniceus — Colon. pl. (158) 5

Alopecurus pratensis — Demonstr. pl. (49) 3; Herbat. Upsal. (50) 7; Stat. pl. (55) 21[as Alopecorus]; Fl. Angl. (56) 10; Calend. fl. (72) [11]; Prodr. fl. Dan. (82) 13; Fl. Belg. (112) 13; Usum hist. nat. (145) 18; Fund. agrost. (152) 11; Fl. Åker. (162) 6; Pand. fl. Ryb. (165) 16

Alpinia — Vir. pl. (13) 26; Gem. arb. (24) 8; Pl. Surin. (177) 5

Alsine — Fl. oecon. (17) 11; Pand. insect. (93) 13; Nom. bot. (107) 11

Alsine alpina, foliis teretibus obtusis, flore albo — Cent. II. pl. (66) 17

Alsine angustifolia caryophylloides multiflora glabra purpurascens, radice astragaliti — Nova pl. gen. 1751 (32) 41

Alsine caryophylloides glabra, florum pediculis longissimis — Cent. II. pl. (66) 18

Alsine fluitans — Fl. Monsp. (74) 29

Alsine foetida — Fl. Monsp. (74) 29

Alsine foliis ellipticis succulentis — Nova pl. gen. 1751 (32) 36

Alsine foliis fasciculatis tenuissimis durisque, petalis integris — Pl. Mart.-Burs. (6) 18

Alsine foliis linearibus acuminatis; petalis florum integris, calyce duplo longioribus — Cent. I. pl. (65) 12

Alsine foliis linearibus integerrimis — Pl. Mart.-Burs. (6) 17

Alsine foliis orbiculatis hirsutis, floribus sessilibus — Nova pl. gen. 1751 (32) 36

Alsine foliis subcordatis, stipulis utrinque quaternis — Nova pl. gen. 1751 (32) 36

Alsine frutescens, caryophylli folio, flore parvo albo — Nova pl. gen. 1751 (32) 41

Alsine gallica — Fl. Monsp. (74) 29

Alsine graminea — Pan Svec. (26) 23

Alsine hirsuta — Fl. Monsp. (74) 29

Alsine littoralis — Fl. Monsp. (74) 29

Alsine media — Hosp. insect. fl. (43) 21; Herbat. Upsal. (50) 10; Stat. pl. (55) 19; Fl. Angl. (56) 14; Cervus (60) 7; Fung. melit. (69) [1]; Fl. Monsp. (74) 13; Prodr. fl. Dan. (82) 16; Fl. Belg. (112) 15; Rar. Norv. (157) 14; Fl. Åker. (162) 10; Pand. fl. Ryb. (165) 18; Esca avium (174) 11

Alsine orientalis altissima, gramineo folio, flore albo — Nova pl. gen. 1751 (32) 41

Alsine pentagyna — Pan Svec. (26) 23

Alsine polygonoides tenuifolia, flosculis ad longitudinem caulis velut in spicam dispositis — Nova pl. gen. 1747 (14) 3

Alsine serrata — Pan Svec. (26) 23

Alsine spuria pusilla repens, foliis saxifragiae aureae — Nova pl. gen. 1751 (32) 38

Alsine vulgaris — Pan Svec. (26) 23

Alsinoides — Nova pl. gen. 1747 (14) 2

Alstroemeria — Pl. Alstr. (121) 8ff.; Nect. fl. (122) 11

Alstroemeria caule adscendente — Pl. Alstr. (121) 10

Alstroemeria caule erecto — Pl. Alstr. (121) 10

Alstroemeria caule volubili — Pl. Alstr. (121) 10

Alstroemeria ligtu — Pl. Alstr. (121) 10

Alstroemeria pelegrina — Pl. Alstr. (121) 10, 11, plate [1]

Alstroemeria salsilla — Pl. Alstr. (121) 10

Althaea — Hort. Upsal. (7) 33; Vir. pl. (13) 12[as Althea], 22, 32[as Althea]; Sapor. med. (31) 12; Nom. bot. (107) 16; Fl. Belg. (112) 10

Althaea africana frutescens — Pl. rar. Afr. (115) 13

Althaea cannabina — Demonstr. pl. (49) 18[as Althea]; Fl. Monsp. (74) 21

Althaea hirsuta — Fl. Monsp. (74) 21

Althaea magna, aceris folio, cortice cannabino, floribus parvis, semina rotatim in summitate caulium, singula singulis utriculis rostratis cooperta ferens — Nova pl. gen. 1751 (32) 31

Althaea officinalis — Demonstr. pl. (49) 18[as Althea]; Pl. officin. (52) 4; Fl. Angl. (56) 20; Calend. fl. (72) [22]; Fl. Monsp. (74) 21; Prodr. fl. Dan. (82) 21; Fl. Belg. (112) 8, 19; Hist. nat. Rossia (144) 21, 31

Althaea theophrasti similis — Cent. II. pl. (66) 26[as Altheae]

Althaea virginiana, ricini folio — Nova pl. gen. 1751 (32) 30[as virginia]

Altica — Fund. entom. (154) 30

Alypum — Euphorbia (36) 29

Alyssum — Hort. Upsal. (7) 34

Alyssum alyssoides — Fl. Palaest. (70) 24[as Alysson]

Alyssum campestre — Fl. Palaest. (70) 24[as Alysson]

Alyssum clypeatum — Fl. Palaest. (70) 24[as Alysson]

Alyssum dioscoridis montanum — Cent. I. pl. (65) 3[as Alysson]

Alyssum graecum frutescens — Fl. Palaest. (70) 24[as Alysson]

Alyssum incanum — Stat. pl. (55) 21; Fl. Angl. (56) 6[as Alysson]; Colon. pl. (158) 7

Alyssum saxatile — Fl. Palaest. (70) 24[as Alysson]

Alyssum scanense — Pan Svec. (26) 28

Alyssum spinosum — Fl. Monsp. (74) 21

Amannia baccifera — Colon. pl. (158) 13

Amannia latifolia — Fund. fr. (123) 12; Siren. lacert. (146) 7

Amara indica — Herb. Amboin. (57) 24

Amara litorea — Herb. Amboin. (57) 19

Amara sylvestris — Herb. Amboin. (57) 24

Amaracus — Marum (175) 5

Amarantho affinis brasiliana, glomeratis parvisque floribus — Cent. II. pl. (66) 13

Amaranthus — Peloria (3) 10; Pl. hybr. (33) 29; Vern. arb. (47) 9; Stat. pl. (55) 5; Herb. Amboin. (57) 21; Chin. Lagerstr. (64) 5; Nom. bot. (107) 18[as Amarantus]; Mac. olit. (113) 20

Amaranthus albus — Fl. Monsp. (74) 27[as Amarantus]; Prodr. fl. Dan. (82) 24; Cul. mut. (88) 4[as Amarantus]

Amaranthus blitum — Pan Svec. (26) 35; Fl. Angl. (56) 24[as Amarantus]; Fl. Monsp. (74) 27[as Amarantus]; Fl. Belg. (112) 22[as Amarantus]

Amaranthus caudatus — Demonstr. pl. (49) 25; Hort. cul. (132) 23

Amaranthus cruentus — Somn. pl. (68) 16

Amaranthus graecizans — Demonstr. pl. (49) 25

Amaranthus hybridus — Demonstr. pl. (49) 25

Amaranthus hypochondriacus — Demonstr. pl. (49) 25

Amaranthus lividus — Demonstr. pl. (49) 25

Amaranthus mangostanus — Cent. I. pl. (65) 32

Amaranthus melancholicus — Demonstr. pl. (49) 25

Amaranthus polygamus — Cent. I. pl. (65) 32

Amaranthus polygonoides — Pl. Jam. (102) 27; Fl. Jam. (105) 21

Amaranthus retroflexus — Demonstr. pl. (49) 25

Amaranthus spicis diandris, ovatis, sessilibus, axillaribus; foliis lanceolatis acutis — Cent. I. pl. (65) 32

Amaranthus spicis triandris, glomeratis, sessilibus, axillaribus, terminalibusque; foliis rhombeis obtusis — Cent. I. pl. (65) 32

Amaranthus spinosus — Demonstr. pl. (49) 25; Herb. Amboin. (57) 21; Fl. Jam. (105) 21

Amaranthus tricolor — Demonstr. pl. (49) 25; Somn. pl. (68) 16

Amaranthus tristis — Demonstr. pl. (49) 25; Herb. Amboin. (57) 21

Amaryllis — Hort. Upsal. (7) 37; Vir. pl. (13) 20; Curios. nat. (18) 17; Hort. acad. (63) 3; Pl. tinct. (97) 5; Mund. invis. (149) 20; Colon. pl. (158) 12; Pl. Surin. (177) 7

Amaryllis atamasca — Demonstr. pl. (49) 9

Amaryllis belladonna — Fl. Jam. (105) 15

Amaryllis capensis — Pl. rar. Afr. (115) 10

Amaryllis formosissima — Demonstr. pl. (49) 9

Amaryllis guttata — Fl. Cap. (99) 13

Amaryllis longifolia — Fl. Cap. (99) 13

Amaryllis lutea — Demonstr. pl. (49) 9; Fl. Palaest. (70) 17

Amaryllis sarniensis — Demonstr. pl. (49) 9; Colon. pl. (158) 12

Amaryllis spatha uniflora remotissima, corolla aequali — Pl. rar. Afr. (115) 10

Amaryllis zeylanica — Herb. Amboin. (57) 22

Ambrosia — Hort. Upsal. (7) 35; Spons. pl. (12) 39; Vern. arb. (47) 9; Fund. agrost. (152) 18

Ambrosia elatior — Demonstr. pl. (49) 25; Fl. Jam. (105) 21

Ambrosia maritima — Calend. fl. (72) [21]

Ameira — Amphib. Gyll. (5) 21; Hort. Upsal. (7) 43

Amellus — Fund. fr. (123) 17; Fl. Jam. (105) 26

Amellus lychnitis — Fund. fr. (123) 22

Amellus umbellatus — Pl. Jam. (102) 24; Fl. Jam. (105) 20

Amerimnon — Fl. Jam. (105) 27

Amethystea — Nova pl. gen. 1747 (14) [vi], 1[as Ametystea], 2

Amethystea caerulea — Demonstr. pl. (49) [1][as coerulea]; Hist. nat. Rossia (144) 23, 27

Amethystina — Anandria (9) 5; Nova pl. gen. 1747 (14) 1

Amethystina montana erecta, foliis exiguis digitatis trifidis serratis, flosculis cum coma in caeruleo janthinis — Nova pl. gen. 1747 (14) 2

Amica nocturna — Herb. Amboin. (57) 22

Ammannia — Hort. Upsal. (7) 36

Ammannia latifolia — Demonstr. pl. (49) 4; Fl. Jam. (105) 13[as Ammania]

Ammi — Hort. Upsal. (7) 35; Odor. med. (40) 12

Ammi majus — Demonstr. pl. (49) 8; Fl. Palaest. (70) 16; Fl. Monsp. (74) 13

Ammiralis aurisiacus — Instr. mus. (51) 11

Ammiralis genuinus — Instr. mus. (51) 11

Ammiralis primarius — Instr. mus. (51) 11

Ammodytes — Surin. Grill. (16) 32, 34; Mors. serp. (119) 14[as Amodytes]; Usum hist. nat. (145) 26

Amoena moesta — Herb. Amboin. (57) 28

Amomum — Vir. pl. (13) 26; Gem. arb. (24) 8; Pl. officin. (52) 14; Nom. bot. (107) 9; Nect. fl. (122) 10; Obs. mat. med. (171) 6

Amomum cardamomum — Pl. officin. (52) 7; Herb. Amboin. (57) 20

Amomum curcuma rotunda — Iter Chin. (161) 7

Amomum grana paradisi — Fl. Cap. (99) 11

Amomum zerumbet — Herb. Amboin. (57) 20; Fl. Jam. (105) 12

Amomum zingiber — Pl. officin. (52) 20; Herb. Amboin. (57) 20; Fl. Cap. (99) 11; Fl. Jam. (105) 9, 12

Amorpha — Nova pl. gen. 1751 (32) 10

Amorpha fruticosa — Demonstr. pl. (49) 19; Somn. pl. (68) 20

Ampacus angustifolius — Herb. Amboin. (57) 10

Ampacus latifolius — Herb. Amboin. (57) 10

Ampelis garrulus — Fund. ornith. (137) 26

Amphisbaena — Hort. Upsal. (7) 43; Mus. Ad.-Frid. (11) [v], 17, 18, 19; Surin. Grill. (16) 13, 14; Taenia (19) 26

Amphisbaena amboinensis, corio quasi reticulato conspicua, squamis rubicundis obducta — Mus. Ad.-Frid. (11) 19

Amphisbaena americana ex fusco et albo variegata — Mus. Ad.-Frid. (11) 17

Amphisbaena annulis abdominalibus 200, caudalibus 30 — Surin. Grill. (16) 13

Amphisbaena ceylanica — Mus. Ad.-Frid. (11) 17

Amygdalus — Ficus (2) 22; Hort. Upsal. (7) 35; Vir. pl. (13) 32; Sem. musc. (28) 13; Pl. escul. (35) 3, 4; Acetaria (77) 9; Pand. insect. (93) 14; Nom. bot. (107) 13; Prol. pl. 1760 (114) 20

Amygdalus amara — Vir. pl. (13) 10; Pan Svec. (26) 7

Amygdalus communis — Demonstr. pl. (49) 13; Pl. officin. (52) 4; Fl. Palaest. (70) 20; Fl. Jam. (105) 24; Fr. escul. (127) 21; Hort. cul. (132) 21

Amygdalus nana — Hist. nat. Rossia (144) 22, 30

Amygdalus persica — Gem. arb. (24) 25; Demonstr. pl. (49) 13; Pl. officin. (52) 15; Fl. Palaest. (70) 20; Fl. Jam. (105) 24; Fr. escul. (127) 12; Hort. cul. (132) 21

Amygdalus sativa — Gem. arb. (24) 25

Amyris — Fl. Jam. (105) 26; Opobals. (135) 10ff.

Amyris balsamifera — Fl. Jam. (105) 15; Opobals. (135) 11ff.

Amyris elemifera — Fl. Jam. (105) 15; Opobals. (135) 10ff.

Amyris foliis bijugis — Opobals. (135) 11

Amyris foliis impari pinnatis — Opobals. (135) 11

Amyris foliis pinnatis, foliolis sessilibus — Opobals. (135) 14

Amyris foliis ternatis, acutis — Opobals. (135) 11

Amyris foliis ternatis integerrimis, pedunculis unifloris lateralibus — Opobals. (135) 13

Amyris foliis ternatis, obtusis — Opobals. (135) 11

Amyris gileadensis — Opobals. (135) 13ff.[as giliadensis]

Amyris hypelate — Fl. Jam. (105) 15

Amyris maritima — Opobals. (135) 11ff.

Amyris opobalsamum — Opobals. (135) 14

Amyris toxifera — Opobals. (135) 11ff.

Anabasis — Nova pl. gen. 1751 (32) 39, 48; Aphyteia (185) 9

Anabasis aphylla — Fl. Palaest. (70) 16

Anabasis aphylla: articulis emarginatis — Pl. rar. Camsch. (30) 14

Anabasis foliis subclavatis — Pl. rar. Camsch. (30) 15

Anacampseros — Anandria (9) 4; Pl. rar. Camsch. (30) 19

Anacampseros americana — Fl. Jam. (105) 17

Anacampseros caule arboreo, foliis cuneiformibus oppositis — Hort. Upsal. (7) 40

Anacampseros foliis acuminatis — Hort. Upsal. (7) 40

Anacardium — Vir. pl. (13) 10; Pl. escul. (35) 4; Pand. insect. (93) 14; Inebr. (117) 13; Fraga (170) 7

Anacardium occidentale — Vir. pl. (13) 4; Pl. officin. (52) 4; Herb. Amboin. (57) 8; Fl. Jam. (105) 16; Fr. escul. (127) 22; Rar. Norv. (157) 12; Colon. pl. (158) 5; Pl. Surin. (177) 8

Anacardium orientale — Vir. pl. (13) 4

Anacyclus creticus — Pl. rar. Afr. (115) 6

Anacyclus valentinus — Metam. pl. (67) 21

Anagallis — Peloria (3) 10; Hort. Upsal. (7) 34; Vern. arb. (47) 9; Stat. pl. (55) 6; Nom. bot. (107) 10

Anagallis arvensis — Demonstr. pl. (49) 5; Stat. pl. (55) 19; Fl. Angl. (56) 12; Fl. Palaest. (70) 14; Fl. Monsp. (74) 11; Prodr. fl. Dan. (82) 15; Fl. Cap. (99) 7, 12; Fl. Belg. (112) 14; Obs. mat. med. (171) 2

Anagallis caerulea — Fl. Monsp. (74) 11

Anagallis capensis — Fl. Cap. (99) 12

Anagallis latifolia — Demonstr. pl. (49) 5

Anagallis rubra — Pan Svec. (26) 17

Anagallis zeylanica, aquatica, foliis longis alternis — Nova pl. gen. 1747 (14) 11

Anagyris — Vir. pl. (13) 31, 35; Gem. arb. (24) 6; Odor. med. (40) 13

Anagyris foetida — Fl. Palaest. (70) 19; Fl. Monsp. (74) 15

Anandria — Anandria (9) 5ff.; Sem. musc. (28) 3

Anapodophyllum — Nova pl. gen. 1751 (32) 9

Anas — Oecon. nat. (20) 31, 32, [37, as 7], 40; Morb. hyeme (38) 3; Migr. avium (79) 12, 16, 23; Instr. peregr. (96) 11; Polit. nat. (109) 13; Fund. ornith. (137) 17, 18; Usum hist. nat. (145) 27

Anas acuta — Migr. avium (79) 24

Anas anser domesticus — Esca avium (174) 6ff.

Anas bernicla — Migr. avium (79) 23

Anas boschas — Calend. fl. (72) [8]; Migr. avium (79) 18, 24

Anas boschas domestica — Esca avium (174) 6ff.

Anas canadensis — Migr. avium (79) 14

Anas caudae rectricibus intermediis recurvis — Mat. med. anim. (29) 9

Anas clangula — Migr. avium (79) 24

Anas cygnus — Migr. avium (79) 23

Anas hiemalis — Migr. avium (79) 24

Anas islandica — Oecon. nat. (20) 40

Anas minor, capite purpureo — Migr. avium (79) 14

Anas mollissima — Fund. ornith. (137) 26

Anas moschata — Fund. ornith. (137) 27

Anas nigra — Migr. avium (79) 24

Anas penelope — Migr. avium (79) 18

Anas querquedula — Migr. avium (79) 25

Anas rostro semicylindrico, corpore supra cinereo, subtus albido, rectricibus margine albis — Mat. med. anim. (29) 9

Anassa — Herb. Amboin. (57) 21

Anastatica — Hort. Upsal. (7) 36; Sem. musc. (28) 12; Siren. lacert. (146) 7; Usum musc. (148) 3

Anastatica hierocuntica — Demonstr. pl. (49) 17[as hierocunthea]; Fl. Palaest. (70) 23

Anblatum — Fung. melit. (69) 3, 6

Anchusa — Vir. pl. (13) 18; Pl. escul. (35) 9, 28; Cul. mut. (88) 4; Nom. bot. (107) 10; Nect. fl. (122) 7

Anchusa angustifolia — Prodr. fl. Dan. (82) 14

Anchusa angustifolia, verticillis longis aculeis armata — Cent. II. pl. (66) 22

Anchusa buglossum — Pan Svec. (26) 16

Anchusa officinalis — Herbat. Upsal. (50) 13; Pl. officin. (52) 6; Stat. pl. (55) 20; Fl. Angl. (56) 6[as officinarum]; Calend. fl. (72) [11]; Fl. Monsp. (74) 11; Prodr. fl. Dan. (82) 14; Pl. tinct. (97) 13; Fl. Belg. (112) 14; Mac. olit. (113) 19; Usum hist. nat. (145) 10; Fl. Åker. (162) 8; Pand. fl. Ryb. (165) 17

Anchusa orientalis — Fl. Palaest. (70) 14

Anchusa sempervirens — Fl. Angl. (56) 12

Anchusa undulata — Fl. Palaest. (70) 14

Andrachne — Hort. Upsal. (7) 37; Vir. pl. (13) 27; Nect. fl. (122) 7

Andrachne telephioides — Demonstr. pl. (49) 26

Andromeda — Spons. pl. (12) 33; Vir. pl. (13) 20; Pan Svec. (26) 9; Fl. Angl. (56) 6; Oves (61) 17; Fr. Svec. (91) [ii]; Erica (163) 3, 4; Ledum (178) [1]

Andromeda caerulea — Pan Svec. (26) 22[as coerulea]; Herbat. Upsal. (50) 6; Stat. pl. (55) 15; Cervus (60) 7; Fl. alp. (71) 16[as coerulea]; Rar. Norv. (157) 10

Andromeda calyculata — Fr. Svec. (91) 5, 21; Hist. nat. Rossia (144) 29; Colon. pl. (158) 7[as calcyculata]

Andromeda daboecia — Erica (163) 4

Andromeda droseroides — Erica (163) 4

Andromeda foliis linearibus obtusis sparsis — Pl. Mart.-Burs. (6) 31

Andromeda foliis ovatis obtusis, corollis corymbosis — Pan Svec. (26) 9

Andromeda foliis ovatis obtusis, corollis corymbosis infundibuliformibus, genitalibus declinatis — Pan Svec. (26) 9; Nova pl. gen. 1751 (32) 19

Andromeda hypnoides — Stat. pl. (55) 15; Cervus (60) 7; Fl. alp. (71) 16; Rar. Norv. (157) 10

Andromeda muscosa — Pan Svec. (26) 22

Andromeda palustris — Gem. arb. (24) 16

Andromeda polifolia — Stat. pl. (55) 15[as Andromaeda]; Fl. Angl. (56) 15; Oves (61) 17; Fung. melit. (69) 2; Prodr. fl. Dan. (82) 17; Fl. Åker. (162) 11

Andromeda tetragona — Stat. pl. (55) 15; Fl. alp. (71) 16; Fr. Svec. (91) 5, 21

Andromeda triquetra — Pan Svec. (26) 22

Andromeda vulgaris — Pan Svec. (26) 22

Andropogon — Pl. Jam. (102) 7; Fund. agrost. (152) 27, 30, 36

Andropogon alopecuroides — Cent. II. pl. (66) 6

Andropogon barbatum — Pl. Jam. (102) 30; Fl. Jam. (105) 22

Andropogon bicorne — Fl. Jam. (105) 22

Andropogon fasciculatum — Fl. Jam. (105) 22

Andropogon gryllus — Cent. II. pl. (66) 33

Andropogon insulare — Pl. Jam. (102) 30; Fl. Jam. (105) 22

Andropogon ischaemum — Fl. Monsp. (74) 28

Andropogon nardus — Fl. Palaest. (70) 31

Andropogon paniculae pedunculis simplicissimis, trifloris: flosculo hermaphrodito aristato ciliato basi barbato — Cent. II. pl. (66) 33

Andropogon ravennae — Fund. agrost. (152) 30

Andropogon schoenanthus — Herb. Amboin. (57) 20; Fl. Palaest. (70) 31

Andropogon virgineum — Fl. Jam. (105) 22

Androsace — Pl. Mart.-Burs. (6) 24; Hort. Upsal. (7) 34; Anandria (9) 4

Androsace carnea — Fl. alp. (71) 13

Androsace caulescens, foliis alternis, pedunculis unifloris — Pl. Mart.-Burs. (6) 24

Androsace halleri — Fl. alp. (71) 13

Androsace lactea — Fl. alp. (71) 13

Androsace maxima — Demonstr. pl. (49) 5

Androsace minor — Pan Svec. (26) 16

Androsace septentrionalis — Herbat. Upsal. (50) 10; Stat. pl. (55) 21[as Androcace]; Fl. Angl. (56) 6; Fl. alp. (71) 13

Androsace villosa — Fl. alp. (71) 13

Androsaemum — Hypericum (186) 8, 13

Andryala foliis inferioribus dentatis, summis integris — Pl. Mart.-Burs. (6) 8

Andryala integrifolia — Fl. Monsp. (74) 24; Pl. rar. Afr. (115) 6

Andryala lanata — Pl. rar. Afr. (115) 6

Anemone — Peloria (3) 9; Pl. Mart.-Burs. (6) [vi]; Hort. Upsal. (7) 34; Anandria (9) 5; Vir. pl. (13) 21, 30; Fl. oecon. (17) 15; Metam. pl. (67) 17; Nom. bot. (107) 14; Prol. pl. 1760 (114) 13, 18; Fund. fr. (123) 11, 12; Prol. pl. 1763 (130) 18; Pand. fl. Ryb. (165) 20

Anemone alpina — Fl. alp. (71) 18

Anemone apennina — Fl. Angl. (56) 18; Fl. alp. (71) 18

Anemone caule dichotomo, foliis sessilibus amplexicaulibus palmatis — Pl. Mart.-Burs. (6) 13; Pl. rar. Camsch. (30) 5

Anemone coronaria — Demonstr. pl. (49) 15; Fl. Palaest. (70) 22; Pl. rar. Afr. (115) 6; Hort. cul. (132) 25

Anemone dichotoma — Hist. nat. Rossia (144) 12, 30

Anemone hepatica — Herbat. Upsal. (50) 7; Pl. officin. (52) 11; Stat. pl. (55) 18; Fl. Angl. (56) 6; Cervus (60) 8; Calend. fl. (72) [9], [10]; Fl. Monsp. (74) 18; Prodr. fl. Dan. (82) 19; Hort. cul. (132) 24, 25; Fl. Åker. (162) 13; Pand. fl. Ryb. (165) 19

Anemone hepatica plena — Demonstr. pl. (49) 15

Anemone lutea — Pan Svec. (26) 25

Anemone narcissifolia — Fl. alp. (71) 18; Hist. nat. Rossia (144) 30

Anemone nemorosa — Pan Svec. (26) 25; Vern. arb. (47) 8; Herbat. Upsal. (50) 7; Pl. officin. (52) 16; Stat. pl. (55) 18; Fl. Angl. (56) 18; Oves (61) 17; Calend. fl. (72) [9], [10]; Fl. Monsp. (74) 18; Migr. avium (79) 34; Prodr. fl. Dan. (82) 19; Fl. Belg. (112) 18; Usum hist. nat. (145) 18, 20; Fl. Åker. (162) 13; Pand. fl. Ryb. (165) 19; Esca avium (174) 13

Anemone nemorosa flore majore — Pl. Mart.-Burs. (6) 12[as Animone]

Anemone oelandica — Pan Svec. (26) 25

Anemone patens — Hist. nat. Rossia (144) 30

Anemone pulsatilla — Herbat. Upsal. (50) 11; Pl. officin. (52) 16; Stat. pl. (55) 22; Fl. Angl. (56) 18; Hort. acad. (63) 10; Calend. fl. (72) [9], [13]; Fl. Monsp. (74) 18; Prodr. fl. Dan. (82) 19; Pl. tinct. (97) 20

Anemone ranunculoides — Demonstr. pl. (49) 15; Calend. fl. (72) [9]; Prodr. fl. Dan. (82) 19; Fl. Belg. (112) 18

Anemone sibirica — Hist. nat. Rossia (144) 30

Anemone sylvestris — Colon. pl. (158) 6

Anemone trifolia — Demonstr. pl. (49) 15

Anemone vernalis — Herbat. Upsal. (50) 16; Stat. pl. (55) 18; Hort. acad. (63) 10; Prodr. fl. Dan. (82) 19; Rar. Norv. (157) 11[as verna]

Anemone virginiana — Demonstr. pl. (49) 15[as virginica]; Calend. fl. (72) [17]

Anemonospermos afra, foliis et facie taraxaci incanis — Pl. hybr. (33) 8

Anemonospermos africana, jacobeae maritimae foliis, flore sulphureo — Pl. hybr. (33) 8

Anemonospermos foliis rigidis tenuiter divisis subtus incanis — Pl. rar. Afr. (115) 24

Anethum — Vir. pl. (13) 19, 31; Odor. med. (40) 13; Pand. insect. (93) 13; Nom. bot. (107) 11; Inebr. (117) 9

Anethum foeniculum — Pl. officin. (52) 10; Fl. Angl. (56) 13; Calend. fl. (72) [22][as faeniculum]; Fl. Monsp. (74) 13; Fl. Cap. (99) 2; Fl. Jam. (105) 24; Fl. Belg. (112) 15; Hort. cul. (132) 14

Anethum graveolens — Hosp. insect. fl. (43) 19; Demonstr. pl. (49) 8; Pl. officin. (52) 4; Fl. Palaest. (70) 16; Hort. cul. (132) 14

Angelica — Vir. pl. (13) 19; Fl. oecon. (17) 7; Pan Svec. (26) 3; Sapor. med. (31) 19; Pl. escul. (35) 28; Odor. med. (40) 14; Pand. insect. (93) 13

Angelica alpina — Pan Svec. (26) 19; Pl. escul. (35) 11

Angelica alpina alpha — Hosp. insect. fl. (43) 19

Angelica archangelica — Demonstr. pl. (49) 8; Pl. officin. (52) 4; Stat. pl. (55) 16; Fl. Angl. (56) 13; Fl. alp. (71) 15, 24; Prodr. fl. Dan. (82) 16; Mac. olit. (113) 14; Rar. Norv. (157) 13; Fl. Åker. (162) 9; Pand. fl. Ryb. (165) 17, 21

Angelica sylvestris — Pan Svec. (26) 19[as sylvatica]; Herbat. Upsal. (50) 19; Pl. officin. (52) 4; Stat. pl. (55) 15; Fl. Angl. (56) 13; Fl. Monsp. (74) 13; Prodr. fl. Dan. (82) 16; Fl. Belg. (112) 15; Pand. fl. Ryb. (165) 17

Angelica sylvestris hirsuta inodora — Pl. Mart.-Burs. (6) 10

Angiopteris — Nova pl. gen. 1751 (32) 10, [13, as 15], 34

Angraecum album — Herb. Amboin. (57) 27

Angraecum caninum — Herb. Amboin. (57) 27

Angraecum flavum — Herb. Amboin. (57) 27

Angraecum furvum — Herb. Amboin. (57) 27

Angraecum nervosum — Herb. Amboin. (57) 27

Angraecum purpureum — Herb. Amboin. (57) 27

Angraecum quintum — Herb. Amboin. (57) 27

Angraecum rubrum — Herb. Amboin. (57) 27

Angraecum scriptum — Herb. Amboin. (57) 27

Angraecum sexatile — Herb. Amboin. (57) 27

Angraecum terrestre — Herb. Amboin. (57) 27

Anguiculus africanus coeruleus — Mus. Ad.-Frid. (11) 25

Anguiculus surinamensis cyaneus — Surin. Grill. (16) 15

Anguilla — Cul. mut. (88) 9; Polit. nat. (109) 12; Usum hist. nat. (145) 26

Anguis — Amphib. Gyll. (5) [1], 2, 4, 8; Mus. Ad.-Frid. (11) 6; Spons. pl. (12) 23; Lepra (140) 10

Anguis annulis abdominalibus 200 annulis caudalibus 30 — Mus. Ad.-Frid. (11) 17

Anguis bicolor elegantissimus malabaricus — Amphib. Gyll. (5) 10

Anguis borneocus, viridis, familiaris, pertenuis — Amphib. Gyll. (5) 7

Anguis cinerea, macula dorsi fusca longitudinaliter dentata — Amphib. Gyll. (5) 6

Anguis coluber — Amphib. Gyll. (5) 8

Anguis conspicillo insignita — Lign. colubr. (21) 6

Anguis de cencoatel americanus venustissimus — Mus. Ad.-Frid. (11) 28

Anguis scutellis abdominalibus 142, caudalibus 74 — Mus. Ad.-Frid. (11) 23

Anguis scutis abdominalibus 118, caudalibus 61 — Amphib. Gyll. (5) 10

Anguis scutis abdominalibus 124, caudalibus 60 — Amphib. Gyll. (5) 12

Anguis scutis abdominalibus 128, squamis caudalibus 46 — Mus. Ad.-Frid. (11) 23

Anguis scutis abdominalibus 144, caudalibus 39 — Amphib. Gyll. (5) 5

Anguis scutis abdominalibus 150, caudalibus 54 — Amphib. Gyll. (5) 9

Anguis scutis abdominalibus 150, squamis caudalibus 54 — Mus. Ad.-Frid. (11) 24

Anguis scutis abdominalibus 152, squamis caudalibus 135 — Mus. Ad.-Frid. (11) 24

Anguis scutis abdominalibus 160, squamis caudalibus 100 — Mus. Ad.-Frid. (11) 24

Anguis scutis abdominalibus 162, caudalibus 150 —
    Amphib. Gyll. (5) 7

Anguis scutis abdominalibus 165, caudalibus 24 —
    Mus. Ad.-Frid. (11) 25

Anguis scutis abdominalibus 165, caudalibus 30 —
    Mus. Ad.-Frid. (11) 20

Anguis scutis abdominalibus 177, caudalibus 85 —
    Amphib. Gyll. (5) 8

Anguis scutis abdominalibus 180, squamis caudalibus
    85 — Mus. Ad.-Frid. (11) 26

Anguis scutis abdominalibus 184, caudalibus 50 —
    Mus. Ad.-Frid. (11) 26

Anguis scutis abdominalibus 186, caudalibus 64 —
    Amphib. Gyll. (5) 14; Mus. Ad.-Frid. (11) 27

Anguis scutis abdominalibus 190, caudalibus 98 —
    Mus. Ad.-Frid. (11) 27

Anguis scutis abdominalibus 196, squamis caudalibus
    67 — Mus. Ad.-Frid. (11) 27

Anguis scutis abdominalibus 207, caudalibus 85 —
    Amphib. Gyll. (5) 13; Mus. Ad.-Frid. (11) 28

Anguis scutis abdominalibus 209, squamis caudalibus
    90 — Mus. Ad.-Frid. (11) 28

Anguis scutis abdominalibus 217, squamis caudalibus
    108 — Mus. Ad.-Frid. (11) 22

Anguis scutis abdominalibus 220, squamis caudalibus
    124 — Mus. Ad.-Frid. (11) 28

Anguis scutis abdominalibus 250, caudalibus 35 —
    Amphib. Gyll. (5) 11; Mus. Ad.-Frid. (11) 26

Anguis scutis abdominalibus 250, squamis caudalibus
    35 — Surin. Grill. (16) 14

Anguis squamis abdominalibus 230, caudalibus 13 —
    Surin. Grill. (16) 13

Anguis squamis abdominalibus 240, caudalibus 13 —
    Mus. Ad.-Frid. (11) 19

Anguis stupidus — Surin. Grill. (16) 20

Anguis vulgaris fuscus, collo flavescente, ventre albis
    maculis distincto — Amphib. Gyll. (5) 8

Anguria indica — Herb. Amboin. (57) 23

Anguria lobata — Pl. Surin. (177) 15

Anil, seu nil indorum color — Nova pl. gen. 1747
    (14) 25

Animal moschiferum — Mat. med. anim. (29) 6

Animal zibethicum — Mat. med. anim. (29) 4

Animalculum cynocephalum ceylanicum tardigradum
    — Mus. Ad.-Frid. (11) 2

Anisifolium — Herb. Amboin. (57) 9

Anisum — Vir. pl. (13) 19

Anisum moluccanum — Herb. Amboin. (57) 9

Anisum stellatum — Opobals. (135) 2

Annona — Pl. escul. (35) 4; Herb. Amboin. (57) 7[as
    Anona]; Nom. bot. (107) 14[as Anona]; Fr. escul.
    (127) 9[as Anona]; Pl. Surin. (177) 10

Annona africana — Demonstr. pl. (49) 15; Fl. Cap.
    (99) 15

Annona discreta — Pl. Surin. (177) 11

Annona jacca — Fr. escul. (127) 9[as Anona]

Annona muricata — Demonstr. pl. (49) 15; Fl. Jam.
    (105) 17; Pl. Surin. (177) 10

Annona reticulata — Herb. Amboin. (57) 7; Fl. Jam.
    (105) 17

Annona squamosa — Herb. Amboin. (57) 7[as
    Anona]; Fl. Jam. (105) 17; Pl. Surin. (177) 10

Annona tuberosa — Herb. Amboin. (57) 7

Anomia — Nat. pelagi (84) 8; Fund. test. (166) 18,
    35, 42, 43

Anomia cepa — Fund. test. (166) 42

Anomia craniolaris — Fund. test. (166) 43

Anonis pusilla glabra fruticans, trifoliis affinis — Pl.
    Mart.-Burs. (6) 29

Anonyma — Nova pl. gen. 1751 (32) 20

Anonyma pedunculis arcuatis — Nova pl. gen. 1751
    (32) 21

Anser — Pan Svec. (26) 11; Migr. avium (79) 23;
    Fund. ornith. (137) 27; Usum hist. nat. (145) 24

Anser domesticus — Mat. med. anim. (29) 9

Anser leucorinchos — Hist. nat. Rossia (144) 16

Anseri bassano affinis fusca avis — Chin. Lagerstr.
    (64) 11

Anseri bassano congener cinereo albus — Chin.
    Lagerstr. (64) 12[as cineraeo]

Anserina — Nom. bot. (107) 14

Anthelminthia quadrifolia, spicis terminalibus et e
    centro frondis — Spigelia (89) 12

Anthemis — Fl. oecon. (17) 20; Gem. arb. (24) 13

Anthemis alpina — Cent. II. pl. (66) 31

Anthemis altissima — Fl. Monsp. (74) 26; Pl. rar.
    Afr. (115) 6

Anthemis arvensis — Pan Svec. (26) 33; Herbat.
    Upsal. (50) 13; Stat. pl. (55) 19; Fl. Angl. (56) 22;
    Fl. Monsp. (74) 26; Prodr. fl. Dan. (82) 23; Fl.
    Belg. (112) 21; Fl. Åker. (162) 18; Esca avium
    (174) 14

Anthemis bellidiastrum — Pl. rar. Afr. (115) 24

Anthemis bellidioides — Fl. Cap. (99) 18

Anthemis capensis — Fl. Cap. (99) 18

Anthemis cotula — Herbat. Upsal. (50) 20; Pl.
    officin. (52) 8; Stat. pl. (55) 20; Fl. Angl. (56) 22;
    Calend. fl. (72) [13]; Fl. Monsp. (74) 26; Specif.
    Canad. (76) 16; Prodr. fl. Dan. (82) 23; Fl. Belg.
    (112) 21; Hist. nat. Rossia (144) 17; Fl. Åker. (162)
    18; Pand. fl. Ryb. (165) 22

Anthemis cretica — Fl. Palaest. (70) 28

Anthemis foetida — Pan Svec. (26) 33

Anthemis foliis dentato-pinnatis linearibus
    integerrimis, caule villoso unifloro, paleis
    sphacelatis, petalis ovatis — Cent. II. pl. (66) 31

Anthemis frondosa — Metam. pl. (67) 21

Anthemis fruticosa — Cent. II. pl. (66) 31; Fl. Cap.
    (99) 18

Anthemis leucantha — Pl. rar. Afr. (115) 23

Anthemis maritima — Fl. Monsp. (74) 26

Anthemis millefolia — Demonstr. pl. (49) 23; Hist. nat. Rossia (144) 33

Anthemis nobilis — Pl. officin. (52) 7; Fl. Angl. (56) 22

Anthemis noveboracensis — Specif. Canad. (76) 16

Anthemis pyrethrum — Demonstr. pl. (49) 23; Fl. Monsp. (74) 26

Anthemis suffruticosa, foliis linearibus triquetris tomentosis indivisis, floribus sessilibus — Cent. II. pl. (66) 31

Anthemis suffruticosa, foliis sublanceolatis, dentatis acutis indivisis — Pl. rar. Afr. (115) 23

Anthemis tinctoria — Demonstr. pl. (49) 23; Stat. pl. (55) 22; Fl. Angl. (56) 22; Calend. fl. (72) [14]; Fl. Monsp. (74) 26; Pl. tinct. (97) 24; Fl. Belg. (112) 21

Anthemis tinctoria alba — Calend. fl. (72) [22]

Anthemis triumfetti — Demonstr. pl. (49) 23; Calend. fl. (72) [13][as triumphetti]

Anthemis valentina — Calend. fl. (72) [15], [22]; Fl. Monsp. (74) 26; Fl. Belg. (112) 21

Anthericum — Hort. Upsal. (7) 33; Fl. oecon. (17) 8; Pan Svec. (26) 9; Fl. Cap. (99) 7; Pl. rar. Afr. (115) 4; Fund. fr. (123) 18

Anthericum album — Pan Svec. (26) 20

Anthericum aloides — Fl. Cap. (99) 9, 13

Anthericum annuum — Demonstr. pl. (49) 10; Fl. Cap. (99) 13

Anthericum asphodeloides — Demonstr. pl. (49) 10; Fl. Cap. (99) 13

Anthericum calyculatum — Pan Svec. (26) 20; Stat. pl. (55) 16; Fl. Angl. (56) 14; Fl. alp. (71) 15; Hist. nat. Rossia (144) 28; Colon. pl. (158) 6

Anthericum frutescens — Fl. Cap. (99) 13

Anthericum liliago — Demonstr. pl. (49) 10; Fl. Monsp. (74) 14; Hort. cul. (132) 24

Anthericum ossifragum — Pan Svec. (26) 20; Vern. arb. (47) 19; Demonstr. pl. (49) 10; Stat. pl. (55) 14; Fl. Angl. (56) 14; Oves (61) 17; Calend. fl. (72) [14]; Prodr. fl. Dan. (82) 16; Fl. Belg. (112) 15; Usum hist. nat. (145) 22

Anthericum ramosum — Demonstr. pl. (49) 10; Fl. Monsp. (74) 14; Prodr. fl. Dan. (82) 16

Antholyza — Vir. pl. (13) 26; Fl. Cap. (99) 6; Pl. rar. Afr. (115) 4; Pl. Alstr. (121) 6; Fund. fr. (123) 18

Antholyza aethiopica — Fl. Cap. (99) 11

Antholyza cunonia — Demonstr. pl. (49) 2; Fl. Cap. (99) 11

Antholyza meriana — Fl. Cap. (99) 11

Antholyza ringens — Fl. Cap. (99) 11

Anthora — Vir. pl. (13) 21

Anthospermum — Fl. Cap. (99) 6

Anthospermum aethiopicum — Fl. Cap. (99) 19

Anthoxanthon — Fl. Angl. (56) 26[under Lapathum]

Anthoxanthum — Vir. pl. (13) 16; Fl. oecon. (17) 2[as Anthoxantum]; Fund. agrost. (152) 22, 27, 36

Anthoxanthum floribus paniculatis — Pl. Mart.-Burs. (6) 2[as Anthoxathum]

Anthoxanthum odoratum — Herbat. Upsal. (50) 8; Fl. Angl. (56) 9; Cervus (60) 7; Fl. Monsp. (74) 8; Prodr. fl. Dan. (82) 13; Fl. Belg. (112) 12; Fl. Åker. (162) 5[as Anthoxantum]; Pand. fl. Ryb. (165) 16

Anthoxanthum vulgare — Pan Svec. (26) 12

Anthyllis — Nova pl. gen. 1747 (14) 12; Fl. oecon. (17) 18

Anthyllis altera italorum — Nova pl. gen. 1747 (14) 9

Anthyllis barba-jovis — Demonstr. pl. (49) 19; Fl. Monsp. (74) 22

Anthyllis foliis pinnatis, foliolis aequalibus — Pl. Mart.-Burs. (6) 27[as Antyllis]

Anthyllis fruticosa, foliis ternatis aequalibus, capitulis terminalibus sessilibus — Cent. II. pl. (66) 27

Anthyllis hermanniae — Fl. Palaest. (70) 25

Anthyllis lotoides — Cent. II. pl. (66) 27

Anthyllis montana — Fl. Monsp. (74) 22

Anthyllis pratensis — Pan Svec. (26) 30

Anthyllis tetraphylla — Demonstr. pl. (49) 19; Fl. Monsp. (74) 22

Anthyllis valentina — Fl. Belg. (112) 10

Anthyllis vulneraria — Herbat. Upsal. (50) 15; Stat. pl. (55) 22[as Anthyllus]; Fl. Angl. (56) 20; Hort. acad. (63) 10; Fl. Monsp. (74) 22; Prodr. fl. Dan. (82) 21; Pl. tinct. (97) 10[as vulneria], 22; Pand. fl. Ryb. (165) 21

Anticholerica — Herb. Amboin. (57) 5, 16

Antidesma — Amphib. Gyll. (5) 3; Anandria (9) 6; Spons. pl. (12) 30; Nova pl. gen. 1747 (14) [vi], 30

Antidesma femina — Nova pl. gen. 1747 (14) 31

Antidesma mas — Nova pl. gen. 1747 (14) 30

Antidesma spicis geminis — Nova pl. gen. 1747 (14) 30

Antirrhinum — Peloria (3) 7; Fl. oecon. (17) 16; Pl. hybr. (33) 7; Fl. Monsp. (74) 7; Nom. bot. (107) 15; Nect. fl. (122) 12; Pand. fl. Ryb. (165) 20

Antirrhinum alpinum — Fl. alp. (71) 20

Antirrhinum arvense — Demonstr. pl. (49) 16; Fl. Angl. (56) 19; Fl. Monsp. (74) 20

Antirrhinum asarina — Metam. pl. (67) 13; Fl. Monsp. (74) 20

Antirrhinum bellidifolium — Metam. pl. (67) 14; Fl. Monsp. (74) 20

Antirrhinum bicorne — Pl. rar. Afr. (115) 11

Antirrhinum bipunctatum — Fl. Monsp. (74) 20

Antirrhinum chalepense — Fl. Palaest. (70) 23[as Anthirrhinum]; Fl. Monsp. (74) 20; Pl. rar. Afr. (115) 6

Antirrhinum cymbalaria — Pl. hybr. (33) 22[as Anthirrhinum … dictum], 27[as … dictum]; Demonstr. pl. (49) 16; Fl. Angl. (56) 19[as cymballaria]; Fl. Belg. (112) 10, 19; Colon. pl. (158) 9[as Antirrhinium]

Antirrhinum elatine — Demonstr. pl. (49) 16; Fl. Angl. (56) 19; Fl. Monsp. (74) 20

Antirrhinum foliis hastatis alternis, caule flaccido — Pl. hybr. (33) 22, 27

Antirrhinum foliis lanceolatis obtusis alteris, caule diffuso ramosissimo — Pl. Mart.-Burs. (6) 18

Antirrhinum foliis lanceolato-linearibus confertis, caule erecto, spicis terminatricibus sessilibus, floribus imbricatis — Peloria (3) 7

Antirrhinum foliis lanceolato-linearibus sparsis villosis: inferioribus quaternis; caule decumbente piloso, floribus spicatis — Cent. I. pl. (65) 16

Antirrhinum foliis linearibus alternis, caule paniculato virgato, floribus racemosis — Cent. I. pl. (65) 17

Antirrhinum foliis linearibus ascendentibus congestis, ramis spica florali densa terminatis — Peloria (3) 7

Antirrhinum foliis linearibus sparsis — Peloria (3) 7

Antirrhinum foliis oppositis oblongis serratis, caule erecto, floribus racemosis, capsulis bicornibus — Pl. rar. Afr. (115) 11

Antirrhinum foliis ovatis alternis, caule flaccido — Pl. hybr. (33) 22

Antirrhinum foliis quaternis subulatis, caulibus erectis — Cent. I. pl. (65) 16

Antirrhinum foliis radicalibus quaternis lanceolatis, caulinis linearibus solitariis, calycibus villosis cauli approximatis — Cent. II. pl. (66) 21

Antirrhinum genistifolium — Hist. nat. Rossia (144) 31

Antirrhinum hirtum — Demonstr. pl. (49) 16

Antirrhinum hybridum — Fl. Angl. (56) 19; Fl. Belg. (112) 19

Antirrhinum linaria — Pan Svec. (26) 27; Hosp. insect. fl. (43) 27; Herbat. Upsal. (50) 17; Pl. officin. (52) 12; Stat. pl. (55) 21[as Anthirrhinum]; Fl. Angl. (56) 19; Cervus (60) 8; Metam. pl. (67) 13[as linuria]; Calend. fl. (72) [13][as Anthirhinum]; Prodr. fl. Dan. (82) 20; Fl. Belg. (112) 19; Rar. Norv. (157) 16; Fl. Åker. (162) 15; Pand. fl. Ryb. (165) 20

Antirrhinum majus — Demonstr. pl. (49) 16; Pl. officin. (52) 4; Metam. pl. (67) 13; Fl. Monsp. (74) 20; Hort. cul. (132) 24

Antirrhinum minus — Demonstr. pl. (49) 16; Herbat. Upsal. (50) 20; Fl. Angl. (56) 19; Prodr. fl. Dan. (82) 20; Fl. Belg. (112) 19

Antirrhinum molle — Demonstr. pl. (49) 16; Cent. I. pl. (65) 16

Antirrhinum monspeliense [error for monspessulanum?] — Fl. Monsp. (74) 20

Antirrhinum monspessulanum — Fl. Angl. (56) 19; see also A. monspeliense

Antirrhinum multicaule — Demonstr. pl. (49) 16

Antirrhinum origanifolium — Fl. alp. (71) 20; Fl. Monsp. (74) 20

Antirrhinum orontium — Demonstr. pl. (49) 16; Fl. Angl. (56) 19; Fl. Monsp. (74) 20; Prodr. fl. Dan. (82) 20; Fl. Belg. (112) 19

Antirrhinum pelisserianum — Fl. Monsp. (74) 20

Antirrhinum saxatile — Cent. I. pl. (65) 16

Antirrhinum sparteum — Demonstr. pl. (49) 16[as spartum]; Cent. I. pl. (65) 17[as spartum]

Antirrhinum spurium — Demonstr. pl. (49) 16; Fl. Monsp. (74) 20; Fl. Cap. (99) 7, 15

Antirrhinum supinum — Fl. Monsp. (74) 20

Antirrhinum triphyllum — Demonstr. pl. (49) 16; Metam. pl. (67) 14

Antirrhinum upsaliense — Pan Svec. (26) 27

Antirrhinum viscosum — Cent. II. pl. (66) 21

Antribus — Fund. entom. (154) 30

Aparine — Vir. pl. (13) 17; Fl. oecon. (17) 4; Nom. bot. (107) 10

Aparine floribus in capillamenta abeuntibus — Fl. Palaest. (70) 13[under Galium, as fl. capillam.]

Aparine foliis lineari lanceolatis acuminatis flaccidis, corollis fructu minoribus — Pl. Mart.-Burs. (6) 25

Aparine parisiense — Pan Svec. (26) 15

Aparine semine verrucoso — Pl. Mart.-Burs. (6) 25

Aparine vulgaris — Pan Svec. (26) 15; Hosp. insect. fl. (43) 16

Aper — Mat. med. anim. (29) 6; Cui bono? (42) 24

Aphaca — Hort. Upsal. (7) 34

Aphanes — Vir. pl. (13) 27; Fund. fr. (123) 23; Fraga (170) [1], 2, 3

Aphanes arvensis — Fl. Angl. (56) 11; Fl. Monsp. (74) 10; Prodr. fl. Dan. (82) 14; Fl. Belg. (112) 13

Aphanes smolandica — Pan Svec. (26) 16

Aphis — Peloria (3) 14; Spons. pl. (12) 13; Oecon. nat. (20) 28, 29, 41; Mirac. insect. (45) 15; Noxa insect. (46) 20, 21, 25, 26; Hort. acad. (63) 19; Pl. tinct. (97) 28; Polit. nat. (109) 8, 10; Mund. invis. (149) 10; Fund. entom. (154) 7, 18, 22, 24

Aphis absinthii — Pand. insect. (93) 18[as absintii]

Aphis aceris — Hosp. insect. fl. (43) 20; Pand. insect. (93) 22

Aphis antennis longis, alis magnis — Hosp. insect. fl. (43) 22

Aphis aquatilis — Pand. insect. (93) 16

Aphis artemisiae — Hosp. insect. fl. (43) 31

Aphis atriplicis — Pand. insect. (93) 22

Aphis atriplicis viridis, oculis atris — Hosp. insect. fl. (43) 39

Aphis betulae — Hosp. insect. fl. (43) 33; Pand. insect. (93) 19

Aphis brassicae — Hosp. insect. fl. (43) 28; Pand. insect. (93) [17, as 38]

Aphis bursana [error for bursaria?] — Pand. insect. (93) 22

Aphis bursaria — see A. bursana

Aphis cardui — Hosp. insect. fl. (43) 30; Pand. insect. (93) 18

Aphis centaureae — Hosp. insect. fl. (43) 31

Aphis cirsii — Pand. insect. (93) 18

Aphis craccae — Pand. insect. (93) [17, as 38]

Aphis cucubali — Hosp. insect. fl. (43) 21; Pand.
  insect. (93) 14

Aphis fusca, albo maculata, caudis rubris — Hosp.
  insect. fl. (43) 37

Aphis jaceae — Pand. insect. (93) 18

Aphis lactucae — Pand. insect. (93) 18

Aphis livida, punctis lateralibus quinque niveis —
  Hosp. insect. fl. (43) 38

Aphis mali — Hosp. insect. fl. (43) 24; Pand. insect.
  (93) 15

Aphis minimus — Cui bono? (42) 9

Aphis nigro plumbea — Hosp. insect. fl. (43) 29

Aphis padi — Pand. insect. (93) 14; Pand. fl. Ryb.
  (165) 10

Aphis pastinacae — Hosp. insect. fl. (43) 19; Pand.
  insect. (93) 13

Aphis pini — Hosp. insect. fl. (43) 36; Pand. insect.
  (93) 21

Aphis plantarum aquaticarum — Hosp. insect. fl. (43)
  16, 26

Aphis populi — Pand. insect. (93) 22

Aphis populi nigrae — Hosp. insect. fl. (43) 38

Aphis populi tremulae — Noxa insect. (46) 21

Aphis populnea — Mirac. insect. (45) 14

Aphis pruni — Hosp. insect. fl. (43) 22

Aphis pyri — Hosp. insect. fl. (43) 23; Pand. insect.
  (93) 15

Aphis quercus — Pand. insect. (93) 20

Aphis ribis — Hosp. insect. fl. (43) 17, 18; Pand.
  insect. (93) 12; Pand. fl. Ryb. (165) 10

Aphis roboris — Pand. insect. (93) 20

Aphis rosae — Hosp. insect. fl. (43) 25; Pand. insect.
  (93) 15

Aphis rumicis — Hosp. insect. fl. (43) 20; Pand.
  insect. (93) 13

Aphis salicis — Noxa insect. (46) 21; Pand. insect.
  (93) 21; Pand. fl. Ryb. (165) 10

Aphis sambuci — Hosp. insect. fl. (43) 19; Pand.
  insect. (93) 13

Aphis serratulae — Hosp. insect. fl. (43) 30

Aphis sonchi — Hosp. insect. fl. (43) 30; Pand.
  insect. (93) 18

Aphis tanaceti — Pand. insect. (93) 18

Aphis tanaceti rufa — Hosp. insect. fl. (43) 31

Aphis tiliae — Hosp. insect. fl. (43) 26; Pand. insect.
  (93) 16

Aphis ulmi — Hosp. insect. fl. (43) 18; Pand. insect.
  (93) 12

Aphis urticae — Pand. insect. (93) 19

Aphis viciae — Noxa insect. (46) 21

Aphrodita nitens — Mus. Ad.-Frid. (11) 47

Aphyllanthes — Fl. Monsp. (74) 7; Fund. agrost.
  (152) 4

Aphyllanthes monspeliensis — Fl. Monsp. (74) 14

Aphyllon — Nova pl. gen. 1751 (32) 12

Aphyteia — Aphyteia (185) 7ff.

Aphyteia hydnora — Aphyteia (185) 10ff.

Apios — Euphorbia (36) 3

Apis — Spons. pl. (12) 50; Oecon. nat. (20) 16, 25,
  39; Lign. colubr. (21) 5; Mat. med. anim. (29) 16;
  Hosp. insect. fl. (43) 13; Noxa insect. (46) 11, 17,
  31; Chin. Lagerstr. (64) 34; Exanth. viva (86) 15;
  Pand. insect. (93) 5, 6, 8; Instr. peregr. (96) 11;
  Polit. nat. (109) 19; Mors. serp. (119) 2; Usum hist.
  nat. (145) 28; Mund. invis. (149) 10; Fund. entom.
  (154) 10, 13, 22, 23, 27; Ledum (178) 12

Apis acervorum — Pand. fl. Ryb. (165) 13

Apis annulata — Pand. fl. Ryb. (165) 13

Apis bicornis — Pand. fl. Ryb. (165) 13

Apis centuncularis — Pand. fl. Ryb. (165) 13

Apis conica — Pand. fl. Ryb. (165) 13

Apis cribraria — Mirac. insect. (45) 16

Apis cunicularia — Pand. fl. Ryb. (165) 13

Apis florisomnis — Pand. fl. Ryb. (165) 13

Apis gregaria — Mat. med. anim. (29) 16

Apis helvola — Pand. fl. Ryb. (165) 13

Apis hortorum — Pand. fl. Ryb. (165) 13

Apis hypnorum — Pand. fl. Ryb. (165) 13

Apis lapidaria — Pand. fl. Ryb. (165) 13

Apis longicornis — Pand. fl. Ryb. (165) 13

Apis lucorum — Pand. fl. Ryb. (165) 13

Apis mellifera — Pand. fl. Ryb. (165) 13[as
  mellifica]; Esca avium (174) 3

Apis muscorum — Pand. fl. Ryb. (165) 13

Apis pratorum — Pand. fl. Ryb. (165) 13

Apis retusa — Pand. fl. Ryb. (165) 13

Apis ruficornis — Pand. fl. Ryb. (165) 13

Apis rybyensis — Pand. fl. Ryb. (165) 13

Apis succincta — Pand. fl. Ryb. (165) 13

Apis sylvarum — Pand. fl. Ryb. (165) 13

Apis terrestris — Pand. fl. Ryb. (165) 13

Apis truncorum — Pand. fl. Ryb. (165) 13

Apis variegata — Pand. fl. Ryb. (165) 13

Apium — Vir. pl. (13) 19, 30; Fl. oecon. (17) 8; Pl.
  escul. (35) 12, 28; Oves (61) 22; Cul. mut. (88) 6;
  Nom. bot. (107) 11; Usum hist. nat. (145) 29

Apium graveolens — Pl. officin. (52) 4; Fl. Angl.
  (56) 13[as graveolans]; Fl. Palaest. (70) 16; Fl.
  Monsp. (74) 13; Prodr. fl. Dan. (82) 16; Cul. mut.
  (88) 7; Fl. Jam. (105) 24; Fl. Belg. (112) 15; Mac.
  olit. (113) 22; Hort. cul. (132) 12

Apium graveolens dulce — Acetaria (77) 14

Apium hortense — Fl. Cap. (99) 2

Apium hortense latifolium, maxima crassissima suavi
  et dulce radice — Cul. mut. (88) 6

Apium officinarum — Stat. pl. (55) 7

Apium palustre — Pan Svec. (26) 19

Apium petroselinum — Pl. officin. (52) 15; Cul. mut. (88) 2, 6; Fl. Jam. (105) 24; Hort. cul. (132) 12

Apium petroselinum radicosum — Mac. olit. (113) 11

Apluda — Fl. Jam. (105) 26; Fund. agrost. (152) 28, 37

Apluda aristata — Cent. II. pl. (66) 7

Apluda flosculis sessilibus aristatis — Cent. II. pl. (66) 7

Apluda mutica — Cent. II. pl. (66) 7; Iter Chin. (161) 12

Apluda zeugites — Pl. Jam. (102) 30[as Aplauda]; Fl. Jam. (105) 22

Apocynum — Vir. pl. (13) 24, 25; Nect. fl. (122) 13

Apocynum arborescens, nerii flore, minus — Cent. II. pl. (66) 12

Apocynum cannabinum — Demonstr. pl. (49) 7; Calend. fl. (72) [17]

Apocynum scandens, amplissimo flore luteo — Pl. Surin. (177) 6

Apocynum scandens, salicis folio, flore amplo plano — Cent. II. pl. (66) 12

Aquifolium indicum — Herb. Amboin. (57) 28

Aquila — Migr. avium (79) 19; Polit. nat. (109) 20; Fund. ornith. (137) 19

Aquilegia — Vir. pl. (13) 21, 24; Pl. hybr. (33) 6; Cui bono? (42) 20; Metam. pl. (67) 17; Pand. insect. (93) 16; Nect. fl. (122) 13, 15; Fund. fr. (123) 23; Cimicifuga (173) 2

Aquilegia alpina — Fl. alp. (71) 18

Aquilegia canadensis — Demonstr. pl. (49) 15; Calend. fl. (72) [11]

Aquilegia nectariis incurvis — Pl. hybr. (33) 12

Aquilegia nectariis rectis, pistillis corolla longioribus — Pl. hybr. (33) 12

Aquilegia officinarum — Pan Svec. (26) 25

Aquilegia sibirica — Calend. fl. (72) [11]

Aquilegia stellata — Peloria (3) 9

Aquilegia vulgaris — Pl. officin. (52) 5; Fl. Angl. (56) 18; Calend. fl. (72) [11]; Fl. Monsp. (74) 18; Prodr. fl. Dan. (82) 19; Fl. Belg. (112) 18; Pl. Alstr. (121) 5; Hort. cul. (132) 24, 25; Colon. pl. (158) 9; Fl. Åker. (162) 13; Pand. fl. Ryb. (165) 19

Aquilegia vulgaris sibirica — Demonstr. pl. (49) 15

Arabis — Hort. Upsal. (7) 33; Sapor. med. (31) 12; Fl. Angl. (56) 6

Arabis alpina — Pan Svec. (26) 29; Stat. pl. (55) 16; Fl. alp. (71) 20; Fl. Monsp. (74) 7, 21; Prodr. fl. Dan. (82) 21; Rar. Norv. (157) 11

Arabis annua — Pan Svec. (26) 29

Arabis capensis — Fl. Cap. (99) 16

Arabis caule nudo — Pl. rar. Camsch. (30) 24

Arabis grandiflora — Hist. nat. Rossia (144) 31

Arabis pendula — Demonstr. pl. (49) 17; Hist. nat. Rossia (144) 31

Arabis thaliana — Herbat. Upsal. (50) 7; Fl. Angl. (56) 20; Hort. acad. (63) 10; Fl. Monsp. (74) 21; Prodr. fl. Dan. (82) 21; Fl. Belg. (112) 19; Fl. Åker. (162) 15; Pand. fl. Ryb. (165) 20

Arabis turrita — Demonstr. pl. (49) 17; Fl. Monsp. (74) 21

Arachis — Somn. pl. (68) 7

Arachis hypogaea — Demonstr. pl. (49) 20; Herb. Amboin. (57) 24; Fl. Jam. (105) 19

Aralia — Pl. Mart.-Burs. (6) [vi]; Hort. Upsal. (7) 35; Nova pl. gen. 1751 (32) 8; Vern. arb. (47) 9; Herb. Amboin. (57) 16; Fl. Jam. (105) 26; Fund. fr. (123) 23

Aralia arborea — Pl. Jam. (102) 11; Fl. Jam. (105) 15

Aralia arborea aculeata — Nova pl. gen. 1751 (32) 25

Aralia canadensis — Calend. fl. (72) [17]

Aralia caule nudo — Pl. Mart.-Burs. (6) 10

Aralia chinensis — Herb. Amboin. (57) 16; Iter Chin. (161) 9

Aralia nudicaulis — Demonstr. pl. (49) 9; Specif. Canad. (76) 7, 14, 27

Aralia racemosa — Demonstr. pl. (49) 9; Specif. Canad. (76) 7, 15, 27

Aralia sarmentosa — Fund. fr. (123) 23

Aralia spinosa — Specif. Canad. (76) 15

Aranea — Oecon. nat. (20) 41; Hosp. insect. fl. (43) 4; Mirac. insect. (45) 12, 18; Noxa insect. (46) 11; Polit. nat. (109) 11; Fund. entom. (154) 19, 23, 26; Esca avium (174) 2

Aranea americana — Mus. Ad.-Frid. (11) 44

Aranea cruce alba — Hosp. insect. fl. (43) 33

Aranea diadema — Pand. fl. Ryb. (165) 16; Esca avium (174) [9, as 17]

Aranea domestica — Esca avium (174) [9, as 17]

Aranea fusca, dorso maculis quinque longitudinalibus sub contiguis nigris: anterioribus longioribus — Mat. med. anim. (29) 16

Aranea labyrinthica — Esca avium (174) 3, [9, as 17]

Aranea maxima ceylanica insigne gerens — Mus. Ad.-Frid. (11) 44

Aranea scenica — Pand. fl. Ryb. (165) 16

Aranea virescens — Pand. fl. Ryb. (165) 16

Araneus hirsutus thorace orbiculato, convexo, centro transversim excavato — Mus. Ad.-Frid. (11) 44; Surin. Grill. (16) 30

Araneus subflavus hirsutus, praelongis pedibus domesticus — Mat. med. anim. (29) 16

Arapabaca brasiliensibus — Spigelia (89) 13

Arapabaca quadrifolia, fructu testiculato — Spigelia (89) 13

Arbor alba — Herb. Amboin. (57) 9

Arbor aluminosa — Herb. Amboin. (57) 13

Arbor bon, cum fructu suo — Pot. coff. (118) 8

Arbor champaccae suberis folio, fructu ligneo, seminibus alatis referto — Nova pl. gen. 1747 (14) 24

Arbor coeli — Herb. Amboin. (57) 14

Arbor conciliorum — Herb. Amboin. (57) 13

Arbor excoecans — Herb. Amboin. (57) 10

Arbor facum major — Herb. Amboin. (57) 12

Arbor facum minor — Herb. Amboin. (57) 12

Arbor glutinosa — Herb. Amboin. (57) 13

Arbor indica maxima, cortice candicante, folio oblongo — Ficus (2) 5

Arbor kauki indorum, floribus odoratis — Nova pl. gen. 1747 (14) 14

Arbor lactoria — Herb. Amboin. (57) 10

Arbor malabarica illa dicta; cujus cortice vescuntur indi defectu foliorum beteles — Nova pl. gen. 1747 (14) 5

Arbor malabariensium, fructu lentisci — Nova pl. gen. 1747 (14) 5

Arbor mirabili umbella — Herb. Amboin. (57) 9

Arbor nigra — Herb. Amboin. (57) 11

Arbor noctis — Herb. Amboin. (57) 12

Arbor nuda — Herb. Amboin. (57) 12

Arbor ovigera — Herb. Amboin. (57) 14

Arbor pallidioribus foliis, fructu conoide ex magno calyce emergente — Nova pl. gen. 1747 (14) 14

Arbor palorum — Herb. Amboin. (57) 12

Arbor pinguis — Herb. Amboin. (57) 10

Arbor radulifera — Herb. Amboin. (57) 14

Arbor rediviva — Herb. Amboin. (57) 4, 13

Arbor regis — Herb. Amboin. (57) 11

Arbor rubra — Herb. Amboin. (57) 12

Arbor rubra reliquae — Herb. Amboin. (57) 12

Arbor siliquosa malabarica, pluribus ad singulos flores lobis — Nova pl. gen. 1747 (14) 30

Arbor spiculorum — Herb. Amboin. (57) 14

Arbor stercoria zeylanica, glandifera — Nova pl. gen. 1747 (14) 3

Arbor toxicaria — Herb. Amboin. (57) 11

Arbor vernicis — Herb. Amboin. (57) 11

Arbor versicolor — Herb. Amboin. (57) 13

Arbor violaria — Herb. Amboin. (57) 10

Arbor zeylanica, floribus odoratis faciem humanam quodammodo referentibus — Nova pl. gen. 1747 (14) 14

Arbor zeylanica, folio caryophylli barbati — Nova pl. gen. 1747 (14) 8

Arbutus — Vir. pl. (13) 20; Fl. oecon. (17) 11; Oecon. nat. (20) 19; Pl. escul. (35) 27, 28; Fl. Angl. (56) 5; Pand. insect. (93) 14; Nom. bot. (107) 13; Erica (163) 3

Arbutus alpina — Pan Svec. (26) 22; Stat. pl. (55) 15; Fl. Angl. (56) 15; Cervus (60) 7; Fl. alp. (71) 16; Fr. escul. (127) 7[as alpinum]; Hist. nat. Rossia (144) 29; Rar. Norv. (157) 10

Arbutus andrachne — Fl. Palaest. (70) 19

Arbutus foliis ovatis integris, petiolis laxis longitudine foliorum — Nova pl. gen. 1751 (32) 28

Arbutus unedo — Fl. Angl. (56) 15; Fl. Palaest. (70) 19; Fl. Monsp. (74) 15; Fr. escul. (127) 8

Arbutus uva-ursi — Gem. arb. (24) 16; Pan Svec. (26) 22; Pl. escul. (35) 15; Hosp. insect. fl. (43) 21; Herbat. Upsal. (50) 6; Pl. officin. (52) 20; Stat. pl. (55) 21; Fl. Angl. (56) 6; Fl. Monsp. (74) 15; Prodr. fl. Dan. (82) 17; Pl. tinct. (97) 17, 29; Fr. escul. (127) 7; Fl. Åker. (162) 11; Pand. fl. Ryb. (165) 18; Esca avium (174) 12; Ledum (178) 7

Arca — Fund. test. (166) 18, 34, 42

Arca antiquata — Iter Chin. (161) 8

Arca barbata — Fund. test. (166) 43

Archangelica — Stat. pl. (55) 7

Arctium — Fl. oecon. (17) 19; Pl. escul. (35) 22, 23, 28; Migr. avium (79) 34; Pand. insect. (93) 18[as Arcticum]; Nom. bot. (107) 17

Arctium lappa — Pan Svec. (26) 32; Hosp. insect. fl. (43) 30; Herbat. Upsal. (50) 10; Pl. officin. (52) 5; Stat. pl. (55) 20; Fl. Angl. (56) 22; Calend. fl. (72) [16]; Fl. Monsp. (74) 24; Prodr. fl. Dan. (82) 22; Fl. Belg. (112) 20; Mac. olit. (113) 14; Fl. Åker. (162) 17[as Actium]; Pand. fl. Ryb. (165) 21; Esca avium (174) 3, 14

Arctium personata — Fl. alp. (71) 21; Hist. nat. Rossia (144) 32[as personatum]

Arctopus — Fl. Cap. (99) 6; Aphyteia (185) 6

Arctopus echinatus — Fl. Cap. (99) 8, 19

Arctotis — Hort. Upsal. (7) 35; Pl. hybr. (33) 6; Fl. Cap. (99) 7, 9, 10; Pl. rar. Afr. (115) 5; Fund. fr. (123) 17

Arctotis angustifolia — Fl. Cap. (99) 18

Arctotis anthemoides — Pl. rar. Afr. (115) 25

Arctotis aspera — Fl. Cap. (99) 18

Arctotis calendulacea — Fl. Cap. (99) 18

Arctotis dentata — Pl. rar. Afr. (115) 25

Arctotis flosculis radiantibus quinquepartitis, foliis pinnatis, dentatis: laciniis bipartitis — Cent. II. pl. (66) 32

Arctotis flosculis radiantibus sterilibus, paleis disco longioribus coloratis; foliis bipinnatis linearibus — Cent. II. pl. (66) 32

Arctotis foliis lanceolatis subtus tomentosis integris laciniatisque — Pl. rar. Afr. (115) 24

Arctotis foliis pinnatis linearibus, flosculis radii sterilibus, paleis flosculos aequantibus — Pl. rar. Afr. (115) 25

Arctotis foliis pinnatis: pinnis villosis pinnatifido-dentatis — Pl. rar. Afr. (115) 25

Arctotis foliis supradecompositis linearibus, paleis flosculo brevioribus — Pl. rar. Afr. (115) 25

Arctotis herbacea, petalis radii 20 tripartitis — Pl. hybr. (33) 8

Arctotis herbacea, radii petalis 12 subintegris — Pl. hybr. (33) 8

Arctotis paleacea — Pl. rar. Afr. (115) 25

Arctotis paradoxa — Cent. II. pl. (66) 32; Fl. Cap. (99) 18

Arctotis ramis decumbentibus, foliis lineari-lanceolatis rigidis subtus argenteis — Pl. rar. Afr. (115) 24

Arctotis superba — Cent. II. pl. (66) 32

Arctotis tristis — Fl. Cap. (99) 18

Ardea — Cui bono? (42) 24; Migr. avium (79) 16, 26; Fund. ornith. (137) 14, 24, 25

Ardea alba — Migr. avium (79) 14

Ardea caerulea — Migr. avium (79) 14

Ardea grus — Migr. avium (79) 19

Ardea pavonia — Fl. Cap. (99) [1]; Fund. ornith. (137) 26

Ardea virescens — Migr. avium (79) 14

Ardea virgo — Fund. ornith. (137) 26

Areca — Inebr. (117) 12

Areca catechu — Pl. officin. (52) 7[as cathecu]; Herb. Amboin. (57) 6; Pl. tinct. (97) 28[as cathecu]; Fl. Jam. (105) 23[as catecu]

Arenaria — Pl. Mart.-Burs. (6) 21; Splachnum (27) 2; Nova pl. gen. 1751 (32) 12; Demonstr. pl. (49) 4

Arenaria bavarica — Cent. II. pl. (66) 17; Fl. alp. (71) 17

Arenaria cerastioides — Fl. Monsp. (74) 16[as cerastoides]

Arenaria ciliata — Fl. alp. (71) 17

Arenaria foliis lanceolato-linearibus scabris, caulibus sterilibus longissimis procumbentibus — Cent. I. pl. (65) 12

Arenaria foliis linearibus erectis, calycibus oblongis striatis — Cent. II. pl. (66) 17

Arenaria foliis ovatis nervosis sessilibus imbricatis acutis — Pl. Mart.-Burs. (6) 21

Arenaria foliis semicylindricis carnosis obtusis, petalis lanceolatis, pedunculis terminalibus subbinatis — Cent. II. pl. (66) 17

Arenaria foliis subulatis, calycibus striatis, germinibus oblongis, floribus corymbosis — Pl. Mart.-Burs. (6) 17

Arenaria laricifolia — Fl. Monsp. (74) 16

Arenaria lateriflora — Hist. nat. Rossia (144) 29

Arenaria montana — Cent. I. pl. (65) 12; Fl. alp. (71) 17[as montona]

Arenaria mucronata — Fl. alp. (71) 17

Arenaria multicaulis — Pan Svec. (26) 23

Arenaria peploides — Stat. pl. (55) 12; Fl. Angl. (56) 16; Prodr. fl. Dan. (82) 18; Fl. Belg. (112) 16

Arenaria plantaginis — Pan Svec. (26) 23

Arenaria portulacae — Pan Svec. (26) 23

Arenaria purpurea — Pan Svec. (26) 23; Stat. pl. (55) 21

Arenaria rubra — Herbat. Upsal. (50) 10; Fl. Angl. (56) 16; Fl. Monsp. (74) 16; Prodr. fl. Dan. (82) 18; Fl. Belg. (112) 16; Fl. Åker. (162) 12

Arenaria rubra alpha — Pand. fl. Ryb. (165) 19

Arenaria rubra beta — Pand. fl. Ryb. (165) 19

Arenaria rubra major — Pand. fl. Ryb. (165) 21

Arenaria rubra maritima — Stat. pl. (55) 12; Fl. Palaest. (70) 19

Arenaria saxatilis — Demonstr. pl. (49) 12; Fl. Angl. (56) 16; Hist. nat. Rossia (144) 29

Arenaria serpyllifolia — Herbat. Upsal. (50) 10; Stat. pl. (55) 18; Fl. Angl. (56) 16; Fl. Monsp. (74) 16; Prodr. fl. Dan. (82) 18; Fl. Belg. (112) 16; Fl. Åker. (162) 12; Pand. fl. Ryb. (165) 19; Esca avium (174) 12

Arenaria stellaria — Demonstr. pl. (49) 12

Arenaria striata — Cent. II. pl. (66) 17; Fl. alp. (71) 17

Arenaria tenuifolia — Demonstr. pl. (49) 12; Fl. Angl. (56) 16; Fl. Monsp. (74) 16

Arenaria tetraquetra — Fl. alp. (71) 17

Arenaria trinervia — Stat. pl. (55) 17; Fl. Angl. (56) 16; Fl. Monsp. (74) 16[as trinenia]; Fl. Belg. (112) 16; Fl. Åker. (162) 12; Pand. fl. Ryb. (165) 19

Arcthusa — Nova pl. gen. 1751 (32) 12, 23, 48

Arethusa bulbosa — Specif. Canad. (76) 11

Arethusa capensis — Pl. rar. Afr. (115) 28

Arethusa radice carnosa, scapo foliato, petalis exterioribus longioribus caudatis — Pl. rar. Afr. (115) 28

Arethusa scapi folio ovali spathaceo lanceolato — Nova pl. gen. 1751 (32) 24[as spataceo]

Arethusa scapo vaginato, spatha diphylla — Nova pl. gen. 1751 (32) 23

Aretia alpina — Fl. alp. (71) 13

Aretia cauliculis teretibus, foliis imbricatis, floribus sessilibus — Pl. Mart.-Burs. (6) 24

Aretia foliis linearibus glabris, scapo pauci-floro — Pl. Mart.-Burs. (6) 20

Aretia villosa scapis unifloris — Pl. Mart.-Burs. (6) 24

Argemone — Hort. Upsal. (7) 34; Vir. pl. (13) 21; Opium (179) 4

Argemone capitulo breviore — Pl. hybr. (33) 13

Argemone mexicana — Demonstr. pl. (49) 14; Fl. Jam. (105) 17

Argemone pyrenaica — Fl. alp. (71) 18

Argentina pinna dorsali pinnae ani opposita — Mus. Ad.-Frid. (11) 42

Argilla caerulescens — Hort. acad. (63) 10

Argilla calcarea — Hort. acad. (63) 10

Argilla nilotica — Hort. acad. (63) 9

Argonauta — Fund. test. (166) 17

Argonauta argo — Fund. test. (166) 36

Argus — Amphib. Gyll. (5) 21

Aries angolensis — Oves (61) 7

Aries cretensis — Oves (61) 7

Aries guineensis seu angolensis — Oves (61) 7

Arisarum amboinicum — Herb. Amboin. (57) 22

Arisarum esculentum — Herb. Amboin. (57) 22

Arisarum fluitans pene nudo, virginianum — Nova pl. gen. 1751 (32) 27[see Arum aquaticum minus …]

Aristida — Fund. agrost. (152) 27, 30, 36

Aristida adscensionis — Pl. Jam. (102) 7[as asscensionis]

Aristida americana — Pl. Jam. (102) 7; Fl. Jam. (105) 13

Aristida plumosa — Fund. agrost. (152) 30

Aristolochia — Hort. Upsal. (7) 33; Mus. Ad.-Frid. (11) 21[as Aristochia]; Spons. pl. (12) 29; Usum hist. nat. (145) 25; Siren. lacert. (146) 8; Erica (163) 2

Aristolochia anguicida — Mors. serp. (119) 19

Aristolochia caulibus infirmis angulosis flexuosis, foliis cordato-oblongis, floribus recurvis solitariis — Rad. senega (23) 11

Aristolochia clematitis — Demonstr. pl. (49) 24; Pl. officin. (52) 5; Fl. Monsp. (74) 27; Fl. Belg. (112) 9, 22

Aristolochia cordata — Fl. Jam. (105) 20[as Aristolachia]

Aristolochia indica — Herb. Amboin. (57) 25

Aristolochia longa — Pl. officin. (52) 5; Fl. Monsp. (74) 27

Aristolochia maurorum — Fl. Palaest. (70) 29

Aristolochia pistolochia — Fl. Monsp. (74) 27

Aristolochia rotunda — Pl. officin. (52) 5; Fl. Monsp. (74) 27

Aristolochia serpentaria — Pl. officin. (52) 18; Mors. serp. (119) 17

Aristolochia trilobata — Fl. Jam. (105) 20[as Aristolachia]

Armeniaca — Hort. Upsal. (7) 35; Pl. escul. (35) 4[as Armoniaca]; Nom. bot. (107) 13

Armodillo americanus — Mus. Ad.-Frid. (11) 3

Armodillus minor americanus — Mus. Ad.-Frid. (11) 3

Armoracia — Vir. pl. (13) 29[as Armoraca]; Sapor. med. (31) 19; Pl. escul. (35) 19; Odor. med. (40) 15; Noxa insect. (46) 19; Cul. mut. (88) 2; Nom. bot. (107) 15; Raphania (126) 13ff.; Var. cib. (156) 18

Arnica — Vir. pl. (13) 23; Vern. arb. (47) 19; Pl. rar. Afr. (115) 5; Usum hist. nat. (145) 22

Arnica afra — Fl. Cap. (99) 18

Arnica coronopifolia — Fl. Cap. (99) 18

Arnica crocea — Fl. Cap. (99) 18

Arnica foliis ellipticis integerrimis villosis, scapo unifloro lanato, calyce radium aequante — Pl. rar. Afr. (115) 22

Arnica gerbera — Fl. Cap. (99) 18

Arnica maritima — Hist. nat. Rossia (144) 33[as maritina]

Arnica montana — Pl. officin. (52) 5; Stat. pl. (55) 16, 22; Fl. alp. (71) 22; Fl. Monsp. (74) 25; Prodr.

fl. Dan. (82) 23; Fl. Belg. (112) 21; Fl. Åker. (162) 18

Arnica piloselloides — Pl. rar. Afr. (115) 22

Arnica scorpioides — Fl. alp. (71) 22; Fl. Monsp. (74) 25

Aronia — Nova pl. gen. 1751 (32) 12[as Aronica], 26

Artedia squamata — Fl. Palaest. (70) 16

Artemisia — Hort. Upsal. (7) 33; Vir. pl. (13) 23, 33[as Arthemisia]; Fl. oecon. (17) 20; Pl. hybr. (33) 29; Pl. escul. (35) 29[as Arthemisia]; Fl. Angl. (56) 6; Herb. Amboin. (57) 21; Migr. avium (79) 32; Pand. insect. (93) 18; Nom. bot. (107) 17; Fund. fr. (123) 23; Febr. interm. (167) 37

Artemisia abrotanum — Hosp. insect. fl. (43) 31; Demonstr. pl. (49) 23; Pl. officin. (52) 3; Calend. fl. (72) [21]; Hort. cul. (132) 24

Artemisia absinthium — Pan Svec. (26) 32; Demonstr. pl. (49) 23; Herbat. Upsal. (50) 20; Pl. officin. (52) 3; Stat. pl. (55) 8, 20; Fl. Angl. (56) 22[as Artimesia]; Cervus (60) 8; Calend. fl. (72) [18]; Fl. Monsp. (74) 25; Prodr. fl. Dan. (82) 23; Fl. Belg. (112) 21; Hist. nat. Rossia (144) 32; Fl. Åker. (162) 17; Pand. fl. Ryb. (165) 21; Esca avium (174) 3, 14

Artemisia aethiopica — Fl. Cap. (99) 17

Artemisia anglica maritima — Fl. Angl. (56) 27

Artemisia annua — Demonstr. pl. (49) 23; Calend. fl. (72) [21]; Hist. nat. Rossia (144) 23, 32

Artemisia caerulescens — Prodr. fl. Dan. (82) 23; Fl. Cap. (99) 7[as coerulescens], 17

Artemisia campestris — Pan Svec. (26) 32; Herbat. Upsal. (50) 11; Stat. pl. (55) 21; Fl. Angl. (56) 22[as Artimesia]; Calend. fl. (72) [18]; Fl. Monsp. (74) 25; Prodr. fl. Dan. (82) 23; Fl. Belg. (112) 21; Hist. nat. Rossia (144) 32; Obs. mat. med. (171) 5

Artemisia carolina — Pan Svec. (26) 32

Artemisia chinensis — Hist. nat. Rossia (144) 32

Artemisia cinerea — Fl. Palaest. (70) 28

Artemisia draco [error for dracunculus?] — Calend. fl. (72) [19]; Mac. olit. (113) 22

Artemisia dracunculus — Demonstr. pl. (49) 23; Acetaria (77) 10; Cul. mut. (88) 3, 6[as dranunculus]; Hort. cul. (132) 18; Hist. nat. Rossia (144) 18, 32; Usum hist. nat. (145) 12; see also A. draco

Artemisia foliis bipinnatis; caule erectiusculo; pedunculis solitariis, unifloris, nudis, filiformibus — Cent. I. pl. (65) 27[as eretiusculo]

Artemisia fruticosa — Fl. Palaest. (70) 28

Artemisia integrifolia — Hist. nat. Rossia (144) 32

Artemisia judaica — Fl. Palaest. (70) 28

Artemisia latifolia — Herb. Amboin. (57) 21

Artemisia maritima — Demonstr. pl. (49) 23; Stat. pl. (55) 8, 12; Fl. Angl. (56) 22[as Artimesia]; Oves (61) 14; Calend. fl. (72) [19]; Prodr. fl. Dan. (82) 23; Fl. Belg. (112) 21

Artemisia maritima gallica — Fl. Monsp. (74) 25

Artemisia nilotica — Cent. I. pl. (65) 27; Fl. Palaest. (70) 28

Artemisia palustris — Hist. nat. Rossia (144) 32

Artemisia pontica — Pl. officin. (52) 3; Calend. fl. (72) [21]; Fl. Cap. (99) 7, 17

Artemisia rupestris — Demonstr. pl. (49) 23; Stat. pl. (55) 23; Calend. fl. (72) [19]; Hist. nat. Rossia (144) 32; Colon. pl. (158) 7

Artemisia santonicum — Pl. officin. (52) 8, 17; Hist. nat. Rossia (144) 32

Artemisia seriphium — Pan Svec. (26) 32

Artemisia tanacetifolia — Hist. nat. Rossia (144) 32

Artemisia tenuifolia narbonensis — Fl. Angl. (56) 27

Artemisia vulgaris — Pan Svec. (26) 32; Pl. escul. (35) 23[as Arthemisia]; Hosp. insect. fl. (43) 31; Herbat. Upsal. (50) 13; Pl. officin. (52) 5; Stat. pl. (55) 18; Fl. Angl. (56) 22[as Artimesia]; Calend. fl. (72) [16]; Fl. Monsp. (74) 25; Prodr. fl. Dan. (82) 23; Fl. Belg. (112) 21; Pl. rar. Afr. (115) 6; Hist. nat. Rossia (144) 32; Fl. Åker. (162) 17; Pand. fl. Ryb. (165) 21

Arum — Peloria (3) 10; Vir. pl. (13) 25, 29, 30; Oecon. nat. (20) 20; Lign. colubr. (21) 15; Gem. arb. (24) 8; Sapor. med. (31) 19; Pl. escul. (35) 24; Pl. Jam. (102) 26; Nom. bot. (107) 17; Fl. Belg. (112) 10; Pl. Surin. (177) 15

Arum aegyptium — Herb. Amboin. (57) 22

Arum aquaticum — Herb. Amboin. (57) 22

Arum aquaticum minus seu arisarum fluitans pene nudo, virginianum — Nova pl. gen. 1751 (32) 27

Arum arborescens — Herb. Amboin. (57) 22

Arum arisarum — Fl. Palaest. (70) 29; Fl. Monsp. (74) 27

Arum auritum — Pl. Jam. (102) 26; Fl. Jam. (105) 20

Arum byzantinum — Fl. Palaest. (70) 29

Arum cannifolium — Pl. Surin. (177) 15

Arum chinense — Chin. Lagerstr. (64) 5

Arum colocasia — Herb. Amboin. (57) 22[as colacasia]; Fl. Palaest. (70) 29; Fl. Jam. (105) 20; Mac. olit. (113) 12

Arum divaricatum — Demonstr. pl. (49) 24; Herb. Amboin. (57) 22

Arum dracunculus — Fl. Palaest. (70) 29; Fl. Monsp. (74) 27

Arum esculentum — Herb. Amboin. (57) 22; Fl. Jam. (105) 20; Mac. olit. (113) 12

Arum fluitans pene nudo — Nova pl. gen. 1751 (32) 27

Arum folio enervi-ovato — Nova pl. gen. 1751 (32) 27

Arum lingulatum — Pl. Jam. (102) 26; Fl. Jam. (105) 20[as lingalatum]

Arum macrorrhizon — Fl. Jam. (105) 20[as macrorhizon]

Arum maculatum — Demonstr. pl. (49) 24; Pl. officin. (52) 5; Fl. Angl. (56) 23; Fl. Monsp. (74) 27; Prodr. fl. Dan. (82) 24; Fl. Belg. (112) 10, 22

Arum ovatum — Herb. Amboin. (57) 22

Arum ovidue — Fl. Palaest. (70) 29

Arum peregrinum — Herb. Amboin. (57) 22; Fl. Jam. (105) 20

Arum proboscideum — Fl. alp. (71) 23

Arum sagittaefolium — Herb. Amboin. (57) 22[as sagittifolium]; Fl. Jam. (105) 20[as sagittifolium]

Arum sativum — Herb. Amboin. (57) 22

Arum sylvestre — Herb. Amboin. (57) 22

Arum tenuifolium — Fl. Palaest. (70) 29; Fl. Monsp. (74) 27

Arum trilobum — Herb. Amboin. (57) 22

Arum triphyllum — Demonstr. pl. (49) 24; Fl. Palaest. (70) 29

Aruncus — Pl. rar. Camsch. (30) 20

Arundarbor aspera — Herb. Amboin. (57) 15

Arundarbor cratium — Herb. Amboin. (57) 15

Arundarbor fera — Herb. Amboin. (57) 15

Arundarbor spiculorum — Herb. Amboin. (57) 15

Arundarbor spinosa — Herb. Amboin. (57) 15

Arundarbor vasaria — Herb. Amboin. (57) 15

Arundastrum — Herb. Amboin. (57) 15

Arundinella — Herb. Amboin. (57) 25

Arundo — Peloria (3) 10; Fl. oecon. (17) 4; Oecon. nat. (20) 35; Pan Svec. (26) 6; Pl. hybr. (33) 7; Cui bono? (42) 17, 18; Nom. bot. (107) 9; Fund. agrost. (152) 15, 16, 17, 18, 23, 29, 30, 33, 37

Arundo arbor — Herb. Amboin. (57) 15

Arundo arbor indica procera verticillata — Herb. Amboin. (57) 15

Arundo arenae mobilis — Pan Svec. (26) 15

Arundo arenaria — Oecon. nat. (20) 22; Stat. pl. (55) 21; Fl. Angl. (56) 11; Fl. Monsp. (74) 9; Prodr. fl. Dan. (82) 13; Fl. Cap. (99) 2; Fl. Belg. (112) 6, 8, 13; Usum musc. (148) 4; Fund. agrost. (152) 7, 8

Arundo calamagrostis — Herbat. Upsal. (50) 19[as calamogrostis]; Stat. pl. (55) 13[as calamogrostis]; Fl. Angl. (56) 11; Fl. Belg. (112) 13; Fund. agrost. (152) 7; Fl. Åker. (162) 7

Arundo donax — Fl. Monsp. (74) 9

Arundo epigejos — Demonstr. pl. (49) 3; Herbat. Upsal. (50) 9; Stat. pl. (55) 18; Prodr. fl. Dan. (82) 13; Fl. Åker. (162) 7

Arundo farcta — Herb. Amboin. (57) 15

Arundo foliorum lateribus convolutis acumine pungente — Pl. hybr. (33) 15

Arundo lacustris — Pan Svec. (26) 15

Arundo panicula coarctata erecta integra, foliis inferne glabris — Pl. hybr. (33) 15

Arundo petraea — Pan Svec. (26) 15[as petrea]

Arundo phragmites — Herbat. Upsal. (50) 13; Stat. pl. (55) 13; Fl. Angl. (56) 11; Fl. Monsp. (74) 9; Prodr. fl. Dan. (82) 13; Pl. tinct. (97) 12; Fl. Belg. (112) 13[as phragmitis]; Usum hist. nat. (145) 10; Fund. agrost. (152) 7; Fl. Åker. (162) 7; Pand. fl. Ryb. (165) 16

Arundo ramosa — Pan Svec. (26) 15

Arundo saccharifera — Herb. Amboin. (57) 20; Iter Chin. (161) 9

Arundo scriptoria — Fl. Palaest. (70) 13

Arundo vallatoria — Herb. Amboin. (57) 15

Arupa — Herb. Amboin. (57) 12

Aryathamnia — Fl. Jam. (105) 27

Asarina — Somn. pl. (68) 7

Asarum — Hort. Upsal. (7) 33; Spons. pl. (12) 35; Vir. pl. (13) 31; Sapor. med. (31) 20; Odor. med. (40) 13, 14; Generat. ambig. (104) 8; Nom. bot. (107) 13; Fl. Belg. (112) 10; Prol. pl. 1760 (114) 15; Pot. theae (142) 10; Purg. indig. (143) 17; Erica (163) 2

Asarum e terra marina, violae luteae vel asarinae foliis; serpentaria nigra — Rad. senega (23) 11

Asarum europaeum — Demonstr. pl. (49) 12; Pl. officin. (52) 5; Stat. pl. (55) 17; Fl. Angl. (56) 16; Calend. fl. (72) [9]; Prodr. fl. Dan. (82) 18; Fl. Belg. (112) 17; Purg. indig. (143) 14[as europeum]; Med. purg. (181) 19

Asarum foliis reniformibus obtusis binis — Med. purg. (181) 19

Asarum hypocistis — Pl. officin. (52) 11; Fung. melit. (69) 3; Fl. Monsp. (74) 17

Asarum officinarum — Pan Svec. (26) 24

Ascaris — Taenia (19) 10, 12, 31, 32, 33, 34; Exanth. viva (86) 14; Spigelia (89) 6; Polit. nat. (109) 13; Hirudo (136) 2; Lepra (140) 10, 11

Ascaris lumbricoides — Spigelia (89) 5

Ascaris vermicularis — Spigelia (89) [4]

Asclepias — Vir. pl. (13) 24, 25; Fl. oecon. (17) 7; Gem. arb. (24) 6; Pl. hybr. (33) 6; Somn. pl. (68) 14; Fl. Cap. (99) 6; Nom. bot. (107) 11; Mors. serp. (119) 2; Nect. fl. (122) 13, 15

Asclepias arborescens — Hort. Upsal. (7) 35

Asclepias curassavica — Demonstr. pl. (49) 7; Hort. acad. (63) 19; Somn. pl. (68) 10; Fl. Jam. (105) 14

Asclepias exaltata — Demonstr. pl. (49) 7; Cent. I. pl. (65) 2

Asclepias flore albo — Pl. hybr. (33) 11

Asclepias foliis lanceolato-ellipticis, caule simplici glabro, nectarii corniculis conniventibus — Demonstr. pl. (49) 7

Asclepias fruticosa — Demonstr. pl. (49) 7; Fl. Cap. (99) 12

Asclepias gigantea — Fl. Palaest. (70) 16; Fl. Jam. (105) 14, 25

Asclepias incarnata — Demonstr. pl. (49) 7

Asclepias nigra — Demonstr. pl. (49) 7; Fl. Monsp. (74) 12

Asclepias nigro flore — Pl. hybr. (33) 11

Asclepias rubra — Calend. fl. (72) [19]

Asclepias sibirica — Hist. nat. Rossia (144) 28

Asclepias syriaca — Demonstr. pl. (49) 7

Asclepias tuberosa — Specif. Canad. (76) 11

Asclepias undulata — Fl. Cap. (99) 12

Asclepias vincetoxicum — Demonstr. pl. (49) 7; Herbat. Upsal. (50) 9; Pl. officin. (52) 11; Stat. pl. (55) 23; Fl. Angl. (56) 6; Fl. Monsp. (74) 12; Prodr. fl. Dan. (82) 15; Fl. Åker. (162) 9; Pand. fl. Ryb. (165) 17

Asclepias vulgaris — Pan Svec. (26) 18

Ascyroides — Hypericum (186) 13

Ascyrum — Hort. Upsal. (7) 34[as Aschyron]; Nova pl. gen. 1751 (32) 10; Hypericum (186) 3, 13[as Ascyron]

Ascyrum hypericoides — Fl. Jam. (105) 19

Asellus asininus seu vulgaris — Mat. med. anim. (29) 18

Asellus pessuntius — Var. cib. (156) 8

Asilus — Oecon. nat. (20) 41; Hosp. insect. fl. (43) 32, 37; Noxa insect. (46) 10, 28; Polit. nat. (109) 11, 12; Fund. entom. (154) 30; Pand. fl. Ryb. (165) 12

Asilus aestuans — Cent. insect. (129) 30

Asilus cinereus, abdominis tribus ultimis segmentis albis — Cent. insect. (129) 30

Asilus crabroniformis — Pand. fl. Ryb. (165) 15; Esca avium (174) 3

Asilus forcipatus — Pand. fl. Ryb. (165) 15

Asilus germanicus — Pand. fl. Ryb. (165) 15

Asilus gibbosus — Pand. fl. Ryb. (165) 15; Esca avium (174) 4

Asilus gilvus — Pand. fl. Ryb. (165) 15

Asilus morio — Pand. fl. Ryb. (165) 15

Asilus oelandicus — Pand. fl. Ryb. (165) 15

Asilus tipuloides — Pand. fl. Ryb. (165) 15; Esca avium (174) [9, as 17]

Asinus — Spons. pl. (12) 25; Fund. fr. (123) 14; Lepra (140) 6

Aspalathus — Hort. Upsal. (7) 34[as Asphalathus]; Anandria (9) 5[as Aspalatus]; Fl. Cap. (99) 8; Pl. rar. Afr. (115) 5; Fund. fr. (123) 18[as Asphalatus]; Opobals. (135) 2[as Aspalatus]; Aphyteia (185) 6[as Aspalatus]

Aspalathus araneosa — Fl. Cap. (99) 17

Aspalathus argentea — Fl. Cap. (99) 17

Aspalathus astroites — Fl. Cap. (99) 16

Aspalathus callosa — Fl. Cap. (99) 17

Aspalathus capitata — Pl. rar. Afr. (115) 14

Aspalathus chenopoda — Fl. Cap. (99) 16

Aspalathus cretica — Fl. Cap. (99) 17

Aspalathus ericifolia — Fl. Cap. (99) 17

Aspalathus foliis fasciculatis linearibus acutis, floribus capitatis, bracteis nudis — Pl. rar. Afr. (115) 14

Aspalathus foliis pinnato-quinatis obcordatis pedunculis capitatis — Pl. rar. Afr. (115) 14

Aspalathus foliis quinis sessilibus, pedunculis spicatis — Pl. rar. Afr. (115) 14

Aspalathus pinnata — Pl. rar. Afr. (115) 14

Aspalathus quinquefolia — Pl. rar. Afr. (115) 14

Aspalathus retroflexa — Fl. Cap. (99) 17

Aspalathus thymifolia — Fl. Cap. (99) 16

Aspalathus tridentata — Fl. Cap. (99) 17

Aspalathus uniflora — Fl. Cap. (99) 17

Aspalathus verrucosa — Fl. Cap. (99) 17

Asparagus — Peloria (3) 10; Vir. pl. (13) 7, 36; Fl.
oecon. (17) 8; Sapor. med. (31) 11; Pl. escul. (35)
10, 11, 13, 22, 23, 28; Hosp. insect. fl. (43) 12;
Noxa insect. (46) 18, 19; Hort. acad. (63) 3, 19;
Cul. mut. (88) 5; Pand. insect. (93) 13; Nom. bot.
(107) 12; Fl. Belg. (112) 8, 10; Prol. pl. 1763 (130)
5

Asparagus acutifolius — Fl. Palaest. (70) 18; Fl.
Monsp. (74) 14

Asparagus aphyllus — Fl. Palaest. (70) 18

Asparagus capensis — Fl. Cap. (99) 13

Asparagus foliis gallii — Fl. Palaest. (70) 18

Asparagus hortensis — Fl. Cap. (99) 2

Asparagus officinalis — Demonstr. pl. (49) 10; Pl.
officin. (52) 5; Fl. Angl. (56) 14; Fl. Monsp. (74)
14; Fl. Jam. (105) 24; Fl. Belg. (112) 15; Mac. olit.
(113) 13; Hort. cul. (132) 18

Asparagus officinalis maritimus — Prodr. fl. Dan.
(82) 16

Asparagus refractus — Fl. Cap. (99) 9

Asparagus retrofractus — Fl. Cap. (99) 13

Asparagus sativus — Hosp. insect. fl. (43) 19

Asparagus scanensis — Pan Svec. (26) 20

Asperugo — Vir. pl. (13) 18

Asperugo procumbens — Herbat. Upsal. (50) 10;
Stat. pl. (55) 20; Fl. Angl. (56) 12; Fl. Monsp. (74)
11; Prodr. fl. Dan. (82) 14; Fl. Belg. (112) 14; Fl.
Åker. (162) 8; Pand. fl. Ryb. (165) 17

Asperugo vulgaris — Pan Svec. (26) 16

Asperula — Vir. pl. (13) 17, 31; Fl. oecon. (17) 4;
Odor. med. (40) 12; Nom. bot. (107) 10

Asperula arvensis — Demonstr. pl. (49) 4; Fl.
Monsp. (74) 10

Asperula caerulea — Pl. rar. Afr. (115) 6

Asperula cruciata villosa — Fl. alp. (71) 13

Asperula cynanchica — Fl. Angl. (56) 11; Fl. Monsp.
(74) 10

Asperula foliis pluribus, floribus sessilibus — Pl.
Mart.-Burs. (6) 25

Asperula odorata — Pan Svec. (26) 15; Demonstr. pl.
(49) 4; Herbat. Upsal. (50) 8; Pl. officin. (52) 12;
Stat. pl. (55) 17; Fl. Angl. (56) 11; Prodr. fl. Dan.
(82) 14; Fl. Åker. (162) 7; Pand. fl. Ryb. (165) 17

Asperula pyrenaica — Fl. alp. (71) 13

Asperula rubeola — Pan Svec. (26) 15

Asperula taurina — Fl. alp. (71) 12

Asperula tinctoria — Demonstr. pl. (49) 4; Herbat.
Upsal. (50) 12; Stat. pl. (55) 23; Pl. tinct. (97) 12;
Hist. nat. Rossia (144) 28

Asphaltus — Fl. Jam. (105) 26

Asphaltus ebenus — Fl. Jam. (105) 8, 19

Asphodelus — Hort. Upsal. (7) 35; Nect. fl. (122) 9

Asphodelus capensis — Fl. Cap. (99) 13

Asphodelus fistulosus — Demonstr. pl. (49) 10

Asphodelus luteus — Demonstr. pl. (49) 10; Fl.
Palaest. (70) 17

Asphodelus ramosus — Pl. officin. (52) 5; Fl.
Palaest. (70) 17; Fl. Monsp. (74) 14

Aspis — Amphib. Gyll. (5) 2; Rad. senega (23) 5

Asplenium — Acrostichum (10) 3, 6, 7, 8

Asplenium adiantum nigrum — Fl. Angl. (56) 25; Fl.
Monsp. (74) 29

Asplenium ceterach — Pl. officin. (52) 7; Fl. Angl.
(56) 25; Fl. Palaest. (70) 32[as ceterac]

Asplenium emarginatum — Fl. Jam. (105) 23

Asplenium erosum — Fl. Jam. (105) 23

Asplenium frondibus ensiformibus integris basi
cordato inflexis, stipitibus hirsutis — Pl. Mart.-
Burs. (6) 27

Asplenium frondibus lanceolatis indivisis: apice
filiformibus radicantibus — Pl. rar. Camsch. (30) 5

Asplenium lingua cervi — Pan Svec. (26) 38

Asplenium marinum — Fl. Angl. (56) 25; Fl. Jam.
(105) 23

Asplenium nidus — Fung. melit. (69) 3

Asplenium onopteris — Fl. Monsp. (74) 29; Fl. Cap.
(99) 19

Asplenium plantagineum — Fl. Jam. (105) 23

Asplenium pygmaeum — Fl. Jam. (105) 23

Asplenium radicans — Fl. Jam. (105) 23

Asplenium rhizophyllum — Hist. nat. Rossia (144)
12, 34

Asplenium ruta muraria — Pan Svec. (26) 38[as
murararia]; Pl. officin. (52) 17; Stat. pl. (55) 23; Fl.
Angl. (56) 25; Fl. Monsp. (74) 29; Prodr. fl. Dan.
(82) 25; Fl. Belg. (112) 23

Asplenium salicifolium — Fl. Jam. (105) 23

Asplenium scolopendrium — Demonstr. pl. (49) 27;
Pl. officin. (52) 17; Fl. Angl. (56) 25; Fl. Monsp.
(74) 29; Prodr. fl. Dan. (82) 25; Fl. Belg. (112) 23

Asplenium serratum — Fl. Jam. (105) 23

Asplenium striatum — Fl. Jam. (105) 23

Asplenium trichomanes — Pan Svec. (26) 38; Herbat.
Upsal. (50) 8; Pl. officin. (52) 4, 19; Stat. pl. (55)
23; Fl. Angl. (56) 25; Fl. Monsp. (74) 29; Fl. Jam.
(105) 23; Fl. Belg. (112) 23; Fl. Åker. (162) 20[as
trichamanes]

Asplenium trichomanes ramosum — Fl. Angl. (56)
25

Asplenium virginianum, polypodii facie —
Acrostichum (10) 13

Aspredo — Mus. Ad.-Frid. (11) [vii], 33

Assa foetida — Odor. med. (40) 12, 14, 15; Cul. mut.
(88) 8

Astacus fluviatilis — Mat. med. anim. (29) 17

Aster — Hort. Upsal. (7) 35; Anandria (9) 12; Nova pl. gen. 1747 (14) 26; Pl. hybr. (33) 29; Fl. Cap. (99) 6; Nom. bot. (107) 17; Fund. fr. (123) 17, 22

Aster aethiopicus pilosellae facie, tomento copioso — Pl. rar. Afr. (115) 22

Aster aethiopicus, stoechadis folio, flore aureo — Pl. rar. Afr. (115) 23[as staechadis]

Aster alpinus — Fl. alp. (71) 22; Fl. Monsp. (74) 25

Aster amellus — Calend. fl. (72) [17]; Fl. Monsp. (74) 25; Hist. nat. Rossia (144) 33

Aster annuus — Demonstr. pl. (49) 23; Calend. fl. (72) [14], [22]

Aster auricomus — Fl. Monsp. (74) 29

Aster bellidioides — Calend. fl. (72) [18]

Aster caeruleus virginicus — Calend. fl. (72) [18]

Aster chinensis — Demonstr. pl. (49) 23

Aster conyzoides fol. fl. max. — Fl. Palaest. (70) 28[under Inula]

Aster crinitus — Pl. rar. Afr. (115) 21

Aster dumosus — Demonstr. pl. (49) 23

Aster foliis integris angustis, flore magno luteo — Pl. rar. Afr. (115) 25

Aster foliis ovatis rugosis subtus tomentosis amplexicaulibus, calycum squamis ovatis patulis — Nova pl. gen. 1747 (14) 26

Aster foliis ovato oblongis acutis subtus tomentosis, calycibus squamis pilo terminatis — Pl. rar. Afr. (115) 21

Aster foliis subfiliformibus scabris, pedunculis nudis, calycibus hemisphaericis — Pl. rar. Afr. (115) 21

Aster foliis subimbricatis recurvatis serrato ciliatis, caule fruticoso — Pl. rar. Afr. (115) 21

Aster foliis subulatis rectis decurrentibus margine scabris, caule fruticoso — Pl. rar. Afr. (115) 22

Aster frutescens luteus mauritanicus — Pl. rar. Afr. (115) 22

Aster fruticosus — Fl. Cap. (99) 18

Aster imbricatus — Pl. rar. Afr. (115) 21

Aster miser — Calend. fl. (72) [18], [22]

Aster mutabilis — Demonstr. pl. (49) 23

Aster novae angliae — Demonstr. pl. (49) 23

Aster omnium maximus helenium dictus — Nova pl. gen. 1747 (14) 26

Aster oppositifolius — Fl. Cap. (99) 18

Aster polifolius — Fl. Cap. (99) 18

Aster puniceus — Demonstr. pl. (49) 23

Aster reflexus — Fl. Cap. (99) 18

Aster salicinus — Herbat. Upsal. (50) 19

Aster sedifolius — Fl. Monsp. (74) 25

Aster sibiricus — Hist. nat. Rossia (144) 33

Aster taxifolius — Pl. rar. Afr. (115) 22

Aster tenellus — Pl. rar. Afr. (115) 21

Aster tradescantii — Demonstr. pl. (49) 23; Calend. fl. (72) [22]; Pl. rar. Afr. (115) 7; Hort. cul. (132) 24

Aster tripolium — Pan Svec. (26) 33; Stat. pl. (55) 12; Fl. Angl. (56) 22; Fl. Monsp. (74) 25; Prodr. fl. Dan. (82) 23; Fl. Belg. (112) 21; Hist. nat. Rossia (144) 33; Pand. fl. Ryb. (165) 21

Asterias — Corallia Balt. (4) 10; Noctiluca (39) 6

Asterias caput medusae — Nat. pelagi (84) 9

Asterias decacnemos — Chin. Lagerstr. (64) 32

Asterias lunata — Chin. Lagerstr. (64) 31, 36

Asterias radiata, radiis 5 geminatis, superioribus pinnatis, inferioribus filiformibus — Chin. Lagerstr. (64) 32

Asterias semiorbiculata — Chin. Lagerstr. (64) 31

Asteriscus afer, imo calyce non folioso — Pl. rar. Afr. (115) 23

Asterocephalus argenteus graminifolius, flore caeruleo — Cent. I. pl. (65) 7

Asteroides alpina, salicis folio — Pl. Mart.-Burs. (6) 23

Asteropterus luteus, laricis foliis — Pl. rar. Afr. (115) 23[as Asteropteus]

Astragalus — Hort. Upsal. (7) 34; Anandria (9) 4; Fl. oecon. (17) 18; Pl. rar. Camsch. (30) 26; Pl. hybr. (33) 29; Cui bono? (42) 20; Fl. Angl. (56) 6; Pand. insect. (93) [17, as 38]

Astragalus acaulis, leguminibus inflatis subglobosis — Pl. rar. Camsch. (30) 25

Astragalus acaulis, scapis folio brevioribus, leguminibus cernuis, foliolis subemarginatis — Cent. II. pl. (66) 29

Astragalus alopecuroides — Demonstr. pl. (49) 20; Calend. fl. (72) [20]; Hist. nat. Rossia (144) 32

Astragalus alpinus — Demonstr. pl. (49) 21; Stat. pl. (55) 16; Fl. alp. (71) 21; Calend. fl. (72) [13]; Rar. Norv. (157) 11

Astragalus alpinus procerior — Fl. alp. (71) 21

Astragalus arenarius — Fl. Angl. (56) 21; Prodr. fl. Dan. (82) 22; Colon. pl. (158) 7[as Asragalus]

Astragalus boeticus — Demonstr. pl. (49) 21; Fl. Monsp. (74) 23[as baeticus]

Astragalus campestris — Colon. pl. (158) 6

Astragalus capitatus — Fl. Palaest. (70) 26

Astragalus capitulis oblongis sessilibus, calycibus et leguminibus lanatis — Pl. rar. Camsch. (30) 26

Astragalus christianus — Fl. Palaest. (70) 26

Astragalus contortuplicatus — Hist. nat. Rossia (144) 32[as contortuplica]

Astragalus depressus — Cent. II. pl. (66) 29; Fl. alp. (71) 21

Astragalus dulcis — Pan Svec. (26) 30

Astragalus galegiformis — Demonstr. pl. (49) 20; Calend. fl. (72) [15]; Hist. nat. Rossia (144) 32

Astragalus glycyphyllos — Hosp. insect. fl. (43) 29[as glycyphyllus]; Demonstr. pl. (49) 20; Stat. pl. (55) 17; Fl. Angl. (56) 21[as glycyphyllus]; Fl. Monsp. (74) 23[as glycyphyllus]; Prodr. fl. Dan. (82) 22[as glycyphyllus]; Fl. Åker. (162) 16[as glycyphyllus]; Esca avium (174) 14

Astragalus grandiflorus — Hist. nat. Rossia (144) 32

Astragalus hamosus — Demonstr. pl. (49) 20; Fl. Monsp. (74) 23

Astragalus hedysaroides — Fl. alp. (71) 21; Hist. nat. Rossia (144) 32

Astragalus incanus — Fl. Monsp. (74) 23

Astragalus lapponicus — Pan Svec. (26) 30

Astragalus microphyllus — Demonstr. pl. (49) 20; Hist. nat. Rossia (144) 32

Astragalus monspessulanus — Demonstr. pl. (49) 21; Fl. Monsp. (74) 23

Astragalus montanus — Demonstr. pl. (49) 21; Fl. alp. (71) 21

Astragalus oelandicus — Pan Svec. (26) 30

Astragalus physodes — Hist. nat. Rossia (144) 32

Astragalus pilosus — Hist. nat. Rossia (144) 32

Astragalus scapis radicalibus, calycibus leguminibusque villosis, foliolis acutis — Pl. Mart.-Burs. (6) 27

Astragalus sesamoides — Fl. Monsp. (74) 23

Astragalus spicatus, siliquis pendulis hirsutis, foliis sericeis — Nova pl. gen. 1747 (14) 25

Astragalus sulcatus — Hist. nat. Rossia (144) 32

Astragalus supinus minor, flosculis albis — Cent. II. pl. (66) 29

Astragalus syriacus — Fl. Palaest. (70) 26; Hist. nat. Rossia (144) 32

Astragalus tragacantha — Pl. officin. (52) 19[as tragantha]; Fl. Palaest. (70) 26

Astragalus tragacanthoides — Hist. nat. Rossia (144) 32

Astragalus trimestris — Demonstr. pl. (49) 21

Astragalus uliginosus — Demonstr. pl. (49) 20; Hist. nat. Rossia (144) 32

Astragalus uralensis — Demonstr. pl. (49) 21; Hist. nat. Rossia (144) 32; Colon. pl. (158) 7

Astragalus vesicarius — Fl. alp. (71) 21

Astrantia major — Fl. alp. (71) 14

Astrantia minor — Fl. alp. (71) 14

Astroites — Corallia Balt. (4) 2

Astronium — Nect. fl. (122) 7

Ateramnus — Fl. Jam. (105) 27[as Atheramnus]

Athamanta — Vir. pl. (13) 19[as Athamantha]; Pl. officin. (52) 9

Athamanta cervaria — Calend. fl. (72) [15]

Athamanta condensata — Demonstr. pl. (49) 8; Calend. fl. (72) [14]; Hist. nat. Rossia (144) 28

Athamanta cretensis — Fl. Monsp. (74) 13

Athamanta daucoides — Pan Svec. (26) 19

Athamanta libanotis — Herbat. Upsal. (50) 17; Stat. pl. (55) 22; Fl. Angl. (56) 13; Fl. Åker. (162) 9; Pand. fl. Ryb. (165) 17

Athamanta meum — Demonstr. pl. (49) 8; Pl. officin. (52) 13; Fl. Angl. (56) 13; Fl. alp. (71) 14[as Athamantha]; Fl. Monsp. (74) 13

Athamanta oreoselinum — Stat. pl. (55) 22; Prodr. fl. Dan. (82) 16

Athamanta sibirica — Demonstr. pl. (49) 8; Hist. nat. Rossia (144) 23, 28

Athamanta sicula — Demonstr. pl. (49) 8; Hist. nat. Rossia (144) 28

Atractylis — Fl. Cap. (99) 6

Atractylis ciliaris — Fl. Cap. (99) 8, 17

Atractylis fruticosa — Fl. Cap. (99) 17

Atragene — Nova pl. gen. 1747 (14) [vi], 21, 22; Herb. Amboin. (57) 23

Atragene alpina — Fl. alp. (71) 18; Hist. nat. Rossia (144) 30

Atragene capensis — Fl. Cap. (99) 15

Atragene sibirica — Hist. nat. Rossia (144) 30

Atraphaxis — Rhabarbarum (41) 5, 6

Atraphaxis undulata — Fl. Cap. (99) 13

Atriplex — Spons. pl. (12) 58; Sapor. med. (31) 11; Rhabarbarum (41) 23; Cul. mut. (88) 2; Pand. insect. (93) 22[as Artiplex]; Nom. bot. (107) 19

Atriplex angustifolia beta — Hosp. insect. fl. (43) 39

Atriplex angustifolia laciniata — Fl. Angl. (56) 26

Atriplex caule herbaceo, divaricato; foliis lanceolatis, obtusis, integris; calycibus femineis pedunculatis — Cent. I. pl. (65) 34

Atriplex caule suffruticoso, procumbente; foliis ovatis, sessilibus, integerrimis: inferioribus subdentatis — Cent. I. pl. (65) 34

Atriplex deltoides — Pan Svec. (26) [37, as 39]

Atriplex divaricata — Prodr. fl. Dan. (82) 25

Atriplex glauca — Cent. I. pl. (65) 34

Atriplex graeca — Fl. Palaest. (70) 32

Atriplex halimus — Pan Svec. (26) [37, as 39]; Demonstr. pl. (49) 27

Atriplex hastata — Stat. pl. (55) 12; Fl. Angl. (56) 25[as Ariplex]; Fl. Monsp. (74) 28; Fl. Belg. (112) 23

Atriplex hortensis — Demonstr. pl. (49) 27; Somn. pl. (68) 14; Cul. mut. (88) 3, 4; Fl. Jam. (105) 24; Mac. olit. (113) 18; Hort. cul. (132) 14; Hist. nat. Rossia (144) 18

Atriplex hortensis rubra — Prodr. fl. Dan. (82) 25

Atriplex laciniata — Pan Svec. (26) [37, as 39]; Fl. Monsp. (74) 28; Prodr. fl. Dan. (82) 25

Atriplex lappulis — Fl. Monsp. (74) 29

Atriplex littoralis — Demonstr. pl. (49) 27; Stat. pl. (55) 12; Fl. Angl. (56) 25[as Ariplex]; Prodr. fl. Dan. (82) 25; Fl. Belg. (112) 23

Atriplex marina valerandi — Fl. Angl. (56) 26

Atriplex maritima — Fl. Angl. (56) 25[as Ariplex]; Fl. Palaest. (70) 32; Calend. fl. (72) [20]; Fl. Belg. (112) 23

Atriplex maritima angustifolia — Fl. Angl. (56) 26

Atriplex maritima halimus dicta, humilis, erecta; folliculis in latitudinem expansis et utrinque recurvis, longo pediculo insidentibus — Cent. I. pl. (65) 34

Atriplex maritima hispanica frutescens et procumbens — Cent. I. pl. (65) 34

Atriplex maritima, semine lato — Cent. I. pl. (65) 34

Atriplex montana incanescens, latiusculo folio non sinuato, fructu in thyrsulis squarrosis nigricante patulo — Nova pl. gen. 1751 (32) 44

Atriplex patula — Herbat. Upsal. (50) 10; Stat. pl. (55) 20; Fl. Angl. (56) 25[as Ariplex]; Fl. Monsp. (74) 28; Prodr. fl. Dan. (82) 25; Fl. Belg. (112) 23; Fl. Åker. (162) 20

Atriplex pedunculata — Fl. Angl. (56) 25[as Ariplex]; Cent. I. pl. (65) 34

Atriplex portulacoides — Demonstr. pl. (49) 27; Stat. pl. (55) 12; Fl. Angl. (56) 25[as Ariplex]; Fl. Monsp. (74) 28; Prodr. fl. Dan. (82) 25; Fl. Belg. (112) 8, 10, 23[as protulacoides]

Atriplex sativa — Pl. officin. (52) 5

Atriplex vulgaris — Pan Svec. (26) [37, as 39]

Atropa — Hort. Upsal. (7) 35; Vir. pl. (13) 19, 37; Nom. bot. (107) 10; Inebr. (117) 12; Mors. serp. (119) 2

Atropa arborescens — Cent. II. pl. (66) 10

Atropa belladonna — Demonstr. pl. (49) 6; Pl. officin. (52) 5; Stat. pl. (55) 8; Calend. fl. (72) [12]; Fl. Monsp. (74) 12; Prodr. fl. Dan. (82) 15; Cimicifuga (173) 9

Atropa caule frutescente, pedunculis confertis, corollis limbo revolutis, foliis ovato-oblongis — Cent. II. pl. (66) 10

Atropa physalodes — Demonstr. pl. (49) 6[as physaloides]

Attagene phrygia — Var. cib. (156) 8

Attelabus — Fund. entom. (154) 29, 30

Attelabus betulae — Pand. insect. (93) 19[as Atelabus]

Attelabus buprestoides — Pand. fl. Ryb. (165) 8

Attelabus ceramboides — Pand. insect. (93) [23, as 31]

Attelabus coryli — Pand. insect. (93) 20[as Attetabus]

Attelabus formicarius — Pand. fl. Ryb. (165) 8

Attelabus mollis — Pand. fl. Ryb. (165) 8

Atunus — Herb. Amboin. (57) 8

Atunus litorea — Herb. Amboin. (57) 12

Atzoyatl mirabilis mexicana — Cent. I. pl. (65) 34

Aura — Polit. nat. (109) 14

Aurantium — Sapor. med. (31) 14; Hort. acad. (63) 2; Nom. bot. (107) 16

Aurata — Cul. mut. (88) 9

Auricula ursi virginiana, floribus albis boraginis instar rostratis, cyclaminum more reflexis — Nova pl. gen. 1751 (32) 26

Auricularia — Vir. pl. (13) 17, 18

Auris canina — Herb. Amboin. (57) 26

Autrenus — Fund. entom. (154) 29

Avena — Peloria (3) 15; Spons. pl. (12) 17; Vir. pl. (13) 32; Fl. oecon. (17) 3, 4; Oecon. nat. (20) 17; Pl. escul. (35) 27; Vern. arb. (47) 13; Fl. Angl. (56) 4; Hort. acad. (63) 2; Pane diaet. (83) 11; Transm. frum. (87) 13ff.; Instr. peregr. (96) 10; Nom. bot. (107) 9; Polit. nat. (109) 13; Usum hist. nat. (145) 9; Fund. agrost. (152) 5, 13, 15, 16, 29, 33, 37; Esca avium (174) 5

Avena elatior — Demonstr. pl. (49) 3; Fl. Angl. (56) 11; Fl. Monsp. (74) 9

Avena fatua — Herbat. Upsal. (50) 15; Stat. pl. (55) 19; Fl. Angl. (56) 11; Fl. Monsp. (74) 9; Prodr. fl. Dan. (82) 13; Fl. Belg. (112) 13; Usum hist. nat. (145) 10; Fund. agrost. (152) 7; Fl. Åker. (162) 7

Avena fatua minor — Fl. Palaest. (70) 13

Avena flavescens — Fl. Angl. (56) 11; Fl. Monsp. (74) 9; Fund. agrost. (152) 7

Avena loeflingiana — Demonstr. pl. (49) 3

Avena nodosa — Pan Svec. (26) 15; Fl. Belg. (112) 13

Avena nuda — Demonstr. pl. (49) 3; Cent. I. pl. (65) 2; Fr. escul. (127) 19; Hort. cul. (132) 8

Avena pratensis — Pan Svec. (26) 14; Stat. pl. (55) 22; Cervus (60) 7; Prodr. fl. Dan. (82) 13; Arb. Svec. (101) 14; Polit. nat. (109) 5; Fund. agrost. (152) 9; Fl. Åker. (162) 7; Pand. fl. Ryb. (165) 16; Esca avium (174) 10

Avena sativa — Demonstr. pl. (49) 3; Pl. officin. (52) 5; Fr. escul. (127) 19; Hort. cul. (132) 8

Avena sibirica — Hist. nat. Rossia (144) 27

Avena spicata — Fl. Angl. (56) 11

Avena volitans — Pan Svec. (26) 15; Pl. escul. (35) 8

Avenca major — Acrostichum (10) 13

Averrhoa bilimbi — Herb. Amboin. (57) 7; Fr. escul. (127) 10

Averrhoa carambola — Herb. Amboin. (57) 7; Fr. escul. (127) 10

Avicennia — Obs. mat. med. (171) 6[as Avicenna]

Avicennia nitida — Pl. Surin. (177) 11

Avicennia officinalis — Pl. officin. (52) 4[as Avicenna]

Axyris — Nova pl. gen. 1751 (32) 43, 48

Axyris amaranthoides — Demonstr. pl. (49) 25

Axyris foliis lanceolatis, tomentosis, floribus femineis lanatis — Nova pl. gen. 1751 (32) 44

Axyris foliis obovatis, floribus capitatis — Nova pl. gen. 1751 (32) 44

Axyris foliis ovatis, caule erecto, spicis conglomeratis — Nova pl. gen. 1751 (32) 44

Axyris foliis ovatis, caule erecto, spicis simplicibus — Nova pl. gen. 1751 (32) 44

Axyris hybrida — Demonstr. pl. (49) 25; Hist. nat. Rossia (144) 34

Axyris prostrata — Hist. nat. Rossia (144) 34

Ayenia — Nect. fl. (122) 6; Fund. fr. (123) 16

Azalea — Vir. pl. (13) 20; Fl. Angl. (56) 6; Fr. Svec. (91) [ii]; Erica (163) 2, 3

Azalea floribus pulcherrimis speciosis rubris, folio oblongo-lanceolatis petiolis admodum crassis semper virentibus — Gem. arb. (24) 17

Azalea foliis lanceolatis integerrimis, non nervosis glabris, corymbis terminalibus — Nova pl. gen. 1751 (32) 20

Azalea fruticosa — Pan Svec. (26) 17

Azalea lapponica — Stat. pl. (55) 15; Fl. alp. (71) 13; Fr. Svec. (91) 5, 21

Azalea procumbens — Stat. pl. (55) 15; Fl. alp. (71) 13; Rar. Norv. (157) 10

Azalea supina — Pan Svec. (26) 17

Azedarach — Ficus (2) 3

Baccharis dioscoridis — Cent. I. pl. (65) 27; Fl. Palaest. (70) 28

Baccharis foliis lato-lanceolatis, dentatis, sessilibus, stipulatis — Cent. I. pl. (65) 27

Baccharis halimifolia — Demonstr. pl. (49) 23

Baccharis tenuifolia — Fl. Cap. (99) 18

Baccifera maderaspatana, ribis more floribus muscosis juli instar — Nova pl. gen. 1747 (14) 30

Bactris — Cent. insect. (129) 9

Bague — Mus. Ad.-Frid. (11) 34

Balaena — Mat. med. anim. (29) 12; Noctiluca (39) [1]; Nat. pelagi (84) 14[as Balena]; Instr. peregr. (96) 11

Balaena fistula in medio capite, dorso caudam versus acuminato — Mat. med. anim. (29) 12

Balaena nahrwal — Mat. med. anim. (29) 12

Balanus — Corallia Balt. (4) 10; Noctiluca (39) 5; Anim. comp. (98) 2

Balaustia — Sapor. med. (31) 15

Balistes capistratos — Chin. Lagerstr. (64) 21

Balistes lineis nigris ab oculis radiantibus — Chin. Lagerstr. (64) 21

Balistes ringens — Chin. Lagerstr. (64) 21[as rigens]

Balistes vetula — Iter Chin. (161) 15

Ballota — Pl. Mart.-Burs. (6) 19; Anandria (9) 4[as Ballote]; Fl. oecon. (17) 16; Fl. Jam. (105) 26

Ballota alba — Demonstr. pl. (49) 16; Fl. Belg. (112) 18

Ballota lanata — Hist. nat. Rossia (144) 30

Ballota nigra — Demonstr. pl. (49) 16; Stat. pl. (55) 20; Fl. Angl. (56) 18; Calend. fl. (72) [16]; Fl. Monsp. (74) 19; Prodr. fl. Dan. (82) 20; Fl. Belg. (112) 18

Ballota scanensis — Pan Svec. (26) 26

Ballota suaveolens — Pl. Jam. (102) 15; Fl. Jam. (105) 18

Balsamina — Vern. arb. (47) 9

Balsamina altera indica repens, hederae arboreae foliis, flore subviridi — Passifl. (8) 16

Balsamita — Vir. pl. (13) 23

Balsamum — Opobals. (135) 2ff.

Balsamum gileadensis — Opobals. (135) 14ff.

Balsamum judaicum — Opobals. (135) 14

Ban — Pot. coff. (118) 8

Bancudus angustifolia — Herb. Amboin. (57) 13

Bancudus latifolia — Herb. Amboin. (57) 13

Bangleum — Herb. Amboin. (57) 20

Banisteria — Nect. fl. (122) 14[as Bannisteria]

Banisteria benghalensis — Fl. Jam. (105) 16

Banisteria fulgens — Fl. Jam. (105) 16

Banisteria lupuloides — Demonstr. pl. (49) 12[as Bannisteria]; Fl. Jam. (105) 16

Baobab — Hort. Upsal. (7) 36[as Bahobab]; Gem. arb. (24) 6[as Bahobab]

Barba caprina — Inebr. (117) 13[as cyprina]

Barba saturni — Herb. Amboin. (57) 27

Barbarea — Vir. pl. (13) 22

Barbilus — Fl. Jam. (105) 27

Bardana — Vir. pl. (13) 23; Sapor. med. (31) 11

Barleria cristata — Iter Chin. (161) 9

Barleria longifolia — Cent. II. pl. (66) 22

Barleria spinis verticillorum senis, foliis ensiformibus longissimis scabris — Cent. II. pl. (66) 22

Barreria — Fl. Cap. (99) 6

Barreria capensis — Fl. Cap. (99) 13

Bartramia — Nova pl. gen. 1747 (14) [vi], 17; Herb. Amboin. (57) 14

Bartramia indica — Demonstr. pl. (49) 11

Bartsia — Pl. Mart.-Burs. (6) [vi]; Nova pl. gen. 1751 (32) 9

Bartsia alpina — Stat. pl. (55) 16; Fl. Angl. (56) 19; Fl. alp. (71) 19; Rar. Norv. (157) 10; Colon. pl. (158) 6

Bartsia foliis alternis — Pl. Mart.-Burs. (6) 20

Bartsia foliis alternis (pinnatifidis) — Pl. rar. Camsch. (30) 24

Bartsia foliis alternis bidentatis — Pl. rar. Camsch. (30) 23

Bartsia lapponica — Pan Svec. (26) 27

Bartsia pallida — Hist. nat. Rossia (144) 31

Bartsia trixago — Fl. Palaest. (70) 23; Fl. Monsp. (74) 20

Bartsia viscosa — Fl. Angl. (56) 5, 19

Basella — Nova pl. gen. 1747 (14) [vi], 12, 13

Basella alba — Demonstr. pl. (49) 9

Basella rubra — Demonstr. pl. (49) 9; Herb. Amboin. (57) 24; Pl. tinct. (97) 15

Basilicum agreste — Herb. Amboin. (57) 21

Basilicum indicum — Herb. Amboin. (57) 21

Batatas — Fl. Cap. (99) 2

Batis — Fl. Jam. (105) 26

Batis maritima — Fl. Jam. (105) 21

Battata — Herb. Amboin. (57) 23[as Batatta]

Battata mammosa — Herb. Amboin. (57) 23[as Batatta]

Bauhinia — Hort. Upsal. (7) 36; Somn. pl. (68) 17; Nect. fl. (122) 5, 7

Bauhinia acuminata — Fl. Jam. (105) 16

Bauhinia bipartita — Demonstr. pl. (49) 11

Bauhinia scandens — Herb. Amboin. (57) 18

Bazella — Hort. Upsal. (7) 36

Beccabunga — Morb. hyeme (38) 8; Scorb. (180) 16

Becchaea frutescens — Iter Chin. (161) 9

Begonia — Herb. Amboin. (57) 24

Begonia obliqua — Fl. Jam. (105) 22

Behen album — Vir. pl. (13) 23

Beidelsar — Hort. Upsal. (7) 35[as Beidalsar]

Belladonna — Odor. med. (40) 15

Belladonna frutescens, flore albo, nicotianae foliis — Cent. II. pl. (66) 10

Bellidiastrum subhirsutum linifolium — Cent. II. pl. (66) 31

Bellis — Peloria (3) 9, 10; Nom. bot. (107) 17

Bellis annua — Fl. Palaest. (70) 28; Fl. Monsp. (74) 25

Bellis folio obtuso — Fl. Monsp. (74) 29

Bellis frutescens africana camphorata — Cent. II. pl. (66) 31

Bellis hortensis — Demonstr. pl. (49) 23

Bellis minor — Vir. pl. (13) 23

Bellis officinarum — Pan Svec. (26) 33

Bellis perennis — Pl. officin. (52) 6; Stat. pl. (55) 14; Fl. Angl. (56) 22; Fl. Monsp. (74) 25; Prodr. fl. Dan. (82) 23; Fl. Belg. (112) 8, 21; Hort. cul. (132) 24, 25

Bellonia — Vir. pl. (13) 27

Berberis — Hort. Upsal. (7) 21; Vir. pl. (13) 33, 36; Fl. oecon. (17) 9; Sapor. med. (31) 14; Pl. escul. (35) 13, 28, 29; Fr. Svec. (91) [ii], 24, 25; Pand. insect. (93) 13; Nom. bot. (107) 12; Polit. nat. (109) 5; Prol. pl. 1760 (114) 8; Nect. fl. (122) 4, 10; Prol. pl. 1763 (130) 8; Usum hist. nat. (145) 17

Berberis indica, aurantiae folio — Nova pl. gen. 1747 (14) 31

Berberis spinosa — Gem. arb. (24) 22; Pan Svec. (26) 20

Berberis vulgaris — Demonstr. pl. (49) 10; Herbat. Upsal. (50) 11; Pl. officin. (52) 6; Fl. Angl. (56) 14; Fl. Palaest. (70) 18; Calend. fl. (72) [10], [12], [13]; Fr. Svec. (91) 4, 14; Pl. tinct. (97) 15; Fl. Belg. (112) 16; Fr. escul. (127) 6; Purg. indig. (143) 9; Colon. pl. (158) 8; Fl. Åker. (162) 10

Bernardia — Fl. Jam. (105) 26

Beroe — Mund. invis. (149) 15

Besleria cristata — Pl. Surin. (177) 11

Beta — Cul. mut. (88) 4; Generat. ambig. (104) 8; Nom. bot. (107) 11

Beta alba — Cul. mut. (88) 2

Beta alba vel pallescens — Cul. mut. (88) 4

Beta pallescens — Cul. mut. (88) 4

Beta perennis — Fl. Palaest. (70) 16

Beta radice rapae — Cul. mut. (88) 7

Beta rubra — Cul. mut. (88) 2; Fl. Cap. (99) 2

Beta rubra, radice rapae — Cul. mut. (88) 5

Beta vulgaris — Demonstr. pl. (49) 7; Pl. officin. (52) 6; Fl. Angl. (56) 6, 13; Fl. Monsp. (74) 12; Cul. mut. (88) 4; Fl. Jam. (105) 24; Mac. olit. (113) 17; Hort. cul. (132) 13, 14

Beta vulgaris rubra — Acetaria (77) 15; Mac. olit. (113) 10

Betonica — Vir. pl. (13) 12; Nom. bot. (107) 14

Betonica alopecuros — Fl. alp. (71) 19

Betonica annua glabra — Fl. Monsp. (74) 19

Betonica annua hirsuta — Fl. Monsp. (74) 19[as hirta]; Prodr. fl. Dan. (82) 20

Betonica coronaria — Cent. I. pl. (65) 11

Betonica hirta — Cent. II. pl. (66) 20; Fl. Belg. (112) 18

Betonica officinalis — Pan Svec. (26) 26; Demonstr. pl. (49) 16; Pl. officin. (52) 6; Fl. Angl. (56) 18; Fl. Palaest. (70) 22; Fl. Monsp. (74) 19; Prodr. fl. Dan. (82) 20

Betonica procumbens, verticillis disjunctis, foliis lineari-lanceolatis — Cent. II. pl. (66) 20

Betula — Betula (1) 1ff.; Spons. pl. (12) 32, 41; Fl. oecon. (17) 22, 23; Oecon. nat. (20) 17; Gem. arb. (24) 11; Sapor. med. (31) 15; Pl. escul. (35) 24, 27; Morb. hyeme (38) 13; Hosp. insect. fl. (43) 13, 40; Noxa insect. (46) 25; Vern. arb. (47) 10, 18, table; Fl. Angl. (56) 6; Oves (61) 18; Mus ind. (62) 14; Migr. avium (79) 29; Fr. Svec. (91) [ii], 24; Pand. insect. (93) 18; Arb. Svec. (101) 30; Nom. bot. (107) 18; Fl. Belg. (112) 8; Inebr. (117) 13

Betula alba — Hosp. insect. fl. (43) 33; Herbat. Upsal. (50) 6; Pl. officin. (52) 6; Stat. pl. (55) 18; Fl. Angl. (56) 24; Calend. fl. (72) [10]; Prodr. fl. Dan. (82) 24; Pl. tinct. (97) 25; Arb. Svec. (101) 7, 9, 15, 17, 24, 30; Fl. Belg. (112) 22; Hist. nat. Rossia (144) 34; Fl. Åker. (162) 19; Pand. fl. Ryb. (165) 22

Betula alnus — Herbat. Upsal. (50) 6; Stat. pl. (55) 14; Fl. Angl. (56) 24; Calend. fl. (72) [10]; Fl. Monsp. (74) 27; Prodr. fl. Dan. (82) 24; Pl. tinct. (97) 25; Arb. Svec. (101) 7, 9, 17, 24; Fl. Belg. (112) 22; Hist. nat. Rossia (144) 34; Fl. Åker. (162) 19; Pand. fl. Ryb. (165) 22

Betula arbor americana, seminibus lithospermi frumentacei aemulis — Betula (1) 5

Betula cortice scabro hinc inde nigro — Betula (1) 3

Betula femina — Betula (1) 3

Betula foliis acuminatis serratis — Betula (1) 2, 5

Betula foliis cordatis serratis — Betula (1) 2

Betula foliis orbiculatis crenatis — Betula (1) 4, 5, 6, 16, plate [1]; Pl. Mart.-Burs. (6) 29

Betula folio candido latiore acuminato — Betula (1) 3

Betula folio rotundiore, ramis pendentibus — Betula (1) 3

Betula fragilis, folio subnigro lanuginoso — Betula (1) 3

Betula humilis rotundifolia — Betula (1) 4, 15

Betula julifera, fructu conoide, viminibus lentis — Betula (1) 5

Betula mas — Betula (1) 2

Betula nana — Betula (1) 4, 9ff.; Hort. Upsal. (7) 33; Oecon. nat. (20) 35; Gem. arb. (24) 10, 31; Pan Svec. (26) 6, 35; Demonstr. pl. (49) 25; Stat. pl. (55) 15; Cervus (60) 19; Fl. alp. (71) 23, 24; Calend. fl. (72) [10]; Prodr. fl. Dan. (82) 24; Fr. Svec. (91) 3, 10, 24; Pl. tinct. (97) 25; Arb. Svec. (101) 29; Hist. nat. Rossia (144) 34; Rar. Norv. (157) 11; Colon. pl. (158) 6; Ledum (178) [1]

Betula nana pumila — Betula (1) 14

Betula nana seu pumila — Betula (1) 4

Betula nana seu pusilla — Betula (1) 14

Betula nana suecorum — Betula (1) 4, 14, 15

Betula nigra virginiana — Betula (1) 5

Betula palustris nana — Betula (1) 4, 15

Betula palustris pumila, foliis parvis rotundis — Betula (1) 4, 15, 16

Betula pumila — Betula (1) 4, 5, 14

Betula pumila, foliis subrotundis — Betula (1) 4, 16

Betula pusilla — Betula (1) 4, 14

Betula saxatilis torminalis, folio oblongo — Betula (1) 3

Betula virgulis erectis — Betula (1) 2

Betula virgulis erectis, foliis latioribus, subtus incanis — Betula (1) 3

Betula virgulis pendulis — Betula (1) 3

Betula vulgaris — Betula (1) 5, 9ff.; Gem. arb. (24) 30; Pan Svec. (26) 35

Betula vulgaris major — Betula (1) 2

Bibio — Fund. entom. (154) 30

Bidens — Fl. oecon. (17) 20; Specif. Canad. (76) 22

Bidens americana trifolia, leucanthemi flore — Cent. I. pl. (65) 29

Bidens apiifolia — Pl. Jam. (102) 22; Fl. Jam. (105) 19[as apifolia]

Bidens atriplicifolia — Cent. II. pl. (66) 30[as atripicifolia]

Bidens bipinnata — Demonstr. pl. (49) 22; Herb. Amboin. (57) 26

Bidens caule paniculato, foliis deltoidibus alternis dentatis petiolatis stipulatis — Cent. II. pl. (66) 30

Bidens cernua — Fl. Angl. (56) 22; Metam. pl. (67) 21; Fl. Monsp. (74) 25; Prodr. fl. Dan. (82) 23; Fl. Belg. (112) 21; Pand. fl. Ryb. (165) 21

Bidens frondosa — Demonstr. pl. (49) 22; Calend. fl. (72) [18][as frondosus]

Bidens nivea — Fl. Jam. (105) 19

Bidens nodiflora, folio tetrahit — Cent. I. pl. (65) 28

Bidens nutans — Pan Svec. (26) 32

Bidens qui verbesina minima — Pl. Mart.-Burs. (6) 24

Bidens seminibus erectis, calycibus subtetraphyllis, foliis linearibus, pedunculis capillaribus — Pl. rar. Afr. (115) 17

Bidens tenella — Pl. rar. Afr. (115) 17[as tenellus]

Bidens tripartita — Pan Svec. (26) 32; Herbat. Upsal. (50) 15[as tripartitus]; Stat. pl. (55) 14; Fl. Angl. (56) 22; Fl. Palaest. (70) 28; Fl. Monsp. (74) 25; Prodr. fl. Dan. (82) 23; Pl. tinct. (97) 23; Fl. Belg. (112) 21; Fl. Åker. (162) 17

Bignonia — Hort. Upsal. (7) 35; Herb. Amboin. (57) 12; Nect. fl. (122) 8; Pl. Surin. (177) 11

Bignonia catalpa — Fl. Jam. (105) 18; Meloe (124) 4

Bignonia leucoxylon — Fl. Jam. (105) 18

Bignonia peruviana — Fl. Jam. (105) 18

Bignonia pinnatifolia — Gem. arb. (24) 20

Bignonia radicans — Demonstr. pl. (49) 17; Fung. melit. (69) 2; Polit. nat. (109) 5

Bignonia trifolia — Fl. Jam. (105) 18

Bilacus — Herb. Amboin. (57) 8

Bilacus taurinus — Herb. Amboin. (57) 8

Bintangor maritima — Herb. Amboin. (57) 10[as maritimum]

Bintangor sylvestris — Herb. Amboin. (57) 10

Biscutella auriculata — Demonstr. pl. (49) 17

Biscutella didyma — Fl. Palaest. (70) 24; Fl. Monsp. (74) 21

Biscutella didyma alpha — Demonstr. pl. (49) 17

Biscutella didyma beta — Demonstr. pl. (49) 17

Biserrula pelecinus — Demonstr. pl. (49) 21

Bistorta — Gem. arb. (24) 5; Sem. musc. (28) 6, 9; Sapor. med. (31) 15; Pl. escul. (35) 14, 27; Rhabarbarum (41) 5, 6; Nom. bot. (107) 12; Fraga (170) 2

Bistorta minor — Pan Svec. (26) 21; Hosp. insect. fl. (43) 21

Bistorta vivipara — Herbat. Upsal. (50) 8

Bixa — Passifl. (8) [iii]; Nom. bot. (107) 14

Bixa orellana — Pl. officin. (52) 14; Herb. Amboin. (57) 9; Pl. tinct. (97) 19; Fl. Jam. (105) 17; Pl. Surin. (177) 10

Blaeria — Erica (163) 3

Blaeria ericoides — Fl. Cap. (99) 12

Blairia — Vir. pl. (13) 20

Blakea — Fl. Jam. (105) 26

Blakea trinervia — Fl. Jam. (105) 17; Pl. Surin. (177) 9

Blakea triplinervia — Pl. Surin. (177) 9

Blasia pusilla — Rar. Norv. (157) 11

Blatta — Oecon. nat. (20) 29; Noxa insect. (46) 12, 13; Instr. peregr. (96) 12; Fund. entom. (154) 21, 25; Ledum (178) 11

Blatta lucifuga — Usum hist. nat. (145) 27

Blatta orientalis — Iter Chin. (161) 10

Blechnum — Fl. Jam. (105) 26

Blechnum occidentale — Fl. Jam. (105) 23

Blennius — Oecon. nat. (20) 27

Blennius pinnis ocularibus brevissimis palmatis, linea laterali curva — Mus. Ad.-Frid. (11) 38

Blennius pinnis ocularibus subulatis, pinnae ani ossiculorum 26 — Mus. Ad.-Frid. (11) 37

Blennius pinnulis duabus ad oculos, pinna ani ossiculorum viginti trium — Mus. Ad.-Frid. (11) 38

Blinbingum sylvestre — Herb. Amboin. (57) 17[as Blimbingum]

Blinbingum teres — Herb. Amboin. (57) 7[as Blimbingum]

Blitum — Ficus (2) 18; Hort. Upsal. (7) 34; Anandria (9) 5; Spons. pl. (12) 48; Pl. hybr. (33) 7; Cul. mut. (88) 2, 4

Blitum capitatum — Demonstr. pl. (49) [1]; Prodr. fl. Dan. (82) 12

Blitum capitellis sparsis lateralibus — Pl. hybr. (33) 14

Blitum capitellis spicatis terminalibus — Pl. hybr. (33) 14[as terminalbus]

Blitum ficus folio — Cent. II. pl. (66) 13

Blitum frutescens — Herb. Amboin. (57) 21

Blitum indicum — Herb. Amboin. (57) 21

Blitum spinosum — Herb. Amboin. (57) 21

Blitum virgatum — Demonstr. pl. (49) [1]; Fl. Monsp. (74) 8; Hist. nat. Rossia (144) 23

Boa — Mors. serp. (119) 4; Var. cib. (156) 4

Boa constrictor — Mors. serp. (119) 3

Bobartia — Nova pl. gen. 1747 (14) [vi], 3, 4; Fund. agrost. (152) 20, 25, 34

Bocconia — Vir. pl. (13) 21, 25; Opium (179) 4

Bocconia frutescens — Fl. Jam. (105) 17

Boerhavia — Hort. Upsal. (7) 36[as Boerhaavia]

Boerhavia diandra — Demonstr. pl. (49) [1]

Boerhavia diffusa — Demonstr. pl. (49) [1]; Fl. Jam. (105) 12, 25

Boerhavia scandens — Fl. Jam. (105) 12

Boicocininga — Mus. Ad.-Frid. (11) 20

Boiguacu — Surin. Grill. (16) 20

Boletus — Vir. pl. (13) 7; Fl. oecon. (17) 29, 30; Pl. escul. (35) 27; Pl. officin. (52) 4; Mund. invis. (149) 15; Med. purg. (181) 24

Boletus dimidiatus quidam fere membranaceus — Pl. Mart.-Burs. (6) 28

Bombax — Chin. Lagerstr. (64) 5; Phalaena (78) [2]

Bombax aculeatum — Fl. Jam. (105) 18, 25

Bombax inerme — Fl. Jam. (105) 18, 25

Bombax pentandrum — Herb. Amboin. (57) 8

Bombylius — Spons. pl. (12) 50

Bombylius medius — Esca avium (174) [9, as 17]

Bombyx — Ficus (2) 17, 27; Spons. pl. (12) 55; Mat. med. anim. (29) 15; Hosp. insect. fl. (43) 12;

Mirac. insect. (45) 19; Metam. pl. (67) 11; Phalaena (78) 3ff.; Exanth. viva (86) 15; Instr. peregr. (96) 11; Polit. nat. (109) 8; Usum hist. nat. (145) 29; Mund. invis. (149) 10

Bon vel ban, arbor — Pot. coff. (118) 8

Bon vel ban ex cujus fructu aegyptii potum — Pot. coff. (118) 8

Boncalus — Herb. Amboin. (57) 12

Bontia daphnoides — Fl. Jam. (105) 18

Borago — Spons. pl. (12) 33[as Borrago]; Vir. pl. (13) 18[as Borrago]; Vern. arb. (47) 9[as Borrago]; Cul. mut. (88) 2, 4; Pand. insect. (93) 12; Nom. bot. (107) 10

Borago africana — Fl. Cap. (99) 12

Borago hortensis — Fl. Angl. (56) 12; Fl. Belg. (112) 14

Borago indica — Demonstr. pl. (49) 5[as Borrago]

Borago officinalis — Hosp. insect. fl. (43) 16[as Borrago]; Demonstr. pl. (49) 5[as Borrago]; Pl. officin. (52) 6[as Borrago]; Calend. fl. (72) [22][as Borrago]; Fl. Jam. (105) 13, 25; Mac. olit. (113) 20; Hort. cul. (132) 23

Borassus — Vir. pl. (13) 26

Borassus flabellifer — Herb. Amboin. (57) 6

Borbonia — Fl. Cap. (99) 6, 8, 9; Fund. fr. (123) 18

Borbonia cordata — Fl. Cap. (99) 16

Borbonia crenata — Fl. Cap. (99) 16

Borbonia ericifolia — Pl. rar. Afr. (115) 14

Borbonia foliis sublinearibus acutis, subtus villosis, capitulis terminalibus — Pl. rar. Afr. (115) 14

Borbonia lanceolata — Fl. Cap. (99) 16

Borbonia tomentosa — Fl. Cap. (99) 16

Borbonia trinervia — Fl. Cap. (99) 16

Borrago — see Borago

Bos — Vir. pl. (13) 16, 17; Oecon. nat. (20) 35, 42; Generat. calc. (22) 2, 5, 7; Pan Svec. (26) 3, 11ff.; Mat. med. anim. (29) 8; Hosp. insect. fl. (43) 9; Noxa insect. (46) 27, 28; Polit. nat. (109) 21

Bos cornibus teretibus flexis — Mat. med. anim. (29) 8

Boschas major — Mat. med. anim. (29) 9

Bostricius — Fund. entom. (154) 29

Botrys — Vern. arb. (47) 9

Bourreria — Fl. Jam. (105) 26[as Boureria]

Bovista — Buxbaumia (85) 9

Brabejum — Fl. Cap. (99) 6

Brabejum stellatifolium — Fl. Cap. (99) 12

Bradypus — Surin. Grill. (16) 9; Oecon. nat. (20) 36; Polit. nat. (109) 16

Bradypus manibus tridactylis, cauda brevi — Surin. Grill. (16) 7

Brama — Usum hist. nat. (145) 26

Brassica — Peloria (3) 10, 16; Spons. pl. (12) 49; Vir. pl. (13) 7, 22, 36; Fl. oecon. (17) 17; Sapor. med. (31) 11; Pl. hybr. (33) 7; Pl. escul. (35) 9, 10, 20, 21, 23, 24, 28; Hosp. insect. fl. (43) 12; Noxa insect. (46) 19; Oves (61) 23; Mus ind. (62) 14; Hort. acad. (63) 3; Metam. pl. (67) 15, 25; Pane diaet. (83) 20; Pand. insect. (93) [17, as 38]; Nom. bot. (107) 15; Polit. nat. (109) 8; Fund. entom. (154) 24[as Brasica]; Scorb. (180) 21

Brassica alpina perennis — Fl. alp. (71) 20

Brassica campestris — Stat. pl. (55) 19; Prodr. fl. Dan. (82) 21; Fl. Belg. (112) 19[as campestre]; Raphania (126) 13ff.; Usum hist. nat. (145) 10; Fl. Åker. (162) 15; Pand. fl. Ryb. (165) 20

Brassica capitata — Vir. pl. (13) 4

Brassica chinensis — Cent. I. pl. (65) 19

Brassica eruca — Demonstr. pl. (49) 18; Pl. officin. (52) 10; Calend. fl. (72) [22]; Cul. mut. (88) 6

Brassica erucastrum — Demonstr. pl. (49) 18; Fl. Angl. (56) 20; Fl. Palaest. (70) 24; Fl. Belg. (112) 19

Brassica fimbriata — Mus ind. (62) 14

Brassica foliis lanceolato-ovatis glabris indivisis dentatis — Anandria (9) 5

Brassica foliis lyratis, caule hirsuto, siliquis glabris — Pl. hybr. (33) 15

Brassica foliis lyratis, caule hirsuto, siliquis retrorsum hispidis — Pl. hybr. (33) 15

Brassica foliis ovalibus, subintegerrimis; floralibus amplexicaulibus, lanceolatis; calycibus unguibus petalorum longioribus — Cent. I. pl. (65) 19

Brassica napus — Pan Svec. (26) 28; Pl. escul. (35) 19; Demonstr. pl. (49) 18; Pl. officin. (52) 14; Fl. Angl. (56) 20; Fl. Monsp. (74) 21; Fl. Belg. (112) 19; Mac. olit. (113) 9; Hort. cul. (132) 12; Usum hist. nat. (145) 10

Brassica oleracea — Demonstr. pl. (49) 18; Pl. officin. (52) 6; Fl. Angl. (56) 20; Metam. pl. (67) 15; Fl. Palaest. (70) 24; Fl. Monsp. (74) 21; Fl. Cap. (99) 2; Fl. Jam. (105) 24; Mac. olit. (113) 9, 17; Hort. cul. (132) 11

Brassica oleracea botrytis — Mac. olit. (113) 15; Fund. fr. (123) 13; Hort. cul. (132) 11

Brassica oleracea capitata — Mac. olit. (113) 17; Fund. fr. (123) 13; Hort. cul. (132) 11

Brassica oleracea gongylodes — Mac. olit. (113) 15; Hort. cul. (132) 11

Brassica oleracea laciniata — Mac. olit. (113) 17; Fund. fr. (123) 13; Hort. cul. (132) 11

Brassica oleracea napobrassica — Hort. cul. (132) 11

Brassica oleracea rubra — Acetaria (77) 14; Mac. olit. (113) 17; Fund. fr. (123) 13

Brassica oleracea sabauda — Mac. olit. (113) 17; Fund. fr. (123) 13; Hort. cul. (132) 11

Brassica oleracea sabellica — Mac. olit. (113) 17; Fund. fr. (123) 13; Hort. cul. (132) 11

Brassica oleracea selenisia — Mac. olit. (113) 15; Fund. fr. (123) 13

Brassica oleracea viridis — Mac. olit. (113) 17; Fund. fr. (123) 13; Hort. cul. (132) 11

Brassica orientalis — Demonstr. pl. (49) 17; Fl. Angl. (56) 20

Brassica orientalis perfoliata — Pl. hybr. (33) 15

Brassica perfoliata — Pan Svec. (26) 28

Brassica rapa — Demonstr. pl. (49) 18; Pl. officin. (52) 16; Fl. Angl. (56) 20; Acetaria (77) 14; Fl. Jam. (105) 24; Fl. Belg. (112) 19; Mac. olit. (113) 9; Hort. cul. (132) 12; Esca avium (174) 13

Brassica sativa — Hosp. insect. fl. (43) 28

Brassica selenisia — Cul. mut. (88) 7[as selenicia]

Brassica vesicaria — Demonstr. pl. (49) 18

Briza — Pl. Jam. (102) 7; Fund. agrost. (152) 5, 23, 28, 31, 37

Briza bipinnata — Fl. Palaest. (70) 12

Briza eragrostis — Demonstr. pl. (49) 3; Fl. Monsp. (74) 9

Briza maxima — Fl. Monsp. (74) 9

Briza media — Herbat. Upsal. (50) 6; Stat. pl. (55) 21; Fl. Angl. (56) 10; Fl. Monsp. (74) 9; Prodr. fl. Dan. (82) 13; Fl. Belg. (112) 13; Fund. agrost. (152) 7; Fl. Åker. (162) 6; Pand. fl. Ryb. (165) 16

Briza minor — Fl. Angl. (56) 10; Fl. Monsp. (74) 9

Briza vulgaris — Pan Svec. (26) 14

Bromelia — Hort. Upsal. (7) 36; Pl. escul. (35) 4

Bromelia ananas — Fl. Cap. (99) 2; Fl. Jam. (105) 15; Fr. escul. (127) 9; Hort. cul. (132) 19; Iter Chin. (161) 9; Obs. mat. med. (171) 3

Bromelia comosa — Herb. Amboin. (57) 21

Bromelia karatas — Demonstr. pl. (49) 9; Usum hist. nat. (145) 16[as caratas]; Siren. lacert. (146) 7

Bromelia pinguin — Fl. Jam. (105) 15

Bromus — Peloria (3) 15; Spons. pl. (12) 17; Fl. oecon. (17) 3; Pl. escul. (35) 7, 27; Migr. avium (79) 34; Transm. frum. (87) 13; Nom. bot. (107) 9; Fund. agrost. (152) 5, 16, 21, 29, 31, 37

Bromus arvensis — Demonstr. pl. (49) 3; Herbat. Upsal. (50) 13; Stat. pl. (55) 19; Fl. Angl. (56) 11; Usum hist. nat. (145) 10; Fund. agrost. (152) 7, 9; Fl. Åker. (162) 7; Pand. fl. Ryb. (165) 16; Esca avium (174) 10

Bromus ciliatus — Demonstr. pl. (49) 3

Bromus cristatus — Hist. nat. Rossia (144) 27

Bromus culmo indiviso: spicis alternis subsessilibus teretibus — Pl. Mart.-Burs. (6) 2; Pl. rar. Camsch. (30) 7

Bromus distachyos — Cent. II. pl. (66) 8; Fl. Palaest. (70) 13; Fl. Monsp. (74) 9

Bromus giganteus — Demonstr. pl. (49) 3; Fl. Angl. (56) 11; Prodr. fl. Dan. (82) 13; Fund. agrost. (152) 7; Fl. Åker. (162) 7

Bromus hordeaceus — Herbat. Upsal. (50) 17

Bromus hordeiformis — Pan Svec. (26) 14

Bromus madritensis — Cent. I. pl. (65) 5

Bromus nutans — Fl. Monsp. (74) 9

Bromus panicula fasciculata, spiculis subsessilibus glabris, aristis patulis — Cent. I. pl. (65) 6[as subsessibilibus]

Bromus panicula fasciculata, spiculis subsessilibus villosis; aristis erectis — Cent. I. pl. (65) 5

Bromus panicula nutante, spiculis linearibus — Pl. Mart.-Burs. (6) 5

Bromus panicula nutante, spiculis ovato-oblongis — Pl. Mart.-Burs. (6) 5

Bromus panicula rariore erecta, spiculis linearibus: intermediis geminis — Cent. I. pl. (65) 5

Bromus panicula spicata rarissima, spiculis linearibus alternis: pedicellis incrassatis — Cent. I. pl. (65) 5

Bromus perennis maxima — Pan Svec. (26) 14

Bromus pinnatus — Stat. pl. (55) 18; Fl. Angl. (56) 11; Fl. Monsp. (74) 9; Fl. Belg. (112) 13; Fl. Åker. (162) 7

Bromus purgans — Demonstr. pl. (49) 3

Bromus rubens — Cent. I. pl. (65) 5

Bromus scoparius — Cent. I. pl. (65) 6; Fl. Palaest. (70) 13

Bromus secalinus — Herbat. Upsal. (50) 12; Stat. pl. (55) 19; Fl. Angl. (56) 11; Fl. Monsp. (74) 9; Prodr. fl. Dan. (82) 13; Pl. tinct. (97) 12; Fl. Belg. (112) 13; Usum hist. nat. (145) 10; Fund. agrost. (152) 7, 9; Fl. Åker. (162) 7; Pand. fl. Ryb. (165) 16; Esca avium (174) 10

Bromus spica brizae — Pan Svec. (26) 14

Bromus spicis duabus erectis — Cent. II. pl. (66) 8

Bromus spiculis distiche imbricatis sessilibus depressis — Pl. rar. Camsch. (30) 6

Bromus squarrosus — Fl. Monsp. (74) 9; Hist. nat. Rossia (144) 27

Bromus sterilis — Fl. Angl. (56) 11; Prodr. fl. Dan. (82) 13; Fl. Belg. (112) 13

Bromus sterilis, erecta panicula, major — Cent. I. pl. (65) 5[as Bromos]

Bromus tectorum — Pan Svec. (26) 14; Demonstr. pl. (49) 3; Herbat. Upsal. (50) 12; Stat. pl. (55) 21; Fl. Angl. (56) 11; Fl. Palaest. (70) 13; Fl. Monsp. (74) 9; Prodr. fl. Dan. (82) 13; Fund. agrost. (152) 7, 9; Fl. Åker. (162) 7

Bromus upsaliensis — Pan Svec. (26) 14

Bromus vulgaris — Pan Svec. (26) 14

Browallia americana — Demonstr. pl. (49) 17

Bruchus — Noxa insect. (46) 15; Fund. entom. (154) 29, 30

Bruchus chinensis fuscus, elytris ferrugineis, scutello albo — Noxa insect. (46) 16

Brunfelsia — Nect. fl. (122) 7[as Brunsfelsia]

Brunia — Fl. Cap. (99) 6, 8; Fund. fr. (123) 18

Brunia abrotanoides — Fl. Cap. (99) 12

Brunia ciliata — Fl. Cap. (99) 12

Brunia lanuginosa — Fl. Cap. (99) 12

Brunia levisanus — Fl. Cap. (99) 12

Brunia nodiflora — Fl. Cap. (99) 12

Brunia uniflora — Fl. Cap. (99) 12

Brunsfelsia — see Brunfelsia

Brya — Fl. Jam. (105) 26

Bryonia — Vern. arb. (47) 9; Stat. pl. (55) 6; Nom. bot. (107) 18[as Bayonia]

Bryonia africana — Demonstr. pl. (49) 25; Fl. Cap. (99) 19

Bryonia alba — Pan Svec. (26) 36; Demonstr. pl. (49) 25; Pl. officin. (52) 6; Stat. pl. (55) 20; Fl. Angl. (56) 24; Calend. fl. (72) [13]; Fl. Monsp. (74) 28; Prodr. fl. Dan. (82) 24; Fl. Belg. (112) 22; Purg. indig. (143) 11; Med. purg. (181) 10

Bryonia cordifolia — Herb. Amboin. (57) 24; Fl. Palaest. (70) 31

Bryonia foliis palmatis quinquepartitis: lobis trifidis bifidisve subtus glanduloso-punctatis — Demonstr. pl. (49) 26

Bryonia foliis palmatis utrinque callososcabris — Med. purg. (181) 10

Bryonia punctata — Demonstr. pl. (49) 26

Bryonia zeylanica — Nect. fl. (122) 4

Bryoniae radix lapidea simplex — Corallia Balt. (4) 17

Bryum — Fl. oecon. (17) 29; Oecon. nat. (20) 19, 25; Splachnum (27) 5, 6; Sem. musc. (28) 6, 7, 14, 17; Cui bono? (42) 14, 15; Buxbaumia (85) 11; Arb. Svec. (101) 15; Usum musc. (148) 5, 10

Bryum aestivum — Usum musc. (148) 5

Bryum ampullaceum, foliis thymi pellucidis, collo strictiore — Nova pl. gen. 1751 (32) 47

Bryum apocarpum — Herbat. Upsal. (50) 11

Bryum argenteum — Prodr. fl. Dan. (82) 26

Bryum caespiticium — Herbat. Upsal. (50) 9[as cespiticium]; Stat. pl. (55) 15

Bryum capsuli nutantibus, foliis subovatis obtusis pellucidis punctatis, caulibus striatis procumbentibus, pedunculis aggregatis — Pl. Mart.-Burs. (6) 28

Bryum extinctorium — Herbat. Upsal. (50) 11

Bryum flexuosum — Herbat. Upsal. (50) 11

Bryum heteromallum — Herbat. Upsal. (50) 11

Bryum hypnoides — Herbat. Upsal. (50) 5; Usum musc. (148) 10

Bryum paludosum — Usum musc. (148) 5

Bryum pomiforme — Herbat. Upsal. (50) 11

Bryum pulvinatum — Herbat. Upsal. (50) 16

Bryum rurale — Sem. musc. (28) 18; Herbat. Upsal. (50) 12; Usum musc. (148) 10

Bryum scoparium — Herbat. Upsal. (50) 11

Bryum squarrosum — Usum musc. (148) 5

Bryum striatum — Herbat. Upsal. (50) 9

Bryum tortuosum — Fl. alp. (71) 24

Bryum truncatulum — Herbat. Upsal. (50) 11; Fl. Palaest. (70) 32

Bryum undulatum — Herbat. Upsal. (50) 11

Bubo — Noctiluca (39) 5; Migr. avium (79) 21

Bubon — Vir. pl. (13) 19; Herb. Amboin. (57) 16; Fl. Cap. (99) 6

Bubon galbanum — Fl. Cap. (99) 12

Bubon gummiferum — Fl. Cap. (99) 12

Bubon macedonicum — Demonstr. pl. (49) 8; Pl. officin. (52) 10[as macedonium], 15

Buccinum — Fund. test. (166) 17, 37

Buccinum cornutum — Fund. test. (166) 23

Buccinum harpa — Fund. test. (166) 37

Buccinum musica — Fund. test. (166) 38

Buccinum rufum — Iter Chin. (161) 13

Buceras — Fl. Jam. (105) 26

Buceros — Polit. nat. (109) 14; Fund. ornith. (137) 14

Buchnera africana — Pl. rar. Afr. (115) 12

Buchnera foliis dentatis oppositis, calycibus subtomentosis fructu longioribus — Pl. rar. Afr. (115) 12[as subtomeutosis]

Bucida — Fl. Jam. (105) 26

Bucida buceras — Pl. Jam. (102) 12; Fl. Jam. (105) 16

Buddleja americana — Pl. Jam. (102) 8; Fl. Jam. (105) 13

Bufo — Amphib. Gyll. (5) [1]; Vir. pl. (13) 35; Mat. med. anim. (29) 11

Bufonia — Nova pl. gen. 1747 (14) [vi], 2, 3

Bufonia tenuifolia — Fl. Angl. (56) 11

Bufonia tenuissima — Fl. Monsp. (74) 10

Buglossum — Acetaria (77) 10

Buglossum angustifolium minor — Pl. Mart.-Burs. (6) 21

Buglossum lanuginosum — Herb. Amboin. (57) 17

Buglossum litoreum — Herb. Amboin. (57) 17

Buglossum sylvestre majus nigrum — Fl. Palaest. (70) 14[under Anchusa]

Bugula hirsuta genevensis — Pl. Mart.-Burs. (6) 22

Bulbocodium autumnale — Fl. Angl. (56) 14

Bulbocodium serotinum — Fl. alp. (71) 15

Bulbocodium vernum — Demonstr. pl. (49) 9

Bulla — Fund. test. (166) 17

Bulla ampullacea — Fund. test. (166) 26, 36

Bulla fluviatilis — Fund. test. (166) 13

Bulla hypnorum — Fund. test. (166) 13

Bulla ovum — Iter Chin. (161) 8

Buna, bunna et bunchos arabum — Pot. coff. (118) 8

Bunias — Hort. Upsal. (7) 34; Cui bono? (42) 20

Bunias cakile — Stat. pl. (55) 12; Fl. Angl. (56) 20; Fl. Palaest. (70) 24[as kakile]; Fl. Monsp. (74) 21[as kakile]; Prodr. fl. Dan. (82) 21; Fl. Belg. (112) 19[as kakile]

Bunias cornuta — Hist. nat. Rossia (144) 31

Bunias erucago — Demonstr. pl. (49) 18; Fl. Monsp. (74) 21

Bunias orientalis — Demonstr. pl. (49) 18; Hist. nat. Rossia (144) 23

Bunias sibirica — Colon. pl. (158) 9

Bunium bulbocastanum — Fl. Angl. (56) 13; Fl. Monsp. (74) 13; Fl. Belg. (112) 10, 15; Mac. olit. (113) 11; Rar. Norv. (157) 9

Bunius — Herb. Amboin. (57) 14

Buphaga — Siren. lacert. (146) 8

Buphthalmum — Fl. oecon. (17) 20[as Buphtalmum]; Pl. Jam. (102) 25; Nom. bot. (107) 17; Fund. fr. (123) 17

Buphthalmum aquaticum — Demonstr. pl. (49) 23; Pl. rar. Afr. (115) 6

Buphthalmum calycibus acute foliosis, foliis lanceolato-linearibus recurvis denticulato-ciliatis — Pl. rar. Afr. (115) 23

Buphthalmum capense — Pl. rar. Afr. (115) 23

Buphthalmum foliis lanceolatis subdenticulatis glabris, calycibus nudis — Pl. Mart.-Burs. (6) 23[as Buphtalmum]

Buphthalmum frutescens — Fl. Jam. (105) 20[as Buphtalmum]

Buphthalmum grandiflorum — Fl. alp. (71) 22[as Buphtalmum]

Buphthalmum helianthoides — Demonstr. pl. (49) 23

Buphthalmum maritimum — Pl. rar. Afr. (115) 6

Buphthalmum pyrethrum — Pl. officin. (52) 16[as Buphtalmum]

Buphthalmum salicifolium — Fl. alp. (71) 22[as Buphtalmum]

Buphthalmum spinosum — Demonstr. pl. (49) 23; Fl. Palaest. (70) 28[as Bupthalmum]; Fl. Monsp. (74) 26; Pl. rar. Afr. (115) 6

Buphthalmum tinctorium — Pan Svec. (26) 33; Herbat. Upsal. (50) 17[as Buphtalmum]

Bupleurum — Vir. pl. (13) 14

Bupleurum angulosum — Fl. alp. (71) 14

Bupleurum difforme — Demonstr. pl. (49) 7; Fl. Cap. (99) 12

Bupleurum frutescens — Cent. I. pl. (65) 9[as fruticescens]

Bupleurum frutescens, foliis linearibus, involucro universali partialibusque — Cent. I. pl. (65) 9

Bupleurum fruticans angustifolium hispanicum — Cent. I. pl. (65) 9

Bupleurum fruticosum — Fl. Monsp. (74) 12

Bupleurum hispanicum arborescens, gramineo folio — Cent. I. pl. (65) 9

Bupleurum longifolium — Fl. alp. (71) 14

Bupleurum odontites — Demonstr. pl. (49) 7[as odontides]; Fl. Palaest. (70) 16; Fl. alp. (71) 14; Fl. Monsp. (74) 12

Bupleurum petraeum — Fl. alp. (71) 14

Bupleurum praealtum — Fl. Monsp. (74) 12

Bupleurum ranunculoides — Fl. alp. (71) 14

Bupleurum rigidum — Fl. Monsp. (74) 12

Bupleurum rotundifolium — Demonstr. pl. (49) 7; Pl. officin. (52) 15; Fl. Angl. (56) 13; Fl. Monsp. (74) 12; Prodr. fl. Dan. (82) 15; Fl. Belg. (112) 15

Bupleurum semicompositum — Demonstr. pl. (49) 7; Cent. I. pl. (65) 2

Bupleurum stellatum — Fl. alp. (71) 14

Bupleurum tenuifolium — Fl. Monsp. (74) 12

Bupleurum tenuissimum — Fl. Angl. (56) 13

Bupleurum umbellis compositis simulque simplicibus — Demonstr. pl. (49) 7

Bupleurum villosum — Fl. Cap. (99) 12

Buprestis — Fund. entom. (154) 29, [31, as 30]

Buprestis ignita — Fund. entom. (154) 5

Buprestis mariana — Esca avium (174) 7

Buprestis quadripunctata — Pand. fl. Ryb. (165) 9

Buprestis rustica — Pand. fl. Ryb. (165) 9

Buprestis viridis — Pand. fl. Ryb. (165) 9

Bursa pastoris — Oves (61) 15; Nom. bot. (107) 15

Bursera — Opobals. (135) [1][as Burseria]; Obs. mat. med. (171) 8

Buteo — Migr. avium (79) 20; Polit. nat. (109) 14

Butomus — Hort. Upsal. (7) 41; Nect. fl. (122) 13

Butomus palustris — Pan Svec. (26) 22

Butomus umbellatus — Herbat. Upsal. (50) 14; Stat. pl. (55) 13; Fl. Angl. (56) 15; Fl. Monsp. (74) 15; Prodr. fl. Dan. (82) 17; Fl. Belg. (112) 16; Fl. Åker. (162) 11

Butonica — Herb. Amboin. (57) 14

Butonica sylvestris — Herb. Amboin. (57) 14

Butonica terrestris — Herb. Amboin. (57) 14

Buxbaumia — Buxbaumia (85) 6ff.; Usum musc. (148) 3

Buxbaumia aphylla — Buxbaumia (85) 10, 15; Rar. Norv. (157) 11

Buxus — Vir. pl. (13) 31, 36; Odor. med. (40) 13; Hosp. insect. fl. (43) 32; Pand. insect. (93) 19; Nom. bot. (107) 18

Buxus arborescens — Demonstr. pl. (49) 25

Buxus oleae folio — Fl. Palaest. (70) 30

Buxus sempervirens — Pl. officin. (52) 6; Fl. Angl. (56) 24; Fl. Monsp. (74) 27; Hort. cul. (132) 26

Buxus suffruticosa — Demonstr. pl. (49) 25

Byrrhus — Fund. entom. (154) 29

Byrrhus pilula — Fund. entom. (154) 29; Pand. fl. Ryb. (165) 7

Byrrhus scrophulariae — Pand. fl. Ryb. (165) 7

Byssus — Spons. pl. (12) 19; Fl. oecon. (17) 30

Byssus jolithus — Pl. tinct. (97) 28; Usum musc. (148) 12, 13

Byssus saxatilis — Usum musc. (148) 12

Byssus violacea lignis adnascens — Noctiluca (39) 5

Byttneria — Fl. Jam. (105) 27[as Butneria]

Caballus — Mat. med. anim. (29) 5

Cacalia — Anandria (9) 13; Fl. Cap. (99) 6, 7, 8; Pl. rar. Afr. (115) 4

Cacalia alpina — Fl. alp. (71) 21; Fl. Monsp. (74) 25

Cacalia anteuphorbium — Demonstr. pl. (49) 22; Fl. Cap. (99) 17

Cacalia ficoidea — Fl. Cap. (99) 17

Cacalia foliis cutaneis acutioribus glabris — Pl. Mart.-Burs. (6) 16

Cacalia hastata — Hist. nat. Rossia (144) 32

Cacalia kleinia — Demonstr. pl. (49) 22; Metam. pl. (67) 14

Cacalia papillaris — Fl. Cap. (99) 17; Aphyteia (185) [5]

Cacalia sonchifolia — Herb. Amboin. (57) 22

Cacalia suaveolens — Demonstr. pl. (49) 22; Calend. fl. (72) [19][as Calcalia], [22]; Hist. nat. Rossia (144) 12

Cacara alba — Herb. Amboin. (57) 23

Cacara bulbosa — Herb. Amboin. (57) 23

Cacara litorea — Herb. Amboin. (57) 23

Cacara nigra — Herb. Amboin. (57) 23

Cacara perennis — Herb. Amboin. (57) 23

Cacara pilosa — Herb. Amboin. (57) 23

Cacara pruritus — Herb. Amboin. (57) 23

Cachrys libanotis — Fl. Monsp. (74) 13

Cactus — Ficus (2) 9; Spons. pl. (12) 56; Vir. pl. (13) 12, 21; Pl. escul. (35) 4; Hosp. insect. fl. (43) 12; Metam. pl. (67) 14; Fung. melit. (69) 2; Pand. insect. (93) 14; Fl. Cap. (99) 9; Nom. bot. (107) 13; Fund. fr. (123) 18, 22; Usum hist. nat. (145) 17

Cactus caule denudato spinoso, foliis ovato-lanceolatis — Hort. Upsal. (7) 38

Cactus cochenillifer — Demonstr. pl. (49) 13; Fl. Jam. (105) 17[as cochenellifer]

Cactus compressus articulatus ramosissimus, articulis ovatis, spinis setaceis — Hort. Upsal. (7) 38

Cactus compressus articulatus ramosus: articulis linearibus inermibus — Hort. Upsal. (7) 38

Cactus compressus articulatus ramosus: articulis subovatis hinc retusis — Hort. Upsal. (7) 38

Cactus curassavicus — Demonstr. pl. (49) 13

Cactus epidendrum — Pl. Surin. (177) 10

Cactus ficus indica — Demonstr. pl. (49) 13

Cactus flagelliformis — Demonstr. pl. (49) 13; Fl. Jam. (105) 17

Cactus grandiflorus — Demonstr. pl. (49) 13

Cactus heptagonus — Demonstr. pl. (49) 13

Cactus lanuginosus — Fl. Jam. (105) 17

Cactus mammillaris — Demonstr. pl. (49) 13; Prol. pl. 1760 (114) 12[as mammilaris]

Cactus octangularis longus erectus: angulis compressis undilatis, spinis lana longioribus — Hort. Upsal. (7) 38

Cactus opuntia — Hosp. insect. fl. (43) 21; Demonstr. pl. (49) 13; Pl. tinct. (97) 29; Fl. Jam. (105) 17; Fr. escul. (127) 9

Cactus parasiticus — Fl. Jam. (105) 17

Cactus pereskia — Demonstr. pl. (49) 13; Fl. Jam. (105) 17

Cactus peruvianus — Demonstr. pl. (49) 13; Fl. Jam. (105) 17

Cactus phyllanthus — Fl. Jam. (105) 17

Cactus quadrangularis longus erectus, angulis compressis — Hort. Upsal. (7) 37

Cactus scandens angulis quinque pluribusque obtusis — Hort. Upsal. (7) 38

Cactus scandens teres, punctis echinatis seriatim ulterius — Hort. Upsal. (7) 38

Cactus sexangularis longus erectus — Hort. Upsal. (7) 38

Cactus subrotundus tectus tuberculis ovatis barbatis — Hort. Upsal. (7) 37

Cactus tereti-compressus articulatus ramosissimus — Hort. Upsal. (7) 38

Cactus tetragonus — Demonstr. pl. (49) 13; Pl. Surin. (177) 10

Cactus triangularis — Demonstr. pl. (49) 13; Fl. Jam. (105) 17; Pl. Surin. (177) 10

Cactus triangularis articulatus (angulis dentatis) — Hort. Upsal. (7) 38

Cactus tuna — Fl. Jam. (105) 17

Cadelium — Herb. Amboin. (57) 23

Caecilia — Mus. Ad.-Frid. (11) 19; Surin. Grill. (16) 12

Caecilia rugis — Surin. Grill. (16) 11

Caesalpinia — Pl. tinct. (97) 29

Caesalpinia brasiliensis — Pl. officin. (52) 6[as Caesalpina]; Pl. tinct. (97) 17; Fl. Jam. (105) 8[as Caesalpina], 16

Caesalpinia officinalis — Fl. Jam. (105) 8[as Caesalpina]

Caesalpinia sappan — Herb. Amboin. (57) 15[as Caesalpina]; Pl. tinct. (97) 17

Caesalpinia vesicaria — Pl. tinct. (97) 17; Fl. Jam. (105) 16; Obs. mat. med. (171) 7[as Caesalpina]

Caju galedupa — Herb. Amboin. (57) 9

Caju lape lape — Herb. Amboin. (57) 12

Calaba — Pl. escul. (35) 4

Caladium aquatile — Herb. Amboin. (57) 22

Calamagrostis — Herb. Amboin. (57) 25; Fund. agrost. (152) 17

Calamintha — Vir. pl. (13) 30[as Calaminthia]

Calamintha aquatica — Cent. II. pl. (66) 20

Calamus — Herb. Amboin. (57) 5, 19, 20; Fund. agrost. (152) 4, 15

Calamus rotang — Pl. tinct. (97) 15

Calappa — Herb. Amboin. (57) 6

Calceolaria — Nect. fl. (122) 12; Purg. indig. (143) 13

Calcitrapa — Obs. mat. med. (171) 5

Calendula — Peloria (3) 10; Fl. oecon. (17) 21; Pl. escul. (35) 23, 29; Hort. acad. (63) 3; Fl. Cap. (99) 7, 10; Nom. bot. (107) 17; Pl. rar. Afr. (115) 5; Fund. fr. (123) 17

Calendula arvensis — Pan Svec. (26) 33

Calendula foliis lanceolatis denticulatis, pedunculis filiformibus — Pl. hybr. (33) 9

Calendula foliis obovatis subdentatis, caule fruticoso — Pl. rar. Afr. (115) 25

Calendula foliis obverse ovatis denticulatis, caule perenni — Pl. rar. Afr. (115) 25

Calendula fruticosa — Pl. rar. Afr. (115) 25

Calendula graminifolia — Fl. Cap. (99) 18

Calendula hortensis — Pl. rar. Afr. (115) 7

Calendula humilis africana, flore intus albo, foris violaceo simplici — Pl. hybr. (33) 9

Calendula hybrida — Fl. Cap. (99) 18

Calendula nudicaulis — Fl. Cap. (99) 18

Calendula officinalis — Hosp. insect. fl. (43) 31; Demonstr. pl. (49) 24; Pl. officin. (52) 6; Fl. Palaest. (70) 29; Calend. fl. (72) [22]; Fl. Monsp. (74) 26; Pl. tinct. (97) 24; Fl. Jam. (105) 24; Fl. Belg. (112) 21; Hort. cul. (132) 23, 25

Calendula pluvialis — Fl. Cap. (99) 18

Calendula prolifera — Prol. pl. 1760 (114) 19

Calla — Vir. pl. (13) 25, 29, 30; Fl. oecon. (17) 21; Gem. arb. (24) 8; Pl. rar. Camsch. (30) 29; Pl. escul. (35) 23, 27; Pane diaet. (83) 17

Calla aethiopica — Demonstr. pl. (49) 25; Fl. Cap. (99) 19

Calla aquatilis, odore allii vehementi praeditae — Pl. rar. Camsch. (30) 29

Calla carsami — Fl. Palaest. (70) 29

Calla europaea — Fl. Belg. (112) 22

Calla palustris — Pan Svec. (26) 34; Herbat. Upsal. (50) 19; Stat. pl. (55) 13; Calend. fl. (72) [19]; Prodr. fl. Dan. (82) 24; Fl. Åker. (162) 18; Pand. fl. Ryb. (165) 22; Esca avium (174) 14

Callicarpa — Nova pl. gen. 1747 (14) [iv], 6; Nova pl. gen. 1751 (32) 8, 12

Callichthys — Mus. Ad.-Frid. (11) [vii][as Callicthys], 38, 39

Calligonum polygonoides — Fl. Palaest. (70) 21[as polygonides]

Callisia gnaphalodes — Pl. rar. Afr. (115) 23

Callitriche — Nova pl. gen. 1751 (32) 42, 43, 48

Callitriche androgyna — Cent. I. pl. (65) 31; Fl. Monsp. (74) 8

Callitriche autumnalis — Prodr. fl. Dan. (82) 12; Fl. Åker. (162) 5

Callitriche foliis omnibus linearibus, apice bifidis — Cent. I. pl. (65) 31

Callitriche foliis superioribus ovalibus — Cent. I. pl. (65) 31

Callitriche hermaphroditica — Cent. I. pl. (65) 31; Fl. Monsp. (74) 8[as hermaphrodita]

Callitriche palustris — Pan Svec. (26) 12; Herbat.
Upsal. (50) 10; Stat. pl. (55) 13; Fl. Angl. (56) 23;
Cent. I. pl. (65) 31

Callitriche verna — Prodr. fl. Dan. (82) 12; Fl. Belg.
(112) 12; Fl. Åker. (162) 5; Pand. fl. Ryb. (165) 16

Callococcus — Fl. Jam. (105) 26

Calophyllum calaba — Herb. Amboin. (57) 10[as
Calaphyllum]; Fr. escul. (127) 13

Calophyllum inophyllum — Herb. Amboin. (57) 10;
Fl. Jam. (105) 17; Fr. escul. (127) 13

Caltha — Pl. Mart.-Burs. (6) 23; Spons. pl. (12) 59;
Vir. pl. (13) 21; Fl. oecon. (17) 15; Pl. escul. (35)
19, 29; Metam. pl. (67) 17; Nom. bot. (107) 14;
Prol. pl. 1760 (114) 13, 14; Fund. fr. (123) 23

Caltha palustris — Pan Svec. (26) 26; Herbat. Upsal.
(50) 7[as Calta]; Stat. pl. (55) 14; Fl. Angl. (56) 18;
Cervus (60) 8; Calend. fl. (72) [10]; Prodr. fl. Dan.
(82) 20; Pl. tinct. (97) 20; Fl. Belg. (112) 18; Fl.
Åker. (162) 14; Pand. fl. Ryb. (165) 20; Esca
avium (174) 13

Caltha palustris plena — Demonstr. pl. (49) 15

Calyx coralliorum langii, ad litora cum plurimis
fragmentis obvius — Corallia Balt. (4) 17

Camara arborescens, salviae folio — Cent. II. pl. (66)
22

Cambogia — Pl. Mart.-Burs. (6) 31; Vir. pl. (13) 21,
25; Nova pl. gen. 1747 (14) [vi], 18

Cambogia gutta — Pl. officin. (52) 11; Pl. tinct. (97)
19

Camellia — Pand. insect. (93) [17, as 38]; Pot. theae
(142) 9, 15

Camelus — Vir. pl. (13) 16; Oecon. nat. (20) 35; Pan
Svec. (26) 6; Bigas insect. (184) 2

Cameraria echites — Fl. Jam. (105) 14

Cameraria latifolia — Fl. Jam. (105) 14

Camerariae an species, foliis latioribus oblongis
subtus argenteis, caule rubro, capsula triloculari —
Nova pl. gen. 1751 (32) 14

Camerariae species, foliis viridibus longioribus,
linearibus pilosis alternis, caule duro ligneo
nonnihil hirsuto — Nova pl. gen. 1751 (32) 14

Camirium — Herb. Amboin. (57) 10

Camocladia pinnatifolia — Fl. Jam. (105) 12

Camolenga — Herb. Amboin. (57) 23

Campanula — Spons. pl. (12) 37, 43; Oecon. nat.
(20) 15; Gem. arb. (24) 13; Pl. hybr. (33) 7, 28, 29;
Pl. escul. (35) 10, 28; Acetaria (77) 11; Pand.
insect. (93) 12; Fl. Cap. (99) 6; Nom. bot. (107) 10;
Nect. fl. (122) 9; Fund. fr. (123) 16; Erica (163) 2

Campanula alliariae folio — Fund. fr. (123) 16

Campanula alpina latifolia, flore pullo — Pl. Mart.-
Burs. (6) 6

Campanula bellidis folio — Fund. fr. (123) 16

Campanula blattariae folio — Fund. fr. (123) 16

Campanula bononiensis — Fl. alp. (71) 13

Campanula calycibus a tergo lamellis quinque notatis
— Pl. Mart.-Burs. (6) 6

Campanula capsulis quinquelocularibus tectis calycis
sinubus reflexis, caule dichotomo — Cent. II. pl.
(66) 10

Campanula caule unifloro — Pl. Mart.-Burs. (6) 6

Campanula cervicaria — Herbat. Upsal. (50) 19;
Prodr. fl. Dan. (82) 15

Campanula cymbalariae folio — Pl. hybr. (33) 27,
28; Fund. fr. (123) 16

Campanula dichotoma — Cent. II. pl. (66) 10; Fl.
Palaest. (70) 15

Campanula echii folio — Fund. fr. (123) 16

Campanula echioides — Pan Svec. (26) 17

Campanula erinus — Fl. Monsp. (74) 11; Pl. rar. Afr.
(115) 6

Campanula fahlunensis — Pan Svec. (26) 17

Campanula fennonica — Pan Svec. (26) 17

Campanula flore sursum spectante — Fl. Palaest. (70)
15

Campanula folii echii — Pl. Mart.-Burs. (6) 6

Campanula fructu duro — Fl. Palaest. (70) 15

Campanula gigantea — Pan Svec. (26) 17

Campanula glomerata — Pan Svec. (26) 17;
Demonstr. pl. (49) 5; Stat. pl. (55) 22; Fl. Angl.
(56) 12; Calend. fl. (72) [14]; Fl. Monsp. (74) 11;
Prodr. fl. Dan. (82) 15; Pand. fl. Ryb. (165) 17

Campanula graminifolia — Fl. alp. (71) 13

Campanula hederacea — Fl. Angl. (56) 12; Fl.
Monsp. (74) 11

Campanula hesperidis folio — Fund. fr. (123) 16

Campanula hirsuta, ocymi folio caulem ambiente,
flore pendulo — Cent. II. pl. (66) 10

Campanula hortensis, rapunculi radice repente — Pl.
Mart.-Burs. (6) 6

Campanula hybrida — Demonstr. pl. (49) [vii], 5

Campanula jacobaeae folio — Fund. fr. (123) 16

Campanula lapsanae folio — Fund. fr. (123) 16

Campanula latifolia — Herbat. Upsal. (50) 8; Stat. pl.
(55) 17; Fl. Angl. (56) 12; Calend. fl. (72) [14]; Fl.
Åker. (162) 8; Pand. fl. Ryb. (165) 17

Campanula leucoji folio — Fund. fr. (123) 16

Campanula lilifolia — Hist. nat. Rossia (144) 28

Campanula linifolia — Fl. Monsp. (74) 11

Campanula lychnidis folio — Fund. fr. (123) 16

Campanula magno flore — Pan Svec. (26) 17

Campanula maxima floribus conglobatis — Fl.
Palaest. (70) 15

Campanula medium — Demonstr. pl. (49) 5; Fl.
Monsp. (74) 11

Campanula patula — Demonstr. pl. (49) 5; Stat. pl.
(55) 20; Fl. Angl. (56) 12; Calend. fl. (72) [12];
Prodr. fl. Dan. (82) 15

Campanula pentagonia — Sem. musc. (28) 4; Fl.
Palaest. (70) 15

Campanula perfoliata — Demonstr. pl. (49) [vii], 5;
Fund. fr. (123) 12

Campanula persicifolia — Herbat. Upsal. (50) 7; Stat. pl. (55) 17; Calend. fl. (72) [15]; Fl. Monsp. (74) 11; Prodr. fl. Dan. (82) 15; Fl. Belg. (112) 14; Fl. Åker. (162) 8; Pand. fl. Ryb. (165) 17

Campanula ptarmicae folio — Fund. fr. (123) 16

Campanula pyramidalis — Demonstr. pl. (49) 5; Calend. fl. (72) [18]; Hort. cul. (132) 23

Campanula rapunculus — Demonstr. pl. (49) 5; Calend. fl. (72) [14]; Fl. Monsp. (74) 11; Prodr. fl. Dan. (82) 15; Mac. olit. (113) 10; Hort. cul. (132) 13

Campanula rhomboidalis — Fl. alp. (71) 13

Campanula rotundifolia — Herbat. Upsal. (50) 7; Stat. pl. (55) 20; Fl. Angl. (56) 12; Calend. fl. (72) [12]; Fl. Monsp. (74) 11; Prodr. fl. Dan. (82) 15; Pl. tinct. (97) 14; Fl. Belg. (112) 14; Fl. Åker. (162) 8; Pand. fl. Ryb. (165) 17

Campanula sibirica — Hist. nat. Rossia (144) 28

Campanula speculum — Fl. Belg. (112) 14; Fund. fr. (123) 12; Prol. pl. 1763 (130) 14

Campanula speculum veneris — Demonstr. pl. (49) 5; Fl. Angl. (56) 12; Fl. Palaest. (70) 15; Fl. Monsp. (74) 11

Campanula thyrsoides — Fl. alp. (71) 13[as tyrsoides]; Fl. Monsp. (74) 11; Prodr. fl. Dan. (82) 15

Campanula trachelium — Pan Svec. (26) 17; Herbat. Upsal. (50) 8; Stat. pl. (55) 17; Fl. Angl. (56) 12; Calend. fl. (72) [15]; Fl. Monsp. (74) 11; Prodr. fl. Dan. (82) 15; Fl. Belg. (112) 14; Fl. Åker. (162) 8

Campanula tragopoginis folio — Fund. fr. (123) 16

Campanula uniflora — Pan Svec. (26) 17; Stat. pl. (55) 16; Fl. alp. (71) 13

Campanula urticae folio — Fund. fr. (123) 16

Campanula vulgaris — Pan Svec. (26) 17

Camphora — Menthae (153) 5, 6

Camphorata — Nova pl. gen. 1747 (14) 8

Camphorata altera — Nova pl. gen. 1747 (14) 9

Camphorata cespitosa tartarica, floribus in glomerulis ad caules cespitosis, foliis ericae brevissimis — Nova pl. gen. 1747 (14) 9

Camphorata glabra — Nova pl. gen. 1747 (14) 9

Camphorata hirsuta — Nova pl. gen. 1747 (14) 9

Camphorosma — Nova pl. gen. 1747 (14) [vi], 8; Fl. Monsp. (74) 7

Camphorosma foliis hirsutis linearibus — Nova pl. gen. 1747 (14) 9

Camphorosma foliis semitriquetris glabris inermibus — Nova pl. gen. 1747 (14) 9

Camphorosma foliis subulatis rigidis glabris — Nova pl. gen. 1747 (14) 9

Camphorosma monspeliaca — Pl. officin. (52) 6; Fl. Palaest. (70) 14; Fl. Monsp. (74) 10

Camunium — Herb. Amboin. (57) 18

Camunium japonense — Herb. Amboin. (57) 18

Camunium sinense — Herb. Amboin. (57) 18

Cananga — Herb. Amboin. (57) 10

Cananga sylvestris — Herb. Amboin. (57) 10

Canarium — Herb. Amboin. (57) 5, 10

Canarium decumanum — Herb. Amboin. (57) 10

Canarium minimum — Herb. Amboin. (57) 10

Canarium odoriferum — Herb. Amboin. (57) 9

Canarium sylvestre — Herb. Amboin. (57) 9

Canarium vulgare — Herb. Amboin. (57) 9

Canarium zephyrinum — Herb. Amboin. (57) 9

Cancer — Spons. pl. (12) 13, 23; Taenia (19) 23; Noxa insect. (46) 30; Pand. insect. (93) 5; Mors. serp. (119) 3; Fund. entom. (154) 10, 17, 18, 19, 21, 22, 23, 26; Var. cib. (156) 5

Cancer arenarius — Cent. insect. (129) 31[as Carenarius]

Cancer astacus — Pand. fl. Ryb. (165) 16

Cancer brachyurus, fronte retusa, testac lateribus transversim striatis — Chin. Lagerstr. (64) 27[as rotusa]

Cancer brachyurus hirsutus, thorace utrinque dentato, pedibus posticis unguibus geminis — Cent. insect. (129) 30

Cancer brachyurus, manuum digitis atris — Mat. med. anim. (29) 17

Cancer brachyurus, thorace inaequali orbiculato ciliato, pedibus dorsalibus quatuor — Cent. insect. (129) 31

Cancer brachyurus, thorace laevi cordato integerrimo, chelis subtus muricatis — Cent. insect. (129) 31

Cancer brachyurus, thorace laevi mutico maculato: margine crenulato, manibus cristatis — Cent. insect. (129) 31

Cancer brachyurus, thorace subquadrato inermi, chela alter magna — Cent. insect. (129) 30

Cancer cordatus — Cent. insect. (129) 31

Cancer dormia — Cent. insect. (129) 30

Cancer epheliticus — Cent. insect. (129) 31

Cancer filiformis — Cent. insect. (129) 32

Cancer gammarus — Fund. entom. (154) 5[as gamarus]

Cancer lanosus — Cent. insect. (129) 30

Cancer linearis medio chelatus, pedibus quatuor — Cent. insect. (129) 32

Cancer macrourus, rostro supra serrato: basi utrinque dente simplici — Mat. med. anim. (29) 17

Cancer marinus — Mat. med. anim. (29) 17

Cancer minutus — Nat. pelagi (84) 11; Iter Chin. (161) 13

Cancer neptuni — Iter Chin. (161) 15

Cancer parasiticus — Cent. insect. (129) 31

Cancer pelagicus — Nat. pelagi (84) 11

Cancer pinnotheres — Nat. pelagi (84) 10[as pinotheres]; Polit. nat. (109) 21

Cancer retusus — Chin. Lagerstr. (64) 27, 36

Cancer vocans — Cent. insect. (129) 30[as vocaus]

Canella — Fl. Jam. (105) 26

Canella alba — Scorb. (180) 17

Canis — Spons. pl. (12) 31; Oecon. nat. (20) 26, 46; Generat. calc. (22) 2; Rad. senega (23) 9; Pan Svec. (26) 7; Morb. hyeme (38) 12; Cui bono? (42) 24; Noxa insect. (46) 29; Cynogr. (54) [1]ff.; Polit. nat. (109) 20, 21

Canis aegyptius — Cynogr. (54) 5

Canis aquaticus — Cynogr. (54) 4, 9

Canis aquaticus aviarius — Spons. pl. (12) 26[as aquatica aviaria]

Canis aquaticus grajus — Spons. pl. (12) 26[as aquatica graja]

Canis aureus — Fl. Cap. (99) [1]

Canis avicularius — Cynogr. (54) 5

Canis cauda incurvata — Mat. med. anim. (29) 3[as incurva]

Canis cauda recta: extremitate alba — Mat. med. anim. (29) 3

Canis cauda recurvata — Mat. med. anim. (29) 3[as recurva]

Canis domesticus — Cynogr. (54) 3, 4; Mus ind. (62) 4

Canis extrarius seu hispanicus — Cynogr. (54) 5

Canis familiaris — Esca avium (174) 12

Canis fricator — Cynogr. (54) 5[as fricatrix]

Canis grajus — Cynogr. (54) 4

Canis hispanicus — Cynogr. (54) 5

Canis lupus — Oecon. nat. (20) 42; Esca avium (174) 12

Canis mastivus seu molossus — Cynogr. (54) 4

Canis meliteus — Cynogr. (54) 5[as melitaeus]; Polit. nat. (109) 20[as melitensis]

Canis molossus — Cynogr. (54) 4

Canis sagax — Cynogr. (54) 4

Canis socius et fidelis — Mat. med. anim. (29) 3

Canis vertagus — Cynogr. (54) 5

Canis vulpes — Oecon. nat. (20) 42; Esca avium (174) 3, 12

Canna — Hort. Upsal. (7) 36; Vir. pl. (13) 26; Gem. arb. (24) 8; Fl. Cap. (99) 4; Nom. bot. (107) 9; Nect. fl. (122) 10; Fund. agrost. (152) 14

Canna angustifolia — Demonstr. pl. (49) [1]; Herb. Amboin. (57) 20; Pl. Surin. (177) 5

Canna capitis bonae spei, spicis juliformibus — Cent. I. pl. (65) 4

Canna glauca — Demonstr. pl. (49) [1]

Canna indica — Demonstr. pl. (49) [1]; Fl. Cap. (99) 11; Fl. Jam. (105) 12, 25

Canna palustris — Herb. Amboin. (57) 15

Cannabina — Nova pl. gen. 1747 (14) 31

Cannabina cretica florifera et fructifera — Nova pl. gen. 1747 (14) 31

Cannabis — Spons. pl. (12) [2], 32, 48; Vir. pl. (13) 36; Odor. med. (40) 13, 16; Migr. avium (79) 32, 33, 34; Arb. Svec. (101) 19; Nom. bot. (107) 19; Fund. fr. (123) 8; Usum hist. nat. (145) 27; Usum musc. (148) 6; Cimicifuga (173) 8; Med. purg. (181) 7

Cannabis foliis pinnatis — Nova pl. gen. 1747 (14) 31

Cannabis foliis simplicibus — Nova pl. gen. 1751 (32) 33

Cannabis indica — Herb. Amboin. (57) 21

Cannabis sativa — Demonstr. pl. (49) 26; Pl. officin. (52) 6; Herb. Amboin. (57) 21; Fl. Palaest. (70) 31; Calend. fl. (72) [16]; Fl. Monsp. (74) 28; Fl. Cap. (99) 2; Inebr. (117) 11[as Canabis]

Cannabis sativa mas — Prodr. fl. Dan. (82) 25

Cannabis virginiana — Nova pl. gen. 1751 (32) 33

Cannacorus — Herb. Amboin. (57) 20

Cantharifera — Herb. Amboin. (57) 20

Cantharis — Curios. nat. (18) 17; Noctiluca (39) 5; Hosp. insect. fl. (43) 35; Meloe (124) 2ff.; Fund. entom. (154) 29, 30, [31, as 30]

Cantharis aenea — Pand. fl. Ryb. (165) 9

Cantharis aptera — Mirac. insect. (45) 19

Cantharis atra — Pand. fl. Ryb. (165) 9

Cantharis bicolor — Cent. insect. (129) 12

Cantharis bipustulata — Pand. fl. Ryb. (165) 9

Cantharis caeruleo-viridis, thorace teretiusculo — Mat. med. anim. (29) 14; Meloe (124) 4

Cantharis fasciata — Meloe (124) 6; Pand. fl. Ryb. (165) 9

Cantharis fusca — Pand. fl. Ryb. (165) 9; Esca avium (174) 7

Cantharis ligni — Noxa insect. (46) 16

Cantharis livida — Pand. fl. Ryb. (165) 9

Cantharis minima — Pand. fl. Ryb. (165) 9

Cantharis navalis — Pand. insect. (93) 20

Cantharis officinarum — Hosp. insect. fl. (43) 17, 19, 38, 39; Noxa insect. (46) 19; Meloe (124) 4

Cantharis rubra, elytris postice violaceis — Cent. insect. (129) 12

Cantharis rufa — Pand. fl. Ryb. (165) 9

Cantharis sanguinea — Esca avium (174) 7

Cantharis testacea — Pand. fl. Ryb. (165) 9

Cantharis viridissima — Pand. fl. Ryb. (165) 9

Cantharis vulgaris officinarum — Mat. med. anim. (29) 14

Caper — Mat. med. anim. (29) 7

Capillus veneris — Herb. Amboin. (57) 26

Capparis — Pl. escul. (35) 19, 20, 29; Nom. bot. (107) 14

Capparis arabica — Fl. Palaest. (70) 21

Capparis cynophallophora — Fl. Jam. (105) 17

Capparis ferruginea — Pl. Jam. (102) 13; Fl. Jam. (105) 17

Capparis siliquosa — Fl. Jam. (105) 17

Capparis spinosa — Demonstr. pl. (49) 14; Pl. officin. (52) 6; Fl. Palaest. (70) 21; Fl. Monsp. (74) 18; Mac. olit. (113) 23

Capra — Vir. pl. (13) 16; Oecon. nat. (20) 36; Pan Svec. (26) 3, 7, 10ff.; Mat. med. lapid. (37) 23; Instr. peregr. (96) 11; Usum hist. nat. (145) 19

Capra cornibus carinatis arcuatis — Mat. med. anim. (29) 7

Capra gazella — Generat. calc. (22) 2

Capraria — Nova pl. gen. 1751 (32) 37, 38; Herb. Amboin. (57) 9

Capraria biflora — Demonstr. pl. (49) 17; Fl. Jam. (105) 18

Capraria durantifolia — Pl. Jam. (102) 15

Capraria foliis alternis, corollis quinquefidis — Nova pl. gen. 1751 (32) 38

Capraria foliis integerrimis — Nova pl. gen. 1751 (32) [13, as 15]

Capraria foliis ternis, corollis quadripartitis — Nova pl. gen. 1751 (32) 37

Capraria gratioloides — Colon. pl. (158) 11

Capraria oppositifolia — Fl. Jam. (105) 18

Caprificus — Ficus (2) 3, 8, 9, 13ff.

Caprificus amboinensis — Herb. Amboin. (57) 13

Caprificus aspera — Herb. Amboin. (57) 13

Caprificus chartaria — Herb. Amboin. (57) 13

Caprificus praecox, fructu ex viridi violaceo, staminibus intus sparsis — Ficus (2) 3

Caprificus praecox, fructu nigricante parvo deciduo — Ficus (2) 3

Caprificus viridis — Herb. Amboin. (57) 13

Caprimulgus — Oecon. nat. (20) 41; Polit. nat. (109) 12; Fund. ornith. (137) 27

Caprimulgus europaeus — Migr. avium (79) 16[as europeus], 17, 36

Capsicum — Hort. Upsal. (7) 36; Passifl. (8) [iii]; Vir. pl. (13) 18; Sapor. med. (31) 19; Odor. med. (40) 15; Usum hist. nat. (145) 27

Capsicum annuum — Demonstr. pl. (49) 6; Pl. officin. (52) 15; Fl. Palaest. (70) 15; Fl. Jam. (105) 14

Capsicum frutescens — Fl. Jam. (105) 14

Capsicum fruticosum — Demonstr. pl. (49) 6; Herb. Amboin. (57) 21; Fl. Jam. (105) 25

Capsicum indicum — Herb. Amboin. (57) 21

Capsicum sylvestre — Herb. Amboin. (57) 17

Carabus — Cui bono? (42) 25; Noxa insect. (46) 30, 31; Polit. nat. (109) 11; Usum hist. nat. (145) 14; Fund. entom. (154) 22, 29, [31, as 30]

Carabus bipunctatus — Pand. fl. Ryb. (165) 9

Carabus caerulescens — Pand. fl. Ryb. (165) 9

Carabus cephalotes — Pand. fl. Ryb. (165) 9

Carabus cupreus — Pand. fl. Ryb. (165) 9

Carabus hortensis — Pand. fl. Ryb. (165) 9

Carabus latus — Pand. fl. Ryb. (165) 9; Esca avium (174) 3, 7

Carabus leucophthalmus — Pand. fl. Ryb. (165) 9[as leucophtalmus]

Carabus sexpunctatus — Pand. fl. Ryb. (165) 9

Carabus ustulatus — Pand. fl. Ryb. (165) 9

Carabus violaceus — Esca avium (174) 7

Carabus vulgaris — Pand. fl. Ryb. (165) 9; Esca avium (174) 3, 7

Carapo — Mus. Ad.-Frid. (11) 39

Carbonaria — Herb. Amboin. (57) 11

Carbonaria altera — Herb. Amboin. (57) 11

Carcapuli — Nova pl. gen. 1747 (14) 19

Cardamine — Vir. pl. (13) 22; Pl. escul. (35) 20, 28; Morb. hyeme (38) 8; Hort. acad. (63) 9; Pand. insect. (93) 16[as Cardomine]

Cardamine africana — Fl. Cap. (99) 16

Cardamine alpina minima — Cent. II. pl. (66) 23

Cardamine amara — Herbat. Upsal. (50) 13; Stat. pl. (55) 14; Fl. Angl. (56) 19; Prodr. fl. Dan. (82) 21; Pand. fl. Ryb. (165) 20

Cardamine asarifolia — Fl. alp. (71) 20

Cardamine bellidifolia — Stat. pl. (55) 16; Fl. Angl. (56) 19[as bellifolia]; Fl. alp. (71) 20; Rar. Norv. (157) 11

Cardamine bellidis folio— Pan Svec. (26) 29

Cardamine chelidonia — Hist. nat. Rossia (144) 31

Cardamine foliis pinnatis, foliolis multifidis — Pl. Mart.-Burs. (6) 6

Cardamine hirsuta — Stat. pl. (55) 21; Fl. Angl. (56) 19; Fl. Monsp. (74) 21; Fl. Belg. (112) 19

Cardamine impatiens — Pan Svec. (26) 29; Demonstr. pl. (49) 17; Herbat. Upsal. (50) 8; Stat. pl. (55) 17; Fl. Angl. (56) 19; Fl. Monsp. (74) 21; Prodr. fl. Dan. (82) 21

Cardamine lanceolatus — Esca avium (174) 14

Cardamine lunaria — Demonstr. pl. (49) 17

Cardamine nudicaulis — Hist. nat. Rossia (144) 31

Cardamine petraea — Fl. Angl. (56) 19; Colon. pl. (158) 7[as petrea]

Cardamine pratensis — Pan Svec. (26) 29; Hosp. insect. fl. (43) 12, 28; Herbat. Upsal. (50) 7; Stat. pl. (55) 14; Fl. Angl. (56) 19; Calend. fl. (72) [11]; Fl. Monsp. (74) 21; Prodr. fl. Dan. (82) 21; Fl. Belg. (112) 19; Fl. Åker. (162) 15; Pand. fl. Ryb. (165) 20; Obs. mat. med. (171) 5[as partensis]; Scorb. (180) 16

Cardamine resedifolia — Fl. alp. (71) 20

Cardamine scanica — Pan Svec. (26) 29

Cardamine sicula, foliis fumariae — Pl. Mart.-Burs. (6) 6

Cardamine stolonifera — Pan Svec. (26) 29

Cardamine trifolia — Pan Svec. (26) 29; Fl. alp. (71) 20

Cardamomum minus — Herb. Amboin. (57) 20

Cardiaca — Anandria (9) 4; Nom. bot. (107) 15

Cardiospermum — Hort. Upsal. (7) 36; Nom. bot. (107) 12

Cardiospermum halicacabum — Fl. Jam. (105) 15[as helicacabum], 26

Cardium — Fund. test. (166) 18, 41

Cardium aculeatum — Fund. test. (166) 41

Cardium echinatum — Fund. test. (166) 43

Cardium pectinatum — Fund. test. (166) 43

Carduus — Vir. pl. (13) 7, 12, 14; Fl. oecon. (17) 20; Oecon. nat. (20) 22; Pl. hybr. (33) 7, 26[as Charduus]; Pl. escul. (35) 28; Hosp. insect. fl. (43) 40; Vern. arb. (47) 9; Migr. avium (79) 34; Pand. insect. (93) 18; Nom. bot. (107) 17; Polit. nat. (109) 5; Prol. pl. 1760 (114) 16; Mund. invis. (149) 20

Carduus acanthoides — Pl. hybr. (33) 23; Demonstr. pl. (49) 22; Fl. Angl. (56) 22; Fl. Monsp. (74) 24; Prodr. fl. Dan. (82) 22; Fl. Belg. (112) 20

Carduus acaulis — Pan Svec. (26) 32; Stat. pl. (55) 15; Fl. Angl. (56) 22; Fl. Monsp. (74) 25; Prodr. fl. Dan. (82) 22; Fl. Belg. (112) 20

Carduus benedictus — Vir. pl. (13) 33; Sapor. med. (31) 18

Carduus capite rotundo tomentoso — Pl. Mart.-Burs. (6) 29

Carduus crispus — Pan Svec. (26) 32; Pl. hybr. (33) 23; Hosp. insect. fl. (43) 30; Herbat. Upsal. (50) 13; Stat. pl. (55) 19; Fl. Angl. (56) 22; Fl. Monsp. (74) 24; Prodr. fl. Dan. (82) 22; Fl. Åker. (162) 17

Carduus cyanoides — Hist. nat. Rossia (144) 32

Carduus eriophorus — Demonstr. pl. (49) 22; Fl. Angl. (56) 22; Calend. fl. (72) [16]; Fl. Monsp. (74) 24

Carduus ferocior — Fl. Monsp. (74) 29

Carduus ficus — Peloria (3) 8

Carduus foliis pinnatifidis linearibus subtus tomentosis, caule inermi unifloro — Cent. II. pl. (66) 30

Carduus helenii folio — Pan Svec. (26) 32

Carduus helenioides — Fl. Angl. (56) 22; Calend. fl. (72) [13]; Hist. nat. Rossia (144) 32

Carduus heterophyllus — Demonstr. pl. (49) 22; Herbat. Upsal. (50) 19; Stat. pl. (55) 21; Fl. Angl. (56) 22; Calend. fl. (72) [12]; Prodr. fl. Dan. (82) 22; Fl. Belg. (112) 20; Prol. pl. 1760 (114) 17[as haeterophyllus]; Hist. nat. Rossia (144) 32; Rar. Norv. (157) 16

Carduus lanceolatus — Pan Svec. (26) 32; Hosp. insect. fl. (43) 30; Herbat. Upsal. (50) 17; Stat. pl. (55) 20; Fl. Angl. (56) 22; Calend. fl. (72) [17]; Prodr. fl. Dan. (82) 22; Fl. Belg. (112) 20; Fl. Åker. (162) 17; Pand. fl. Ryb. (165) 21

Carduus marianus — Demonstr. pl. (49) 22; Pl. officin. (52) 7; Fl. Angl. (56) 22; Fl. Monsp. (74) 25; Prodr. fl. Dan. (82) 22

Carduus mollior primus — Cent. II. pl. (66) 30

Carduus mollis — Cent. II. pl. (66) 30; Fl. Palaest. (70) 27

Carduus mollis, laciniato folio — Cent. II. pl. (66) 30

Carduus monspessulanus — Fl. Monsp. (74) 24

Carduus nutans — Pan Svec. (26) 32; Pl. hybr. (33) 24; Hosp. insect. fl. (43) 30; Demonstr. pl. (49) 22; Stat. pl. (55) 20; Fl. Angl. (56) 22; Calend. fl. (72) [16]; Fl. Monsp. (74) 24; Fl. Belg. (112) 20

Carduus orientalis acaulos incanus et tomentosus, dentis leonis folio — Cent. I. pl. (65) 30

Carduus palustris — Pan Svec. (26) 32; Pl. escul. (35) 23; Herbat. Upsal. (50) 16; Stat. pl. (55) 15; Fl. Angl. (56) 22; Prodr. fl. Dan. (82) 22; Fl. Belg. (112) 20; Fl. Åker. (162) 17

Carduus pratensis, asphodeli radice, foliis profunde et tenuitur laciniatis — Pl. Mart.-Burs. (6) 28

Carduus serratuloides — Demonstr. pl. (49) 22; Hist. nat. Rossia (144) 32

Carduus spinosissimus — Calend. fl. (72) [16]

Carduus stellatus, foliis integris serratis — Cent. I. pl. (65) 29; Metam. pl. (67) 20

Carduus syriacus — Demonstr. pl. (49) 22; Fl. Palaest. (70) 27

Carduus tataricus — Demonstr. pl. (49) 22; Calend. fl. (72) [14]; Prol. pl. 1760 (114) 17; Hist. nat. Rossia (144) 32

Carduus tomentosus pyrenaicus, floribus purpureis glomeratis — Pl. Mart.-Burs. (6) 29

Carduus tuberosus — Fl. Monsp. (74) 25

Carex — Hort. Upsal. (7) 41; Spons. pl. (12) 39; Vir. pl. (13) 17; Fl. oecon. (17) 21; Ping. anim. (108) 17; Fund. agrost. (152) 4, 16, 29, 38

Carex acuta — Herbat. Upsal. (50) 8; Stat. pl. (55) 14; Fl. Angl. (56) 24; Fl. Monsp. (74) 27; Prodr. fl. Dan. (82) 24; Fl. Belg. (112) 22; Fund. agrost. (152) 7; Fl. Åker. (162) 19; Pand. fl. Ryb. (165) 22

Carex acuta, maxima — Fl. Palaest. (70) 30

Carex alpina, capitulis albis: squamis triquetris et pulchre lucentibus — Cent. II. pl. (66) 32

Carex amboinica — Herb. Amboin. (57) 25

Carex arenaria — Pan Svec. (26) 35; Stat. pl. (55) 21; Hort. acad. (63) 10; Fund. agrost. (152) 7

Carex atrata — Pan Svec. (26) 35[as atra]; Stat. pl. (55) 16; Fl. alp. (71) 23; Hist. nat. Rossia (144) 33; Fund. agrost. (152) 7; Rar. Norv. (157) 11

Carex baldensis — Cent. II. pl. (66) 32

Carex brizoides — Cent. I. pl. (65) 31

Carex canescens — Pan Svec. (26) 35; Fl. Angl. (56) 23; Fund. agrost. (152) 7

Carex capillaris — Pan Svec. (26) 35[as capillacea]; Herbat. Upsal. (50) 14; Fund. agrost. (152) 7; Pand. fl. Ryb. (165) 22

Carex cespitosa — Pan Svec. (26) 35; Herbat. Upsal. (50) 8; Stat. pl. (55) 14; Hist. nat. Rossia (144) 34; Fund. agrost. (152) 7[as caespitosa], 9[as caespitosa]; Fl. Åker. (162) 19; Pand. fl. Ryb. (165) 22[as caespitosa]

Carex coerulea — Pan Svec. (26) 35

Carex cyperoides — Pan Svec. (26) 35

Carex dactyloidea — Pan Svec. (26) 35

Carex digitata — Demonstr. pl. (49) 25; Fl. Belg. (112) 22; Fl. Åker. (162) 19

Carex dioica — Pan Svec. (26) 34; Stat. pl. (55) 14; Fl. Angl. (56) 23; Fl. Belg. (112) 22; Fund. agrost. (152) 7; Fl. Åker. (162) 19

Carex echinata — Pan Svec. (26) 35

Carex elongata — Fund. agrost. (152) 7

Carex ferruginea — Pan Svec. (26) 35

Carex fibrata radice, angustifolia; caule exquisite triangulari — Cent. I. pl. (65) 31

Carex filiformis — Pan Svec. (26) 35; Fund. agrost. (152) 7; Rar. Norv. (157) 11

Carex flava — Fl. Angl. (56) 23; Fl. Monsp. (74) 27; Prodr. fl. Dan. (82) 24; Fl. Belg. (112) 22; Fund. agrost. (152) 7; Fl. Åker. (162) 19

Carex flavescens — Pan Svec. (26) 35; Fund. agrost. (152) 7

Carex folio molle — Fl. Angl. (56) 29

Carex globularis — Fund. agrost. (152) 7; Esca avium (174) 14

Carex globulosa — Pan Svec. (26) 35

Carex hirta — Pan Svec. (26) 35; Herbat. Upsal. (50) 15; Fl. Angl. (56) 24; Fl. Belg. (112) 22; Fl. Åker. (162) 19

Carex inflata — Pan Svec. (26) 35

Carex lagopodoides — Pan Svec. (26) 35

Carex leporina — Fl. Angl. (56) 23; Fl. Monsp. (74) 27; Prodr. fl. Dan. (82) 24; Fl. Belg. (112) 22; Fund. agrost. (152) 7; Fl. Åker. (162) 19; Pand. fl. Ryb. (165) 22

Carex limosa — Pan Svec. (26) 35; Herbat. Upsal. (50) 16, 19; Stat. pl. (55) 15; Hist. nat. Rossia (144) 33; Fund. agrost. (152) 7; Fl. Åker. (162) 19

Carex loliacea — Fund. agrost. (152) 7; Fl. Åker. (162) 19

Carex muricata — Herbat. Upsal. (50) 15; Fl. Angl. (56) 23; Fl. Monsp. (74) 27; Hist. nat. Rossia (144) 33; Fund. agrost. (152) 7; Fl. Åker. (162) 19

Carex nigra verna vulgaris — Pl. Mart.-Burs. (6) 3

Carex obesa — Pan Svec. (26) 35

Carex pallescens — Fl. Angl. (56) 24; Hist. nat. Rossia (144) 34; Fl. Åker. (162) 19

Carex pallida — Pan Svec. (26) 35

Carex palustre elatius — Fl. Angl. (56) 29

Carex panicea — Pan Svec. (26) 35; Herbat. Upsal. (50) 16; Fl. Angl. (56) 24; Hist. nat. Rossia (144) 34[as panicaea]; Fund. agrost. (152) 7; Fl. Åker. (162) 19

Carex paniculata — Cent. I. pl. (65) 32

Carex pilulifera — Fl. Angl. (56) 23

Carex pseudocyperus — Fl. Angl. (56) 24; Prodr. fl. Dan. (82) 24; Fl. Belg. (112) 22

Carex pulicaris — Stat. pl. (55) 15; Fl. Angl. (56) 23; Fl. Belg. (112) 22; Fund. agrost. (152) 7

Carex racemo composito — Cent. I. pl. (65) 32

Carex racemosa — Pan Svec. (26) 35

Carex remota — Fl. Angl. (56) 24; Cent. I. pl. (65) 31

Carex saxatilis — Fl. alp. (71) 23; Fund. agrost. (152) 7

Carex simplex — Pan Svec. (26) 34

Carex spadiceo viridis — Fl. Angl. (56) 29

Carex spica composita, disticha, nuda; spiculis androgynis, oblongis, contiguis, patentibus; culmo nudo — Cent. I. pl. (65) 31

Carex spica composita, spiculis androgynis: inferioribus remotioribus, folioli longiori instructis, culmo triquetro — Pl. Mart.-Burs. (6) 3

Carex spica composita, spiculis ovatis sessilibus approximatis alternis androgynis nudis — Pl. Mart.-Burs. (6) 3

Carex spica compressa — Fl. Angl. (56) 29

Carex spica divulsa — Fl. Angl. (56) 29

Carex spica longissime distanti — Fl. Angl. (56) 29

Carex spica mascula oblonga, femineis sessilibus oblongis: inferiore foliolo proprio breviore — Pl. Mart.-Burs. (6) 3[as faemineis]

Carex spica monoclina paludosa — Pan Svec. (26) 34

Carex spica multifera — Fl. Angl. (56) 29

Carex spica paniculata — Cent. I. pl. (65) 32

Carex spica pendula longiore — Fl. Angl. (56) 29

Carex spica recurva — Fl. Angl. (56) 29

Carex spicis 3 subrotundis — Fl. Angl. (56) 29

Carex spicis androgynis ovatis triquetris ternis congestis terminalibus sessilibus, involucro diphyllo — Cent. II. pl. (66) 32

Carex spicis androgynis terminatricibus petiolatis: florentibus erectis, fructiferis pendulis — Pl. Mart.-Burs. (6) 3

Carex spicis compactis — Fl. Angl. (56) 29

Carex spicis in foliorum alis sessilibus — Cent. I. pl. (65) 31

Carex spicis masculis pluribus, femineis pedunculatis, capsulis inflatis acuminatis — Pl. Mart.-Burs. (6) 3

Carex spicis ovatis, subsessilibus, remotis, androgynis; foliis caulinis culmum aequantibus — Cent. I. pl. (65) 31

Carex spicis pendulis: mascula erecta, femineis oblongis distichis, capsulis nudis acuminatis — Pl. Mart.-Burs. (6) 3

Carex spicis teretibus — Fl. Angl. (56) 29

Carex spicis teretibus, acutis, alternis, se contingentibus — Cent. I. pl. (65) 31

Carex spiculis subovatis sessilibus distinctis, capsulis acutis divergentibus aculeatis — Pl. Mart.-Burs. (6) 4

Carex sylvarum tenuius — Fl. Angl. (56) 29

Carex uliginosa — Stat. pl. (55) 14; Fund. agrost. (152) 7

Carex vesicaria — Herbat. Upsal. (50) 8; Stat. pl. (55) 14; Fl. Angl. (56) 23; Cervus (60) 8, 10; Prodr. fl. Dan. (82) 24; Fl. Belg. (112) 22; Hist.

46

nat. Rossia (144) 34; Fund. agrost. (152) 7; Fl. Åker. (162) 19; Pand. fl. Ryb. (165) 22

Carex vulpina — Stat. pl. (55) 14; Fl. Angl. (56) 23; Fl. Monsp. (74) 27; Fl. Belg. (112) 22; Hist. nat. Rossia (144) 33; Fund. agrost. (152) 7; Fl. Åker. (162) 19; Pand. fl. Ryb. (165) 22

Carica — Ficus (2) 9, 23, 27; Vir. pl. (13) 10; Pl. escul. (35) 4; Pand. insect. (93) 22; Fund. fr. (123) 8; Reform. bot. (125) 7; Dulcamara (164) 7

Carica papaya — Herb. Amboin. (57) 7; Fl. Jam. (105) 22; Fr. escul. (127) 10; Pl. Surin. (177) 16

Carica posoposa — Fl. Jam. (105) 22

Carigue — Mus. Ad.-Frid. (11) 2

Carigueija brasiliensibus — Mus. Ad.-Frid. (11) 2

Carlina — Hort. Upsal. (7) 35; Vir. pl. (13) 12, 23

Carlina acaulis — Demonstr. pl. (49) 22; Pl. officin. (52) 7; Fl. Monsp. (74) 25; Mac. olit. (113) 16; Fr. escul. (127) 22

Carlina acaulos, magno flore — Pl. Mart.-Burs. (6) 29

Carlina atractyloides — Pl. rar. Afr. (115) 17[as atractydois]

Carlina caule subramoso, calycibus spinis ciliatis — Pl. rar. Afr. (115) 17

Carlina corymbosa — Fl. Monsp. (74) 25

Carlina lanata — Fl. Monsp. (74) 25

Carlina polycephalos, polyacanthae vulgari similis, aethiopica — Pl. rar. Afr. (115) 17[as polyachanthae]

Carlina pyrenaica — Fl. alp. (71) 21

Carlina racemosa — Fl. Monsp. (74) 25

Carlina sylvestris — Pan Svec. (26) 32

Carlina vulgaris — Herbat. Upsal. (50) 10; Stat. pl. (55) 21; Fl. Angl. (56) 22; Prodr. fl. Dan. (82) 23; Fl. Belg. (112) 21; Fl. Åker. (162) 17

Carpesium — Hort. Upsal. (7) 37; Nova pl. gen. 1747 (14) [iv]

Carpesium cernuum — Demonstr. pl. (49) 23; Calend. fl. (72) [18]; Fl. Monsp. (74) 25

Carpinus — Spons. pl. (12) 41; Fl. oecon. (17) 24; Gem. arb. (24) 6; Pan Svec. (26) 36; Hosp. insect. fl. (43) 13, 40; Mirac. insect. (45) 14; Fr. Svec. (91) 24; Pand. insect. (93) 20; Arb. Svec. (101) 17, 26, 30; Nom. bot. (107) 18; Usum musc. (148) 12

Carpinus betulus — Demonstr. pl. (49) 25; Stat. pl. (55) 22; Fl. Angl. (56) 24; Calend. fl. (72) [10]; Fl. Monsp. (74) 27; Prodr. fl. Dan. (82) 24; Pl. tinct. (97) 26; Arb. Svec. (101) 7, 9, 23; Fl. Åker. (162) 19

Carpinus ostrya — Gem. arb. (24) 30; Hosp. insect. fl. (43) 35

Carpio — Usum hist. nat. (145) 27

Carpobalsamum — Opobals. (135) 15

Carthamus — Vir. pl. (13) 23

Carthamus carduncellus — Fl. Monsp. (74) 25

Carthamus caule niveo — Fl. Palaest. (70) 27

Carthamus lanatus — Fl. Palaest. (70) 27; Fl. Monsp. (74) 25

Carthamus tinctorius — Demonstr. pl. (49) 22; Pl. officin. (52) 7[as Carthamns]; Herb. Amboin. (57) 21; Fl. Palaest. (70) 27; Pl. tinct. (97) 23; Fl. Jam. (105) 24

Carum — Vir. pl. (13) 19; Fl. oecon. (17) 8; Pl. escul. (35) 12, 28, 29; Herb. Amboin. (57) 21; Nom. bot. (107) 11

Carum carvi — Demonstr. pl. (49) 8; Pl. officin. (52) 7; Stat. pl. (55) 20; Fl. Angl. (56) 13; Prodr. fl. Dan. (82) 16; Fl. Belg. (112) 15; Mac. olit. (113) 11; Fl. Åker. (162) 9; Pand. fl. Ryb. (165) 18; Esca avium (174) 11

Carum officinarum — Pan Svec. (26) 19

Carum peregrinum — Demonstr. pl. (49) 8

Caryophyllaster — Herb. Amboin. (57) 15

Caryophyllaster litoreus — Herb. Amboin. (57) 17

Caryophyllata — Sapor. med. (31) 15

Caryophyllus — Vir. pl. (13) 21, 30; Sapor. med. (31) 19; Odor. med. (40) 15; Herb. Amboin. (57) 8; Nom. bot. (107) 14; Usum hist. nat. (145) 15

Caryophyllus aromaticus — Pl. officin. (52) 4, 7; Herb. Amboin. (57) 8

Caryophyllus fruticosus flore laciniato — Fl. Palaest. (70) 19[under Dianthus]

Caryophyllus minor, folio viride nigricante, repens, flore argenteis punctis notato — Cent. I. pl. (65) 11

Caryophyllus saxatilis, ericae foliis, umbellatis corymbis — Nova pl. gen. 1751 (32) 41

Caryophyllus saxatilis, polygoni minoris folio et facie — Cent. II. pl. (66) 18

Caryophyllus simplex supinus latifolius — Cent. I. pl. (65) 11

Caryota — Vir. pl. (13) 26

Caryota urens — Herb. Amboin. (57) 6

Cascarilla — Vir. pl. (13) 27

Cassia — Hort. Upsal. (7) 36; Spons. pl. (12) 12, 32, 38; Vir. pl. (13) 31; Gem. arb. (24) 6; Sapor. med. (31) 16; Odor. med. (40) 13; Hosp. insect. fl. (43) 13; Herb. Amboin. (57) 11, 16; Somn. pl. (68) 20; Pand. insect. (93) 14; Pl. Jam. (102) 12; Nect. fl. (122) 4; Fund. fr. (123) 16; Med. purg. (181) 3

Cassia absus — Fl. Palaest. (70) 19

Cassia alata — Fl. Jam. (105) 16; Obs. mat. med. (171) 4; Pl. Surin. (177) 8

Cassia bicapsularis — Demonstr. pl. (49) 11; Pl. Surin. (177) 8

Cassia biflora — Pl. Jam. (102) 12; Fl. Jam. (105) 16

Cassia chamaecrista — Fl. Jam. (105) 16; Pl. rar. Afr. (115) 6

Cassia emarginata — Fl. Jam. (105) 16

Cassia fistula — Demonstr. pl. (49) 11; Pl. officin. (52) 7; Herb. Amboin. (57) 9; Fl. Palaest. (70) 19; Fl. Jam. (105) 16; Fr. escul. (127) 17; Rar. Norv. (157) 12; Colon. pl. (158) 5; Med. purg. (181) 3, 22

Cassia fistula sylvestris — Herb. Amboin. (57) 9

Cassia flexuosa — Demonstr. pl. (49) 11

Cassia foliis quinquelobis acuminatis glabris, petiolis eglandulosis — Med. purg. (181) 22[as accuminatis]

Cassia foliis sejugis subovatis, petiolis eglandulatis — Med. purg. (181) 7

Cassia glandulosa — Fl. Jam. (105) 16

Cassia javanica — Fl. Jam. (105) 16, 25; Pl. Surin. (177) 8

Cassia mimosoides — Fl. Jam. (105) 16

Cassia occidentalis — Demonstr. pl. (49) 11; Fl. Jam. (105) 16

Cassia pilosa — Fl. Jam. (105) 16

Cassia planisiliqua — Fl. Palaest. (70) 19

Cassia procumbens — Herb. Amboin. (57) 28; Fl. Jam. (105) 16

Cassia senna — Pl. officin. (52) 18; Fl. Palaest. (70) 19; Med. purg. (181) 3, 7

Cassia serpens — Fl. Jam. (105) 16

Cassia sophera — Demonstr. pl. (49) 11; Herb. Amboin. (57) 22

Cassia tagera — Fl. Jam. (105) 16

Cassia tora — Herb. Amboin. (57) 22; Fl. Jam. (105) 16, 25; Pl. Surin. (177) 8[as thora]

Cassia viminea — Pl. Jam. (102) 12; Fl. Jam. (105) 16

Cassida — Hosp. insect. fl. (43) 12; Mirac. insect. (45) 18; Noxa insect. (46) 12; Pand. insect. (93) 7; Fund. entom. (154) 18

Cassida bicornis — Cent. insect. (129) 7, 9

Cassida bipustulata — Cent. insect. (129) 9

Cassida cinerea — Hosp. insect. fl. (43) 27

Cassida cyanea, elytris angulo antico spina truncata — Cent. insect. (129) 9

Cassida ferruginea, elytris angulo antico spina porrecta — Cent. insect. (129) 9

Cassida leucophaea — Cent. insect. (129) 10

Cassida nebulosa — Pand. insect. (93) 18

Cassida nobilis — Pand. fl. Ryb. (165) 7

Cassida spinifex — Cent. insect. (129) 9

Cassida testacea margine punctisque flavis — Cent. insect. (129) 10

Cassida viridis — Hosp. insect. fl. (43) 27, 30; Pand. insect. (93) 11, 16, 18

Cassida viridis, elytris maculis lateralibus duabus sanguineis — Cent. insect. (129) 9

Cassine — Vir. pl. (13) 27; Pot. theae (142) 15

Cassine maurocenia — Fl. Cap. (99) 13

Cassine peragua — Pl. officin. (52) 15; Fl. Cap. (99) 13

Cassuvium — Herb. Amboin. (57) 8

Cassuvium sylvestre — Herb. Amboin. (57) 8

Cassytha — Polit. nat. (109) 5; Aphyteia (185) 9[as Cassyta]

Cassytha filiformis — Herb. Amboin. (57) 25; Fung. melit. (69) 2

Castanea — Hort. Upsal. (7) 35; Vir. pl. (13) 32; Pl. escul. (35) 4, 24; Nom. bot. (107) 18

Castor — Oecon. nat. (20) 36; Mat. med. anim. (29) 4; Mus ind. (62) 6ff.; Arb. Svec. (101) 25

Castor cauda ovata plana — Mat. med. anim. (29) 4

Castus — Nect. fl. (122) 10

Casuarina litorea — Herb. Amboin. (57) 12[as Casaarina]

Casuarius — Fund. ornith. (137) 19

Catananche caerulea — Pl. hybr. (33) 29[as coerulea]; Fl. Monsp. (74) 24[as Catanance]

Catananche flava — Pl. hybr. (33) 29

Catananche lutea — Demonstr. pl. (49) 22

Catappa — Herb. Amboin. (57) 8

Cataputia — Euphorbia (36) 3

Cataputia minor — Euphorbia (36) 20

Catesbaea — Nova pl. gen. 1751 (32) 8; Nect. fl. (122) 7

Catodon fistula in cervice — Mat. med. anim. (29) 13

Catonia — Fl. Jam. (105) 27

Catti marus — Herb. Amboin. (57) 14

Caucalis — Hort. Upsal. (7) 34

Caucalis carolina — Pan Svec. (26) 18

Caucalis leptophylla — Fl. Angl. (56) 13; Fl. Monsp. (74) 13; Prodr. fl. Dan. (82) 15

Caucalis major — Acetaria (77) 14

Caucalis maritima — Fl. Monsp. (74) 29

Caucalis platycarpos — Demonstr. pl. (49) 8

Caucalis platyphylla — Fl. Monsp. (74) 13

Cauda felis — Herb. Amboin. (57) 16

Cauda felis agrestis — Herb. Amboin. (57) 16

Caudisona — Rad. senega (23) 5ff.

Cavia cobaija — Mus ind. (62) 10

Ceanothus — Nova pl. gen. 1747 (14) [iv]; Nova pl. gen. 1751 (32) 8; Cui bono? (42) 21; Specif. Canad. (76) 24

Ceanothus africanus — Fl. Cap. (99) 12

Ceanothus americanus — Demonstr. pl. (49) 6; Pl. officin. (52) 7; Specif. Canad. (76) 13; Obs. mat. med. (171) 3

Cecropia peltata — Pl. Jam. (102) 28; Fl. Jam. (105) 21; Obs. mat. med. (171) 6; Pl. Surin. (177) 16

Cedrela — Fl. Jam. (105) 8, 26

Cedrela mahagoni — Fl. Jam. (105) 14

Cedrela odorata — Fl. Jam. (105) 14

Cedrus — Hort. Upsal. (7) 35; Nom. bot. (107) 18; Usum musc. (148) 10

Celastrus — Vir. pl. (13) 27

Celastrus buxifolius — Fl. Cap. (99) 12

Celastrus inermis, foliis ovatis, serratis, trinerviis — Specif. Canad. (76) 24

Celastrus pyracanthus — Demonstr. pl. (49) 6; Fl. Cap. (99) 12

Celastrus scandens — Demonstr. pl. (49) 6

Cellepora — Corallia Balt. (4) 10

Celosia — Hort. Upsal. (7) 36; Spons. pl. (12) 45; Stat. pl. (55) 5; Nect. fl. (122) 9

Celosia cristata — Demonstr. pl. (49) 7; Herb. Amboin. (57) 21; Somn. pl. (68) 16

Celosia paniculata — Fl. Jam. (105) 14, 26

Celsia — Hort. Upsal. (7) 35

Celtis — Hort. Upsal. (7) 35; Spons. pl. (12) 30; Herb. Amboin. (57) 17; Nom. bot. (107) 19

Celtis australis — Demonstr. pl. (49) 26; Fl. Monsp. (74) 28

Cenchris — Surin. Grill. (16) 34

Cenchris scutis abdominalibus 240, scutis caudalibus 64 — Surin. Grill. (16) 20

Cenchrus — Fund. agrost. (152) 25, 34

Cenchrus capitatus — Demonstr. pl. (49) 26; Fl. Monsp. (74) 28

Cenchrus echinatus — Fl. Jam. (105) 22

Cenchrus lappaceus — Fund. agrost. (152) 32

Cenchrus racemosus — Fl. Monsp. (74) 28; Fl. Jam. (105) 22; Fund. agrost. (152) 32

Centaurea — Pl. Mart.-Burs. (6) 23; Hort. Upsal. (7) 34; Anandria (9) 5; Vir. pl. (13) 23[as Centauria], 33, 36; Fl. oecon. (17) 21; Pl. hybr. (33) 18, 19; Obst. med. (34) 6; Cui bono? (42) 20; Fl. Monsp. (74) 7; Migr. avium (79) 34; Pand. insect. (93) 18; Nom. bot. (107) 17; Fund. fr. (123) 21

Centaurea alpina — Hort. cul. (132) 24

Centaurea aspera — Fl. Monsp. (74) 26

Centaurea behen — Pl. officin. (52) 5; Fl. Palaest. (70) 29

Centaurea benedicta — Febr. interm. (167) 37

Centaurea calcitrapa — Demonstr. pl. (49) 24; Fl. Angl. (56) 22; Metam. pl. (67) 20[as calcetrapa]; Fl. Palaest. (70) 28; Fl. Monsp. (74) 26; Fl. Belg. (112) 10, 21; Obs. mat. med. (171) 5

Centaurea calcitrapoides — Cent. I. pl. (65) 29; Fl. Monsp. (74) 26

Centaurea calycibus simplicissime spinosis: dentibus duobus oppositis, foliis lanceolatis integris decurrentibus — Cent. I. pl. (65) 30

Centaurea calycibus simplicissime spinosis, foliis dentato-pinnatis villosis, caule nullo — Cent. I. pl. (65) 30

Centaurea calycibus squamosis, foliis lanceolatis radicalibus sinuato-dentatis, ramis angulatis — Pl. Mart.-Burs. (6) 23

Centaurea calycibus subduplicato-spinosis, foliis amplexicaulibus lanceolatis serratis — Cent. I. pl. (65) 29

Centaurea calycibus subulato spinosis, foliis decurrentibus inermibus lanceolatis: inferioribus dentatis — Pl. Mart.-Burs. (6) 29

Centaurea capillata — Hist. nat. Rossia (144) 33

Centaurea centaurium — Fl. alp. (71) 22

Centaurea collina — Fl. Monsp. (74) 26

Centaurea conifera — Fl. Monsp. (74) 7, 26

Centaurea crocodylium — Fl. Palaest. (70) 29

Centaurea crupina — Demonstr. pl. (49) 24; Fl. Palaest. (70) 29; Fl. Monsp. (74) 26

Centaurea cyanus — Pan Svec. (26) 33; Demonstr. pl. (49) 24; Herbat. Upsal. (50) 13; Pl. officin. (52) 9; Stat. pl. (55) 19; Fl. Angl. (56) 22; Calend. fl. (72) [13]; Fl. Monsp. (74) 26; Prodr. fl. Dan. (82) 23; Pl. tinct. (97) 24; Fl. Belg. (112) 21; Hort. cul. (132) 23, 25; Usum hist. nat. (145) 10; Fl. Åker. (162) 18; Pand. fl. Ryb. (165) 22; Esca avium (174) 14

Centaurea eriophora — Demonstr. pl. (49) 24

Centaurea erucifolia — Fl. Palaest. (70) 28

Centaurea galactites — Fl. Palaest. (70) 29; Fl. Monsp. (74) 26

Centaurea glastifolia — Demonstr. pl. (49) 24; Calend. fl. (72) [17]; Hist. nat. Rossia (144) 33

Centaurea jacea — Pan Svec. (26) 33; Hosp. insect. fl. (43) 31; Herbat. Upsal. (50) 7; Stat. pl. (55) 18; Fl. Angl. (56) 22; Calend. fl. (72) [15]; Fl. Monsp. (74) 26; Prodr. fl. Dan. (82) 23; Pl. tinct. (97) 24; Fl. Belg. (112) 21; Fl. Åker. (162) 18; Pand. fl. Ryb. (165) 22

Centaurea maxima — Pan Svec. (26) 33

Centaurea melitensis — Fl. Monsp. (74) 26

Centaurea montana — Demonstr. pl. (49) 24; Fl. alp. (71) 22; Fl. Monsp. (74) 26

Centaurea moschata — Fl. Palaest. (70) 29; Hist. nat. Rossia (144) 23

Centaurea moschata lutea — Demonstr. pl. (49) 24[as moscata]

Centaurea moschata purpurea — Demonstr. pl. (49) 24[as moscata]

Centaurea nigra — Calend. fl. (72) [14]

Centaurea orientalis — Demonstr. pl. (49) 24; Calend. fl. (72) [17]; Hist. nat. Rossia (144) 33

Centaurea paniculata — Fl. Monsp. (74) 26; Hist. nat. Rossia (144) 23

Centaurea phrygia — Demonstr. pl. (49) 24; Calend. fl. (72) [12], [16]; Fl. Monsp. (74) 26; Prodr. fl. Dan. (82) 23; Colon. pl. (158) 7

Centaurea pullata — Fl. Monsp. (74) 26

Centaurea pumila — Cent. I. pl. (65) 30[as pumilis]; see also C. pumilio

Centaurea pumilio [error for pumila?] — Fl. Palaest. (70) 29

Centaurea rhapontica — Fl. alp. (71) 22

Centaurea salmantica — Demonstr. pl. (49) 24; Fl. Monsp. (74) 26

Centaurea scabiosa — Herbat. Upsal. (50) 17; Pl. officin. (52) 3; Stat. pl. (55) 18; Fl. Angl. (56) 22; Calend. fl. (72) [17]; Fl. Monsp. (74) 26; Prodr. fl. Dan. (82) 23; Usum hist. nat. (145) 10; Fl. Åker. (162) 18; Pand. fl. Ryb. (165) 22

Centaurea seridis — Fl. Monsp. (74) 26

Centaurea sibirica — Hist. nat. Rossia (144) 33

Centaurea solstitialis — Demonstr. pl. (49) 24; Fl. Angl. (56) 22; Fl. Monsp. (74) 26

Centaurea splendens — Hist. nat. Rossia (144) 33

Centaurea strepens — Fl. Monsp. (74) 26

Centaurea verutum — Cent. I. pl. (65) 30; Fl. Palaest. (70) 28

Centaurium foliis binis oppositis angustis linearibus, flore magno rubente — Cent. II. pl. (66) 12

Centaurium luteum minimum — Fl. Angl. (56) 27

Centaurium minus spicatum, angustissimo folio, seu scopiarium marilandium novum — Nova pl. gen. 1751 (32) 15

Centaurium zeylanicum minus, flore luteo — Nova pl. gen. 1747 (14) 7

Centella glabrata — Pl. rar. Afr. (115) 28

Centella villosa — Pl. rar. Afr. (115) 28

Centriscus — Pand. insect. (93) 3

Centunculus — Hort. Upsal. (7) 41

Centunculus foliis alternis ovatis — Pl. Mart.-Burs. (6) 22

Centunculus minimus — Pan Svec. (26) 15; Fung. melit. (69) 2; Fl. Åker. (162) 7

Cepa — Vir. pl. (13) 7, 20; Fl. oecon. (17) 8; Sapor. med. (31) 19; Pl. escul. (35) 28, 29; Odor. med. (40) 14; Cul. mut. (88) 2; Nom. bot. (107) 12; Usum hist. nat. (145) 25

Cepa aegyptiorum radice rapae — Cul. mut. (88) 8

Cepa pratensis — Pan Svec. (26) 20

Cepa sectilis — Pan Svec. (26) 20; Pl. escul. (35) 12

Cepa sylvestris — Pl. escul. (35) 12; Herb. Amboin. (57) 28

Cepa vulgaris — Fl. Cap. (99) 2

Cephalanthus — Hort. Upsal. (7) 35; Gem. arb. (24) 21; Herb. Amboin. (57) 11

Cephalanthus occidentalis — Demonstr. pl. (49) 4

Cephalanthus orientalis — Herb. Amboin. (57) 12; Fl. Cap. (99) 11

Cerambyx — Oecon. nat. (20) 25; Noxa insect. (46) 13, 14, 16; Pand. insect. (93) 7; Polit. nat. (109) 21; Fund. entom. (154) 18, 30, [31, as 30]

Cerambyx aedilis — Pand. fl. Ryb. (165) 8

Cerambyx bajulus — Pand. fl. Ryb. (165) 8

Cerambyx coriarius — Esca avium (174) 6

Cerambyx fur — Pane diaet. (83) 17

Cerambyx hispidus — Pand. fl. Ryb. (165) 8

Cerambyx inquisitor — Pand. fl. Ryb. (165) 8

Cerambyx nebulosus — Pand. insect. (93) 21

Cerambyx noctis — Pand. fl. Ryb. (165) 8

Cerambyx rusticus — Pand. fl. Ryb. (165) 8

Cerambyx sutor — Pand. fl. Ryb. (165) 8; Esca avium (174) 6

Cerambyx testaceus, elytrorum fascia duplici albida, thorace spinoso — Noxa insect. (46) 13[as dupplici]

Cerambyx testaceus, elytrorum fascia gemina albida, thorace spinoso — Hosp. insect. fl. (43) 36

Cerambyx undatus — Pand. fl. Ryb. (165) 8

Cerambyx violaceus — Pand. fl. Ryb. (165) 8

Cerambyx viridi caerulescens — Hosp. insect. fl. (43) 37

Cerastium — Oecon. nat. (20) 29; Mirac. insect. (45) 16; Metam. pl. (67) 24; Pand. insect. (93) 14

Cerastium alpinum — Stat. pl. (55) 16; Fl. alp. (71) 17; Rar. Norv. (157) 10

Cerastium aquaticum — Fl. Angl. (56) 16; Prodr. fl. Dan. (82) 18; Fl. Belg. (112) 17; Fl. Åker. (162) 12

Cerastium arvense — Fl. Angl. (56) 16; Prodr. fl. Dan. (82) 18; Fl. Belg. (112) 8, 17

Cerastium dichotomum — Demonstr. pl. (49) 12

Cerastium glabrum, caule stricto, foliis lanceolatis, pedunculis longissimis, capsulis globosis — Cent. II. pl. (66) 18

Cerastium hirsutum magno flore — Fl. Angl. (56) 28

Cerastium lapponicum — Pan Svec. (26) 23

Cerastium latifolium — Fl. Angl. (56) 16; Fl. alp. (71) 17

Cerastium manticum — Cent. II. pl. (66) 18

Cerastium maximum — Hist. nat. Rossia (144) 29

Cerastium pentandrum — Pan Svec. (26) 23; Herbat. Upsal. (50) 10

Cerastium perfoliatum — Demonstr. pl. (49) 12

Cerastium scanicum — Pan Svec. (26) 23

Cerastium semidecandrum — Stat. pl. (55) 21; Fl. Angl. (56) 16; Fl. Monsp. (74) 16; Prodr. fl. Dan. (82) 18

Cerastium strictum — Fl. alp. (71) 17

Cerastium tomentosum — Fl. Angl. (56) 16; Fl. Monsp. (74) 16

Cerastium viscosum — Pan Svec. (26) 23; Hosp. insect. fl. (43) 21; Herbat. Upsal. (50) 10; Stat. pl. (55) 21; Fl. Angl. (56) 16; Fl. Monsp. (74) 16; Fl. Belg. (112) 17; Fl. Åker. (162) 12; Pand. fl. Ryb. (165) 19

Cerastium vulgatum — Fl. Monsp. (74) 16; Prodr. fl. Dan. (82) 18; Fl. Belg. (112) 8, 17; Pand. fl. Ryb. (165) 19

Cerasus — Spons. pl. (12) 42; Vir. pl. (13) 21, 33, 36; Sapor. med. (31) 12, 14; Pl. escul. (35) 17, 28; Hosp. insect. fl. (43) 40; Noxa insect. (46) 20; Vern. arb. (47) 10, table; Calend. fl. (72) [15]; Pl. Jam. (102) 10; Nom. bot. (107) 13; Pot. theae (142) 16

Cerasus avium — Colon. pl. (158) 8

Cerasus mahaleb — Gem. arb. (24) 25

Cerasus padus — Herbat. Upsal. (50) 7[as Ceresus]

Cerasus sativa — Hosp. insect. fl. (43) 21

Cerasus vulgaris — Gem. arb. (24) 26

Ceratocarpus — Nova pl. gen. 1747 (14) [vi], 28; Sem. musc. (28) 12; Hist. nat. Rossia (144) 24; Siren. lacert. (146) 7

Ceratonia — Hort. Upsal. (7) 37; Vir. pl. (13) 32; Pl. escul. (35) 4; Pand. insect. (93) 22; Nom. bot. (107) 18; Inebr. (117) 13

Ceratonia siliqua — Demonstr. pl. (49) 26; Pl. officin. (52) 9, 18; Fl. Palaest. (70) 31; Fr. escul. (127) 17

Ceratophyllum aquaticum — Pan Svec. (26) 35

Ceratophyllum demersum — Stat. pl. (55) 12; Fl. Angl. (56) 24; Fl. Monsp. (74) 27; Prodr. fl. Dan. (82) 24; Fl. Jam. (105) 21, 25; Fl. Belg. (112) 22; Colon. pl. (158) 6; Fl. Åker. (162) 19

Ceratospermum — Nova pl. gen. 1747 (14) 28

Cerbera — Vir. pl. (13) 10, 25

Cerbera manghas — Demonstr. pl. (49) 7; Herb. Amboin. (57) 10

Cerbera thevetia — Pl. Surin. (177) 7

Cercis — Hort. Upsal. (7) 37; Fl. Monsp. (74) 7; Nect. fl. (122) 7

Cercis canadensis — Demonstr. pl. (49) 11

Cercis siliquastrum — Fl. Palaest. (70) 19; Fl. Monsp. (74) 15[as Cerus]

Cercopithecus — Anthrop. (111) 5

Cercopithecus ceilonicus seu tardigradus dictus major — Mus. Ad.-Frid. (11) 2

Cerefolium — Acetaria (77) 10; Nom. bot. (107) 11

Cereus — Spons. pl. (12) 56

Cerinthe — Hort. Upsal. (7) 34; Vir. pl. (13) 18; Nom. bot. (107) 10

Cerinthe echioides — Cent. I. pl. (65) 7; Fl. Monsp. (74) 11

Cerinthe foliis lanceolatis hispidis, seminibus quaternis distinctis, fructibus pendulis — Cent. I. pl. (65) 7

Cerinthe maculata — Demonstr. pl. (49) 5

Cerinthe major — Demonstr. pl. (49) 5

Cerinthe minor — Demonstr. pl. (49) 5

Cerinthe orientalis — Cent. I. pl. (65) 7; Fl. Palaest. (70) 14

Cerocoma — Fund. entom. (154) 30

Certhia — Migr. avium (79) 17, 23; Polit. nat. (109) 14

Cerva — Mat. med. anim. (29) 7

Cervaria — Nova pl. gen. 1747 (14) [vi], 31, 32

Cervispina — Vir. pl. (13) 27

Cervus — Vir. pl. (13) 16; Oecon. nat. (20) 26; Pan Svec. (26) 3; Mat. med. anim. (29) 7; Morb. hyeme (38) 3; Cui bono? (42) 24; Noxa insect. (46) 28, 29; Cervus (60) 4ff.; Metam. pl. (67) [5]; Polit. nat. (109) 21; Fund. fr. (123) 8; Usum hist. nat. (145) 24

Cervus alces — Fund. fr. (123) 8

Cervus cornibus acaulibus palmatis — Mat. med. anim. (29) 6

Cervus cornibus ramosis teretibus incurvatis — Mat. med. anim. (29) 7

Cervus cornibus ramosis teretibus: summitatibus palmatis — Mat. med. anim. (29) 7; Cervus (60) 3

Cervus dama — Fund. fr. (123) 8

Cervus elaphus — Fund. fr. (123) 8

Cervus mirabilis — Cervus (60) 4

Cervus palmatus — Cervus (60) 4

Cervus rangifer — Cervus (60) 4

Cervus tarandus — Usum musc. (148) 9

Cervus vulgaris — Cervus (60) 17

Cestrum nocturnum — Fl. Jam. (105) 14

Cestrum vespertinum — Pl. Surin. (177) 6

Cete — Mat. med. anim. (29) 13

Ceterach — Acrostichum (10) 6

Chaa — Pot. theae (142) 3

Chaerophyllum — Fl. oecon. (17) 7; Pand. insect. (93) 13

Chaerophyllum bulbosum — Demonstr. pl. (49) 8; Calend. fl. (72) [13]

Chaerophyllum cicutaria — Pan Svec. (26) 19; Hosp. insect. fl. (43) 19

Chaerophyllum geniculatum — Pan Svec. (26) 19

Chaerophyllum hirsutum — Fl. alp. (71) 15; Fl. Monsp. (74) 13

Chaerophyllum sylvestre — Pl. officin. (52) 8; Stat. pl. (55) 20[as Caerophyllum]; Fl. Angl. (56) 13; Calend. fl. (72) [11], [15]; Fl. Monsp. (74) 13; Prodr. fl. Dan. (82) 16; Pl. tinct. (97) 14; Fl. Belg. (112) 15; Fl. Åker. (162) 9; Pand. fl. Ryb. (165) 18; Esca avium (174) 11

Chaerophyllum temulentum — Fl. Angl. (56) 13; Prodr. fl. Dan. (82) 16; Fl. Belg. (112) 15

Chaerophyllum temulum — Demonstr. pl. (49) 8; Herbat. Upsal. (50) 10

Chaetodon argenteus — Chin. Lagerstr. (64) 23

Chaetodon griseus, fascia frontali apiceque caudae albis — Chin. Lagerstr. (64) 23

Chaetodon pinnatus — Chin. Lagerstr. (64) 23

Chaetodon pinnis ventralibus ex spinis duabus — Chin. Lagerstr. (64) 23

Chama — Fund. test. (166) 18, 42

Chama gigas — Fund. test. (166) 42, 43

Chama hippopus — Iter Chin. (161) 8

Chama lazarus — Cent. insect. (129) 32[as Cama]

Chamaebalanus japonica — Herb. Amboin. (57) 24

Chamaebuxus flore coluteae — Rad. senega (23) 18

Chamaebuxus flore coluteo flavescente — Rad. senega (23) 18

Chamaecissus angustifolia — Pl. Mart.-Burs. (6) 30

Chamaecistus ericae folio, luteus elatior — Cent. I. pl. (65) 14

Chamaedaphne — Nova pl. gen. 1751 (32) 12, 24, 25

Chamaedaphne foliis tini, floribus bullatis — Nova pl. gen. 1751 (32) 19

Chamaedryfolia tomentosa mascatensis — Opobals. (135) 18

51

Chamaedrys incana maritima frutescens, foliis lanceolatis — Marum (175) 6

Chamaedrys spuria adfinis rotundifolia scutellata — Cent. I. pl. (65) 3

Chamaeficus — Ficus (2) 2

Chamaejasme — Nova pl. gen. 1747 (14) 16

Chamaejasme radice mandragorae — Nova pl. gen. 1747 (14) 16

Chamaeleo ceilonicus, subcrocei coloris — Mus. Ad.-Frid. (11) 13

Chamaeleo orientalis ex amboina — Mus. Ad.-Frid. (11) 13

Chamaeleo promontorii bonae spei, coeruleo alboque colore, marmoris instar variegatus — Mus. Ad.-Frid. (11) 13

Chamaeleo pullus amboinensis — Mus. Ad.-Frid. (11) 13

Chamaeleon — Mus. Ad.-Frid. (11) 13

Chamaemelum alpinum saxatile perenne, flore albo singulare, calyce nigricante — Cent. II. pl. (66) 31

Chamaemelum inodorum annuum — Fl. Angl. (56) 27

Chamaemelum marinum — Fl. Angl. (56) 27

Chamaemelum pumilum, foliis angustis pinnatis — Pl. rar. Afr. (115) 25

Chamaepitys — Nom. bot. (107) 14[as Chumaepithys]

Chamaepitys moschata foliis serratis — Pl. Mart.-Burs. (6) 21

Chamaerops — Vir. pl. (13) 26[as Chamerops]; Fl. Jam. (105) 23

Chamaerops humilis — Demonstr. pl. (49) 27

Chamaesyce — Euphorbia (36) 3[as Chamesyce], 16

Chamaesyce arbor — Ficus (2) 2

Chamaesyce villosa major, cauliculis viridibus — Euphorbia (36) 16

Chamepithyn — Hypericum (186) 13

Chamomilla — Vir. pl. (13) 23, 33; Sapor. med. (31) 18; Nom. bot. (107) 17

Chaos protheus — Mund. invis. (149) 18

Chaos redivivus — Siren. lacert. (146) 8

Chara — Morb. hyeme (38) 8

Chara flexilis — Stat. pl. (55) 12

Chara hispida — Stat. pl. (55) 12

Chara tomentosa — Stat. pl. (55) 12

Chara vulgaris — Herbat. Upsal. (50) 10; Prodr. fl. Dan. (82) 26

Characias — Euphorbia (36) [2]

Charadrius apricarius — Migr. avium (79) 28

Charadrius hiaticula — Migr. avium (79) 18, 28

Charadrius morinellus — Fund. ornith. (137) 25

Charadrius pluvialis — Migr. avium (79) 18, 28

Charandrius spinosus — Polit. nat. (109) 21

Chavaria — Fund. ornith. (137) 25

Cheiranthus — Hort. Upsal. (7) 34; Spons. pl. (12) 59; Odor. med. (40) 12; Hosp. insect. fl. (43) 28; Pand. insect. (93) [17, as 38]; Nom. bot. (107) 15

Cheiranthus africanus — Pl. rar. Afr. (115) 13

Cheiranthus caule ramoso diffuso; foliis lanceolatis, acutiusculis; antheris eminentibus — Cent. I. pl. (65) 19

Cheiranthus cheiri — Demonstr. pl. (49) 17; Pl. officin. (52) 7; Fl. Angl. (56) 20; Fl. Monsp. (74) 21; Fl. Belg. (112) 19; Pl. Alstr. (121) 5; Hort. cul. (132) 24[as cheri], 25

Cheiranthus erysimoides — Demonstr. pl. (49) 17; Fl. Palaest. (70) 24

Cheiranthus fenestralis — Demonstr. pl. (49) 17

Cheiranthus foliis lanceolatis integerrimis subhirsutis acutis, siliquis compressis, caule herbaceo — Pl. rar. Afr. (115) 13

Cheiranthus fruticulosus — Demonstr. pl. (49) 17; Fl. Monsp. (74) 21

Cheiranthus incanus — Demonstr. pl. (49) 17; Pl. Alstr. (121) 5; Hort. cul. (132) 24, 25

Cheiranthus incanus albus — Calend. fl. (72) [22]

Cheiranthus maritimus — Demonstr. pl. (49) 17; Cent. I. pl. (65) 19

Cheiranthus maritimus folio sinuato — Fl. Angl. (56) 27

Cheiranthus sinuatus — Fl. Monsp. (74) 21

Chelidonium — Vir. pl. (13) 4, 21, 25, 36; Pl. hybr. (33) 6, 13; Pand. insect. (93) 16; Nom. bot. (107) 14; Opium (179) 4

Chelidonium corniculatum — Demonstr. pl. (49) 14; Fl. Monsp. (74) 18

Chelidonium glaucium — Demonstr. pl. (49) 14[as glaucum]; Fl. Angl. (56) 17; Fl. Palaest. (70) 21; Fl. Monsp. (74) 18; Prodr. fl. Dan. (82) 19

Chelidonium hispidum, pedunculis unifloris — Pl. hybr. (33) 13

Chelidonium hybridum — Demonstr. pl. (49) 14; Fl. Angl. (56) 17; Fl. Monsp. (74) 18

Chelidonium majus — Herbat. Upsal. (50) 10; Pl. officin. (52) 8; Stat. pl. (55) 20; Fl. Angl. (56) 17; Calend. fl. (72) [11]; Fl. Monsp. (74) 18; Prodr. fl. Dan. (82) 19; Fl. Belg. (112) 18; Fl. Åker. (162) 13; Pand. fl. Ryb. (165) 19; Febr. interm. (167) 29; Esca avium (174) 13

Chelidonium majus quernum — Demonstr. pl. (49) 14

Chelidonium vulgare — Pan Svec. (26) 25

Chelone — Nova pl. gen. 1751 (32) 10, 12; Nect. fl. (122) 7, 8

Chelone acadiensis — Specif. Canad. (76) 22

Chenopodium — Vir. pl. (13) 31, 32, 35; Fl. oecon. (17) 7; Sapor. med. (31) 13; Pl. hybr. (33) 7, 29; Pl. escul. (35) 28; Pand. insect. (93) 12

Chenopodium album — Herbat. Upsal. (50) 13; Stat. pl. (55) 19; Fl. Angl. (56) 13; Prodr. fl. Dan. (82) 15; Fl. Belg. (112) 14; Fl. Åker. (162) 9

Chenopodium ambrosioides — Demonstr. pl. (49) 7;
Calend. fl. (72) [22]

Chenopodium anthelminticum — Specif. Canad. (76)
25

Chenopodium aristatum — Demonstr. pl. (49) 7;
Hist. nat. Rossia (144) 28

Chenopodium bonus henricus — Pl. escul. (35) 10;
Herbat. Upsal. (50) 20; Pl. officin. (52) 6; Stat. pl.
(55) 20; Fl. Angl. (56) 13; Cervus (60) 7; Fl.
Monsp. (74) 12[as hinricus]; Prodr. fl. Dan. (82)
15; Fl. Belg. (112) 14[as hinricus]; Mac. olit. (113)
14[as hinricus]; Fl. Åker. (162) 9; Pand. fl. Ryb.
(165) 17

Chenopodium botrys — Demonstr. pl. (49) 7; Pl.
officin. (52) 6

Chenopodium erectum chrysanthemo folio — Fl.
Angl. (56) 26

Chenopodium ficus folio — Fl. Angl. (56) 26

Chenopodium foliis deltoideis sinuato-dentatis
rugosis glabris uniformibus, racemis terminalibus
— Cent. II. pl. (66) 12

Chenopodium folio oblongo integro — Fl. Angl. (56)
26

Chenopodium folio subrotundo — Fl. Angl. (56) 26

Chenopodium fruticosum — Hort. Upsal. (7) 35;
Demonstr. pl. (49) 7; Fl. Angl. (56) 13; Fl. Palaest.
(70) 16

Chenopodium glaucum — Fl. Angl. (56) 13; Prodr.
fl. Dan. (82) 15; Fl. Belg. (112) 14; Fl. Åker. (162)
9

Chenopodium henricus — Pan Svec. (26) 18

Chenopodium hirsutum — Prodr. fl. Dan. (82) 15

Chenopodium hispanicum procerius, folio deltoide —
Cent. II. pl. (66) 13

Chenopodium hybridum — Fl. Angl. (56) 13; Prodr.
fl. Dan. (82) 15

Chenopodium kali semine — Pan Svec. (26) 18

Chenopodium lundinense — Pan Svec. (26) 18

Chenopodium maritimum — Stat. pl. (55) 12; Fl.
Angl. (56) 13; Fl. Palaest. (70) 16; Prodr. fl. Dan.
(82) 15; Fl. Belg. (112) 14

Chenopodium murale — Fl. Angl. (56) 13; Calend.
fl. (72) [22]; Fl. Belg. (112) 14

Chenopodium oleo folio — Fl. Angl. (56) 26

Chenopodium polyspermum — Pan Svec. (26) 18;
Herbat. Upsal. (50) 15; Stat. pl. (55) 19; Fl. Angl.
(56) 13; Prodr. fl. Dan. (82) 15; Fl. Åker. (162) 9

Chenopodium procumbes lucidum — Fl. Angl. (56)
26

Chenopodium purpurascens — Pan Svec. (26) 18;
Hosp. insect. fl. (43) 18

Chenopodium repandifolium — Pan Svec. (26) 18

Chenopodium rubrum — Pl. hybr. (33) 14; Vern. arb.
(47) 9; Demonstr. pl. (49) [vii], 7; Pl. officin. (52)
5; Stat. pl. (55) 20; Fl. Angl. (56) 13; Fl. Monsp.
(74) 12; Prodr. fl. Dan. (82) 15; Fl. Belg. (112) 14;
Fl. Åker. (162) 9; Pand. fl. Ryb. (165) 17

Chenopodium scoparium — Fl. Palaest. (70) 16

Chenopodium segetum — Pan Svec. (26) 18

Chenopodium serotinum — Cent. II. pl. (66) 12

Chenopodium stramonifolium — Pan Svec. (26) 18;
Pl. hybr. (33) 28

Chenopodium upsaliense — Pan Svec. (26) 18

Chenopodium urbanum [error for urbicum?] — Esca
avium (174) 11

Chenopodium urbicum — Herbat. Upsal. (50) 20;
Stat. pl. (55) 20; Fl. Angl. (56) 13; Prodr. fl. Dan.
(82) 15; see also C. urbanum

Chenopodium viride — Pan Svec. (26) 18; Pl. hybr.
(33) 28; Stat. pl. (55) 19; Fl. Palaest. (70) 16;
Prodr. fl. Dan. (82) 15; Fl. Åker. (162) 9; Pand. fl.
Ryb. (165) 17

Chenopodium vulvaria — Pan Svec. (26) 18;
Demonstr. pl. (49) 7; Pl. officin. (52) 20; Stat. pl.
(55) 19; Fl. Angl. (56) 13; Prodr. fl. Dan. (82) 15;
Colon. pl. (158) 5; Fl. Åker. (162) 9

Cherleria — Pl. Mart.-Burs. (6) 24

Cherleria ledoides — Fl. alp. (71) 17

Chermes — Spons. pl. (12) 13; Oecon. nat. (20) 28,
29; Gem. arb. (24) 11; Cui bono? (42) 10; Hosp.
insect. fl. (43) 32, 39; Mirac. insect. (45) 15; Noxa
insect. (46) 26, 30; Mund. invis. (149) 10; Fund.
entom. (154) 18, 19

Chermes abietis — Hosp. insect. fl. (43) 36; Mirac.
insect. (45) 15; Pand. insect. (93) 21

Chermes aceris — Hosp. insect. fl. (43) 20; Pand.
insect. (93) [23, as 31]

Chermes alni — Hosp. insect. fl. (43) 33; Pand.
insect. (93) 19

Chermes betulae — Hosp. insect. fl. (43) 33; Pand.
insect. (93) 19

Chermes buxi — Pand. insect. (93) 19

Chermes calthae — Pand. fl. Ryb. (165) 10

Chermes cerastii — Hosp. insect. fl. (43) 21; Pand.
insect. (93) 14

Chermes fagi — Hosp. insect. fl. (43) 35; Pand.
insect. (93) 20

Chermes ficus — Pand. insect. (93) [23, as 31]

Chermes fraxini — Hosp. insect. fl. (43) 39; Pand.
insect. (93) [23, as 31]

Chermes graminis — Pand. insect. (93) 11

Chermes grisea, abdomine brevi: striis transversi
albis — Hosp. insect. fl. (43) 23

Chermes pyri — Pand. insect. (93) 15

Chermes quercus — Pand. insect. (93) 20

Chermes salicis — Hosp. insect. fl. (43) 37; Pand.
insect. (93) 21

Chermes tinctoria — Hosp. insect. fl. (43) 13

Chermes ulmi — Hosp. insect. fl. (43) 18; Pand.
insect. (93) 12

Chermes urticae — Hosp. insect. fl. (43) 32; Pand.
insect. (93) 19

Chersea — Amphib. Gyll. (5) 3[as Chersaea]

Chimaera — Fl. Cap. (99) [1]

China — Sapor. med. (31) 18

Chiococca — Fl. Jam. (105) 26

Chiococca racemosa — Fl. Jam. (105) 13; Pl. Surin. (177) 6

Chionanthus — Nova pl. gen. 1751 (32) 7

Chironia — Fl. Cap. (99) 6; Fund. fr. (123) 18

Chironia baccifera — Fl. Cap. (99) 12

Chironia caryophylloides — Cent. II. pl. (66) 12; Fl. Cap. (99) 12

Chironia frutescens — Fl. Cap. (99) 12

Chironia fruticosa, calycibus inflatis rotundatis — Cent. II. pl. (66) 12

Chironia herbacea, foliis lanceolatis — Pl. rar. Afr. (115) 9

Chironia jasminoides — Pl. rar. Afr. (115) 9

Chironia linoides — Fl. Cap. (99) 12

Chiton — Fund. test. (166) 18, 40

Chiton aculeatus — Fund. test. (166) 31, 40

Chiton corpore punctato, testis octo — Chin. Lagerstr. (64) 32

Chiton punctatum — Chin. Lagerstr. (64) 32

Chloroxylon — Fl. Jam. (105) 26

Chondrilla — Vir. pl. (13) 25

Chondrilla altera — Cent. I. pl. (65) 26

Chondrilla bulbosa syriaca, foliis latioribus — Cent. I. pl. (65) 26

Chondrilla juncea — Fl. Palaest. (70) 27; Fl. Monsp. (74) 24; Hist. nat. Rossia (144) 32

Chondrilla viscosa humilis — Fl. Angl. (56) 26

Christophoriana — Cimicifuga (173) 5, 6

Christophoriana americana procerior et longius spicata — Cimicifuga (173) 5

Christophoriana americana racemosa baccis niveis — Pl. hybr. (33) 16

Christophoriana vulgaris, nostras, racemosa et ramosa — Cimicifuga (173) 5

Chrysanthemum — Nom. bot. (107) 17

Chrysanthemum alpinum — Fl. alp. (71) 22[as Crysanthemum]; Fl. Monsp. (74) 26

Chrysanthemum arcticum — Hist. nat. Rossia (144) 33

Chrysanthemum conyzoides aethiopicum, capitulo aphyllo, foliis majoranae — Pl. rar. Afr. (115) 18[as Crysanthemum]

Chrysanthemum conyzoides nodiflorum, semine rostrato bidente — Cent. I. pl. (65) 28

Chrysanthemum coronarium — Demonstr. pl. (49) 23; Fl. Palaest. (70) 28; Calend. fl. (72) [14], [22]; Fl. Monsp. (74) 26; Hort. cul. (132) 23, 25

Chrysanthemum corymbiferum — Fl. Monsp. (74) 26

Chrysanthemum corymbosum — Hist. nat. Rossia (144) 33

Chrysanthemum creticum — Pl. rar. Afr. (115) 7

Chrysanthemum ericoides coronatum capitis bonae spei — Cent. I. pl. (65) 8

Chrysanthemum flosculosum — Fl. Cap. (99) 18

Chrysanthemum foliis amplexicaulibus, superne serratis, inferne dentatis — Pl. Mart.-Burs. (6) 22

Chrysanthemum foliorum pinnis brevissimis dentatis — Cent. II. pl. (66) 32; Pl. rar. Afr. (115) 26

Chrysanthemum graminifolium — Fl. Monsp. (74) 25

Chrysanthemum indicum — Herb. Amboin. (57) 21

Chrysanthemum leucanthemum — Pan Svec. (26) 33; Herbat. Upsal. (50) 7; Pl. officin. (52) 6[as Crysanthemum]; Stat. pl. (55) 21; Fl. Angl. (56) 22; Calend. fl. (72) [12]; Fl. Monsp. (74) 25; Prodr. fl. Dan. (82) 23; Fl. Belg. (112) 21; Fl. Åker. (162) 18; Pand. fl. Ryb. (165) 21

Chrysanthemum luteum — Pan Svec. (26) 33

Chrysanthemum monspeliense — Fl. Monsp. (74) 26

Chrysanthemum montanum — Fl. Monsp. (74) 25

Chrysanthemum repens — Pl. Jam. (102) 25

Chrysanthemum segetum — Demonstr. pl. (49) 23; Stat. pl. (55) 19; Fl. Angl. (56) 22; Calend. fl. (72) [14], [22]; Fl. Monsp. (74) 26; Prodr. fl. Dan. (82) 23; Fl. Belg. (112) 21; Raphania (126) 17; Usum hist. nat. (145) 10; Colon. pl. (158) 5[as Crysanthemum]

Chrysanthemum serotinum — Demonstr. pl. (49) 23; Calend. fl. (72) [21]

Chrysis cyanea — Pand. fl. Ryb. (165) 13

Chrysis fulgida — Pand. fl. Ryb. (165) 13

Chrysis ignita — Pand. fl. Ryb. (165) 13

Chrysobalanus — Pl. escul. (35) 4

Chrysobalanus icaco — Herb. Amboin. (57) 8; Fl. Jam. (105) 17; Fr. escul. (127) 13

Chrysocoma — Hort. Upsal. (7) 35; Fl. Cap. (99) 8

Chrysocoma aethiopica, plantaginis folio — Pl. rar. Afr. (115) 19

Chrysocoma biflora — Hist. nat. Rossia (144) 32

Chrysocoma cernua — Demonstr. pl. (49) 22; Fl. Cap. (99) 17

Chrysocoma ciliata — Fl. Cap. (99) 17

Chrysocoma coma aurea — Demonstr. pl. (49) 22; Fl. Cap. (99) 17[as comaurea]

Chrysocoma foliis oppositis obovatis, floribus fasciculatis pedunculatis — Pl. rar. Afr. (115) 18

Chrysocoma linosyris — Fl. Monsp. (74) 25; Colon. pl. (158) 6

Chrysocoma oppositifolia — Pl. rar. Afr. (115) 18

Chrysocoma scoparia — Pl. Jam. (102) 21; Fl. Jam. (105) 19

Chrysocoma syriaca, flore atro rubente — Cent. I. pl. (65) 27

Chrysocoma villosa — Hist. nat. Rossia (144) 32

Chrysogonum — Fund. fr. (123) 17

Chrysogonum peruvianum — Demonstr. pl. (49) 24

Chrysomela — Oecon. nat. (20) 28; Hosp. insect. fl. (43) 21, 26, 37; Noxa insect. (46) 19, 21; Pand. insect. (93) 20; Polit. nat. (109) 8; Hort. cul. (132) 11; Fund. agrost. (152) 10; Fund. entom. (154) 19, 29[as Crysomela], 30

Chrysomela aenei coloris — Hosp. insect. fl. (43) 38

Chrysomela alni — Hosp. insect. fl. (43) 33; Pand. fl. Ryb. (165) 8; Esca avium (174) 6

Chrysomela armoraciae — Hosp. insect. fl. (43) 28; Pand. insect. (93) 16[as armoracic.]

Chrysomela asparagi — Hosp. insect. fl. (43) 19; Noxa insect. (46) 18; Pand. insect. (93) 13

Chrysomela atricilla — Pand. fl. Ryb. (165) 8

Chrysomela aurata — Hosp. insect. fl. (43) 29

Chrysomela beccabungae — Pand. insect. (93) 11[as Crhysomela]

Chrysomela betulae — Hosp. insect. fl. (43) 33; Pand. insect. (93) 19; Pand. fl. Ryb. (165) 8

Chrysomela boleti — Pand. insect. (93) [23, as 31]

Chrysomela caprea — Pand. insect. (93) 22; Pand. fl. Ryb. (165) 8[as capraea]

Chrysomela castanea — Cent. insect. (129) 11

Chrysomela cichorii — Meloe (124) 6

Chrysomela collaris — Pand. insect. (93) 22; Pand. fl. Ryb. (165) 8

Chrysomela coryli — Pand. insect. (93) 20

Chrysomela decempunctata — Pand. insect. (93) 13, 22

Chrysomela fastuosa — Pand. fl. Ryb. (165) 8

Chrysomela gibbosa — Cent. insect. (129) 7[as Crysomela], 10

Chrysomela gorterae — Cent. insect. (129) 11

Chrysomela graminis — Pand. insect. (93) 11; Pand. fl. Ryb. (165) 8

Chrysomela haemorrhoidalis — Pand. insect. (93) 19; Pand. fl. Ryb. (165) 8

Chrysomela helxines — Pand. insect. (93) 11, 13; Pand. fl. Ryb. (165) 8

Chrysomela hyoscyami — Pand. insect. (93) 12, [17, as 38]; Pand. fl. Ryb. (165) 8

Chrysomela hypochaeridis — Pand. insect. (93) 18; Pand. fl. Ryb. (165) 8

Chrysomela marginata — Pand. insect. (93) 16; Pand. fl. Ryb. (165) 8

Chrysomela marginella — Pand. fl. Ryb. (165) 8; Esca avium (174) 6

Chrysomela merdigera — Pand. insect. (93) 13; Pand. fl. Ryb. (165) 8

Chrysomela nemorum — Pand. insect. (93) 12, 16; Pand. fl. Ryb. (165) 8

Chrysomela nigra — Hosp. insect. fl. (43) 23; Arb. Svec. (101) 20[as Crysomela]

Chrysomela nigro-aenea — Hosp. insect. fl. (43) 19

Chrysomela nucum — Pand. insect. (93) 20

Chrysomela nymphaeae — Hosp. insect. fl. (43) 26; Pand. insect. (93) 16

Chrysomela oblongiuscula nigra, thorace testaceo, elytris punctis quatuor flavis — Cent. insect. (129) 11

Chrysomela oblongiuscula viridi aenea punctatissima, pedibus ferrugineis — Cent. insect. (129) 11

Chrysomela octopunctata — Cent. insect. (129) 11

Chrysomela ovalis castanea, elytris margine exteriore testaceo — Cent. insect. (129) 11

Chrysomela ovata nigra, elytris testaceis nigro punctatis: fascia media posticaque nigris — Cent. insect. (129) 10

Chrysomela ovata rufa, elytris fasciis tribus atro caeruleis undulatis — Cent. insect. (129) 10

Chrysomela pallida — Pand. insect. (93) 21

Chrysomela phellandrii — Pand. insect. (93) 13; Pand. fl. Ryb. (165) 8

Chrysomela pini — Pand. insect. (93) 21

Chrysomela polita — Pand. insect. (93) 21, 22; Esca avium (174) 3, 6

Chrysomela polygoni — Pand. insect. (93) 13; Pand. fl. Ryb. (165) 8

Chrysomela populi — Hosp. insect. fl. (43) 38; Noxa insect. (46) 25; Pand. insect. (93) 22; Fund. entom. (154) [31, as 30]; Pand. fl. Ryb. (165) 8

Chrysomela punctatissima — Cent. insect. (129) 11

Chrysomela quadripunctata — Esca avium (174) 6

Chrysomela rubra — Hosp. insect. fl. (43) 19

Chrysomela sericea — Pand. insect. (93) 22; Pand. fl. Ryb. (165) 8

Chrysomela staphylaea — Pand. fl. Ryb. (165) 8

Chrysomela subcylindrica atra glaberrima, thorace elytrisque punctis 4 flavescentibus — Cent. insect. (129) 11

Chrysomela tanaceti — Hosp. insect. fl. (43) 31; Pand. insect. (93) 18; Pand. fl. Ryb. (165) 8

Chrysomela thorace nitido caput occultante — Hosp. insect. fl. (43) 35

Chrysomela tridentata — Pand. insect. (93) 12

Chrysomela undulata — Cent. insect. (129) 10

Chrysomela viminalis — Pand. insect. (93) 21; Pand. fl. Ryb. (165) 8

Chrysomela viridi-caerulea, elytris testaceis — Hosp. insect. fl. (43) 35

Chrysomela viridis, elytris griseis, thorace pone tridentato — Hosp. insect. fl. (43) 17

Chrysomela vitellinae — Pand. insect. (93) 21[as vitellina], 22[as vitellina]; Pand. fl. Ryb. (165) 8

Chrysophyllum — Pl. escul. (35) 4

Chrysophyllum cainito — Fr. escul. (127) 10

Chrysophyllum oliviforme — Fl. Jam. (105) 14

Chrysosplenii foliis planta aquatica, flore flavo pentapetalo — Nova pl. gen. 1751 (32) 39

Chrysosplenium — Hort. Upsal. (7) 33[as Crysosplenium]; Vir. pl. (13) 30[as Chrysosphenium]; Erica (163) 2

Chrysosplenium alternifolium — Stat. pl. (55) 14; Fl. Angl. (56) 15; Prodr. fl. Dan. (82) 17; Fl. Åker. (162) 11[as Chysosplen.]; Pand. fl. Ryb. (165) 19

Chrysosplenium cornubiense — Nova pl. gen. 1751 (32) 38

Chrysosplenium foliis alternis — Pl. hybr. (33) 28

Chrysosplenium oppositifolium — Fl. Angl. (56) 15; Fl. Monsp. (74) 16

Chrysosplenium sylvaticum — Pan Svec. (26) 21

Chytraculia — Fl. Jam. (105) 26[as Chytracula]

Cicada — Oecon. nat. (20) 26, 28; Mirac. insect. (45) 17; Noxa insect. (46) 26; Pand. insect. (93) 5, 7; Polit. nat. (109) 8; Fund. entom. (154) 18, 30

Cicada bifasciata — Pand. fl. Ryb. (165) 10

Cicada coleoptrata — Pand. fl. Ryb. (165) 10

Cicada cornuta — Pand. insect. (93) 18, 22

Cicada flammea — Cent. insect. (129) 16

Cicada flava — Hosp. insect. fl. (43) 25

Cicada fronte rostrata adscendcnte tereti truncata — Cent. insect. (129) 16

Cicada interrupta — Pand. fl. Ryb. (165) 10

Cicada laternaria — Noctiluca (39) 5; Mirac. insect. (45) 19

Cicada orni — Pand. insect. (93) [23, as 31]

Cicada rosae — Pand. insect. (93) 15

Cicada spumaria — Pand. fl. Ryb. (165) 10

Cicada thorace bicorni — Hosp. insect. fl. (43) 37

Cicada truncata — Cent. insect. (129) 16

Cicada ulmi — Hosp. insect. fl. (43) 18; Pand. insect. (93) 12

Cicada viridi-albicans, alis deflexis compressis, postice truncatis — Cent. insect. (129) 16[as iridi-albicans]

Cicada viridis — Pand. fl. Ryb. (165) 10

Cicadaria — Herb. Amboin. (57) 15

Cicer — Vir. pl. (13) 23; Pl. escul. (35) 21; Nom. bot. (107) 16

Cicer arietinum — Demonstr. pl. (49) 20; Pl. officin. (52) 8; Fl. Palaest. (70) 25; Fr. escul. (127) 18

Cicer arvensis — Pan Svec. (26) 30

Cicer sativum — Fl. Cap. (99) 2

Cichorium — Peloria (3) 10; Vir. pl. (13) 23, 29, 36; Fl. oecon. (17) 19; Pl. escul. (35) 22, 27, 28; Stat. pl. (55) 8; Hort. acad. (63) 19; Phalaena (78) 5; Pand. insect. (93) 18; Nom. bot. (107) 17; Obs. mat. med. (171) 5

Cichorium endivia — Demonstr. pl. (49) 22; Pl. officin. (52) 9; Fl. Palaest. (70) 27; Acetaria (77) 13; Fl. Cap. (99) 2; Fl. Jam. (105) 24; Mac. olit. (113) 21; Hort. cul. (132) 14

Cichorium intybus — Demonstr. pl. (49) 22; Pl. officin. (52) 8; Stat. pl. (55) 20; Fl. Angl. (56) 22; Calend. fl. (72) [16]; Fl. Monsp. (74) 24; Prodr. fl. Dan. (82) 22; Fl. Belg. (112) 20; Mac. olit. (113) 21; Hort. cul. (132) 14

Cichorium scanense — Pan Svec. (26) 32

Cichorium spinosum — Fl. Palaest. (70) 27; Calend. fl. (72) [16]

Cicindela — Noctiluca (39) 5; Noxa insect. (46) 30; Polit. nat. (109) 19; Fund. entom. (154) 29, [31, as 30]

Cicindela aequinoctialis — Cent. insect. (129) 12

Cicindela aquatica — Pand. fl. Ryb. (165) 9

Cicindela campestris — Pand. fl. Ryb. (165) 9; Esca avium (174) 3

Cicindela carolina — Cent. insect. (129) 12

Cicindela cyanea nitida, elytrorum apicibus antennis pedibusque flavis — Cent. insect. (129) 12

Cicindela flava elytris fasciis duabus nigris latis — Cent. insect. (129) 12

Cicindela sylvatica — Pand. fl. Ryb. (165) 9

Ciconia — Oecon. nat. (20) 44; Calend. fl. (72) [10]; Migr. avium (79) 12, 13, 18, 19, 37; Polit. nat. (109) 13; Usum hist. nat. (145) 25

Ciconia alba — Migr. avium (79) 26

Ciconia nigra — Migr. avium (79) 27

Cicuta — Vir. pl. (13) 12, 29; Fl. oecon. (17) 7; Oecon. nat. (20) 36; Pan Svec. (26) 7, 38; Odor. med. (40) 16; Nom. bot. (107) 11; Mors. serp. (119) 2; Usum hist. nat. (145) 18, 19, 20; Cimicifuga (173) 9

Cicuta aquatica — Pan Svec. (26) 19; Oves (61) 18

Cicuta minor hirsuta, semine parvo — Cent. I. pl. (65) 9

Cicuta virosa — Demonstr. pl. (49) 8; Herbat. Upsal. (50) 16; Pl. officin. (52) 8; Stat. pl. (55) 13; Fl. Angl. (56) 13; Fl. Palaest. (70) 16; Prodr. fl. Dan. (82) 16; Fl. Belg. (112) 15; Rar. Norv. (157) 14

Cicutaria latifolia dicta foetida — Pl. Mart.-Burs. (6) 11

Cimex — Oecon. nat. (20) 28; Pl. rar. Camsch. (30) 22; Cui bono? (42) 10, 24; Hosp. insect. fl. (43) 30, 32; Noxa insect. (46) 10, 15; Oves (61) 19; Instr. peregr. (96) 12; Usum hist. nat. (145) 27; Siren. lacert. (146) 7; Fund. entom. (154) 7, 18, 21, 22, 26; Ledum (178) 11; Bigas insect. (184) 2

Cimex abietis — Pand. insect. (93) 21

Cimex acuminatus — Pand. fl. Ryb. (165) 10

Cimex apterus — Pand. insect. (93) [17, as 38]

Cimex baccarum — Pand. fl. Ryb. (165) 10; Esca avium (174) 7

Cimex betulae — Pand. insect. (93) 19; Pand. fl. Ryb. (165) 10

Cimex caeruleus — Pand. fl. Ryb. (165) 10

Cimex cardui — Pand. insect. (93) 18; Pand. fl. Ryb. (165) 10

Cimex corticalis — Pand. fl. Ryb. (165) 10

Cimex coryli — Pand. insect. (93) 20

Cimex cristatus — Cent. insect. (129) 7, 16

Cimex dolabratus — Pand. fl. Ryb. (165) 10

Cimex domesticus — Pl. rar. Camsch. (30) 22; Cui bono? (42) 24

Cimex femoribus dentatis — Hosp. insect. fl. (43) 36

Cimex filicis — Pand. insect. (93) [23, as 31]

Cimex griseus — Pand. fl. Ryb. (165) 10

Cimex haemorrhous — Cent. insect. (129) 17

Cimex hyoscyami — Pand. insect. (93) 12; Pand. fl. Ryb. (165) 10; Esca avium (174) 7

Cimex ictericus — Cent. insect. (129) 16

Cimex juniperinus — Pand. insect. (93) 22; Pand. fl. Ryb. (165) 10

Cimex lacustris — Pand. fl. Ryb. (165) 10

Cimex lectularius — Fund. entom. (154) 26; Pand. fl. Ryb. (165) 10

Cimex nobilis — Cent. insect. (129) 17

Cimex oblongiusculus testaceus, thorace angulato-spinoso, femoribus denticulatis, alis nigris — Cent. insect. (129) 17

Cimex oblongus — Hosp. insect. fl. (43) 36

Cimex oblongus niger, thorace spinoso, abdomine rufo, elytris testaceis punctis linearibus quinque nigris — Cent. insect. (129) 17

Cimex oblongus thoracis elytrorumque margine exteriore femorumque basi sanguineis — Cent. insect. (129) 17

Cimex oleraceus — Pand. fl. Ryb. (165) 10; Esca avium (174) 7

Cimex ovatus, supra incarnatus subtus flavus, thorace acute spinoso — Cent. insect. (129) 16

Cimex pini — Pand. insect. (93) 21

Cimex populi — Pand. insect. (93) 22

Cimex rostro arcuato, antennis setaceis fusco ferrugineis, scutello cristato — Cent. insect. (129) 16

Cimex ruber — Hosp. insect. fl. (43) 16

Cimex scaber — Cent. insect. (129) 17

Cimex scutatus viridi-auratus nigro-maculatus — Cent. insect. (129) 17

Cimex stockerus — Iter Chin. (161) 12

Cimex striatus — Pand. insect. (93) 12

Cimex succinctus — Cent. insect. (129) 17

Cimex ulmi — Hosp. insect. fl. (43) 18; Pand. insect. (93) 12

Cimicifuga — Pl. rar. Camsch. (30) 21; Usum hist. nat. (145) 28; Obs. mat. med. (171) 5; Cimicifuga (173) [1]ff.

Cimicifuga foetida — Obs. mat. med. (171) 6

Cimicifuga foetida, christophorianae foliis, floribus in thyrso stamineis luteolis, semine in corniculis villoso rufo — Usum hist. nat. (145) 27

Cinchona — Passifl. (8) [iii][as Cincona]; Vir. pl. (13) 8, 33; Nom. bot. (107) 10; Dulcamara (164) 4

Cinchona officinalis — Pl. officin. (52) 8; Febr. interm. (167) 34

Cinclus — Mus ind. (62) 22

Cineraria — Fund. fr. (123) 17

Cineraria amelloides — Fund. fr. (123) 22

Cingulum terrae — Herb. Amboin. (57) 27

Cinna — Fund. agrost. (152) 27, 31, 37

Cinna arundinacea — Demonstr. pl. (49) [1]; Calend. fl. (72) [17]

Cinnamomum — Vir. pl. (13) 29[as Cinamomum], 34[as Cinamomum]; Pl. escul. (35) 13; Odor. med. (40) 15; Usum hist. nat. (145) 15

Circaea — Hort. Upsal. (7) 33; Erica (163) 2

Circaea alpina — Fl. alp. (71) 12; Fl. Monsp. (74) 8; Prodr. fl. Dan. (82) 12; Fl. Åker. (162) 5; Pand. fl. Ryb. (165) 16

Circaea canadensis — Demonstr. pl. (49) [1]; Calend. fl. (72) [16]

Circaea lutetiana — Stat. pl. (55) 17; Fl. Angl. (56) 9; Fl. Monsp. (74) 8; Prodr. fl. Dan. (82) 12; Fl. Belg. (112) 12; Pl. rar. Afr. (115) 6

Circaea utraque — Pan Svec. (26) 12

Cirlus tungusicus — Hist. nat. Rossia (144) 16

Cissampelos — Pl. officin. (52) 14

Cissampelos pareira — Fl. Jam. (105) 22

Cissus — Nova pl. gen. 1747 (14) [vi], 6; Herb. Amboin. (57) 25; Fl. Jam. (105) 27

Cissus sicyoides — Fl. Jam. (105) 13

Cissus trifoliata — Fl. Jam. (105) 13

Cissus vitiginea — Herb. Amboin. (57) 24

Cistella — Fund. entom. (154) 29

Cisto affinis flore purpureo — Hist. nat. Rossia (144) 10

Cistus — Pl. Mart.-Burs. (6) 30; Hort. Upsal. (7) 35; Pl. officin. (52) 11; Fl. Angl. (56) 28; Fung. melit. (69) 3; Fl. Monsp. (74) 7; Pand. insect. (93) 16

Cistus albida — Fl. Monsp. (74) 18

Cistus apenninus — Fl. alp. (71) 18

Cistus arabicus — Cent. I. pl. (65) 14; Fl. Palaest. (70) 21

Cistus arborescens exstipulata, foliis lanceolato-linearibus trinerviis hirtis — Cent. I. pl. (65) 14

Cistus chamaerododendros mariana laurifolia, floribus expansis summo ramulo in umbellam plurimis — Nova pl. gen. 1751 (32) 19

Cistus creticus — Fl. Palaest. (70) 21

Cistus crispa — Fl. Monsp. (74) 18

Cistus flore albo — Fl. Monsp. (74) 29

Cistus fumana — Pan Svec. (26) 25; Stat. pl. (55) 23; Cent. I. pl. (65) 14; Fl. Monsp. (74) 18

Cistus guttatus — Demonstr. pl. (49) [vii], 14; Fl. Angl. (56) 17; Fl. Monsp. (74) 18; Fl. Belg. (112) 10, 18; Fund. fr. (123) 12

Cistus helianthemum — Hosp. insect. fl. (43) 26; Herbat. Upsal. (50) 15; Fl. Angl. (56) 17; Hort. acad. (63) 10; Fl. Monsp. (74) 18; Prodr. fl. Dan. (82) 19; Pand. fl. Ryb. (165) 19

Cistus hirtus — Cent. I. pl. (65) 14[as hirta]

Cistus incana — Fl. Palaest. (70) 21; Fl. Monsp. (74) 29[as incanus]

Cistus ladanifera — Fl. Monsp. (74) 18

Cistus laevipes — Cent. I. pl. (65) 14; Fl. Monsp. (74) 18

Cistus laurifolia — Fl. Monsp. (74) 18

Cistus ledifolius — Demonstr. pl. (49) 14; Fl. Monsp. (74) 18

Cistus ledon — Ledum (178) 3

Cistus ledon, foliis rosmarini ferrugineis — Ledum (178) 5

Cistus ledon hirsutum — Cent. I. pl. (65) 14

Cistus monspeliensis — Demonstr. pl. (49) 14; Fl. Monsp. (74) 18

Cistus nummularius — Fl. Monsp. (74) 18

Cistus oelandicus — Pan Svec. (26) 25; Stat. pl. (55) 22; Colon. pl. (158) 6

Cistus pilosus — Fl. Monsp. (74) 18

Cistus salicifolius — Demonstr. pl. (49) [vii], 14; Fund. fr. (123) 12

Cistus salvifolia — Fl. Monsp. (74) 18

Cistus sempervivens laurifolia, floribus eleganter bullatis — Nova pl. gen. 1751 (32) 20

Cistus serpillifolius — Fl. alp. (71) 18; Fl. Monsp. (74) 18

Cistus suffruticosus adscendens exstipulatus, foliis alternis linearibus glabris, pedunculis racemosis — Cent. I. pl. (65) 14

Cistus suffruticosus stipulatus, foliis alternis lanceolatis planis laevibus — Cent. I. pl. (65) 14

Cistus surrejanus — Fl. Angl. (56) 5, 17

Cistus thymifolius — Fl. Monsp. (74) 18

Cistus trifoliatus — Pl. Surin. (177) 5

Cistus tuberaria — Fl. Monsp. (74) 18

Cistus vulgaris — Pan Svec. (26) 25

Citharexylon — Nova pl. gen. 1747 (14) [vi], 22

Citharexylon americanum alterum, foliis ad marginem dentatis — Nova pl. gen. 1747 (14) 22

Citharexylon caudatum — Fl. Jam. (105) 18

Citharexylon cinereum — Pl. Surin. (177) 11

Citharexylon fruticosum — Fl. Jam. (105) 18

Citrus — Hort. Upsal. (7) 37; Vir. pl. (13) 10, 31; Gem. arb. (24) 6; Sapor. med. (31) 14; Pl. escul. (35) 13, 29; Hosp. insect. fl. (43) 29; Pl. officin. (52) 12; Herb. Amboin. (57) 5; Hort. acad. (63) 2; Metam. pl. (67) 25; Acetaria (77) 7; Pand. insect. (93) [17, as 38]; Nom. bot. (107) 16

Citrus aurantium — Demonstr. pl. (49) 21; Pl. officin. (52) 5, 14; Herb. Amboin. (57) 9; Fl. Palaest. (70) 26; Fl. Jam. (105) 24; Fr. escul. (127) 15; Hort. cul. (132) 21; Iter Chin. (161) 9

Citrus decumanus — Iter Chin. (161) 9; Pl. Surin. (177) 13

Citrus medica — Demonstr. pl. (49) 21; Pl. officin. (52) 8; Herb. Amboin. (57) 9; Fl. Palaest. (70) 26; Fl. Jam. (105) 24; Fr. escul. (127) 15; Hort. cul. (132) 21

Cladium — Fl. Jam. (105) 27

Clandestina — Fung. melit. (69) 6

Clathroides — Buxbaumia (85) 9

Clavaria — Aphyteia (185) 7

Claytonia — Spons. pl. (12) 38; Nova pl. gen. 1751 (32) 8; Cui bono? (42) 20

Claytonia foliis linearibus — Pl. rar. Camsch. (30) 5

Claytonia sibirica — Demonstr. pl. (49) 7; Hist. nat. Rossia (144) 28

Claytonia virginica — Hist. nat. Rossia (144) 12

Clematis — Hort. Upsal. (7) 33; Passifl. (8) 4; Vir. pl. (13) 21

Clematis aquatica trifoliata late scandens, floribus albis odoratis — Cent. I. pl. (65) 15

Clematis dioica — Pl. Jam. (102) 14; Fl. Jam. (105) 17

Clematis erecta — Calend. fl. (72) [13]; Obs. mat. med. (171) 4

Clematis flammula — Fl. Monsp. (74) 18

Clematis foliis ternatis: foliolis cordatis scandentibus serrato-angulatis — Cent. I. pl. (65) 15

Clematis indica alia, flore minore pallido — Passifl. (8) 8

Clematis indica alia polyphylla, flore crispato — Passifl. (8) 24

Clematis indica, flore clavato suave rubente, fructu hexagono coccineo, folio bicorni — Passifl. (8) 13

Clematis indica, flore minimo pallido — Passifl. (8) 18

Clematis indica, flore puniceo, folio lunato — Passifl. (8) 13

Clematis indica, foliis persicae, fructu periclymeni — Lign. colubr. (21) 16

Clematis indica, folio angusto trifido, fructu olivae-formi — Passifl. (8) 17

Clematis indica, folio hederaceo, major, fructu olivae-formi — Passifl. (8) 16

Clematis indica, fructu citriformi, foliis oblongis — Passifl. (8) 10

Clematis indica hirsuta foetida — Passifl. (8) 19

Clematis indica latifolia, flore clavato, fructu maliforme — Passifl. (8) 10

Clematis indica polyanthos odoratissima — Passifl. (8) 11

Clematis indica polyphylla major, flore clavato, fructu colocynthiis — Passifl. (8) 24[as colocyntiis]

Clematis integrifolia — Demonstr. pl. (49) 15; Calend. fl. (72) [13]; Hort. cul. (132) 24; Hist. nat. Rossia (144) 23

Clematis murucuja pyriformis major — Passifl. (8) 25

Clematis murucuja pyriformis minor — Passifl. (8) 8

Clematis non crenata americana triphylla, ex codice bentingiano — Passifl. (8) 27

Clematis orientalis — Fl. Palaest. (70) 22

Clematis pappis brevissimis — Fl. Palaest. (70) 22

Clematis passiflora, flore luteo — Passifl. (8) 15

Clematis passiflora flore roseo, triphyllo — Passifl. (8) 21

Clematis passiflora pentaphylla angustifolia — Passifl. (8) 29[as angusti folia]

Clematis passiflora pentaphylla flore caeruleo punctato — Passifl. (8) 28

Clematis passiflora pentaphylla, flore caeruleo punctato — Passifl. (8) 22

Clematis passionalis — Passifl. (8) 4

Clematis passionalis bifido folio — Passifl. (8) 26

Clematis passionalis flore campanulato — Passifl. (8) 28

Clematis passionalis triphyllos flore luteo — Passifl. (8) 16

Clematis passionalis triphyllos, flore roseo — Passifl. (8) 27

Clematis pentaphylla, flore roseo clavato — Passifl. (8) 22, 28

Clematis quinquefolia americana seu flos passionis — Passifl. (8) 22[as quinque folia]

Clematis recta — Demonstr. pl. (49) 15; Fl. Monsp. (74) 3

Clematis seu flos passionis, flore luteo — Passifl. (8) 16

Clematis seu flos passionis, flore viridi — Passifl. (8) 16

Clematis seu flos passionis hederae folio, floribus parvis herbaceis, fructu minimo nigro — Passifl. (8) 16

Clematis trifolia altera, flore ex purpura nigricante — Passifl. (8) 27

Clematis trifolia seu flos passionalis, flore viridi — Passifl. (8) 21

Clematis viorna — Demonstr. pl. (49) 15

Clematis virginiana — Passifl. (8) 21; Cent. I. pl. (65) 15; Calend. fl. (72) [19]

Clematis virginiana pannonicae similis — Cent. I. pl. (65) 15

Clematis vitalba — Demonstr. pl. (49) 15; Fl. Angl. (56) 18; Calend. fl. (72) [19]; Fl. Monsp. (74) 18; Fl. Belg. (112) 9, 18

Clematis zeylanica, floribus obsoletis parvis — Nova pl. gen. 1747 (14) 22

Clematis zeylanica hermanni — Nova pl. gen. 1747 (14) 22

Clematitis indica foliis lentiscinis, candidis maculis adspersis — Lign. colubr. (21) 18

Clematitis indica spinosa, foliis luteis — Lign. colubr. (21) 17

Clematitis malabariensis altera, radice serpente — Lign. colubr. (21) 15

Clematitis malabariensis, folio vitis, colore dracunculi — Lign. colubr. (21) 15

Cleome — Hort. Upsal. (7) 37

Cleome arabica — Cent. I. pl. (65) 20; Fl. Palaest. (70) 24

Cleome dodecandra — Fl. Jam. (105) 18

Cleome floribus hexandris, foliis simplicibus subrotundo ovatis, siliquis gladiatis — Cent. I. pl. (65) 20

Cleome gigantea — Obs. mat. med. (171) 5

Cleome gynandra — Fl. Palaest. (70) 24; Fl. Jam. (105) 18

Cleome icosandra — Herb. Amboin. (57) 21

Cleome pentaphylla — Fl. Jam. (105) 18; Pl. Surin. (177) 11

Cleome violacea — Demonstr. pl. (49) 18

Cleome viscosa — Herb. Amboin. (57) 22

Clerodendron — Herb. Amboin. (57) 17

Clerodendrum foliis simplicibus, lanceolatis integerrimis — Cent. II. pl. (66) 23

Clerodendrum fortunatum — Cent. II. pl. (66) 23[as fortunata]; Iter Chin. (161) 12

Clerus — Fund. entom. (154) 29

Clethra — Nova pl. gen. 1751 (32) 9

Cliffortia — Vir. pl. (13) 27; Fl. Cap. (99) 6, 9; Fund. fr. (123) 18

Cliffortia ilicifolia — Fl. Cap. (99) 19

Cliffortia polygonifolia — Fl. Cap. (99) 19

Cliffortia ruscifolia — Fl. Cap. (99) 19

Cliffortia trifoliata — Fl. Cap. (99) 19

Clinopodium — Hort. Upsal. (7) 35[as Clinapodium]; Vir. pl. (13) 29; Metam. pl. (67) 21

Clinopodium montanum — Pan Svec. (26) 26

Clinopodium rugosum — Fl. Jam. (105) 18

Clinopodium vulgare — Herbat. Upsal. (50) 8; Pl. officin. (52) 3; Stat. pl. (55) 23; Fl. Angl. (56) 18; Calend. fl. (72) [16]; Fl. Monsp. (74) 19; Prodr. fl. Dan. (82) 20; Fl. Åker. (162) 14

Clio — Nat. pelagi (84) 10

Clitoria brasiliana — Fl. Jam. (105) 19

Clitoria foliis pinnatis, caule decumbente — Nova pl. gen. 1751 (32) 32

Clitoria ternatea — Herb. Amboin. (57) 19

Clitoria virginiana — Fl. Jam. (105) 19

Clompanus major — Herb. Amboin. (57) 14

Clompanus minor — Herb. Amboin. (57) 14

Clupea — Noctiluca (39) 5; Chin. Lagerstr. (64) 26; Lepra (140) 11

Clupea chinensis — Iter Chin. (161) 10

Clupea encrasicolus — Cul. mut. (88) 9

Clupea harengus — Rar. Norv. (157) 17

Clupea tropica — Nat. pelagi (84) 12

Clusia — Nect. fl. (122) 10

Clusia foliis cordatis lanceolatis crenatis — Passifl. (8) [iii]

Clusia major — Fl. Jam. (105) 22

Clutia — Vir. pl. (13) 27; Lign. colubr. (21) 5; Fl. Cap. (99) 6; Nect. fl. (122) 7; Fund. fr. (123) 8, 18

Clutia alternifolia — Fl. Cap. (99) 19

Clutia cascarilla — Pl. officin. (52) 7; Pl. Jam. (102) 29; Fl. Jam. (105) 22

Clutia eluteria — Pl. Jam. (102) 29; Fl. Jam. (105) 22[as elateria]

Clutia pulchella — Demonstr. pl. (49) 26; Fl. Cap. (99) 19

Clymenum flore maximo — Fl. Palaest. (70) 25[under Lathyrus]

Clypearia maritima — Herb. Amboin. (57) 14

Clypearia rubra — Herb. Amboin. (57) 14

Clypeola — Hort. Upsal. (7) 34

Clypeola campestris — Fl. Monsp. (74) 21

Clypeola jonthlaspi — Fl. Monsp. (74) 21

Clypeola maritima — Fl. Monsp. (74) 21

Clypeola minor — Fl. Monsp. (74) 21

Cneorum — Fl. Monsp. (74) 7; Erica (163) 2

Cneorum tricoccum — Demonstr. pl. (49) 2; Fl. Monsp. (74) 8

Cnicus — Fl. oecon. (17) 21; Pl. escul. (35) 23, 28; Cui bono? (42) 20; Pand. insect. (93) 18

Cnicus acanthifolius — Pan Svec. (26) 33

Cnicus acarna — Fl. Monsp. (74) 25

Cnicus benedictus — Demonstr. pl. (49) 22; Pl. officin. (52) 7; Fl. Palaest. (70) 27; Fl. Jam. (105) 24

Cnicus centauroides — Fl. alp. (71) 21

Cnicus cernuus — Demonstr. pl. (49) 22; Calend. fl. (72) [16]; Hist. nat. Rossia (144) 23, 32

Cnicus indicus — Herb. Amboin. (57) 21

Cnicus oleraceus — Demonstr. pl. (49) 22; Stat. pl. (55) 17; Prodr. fl. Dan. (82) 22; Fl. Belg. (112) 21; Mac. olit. (113) 18; Colon. pl. (158) 8; Fl. Åker. (162) 17

Cnicus spinosissimus — Fl. alp. (71) 21

Cobella — Amphib. Gyll. (5) 9; Surin. Grill. (16) 18

Cobella americana — Hort. Upsal. (7) 43

Cobra de capello — Amphib. Gyll. (5) 3, 4; Lign. colubr. (21) 7

Cobra de capello femina sine perspicillo — Lign. colubr. (21) 7

Cobras de capello — Lign. colubr. (21) 6

Coccinella — Cui bono? (42) 9; Noxa insect. (46) 14, 15

Coccinella bipunctata — Pand. fl. Ryb. (165) 7; Esca avium (174) 6

Coccinella bipustulata — Pand. insect. (93) 15; Pand. fl. Ryb. (165) 7

Coccinella coleoptris rubris immaculatis, thorace capiteque nigris — Cent. insect. (129) 10

Coccinella decempustulata — Pand. fl. Ryb. (165) 8

Coccinella elytris sanguineis immaculatis, thorace maculis nigris — Cent. insect. (129) 10

Coccinella lineis albis — Hosp. insect. fl. (43) 38

Coccinella nigra — Hosp. insect. fl. (43) 25

Coccinella novempunctata — Pand. insect. (93) 22[as Coccionella]

Coccinella quadripustulata — Pand. fl. Ryb. (165) 7

Coccinella quatuordecimguttata — Pand. insect. (93) 22[as Coccionella]; Esca avium (174) 6

Coccinella quatuordecimpunctata — Pand. fl. Ryb. (165) 7

Coccinella quatuordecimpustulata — Pand. fl. Ryb. (165) 8

Coccinella quinquepunctata — Pand. fl. Ryb. (165) 7

Coccinella rubra — Hosp. insect. fl. (43) 33

Coccinella sanguinea — Cent. insect. (129) 10

Coccinella septempunctata — Pand. fl. Ryb. (165) 7; Esca avium (174) 6

Coccinella sexpustulata — Pand. fl. Ryb. (165) 7

Coccinella surinamensis — Cent. insect. (129) 10

Coccinella tinctoria — Hosp. insect. fl. (43) 12

Coccinella tredecimpunctata — Pand. insect. (93) 16; Pand. fl. Ryb. (165) 7

Coccinella villosa — Hosp. insect. fl. (43) 27

Coccionella — Fl. Jam. (105) 8; Polit. nat. (109) 10; Meloe (124) 10

Coccocypselum — Fl. Jam. (105) 27[as Coccocipsilon]

Coccoloba — Fl. Jam. (105) 26

Coccoloba excoriata — Fl. Jam. (105) 15

Coccoloba pubescens — Fl. Jam. (105) 15[as pubesceus]

Coccoloba tenuifolia — Pl. Jam. (102) 12; Fl. Jam. (105) 15

Coccoloba uvifera — Fl. Jam. (105) 15

Coccoloba venosa — Fl. Jam. (105) 15

Coccothraustes capensis ruber, rostro hiante — Chin. Lagerstr. (64) 15

Coccothraustes indica cristata — Chin. Lagerstr. (64) 15

Coccothraustes rubra — Chin. Lagerstr. (64) 15

Coccus — Taenia (19) 23; Oecon. nat. (20) 28; Hosp. insect. fl. (43) 18, 26, 35; Noxa insect. (46) 20; Hort. acad. (63) 19; Pl. tinct. (97) 10; Polit. nat. (109) 8; Usum hist. nat. (145) 28; Mund. invis. (149) 10; Fund. entom. (154) 5, 18, 19, 22, 24, 28

Coccus aonidum — Pand. insect. (93) [17, as 38]

Coccus aquaticus — Hosp. insect. fl. (43) 26

Coccus betulae — Hosp. insect. fl. (43) 33; Pand. insect. (93) 19

Coccus cacti — Mat. med. anim. (29) 15; Pand. insect. (93) 14; Pl. tinct. (97) 10, 29

Coccus capensis — Cent. insect. (129) 17

Coccus carpini — Hosp. insect. fl. (43) 35; Pand. insect. (93) 20

Coccus coccionella officinalis — Hosp. insect. fl. (43) 21

Coccus coryli — Pand. insect. (93) 20

Coccus hesperidum — Hosp. insect. fl. (43) 29; Pand. insect. (93) [17, as 38]

Coccus ilicis — Mat. med. anim. (29) 15; Pand. insect. (93) 20; Pl. tinct. (97) 29; Mund. invis. (149) 19

Coccus ovalis subtomentosus conico-gibbus apice operculato — Cent. insect. (129) 17

Coccus oxyacanthae — Pand. insect. (93) 15

Coccus phalaridis — Pand. insect. (93) 11; Pl. tinct. (97) 10

Coccus pilosellae — Pand. insect. (93) 18

Coccus polonias — Hosp. insect. fl. (43) 12[as polonicus], 21[as polonicus]; Pand. insect. (93) 14[as polonicus], 16[as polonicus]; Pl. tinct. (97) 29[as polonicus]; Hypericum (186) 14

Coccus quercus — Mat. med. anim. (29) 15; Pand. insect. (93) 20; Pl. tinct. (97) 10

Coccus rusci — Pand. insect. (93) 22

Coccus salici — Pand. insect. (93) 21[as salicis]; Pl. tinct. (97) 10

Coccus scleranthi — Pl. tinct. (97) 10

Coccus tiliae — Pand. insect. (93) 16

Coccus tinctorius — Hosp. insect. fl. (43) 26, 30

Coccus ulmi — Pand. insect. (93) 12; Pl. tinct. (97) 10, 29

Coccus uvae ursi — Pand. insect. (93) 14; Pl. tinct. (97) 10

Coccus vitis — Pand. insect. (93) 12

Cochlea — Taenia (19) 5, 24, 28; Generat. calc. (22) 2

Cochlea pomatia edulis — Mat. med. anim. (29) 19

Cochlea testa ovata quinque spiratum, pomatia dicta — Mat. med. anim. (29) 19

Cochlearia — Vir. pl. (13) 22, 30; Fl. oecon. (17) 17; Sapor. med. (31) 19; Pl. hybr. (33) 7; Pl. escul. (35) 28, 29; Pand. insect. (93) 16; Nom. bot. (107) 15; Raphania (126) 14; Scorb. (180) 16[as Cochleria], 17

Cochlearia anglica — Fl. Belg. (112) 19

Cochlearia armoracia — Pan Svec. (26) 28; Pl. escul. (35) 19[as Coclearia]; Hosp. insect. fl. (43) 28; Demonstr. pl. (49) 17; Pl. officin. (52) 5; Fl. Angl. (56) 19; Prodr. fl. Dan. (82) 20; Cul. mut. (88) 8; Fl. Jam. (105) 24; Fl. Belg. (112) 19; Hort. cul. (132) 18

Cochlearia coronopus — Pan Svec. (26) 28; Stat. pl. (55) 20; Fl. Angl. (56) 19; Fl. Monsp. (74) 21; Prodr. fl. Dan. (82) 20

Cochlearia danica — Pan Svec. (26) 28; Stat. pl. (55) 12; Fl. Angl. (56) 19; Prodr. fl. Dan. (82) 20; Rar. Norv. (157) 11

Cochlearia draba — Fl. Palaest. (70) 23

Cochlearia foliis caulinis cordato-sagittatis amplexicaulibus — Pl. hybr. (33) 15

Cochlearia foliis radicalibus subrotundis, caulinis oblongis sinuatis — Pl. hybr. (33) 15

Cochlearia folio sinuato — Fl. Angl. (56) 27

Cochlearia glastifolia — Hort. Upsal. (7) 35; Demonstr. pl. (49) 17

Cochlearia groenlandica — Fl. Angl. (56) 19; Prodr. fl. Dan. (82) 20

Cochlearia officinalis — Demonstr. pl. (49) 17; Pl. officin. (52) 8; Fl. Angl. (56) 19; Acetaria (77) 15; Prodr. fl. Dan. (82) 20; Fl. Belg. (112) 19; Mac. olit. (113) 22; Hort. cul. (132) 13

Cochlearia saxatilis — Fl. alp. (71) 20; Fl. Monsp. (74) 7, 20

Cochlearia vulgaris — Pan Svec. (26) 28; Pl. escul. (35) 19

Cocos — Vir. pl. (13) 26[as Cocus]; Pl. escul. (35) 4[as Cocus]; Chin. Lagerstr. (64) 5

Cocos nucifera — Herb. Amboin. (57) 6; Fl. Jam. (105) 23; Fr. escul. (127) 20[as Cocus]; Rar. Norv. (157) 13; Colon. pl. (158) 5; Pl. Surin. (177) 17

Cocothraustes — Oecon. nat. (20) 18

Codiaeum chrysostictum — Herb. Amboin. (57) 16

Codiaeum sylvestre — Herb. Amboin. (57) 16

Codiaeum teniosum — Herb. Amboin. (57) 16

Cofassus — Herb. Amboin. (57) 11

Cofassus citrina — Herb. Amboin. (57) 11

Coffe — Pot. coff. (118) 7

Coffe frutex, ex cujus fructu fit potus — Pot. coff. (118) 7

Coffea — Hort. Upsal. (7) 36; Vir. pl. (13) 28; Pl. escul. (35) 24, 29; Cui bono? (42) 4; Fl. Jam. (105) 9; Pot. coff. (118) 2ff.; Fund. fr. (123) 23; Usum hist. nat. (145) 15

Coffea arabica — Pl. officin. (52) 8; Fl. Palaest. (70) 15; Fl. Jam. (105) 14; Pot. coff. (118) 7, plate [1]; Pot. theae (142) 16; Pl. Surin. (177) 6

Coffea floribus tetrandris, fructibus monospermis — Pot. coff. (118) 7

Coffea occidentalis — Pot. coff. (118) 7

Coix — Hort. Upsal. (7) 36; Spons. pl. (12) 39; Fund. agrost. (152) 25, 34

Coix dactyloides — Demonstr. pl. (49) 25

Coix lacryma — Herb. Amboin. (57) 20; Fl. Jam. (105) 21

Coix lacryma jobi — Demonstr. pl. (49) 25

Colchicum — Hort. Upsal. (7) 33; Spons. pl. (12) 28; Vern. arb. (47) 9; Calend. fl. (72) [17], [19], [20]; Nom. bot. (107) 12; Fund. fr. (123) 12

Colchicum autumnale — Demonstr. pl. (49) 11; Fl. Angl. (56) 15; Calend. fl. (72) [19], [22]; Fl. Monsp. (74) 15; Hort. cul. (132) 24; Obs. mat. med. (171) 3

Colchicum illyricum — Obs. mat. med. (171) 6

Coldenia — Nova pl. gen. 1747 (14) [vi], 9, 10

Collinsonia — Nova pl. gen. 1747 (14) [33][as Collisonia]; Nova pl. gen. 1751 (32) 7; Pl. officin. (52) 8; Nect. fl. (122) 7

Collinsonia canadensis — Demonstr. pl. (49) 2; Calend. fl. (72) [19]; Specif. Canad. (76) 8, 14, 27; Obs. mat. med. (171) 2

Collurio — Migr. avium (79) 21

Colocasia — Hort. Upsal. (7) 36

Colocynthis — Vir. pl. (13) 30, 31, 35; Sapor. med. (31) 18; Odor. med. (40) 13[as Colocyntis], 14[as Colocyntis]; Nom. bot. (107) 18

Colocynthis pumila echinata arabica, striis duodecim luteis et viridibus variegata — Cent. I. pl. (65) 33

Coluber — Amphib. Gyll. (5) 3, 8; Surin. Grill. (16) 17, 32; Curios. nat. (18) 17; Taenia (19) 26; Lign. colubr. (21) 5ff.; Calend. fl. (72) [8]; Arb. Svec. (101) 25; Mors. serp. (119) 14, 17, 18; Lepra (140) 12; Usum hist. nat. (145) 26

Coluber ammodytes — Mors. serp. (119) 14

Coluber aspis — Mors. serp. (119) 13, 14

Coluber atropos — Mors. serp. (119) 14

Coluber atrox — Mors. serp. (119) 14

Coluber berus — Mors. serp. (119) 4, 5, 12, 14, 16; Lepra (140) 12

Coluber chersea — Mors. serp. (119) 13, 14, 16

Coluber corallinus — Mors. serp. (119) 14

Coluber dipsas — Mors. serp. (119) 13, 14

Coluber lacteus — Mors. serp. (119) 14

Coluber leberis — Mors. serp. (119) 14

Coluber lebetinus — Mors. serp. (119) 14

Coluber mycterizans — Mors. serp. (119) 14[as mycteriznas]

Coluber naja — Ambros. (100) 8; Mors. serp. (119) 14, 17, 18

Coluber natrix — Migr. avium (79) 12

Coluber niveus — Mors. serp. (119) 14

Coluber prester — Mors. serp. (119) 14, 16

Coluber scutis abdominalibus 119, squamis caudalibus 110 — Surin. Grill. (16) 15

Coluber scutis abdominalibus 142, squamis caudalibus 32 — Surin. Grill. (16) 32

Coluber scutis abdominalibus 145, squamis caudalibus 36 — Mat. med. anim. (29) 12

Coluber scutis abdominalibus 150, squamis caudalibus 50 — Surin. Grill. (16) 18

Coluber scutis abdominalibus 155, squamis caudalibus 94 — Surin. Grill. (16) 16

Coluber scutis abdominalibus 164, squamis caudalibus 150 — Surin. Grill. (16) 17

Coluber scutis abdominalibus 176, squamis caudalibus 60 — Mat. med. anim. (29) 12

Coluber scutis abdominalibus 190, squamis caudalibus 42 — Surin. Grill. (16) 19

Coluber scutis abdominalibus 193, squamis caudalibus 98 — Lign. colubr. (21) 6

Coluber scutis abdominalibus 208, squamis caudalibus 90 — Surin. Grill. (16) 18

Coluber severus — Mors. serp. (119) 14

Coluber stolatus — Mors. serp. (119) 14

Coluber vipera — Mors. serp. (119) 14

Columba — Oecon. nat. (20) 31, 43; Migr. avium (79) 30; Polit. nat. (109) 13, 14, 19

Columba caerulescens, collo nitido, macula duplici alarum nigricante — Mat. med. anim. (29) 10

Columba capensis — Chin. Lagerstr. (64) 13; Iter Chin. (161) 6

Columba caudata — Migr. avium (79) 15

Columba domestica seu vulgaris — Mat. med. anim. (29) 10

Columba oenas — Migr. avium (79) 30

Columba palumbus — Migr. avium (79) 30

Columba rupicola — Hist. nat. Rossia (144) 16

Columba vulgaris — Mat. med. anim. (29) 10

Columellus — Corallia Balt. (4) 17

Columellus seu fungites minor lapidi calcario griseo immersus — Corallia Balt. (4) 15

Columellus striatus seu bryoniae radix lapidea simplex — Corallia Balt. (4) 17

Columellus turbinatus major, superna facie excavatus et radiis coralliis propriis stellatus est — Corallia Balt. (4) 17

Columellus turbinatus minimus — Corallia Balt. (4) 17

Columellus turbinatus minor luidii numero 134 seu calyx coralliorum langii, ad litora cum plurimis fragmentis obvius — Corallia Balt. (4) 17

Columnea — Fl. Jam. (105) 27

Colutea — Hort. Upsal. (7) 35[as Coluthea]; Nom. bot. (107) 16

Colutea arborea — Somn. pl. (68) 17

Colutea arborescens — Demonstr. pl. (49) 19; Fl. Monsp. (74) 22

Colutea frutescens — Demonstr. pl. (49) 19; Fl. Cap. (99) 17

Colutea fruticosa — Somn. pl. (68) 17; Fl. Cap. (99) 9

Colutea herbacea — Fl. Cap. (99) 17

Colutea scorpioides maritima, glauco folio — Cent. I. pl. (65) 23

Colutea siliquosa glabra, ternis quinisve foliis, maderaspatana, semine rubello — Nova pl. gen. 1747 (14) 25

Colutea vesicaria — Fl. Palaest. (70) 25

Coluteae affinis fruticosa, floribus spicatis purpurascentibus, siliquis incurvis ex cujus tinctura indigo conficitur — Nova pl. gen. 1747 (14) 24[as siliguis]

Colymbus — Oecon. nat. (20) 31, 32, 40; Polit. nat. (109) 13; Fund. ornith. (137) 17

Colymbus arcticus — Cynogr. (54) 9; Migr. avium (79) 16, 25

Colymbus auritus — Migr. avium (79) 25

Colymbus minimus — Splachnum (27) 2

Colymbus minor — Cervus (60) 12

Coma aurea africana fruticosa omnium maxima, foliis tomentosis et incanis — Cent. II. pl. (66) 31

Comaroides alpina argentea sericea, persici flore — Cent. II. pl. (66) 19

Comarum — Vir. pl. (13) 27; Pan Svec. (26) 3; Nect. fl. (122) 6; Fund. fr. (123) 20, 23; Fraga (170) [1]

Comarum palustre — Pan Svec. (26) 24; Herbat. Upsal. (50) 18; Stat. pl. (55) 14; Fl. Angl. (56) 17; Prodr. fl. Dan. (82) 19; Pl. tinct. (97) 19; Fl. Belg. (112) 17; Fl. Åker. (162) 13; Pand. fl. Ryb. (165) 19

Combilium — Herb. Amboin. (57) 23

Cominia — Fl. Jam. (105) 26

Commelina — Hort. Upsal. (7) 36; Vir. pl. (13) 26; Herb. Amboin. (57) 25; Nect. fl. (122) 9; Fund. fr. (123) 16

Commelina africana — Demonstr. pl. (49) 3; Fl. Cap. (99) 11

Commelina communis — Fl. Jam. (105) 12; Pl. Surin. (177) 5

Commelina communissima — Demonstr. pl. (49) 3

Commelina nudiflora — Fl. Jam. (105) 12

Commelina tuberosa — Demonstr. pl. (49) 3

Commelina zanonia — Fl. Jam. (105) 12

Complanus funicularis — Herb. Amboin. (57) 19

Concha — Generat. calc. (22) 2; Mat. med. lapid. (37) 24

Concha anatifera — Corallia Balt. (4) 10; Taenia (19) 5

Concha margarifera — Mat. med. anim. (29) 19

Concha testa subrotunda rugosa substriata: valvis inaequalibus, cardine obliterato — Mat. med. anim. (29) 19

Concha valvis aequalibus inaequaliter mediocriter et laeviter umbonata — Mat. med. anim. (29) 19

Condondum — Herb. Amboin. (57) 8

Condondum moluccanum — Herb. Amboin. (57) 8[as malacc.]

Conferva — Taenia (19) 3, 4; Oecon. nat. (20) 19; Stat. pl. (55) 12; Somn. pl. (68) 5; Usum musc. (148) 10

Conferva aegagropila — Prodr. fl. Dan. (82) 26

Conferva reticulata — Herbat. Upsal. (50) 14; Prodr. fl. Dan. (82) 26

Conferva rivularis — Herbat. Upsal. (50) 10

Conger brasiliensibus — Mus. Ad.-Frid. (11) 40

Conium — Fl. Cap. (99) 6

Conium africanum — Fl. Cap. (99) 12

Conium arvense — Pan Svec. (26) 18

Conium maculatum — Herbat. Upsal. (50) 13; Stat. pl. (55) 19; Fl. Angl. (56) 13; Prodr. fl. Dan. (82) 16; Fl. Belg. (112) 15; Fl. Åker. (162) 9; Obs. mat. med. (171) 3

Connarus — Nova pl. gen. 1747 (14) [vi], 23; Herb. Amboin. (57) 9

Conocarpus erecta — Fl. Jam. (105) 14

Conocarpus procumbens — Fl. Jam. (105) 14

Conocarpus racemosus — Pl. Surin. (177) 5

Conops calcitrans — Usum hist. nat. (145) 21; Pand. fl. Ryb. (165) 15; Esca avium (174) [9, as 17]

Conops ferruginea — Pand. fl. Ryb. (165) 15

Conops flavipes — Pand. fl. Ryb. (165) 15

Conops irritans — Usum hist. nat. (145) 21

Conops macrocephala — Pand. fl. Ryb. (165) 15; Esca avium (174) [9, as 17]

Conops testacea — Pand. fl. Ryb. (165) 15

Consolida major — Sapor. med. (31) 12

Constrictor — Surin. Grill. (16) 20

Contorta — Herb. Amboin. (57) 17, 18, 19, 24, 25

Conus — Fund. test. (166) 17, 23, 24, 27, 28

Conus basi punctato-scaber — Instr. mus. (51) 11

Conus striatus — Iter Chin. (161) 8

Convallaria — Vir. pl. (13) 20, 31; Fl. oecon. (17) 9; Pan Svec. (26) 3; Sapor. med. (31) 20; Pl. escul. (35) 27, 28; Odor. med. (40) 13, 14; Pand. insect. (93) 13; Nom. bot. (107) 12; Usum hist. nat. (145) 22

Convallaria altissimum — Pan Svec. (26) 20

Convallaria bifolia — Herbat. Upsal. (50) 16; Stat. pl. (55) 15; Fl. Monsp. (74) 14; Prodr. fl. Dan. (82) 16; Fl. Belg. (112) 15; Hist. nat. Rossia (144) 29; Fl. Åker. (162) 10; Pand. fl. Ryb. (165) 18

Convallaria cordifolia — Pan Svec. (26) 20

Convallaria fruticosa — Cent. I. pl. (65) 2

Convallaria fruticosa, foliis petiolatis sparsis lanceolatis, racemis ramosis, caule fruticoso — Herb. Amboin. (57) 16

Convallaria lilium convallium — Pan Svec. (26) 20[as concallium]; Hosp. insect. fl. (43) 19

Convallaria majalis — Herbat. Upsal. (50) 7; Pl. officin. (52) 12; Stat. pl. (55) 22; Fl. Angl. (56) 14; Calend. fl. (72) [11]; Fl. Monsp. (74) 14; Prodr. fl. Dan. (82) 16; Fl. Belg. (112) 15; Hist. nat. Rossia (144) 29; Rar. Norv. (157) 15; Fl. Åker. (162) 10; Pand. fl. Ryb. (165) 18

Convallaria multiflora — Stat. pl. (55) 23[as multiflorum]; Fl. Angl. (56) 14[as multiflorum]; Fl. Monsp. (74) 14; Prodr. fl. Dan. (82) 16

Convallaria polygonatum — Pan Svec. (26) 20; Pl. escul. (35) 13; Herbat. Upsal. (50) 7; Pl. officin. (52) 18; Stat. pl. (55) 23; Fl. Angl. (56) 14; Fl. Monsp. (74) 14; Prodr. fl. Dan. (82) 16; Fl. Belg. (112) 15; Hist. nat. Rossia (144) 29; Fl. Åker. (162) 10; Pand. fl. Ryb. (165) 18; Esca avium (174) 11

Convallaria verticillata — Pan Svec. (26) 20[as verticellatum]; Demonstr. pl. (49) 10; Stat. pl. (55) 17; Fl. Monsp. (74) 14; Prodr. fl. Dan. (82) 16

Convolvulus — Hort. Upsal. (7) 35, 36; Fl. oecon. (17) 5; Vern. arb. (47) 9; Pl. officin. (52) 13; Herb. Amboin. (57) 23, 24; Pand. insect. (93) 12; Pl. Jam. (102) 9; Nom. bot. (107) 10; Erica (163) 2; Obs. mat. med. (171) 7; Med. purg. (181) 16

Convolvulus althaeoides — Fl. Palaest. (70) 14; Fl. Monsp. (74) 11

Convolvulus arvensis — Pan Svec. (26) 17; Hosp. insect. fl. (43) 16; Herbat. Upsal. (50) 13; Stat. pl. (55) 18[as Convolvolus]; Fl. Angl. (56) 12; Cervus

(60) 7; Calend. fl. (72) [14]; Fl. Monsp. (74) 11; Prodr. fl. Dan. (82) 15; Fl. Belg. (112) 14; Usum hist. nat. (145) 10; Fl. Åker. (162) 8; Pand. fl. Ryb. (165) 17[as Convonvulus]

Convolvulus batatas — Herb. Amboin. (57) 23[as battatus]; Fl. Palaest. (70) 14; Fl. Jam. (105) 14[as Convolvolus]; Mac. olit. (113) 12

Convolvulus brasilianus — Fl. Jam. (105) 14[as Convolvolus]

Convolvulus caeruleus — Herb. Amboin. (57) 24

Convolvulus cairicum — Fl. Palaest. (70) 14

Convolvulus cantabrica — Demonstr. pl. (49) 5[as Convolvolus]; Fl. Monsp. (74) 11

Convolvulus caule volubili, foliis difformibus cordatis angulatis oblongis lanceolatisque, pedunculis unifloris — Med. purg. (181) 16

Convolvulus cneorum — Fl. Palaest. (70) 14

Convolvulus dorycnium — Fl. Palaest. (70) 14

Convolvulus foetidus — Herb. Amboin. (57) 24

Convolvulus foliis cordatis obtusis mucronatis villosis, pedunculis unifloris, caule diffuso — Cent. II. pl. (66) 9

Convolvulus foliis lanceolatis, villosis, pedunculis filiformibus villosis multifloris longis, caule erecto — Cent. II. pl. (66) 10

Convolvulus foliis quadratis angulatis, caule membranaceo-quadrangulari, pedunculis multifloris — Med. purg. (181) 15

Convolvulus foliis reniformibus — Pl. Mart.-Burs. (6) 16

Convolvulus foliis reniformibus, pedunculis unifloris — Med. purg. (181) 16

Convolvulus foliis sagittatis postice truncatis, pedunculis teretibus subtrifloris — Med. purg. (181) 14

Convolvulus foliis variis — Purg. indig. (143) 15

Convolvulus gangeticus — Cent. II. pl. (66) 9

Convolvulus hederaceus — Demonstr. pl. (49) 5[as Convolvolus]; Fl. Palaest. (70) 14; Fl. Jam. (105) 14[as Convolvolus]

Convolvulus jalapa — Med. purg. (181) 16

Convolvulus jamaicensis — Fl. Jam. (105) 14[as Convolvolus]

Convolvulus laevis major — Herb. Amboin. (57) 24

Convolvulus laevis minor — Herb. Amboin. (57) 24

Convolvulus lineatus — Fl. Monsp. (74) 11

Convolvulus linifolius — Cent. II. pl. (66) 10; Fl. Jam. (105) 14[as Convolvolus]

Convolvulus marinus — Herb. Amboin. (57) 24

Convolvulus maximus — Pan Svec. (26) 17

Convolvulus mechoacanna — Purg. indig. (143) 10; Med. purg. (181) 23

Convolvulus medium — Herb. Amboin. (57) 24

Convolvulus nummularius — Fl. Jam. (105) 14[as Convolvolus]

Convolvulus panduratus — Fl. Jam. (105) 14[as Convolvolus]

Convolvulus pedunculis unifloris, foliis ovalibus tomentosis — Pl. rar. Camsch. (30) 9

Convolvulus peltatus — Herb. Amboin. (57) 24

Convolvulus pentaphyllus — Pl. Surin. (177) 5

Convolvulus pes caprae — Herb. Amboin. (57) 24; Fl. Jam. (105) 14[as Convolvolus]; Iter Chin. (161) 12[as capra]

Convolvulus polygonum — Herbat. Upsal. (50) 13

Convolvulus quinquefolius — Fl. Jam. (105) 14[as Convolvolus]

Convolvulus riparius — Herb. Amboin. (57) 24

Convolvulus scammonia — Pl. officin. (52) 17; Fl. Palaest. (70) 14; Purg. indig. (143) 10; Med. purg. (181) 14

Convolvulus sepium — Demonstr. pl. (49) 5[as Convolvolus]; Fl. Angl. (56) 12; Calend. fl. (72) [15]; Fl. Monsp. (74) 11; Prodr. fl. Dan. (82) 15; Fl. Belg. (112) 14; Purg. indig. (143) 9, 10; Med. purg. (181) 14

Convolvulus siculus — Demonstr. pl. (49) 5[as Convolvolus]; Fl. Palaest. (70) 14[as siculum]

Convolvulus soldanella — Pl. officin. (52) 18; Fl. Angl. (56) 6, 12; Fl. Monsp. (74) 11; Fl. Belg. (112) 8, 10, 14; Purg. indig. (143) 10; Med. purg. (181) 16

Convolvulus tomentosus — Fl. Jam. (105) 14[as Convolvolus]

Convolvulus tricolor — Demonstr. pl. (49) 5[as Convolvolus]; Hort. cul. (132) 23

Convolvulus turpethum — Pl. officin. (52) 19; Purg. indig. (143) 10; Med. purg. (181) 15

Conyza — Chin. Lagerstr. (64) 5

Conyza arborescens — Pl. Jam. (102) 23; Fl. Jam. (105) 20; Pl. Surin. (177) 14

Conyza bifrons — Metam. pl. (67) 21; Fl. alp. (71) 22

Conyza chinensis — Herb. Amboin. (57) 22

Conyza cinerea — Calend. fl. (72) [19]; Pl. Jam. (102) 23

Conyza dioscoridis — Cent. I. pl. (65) 28

Conyza femina theophrasti, minor dioscoridis — Cent. I. pl. (65) 28

Conyza fruticosa flore pallido-purpureo — Pl. Jam. (102) 23

Conyza major altera — Cent. I. pl. (65) 27

Conyza minor vera — Cent. I. pl. (65) 28

Conyza odorata — Pl. Jam. (102) 23; Fl. Jam. (105) 20

Conyza raguzina — Metam. pl. (67) 21

Conyza squarrosa — Demonstr. pl. (49) 23; Fl. Angl. (56) 22; Calend. fl. (72) [17]; Fl. Monsp. (74) 25; Prodr. fl. Dan. (82) 23; Fl. Belg. (112) 21

Copaifera — Opobals. (135) 2

Copaiva — Opobals. (135) 2

Copris — Fund. entom. (154) 29

Corallaria parvifolia — Herb. Amboin. (57) 14

Corallia — Noctiluca (39) 2

Corallina — Corallia Balt. (4) 36, 38

Corallina astaci corniculorum aemula — Corallia
Balt. (4) 8

Corallina marina abietis forma — Corallia Balt. (4) 9

Corallina minus ramosa, alterna vice denticulata —
Corallia Balt. (4) 9

Corallina muscosa, alterna vice denticulata, ramulis
in creberrima capillamenta sparsis — Corallia Balt.
(4) 9

Corallina muscosa, dentaculis bijugis unum latus
spectantibus — Corallia Balt. (4) 9

Corallina muscosa denticulata procumbens, caule
tenuissimo, denticellis ex adverso sitis — Corallia
Balt. (4) 9

Corallina muscosa pennata, ramulis et capillamentis
falcatis — Corallia Balt. (4) 9

Corallina pumila erecta ramosior — Corallia Balt. (4)
9

Corallina pumila repens, minus ramosa — Corallia
Balt. (4) 9

Corallium — Corallia Balt. (4) 27, 28, 35; Chin.
Lagerstr. (64) [1], 34

Corallium alabastrinum, polymorphon — Chin.
Lagerstr. (64) 35

Corallium albidum, superficie figuris astriformibus
propemodum obliteratis, quae extersio aquarum
fluctibus est adscribenda — Corallia Balt. (4) 21

Corallium album oculatum officinarum — Mat. med.
anim. (29) 20

Corallium album punctatum rugosum, aliquando
tamen laeve, furcatum et ramosum — Corallia
Balt. (4) 27

Corallium chinense — Chin. Lagerstr. (64) 35, 36

Corallium laterulatum — Corallia Balt. (4) 36

Corallium rubrum — Mat. med. anim. (29) 20

Corallodendron — Hort. Upsal. (7) 36

Corallorhiza — Betula (1) 12

Corax — Fund. ornith. (137) 18

Corchorus — Fl. Jam. (105) 26

Corchorus aestuans — Fl. Jam. (105) 17

Corchorus capsularis — Herb. Amboin. (57) 21

Corchorus capsulis linearibus teretibus, foliis
subcoriatis serratis: infima serratura setacea — Pl.
Jam. (102) 14

Corchorus coreta — Pl. Jam. (102) 14; Fl. Jam. (105)
17

Corchorus olitorius — Demonstr. pl. (49) 14; Herb.
Amboin. (57) 21; Fl. Palaest. (70) 21; Pl. Jam.
(102) 14

Corchorus siliquosus — Demonstr. pl. (49) 14; Pl.
Jam. (102) 14

Cordia — Pl. escul. (35) 4; Fl. Jam. (105) 26

Cordia bourreria — Pl. Jam. (102) 10; Fl. Jam. (105)
14[as boureria]

Cordia callococca — Fl. Jam. (105) 14

Cordia gerascanthus — Fl. Jam. (105) 14

Cordia macrophylla — Fl. Jam. (105) 14

Cordia myxa — Pl. officin. (52) 17; Herb. Amboin.
(57) 13; Fl. Palaest. (70) 15; Fr. escul. (127) 14

Cordia sebestena — Herb. Amboin. (57) 10; Fl. Jam.
(105) 14; Fr. escul. (127) 14

Cordylus — Hort. Upsal. (7) 43

Coregonus thymallus — Cervus (60) 15

Coreopsis — Hort. Upsal. (7) 35; Nova pl. gen. 1751
(32) 10; Fund. fr. (123) 17

Coreopsis alata — Calend. fl. (72) [21]

Coreopsis alba — Fl. Jam. (105) 20

Coreopsis alternifolia — Demonstr. pl. (49) 24

Coreopsis baccata — Pl. Surin. (177) 14

Coreopsis bidens — Metam. pl. (67) 21; Prodr. fl.
Dan. (82) 23; Pand. fl. Ryb. (165) 21

Coreopsis foliis pinnatis serratis, radio diversicolore
— Cent. I. pl. (65) 29

Coreopsis leucanthema — Cent. I. pl. (65) 29

Coreopsis reptans — Pl. Jam. (102) 25; Fl. Jam. (105)
20

Coreopsis tripteris — Demonstr. pl. (49) 24; Calend.
fl. (72) [18], [22]

Coreopsis verbesina minima — Prodr. fl. Dan. (82)
23

Coreopsis verticillata — Prol. pl. 1760 (114) 5[as
verticilata]

Coreta — Pl. Jam. (102) 14; Fl. Jam. (105) 26

Coriandrum — Vir. pl. (13) 31; Odor. med. (40) 13

Coriandrum sativum — Demonstr. pl. (49) 8; Pl.
officin. (52) 8; Fl. Palaest. (70) 16; Pl. rar. Afr.
(115) 6; Hort. cul. (132) 16

Coriandrum testiculatum — Fl. Monsp. (74) 13

Coriaria — Hort. Upsal. (7) 35; Vir. pl. (13) 37;
Sapor. med. (31) 15; Erica (163) 2

Coriaria monspeliaca — Gem. arb. (24) 15

Coriaria myrtifolia — Demonstr. pl. (49) 26; Fl.
Monsp. (74) 7, 28

Corion — Nova pl. gen. 1751 (32) 12; Hypericum
(186) 13

Coris — Hort. Upsal. (7) 41; Vir. pl. (13) 33; Fl.
Monsp. (74) 7

Coris monspeliensis — Demonstr. pl. (49) 6; Pl.
officin. (52) 8; Fl. Monsp. (74) 11

Corispermum — Hort. Upsal. (7) 34; Nova pl. gen.
1751 (32) 43

Corispermum floribus lateralibus — Nova pl. gen.
1751 (32) 43

Corispermum foliis oppositis — Nova pl. gen. 1751
(32) 43; Cent. I. pl. (65) 31

Corispermum hyssopifolium — Demonstr. pl. (49)
[1]; Fl. Monsp. (74) 8; Hist. nat. Rossia (144) 23

Corispermum spicis squarrosis — Nova pl. gen. 1751 (32) 43

Corius — Herb. Amboin. (57) 11

Cornelia verticillata — Colon. pl. (158) 13

Cornix — Oecon. nat. (20) 32; Morb. hyeme (38) 13; Cui bono? (42) 12; Cynogr. (54) 9; Polit. nat. (109) 14; Fund. ornith. (137) 18; Usum hist. nat. (145) 17

Cornucopiac — Fund. agrost. (152) 21, 26, 30, 35

Cornucopiae cucullatum — Fl. Palaest. (70) 12

Cornus — Pl. Mart.-Burs. (6) [vi]; Hort. Upsal. (7) 35; Vir. pl. (13) 12, 27; Fl. oecon. (17) 4, 5; Pl. escul. (35) 4, 28; Fr. Svec. (91) [ii], 24; Nom. bot. (107) 10; Inebr. (117) 13; Fund. fr. (123) 23

Cornus femina — Pan Svec. (26) 16

Cornus herbacea — Peloria (3) 9; Pl. Mart.-Burs. (6) 15; Hort. Upsal. (7) 33; Pan Svec. (26) 16; Pl. escul. (35) 9; Fl. Angl. (56) 11; Rar. Norv. (157) 5, 11; Ledum (178) [1]

Cornus herbacea ramis nullis — Pl. Mart.-Burs. (6) 15

Cornus mas — Demonstr. pl. (49) 4; Fl. Monsp. (74) 10

Cornus mascula — Fr. escul. (127) 12

Cornus sanguinea — Demonstr. pl. (49) 4; Fl. Angl. (56) 11; Prodr. fl. Dan. (82) 14; Fr. Svec. (91) 3, 8; Fl. Belg. (112) 13

Cornus suecica — Fl. alp. (71) 13; Prodr. fl. Dan. (82) 14; Fr. escul. (127) 12

Cornus sylvestris, foliis croceum colorem tingentibus — Nova pl. gen. 1747 (14) 16

Cornus virga sanguinea — Fl. Monsp. (74) 10

Corona ariadnes — Herb. Amboin. (57) 24

Corona imperialis — Spons. pl. (12) 44; Vir. pl. (13) 20, 31; Nect. fl. (122) 11

Coronaria — Spons. pl. (12) 55

Coronilla — Hort. Upsal. (7) 35; Fl. Monsp. (74) 7; Nom. bot. (107) 16

Coronilla coronata — Fl. Monsp. (74) 23; Pl. rar. Afr. (115) 6

Coronilla emerus — Pan Svec. (26) 30; Demonstr. pl. (49) 20; Fl. Monsp. (74) 23; Fr. Svec. (91) 4, 19; Pl. rar. Afr. (115) 6; Colon. pl. (158) 7

Coronilla fruticosa procumbens, foliolis obcordatis, leguminibus teretibus — Cent. I. pl. (65) 23

Coronilla glauca — Cent. I. pl. (65) 23

Coronilla juncea — Fl. Monsp. (74) 23

Coronilla maritima, glauco folio — Cent. I. pl. (65) 23

Coronilla minima — Cent. II. pl. (66) 28; Fl. Monsp. (74) 23

Coronilla monilis — Pl. Surin. (177) 13

Coronilla procumbens, leguminibus angulatis articulatis nodosis — Cent. II. pl. (66) 28

Coronilla securidaca — Demonstr. pl. (49) 20; Fl. Monsp. (74) 23

Coronilla valentina — Fl. Monsp. (74) 23

Coronilla varia — Fl. Monsp. (74) 23; Prodr. fl. Dan. (82) 22; Pl. rar. Afr. (115) 6

Coronopus — Vir. pl. (13) 30

Coronopus sylvestris hirsutioris — Pl. Mart.-Burs. (6) 15

Corrigiola — Hort. Upsal. (7) 41

Corrigiola caule fasciculis florum terminato — Pl. Mart.-Burs. (6) 7

Corrigiola litoralis — Demonstr. pl. (49) 9; Calend. fl. (72) [15][as littoralis]; Fl. Monsp. (74) 13; Fl. Belg. (112) 15

Cortex caryophylloides — Herb. Amboin. (57) 9

Cortex consolidans — Herb. Amboin. (57) 18

Cortex oninius — Herb. Amboin. (57) 9

Cortex papetarius — Herb. Amboin. (57) 15

Cortex piscatorum — Herb. Amboin. (57) 17

Cortex saponarius — Herb. Amboin. (57) 17

Cortusa calycibus corollam excedentibus — Pl. rar. Camsch. (30) 8

Cortusa foliis cordatis petiolatis — Pl. hybr. (33) 12[as folis]

Cortusa gmelini — Hist. nat. Rossia (144) 28

Cortusa matthioli — Fl. alp. (71) 13; Hist. nat. Rossia (144) 28

Corus malabarica, folio cuspidato ossiculo tomentoso obsito — Nova pl. gen. 1747 (14) 20

Corvus — Oecon. nat. (20) 32, 41, 45; Morb. hyeme (38) 13; Cynogr. (54) 9; Migr. avium (79) 21; Polit. nat. (109) 16, 21

Corvus caryocatactes — Migr. avium (79) 21; Polit. nat. (109) 15

Corvus cauda cuneiformi — Mat. med. anim. (29) 8

Corvus corax — Migr. avium (79) 21; Polit. nat. (109) 14; Fund. ornith. (137) 26

Corvus cornix — Migr. avium (79) 22; Fund. ornith. (137) 26

Corvus frugilegus — Migr. avium (79) 21

Corvus garrulus — Migr. avium (79) 21

Corvus glandarius — Migr. avium (79) 21; Polit. nat. (109) 15

Corvus infaustus — Migr. avium (79) 21

Corvus monedula — Migr. avium (79) 22

Corvus pica — Migr. avium (79) 21; Arb. Svec. (101) 20; Esca avium (174) 3

Corydalis — Erica (163) 2

Corylus — Spons. pl. (12) 28, 32, 41, 50; Vir. pl. (13) 32; Fl. oecon. (17) 24; Gem. arb. (24) 6; Pl. escul. (35) 24, 28; Hosp. insect. fl. (43) 40; Vern. arb. (47) 10, table; Calend. fl. (72) [20]; Fr. Svec. (91) [ii], 23, 24; Pand. insect. (93) 20; Arb. Svec. (101) 17, 21, 24; Nom. bot. (107) 18; Polit. nat. (109) 8; Usum musc. (148) 7

Corylus avellana — Gem. arb. (24) 30; Pan Svec. (26) 36; Hosp. insect. fl. (43) 35; Herbat. Upsal. (50) 7; Pl. officin. (52) 8; Stat. pl. (55) 17[as Coryllus]; Fl. Angl. (56) 24; Calend. fl. (72) [9],

[10]; Fl. Monsp. (74) 27; Prodr. fl. Dan. (82) 24; Fr. Svec. (91) 3, 6; Fl. Cap. (99) 2; Fl. Jam. (105) 24; Fl. Belg. (112) 22; Fr. escul. (127) 21; Fl. Åker. (162) 19; Pand. fl. Ryb. (165) 22

Corylus avellana hispanica — Demonstr. pl. (49) 25

Corylus avellana virginica — Demonstr. pl. (49) 25

Corylus sylvestris — Noxa insect. (46) 13

Corymbium — Fl. Cap. (99) 6, 9

Corymbium africanum — Fl. Cap. (99) 18

Corypha — Spons. pl. (12) 55; Vir. pl. (13) 26; Fl. Jam. (105) 23

Corypha umbraculifera — Herb. Amboin. (57) 6; Fr. escul. (127) 13

Coryphaena — Nat. pelagi (84) 11, 13; Polit. nat. (109) 14[as Coryphena]

Coryphaena equiselis — Nat. pelagi (84) 11

Coryphaena hippuris — Nat. pelagi (84) 11; Iter Chin. (161) 14[as hippurus]

Coryphaena pompylus — Nat. pelagi (84) 11

Coryspermum — Anandria (9) 5

Coryza — Fund. entom. (154) 30

Cossus — Oecon. nat. (20) 25

Costus — Hort. Upsal. (7) 36; Vir. pl. (13) 26

Costus arabicus — Pl. officin. (52) 8; Pl. Surin. (177) 5

Cotinus — Vir. pl. (13) 27; Sapor. med. (31) 15; Nom. bot. (107) 11

Cottus gobio — Usum hist. nat. (145) 27

Cotula — Vir. pl. (13) 31, 35; Odor. med. (40) 13; Nom. bot. (107) 17; Cimicifuga (173) 9

Cotula coronopifolia — Demonstr. pl. (49) 23; Calend. fl. (72) [22]; Fl. Cap. (99) 18

Cotula turbinata — Fl. Cap. (99) 18

Cotula verbesina — Pl. Jam. (102) 24; Fl. Jam. (105) 20

Coturnix — Vir. pl. (13) 7

Cotyledon — Fl. Cap. (99) 7; Pl. rar. Afr. (115) 4; Pl. Alstr. (121) 5; Nect. fl. (122) 13

Cotyledon aizoon — Demonstr. pl. (49) 12

Cotyledon altera montana — Cent. I. pl. (65) 12

Cotyledon foliis laciniatis — Hort. Upsal. (7) 40

Cotyledon hemisphaerica — Fl. Cap. (99) 14

Cotyledon hispanica — Demonstr. pl. (49) 12

Cotyledon hybrida — Demonstr. pl. (49) 12

Cotyledon laciniata — Herb. Amboin. (57) 21

Cotyledon orbiculata — Demonstr. pl. (49) 12; Fl. Cap. (99) 4, 14

Cotyledon rupestris — Demonstr. pl. (49) 12

Cotyledon serrata — Hist. nat. Rossia (144) 29

Cotyledon spinosa — Hist. nat. Rossia (144) 29

Cotyledon umbilicus — Fl. Angl. (56) 16; Fl. Palaest. (70) 19; Fl. Monsp. (74) 16; Fl. Belg. (112) 17

Crabro — Noxa insect. (46) 31; Fund. entom. (154) 30, [31, as 30]

Cracca — Nova pl. gen. 1751 (32) 12, 31, 48

Cracca leguminibus binis lateralibus glabris, foliolis emarginatis subtus sericeis, caule fruticoso — Nova pl. gen. 1751 (32) 32

Cracca leguminibus retrofalcatis compressis villosis spicalis, calycibus lanatis, foliolis ovali-oblongis acuminatis — Nova pl. gen. 1751 (32) 31

Cracca leguminibus retrofalcatis villosis pendulis, raremosis lateralibus, foliis glabris lanceolatis — Nova pl. gen. 1751 (32) 32

Cracca leguminibus strictis adscendentibus glabris racemosis terminalibus, stipulis subulatis, foliis oblongis glabris — Nova pl. gen. 1751 (32) 32

Cracca leguminibus strictis adscendentibus glabris, stipulis lanceolatis, foliolis oblongis glabris striatis — Nova pl. gen. 1751 (32) 32

Cracca spicis lateralibus pedunculatis, leguminibus strictis pendulis, foliis emarginatis subtus villosis — Nova pl. gen. 1751 (32) 32

Cracca virginiana — Demonstr. pl. (49) 20

Crambe — Hort. Upsal. (7) 35; Fl. oecon. (17) 17; Pl. escul. (35) 20, 28; Metam. pl. (67) 15

Crambe hispanica — Demonstr. pl. (49) 18; Fl. Palaest. (70) 24

Crambe maritima — Pan Svec. (26) 29; Demonstr. pl. (49) 18; Stat. pl. (55) 12; Fl. Angl. (56) 20; Metam. pl. (67) 15; Fl. Palaest. (70) 24; Fl. Monsp. (74) 21; Prodr. fl. Dan. (82) 21

Craniolaria — Nect. fl. (122) 7

Crassula — Metam. pl. (67) 14; Fl. Cap. (99) 7, 10; Pl. rar. Afr. (115) 4; Pl. Alstr. (121) 5; Nect. fl. (122) 13

Crassula arborea — Fl. Cap. (99) 13

Crassula arborescens portlandicae facie — Fl. Cap. (99) 8

Crassula caule erecto dichotomo, foliis ovato-lanceolatis, pedunculis unifloris — Pl. rar. Afr. (115) 9

Crassula caule erecto, foliis oppositis obovatis strigosis, ramis dichotomis, pecunculis unifloris — Pl. rar. Afr. (115) 10

Crassula caule herbaceo dichotomo, foliis cordatis sessilibus, pedunculis unifloris — Pl. rar. Afr. (115) 9

Crassula centauroides — Pl. rar. Afr. (115) 9

Crassula ciliata — Fl. Cap. (99) 13

Crassula coccinea — Fl. Cap. (99) 8, 13

Crassula cultrata — Fl. Cap. (99) 13

Crassula dichotoma — Pl. rar. Afr. (115) 9

Crassula foliis oppositis imbricatis ovatis gibbis caulem obtegentibus, floribus sessilibus — Pl. rar. Afr. (115) 10

Crassula minima — Pan Svec. (26) 19

Crassula muscosa — Pl. rar. Afr. (115) 10

Crassula nudicaulis — Fl. Cap. (99) 13

Crassula orbiculata — Fl. Cap. (99) 13

Crassula pellucida — Fl. Cap. (99) 13

Crassula perfoliata — Fl. Cap. (99) 13

Crassula punctata — Fl. Cap. (99) 13

Crassula strigosa — Pl. rar. Afr. (115) 10

Crassula subulata — Fl. Cap. (99) 13

Crassula tetragona — Fl. Cap. (99) 13

Crataegus — Vir. pl. (13) 21[as Crategus]; Fl. oecon. (17) 12; Pl. escul. (35) 27, 28; Cui bono? (42) 20; Vern. arb. (47) 10; Fr. Svec. (91) [ii]; Pand. insect. (93) 15; Nom. bot. (107) 13; Inebr. (117) 13; Fund. fr. (123) 18

Crataegus aria — Herbat. Upsal. (50) 13[as aira]; Fl. Angl. (56) 17; Fl. alp. (71) 18; Calend. fl. (72) [10], [12]; Fl. Monsp. (74) 17; Prodr. fl. Dan. (82) 18; Arb. Svec. (101) 7, 9, 19, 30; Fr. escul. (127) 5; Hort. cul. (132) 21; Fl. Åker. (162) 12; Pand. fl. Ryb. (165) 19; Ledum (178) [1]

Crataegus aria suecica — Pl. officin. (52) 18

Crataegus azarolus — Fl. Palaest. (70) 20; Fl. Monsp. (74) 17

Crataegus coccinea — Demonstr. pl. (49) 13

Crataegus foliis ovatis inaequaliter serratis — Pl. Mart.-Burs. (6) 30[as Crategus]

Crataegus foliis ovatis repando angulatis serratis — Pl. Mart.-Burs. (6) 30[as Crategus]

Crataegus oxyacantha — Gem. arb. (24) 24; Pan Svec. (26) 24; Pl. escul. (35) 16; Hosp. insect. fl. (43) 23[as oxyocantha]; Noxa insect. (46) 20[as oxyocantha]; Demonstr. pl. (49) 13; Herbat. Upsal. (50) 8; Stat. pl. (55) 22; Fl. Angl. (56) 17; Fl. Palaest. (70) 20; Calend. fl. (72) [10]; Fl. Monsp. (74) 17; Prodr. fl. Dan. (82) 18; Fr. Svec. (91) 3, 13, 23, 25, 26; Fl. Belg. (112) 17; Fl. Åker. (162) 12; Pand. fl. Ryb. (165) 19

Crataegus scandica — Gem. arb. (24) 24; Pan Svec. (26) 24; Pl. escul. (35) 16

Crataegus suecica — Demonstr. pl. (49) 13

Crataegus tomentosa — Demonstr. pl. (49) 13

Crataegus torminalis — Fl. Angl. (56) 17; Fl. Monsp. (74) 17

Crataeogonum amboinicum — Herb. Amboin. (57) 26[as Crataegomum]

Crataeva marmelos — Herb. Amboin. (57) 8; Fl. Jam. (105) 16

Crataeva tapia — Herb. Amboin. (57) 8; Fl. Jam. (105) 16

Crepis — Hort. Upsal. (7) 34; Vir. pl. (13) 25

Crepis alpina — Demonstr. pl. (49) 22; Fl. alp. (71) 21

Crepis barbata — Fl. Monsp. (74) 24

Crepis biennis — Demonstr. pl. (49) 22; Fl. Angl. (56) 21; Calend. fl. (72) [14]; Fl. Monsp. (74) 24; Prodr. fl. Dan. (82) 22

Crepis foetida — Fl. Monsp. (74) 24

Crepis foliis lanceolatis hastatis sessilibus; inferioribus dentatis — Pl. Mart.-Burs. (6) 8[as cessilibus]

Crepis hirta — Fl. Monsp. (74) 24

Crepis nudicaulis — Fl. Monsp. (74) 24

Crepis rubra — Demonstr. pl. (49) 22; Fl. Monsp. (74) 24

Crepis sibirica — Demonstr. pl. (49) 22; Calend. fl. (72) [13]; Hist. nat. Rossia (144) 23, 32

Crepis tectorum — Pan Svec. (26) 31; Herbat. Upsal. (50) 12; Stat. pl. (55) 23; Fl. Angl. (56) 21; Prodr. fl. Dan. (82) 22; Fl. Belg. (112) 20; Fl. Åker. (162) 17

Crepis vesicaria — Fl. Palaest. (70) 27

Crescentia cujete — Fl. Jam. (105) 18; Pl. Surin. (177) 11

Cressa — Nova pl. gen. 1747 (14) [vi], 12

Cressa cretica — Fl. Monsp. (74) 7, 12

Crinum — Vir. pl. (13) 20

Crinum africanum — Demonstr. pl. (49) 9; Fl. Cap. (99) 13

Crinum americanum — Pl. Surin. (177) 7

Crinum asiaticum — Herb. Amboin. (57) 28

Crioseris — Fund. entom. (154) 29

Crista galli pratensis humilior, coma fusca — Pl. hybr. (33) 26

Crista pavonis — Herb. Amboin. (57) 15

Crithmum — Hort. Upsal. (7) 35; Vir. pl. (13) 32; Nom. bot. (107) 11

Crithmum indicum — Herb. Amboin. (57) 28

Crithmum maritimum — Fl. Angl. (56) 6, 13; Fl. Monsp. (74) 13; Fl. Belg. (112) 8, 10, 15

Crithmum pyrenaicum — Fl. alp. (71) 14

Crocodilus — Amphib. Gyll. (5) 15, 16; Hort. Upsal. (7) 43; Oecon. nat. (20) 28; Fl. Cap. (99) [1]

Crocodilus lacertorum omnium maximus, africanus — Amphib. Gyll. (5) 16

Crocodilus leviathan jobi — Amphib. Gyll. (5) 16

Crocodilus qui per totam indiam, cayman audit — Amphib. Gyll. (5) 16

Crocus — Hort. Upsal. (7) 33; Vir. pl. (13) 4, 31, 36; Pl. escul. (35) 23, 29; Odor. med. (40) 12, 14, 16; Cui bono? (42) 18; Fl. alp. (71) 26; Nom. bot. (107) 9; Inebr. (117) 9, 13, 23; Fund. fr. (123) 12; Usum hist. nat. (145) 29; Menthae (153) 6

Crocus bulbocodium — Demonstr. pl. (49) 2; Fl. Palaest. (70) 11; Fl. alp. (71) 12

Crocus sativus — Demonstr. pl. (49) 2; Fl. Palaest. (70) 11; Fl. alp. (71) 12; Calend. fl. (72) [9]; Fl. Monsp. (74) 8; Migr. avium (79) 20; Pl. tinct. (97) 12; Hort. cul. (132) 10, 24

Crocus sativus autumnalis — Hort. cul. (132) 10[as auctumnalis]

Crocus sativus officinalis — Pl. officin. (52) 8

Crocus sativus vernalis — Hort. cul. (132) 10

Crocus sativus vernus — Demonstr. pl. (49) 2

Crocus vernus — Vern. arb. (47) 8

Crossopetalum — Fl. Jam. (105) 26

Crotalaria — Herb. Amboin. (57) 21

Crotalaria amplexicaulis — Pl. rar. Afr. (115) 16

Crotalaria foliis caulinis amplexicaulibus cordatis alternis, floribus oppositis reniformibus — Pl. rar. Afr. (115) 16

Crotalaria foliis petiolatis ovatis margine scabris — Pl. rar. Afr. (115) 15

Crotalaria foliis simplicibus ovatis acutis villosis subsessilibus, floribus subsessilibus — Pl. rar. Afr. (115) 16

Crotalaria imbricata — Pl. rar. Afr. (115) 16

Crotalaria incana — Demonstr. pl. (49) 19; Fl. Jam. (105) 19

Crotalaria juncea — Demonstr. pl. (49) 19

Crotalaria perforata — Pl. rar. Afr. (115) 15

Crotalaria retusa — Herb. Amboin. (57) 21

Crotalaria sagittalis — Pl. Surin. (177) 13

Crotalaria villosa — Fl. Cap. (99) 17

Crotalophorus — Surin. Grill. (16) 25; Oecon. nat. (20) 38; Lign. colubr. (21) 10; Rad. senega (23) 6ff.

Crotalophorus scutis abdominalibus 165, scutis caudalibus 28 — Rad. senega (23) 7

Crotalophorus scutis abdominalibus 172, scutis caudalibus 21, paribusque squamarum 3 — Surin. Grill. (16) 23

Crotalophorus scutis abdominalibus 172, scutis caudalibus 81, squammisque 3 — Rad. senega (23) 6

Crotalus — Mors. serp. (119) 4, 5, 6, 14, 17

Crotalus horridus — Ambros. (100) 8

Croton — Vir. pl. (13) 27; Herb. Amboin. (57) 16, 19; Pl. Jam. (102) 29

Croton aromaticum — Herb. Amboin. (57) 14

Croton flavens — Pl. Jam. (102) 28; Fl. Jam. (105) 21

Croton foliis lineari-lanceolatis glabris subtus argenteis — Pl. Jam. (102) 29

Croton glabellum — Pl. Jam. (102) 27; Fl. Jam. (105) 21

Croton glandulosum — Pl. Jam. (102) 27; Fl. Jam. (105) 21

Croton humile — Pl. Jam. (102) 28; Fl. Jam. (105) 21

Croton lacciferum — Herb. Amboin. (57) 14; Pl. tinct. (97) 29; Obs. mat. med. (171) 8

Croton lucidum — Pl. Jam. (102) 28; Fl. Jam. (105) 21

Croton moluccanum — Pl. Jam. (102) 28

Croton tiglium — Pl. officin. (52) 15, 19; Herb. Amboin. (57) 16; Pl. Jam. (102) 28

Croton tinctorium — Pl. officin. (52) 11[as tinctorum]; Fl. Monsp. (74) 28; Pl. tinct. (97) 26; Colon. pl. (158) 10; Opium (179) 10

Croton variegatum — Herb. Amboin. (57) 16

Crotophaga — Polit. nat. (109) 14[as Crotophagus]; Siren. lacert. (146) 8

Crucianella — Hort. Upsal. (7) 34; Pl. hybr. (33) 28; Fl. Monsp. (74) 7; Pot. coff. (118) 7

Crucianella angustifolia — Demonstr. pl. (49) 4; Fl. Monsp. (74) 10

Crucianella fruticosa flore flavescente — Fl. Palaest. (70) 13

Crucianella latifolia — Fl. Monsp. (74) 10

Crucianella maritima — Fl. Monsp. (74) 10

Crucianella monspeliaca — Fl. Palaest. (70) 13; Fl. Monsp. (74) 10

Crucianella patula — Demonstr. pl. (49) [vii], 4; Cent. I. pl. (65) 2

Crucianella patula, foliis senis, floribus sparsis — Demonstr. pl. (49) 4

Crucianella spicata — Pl. rar. Afr. (115) 6

Crusta arborum — Herb. Amboin. (57) 19

Crusta ollae — Herb. Amboin. (57) 24

Cucubalus — Splachnum (27) 3

Cucubalus acaulis — Stat. pl. (55) 16; Fl. Angl. (56) 16; Fl. alp. (71) 17; Fl. Monsp. (74) 7, 16

Cucubalus baccatus [error for baccifer?] — Calend. fl. (72) [17]

Cucubalus baccifer — Demonstr. pl. (49) 12[as bacciferus]; Fl. Angl. (56) 16; Fl. Monsp. (74) 16[as bacciferus]; Prodr. fl. Dan. (82) 18; Fl. Belg. (112) 16; see also C. baccatus

Cucubalus behen — Pan Svec. (26) 23; Demonstr. pl. (49) 12; Stat. pl. (55) 22; Fl. Monsp. (74) 16; Prodr. fl. Dan. (82) 18; Rar. Norv. (157) 15

Cucubalus calycibus subovatis glabris reticulato venosis, capsulis trilocularibus — Anandria (9) 13

Cucubalus caule simplicissimo unifloro, corolla inclusa — Anandria (9) 13

Cucubalus dioicus — Pan Svec. (26) 23; Hosp. insect. fl. (43) 21

Cucubalus giganteus — Demonstr. pl. (49) 12

Cucubalus lapponicus uniflorus — Pan Svec. (26) 23

Cucubalus ocymoides — Pan Svec. (26) 23

Cucubalus otites — Fl. Angl. (56) 16; Fl. Monsp. (74) 16; Hist. nat. Rossia (144) 29

Cucubalus reflexus — Demonstr. pl. (49) 12; Fl. Monsp. (74) 16

Cucubalus tataricus — Demonstr. pl. (49) 12; Calend. fl. (72) [17]

Cucubalus viscosus — Demonstr. pl. (49) 12; Fl. Angl. (56) 16; Colon. pl. (158) 7

Cucujus — Fund. entom. (154) 29, [31, as 30]

Cucullaria — Cent. I. pl. (65) 34

Cuculus — Oecon. nat. (20) 33; Calend. fl. (72) [16]; Migr. avium (79) 21, 22, 27, 33; Polit. nat. (109) 14; Fund. ornith. (137) 19

Cuculus americanus — Migr. avium (79) 14

Cuculus canorus — Calend. fl. (72) [10]; Migr. avium (79) 14, 22; Fund. ornith. (137) 26, 27

Cucumis — Passifl. (8) 4, 6; Spons. pl. (12) 47; Vern. arb. (47) 9; Demonstr. pl. (49) [vii]; Stat. pl. (55) 5; Hort. acad. (63) 3; Nom. bot. (107) 18

Cucumis acutangulus — Herb. Amboin. (57) 24

Cucumis anguria — Demonstr. pl. (49) 25; Fl. Jam. (105) 21

Cucumis chate — Fl. Palaest. (70) 30[as cate]; Fr. escul. (127) 16

Cucumis colocynthis — Pl. officin. (52) 8; Fl. Palaest. (70) 30; Med. purg. (181) 10

Cucumis dudaim — Demonstr. pl. (49) 25; Fl. Palaest. (70) 30; Fr. escul. (127) 16

Cucumis flexuosus — Fl. Palaest. (70) 30

Cucumis flos passionis dictus, hederaceo folio, flore ex luteo viridanti — Passifl. (8) 16

Cucumis flos passionis dictus pentaphyllus, flore clavato — Passifl. (8) 22

Cucumis flos passionis dictus triphyllus, flore roseo clavato — Passifl. (8) 21

Cucumis flos passionis quajavas, folio majori — Passifl. (8) 25

Cucumis flos passionis quajavas, folio minori — Passifl. (8) 8

Cucumis foliis cordatis, quinquelobis, denticulatis, obtusis; pomis globosis, spinoso-muricatis — Cent. I. pl. (65) 33

Cucumis foliis multifidis, pomis globosis glabris — Med. purg. (181) 10

Cucumis melo — Demonstr. pl. (49) 25; Pl. officin. (52) 13; Fl. Palaest. (70) 30; Fl. Jam. (105) 21, 24; Fr. escul. (127) 15; Hort. cul. (132) 16

Cucumis murinus — Herb. Amboin. (57) 24

Cucumis prophetarum — Cent. I. pl. (65) 33; Fl. Palaest. (70) 30

Cucumis sativus — Demonstr. pl. (49) 25; Pl. officin. (52) 9; Herb. Amboin. (57) 24; Acetaria (77) 15; Fl. Jam. (105) 21, 24; Fr. escul. (127) 16; Hort. cul. (132) 15; Scorb. (180) 21

Cucumis sinensis — Herb. Amboin. (57) 23

Cucumis trilobus — Fl. Jam. (105) 21

Cucumis triphyllus, flore ex purpura nigricante — Passifl. (8) 27

Cucumis vulgaris — Fl. Cap. (99) 2

Cucurbita — Spons. pl. (12) 47; Pl. escul. (35) 4; Nom. bot. (107) 18; Pl. Surin. (177) 16

Cucurbita citrullus — Pl. officin. (52) 8; Herb. Amboin. (57) 23; Fl. Palaest. (70) 30; Fl. Jam. (105) 21, 24; Fr. escul. (127) 16; Hort. cul. (132) 16; Iter Chin. (161) 9

Cucurbita lagenaria — Pl. officin. (52) 9[as laginaria]; Herb. Amboin. (57) 23; Fl. Cap. (99) 2; Fl. Jam. (105) 21; Nect. fl. (122) 4; Fr. escul. (127) 16; Rar. Norv. (157) 12; Pl. Surin. (177) 16

Cucurbita malabatri foliis scandens — Obs. mat. med. (171) 8

Cucurbita pepo — Demonstr. pl. (49) 25; Herb. Amboin. (57) 23; Fr. escul. (127) 16; Hort. cul. (132) 16

Cucurbita vulgaris — Herb. Amboin. (57) 23

Cudranus — Herb. Amboin. (57) 18

Cujavillus — Herb. Amboin. (57) 7

Cujavis agrestis — Herb. Amboin. (57) 7[as Cujavus]

Cujavis domestica — Herb. Amboin. (57) 7[as Cujavus]

Culex — Ficus (2) [iv], 15, 17; Oecon. nat. (20) 29, 40, 45; Cui bono? (42) 24; Mirac. insect. (45) 7; Noxa insect. (46) 10, 11, 28, 29; Cervus (60) 5, 11, 12, 13; Migr. avium (79) 29; Nat. pelagi (84) 10; Pand. insect. (93) 7; Polit. nat. (109) 11, 12, 13; Fund. entom. (154) 7; Esca avium (174) 2

Culex lanigerus — Hosp. insect. fl. (43) 27

Culex pipiens — Migr. avium (79) 12; Pand. fl. Ryb. (165) 15

Culex pulicaris — Pand. fl. Ryb. (165) 15

Cuminum — Vir. pl. (13) 19; Ping. anim. (108) 15

Cuminum cyminum — Pl. officin. (52) 9; Fl. Palaest. (70) 16

Cuniculus — Mus ind. (62) 6ff.; Usum hist. nat. (145) 24

Cuniculus americanus guineensis porcelli pilis et voce — Mus ind. (62) 10

Cuniculus dauricus caudatus — Hist. nat. Rossia (144) 16

Cuniculus indicus — Mus ind. (62) 10

Cunila — Hort. Upsal. (7) 34

Cunonia — Fl. Cap. (99) 6

Cunonia stipularis — Fl. Cap. (99) 14

Cupania americana — Fl. Jam. (105) 14

Cuphea — Fl. Jam. (105) 27

Cupressus — Hort. Upsal. (7) 37; Vir. pl. (13) 24; Oecon. nat. (20) 15; Gem. arb. (24) 6; Arb. Svec. (101) 14, 30; Nom. bot. (107) 18

Cupressus fructu quadrivalvi, foliis equiseti instar articulatis — Cent. I. pl. (65) 33

Cupressus sempervirens — Demonstr. pl. (49) 25; Pl. officin. (52) 9; Fl. Palaest. (70) 30; Fl. Monsp. (74) 28

Curculio — Oecon. nat. (20) 28; Cui bono? (42) 10; Hosp. insect. fl. (43) 9, 12, 22, 30, 32, 37; Noxa insect. (46) 14, 15, 19, 20, 21, 22, 27; Pand. insect. (93) 4, 7; Polit. nat. (109) 8; Fund. entom. (154) 6, 18

Curculio abietis — Pand. insect. (93) 21; Pand. fl. Ryb. (165) 8

Curculio alliariae — Pand. insect. (93) [17, as 38]

Curculio alni — Pand. insect. (93) 19

Curculio argentatus — Pand. insect. (93) 19; Pand. fl. Ryb. (165) 8; Esca avium (174) 6

Curculio ater, fasciis duabus albis: antica latiore — Hosp. insect. fl. (43) 37

Curculio bacchus — Pand. insect. (93) 12

Curculio beccabungae — Pand. insect. (93) 11

Curculio betulae — Noxa insect. (46) 25; Pand. insect. (93) 19

Curculio bipunctatus — Pand. insect. (93) 22

Curculio caput vulpis — Hosp. insect. fl. (43) 33

Curculio cerasi — Pand. insect. (93) 14; Pand. fl. Ryb. (165) 8

Curculio chinensis — Pand. insect. (93) [17, as 38]

Curculio fagi — Hosp. insect. fl. (43) 35; Noxa insect. (46) 25; Pand. insect. (93) 20

Curculio frumentarius — Pand. insect. (93) 11

Curculio granarius — Pand. insect. (93) 11

Curculio inauratus — Hosp. insect. fl. (43) 33

Curculio inauratus, abdomine virescente; antennis nigris — Hosp. insect. fl. (43) 38

Curculio incanus — Pand. fl. Ryb. (165) 8

Curculio lapathi — Pand. fl. Ryb. (165) 8

Curculio ligustici — Hosp. insect. fl. (43) 19; Pand. insect. (93) 13

Curculio lineatus — Pand. fl. Ryb. (165) 8

Curculio lividus — Hosp. insect. fl. (43) 33

Curculio longirostris cyaneus, elytrorum lateribus antice gibbis — Cent. insect. (129) 12

Curculio longirostris oblongus niger, elytris maculis quatuor ferrugineis, femoribus muticis — Cent. insect. (129) 12

Curculio nebulosus — Pand. insect. (93) 22

Curculio nigricans, postice lateribusque albidus — Hosp. insect. fl. (43) 20

Curculio nucum — Polit. nat. (109) 8

Curculio oryza — Cent. insect. (129) 12

Curculio ovatus — Pand. fl. Ryb. (165) 8

Curculio palmarum — Pand. insect. (93) [23, as 31]

Curculio paraplecticus — Hosp. insect. fl. (43) 19; Pand. insect. (93) 13; Usum hist. nat. (145) 23

Curculio pini — Pand. insect. (93) 21; Pand. fl. Ryb. (165) 8

Curculio populi — Pand. insect. (93) 22

Curculio pyri — Hosp. insect. fl. (43) 23; Pand. insect. (93) 15

Curculio quercus — Pand. insect. (93) 20

Curculio rumicis — Hosp. insect. fl. (43) 20; Pand. insect. (93) 13; Pand. fl. Ryb. (165) 8

Curculio scrophulariae — Hosp. insect. fl. (43) 17, 27; Pand. insect. (93) 12, 16; Polit. nat. (109) 8; Fund. fr. (123) 19

Curculio segetis — Pand. insect. (93) 11; Pand. fl. Ryb. (165) 8

Curculio surinamensis — Cent. insect. (129) 12

Curculio viridi-nitens, subtus nigro caerulescens, thorace bicorni — Hosp. insect. fl. (43) 35

Curculio viridis — Hosp. insect. fl. (43) 33

Curcuma — Vir. pl. (13) 4, 26; Gem. arb. (24) 8; Herb. Amboin. (57) 20; Nect. fl. (122) 10; Pl. Surin. (177) 5

Curcuma longa — Pl. officin. (52) 9; Herb. Amboin. (57) 20; Pl. tinct. (97) 11

Curcuma rotunda — Pl. tinct. (97) 11

Curcuma rotunda figura tenus — Herb. Amboin. (57) 20

Curruca — Migr. avium (79) 17

Cuscuta — Vir. pl. (13) 12; Fl. oecon. (17) 5; Stat. pl. (55) 23; Nom. bot. (107) 10; Polit. nat. (109) 5; Nect. fl. (122) 11; Aphyteia (185) 9, 12

Cuscuta americana — Fl. Jam. (105) 13

Cuscuta epithymum — Fl. Monsp. (74) 10

Cuscuta europaea — Herbat. Upsal. (50) 10; Pl. officin. (52) 9; Fl. Angl. (56) 11[as europea]; Fung. melit. (69) 2; Fl. Palaest. (70) 14; Fl. Monsp. (74) 10; Prodr. fl. Dan. (82) 14; Pl. tinct. (97) 13; Fl. Belg. (112) 13; Fl. Åker. (162) 7; Pand. fl. Ryb. (165) 17

Cuscuta europaea epithymum — Pl. officin. (52) 9; Prodr. fl. Dan. (82) 14

Cuscuta foliis subcordatis — Nova pl. gen. 1747 (14) 13

Cuscuta parasitica — Pan Svec. (26) 16

Cussambium — Herb. Amboin. (57) 7

Cussuta — Herb. Amboin. (57) 25

Cyanella — Fl. Cap. (99) 9; Pl. rar. Afr. (115) 4

Cyanella capensis — Fl. Cap. (99) 13

Cyanus — Pl. hybr. (33) 7; Nom. bot. (107) 17

Cyanus arborescens minor, foliis majoranae — Pl. rar. Afr. (115) 18

Cyanus floridus odoratus turcicus seu orientalis major, flore albo — Pl. hybr. (33) 18

Cyanus floridus odoratus turcicus seu orientalis major, flore luteo — Pl. hybr. (33) 18

Cyanus orientalis major moschatus, flore purpureo — Pl. hybr. (33) 18

Cycas — Spons. pl. (12) 30; Chin. Lagerstr. (64) 5

Cycas circinalis — Herb. Amboin. (57) 6; Pane diaet. (83) 20

Cyclamen — Peloria (3) 10; Hort. Upsal. (7) 37; Spons. pl. (12) 43; Nom. bot. (107) 10; Fund. fr. (123) 12

Cyclamen corollis retroflexis — Med. purg. (181) 19

Cyclamen europaeum — Demonstr. pl. (49) 5; Pl. officin. (52) 9; Fl. Palaest. (70) 14; Calend. fl. (72) [19]; Fl. Monsp. (74) 11; Med. purg. (181) 19

Cydonia — Vir. pl. (13) 33; Sapor. med. (31) 12, 15; Nom. bot. (107) 13

Cymbalaria — Metam. pl. (67) 14

Cymbium — Nat. pelagi (84) 10

Cynanchum — Vir. pl. (13) 25; Mors. serp. (119) 2; Nect. fl. (122) 13

Cynanchum acutum — Demonstr. pl. (49) 7; Fl. Monsp. (74) 12

Cynanchum caule volubili, foliis cordato-lanceolatis glabris — Pl. hybr. (33) 11

Cynanchum creticum — Fl. Palaest. (70) 16

Cynanchum monspeliacum — Fl. Palaest. (70) 15; Calend. fl. (72) [18]; Fl. Monsp. (74) 12

Cynanchum tuberosum — Demonstr. pl. (49) 7

Cynanchum viminale — Aphyteia (185) 9

Cynara — Pl. hybr. (33) 7, 26; Pl. escul. (35) 23; Hort. acad. (63) 3, 19; Pand. insect. (93) 18; Nom. bot. (107) 17

Cynara cardunculus — Fl. Palaest. (70) 27; Acetaria (77) 14; Fl. Jam. (105) 24; Mac. olit. (113) 14; Hort. cul. (132) 19

Cynara hortensis foliis non aculeatis — Pl. hybr. (33) 26

Cynara humilis — Demonstr. pl. (49) 22

Cynara inermis — Pl. hybr. (33) 26

Cynara scolymus — Hosp. insect. fl. (43) 30; Demonstr. pl. (49) 22; Fl. Monsp. (74) 25; Fl. Jam. (105) 24; Mac. olit. (113) 15; Fr. escul. (127) 22; Hort. cul. (132) 19

Cynips — Hosp. insect. fl. (43) 23, 25, 37; Mirac. insect. (45) 12, 14, 15

Cynips amerinae — Pl. tinct. (97) 28

Cynips bedeguar — Hosp. insect. fl. (43) 25

Cynips fagi — Pand. insect. (93) 20

Cynips ficus — Hosp. insect. fl. (43) 39

Cynips foliorum — Hosp. insect. fl. (43) 26

Cynips glechomae — Pand. insect. (93) 16

Cynips granularia — Hosp. insect. fl. (43) 34

Cynips hieracii — Hosp. insect. fl. (43) 30; Pand. insect. (93) 18

Cynips nigra, pedibus albidis, femoribus fuscis — Hosp. insect. fl. (43) 35

Cynips psenes — Pand. insect. (93) [23, as 31]

Cynips pyri — Pand. insect. (93) 15

Cynips quercus — Mat. med. anim. (29) 15[as querci]; Hosp. insect. fl. (43) 34

Cynips quercus baccarium — Pand. insect. (93) 20

Cynips quercus folii — Pand. insect. (93) 20; Pl. tinct. (97) 28

Cynips quercus gemmae — Pand. insect. (93) 20

Cynips quercus pedunculi — Pand. insect. (93) 20

Cynips quercus petioli — Pand. insect. (93) 20

Cynips quercus radicis — Pand. insect. (93) 20

Cynips radicis — Hosp. insect. fl. (43) 35

Cynips rosae — Mat. med. anim. (29) 16; Pand. insect. (93) 15

Cynips rosae salicis — Hosp. insect. fl. (43) 37

Cynips salicis strobili — Pand. insect. (93) 21; Pl. tinct. (97) 28

Cynips strumae glechomae — Hosp. insect. fl. (43) 27

Cynips sycomori — Pand. insect. (93) [23, as 31][as cycomori]

Cynips sycomori fusca, aculeo longitudine corporis — Hosp. insect. fl. (43) 39

Cynips tiliae — Pand. insect. (93) 16

Cynips viminalis — Pand. insect. (93) 21; Pl. tinct. (97) 28

Cynoglossa media altera, virente folio, rubro flore, montana frigidarum regionum — Demonstr. pl. (49) 5[as vivente, corr. p. 27]

Cynoglossum — Vir. pl. (13) 18, 31; Oecon. nat. (20) 17; Pand. insect. (93) 11; Nom. bot. (107) 10

Cynoglossum apenninum — Demonstr. pl. (49) 5; Fl. alp. (71) 13[as apennininum]; Fl. Monsp. (74) 11

Cynoglossum cheirifolium — Fl. Monsp. (74) 11

Cynoglossum linifolium — Demonstr. pl. (49) 5

Cynoglossum majus vulgare — Pl. Mart.-Burs. (6) 22

Cynoglossum montanum — Demonstr. pl. (49) 5

Cynoglossum officinale — Demonstr. pl. (49) 5; Herbat. Upsal. (50) 20; Pl. officin. (52) 9; Stat. pl. (55) 20; Fl. Angl. (56) 12; Fl. Palaest. (70) 14; Fl. Monsp. (74) 11; Prodr. fl. Dan. (82) 14; Fl. Åker. (162) 8; Pand. fl. Ryb. (165) 17

Cynoglossum omphaloides — Demonstr. pl. (49) 5; Calend. fl. (72) [9][as omphalodes]

Cynoglossum sempervirens — Fl. Angl. (56) 27

Cynoglossum virens — Fl. Monsp. (74) 29

Cynoglossum vulgare — Pan Svec. (26) 16; Hosp. insect. fl. (43) 16; Fl. Belg. (112) 14

Cynometra — Nova pl. gen. 1747 (14) [iv]

Cynometra cauliflora — Herb. Amboin. (57) 8

Cynometra ramiflora — Herb. Amboin. (57) 8

Cynomolgos — Fl. Cap. (99) [1]

Cynomorium — Pl. officin. (52) 13; Herb. Amboin. (57) 8; Somn. pl. (68) 6; Fung. melit. (69) 2, 3, 6, 7, 8; Pl. tinct. (97) 10; Fl. Jam. (105) 9; Aphyteia (185) 7, 9

Cynomorium coccineum — Fung. melit. (69) 5; Fl. Jam. (105) 20[as Cynomorion], 25; Colon. pl. (158) 11

Cynomorium purpureum officinale — Fung. melit. (69) 5

Cynomorium sylvestre — Herb. Amboin. (57) 8

Cynops — Fund. entom. (154) 28

Cynorrhynchium — Nova pl. gen. 1751 (32) 9, 12

Cynosurus — Fl. oecon. (17) 3; Fund. agrost. (152) 29, 32, 35

Cynosurus aegyptius — Herb. Amboin. (57) 25; Fl. Cap. (99) 11; Fl. Jam. (105) 13[as aegypticus]; Hist. nat. Rossia (144) 27; Fund. agrost. (152) 33

Cynosurus aureus — Demonstr. pl. (49) 3; Fl. Palaest. (70) 12; Fund. agrost. (152) 32

Cynosurus bracteis pinnatifidis — Pl. Mart.-Burs. (6) [1]

Cynosurus caeruleus — Pan Svec. (26) 14; Herbat. Upsal. (50) 10; Stat. pl. (55) 14; Fl. Angl. (56) 10; Fl. Monsp. (74) 9; Fund. agrost. (152) 33; Pand. fl. Ryb. (165) 16

Cynosurus coracanus — Fund. agrost. (152) 33

Cynosurus cristatus — Pan Svec. (26) 14; Herbat. Upsal. (50) 10; Fl. Angl. (56) 10; Fl. Monsp. (74) 9; Prodr. fl. Dan. (82) 13; Fl. Belg. (112) 13; Fund. agrost. (152) 7, 32; Fl. Åker. (162) 6; Esca avium (174) 10

Cynosurus durus — Fund. agrost. (152) 33

Cynosurus echinatus — Fl. Angl. (56) 10; Fl. Palaest. (70) 12; Fl. Monsp. (74) 9; Fund. agrost. (152) 32

Cynosurus glomeratus — Herbat. Upsal. (50) 13

Cynosurus indicus — Fl. Jam. (105) 13; Fund. agrost. (152) 33

Cynosurus lima — Demonstr. pl. (49) 3; Fund. agrost. (152) 32

Cynosurus paniceus — Demonstr. pl. (49) 3; Stat. pl. (55) 19; Fl. Angl. (56) 10; Fl. Monsp. (74) 9; Prodr. fl. Dan. (82) 13; Fl. Belg. (112) 13

Cynosurus paniculatus — Pan Svec. (26) 14

Cynosurus virgatus — Pl. Jam. (102) 7; Fl. Jam. (105) 13

Cyperoides angustifolium, spicis sessilibus in foliorum alis — Cent. I. pl. (65) 31

Cyperus — Hort. Upsal. (7) 41; Herb. Amboin. (57) 25; Nom. bot. (107) 9; Fund. agrost. (152) 13, 14, 15, 29, 38; Pl. Surin. (177) 5

Cyperus alpinus longus inodorus, panicula ferruginea minus sparsa — Cent. I. pl. (65) 32

Cyperus aquaticus italicus procerior, locustis tenuissimis in racemum dense congestis — Cent. II. pl. (66) 5

Cyperus caespitosus — Fl. Jam. (105) 12

Cyperus capitulis glomeratim congestis, seminibus aristatis — Cent. II. pl. (66) 5

Cyperus culmo triquetro folioso, umbella foliosa glomerata, spicis striatis squarrosis — Cent. II. pl. (66) 6

Cyperus culmo triquetro nudo, umbella diphylla composita, spiculis alterno digitatis lanceolatis, glumis mucronatis — Cent. II. pl. (66) 6

Cyperus culmo triquetro nudo, umbella foliosa supradecomposita, spicis digitalibus imbricatis: spiculis subulatis — Cent. II. pl. (66) 5

Cyperus culmo triquetro nudo, umbella triphylla supradecomposita, spicis conglomerato-rotundatis, spiculis subulatis — Cent. II. pl. (66) 5

Cyperus culmo triquetro subnudo, umbella diphylla simplici trifida, spicis capitatis: intermedia sessili — Cent. II. pl. (66) 6[as cupitatis]

Cyperus difformis — Cent. II. pl. (66) 6

Cyperus dulcis — Herb. Amboin. (57) 25

Cyperus elatus — Cent. II. pl. (66) 5

Cyperus elegans — Fl. Jam. (105) 12

Cyperus esculentus — Fl. Palaest. (70) 12; Fl. Monsp. (74) 9; Mac. olit. (113) 12

Cyperus flavescens — Fl. Monsp. (74) 9

Cyperus fuscus — Fl. Monsp. (74) 9; Fl. Belg. (112) 8, 12

Cyperus glomeratus — Cent. II. pl. (66) 5; Colon. pl. (158) 12

Cyperus haspan — Fl. Cap. (99) 11

Cyperus ligularis — Pl. Jam. (102) [5]; Fl. Jam. (105) 12

Cyperus longus — Pl. officin. (52) 9; Fl. Angl. (56) 10; Herb. Amboin. (57) 25; Fl. Monsp. (74) 9

Cyperus longus inodorus sylvaticus — Cent. I. pl. (65) 32

Cyperus minimus — Fl. Cap. (99) 11

Cyperus odoratus — Fl. Jam. (105) 12

Cyperus papyrus — Fl. Palaest. (70) 12

Cyperus pumilus — Cent. II. pl. (66) 6; Fl. Jam. (105) 12

Cyperus rotundus — Pl. officin. (52) 9; Herb. Amboin. (57) 25; Fl. Palaest. (70) 12

Cyperus squarrosus — Cent. II. pl. (66) 6

Cypraea — Generat. calc. (22) 2; Fund. test. (166) 5, 9, 17, 27, 29, 37

Cypraea caurica — Fund. test. (166) 37

Cypraea globulus — Fund. test. (166) 37

Cypraea lynx — Fund. test. (166) 36

Cypraea moneta — Fund. test. (166) 9, 37

Cyprinus — Mat. med. anim. (29) 14; Morb. hyeme (38) 3; Instr. mus. (51) 5; Lepra (140) 11

Cyprinus aspius — Calend. fl. (72) [9]

Cyprinus auratus — Chin. Lagerstr. (64) 27[as auraeus]; Siren. lacert. (146) 8; Iter Chin. (161) 10

Cyprinus auratus chinensium — Hort. Upsal. (7) 43

Cyprinus brama — Calend. fl. (72) [11]

Cyprinus carpio — Cul. mut. (88) 9

Cyprinus chinensis — Curios. nat. (18) 17

Cyprinus cirrhis quatuor, ossiculo tertio pinnarum dorsi anique uncinatis — Mat. med. anim. (29) 14

Cyprinus pelagicus — Nat. pelagi (84) 12

Cyprinus pinna ani duplici, caudae bifurca — Mus. Ad.-Frid. (11) 43

Cyprinus rutilus — Calend. fl. (72) [11]

Cypripedium — Peloria (3) 10; Vir. pl. (13) 24; Nom. bot. (107) 17

Cypripedium bulbosum — Stat. pl. (55) 16; Fl. alp. (71) 23; Hist. nat. Rossia (144) 33

Cypripedium calceolus — Pan Svec. (26) 34; Fl. Angl. (56) 23; Cervus (60) 8; Prodr. fl. Dan. (82) 24; Hist. nat. Rossia (144) 33

Cypripedium folio caulino ovato-oblongo terminali lanceolato plano — Nova pl. gen. 1751 (32) 24

Cypripedium lapponicum — Pan Svec. (26) 34

Cypripedium myodes — Pan Svec. (26) 34

Cypripedium radice fibrosa, folio ovato-oblongo caulino — Nova pl. gen. 1751 (32) 24

Cyprus alcanna — Herb. Amboin. (57) 15

Cytinus — Aphyteia (185) 9

Cytisus — Fl. Monsp. (74) 7

Cytisus aethiopicus — Fl. Cap. (99) 17[as Cytiscus]

Cytisus argenteus — Fl. Monsp. (74) 23

Cytisus cajan — Herb. Amboin. (57) 23; Fl. Jam. (105) 19; Pl. Surin. (177) 13

Cytisus hirsutus — Fl. Palaest. (70) 25; Fl. Monsp. (74) 22; Hist. nat. Rossia (144) 31

Cytisus laburnum — Gem. arb. (24) 28; Demonstr. pl. (49) 20; Fl. alp. (71) 21

Cytisus monspessulana, medicae folio, siliquis dense congestis et villosis — Cent. I. pl. (65) 22

Cytisus monspessulans — Fl. Monsp. (74) 22

Cytisus nigricans — Fl. Monsp. (74) 22

Cytisus psoraloides — Pl. rar. Afr. (115) 15

Cytisus sessilifolius — Fl. Monsp. (74) 22

Cytisus spicis pubescentibus, ramis angulatis, foliolis lanceolatis, caule suffruticoso — Pl. rar. Afr. (115) 15[as laceolatis … sufruticoso]

Cytisus supinus — Hist. nat. Rossia (144) 31

Cytisus sylvestris candicans — Cent. I. pl. (65) 22

Dabanus — Herb. Amboin. (57) 11

Dactylis — Vir. pl. (13) 32; Sapor. med. (31) 16; Noctiluca (39) 5; Fund. agrost. (152) 27, 36

Dactylis cynosuroides — Demonstr. pl. (49) 3; Fl. Angl. (56) 10; Calend. fl. (72) [17]; Fund. agrost. (152) 33; Colon. pl. (158) 10

Dactylis glomerata — Cynogr. (54) 10; Stat. pl. (55) 20; Fl. Angl. (56) 10; Cervus (60) 7; Fl. Palaest. (70) 12; Fl. Monsp. (74) 9; Prodr. fl. Dan. (82) 13; Fl. Belg. (112) 13; Fund. agrost. (152) 7, 33; Fl. Åker. (162) 6; Pand. fl. Ryb. (165) 16

Daedonea — Fl. Jam. (105) 27

Dais — Nect. fl. (122) 7

Dalea — Fl. Jam. (105) 26, 27

Dalechampia — Vir. pl. (13) 27

Dammara alba — Herb. Amboin. (57) 10

Dammara celebica — Herb. Amboin. (57) 10

Dammara nigra — Herb. Amboin. (57) 10

Dammara zeylanica — Herb. Amboin. (57) 10[as zelanica]

Daphne — Hort. Upsal. (7) 33; Vir. pl. (13) 30; Fl. oecon. (17) 10; Gem. arb. (24) 9; Vern. arb. (47) 8; Fr. Svec. (91) [ii]; Nom. bot. (107) 12; Prol. pl. 1760 (114) 13, 14

Daphne alpina — Fl. alp. (71) 16

Daphne cneorum — Fl. alp. (71) 16; Fl. Monsp. (74) 15

Daphne gnidium — Fl. Monsp. (74) 7, 15

Daphne laureola — Gem. arb. (24) 17; Demonstr. pl. (49) 11; Pl. officin. (52) 13; Fl. Angl. (56) 15; Fl. Monsp. (74) 15

Daphne mezereum — Herbat. Upsal. (50) 8; Pl. officin. (52) 8; Stat. pl. (55) 17; Calend. fl. (72) [9]; Fl. Monsp. (74) 15; Prodr. fl. Dan. (82) 17; Fr. Svec. (91) 4, 19; Prol. pl. 1763 (130) 18; Rar. Norv. (157) 15; Fl. Åker. (162) 11; Pand. fl. Ryb. (165) 18; Esca avium (174) 12

Daphne rubra — Pan Svec. (26) 21

Daphne squarrosa — Fl. Cap. (99) 14

Daphne thymelaea — Fl. Monsp. (74) 15

Dasypus — Mus. Ad.-Frid. (11) 3

Datisca — Nova pl. gen. 1747 (14) [vi], 31

Datisca cannabina — Demonstr. pl. (49) 26; Calend. fl. (72) [17]; Pl. tinct. (97) 26[as canabina]

Datisca hirta — Pl. tinct. (97) 26

Datura — Vir. pl. (13) 19, 31; Fl. oecon. (17) 5; Vern. arb. (47) 9; Nom. bot. (107) 10; Inebr. (117) 11; Mors. serp. (119) 2

Datura cochinensis spinosissima — Demonstr. pl. (49) 6

Datura erecta — Pan Svec. (26) 17

Datura ferox — Demonstr. pl. (49) 6; Cent. I. pl. (65) 2; Fl. Palaest. (70) 15

Datura metel — Demonstr. pl. (49) 6; Herb. Amboin. (57) 21; Fl. Cap. (99) 12

Datura pericarpiis erectis ovatis — Pl. hybr. (33) 28

Datura pericarpiis spinosis erectis: spinis inferioribus minoribus — Demonstr. pl. (49) 6

Datura stramonium — Demonstr. pl. (49) 6; Pl. officin. (52) 9; Stat. pl. (55) 20; Fl. Angl. (56) 12; Somn. pl. (68) 16; Fl. Monsp. (74) 12; Prodr. fl. Dan. (82) 15; Fl. Jam. (105) 14; Fl. Belg. (112) 14; Colon. pl. (158) 9; Fl. Åker. (162) 8; Pand. fl. Ryb. (165) 17

Daucus — Vir. pl. (13) 14; Fl. oecon. (17) 7; Pl. escul. (35) 22, 28; Mus ind. (62) 14, 15; Hort. acad. (63) 3; Generat. ambig. (104) 8; Nom. bot. (107) 11; Usum hist. nat. (145) 27

Daucus carota — Demonstr. pl. (49) 8; Herbat. Upsal. (50) 15; Pl. officin. (52) 9; Stat. pl. (55) 22; Fl. Angl. (56) 13; Calend. fl. (72) [15]; Fl. Monsp. (74) 13; Prodr. fl. Dan. (82) 16; Fl. Jam. (105) 24; Fl. Belg. (112) 15; Mac. olit. (113) 9; Hort. cul. (132) 12; Fl. Åker. (162) 9

Daucus gingidium — Fl. Monsp. (74) 13

Daucus sativa — Pl. escul. (35) 11

Daucus sylvestris — Pan Svec. (26) 18; Pl. escul. (35) 11

Daucus visnaga — Fl. Palaest. (70) 16; Fl. Monsp. (74) 13

Delima — Nova pl. gen. 1747 (14) [vi], 19, 20

Delphinium — Anandria (9) 4[as Delphium]; Vir. pl. (13) 14, 21; Cryst. gen. (15) 20; Pl. rar. Camsch. (30) 22; Pl. hybr. (33) 6; Cui bono? (42) 20; Hort. acad. (63) 3; Metam. pl. (67) 17; Pand. insect. (93) 16; Nom. bot. (107) 14; Nect. fl. (122) 12; Fund. fr. (123) 12, 23; Cimicifuga (173) 2, 9

Delphinium aconitum — Fund. fr. (123) 15

Delphinium ajacis — Demonstr. pl. (49) 14; Calend. fl. (72) [14]; Nect. fl. (122) 12; Hort. cul. (132) 23, 24, 25

Delphinium ambiguum — Nect. fl. (122) 12

Delphinium consolida — Herbat. Upsal. (50) 13; Pl. officin. (52) 8; Stat. pl. (55) 19; Fl. Angl. (56) 18; Fl. Monsp. (74) 18; Prodr. fl. Dan. (82) 19; Pl. tinct. (97) 20; Fl. Belg. (112) 18; Nect. fl. (122) 12; Usum hist. nat. (145) 10; Fl. Åker. (162) 13; Pand. fl. Ryb. (165) 19

Delphinium elatum — Demonstr. pl. (49) 14, 15; Calend. fl. (72) [13], [14]; Pl. Alstr. (121) 6; Hort. cul. (132) 24; Hist. nat. Rossia (144) 23, 30

Delphinium elatum aconiti — Calend. fl. (72) [16]

Delphinium grandiflorum — Demonstr. pl. (49) 14; Calend. fl. (72) [14]; Pl. Alstr. (121) 6; Hist. nat. Rossia (144) 23, 30

Delphinium hybridum — Pl. hybr. (33) 10; Demonstr. pl. (49) 15; Fund. fr. (123) 15

Delphinium monstrosum — Demonstr. pl. (49) 14

Delphinium nectariis diphyllis, foliis peltatis multipartitis acutis — Pl. hybr. (33) 10

Delphinium peregrinum — Fl. Palaest. (70) 21; Calend. fl. (72) [19]

Delphinium regale — Hosp. insect. fl. (43) 26

Delphinium segetum — Pan Svec. (26) 25

Delphinium staphisagria — Pl. officin. (52) 18[as Delphinum]; Fl. Monsp. (74) 18; Nect. fl. (122) 12

Delphinus — Nat. pelagi (84) 14

Delphinus delphis — Iter Chin. (161) 14

Dens leonis angustiori folio — Pl. Mart.-Burs. (6) 8

Dens leonis folio subtus incano — Pl. Jam. (102) 23

Dens leonis tenuissimo folio — Pl. Mart.-Burs. (6) 8

Dentale laeve album, altera extremitate rufescens — Mat. med. anim. (29) 19

Dentalium — Corallia Balt. (4) 8; Fund. test. (166) 17

Dentalium testa subcylindracea laevi arcuata, hinc angustiore — Mat. med. anim. (29) 19

Dentaria — Hort. Upsal. (7) 33; Gem. arb. (24) 5; Sem. musc. (28) 6; Obst. med. (34) 7; Pand. insect. (93) 16; Prol. pl. 1763 (130) 16

Dentaria bulbifera — Pan Svec. (26) 29; Hosp. insect. fl. (43) 28; Demonstr. pl. (49) 17; Herbat. Upsal. (50) 8; Stat. pl. (55) 17; Fl. Angl. (56) 6; Prodr. fl. Dan. (82) 21; Pand. fl. Ryb. (165) 20

Dentaria pentaphyllos — Fl. alp. (71) 20; Fl. Monsp. (74) 21

Dermestes — Oecon. nat. (20) 25, 29; Hosp. insect. fl. (43) 9; Noxa insect. (46) 12, 13, 14, 15, 16; Instr. mus. (51) 8; Migr. avium (79) 23; Pand. insect. (93) 4; Fund. fr. (123) 19; Bigas insect. (184) 3

Dermestes bactris — Cent. insect. (129) 9

Dermestes capucinus — Fund. entom. (154) 29

Dermestes eustatius — Pand. insect. (93) [23, as 31]

Dermestes fenestralis — Pand. fl. Ryb. (165) 7

Dermestes ferrugineus — Pand. fl. Ryb. (165) 7

Dermestes gleditsiae — Cent. insect. (129) 9

Dermestes lardarius — Pand. fl. Ryb. (165) 7

Dermestes niger — Pand. fl. Ryb. (165) 7

Dermestes obsolete tomentosus subincanus, antennis filiformibus, elytris laeviusculis, femoribus posticis gibbosis — Cent. insect. (129) 9

Dermestes pedicularis — Esca avium (174) 3

Dermestes pellio — Pand. fl. Ryb. (165) 7

Dermestes piniperda — Pand. insect. (93) 21; Prol. pl. 1760 (114) 2

Dermestes pisorum — Pand. insect. (93) [17, as 38]; Polit. nat. (109) 18

Dermestes praemorsus — Hosp. insect. fl. (43) 36

Dermestes psyllius — Pand. fl. Ryb. (165) 7

Dermestes pulicarius — Pand. fl. Ryb. (165) 7

Dermestes scarabaeoides — Pand. fl. Ryb. (165) 7

Dermestes subtomentosus piceus, antennis filiformibus, elytris striatis, femoribus posticis gibbosis — Cent. insect. (129) 9

Dermestes typographus — Pand. insect. (93) 21; Pand. fl. Ryb. (165) 7

Diana — Fl. Cap. (99) [1]

Dianthera — Nova pl. gen. 1751 (32) 7

Dianthera comata — Fl. Jam. (105) 12

Dianthus — Peloria (3) 9; Hort. Upsal. (7) 33; Spons. pl. (12) 38, 55, 59; Odor. med. (40) 12; Hort. acad. (63) 3; Fl. Monsp. (74) 7; Nom. bot. (107) 13

Dianthus arenarius — Demonstr. pl. (49) 12; Stat. pl. (55) 21; Hort. acad. (63) 10; Fl. Monsp. (74) 16; Prodr. fl. Dan. (82) 18; Fl. Åker. (162) 12

Dianthus armeria — Fl. Angl. (56) 16; Calend. fl. (72) [16]; Fl. Monsp. (74) 16; Prodr. fl. Dan. (82) 18

Dianthus barbatus — Demonstr. pl. (49) 12; Calend. fl. (72) [13]; Hort. cul. (132) 24

Dianthus carthusianorum — Fl. Monsp. (74) 16; Pl. Alstr. (121) 5

Dianthus caryophyllus — Demonstr. pl. (49) 12; Pl. officin. (52) 19; Fl. Palaest. (70) 19; Fl. Jam. (105) 24[as carophyllus]; Pl. Alstr. (121) 5; Hort. cul. (132) 24, 25

Dianthus chemensis [error for chinensis?] — Pan Svec. (26) 22

Dianthus chinensis — Demonstr. pl. (49) 12; see also D. chemensis

Dianthus coronarius — Calend. fl. (72) [16]

Dianthus deltoides — Herbat. Upsal. (50) 19; Fl. Angl. (56) 16; Calend. fl. (72) [14]; Fl. Monsp. (74) 16; Prodr. fl. Dan. (82) 18; Fl. Åker. (162) 12; Pand. fl. Ryb. (165) 19

Dianthus flore roseo — Fl. alp. (71) 17

Dianthus foliis subsolitariis, squamis calycinis longitudine tubi; corollis multifidis; caule erecto — Cent. I. pl. (65) 11

Dianthus glaucus — Demonstr. pl. (49) 12; Fl. Angl. (56) 5, 16

Dianthus gotlandicus — Pan Svec. (26) 22

Dianthus hortensis — Hosp. insect. fl. (43) 21

Dianthus hyssopifolius — Cent. I. pl. (65) 11

Dianthus monspeliacus — Calend. fl. (72) [17]; Fl. Monsp. (74) 16

Dianthus plumarius — Demonstr. pl. (49) 12; Calend. fl. (72) [12]; Prodr. fl. Dan. (82) 18

Dianthus prolifer — Fl. Angl. (56) 16; Fl. Monsp. (74) 16[as proliferus]

Dianthus saxifragus — Fl. Monsp. (74) 16

Dianthus scanensis — Pan Svec. (26) 22

Dianthus superbus — Calend. fl. (72) [17]; Fl. Monsp. (74) 16; Prodr. fl. Dan. (82) 18; Colon. pl. (158) 7

Dianthus sylvestris — Fl. Angl. (56) 28

Dianthus virgineus — Calend. fl. (72) [15]; Fl. Monsp. (74) 16

Dianthus vulgaris — Pan Svec. (26) 22

Diapensia — Pl. Mart.-Burs. (6) 24; Fl. Angl. (56) 6

Diapensia helvetica — Fl. alp. (71) 13

Diapensia lapponica — Pan Svec. (26) 17; Stat. pl. (55) 16; Fl. alp. (71) 13; Rar. Norv. (157) 10

Diaperis — Fund. entom. (154) 30

Diconangia — Nova pl. gen. 1751 (32) 8, 12[as Diconangias]

Dictamnus — Oecon. nat. (20) 17; Nect. fl. (122) 14; Erica (163) 2

Dictamnus albus — Pl. officin. (52) 9; Calend. fl. (72) [12]; Fl. Monsp. (74) 15; Hort. cul. (132) 24

Didelphis — Mus. Ad.-Frid. (11) [v]

Didelphis mammis extra abdomen — Mus. Ad.-Frid. (11) 2

Didelphis mammis intra abdomen — Mus. Ad.-Frid. (11) 2

Didus — Fund. ornith. (137) 10, 16

Diervilla — Hort. Upsal. (7) 35; Vir. pl. (13) 28; Nova pl. gen. 1751 (32) 8; Cui bono? (42) 21; Calend. fl. (72) [9]

Diervilla acadiensis — Gem. arb. (24) 18

Digitalis — Hort. Upsal. (7) 34; Nom. bot. (107) 15[as Digitatis]

Digitalis alba — Calend. fl. (72) [15]

Digitalis ferruginea — Demonstr. pl. (49) 17

Digitalis lutea — Demonstr. pl. (49) 16; Fl. Monsp. (74) 20

Digitalis purpurea — Demonstr. pl. (49) 16; Fl. Angl. (56) 19; Fl. Monsp. (74) 20; Fl. Belg. (112) 19; Fund. fr. (123) 17; Hort. cul. (132) 23; Rar. Norv. (157) 9

Digitalis rubra — Calend. fl. (72) [15]; Fund. fr. (123) 16, 17

Digitalis thapsus — Fund. fr. (123) 16, 17

Dillenia — Pl. escul. (35) 4

Dillenia indica — Herb. Amboin. (57) 9

Dillenia syalita — Fr. escul. (127) 11

Diodia — Nova pl. gen. 1751 (32) 8

Dioica triandra tricocca — Herb. Amboin. (57) 10

Diomedea — Polit. nat. (109) 13

Diomedea demersa — Fund. ornith. (137) 10, 16; see also D. submersa

Diomedea exulans — Nat. pelagi (84) 13; Fund. ornith. (137) 16[as exulante]

Diomedea submersa [error for demersa?] — Nat. pelagi (84) 13

Diopsis — Bigas insect. (184) 5ff.

Diopsis ichneumonea — Bigas insect. (184) 5ff.

Dioscorea — Hort. Upsal. (7) 36; Gem. arb. (24) 5; Herb. Amboin. (57) 5; Pane diaet. (83) 20

Dioscorea aculeata — Herb. Amboin. (57) 23; Fl. Jam. (105) 22

Dioscorea bulbifera — Herb. Amboin. (57) 23; Fl. Jam. (105) 22

Dioscorea hirsuta — Fl. Cap. (99) 19

Dioscorea oppositifolia — Herb. Amboin. (57) 22, 23

Dioscorea pentaphylla — Herb. Amboin. (57) 23

Dioscorea sativa — Herb. Amboin. (57) 25[as Discorea]; Fl. Palaest. (70) 31; Fl. Jam. (105) 22

Dioscorea sativa: bulbifera — Mac. olit. (113) 12

Dioscorea triphylla — Herb. Amboin. (57) 23

Dioscorea villosa — Herb. Amboin. (57) 24

Diosma — Fl. Cap. (99) 6, 8, 9; Nect. fl. (122) 14; Fund. fr. (123) 16, 18

Diosma ciliata — Fl. Cap. (99) 12

Diosma crenata — Fl. Cap. (99) 12

Diosma crenulata — Cent. II. pl. (66) 11

Diosma ericoides — Fl. Cap. (99) 12

Diosma foliis lanceolato-ovalibus crenatis — Cent. II. pl. (66) 11

Diosma hirsuta — Fl. Cap. (99) 12

Diosma lanceolata — Fl. Cap. (99) 12

Diosma linifolia — Fl. Cap. (99) 12

Diosma oppositifolia — Fl. Cap. (99) 12

Diosma pulchella — Fl. Cap. (99) 12

Diosma rubra — Fl. Cap. (99) 12

Diospyros — Vir. pl. (13) 20[incl. as Diospyrus]; Nova pl. gen. 1751 (32) 12; Pl. escul. (35) 4; Herb. Amboin. (57) 11; Erica (163) 3

Diospyros lotus — Fr. escul. (127) 10

Diospyros virginiana — Fr. escul. (127) 10

Dipsacus — Hort. Upsal. (7) 34; Pl. hybr. (33) 7; Pand. insect. (93) 11; Nom. bot. (107) 10

Dipsacus capitulis florum conicis — Pl. hybr. (33) 20

Dipsacus foliis petiolatis appendiculatis — Pl. hybr. (33) 20

Dipsacus folio laciniato — Pl. hybr. (33) 20

Dipsacus fullonum — Demonstr. pl. (49) 4; Fl. Angl. (56) 11; Calend. fl. (72) [17]; Fl. Monsp. (74) 10; Prodr. fl. Dan. (82) 14; Fl. Belg. (112) 13

Dipsacus laciniatus — Demonstr. pl. (49) 4

Dipsacus pilosus — Demonstr. pl. (49) 4; Fl. Angl. (56) 11; Calend. fl. (72) [17]; Fl. Monsp. (74) 10; Prodr. fl. Dan. (82) 14; Fl. Belg. (112) 13

Dirca — Nova pl. gen. 1751 (32) [13, as 15], 17, 18, 48

Dodartia orientalis — Demonstr. pl. (49) 17; Calend. fl. (72) [15]; Hist. nat. Rossia (144) 23

Dodecas — Pl. Surin. (177) 4, 9

Dodecatheon — Nova pl. gen. 1751 (32) 8, 25, 26, 48

Dodecatheon meadia — Demonstr. pl. (49) 5; Calend. fl. (72) [11], [14]; Hort. cul. (132) 24

Dolichos — Pl. officin. (52) 18; Fl. Jam. (105) 26

Dolichos capensis — Pl. rar. Afr. (115) 17

Dolichos caule volubili, pedunculis multifloris erectis, leguminibus pendulis cylindricis torulosis — Cent. II. pl. (66) 28

Dolichos caule volubili, pedunculis subbifloris, leguminis ellipticis compressis, foliis glabris — Pl. rar. Afr. (115) 17

Dolichos ensiformis — Fl. Jam. (105) 19; Pl. Surin. (177) 13

Dolichos erosus — Herb. Amboin. (57) 23[as Dolichus]

Dolichos filiformis — Pl. Jam. (102) 19; Fl. Jam. (105) 19

Dolichos lablab — Demonstr. pl. (49) 20; Herb. Amboin. (57) 23[as Dolichus]; Fl. Palaest. (70) 25

Dolichos lignosus — Demonstr. pl. (49) 20; Herb. Amboin. (57) 23[as Dolichus]

Dolichos minimus — Fl. Jam. (105) 19

Dolichos pruriens — Cent. I. pl. (65) 2; Fl. Jam. (105) 19

Dolichos pruriens, caule volubili, leguminibus racemosis hirtis flexuosis — Herb. Amboin. (57) 23[as Dolichus]

Dolichos repens — Pl. Jam. (102) 19; Fl. Jam. (105) 19

Dolichos sinensis — Cent. II. pl. (66) 28

Dolichos soja — Fr. escul. (127) 18[as soija]

Dolichos tetragonolobus — Cent. I. pl. (65) 2

Dolichos tetragonolobus, leguminibus membranaceo quadrangulatis — Herb. Amboin. (57) 23[as Dolichus]

Dolichos trilobus — Iter Chin. (161) 7

Dolichos unguiculatus — Demonstr. pl. (49) 20

Domina serpentum — Mus. Ad.-Frid. (11) 20; Surin. Grill. (16) 23

Donax — Fund. test. (166) 18, 41

Donax scripta — Fund. test. (166) 41

Doronicum — Anandria (9) 12; Vir. pl. (13) 23, 31; Fl. oecon. (17) 20; Odor. med. (40) 13

Doronicum arnica — Pan Svec. (26) 32

Doronicum bellidiastrum — Fl. Palaest. (70) 28; Fl. alp. (71) 22; Fl. Monsp. (74) 25

Doronicum foliis alternis lanceolatis obtusis integerrimis, caule unifloro — Pl. Mart.-Burs. (6) 14

Doronicum incanum — Fl. alp. (71) 22; Fl. Monsp. (74) 25

Doronicum longifolium hirsutie asperum — Pl. Mart.-Burs. (6) 14

Doronicum pardalianches — Pl. officin. (52) 9; Fl. alp. (71) 22; Fl. Monsp. (74) 25

Doronicum plantagineum — Fl. Monsp. (74) 25

Doronicum primum — Pl. Mart.-Burs. (6) 14

Dorstenia — Ficus (2) 11, 12; Passifl. (8) [iii]; Mus. Ad.-Frid. (11) 21; Sem. musc. (28) 3

Dorstenia contrajerva — Pl. officin. (52) 8

Dorychnium majus — Pl. Mart.-Burs. (6) 25

Draba — Spons. pl. (12) 11; Fl. oecon. (17) 16

Draba alpina — Stat. pl. (55) 16; Fl. alp. (71) 20; Fl. Monsp. (74) 20; Rar. Norv. (157) 11

Draba chalepensis repens humilior, foliis minus cinereis et quasi viridibus — Cent. II. pl. (66) 23

Draba hirta — Rar. Norv. (157) 11

Draba incana — Fl. Angl. (56) 19; Fl. alp. (71) 20; Rar. Norv. (157) 11

Draba intorta — Pan Svec. (26) 28

Draba lapponica — Pan Svec. (26) 28

Draba muralis — Pan Svec. (26) 28; Herbat. Upsal. (50) 7; Stat. pl. (55) 17; Fl. Angl. (56) 19; Fl. Monsp. (74) 20

Draba nemorosa — Demonstr. pl. (49) 17

Draba nudicaulis — Pan Svec. (26) 28

Draba palustris siliquosa major alpina, bursae pastoris folio — Cent. II. pl. (66) 24

Draba pyrenaica — Fl. alp. (71) 20

Draba verna — Herbat. Upsal. (50) 7; Stat. pl. (55) 21; Fl. Angl. (56) 19; Somn. pl. (68) 22; Calend. fl. (72) [9]; Fl. Monsp. (74) 20; Prodr. fl. Dan. (82) 20; Fl. Belg. (112) 19; Fl. Åker. (162) 15; Pand. fl. Ryb. (165) 20[as verva]

Draco — Fund. ornith. (137) 10

Draco volans — Amphib. Gyll. (5) 15, 20; Hort. Upsal. (7) 43

Dracocephalum — Hort. Upsal. (7) 34; Anandria (9) 4[as Dracocephalon]; Vir. pl. (13) 22; Pl. hybr. (33) 7; Cui bono? (42) 20

Dracocephalum canariense — Demonstr. pl. (49) 16; Pl. officin. (52) 13

Dracocephalum canescens — Demonstr. pl. (49) 16

Dracocephalum floribus oppositis, bracteis lanceolatis integerrimis, foliis lanceolatis mucronatis dentatis — Cent. II. pl. (66) 20

Dracocephalum floribus verticillatis, bracteis oblongis integerrimis, corollis vix calycem aequantibus — Pl. hybr. (33) 14[as Dracocepalum]

Dracocephalum foliis ex lanceolato-linearibus rarius dentatis — Cent. II. pl. (66) 20[as Dracocephalon]

Dracocephalum foliis verticillatis, bracteis longis ovatis integerrimis, corollis calyce multoties majoribus — Pl. hybr. (33) 14

Dracocephalum grandiflorum — Hist. nat. Rossia (144) 23, 31

Dracocephalum moldavica — Demonstr. pl. (49) 16; Pl. officin. (52) 13

Dracocephalum nutans — Demonstr. pl. (49) 16; Hist. nat. Rossia (144) 23, 31

Dracocephalum peltatum — Demonstr. pl. (49) 16

Dracocephalum peregrinum — Cent. II. pl. (66) 20; Hist. nat. Rossia (144) 23, 31

Dracocephalum pinnatum — Hist. nat. Rossia (144) 31

Dracocephalum ruyschiana — Demonstr. pl. (49) 16; Hist. nat. Rossia (144) 31; Colon. pl. (158) 7

Dracocephalum thymiflorum — Demonstr. pl. (49) 16; Hist. nat. Rossia (144) 31

Dracocephalum virginicum — Demonstr. pl. (49) 16

Dracontium — Vir. pl. (13) 10, 25; Nova pl. gen. 1747 (14) 27; Gem. arb. (24) 8; Pl. rar. Camsch. (30) 29; Nova pl. gen. 1751 (32) 12; Odor. med. (40) 13; Herb. Amboin. (57) 22

Dracontium foliis lanceolatis — Pl. rar. Camsch. (30) 29

Dracontium polyphyllum — Herb. Amboin. (57) 22

Dracunculus — Lign. colubr. (21) 15; Cul. mut. (88) 2

Dracunculus alatus — Amphib. Gyll. (5) 20

Dracunculus amboinicus — Herb. Amboin. (57) 22

Drosera — Fl. oecon. (17) 8; Pan Svec. (26) 9; Nom. bot. (107) 11; Erica (163) 2

Drosera capensis — Fl. Cap. (99) 13

Drosera caule folioso simplici, foliis lanceolatis — Pl. rar. Afr. (115) 9

Drosera cistiflora — Pl. rar. Afr. (115) 9

Drosera foliis ad caulem oblongis alternis, flore ampla purpureo — Pl. rar. Afr. (115) 9

Drosera longifolia — Herbat. Upsal. (50) 16; Stat. pl. (55) 15; Fl. Angl. (56) 14; Prodr. fl. Dan. (82) 16; Fl. Belg. (112) 15

Drosera oblongifolia — Pan Svec. (26) 19

Drosera perennis — Fl. Angl. (56) 28

Drosera rotundifolia — Pan Svec. (26) 19; Herbat. Upsal. (50) 6; Pl. officin. (52) 16; Stat. pl. (55) 15; Fl. Angl. (56) 14; Fl. Monsp. (74) 14; Prodr. fl. Dan. (82) 16; Fl. Belg. (112) 15; Rar. Norv. (157) 15; Fl. Åker. (162) 10

Drupina — Pl. Surin. (177) 4

Drupina cristata — Pl. Surin. (177) 11

Dryas — Vir. pl. (13) 27; Pl. hybr. (33) 7, 26; Fl. Angl. (56) 5; Fund. fr. (123) 20, 23; Fraga (170) [1], 3

Dryas lapponica — Pan Svec. (26) 25

Dryas octopetala — Stat. pl. (55) 15; Fl. Angl. (56) 17; Cervus (60) 7; Fl. alp. (71) 18; Hist. nat. Rossia (144) 30; Rar. Norv. (157) 10

Dryas pentapetala — Fl. Angl. (56) 17; Fl. alp. (71) 18; Hist. nat. Rossia (144) 30

Dryas pentapetala, foliis pinnatis — Pl. rar. Camsch. (30) 20; Pl. hybr. (33) 26

Dryopteris lobelii — Acrostichum (10) 6

Dryopteris triplex — Herb. Amboin. (57) 26

Drypis theophrasti — Cent. II. pl. (66) 13

Dulcamara — Sapor. med. (31) 20; Purg. indig. (143) 17; Dulcamara (164) 5ff.

Duracina durio — Fr. escul. (127) 10

Durio — Herb. Amboin. (57) 7

Dytiscus — Noxa insect. (46) 30; Pand. insect. (93) 5; Fund. entom. (154) 18, 19, 30; Bigas insect. (184) 3, 7

Dytiscus bipustulatus — Pand. fl. Ryb. (165) 9

Dytiscus caraboides — Bigas insect. (184) 7

Dytiscus cinereus — Pand. fl. Ryb. (165) 9

Dytiscus fuscipes — Bigas insect. (184) 7

Dytiscus luridus — Bigas insect. (184) 7

Dytiscus minutus — Pand. fl. Ryb. (165) 9

Dytiscus palustris — Pand. fl. Ryb. (165) 9

Dytiscus piceus — Bigas insect. (184) 7

Dytiscus scarabaeoides — Bigas insect. (184) 7

Dytiscus semistriatus — Pand. fl. Ryb. (165) 9

Dytiscus striatus — Pand. fl. Ryb. (165) 9

Ebenus — Pl. officin. (52) 9; Herb. Amboin. (57) 11; Opobals. (135) 2

Ebenus alba — Herb. Amboin. (57) 11

Ebenus molucca — Herb. Amboin. (57) 11

Ebulus — Hort. Upsal. (7) 33; Odor. med. (40) 13, 14

Ecastaphyllum — Fl. Jam. (105) 26

Echeneis — Mus. Ad.-Frid. (11) 41; Nat. pelagi (84) 11[as Echineis]; Iter Chin. (161) 6[as Echineis]

Echinometra — Corallia Balt. (4) 21

Echinophora spinosa — Fl. Angl. (56) 13; Fl. Monsp. (74) 12

Echinops — Hort. Upsal. (7) 33; Mund. invis. (149) 20

Echinops corymbiferus — Fl. Palaest. (70) 27

Echinops ritro — Fl. Palaest. (70) 27; Fl. Monsp. (74) 24; Hist. nat. Rossia (144) 32

Echinops sphaerocephalus — Demonstr. pl. (49) 22; Calend. fl. (72) [17]; Hort. cul. (132) 24

Echinops strigosus — Demonstr. pl. (49) 22; Calend. fl. (72) [16]

Echinus — Corallia Balt. (4) 10[as Echinnus]; Fund. test. (166) 22

Echites — Fl. Jam. (105) 26

Echites angularis — Pl. Surin. (177) 7

Echium — Vir. pl. (13) 18[as Echinm]; Fl. oecon. (17) 5; Vern. arb. (47) 9; Stat. pl. (55) 6; Fl. Cap. (99) 6; Nom. bot. (107) 10

Echium creticum — Fl. Palaest. (70) 14

Echium fruticosum — Fl. Cap. (99) 12

Echium italicum — Fl. Palaest. (70) 14; Fl. Monsp. (74) 11

Echium laevigatum — Fl. Cap. (99) 12

Echium lycopsis — Fl. Angl. (56) 12

Echium maculatum — Fl. Monsp. (74) 11

Echium majus et asperius, flore dilute purpureo — Pl. Mart.-Burs. (6) 21

Echium orientale — Fl. Palaest. (70) 14

Echium rosmarini folio — Pl. Mart.-Burs. (6) 21

Echium scanense — Pan Svec. (26) 16

Echium scorpioides minus, flosculis luteis — Pl. Mart.-Burs. (6) 21

Echium vulgare — Demonstr. pl. (49) 5; Stat. pl. (55) 20, 22; Fl. Angl. (56) 12; Calend. fl. (72) [22]; Fl. Monsp. (74) 11; Prodr. fl. Dan. (82) 14; Fl. Belg. (112) 14; Pand. fl. Ryb. (165) 17

Ecliptica — Herb. Amboin. (57) 26

Ehretia — Fl. Jam. (105) 26

Ehretia tinifolia — Pl. Jam. (102) 10; Fl. Jam. (105) 14[as Erethia]

Ekawerya — Lign. colubr. (21) 9ff.

Ekawerya, periclymenum zeylanicum herbaceum, foliis variegatis, diversicoloribus maculis ornatus — Lign. colubr. (21) 14ff.

Elaeagnus angustifolius — Fl. Palaest. (70) 14

Elaeagnus foliis ellipticis — Cent. II. pl. (66) 9

Elaeagnus mathioli, incolis seisefun — Cent. II. pl. (66) 9

Elaeagnus spinosa — Cent. II. pl. (66) 9; Fl. Palaest. (70) 14[as spinosus]

Elaeocarpus — Nova pl. gen. 1747 (14) [vi], 19

Elaeocarpus serrata — Herb. Amboin. (57) 13; see also Ellocarpus s.

Elajocarpos folio lauri serrato, floribus spicatis — Nova pl. gen. 1747 (14) 19

Elater — Fund. entom. (154) 18

Elater aeneus — Pand. fl. Ryb. (165) 9

Elater aterrimus — Pand. fl. Ryb. (165) 9

Elater balteatus — Pand. fl. Ryb. (165) 9

Elater brunneus — Pand. fl. Ryb. (165) 9

Elater castaneus — Pand. fl. Ryb. (165) 9

Elater cruciatus — Pand. fl. Ryb. (165) 9

Elater fasciatus — Esca avium (174) 7

Elater ferrugineus, elytris mucronatis — Cent. insect. (129) 12

Elater ligneus — Cent. insect. (129) 12

Elater murinus — Pand. fl. Ryb. (165) 9[as murinns]; Esca avium (174) 3

Elater obscurus — Pand. fl. Ryb. (165) 9

Elater pectinicornis — Pand. fl. Ryb. (165) 9

Elater sanguineus — Pand. fl. Ryb. (165) 9; Esca avium (174) 3

Elater sputator — Pand. fl. Ryb. (165) 9

Elater tessellatus — Pand. fl. Ryb. (165) 9

Elaterium — Sapor. med. (31) 18; Odor. med. (40) 14

Elatine — Morb. hyeme (38) 8

Elatine alsinastrum — Stat. pl. (55) 13; Fl. Angl. (56) 15; Fl. Monsp. (74) 15

Elatine hydropiper — Herbat. Upsal. (50) 18; Stat. pl. (55) 13; Prodr. fl. Dan. (82) 17; Fl. Åker. (162) 11

Elatine minima — Pan Svec. (26) 22

Elengi — Nova pl. gen. 1747 (14) 14

Elephantopus — Hort. Upsal. (7) 36

Elephantopus scaber — Fl. Jam. (105) 19; Iter Chin. (161) 7[as Elephanthopus]

Elephantopus tomentosus — Fl. Jam. (105) 19, 25

Elephas — Spons. pl. (12) 16; Vir. pl. (13) 16; Oecon. nat. (20) 31, 34; Mat. med. anim. (29) 5; Mus ind. (62) 7, 8; Fl. Cap. (99) [1]; Polit. nat. (109) 16

Ellisia — Fl. Jam. (105) 26

Ellisia aculeata — Fl. Jam. (105) 18

Ellisia acuta — Pl. Jam. (102) 16

Ellocarpus serrata [error for Elaeocarpus?] — Fr. escul. (127) 13

Eluteria — Vir. pl. (13) 27

Elvela mitra — Herbat. Upsal. (50) 9

Elymus — Nova pl. gen. 1751 (32) 10, 12, 32, 34, 48; Pl. hybr. (33) 15; Cui bono? (42) 17; Fund. agrost. (152) 25, 32, 34

Elymus arenarius — Demonstr. pl. (49) 3; Stat. pl. (55) 21; Fl. Angl. (56) 11; Hort. acad. (63) 10; Calend. fl. (72) [13]; Prodr. fl. Dan. (82) 13; Fl. Belg. (112) 6, 8, 13; Usum musc. (148) 4; Fund. agrost. (152) 7, 8

Elymus aristis spiculis longioribus — Nova pl. gen. 1751 (32) 35

Elymus canadensis — Demonstr. pl. (49) 3

Elymus caninus — Fl. Åker. (162) 7

Elymus caput medusae — Demonstr. pl. (49) 4

Elymus foliis mucronatis pungentibus — Nova pl. gen. 1751 (32) 35

Elymus involucris reflexo-patentibus — Nova pl. gen. 1751 (32) 35

Elymus maritimus — Pan Svec. (26) 15

Elymus philadelphicus — Cent. I. pl. (65) 6

Elymus sibiricus — Demonstr. pl. (49) 3; Hist. nat. Rossia (144) 28

Elymus spica erecta, involucris spicula longioribus — Nova pl. gen. 1751 (32) 35

Elymus spica flaccido-pendula, spiculis geminis — Nova pl. gen. 1751 (32) 35

Elymus spica nutante, spiculis inferioribus ternis, superioribus geminis — Nova pl. gen. 1751 (32) 35

Elymus spica pendula; spiculis sexfloris: inferioribus ternatis, superioribus binatis — Cent. I. pl. (65) 6

Elymus spicula flaccido-pendula — Nova pl. gen. 1751 (32) 35

Elymus virginicus — Demonstr. pl. (49) 3

Emberiza citrinella — Migr. avium (79) 32

Emberiza grisea, pectore gulaque caerulaeis, abdomine albo — Chin. Lagerstr. (64) 19

Emberiza hortulana — Migr. avium (79) 18[as hortulanus], 32

Emberiza mixta — Chin. Lagerstr. (64) 19

Emberiza nivalis — Migr. avium (79) 17, 32; Fund. ornith. (137) 18, 26

Emberiza remigibus rectricibusque nigris, pectore viridi-caerulescente — Surin. Grill. (16) 10[as Embriza]

Emberiza seu hortulanus carolinianus — Oecon. nat. (20) 40[as Embriza]

Emerus — Fr. Svec. (91) [ii]

Empetrum — Peloria (3) 10; Vir. pl. (13) 37; Fl. oecon. (17) 28; Pl. escul. (35) 26, 28; Morb. hyeme (38) 12; Fr. Svec. (91) [ii]

Empetrum acetosum — Herb. Amboin. (57) 24

Empetrum nigrum — Pan Svec. (26) [37, as 39]; Herbat. Upsal. (50) 6; Stat. pl. (55) 15; Fl. Angl. (56) 24; Calend. fl. (72) [9]; Prodr. fl. Dan. (82) 25; Fr. Svec. (91) 5, 21; Pl. tinct. (97) 26; Fl. Belg. (112) 23; Pand. fl. Ryb. (165) 22; Ledum (178) 7

Empis livida — Pand. fl. Ryb. (165) 15

Empis pennipes — Pand. fl. Ryb. (165) 15

Empis stercorea — Pand. fl. Ryb. (165) 15

Endivia — Sapor. med. (31) 11; Scorb. (180) 21

Enula — Nova pl. gen. 1747 (14) 25, 26; see also Inula

Ephedra — Oecon. nat. (20) 15; Aphyteia (185) 9

Ephedra distachya — Fl. Palaest. (70) 31; Fl. Monsp. (74) 28

Ephedra monostachya — Hist. nat. Rossia (144) 34

Ephemera — Mirac. insect. (45) 19; Fund. entom. (154) 20, 21

Ephemera culiciformis — Esca avium (174) 8

Ephemera horaria — Pand. fl. Ryb. (165) 11

Ephemera vulgata — Pand. fl. Ryb. (165) 11; Esca avium (174) 8

Epidendrum — Passifl. (8) [iii][as Epidendron]; Vir. pl. (13) 24; Cryst. gen. (15) 6[as Epidendron]; Herb. Amboin. (57) 5, 27; Pand. insect. (93) 18; Polit. nat. (109) 5[as Epidendron]; Nect. fl. (122) 10; Pl. Surin. (177) 14

Epidendrum amabile — Herb. Amboin. (57) 27

Epidendrum guttatum — Fl. Jam. (105) 20[as Epidendron]

Epidendrum nodosum — Fl. Jam. (105) 20[as Epidendron]

Epidendrum pusillum — Pl. Surin. (177) 14

Epidendrum scandens foliis ovato oblongis nervosis sessilibus caulinis, cirrhis spiralibus — Pot. choc. (141) 5[as sessibilis]

Epidendrum vanilla — Pl. officin. (52) 19[as Epidendron]; Fung. melit. (69) 2; Fl. Jam. (105) 20[as Epidendron]; Fr. escul. (127) 17[as Epidendron]; Pot. choc. (141) 5

Epigaea — Nova pl. gen. 1751 (32) 12, 27, 28, 48; Erica (163) 3

Epilobium — Fl. oecon. (17) 9; Pan Svec. (26) 3; Nova pl. gen. 1751 (32) 47; Pl. escul. (35) 27, 28; Pand. insect. (93) 13; Nect. fl. (122) 6

Epilobium alpinum — Stat. pl. (55) 16; Fl. Angl. (56) 15; Fl. alp. (71) 16; Fl. Monsp. (74) 15

Epilobium angustifolium — Hosp. insect. fl. (43) 20; Herbat. Upsal. (50) 9; Stat. pl. (55) 23; Fl. Angl. (56) 15; Calend. fl. (72) [13]; Fl. Monsp. (74) 15; Prodr. fl. Dan. (82) 17; Transm. frum. (87) 3; Fl. Belg. (112) 16; Mac. olit. (113) 14; Fl. Åker. (162) 11; Pand. fl. Ryb. (165) 18

Epilobium hirsutum — Pan Svec. (26) 21; Demonstr. pl. (49) 11; Fl. Angl. (56) 15; Calend. fl. (72) [16]; Fl. Monsp. (74) 15; Prodr. fl. Dan. (82) 17; Fl. Belg. (112) 8, 16; Pl. rar. Afr. (115) 6

Epilobium irregulare — Pan Svec. (26) 21; Pl. escul. (35) 13

Epilobium lapponicum — Pan Svec. (26) 21

Epilobium latifolium — Hist. nat. Rossia (144) 29

Epilobium montanum — Pan Svec. (26) 21; Herbat. Upsal. (50) 9; Stat. pl. (55) 23; Fl. Angl. (56) 15; Calend. fl. (72) [13]; Prodr. fl. Dan. (82) 17; Fl. Belg. (112) 16; Fl. Åker. (162) 11; Pand. fl. Ryb. (165) 18

Epilobium palustre — Pan Svec. (26) 21; Hosp. insect. fl. (43) 20; Herbat. Upsal. (50) 16; Stat. pl. (55) 14; Fl. Angl. (56) 15; Fl. Monsp. (74) 15; Prodr. fl. Dan. (82) 17; Fl. Belg. (112) 16; Fl. Åker. (162) 11; Pand. fl. Ryb. (165) 18

Epilobium tetragonum — Demonstr. pl. (49) 11; Fl. Angl. (56) 15; Fl. Monsp. (74) 15; Prodr. fl. Dan. (82) 17

Epimedium — Hort. Upsal. (7) 33; Spons. pl. (12) 33; Vir. pl. (13) 24; Nect. fl. (122) 13; Fund. fr. (123) 21[as Epidemium]

Epimedium alpinum — Demonstr. pl. (49) 4; Fl. alp. (71) 13; Calend. fl. (72) [11]

Equa — Mat. med. anim. (29) 5

Equisetum — Acrostichum (10) 3, 5, 8; Fl. oecon. (17) 28; Cui bono? (42) 18; Herb. Amboin. (57) 12; Cervus (60) 9; Nom. bot. (107) 19; Fl. Belg. (112) 10; Usum hist. nat. (145) 20, 22

Equisetum amboinicum — Herb. Amboin. (57) 27

Equisetum arvense — Pan Svec. (26) [37, as 39]; Herbat. Upsal. (50) 14; Pl. officin. (52) 9; Stat. pl. (55) 21; Fl. Angl. (56) 25; Oves (61) 16; Fl. Monsp. (74) 29; Prodr. fl. Dan. (82) 25; Fl. Belg. (112) 23; Fl. Åker. (162) 20; Pand. fl. Ryb. (165) 22

Equisetum fluviatile — Pan Svec. (26) [37, as 39]; Herbat. Upsal. (50) 14; Stat. pl. (55) 13; Fl. Angl. (56) 25; Fl. Monsp. (74) 29; Prodr. fl. Dan. (82) 25; Fl. Belg. (112) 23; Pand. fl. Ryb. (165) 23; Esca avium (174) 15

Equisetum giganteum — Fl. Jam. (105) 22

Equisetum glabrum — Pan Svec. (26) [37, as 39]

Equisetum hyemale — Herbat. Upsal. (50) 6; Stat. pl. (55) 18; Fl. Angl. (56) 25; Fl. Monsp. (74) 29; Prodr. fl. Dan. (82) 25; Fl. Belg. (112) 23; Pand. fl. Ryb. (165) 23

Equisetum limosum — Herbat. Upsal. (50) 19, 20; Stat. pl. (55) 15; Fl. Angl. (56) 25; Prodr. fl. Dan. (82) 25

Equisetum palustre — Pan Svec. (26) [37, as 39]; Herbat. Upsal. (50) 14; Stat. pl. (55) 14; Fl. Angl. (56) 25; Fl. Jam. (105) 22; Fl. Belg. (112) 23; Fl. Åker. (162) 20

Equisetum scabrum — Pan Svec. (26) [37, as 39]

Equisetum sylvaticum — Pan Svec. (26) [37, as 39]; Herbat. Upsal. (50) 19; Stat. pl. (55) 18; Fl. Angl. (56) 25; Fl. Monsp. (74) 29; Prodr. fl. Dan. (82) 25; Fl. Belg. (112) 23; Pand. fl. Ryb. (165) 22

Equus — Spons. pl. (12) 16, 25; Vir. pl. (13) 16, 28; Oecon. nat. (20) 36, 42, 43; Generat. calc. (22) 2; Pan Svec. (26) 2, 3, 7, 10ff.; Mat. med. anim. (29) 5; Hosp. insect. fl. (43) 9; Noxa insect. (46) 27, 28; Mus ind. (62) 22; Instr. peregr. (96) 11; Generat. ambig. (104) 14; Polit. nat. (109) 21; Fund. fr. (123) 14; Usum hist. nat. (145) 19; Esca avium (174) 3, 4

Equus cauda undique setosa — Mat. med. anim. (29) 5

Eragrostis major — Pl. Mart.-Burs. (6) [1]

Eranthemum — Nova pl. gen. 1747 (14) [vi], 1; Fl. Cap. (99) 6

Eranthemum capense — Fl. Cap. (99) 11

Erebinthus — Nova pl. gen. 1751 (32) 12, 31

Erica — Spons. pl. (12) 33; Vir. pl. (13) 20; Fl. oecon. (17) 10; Gem. arb. (24) 6; Pl. hybr. (33) 29; Morb. hyeme (38) 12; Oves (61) 15; Pand. insect. (93) 13; Fl. Cap. (99) 7, 9; Arb. Svec. (101) 10; Nom. bot. (107) 12; Pl. rar. Afr. (115) 5; Fund. fr. (123) 18, 21, 22; Erica (163) [1]ff.; Aphyteia (185) 6

Erica abietina — Fl. Cap. (99) 14; Erica (163) 5, 7, 9

Erica absinthioides — Erica (163) 5, 7, 10

Erica aethiopica — Fl. Cap. (99) 14

Erica africana, flore rubro pleno — Pl. rar. Afr. (115) 11

Erica albens — Erica (163) 5, 7, 10

Erica antheris bifidis inclusis, calycibus trifloris inflatis inflexis, foliis ternis laevibus — Pl. rar. Afr. (115) 11

Erica antheris bifidis inclusis, corollis maximis, foliis ternis linearibus laevibus — Pl. rar. Afr. (115) 11

Erica arborea — Fl. Monsp. (74) 15; Fl. Belg. (112) 9, 16; Erica (163) 5, 7, 9

Erica articularis — Erica (163) 5, 7, 9

Erica australis — Erica (163) 5, 7, 9

Erica baccans — Erica (163) 5, 7, 9

Erica bergiana — Erica (163) 5, 7, 9

Erica bruniades — Fl. Cap. (99) 14; Erica (163) 5, 7, 10

Erica caffra — Fl. Cap. (99) 14; Erica (163) 5, 7, 9

Erica calycina — Erica (163) 5, 7, 9

Erica capitata — Fl. Cap. (99) 14; Erica (163) 5, 7, 10

Erica carnea — Erica (163) 7

Erica cerinthoides — Erica (163) 5, 7, 10

Erica ciliaris — Erica (163) 5, 7, 10

Erica cinerea — Fl. Angl. (56) 15; Fl. Monsp. (74) 15; Prodr. fl. Dan. (82) 17; Fl. Belg. (112) 9, 16; Rar. Norv. (157) 9; Colon. pl. (158) 8; Erica (163) 4, 5, 7, 9

Erica coccinea — Fl. Cap. (99) 14; Erica (163) 5, 7, 10

Erica comosa — Erica (163) 5, 7, 10

Erica corifolia — Fl. Cap. (99) 14; Erica (163) 5, 7, 9

Erica coris folio tertia — Pl. Mart.-Burs. (6) 31

Erica cubica — Erica (163) 5, 6, 7, 10

Erica cubitalis — Erica (163) 5, 7

Erica curviflora — Fl. Cap. (99) 14; Erica (163) 5, 7, 10

Erica daboeci — Fl. Angl. (56) 29

Erica depressa — Erica (163) 5, 7, 9

Erica empetrifolia — Fl. Cap. (99) 14; Erica (163) 5, 7, 9

Erica fagis — Polit. nat. (109) 5

Erica fastigiata — Erica (163) 5, 6, 10

Erica foliis subulatis ciliatis quaternis, corollis globoso-ovatis terminatricibus confertis — Pl. Mart.-Burs. (6) 31

Erica glutinosa — Erica (163) 4

Erica gnaphaloides — Fl. Cap. (99) 14; Erica (163) 5[as gnaphalodes], 7[as gnaphalodes], 9[as gnaphalodes]

Erica granulata — Erica (163) 5, 7, 10

Erica halicacaba — Pl. rar. Afr. (115) 11; Erica (163) 5, 7, 9

Erica herbacea — Erica (163) 5, 7, 10

Erica imbricata — Erica (163) 5, 7, 10

Erica lutea — Erica (163) 5, 9

Erica mammosa — Erica (163) 5, 7, 9

Erica mauritanica — Fl. Cap. (99) 14

Erica mediterranea — Erica (163) 5, 7, 10

Erica melanthera — Erica (163) 5, 6, 10

Erica mucosa — Erica (163) 5, 7, 9

Erica multiflora — Fl. Angl. (56) 15; Fl. Monsp. (74) 15; Fl. Belg. (112) 9, 16; Erica (163) 5, 7, 10

Erica myricae folio — Fl. Angl. (56) 29

Erica nigrita — Erica (163) 5, 7, 9

Erica nudiflora — Erica (163) 5, 7, 10

Erica orientalis — Fl. Palaest. (70) 18

Erica paniculata — Erica (163) 5, 7, 9

Erica parviflora — Fl. Cap. (99) 14

Erica parvifolia — Erica (163) 7

Erica pentaphyllea — Erica (163) 5, 7, 9

Erica persoluta — Erica (163) 5, 7, 9

Erica petiveri — Erica (163) 5, 7, 10

Erica physodes — Fl. Cap. (99) 9[as physodea], 14; Erica (163) 5, 7, 9

Erica pilulifera — Fl. Cap. (99) 14; Erica (163) 5, 7, 9

Erica planifolia — Erica (163) 5, 7, 9

Erica plukenetii — Fl. Cap. (99) 14; Erica (163) 5, 7, 10

Erica pubescens — Erica (163) 5, 7, 9

Erica purpurascens — Erica (163) 5, 10

Erica ramentacea — Erica (163) 5, 7, 9

Erica regerminans — Erica (163) 5, 7, 9

Erica scoparia — Fl. Monsp. (74) 15[as scopavia]; Fl. Belg. (112) 16; Erica (163) 4, 5, 7, 9

Erica spumosa — Pl. rar. Afr. (115) 11; Erica (163) 5, 7, 10

Erica subdivaricata — Erica (163) 5

Erica tenella — Oves (61) 15

Erica tenuifolia — Fl. Cap. (99) 14; Erica (163) 5, 7, 10

Erica tetralix — Pan Svec. (26) 21; Stat. pl. (55) 15; Fl. Angl. (56) 15; Prodr. fl. Dan. (82) 17; Erica (163) 4, 5, 7, 9

Erica triflora — Fl. Cap. (99) 14; Erica (163) 5, 7, 9; see also E. trifolia

Erica trifolia [error for triflora?] — Erica (163) 7

Erica tubiflora — Erica (163) 5, 7, 10

Erica umbellata — Erica (163) 5, 7, 10

Erica vagans — Erica (163) 5, 7, 10

Erica viridipurpurea — Fl. Monsp. (74) 15; Erica (163) 5[as viridipurpurascens], 7[as viridipurpurascens], 9[as viridipurpurascens]

Erica viscaria — Erica (163) 5, 7, 10

Erica vulgaris — Pan Svec. (26) 21; Hosp. insect. fl. (43) 20; Herbat. Upsal. (50) 13; Stat. pl. (55) 18; Fl. Angl. (56) 15; Cervus (60) 7; Fl. Monsp. (74) 15; Prodr. fl. Dan. (82) 17; Fl. Belg. (112) 16; Fl. Åker. (162) 11; Erica (163) 4, 5, 7, 9, 11; Pand. fl. Ryb. (165) 18

Erigeron — Hort. Upsal. (7) 35, 41; Fl. Angl. (56) 6; Specif. Canad. (76) 7

Erigeron acre — Pan Svec. (26) 33; Hosp. insect. fl. (43) 31; Demonstr. pl. (49) 23; Herbat. Upsal. (50) 19; Stat. pl. (55) 21; Fl. Angl. (56) 22; Cervus (60) 8; Fl. Monsp. (74) 25; Prodr. fl. Dan. (82) 23; Fl. Belg. (112) 21; Fl. Åker. (162) 17; Pand. fl. Ryb. (165) 21

Erigeron alpinum — Fl. alp. (71) 22

Erigeron bonariense — Demonstr. pl. (49) 23; Fl. Jam. (105) 20

Erigeron canadense — Demonstr. pl. (49) 23; Fl. Angl. (56) 22; Calend. fl. (72) [16]; Fl. Monsp. (74) 25; Pl. Jam. (102) 23; Fl. Belg. (112) 21; Colon. pl. (158) 10

Erigeron gramineum — Hist. nat. Rossia (144) 33

Erigeron graveolens — Cent. I. pl. (65) 28; Fl. Monsp. (74) 25

Erigeron jamaicense — Pl. Jam. (102) 23; Fl. Jam. (105) 20

Erigeron lapponicum — Pan Svec. (26) 33

Erigeron palustris — Pan Svec. (26) 33

Erigeron philadelphicum — Specif. Canad. (76) 8

Erigeron ramis lateralibus multifloris, calycibus squarrosis — Cent. I. pl. (65) 28

Erigeron siculum — Fl. Palaest. (70) 28; Fl. Monsp. (74) 25

Erigeron tuberosum — Fl. Monsp. (74) 25; Pl. rar. Afr. (115) 7

Erigeron uniflorum — Demonstr. pl. (49) 23; Stat. pl. (55) 16; Fl. alp. (71) 22; Rar. Norv. (157) 11

Erigeron viscosum — Demonstr. pl. (49) 23; Fl. Monsp. (74) 25

Erinaceus — Oecon. nat. (20) 38; Morb. hyeme (38) [2]; Polit. nat. (109) 15, 17

Erinaceus loricatus, cingulis septenis, palmis tetradactylis, plantis pentadactylis — Mus. Ad.-Frid. (11) 3

Erinosyce — Ficus (2) 9[as Erinocyse], 13

Erinosyce grosso et ficu longiusculis et viridibus — Ficus (2) 3

Erinosyce grosso et ficu luteolis cum placenta violacea — Ficus (2) 3

Erinosyce grosso viridi turbinato parvo, ficu atro violaceo — Ficus (2) 3

Erinus alpinus — Fl. alp. (71) 20; Fl. Monsp. (74) 20

Erinus pyrenaicus — Fl. alp. (71) 20

Eriocaulon — Nova pl. gen. 1751 (32) 7

Eriocaulon setaceum — Herb. Amboin. (57) 25

Eriocephalus africanus — Fl. Cap. (99) 18

Eriocephalus foliis linearibus indivisis — Pl. rar. Afr. (115) 26

Eriocephalus racemosus — Pl. rar. Afr. (115) 26

Eriophorum — Hort. Upsal. (7) 41; Fl. oecon. (17) 2; Oecon. nat. (20) [5, as 7]; Nom. bot. (107) 9; Fund. agrost. (152) 4, 29, 31, 38; Ledum (178) 7

Eriophorum alpinum — Demonstr. pl. (49) 3; Herbat. Upsal. (50) 16; Stat. pl. (55) 15[as Eriophoron]; Fl. alp. (71) 12; Fund. agrost. (152) 7

Eriophorum polystachion — Pan Svec. (26) 13; Herbat. Upsal. (50) 6; Stat. pl. (55) 15[as Eriophoron]; Fl. Angl. (56) 10; Fl. Monsp. (74) 9; Prodr. fl. Dan. (82) 13; Fl. Belg. (112) 12; Fund. agrost. (152) 7; Fl. Åker. (162) 6; Pand. fl. Ryb. (165) 16

Eriophorum schoenolagurus — Pan Svec. (26) 13

Eriophorum triqueter — Pan Svec. (26) 13

Eriophorum vaginatum — Herbat. Upsal. (50) 6; Stat. pl. (55) 15[as Eriophoron]; Fl. Angl. (56) 10; Fl. alp. (71) 12; Prodr. fl. Dan. (82) 13; Fund. agrost. (152) 7; Fl. Åker. (162) 6; Pand. fl. Ryb. (165) 16

Eriophorus javana — Herb. Amboin. (57) 8

Eriphia — Fl. Jam. (105) 27

Erithalis — Fl. Jam. (105) 26

Erithalis fruticosa — Fl. Jam. (105) 14

Eruca — Cui bono? (42) 25; Cul. mut. (88) 2, 6; Nom. bot. (107) 15; Fund. entom. (154) 25

Eruca hirsuta, hieracii asperi folio, floribus albis, nigris lineis depictis — Raphania (126) 19

Eruca inodora — Pl. Mart.-Burs. (6) 6

Eruca perennis — Fl. Monsp. (74) 29

Eruca seu scolopendra marina corallina multipes — Mus. Ad.-Frid. (11) 47

Eruca sylvestris, flore albo, italica — Cent. II. pl. (66) 25

Eruca tenuifolia perennis — Cent. I. pl. (65) 18

Ervum — Pl. escul. (35) 21; Nom. bot. (107) 16

Ervum arvense — Pan Svec. (26) 30

Ervum ervilia — Pl. officin. (52) 14; Fl. Monsp. (74) 22; Pl. rar. Afr. (115) 6

Ervum hirsutum — Herbat. Upsal. (50) 13; Stat. pl. (55) 19; Fl. Angl. (56) 21; Fl. Monsp. (74) 22; Prodr. fl. Dan. (82) 22; Fl. Belg. (112) 20; Fl. Åker. (162) 16; Pand. fl. Ryb. (165) 21; Esca avium (174) 14

Ervum lens — Demonstr. pl. (49) 20; Pl. officin. (52) 12; Fl. Palaest. (70) 25; Fl. Monsp. (74) 22; Fr. escul. (127) 18; Hort. cul. (132) 17

Ervum monanthos — Demonstr. pl. (49) 20[as monanthus]; Hist. nat. Rossia (144) 31

Ervum pedunculis cirrhosis subunifloris, petiolis mucronatis, foliolis obtusis — Cent. II. pl. (66) 28

Ervum pedunculis subbifloris, seminibus globosis quaternis — Pl. Mart.-Burs. (6) 26

Ervum soloniense — Cent. II. pl. (66) 28; Fl. Monsp. (74) 22

Ervum tetraspermum — Stat. pl. (55) 19; Fl. Angl. (56) 21; Prodr. fl. Dan. (82) 22; Fl. Åker. (162) 16; Pand. fl. Ryb. (165) 21[as tatraspermum]; Esca avium (174) 14

Eryngium — Hort. Upsal. (7) 33; Vir. pl. (13) 14; Fl. oecon. (17) 7; Gem. arb. (24) 13; Pl. escul. (35) 28; Nom. bot. (107) 11

Eryngium alpinum — Fl. alp. (71) 14, 24

Eryngium amethystinum — Fl. alp. (71) 14[as ametystinum], 24[as ametystinum]; Calend. fl. (72) [18]

Eryngium aquaticum — Mors. serp. (119) 17

Eryngium campestre — Pl. officin. (52) 10; Fl. Angl. (56) 13; Fl. Monsp. (74) 12; Prodr. fl. Dan. (82) 15; Fl. Belg. (112) 10, 15

Eryngium foetidum — Fl. Jam. (105) 14; Mors. serp. (119) 17; Obs. mat. med. (171) 3; Pl. Surin. (177) 7

Eryngium foliis omnibus trifidis pinnatis, involucris trifidis pinnatis — Demonstr. pl. (49) 8

Eryngium foliis radicalibus cordatis: caulinis palmatis auriculis reflexis retroflexisque, paleis tricuspidatis — Demonstr. pl. (49) 8

Eryngium maritimum — Pan Svec. (26) 18; Pl. escul. (35) 11; Demonstr. pl. (49) 8; Stat. pl. (55) 12; Fl. Angl. (56) 13; Fl. Monsp. (74) 12; Acetaria (77) 14; Prodr. fl. Dan. (82) 15; Fl. Belg. (112) 8, 15; Mac. olit. (113) 14

Eryngium minus trifidum hispanicum — Demonstr. pl. (49) 8

Eryngium planum — Demonstr. pl. (49) 8; Calend. fl. (72) [17]

Eryngium tricuspidatum — Demonstr. pl. (49) 8; Cent. I. pl. (65) 2; Fl. Palaest. (70) 16

Eryngium trifidum — Demonstr. pl. (49) 8; Cent. I. pl. (65) 2

Erysimum — Pl. Mart.-Burs. (6) 7; Vir. pl. (13) 22; Fl. oecon. (17) 17; Pl. escul. (35) 28; Cent. I. pl. (65) 20; Pand. insect. (93) [17, as 38]; Nom. bot. (107) 15

Erysimum alliaria — Pan Svec. (26) 29; Herbat. Upsal. (50) 17; Pl. officin. (52) 4; Stat. pl. (55) 20; Fl. Angl. (56) 20; Calend. fl. (72) [11]; Fl. Monsp. (74) 21; Prodr. fl. Dan. (82) 21; Fl. Belg. (112) 19; Fl. Åker. (162) 15

Erysimum angustifolium majus — Cent. I. pl. (65) 18

Erysimum barbarea — Pan Svec. (26) 29; Pl. escul. (35) 20[as barbaraea]; Demonstr. pl. (49) 17; Herbat. Upsal. (50) 14[as barbaraea]; Fl. Angl. (56) 20; Fl. Monsp. (74) 21[as barbaraea]; Acetaria (77) 15[as barbaraea]; Prodr. fl. Dan. (82) 21; Fl. Belg. (112) 19; Mac. olit. (113) 22[as barbaraea]; Hort. cul. (132) 14; Fl. Åker. (162) 15[as barbaraea]; Scorb. (180) 17

Erysimum cheiranthoides — Demonstr. pl. (49) 17; Herbat. Upsal. (50) 12; Stat. pl. (55) 19; Fl. Angl. (56) 19; Calend. fl. (72) [22][as cheirantoides]; Prodr. fl. Dan. (82) 21; Fl. Belg. (112) 19; Fl. Åker. (162) 15[as cheirantoides]

Erysimum foliis lanceolatis: radicalibus, repando dentatis, siliquis racemosis subsessilibus, corollis brevissimis — Demonstr. pl. (49) 17

Erysimum foliis lanceolatis serratis — Cent. I. pl. (65) 18

Erysimum foliis pinnatis: extrema pinna triangula dentata, petiolis longis hirsutis — Cent. I. pl. (65) 18

Erysimum foliis subincanis, siliquis brevissimus — Cent. I. pl. (65) 20

Erysimum hieracifolium — Cent. I. pl. (65) 18

Erysimum hirsutum, siliquis erucae — Cent. I. pl. (65) 18

Erysimum irio — Pan Svec. (26) 29; Herbat. Upsal. (50) 15

Erysimum leucoji folio — Pan Svec. (26) 28

Erysimum officinale — Herbat. Upsal. (50) 17; Pl. officin. (52) 10; Stat. pl. (55) 20; Fl. Angl. (56) 19; Fl. Monsp. (74) 21; Prodr. fl. Dan. (82) 21; Fl. Belg. (112) 19; Fl. Åker. (162) 15

Erysimum orientale, sonchi folio, flore sulphureo, siliquis longissimis — Cent. II. pl. (66) 24

Erysimum repandum — Demonstr. pl. (49) 17; Cent. I. pl. (65) 2

Erysimum vulgare — Pan Svec. (26) 28

Erysiphe — Mund. invis. (149) 16

Erythrina — Gem. arb. (24) 6; Rar. Norv. (157) 13

Erythrina corallodendrum — Demonstr. pl. (49) 19; Herb. Amboin. (57) 10[as corallodendron]; Fl. Jam. (105) 19[as corallodendron], 25[as corallodendron]

Erythrina corallodendrum occidentalis — Demonstr. pl. (49) 19

Erythrina corallodendrum orientalis — Demonstr. pl. (49) 19

Erythrina crista galli — Pl. Surin. (177) 12

Erythrina variegata — Herb. Amboin. (57) 10

Erythronium — Spons. pl. (12) 43; Nect. fl. (122) 11

Erythronium dens canis — Fl. alp. (71) 15; Hist. nat. Rossia (144) 28

Erythroxylon — Fl. Jam. (105) 26; Nect. fl. (122) 11

Erythroxylon areolatum — Pl. Jam. (102) 12; Fl. Jam. (105) 16[as Erytroxyl.]

Eschara marina imperati lapidea gothlandica — Corallia Balt. (4) 38

Esculus — see Aesculus

Esox — Noctiluca (39) 5

Esox lucius — Calend. fl. (72) [8]

Esox rostro plagioplateo — Mat. med. anim. (29) 13

Esula — Euphorbia (36) 3, 5

Esula esculenta — Herb. Amboin. (57) 26

Esula exigua — Euphorbia (36) 20

Esula exigua, foliis obtusis — Euphorbia (36) 20

Esula major — Euphorbia (36) 20, 28

Esula minima tragi — Euphorbia (36) 20

Esula minor — Euphorbia (36) 29

Esula minor altera, floribus rubris — Euphorbia (36) 23

Esula palustris — Euphorbia (36) 28

Esula rotunda — Euphorbia (36) 19

Esula rotundifolia non crenata — Euphorbia (36) 19

Esula solisequia — Euphorbia (36) 26[as solisequa]

Ethusa — see Aethusa

Eugenia — Vir. pl. (13) 21; Pl. escul. (35) 4; Herb. Amboin. (57) 7, 12, 14

Eugenia acutangula — Herb. Amboin. (57) 14

Eugenia jambos — Herb. Amboin. (57) 7; Fr. escul. (127) 14

Eugenia malaccensis — Herb. Amboin. (57) 7

Eugenia racemosa — Herb. Amboin. (57) 7, 14

Euonymo affinis arbor orientalis nucifera, flore roseo — Pot. theae (142) 3

Euonymo similis aegyptiaca, fructu baccis lauri simili — Pot. coff. (118) 8

Euonymus — Hort. Upsal. (7) 21; Vir. pl. (13) 27; Fl. oecon. (17) 5; Noxa insect. (46) 19; Calend. fl. (72) [20]; Fr. Svec. (91) [ii], 23, 25; Pand. insect. (93) 12; Nom. bot. (107) 11

Euonymus europaeus — Demonstr. pl. (49) 6; Fl. Angl. (56) 12; Calend. fl. (72) [10]; Fl. Monsp. (74) 5, 12; Prodr. fl. Dan. (82) 15; Fr. Svec. (91) 3, 6[as europeus]; Fl. Belg. (112) 14

Euonymus latifolius — Demonstr. pl. (49) 6

Euonymus virginianus — Hort. Upsal. (7) 35

Euonymus vulgaris — Gem. arb. (24) 19; Pan Svec. (26) 16; Hosp. insect. fl. (43) 16

Eupatoria virginiana — Vern. arb. (47) 9

Eupatorium — Hort. Upsal. (7) 35; Vir. pl. (13) 23; Specif. Canad. (76) 22; Pl. Jam. (102) 23; Fl. Jam. (105) 26, 27; Fund. fr. (123) 18

Eupatorium cannabinum — Pan Svec. (26) 32; Hosp. insect. fl. (43) 31; Demonstr. pl. (49) 22; Pl. officin. (52) 10; Stat. pl. (55) 13; Fl. Angl. (56) 22; Calend. fl. (72) [16]; Fl. Monsp. (74) 25; Prodr. fl. Dan. (82) 23; Fl. Belg. (112) 21; Purg. indig. (143) 8

Eupatorium coelestinum — Fl. Jam. (105) 19

Eupatorium dalea — Fl. Jam. (105) 19

Eupatorium enulifolium — Demonstr. pl. (49) 22

Eupatorium foliis quinis, lanceolatis, aequaliter serratis, petiolatis, venosis — Cent. I. pl. (65) 27

Eupatorium hastatum — Pl. Jam. (102) 22; Fl. Jam. (105) 19

Eupatorium houstonianum — Pl. Jam. (102) 22

Eupatorium hyssopifolium — Pl. Jam. (102) 22

Eupatorium ivaefolium — Pl. Jam. (102) 22[as ivifolium]; Fl. Jam. (105) 19

Eupatorium maculatum — Cent. I. pl. (65) 27; Calend. fl. (72) [19]

Eupatorium odoratum — Pl. Jam. (102) 22; Fl. Jam. (105) 19[as odorum]

Eupatorium perfoliatum — Calend. fl. (72) [18]; Specif. Canad. (76) 14

Eupatorium purpureum — Demonstr. pl. (49) 22; Cent. I. pl. (65) 27; Calend. fl. (72) [18]; Specif. Canad. (76) 16

Eupatorium scandens — Pl. Jam. (102) 22; Pl. Surin. (177) 14

Euphorbia — Hort. Upsal. (7) 37; Spons. pl. (12) 56; Vir. pl. (13) 12, 21, 25, 27; Oecon. nat. (20) 17, 36; Pan Svec. (26) 7; Pl. hybr. (33) 29; Euphorbia (36) [1], 3ff.; Fl. Angl. (56) 5; Metam. pl. (67) 14; Fl. Monsp. (74) 7; Pand. insect. (93) 14; Aer habit. (106) 20; Nom. bot. (107) 13; Pl. rar. Afr. (115) 4; Mors. serp. (119) 2; Pl. Alstr. (121) 5; Usum hist. nat. (145) 17; Febr. interm. (167) 51; Aphyteia (185) 8, 9

Euphorbia aculeata nuda: angulis tuberosis, spinis interstinctis — Euphorbia (36) 9

Euphorbia aculeata nuda multangularis, aculeis geminatis — Hort. Upsal. (7) 38[as gemminatis]; Euphorbia (36) 7

Euphorbia aculeata nuda multangularis, spinis solitariis subulatis — Euphorbia (36) 8

Euphorbia aculeata nuda quadrangularis — Hort. Upsal. (7) 38

Euphorbia aculeata nuda quinquangularis, aculeis geminatis — Euphorbia (36) 7

Euphorbia aculeata nuda septemangularis, spinis solitariis subulatis floriferis — Euphorbia (36) 9

Euphorbia aculeata seminuda, angulis oblique tuberculatis — Hort. Upsal. (7) 39; Euphorbia (36) 9

Euphorbia aculeata subnuda triangularis articulata, ramis patentibus — Euphorbia (36) 6

Euphorbia aculeata triangularis subnuda articulata, ramis patentibus — Hort. Upsal. (7) 38

Euphorbia amygdaloides — Fl. Angl. (56) 17; Fl. Monsp. (74) 17

Euphorbia canariensis — Demonstr. pl. (49) 13

Euphorbia canariensis quadrilatera et quinquelatera, cerei effigie, ad angulos per crebra intervalla spinis rectis atronitentibus gazellae cornua referentibus armata — Euphorbia (36) 7

Euphorbia canescens — Pl. Surin. (177) 9

Euphorbia caput medusae — Demonstr. pl. (49) 13; Fl. Cap. (99) 8, 14; Aphyteia (185) [5]

Euphorbia cereifolia — Fl. Cap. (99) 14

Euphorbia chamaesyce — Fl. Palaest. (70) 20; Fl. Monsp. (74) 17; Fl. Jam. (105) 17[as camaesyce], 25; Fl. Belg. (112) 17; Hist. nat. Rossia (144) 29

Euphorbia characias — Fl. Angl. (56) 17[as chararias]; Fl. Monsp. (74) 17

Euphorbia cyparissias — Fl. Monsp. (74) 17; Fl. Belg. (112) 10, 17

Euphorbia dichotoma, foliis crenulatis subrotundis, floribus solitariis axillaribus, caulibus procumbentibus — Euphorbia (36) 16

Euphorbia dichotoma, foliis integerrimis lanceolatis, pedunculis axillaribus unifloris folia aequantibus, caule erecto — Euphorbia (36) 17

Euphorbia dichotoma, foliis integerrimis ovalibus retusis, pedunculis axillaribus unifloris folia aequantibus, caule erecto — Euphorbia (36) 18

Euphorbia dichotoma, foliis integerrimis semicordatis, floribus solitariis axillaribus, caulibus procumbentibus — Euphorbia (36) 16

Euphorbia dichotoma, foliis serratis axillaribus ovali oblongis, corymbis terminalibus, ramis divaricatis — Euphorbia (36) 13[as folliis]

Euphorbia dichotoma, foliis serratis ovali-oblongis, capitulis axillaribus glomeratis subsessilibus, caulibus procumbentibus — Euphorbia (36) 15

Euphorbia dichotoma, foliis serratis ovali-oblongis, pedunculis bicapitatis axillaribus, caule erecto — Euphorbia (36) 15

Euphorbia dichotoma, foliis serrulatis ovatis, acuminatis, pedunculis capitatis axillaribus, caulibus pilosis — Euphorbia (36) 14

Euphorbia dichotoma, foliis serrulatis ovatis, obtusis trinervis, panicula terminali, caulibus simplicibus — Euphorbia (36) 14

Euphorbia dulcis — Fl. Monsp. (74) 17

Euphorbia esula — Demonstr. pl. (49) 13; Fl. Monsp. (74) 17

Euphorbia exigua — Fl. Angl. (56) 16; Fl. Monsp. (74) 17; Fl. Belg. (112) 17

Euphorbia foliis crenatis, umbella universali quinquefida, pentaphylla, partialibus trifidis, propriis triphyllis — Euphorbia (36) 26

Euphorbia foliis lanceolatis, umbella universali multifida polyphylla, partialibus trifidis triphyllis, propriis dichotomis — Euphorbia (36) 28

Euphorbia foliis obverse ovatis integerrimis, umbella universali trifida triphylla, partialibus dichotomis diphyllis — Euphorbia (36) 19

Euphorbia foliis oppositis integerrimis lanceolatis obtusis, floribus solitariis axillaribus, caulibus procumbentibus — Euphorbia (36) 17

Euphorbia foliis oppositis subcordatis petiolatis emarginatis integerrimis, petiolis folio longioribus, caule fruticoso — Euphorbia (36) 13

Euphorbia fruticosa — Pan Svec. (26) 25[as fructicosa]

Euphorbia germanica — Somn. pl. (68) 22

Euphorbia helioscopia — Herbat. Upsal. (50) 15; Stat. pl. (55) 19; Fl. Angl. (56) 16; Calend. fl. (72) [22]; Fl. Monsp. (74) 17; Prodr. fl. Dan. (82) 18; Fl. Belg. (112) 17; Fl. Åker. (162) 12

Euphorbia hirta — Herb. Amboin. (57) 26; Fl. Jam. (105) 17

Euphorbia hyberna — Fl. alp. (71) 17; Hist. nat. Rossia (144) 30

Euphorbia hypericifolia — Fl. Jam. (105) 17

Euphorbia hyssopifolia — Fl. Jam. (105) 17

Euphorbia inermis, foliis alternis lanceolatis amplexicaulibus subserratis, umbella universali quinquefida pentaphylla, partialibus bifidis — Euphorbia (36) 25

Euphorbia inermis, foliis alternis linearibus acutis, partialibus umbellulae ovato-rhombeis, petalis bicornibus — Euphorbia (36) 22

Euphorbia inermis, foliis alternis linearibus acutis, umbella universali trifida triphylla, partialibus dichotomis diphyllis — Euphorbia (36) 19

Euphorbia inermis, foliis confertis linearibus, umbella universali multifida, partialibus dichotomis, foliolis subrotundis — Pl. Mart.-Burs. (6) 24[as dicothomis]; Euphorbia (36) 29

Euphorbia inermis, foliis confertis: superioribus reflexis latioribus lanceolatis, umbella universali trifida, partialibus bifidis — Euphorbia (36) 30

Euphorbia inermis, foliis denticulatis: caulinis lanceolatis, umbellularum cordatis — Euphorbia (36) 26

Euphorbia inermis, foliis lanceolatis, involucro universali quinquefido lanceolato, partiali tetraphyllo subrotundo, propriis diphyllis — Euphorbia (36) 25

Euphorbia inermis, foliis lanceolatis obtusis alternis, ramis floriferis dichotomis, petalis maximis subrotundis — Euphorbia (36) 24

Euphorbia inermis, foliis lanceolatis, umbella universali multifida, partialibus dichotomis, involucris semibifidis perfoliatis — Euphorbia (36) 27

Euphorbia inermis, foliis lanceolatis, umbella universali partialiumque prima quinquefidis, secunda trifida, reliquis bifidis — Euphorbia (36) 25

Euphorbia inermis, foliis lanceolato-linearibus; involucri universalis foliolis quinis ovato-acutis, partialis, semiorbiculatis — Euphorbia (36) 28

Euphorbia inermis, foliis linearibus, umbella universali trifida triphylla, partialibus trifidis, propriis dichotomis diphyllis, foliolis subrotundis — Euphorbia (36) 21

Euphorbia inermis, foliis oblongis obtusis emarginatis — Euphorbia (36) 18

Euphorbia inermis, foliis obtusis subcordatis integerrimis petiolatis, caule ramoso erecto — Euphorbia (36) 13

Euphorbia inermis, foliis oppositis lanceolatis integerrimis, umbella universali quadrifida tetraphylla, ulterioribus dichotomis — Euphorbia (36) 20

Euphorbia inermis, foliis oppositis lanceolatis, umbella universali quadrifida tetraphylla, partialibus dichotomis diphyllis — Euphorbia (36) 20

Euphorbia inermis, foliis oppositis oblique cordatis, obtusis serratis, pedunculis multifloris — Euphorbia (36) 15

Euphorbia inermis, foliis oppositis oblique-cordatis, serrulatis uniformibus, ramis alternis, floribus solitariis — Euphorbia (36) 16

Euphorbia inermis, foliis oppositis ovalibus serratis uniformibus, pedunculis capitatis, axillaribus — Euphorbia (36) 15

Euphorbia inermis, foliis ovalibus oppositis serratis uniformibus, ramis alternis, caule teretiusculo — Euphorbia (36) 13

Euphorbia inermis, foliis serratis petiolatis difformibus ovatis lanceolatis panduriformibus — Euphorbia (36) 12

Euphorbia inermis, foliis subrotundis crenatis — Euphorbia (36) 26

Euphorbia inermis fruticosa, foliis distiche alternis ovatis — Euphorbia (36) 12

Euphorbia inermis fruticosa, foliis lanceolatis, involucro universali quinquefido, partialibus trifidis, reliquis dichotomis — Euphorbia (36) 24

Euphorbia inermis fruticosa, foliis lanceolatis oppositis integerrimis, floribus solitariis terminalibus, involucris triphyllis — Euphorbia (36) 21

Euphorbia inermis fruticosa nuda filiformis volubilis, cicatricibus oppositis — Hort. Upsal. (7) 39

Euphorbia inermis fruticosa subnuda filiformis erecta, ramis patulis determinate confertis — Hort. Upsal. (7) 39

Euphorbia inermis fruticosa subnuda filiformis flaccida, foliolis alternis — Hort. Upsal. (7) 39

Euphorbia inermis herbacea ramosa, foliis subcordatis integerrimis petiolo brevioribus, floribus solitariis — Euphorbia (36) 13

Euphorbia inermis imbricata tuberculis foliolo lineari instructis — Euphorbia (36) 10

Euphorbia inermis nuda fruticosa filiformis volubilis, cicatricibus oppositis — Euphorbia (36) 11

Euphorbia inermis subnuda fruticosa filiformis erecta, ramis patulis determinate confertis — Euphorbia (36) 11

Euphorbia inermis subnuda fruticosa filiformis flaccida, foliis alternis — Euphorbia (36) 8

Euphorbia inermis tecta tuberculis imbricatis foliolo lineari instructis — Hort. Upsal. (7) 39

Euphorbia ipecacuanha — Viola ipecac. (176) [4]

Euphorbia lathyris — Demonstr. pl. (49) 13[as lathyrus]; Pl. officin. (52) 7[as lathyrus]; Hort. acad. (63) 19[as latyrus]; Somn. pl. (68) 10; Fl. Monsp. (74) 17

Euphorbia mammillaris — Fl. Cap. (99) 14

Euphorbia mauritanica — Fl. Cap. (99) 14

Euphorbia myrtifolia — Fl. Jam. (105) 17

Euphorbia neriifolia — Demonstr. pl. (49) 13; Herb. Amboin. (57) 16

Euphorbia officinarum — Demonstr. pl. (49) 13; Pl. officin. (52) 10; Fl. Cap. (99) 14[as officinalis]

Euphorbia palustris — Demonstr. pl. (49) 13; Pl. officin. (52) 10; Stat. pl. (55) 15; Fl. Belg. (112) 17; Colon. pl. (158) 6

Euphorbia paralias — Demonstr. pl. (49) 13[as paralius]; Fl. Angl. (56) 17[as paralius]; Fl. Monsp. (74) 17; Fl. Belg. (112) 8, 17

Euphorbia peplis — Pan Svec. (26) 25; Herbat. Upsal. (50) 15; Fl. Angl. (56) 16; Fl. Monsp. (74) 17; Fl. Belg. (112) 17

Euphorbia peplus — Stat. pl. (55) 19; Fl. Angl. (56) 16; Fl. Palaest. (70) 20; Calend. fl. (72) [22]; Fl. Monsp. (74) 17; Prodr. fl. Dan. (82) 18; Fl. Åker. (162) 12

Euphorbia pilosa — Demonstr. pl. (49) 13; Hist. nat. Rossia (144) 30

Euphorbia pithyusa — Fl. Monsp. (74) 17

Euphorbia platyphyllos — Fl. Angl. (56) 16; Fl. Monsp. (74) 17; Fl. Belg. (112) 17

Euphorbia portlandica — Fl. Angl. (56) 16; Fl. Palaest. (70) 20

Euphorbia procumbens, ramulis alternis, foliis lanceolato-linearibus, floribus solitariis — Euphorbia (36) 17

Euphorbia quinquefida bifida, involucellis ovatis mucronatis, foliis lanceolatis: infimis involutis, retrorsum imbricatis — Euphorbia (36) 23

Euphorbia sagittalis — Demonstr. pl. (49) 13

Euphorbia segetalis — Fl. Angl. (56) 16; Fl. Monsp. (74) 17

Euphorbia serrata — Fl. Palaest. (70) 20; Fl. Monsp. (74) 17

Euphorbia solisequia — Pan Svec. (26) 25; Hosp. insect. fl. (43) 26

Euphorbia sylvatica — Fl. Monsp. (74) 17

Euphorbia tuberosa — Fl. Cap. (99) 14

Euphorbia umbella multifida dichotoma, involucellis perfoliatis emarginatis, foliis integerrimis, caule frutescente — Euphorbia (36) 27

Euphorbia umbella multifida dichotoma, involucellis perfoliatis orbiculatis, foliis obtusis — Euphorbia (36) 27

Euphorbia umbella multifida dichotoma, involucellis perfoliatis subcordatis, foliis lanceolatis integerrimis — Euphorbia (36) 27

Euphorbia umbella multifida dichotoma, involucellis subcordatis, primariis triphyllis, caule arborescente — Euphorbia (36) 30

Euphorbia umbella multifida dichotoma, involucellis subcordatis, ramis sterilibus, foliis setaceis caulinis lanceolatis — Euphorbia (36) 29

Euphorbia umbella multifida dichotoma, involucellis subcordatis, ramis sterilibus, foliis uniformibus — Euphorbia (36) 28

Euphorbia umbella multifida trifida dichotoma, involucellis ovatis, foliis lanceolatis, ramis sterilibus — Euphorbia (36) 28

Euphorbia umbella quadrifida dichotoma, foliis oppositis integerrimis — Euphorbia (36) 20

Euphorbia umbella quinquefida bifida, involucellis obverse cordatis — Euphorbia (36) 21

Euphorbia umbella quinquefida bifida, involucellis subovatis, foliis lanceolatis obtusis integerrimis — Euphorbia (36) 23

Euphorbia umbella quinquefida dichotoma, involucellis diphyllis reniformibus, foliis amplexicaulibus cordatis serratis — Euphorbia (36) 26

Euphorbia umbella quinquefida dichotoma, involucellis foliisque oblongis obtusis, petalis membranaceis — Euphorbia (36) 23

Euphorbia umbella quinquefida dichotoma, involucellis ovatis, foliis cuneiformibus, serratis — Euphorbia (36) 26

Euphorbia umbella quinquefida dichotoma, involucellis ovato-lanceolatis mucronatis, foliis inferioribus capillaceis — Euphorbia (36) 23

Euphorbia umbella quinquefida dichotoma, involucellis semiorbiculatis, foliis lineari-lanceolatis, ramis floriferis — Euphorbia (36) 22

Euphorbia umbella quinquefida, quadrifida, dichotoma, involucellis subrotundis ovatis, foliis lanceolatis — Euphorbia (36) 25

Euphorbia umbella quinquefida trifida dichotoma, involucellis ovatis, foliis lanceolatis, capsulis lunatis — Euphorbia (36) 24

Euphorbia umbella quinquefida trifida dichotoma, involucellis primariis tetraphyllis, foliis sessilibus serrulatis — Euphorbia (36) 25

Euphorbia umbella quinquefida trifida dichotoma, involucellis subovatis, foliis lanceolatis, serrulatis, capsulis verrucosis — Euphorbia (36) 21

Euphorbia umbella sexifida bifida, involucellis cordato-reniformibus, foliis sursum imbricatis — Euphorbia (36) 31[as sexfida]

Euphorbia umbella sexifida dichotoma, involucellis ovalibus, foliis oblongis integerrimis, ramis nullis capsulis verrucosis — Euphorbia (36) 29[as folliis]

Euphorbia umbella suboctifida bifida, involucellis subcordatis, foliis spathulatis patentibus carnosis margine scabris — Euphorbia (36) 30

Euphorbia umbella subquinquefida simplici, involucellis ovatis: primariis triphyllis, foliis oblongis integerrimis, caule fruticoso — Euphorbia (36) 21

Euphorbia umbella trifida dichotoma, involucellis cordato-falcatis acutis, foliis lanceolatis obtusiusculis — Euphorbia (36) 19[as dichothoma]

Euphorbia umbella trifida dichotoma, involucellis lanceolatis, foliis linearibus — Euphorbia (36) 19

Euphorbia umbella trifida dichotoma, involucris ovatis, foliis integerrimis ovatis petiolatis — Euphorbia (36) 18

Euphorbia umbella trifida involucro tetraphyllo, caule nudo, foliis oblongis emarginatis — Euphorbia (36) 18

Euphorbia verrucosa — Demonstr. pl. (49) 13; Fl. Angl. (56) 16; Fl. Monsp. (74) 17

Euphorbia viminalis — Demonstr. pl. (49) 13; Fl. Palaest. (70) 20; Fl. Cap. (99) 14

Euphorbio-tithymalus spinosus, caule rotundo et anguloso, nerii foliis latioribus et angustioribus — Euphorbia (36) 9

Euphorbium — Euphorbia (36) 8

Euphorbium afrum spinosum, foliis latioribus non spinosis — Euphorbia (36) 9

Euphorbium anacanthum squamosum, lobis florum tridentatis — Euphorbia (36) 10

Euphorbium antiquorum verum — Euphorbia (36) 7

Euphorbium aphyllum angulosum, florum coma densissima — Euphorbia (36) 8

Euphorbium cerei effigie, caulibus crassioribus, spinis validioribus armatum — Euphorbia (36) 8

Euphorbium cerei effigie, caulibus gracilioribus — Euphorbia (36) 8

Euphorbium erectum aphyllum, ramis rotundis, tuberculis tetragonis — Euphorbia (36) 10

Euphorbium heptagonum, spinis longissimis, in apice frugiferis — Euphorbia (36) 9

Euphorbium humile procumbens, ramis simplicibus copiosis, caule crassissimo, tuberoso — Euphorbia (36) 10

Euphorbium polygonum, aculeis longioribus ex tuberculorum internodiis prodeuntibus — Euphorbia (36) 9

Euphorbium polygonum spinosum, cerei effigie — Euphorbia (36) 8

Euphorbium procumbens, ramis geminatis, caule glabro oblongo cinereo — Euphorbia (36) 11

Euphorbium procumbens, ramis plurimis simplicibus squamosis, foliis deciduis — Euphorbia (36) 10

Euphorbium spinosum, amplo nerii folio — Euphorbia (36) 9

Euphorbium trigonum et tetragonum spinosum, ramis compressis — Euphorbia (36) 7

Euphorbium trigonum spinosum rotundifolium — Euphorbia (36) 7

Euphrasia — Cent. II. pl. (66) 22; Nom. bot. (107) 15

Euphrasia latifolia — Fl. Monsp. (74) 20

Euphrasia lignosa praealta, amplo linariae aut dracunculi hortensis folio — Pl. Mart.-Burs. (6) 19

Euphrasia linifolia — Fl. Monsp. (74) 20

Euphrasia lutea — Fl. Monsp. (74) 20

Euphrasia minor — Pl. Mart.-Burs. (6) 19

Euphrasia odontites — Pan Svec. (26) 27; Herbat. Upsal. (50) 13; Stat. pl. (55) 22; Fl. Angl. (56) 19; Fl. Monsp. (74) 20; Prodr. fl. Dan. (82) 20; Fl. Belg. (112) 19; Pand. fl. Ryb. (165) 20

Euphrasia officinalis — Pl. Mart.-Burs. (6) 19; Herbat. Upsal. (50) 6; Pl. officin. (52) 10; Fl. Angl. (56) 19; Calend. fl. (72) [12]; Fl. Monsp. (74) 20; Prodr. fl. Dan. (82) 20; Fl. Belg. (112) 19; Fl. Åker. (162) 15; Pand. fl. Ryb. (165) 20

Euphrasia vulgaris — Pan Svec. (26) 27

Exacum — Nova pl. gen. 1747 (14) [vi], 6, 7; Fl. Cap. (99) 6

Exacum sessile — Fl. Cap. (99) 12

Exocoetus — Mus. Ad.-Frid. (11) 42

Exocoetus volans — Nat. pelagi (84) 11

Faba — Vir. pl. (13) 23, 31, 32; Cul. mut. (88) 2, 6; Instr. peregr. (96) 10; Nom. bot. (107) 16

Faba americana — Rar. Norv. (157) 13

Faba ignatii — Sapor. med. (31) 18

Faba indica — Rar. Norv. (157) 13

Faba marina — Herb. Amboin. (57) 18

Fagara — Fl. Jam. (105) 26

Fagara octandra — Obs. mat. med. (171) 7

Fagara pterota — Pl. Jam. (102) 8; Fl. Jam. (105) 13

Fagonia — Cryst. gen. (15) 20

Fagonia arabica — Fl. Palaest. (70) 19

Fagonia cretica — Fl. Palaest. (70) 19

Fagopyrum — Sapor. med. (31) 16; Pl. escul. (35) 15; Vern. arb. (47) 9; Pane diaet. (83) 11; Nom. bot. (107) 12

Fagus — Spons. pl. (12) 41; Vir. pl. (13) 7; Fl. oecon. (17) 24; Gem. arb. (24) 30; Pan Svec. (26) 36; Pl. escul. (35) 24, 27, 29; Hosp. insect. fl. (43) 40; Noxa insect. (46) 25; Vern. arb. (47) 9, 10; Hort. acad. (63) 14; Chin. Lagerstr. (64) 5; Pand. insect. (93) 20; Nom. bot. (107) 18; Ping. anim. (108) 16; Polit. nat. (109) 5; Prol. pl. 1763 (130) 6; Usum musc. (148) 7, 12; Erica (163) 12

Fagus castanea — Hosp. insect. fl. (43) 35; Pl. officin. (52) 7; Fl. Monsp. (74) 27; Pane diaet. (83) 20; Fr. escul. (127) 21

Fagus sylvatica — Hosp. insect. fl. (43) 35; Demonstr. pl. (49) 25; Pl. officin. (52) 10; Stat. pl. (55) 17; Fl. Angl. (56) 24; Calend. fl. (72) [10]; Fl. Monsp. (74) 27; Prodr. fl. Dan. (82) 24; Arb. Svec. (101) 7, 9, 22; Fl. Belg. (112) 22; Prol. pl. 1763 (130) 8; Fl. Åker. (162) 19

Falcata — Hort. Upsal. (7) 35

Falco — Oecon. nat. (20) 44; Noxa insect. (46) 31; Migr. avium (79) 19, 20; Instr. peregr. (96) 11; Polit. nat. (109) 16; Fund. ornith. (137) 25; Usum hist. nat. (145) 25

Falco aeruginosus — Migr. avium (79) 19

Falco tinnunculus — Calend. fl. (72) [9][as tinunculus]; Migr. avium (79) 34; Fund. ornith. (137) 26

Fasciola — Taenia (19) 10, 11; Hirudo (136) 2; Lepra (140) 11

Fasciola hepatica — Usum hist. nat. (145) 22; Rar. Norv. (157) 18

Fasciola nigra — Rar. Norv. (157) 18

Fascum acaulon — Herbat. Upsal. (50) 18

Felis — Oecon. nat. (20) 46; Mat. med. anim. (29) 3; Morb. hyeme (38) 12; Polit. nat. (109) 18; Menthae (153) 5

Felis cauda elongata, auribus aequalibus — Mat. med. anim. (29) 3

Felis lynx — Usum hist. nat. (145) 23

Felis tigris — Usum hist. nat. (145) 23

Feniseca — Calend. fl. (72) [15][as Faeniseca], [16][as Foeniseca], [17][as Foeniseca]

Ferraria — Fl. Cap. (99) 9; Aphyteia (185) 6

Ferrum equinum gallicum, siliquis in summitate — Cent. II. pl. (66) 28

Ferrum equinum volubile — Passifl. (8) 26

Ferula — Gem. arb. (24) 13; Obs. mat. med. (171) 8

Ferula assa foetida — Pl. officin. (52) 5

Ferula canadensis — Demonstr. pl. (49) 8

Ferula communis — Fl. Monsp. (74) 13

Ferula nodiflora — Fl. Monsp. (74) 13

Festuca — Vir. pl. (13) 17; Fl. oecon. (17) 3; Oecon. nat. (20) 36; Pan Svec. (26) 6, 10, 11; Splachnum (27) 2[as Ffstuca]; Pl. escul. (35) 27; Cui bono? (42) 17; Fl. alp. (71) 8; Pand. insect. (93) 11; Anim. comp. (98) 6; Pl. Jam. (102) 7; Fund. agrost. (152) 16, 29, 31, 37

Festuca altera, capitulis duris — Pl. Mart.-Burs. (6) 5

Festuca amethystina — Fl. Angl. (56) 11

Festuca aquatica — Pl. escul. (35) 7

Festuca avenaceum dumetorum — Fl. Angl. (56) 29

Festuca barbata — Demonstr. pl. (49) 3; Cent. I. pl. (65) 2

Festuca bromoides — Fl. Angl. (56) 11

Festuca culmo spicato, spiculis multifloris — Pl. rar. Camsch. (30) 6

Festuca decumbens — Stat. pl. (55) 14; Fl. Angl. (56) 10; Prodr. fl. Dan. (82) 13; Fund. agrost. (152) 7; Esca avium (174) 10

Festuca duriuscula — Fl. Angl. (56) 10

Festuca elatior — Stat. pl. (55) 21; Fl. Angl. (56) 29; Prodr. fl. Dan. (82) 13; Fund. agrost. (152) 7, 31; Fl. Åker. (162) 6; Esca avium (174) 10

Festuca fluitans — Herbat. Upsal. (50) 14; Stat. pl. (55) 13; Fl. Angl. (56) 10; Fl. Monsp. (74) 9; Prodr. fl. Dan. (82) 13; Fl. Belg. (112) 13; Fund. agrost. (152) 7, 31; Fl. Åker. (162) 7; Esca avium (174) 10

Festuca fusca — Fl. Palaest. (70) 13

Festuca graminea arvensis minor — Pl. Mart.-Burs. (6) 5

Festuca graminea, effusa juba — Pl. Mart.-Burs. (6) 4

Festuca marginibus agrorum — Pan Svec. (26) 14

Festuca myuros — Fl. Angl. (56) 11[as myurus]; Fl. Palaest. (70) 12

Festuca natans — Pan Svec. (26) 14; Fr. escul. (127) 20

Festuca ovina — Pan Svec. (26) 14; Herbat. Upsal. (50) 10[as Festua]; Stat. pl. (55) 16, 21; Fl. Angl. (56) 10; Oves (61) 15; Prodr. fl. Dan. (82) 13; Arb. Svec. (101) 10; Fl. Belg. (112) 13; Usum hist. nat. (145) 21; Fund. agrost. (152) 6, 7, 10; Fl. Åker. (162) 6; Erica (163) 12; Pand. fl. Ryb. (165) 16

Festuca ovina vivipara — Demonstr. pl. (49) 3; Fl. alp. (71) 12

Festuca panicula contracta, spiculis linearibus; calyce flosculis longiore, foliis basi barbatis — Demonstr. pl. (49) 3

Festuca panicula secunda coarctata aristata, culmo tetragono nudiusculo, foliis setaceis — Pl. Mart.-Burs. (6) [1]

Festuca panicula secunda scabra, spiculis septifloris aristatis, flosculo ultimo mutico, culmo laevi — Pl. Mart.-Burs. (6) 2[as Festicca]

Festuca paniculis confertis — Fl. Angl. (56) 29

Festuca reptatrix — Fl. Palaest. (70) 13

Festuca rubra — Pan Svec. (26) 14; Herbat. Upsal. (50) 14; Fl. Monsp. (74) 9; Fl. Åker. (162) 6; Pand. fl. Ryb. (165) 16

Festuca spicis erectis — Fl. Angl. (56) 29

Festuca triticea — Pan Svec. (26) 14

Festuca vivipara — Pan Svec. (26) 14

Fevillea — Nect. fl. (122) 8[as Fewillea]

Fevillea cordifolia — Fl. Jam. (105) 22

Fiber seu castor — Mat. med. anim. (29) 4

Ficaria — Ficus (2) 17

Ficedula — Vir. pl. (13) 7; Migr. avium (79) 33

Ficoides africana annua minima muscosa — Pl. rar. Afr. (115) 10

Ficus — Ficus (2) [iv]ff.; Peloria (3) 14; Hort. Upsal. (7) 35; Spons. pl. (12) [2], 50; Vir. pl. (13) 7, 10,

25, 32; Sem. musc. (28) 3; Sapor. med. (31) 16; Pl. escul. (35) 3, 4; Vern. arb. (47) 9; Pl. officin. (52) 4; Herb. Amboin. (57) 13, 17; Phalaena (78) 5; Pand. insect. (93) [23, as 31]; Nom. bot. (107) 19; Inebr. (117) 13; Nect. fl. (122) 4; Opobals. (135) [1]; Fraga (170) 7

Ficus americana, folio citri obtuso, fructu sanguineo — Ficus (2) 4

Ficus americana, folio citri subrotundo, fructu umbilicato — Ficus (2) 5

Ficus americana, folio latiori venoso — Ficus (2) 6

Ficus arbor americana, arbuti foliis non serrata, fructu pisi magnitudine, funiculis e ramis ad terram demissis prolifera — Ficus (2) 4

Ficus benghalensis — Herb. Amboin. (57) 13

Ficus benghalensis, folio subrotundo, fructu orbiculato — Ficus (2) 5

Ficus carica — Hosp. insect. fl. (43) 39; Demonstr. pl. (49) 27; Pl. officin. (52) 7; Fl. Palaest. (70) 32; Calend. fl. (72) [19]; Fl. Monsp. (74) 29; Fl. Jam. (105) 24; Fr. escul. (127) 7; Hort. cul. (132) 21

Ficus communis — Ficus (2) 1

Ficus cypria — Ficus (2) 3

Ficus dactyloides major, folio subtus argenteo — Ficus (2) 7

Ficus foliis cordatis integerrimis acuminatis — Ficus (2) 6

Ficus foliis cordatis repandis, fructu sessili — Ficus (2) 3

Ficus foliis cordatis subrotundis integerrimis — Ficus (2) 3

Ficus foliis lanceolatis integerrimis — Ficus (2) 6

Ficus foliis lauri, fructu maximo vel minori — Ficus (2) 5

Ficus foliis ovatis acutis integerrimis, caule arboreo, fructu racemoso — Ficus (2) 6

Ficus foliis ovatis acutis integerrimis, caule repente — Ficus (2) 6

Ficus foliis ovatis integerrimis obtusis — Ficus (2) 5

Ficus foliis ovatis obtusis integerrimis, caule inferne radicato — Ficus (2) 5

Ficus foliis ovato-cordatis integris, fructu racemoso — Ficus (2) 3

Ficus foliis palmatis — Ficus (2) 1

Ficus foliis robustioribus et ramis erectioribus — Ficus (2) 2

Ficus folio citri acutiore, fructu viridi — Ficus (2) 7

Ficus folio mori, fructum in caudice ferens — Ficus (2) 3

Ficus folio sycomori, fructum non in caudice gerens — Ficus (2) 3

Ficus humilis — Ficus (2) 2, 7

Ficus indica — Ficus (2) 4; Herb. Amboin. (57) 13; Fl. Jam. (105) 22

Ficus indica arcuata — Ficus (2) 4

Ficus indica, fibris ex ipso trunco exeuntibus eique accrescentibus augens — Ficus (2) 5

Ficus indica, foliis mali cotoneae similibus, fructu ficubus simili in goa — Ficus (2) 4

Ficus indica, folio acuminato minore atrovirente, fructu sphaerico, pallide luteo, cerasi magnitudine in summitate aperto — Ficus (2) 5

Ficus indica, folio oblongo, fructu minore pallide luteo sphaerico — Ficus (2) 5

Ficus indica maxima, cortice nigricante, folio oblongo, funiculis e summis ramis demissis, et radices agentibus se propagans, fructu caprificus — Ficus (2) 5

Ficus indica maxima, folio oblongo, funiculis, e summis ramis demissis, radices agentibus, se propagans, fructu minori sphaerico sanguineo — Ficus (2) 4

Ficus malabarica, foliis asperis, fructu rotundo lanuginoso majore — Ficus (2) 6

Ficus malabarica, foliis rigidis, fructu rotundo lanuginoso flavescente cerasi magnitudine — Ficus (2) 6

Ficus malabarica folio et fructu minore — Ficus (2) 6

Ficus malabarica, folio mali cotoneae, fructu exiguo plano rotundo sanguineo — Ficus (2) 6

Ficus malabarica, fructu ribesii forma et magnitudine — Ficus (2) 5

Ficus malabarica semel in anno fructifera, fructu minimo — Ficus (2) 6

Ficus malabariensis, folio crassiusculo majori, fructu gemino intense rubente — Ficus (2) 5

Ficus malabariensis, folio cuspidato, fructu rotundo parvo gemino — Ficus (2) 6

Ficus malabariensis, folio oblongo acuminato, fructu vulgari aemulo — Ficus (2) 6

Ficus nunquam maturescens — Ficus (2) 3

Ficus nymphaeae folio — Ficus (2) 3

Ficus perforata — Pl. Surin. (177) 17

Ficus pharaonis — Ficus (2) 3

Ficus pumila — Ficus (2) 2, 7; Herb. Amboin. (57) 13

Ficus quae arbor peregrina, fructum ficui similem gerens — Ficus (2) 6

Ficus racemosa — Herb. Amboin. (57) 13

Ficus religiosa — Herb. Amboin. (57) 13

Ficus sativa — Ficus (2) 1, 16; Gem. arb. (24) 31

Ficus sativa, fructu atro-rubente, polline caesio asperso — Ficus (2) 2

Ficus sativa, fructu flavescente intus et extra — Ficus (2) 2

Ficus sativa, fructu flavescente intus suave rubente — Ficus (2) 2

Ficus sativa, fructu globoso albido omnium minimo — Ficus (2) 2

Ficus sativa, fructu globoso albo mellifluo — Ficus (2) 1, 20

Ficus sativa, fructu globoso atro rubente intus purpureo: cute firma — Ficus (2) 2

Ficus sativa, fructu longo majori nigro intus albo serotino — Ficus (2) 2

Ficus sativa, fructu longo majori nigro intus purpurascente — Ficus (2) 2

Ficus sativa, fructu majori violaceo oblongo: cute lacera — Ficus (2) 2

Ficus sativa, fructu minori violaceo oblongo: cute lacera — Ficus (2) 2

Ficus sativa, fructu oblongo albo mellifluo — Ficus (2) 1, 20

Ficus sativa, fructu parvo fusco intus rubente — Ficus (2) 2

Ficus sativa, fructu parvo serotino albido intus roseo mellifluo: cute lacera — Ficus (2) 2, 20

Ficus sativa, fructu praecoci albido fugaci — Ficus (2) 2

Ficus sativa, fructu praecoci, pallide virenti, intus roseo — Ficus (2) 1

Ficus sativa, fructu praecoci subrotundo albido striato intus roseo — Ficus (2) 1

Ficus sativa, fructu violaceo longo intus rubente — Ficus (2) 2, 20

Ficus sativa, fructu viridi: longo pediculo insidente — Ficus (2) 2

Ficus semel quotannis ferens poma conica grandiuscula et viridia — Ficus (2) 2

Ficus semel quotannis ferens poma parva luteola — Ficus (2) 2

Ficus septica — Herb. Amboin. (57) 13

Ficus sycomorus — Fl. Palaest. (70) 32[as cycomorus]; Fr. escul. (127) 8

Ficus sycomorus foliis minoribus — Ficus (2) 4

Ficus sylvestris — Ficus (2) 2

Ficus sylvestris procumbens, folio simplici — Ficus (2) 6

Ficus trigonata — Pl. Surin. (177) 17

Filago — Fund. fr. (123) 23

Filago acaulis — Demonstr. pl. (49) 24

Filago arvensis — Fl. Monsp. (74) 26; Fl. Belg. (112) 21

Filago dichotoma — Demonstr. pl. (49) 24

Filago gallica — Fl. Angl. (56) 23; Fl. Monsp. (74) 26

Filago germanica — Fl. Belg. (112) 21

Filago maritima — Fl. Angl. (56) 23; Fl. Monsp. (74) 26

Filago montana — Fl. Angl. (56) 23; Fl. Monsp. (74) 26; Prodr. fl. Dan. (82) 23; Pand. fl. Ryb. (165) 22

Filago pygmaea — Fl. Monsp. (74) 26

Filago pyramidata — Fl. Angl. (56) 23; Fl. Monsp. (74) 26; Prodr. fl. Dan. (82) 23

Filicifolia phyllitis parva saxatilis virginiana per summitates foliorum radicosa — Pl. rar. Camsch. (30) 5

Filicis humilis species segmentis longis et angustis — Acrostichum (10) 12

Filicula — Acrostichum (10) 7

Filicula saxatilis corniculata — Acrostichum (10) 10[as saxalis]

Filipendula — Fl. oecon. (17) 13; Pan Svec. (26) 2; Pl. rar. Camsch. (30) 20; Pl. escul. (35) 27; Nom. bot. (107) 13; Ping. anim. (108) 15

Filipendula molon — Pan Svec. (26) 24; Pl. escul. (35) 17; Hosp. insect. fl. (43) 24

Filipendula ulmaria — Pan Svec. (26) 24; Hosp. insect. fl. (43) 24; Cervus (60) 7

Filix — Acrostichum (10) 7; Nom. bot. (107) 19

Filix africana floridae similis in ambitu foliorum argute denticulata — Acrostichum (10) 16

Filix albissimo pulvere conspersa — Acrostichum (10) 13

Filix amboinica — Herb. Amboin. (57) 26

Filix americana aurea maxima non ramosa, alis integris alternis planis — Acrostichum (10) 14

Filix aquatica — Herb. Amboin. (57) 26

Filix arborea — Acrostichum (10) 10

Filix calamaria — Herb. Amboin. (57) 27

Filix corniculata — Acrostichum (10) 10

Filix esculenta — Herb. Amboin. (57) 26

Filix florida — Acrostichum (10) 7; Herb. Amboin. (57) 26

Filix foemina — Acrostichum (10) 6, 8

Filix jamaicensis non ramosa trifolia angustifolia, caule levi — Acrostichum (10) 15

Filix mariana, osmundae facie, racemifera — Nova pl. gen. 1751 (32) 34

Filix mariana, pinnulis seminiferis angustissimis — Acrostichum (10) 15

Filix mas — Acrostichum (10) 6, 8

Filix minor ruffa lanugine tota obducta, in pinnas tantum divisa raras non crenatas subrotundas — Acrostichum (10) 17

Filix non ramosa, foliis integris non serratis, maxima, indiae orientalis — Acrostichum (10) 14

Filix non ramosa major, caule nigro, surculis raris, pinnulis angustis raris longis dentatis — Acrostichum (10) 16

Filix non ramosa minima, caule nigro, surculis raris, pinnulis angustis raris brevibus acutis, subtus niveis — Acrostichum (10) 13

Filix non ramosa minor, caule nigro, surculis raris, pinnulis angustis dentatis raris brevibus acutis, subtus niveis — Acrostichum (10) 13

Filix palustris aurea, foliis linguae cervinae — Acrostichum (10) 14

Filix polypodium dicta minima jamaicensis, foliis aversa parte pulvere, asplenii ritu, circumquaque respersis — Acrostichum (10) 12

Filix polypodium dicta minima virginiana platyneuros — Acrostichum (10) 13

Filix pulverulenta, pinnis obtuse dentatis — Acrostichum (10) 16

Filix saxatilis — Acrostichum (10) 10

Filix scandens, nummulariae folio — Acrostichum (10) 9

Filix simpliciter pinnatis foliis — Acrostichum (10) 14

Flagellaria — Vir. pl. (13) 16; Nova pl. gen. 1747 (14) [vi], 13; Fund. agrost. (152) 4

Flagellaria indica — Herb. Amboin. (57) 20

Flamma sylvarum — Herb. Amboin. (57) 16

Flamma sylvarum peregrinorum — Herb. Amboin. (57) 16

Flammula — Pan Svec. (26) 9; Raphania (126) 14

Flori passionis seu granadillae affinis coanenepilli — Passifl. (8) 26

Flos ambervalis, floribus luteis in capitulum oblongum congestis — Rad. senega (23) 17

Flos caeruleus — Herb. Amboin. (57) 19

Flos cardinalis — Herb. Amboin. (57) 24

Flos convolutus — Herb. Amboin. (57) 16

Flos cuspidum — Herb. Amboin. (57) 10

Flos festalis — Herb. Amboin. (57) 15

Flos flavus — Herb. Amboin. (57) 16

Flos globosus — Herb. Amboin. (57) 22

Flos horarius — Herb. Amboin. (57) 15

Flos impius — Herb. Amboin. (57) 22

Flos manilhanus — Herb. Amboin. (57) 16

Flos manorae — Herb. Amboin. (57) 19

Flos passionalis, flore viridi — Passifl. (8) 21

Flos passionis — Passifl. (8) 3ff.

Flos passionis albus, folio ibisci sericeo trilobato — Passifl. (8) 18

Flos passionis albus reticulatus — Passifl. (8) 19

Flos passionis altheae foliis magis serratis — Passifl. (8) 18

Flos passionis altheae folio lanuginoso, flore decapetalo parvo albo, filamentis purpuro-violaceis — Passifl. (8) 18

Flos passionis altheae folio lanuginoso, foetidus, flore decapetalo et filamentis ex albo et purpureo colore variegatis — Passifl. (8) 19

Flos passionis altheae folio lanuginoso longiore, foetidus, flore decapetalo et filamentis niveis, fructu vesicario — Passifl. (8) 19

Flos passionis campanulatus pentaphyllus — Passifl. (8) 28

Flos passionis curassavicus, folio glabro trilobato et angusto, flore flavescente omnium minimo — Passifl. (8) 20

Flos passionis curassavicus, hederae folio hirsuto, flore albo — Passifl. (8) 18

Flos passionis curassavicus, hederae hirsuto folio, flore purpureo variegato — Passifl. (8) 19

Flos passionis flore et fructu omnium minimis — Passifl. (8) 20

Flos passionis, flore luteo — Passifl. (8) 16

Flos passionis, flore viridi — Passifl. (8) 16

Flos passionis folii media lacinia quasi abscissa, flore minore carneo — Passifl. (8) 13

Flos passionis foliis integris glabris, macula lutea in medio secundum longitudinem notatis — Passifl. (8) 25

Flos passionis foliis trilobis, lobis in acutum mucronem abeuntibus — Passifl. (8) 27

Flos passionis folio hederaceo anguloso foetido — Passifl. (8) 19

Flos passionis folio tripartito — Passifl. (8) 19

Flos passionis fructu rubicundissimo, folio vitis non inciso — Passifl. (8) 29

Flos passionis hederae folio, floribus parvis herbaceis, fructu minimo nigro — Passifl. (8) 16

Flos passionis hirsuto folio, flore purpureo variegato — Passifl. (8) 19

Flos passionis major pentaphyllus — Passifl. (8) 23

Flos passionis minor, foliis in tres lacinias non serratas profundius divisis, flore luteo — Passifl. (8) 17

Flos passionis minor, folio in tres lacinias non serratas minus profundas diviso — Passifl. (8) 16

Flos passionis pentaphyllus major angustifolius sempervirens — Passifl. (8) 29

Flos passionis perfoliatus, seu periclymeni perfoliati folio — Passifl. (8) 12

Flos passionis sparius malabaricus — Passifl. (8) 30

Flos passionis trifido folio angusto, flore amplo decapetalo albo, filamentis purpuro caeruleis — Passifl. (8) 27

Flos passionis trifido folio, flore minimo pentapetalo viridi, fructu minimo nigro molli — Passifl. (8) 20

Flos pergulanus — Herb. Amboin. (57) 19

Flos susannae — Herb. Amboin. (57) 22

Flos triplicatus — Herb. Amboin. (57) 27

Flustra — Mund. invis. (149) 8

Foeniculum — Acetaria (77) 10; Nom. bot. (107) 11

Foeniculum fasciatum — Cul. mut. (88) 7

Foenum-graecum — Sapor. med. (31) 12

Folium acidum majus — Herb. Amboin. (57) 12

Folium acidum minus — Herb. Amboin. (57) 12

Folium baggea maritimum — Herb. Amboin. (57) 18

Folium baggea verum — Herb. Amboin. (57) 18

Folium bracteatum — Herb. Amboin. (57) 16

Folium buccinatum — Herb. Amboin. (57) 20

Folium calcosum — Herb. Amboin. (57) 17

Folium caussonis — Herb. Amboin. (57) 24[as causonis]

Folium crocodili — Herb. Amboin. (57) 17

Folium hircinum — Herb. Amboin. (57) 14

Folium intinctus — Herb. Amboin. (57) 14

Folium linguae — Herb. Amboin. (57) 18

Folium lunatum — Herb. Amboin. (57) 18

Folium mappae — Herb. Amboin. (57) 14

Folium mensarium — Herb. Amboin. (57) 20

Folium petolatum — Herb. Amboin. (57) 27[petiolatum?]

Folium politorium — Herb. Amboin. (57) 17

Folium polypi — Herb. Amboin. (57) 16

Folium principissae — Nova pl. gen. 1747 (14) 11; Herb. Amboin. (57) 17

Folium tinctorum — Herb. Amboin. (57) 26

Folium urens — Herb. Amboin. (57) 15

Fontinalis — Splachnum (27) 5, 6; Sem. musc. (28) 6, 17

Fontinalis antipyretica — Herbat. Upsal. (50) 13; Stat. pl. (55) 13; Prodr. fl. Dan. (82) 25; Usum musc. (148) 10

Fontinalis minor — Prodr. fl. Dan. (82) 25

Forficula — Noxa insect. (46) 10; Pand. insect. (93) 6; Fund. entom. (154) 21

Forficula auriculata — Pand. fl. Ryb. (165) 10

Formica — Oecon. nat. (20) 26; Lign. colubr. (21) 5; Noxa insect. (46) 10, 13, 22; Chin. Lagerstr. (64) 34; Pand. insect. (93) 8; Pl. tinct. (97) 29; Polit. nat. (109) 21; Usum hist. nat. (145) 25, 27; Mund. invis. (149) 10; Fund. entom. (154) 22, 23, 24

Formica binodis — Cent. insect. (129) 30

Formica caespitum — Pand. fl. Ryb. (165) 14

Formica fusca — Pand. fl. Ryb. (165) 14; Esca avium (174) 8

Formica herculeana — Esca avium (174) 8

Formica leone — Metam. pl. (67) 6

Formica media rubra — Mat. med. anim. (29) 16

Formica nigra — Pand. fl. Ryb. (165) 14

Formica nigra, abdomine glaberrimo segmentis duobus primis subglobosis — Cent. insect. (129) 30

Formica obsoleta — Pand. fl. Ryb. (165) 14

Formica rubra — Pand. fl. Ryb. (165) 14; Esca avium (174) 8

Formica rufa — Mat. med. anim. (29) 16; Pand. fl. Ryb. (165) 13; Esca avium (174) 3, 8

Formicaleo — Fund. entom. (154) 29

Forsskålea — Opobals. (135) 17

Forsskålea tenacissima — Opobals. (135) 18

Fragaria — Ficus (2) 12, 18; Vir. pl. (13) 21, 27, 33; Fl. oecon. (17) 14; Sapor. med. (31) 15; Pl. escul. (35) 18, 28; Calend. fl. (72) [13]; Pand. insect. (93) 16; Nom. bot. (107) 14; Prol. pl. 1760 (114) 5; Nect. fl. (122) 6; Fund. fr. (123) 20, 23; Fraga (170) [1]ff.

Fragaria caule decumbente ramis floriferis laxis — Fraga (170) 4

Fragaria chiloensis — Fr. escul. (127) 4; Fraga (170) 4

Fragaria flagellis reptantibus — Fraga (170) 4

Fragaria muricata — Fraga (170) 5

Fragaria pratensis — Fr. escul. (127) 4

Fragaria sativa — Demonstr. pl. (49) 14

Fragaria sterilis — Fl. Angl. (56) 17; Fl. Monsp. (74) 18; Fraga (170) 4

Fragaria vesca — Herbat. Upsal. (50) 7; Pl. officin. (52) 10; Fl. Angl. (56) 17; Fl. Monsp. (74) 18; Prodr. fl. Dan. (82) 19; Fl. Cap. (99) 2; Fl. Jam. (105) 24; Fl. Belg. (112) 17; Fr. escul. (127) 3; Hort. cul. (132) 19; Fl. Åker. (162) 13; Pand. fl. Ryb. (165) 19; Fraga (170) 3, 4, 5; Esca avium (174) 13

Fragaria vesca pratensis — Fraga (170) 5, 6

Fragaria vesca sylvestris — Fraga (170) 5, 6

Fragaria vulgaris — Pan Svec. (26) 24; Hosp. insect. fl. (43) 25

Fragarius niger — Herb. Amboin. (57) 17

Fragarius ruber — Herb. Amboin. (57) 17

Frangula — Vir. pl. (13) 27; Vern. arb. (47) 10; Arb. Svec. (101) 21; Prol. pl. 1760 (114) 4

Frankenia — Erica (163) 2

Frankenia hirsuta — Fl. Palaest. (70) 18

Frankenia laevis — Fl. Angl. (56) 14; Fl. Monsp. (74) 14

Frankenia pulverulenta — Demonstr. pl. (49) 10; Fl. Angl. (56) 6, 14; Fl. Palaest. (70) 18; Calend. fl. (72) [16]; Fl. Monsp. (74) 14

Fraxinus — Spons. pl. (12) 41; Fl. oecon. (17) 28; Oecon. nat. (20) 17; Hosp. insect. fl. (43) 40; Vern. arb. (47) 10, 11, table; Oves (61) 18; Calend. fl. (72) [10], [20]; Pand. insect. (93) [23, as 31]; Arb. Svec. (101) 17, 30; Nom. bot. (107) 19; Prol. pl. 1763 (130) 8; Usum musc. (148) 12

Fraxinus americana — Demonstr. pl. (49) 27

Fraxinus apetala — Gem. arb. (24) 19; Pan Svec. (26) [37, as 39]; Hosp. insect. fl. (43) 39

Fraxinus excelsior — Pl. officin. (52) 10[as exelsior]; Stat. pl. (55) 17; Fl. Angl. (56) 25; Calend. fl. (72) [10]; Fl. Monsp. (74) 29; Prodr. fl. Dan. (82) 25; Pl. tinct. (97) 26; Arb. Svec. (101) 8, 17; Fl. Belg. (112) 23; Meloe (124) 4; Fl. Åker. (162) 20; Pand. fl. Ryb. (165) 22; Febr. interm. (167) 42

Fraxinus foliolis serratis, floribus corollatis — Med. purg. (181) 24

Fraxinus ornus — Demonstr. pl. (49) 27; Pl. officin. (52) 12; Med. purg. (181) 24

Fraxinus petalodes — Gem. arb. (24) 19

Fringilla — Oecon. nat. (20) 40; Morb. hyeme (38) 3; Migr. avium (79) 33; Usum hist. nat. (145) 25

Fringilla canaria — Fund. fr. (123) 14

Fringilla cannabina — Migr. avium (79) 34

Fringilla carduelis — Migr. avium (79) 34

Fringilla coelebs — Migr. avium (79) 33[as celebs]

Fringilla domestica — Migr. avium (79) 34

Fringilla hiemalis — Migr. avium (79) 15

Fringilla linaria — Migr. avium (79) 34

Fringilla montifringilla — Migr. avium (79) 34

Fringilla oryzivora — Migr. avium (79) 15

Fringilla purpurea — Migr. avium (79) 16

Fringilla spinus — Migr. avium (79) 34; Fund. fr. (123) 14

Fritillaria — Hort. Upsal. (7) 33; Spons. pl. (12) 29, 32, 43, 44; Vir. pl. (13) 20; Hort. acad. (63) 3; Prol. pl. 1760 (114) 13; Nect. fl. (122) 11

Fritillaria imperialis — Demonstr. pl. (49) 10; Calend. fl. (72) [10], [11]; Pl. Alstr. (121) 5; Hort. cul. (132) 23; Cimicifuga (173) 9

Fritillaria meleagris — Demonstr. pl. (49) 10; Herbat. Upsal. (50) 14; Calend. fl. (72) [10], [11]; Pl. rar. Afr. (115) 6; Pl. Alstr. (121) 5; Hort. cul. (132) 23; Colon. pl. (158) 9; Fl. Åker. (162) 10

Fritillaria persica — Demonstr. pl. (49) 10; Pl. Alstr. (121) 5

Fritillaria pyrenaica — Demonstr. pl. (49) 10; Fl. alp. (71) 15

Fritillaria regia — Fl. Cap. (99) 13

Fructus bobae — Herb. Amboin. (57) 13

Fructus musculiformis — Herb. Amboin. (57) 10

Frutex aquosus femina — Herb. Amboin. (57) 16

Frutex aquosus mas — Herb. Amboin. (57) 16

Frutex baccifer, fructu ad singulos flores multiplici — Nova pl. gen. 1747 (14) 21

Frutex carbonarius — Herb. Amboin. (57) 17

Frutex carbonarius asper — Herb. Amboin. (57) 17

Frutex ceramicus — Herb. Amboin. (57) 17

Frutex cerasiformis — Herb. Amboin. (57) 17

Frutex excaecans — Herb. Amboin. (57) 17

Frutex globulorum — Herb. Amboin. (57) 19

Frutex indicus baccifer, fructu oblongo polyspermo — Nova pl. gen. 1747 (14) 11

Frutex indicus sarmentosus, foliis hispidis rigidis — Nova pl. gen. 1747 (14) 20

Frutex lintearius — Herb. Amboin. (57) 17

Fucus — Spons. pl. (12) 28; Vir. pl. (13) 12; Fl. oecon. (17) 29; Oecon. nat. (20) 4, 19, 27; Pl. escul. (35) 26, 29; Hort. acad. (63) 11; Anim. comp. (98) 2, 4; Nom. bot. (107) 19; Rar. Norv. (157) 4

Fucus abrotanifolius — Rar. Norv. (157) 12

Fucus aculeatus — Rar. Norv. (157) 12

Fucus alatus — Rar. Norv. (157) 12

Fucus barbatus — Fl. Palaest. (70) 32

Fucus bifurcatus — Rar. Norv. (157) 12

Fucus buccinalis — Aphyteia (185) 6

Fucus canaliculatus — Rar. Norv. (157) 12

Fucus caprinus — Rar. Norv. (157) 12

Fucus ceranoides — Stat. pl. (55) 12; Prodr. fl. Dan. (82) 26; Rar. Norv. (157) 11

Fucus ciliatus — Rar. Norv. (157) 12

Fucus concatenatus — Rar. Norv. (157) 12

Fucus confervoides — Rar. Norv. (157) 12

Fucus crispus — Rar. Norv. (157) 12

Fucus cristatus — Rar. Norv. (157) 12

Fucus dentatus — Rar. Norv. (157) 12

Fucus digitatus — Rar. Norv. (157) 12

Fucus discors — Rar. Norv. (157) 12

Fucus distichus — Rar. Norv. (157) 12

Fucus esculentus — Rar. Norv. (157) 12

Fucus excisus — Rar. Norv. (157) 11

Fucus fastigiatus — Stat. pl. (55) 12; Prodr. fl. Dan. (82) 26; Rar. Norv. (157) 12

Fucus filum — Stat. pl. (55) 12; Prodr. fl. Dan. (82) 26; Rar. Norv. (157) 12

Fucus foeniculaceus — Fl. Palaest. (70) 32; Rar. Norv. (157) 12[as foeniculatus]

Fucus furcellatus — Rar. Norv. (157) 12

Fucus hirsutus — Rar. Norv. (157) 12

Fucus hyperboreus — Rar. Norv. (157) 12

Fucus indicus teres, setam piscatoriam referens, longissimus — Chin. Lagerstr. (64) 35

Fucus inflatus — Stat. pl. (55) 12; Prodr. fl. Dan. (82) 26; Rar. Norv. (157) 11

Fucus lanosus — Rar. Norv. (157) 12

Fucus loreus — Rar. Norv. (157) 12

Fucus lycopodioides — Rar. Norv. (157) 12

Fucus marinus scruposus albidus angustior compressus, extremitatibus quasi abscissis — Corallia Balt. (4) 9

Fucus natans — Herb. Amboin. (57) 6, 28; Nat. pelagi (84) 7, 9, 11, 12; Iter Chin. (161) 7, 15

Fucus nodosus — Stat. pl. (55) 12; Prodr. fl. Dan. (82) 26; Rar. Norv. (157) 12; Pand. fl. Ryb. (165) 23

Fucus ovinus — Rar. Norv. (157) 12

Fucus palmatus — Stat. pl. (55) 12; Rar. Norv. (157) 12

Fucus pennam referens — Noctiluca (39) 5

Fucus pinnatus — Rar. Norv. (157) 12

Fucus plumosus — Rar. Norv. (157) 12

Fucus purpureus humilis tenuiter divisus geniculatus — Pl. Mart.-Burs. (6) 28

Fucus ramentaceus — Rar. Norv. (157) 12

Fucus rubens — Rar. Norv. (157) 12

Fucus saccharinus — Stat. pl. (55) 12; Prodr. fl. Dan. (82) 26; Rar. Norv. (157) 12

Fucus sanguineus — Rar. Norv. (157) 12

Fucus selaginoides — Rar. Norv. (157) 12

Fucus serratus — Stat. pl. (55) 12; Prodr. fl. Dan. (82) 26; Rar. Norv. (157) 11

Fucus seu alga marina graminea angustifolia seminifera ramosior — Nova pl. gen. 1747 (14) 27

Fucus siliquosus — Stat. pl. (55) 12; Prodr. fl. Dan. (82) 26; Rar. Norv. (157) 12

Fucus spermophorus — Rar. Norv. (157) 12

Fucus spiralis — Stat. pl. (55) 12; Rar. Norv. (157) 11

Fucus telam linteam, sericeamve textura sua aemulans — Corallia Balt. (4) 9

Fucus tendo — Chin. Lagerstr. (64) 35, 36

Fucus vesiculosus — Stat. pl. (55) 12; Prodr. fl. Dan. (82) 26; Rar. Norv. (157) 11

Fucus virgatus — Rar. Norv. (157) 12

Fucus vittatus — Rar. Norv. (157) 12

Fulgora — Siren. lacert. (146) 8

Fulgora candelaria — Iter Chin. (161) 10

Fulica — Fund. ornith. (137) 19

Fulica atra — Migr. avium (79) 29

Fumaria — Hort. Upsal. (7) 34; Vir. pl. (13) 33; Sapor. med. (31) 18; Nom. bot. (107) 16; Prol. pl. 1760 (114) 9; Nect. fl. (122) 12; Erica (163) 2

Fumaria bulbosa — Pan Svec. (26) 29; Pl. rar. Camsch. (30) 23; Herbat. Upsal. (50) 8; Pl. officin. (52) 5; Stat. pl. (55) 17; Fl. Angl. (56) 6; Calend. fl. (72) [10]; Fl. Monsp. (74) 22; Fl. Belg. (112) 20; Hort. cul. (132) 24; Fl. Åker. (162) 16

Fumaria bulbosa cava — Demonstr. pl. (49) 19; Calend. fl. (72) [9]; Prodr. fl. Dan. (82) 21

Fumaria bulbosa radice cava — Metam. pl. (67) 18

Fumaria bulbosa radice non cava — Metam. pl. (67) 18

Fumaria bulbosa solida — Demonstr. pl. (49) 19; Calend. fl. (72) [9]; Prodr. fl. Dan. (82) 21

Fumaria canadensis — Pl. hybr. (33) 13

Fumaria capnoides — Demonstr. pl. (49) 19

Fumaria capreolata — Fl. Palaest. (70) 25; Fl. Monsp. (74) 22

Fumaria claviculata — Fl. Angl. (56) 20; Fl. Belg. (112) 9, 20

Fumaria cucullaria — Nect. fl. (122) 12

Fumaria officinalis — Pan Svec. (26) 29[as officinarum]; Herbat. Upsal. (50) 13; Pl. officin. (52) 10; Stat. pl. (55) 19; Fl. Angl. (56) 20; Fl. Monsp. (74) 22; Prodr. fl. Dan. (82) 21; Fl. Belg. (112) 20; Fl. Åker. (162) 16; Pand. fl. Ryb. (165) 21

Fumaria sempervirens — Demonstr. pl. (49) 19

Fumaria solida — Calend. fl. (72) [10]

Fumaria spectabilis — Hist. nat. Rossia (144) 24[as Femaria], 31

Fumaria tenuifolia — Fl. Monsp. (74) 22

Fumaria vesicaria — Demonstr. pl. (49) 19; Fl. Cap. (99) 9, 16

Fungites — Corallia Balt. (4) 2, 15, 16, 19, 22

Fungites alius gothlandicus, brevi pediculo et magno latoque pileolo conspicuus, cujus orificium sive cavitas, madrepora placentiformi sive eschara marina tenui reticulari obtegitur — Corallia Balt. (4) 17

Fungites cinerei coloris, cujus striatum capitulum nitide super lapidem calcarium fuscum expanditur et explicatur — Corallia Balt. (4) 15

Fungites elegans major, oris profunde crenatis, intusque reflexis, ex gothlandia — Corallia Balt. (4) 16

Fungites gothlandicus brevi pediculo et magno amploque pileolo, cujus superficies tota figuris astriformibus subtilissimis, et propemodum obliteratis obducitur — Corallia Balt. (4) 21

Fungites gothlandicus magnus, pileolo amplo, lato, admodumque expanso, sed pediculo brevi donatus — Corallia Balt. (4) 16

Fungites gothlandicus major, longo et incurvato pediculo, cujus pileoli orificium stalactite infarctum est — Corallia Balt. (4) 17

Fungites gothlandicus major, parvo pediculo, cujus pileoli orificium lapide calcario communi infarctum et repletum — Corallia Balt. (4) 16

Fungites gothlandicus maximus, circumferentia sua 14 pollices capiens, ex meris lamellis tenuioribus ac striatis compositus; in cujus protuberante capitulo, cavitas adeo coarctatur, ut digiti minimi apicem vix admittat — Corallia Balt. (4) 16

Fungites major orbicularis, amplo pileoli orificio, cujus crenati et tenues margines praeter morem valde extant, et circa centrum in altum elevantur — Corallia Balt. (4) 16

Fungites major orbicularis gothlandicus — Corallia Balt. (4) 16

Fungites mediae magnitudinis candidus ac elegans, levioribus quidem, ast nitidissimis striis, a centro profundiori ad marginem elatiorem, amplum ac reflexum, procurrentibus, brevique petiolo conspicuus — Corallia Balt. (4) 16

Fungites mediae magnitudinis subrotundus, laevis, gothlandicus, cujus pileoli orificium rotundum et profunde striatum, pediculus autem valde brevis — Corallia Balt. (4) 15

Fungites minor lapidi calcario griseo immersus — Corallia Balt. (4) 15

Fungus — Pl. rar. Camsch. (30) 22; Nom. bot. (107) 19

Fungus laricis — Med. purg. (181) 24

Fungus mauritanicus verrucosus ruber — Fung. melit. (69) 5

Fungus melitensis — Fung. melit. (69) 5, 8

Fungus typhoides coccineus — Fung. melit. (69) 5

Fungus typhoides coccineus tuberosus melitensis — Fung. melit. (69) 5

Fungus typhoides liburnensis — Fung. melit. (69) 5

Funis butonicus — Herb. Amboin. (57) 19

Funis convolutus — Herb. Amboin. (57) 19

Funis crepitans — Herb. Amboin. (57) 24

Funis eratium — Herb. Amboin. (57) 18

Funis felleus — Herb. Amboin. (57) 19

Funis gnemoniformis — Herb. Amboin. (57) 18

Funis muraenarum — Herb. Amboin. (57) 19[as muraenarnm]

Funis musarius — Herb. Amboin. (57) 19

Funis papius — Herb. Amboin. (57) 18

Funis quadrifidus — Herb. Amboin. (57) 18

Funis toaccae — Herb. Amboin. (57) 25

Funis uncatus lanosus — Herb. Amboin. (57) 19

Funis uncatus latifolius — Herb. Amboin. (57) 19

Funis urens — Herb. Amboin. (57) 18

Funis viminalis — Herb. Amboin. (57) 18

Furia — Hirudo (136) 2

Furia infernalis — Exanth. viva (86) 14

Furunculus myodes — Hist. nat. Rossia (144) 16

Gadus — Noctiluca (39) 5; Var. cib. (156) 17

Gajanus — Herb. Amboin. (57) 8

Gajatus — Herb. Amboin. (57) 16

Galactia — Fl. Jam. (105) 26

Galanga — Sapor. med. (31) 19; Odor. med. (40) 15; Herb. Amboin. (57) 5

Galanga major — Herb. Amboin. (57) 20

Galanga malaccensis — Herb. Amboin. (57) 20

Galanga minor — Herb. Amboin. (57) 20

Galanthus — Hort. Upsal. (7) 33; Spons. pl. (12) 33, 43, 46; Vir. pl. (13) 20; Vern. arb. (47) 8; Nom. bot. (107) 12; Prol. pl. 1760 (114) 13

Galanthus nivalis — Calend. fl. (72) [9]; Migr. avium (79) 20; Hort. cul. (132) 23

Galanthus nivalis plena — Demonstr. pl. (49) 9

Galberya — Nova pl. gen. 1747 (14) 6

Galega — Hort. Upsal. (7) 35

Galega cinerea — Pl. Jam. (102) 19; Fl. Jam. (105) 19

Galega officinalis — Demonstr. pl. (49) 19; Pl. officin. (52) 10; Fl. Palaest. (70) 25; Fl. Cap. (99) 17

Galega tinctoria — Pl. tinct. (97) 22

Galenia — Fl. Cap. (99) 6

Galenia africana — Fl. Cap. (99) 14

Galeopsis — Vir. pl. (13) 29; Pand. insect. (93) 16; Nect. fl. (122) 7; Mund. invis. (149) 16

Galeopsis galeobdolon — Stat. pl. (55) 17; Fl. Angl. (56) 18; Prodr. fl. Dan. (82) 20; Fl. Belg. (112) 18

Galeopsis ladanum — Pan Svec. (26) 27; Hosp. insect. fl. (43) 27; Herbat. Upsal. (50) 10; Fl. Angl. (56) 18; Fl. Monsp. (74) 19; Prodr. fl. Dan. (82) 20; Fl. Belg. (112) 18; Usum hist. nat. (145) 10; Fl. Åker. (162) 14; Pand. fl. Ryb. (165) 20

Galeopsis tetrahit — Pan Svec. (26) 27; Herbat. Upsal. (50) 10; Stat. pl. (55) 19; Fl. Angl. (56) 18; Metam. pl. (67) 21; Prodr. fl. Dan. (82) 20; Fl. Belg. (112) 18; Fl. Åker. (162) 14; Pand. fl. Ryb. (165) 20; Esca avium (174) 13

Galericula — Fund. entom. (154) 29

Galium — Pl. Mart.-Burs. (6) 25; Vir. pl. (13) 17, 18; Nova pl. gen. 1747 (14) 8; Fl. oecon. (17) 4; Pand. insect. (93) 11; Nom. bot. (107) 10

Galium album vulgare — Pl. Mart.-Burs. (6) 25

Galium aparine — Herbat. Upsal. (50) 10; Stat. pl. (55) 19[as Gallium]; Fl. Angl. (56) 11; Fl. Palaest. (70) 13; Fl. Monsp. (74) 10; Prodr. fl. Dan. (82) 14;

Fl. Belg. (112) 13; Fl. Åker. (162) 7; Pand. fl. Ryb. (165) 17; Esca avium (174) 11

Galium boreale — Fl. Angl. (56) 11; Prodr. fl. Dan. (82) 14; Pl. tinct. (97) 12; Fl. Åker. (162) 7; Pand. fl. Ryb. (165) 17

Galium cruciata — Pan Svec. (26) 15

Galium foliis octonis lineari-lanceolatis, margine asperis acutis, panicula terminatrice — Pl. Mart.-Burs. (6) 25

Galium foliis pluribus acutis, caule flaccido — Pl. Mart.-Burs. (6) 25

Galium glaucum — Fl. Monsp. (74) 10

Galium hierosolymitanum — Fl. Palaest. (70) 13

Galium hierosolymitanum foliis denis lanceolato-linearibus, umbellis fastigiatis, fructibus glabris — Fl. Palaest. (70) 13

Galium luteum — Pan Svec. (26) 15

Galium minutum — Demonstr. pl. (49) 4; Hist. nat. Rossia (144) 28

Galium mollugo — Demonstr. pl. (49) 4; Herbat. Upsal. (50) 7; Fl. Angl. (56) 11; Fl. Monsp. (74) 10; Prodr. fl. Dan. (82) 14; Fl. Belg. (112) 13; Fl. Åker. (162) 7

Galium palustre — Herbat. Upsal. (50) 6; Stat. pl. (55) 15; Fl. Angl. (56) 11; Prodr. fl. Dan. (82) 14; Fl. Belg. (112) 13; Fl. Åker. (162) 7; Pand. fl. Ryb. (165) 17

Galium parisiense — Demonstr. pl. (49) 4; Fl. Angl. (56) 11; Fl. Palaest. (70) 13; Fl. Monsp. (74) 10; Fl. Belg. (112) 13

Galium quadrifolium — Pan Svec. (26) 15

Galium rotundifolium — Fl. alp. (71) 12

Galium saxatile — Prodr. fl. Dan. (82) 14

Galium staekense — Pan Svec. (26) 15

Galium trifidum — Rar. Norv. (157) 9

Galium uliginosum — Stat. pl. (55) 15; Fl. Angl. (56) 11; Fl. Monsp. (74) 10; Prodr. fl. Dan. (82) 14; Fl. Åker. (162) 7; Pand. fl. Ryb. (165) 17

Galium verum — Herbat. Upsal. (50) 6; Pl. officin. (52) 10; Fl. Angl. (56) 11; Calend. fl. (72) [15]; Fl. Monsp. (74) 10; Prodr. fl. Dan. (82) 14; Pl. tinct. (97) 12; Fl. Belg. (112) 13; Fl. Åker. (162) 7; Pand. fl. Ryb. (165) 17

Gallina — Metam. pl. (67) 22

Gallina domestica — Mat. med. anim. (29) 10

Gallina frislandica — Spons. pl. (12) 26; Metam. pl. (67) 21

Gallinaria — Herb. Amboin. (57) 22

Gallopavo — Usum hist. nat. (145) 25

Gallus — Oecon. nat. (20) 26; Pan Svec. (26) 7; Noxa insect. (46) 29, 31; Fund. ornith. (137) 19, 26

Gallus cauda compressa ascendente — Mat. med. anim. (29) 10

Gallus gallinaceus — Spons. pl. (12) 26; Mat. med. anim. (29) 10

Gandasulum — Herb. Amboin. (57) 20

Gandola — Herb. Amboin. (57) 24

Ganitrum oblongum — Herb. Amboin. (57) 13

Ganitrus — Herb. Amboin. (57) 13

Ganja agrestis — Herb. Amboin. (57) 21

Ganja sativa — Herb. Amboin. (57) 21

Garcinia — Pl. escul. (35) 4; Herb. Amboin. (57) 11

Garcinia celebica — Cent. I. pl. (65) 2[as celibica]

Garcinia celebica foliis lanceolatis, pedunculis trifloris — Herb. Amboin. (57) 7

Garcinia mangostana — Fr. escul. (127) 10

Garcinia mangostana foliis ovatis, pedunculis unifloris — Herb. Amboin. (57) 7

Garidella — Hort. Upsal. (7) 35; Nect. fl. (122) 13, 15; Fund. fr. (123) 23

Garidella nigellastrum — Demonstr. pl. (49) 12

Garosmos — Nova pl. gen. 1751 (32) 12

Gasterosteus — Taenia (19) 11; Fund. ornith. (137) 10

Gasterosteus ductor — Iter Chin. (161) 6

Gaultheria — Nova pl. gen. 1751 (32) 9, [13, as 15], 20, 21, 48[as Gaulteria]; Nect. fl. (122) 8; Erica (163) 3[as Gaulteria]

Gaura — Nova pl. gen. 1751 (32) 47, 48; Nect. fl. (122) 7

Gazella — Fl. Cap. (99) [1]; Fund. ornith. (137) 25

Gecko — Amphib. Gyll. (5) 15[as Gekco]; Hort. Upsal. (7) 43[as Gecco]

Gecko ceilonicus maximus, brevi cauda, amphibius — Amphib. Gyll. (5) 27

Gelala alba — Herb. Amboin. (57) 10

Gelala aquatica — Herb. Amboin. (57) 10

Gelala litorea — Herb. Amboin. (57) 10

Gendarussa femina — Herb. Amboin. (57) 16

Gendarussa vulgaris — Herb. Amboin. (57) 16

Genipa — Pl. escul. (35) 4

Genipa americana — Pl. tinct. (97) 13; Fr. escul. (127) 11

Genista — Hort. Upsal. (7) 35; Fl. oecon. (17) 17; Fl. Monsp. (74) 7; Fr. Svec. (91) [ii]; Pand. insect. (93) [17, as 38]; Nom. bot. (107) 16

Genista africana, ericae folio, floribus parvis luteis, in capitula congestis — Pl. rar. Afr. (115) 14

Genista africana, pinastri foliis, floribus spicatis luteis — Pl. rar. Afr. (115) 14

Genista anglica — Fl. Angl. (56) 20; Fl. Belg. (112) 10, 20

Genista canariensis — Obs. mat. med. (171) 7

Genista candicans — Cent. I. pl. (65) 22

Genista foliis genistae hispanicae: superioribus junceis — Pl. rar. Afr. (115) 14

Genista foliis genistae tinctoriae majoribus — Pl. rar. Afr. (115) 14

Genista foliis lanceolatis, ramis teretibus striatis — Pl. Mart.-Burs. (6) 29

Genista foliis ternatis, subtus villosis; pedunculis lateralibus subquinquefloris foliatis; leguminibus hirsutis — Cent. I. pl. (65) 22

Genista germanica — Prodr. fl. Dan. (82) 21; Fl. Belg. (112) 9, 20

Genista hispanica — Fl. Monsp. (74) 22

Genista juncea — Pl. rar. Afr. (115) 6

Genista perfoliata, orbiculatis foliis — Pl. rar. Afr. (115) 16

Genista pilosa — Demonstr. pl. (49) 19; Stat. pl. (55) 21; Fl. Monsp. (74) 22; Prodr. fl. Dan. (82) 21; Fr. Svec. (91) 4, 20

Genista procumbens — Gem. arb. (24) 22; Pan Svec. (26) 30

Genista sagittalis — Fl. Monsp. (74) 22; Pl. rar. Afr. (115) 6

Genista spartium caeruleum — Pl. rar. Afr. (115) 15

Genista tinctoria — Gem. arb. (24) 22; Pan Svec. (26) 30; Demonstr. pl. (49) 19; Pl. officin. (52) 10[as Ginista]; Stat. pl. (55) 21; Fl. Angl. (56) 20; Fl. Monsp. (74) 22; Prodr. fl. Dan. (82) 21; Fr. Svec. (91) 4, 20; Pl. tinct. (97) 22; Fl. Belg. (112) 20; Purg. indig. (143) 9; Colon. pl. (158) 8

Gentiana — Vir. pl. (13) 33, 36; Sapor. med. (31) 18; Pl. hybr. (33) 11; Nom. bot. (107) 11; Fund. fr. (123) 23

Gentiana acaulis — Fl. alp. (71) 14

Gentiana alpinula — Pan Svec. (26) 18

Gentiana amarella — Pan Svec. (26) 18; Herbat. Upsal. (50) 13; Pl. officin. (52) 10; Fl. Angl. (56) 13; Prodr. fl. Dan. (82) 15; Fl. Åker. (162) 9; Febr. interm. (167) 36

Gentiana aquatica — Hist. nat. Rossia (144) 28

Gentiana asclepiadea — Fl. alp. (71) 14

Gentiana autumnalis ramosa — Pl. Mart.-Burs. (6) 14

Gentiana bavarica — Fl. alp. (71) 14

Gentiana campestris — Stat. pl. (55) 22; Fl. Angl. (56) 13; Fl. Monsp. (74) 12; Prodr. fl. Dan. (82) 15; Rar. Norv. (157) 10; Fl. Åker. (162) 9; Pand. fl. Ryb. (165) 17

Gentiana caule ramisque ramosissimis, foliis subulatis minimis — Nova pl. gen. 1751 (32) 15

Gentiana centaurium — Pan Svec. (26) 18; Pl. officin. (52) 7; Stat. pl. (55) 14; Fl. Angl. (56) 13; Fl. Palaest. (70) 16; Fl. Monsp. (74) 12; Prodr. fl. Dan. (82) 15; Fl. Belg. (112) 14; Pand. fl. Ryb. (165) 17, 21[as centaurinm]; Febr. interm. (167) 37

Gentiana centaurium pollicare — Prodr. fl. Dan. (82) 15

Gentiana ciliata — Fl. alp. (71) 14; Rar. Norv. (157) 10

Gentiana corollis hypocrateriformibus, fauce barbatis — Pl. Mart.-Burs. (6) 14

Gentiana cruciata — Fl. alp. (71) 14; Calend. fl. (72) [18]; Fl. Monsp. (74) 12; Fl. Belg. (112) 10, 14

Gentiana filiformis — Fl. Monsp. (74) 12

Gentiana foliis margine membranaceis basi coadunatis — Pl. rar. Camsch. (30) 11

Gentiana humilis aquatica verna — Pl. rar. Camsch. (30) 11

Gentiana lutea — Pl. officin. (52) 10; Fl. alp. (71) 14; Fl. Monsp. (74) 12; Rar. Norv. (157) 13

Gentiana nivalis — Stat. pl. (55) 16; Fl. alp. (71) 14; Rar. Norv. (157) 10

Gentiana officinarum — Pan Svec. (26) 18

Gentiana perfoliata — Fl. Angl. (56) 13; Fl. Monsp. (74) 12; Fl. Belg. (112) 14; Fund. fr. (123) 19

Gentiana pilosa — Colon. pl. (158) 8

Gentiana pneumonanthe — Pan Svec. (26) 18; Vern. arb. (47) 19; Stat. pl. (55) 14; Fl. Angl. (56) 13; Calend. fl. (72) [17]; Prodr. fl. Dan. (82) 15; Fl. Belg. (112) 8, 14

Gentiana punctata — Fl. alp. (71) 14; Hist. nat. Rossia (144) 28

Gentiana purpurea — Fl. alp. (71) 14; Rar. Norv. (157) 9, 10

Gentiana quadrifolia — Fund. fr. (123) 19

Gentiana spicata — Fl. Monsp. (74) 12

Gentiana utriculosa — Fl. alp. (71) 14

Gentiana verna — Fl. alp. (71) 14

Gentianella alpina verna major, corolla alba — Pl. Mart.-Burs. (6) 14

Gentianella brevi folio — Pl. Mart.-Burs. (6) 14

Gentianella utriculis ventricosis — Pl. Mart.-Burs. (6) 14

Geranium — Hort. Upsal. (7) 37; Spons. pl. (12) 35; Vir. pl. (13) 12; Gem. arb. (24) 6; Pan Svec. (26) 3; Pl. hybr. (33) 7, 25, 29; Pand. insect. (93) [17, as 38]; Fl. Cap. (99) 6, 7, 9; Generat. ambig. (104) 13; Nom. bot. (107) 15; Pl. rar. Afr. (115) 4, 5, 7; Fund. fr. (123) 17, 22; Aphyteia (185) 6

Geranium acetosum — Fl. Cap. (99) 16

Geranium africanum carnosum, petalis angustis albicantibus — Cent. I. pl. (65) 20

Geranium africanum tenuifolium robertiani divisuris — Pl. rar. Afr. (115) 13

Geranium alchimilloides — Demonstr. pl. (49) 18; Fl. Cap. (99) 16

Geranium alpinum longius radicatum — Cent. II. pl. (66) 26

Geranium althaeoides — Fl. Cap. (99) 16

Geranium apulum coriandrifolium — Cent. I. pl. (65) 21

Geranium argenteum — Cent. II. pl. (66) 25; Fl. alp. (71) 20

Geranium argenteum alpinum — Cent. II. pl. (66) 26

Geranium argenteum montis baldi — Cent. II. pl. (66) 26

Geranium auritum — Fl. Cap. (99) 16

Geranium batrachioides — Pan Svec. (26) 29; Hosp. insect. fl. (43) 28

Geranium batrachioides bohemicum, capsulis nigris hirsutis — Cent. II. pl. (66) 25

Geranium batrachioides gratia dei germanorum — Pl. Mart.-Burs. (6) 13

Geranium batrachioides minus annuum purpureo-caeruleum — Cent. II. pl. (66) 25

Geranium batrachioides palustre, flore sanguineo — Cent. II. pl. (66) 25

Geranium betulinum — Fl. Cap. (99) 16

Geranium bohemicum — Cent. II. pl. (66) 25

Geranium bohemicum batrachioides annuum — Cent. II. pl. (66) 25

Geranium calycibus monophyllis, caule carnoso gibboso, foliis pinnatifidis, petalis linearibus — Cent. I. pl. (65) 20

Geranium calycibus monophyllis florentibus erectis, foliis subcordatis — Spons. pl. (12) 38

Geranium capitatum — Demonstr. pl. (49) 18

Geranium capitulatum — Fl. Cap. (99) 16

Geranium carnosum — Cent. I. pl. (65) 20; Fl. Cap. (99) 16

Geranium ciconium — Cent. I. pl. (65) 21

Geranium cicutae folio, acu longissima — Cent. I. pl. (65) 21

Geranium cicutarium — Pan Svec. (26) 29; Herbat. Upsal. (50) 20; Stat. pl. (55) 19; Fl. Angl. (56) 20; Fl. Monsp. (74) 21; Prodr. fl. Dan. (82) 21; Fl. Belg. (112) 19; Fl. Åker. (162) 16; Pand. fl. Ryb. (165) 20

Geranium cicutarium moschatum — Pl. officin. (52) 10

Geranium columbinum — Demonstr. pl. (49) 18; Fl. Angl. (56) 20, 28; Fl. Palaest. (70) 24; Calend. fl. (72) [22]; Fl. Monsp. (74) 21

Geranium cucullatum — Fl. Cap. (99) 16

Geranium dissectum — Cent. I. pl. (65) 21; Calend. fl. (72) [22]; Fl. Monsp. (74) 21; Prodr. fl. Dan. (82) 21

Geranium foetidum — Fl. Monsp. (74) 21

Geranium foliis ad nervum quinquefidis, pediculis brevioribus, caule erecto — Cent. I. pl. (65) 21

Geranium fructu hirsuto — Pan Svec. (26) 29

Geranium fulgidum — Fl. Cap. (99) 16

Geranium gibbosum — Fl. Cap. (99) 16

Geranium glaucophyllum — Fl. Cap. (99) 16

Geranium glaucum — Demonstr. pl. (49) 18

Geranium gratia dei — Pan Svec. (26) 29

Geranium grossularioides — Fl. Cap. (99) 16

Geranium gruinum — Fl. Monsp. (74) 21

Geranium incanum — Pl. rar. Afr. (115) 13

Geranium incarnatum — Fl. Cap. (99) 16

Geranium inquinans — Demonstr. pl. (49) 18; Fl. Cap. (99) 16

Geranium lucidum — Pan Svec. (26) 29; Demonstr. pl. (49) 18; Stat. pl. (55) 17; Fl. Angl. (56) 20; Fl. Monsp. (74) 21; Colon. pl. (158) 7

Geranium macrorrhizum — Prodr. fl. Dan. (82) 21[as macrorhizon]

Geranium maculatum — Hist. nat. Rossia (144) 31

Geranium majus, foliis imis longis, ad usque pediculum divisis — Cent. I. pl. (65) 21

Geranium malacoides — Demonstr. pl. (49) 18; Fl. Angl. (56) 20; Calend. fl. (72) [16]; Fl. Monsp. (74) 21

Geranium malvaceum — Pan Svec. (26) 29

Geranium molle — Demonstr. pl. (49) 18; Fl. Angl. (56) 20; Calend. fl. (72) [12]; Fl. Monsp. (74) 21

Geranium moschatum — Odor. med. (40) 12; Demonstr. pl. (49) 18; Fl. Angl. (56) 20; Ambros. (100) 14; Fl. Belg. (112) 19

Geranium moschatum, cicutae folio — Pl. hybr. (33) 25

Geranium myrrhifolium — Demonstr. pl. (49) 18[as myrrifolium]; Fl. Cap. (99) 16

Geranium nodosum — Fl. Angl. (56) 20; Fl. Monsp. (74) 21

Geranium noveboracense — Specif. Canad. (76) 15

Geranium odoratissimum — Fl. Cap. (99) 16

Geranium palustre — Cent. II. pl. (66) 25; Prodr. fl. Dan. (82) 21

Geranium papilionaceum — Fl. Cap. (99) 16

Geranium pedunculis bifloris, calycibus aristatis, petalis integris, pericarpiis hirsutis, foliis subdigitatis — Pl. rar. Afr. (115) 13

Geranium pedunculis bifloris, foliis multipartitis: laciniis linearibus — Pl. rar. Afr. (115) 13

Geranium pedunculis bifloris, foliis peltatis multifidis, caule erecto — Pl. Mart.-Burs. (6) 24

Geranium pedunculis bifloris, foliis quinquelobis: lobis medio dilatatis, petalis emarginatis reticulatis — Cent. I. pl. (65) 21

Geranium pedunculis bifloris, foliis quinquepartito-multifidis, caule glabro erectiusculo — Cent. I. pl. (65) 21

Geranium pedunculis bifloris longissimis declinatis, petalis integris, foliis quinquelobis incisis — Cent. II. pl. (66) 25

Geranium pedunculis bifloris, petalis emarginatis, arillis hirtis, cotyledonibus trifidis: medio truncato — Cent. II. pl. (66) 25

Geranium pedunculis bifloris, petalis emarginatis, foliis peltatis septempartitis trifidis tomentoso-sericeis — Cent. II. pl. (66) 25

Geranium pedunculis longissimis — Pan Svec. (26) 29

Geranium pedunculis submultifloris; calycibus pentaphyllis; floribus pentandris; foliis pinnatis pinnatifidis obtusis — Cent. I. pl. (65) 21

Geranium pedunculis unifloris — Spons. pl. (12) 33

Geranium peltatum — Fl. Cap. (99) 16

Geranium phaeum — Demonstr. pl. (49) 18; Fl. Angl. (56) 20; Fl. alp. (71) 20; Calend. fl. (72) [11]

Geranium pinnatum — Fl. Cap. (99) 16

Geranium pratense — Herbat. Upsal. (50) 8; Stat. pl. (55) 20; Fl. Angl. (56) 20; Calend. fl. (72) [12]; Prodr. fl. Dan. (82) 21; Fl. Åker. (162) 16

Geranium rapaceum — Fl. Cap. (99) 16

Geranium robertianum — Pan Svec. (26) 29; Odor. med. (40) 13; Demonstr. pl. (49) 18; Herbat. Upsal. (50) 9; Pl. officin. (52) 10; Stat. pl. (55) 23; Fl. Angl. (56) 20; Fl. Monsp. (74) 21; Prodr. fl. Dan. (82) 21; Med. grav. (92) 13; Fl. Belg. (112) 19; Menthae (153) 6; Fl. Åker. (162) 16; Pand. fl. Ryb. (165) 20; Cimicifuga (173) 8

Geranium romanum versicolor seu striatum — Cent. I. pl. (65) 21

Geranium rotundifolium — Fl. Palaest. (70) 24; Calend. fl. (72) [22]; Fl. Monsp. (74) 21; Prodr. fl. Dan. (82) 21; Fl. Belg. (112) 19; Fl. Åker. (162) 16; Pand. fl. Ryb. (165) 20

Geranium sanguineum — Pan Svec. (26) 29; Demonstr. pl. (49) 18; Herbat. Upsal. (50) 8; Stat. pl. (55) 22; Fl. Angl. (56) 20; Fl. Monsp. (74) 21; Prodr. fl. Dan. (82) 21; Pand. fl. Ryb. (165) 20

Geranium sanguineum majus — Cent. II. pl. (66) 25

Geranium scabrum — Fl. Cap. (99) 16

Geranium sibiricum — Demonstr. pl. (49) 18; Hist. nat. Rossia (144) 31

Geranium striatum — Somn. pl. (68) 22

Geranium sylvaticum — Demonstr. pl. (49) 18; Stat. pl. (55) 18; Fl. Angl. (56) 20; Calend. fl. (72) [11], [12]; Prodr. fl. Dan. (82) 21; Fl. Åker. (162) 15; Ledum (178) 8

Geranium triste — Demonstr. pl. (49) 18; Fl. Cap. (99) 16

Geranium uniflorum — Calend. fl. (72) [12]

Geranium versicolor — Cent. I. pl. (65) 21

Geranium vitifolium — Demonstr. pl. (49) 18; Fl. Cap. (99) 16

Geranium zonale — Demonstr. pl. (49) 18; Fl. Cap. (99) 16

Gerardia delphinifolia — Cent. II. pl. (66) 21

Gerardia foliis linearibus pinnatifidis, caule subramoso — Cent. II. pl. (66) 21

Gerascanthus — Fl. Jam. (105) 26[as Gerascantus]

Gesneria acaulis — Pl. Jam. (102) 15; Fl. Jam. (105) 18

Gesneria tomentosa — Fl. Jam. (105) 18

Gethyllis — Fl. Cap. (99) 6

Gethyllis afra — Fl. Cap. (99) 14

Geum — Peloria (3) 10; Spons. pl. (12) 60; Vir. pl. (13) 27; Fl. oecon. (17) 14; Pl. rar. Camsch. (30) 21; Pl. hybr. (33) 26; Pl. escul. (35) 29; Cui bono? (42) 21; Nom. bot. (107) 14; Prol. pl. 1760 (114) 14, 18; Nect. fl. (122) 6; Fund. fr. (123) 20, 23; Fraga (170) [1], 3

Geum caryophyllatum — Pl. escul. (35) 18

Geum floribus nutantibus, fructu oblongo, seminum cauda molli plumosa — Specif. Canad. (76) 23

Geum montanum — Fl. alp. (71) 18; Fl. Monsp. (74) 18

Geum reptans — Fl. alp. (71) 18

Geum rivale — Pan Svec. (26) 25; Herbat. Upsal. (50) 7; Pl. officin. (52) 10; Stat. pl. (55) 14; Fl. Angl. (56) 17; Specif. Canad. (76) 26, 28; Prodr. fl. Dan. (82) 19; Prol. pl. 1760 (114) 12; Fl. Åker. (162) 13; Pand. fl. Ryb. (165) 19; Febr. interm. (167) 41

Geum suaveolens — Pan Svec. (26) 25

Geum urbanum — Herbat. Upsal. (50) 10; Pl. officin. (52) 7; Stat. pl. (55) 17; Fl. Angl. (56) 17; Calend. fl. (72) [12]; Fl. Monsp. (74) 18; Prodr. fl. Dan. (82) 19; Fl. Belg. (112) 17; Fl. Åker. (162) 13

Geum virginicum — Demonstr. pl. (49) 14

Gigalobium — Fl. Jam. (105) 26

Gladiolus — Hort. Upsal. (7) 33; Vir. pl. (13) 26; Fl. Monsp. (74) 7; Fl. Cap. (99) 7, 9; Pl. rar. Afr. (115) 4; Pl. Alstr. (121) 6; Fund. fr. (123) 18

Gladiolus alatus — Pl. rar. Afr. (115) 8[as Gladgolus]

Gladiolus alopecuroides — Cent. II. pl. (66) 5; Fl. Cap. (99) 11

Gladiolus angustus — Fl. Cap. (99) 11

Gladiolus capitatus — Fl. Cap. (99) 11

Gladiolus communis — Demonstr. pl. (49) 2; Fl. Palaest. (70) 12; Calend. fl. (72) [14]; Fl. Monsp. (74) 8; Hort. cul. (132) 24[as Gladiosus]

Gladiolus foliis ensiformibus, petalis lateralibus latissimis — Pl. rar. Afr. (115) 8[as Gladgolus]

Gladiolus foliis linearibus, spica disticha imbricata — Cent. II. pl. (66) 5

Gladiolus imbricatus — Hist. nat. Rossia (144) 27

Gladiolus odoratus — Herb. Amboin. (57) 20

Gladiolus ramosus — Fl. Cap. (99) 11

Gladiolus spicatus — Fl. Cap. (99) 11

Glandaria — Oecon. nat. (20) 39

Glans iberica — Var. cib. (156) 8

Glans terrestris — Herb. Amboin. (57) 23

Glastivida prima e candia — Cent. II. pl. (66) 10

Glaucium — Hort. Upsal. (7) 34

Glaux maritima — Herbat. Upsal. (50) 14; Stat. pl. (55) 12; Fl. Angl. (56) 12; Prodr. fl. Dan. (82) 15; Fl. Belg. (112) 14; Pand. fl. Ryb. (165) 17, 21

Glaux palustris — Pan Svec. (26) 18

Glechoma — Fl. oecon. (17) 16; Mirac. insect. (45) 16; Metam. pl. (67) 13[as Glecoma], 24[as Glecoma]; Pand. insect. (93) 16; Pl. tinct. (97) 10; Nom. bot. (107) 14

Glechoma arvensis — Fl. Angl. (56) 18; Prodr. fl. Dan. (82) 20[as Glecoma]; Fl. Belg. (112) 18

Glechoma belgica — Fl. Belg. (112) 9[as Glecoma]

Glechoma hedera terrestris — Pan Svec. (26) 26[as terrastris]; Hosp. insect. fl. (43) 27

Glechoma hederacea — Herbat. Upsal. (50) 8; Pl. officin. (52) 11; Stat. pl. (55) 17; Fl. Angl. (56) 18; Fl. Monsp. (74) 19[as Glecoma]; Prodr. fl. Dan.

(82) 20[as Glecoma]; Fl. Jam. (105) 25; Fl. Belg. (112) 18; Fl. Åker. (162) 14[as Glecoma]; Pand. fl. Ryb. (165) 20[as Glecoma]; Esca avium (174) 13

Gleditsia — Hort. Upsal. (7) 37[as Gleditschia]; Gem. arb. (24) 6, 9; Nova pl. gen. 1751 (32) 10, 12; Cent. insect. (129) 9; Prol. pl. 1763 (130) 8[as Gleditschia]

Gleditsia triacanthos — Demonstr. pl. (49) 27; Somn. pl. (68) 21[as Gleditzia triacantha]

Glinus — Nect. fl. (122) 8

Glinus lotoides — Fl. Palaest. (70) 20

Glis montanus — Hist. nat. Rossia (144) 16

Globba — Herb. Amboin. (57) 5

Globba acris — Herb. Amboin. (57) 27

Globba crispa — Herb. Amboin. (57) 27

Globba longa — Herb. Amboin. (57) 27

Globba sylvestris — Herb. Amboin. (57) 27

Globba uviformis — Herb. Amboin. (57) 27

Globularia — Hort. Upsal. (7) 33

Globularia alypum — Fl. Monsp. (74) 7[as alypus], 10

Globularia cordifolia — Fl. alp. (71) 12

Globularia foliis radicalibus cuneiformibus retusodentatis, denticulo intermedio minimo — Pl. Mart.-Burs. (6) 22

Globularia gotlandica — Pan Svec. (26) 15

Globularia nudicaulis — Fl. alp. (71) 12

Globularia vulgaris — Demonstr. pl. (49) 4; Stat. pl. (55) 23; Calend. fl. (72) [11]; Fl. Monsp. (74) 10; Fl. Belg. (112) 13

Globuli majores — Herb. Amboin. (57) 19

Gloriosa — Vir. pl. (13) 20, 31; Nect. fl. (122) 11; Mund. invis. (149) 20

Glycine — Fl. Jam. (105) 26

Glycine abrus — Demonstr. pl. (49) 20; Herb. Amboin. (57) 19; Somn. pl. (68) 20[as Glyzine]; Fl. Palaest. (70) 26; Fl. Jam. (105) 19, 25[as abres]

Glycine bituminosa — Fl. Cap. (99) 17

Glycine bracteata — Demonstr. pl. (49) 20

Glycine galactia — Fl. Jam. (105) 19

Glycyrrhiza — Hort. Upsal. (7) 35[as Glycyrhiza]; Nom. bot. (107) 16

Glycyrrhiza echinata — Demonstr. pl. (49) 20; Calend. fl. (72) [17]

Glycyrrhiza glabra — Demonstr. pl. (49) 20; Pl. officin. (52) 12; Fl. Angl. (56) 21

Gmelina asiatica — Herb. Amboin. (57) 9

Gnaphalio montano affinis aegyptiaca — Cent. I. pl. (65) 27

Gnaphalium — Vir. pl. (13) 23; Sapor. med. (31) 9; Pl. hybr. (33) 29; Oves (61) 14; Fl. Cap. (99) 6, 7, 9; Nom. bot. (107) 17; Pl. rar. Afr. (115) 5; Aphyteia (185) 6

Gnaphalium aegyptiacum, latiore flore ramosius, flore ex albicante purpureo — Cent. I. pl. (65) 27

Gnaphalium alpinum — Demonstr. pl. (49) 23; Stat. pl. (55) 16; Fl. alp. (71) 22

Gnaphalium arborescens — Pl. rar. Afr. (115) 18

Gnaphalium arenarium — Pl. officin. (52) 18; Stat. pl. (55) 21; Hort. acad. (63) 10; Prodr. fl. Dan. (82) 23; Colon. pl. (158) 8

Gnaphalium candidissimum — Fl. Palaest. (70) 28

Gnaphalium caule fruticoso tomentoso, foliis linearibus, calycibus extus nudibus, intus incarnatis — Pl. rar. Afr. (115) 19

Gnaphalium caule ramoso diffuso, floribus confertis lana tectis — Demonstr. pl. (49) 24

Gnaphalium caulibus ramosissimis diffusis, calycibus subfasciculatis sessilibus: squamis intimis nudis subulatis recurvis — Pl. rar. Afr. (115) 20

Gnaphalium coronatum — Fl. Cap. (99) 17

Gnaphalium cylindriflorum — Pl. rar. Afr. (115) 19

Gnaphalium cymosum — Fl. Cap. (99) 17

Gnaphalium dentatum — Fl. Cap. (99) 17

Gnaphalium dioicum — Pan Svec. (26) 32; Herbat. Upsal. (50) 10; Pl. officin. (52) 10; Stat. pl. (55) 21; Fl. Angl. (56) 22; Hort. acad. (63) 10; Fl. Monsp. (74) 25; Prodr. fl. Dan. (82) 23; Fl. Belg. (112) 21; Fl. Åker. (162) 17; Pand. fl. Ryb. (165) 21

Gnaphalium ericoides — Pl. rar. Afr. (115) 19

Gnaphalium filago sylvatica — Pan Svec. (26) 32

Gnaphalium foetidum — Demonstr. pl. (49) 23; Fl. Cap. (99) 17

Gnaphalium foliis decurrentibus, lanceolatis, utrinque tomentosis, planis, apiculo nudo terminatis — Cent. I. pl. (65) 27

Gnaphalium foliis lanceolatis nudis trinerviis reticulato venosis — Pl. rar. Afr. (115) 19

Gnaphalium foliis linearibus acutis nudis subtus tomentosis, floribus subcapitatis, caule arboreo — Pl. rar. Afr. (115) 18

Gnaphalium foliis linearibus, caule fruticoso ramoso, corymbo composito terminatrice — Pl. Mart.-Burs. (6) 22

Gnaphalium foliis oblongis tomentosis, corymbis inaequalibus, calycibus glabris cylindricis sessilibus — Pl. rar. Afr. (115) 19

Gnaphalium foliis semiamplexicaulibus lanceolatis denticulatis supra nudis — Pl. rar. Afr. (115) 19

Gnaphalium foliis thymi incanis dense stipatum — Pl. rar. Afr. (115) 20

Gnaphalium foliis villosis, calycibus extus incarnatis, intus niveis acutis — Pl. rar. Afr. (115) 19

Gnaphalium folio oblongo acuto molli, floribus ferrugineis — Pl. rar. Afr. (115) 19

Gnaphalium glomeratum — Pl. rar. Afr. (115) 20

Gnaphalium glutinosum — Fl. Palaest. (70) 28

Gnaphalium grandiflorum — Fl. Cap. (99) 17

Gnaphalium helianthemifolium — Fl. Cap. (99) 17

Gnaphalium ignescens — Demonstr. pl. (49) 23

Gnaphalium imbricatum — Fl. Cap. (99) 17

Gnaphalium impia — Pan Svec. (26) 32

Gnaphalium lapponicum — Pan Svec. (26) 32

Gnaphalium leontopodium — Fl. alp. (71) 21; Hist. nat. Rossia (144) 32[as leonthopodium]

Gnaphalium luteo-album — Fl. Angl. (56) 22; Fl. Monsp. (74) 25; Prodr. fl. Dan. (82) 23

Gnaphalium margaritaceum — Demonstr. pl. (49) 23; Fl. Angl. (56) 5, 22; Calend. fl. (72) [17]; Specif. Canad. (76) 12; Hort. cul. (132) 24; Colon. pl. (158) 10

Gnaphalium montanum — Herbat. Upsal. (50) 9

Gnaphalium muricatum — Fl. Cap. (99) 17; Cent. insect. (129) 17

Gnaphalium niveum — Fl. Cap. (99) 17

Gnaphalium nudifolium — Pl. rar. Afr. (115) 19[as nudifalium]

Gnaphalium obtusifolium — Demonstr. pl. (49) 23

Gnaphalium orientale — Demonstr. pl. (49) 23; Fl. Cap. (99) 17; Hort. cul. (132) 24

Gnaphalium palustris — Pan Svec. (26) 32

Gnaphalium patulum — Fl. Cap. (99) 17

Gnaphalium petiolatum — Fl. Cap. (99) 17

Gnaphalium rutilans — Fl. Cap. (99) 17

Gnaphalium sanguineum — Cent. I. pl. (65) 27; Fl. Palaest. (70) 28

Gnaphalium saxatile — Fl. Palaest. (70) 28; Pl. rar. Afr. (115) 7

Gnaphalium scabrum — Fl. Cap. (99) 17

Gnaphalium scanensis — Pan Svec. (26) 32

Gnaphalium serratum — Pl. rar. Afr. (115) 19

Gnaphalium sordidum — Fl. Monsp. (74) 25; Fl. Belg. (112) 21

Gnaphalium stellatum — Pl. rar. Afr. (115) 19

Gnaphalium stoechas — Pan Svec. (26) 32; Fl. Palaest. (70) 28; Fl. Monsp. (74) 25[as staechas]

Gnaphalium sylvaticum — Herbat. Upsal. (50) 19; Stat. pl. (55) 18; Fl. Angl. (56) 22; Fl. Monsp. (74) 25; Prodr. fl. Dan. (82) 23; Fl. Jam. (105) 19, 25; Fl. Belg. (112) 21; Fl. Åker. (162) 17; Pand. fl. Ryb. (165) 21

Gnaphalium teretifolium — Fl. Cap. (99) 17

Gnaphalium tomentosum — Pl. rar. Afr. (115) 19

Gnaphalium uliginosum — Herbat. Upsal. (50) 10; Stat. pl. (55) 14; Fl. Angl. (56) 22; Fl. Palaest. (70) 28; Fl. Monsp. (74) 25; Prodr. fl. Dan. (82) 23; Fl. Åker. (162) 17; Pand. fl. Ryb. (165) 21

Gnaphalium undulatum — Fl. Cap. (99) 17

Gnaphalium upsaliensis — Pan Svec. (26) 32

Gnaphalium virgatum — Pl. Jam. (102) 22; Fl. Jam. (105) 19

Gnemon domestica — Herb. Amboin. (57) 8

Gnemon funicularis — Herb. Amboin. (57) 18

Gnemon sylvestris — Herb. Amboin. (57) 8

Gnidia — Sapor. med. (31) 19[as Gnidium]; Fl. Cap. (99) 6[as Gnidium]

Gnidia oppositifolia — Fl. Cap. (99) 14

Gnidia pinifolia — Fl. Cap. (99) 14

Gnidia tomentosa — Fl. Cap. (99) 14

Gobius dentibus maxillae inferioris horizontalibus — Chin. Lagerstr. (64) 25

Gobius nebulosus — Chin. Lagerstr. (64) 25

Gobius pectinirostris — Chin. Lagerstr. (64) 25, 36; Iter Chin. (161) 7

Gobius pinna ani radiis novem — Chin. Lagerstr. (64) 25

Gomphrena — Hort. Upsal. (7) 36; Nect. fl. (122) 9

Gomphrena brasiliana — Cent. II. pl. (66) 13

Gomphrena foliis ovato-oblongis, caule erecto, capitulis pedunculatis globosis aphyllis — Cent. II. pl. (66) 13

Gomphrena globosa — Demonstr. pl. (49) 7; Herb. Amboin. (57) 22[as Gomphraena]; Fl. Jam. (105) 14; Hort. cul. (132) 23

Gomphrena polygonoides — Fl. Jam. (105) 14

Gomphrena sessilis — Herb. Amboin. (57) 26[as Gomphraena]; Fl. Palaest. (70) 16

Gordius — Taenia (19) 4, 10, 11; Splachnum (27) 2; Migr. avium (79) 8; Hirudo (136) 2; Lepra (140) 10, 11; Siren. lacert. (146) 8; Mund. invis. (149) 15; Ledum (178) 15

Gordius marinus — Rar. Norv. (157) 17

Gordius spiralis — Lepra (140) 14

Gorgonia — Corallia Balt. (4) 2; Siren. lacert. (146) 8; Mund. invis. (149) 8, 20

Gorgonia abies — Iter Chin. (161) 13

Gorgonia anceps — Iter Chin. (161) 13

Gorgonia flabellum — Mund. invis. (149) 8[as fabellum]

Gorgonia ventalina — Iter Chin. (161) 13

Gorteria — Fl. Cap. (99) 6[as Gortera], 9[as Gortera], 10[as Gortera]; Pl. rar. Afr. (115) 5[as Gortheria]; Fund. fr. (123) 17

Gorteria ciliaris — Aphyteia (185) [5]

Gorteria foliis caulinis subulatis dentato-spinosis recurvatis, floribus terminalibus sessilibus — Pl. rar. Afr. (115) 23

Gorteria personata — Fl. Cap. (99) 18[as Gortera]

Gorteria squarrosa — Pl. rar. Afr. (115) 23

Gossypium — Hort. Upsal. (7) 37; Phalaena (78) [2]; Pand. insect. (93) [17, as 38]; Fl. Jam. (105) 9; Nom. bot. (107) 16; Nect. fl. (122) 4

Gossypium arboreum — Herb. Amboin. (57) 15; Pl. Surin. (177) 12

Gossypium barbadense — Demonstr. pl. (49) 19; Fl. Jam. (105) 19

Gossypium capas — Herb. Amboin. (57) 15

Gossypium daemonis — Herb. Amboin. (57) 15

Gossypium herbaceum — Demonstr. pl. (49) 19; Pl. officin. (52) 6, 10; Herb. Amboin. (57) 15; Fl. Palaest. (70) 24

Gossypium latifolium — Herb. Amboin. (57) 15

Gossypium religiosum — Pl. Surin. (177) 12

Graculus — Polit. nat. (109) 14

Gramen — Peloria (3) 10; Pl. Jam. (102) 7; Fund. agrost. (152) 16

Gramen aciculatum — Herb. Amboin. (57) 25

Gramen alopecurus maximus — Fl. Angl. (56) 28

Gramen alpinum pratense, panicula duriore laxa spadicea, locustis majoribus — Pl. Mart.-Burs. (6) 2

Gramen arguens — Herb. Amboin. (57) 25

Gramen arundinaceum aquaticum — Fl. Angl. (56) 28

Gramen barcinense, panicula densa aurea — Pl. Mart.-Burs. (6) 2[as barcinonense]

Gramen bromoides pumilum, locustis erectis majoribus aristatis — Cent. I. pl. (65) 5

Gramen bulbosum ex alepo — Cent. II. pl. (66) 8

Gramen capitatum — Herb. Amboin. (57) 25

Gramen carinosum — Herb. Amboin. (57) 25

Gramen cristatum tartaricum, spica latiore et breviore — Pl. rar. Camsch. (30) 6

Gramen cyperoides elegans, spica composita asperiore — Cent. I. pl. (65) 31

Gramen cyperoides palustre majus, spica diversa — Pl. Mart.-Burs. (6) 3

Gramen cyperoides palustre, spica longiore laxa — Cent. I. pl. (65) 32

Gramen cyperoides pumilum elegans e maderaspata — Cent. II. pl. (66) 6[as maderaspatan]

Gramen cyperoides spica pendula longiori et angustiori — Pl. Mart.-Burs. (6) 3

Gramen dactylon spica gemina — Pl. Mart.-Burs. (6) 5

Gramen essexiense — Colon. pl. (158) 10

Gramen exile duriusculum in muris et aridis proveniens — Cent. I. pl. (65) 5

Gramen filiceum rigidiusculum — Cent. I. pl. (65) 5

Gramen foliis pungentibus — Fl. Angl. (56) 28

Gramen foliolis junceis oblongis, radice alba — Pl. Mart.-Burs. (6) 2

Gramen foliolis junceis, radice alba — Fl. Angl. (56) 28[as juncus]

Gramen gross. accedens — Fl. Monsp. (74) 29

Gramen hirsutum indicum, glomeratis capitulis lagopi aemulis, gluma e squamis plurimis purpurascentibus arista una donatis compactili — Cent. II. pl. (66) 7

Gramen junceum — Pl. Mart.-Burs. (6) 3

Gramen junceum e monte baldo — Cent. II. pl. (66) 32

Gramen junceum, folio et spica junci, minus — Pl. Mart.-Burs. (6) 2

Gramen junceum montanum, capite squamoso — Cent. II. pl. (66) 32

Gramen junceum reptans — Pl. Mart.-Burs. (6) [1]

Gramen latifolium, spica triticea latiori compacta — Pl. Mart.-Burs. (6) 4

Gramen loliaceum minus — Fl. Monsp. (74) 29

Gramen loliaceum minus supinum, spica multiplici — Pl. Mart.-Burs. (6) 4

Gramen loliaceum murorum duriusculum, spica erecta rigida — Cent. I. pl. (65) 5

Gramen loliaceum supinum — Fl. Monsp. (74) 29

Gramen myosuroides nodosum — Fl. Angl. (56) 28

Gramen nemorosum — Fl. Angl. (56) 29

Gramen nodosum pratense, panicula fusca nigricante — Pl. Mart.-Burs. (6) [1]

Gramen palustre aculeatum germanicum vel minore — Pl. Mart.-Burs. (6) 4

Gramen panicula molli rubente — Cent. I. pl. (65) 5

Gramen panicula multiplici — Pl. Mart.-Burs. (6) [1]; Cent. I. pl. (65) 5; Fl. Monsp. (74) 30

Gramen paniculatum latifolium — Fl. Monsp. (74) 30

Gramen paniculatum molle — Fl. Angl. (56) 28

Gramen paniculatum rubrum — Fl. Monsp. (74) 30

Gramen paniculatum supinum — Fl. Monsp. (74) 30

Gramen paniculis elegantissimis; minimum — Pl. Mart.-Burs. (6) [1]

Gramen paniculis elegantissimis, sive eragrostis major — Pl. Mart.-Burs. (6) [1]

Gramen phoenicoides — Fl. Monsp. (74) 29

Gramen polytrichum — Herb. Amboin. (57) 25

Gramen pratense, spica subflavescente — Pl. Mart.-Burs. (6) [1]

Gramen repens — Herb. Amboin. (57) 25

Gramen secalinum bulbosa radice — Cent. II. pl. (66) 8

Gramen secalinum chalepense, radice tuberosa — Cent. II. pl. (66) 8

Gramen sparteum 1, panicula comosa — Cent. I. pl. (65) 6

Gramen sparteum festuceum — Cent. II. pl. (66) 33

Gramen sparteum juncifolium — Pl. Mart.-Burs. (6) 2

Gramen sparteum, panicula arundinacea fusca — Pl. Mart.-Burs. (6) 2

Gramen sparteum, panicula flavescente — Pl. Mart.-Burs. (6) 2

Gramen sparteum secundum, panicula brevi, folliculo inclusa — Cent. I. pl. (65) 4

Gramen spica brizae minus — Cent. II. pl. (66) 8; Fl. Palaest. (70) 13

Gramen spica foliacea — Fl. Angl. (56) 28[as foliaceua.]

Gramen spicatum alopecurus — Fl. Monsp. (74) 29

Gramen spicatum maritimum — Fl. Monsp. (74) 29

Gramen spicatum molle — Fl. Monsp. (74) 29

Gramen spicatum parvum — Fl. Monsp. (74) 29

Gramen spicatum plumosum — Fl. Monsp. (74) 29

Gramen spicatum reclinatum — Fl. Monsp. (74) 29

Gramen spicatum sparteum — Fl. Monsp. (74) 29

Gramen spicatum tomentosum — Fl. Monsp. (74) 29[as tomentisum]

Gramen supplex — Herb. Amboin. (57) 25

Gramen triplici spica muticae simili, angustifolium — Cent. I. pl. (65) 6

Gramen triticeum, spica latiore compacta cristatum — Pl. rar. Camsch. (30) 6

Gramen typhinum nodosum — Fl. Angl. (56) 28

Gramen typhinum phalaroides majus bulbosum aquaticum — Cent. I. pl. (65) 4

Gramen vaccinum — Herb. Amboin. (57) 25

Granadilla — Passifl. (8) 3ff.

Granadilla americana, folio oblongo leviter serrato, petalis ex viridi rubescentibus — Passifl. (8) 7

Granadilla americana, fructu subrotundo, corolla floris erecta: petalis amoene fulvis, foliis integris — Passifl. (8) 8

Granadilla androsaemi foliis, fructu jujubino — Passifl. (8) 7

Granadilla bicornis, flore candido, filamentis intortis — Passifl. (8) 14

Granadilla flore albo — Passifl. (8) 19

Granadilla flore albo, fructu reticulato — Passifl. (8) 19

Granadilla flore cupreo, fructu oliviformi — Passifl. (8) 9

Granadilla flore suave rubente, folio bicorni — Passifl. (8) 13

Granadilla foetida, folio tricuspidi villoso, flore albo — Passifl. (8) 19

Granadilla foetida, folio tricuspidi villoso, flore purpureo, variegato — Passifl. (8) 19

Granadilla folio amplotricuspidi, fructu olivae-formi — Passifl. (8) 16

Granadilla folio anguloso hederaceo foetido, flore albo — Passifl. (8) 18

Granadilla folio glabro tricuspidi et angusto, flore virescente minimo — Passifl. (8) 20

Granadilla folio hastato holosericeo, petalis candicantibus: fimbriis ex purpureo et luteo variis — Passifl. (8) 17

Granadilla folio hederaceo, flore albo, fructu globoso villoso — Passifl. (8) 28

Granadilla folio hederaceo, flore et fructu minimis — Passifl. (8) 18

Granadilla folio hederaceo, flore luteo minore — Passifl. (8) 15

Granadilla folio tricuspidi, flore ex purpura nigricante — Passifl. (8) 27

Granadilla folio tricuspidi, flore magno flavescente — Passifl. (8) 27

Granadilla folio tricuspidi, flore parvo flavescente — Passifl. (8) 15

Granadilla folio tricuspidi obtuso et oculato — Passifl. (8) 15

Granadilla folio vario — Passifl. (8) 28

Granadilla fructu citriformi, foliis oblongis — Passifl. (8) 10

Granadilla fructu minore corymboso — Passifl. (8) 11

Granadilla fructu rubente, folio bicorni — Passifl. (8) 26

Granadilla hederae similis — Passifl. (8) 21

Granadilla heterophylla, flore albo — Passifl. (8) 28

Granadilla hispanis, flos passionis italis — Passifl. (8) 21

Granadilla latifolia, fructu maliformi — Passifl. (8) 10

Granadilla magna — Passifl. (8) 25

Granadilla pentaphylla, latioribus foliis, flore caeruleo magno — Passifl. (8) 23

Granadilla pentaphyllos, flore caeruleo magno — Passifl. (8) 22

Granadilla polyphyllos, flore crispo — Passifl. (8) 24

Granadilla polyphyllos, fructu colocyntidis — Passifl. (8) 23

Granadilla polyphyllos, fructu ovato — Passifl. (8) 28

Granadilla polyphyllos lanceolata — Passifl. (8) 29

Granadilla pomifera, tiliae folio — Passifl. (8) 9

Granadilla pumila, flore parvo luteo — Passifl. (8) 15

Granadilla surinamensis, folio oblongo serrato — Passifl. (8) 7[as sirinamensis]

Granadilla surinamensis, folio ulmi — Passifl. (8) 25[as sirinamensis]

Granadilla triphylla, flore roseo — Passifl. (8) 21

Granadillae affinis coanenepilli — Passifl. (8) 26

Granatum — Sapor. med. (31) 15

Granatum litoreum — Herb. Amboin. (57) 12

Granum moluccum — Herb. Amboin. (57) 16

Granum moschatum — Herb. Amboin. (57) 15

Gratiola — Spons. pl. (12) 37; Vir. pl. (13) 7, 31; Sapor. med. (31) 20; Fl. Jam. (105) 26; Nom. bot. (107) 9; Fl. Belg. (112) 10; Pot. theae (142) 10; Purg. indig. (143) 17

Gratiola foliis lanceolatis, floribus pedunculatis — Med. purg. (181) 14

Gratiola monieria — Fl. Jam. (105) 12

Gratiola officinalis — Demonstr. pl. (49) [1]; Pl. officin. (52) 11; Fl. Monsp. (74) 8; Fl. Belg. (112) 8, 12; Purg. indig. (143) 14; Med. purg. (181) 14

Grewia — Hort. Upsal. (7) 35; Nova pl. gen. 1747 (14) 20; Nect. fl. (122) 11

Grewia occidentalis — Fl. Cap. (99) 19

Grias cauliflora — Fr. escul. (127) 13

Grielum — Aphyteia (185) 6

Grossularia — Vir. pl. (13) 12; Hosp. insect. fl. (43) 40; Noxa insect. (46) 20; Vern. arb. (47) 10, table; Fr. Svec. (91) 24, 25; Usum hist. nat. (145) 17

Grossularia domestica — Herb. Amboin. (57) 13

Grossularia sylvestris — Herb. Amboin. (57) 13

Grossularia zeylanica, baciis minoribus, acidiusculis — Nova pl. gen. 1747 (14) 30

Grus — Migr. avium (79) 9, 17, 26; Polit. nat. (109) 21

Grus daurica — Hist. nat. Rossia (144) 16

Grus melica — Var. cib. (156) 8

Gryllus — Surin. Grill. (16) 29; Oecon. nat. (20) 26; Hosp. insect. fl. (43) 9; Noxa insect. (46) 11, 13, 23, 24; Pand. insect. (93) 5, 8; Instr. peregr. (96) 12; Polit. nat. (109) 8, 18; Meloe (124) 10; Fund. entom. (154) 18, 19, 21, 22, 26, 30, [31, as 30]; Var. cib. (156) 5; Esca avium (174) 7; Bigas insect. (184) 2

Gryllus acheta thorace rotundato, corpore nigro nebuloso, elytris convolutis albidis — Cent. insect. (129) 16

Gryllus acrida — Fund. entom. (154) [31, as 30]

Gryllus acrida viridis, capite prominuto, antennis compressis longitudine thoracis — Cent. insect. (129) 15

Gryllus alarum rudimentis ocello atro oculis aureis — Cent. insect. (129) 15

Gryllus apterus, thorace spinoso, femoribus punctatis — Mus. Ad.-Frid. (11) 43

Gryllus biguttatus — Pand. fl. Ryb. (165) 10[as biguttulus]; Esca avium (174) 3, 4[as biguttulus], 7[as biguttulus]

Gryllus brachypterus — Cent. insect. (129) 7, 14

Gryllus brevicornis — Cent. insect. (129) 15

Gryllus carolinus — Cent. insect. (129) 13

Gryllus cinerarius — Cent. insect. (129) 14

Gryllus convolutus — Cent. insect. (129) 16

Gryllus crista thoracis quadrifida — Surin. Grill. (16) 27

Gryllus domesticus — Usum hist. nat. (145) 27; Pand. fl. Ryb. (165) 10

Gryllus elephas — Cent. insect. (129) 15

Gryllus ensifer — Hosp. insect. fl. (43) 26

Gryllus ex aegypto — Surin. Grill. (16) 27

Gryllus grossus — Pand. fl. Ryb. (165) 10

Gryllus gryllo-talpa — Noxa insect. (46) 18

Gryllus irroratus — Cent. insect. (129) 14

Gryllus javanus — Cent. insect. (129) 15

Gryllus locusta — Fund. entom. (154) [31, as 30]

Gryllus locusta cinereus, thoracis carina margineque postico elytrorumque margine dorsali flavis — Cent. insect. (129) 15

Gryllus locusta thorace spinis muricato cinctoque, corpore aptero — Cent. insect. (129) 15

Gryllus lunus — Cent. insect. (129) 14

Gryllus mantis elytris ovatis angulatis brevissimis, alis longitudine abdominis — Cent. insect. (129) 14

Gryllus mantis thorace laevi, elytris viridibus alis apice striatis, vertice subulato, antennis pectinatis — Cent. insect. (129) 13

Gryllus mantis thorace laevi subcarinato, elytris viridibus punctis ferrugineis vagis — Cent. insect. (129) 14

Gryllus mantis thorace subciliato subcarinato, elytris albidis fusco-nebulosis — Cent. insect. (129) 13

Gryllus maxillis atris — Noxa insect. (46) 23

Gryllus orientalis — Surin. Grill. (16) 27

Gryllus pedestris — Siren. lacert. (146) 7; Fund. entom. (154) 22; Esca avium (174) 7

Gryllus perspicillatus — Cent. insect. (129) 7, 15; Siren. lacert. (146) 7

Gryllus spinulosus — Cent. insect. (129) 15

Gryllus stridulus — Pand. fl. Ryb. (165) 10; Esca avium (174) 7

Gryllus succinctus — Cent. insect. (129) 15

Gryllus tettigonia — Fund. entom. (154) 30[as tetttigonia]

Gryllus tettigonia antennis longissimis, elytris deflexis — Cent. insect. (129) 14

Gryllus tettigonia cinerea, elytris fusco maculatis — Cent. insect. (129) 15

Gryllus tettigonia thoracis segmento posteriore crista semiorbiculata elytris nigris fasciis albis — Cent. insect. (129) 14

Gryllus thorace lineari alarum longitudine; margine denticulis ciliato — Surin. Grill. (16) 29

Gryllus unicornis — Cent. insect. (129) 13

Gryllus verrucivorus — Pand. fl. Ryb. (165) 10; Esca avium (174) 7

Gryllus viridulus — Pand. fl. Ryb. (165) 10; Esca avium (174) 7

Gryphus — Siren. lacert. (146) 8

Guaiacum — Passifl. (8) [iii]; Fl. Jam. (105) 8

Guaiacum afrum — Fl. Cap. (99) 14

Guaiacum officinale — Pl. officin. (52) 11; Pane diaet. (83) 20; Fl. Jam. (105) 16

Guaiacum sanctum — Pl. officin. (52) 17

Guamajacuguara — Mus. Ad.-Frid. (11) 32

Guettarda — Fl. Jam. (105) 27[as Guettardia]

Guettarda speciosa — Fl. Jam. (105) 21

Guidonia — Nova pl. gen. 1747 (14) 17; Fl. Jam. (105) 26

Guidonia nucis juglandis folio, major — Nova pl. gen. 1747 (14) 18

Guidonia nucis juglandis folio, minor — Nova pl. gen. 1747 (14) 18

Guilandina — Hort. Upsal. (7) 37; Herb. Amboin. (57) 19

Guilandina bonduc — Fl. Jam. (105) 16, 25

Guilandina moringa — Demonstr. pl. (49) 11, 27; Pl. officin. (52) 5, 14; Herb. Amboin. (57) 8[as Guilandi]; Fl. Palaest. (70) 19; Fl. Jam. (105) 16[as morhinga], 25[as morhinga]

Gulo — Cervus (60) 18

Gumira litorea — Herb. Amboin. (57) 14

Gundelia — Mund. invis. (149) 20

Gundelia tournefortii — Fl. Palaest. (70) 27

Gunnera — Aphyteia (185) 6

Gunnera perpensa — Rar. Norv. (157) 18

Gustavia — Pl. Surin. (177) 4, 18

Gustavia angusta — Pl. Surin. (177) 12, 17, 18

Gymnotus — Mus. Ad.-Frid. (11) 39; Surin. Grill. (16) 26

Gymnotus electricus — Siren. lacert. (146) 8[as electicus]

Gypsophila — Nova pl. gen. 1751 (32) 40, 48

Gypsophila aggregata — Fl. Monsp. (74) 7, 16

Gypsophila altissima — Demonstr. pl. (49) 12; Hist. nat. Rossia (144) 29

Gypsophila fastigiata — Demonstr. pl. (49) 12; Stat. pl. (55) 23; Calend. fl. (72) [14]; Pl. tinct. (97) 18; Colon. pl. (158) 7

Gypsophila foliis lanceolatis scabris, corollis recurvatis — Nova pl. gen. 1751 (32) 41

Gypsophila foliis lanceolatis, staminibus pistillo brevioribus — Nova pl. gen. 1751 (32) 41

Gypsophila foliis lanceolatis subtrinerviis — Nova pl. gen. 1751 (32) 41

Gypsophila foliis lanceolatis subtrinerviis tomentosis, caule pubescente — Cent. I. pl. (65) 11

Gypsophila foliis lanceolato-linearibus subtriquetris laevibus obtusis — Nova pl. gen. 1751 (32) 42

Gypsophila foliis lineari-lanceolatis planis, caule dichotomo, petalis emarginatis — Nova pl. gen. 1751 (32) 42

Gypsophila foliis linearibus planis, caule dichotomo, petalis crenatis — Nova pl. gen. 1751 (32) 42[as Gypsophita]

Gypsophila foliis mucronatis, floribus aggregatis — Nova pl. gen. 1751 (32) 41

Gypsophila muralis — Stat. pl. (55) 22

Gypsophila paniculata — Demonstr. pl. (49) 12; Hist. nat. Rossia (144) 29

Gypsophila prostrata — Demonstr. pl. (49) 12

Gypsophila repens — Demonstr. pl. (49) 12; Fl. alp. (71) 17; Hist. nat. Rossia (144) 29

Gypsophila rigida — Fl. Monsp. (74) 16

Gypsophila struthium — Pl. tinct. (97) 18; Obs. mat. med. (171) 4[as strutium]

Gypsophila tomentosa — Cent. I. pl. (65) 11

Gyrinus natator — Pand. fl. Ryb. (165) 7

Haedus ambraccius — Var. cib. (156) 8

Haemanthus — Hort. Upsal. (7) 37; Fl. Cap. (99) 6, 9; Pl. rar. Afr. (115) 4; Fund. fr. (123) 18

Haemanthus coccineus — Fl. Cap. (99) 4, 13

Haemanthus puniceus — Demonstr. pl. (49) 10; Fl. Cap. (99) 13

Haematopus ostralegus — Migr. avium (79) 29

Haematoxylum — Passifl. (8) [iii][as Hematoxylon]; Fl. Jam. (105) 8[as Haematoxylon]; Nom. bot. (107) 12

Haematoxylum campechianum — Pl. officin. (52) 6[as Haematoxylon campescanum]; Pl. tinct. (97) 17[as Haemathoxylon campechianam]; Fl. Jam. (105) 16[as Haematoxylon]

Halecus litorea — Herb. Amboin. (57) 14

Halecus terrestris — Herb. Amboin. (57) 14

Halesia — Fl. Jam. (105) 27

Halex — Var. cib. (156) 17

Haliaetus — Migr. avium (79) 20; Polit. nat. (109) 14[as Halietus]

Halicacabus baccifer — Herb. Amboin. (57) 26

Halicacabus indicus — Herb. Amboin. (57) 26

Halimus — Fung. melit. (69) 10; Fl. Jam. (105) 26

Haliotis — Fund. test. (166) 17, 25

Haliotis parva — Fund. test. (166) 39

Halleria lucida — Fl. Cap. (99) 15

Hamadryas — Fl. Cap. (99) [1]

Hamamelis — Nova pl. gen. 1751 (32) 8, 12; Nect. fl. (122) 11

Hamamelis virginiana — Specif. Canad. (76) 26

Hansape — Nova pl. gen. 1747 (14) 10

Harengus — Noxa insect. (46) 30

Harpyja — Polit. nat. (109) 14[as Harpya]

Hartogia — Nect. fl. (122) 8

Hartogia capensis — Fl. Cap. (99) 12

Hasselquistia aegyptiaca — Cent. I. pl. (65) 9; Fl. Palaest. (70) 16

Haut — Surin. Grill. (16) 7

Hay — Surin. Grill. (16) 7

Hebenaster — Herb. Amboin. (57) 11

Hebenstretia — Fl. Cap. (99) 6, 8

Hebenstretia dentata — Fl. Cap. (99) 16

Hebenstretia integrifolia — Fl. Cap. (99) 16

Hedera — Hort. Upsal. (7) 33; Spons. pl. (12) 10; Fl. oecon. (17) 6; Gem. arb. (24) 6; Sapor. med. (31) 9; Nova pl. gen. 1751 (32) 12; Metam. pl. (67) 13; Fr. Svec. (91) [ii]; Nom. bot. (107) 11; Polit. nat. (109) 5; Fl. Belg. (112) 10

Hedera arbor folio hastato — Pl. Jam. (102) 11

Hedera arborea — Spons. pl. (12) 10

Hedera helix — Demonstr. pl. (49) 7; Pl. officin. (52) 11; Stat. pl. (55) 17; Fl. Angl. (56) 12; Fung. melit. (69) 2; Fl. Palaest. (70) 15; Fl. Monsp. (74) 12; Prodr. fl. Dan. (82) 15; Fr. Svec. (91) 4, 18; Fl. Belg. (112) 14; Fl. Åker. (162) 9

Hedera humi repens — Spons. pl. (12) 10

Hedera indica, folio simplici integro, claviculata, racemosa, racemis laxis, uvis rotundis nigris — Nova pl. gen. 1747 (14) 6

Hedera major sterilis — Spons. pl. (12) 10

Hedera murucuja vesicaria lanuginosa, odoris gravis — Passifl. (8) 20

Hedera poetica — Spons. pl. (12) 10

Hedera quinquefolia — Demonstr. pl. (49) 7

Hedera repens — Pan Svec. (26) 17

Hedyosmos — Nova pl. gen. 1751 (32) 12

Hedyotis — Nova pl. gen. 1747 (14) [vi], 7

Hedyotis auricularia — Menthae (153) 11; Obs. mat. med. (171) 4

Hedyotis foliis lanceolatis, petiolatis, corymbis terminantibus involucratis — Nova pl. gen. 1747 (14) 8

Hedyotis foliis lanceolato-ovatis, floribus verticillatis — Vir. pl. (13) 18; Nova pl. gen. 1747 (14) 8

Hedyotis fruticosa — Iter Chin. (161) 9

Hedyotis stellata — Nova pl. gen. 1747 (14) 8

Hedysarum — Vir. pl. (13) 23; Pl. hybr. (33) 29; Cui bono? (42) 20; Fl. Angl. (56) 5; Fl. Jam. (105) 26; Nom. bot. (107) 16; Fund. fr. (123) 18

Hedysarum alhagi — Demonstr. pl. (49) 20; Fl. Palaest. (70) 25

Hedysarum alpinum — Demonstr. pl. (49) 20; Fl. alp. (71) 21; Hist. nat. Rossia (144) 23, 31

Hedysarum barbatum — Pl. Jam. (102) 20; Fl. Jam. (105) 19

Hedysarum biarticulatum — Iter Chin. (161) 9

Hedysarum canadense — Hort. Upsal. (7) 37; Somn. pl. (68) 19

Hedysarum canescens — Demonstr. pl. (49) 20; Fl. Jam. (105) 19

Hedysarum caput galli — Fl. Palaest. (70) 26; Fl. Monsp. (74) 23

Hedysarum coronarium — Demonstr. pl. (49) 20; Somn. pl. (68) 17; Fl. Palaest. (70) 26; Hort. cul. (132) 24

Hedysarum diphyllum — Fl. Jam. (105) 19

Hedysarum ecastaphyllum — Pl. Jam. (102) 20; Fl. Jam. (105) 19

Hedysarum flexuosum — Demonstr. pl. (49) 20

Hedysarum gangeticum — Herb. Amboin. (57) 28; Pl. Jam. (102) 20

Hedysarum hamatum — Pl. Jam. (102) 20; Fl. Jam. (105) 19

Hedysarum hamatum viscosa — Pl. Jam. (102) 20

Hedysarum onobrychis — Demonstr. pl. (49) 20; Fl. Angl. (56) 21; Hort. acad. (63) 11; Fl. Monsp. (74) 23; Prodr. fl. Dan. (82) 22; Hist. nat. Rossia (144) 31

Hedysarum pulchellum — Demonstr. pl. (49) 20

Hedysarum spinosum — Demonstr. pl. (49) 20

Hedysarum umbellatum — Herb. Amboin. (57) 17

Hedysarum virginicum — Demonstr. pl. (49) 20

Helenia — Nova pl. gen. 1751 (32) 10

Heleniastrum — Nova pl. gen. 1751 (32) 10

Helenium — Hort. Upsal. (7) 35; Anandria (9) 12; Nova pl. gen. 1747 (14) 25

Helenium autumnale — Demonstr. pl. (49) 23

Helenium fruticosum afrum, foliis creberrimis pinum aemulantibus — Pl. rar. Afr. (115) 22

Helenium seu enula campana — Nova pl. gen. 1747 (14) 26

Helenium vulgare — Nova pl. gen. 1747 (14) 26

Helianthemum tenuifolium glabrum erectum, luteo flore — Cent. I. pl. (65) 14

Helianthus — Peloria (3) 9; Spons. pl. (12) 33[as Helicanthus]; Pl. hybr. (33) 7, 29; Stat. pl. (55) 5; Nom. bot. (107) 17; Fund. fr. (123) 17

Helianthus annuus — Vern. arb. (47) 9; Demonstr. pl. (49) 23; Calend. fl. (72) [17], [22]; Mac. olit. (113) 16; Pl. Alstr. (121) 5; Hort. cul. (132) 23, 25

Helianthus calycibus squarrosis, undulatis, frondosis; radiis octopetalis — Cent. I. pl. (65) 28

Helianthus decapetalus — Demonstr. pl. (49) 24

Helianthus divaricatus — Demonstr. pl. (49) 24; Calend. fl. (72) [17]

Helianthus frondosus — Cent. I. pl. (65) 28; Calend. fl. (72) [18]

Helianthus giganteus — Demonstr. pl. (49) 24; Calend. fl. (72) [18]

Helianthus multiflorus — Demonstr. pl. (49) 23; Pl. rar. Afr. (115) 7

Helianthus radice annua — Pl. hybr. (33) 17

Helianthus radice tereti inflexa perenni — Pl. hybr. (33) 17

Helianthus radice tuberosa — Pl. hybr. (33) 17

Helianthus tuberosus — Demonstr. pl. (49) 24; Calend. fl. (72) [21]; Mac. olit. (113) 12[as Hellianthus]; Hort. cul. (132) 17

Heliconia bihai — Pl. Surin. (177) 6

Helicteres — Nect. fl. (122) 9[as Helicteris]

Helicteres isora — Fl. Jam. (105) 20[as Helioteres]

Heliotropium — Hort. Upsal. (7) 35; Vir. pl. (13) 18; Vern. arb. (47) 9

Heliotropium arborescens — Fl. Jam. (105) 13

Heliotropium arboreum maritimum tomentosum — Pl. Jam. (102) 8

Heliotropium curassavicum — Fl. Jam. (105) 13; Pl. rar. Afr. (115) 6

Heliotropium europaeum — Demonstr. pl. (49) 5; Fl. Palaest. (70) 14; Fl. Monsp. (74) 10

Heliotropium fruticosum — Pl. Jam. (102) 8; Fl. Jam. (105) 13

Heliotropium gnaphalodes — Pl. Jam. (102) 8; Fl. Jam. (105) 13

Heliotropium indicum — Demonstr. pl. (49) 5; Fl. Jam. (105) 13; Pl. Surin. (177) 5

Helix — Nova pl. gen. 1751 (32) 12; Var. cib. (156) 5; Fund. test. (166) 17, 36

Helix arbustorum — Fund. test. (166) 7

Helix auricularia — Fund. test. (166) 36; Esca avium (174) 10

Helix citrina — Fund. test. (166) 38

Helix decollata — Fund. test. (166) 36

Helix fragilis — Esca avium (174) 10

Helix lapicida — Fund. test. (166) 7; Esca avium (174) 10

Helix lusitanica — Fund. test. (166) 36

106

Helix nemoralis — Usum musc. (148) 7; Esca avium (174) 10

Helix pomatia — Fund. test. (166) 3, 28

Helix vivipara — Fund. test. (166) 16; Esca avium (174) 10

Helleborine mariana, bupleurifolio angustissimo, purpurascente flore; caule aphyllo — Nova pl. gen. 1751 (32) 24

Helleborine mariana monanthos, flore longo purpurascente liliaceo — Nova pl. gen. 1751 (32) 24

Helleborine virginiana, ophioglossi folio — Nova pl. gen. 1751 (32) 24

Helleborus — Hort. Upsal. (7) 36; Anandria (9) 4; Spons. pl. (12) 30, 32; Vir. pl. (13) 7, 21, 25, 31; Pan Svec. (26) 3; Odor. med. (40) 13; Nom. bot. (107) 14; Prol. pl. 1760 (114) 13, 14; Mors. serp. (119) 2; Nect. fl. (122) 13, 15; Fund. fr. (123) 16, 23; Cimicifuga (173) 2

Helleborus aconiti folio, flore globoso croceo — Peloria (3) 9

Helleborus foetidus — Fl. Angl. (56) 18; Fl. Palaest. (70) 22; Fl. Monsp. (74) 19; Obs. mat. med. (171) 4

Helleborus foliis ternatis, scapo unifloro — Pl. rar. Camsch. (30) 22

Helleborus hyemalis — Demonstr. pl. (49) 15

Helleborus niger — Demonstr. pl. (49) 15; Pl. officin. (52) 11; Fl. Palaest. (70) 22; Fl. alp. (71) 19; Med. purg. (181) 18

Helleborus scapo subbifloro subnudo, foliis pedatis — Med. purg. (181) 18

Helleborus trifolius — Hist. nat. Rossia (144) 30

Helleborus trollius — Pan Svec. (26) 26

Helleborus viridis — Demonstr. pl. (49) 15; Fl. Angl. (56) 18; Hort. cul. (132) 24

Helonias — Nova pl. gen. 1751 (32) 9, [13, as 15], 17, 48; Fung. melit. (69) 2

Helonias bullata — Specif. Canad. (76) 10

Helxine — Hort. Upsal. (7) 34; Anandria (9) 5; Vir. pl. (13) 32; Fl. oecon. (17) 10, 11; Pl. escul. (35) 27; Rhabarbarum (41) 5, 6, 17; Demonstr. pl. (49) [vii]; Stat. pl. (55) 6; Oves (61) 18; Instr. peregr. (96) 10

Helxine caule tetragono aculeato — Specif. Canad. (76) 22

Helxine sativum — Pan Svec. (26) 21; Hosp. insect. fl. (43) 21

Helxine scandens — Pan Svec. (26) 21; Pl. escul. (35) 15

Hemerobius — Cui bono? (42) 9; Metam. pl. (67) 6; Polit. nat. (109) 12; Fund. entom. (154) 30

Hemerobius albus — Pand. fl. Ryb. (165) 12

Hemerobius antennis pectinatis, alis albidis signaturis nervisque fuscis albo articulatis — Cent. insect. (129) 29

Hemerobius chrysops — Polit. nat. (109) 10[as Haemerobius crysops]; Esca avium (174) 8

Hemerobius pectinicornis — Cent. insect. (129) 29

Hemerobius perla — Polit. nat. (109) 10[as Haemerobius]; Fund. entom. (154) 20, 25; Pand. fl. Ryb. (165) 12

Hemerocallis — Hort. Upsal. (7) 33; Pl. Alstr. (121) 8ff.

Hemerocallis flava — Pl. hybr. (33) 28; Calend. fl. (72) [13]; Hort. cul. (132) 24[as flavus]; Hist. nat. Rossia (144) 29; Hypericum (186) 7

Hemerocallis fulva — Pl. hybr. (33) 28; Calend. fl. (72) [17], [18]; Hort. cul. (132) 24[as fulvus]; Hypericum (186) 7

Hemerocallis liliastrum — Demonstr. pl. (49) 10[as Hemerocaliis]; Fl. alp. (71) 15

Hemerocallis lilio-asphodelus flavus — Demonstr. pl. (49) 10[as Hemerocaliis]

Hemimeris bonae spei — Pl. rar. Afr. (115) 8

Hemionitis — Acrostichum (10) 3, 6, 7, 8

Hemionitis lanceolata — Fl. Jam. (105) 23

Hemionitis palmata — Fl. Jam. (105) 23

Hemionitis parasita — Fl. Jam. (105) 23

Hepatica — Peloria (3) 9; Spons. pl. (12) 59; Gem. arb. (24) 5; Vern. arb. (47) 8; Prol. pl. 1763 (130) 18; Pand. fl. Ryb. (165) 20

Hepatica verna — Pan Svec. (26) 25

Heracleum — Hort. Upsal. (7) 34; Anandria (9) 5; Fl. oecon. (17) 7; Obst. med. (34) 6; Pl. escul. (35) 27, 28, 29; Cui bono? (42) 20; Noxa insect. (46) 22; Pand. insect. (93) 13; Nom. bot. (107) 11

Heracleum alpinum — Fl. alp. (71) 15, 24

Heracleum angustifolium — Pand. fl. Ryb. (165) 17[as augustifolium]

Heracleum austriacum — Fl. alp. (71) 15, 24

Heracleum branca ursi — Pl. escul. (35) 11

Heracleum panaces — Fl. alp. (71) 15, 24; Calend. fl. (72) [12]; Hist. nat. Rossia (144) 23, 28

Heracleum panax — Demonstr. pl. (49) 8

Heracleum sibiricum — Demonstr. pl. (49) 8; Hist. nat. Rossia (144) 23, 28

Heracleum sphondylium — Herbat. Upsal. (50) 8; Stat. pl. (55) 20; Fl. Angl. (56) 13; Calend. fl. (72) [14][as spondylium]; Fl. Monsp. (74) 13; Prodr. fl. Dan. (82) 16; Fl. Belg. (112) 15; Fl. Åker. (162) 9; Pand. fl. Ryb. (165) 17; Obs. mat. med. (171) 3

Heracleum sphondylium hirsutum foliis angustioribus — Metam. pl. (67) 19

Heracleum sphondylium vulgare hirsutum — Metam. pl. (67) 19

Heracleum vulgare — Pan Svec. (26) 19; Hosp. insect. fl. (43) 18

Herba crinium — Herb. Amboin. (57) 15[as crinalium]

Herba memoriae — Herb. Amboin. (57) 26

Herba moeroris alba — Herb. Amboin. (57) 26

Herba moeroris rubra — Herb. Amboin. (57) 26

Herba sentiens — Herb. Amboin. (57) 22

Herba spiralis — Herb. Amboin. (57) 28

Herba supplex — Herb. Amboin. (57) 27

Herba urinalis — Peloria (3) 7

Herba veterum sapientum — Acetaria (77) 10

Herba vitiliginum — Herb. Amboin. (57) 26

Heritinandel — Amphib. Gyll. (5) 3

Hermannia — Hort. Upsal. (7) 37; Pl. hybr. (33) 29; Fl. Cap. (99) 6, 8, 9; Nect. fl. (122) 5, 10; Fund. fr. (123) 18

Hermannia alnifolia — Fl. Cap. (99) 16

Hermannia althaeaefolia — Demonstr. pl. (49) 18[as altheaefolia]; Fl. Cap. (99) 16[as althaeifolia]

Hermannia foliis lanceolatis integris tridentatis — Pl. rar. Afr. (115) 13

Hermannia foliis ternatis petiolatis — Pl. rar. Afr. (115) 13

Hermannia grossularifolia — Fl. Cap. (99) 16

Hermannia hyssopifolia — Demonstr. pl. (49) 18; Fl. Cap. (99) 16

Hermannia lavendulifolia — Fl. Cap. (99) 16

Hermannia pinnata — Fl. Cap. (99) 16

Hermannia trifoliata — Fl. Cap. (99) 16

Hermannia trifurcata — Pl. rar. Afr. (115) 13[as trifurca]

Hermannia triphylla — Pl. rar. Afr. (115) 13

Herminium — Vir. pl. (13) 24

Herminium bifolium — Pan Svec. (26) 34

Herminium monorchis — Pan Svec. (26) 34

Hernandia — Herb. Amboin. (57) 5; Nect. fl. (122) 4

Hernandia ovigera — Cent. I. pl. (65) 2

Hernandia ovigera, foliis ovatis basi petiolatis — Herb. Amboin. (57) 14

Hernandia sonora — Herb. Amboin. (57) 11; Fl. Jam. (105) 21[as Hernandria]

Herniaria — Erica (163) 2

Herniaria caulibus fruticosis, floribus quadrifidis — Cent. I. pl. (65) 8

Herniaria fruticosa — Cent. I. pl. (65) 8; Fl. Monsp. (74) 12

Herniaria fruticosa, viticulis lignosis — Cent. I. pl. (65) 8

Herniaria glabra — Pan Svec. (26) 18; Herbat. Upsal. (50) 10; Pl. officin. (52) 11; Stat. pl. (55) 21; Fl. Angl. (56) 13; Fl. Monsp. (74) 12; Prodr. fl. Dan. (82) 15; Fl. Belg. (112) 14; Fl. Åker. (162) 9

Herniaria hirsuta — Demonstr. pl. (49) 7; Fl. Angl. (56) 13

Herniaria lenticulata — Fl. Angl. (56) 13

Herniaria vulgaris — Demonstr. pl. (49) 7

Hesperis — Peloria (3) 10; Hort. Upsal. (7) 34; Calend. fl. (72) [10]; Nom. bot. (107) 15

Hesperis africana — Demonstr. pl. (49) 17; Fl. Cap. (99) 16

Hesperis caule simplici, foliis ovato-lanceolatis denticulatis — Pl. Mart.-Burs. (6) 16

Hesperis flore albo minimo, siliqua longa, folio profunde dentato — Cent. II. pl. (66) 24

Hesperis maritima supina exigua — Cent. I. pl. (65) 19

Hesperis matronalis — Demonstr. pl. (49) 17; Fl. Angl. (56) 20; Calend. fl. (72) [11]; Fl. Monsp. (74) 21; Prodr. fl. Dan. (82) 21; Pl. Alstr. (121) 5; Hort. cul. (132) 24; Hist. nat. Rossia (144) 21

Hesperis sibirica — Demonstr. pl. (49) 17; Hist. nat. Rossia (144) 31

Hesperis tristis — Demonstr. pl. (49) 17; Hort. cul. (132) 23

Hesperis verna — Fl. Monsp. (74) 21

Heuchera — Pl. rar. Camsch. (30) 5; Nova pl. gen. 1751 (32) 8

Heuchera americana — Hist. nat. Rossia (144) 12

Hibiscus — Hort. Upsal. (7) 37; Gem. arb. (24) 6; Pl. hybr. (33) 29; Chin. Lagerstr. (64) 5; Pand. insect. (93) [17, as 38]; Nect. fl. (122) 4

Hibiscus abelmoschus — Demonstr. pl. (49) 19; Pl. officin. (52) 3; Herb. Amboin. (57) 15[as abelmosch]; Fl. Jam. (105) 19

Hibiscus africanus — Demonstr. pl. (49) 19

Hibiscus cancellatus — Pl. Surin. (177) 12

Hibiscus esculentus — Fl. Palaest. (70) 24; Fl. Jam. (105) 19; Pl. Surin. (177) 12

Hibiscus fraternus — Pl. Surin. (177) 12

Hibiscus malvaviscus — Fl. Jam. (105) 19

Hibiscus manihot — Demonstr. pl. (49) 19

Hibiscus moscheutos — Cui bono? (42) 22; Demonstr. pl. (49) 19

Hibiscus mutabilis — Demonstr. pl. (49) 19; Herb. Amboin. (57) 15; Fl. Cap. (99) 2; Fl. Jam. (105) 19

Hibiscus palustris — Demonstr. pl. (49) 19

Hibiscus pentacarpos — Demonstr. pl. (49) 19; Colon. pl. (158) 11[as pentacarpus]

Hibiscus populneus — Demonstr. pl. (49) 19; Herb. Amboin. (57) 10; Fl. Jam. (105) 19

Hibiscus rosa chinensis — Herb. Amboin. (57) 15

Hibiscus sabdariffa — Demonstr. pl. (49) 19; Somn. pl. (68) 16; Inebr. (117) 11

Hibiscus salicifolius — Pl. Surin. (177) 12

Hibiscus sororius — Pl. Surin. (177) 12

Hibiscus surattensis — Herb. Amboin. (57) 15

Hibiscus syriacus — Hort. Upsal. (7) 35[as cyriacus]; Demonstr. pl. (49) 19; Calend. fl. (72) [18]

Hibiscus tiliaceus — Herb. Amboin. (57) 10; Fl. Jam. (105) 19[as tilaceus]; Pl. Surin. (177) 12

Hibiscus trionum — Demonstr. pl. (49) 19; Fl. Cap. (99) 9, 16

Hibiscus virginicus — Demonstr. pl. (49) 19; Colon. pl. (158) 11

Hibiscus vitifolius — Demonstr. pl. (49) 19

Hibiscus zeylanicus — Herb. Amboin. (57) 15

Hieracium — Peloria (3) 10; Spons. pl. (12) 47; Vir. pl. (13) 25; Fl. oecon. (17) 19; Mirac. insect. (45) 15; Fl. alp. (71) 24; Pand. insect. (93) 18; Pl. tinct. (97) 10; Nom. bot. (107) 17

Hieracium alpinum — Stat. pl. (55) 16; Fl. Angl. (56) 21; Fl. alp. (71) 21; Rar. Norv. (157) 11

Hieracium amplexicaule — Fl. alp. (71) 21

Hieracium aphyllum — Fl. Monsp. (74) 30

Hieracium aurantiacum — Demonstr. pl. (49) 22; Fl. alp. (71) 21; Hort. cul. (132) 24

Hieracium auricula — Herbat. Upsal. (50) 17; Prodr. fl. Dan. (82) 22; Fl. Åker. (162) 17; Pand. fl. Ryb. (165) 21

Hieracium blattarioides — Fl. alp. (71) 21

Hieracium bulbosum — Fl. Monsp. (74) 30

Hieracium capense — Pl. rar. Afr. (115) 17[as Hiercium]

Hieracium capillaceum — Fl. Monsp. (74) 30

Hieracium castorei odore — Fl. Angl. (56) 26

Hieracium caule ramoso, foliis radicalibus ovatis dentatis: caulino minore — Pl. Mart.-Burs. (6) 9

Hieracium caule unifloro, calyce villoso — Pl. Mart.-Burs. (6) 9

Hieracium cerinthoides — Demonstr. pl. (49) 22; Fl. alp. (71) 21

Hieracium chondrilloides — Fl. alp. (71) 21

Hieracium cichoraceum — Pan Svec. (26) 31

Hieracium dentatum — Fl. Monsp. (74) 30

Hieracium dentis leonis folio obtuso, majus — Pl. Mart.-Burs. (6) 8

Hieracium dubium — Herbat. Upsal. (50) 17

Hieracium falcatum — Pl. hybr. (33) 13

Hieracium flore singulari — Fl. Angl. (56) 27

Hieracium foliis integris lanceolatis, scapo nudo multifloro — Pl. Mart.-Burs. (6) 9

Hieracium foliis lanceolatis amplexicaulibus dentatis, floribus solitariis, calycibus laxis — Pl. Mart.-Burs. (6) 9[as lanceotatis]

Hieracium foliis lyratis obtusis dentatis, scapo nudo multifloro — Cent. II. pl. (66) 30

Hieracium foliis oblongis dentatis scabris, caule nudo multifloro, pedunculis serioribus altioribus — Pl. rar. Afr. (115) 17[as Hiercium]

Hieracium foliis oblongo-ovatis, hirsutis, sessilibus, subdentatis; pedunculis multifloris — Cent. I. pl. (65) 26

Hieracium foliis obverse ovatis lanceolatis retrorsum dentatis, caule simplici, floribus terminatricibus confertis — Pl. Mart.-Burs. (6) 8

Hieracium fruticosum — Pan Svec. (26) 31; Demonstr. pl. (49) 22

Hieracium fruticosum alpinum — Fl. Angl. (56) 27

Hieracium fruticosum latifolium glabrum — Fl. Angl. (56) 27

Hieracium gmelini — Hist. nat. Rossia (144) 32

Hieracium hedypnoides — Fl. Monsp. (74) 24

Hieracium incanum — Fl. alp. (71) 21

Hieracium lanuginosum — Fl. Monsp. (74) 30

Hieracium lapponicum — Pan Svec. (26) 31

Hieracium lyratum — Hist. nat. Rossia (144) 32

Hieracium minimum falcatum — Pl. Mart.-Burs. (6) 8

Hieracium montanum angustifolium — Fl. Angl. (56) 27

Hieracium montanum latifolium glabrum minor — Fl. Angl. (56) 26

Hieracium montanum tomentosum — Cent. I. pl. (65) 26

Hieracium murorum — Demonstr. pl. (49) 22; Herbat. Upsal. (50) 9; Stat. pl. (55) 18; Fl. Angl. (56) 21; Metam. pl. (67) 24; Fl. Monsp. (74) 24; Prodr. fl. Dan. (82) 22; Fl. Belg. (112) 20; Fl. Åker. (162) 17

Hieracium murorum laciniatum — Fl. Monsp. (74) 30

Hieracium murorum sylvaticum — Fl. Angl. (56) 21

Hieracium narbonense rotundifolium caule aphyllo — Pl. Mart.-Burs. (6) 8

Hieracium paludosum — Herbat. Upsal. (50) 19

Hieracium pilosella — Hosp. insect. fl. (43) 29; Herbat. Upsal. (50) 10; Pl. officin. (52) 5; Stat. pl. (55) 21; Fl. Angl. (56) 21; Fl. Monsp. (74) 24; Prodr. fl. Dan. (82) 22; Pl. tinct. (97) 29; Fl. Belg. (112) 20; Fl. Åker. (162) 17

Hieracium pilosella major multiflorum — Pan Svec. (26) 31

Hieracium pilosella minor multiflorum — Pan Svec. (26) 31

Hieracium pilosella officinarum — Pan Svec. (26) 31

Hieracium porrifolium — Fl. alp. (71) 21

Hieracium praemorsum — Herbat. Upsal. (50) 8; Fl. Monsp. (74) 24; Prodr. fl. Dan. (82) 22; Pand. fl. Ryb. (165) 21

Hieracium pulmonaria — Pan Svec. (26) 31; Hosp. insect. fl. (43) 30

Hieracium pulmonaria angustifolia — Fl. Angl. (56) 27

Hieracium pyrenaicum — Fl. alp. (71) 21

Hieracium sabaudum — Demonstr. pl. (49) 22[as subacidum; corr. subaudum, p. 27]; Fl. Angl. (56) 21; Prodr. fl. Dan. (82) 22

Hieracium sanctum — Cent. II. pl. (66) 30; Fl. Palaest. (70) 27

Hieracium saxatile — Fl. Angl. (56) 27

Hieracium thalii upsaliense — Pan Svec. (26) 31

Hieracium tomentosum — Cent. I. pl. (65) 26

Hieracium umbellatum — Demonstr. pl. (49) 22; Herbat. Upsal. (50) 9; Stat. pl. (55) 21; Fl. Angl. (56) 21; Fl. Monsp. (74) 24; Prodr. fl. Dan. (82) 22; Pl. tinct. (97) 23; Fl. Belg. (112) 20; Fl. Åker. (162) 17; Pand. fl. Ryb. (165) 21

Hieracium umbellatum sabaudum — Calend. fl. (72) [17]

Hinnulus — Mat. med. anim. (29) 7

Hippelaphus — Cervus (60) 4

Hippobosca — Noxa insect. (46) 11, 27, 28, 30; Cynogr. (54) 21; Polit. nat. (109) 21

Hippobosca aptera — Oves (61) 22

Hippobosca avicularia — Pand. fl. Ryb. (165) 16

Hippobosca equina — Pand. fl. Ryb. (165) 16

Hippocampus — Mus. Ad.-Frid. (11) 43; Nat. pelagi (84) 11

Hippocampus aculeatus — Mus. Ad.-Frid. (11) 43

Hippocastanum — Arb. Svec. (101) 18

Hippocrepis — Hort. Upsal. (7) 34; Fl. Angl. (56) 5; Nom. bot. (107) 16

Hippocrepis comosa — Fl. Angl. (56) 21; Hort. acad. (63) 11; Fl. Monsp. (74) 23

Hippocrepis leguminibus solitariis sessilibus — Pl. Mart.-Burs. (6) 27

Hippocrepis multisiliquosa — Demonstr. pl. (49) 20[as multisiliqua]; Fl. Monsp. (74) 23

Hippocrepis perpusillus — Fl. Monsp. (74) 23

Hippogrostis amboinica — Herb. Amboin. (57) 25

Hippomane — Vir. pl. (13) 35; Fl. Jam. (105) 26; Aer habit. (106) 19; Nect. fl. (122) 4

Hippomane biglandulosa — Pl. Surin. (177) 15

Hippomane mancinella — Fl. Jam. (105) 20

Hippophae — Spons. pl. (12) 41; Fl. oecon. (17) 26; Cui bono? (42) 20; Fr. Svec. (91) [ii], 24, 25; Nom. bot. (107) 18; Usum hist. nat. (145) 17

Hippophae maritima — Gem. arb. (24) 22; Pan Svec. (26) 36

Hippophae rhamnoides — Stat. pl. (55) 12; Fl. Angl. (56) 24; Calend. fl. (72) [10]; Prodr. fl. Dan. (82) 25; Fr. Svec. (91) 3, 13; Fl. Belg. (112) 23; Fr. escul. (127) 7; Rar. Norv. (157) 17

Hippopotamus — Vir. pl. (13) 16; Mat. med. anim. (29) 5; Fl. Cap. (99) [1]

Hippuris — Hort. Upsal. (7) 41; Morb. hyeme (38) 8

Hippuris aquatica — Pan Svec. (26) 12

Hippuris vulgaris — Herbat. Upsal. (50) 11; Stat. pl. (55) 13; Fl. Angl. (56) 9; Fl. Monsp. (74) 8; Prodr. fl. Dan. (82) 12; Fl. Belg. (112) 12; Fl. Åker. (162) 5

Hirudo — Taenia (19) 10, 25; Chin. Lagerstr. (64) 29; Hirudo (136) 2ff.; Usum hist. nat. (145) 29

Hirudo complanata — Hirudo (136) 3

Hirudo depressa fusca, lineis flavis dorsalibus sex: intermediis immaculatis; subtus cinerea nigro maculata — Hirudo (136) 4

Hirudo depressa fusca: margine laterali flavo — Mat. med. anim. (29) 18

Hirudo geometra — Hirudo (136) 3

Hirudo indica — Hirudo (136) 3

Hirudo maxime in anglia vulgaris — Mat. med. anim. (29) 18

Hirudo medicinalis — Hirudo (136) 3, 4

Hirudo muricata — Chin. Lagerstr. (64) 29; Hirudo (136) 3

Hirudo octoculata — Hirudo (136) 3

Hirudo sanguisuga — Hirudo (136) 3; Esca avium (174) [9, as 17]

Hirudo stagnalis — Hirudo (136) 3

Hirundo — Mus. Ad.-Frid. (11) 42; Oecon. nat. (20) 39, 41; Morb. hyeme (38) 3, 13; Calend. fl. (72) [9], [10], [19]; Migr. avium (79) 18, 33, 34, 35, 36; Polit. nat. (109) 12; Prol. pl. 1760 (114) 6; Esca avium (174) 3

Hirundo apus — Migr. avium (79) 36

Hirundo daurica — Hist. nat. Rossia (144) 16

Hirundo dorso nigro caerulescente, rectricibus immaculatis — Mat. med. anim. (29) 11

Hirundo marina major, capite albo — Chin. Lagerstr. (64) 12[as abbo]

Hirundo purpurea — Migr. avium (79) 16

Hirundo ruricola — Migr. avium (79) 35

Hirundo sylvestris — Mat. med. anim. (29) 11

Hirundo urbica — Migr. avium (79) 35

Hispa — Fund. entom. (154) 29

Hispa clavicornis — Pand. fl. Ryb. (165) 8

Hister — Fund. entom. (154) 29

Hister unicolor — Pand. fl. Ryb. (165) 7

Holcus — Odor. med. (40) 12; Fund. agrost. (152) 5, 28, 33, 37

Holcus lanatus — Demonstr. pl. (49) 26; Stat. pl. (55) 22; Fl. Angl. (56) 25; Calend. fl. (72) [15]; Fl. Monsp. (74) 28; Prodr. fl. Dan. (82) 25; Fl. Belg. (112) 23; Fund. agrost. (152) 7, 31

Holcus latifolius — Fund. agrost. (152) 31

Holcus mollis — Fl. Belg. (112) 23

Holcus odoratus — Demonstr. pl. (49) 26; Stat. pl. (55) 14; Exanth. viva (86) 8; Hist. nat. Rossia (144) 34; Pand. fl. Ryb. (165) 22

Holcus saccharatus — Demonstr. pl. (49) 26; Herb. Amboin. (57) 20

Holcus sorghum — Fl. Palaest. (70) 31; Pane diaet. (83) 20; Fl. Jam. (105) 22; Fr. escul. (127) 20

Holcus spicatus — Fr. escul. (127) 20

Holosteum alterum — Acrostichum (10) 10

Holosteum cordatum — Fl. Jam. (105) 13

Holosteum creticum alterum — Pl. Mart.-Burs. (6) 14[as Holostium]

Holosteum petraeum — Acrostichum (10) 10[as Holostium]

Holothuria physalis — Iter Chin. (161) 15

Holothuria velificans — Nat. pelagi (84) 9

Homo — Curios. nat. (18) [1]ff.; Oecon. nat. (20) 46; Generat. calc. (22) 2ff.; Pan Svec. (26) 7, 38; Mat. med. anim. (29) [2]; Polit. nat. (109) 16, 22

Homo caudatus vulgo dictus — Anthrop. (111) 9

Homo nocturnus — Anthrop. (111) 11

Homo sylvestris — Anthrop. (111) 7

110

Hordeum — Peloria (3) 15; Spons. pl. (12) 17, 42; Vir. pl. (13) 32; Oecon. nat. (20) 17; Pl. escul. (35) 5; Hosp. insect. fl. (43) 12; Noxa insect. (46) 23; Vern. arb. (47) 13, 18, table; Fl. Angl. (56) 4; Mus ind. (62) 14; Hort. acad. (63) 2; Calend. fl. (72) [10], [15]; Pane diaet. (83) 11; Transm. frum. (87) 13; Pand. insect. (93) 11; Instr. peregr. (96) 10; Fl. Cap. (99) 2; Nom. bot. (107) 9; Inebr. (117) 13; Raphania (126) 12ff.; Usum hist. nat. (145) 9, 11; Mund. invis. (149) 14; Fund. agrost. (152) 5, 15, 16, 18, 25, 32, 34; Esca avium (174) 4, 5

Hordeum bulbosum — Cent. II. pl. (66) 8; Fl. Palaest. (70) 13; Fund. agrost. (152) 17

Hordeum communis — Calend. fl. (72) [9]

Hordeum distichon — Fl. Palaest. (70) 13; Fr. escul. (127) 19; Hort. cul. (132) 8; Hist. nat. Rossia (144) 20[as distichum]

Hordeum flosculis omnibus fertilibus aristatis, involucris setaceis basi ciliatis — Cent. II. pl. (66) 8

Hordeum hexastichon — Fr. escul. (127) 19; Hort. cul. (132) 8

Hordeum murinum — Pan Svec. (26) 15; Stat. pl. (55) 20; Fl. Angl. (56) 11; Fl. Palaest. (70) 13; Fl. Monsp. (74) 9; Prodr. fl. Dan. (82) 14; Fl. Belg. (112) 13; Fund. agrost. (152) 7; Colon. pl. (158) 7; Fl. Åker. (162) 7

Hordeum vulgare — Pl. officin. (52) 11; Calend. fl. (72) [18]; Hort. cul. (132) 8

Hordeum zeocriton — Hort. cul. (132) 8

Horminum — Sapor. med. (31) 12; Odor. med. (40) 16; Metam. pl. (67) 14; Inebr. (117) 23; Marum (175) 13

Horminum foliosum — Fl. Cap. (99) 15

Horminum pratense niveum, foliis incanis — Demonstr. pl. (49) 2

Horminum pyrenaicum — Fl. alp. (71) 19

Hortulanus carolinianus — Oecon. nat. (20) 40

Hottonia — Hort. Upsal. (7) 41

Hottonia palustris — Pan Svec. (26) 17; Stat. pl. (55) 13; Fl. Angl. (56) 12; Fl. Monsp. (74) 11; Prodr. fl. Dan. (82) 15; Fl. Belg. (112) 14; Fl. Åker. (162) 8; Pand. fl. Ryb. (165) 17

Houstonia — Nova pl. gen. 1751 (32) 8

Humulus — Ficus (2) 18; Spons. pl. (12) [2], 13, 48; Vir. pl. (13) 33, 36; Fl. oecon. (17) 27; Pl. escul. (35) 25, 28; Hosp. insect. fl. (43) 12; Noxa insect. (46) 19; Oves (61) 18, 24; Pand. insect. (93) 22; Nom. bot. (107) 19; Inebr. (117) 13; Fund. fr. (123) 8; Usum hist. nat. (145) 14; Mund. invis. (149) 16; Erica (163) [14, as 10]; Fraga (170) 7; Ledum (178) 2, 3

Humulus lupulus — Hosp. insect. fl. (43) 38; Demonstr. pl. (49) 26; Pl. officin. (52) 12; Fl. Angl. (56) 24; Calend. fl. (72) [15], [18]; Fl. Monsp. (74) 28; Prodr. fl. Dan. (82) 25; Fl. Belg. (112) 23; Mac. olit. (113) 15; Hort. cul. (132) 9; Hist. nat. Rossia (144) 18; Colon. pl. (158) 8

Humulus salictarius — Pan Svec. (26) [37, as 39]

Hura crepitans — Demonstr. pl. (49) 25; Fl. Jam. (105) 21; Pl. Surin. (177) 15[as Hurra]

Huso germanorum — Mat. med. anim. (29) 13

Hyacinthus — Hort. Upsal. (7) 33; Vir. pl. (13) 14, 20; Cryst. gen. (15) 20; Cui bono? (42) 20; Pand. insect. (93) 13; Prol. pl. 1760 (114) 10; Pl. rar. Afr. (115) 4; Nect. fl. (122) 14

Hyacinthus amethystinus — Hist. nat. Rossia (144) 23[as amethestinus]

Hyacinthus botryoides — Demonstr. pl. (49) 10; Fl. Palaest. (70) 18; Calend. fl. (72) [10], [11]; Fl. Monsp. (74) 14; Prodr. fl. Dan. (82) 16; Pl. Alstr. (121) 5; Hort. cul. (132) 23

Hyacinthus caudatus — Fl. Cap. (99) 9, 13

Hyacinthus caule nudo, foliis linguiformibus acuminatis dentatis — Nova pl. gen. 1751 (32) 16

Hyacinthus cernuus — Demonstr. pl. (49) 10

Hyacinthus comosus — Fl. Palaest. (70) 18; Fl. Monsp. (74) 14

Hyacinthus floridanus spicatus, foliis tantum circa radicem brevibus, elato caule, floribus albis parvis striatis et velut lanugine seu pube elegantissime crispatis — Nova pl. gen. 1751 (32) 16

Hyacinthus muscari — Demonstr. pl. (49) 10; Pl. Alstr. (121) 5

Hyacinthus non scriptus — Demonstr. pl. (49) 10; Fl. Angl. (56) 14; Pl. Alstr. (121) 5

Hyacinthus orchioides — Fl. Cap. (99) 13

Hyacinthus orientalis — Demonstr. pl. (49) 10; Fl. Palaest. (70) 18; Fl. Cap. (99) 13; Hort. cul. (132) 23

Hyacinthus serotinus — Demonstr. pl. (49) 10; Calend. fl. (72) [17]; Fl. Monsp. (74) 14

Hyaena — Cynogr. (54) 3; Usum hist. nat. (145) 23

Hybanthus — Nect. fl. (122) 12[as Hybantus]; Purg. indig. (143) 13

Hydnora africana — Aphyteia (185) 9

Hydnum — Mac. olit. (113) 16

Hydra — Spons. pl. (12) 17, 18; Curios. nat. (18) 5; Taenia (19) 5; Oecon. nat. (20) 30; Sem. musc. (28) 16; Pl. hybr. (33) 2; Anim. comp. (98) 4; Prol. pl. 1763 (130) 18; Lepra (140) 9; Siren. lacert. (146) 8; Mund. invis. (149) 5, 9

Hydrangea — Nova pl. gen. 1751 (32) 9

Hydrargyra — Usum hist. nat. (145) 29

Hydrastis — Usum musc. (148) 11

Hydrocharis — Hort. Upsal. (7) [42]; Spons. pl. (12) 44

Hydrocharis morsus — Fl. Belg. (112) 23

Hydrocharis morsus ranae — Herbat. Upsal. (50) 11; Stat. pl. (55) 13; Fl. Angl. (56) 25; Fl. Monsp. (74) 28; Prodr. fl. Dan. (82) 25; Fl. Åker. (162) 20

Hydrocharis palustris — Pan Svec. (26) [37, as 39]

Hydrocotyle — Vir. pl. (13) 14

Hydrocotyle aquatica — Pan Svec. (26) 18

Hydrocotyle asiatica — Herb. Amboin. (57) 24; Fl. Jam. (105) 15, 25

Hydrocotyle foliis peltatis — Pl. hybr. (33) 28

Hydrocotyle foliis reniformibus crenatis — Pl. hybr. (33) 28

Hydrocotyle umbellata — Fl. Jam. (105) 15

Hydrocotyle vulgaris — Stat. pl. (55) 14; Fl. Angl. (56) 13; Fl. Monsp. (74) 12; Prodr. fl. Dan. (82) 15; Fl. Belg. (112) 15

Hydrophilus — Fund. entom. (154) 30; Bigas insect. (184) 7

Hydrophyllum — Nova pl. gen. 1751 (32) 8; Metam. pl. (67) 14; Nect. fl. (122) 11, 12

Hydrophyllum spicatum — Fl. Åker. (162) 19

Hydrophyllum virginianum — Calend. fl. (72) [13]

Hydroum — Bigas insect. (184) 3, 7

Hymenaea — Hort. Upsal. (7) 37; Passifl. (8) [iii][as Hymenea]; Spons. pl. (12) 12[as Hymenea]; Pl. officin. (52) 4; Opobals. (135) [1]

Hymenaea courbaril — Somn. pl. (68) 17[as Hymemaea]; Pane diaet. (83) 20; Fl. Jam. (105) 16; Fr. escul. (127) 17

Hyobanche — Aphyteia (185) 9

Hyoscyamus — Vir. pl. (13) 19, 31; Fl. oecon. (17) 5; Odor. med. (40) 13, 16; Hosp. insect. fl. (43) 40[as Hyoschyamus]; Pand. insect. (93) 12; Nom. bot. (107) 10; Mors. serp. (119) 2; Nect. fl. (122) 5[as Hyoschyamus]; Usum hist. nat. (145) 28; Febr. interm. (167) 54; Esca avium (174) 2, 7

Hyoscyamus albus — Fl. Palaest. (70) 15; Fl. Monsp. (74) 12; Pl. rar. Afr. (115) 6

Hyoscyamus aureus — Fl. Palaest. (70) 15; Fl. Monsp. (74) 12

Hyoscyamus niger — Herbat. Upsal. (50) 20; Pl. officin. (52) 11; Stat. pl. (55) 20; Fl. Monsp. (74) 12; Prodr. fl. Dan. (82) 15; Inebr. (117) 12[as nigra]; Fl. Åker. (162) 8; Pand. fl. Ryb. (165) 17; Cimicifuga (173) 9

Hyoscyamus physalodes — Inebr. (117) 12[as physaloides]; Hist. nat. Rossia (144) 28[as physaloides]; Usum hist. nat. (145) 28[as physaloides], plate [1][as Hyoschyamus physaloides]

Hyoscyamus scopolia — Colon. pl. (158) 12

Hyoscyamus vulgaris — Pan Svec. (26) 17; Hosp. insect. fl. (43) 16[as Hyoschyamus]; Fl. Angl. (56) 12; Fl. Belg. (112) 14[as Hyoschyamus]

Hyoseris — Vir. pl. (13) 25

Hyoseris cretica — Demonstr. pl. (49) 22

Hyoseris foetida — Fl. alp. (71) 21; Fl. Monsp. (74) 24

Hyoseris foliis glabris hastato pinnatis — Pl. Mart.-Burs. (6) 8

Hyoseris hedypnois — Demonstr. pl. (49) 22; Fl. Monsp. (74) 24

Hyoseris minima — Stat. pl. (55) 22; Fl. Angl. (56) 21; Prodr. fl. Dan. (82) 22; Fl. Belg. (112) 9, 20; Colon. pl. (158) 8; Fl. Åker. (162) 17

Hyoseris radiata — Demonstr. pl. (49) 22; Fl. Monsp. (74) 24

Hyoseris rhagadioloides — Demonstr. pl. (49) 22

Hyoseris scanica — Pan Svec. (26) 31

Hypecoum — Hort. Upsal. (7) 34; Vir. pl. (13) 25[as Hypechoum]

Hypecoum erectum — Hist. nat. Rossia (144) 24[as Hypecoon]

Hypecoum procumbens — Fl. Palaest. (70) 14[as Hipecoum]; Fl. Monsp. (74) 10

Hypelate — Fl. Jam. (105) 26[as Hypetale]

Hypericoides — Hypericum (186) 3

Hypericon — Hypericum (186) 13

Hypericum — Fl. oecon. (17) 19; Obst. med. (34) 7; Cui bono? (42) 20; Nom. bot. (107) 16; Hypericum (186) [2]ff.

Hypericum aegyptiacum — Hypericum (186) 6

Hypericum alium — Pl. Surin. (177) 13

Hypericum anceps — Pan Svec. (26) 31

Hypericum androsaemum — Gem. arb. (24) 15; Fl. Angl. (56) 21; Fl. Monsp. (74) 23; Hypericum (186) 5

Hypericum ascyron — Demonstr. pl. (49) 21; Calend. fl. (72) [14], [16]; Hort. cul. (132) 24; Hist. nat. Rossia (144) 23[as ascriron], 32; Hypericum (186) 4

Hypericum bacciferum — Hypericum (186) 4, 12

Hypericum balearicum — Hypericum (186) 4

Hypericum barbatum — Hypericum (186) 6

Hypericum caijanense — Hypericum (186) 4

Hypericum cajense — Pl. Surin. (177) 13

Hypericum calycinum — Hypericum (186) 4

Hypericum canadense — Hypericum (186) 5

Hypericum canariense — Hypericum (186) 5

Hypericum caule ancipiti, foliis quasi poris perforatis — Hypericum (186) 5

Hypericum caule pubescente — Hypericum (186) 6

Hypericum caule quadrangulo, foliis absque poris pellucidis — Hypericum (186) 5

Hypericum caule scabro — Hypericum (186) 5

Hypericum caulibus suffruticosis, compressis — Hypericum (186) 6

Hypericum centaurii minoris facie, floribus minutissimis — Hypericum (186) 5

Hypericum chinense — Hypericum (186) 6

Hypericum coris — Fl. Palaest. (70) 27; Hypericum (186) 6

Hypericum corollis hirsutis, foliis subtus incanis, bacca — Hypericum (186) 4

Hypericum corollis hirsutis, foliis utrinque glabris, bacca — Hypericum (186) 4

Hypericum crispum — Hypericum (186) 5

Hypericum elodes — Fl. Angl. (56) 28[as eloides]; Hypericum (186) 6

Hypericum ericoides — Hypericum (186) 5

Hypericum filiforme, procumbens — Hypericum (186) 5

Hypericum flore foliis majore — Hypericum (186) 5

Hypericum floribus pentagynis, foliis lanceolatis serratis — Nova pl. gen. 1747 (14) 24

Hypericum floribus pentagynis, subumbellatis, caule fruticoso, ramis teretibus, foliis ovatis, acutis — Hypericum (186) 4

Hypericum floribus trigynis; caule tereti repente; foliis lanceolato-linearibus, obtusis — Cent. I. pl. (65) 26

Hypericum floribus trigynis; caule tereti, suffruticoso, muricato; foliis oblongis — Cent. I. pl. (65) 25

Hypericum floribus trigynis, ramis simplicibus, foliis imbricatis, ovatis — Hypericum (186) 5

Hypericum foliis acutis, capsula — Hypericum (186) 4

Hypericum foliis amplexicaulibus, cordatis, glabris — Hypericum (186) 6

Hypericum foliis cordato-orbiculatis, imbricatis — Hypericum (186) 6

Hypericum foliis crenatis, sagittatis — Hypericum (186) 5

Hypericum foliis linearibus, caule ancipiti — Hypericum (186) 5

Hypericum foliis linearibus, imbricatis — Hypericum (186) 5

Hypericum foliis linearibus, obtusis, caule repente — Hypericum (186) 5

Hypericum foliis obtusis, capsula — Hypericum (186) 4

Hypericum foliis ramisque cicatrisatis — Hypericum (186) 4

Hypericum foliis semidecurrentibus — Hypericum (186) 5

Hypericum foliis subtus tomentosis, caule tetragono — Hypericum (186) 5

Hypericum foliis subverticillatis — Hypericum (186) 6

Hypericum foliis tomentosis — Hypericum (186) 6

Hypericum foliis undulatis — Hypericum (186) 5

Hypericum fructu baccato — Hypericum (186) 5

Hypericum guineense — Hypericum (186) 4

Hypericum hircinum — Odor. med. (40) 13; Fl. Palaest. (70) 27; Med. grav. (92) 13; Hypericum (186) 5

Hypericum hirsutum — Demonstr. pl. (49) 21; Herbat. Upsal. (50) 12; Stat. pl. (55) 23; Fl. Angl. (56) 21; Fl. Palaest. (70) 27; Calend. fl. (72) [15]; Fl. Monsp. (74) 24; Prodr. fl. Dan. (82) 22; Fl. Belg. (112) 20; Hypericum (186) 6

Hypericum humifusum — Fl. Angl. (56) 21; Fl. Monsp. (74) 24; Prodr. fl. Dan. (82) 22; Fl. Belg. (112) 20; Hypericum (186) 5, 6

Hypericum kalmianum — Hypericum (186) 4

Hypericum laeve — Hypericum (186) 6

Hypericum mexicanum — Hypericum (186) 5

Hypericum monogynum — Hypericum (186) 6

Hypericum montanum — Fl. Monsp. (74) 24; Fl. Åker. (162) 16; Hypericum (186) 6

Hypericum nummularium — Fl. alp. (71) 21; Hypericum (186) 6

Hypericum olympicum — Fl. alp. (71) 21; Hypericum (186) 5

Hypericum orientale — Hypericum (186) 5

Hypericum orientale, caule aspero purpureo — Cent. I. pl. (65) 25

Hypericum orientale, polygoni folio — Cent. I. pl. (65) 26

Hypericum panicula subdichotoma — Hypericum (186) 5

Hypericum paniculatum, caule ancipiti — Hypericum (186) 5

Hypericum perfoliatum — Hypericum (186) 5

Hypericum perforatum — Herbat. Upsal. (50) 9; Pl. officin. (52) 11; Stat. pl. (55) 22; Fl. Angl. (56) 21; Calend. fl. (72) [15]; Fl. Monsp. (74) 24; Prodr. fl. Dan. (82) 22; Pl. tinct. (97) 22; Fl. Belg. (112) 20; Rar. Norv. (157) 16; Fl. Åker. (162) 16; Pand. fl. Ryb. (165) 21; Hypericum (186) 5, 6, 12

Hypericum petiolatum — Hypericum (186) 5

Hypericum pistillis flore longioribus, odore hircino — Hypericum (186) 5

Hypericum prolificum — Hypericum (186) 5

Hypericum pulchrum — Fl. Angl. (56) 21; Prodr. fl. Dan. (82) 22; Hypericum (186) 6

Hypericum quadrangulum — Pan Svec. (26) 31[as quadrangulare]; Stat. pl. (55) 20[as quadrangulare]; Fl. Angl. (56) 21; Fl. Monsp. (74) 24; Prodr. fl. Dan. (82) 22; Fl. Belg. (112) 20; Fl. Åker. (162) 16; Pand. fl. Ryb. (165) 21[as quadrangulare]; Hypericum (186) 5[as quadrangulare], 6[as quadrangulare], 7[as quadrangulare]

Hypericum repens — Cent. I. pl. (65) 26; Fl. Palaest. (70) 27; Hypericum (186) 5

Hypericum scabrum — Cent. I. pl. (65) 25; Hypericum (186) 5

Hypericum stipulis geminis, foliis lanceolatis — Hypericum (186) 4

Hypericum teres — Pan Svec. (26) 31

Hypericum tomentosum — Fl. Monsp. (74) 24; Hypericum (186) 6, 12

Hypericum villosum — Hypericum (186) 6

Hypericum virginicum — Hypericum (186) 5

Hypnum — Fl. oecon. (17) 29; Oecon. nat. (20) 20, 25; Splachnum (27) 5, 6; Sem. musc. (28) 6, 14, 17; Cui bono? (42) 14; Buxbaumia (85) 15; Arb. Svec. (101) 10, 15; Usum musc. (148) 3, 5, 10

Hypnum abietinum — Herbat. Upsal. (50) 11; Pand. fl. Ryb. (165) 23

Hypnum aduncum — Herbat. Upsal. (50) 11; Usum musc. (148) 5

Hypnum alopecurum — Herbat. Upsal. (50) 17

Hypnum bryoides — Herbat. Upsal. (50) 11

Hypnum complanatum — Herbat. Upsal. (50) 9; Prodr. fl. Dan. (82) 26

Hypnum crista castrensis — Herbat. Upsal. (50) 11

Hypnum cupressiforme — Herbat. Upsal. (50) 11

Hypnum curtipendulum — Herbat. Upsal. (50) 11

Hypnum cuspidatum — Usum musc. (148) 5

Hypnum dendroides — Herbat. Upsal. (50) 8; Pand. fl. Ryb. (165) 23

Hypnum parietinum — Herbat. Upsal. (50) 11; Usum musc. (148) 10

Hypnum proliferum — Herbat. Upsal. (50) 11; Stat. pl. (55) 18; Prodr. fl. Dan. (82) 26; Usum musc. (148) 10; Pand. fl. Ryb. (165) 23

Hypnum purum — Herbat. Upsal. (50) 11

Hypnum riparium — Usum musc. (148) 5

Hypnum scorpioides — Herbat. Upsal. (50) 20; Usum musc. (148) 5

Hypnum sericeum — Herbat. Upsal. (50) 9

Hypnum taxifolium — Herbat. Upsal. (50) 11

Hypnum triquetrum — Herbat. Upsal. (50) 11; Pand. fl. Ryb. (165) 23

Hypnum velutinum — Herbat. Upsal. (50) 11

Hypochaeris — Vir. pl. (13) 25[as Hypocheris]; Pl. escul. (35) 21, 28; Pand. insect. (93) 18

Hypochaeris achyrophorus — Demonstr. pl. (49) 22

Hypochaeris glabra — Fl. Angl. (56) 22; Fl. Monsp. (74) 24[as Hypochoeris]

Hypochaeris maculata — Hosp. insect. fl. (43) 29[as Hypochoeris]; Herbat. Upsal. (50) 8; Pl. officin. (52) 3; Stat. pl. (55) 22[as Hypocheris]; Fl. Angl. (56) 21; Calend. fl. (72) [13]; Fl. Monsp. (74) 24[as Hypochoeris]; Prodr. fl. Dan. (82) 22; Mac. olit. (113) 18[as Hypochoeris]; Fl. Åker. (162) 17; Pand. fl. Ryb. (165) 21

Hypochaeris pratensis — Pan Svec. (26) 31

Hypochaeris radicata — Fl. Angl. (56) 21; Fl. Monsp. (74) 24[as Hypochoeris]; Fl. Belg. (112) 9[as Hypocheris], 20; Colon. pl. (158) 8; Fl. Åker. (162) 17

Hypocistis — Sapor. med. (31) 15; Somn. pl. (68) 6; Fung. melit. (69) 3; Pl. tinct. (97) 10; Aphyteia (185) 9[as Hypocistus]

Hypopitys — Betula (1) 12[as Hypopitus]; Fung. melit. (69) 3[as Hypopithys], 6[as Hypopithys]

Hypoxis decumbens — Pl. Jam. (102) 11; Fl. Jam. (105) 15

Hyssopus — Vir. pl. (13) 29; Sapor. med. (31) 18; Cui bono? (42) 20; Nom. bot. (107) 14; Fund. fr. (123) 22; Usum musc. (148) 10

Hyssopus lophanthus — Demonstr. pl. (49) 15[as lophantus]; Hist. nat. Rossia (144) 23, 30

Hyssopus nepetoides — Demonstr. pl. (49) 15[as nepethoides]

Hyssopus officinalis — Demonstr. pl. (49) 15; Pl. officin. (52) 11; Calend. fl. (72) [16]; Hort. cul. (132) 24

Hyssopus salomonis — Usum musc. (148) 10

Hystrix — Generat. calc. (22) 2

Hystrix cristata — Fl. Cap. (99) [1]

Hystrix piscis — Mus. Ad.-Frid. (11) 32

Iberis — Hort. Upsal. (7) 36

Iberis amara — Fl. Monsp. (74) 21

Iberis arabica — Cent. I. pl. (65) 17; Fl. Palaest. (70) 23

Iberis badensis — Cent. I. pl. (65) 17

Iberis cretica — Demonstr. pl. (49) 17; Fl. Monsp. (74) 21

Iberis foliis cordatis: superioribus amplexicaulibus — Cent. I. pl. (65) 17

Iberis foliis lanceolato-linearibus carnosis acutis integerrimis ciliatis, ramulis suffructicosis — Cent. II. pl. (66) 23

Iberis foliis linearibus pinnatifidis — Cent. I. pl. (65) 18

Iberis herbacea, foliis ovatis glabris aveniis integerrimis, siliculis basi apiceque bilobis — Cent. I. pl. (65) 17

Iberis nudicaulis — Stat. pl. (55) 21; Fl. Angl. (56) 19; Hort. acad. (63) 10; Fl. Monsp. (74) 21; Prodr. fl. Dan. (82) 20; Fl. Belg. (112) 19; Fl. Åker. (162) 15

Iberis odorata — Fl. alp. (71) 20

Iberis pinnata — Pan Svec. (26) 28; Cent. I. pl. (65) 18; Fl. Monsp. (74) 7, 21

Iberis racemosa — Calend. fl. (72) [22]

Iberis rotundifolia — Fl. alp. (71) 20

Iberis saxatilis — Cent. II. pl. (66) 23

Iberis semperflorens — Demonstr. pl. (49) 17

Iberis umbellata — Demonstr. pl. (49) 17

Ibyaru — Mus. Ad.-Frid. (11) 17

Ichneumon — Ficus (2) 17; Mirac. insect. (45) 17, 18; Pand. insect. (93) 7; Fl. Cap. (99) [1]; Fund. entom. (154) 28, 33; Iter Chin. (161) 9

Ichneumon aphidum — Polit. nat. (109) 10

Ichneumon assectator — Pand. fl. Ryb. (165) 12

Ichneumon bedeguaris — Pand. insect. (93) 15

Ichneumon cinctus — Pand. fl. Ryb. (165) 12

Ichneumon circumflexus — Pand. fl. Ryb. (165) 12

Ichneumon comitator — Pand. fl. Ryb. (165) 12

Ichneumon compunctor — Pand. fl. Ryb. (165) 12

Ichneumon constrictorius — Pand. fl. Ryb. (165) 12

Ichneumon culpatorius — Pand. fl. Ryb. (165) 12

Ichneumon cyniphidis — Pand. insect. (93) 21

Ichneumon deliratorius — Pand. fl. Ryb. (165) 12

Ichneumon extensorius — Pand. fl. Ryb. (165) 12

Ichneumon glomeratus — Pand. insect. (93) 21

Ichneumon incubitor — Pand. fl. Ryb. (165) 12

Ichneumon inculcator — Pand. fl. Ryb. (165) 12

Ichneumon jaculator — Pand. fl. Ryb. (165) 12

Ichneumon juniperi — Pand. insect. (93) 22

Ichneumon luctatorius — Pand. fl. Ryb. (165) 12

Ichneumon luteus — Pand. fl. Ryb. (165) 12

Ichneumon mandator — Pand. fl. Ryb. (165) 12

Ichneumon manifestator — Pand. fl. Ryb. (165) 12

Ichneumon moderator — Pand. insect. (93) 21; Polit. nat. (109) 10

Ichneumon molitorius — Pand. fl. Ryb. (165) 12

Ichneumon reluctator — Pand. fl. Ryb. (165) 12

Ichneumon resinellae — Pand. insect. (93) 21

Ichneumon sarcitorius — Pand. fl. Ryb. (165) 12

Ichneumon strobilellae — Pand. insect. (93) 21; Polit. nat. (109) 10

Ichneumon titillator — Pand. fl. Ryb. (165) 12; Esca avium (174) 8

Ichneumon triglochidis — Hosp. insect. fl. (43) 38

Ichneumon venator — Pand. fl. Ryb. (165) 12

Ichneumon volutatorius — Pand. fl. Ryb. (165) 12

Ichthyotonos litorea — Herb. Amboin. (57) 15

Ichthyotonos montana — Herb. Amboin. (57) 15

Icthyometra — Fl. Jam. (105) 27[as Ictyomethra]

Ignatia — Pl. Surin. (177) 4, 6

Ignavus — Surin. Grill. (16) 7, 9

Ignavus americanus major hirsutus, pilis longis et griseis — Surin. Grill. (16) 7

Ignavus gracilis americanus — Surin. Grill. (16) 7

Ignavus seu per antiphrasin agilis — Surin. Grill. (16) 7

Iguana — Amphib. Gyll. (5) 18; Hort. Upsal. (7) 43; Chin. Lagerstr. (64) 6

Ilex — Hort. Upsal. (7) 36; Vir. pl. (13) 7; Nom. bot. (107) 10; Polit. nat. (109) 5

Ilex aquifolium — Gem. arb. (24) 22; Demonstr. pl. (49) 4[as agrifolium]; Fl. Angl. (56) 11; Fl. Palaest. (70) 30[as aquifolia, under Quercus]; Fl. Monsp. (74) 10[as agrifolium]; Prodr. fl. Dan. (82) 14; Fr. Svec. (91) 26; Fl. Belg. (112) 13; Rar. Norv. (157) 9; Colon. pl. (158) 8[as aquifolum]

Ilex baccifera — Mund. invis. (149) 20

Illa — Nova pl. gen. 1747 (14) 5

Illecebra — Febr. interm. (167) 19

Illecebrum capitatum — Fl. Monsp. (74) 7, 12

Illecebrum cymosum — Fl. Monsp. (74) 12

Illecebrum paronychia — Fl. Palaest. (70) 15; Fl. Monsp. (74) 12

Illecebrum verticillatum — Demonstr. pl. (49) 7; Fl. Angl. (56) 12; Fl. Belg. (112) 9, 14

Illicium — Opobals. (135) 2

Impatiens — Vir. pl. (13) 25; Pl. hybr. (33) 29; Vern. arb. (47) 8, 9; Demonstr. pl. (49) [vii]; Stat. pl. (55)

6; Pand. insect. (93) 18; Nom. bot. (107) 17; Nect. fl. (122) 14

Impatiens balsamina — Herb. Amboin. (57) 21; Fl. Jam. (105) 20; Hort. cul. (132) 23, 25

Impatiens nemorum — Pan Svec. (26) 34

Impatiens noli me tangere — Fl. Åker. (162) 18

Impatiens noli tangere — Hosp. insect. fl. (43) 31; Demonstr. pl. (49) 24; Stat. pl. (55) 17; Fl. Angl. (56) 23; Calend. fl. (72) [17]; Prodr. fl. Dan. (82) 24; Fl. Belg. (112) 21; Pand. fl. Ryb. (165) 22

Imperatoria — Hort. Upsal. (7) 33; Vir. pl. (13) 19; Nom. bot. (107) 11

Imperatoria ostruthium — Demonstr. pl. (49) 8[as ostruthion]; Pl. officin. (52) 11[as ostrutium]; Fl. alp. (71) 15; Fl. Monsp. (74) 13[as ostrutium]; Prodr. fl. Dan. (82) 16

Imperatoria tenuifolia — Fl. alp. (71) 15

Indicum — Herb. Amboin. (57) 21

Indigo — Hort. Upsal. (7) 37

Indigofera — Nova pl. gen. 1747 (14) [vi], 24; Nom. bot. (107) 16

Indigofera foliis ternatis, racemis elongatis, leguminibus cernuis — Pl. rar. Afr. (115) 15

Indigofera leguminibus arcuatis incanis, racemis folio brevioribus — Nova pl. gen. 1747 (14) 24

Indigofera leguminibus compressis pendulis, foliis ternatis lanceolatis — Cent. II. pl. (66) 29

Indigofera leguminibus horizontalibus teretibus, foliis pinnatis ternatisque — Nova pl. gen. 1747 (14) 25

Indigofera leguminibus pendulis lanatis tetragonis — Nova pl. gen. 1747 (14) 25

Indigofera tinctoria — Demonstr. pl. (49) 20; Pl. officin. (52) 11; Herb. Amboin. (57) 21; Pl. tinct. (97) 21; Fl. Jam. (105) 8, 19; Pl. Surin. (177) 13

Indigofera trifoliata — Cent. II. pl. (66) 29; Pl. rar. Afr. (115) 15

Inula — Nova pl. gen. 1747 (14) [vi], 25, 26; Fl. oecon. (17) 20; Fl. Jam. (105) 26; Nom. bot. (107) 17; Fund. fr. (123) 17[as Enula]

Inula aromatica — Pl. rar. Afr. (115) 22

Inula britannica — Prodr. fl. Dan. (82) 23

Inula campana — Nova pl. gen. 1747 (14) 26[as Enula]

Inula crithmoides — Demonstr. pl. (49) 23; Fl. Angl. (56) 6, 22; Calend. fl. (72) [19]; Fl. Monsp. (74) 25

Inula dysenterica — Pan Svec. (26) 33; Demonstr. pl. (49) 23; Pl. officin. (52) 8; Fl. Angl. (56) 22; Calend. fl. (72) [17], [22]; Fl. Monsp. (74) 25; Prodr. fl. Dan. (82) 23; Fl. Belg. (112) 21; Hist. nat. Rossia (144) 33; Colon. pl. (158) 7; Obs. mat. med. (171) 5

Inula foetida — Fl. Cap. (99) 18

Inula foliis linearibus integerrimis tomentosis sparsis, caule fruticoso — Pl. rar. Afr. (115) 22

Inula foliis ovatis rugosis, subtus tomentosis — Nova pl. gen. 1747 (14) 26

Inula foliis subulato-linearibus triquetris confertissimis, caule fruticoso — Pl. rar. Afr. (115) 22[as con ertissimis]

Inula germanica — Hist. nat. Rossia (144) 33

Inula helenium — Pan Svec. (26) 33; Hosp. insect. fl. (43) 31; Demonstr. pl. (49) 23; Pl. officin. (52) 9; Fl. Angl. (56) 22; Calend. fl. (72) [17]; Prodr. fl. Dan. (82) 23; Fl. Belg. (112) 21; Hist. nat. Rossia (144) 33

Inula montana — Fl. alp. (71) 22; Fl. Monsp. (74) 25

Inula oculus christi — Demonstr. pl. (49) 23; Calend. fl. (72) [13]; Prodr. fl. Dan. (82) 23; Fl. Belg. (112) 21

Inula pinifolia — Pl. rar. Afr. (115) 22

Inula pulicaria — Demonstr. pl. (49) 23; Stat. pl. (55) 14; Fl. Angl. (56) 22; Calend. fl. (72) [16]; Fl. Monsp. (74) 25; Prodr. fl. Dan. (82) 23; Fl. Belg. (112) 21

Inula salicina — Stat. pl. (55) 15; Calend. fl. (72) [16]; Fl. Monsp. (74) 25; Prodr. fl. Dan. (82) 23; Hist. nat. Rossia (144) 33

Inula salicis folio — Pan Svec. (26) 33

Inula trixis — Pl. Jam. (102) 23; Fl. Jam. (105) 20

Involucrum — Herb. Amboin. (57) 27

Involucrum cusci — Herb. Amboin. (57) 16

Ipecacahuana — Viola ipecac. (176) 5ff.

Ipecacoanha — Viola ipecac. (176) 5

Ipomoea — Hort. Upsal. (7) 35

Ipomoea aegyptia — Somn. pl. (68) 19

Ipomoea alba — Fl. Jam. (105) 13

Ipomoea coccinea — Demonstr. pl. (49) 5; Fl. Jam. (105) 13

Ipomoea foliis palmatis, floribus aggregatis — Sem. musc. (28) 4

Ipomoea pes tigridis — Demonstr. pl. (49) [vii], 5; Fund. fr. (123) 12

Ipomoea quamoclit — Demonstr. pl. (49) 5; Herb. Amboin. (57) 24; Fl. Jam. (105) 13

Ipomoea quinqueloba — Fl. Jam. (105) 13

Ipomoea serpens — Fl. Jam. (105) 13

Ipomoea triloba — Demonstr. pl. (49) 5

Ipomoea tuberosa — Fl. Jam. (105) 14

Ipomoea verticillata — Pl. Jam. (102) 9; Fl. Jam. (105) 13

Iresine — Fl. Jam. (105) 26; Nect. fl. (122) 8

Iresine celosia — Fl. Jam. (105) 22

Irion — Fl. Jam. (105) 27

Iris — Hort. Upsal. (7) 33, 41; Spons. pl. (12) 37; Vir. pl. (13) 26; Pl. hybr. (33) 7; Pl. officin. (52) 11; Nom. bot. (107) 9; Nect. fl. (122) 14

Iris angustifolia prunum revolens minor — Pl. hybr. (33) 23

Iris biflora — Demonstr. pl. (49) 2; Hort. cul. (132) 24

Iris corollis barbatis, foliis repandis — Cent. I. pl. (65) 4

Iris foetidissima — Fl. Angl. (56) 10; Fl. Palaest. (70) 12; Calend. fl. (72) [15]; Fl. Monsp. (74) 8; Fl. Belg. (112) 8, 12

Iris germanica — Demonstr. pl. (49) 2; Pl. officin. (52) 11[as germannica]; Calend. fl. (72) [12]; Fl. Monsp. (74) 8; Prodr. fl. Dan. (82) 13; Pl. tinct. (97) 11; Pl. Alstr. (121) [4]; Hort. cul. (132) 24

Iris graminea — Demonstr. pl. (49) 2; Hist. nat. Rossia (144) 27

Iris humilis pyrenaica, foliis repandis, e luteo virescentibus — Cent. I. pl. (65) 4

Iris humilis pyrenaica, foliis repandis virescentibus cum lineis caeruleis — Cent. I. pl. (65) 4

Iris mariscus — Fl. Monsp. (74) 8

Iris narbonensis — Fl. Monsp. (74) 30

Iris palustris — Pan Svec. (26) 13

Iris perpusilla — Fl. Monsp. (74) 30

Iris persica — Demonstr. pl. (49) 2

Iris pratensis angustifolia, folio foetido — Pl. hybr. (33) 23

Iris pratensis angustifolia non foetida altior — Pl. hybr. (33) 23

Iris pseudacorus — Demonstr. pl. (49) 2; Herbat. Upsal. (50) 14; Pl. officin. (52) 3; Stat. pl. (55) 13; Fl. Angl. (56) 10; Calend. fl. (72) [12]; Fl. Monsp. (74) 8; Prodr. fl. Dan. (82) 13; Fl. Belg. (112) 12; Fl. Åker. (162) 5

Iris pumila — Fl. Monsp. (74) 8

Iris pyrenaica — Cent. I. pl. (65) 4; Fl. alp. (71) 12; Fl. Monsp. (74) 8

Iris sibirica — Demonstr. pl. (49) 2; Calend. fl. (72) [12]; Hort. cul. (132) 24; Hist. nat. Rossia (144) 27

Iris spuria — Demonstr. pl. (49) 2; Hort. cul. (132) 24

Iris susiana — Demonstr. pl. (49) 2; Fl. Palaest. (70) 12; Pl. Alstr. (121) 5

Iris tuberosa — Demonstr. pl. (49) 2; Pl. officin. (52) 11; Fl. Palaest. (70) 12; Obs. mat. med. (171) 6

Iris variegata — Demonstr. pl. (49) 2; Calend. fl. (72) [12]; Hort. cul. (132) 24

Iris versicolor — Specif. Canad. (76) 26

Iris virginica — Demonstr. pl. (49) 2

Iris xiphium — Demonstr. pl. (49) 2

Irsiola — Fl. Jam. (105) 27

Isatis — Hort. Upsal. (7) 34; Fl. oecon. (17) 17; Nom. bot. (107) 15

Isatis aegyptiaca — Fl. Palaest. (70) 24

Isatis lepidii folio — Fl. Palaest. (70) 24

Isatis lusitanica — Demonstr. pl. (49) 18; Fl. Palaest. (70) 24

Isatis maritima — Pan Svec. (26) 28

Isatis tinctoria — Demonstr. pl. (49) 18; Stat. pl. (55) 12; Fl. Angl. (56) 20; Calend. fl. (72) [14]; Prodr. fl. Dan. (82) 21; Pl. tinct. (97) 21; Colon. pl. (158) 7

Ischaemum — Fund. agrost. (152) 16, 26, 35

Isis — Mund. invis. (149) 8

Isis hippuris — Mund. invis. (149) 8; Iter Chin. (161) 8

Isnardia palustris — Pl. Jam. (102) 8; Fl. Jam. (105) 13[as Isnarda], 25[as Isnarda]; Colon. pl. (158) 6[as Isnarda]

Isoetes — Nova pl. gen. 1751 (32) 46, 48; Morb. hyeme (38) 8; Mirac. insect. (45) 11

Isoetes lacustris — Stat. pl. (55) 12; Fl. Angl. (56) 25[as Isoetis]; Fl. alp. (71) 23; Rar. Norv. (157) 11; Fl. Åker. (162) 20

Isopyrum — Hort. Upsal. (7) 34; Anandria (9) 4; Nect. fl. (122) 13; Fund. fr. (123) 23

Isopyrum aquilegioides — Fl. alp. (71) 19[as aquilegiodes]

Isopyrum fumarioides — Demonstr. pl. (49) 15; Hist. nat. Rossia (144) 23

Isopyrum thalictroides — Fl. alp. (71) 19

Ispida supra ferruginea — Chin. Lagerstr. (64) 10[as ferruginiaea]

Ispida viridis — Chin. Lagerstr. (64) 10

Itea — Nova pl. gen. 1751 (32) 8, 12

Iva — Nova pl. gen. 1751 (32) 44, 48

Iva annua — Somn. pl. (68) 15; Calend. fl. (72) [21]

Iva foliis lanceolatis, caule fruticoso — Nova pl. gen. 1751 (32) 45

Iva foliis lanceolato-ovatis, caule annuo — Nova pl. gen. 1751 (32) 45

Ixia — Vir. pl. (13) 26; Fl. Cap. (99) 7, 8, 9; Pl. rar. Afr. (115) 4; Pl. Alstr. (121) 6; Fund. fr. (123) 18

Ixia africana — Fl. Cap. (99) 11

Ixia alba — Fl. Cap. (99) 11

Ixia bulbifera — Cent. II. pl. (66) 4; Fl. Cap. (99) 11

Ixia chinensis — Hort. Upsal. (7) 37; Demonstr. pl. (49) 2

Ixia corymbosa — Cent. II. pl. (66) 4; Fl. Cap. (99) 11

Ixia floribus corymbosis pedunculatis, caule ancipiti — Cent. II. pl. (66) 4

Ixia foliis ensiformibus, caule dichotomo — Anandria (9) 5

Ixia foliis ensiformibus plicatis villosis — Cent. II. pl. (66) 4

Ixia foliis lineari-ensiformibus, axillis bulbiferis, floribus alternis: staminibus lateralibus — Cent. II. pl. (66) 4

Ixia plicata — Cent. II. pl. (66) 4

Ixora — Vir. pl. (13) 28; Nova pl. gen. 1747 (14) 5

Ixora americana — Pl. Jam. (102) 8; Fl. Jam. (105) 13

Ixora coccinea — Herb. Amboin. (57) 16; Iter Chin. (161) 9

Jaboti — Amphib. Gyll. (5) 34

Jacea — Migr. avium (79) 32

Jacea ciliis pilosis — Fl. Monsp. (74) 30

Jacea maxima — Fl. Palaest. (70) 29[under Centaurea]

Jacea odorata — Fl. Monsp. (74) 30

Jacea sicula — Fl. Monsp. (74) 30

Jacobaea aethiopica, laricis folio — Pl. rar. Afr. (115) 22

Jacobaea africana, stoebes facie, flore ampliore, petalis radialibus trifidis — Cent. II. pl. (66) 32

Jacobaea senecio — Stat. pl. (55) 19

Jacobaea senecionis folio incano perennis — Pl. Mart.-Burs. (6) 10

Jacobaea spicata monomopatensis — Pl. rar. Afr. (115) 21

Jacobaea vulgaris flore nudo — Metam. pl. (67) 21

Jacobaeastrum — Anandria (9) 5

Jacove — Amphib. Gyll. (5) 16

Jacquinia — Fl. Jam. (105) 27[as Jaquinia]

Jambolana — Herb. Amboin. (57) 7

Jambolifera — Nova pl. gen. 1747 (14) [vi], 15

Jambolifera pedunculata — Herb. Amboin. (57) 7

Jambolines — Nova pl. gen. 1747 (14) 15

Jambosa aquea — Herb. Amboin. (57) 7

Jambosa ceramica — Herb. Amboin. (57) 7

Jambosa domestica — Herb. Amboin. (57) 7

Jambosa litorea — Herb. Amboin. (57) 12

Jambosa nigra — Herb. Amboin. (57) 7

Jambosa sylvestris alba — Herb. Amboin. (57) 7

Jambosa sylvestris parvifolia — Herb. Amboin. (57) 7

Jasione — Gem. arb. (24) 13

Jasione campestris — Pan Svec. (26) 33

Jasione montana — Stat. pl. (55) 21; Fl. Angl. (56) 23; Fl. Monsp. (74) 26; Prodr. fl. Dan. (82) 23; Fl. Belg. (112) 21; Pand. fl. Ryb. (165) 22

Jasminum — Hort. Upsal. (7) 36; Vir. pl. (13) 31[as Jasminium]; Odor. med. (40) 12; Pand. insect. (93) 11; Pl. Jam. (102) 10; Nom. bot. (107) 9

Jasminum arabicum, castaneae folio, flore albo odoratissimo, cujus fructus coffe in officinis dicitur belgis — Pot. coff. (118) 7

Jasminum arabicum, lauri folio, cujus semen apud nos caffe dicitur — Pot. coff. (118) 7

Jasminum arborescens, lauri foliis, flore albo odoratissimo — Pot. coff. (118) 7

Jasminum castaneae folio, flore odoratissimo, rubro fructu (qui Coffe) duro — Pot. coff. (118) 8

Jasminum foliis oppositis pinnatis — Pl. hybr. (33) 16

Jasminum fruticans — Fl. Palaest. (70) 11; Fl. Monsp. (74) 8

Jasminum fruticosum — Demonstr. pl. (49) [1]

Jasminum grandiflorum — Fl. Palaest. (70) 11; Opobals. (135) 15

Jasminum litoreum — Herb. Amboin. (57) 19

Jasminum odoratissimum — Gem. arb. (24) 15; Demonstr. pl. (49) [1]

Jasminum officinale — Pl. officin. (52) 11; Fl. Jam. (105) 24; Hort. cul. (132) 26; Opobals. (135) 15

Jatropha — Ficus (2) 9; Hort. Upsal. (7) 37; Spons. pl. (12) 39; Vir. pl. (13) 27[as Jatrophia]; Gem. arb. (24) 6; Pand. insect. (93) 20; Nect. fl. (122) 4; Reform. bot. (125) 7; Cent. insect. (129) 25; Pot. theae (142) 10

Jatropha curcas — Demonstr. pl. (49) 25; Pl. officin. (52) 16; Fl. Jam. (105) 21; Pl. Surin. (177) 15

Jatropha foliis palmatis dentatis retrorsum aculeatis — Spons. pl. (12) 40

Jatropha gossypifolia — Demonstr. pl. (49) 25; Fl. Jam. (105) 21; Pl. Surin. (177) 15

Jatropha manihot — Pane diaet. (83) 20; Fl. Jam. (105) 21

Jatropha multifida — Fl. Jam. (105) 21

Jatropha urens — Demonstr. pl. (49) 25, 27

Jatus — Herb. Amboin. (57) 11

Juglans — Ficus (2) 22; Hort. Upsal. (7) 36; Spons. pl. (12) 41; Vir. pl. (13) 31, 35, 36; Pl. escul. (35) 4; Odor. med. (40) 13; Vern. arb. (47) 9; Fl. Angl. (56) 4; Pand. insect. (93) 20; Aer habit. (106) 20; Nom. bot. (107) 18; Fr. escul. (127) 21

Juglans alba — Demonstr. pl. (49) 25

Juglans baccata — Fl. Jam. (105) 21

Juglans europaea — Gem. arb. (24) 23

Juglans nigra — Demonstr. pl. (49) 25

Juglans regia — Demonstr. pl. (49) 25; Pl. officin. (52) 11; Fl. Palaest. (70) 30; Fl. Jam. (105) 24

Jujuba — Sapor. med. (31) 12

Julis — Cul. mut. (88) 9

Julus — Metam. pl. (67) 9; Fund. entom. (154) 19

Julus crassus — Chin. Lagerstr. (64) 28

Julus fuscus — Chin. Lagerstr. (64) 28

Julus ovatus — Chin. Lagerstr. (64) 29, 36

Julus pedibus utrinque 20 — Chin. Lagerstr. (64) 29

Julus pedibus utrinque 96 — Chin. Lagerstr. (64) 28

Julus pedibus utrinque 128 — Chin. Lagerstr. (64) 28

Julus terrestris — Pand. fl. Ryb. (165) 16; Esca avium (174) 3, [9, as 17]

Juncago — Pl. Mart.-Burs. (6) [vii]; Fund. agrost. (152) 15

Juncaria — Nova pl. gen. 1747 (14) 32

Juncaria salmanticensis — Nova pl. gen. 1747 (14) 32

Juncus — Pl. Mart.-Burs. (6) [1]; Hort. Upsal. (7) 41; Vir. pl. (13) 16; Fl. oecon. (17) 9; Pan Svec. (26) 9; Cui bono? (42) 18; Nom. bot. (107) 12; Prol. pl. 1760 (114) 14; Fund. agrost. (152) 4, 13, 14, 15

Juncus acutus — Fl. Angl. (56) 14; Fl. Monsp. (74) 14

Juncus africanus, pectinato capite — Acrostichum (10) 11

Juncus articulatus — Stat. pl. (55) 14; Fl. Angl. (56) 14; Fl. Monsp. (74) 14; Prodr. fl. Dan. (82) 17

Juncus articulosus — Pan Svec. (26) 20

Juncus biglumis — Stat. pl. (55) 16; Fl. alp. (71) 15; Rar. Norv. (157) 10

Juncus bufonius — Pan Svec. (26) 20; Herbat. Upsal. (50) 14; Stat. pl. (55) 14; Fl. Angl. (56) 14; Fl. Monsp. (74) 14; Prodr. fl. Dan. (82) 17; Fl. Åker. (162) 10; Pand. fl. Ryb. (165) 18

Juncus bulbosus — Herbat. Upsal. (50) 14; Fl. Angl. (56) 14; Prodr. fl. Dan. (82) 17; Hist. nat. Rossia (144) 29; Fl. Åker. (162) 10; Pand. fl. Ryb. (165) 18

Juncus campestris — Stat. pl. (55) 22; Fl. Angl. (56) 14; Prodr. fl. Dan. (82) 17; Fl. Åker. (162) 10; Pand. fl. Ryb. (165) 18; Esca avium (174) 12

Juncus capitulo laterali — Pan Svec. (26) 20

Juncus cespitosus — Pan Svec. (26) 20

Juncus conglomeratus — Stat. pl. (55) 15; Fl. Angl. (56) 14; Prodr. fl. Dan. (82) 17; Fl. Åker. (162) 10

Juncus e capite bonae spei, paniculis fuscis juliformibus — Cent. I. pl. (65) 4

Juncus effusus — Herbat. Upsal. (50) 16; Stat. pl. (55) 15; Fl. Angl. (56) 14; Fl. Palaest. (70) 18; Fl. Monsp. (74) 14; Prodr. fl. Dan. (82) 17; Fl. Åker. (162) 10

Juncus elegantissimus, capitulis pectinatis — Acrostichum (10) 11

Juncus filiformis — Pan Svec. (26) 20; Stat. pl. (55) 15; Fl. Angl. (56) 14; Prodr. fl. Dan. (82) 17; Fl. Åker. (162) 10

Juncus glomeratus — Fl. Monsp. (74) 14; Rar. Norv. (157) 10

Juncus gluma biflora terminali — Splachnum (27) 3, [16]

Juncus inflexus — Fl. Monsp. (74) 14

Juncus panicula laterali — Pan Svec. (26) 20

Juncus pilosus — Herbat. Upsal. (50) 11; Stat. pl. (55) 18; Fl. Angl. (56) 14; Fl. Monsp. (74) 14; Prodr. fl. Dan. (82) 17; Fl. Åker. (162) 10; Pand. fl. Ryb. (165) 18; Esca avium (174) 11

Juncus psyllii — Pan Svec. (26) 20

Juncus spicatus alpinus — Pan Svec. (26) 20

Juncus squarrosus — Stat. pl. (55) 15; Fl. Angl. (56) 14; Fl. Monsp. (74) 14

Juncus sylvaticus — Pan Svec. (26) 20

Juncus trifidus — Pan Svec. (26) 20; Stat. pl. (55) 16; Fl. alp. (71) 15; Rar. Norv. (157) 10

Juncus triflorus — Pan Svec. (26) 20

Juncus triglumis — Stat. pl. (55) 16; Fl. alp. (71) 15; Rar. Norv. (157) 10

Juncus valantii — Pan Svec. (26) 20

Jungermannia — Spons. pl. (12) 28; Sem. musc. (28) 15; Cui bono? (42) 26; Usum musc. (148) 2

Jungermannia alpina — Fl. alp. (71) 24

Jungermannia ciliaris — Herbat. Upsal. (50) 11

Jungermannia julacea — Fl. alp. (71) 24

Jungermannia pusilla — Herbat. Upsal. (50) 18

Jungermannia resupinata — Herbat. Upsal. (50) 9

Jungermannia trichophylla — Herbat. Upsal. (50) 5

Juniperus — Spons. pl. (12) 39, 49; Vir. pl. (13) 24; Fl. oecon. (17) 27; Oecon. nat. (20) 15, 18, 29; Pl. escul. (35) 26, 27, 28; Morb. hyeme (38) 12; Mirac. insect. (45) 15; Pl. officin. (52) 14, 17, 19; Cervus (60) 12; Metam. pl. (67) 24; Calend. fl. (72) [11]; Migr. avium (79) 29, 36; Transm. frum. (87) 3, 7; Fr. Svec. (91) 23, 24; Pand. insect. (93) 22; Arb. Svec. (101) 19; Nom. bot. (107) 19; Fund. agrost. (152) 9

Juniperus barbadensis — Demonstr. pl. (49) 26; Fl. Jam. (105) 22

Juniperus communis — Hosp. insect. fl. (43) 38; Herbat. Upsal. (50) 11; Pl. officin. (52) 11; Stat. pl. (55) 18; Fl. Angl. (56) 25; Calend. fl. (72) [11]; Fl. Monsp. (74) 28; Prodr. fl. Dan. (82) 25; Arb. Svec. (101) 8, 14, 30; Fl. Belg. (112) 23; Fr. escul. (127) 7; Hist. nat. Rossia (144) 34; Fl. Åker. (162) 20; Pand. fl. Ryb. (165) 22; Esca avium (174) 14

Juniperus frutex — Pan Svec. (26) [37, as 39]

Juniperus fruticosa — Fl. Cap. (99) 2

Juniperus kedros ligno odoratissimo — Fl. Palaest. (70) 31

Juniperus lycia — Hist. nat. Rossia (144) 34

Juniperus oxycedrus — Fl. Monsp. (74) 28

Juniperus phoenicea — Fl. Palaest. (70) 31; Fl. Monsp. (74) 28

Juniperus sabina — Pl. officin. (52) 17; Fl. Angl. (56) 25; Fr. Svec. (91) 5; Hist. nat. Rossia (144) 34

Juniperus sativa — Demonstr. pl. (49) 26

Junius articulatus — Fl. Belg. (112) 16

Junius bufonius — Fl. Belg. (112) 16

Junius bulbosus — Fl. Belg. (112) 16

Junius campestris — Fl. Belg. (112) 16

Junius conglomeratus — Fl. Belg. (112) 15

Junius effusus — Fl. Belg. (112) 15

Junius inflexus — Fl. Belg. (112) 16

Junius squarrosus — Fl. Belg. (112) 16

Jurucua brasiliensibus — Amphib. Gyll. (5) 31

Jussiaea erecta — Fl. Jam. (105) 16[as Jussicea]; Pl. Surin. (177) 9

Jussiaea purpurea — Herb. Amboin. (57) 26

Jussiaea suffruticosa — Herb. Amboin. (57) 26

Jussiea — Hort. Upsal. (7) 37

Justicia — Gem. arb. (24) 6

Justicia adhatoda — Demonstr. pl. (49) [1]

Justicia assurgens — Pl. Jam. (102) [5]; Fl. Jam. (105) 12[as adsurgens]

Justicia diffusa, spicis axillaribus sessilibus tomentosis secundis dorso imbricatis bracteis semilanceolatis — Cent. II. pl. (66) 3

Justicia foliis ovatis, racemis simplicibus longis, floribus alternis secundis, bracteis obsoletis — Cent. II. pl. (66) 3

Justicia gangetica — Cent. II. pl. (66) 3

Justicia nasuta — Herb. Amboin. (57) 16

Justicia pectinata — Cent. II. pl. (66) 3

Justicia sexangularis — Pl. Jam. (102) [5]

Jynx — Fund. ornith. (137) 27

Jynx torquilla — Migr. avium (79) 22

Kaempferia — Hort. Upsal. (7) 37[as Kaempheria]; Vir. pl. (13) 26[as Kempferia]; Gem. arb. (24) 8; Pl. officin. (52) 10; Obs. mat. med. (171) 6

Kaempferia galanga — Herb. Amboin. (57) 20

Kaempferia rotunda — Herb. Amboin. (57) 20

Kali bacciferum: foliis clavatis — Pl. rar. Camsch. (30) 15

Kali bacciferum salicorniae facie — Pl. rar. Camsch. (30) 14

Kali floridum repens aizooides neapolitanum — Hort. Upsal. (7) 40

Kali spinosum cochleatum — Cent. II. pl. (66) 13

Kali spinosum foliis longioribus et angustioribus — Cent. II. pl. (66) 13

Kalmia — Nova pl. gen. 1751 (32) 9, [13, as 15], 18, 48; Nect. fl. (122) 13; Erica (163) 3

Kalmia angustifolia — Oves (61) 17; Usum hist. nat. (145) 22

Kalmia foliis ovatis, corymbis terminalibus — Nova pl. gen. 1751 (32) 19

Kalmia foliis sublanceolatis, corymbis lateralibus — Nova pl. gen. 1751 (32) 20

Kalmia latifolia — Oves (61) 17; Usum hist. nat. (145) 22

Kauken indorum — Nova pl. gen. 1747 (14) 14

Kauki indorum — Nova pl. gen. 1747 (14) 14

Kermes — Mat. med. anim. (29) 15

Kiggelaria — Nect. fl. (122) 11, 15

Kiggelaria africana — Fl. Cap. (99) 4, 19

Kleinia — Hort. Upsal. (7) 35; Odor. med. (40) 12

Kleinia caule herbaceo, foliis hastato-sagittatis denticulatis, petiolis superne dilatatis — Pl. rar. Camsch. (30) 5

Knautia — Hort. Upsal. (7) 34; Nova pl. gen. 1751 (32) 8

Knautia orientalis — Demonstr. pl. (49) 4; Fl. Palaest. (70) 13

Knoxia — Nova pl. gen. 1751 (32) 36, 48

Knoxia scandens — Fl. Jam. (105) 13

Koenigia islandica — Rar. Norv. (157) 10

Krameria — Cent. insect. (129) 11

Labrus — Usum hist. nat. (145) 27

Labrus aristatus — Iter Chin. (161) 14

119

Labrus immaculatus, pinnae dorsalis radiis spinosis decem — Mus. Ad.-Frid. (11) 36

Labrus oblongus, pinnae dorsalis unico radio inermi — Mus. Ad.-Frid. (11) 37

Labrus rostro reflexo, fasciis lateralibus tribus fuscis — Mus. Ad.-Frid. (11) 34

Labrus rostro reflexo, ocello purpureo iride alba juxta caudam — Mus. Ad.-Frid. (11) 35

Labrusca — Chin. Lagerstr. (64) 6

Labrusca molucca — Herb. Amboin. (57) 24

Lacca herba — Herb. Amboin. (57) 21

Lacca lignum — Herb. Amboin. (57) 18

Lacerta — Amphib. Gyll. (5) [1], 15, 18; Mus. Ad.-Frid. (11) 6; Surin. Grill. (16) 33; Oecon. nat. (20) 28; Polit. nat. (109) 12; Lepra (140) 10; Siren. lacert. (146) 13ff.

Lacerta africana guineensis — Amphib. Gyll. (5) 24

Lacerta africana volans — Amphib. Gyll. (5) 20

Lacerta agilis — Esca avium (174) 3

Lacerta amboinensis taeniolis fimbriatis — Amphib. Gyll. (5) 24

Lacerta americana cum cauda longissima — Amphib. Gyll. (5) 23

Lacerta americana maculata — Amphib. Gyll. (5) 21

Lacerta americana minor coerulea — Amphib. Gyll. (5) 21

Lacerta aquatica — Usum hist. nat. (145) 25; Siren. lacert. (146) 13

Lacerta cauda ancipiti, pedibus triungulatis, palmis pentadactylis, plantis palmatis tetradactylis — Amphib. Gyll. (5) 16

Lacerta cauda longa, pedibus pentadactylis, dorso antice dentato, capite pone denticulato — Mus. Ad.-Frid. (11) 12

Lacerta cauda tereti brevi, pedibus pentadactylis, digitis duobus tribusque coadunatis — Mus. Ad.-Frid. (11) 13; Surin. Grill. (16) 25

Lacerta cauda tereti, collo crassitie capitis, pedibus pentadactylis marginatis — Mat. med. anim. (29) 11

Lacerta cauda tereti, corpore duplo longiore, pedibus pentadactylis, crista gulae integerrima, dorso levi — Mus. Ad.-Frid. (11) 9

Lacerta cauda tereti, corpore duplo longiore, pedibus pentadactylis, crista nulla, hypochondriis plicatis — Amphib. Gyll. (5) 22; Surin. Grill. (16) 25

Lacerta cauda tereti, corpore duplo longiore, pedibus pentadactylis, crista nulla, scutis abdominalibus 30 — Amphib. Gyll. (5) 21; Mus. Ad.-Frid. (11) 15[as pantadactylis]

Lacerta cauda tereti, corpore longo, pedibus pentadactylis, gula subcristata, antice dentata, dorso levi — Mus. Ad.-Frid. (11) 11

Lacerta cauda tereti, corpore sesqui longiore, pedibus pentadactylis, dorso lineis longitudinalibus striato — Amphib. Gyll. (5) 24[as pendactylis]

Lacerta cauda tereti, corpore triplo longiore, pedibus pentadactylis, gula subcristata — Amphib. Gyll. (5) 23; Mus. Ad.-Frid. (11) 11

Lacerta cauda tereti longa, pedibus pentadactylis, dorso antice denticulato, collo capiteque pone aculeato — Mus. Ad.-Frid. (11) 11[as aculiato]

Lacerta cauda tereti, pedibus inermibus, palmis tetradactylis, plantis pentadactylis, corpore nudo punctis perforato — Amphib. Gyll. (5) 25

Lacerta cauda tereti, pedibus pentadactylis, alis femore connexis, crista gulae triplici — Amphib. Gyll. (5) 20

Lacerta cauda tereti, pedibus pentadactylis, crista dorsi longitudinali, gulae pendula antice dentata — Amphib. Gyll. (5) 18; Mus. Ad.-Frid. (11) 10

Lacerta cauda tereti, pedibus pentadactylis, crista gulae pendula antice dentata, dorsi sutura denticulata — Mus. Ad.-Frid. (11) 10

Lacerta cauda tereti, pedibus pentadactylis, digitis utrinque cristatis subtus lunulato-imbricatis, corpore verrucoso — Amphib. Gyll. (5) 27; Mus. Ad.-Frid. (11) 15

Lacerta cauda tereti, pedibus pentadactylis, squamis rotundatis levissimis subgriseis, lateralibus subfuscis — Mus. Ad.-Frid. (11) 16

Lacerta cauda verticillata, pedibus subpentadactylis squamis quadratis — Mus. Ad.-Frid. (11) 16

Lacerta cauda verticillata, squamis denticulatis, pedibus pentadactylis — Amphib. Gyll. (5) 26; Mus. Ad.-Frid. (11) 15

Lacerta ceilonica coerulea — Mus. Ad.-Frid. (11) 12

Lacerta ceilonica crocodili capite, maxima et ex griseo et nigro varia stellulisque albis transversim sitis notata, cauda longa — Amphib. Gyll. (5) 21; Mus. Ad.-Frid. (11) 16

Lacerta ceilonica lemniscata et pectinata coerulea, kolotes et askalotes graecis dicta, aliis ophiomachus seu pugnatrix coerulea — Mus. Ad.-Frid. (11) 12

Lacerta chalcidica — Mus. Ad.-Frid. (11) 16

Lacerta chalcidica marmorata ex gallecia — Amphib. Gyll. (5) 23[as chalcitica … gallaecia]; Mus. Ad.-Frid. (11) 11[as gallaecia]

Lacerta iguana — Siren. lacert. (146) 13

Lacerta indica — Amphib. Gyll. (5) 27

Lacerta indica squamis et verrucis rotundis, digitis latis interne rugosis — Amphib. Gyll. (5) 27

Lacerta palustris — Siren. lacert. (146) 13

Lacerta punctata — Siren. lacert. (146) 13

Lacerta salamandra — Siren. lacert. (146) 13

Lacerta seu leguana surinamensis pectinata et strumosa coerulea foemina — Amphib. Gyll. (5) 18

Lacerta surinamensis major — Amphib. Gyll. (5) 21

Lacerta teguixin — Amphib. Gyll. (5) 22

Lacerta volans indica — Amphib. Gyll. (5) 20; Mus. Ad.-Frid. (11) 9

Lacertus africanus, cauda spinosa, mas et foemina —
Amphib. Gyll. (5) 26; Mus. Ad.-Frid. (11) 15[as
african]

Lacertus amboinensis pectinatus et strumosus
maximus, senembi et iguana, dictus, amphibius —
Amphib. Gyll. (5) 18

Lacertus americanus lemniscatus — Amphib. Gyll.
(5) 24

Lacertus americanus pectinatus et strumosus —
Amphib. Gyll. (5) 18

Lacertus ceilonicus amphibius seu leguana soa ajer
dicta — Mus. Ad.-Frid. (11) 12

Lacertus indicus — Amphib. Gyll. (5) 18, 21

Lacertus omnium maximus — Amphib. Gyll. (5) 16

Lacertus volans — Amphib. Gyll. (5) 20

Lachnaea — Fl. Cap. (99) 6[as Lachnea]

Lachnaea conglomerata — Fl. Cap. (99) 14

Lachnaea eriocephala — Fl. Cap. (99) 14

Lacryma jobi — Herb. Amboin. (57) 20; Fund.
agrost. (152) 15

Lacryma jobi, gramineis foliis in capreolos
definentibus — Nova pl. gen. 1747 (14) 13

Lactaria salubris — Herb. Amboin. (57) 10

Lactuca — Peloria (3) 10; Hort. Upsal. (7) 34;
Anandria (9) 4; Vir. pl. (13) 23, 25, 36; Sapor.
med. (31) 11; Pl. escul. (35) 26; Hosp. insect. fl.
(43) 12; Noxa insect. (46) 18; Vern. arb. (47) 9;
Mus ind. (62) 14; Hort. acad. (63) 3; Acetaria (77)
10ff.; Phalaena (78) 5; Pand. insect. (93) 18; Nom.
bot. (107) 17; Polit. nat. (109) 8; Fund. entom.
(154) [31, as 30]; Scorb. (180) 21

Lactuca capitata e rubro variegata — Acetaria (77) 10

Lactuca capitata praecox rubra — Acetaria (77) 10

Lactuca carolina — Pan Svec. (26) 31

Lactuca crispa — Acetaria (77) 10

Lactuca foliis hastato linearibus sessilibus, rachi
dorsali aculeato, dicenda — Pl. Mart.-Burs. (6)
7[as cessilibus]

Lactuca foliis verticalibus carina aculeatis — Cent. II.
pl. (66) 29

Lactuca intybacea — Acetaria (77) 10

Lactuca maculosa — Acetaria (77) 10

Lactuca perennis — Fl. Monsp. (74) 24

Lactuca romana longa dulcis — Acetaria (77) 10

Lactuca saligna — Demonstr. pl. (49) 22; Fl. Monsp.
(74) 24

Lactuca sativa — Hosp. insect. fl. (43) 29; Demonstr.
pl. (49) 22; Pl. officin. (52) 11; Acetaria (77) 10;
Fl. Jam. (105) 24; Mac. olit. (113) 20; Hort. cul.
(132) 14

Lactuca sativa capitata — Hort. cul. (132) 14

Lactuca sativa crispa — Hort. cul. (132) 14

Lactuca scariola — Fl. Monsp. (74) 24

Lactuca serriola — Cent. II. pl. (66) 29; Fl. Palaest.
(70) 27[as seriola]; Acetaria (77) 11; Fl. Belg.
(112) 20[as seriola]

Lactuca suecica hypocrateriformis — Acetaria (77)
10

Lactuca suecica oblonga — Acetaria (77) 10

Lactuca suecica virescens — Acetaria (77) 10

Lactuca sylvestris altera, angusto saligno folio, costa
albicante — Pl. Mart.-Burs. (6) 7

Lactuca sylvestris annua costa spinosa, folio integro
colore caesio — Cent. II. pl. (66) 29

Lactuca sylvestris costa spinosa — Pl. Mart.-Burs.
(6) 7; Cent. II. pl. (66) 29

Lactuca sylvestris italica costa spinosa, sanguineis
maculis adspersa — Cent. II. pl. (66) 29

Lactuca sylvestris laciniata — Cent. II. pl. (66) 29

Lactuca sylvestris latifolia — Fl. Angl. (56) 26

Lactuca virosa — Demonstr. pl. (49) 22; Fl. Angl.
(56) 21; Fl. Monsp. (74) 24; Acetaria (77) 11, 12;
Prodr. fl. Dan. (82) 22; Med. grav. (92) 9; Opium
(179) 8

Laedendo odore — Ledum (178) 3

Laetia — Fl. Jam. (105) 26

Laetia americana — Fl. Jam. (105) 17

Laetia thamnia — Pl. Jam. (102) 31; Fl. Jam. (105)
17

Lagansa — Herb. Amboin. (57) 21

Lagoecia — Fund. fr. (123) 21

Lagoecia cuminoides — Fl. Palaest. (70) 15

Lagondium litoreum — Herb. Amboin. (57) 15

Lagondium vulgare — Herb. Amboin. (57) 15

Lagopus — Betula (1) 19; Oecon. nat. (20) 35; Pan
Svec. (26) 6

Lagurus — Hort. Upsal. (7) 34; Fund. agrost. (152) 5,
27, 30, 36

Lagurus nardus — Pl. officin. (52) 14, 18

Lagurus oblongus — Fl. Belg. (112) 13

Lagurus ovatus — Fl. Palaest. (70) 13; Fl. Monsp.
(74) 9

Lagurus schoenanthus — Pl. officin. (52) 17

Laharus — Herb. Amboin. (57) 11

Lamium — Fl. alp. (71) 26; Nom. bot. (107) 15;
Nect. fl. (122) 7

Lamium album — Herbat. Upsal. (50) 10; Pl. officin.
(52) 12; Stat. pl. (55) 20; Fl. Angl. (56) 18; Fl.
Palaest. (70) 23; Fl. Monsp. (74) 19; Prodr. fl. Dan.
(82) 20; Fl. Belg. (112) 18; Fl. Åker. (162) 14;
Pand. fl. Ryb. (165) 20

Lamium amplexicaule — Pan Svec. (26) 27;
Demonstr. pl. (49) [vii]; Herbat. Upsal. (50) 12;
Stat. pl. (55) 19; Fl. Angl. (56) 18; Fl. Monsp. (74)
19; Prodr. fl. Dan. (82) 20; Fl. Belg. (112) 18;
Fund. fr. (123) 12; Prol. pl. 1763 (130) 14; Fl.
Åker. (162) 14; Pand. fl. Ryb. (165) 20

Lamium galeobdolon — Fl. Monsp. (74) 19

Lamium perenne — Pan Svec. (26) 27

Lamium purpureum — Herbat. Upsal. (50) 15; Stat.
pl. (55) 19; Fl. Angl. (56) 18; Fl. Palaest. (70) 23;
Fl. Monsp. (74) 19; Prodr. fl. Dan. (82) 20; Fl.

Belg. (112) 18; Fl. Åker. (162) 14; Pand. fl. Ryb. (165) 20; Esca avium (174) 13

Lamium rubrum — Pan Svec. (26) 27

Lampujum — Herb. Amboin. (57) 20[as Lampurjum]

Lampyris — Fund. entom. (154) 22

Lampyris noctiluca — Pand. fl. Ryb. (165) 9

Lampyris sanguinea — Pand. fl. Ryb. (165) 9

Lanarius — Migr. avium (79) 20

Lanius — Herb. Amboin. (57) 14; Migr. avium (79) 21; Polit. nat. (109) 14, 21; Fund. ornith. (137) 24

Lanius excubitor — Usum hist. nat. (145) 25

Lansium — Herb. Amboin. (57) 7

Lansium sylvestre — Herb. Amboin. (57) 7

Lantana — Hort. Upsal. (7) 37

Lantana aculeata — Fl. Jam. (105) 18

Lantana annua — Cent. II. pl. (66) 22

Lantana camara — Fl. Jam. (105) 18; Pl. Surin. (177) 11

Lantana foliis oppositis, caule inermi, floribus capitato-umbellatis involucrato-foliosis — Cent. II. pl. (66) 22

Lantana involucrata — Cent. II. pl. (66) 22

Lapathum — Sapor. med. (31) 15; Rhabarbarum (41) 17

Lapathum aureum — Fl. Angl. (56) 26

Lapathum bardanae folio undulato glabro — Rhabarbarum (41) 6

Lapathum minimum — Fl. Angl. (56) 26

Lapathum sanguineum — Vir. pl. (13) 4

Lapathum viride — Fl. Angl. (56) 26

Lapillus numismalis — Corallia Balt. (4) 19

Lapis calcarius, coralloides, radiatus, gothlandicus, cujus superficies densas, elevatas et a centro ad peripheriam excurrentes lineolas radiatas exhibet — Corallia Balt. (4) 31

Lappula benghalensis tetraspermos, ribesii folio, echinis orbicularibus ad foliorum ortum plurimis simul sessilibus — Nova pl. gen. 1747 (14) 17

Lapsana — Pl. hybr. (33) 13; Pl. escul. (35) 22, 28

Lapsana apula — Raphania (126) 19[as Lampsana]

Lapsana chondrilloides — Demonstr. pl. (49) 22; Fl. Monsp. (74) 24

Lapsana communis — Herbat. Upsal. (50) 10; Stat. pl. (55) 19; Fl. Angl. (56) 22; Fl. Monsp. (74) 24; Acetaria (77) 15; Prodr. fl. Dan. (82) 22; Fl. Belg. (112) 20; Usum hist. nat. (145) 10; Fl. Åker. (162) 17; Pand. fl. Ryb. (165) 21; Esca avium (174) 14

Lapsana flore melino — Raphania (126) 19

Lapsana rhagadiolus — Demonstr. pl. (49) 22

Lapsana stellata — Demonstr. pl. (49) 22; Fl. Monsp. (74) 24

Lapsana vulgaris — Pan Svec. (26) 31

Laria — Fund. entom. (154) 29

Larix — Nom. bot. (107) 18

Larus — Oecon. nat. (20) [37, as 7], 41; Metam. pl. (67) [5]; Migr. avium (79) 16, 26; Polit. nat. (109) 13; Iter Chin. (161) 6

Larus parasiticus — Migr. avium (79) 12; Fund. ornith. (137) 26

Larva oblonga pedibus 16 corpore spinis distinctis armato — Mus. Ad.-Frid. (11) 48

Larva oblonga pedibus 16 veris 4 praeterea sparsis corpore glabro; pone commaculato — Mus. Ad.-Frid. (11) 48

Larva ovata pedibus 16 lana erecta — Mus. Ad.-Frid. (11) 48

Laserpitium — Vir. pl. (13) 19

Laserpitium chironium — Fl. Monsp. (74) 13

Laserpitium exoticum, lobis angustissimus integris — Cent. II. pl. (66) 13

Laserpitium foliolis lineari-lanceolatis venosostriatis distinctis — Cent. II. pl. (66) 13

Laserpitium gallicum — Fl. Monsp. (74) 13

Laserpitium latifolium — Herbat. Upsal. (50) 8; Pl. officin. (52) 10; Fl. Angl. (56) 6; Fl. Palaest. (70) 16; Fl. Monsp. (74) 13; Pand. fl. Ryb. (165) 17

Laserpitium majus — Pan Svec. (26) 19

Laserpitium peucedanoides — Cent. II. pl. (66) 13

Laserpitium peucedanoides, foliorum segmentis angustissimis — Cent. II. pl. (66) 13

Laserpitium siler — Pl. officin. (52) 18; Fl. alp. (71) 14; Fl. Monsp. (74) 13

Laserpitium trilobum — Fl. Monsp. (74) 13[as trilobium]

Lathraea — Obst. med. (34) 7; Vern. arb. (47) 8; Somn. pl. (68) 6[as Latraea]; Pl. tinct. (97) 10; Nect. fl. (122) 7

Lathraea anblatum — Stat. pl. (55) 17; Fl. Angl. (56) 19

Lathraea clandestina — Fung. melit. (69) 3; Pl. rar. Afr. (115) 6; Aphyteia (185) 9

Lathraea squamaria — Pan Svec. (26) 27; Herbat. Upsal. (50) 8; Fl. Monsp. (74) 20; Prodr. fl. Dan. (82) 20; Hist. nat. Rossia (144) 31[as Lathrea]

Lathyris — Euphorbia (36) 3, 20

Lathyris major — Euphorbia (36) 20

Lathyroides — Anandria (9) 4

Lathyrus — Hort. Upsal. (7) 33; Vir. pl. (13) 23; Fl. oecon. (17) 18; Pl. escul. (35) 21; Nom. bot. (107) 16

Lathyrus amphicarpos — Fl. Palaest. (70) 25; Fl. Monsp. (74) 22

Lathyrus angulatus — Fl. Angl. (56) 20; Fl. Monsp. (74) 22

Lathyrus angustissimo folio, semine anguloso — Pl. Mart.-Burs. (6) 26

Lathyrus angustissimo sive capillaceo folio — Pl. Mart.-Burs. (6) 26

Lathyrus annuus — Demonstr. pl. (49) 20; Cent. I. pl. (65) 2; Fl. Monsp. (74) 22

Lathyrus aphaca — Fl. Angl. (56) 20; Fl. Monsp. (74) 22; Prodr. fl. Dan. (82) 21

Lathyrus arabicus — Fl. Palaest. (70) 25

Lathyrus articulatus — Demonstr. pl. (49) 20; Fl. Monsp. (74) 22

Lathyrus biflorus — Fl. Palaest. (70) 25

Lathyrus bithynicus — Demonstr. pl. (49) 20

Lathyrus capillaceo folio — Pl. Mart.-Burs. (6) 26

Lathyrus cicera — Demonstr. pl. (49) 20; Fl. Monsp. (74) 22

Lathyrus clymenum — Pan Svec. (26) 30; Demonstr. pl. (49) 20

Lathyrus collium — Pan Svec. (26) 30

Lathyrus foliis solitariis cirrho terminatis — Pl. Mart.-Burs. (6) 26

Lathyrus heterophyllus — Fl. Monsp. (74) 22

Lathyrus hirsutus — Fl. Angl. (56) 20; Fl. Monsp. (74) 22

Lathyrus hispanicus flore luteo — Demonstr. pl. (49) 20

Lathyrus humilior — Fl. Monsp. (74) 30

Lathyrus inconspicuus — Demonstr. pl. (49) 20

Lathyrus latifolius — Demonstr. pl. (49) 20; Fl. Angl. (56) 20; Calend. fl. (72) [14]; Fl. Monsp. (74) 22, 30; Prodr. fl. Dan. (82) 21; Fl. Belg. (112) 20; Fl. Åker. (162) 16

Lathyrus moschatus — Odor. med. (40) 12[as Latyrus]; Ambros. (100) 14

Lathyrus nissolia — Fl. Angl. (56) 20; Metam. pl. (67) 13; Fl. Monsp. (74) 22

Lathyrus odoratus — Somn. pl. (68) 17; Calend. fl. (72) [22]; Hort. cul. (132) 23

Lathyrus odoratus siculus — Demonstr. pl. (49) 20

Lathyrus odoratus zeylanicus — Demonstr. pl. (49) 20

Lathyrus palustris — Herbat. Upsal. (50) 18; Stat. pl. (55) 14; Fl. Angl. (56) 20; Calend. fl. (72) [12]; Esca avium (174) 14

Lathyrus pedunculis bifloris, cirrhis diphyllis, foliolis ensiformibus, leguminibus glabris, stipulis bipartitis — Demonstr. pl. (49) 20

Lathyrus pedunculis bifloris, cirrhis diphyllis, foliolis lanceolatis — Pl. Mart.-Burs. (6) 26

Lathyrus pedunculis unifloris, cirrhis diphyllis, radicibus etiam sub terra fructificantibus — Pl. Mart.-Burs. (6) 26

Lathyrus pedunculis unifloris, petiolis tetraphyllis, stipulis setaceis, caule ancipiti — Pl. Mart.-Burs. (6) 26

Lathyrus pedunculis unifloris seta terminatis, cirrhis diphyllis, foliis setaceo-linearibus — Pl. Mart.-Burs. (6) 26

Lathyrus pisiformis — Demonstr. pl. (49) 20

Lathyrus pratensis — Pan Svec. (26) 30[as pratensus]; Herbat. Upsal. (50) 6; Stat. pl. (55) 20; Fl. Angl. (56) 20; Fl. Monsp. (74) 22; Prodr. fl.

Dan. (82) 21; Fl. Belg. (112) 20; Fl. Åker. (162) 16; Pand. fl. Ryb. (165) 21; Esca avium (174) 14

Lathyrus sativus — Demonstr. pl. (49) 20; Fl. Palaest. (70) 25

Lathyrus setifolius — Fl. Monsp. (74) 22[as setisotius]

Lathyrus subterraneus — Somn. pl. (68) 7[as Latyrus]

Lathyrus sylvestris — Stat. pl. (55) 22; Fl. Angl. (56) 20; Fl. Monsp. (74) 22; Prodr. fl. Dan. (82) 21; Esca avium (174) 14

Lathyrus tingitanus — Demonstr. pl. (49) 20

Lathyrus tuberosus — Demonstr. pl. (49) 20; Calend. fl. (72) [16]; Fl. Monsp. (74) 22; Prodr. fl. Dan. (82) 21; Fl. Belg. (112) 20; Mac. olit. (113) 11; Hort. cul. (132) 17; Usum hist. nat. (145) 12

Lathyrus westrogothicus — Pan Svec. (26) 30

Lauraster amboinensis — Herb. Amboin. (57) 9

Laurifolia — Siren. lacert. (146) 7

Laurocerasus — Hort. acad. (63) 2

Laurus — Hort. Upsal. (7) 36; Odor. med. (40) 12; Pl. officin. (52) 12; Herb. Amboin. (57) 9, 12; Hort. acad. (63) 2; Fl. Jam. (105) 26; Nom. bot. (107) 12; Nect. fl. (122) 7; Usum hist. nat. (145) 29; Obs. mat. med. (171) 8

Laurus benzoin — Pl. officin. (52) 6[as benzoe]

Laurus camphora — Pl. officin. (52) 6; Fl. Cap. (99) 2

Laurus cassia — Pl. officin. (52) 7

Laurus chloroxylon — Fl. Jam. (105) 15

Laurus cinnamomum — Pl. officin. (52) 8; Pl. Surin. (177) 8

Laurus culilaban — Herb. Amboin. (57) 9[as culilawan]; Obs. mat. med. (171) 3[as culilawan]

Laurus foliis enervibus obverse ovatis obtusis — Passifl. (8) [iii]

Laurus foliis trilobis — Passifl. (8) [iii]

Laurus indica — Fl. Jam. (105) 15

Laurus indica serratifolia inodora, fructu olivae magnitudine et forma, nucleis crispis lapideis — Nova pl. gen. 1747 (14) 19

Laurus nobilis — Demonstr. pl. (49) 11; Pl. officin. (52) 12; Fl. Monsp. (74) 15; Hort. cul. (132) 21

Laurus persea — Fl. Jam. (105) 15; Fr. escul. (127) 14

Laurus sassafras — Pl. officin. (52) 17

Laurus vulgaris — Gem. arb. (24) 17

Laurus winterana — Pl. officin. (52) 6, 20

Lavandula — Hort. Upsal. (7) 36[as Lavendula]; Vir. pl. (13) 29, 34; Stat. pl. (55) 8[as Lavendula]; Fl. Monsp. (74) 7; Nom. bot. (107) 14[as Lavendula]; Menthae (153) 7; Marum (175) 13

Lavandula multifida — Demonstr. pl. (49) 16

Lavandula spica — Demonstr. pl. (49) 16; Pl. officin. (52) 12, 18; Fl. Monsp. (74) 19; Fl. Jam. (105) 24; Hort. cul. (132) 15

Lavandula stoechas — Pl. officin. (52) 18; Fl. Monsp. (74) 19

Lavatera — Hort. Upsal. (7) 36; Gem. arb. (24) 6

Lavatera americana — Pl. Jam. (102) 16; Fl. Jam. (105) 18[as Lavaterra]

Lavatera arborea — Demonstr. pl. (49) 19; Fl. Angl. (56) 20

Lavatera foliis septemangularibus, obtusis, plicatis, villosis, caule fruticoso, floribus ad alas confertis — Spons. pl. (12) 55

Lavatera olbia — Fl. Monsp. (74) 21[as albia]

Lavatera thuringiaca — Demonstr. pl. (49) 19; Fl. Palaest. (70) 24; Calend. fl. (72) [16]; Fl. Monsp. (74) 21

Lavatera triloba — Demonstr. pl. (49) 19

Lavatera trimestris — Demonstr. pl. (49) 19; Fl. Monsp. (74) 21; Hort. cul. (132) 23

Lavendula — see Lavandula

Lawsonia inermis — Pl. officin. (52) 4; Fl. Palaest. (70) 18; Pl. tinct. (97) 16

Lawsonia spinosa — Demonstr. pl. (49) 11; Herb. Amboin. (57) 15

Lechea — Nova pl. gen. 1751 (32) 7, [13, as 15], 48

Lechea foliis lineari-lanceolatis, floribus paniculatis — Nova pl. gen. 1751 (32) [13, as 15]

Lechea foliis ovato-lanceolatis, floribus lateralibus — Nova pl. gen. 1751 (32) 14

Lecythis — Nect. fl. (122) 14

Lecythis ollaria — Pl. Surin. (177) 10

Ledon 4 — Cent. I. pl. (65) 14

Ledum — Vir. pl. (13) 20; Fl. oecon. (17) 11; Pan Svec. (26) 9; Fr. Svec. (91) [ii]; Pand. insect. (93) 14; Usum hist. nat. (145) 27; Usum musc. (148) 11, 12; Erica (163) 3; Cimicifuga (173) 8; Ledum (178) 2ff.

Ledum foliis linearibus subtus hirsutis, floribus corymbosis — Ledum (178) 5

Ledum foliis rosmarini alterum — Ledum (178) 5[as rorismarini]

Ledum graveolens — Pan Svec. (26) 22

Ledum lauro-cerasi folio — Gem. arb. (24) 17

Ledum palustre — Herbat. Upsal. (50) 6; Pl. officin. (52) 16; Stat. pl. (55) 15; Prodr. fl. Dan. (82) 17; Fr. Svec. (91) 4, 20; Fl. Åker. (162) 11; Pand. fl. Ryb. (165) 18; Ledum (178) 5

Ledum rosmarini foliis — Ledum (178) 5[as rorismarini]

Ledum rosmarini folio — Gem. arb. (24) 17

Ledum silesiacum — Ledum (178) 5

Leguana pectinata et strumosa asiatica — Amphib. Gyll. (5) 18

Leguana soa ajer dicta — Mus. Ad.-Frid. (11) 12

Leguana surinamensis pectinata et strumosa coerulea foemina — Amphib. Gyll. (5) 18

Leleba — Herb. Amboin. (57) 15

Lemma — Spons. pl. (12) 19, 28

Lemna — Fl. oecon. (17) 29; Noxa insect. (46) 24; Pand. insect. (93) 22; Nom. bot. (107) 18; Polit. nat. (109) 12

Lemna aquatica — Hosp. insect. fl. (43) 39

Lemna gibba — Stat. pl. (55) 13; Fl. Belg. (112) 22; Fl. Åker. (162) 18

Lemna minor — Stat. pl. (55) 13; Fl. Angl. (56) 23; Fl. Monsp. (74) 27; Prodr. fl. Dan. (82) 24; Fl. Jam. (105) 21, 25; Fl. Belg. (112) 22; Fl. Åker. (162) 18

Lemna polyrhiza — Herbat. Upsal. (50) 10[as polyrrhiza]; Stat. pl. (55) 13; Fl. Angl. (56) 23[as polyrrhiza]; Prodr. fl. Dan. (82) 24[as polyrrhiza]; Fl. Belg. (112) 22; Fl. Åker. (162) 18[as polyrrhiza]; Pand. fl. Ryb. (165) 22

Lemna trisulca — Stat. pl. (55) 13; Fl. Angl. (56) 23; Fl. Monsp. (74) 27; Prodr. fl. Dan. (82) 24; Fl. Belg. (112) 22

Lemniscata — Hort. Upsal. (7) 43

Lemur — Polit. nat. (109) 16

Lemur mungoz — Iter Chin. (161) 10[as mongos]

Lens — Instr. peregr. (96) 10; Nom. bot. (107) 16

Lens lapidea striata, utrinque convexa — Corallia Balt. (4) 19

Lens phaseoloides — Herb. Amboin. (57) 18

Lenticula palustris angustifolia, folio in apice dissecto — Cent. I. pl. (65) 31

Lenticula palustris indica, foliis subrotundis binis capillamentis ad imum barbatis — Nova pl. gen. 1751 (32) 40

Lentiscus — Mirac. insect. (45) 15; Fung. melit. (69) 10; Fl. Monsp. (74) 7

Leo — Curios. nat. (18) 11; Oecon. nat. (20) 35, 42, 43; Fl. Cap. (99) [1]; Polit. nat. (109) 20; Usum hist. nat. (145) 23

Leontice — Nect. fl. (122) 11

Leontice chrysogonum — Fl. Palaest. (70) 17

Leontice leontopetalum — Fl. Palaest. (70) 17

Leontodon — Vir. pl. (13) 25, 36; Fl. oecon. (17) 19; Pl. escul. (35) 22, 28; Fl. Angl. (56) 27; Hort. acad. (63) 19; Phalaena (78) 5; Pand. insect. (93) 18; Pl. Jam. (102) 23; Nom. bot. (107) 17; Ping. anim. (108) 15

Leontodon aureum — Fl. Jam. (105) 19

Leontodon autumnale — Herbat. Upsal. (50) 7; Stat. pl. (55) 21; Fl. Angl. (56) 21[as Leonthodon]; Fl. Monsp. (74) 24; Prodr. fl. Dan. (82) 22; Fl. Belg. (112) 20; Pl. rar. Afr. (115) 6; Fl. Åker. (162) 17; Esca avium (174) 14

Leontodon bulbosum — Fl. Monsp. (74) 24

Leontodon calyce inferne reflexo — Pl. Mart.-Burs. (6) 7

Leontodon chondrilloides — Pan Svec. (26) 31

Leontodon foliis ensiformibus, integris, hirsutis; calyce erecto, simplici — Cent. I. pl. (65) 26

Leontodon hispidum — Fl. Monsp. (74) 24; Colon. pl. (158) 8; Pand. fl. Ryb. (165) 21[as Leonthodon]

Leontodon lanatum — Cent. I. pl. (65) 26; Fl. Palaest. (70) 27

Leontodon taraxaconoides — Pan Svec. (26) 31

Leontodon taraxacum — Pan Svec. (26) 31; Pl. escul. (35) 21; Hosp. insect. fl. (43) 29; Herbat. Upsal. (50) 10; Pl. officin. (52) 19; Stat. pl. (55) 19; Fl. Angl. (56) 21[as Leonthodon]; Fl. Monsp. (74) 24; Acetaria (77) 12; Prodr. fl. Dan. (82) 22; Fl. Belg. (112) 20; Mac. olit. (113) 21; Fl. Åker. (162) 17; Pand. fl. Ryb. (165) 21[as Leonthodon]; Esca avium (174) 14

Leontodon tuberosum — Fl. Monsp. (74) 24

Leonurus — Hort. Upsal. (7) 34; Anandria (9) 4; Mund. invis. (149) 20

Leonurus cardiaca — Pan Svec. (26) 27; Herbat. Upsal. (50) 20; Pl. officin. (52) 7; Stat. pl. (55) 20; Fl. Angl. (56) 18; Calend. fl. (72) [16]; Prodr. fl. Dan. (82) 20; Fl. Belg. (112) 18; Fl. Åker. (162) 14; Pand. fl. Ryb. (165) 20

Leonurus galeobdolon — Pan Svec. (26) 27

Leonurus sibiricus — Hist. nat. Rossia (144) 30

Lepas — Fund. test. (166) 18, 33, 35, 40

Lepas anatifera — Nat. pelagi (84) 9; Fund. test. (166) 40

Lepas balanus — Nat. pelagi (84) 9

Lepidium — Vir. pl. (13) 22; Fl. oecon. (17) 17; Sapor. med. (31) 19; Pl. escul. (35) 29; Noxa insect. (46) 19; Cul. mut. (88) 2, 8; Nom. bot. (107) 15; Raphania (126) 13

Lepidium alpinum — Cent. II. pl. (66) 23

Lepidium cardamine — Cent. I. pl. (65) 17

Lepidium chalepense — Cent. II. pl. (66) 23; Fl. Palaest. (70) 23

Lepidium draba — Cent. II. pl. (66) 23; Fl. Monsp. (74) 20

Lepidium foliis pinnatis integerrimis scapo subradicato, siliculis lanceolatis mucronatis — Cent. II. pl. (66) 23

Lepidium foliis radicalibus pinnatis, caulinis lyratis — Cent. I. pl. (65) 17

Lepidium foliis sagittatis sessilibus dentatis — Cent. II. pl. (66) 23

Lepidium iberis — Fl. Monsp. (74) 20; Obs. mat. med. (171) 5

Lepidium latifolium — Demonstr. pl. (49) 17; Fl. Angl. (56) 19; Fl. Palaest. (70) 23; Calend. fl. (72) [16]; Fl. Monsp. (74) 20; Cul. mut. (88) 7; Fl. Belg. (112) 19; Obs. mat. med. (171) 5

Lepidium nasturtium — Pl. officin. (52) 14; Mac. olit. (113) 22

Lepidium nasturtium alpinum — Fl. alp. (71) 20

Lepidium nudicaule — Fl. Monsp. (74) 7, 20

Lepidium oelandicum — Pan Svec. (26) 28

Lepidium osiris — Pan Svec. (26) 28

Lepidium perenne — Pan Svec. (26) 28; Pl. escul. (35) 19

Lepidium perfoliatum — Fl. Palaest. (70) 23

Lepidium petraeum — Demonstr. pl. (49) 17[as petreum]; Stat. pl. (55) 21; Fl. Angl. (56) 19; Cent. II. pl. (66) 23; Fl. Monsp. (74) 20; Fl. Belg. (112) 19

Lepidium procumbens — Fl. Monsp. (74) 7, 20

Lepidium ruderale — Herbat. Upsal. (50) 17; Stat. pl. (55) 20; Fl. Angl. (56) 19; Fl. Monsp. (74) 20; Prodr. fl. Dan. (82) 20; Fl. Belg. (112) 19

Lepidium sativum — Demonstr. pl. (49) 17; Prodr. fl. Dan. (82) 20; Cul. mut. (88) 6; Hort. cul. (132) 15

Lepidium virginicum — Demonstr. pl. (49) 17; Fl. Jam. (105) 18[as Lepidum virginianum]

Lepidocarpodendron foliis sericeis brevibus confertissimis, fructu gracili longo — Pl. rar. Afr. (115) 8[as Lepidocarpodendrum]

Lepisma — Fund. entom. (154) 21

Lepisma saccharina — Pand. fl. Ryb. (165) 16

Leptostachya — Nova pl. gen. 1751 (32) 12, 33, 34

Leptura — Noxa insect. (46) 16; Fund. entom. (154) 6, 30

Leptura aquatica — Pand. insect. (93) 13, 16; Esca avium (174) 6

Leptura collaris — Esca avium (174) 7

Leptura deaurata — Hosp. insect. fl. (43) 19, 26

Leptura melanura — Pand. fl. Ryb. (165) 9; Esca avium (174) 6

Leptura quadrifasciata — Pand. fl. Ryb. (165) 9

Leptura rubra — Pand. fl. Ryb. (165) 9; Esca avium (174) 6

Leptura sanguinolenta — Pand. fl. Ryb. (165) 9

Leptura testacea — Pand. fl. Ryb. (165) 9

Leptura violacea — Hosp. insect. fl. (43) 26

Leptura virens — Pand. fl. Ryb. (165) 9

Leptura virginea — Pand. fl. Ryb. (165) 9; Esca avium (174) 7

Lepus — Oecon. nat. (20) 42; Mat. med. anim. (29) 4; Morb. hyeme (38) 5, 12, 13; Cui bono? (42) 24; Mus ind. (62) 6ff.; Polit. nat. (109) 14, 19; Usum hist. nat. (145) 23, 24, 29

Lepus capensis — Fl. Cap. (99) [1]

Lepus cauda abrupta, pupillis atris — Mat. med. anim. (29) 4

Lernaea — Sem. musc. (28) 16[as Lernea]; Usum hist. nat. (145) 29[as Lernea]

Lernaea carassi — Chin. Lagerstr. (64) 33

Leucadendron — Pl. hybr. (33) 29; Incr. bot. (48) 11; Fl. Cap. (99) 6[as Leucadendrum], 7[as Leucadendrum], 9[as Leucadendrum]; Pl. rar. Afr. (115) 5; Fund. fr. (123) 18

Leucadendron acaulon — Fl. Cap. (99) 11[as Leucadendrum]

Leucadendron cancellatum — Fl. Cap. (99) 11[as Leucadendrum]

Leucadendron cinaroides — Fl. Cap. (99) 11[as Leucadendrum]

Leucadendron conocarpodendron — Fl. Cap. (99) 11[as Leucadendrum]

Leucadendron cucullatum — Fl. Cap. (99) 11[as Leucadendrum]

Leucadendron cyanoides — Fl. Cap. (99) 11[as Leucadendrum]

Leucadendron foliis lanceolatis apice callosis, caule hirsuto, floribus sparsis axillaribus — Pl. rar. Afr. (115) 8

Leucadendron hirtum — Pl. rar. Afr. (115) 8

Leucadendron hypophyllocarpodendron — Fl. Cap. (99) 11[as Leucadendrum]

Leucadendron lepidocarpodendron — Fl. Cap. (99) 11[as Leucadendrum]

Leucadendron proteoides — Fl. Cap. (99) 11[as Leucadendrum]

Leucadendron racemosum — Fl. Cap. (99) 11[as Leucadendrum]

Leucadendron repens — Fl. Cap. (99) 11[as Leucadendrum]

Leucadendron scolymocephalum — Fl. Cap. (99) 11[as Leucadendrum scolymocephalus]

Leucadendron serraria — Fl. Cap. (99) 11[as Leucadendrum]

Leucanthemum fruticosum, foliis crassis — Pl. rar. Afr. (115) 24

Leucojum — Hort. Upsal. (7) 33; Spons. pl. (12) 33, 43, 59; Vir. pl. (13) 20; Vern. arb. (47) 8; Fl. Monsp. (74) 7; Nom. bot. (107) 12; Prol. pl. 1760 (114) 13

Leucojum africanum, caeruleo flore, latifolium — Pl. rar. Afr. (115) 13

Leucojum creticum spinosum incanum luteum — Cent. II. pl. (66) 10

Leucojum luteum sylvestre hieracifolium — Cent. I. pl. (65) 18

Leucojum maritimum parvum, folio virente crassiusculo — Cent. I. pl. (65) 19

Leucojum spinosum — Cent. II. pl. (66) 10

Leucojum sylvestre inodorum, flore parvo pallidiore — Cent. I. pl. (65) 19

Leucojum vernale — Calend. fl. (72) [9]; Migr. avium (79) 20

Leucojum vernum — Pl. Alstr. (121) [4]; Hort. cul. (132) 23

Leucojum vernum polyanthemum — Demonstr. pl. (49) 9[as polyanthus]; Fl. Monsp. (74) 14

Leuconymphaea minor — Fl. Belg. (112) 9

Levisticum — Vir. pl. (13) 8

Levisticum indicum — Herb. Amboin. (57) 21

Libanotis tenuifolia germanica — Pl. Mart.-Burs. (6) 11

Libellula — Oecon. nat. (20) 41; Cui bono? (42) 25; Noxa insect. (46) 31; Metam. pl. (67) 6; Calend. fl. (72) [11]; Polit. nat. (109) 11, 19; Fund. entom. (154) 20, 21, 23

Libellula aenea — Esca avium (174) 8

Libellula alis hyalinis: posticis tota basi fuscis — Cent. insect. (129) 28

Libellula alis patentibus fusco-caerulescente flavoque variegatis apice hyalinis — Cent. insect. (129) 28

Libellula carolina — Cent. insect. (129) 28

Libellula depressa — Pand. fl. Ryb. (165) 11

Libellula flaveola — Pand. fl. Ryb. (165) 11

Libellula grandis — Pand. fl. Ryb. (165) 11

Libellula puella — Fund. entom. (154) 20

Libellula puella alpha — Pand. fl. Ryb. (165) 11

Libellula puella delta — Pand. fl. Ryb. (165) 11

Libellula variegata — Cent. insect. (129) 28

Libellula virgo — Fund. entom. (154) 20; Esca avium (174) 8

Libellula virgo delta — Pand. fl. Ryb. (165) 11

Libellula virgo gamma — Pand. fl. Ryb. (165) 11

Libellula vulgatissima — Esca avium (174) 8

Libelluloides — Fund. entom. (154) 30

Lichen — Vir. pl. (13) 12; Fl. oecon. (17) 29; Oecon. nat. (20) 20, 24, 25, 34; Pan Svec. (26) 5; Sem. musc. (28) 15, 16; Pl. escul. (35) 27; Cui bono? (42) 15, 16; Usum hist. nat. (145) 22; Mund. invis. (149) 14

Lichen aphtosus — Pl. officin. (52) 13; Purg. indig. (143) 12

Lichen arcticus — Fl. alp. (71) 24

Lichen atro-virens — Herbat. Upsal. (50) 16

Lichen calcareus — Usum musc. (148) 12

Lichen candelarius — Pand. insect. (93) [23, as 31]; Pl. tinct. (97) 28

Lichen caninus — Herbat. Upsal. (50) 11; Pl. officin. (52) 13; Prodr. fl. Dan. (82) 26; Usum musc. (148) 14

Lichen caperatus — Prodr. fl. Dan. (82) 26

Lichen capillaceo folio elatior, pelvi ruberrima — Splachnum (27) 8, 11

Lichen carpineus — Usum musc. (148) 12

Lichen centrifugus — Herbat. Upsal. (50) 6; Pand. fl. Ryb. (165) 23

Lichen chalybeiformis — Pand. fl. Ryb. (165) 23

Lichen ciliaris — Pand. fl. Ryb. (165) 23

Lichen ciliatus — Pl. escul. (35) 26

Lichen cocciferus — Pl. officin. (52) 13

Lichen cornutus — Herbat. Upsal. (50) 13

Lichen croceus — Fl. alp. (71) 24

Lichen deustus — Herbat. Upsal. (50) 6

Lichen fagineus — Usum musc. (148) 12

Lichen falunensis — Herbat. Upsal. (50) 16

Lichen floridus — Prodr. fl. Dan. (82) 26

Lichen foliaceus ciliatus, peltis cylindricis rectis sparsis perforatis truncatis: duplici circulo — Splachnum (27) 2

Lichen foliaceus repens lobatus obtusus planus, verrucis sparsis, pelta marginali adscendente — Taenia (19) 10

Lichen fragilis — Herbat. Upsal. (50) 16

Lichen fraxineus — Usum musc. (148) 12; Pand. fl. Ryb. (165) 23

Lichen fruticulosus solidus tectus, foliolis crustaceis — Pl. Mart.-Burs. (6) 28

Lichen fuciformis — Usum musc. (148) 13[as fusiformis]

Lichen gelidus — Rar. Norv. (157) 10

Lichen hirtus — Herbat. Upsal. (50) 11; Prodr. fl. Dan. (82) 26; Pand. fl. Ryb. (165) 23

Lichen islandicus — Vir. pl. (13) 24; Herbat. Upsal. (50) 6; Pl. officin. (52) 13; Stat. pl. (55) 21; Pane diaet. (83) 20; Usum musc. (148) 14; Rar. Norv. (157) 14; Erica (163) 11, 12

Lichen judaicus — Fl. Palaest. (70) 32

Lichen juniperinus — Herbat. Upsal. (50) 11; Pl. tinct. (97) 27; Usum musc. (148) 13, 14

Lichen lanatus — Herbat. Upsal. (50) 16

Lichen nivalis — Herbat. Upsal. (50) 10; Stat. pl. (55) 21; Fl. alp. (71) 24

Lichen olivaceus — Herbat. Upsal. (50) 16

Lichen omphalodes — Herbat. Upsal. (50) 6

Lichen parellus — Usum musc. (148) 13

Lichen parietinus — Prodr. fl. Dan. (82) 26; Pl. tinct. (97) 27; Usum musc. (148) 13; Rar. Norv. (157) 17

Lichen pascalis — Herbat. Upsal. (50) 6

Lichen physodes — Pand. fl. Ryb. (165) 23[as physoides]

Lichen plicatus — Herbat. Upsal. (50) 11; Pl. officin. (52) 13; Usum musc. (148) 14

Lichen prunastri — Usum musc. (148) 12, 13

Lichen pulmonarius — Pl. officin. (52) 16; Prodr. fl. Dan. (82) 26; Usum musc. (148) 13

Lichen pustulatus — Herbat. Upsal. (50) 6; Usum musc. (148) 13

Lichen pyxidatus — Prodr. fl. Dan. (82) 26

Lichen rangiferinus — Herbat. Upsal. (50) 6; Cervus (60) 5, 8; Fl. alp. (71) 4; Usum hist. nat. (145) 22; Usum musc. (148) 7, 8, 14; Erica (163) 12

Lichen rangiferinus sylvaticus — Prodr. fl. Dan. (82) 26

Lichen roccella — Pl. tinct. (97) 27; Obs. mat. med. (171) 6

Lichen sanguinarius — Herbat. Upsal. (50) 16

Lichen saxatilis — Herbat. Upsal. (50) 6; Pl. officin. (52) 20; Pl. tinct. (97) 27; Usum musc. (148) 12, 13; Pand. fl. Ryb. (165) 23

Lichen stygius — Herbat. Upsal. (50) 16; Usum musc. (148) 13

Lichen subulatus — Herbat. Upsal. (50) 13

Lichen tartareus — Herbat. Upsal. (50) 10; Pl. tinct. (97) 27; Usum musc. (148) 13

Lichen upsaliensis — Herbat. Upsal. (50) 10; Stat. pl. (55) 21

Lichen velleus — Herbat. Upsal. (50) 6; Usum musc. (148) 14

Lichen venosus — Herbat. Upsal. (50) 11

Lichen vulpinus — Usum musc. (148) 12, 13; Rar. Norv. (157) 17

Lichenastrum — Buxbaumia (85) 9

Lichenastrum imbricatum — Sem. musc. (28) 15

Lichenella — Fund. entom. (154) 22

Lichenoides foliorum laciniis crinitis — Splachnum (27) 2

Licuala — Herb. Amboin. (57) 6

Lignum aquatile — Herb. Amboin. (57) 17

Lignum clavorum — Herb. Amboin. (57) 12

Lignum colubrinum — Lign. colubr. (21) 11ff.; Herb. Amboin. (57) 9

Lignum colubrinum primum et laudatissimum — Lign. colubr. (21) 11ff.

Lignum colubrinum secundum — Lign. colubr. (21) 11ff.

Lignum colubrinum tertium — Lign. colubr. (21) 11ff.

Lignum corneum — Herb. Amboin. (57) 11

Lignum emanum — Herb. Amboin. (57) 11

Lignum equinum — Herb. Amboin. (57) 12

Lignum eurinum — Herb. Amboin. (57) 12

Lignum laeve — Herb. Amboin. (57) 12

Lignum laeve alterum — Herb. Amboin. (57) 12

Lignum longaevitatis — Herb. Amboin. (57) 15

Lignum momentaneum — Herb. Amboin. (57) 13

Lignum moschatum — Herb. Amboin. (57) 8

Lignum murinum — Herb. Amboin. (57) 11

Lignum nucosum — Herb. Amboin. (57) 14

Lignum papuanum — Herb. Amboin. (57) 9

Lignum salus minus — Herb. Amboin. (57) 12

Lignum sappan — Herb. Amboin. (57) 15

Lignum scholare — Herb. Amboin. (57) 10, 18

Lignum stercoris — Nova pl. gen. 1747 (14) 29

Liguana senembi in nova hispania, tamacolin dicta, pectinata et strumosa — Amphib. Gyll. (5) 18

Ligula intestinorum — Taenia (19) 11

Ligularia — Herb. Amboin. (57) 16

Ligusticum — Vir. pl. (13) 14, 19; Odor. med. (40) 14; Noxa insect. (46) 21; Pand. insect. (93) 13; Nom. bot. (107) 11

Ligusticum austriacum — Fl. alp. (71) 15

Ligusticum cornubiense — Cent. II. pl. (66) 13

Ligusticum foliis decompositis incisis: radicalibus ternatis lanceolatis integerrimis — Cent. II. pl. (66) 13

Ligusticum foliis multiplicato-pinnatis, foliolis pinnatis incisis — Pl. Mart.-Burs. (6) 11

Ligusticum levisticum — Demonstr. pl. (49) 8; Pl. officin. (52) 12; Fl. Palaest. (70) 16; Calend. fl. (72) [14]; Fl. Monsp. (74) 13; Prodr. fl. Dan. (82) 16; Fl. Belg. (112) 15; Usum hist. nat. (145) 25

Ligusticum peleponnesiacum — Fl. alp. (71) 15[as peleponesiacum]; Fl. Monsp. (74) 13[as peloponesiacum]

Ligusticum scoticum — Pan Svec. (26) 19; Demonstr. pl. (49) 8; Stat. pl. (55) 12[as scothicum]; Fl. Angl. (56) 13[as scothicum]; Calend. fl. (72) [15]; Prodr. fl. Dan. (82) 16; Colon. pl. (158) 8

Ligusticum vulgare — Hosp. insect. fl. (43) 19

Ligustrum — Hort. Upsal. (7) 33; Fl. oecon. (17) [1]; Noxa insect. (46) 19; Calend. fl. (72) [10]; Fr. Svec. (91) [ii], 23, 24, 25; Pand. insect. (93) 11; Nom. bot. (107) 9

Ligustrum vulgare — Gem. arb. (24) 15; Pan Svec. (26) 12; Demonstr. pl. (49) [1]; Fl. Angl. (56) 9; Fl. Monsp. (74) 8; Fr. Svec. (91) 3, 8; Pl. tinct. (97) 11; Fl. Belg. (112) 12; Meloe (124) 4; Hort. cul. (132) 26; Colon. pl. (158) 8; Fl. Åker. (162) 5

Lilioasphodelus — Pl. Alstr. (121) 8

Lilium — Hort. Upsal. (7) 33; Anandria (9) 4; Vir. pl. (13) 20, 31; Curios. nat. (18) 7; Gem. arb. (24) 5, 11; Sem. musc. (28) 6; Odor. med. (40) 12; Cui bono? (42) 20; Noxa insect. (46) 21; Hort. acad. (63) 3; Pand. insect. (93) 13; Nom. bot. (107) 12; Nect. fl. (122) 11, 14

Lilium album — Pl. officin. (52) 12; Calend. fl. (72) [17]

Lilium alstroemeri — Pl. Alstr. (121) 8

Lilium bulbiferum — Demonstr. pl. (49) 10; Pl. Alstr. (121) 5; Prol. pl. 1763 (130) 16; Hort. cul. (132) 23; Hist. nat. Rossia (144) 28; Colon. pl. (158) 9

Lilium bulbiferum oviparum — Calend. fl. (72) [16]

Lilium bulbiferum viviparum — Calend. fl. (72) [12], [15]

Lilium camschatcense — Hist. nat. Rossia (144) 28[as kamtschatcense]

Lilium candidum — Demonstr. pl. (49) 9; Fl. Palaest. (70) 17; Hort. cul. (132) 23

Lilium chalcedonicum — Demonstr. pl. (49) 10

Lilium foliis verticillatis: floribus erectis: corollis campanulatis — Pl. rar. Camsch. (30) 15

Lilium jacobaeum — Curios. nat. (18) 17

Lilium javanicum — Herb. Amboin. (57) 28

Lilium martagon — Vir. pl. (13) 20; Demonstr. pl. (49) 10; Calend. fl. (72) [14]; Fl. Monsp. (74) 14; Pl. Alstr. (121) 5; Hort. cul. (132) 23; Hist. nat. Rossia (144) 28

Lilium martagon album — Calend. fl. (72) [15]

Lilium pomponium — Demonstr. pl. (49) 10; Calend. fl. (72) [13]; Hist. nat. Rossia (144) 28

Limax — Taenia (19) 24, 25, 28; Oves (61) 20

Limax ater — Esca avium (174) [9, as 17]

Limax cinerea — Esca avium (174) [9, as 17]

Limax ovatus lividus margine acuto — Taenia (19) 24

Limeum — Fl. Cap. (99) 6; Nect. fl. (122) 9

Limeum capense — Fl. Cap. (99) 13

Limnia — Anandria (9) 4; Spons. pl. (12) 38

Limodorum — Nova pl. gen. 1751 (32) 10

Limodorum tuberosum — Fl. Jam. (105) 20

Limon — Nom. bot. (107) 16

Limonellus — Herb. Amboin. (57) 18

Limonia — Sapor. med. (31) 14

Limonium — Gem. arb. (24) 13

Limonium minus, bellidis folio, flagellis foeniculaceis — Pl. Mart.-Burs. (6) 15

Limonium parvum, bellidis minoris folio — Pl. Mart.-Burs. (6) 15

Limosella — Betula (1) 12; Morb. hyeme (38) 8

Limosella aquatica — Herbat. Upsal. (50) 18; Stat. pl. (55) 13; Fl. Angl. (56) 19; Prodr. fl. Dan. (82) 20; Fl. Belg. (112) 19; Rar. Norv. (157) 11; Fl. Åker. (162) 15

Limosella palustris — Pan Svec. (26) 27

Linagrostis — Fund. agrost. (152) 14, 15

Linaria — Peloria (3) 7ff.; Metam. pl. (67) 14; Migr. avium (79) 34

Linaria altera botryoides montana — Nova pl. gen. 1747 (14) 17

Linaria foliis confertis linearibus carnosis — Cent. I. pl. (65) 16

Linaria foliis copiosis oblongis dentatis, capsula corniculata reflexa — Pl. rar. Afr. (115) 12

Linaria longicauda — Hist. nat. Rossia (144) 16

Linaria lutea vulgaris — Peloria (3) 7[as Linearia]

Linaria maritima foliis succulentis — Cent. I. pl. (65) 16

Linaria valentina saxatilis et perennis villosa, flore luteo — Cent. I. pl. (65) 16

Linaria vulgaris — Peloria (3) 7

Linaria vulgaris lutea, flore majore — Peloria (3) 7

Lingoum — Herb. Amboin. (57) 10

Lingua cervina — Acrostichum (10) 5, 6, 7

Lingua cervina aurea — Acrostichum (10) 14

Lingua cervina scandens, citrei foliis, minor — Acrostichum (10) 10

Lingua cervina triphylla angusta et leviter serrata — Acrostichum (10) 15

Linnaea — Fl. oecon. (17) 16; Gem. arb. (24) 18; Pan Svec. (26) 27

Linnaea borealis — Demonstr. pl. (49) 17; Herbat. Upsal. (50) 18; Pl. officin. (52) 12; Stat. pl. (55) 18; Cervus (60) 8; Fl. alp. (71) 20; Fl. Monsp. (74) 20; Hist. nat. Rossia (144) 31; Rar. Norv. (157) 5, 11, 13, 16; Fl. Åker. (162) 15

Linum — Cui bono? (42) 20; Phalaena (78) [2]; Fl. Cap. (99) 6; Arb. Svec. (101) 19; Nom. bot. (107) 11; Usum hist. nat. (145) 15

Linum africanum — Fl. Cap. (99) 13

Linum campanulatum — Fl. Monsp. (74) 14

Linum catharticum — Pan Svec. (26) 19; Herbat. Upsal. (50) 19; Pl. officin. (52) 12; Stat. pl. (55)

21; Fl. Angl. (56) 14; Fl. Monsp. (74) 14; Prodr. fl. Dan. (82) 16; Fl. Belg. (112) 15[as catarthicum]; Purg. indig. (143) 8; Fl. Åker. (162) 10; Pand. fl. Ryb. (165) 18

Linum hirsutum — Fl. Palaest. (70) 17

Linum laricis folio — Fl. alp. (71) 15

Linum maritimum — Fl. Monsp. (74) 14

Linum montanum latifolium perenne, floribus luteis umbellatim compactis — Pl. Mart.-Burs. (6) 18

Linum narbonense — Fl. Monsp. (74) 14

Linum nodiflorum — Fl. Palaest. (70) 17

Linum perenne — Hort. Upsal. (7) 35; Demonstr. pl. (49) 9; Fl. Angl. (56) 14; Calend. fl. (72) [13]; Hist. nat. Rossia (144) 28

Linum perenne, ramis foliisque alternis lineari lanceolatis — Pl. Mart.-Burs. (6) 18

Linum quadrifolium — Fl. Cap. (99) 13

Linum radiola — Pan Svec. (26) 19[as rhadiola]; Stat. pl. (55) 14; Fl. Angl. (56) 14; Prodr. fl. Dan. (82) 16; Fl. Belg. (112) 15

Linum strictum — Fl. Monsp. (74) 14

Linum sylvestre coeruleo folio acuto — Pl. Mart.-Burs. (6) 18

Linum sylvestre latifolium, flore albicante — Cent. I. pl. (65) 11

Linum tenuifolium — Fl. Angl. (56) 14; Fl. Monsp. (74) 14

Linum trigynum — Fl. Monsp. (74) 14

Linum usitatissimum — Demonstr. pl. (49) 9[as usitatum]; Pl. officin. (52) 12; Fl. Angl. (56) 14[as usitatum]; Fl. Palaest. (70) 17; Fl. Monsp. (74) 14

Liquidambar — Nova pl. gen. 1751 (32) 12

Liquidambar styraciflua — Pl. officin. (52) 18

Liquiritia — Sapor. med. (31) 16

Liriodendron — Hort. Upsal. (7) 36; Nova pl. gen. 1751 (32) 9[as Liriodendrum]

Liriodendron tulipifera — Specif. Canad. (76) 11[as Liriodendrum]; Prol. pl. 1763 (130) 16

Lisianthus — Fl. Jam. (105) 27

Lisianthus biflorus — Fl. Jam. (105) 14

Lithodendron — Corallia Balt. (4) 2

Lithonthlaspi tertium fruticosius, vermiculato acuto folio — Cent. II. pl. (66) 24

Lithophyton — Corallia Balt. (4) 2

Lithospermum — Vir. pl. (13) 18; Fl. oecon. (17) 5; Sapor. med. (31) 9; Nom. bot. (107) 10; Mund. invis. (149) 16

Lithospermum amboinicum — Herb. Amboin. (57) 25

Lithospermum annuum — Pan Svec. (26) 16

Lithospermum arvense — Herbat. Upsal. (50) 12; Stat. pl. (55) 19; Fl. Angl. (56) 12; Fl. Monsp. (74) 11; Prodr. fl. Dan. (82) 14; Fl. Belg. (112) 14; Usum hist. nat. (145) 10; Fl. Åker. (162) 8; Pand. fl. Ryb. (165) 17[as arverse]

Lithospermum fruticosum — Fl. Monsp. (74) 11

Lithospermum officinale — Pan Svec. (26) 16[as officinarum]; Demonstr. pl. (49) 5; Pl. officin. (52) 12; Fl. Angl. (56) 12; Fl. Monsp. (74) 11; Prodr. fl. Dan. (82) 14; Fl. Belg. (112) 14; Fl. Åker. (162) 8

Lithospermum purpureum caeruleum — Fl. Monsp. (74) 11

Lithospermum purpurocaeruleum — Fl. Angl. (56) 12

Lithospermum seminibus laevibus, corollis calycem multoties superantibus — Pl. Mart.-Burs. (6) 22

Lithospermum seminibus rugosis, corollis vix calycem superantibus — Pl. Mart.-Burs. (6) 22

Lithospermum tinctorium — Pl. officin. (52) 4; Fl. Monsp. (74) 11; Pl. tinct. (97) 13

Lituus — Corallia Balt. (4) 10

Lobelia — Oecon. nat. (20) 19; Pl. hybr. (33) 29; Cui bono? (42) 21; Specif. Canad. (76) 13, 20, 21, 22, 24; Fl. Cap. (99) 6, 7; Fund. fr. (123) 18; Viola ipecac. (176) 8; Pl. Surin. (177) 14

Lobelia assurgens — Pl. Jam. (102) 25; Fl. Jam. (105) 20

Lobelia bulbosa — Fl. Cap. (99) 19

Lobelia cardinalis — Fl. Jam. (105) 20; Hort. cul. (132) 24

Lobelia cheiranthus — Fl. Cap. (99) 19

Lobelia comosa — Fl. Cap. (99) 19

Lobelia coronopifolia — Fl. Cap. (99) 19

Lobelia dortmanna — Pan Svec. (26) 33; Herbat. Upsal. (50) 12; Stat. pl. (55) 13; Hist. nat. Rossia (144) 33; Rar. Norv. (157) 11; Fl. Åker. (162) 18[as dortmannia]; Ledum (178) [1]

Lobelia erinoides — Fl. Cap. (99) 18

Lobelia erinus — Fl. Cap. (99) 18

Lobelia hirsuta — Fl. Cap. (99) 18

Lobelia hirta — Fl. Cap. (99) 18

Lobelia inflata — Demonstr. pl. (49) 24

Lobelia longiflora — Fl. Jam. (105) 20; Obs. mat. med. (171) 6; Viola ipecac. (176) 8

Lobelia lutea — Fl. Cap. (99) 18

Lobelia paniculata — Fl. Cap. (99) 18

Lobelia phyteuma — Fl. Cap. (99) 18

Lobelia pinifolia — Fl. Cap. (99) 18

Lobelia plumieri — Herb. Amboin. (57) 17; Iter Chin. (161) 12

Lobelia siphilitica — Specif. Canad. (76) 12, 17, 27; Obs. mat. med. (171) 5

Lobus litoralis — Herb. Amboin. (57) 18

Lobus peregrinus cartilagineus — Rar. Norv. (157) 13

Lobus quadrangularis — Herb. Amboin. (57) 23

Locusta — Hosp. insect. fl. (43) 9; Nom. bot. (107) 9; Fund. entom. (154) 30

Locusta talpa lapensis, pedibus longis — Mus. Ad.-Frid. (11) 43

Loeflingia hispanica — Demonstr. pl. (49) 2; Fung. melit. (69) 2

Lolium — Vir. pl. (13) 17; Fl. oecon. (17) 4; Pl. escul. (35) 27; Cui bono? (42) 17; Transm. frum. (87) 13; Nom. bot. (107) 9; Raphania (126) 10; Fund. agrost. (152) 16, 25, 34

Lolium annuum — Stat. pl. (55) 19; Fl. Angl. (56) 11; Inebr. (117) 13

Lolium perenne — Pan Svec. (26) 15; Herbat. Upsal. (50) 13; Stat. pl. (55) 20; Fl. Angl. (56) 11; Fl. Monsp. (74) 9; Prodr. fl. Dan. (82) 13; Fl. Belg. (112) 13; Fl. Åker. (162) 7; Esca avium (174) 11

Lolium spicis muticis, radice perenni — Pl. Mart.-Burs. (6) 4

Lolium temulentum — Pan Svec. (26) 15; Pl. escul. (35) 8; Demonstr. pl. (49) 3; Fl. Monsp. (74) 9[as temulum]; Prodr. fl. Dan. (82) 13; Fl. Belg. (112) 13; Usum hist. nat. (145) 10; Fund. agrost. (152) 5, 7, 9; Esca avium (174) 11

Lomba — Herb. Amboin. (57) 27

Lonchitis — Acrostichum (10) 3, 6, 7, 8

Lonchitis amboinica — Herb. Amboin. (57) 26

Lonchitis hirsuta — Fl. Jam. (105) 23

Lonchitis juxta nervum pulverulenta — Acrostichum (10) 8

Lonchitis palustris maxima — Acrostichum (10) 14

Lonchitis pedata — Fl. Jam. (105) 23

Lonicera — Hort. Upsal. (7) 33; Vir. pl. (13) 28; Fl. oecon. (17) 6; Cui bono? (42) 20; Pl. officin. (52) 11; Fr. Svec. (91) [ii]; Pand. insect. (93) 12; Nom. bot. (107) 10; Nect. fl. (122) 12; Viola ipecac. (176) 5

Lonicera alpigena — Fl. alp. (71) 14; Prodr. fl. Dan. (82) 15; Hort. cul. (132) 22

Lonicera caerulea — Fl. Monsp. (74) 11; Fr. Svec. (91) 3, 7

Lonicera caprifolium — Pan Svec. (26) 17; Hosp. insect. fl. (43) 17; Demonstr. pl. (49) 5; Fl. Monsp. (74) 11; Fr. Svec. (91) 5, 22, 24; Meloe (124) 4; Hort. cul. (132) 26

Lonicera diervilla — Demonstr. pl. (49) 5; Pl. officin. (52) 9; Calend. fl. (72) [13]; Specif. Canad. (76) 25

Lonicera foliis subovatis, germine bifloro, corollis interne hirsutis, stylo bifido — Nova pl. gen. 1751 (32) 25

Lonicera nigra — Fl. Monsp. (74) 11

Lonicera perfoliata — Calend. fl. (72) [9], [12]; Fl. Monsp. (74) 5

Lonicera periclymenum — Demonstr. pl. (49) 5; Pl. officin. (52) 6; Fl. Angl. (56) 12; Fl. Monsp. (74) 11; Prodr. fl. Dan. (82) 15; Fr. Svec. (91) 4, 17, 22, 24; Fl. Belg. (112) 14

Lonicera periclymenum italicum — Gem. arb. (24) 18

Lonicera periclymenum serotinum — Calend. fl. (72) [16]

Lonicera pyrenaica — Fl. alp. (71) 14

Lonicera ruthenica — Gem. arb. (24) 18

Lonicera serotinum — Demonstr. pl. (49) 5

Lonicera symphoricarpos — Obs. mat. med. (171) 3

Lonicera tatarica — Demonstr. pl. (49) 5; Calend. fl. (72) [12]; Fr. Svec. (91) 5, 22; Hist. nat. Rossia (144) 22

Lonicera xylosteum — Gem. arb. (24) 18; Pan Svec. (26) 17; Hosp. insect. fl. (43) 17; Herbat. Upsal. (50) 7; Stat. pl. (55) 23; Fl. Angl. (56) 6; Fl. Monsp. (74) 11; Fr. Svec. (91) 3, 7, 22, 23, 24, 25; Meloe (124) 4; Fl. Åker. (162) 8; Esca avium (174) 11

Lontarus altera — Herb. Amboin. (57) 6

Lontarus domestica — Herb. Amboin. (57) 6

Lontarus sylvestris — Herb. Amboin. (57) 6

Lophanthus — Anandria (9) 5; Fund. fr. (123) 22

Lophius histrionius — Nat. pelagi (84) 12

Lophius pinnis dorsalibus tribus — Chin. Lagerstr. (64) 20

Lophius tumidus — Chin. Lagerstr. (64) 20, 33

Loranthus — Polit. nat. (109) 5; Aphyteia (185) 10

Loranthus americanus — Pl. Jam. (102) 11; Fl. Jam. (105) 15

Loranthus occidentalis — Pl. Jam. (102) 11; Fl. Jam. (105) 15

Lotus — Fl. oecon. (17) 18; Pand. insect. (93) [17, as 38]; Inebr. (117) 13

Lotus aethiopicus — Fl. Cap. (99) 17

Lotus africana annua hirsuta, floribus luteis — Pl. rar. Afr. (115) 16

Lotus angustissimus — Fl. Palaest. (70) 26; Fl. Monsp. (74) 23[as angustissima]; Pl. rar. Afr. (115) 6[as angustissima]

Lotus candidans — Fl. Monsp. (74) 30

Lotus conjugata — Demonstr. pl. (49) 21

Lotus corniculata — Hosp. insect. fl. (43) 29; Herbat. Upsal. (50) 13; Stat. pl. (55) 20; Fl. Angl. (56) 21; Fl. Monsp. (74) 23; Prodr. fl. Dan. (82) 22; Pl. tinct. (97) 10[as corniculatus], 22; Fl. Belg. (112) 20; Fl. Åker. (162) 16; Pand. fl. Ryb. (165) 21; Esca avium (174) 14

Lotus cretica — Pl. rar. Afr. (115) 6

Lotus dorycnium — Fl. Monsp. (74) 23

Lotus erecta — Fl. Monsp. (74) 23

Lotus flore majore — Fl. Angl. (56) 28

Lotus foliis tenuissimis — Fl. Monsp. (74) 30

Lotus fruticosior — Fl. Angl. (56) 28

Lotus graeca — Fl. Palaest. (70) 26

Lotus haemorrhoidalis — Fl. Palaest. (70) 26

Lotus hirsuta — Fl. Monsp. (74) 23; Pl. rar. Afr. (115) 6

Lotus maritima — Pan Svec. (26) 30[as maritimus]; Demonstr. pl. (49) 21; Stat. pl. (55) 12; Fl. Monsp. (74) 23; Prodr. fl. Dan. (82) 22

Lotus ornithopodioides — Somn. pl. (68) 11[as ornitopodioides], 18[as ornitopodioides]

Lotus peregrina — Fl. Monsp. (74) 23

Lotus prostratus — Fl. Cap. (99) 17

Lotus recta — Fl. Monsp. (74) 23

Lotus tetragonolobus — Demonstr. pl. (49) 21; Fl. Angl. (56) 21; Somn. pl. (68) 18[as tetragonolovus]

Lotus vulgaris — Pan Svec. (26) 30

Loxia — Oecon. nat. (20) 18

Loxia caerula — Chin. Lagerstr. (64) 18[as coerulaea]

Loxia cardinalis — Chin. Lagerstr. (64) 15

Loxia chloris — Migr. avium (79) 32

Loxia coccothraustes — Migr. avium (79) 32; Polit. nat. (109) 15[as coccotraustes]

Loxia curvirostra — Polit. nat. (109) 15

Loxia enucleator — Migr. avium (79) 32; Fund. ornith. (137) 27[as enuceator]

Loxia erythrocephala — Chin. Lagerstr. (64) 16

Loxia flava, dorso virescente, capite fulvo — Chin. Lagerstr. (64) 17

Loxia flavicans — Chin. Lagerstr. (64) 17

Loxia fusca — Chin. Lagerstr. (64) 19

Loxia fusca, temporibus albis — Chin. Lagerstr. (64) 17

Loxia nigra, capite gulaque coccineis, pectore abdomineque albis — Chin. Lagerstr. (64) 16

Loxia oryzae — Chin. Lagerstr. (64) 17

Loxia pyrrhula — Migr. avium (79) 32; Esca avium (174) 3

Loxia remigibus a tertia ad novam, basi omnino albis — Chin. Lagerstr. (64) 19

Loxia remigibus rectricibusque nigris — Chin. Lagerstr. (64) 17

Loxia rostro pedibusque sanguineis corpore supra griseo, subtus pallido — Chin. Lagerstr. (64) 16[as grisaeo]

Loxia rubra, fronte nigrae — Chin. Lagerstr. (64) 15

Loxia sanguinirostris — Chin. Lagerstr. (64) 16

Loxia viridi coerulea, remigibus rectricibusque nigris — Chin. Lagerstr. (64) 18[as coeruloea]

Lucanus — Fund. entom. (154) 29

Lucanus caraboides — Pand. fl. Ryb. (165) 7

Lucanus cervus — Esca avium (174) 6

Lucius — Oecon. nat. (20) 41; Mat. med. anim. (29) 13; Lepra (140) 10; Usum hist. nat. (145) 27

Ludwigia — Nova pl. gen. 1751 (32) 8

Luffa — Pl. Surin. (177) 4

Luffa arabum — Pl. Surin. (177) 16

Lumbricus — Taenia (19) 10ff.; Splachnum (27) 2; Migr. avium (79) 8; Spigelia (89) 6; Polit. nat. (109) 12, 13, 17, 18; Hirudo (136) 2; Lepra (140) 10; Usum hist. nat. (145) 29; Hypericum (186) 11

Lumbricus laevis — Mat. med. anim. (29) 18

Lumbricus latus — Taenia (19) 13, 16, 17, 21

Lumbricus latus seu taenia intestinorum — Taenia (19) 17

Lumbricus terrestris — Spigelia (89) 5; Esca avium (174) [9, as 17]

Lumbricus terrestris major — Mat. med. anim. (29) 18

Lunaria — Hort. Upsal. (7) 34; Acrostichum (10) 7; Hort. acad. (63) 9

Lunaria annua — Prodr. fl. Dan. (82) 20; Fl. Åker. (162) 15

Lunaria rediviva — Stat. pl. (55) 17

Lunaria scanensis — Pan Svec. (26) 28

Lupinaster — Anandria (9) 4

Lupinus — Hort. Upsal. (7) 34; Vir. pl. (13) 23

Lupinus albus — Demonstr. pl. (49) 19; Pl. officin. (52) 12; Somn. pl. (68) 19; Fr. escul. (127) 19

Lupinus angustifolius — Demonstr. pl. (49) 19; Fl. Palaest. (70) 25

Lupinus calycibus alternis appendiculatis, foliis simplicibus oblongis villosis — Pl. rar. Afr. (115) 16

Lupinus calycibus alternis appendiculatis: labio superiore bipartito, inferiore tridentato, leguminibus lanatis — Cent. I. pl. (65) 23

Lupinus calycibus verticillatis, labio inferiore integerrimo — Pl. Mart.-Burs. (6) 27

Lupinus hirsutus — Fl. Monsp. (74) 22

Lupinus integrifolius — Pl. rar. Afr. (115) 16

Lupinus lanuginosus latifolius humilis, flore caeruleo-purpurascente, stoloniferus — Cent. I. pl. (65) 23

Lupinus luteus — Demonstr. pl. (49) 19; Fl. Monsp. (74) 22

Lupinus purpureus — Fl. Monsp. (74) 30

Lupinus stoloniferus — Cent. I. pl. (65) 23; Fl. Palaest. (70) 25

Lupinus varius — Demonstr. pl. (49) 19; Fl. Palaest. (70) 25; Fl. Monsp. (74) 22

Lupulus — Sapor. med. (31) 18; Pl. escul. (35) 25; Usum hist. nat. (145) 14

Lupus — Oecon. nat. (20) 26, 43, 45; Mat. med. anim. (29) 3; Morb. hyeme (38) 12; Noctiluca (39) 5; Noxa insect. (46) 30; Ambros. (100) 13; Polit. nat. (109) 20; Usum hist. nat. (145) 23; Usum musc. (148) 12

Lupus aureus — Cynogr. (54) 3

Lupus vulgaris — Cynogr. (54) 3

Luscinia — Migr. avium (79) 17; Usum hist. nat. (145) 25

Luteola — Nom. bot. (107) 13

Lutra — Oecon. nat. (20) 36; Polit. nat. (109) 15; Usum hist. nat. (145) 24

Lychnidea villosa, foliis oblongis dentatis, flor spicatis — Pl. rar. Afr. (115) 12

Lychnis — Spons. pl. (12) 46, 55, 59; Fl. Angl. (56) 6; Pand. insect. (93) 14; Fund. fr. (123) 23

Lychnis alpina — Demonstr. pl. (49) 12; Stat. pl. (55) 16; Fl. alp. (71) 17; Hist. nat. Rossia (144) 29; Rar. Norv. (157) 10

131

Lychnis apetala — Stat. pl. (55) 16; Metam. pl. (67) 22; Fl. alp. (71) 17; Hist. nat. Rossia (144) 29

Lychnis aquatica — Pan Svec. (26) 23

Lychnis chalcedonica — Demonstr. pl. (49) 12; Calend. fl. (72) [15]; Prodr. fl. Dan. (82) 18; Hort. cul. (132) 24, 25[as chalcedoniaca]; Hist. nat. Rossia (144) 29

Lychnis coronaria — Calend. fl. (72) [14]

Lychnis cretica angustifolia, floribus pediculis longissimis insidentibus, capsula pyramidata — Pl. Mart.-Burs. (6) 17

Lychnis dioica — Demonstr. pl. (49) 12; Stat. pl. (55) 21; Fl. Angl. (56) 16; Metam. pl. (67) 22, 23; Calend. fl. (72) [22]; Fl. Monsp. (74) 16; Prodr. fl. Dan. (82) 18; Fl. Belg. (112) 17; Fl. Åker. (162) 12; Pand. fl. Ryb. (165) 19

Lychnis flore albo minimo — Cent. II. pl. (66) 17

Lychnis flos cuculi — Herbat. Upsal. (50) 14; Stat. pl. (55) 14; Fl. Angl. (56) 16; Fl. Monsp. (74) 16; Prodr. fl. Dan. (82) 18; Fl. Belg. (112) 17; Prol. pl. 1763 (130) 5; Fl. Åker. (162) 12; Pand. fl. Ryb. (165) 19

Lychnis minima muralis — Betula (1) 12

Lychnis montana viscosa latifolia — Fl. Angl. (56) 28

Lychnis sibirica — Hist. nat. Rossia (144) 29

Lychnis viscaria — Stat. pl. (55) 22; Calend. fl. (72) [11]; Prodr. fl. Dan. (82) 18; Fl. Åker. (162) 12; Pand. fl. Ryb. (165) 19

Lychnis viscosa — Fl. Angl. (56) 16

Lychniscabiosa — Nova pl. gen. 1751 (32) 8[as Lychni Scabiosa]

Lycium — Hort. Upsal. (7) 36; Metam. pl. (67) 13

Lycium africanum — Demonstr. pl. (49) 6

Lycium afrum — Fl. Palaest. (70) 15; Fl. Cap. (99) 12

Lycium barbarum — Demonstr. pl. (49) 6; Fr. Svec. (91) 24; Fl. Cap. (99) 12

Lycium capsulare — Cent. II. pl. (66) 11

Lycium europaeum — Fl. Palaest. (70) 15; Fl. Monsp. (74) 12

Lycium foliis lanceolatis tenuibus glabris, pedunculis calycibusque pubescentibus, pericarpiis capsularibus — Cent. II. pl. (66) 11

Lycium foliis ovalibus — Fl. Palaest. (70) 15

Lycium gallicum — Fl. Monsp. (74) 30

Lycoperdon — Fl. oecon. (17) 30; Sapor. med. (31) 9; Pl. escul. (35) 27[as Lycoperdum], 29[as Lycoperdum]; Mund. invis. (149) 12, 15, 22

Lycoperdon bovista — Pl. officin. (52) 8; Prodr. fl. Dan. (82) 26; Pand. fl. Ryb. (165) 23

Lycoperdon stellatum — Herbat. Upsal. (50) 11

Lycoperdon tuber — Pl. officin. (52) 6; Mac. olit. (113) 13

Lycopersicum — Pl. escul. (35) 4; Vern. arb. (47) 9; Nom. bot. (107) 11[as Lycopersicon]

Lycopodioides — Sem. musc. (28) 6, 16; Pl. rar. Camsch. (30) 29

Lycopodium — Acrostichum (10) 6; Spons. pl. (12) 27; Fl. oecon. (17) 28; Splachnum (27) 5, 6; Sem. musc. (28) 6, 8, 13, 15, 16; Sapor. med. (31) 9; Cui bono? (42) 14; Buxbaumia (85) 14; Usum musc. (148) 4, 6, 14

Lycopodium alpinum — Fl. Angl. (56) 25; Fl. alp. (71) 23; Prodr. fl. Dan. (82) 25; Rar. Norv. (157) 11

Lycopodium annotinum — Herbat. Upsal. (50) 11, 19; Stat. pl. (55) 18; Fl. Angl. (56) 25; Usum musc. (148) 9[as Elycopodium]; Fl. Åker. (162) 20

Lycopodium canaliculatum — Herb. Amboin. (57) 27

Lycopodium caule erecto dichotomo — Sem. musc. (28) 8

Lycopodium cernuum — Herb. Amboin. (57) 27

Lycopodium clavatum — Herbat. Upsal. (50) 6; Pl. officin. (52) 13; Stat. pl. (55) 18; Fl. Angl. (56) 25; Prodr. fl. Dan. (82) 25; Usum musc. (148) 9[as Elycopodium], 13; Pand. fl. Ryb. (165) 23

Lycopodium complanatum — Herbat. Upsal. (50) 6; Stat. pl. (55) 18; Pl. tinct. (97) 27; Rar. Norv. (157) 11; Pand. fl. Ryb. (165) 23

Lycopodium denticulatum — Fl. Angl. (56) 25

Lycopodium elevatum — Fl. Åker. (162) 20

Lycopodium helveticum — Fl. alp. (71) 23

Lycopodium inundatum — Stat. pl. (55) 13; Fl. Angl. (56) 25

Lycopodium phlegmaria — Herb. Amboin. (57) 27

Lycopodium plumosum — Herb. Amboin. (57) 27

Lycopodium repens dichotomum, foliis quadrifariam imbricatis, spicis sessilibus — Pl. rar. Camsch. (30) 29

Lycopodium rupestre — Hist. nat. Rossia (144) 12, 34

Lycopodium rupestre pilosum et incanum, spicis acute quadrangulatis — Pl. rar. Camsch. (30) 5

Lycopodium selaginoides — Fl. Angl. (56) 25

Lycopodium selago — Herbat. Upsal. (50) 6; Pl. officin. (52) 13; Stat. pl. (55) 18; Fl. Angl. (56) 25; Purg. indig. (143) 12; Usum musc. (148) 12; Fl. Åker. (162) 20; Pand. fl. Ryb. (165) 23; Esca avium (174) 4

Lycopodium spica sessili tetragona: squamis carinatis mucronatis — Pl. rar. Camsch. (30) 5

Lycopodium spicis solitariis sessilibus, foliis aculeato-ciliatis, capsulis tetraspermis — Acrostichum (10) 6[as sesilibus]

Lycopsis — Hort. Upsal. (7) 34; Vir. pl. (13) 18

Lycopsis arvensis — Pan Svec. (26) 16; Herbat. Upsal. (50) 12; Stat. pl. (55) 19; Fl. Angl. (56) 12; Fl. Monsp. (74) 11; Prodr. fl. Dan. (82) 14; Fl. Belg. (112) 14; Fl. Åker. (162) 8; Pand. fl. Ryb. (165) 17

Lycopsis foliis repando dentatis — Pl. Mart.-Burs. (6) 22

Lycopsis variegata — Demonstr. pl. (49) 5

Lycopsis vesicaria — Demonstr. pl. (49) 5; Fl. Monsp. (74) 11

Lycopus — Vir. pl. (13) 29; Nova pl. gen. 1747 (14) 2; Fl. oecon. (17) 2; Hosp. insect. fl. (43) 12; Specif. Canad. (76) 22; Pand. insect. (93) 11

Lycopus europaeus — Herbat. Upsal. (50) 18; Stat. pl. (55) 13; Fl. Angl. (56) 9; Fl. Monsp. (74) 8; Prodr. fl. Dan. (82) 13; Pl. tinct. (97) 10, 11; Fl. Belg. (112) 12; Fl. Åker. (162) 5; Pand. fl. Ryb. (165) 16

Lycopus palustris — Pan Svec. (26) 12

Lygeum — Fund. agrost. (152) 4, 21, 22, 26, 35

Lygeum spartum — Cent. I. pl. (65) 4

Lygistum — Fl. Jam. (105) 26

Lyra volans — Nat. pelagi (84) 11

Lysimachia — Peloria (3) 10; Nom. bot. (107) 10

Lysimachia atropurpurea — Calend. fl. (72) [15]

Lysimachia axillaris — Pan Svec. (26) 17

Lysimachia foliis ovali-oblongis, pedunculis unifloris, caule repente — Cent. II. pl. (66) 9

Lysimachia linum stellatum — Fung. melit. (69) 2; Fl. Monsp. (74) 7, 11

Lysimachia monnieri — Cent. II. pl. (66) 9

Lysimachia nemorum — Fl. Angl. (56) 12[as Lysmachia]; Prodr. fl. Dan. (82) 15

Lysimachia nummularia — Pan Svec. (26) 17; Demonstr. pl. (49) 5; Pl. officin. (52) 14; Fl. Angl. (56) 12[as Lysmachia]; Calend. fl. (72) [15]; Fl. Monsp. (74) 11; Prodr. fl. Dan. (82) 15; Fl. Belg. (112) 14

Lysimachia punctata — Fl. Belg. (112) 9, 14

Lysimachia tenella — Fl. Monsp. (74) 11

Lysimachia thyrsiflora — Demonstr. pl. (49) 5; Stat. pl. (55) 13; Fl. Angl. (56) 12[as Lysmachia]; Prodr. fl. Dan. (82) 15; Fl. Belg. (112) 14; Fl. Åker. (162) 8

Lysimachia vulgaris — Pan Svec. (26) 17; Demonstr. pl. (49) 5; Herbat. Upsal. (50) 14; Stat. pl. (55) 13; Fl. Angl. (56) 12[as Lysmachia]; Calend. fl. (72) [15]; Fl. Monsp. (74) 11; Prodr. fl. Dan. (82) 15; Pl. tinct. (97) 13; Fl. Belg. (112) 14; Fl. Åker. (162) 8; Pand. fl. Ryb. (165) 17

Lysimachiae spicatae purpureae affinis, flosculis in cacumine plurimis quasi in nodos junctis — Nova pl. gen. 1747 (14) 12

Lythrum — Pl. Mart.-Burs. (6) 20; Fl. Jam. (105) 26; Nect. fl. (122) 7; Fund. fr. (123) 23

Lythrum hyssopifolia — Hort. Upsal. (7) 41; Demonstr. pl. (49) 13[as hyssopifolium]; Fl. Monsp. (74) 17; Fl. Belg. (112) 8, 17

Lythrum melanium — Fl. Jam. (105) 17

Lythrum palustre — Pan Svec. (26) 24

Lythrum parsonsia — Fl. Jam. (105) 17

Lythrum salicaria — Herbat. Upsal. (50) 14; Stat. pl. (55) 13; Fl. Angl. (56) 16; Fl. Palaest. (70) 20; Calend. fl. (72) [14]; Fl. Monsp. (74) 17; Prodr. fl. Dan. (82) 18; Fl. Belg. (112) 17; Fl. Åker. (162) 12; Pand. fl. Ryb. (165) 19; Obs. mat. med. (171) 4

Lythrum thymifolia — Fl. Monsp. (74) 17

Lythrum virgatum — Hist. nat. Rossia (144) 29

Machilus — Herb. Amboin. (57) 12[as Machillus]

Macrocnemum jamaicense — Pl. Jam. (102) 31; Fl. Jam. (105) 14[as Macrocn. jamaicensi]

Mactra — Fund. test. (166) 18, 34, 41

Mactra stultorum — Fund. test. (166) 41

Macuerus — Herb. Amboin. (57) 27

Madrepora — Corallia Balt. (4) 2, 3, 4, 10, 27; Taenia (19) 14; Chin. Lagerstr. (64) 34, 35; Nat. pelagi (84) 8; Mund. invis. (149) 9

Madrepora aggregata, stellis angulosis, concavis; radiis quatuor altioribus — Corallia Balt. (4) 26

Madrepora aggregata, stellis cylindricis duodecim radiatis, cum intermixtis majusculis, convexis, cavis — Chin. Lagerstr. (64) 34

Madrepora cancellata — Iter Chin. (161) 8

Madrepora composita, corporibus proliferis e centro pluribus, undique coadunatis; stella convexa, centro-concava — Corallia Balt. (4) 21

Madrepora composita, corporibus proliferis e centro solitariis, coadunatis stellae margine dilatato — Corallia Balt. (4) 24

Madrepora composita, corporibus proliferis e centro solitariis, membrana reflexa coadunatis stellatis — Corallia Balt. (4) 25

Madrepora composita, corporibus proliferis e disco pluribus, margine coadunatis; stellis truncatis, centro cylindraceo-concavis — Corallia Balt. (4) 22

Madrepora composita, cylindris flexuosis, scabris, cortice hinc inde coalitis — Corallia Balt. (4) 26

Madrepora fungites — Mund. invis. (149) 9; Iter Chin. (161) 8

Madrepora muricata — Iter Chin. (161) 8

Madrepora polygama — Anim. comp. (98) 8

Madrepora polygona — Chin. Lagerstr. (64) 34, 36

Madrepora simplex, orbicularis, plana; stella convexa — Corallia Balt. (4) 19

Madrepora simplex ramosa, ramis teretibus laevibus tubulosis: lamellis integris — Mat. med. anim. (29) 20

Madrepora simplex, turbinata, laevis; stella concava — Corallia Balt. (4) 15

Magnolia — Nova pl. gen. 1751 (32) 9; Herb. Amboin. (57) 10

Mahagoni — Opobals. (135) 2

Majana rubra — Herb. Amboin. (57) 22

Majorana — Nom. bot. (107) 15

Majorana aurea — Herb. Amboin. (57) 22

Majorana cretica — Marum (175) 6

Majorana foetida — Herb. Amboin. (57) 26

Majorana syriaca vel cretica — Marum (175) 6

Malacodendron — Nova pl. gen. 1751 (32) 10, 12

Malaparius — Herb. Amboin. (57) 14

Malpighia — Hort. Upsal. (7) 37; Gem. arb. (24) 6; Nect. fl. (122) 14; Fr. escul. (127) 10; Pl. Surin. (177) 9[as Malpigia]

Malpighia aquifolia — Fl. Jam. (105) 16[as Malpigia]

Malpighia bannisterioides — Pl. Surin. (177) 9[as Malpigia]

Malpighia crassifolia — Fl. Jam. (105) 16[as Malpigia]

Malpighia glabra — Demonstr. pl. (49) 12; Fl. Jam. (105) 16[as Malpigia]

Malpighia urens — Fl. Jam. (105) 16[as Malpigia]

Malum granatum — Herb. Amboin. (57) 9

Malum indicum — Herb. Amboin. (57) 9

Malus — Vir. pl. (13) 36; Sem. musc. (28) 3; Pl. escul. (35) 16, 27, 28, 29; Vern. arb. (47) 10, table; Metam. pl. (67) 17; Arb. Svec. (101) 30; Nom. bot. (107) 13; Inebr. (117) 13

Malus pomifera absque floribus — Sem. musc. (28) 4

Malva — Spons. pl. (12) 33, 35; Vir. pl. (13) 12, 22, 32; Fl. oecon. (17) 17; Sapor. med. (31) 12; Pl. hybr. (33) 7; Pl. escul. (35) 28; Metam. pl. (67) 19; Cul. mut. (88) 2, 3, 4, 5; Pand. insect. (93) [17, as 38]; Pl. Jam. (102) 17; Nom. bot. (107) 15

Malva africana frutescens, flore parvo corneo unguiculis atro-rubentibus — Cent. II. pl. (66) 27

Malva africana frutescens, flore rubro — Cent. II. pl. (66) 27

Malva alcea — Pan Svec. (26) 29; Hosp. insect. fl. (43) 28; Demonstr. pl. (49) 19; Calend. fl. (72) [16][as alcaea], [22]; Prodr. fl. Dan. (82) 21; Pl. Alstr. (121) 5

Malva capensis — Fl. Cap. (99) 16

Malva carolina — Demonstr. pl. (49) 18

Malva caule erecto, foliis angulatis, floribus axillaribus glomeratis — Pl. hybr. (33) 25

Malva caule erecto, foliis multipartitis — Pl. hybr. (33) 24

Malva caule erecto herbaceo, foliis lobatis, spicis secundis axillaribus, seminibus laevibus — Cent. II. pl. (66) 27

Malva caule fruticoso hirto, foliis lobatis hirtis, floribus solitariis, pedunculo subnutante — Cent. II. pl. (66) 27

Malva caule patulo, foliis angulatis, floribus axillaribus glomeratis, calycibus glabris patentibus — Demonstr. pl. (49) 18

Malva coromandeliana — Demonstr. pl. (49) 18; Fl. Jam. (105) 18[as coromandelia]

Malva crispa — Demonstr. pl. (49) 18; Calend. fl. (72) [22]; Hort. cul. (132) 23

Malva flore parvo caeruleo — Fl. Angl. (56) 27

Malva foliis angulatis crispis, floribus axillaribus glomeratis — Pl. hybr. (33) 25

Malva foliis radicalibus quinquepartitis trilobis, pedunculis folio caulino longioribus, caule subdecumbente — Cent. I. pl. (65) 21

Malva foliis radicalibus reniformibus incisis, caulinis quinquepartitis pinnato-multifidis — Pl. hybr. (33) 24

Malva glomerata — Calend. fl. (72) [22]

Malva hispanica — Demonstr. pl. (49) 18

Malva limensis — Cent. II. pl. (66) 27

Malva major — Pl. escul. (35) 20

Malva mauritiana — Demonstr. pl. (49) 18; Calend. fl. (72) [22]; Hort. cul. (132) 23

Malva moschata — Odor. med. (40) 12; Demonstr. pl. (49) 19; Calend. fl. (72) [13]; Ambros. (100) 14; Hort. cul. (132) 24

Malva parviflora — Demonstr. pl. (49) 18; Cent. I. pl. (65) 2; Fl. Monsp. (74) 21

Malva peruviana — Demonstr. pl. (49) 18; Cent. II. pl. (66) 27; Somn. pl. (68) 15

Malva procumbens — Pl. escul. (35) 20

Malva repens — Pan Svec. (26) 29

Malva rotundifolia — Demonstr. pl. (49) 19; Herbat. Upsal. (50) 20; Pl. officin. (52) 12; Stat. pl. (55) 20; Fl. Angl. (56) 20[as rotundlfolia]; Fl. Monsp. (74) 21; Prodr. fl. Dan. (82) 21; Fl. Jam. (105) 24; Fl. Belg. (112) 19; Mac. olit. (113) 19; Fl. Åker. (162) 16; Pand. fl. Ryb. (165) 20; Esca avium (174) 13

Malva scabrosa — Cent. II. pl. (66) 27

Malva scanica — Pan Svec. (26) 29

Malva scariosa — Calend. fl. (72) [18]; Fl. Cap. (99) 16

Malva spicata — Pl. Jam. (102) 17; Fl. Jam. (105) 19

Malva strigosa — Fl. Jam. (105) 18

Malva suaveolens — Pan Svec. (26) 29

Malva sylvestris — Hosp. insect. fl. (43) 28; Demonstr. pl. (49) 18; Stat. pl. (55) 20; Fl. Angl. (56) 20; Fl. Monsp. (74) 21; Prodr. fl. Dan. (82) 21; Fl. Belg. (112) 19

Malva tomentosa — Demonstr. pl. (49) 18

Malva tournefortiana — Cent. I. pl. (65) 21

Malva verticillata — Demonstr. pl. (49) 18; Pl. rar. Afr. (115) 6

Mamanira — Herb. Amboin. (57) 17

Mamanira alba — Herb. Amboin. (57) 17

Mammea — Pl. escul. (35) 4

Mammea americana — Fr. escul. (127) 10; Pl. Surin. (177) 10

Mammea asiatica — Fr. escul. (127) 10

Mandragora — Vir. pl. (13) 19; Odor. med. (40) 16; Febr. interm. (167) 54

Mandragora officinarum — Pl. officin. (52) 12[as officinalis]; Fl. Palaest. (70) 15

Manga domestica — Herb. Amboin. (57) 7

Manga foetida — Herb. Amboin. (57) 7

Manga sylvestris — Herb. Amboin. (57) 7

Mangifera — Herb. Amboin. (57) 12

Mangifera indica — Herb. Amboin. (57) 7; Fr. escul. (127) 13

Mangium album — Herb. Amboin. (57) 13

Mangium candelarium — Herb. Amboin. (57) 13

Mangium caryophylloides — Herb. Amboin. (57) 13

Mangium caseolare — Herb. Amboin. (57) 13

Mangium celsum — Herb. Amboin. (57) 12

Mangium corniculatum — Herb. Amboin. (57) 13

Mangium digitatum — Herb. Amboin. (57) 13

Mangium ferreum — Herb. Amboin. (57) 13

Mangium floridum — Herb. Amboin. (57) 13

Mangium minus — Herb. Amboin. (57) 12

Mangium montanum — Herb. Amboin. (57) 13

Mangium sylvestre — Herb. Amboin. (57) 12

Mangostana — Herb. Amboin. (57) 7

Mangostana celebica — Herb. Amboin. (57) 7

Manis — Polit. nat. (109) 16

Manis squamosa — Chin. Lagerstr. (64) 8

Mantes — Surin. Grill. (16) 29

Manumal — Nova pl. gen. 1747 (14) 14

Maranta — Vir. pl. (13) 26; Gem. arb. (24) 8; Herb. Amboin. (57) 20

Maranta arundinacea — Fl. Jam. (105) 12

Maranta galanga — Obs. mat. med. (171) 6

Marcgravia umbellata — Fl. Jam. (105) 17; Pl. Surin. (177) 10

Marchantia — Sem. musc. (28) 15, 16; Buxbaumia (85) 8; Usum musc. (148) 2

Marchantia hemisphaerica — Herbat. Upsal. (50) 9

Marchantia polymorpha — Herbat. Upsal. (50) 9; Prodr. fl. Dan. (82) 26; Pand. fl. Ryb. (165) 23

Margaritaria — Pl. Surin. (177) 4

Margaritaria alternifolia — Pl. Surin. (177) 16

Margaritaria oppositifolia — Pl. Surin. (177) 16

Maritacaca — Mus. Ad.-Frid. (11) 2

Marmota — Mus ind. (62) 8

Maroc seu clematis virginiana — Passifl. (8) 21

Marrubium — Hort. Upsal. (7) 36; Oves (61) 14; Nom. bot. (107) 15

Marrubium africanum — Fl. Cap. (99) 15

Marrubium album — Stat. pl. (55) 19; Herb. Amboin. (57) 22

Marrubium hispanicum — Demonstr. pl. (49) 16

Marrubium nigrum — Oves (61) 14

Marrubium peregrinum — Fl. Palaest. (70) 23

Marrubium pseudodictamnus — Demonstr. pl. (49) 16[as pseudodictamus]; Fl. alp. (71) 19

Marrubium vulgare — Pan Svec. (26) 26; Herbat. Upsal. (50) 20[as Marubium]; Pl. officin. (52) 12; Fl. Angl. (56) 18; Fl. Monsp. (74) 19; Prodr. fl. Dan. (82) 20; Fl. Belg. (112) 18; Fl. Åker. (162) 14

Marsilea — Acrostichum (10) 6

Marsilea foliis subulatis semicylindricis articulatis — Nova pl. gen. 1751 (32) 46

Marsilea natans — Fl. Monsp. (74) 29

Marsilea quadrifolia — Fl. Jam. (105) 23, 25; Hist. nat. Rossia (144) 34[as Marsilaea]; Colon. pl. (158) 6

Marsupialis americana — Mus. Ad.-Frid. (11) 2

Martagon album — Calend. fl. (72) [17]

Martagon vulgare — Calend. fl. (72) [16]

Martes — Usum hist. nat. (145) 23

Martynia — Hort. Upsal. (7) 37; Nect. fl. (122) 8, 12

Martynia annua — Colon. pl. (158) 9

Marum — Vir. pl. (13) 22, 34, 35; Usum hist. nat. (145) 23; Marum (175) 5ff.

Marum cortusi — Marum (175) 5, 6

Marum creticum — Marum (175) 6

Marum syriacum — Marum (175) 6

Marum syriacum, vel creticum — Marum (175) 6

Marum syriacum, vel verum — Marum (175) 5

Marum verum — Marum (175) 5

Marum verum, cortusi — Marum (175) 6

Marum verum syriacum — Marum (175) 7

Marum vulgare — Marum (175) 5

Massa lapidea ex ramulis corallinis punctatis tam rectis quam inclinatis, saepe etiam ramosis constans, et ad instar vermiculorum uncialis longitudinis, crassitie lumbricis junioribus simili sibi invicem stipatis — Corallia Balt. (4) 29

Mastichina — Marum (175) 6

Matricaria — Peloria (3) 9; Spons. pl. (12) 59; Vir. pl. (13) 23, 33; Fl. oecon. (17) 20; Nom. bot. (107) 17

Matricaria alpina chamaemeli foliis — Pl. Mart.-Burs. (6) 10

Matricaria chamomilla — Pl. officin. (52) 7; Stat. pl. (55) 19; Fl. Angl. (56) 22; Fl. Palaest. (70) 28; Calend. fl. (72) [12], [22]; Fl. Monsp. (74) 26; Prodr. fl. Dan. (82) 23; Fl. Belg. (112) 21; Hist. nat. Rossia (144) 33[as Martricaria]; Usum hist. nat. (145) 10; Fl. Åker. (162) 18; Pand. fl. Ryb. (165) 22

Matricaria chamomilla nobile — Pan Svec. (26) 33

Matricaria chamomilla vulgare — Pan Svec. (26) 33

Matricaria inodora — Calend. fl. (72) [22]; Fl. Monsp. (74) 26; Prodr. fl. Dan. (82) 23; Fl. Åker. (162) 18

Matricaria inodora maritima — Prodr. fl. Dan. (82) 23

Matricaria maritima — Fl. Angl. (56) 22

Matricaria nuda — Demonstr. pl. (49) 23

Matricaria parthenium — Demonstr. pl. (49) 23; Pl. officin. (52) 12; Fl. Angl. (56) 22; Calend. fl. (72) [14], [22]; Fl. Belg. (112) 21; Hort. cul. (132) 24[as parthenicum], 25

Matricaria plena — Demonstr. pl. (49) 23

Matricaria recutita — Hist. nat. Rossia (144) 33[as Martricaria]

Matricaria sinensis — Herb. Amboin. (57) 21

Matricaria suaveolens — Fl. Åker. (162) 18

Matthiola — Polit. nat. (109) 5

Maurocenia — Vir. pl. (13) 27

Maurus — Fl. Cap. (99) [1]

Mays — Fund. agrost. (152) 15

Mazama — Generat. calc. (22) 2

Meadia — Nova pl. gen. 1751 (32) 26

Medeola — Nova pl. gen. 1751 (32) 9; Demonstr. pl. (49) 10

Medeola asparagoides — Demonstr. pl. (49) 11; Fl. Cap. (99) 13

Medicago — Hort. Upsal. (7) 34; Vir. pl. (13) 23; Fl. oecon. (17) 19; Gem. arb. (24) 6; Pan Svec. (26) 31; Oves (61) 14; Pand. insect. (93) [17, as 38]; Nom. bot. (107) 16

Medicago arborea — Demonstr. pl. (49) 21

Medicago biennis — Pan Svec. (26) 31

Medicago circinata — Fl. Palaest. (70) 26

Medicago falcata — Hosp. insect. fl. (43) 29; Herbat. Upsal. (50) 17; Stat. pl. (55) 22; Fl. Angl. (56) 21; Oves (61) 18; Calend. fl. (72) [13]; Fl. Monsp. (74) 23; Prodr. fl. Dan. (82) 22; Fl. Belg. (112) 20

Medicago leguminibus cochleatis, stipulis dentatis caule diffuso — Pl. Mart.-Burs. (6) 25

Medicago lupulina — Herbat. Upsal. (50) 17; Stat. pl. (55) 21; Fl. Angl. (56) 21; Fl. Monsp. (74) 23; Prodr. fl. Dan. (82) 22; Fl. Åker. (162) 16; Pand. fl. Ryb. (165) 21

Medicago marina — Fl. Monsp. (74) 23

Medicago minima — Fl. Angl. (56) 21

Medicago polymorpha — Demonstr. pl. (49) 21; Somn. pl. (68) 18; Pl. rar. Afr. (115) 6

Medicago polymorpha arabica — Fl. Angl. (56) 21; Fl. Monsp. (74) 23

Medicago polymorpha ciliaris — Fl. Monsp. (74) 23

Medicago polymorpha coronata — Fl. Monsp. (74) 23

Medicago polymorpha echinata — Fl. Palaest. (70) 26

Medicago polymorpha hirsuta — Fl. Monsp. (74) 23

Medicago polymorpha laciniata — Fl. Monsp. (74) 23

Medicago polymorpha orbiculata — Fl. Monsp. (74) 23

Medicago polymorpha rigidula — Fl. Monsp. (74) 23

Medicago polymorpha scuta [error for scutellata?] — Fl. Monsp. (74) 23

Medicago polymorpha turbinata — Fl. Monsp. (74) 23

Medicago radiata — Fl. Palaest. (70) 26; Pl. rar. Afr. (115) 6

Medicago sativa — Usum hist. nat. (145) 18

Medusa — Corallia Balt. (4) 2; Curios. nat. (18) 5; Noctiluca (39) 6; Odor. med. (40) 6; Chin. Lagerstr. (64) 34; Nat. pelagi (84) 15; Mors. serp. (119) 2

Medusa corpore orbiculato seu conico, tentaculis filiformibus — Corallia Balt. (4) 10

Medusa orbicularis — Chin. Lagerstr. (64) 30, 36

Medusa orbicularis, supra plana, subtus sulcata, villosa — Chin. Lagerstr. (64) 30

Medusa velella — Nat. pelagi (84) 10; Iter Chin. (161) 15

Melaleuca leucadendron — Obs. mat. med. (171) 5

Melampodium — Fund. fr. (123) 17

Melampyrum — Fl. oecon. (17) 16; Pl. escul. (35) 27; Nom. bot. (107) 15

Melampyrum arvense — Pan Svec. (26) 27; Pl. escul. (35) 19[as arverse]; Demonstr. pl. (49) 16; Stat. pl. (55) 19; Fl. Angl. (56) 19; Fl. Monsp. (74) 20; Prodr. fl. Dan. (82) 20; Fl. Belg. (112) 19; Usum hist. nat. (145) 10; Colon. pl. (158) 5

Melampyrum caeruleum — Pan Svec. (26) 27

Melampyrum cristatum — Stat. pl. (55) 23; Fl. Angl. (56) 19; Fl. Monsp. (74) 20; Prodr. fl. Dan. (82) 20; Fl. Åker. (162) 15; Pand. fl. Ryb. (165) 20

Melampyrum nemorosum — Herbat. Upsal. (50) 15; Stat. pl. (55) 17[as nemorum]; Fl. Monsp. (74) 20; Prodr. fl. Dan. (82) 20; Pand. fl. Ryb. (165) 20

Melampyrum pratense — Stat. pl. (55) 21; Fl. Angl. (56) 19; Fl. Monsp. (74) 20; Prodr. fl. Dan. (82) 20; Fl. Belg. (112) 19; Fl. Åker. (162) 15; Pand. fl. Ryb. (165) 20; Esca avium (174) 13

Melampyrum ringens — Pan Svec. (26) 27

Melampyrum sylvaticum — Herbat. Upsal. (50) 15; Stat. pl. (55) 18; Fl. Angl. (56) 19; Fl. Monsp. (74) 20; Rar. Norv. (157) 11; Fl. Åker. (162) 15; Pand. fl. Ryb. (165) 20

Melampyrum tetragonum — Pan Svec. (26) 27

Melampyrum vulgare — Pan Svec. (26) 27

Melanthium — Nova pl. gen. 1747 (14) [vi], 13; Nova pl. gen. 1751 (32) 9; Nect. fl. (122) 11

Melanthium petalis punctatis, foliis maculatis — Pl. rar. Afr. (115) 10

Melanthium petalis sessilibus — Pl. rar. Camsch. (30) 16

Melanthium petalis unguiculatis — Pl. rar. Camsch. (30) 17

Melanthium punctatum — Pl. rar. Afr. (115) 10

Melanthium sibiricum — Hist. nat. Rossia (144) 29

Melanurus — Mus. Ad.-Frid. (11) 36[as Medanurus]

Melastoma — Vir. pl. (13) 20; Pl. tinct. (97) 18; Fr. escul. (127) 11[as Melostoma]; Pl. Surin. (177) 8

Melastoma acinodendron — Fl. Jam. (105) 16

Melastoma aspera — Herb. Amboin. (57) 17

Melastoma hirta — Fl. Jam. (105) 16

Melastoma holosericea — Fl. Jam. (105) 16[as holoserica]

Melastoma laevigata — Fl. Jam. (105) 16

Melastoma malabathrica — Herb. Amboin. (57) 19

Melastoma octandra — Herb. Amboin. (57) 17, 19

Melastoma parviflora — Fl. Jam. (105) 16

Melastoma scabrosa — Fl. Jam. (105) 16

Melastoma sessilifolia — Fl. Jam. (105) 16

Meleagris — Vir. pl. (13) 17; Rad. senega (23) 9; Polit. nat. (109) 21; Fund. ornith. (137) 19

Meleagris gallopavo — Calend. fl. (72) [9]; Esca avium (174) 6ff.

Meles — Oecon. nat. (20) 38; Morb. hyeme (38) [2]; Usum hist. nat. (145) 24

Meles unguibus anticis longissimis — Mat. med. anim. (29) 4

Meles unguibus uniformibus — Mat. med. anim. (29) 4

Melia — Nect. fl. (122) 9

Melia azedarach — Demonstr. pl. (49) 11; Fl. Palaest. (70) 19[as azederach]

Melia seu azedarach — Ficus (2) 3

Melianthus — Hort. Upsal. (7) 36; Vir. pl. (13) 24; Odor. med. (40) 13; Fl. Cap. (99) 6, 9; Nect. fl. (122) 7; Cimicifuga (173) 9

Melianthus major — Gem. arb. (24) 26; Demonstr. pl. (49) 17; Fl. Cap. (99) 16

Melianthus minor — Fl. Cap. (99) 16

Melianthus roridus multiflorus — Calend. fl. (72) [17]

Melica — Hort. Upsal. (7) 34; Fund. agrost. (152) 28, 31, 37

Melica altissima — Demonstr. pl. (49) 3; Hist. nat. Rossia (144) 27

Melica ciliata — Pan Svec. (26) 13; Stat. pl. (55) 23; Fl. Monsp. (74) 9; Prodr. fl. Dan. (82) 13; Fund. agrost. (152) 7

Melica nutans — Pan Svec. (26) 13; Herbat. Upsal. (50) 7; Stat. pl. (55) 23; Fl. Angl. (56) 10; Fl. Monsp. (74) 9; Prodr. fl. Dan. (82) 13; Fund. agrost. (152) 7; Fl. Åker. (162) 6; Esca avium (174) 10

Melicoccus — Fl. Jam. (105) 26

Melilobus — Nova pl. gen. 1751 (32) 10, 12

Melilotus — Vir. pl. (13) 31; Nom. bot. (107) 16

Melilotus cretica humillima humifusa, flore albo magno — Cent. I. pl. (65) 24

Melissa — Vir. pl. (13) 29, 30, 34; Fl. Monsp. (74) 7; Acetaria (77) 10; Pand. insect. (93) 16; Nom. bot. (107) 15; Inebr. (117) 13, 23; Menthae (153) 6, 7

Melissa calamintha — Pl. officin. (52) 6; Fl. Angl. (56) 18; Fl. Monsp. (74) 19

Melissa floribus verticillatis, subsessilibus secundum longitudinem caulis — Vir. pl. (13) 17

Melissa lotoria — Herb. Amboin. (57) 22

Melissa nepeta — Fl. Angl. (56) 18; Fl. Monsp. (74) 20; Fl. Belg. (112) 18

Melissa officinalis — Hosp. insect. fl. (43) 27; Demonstr. pl. (49) 16; Pl. officin. (52) 13; Fl. Palaest. (70) 23; Calend. fl. (72) [17]; Fl. Monsp. (74) 19; Fl. Jam. (105) 24; Hort. cul. (132) 18

Melissa pulegioides — Demonstr. pl. (49) 16

Melittis — Hort. Upsal. (7) 36

Melittis melissophyllum — Fl. Angl. (56) 18; Fl. Monsp. (74) 20

Melo — Spons. pl. (12) 47; Pl. escul. (35) 4; Hort. acad. (63) 3; Nom. bot. (107) 18; Marum (175) 10

Melocactus — Spons. pl. (12) 56

Melochia — Hort. Upsal. (7) 37

Melochia corchorifolia — Fl. Jam. (105) 18

Melochia depressa — Fl. Jam. (105) 18

Melochia frutescens — Pl. Jam. (102) 16

Melochia pyramidata — Fl. Jam. (105) 18

Melochia tomentosa — Pl. Jam. (102) 16; Fl. Jam. (105) 18

Meloe — Hosp. insect. fl. (43) 20; Polit. nat. (109) 8; Meloe (124) 3ff.; Fund. entom. (154) 22, [31, as 30]

Meloe alatus — Fund. entom. (154) 30[as alata]

Meloe alatus niger, coleopteris luteis: maculis duabus nigris posticis — Meloe (124) 6

Meloe alatus niger, thorace hirsuto, elytris fasciis tribus flavis — Meloe (124) 6

Meloe alatus viridissimus nitens, antennis nigris — Meloe (124) 4

Meloe bimaculatus — Meloe (124) 6

Meloe chrysomeloides — Cent. insect. (129) 13

Meloe cichorii — Pand. insect. (93) 18; Meloe (124) 6, 7

Meloe floralis — Pand. insect. (93) 18

Meloe monoceros — Fund. entom. (154) 30

Meloe proscarabaeus — Pand. insect. (93) 13, 22; Pand. fl. Ryb. (165) 9

Meloe schaefferi — Meloe (124) 6; Fund. entom. (154) 30

Meloe vesicatorius — Pand. insect. (93) 13, 22, [23, as 31]; Meloe (124) 4, 7

Melolontha — Fund. entom. (154) 30

Melongena — Nom. bot. (107) 11

Melothria — Hort. Upsal. (7) 37; Nova pl. gen. 1751 (32) 7, 12

Melothria pendula — Demonstr. pl. (49) 2; Fl. Jam. (105) 12

Memecylon — Nova pl. gen. 1747 (14) [vi], 16; Nova pl. gen. 1751 (32) 12, 27[as Memecylum]

Memecylon foliis ovatis — Nova pl. gen. 1747 (14) 16

Menispermum — Hort. Upsal. (7) 36; Nova pl. gen. 1751 (32) 9; Usum hist. nat. (145) 29

Menispermum canadense — Demonstr. pl. (49) 11

Menispermum carolinum — Herb. Amboin. (57) 18

Menispermum cocculus — Pl. officin. (52) 8; Herb. Amboin. (57) 18

Menispermum flavum — Cent. I. pl. (65) 2

Menispermum flavum, foliis ovatis glabris — Herb. Amboin. (57) 18

Mentha — Pl. Mart.-Burs. (6) 20; Vir. pl. (13) 17, 18; Nova pl. gen. 1747 (14) 8; Fl. oecon. (17) 16; Pl. hybr. (33) 7; Hosp. insect. fl. (43) 12; Fl. Angl. (56) 5; Metam. pl. (67) 19; Pand. insect. (93) 16; Nom. bot. (107) 14; Menthae (153) [2]ff.

Mentha aquatica — Vir. pl. (13) 17, 30; Pan Svec. (26) 26; Herbat. Upsal. (50) 9; Pl. officin. (52) 13; Stat. pl. (55) 14; Fl. Angl. (56) 18; Fl. Monsp. (74) 19; Prodr. fl. Dan. (82) 20; Fl. Belg. (112) 18; Menthae (153) 3; Fl. Åker. (162) 14; Pand. fl. Ryb. (165) 20

Mentha aquatica exigua — Cent. II. pl. (66) 20

Mentha aromatica — Fl. Angl. (56) 27

Mentha arvensis — Pan Svec. (26) 26; Hosp. insect. fl. (43) 27; Herbat. Upsal. (50) 18; Stat. pl. (55) 18; Fl. Angl. (56) 18; Prodr. fl. Dan. (82) 20; Fl. Belg. (112) 18; Menthae (153) 3, 8; Fl. Åker. (162) 14; Pand. fl. Ryb. (165) 20

Mentha auricularia — Menthae (153) [2], 3, 11; Obs. mat. med. (171) 4

Mentha canadensis — Menthae (153) 3

Mentha canariensis — Menthae (153) 3, 4

Mentha cervina — Fl. Monsp. (74) 19; Menthae (153) 3, 4

Mentha ceylanica aquatica inodora latifolia — Vir. pl. (13) 18

Mentha crispa — Vir. pl. (13) 30; Demonstr. pl. (49) 16; Pl. officin. (52) 13; Herb. Amboin. (57) 21; Calend. fl. (72) [17]; Hort. cul. (132) 24[as Menta]; Hist. nat. Rossia (144) 30; Menthae (153) 3, 4, 5

Mentha crispa verticillata — Fl. Angl. (56) 27

Mentha exigua — Cent. II. pl. (66) 20; Menthae (153) 3

Mentha floribus capitatis, foliis ovatis serratis petiolatis — Pl. hybr. (33) 24

Mentha floribus spicatis, foliis cordatis dentatis undulatis sessilibus — Pl. hybr. (33) 24

Mentha floribus spicatis, foliis oblongis serratis — Pl. hybr. (33) 24[as Menta]

Mentha floribus verticillatis, foliis lanceolato-ovatis glabris acutis integerrimis — Cent. II. pl. (66) 20

Mentha foetida — Demonstr. pl. (49) 16

Mentha gentilis — Fl. Angl. (56) 18; Calend. fl. (72) [16]; Menthae (153) 3

Mentha hirsuta — Menthae (153) 3

Mentha hortensis 4 — Cent. II. pl. (66) 20

Mentha longifolia — Fl. Monsp. (74) 19

Mentha piperita — Fl. Angl. (56) 5, 18; Menthae (153) 3, 5

Mentha pulegium — Pl. officin. (52) 16; Fl. Angl. (56) 18; Fl. Monsp. (74) 19; Prodr. fl. Dan. (82) 20; Fl. Belg. (112) 18; Menthae (153) 3, 4

Mentha rotundifolia — Menthae (153) [2]

Mentha sativa — Menthae (153) 3

Mentha spicata — Demonstr. pl. (49) 16; Pl. officin. (52) 13; Fl. Angl. (56) 18; Calend. fl. (72) [16]; Fl. Monsp. (74) 19; Fl. Jam. (105) 18, 25; Fl. Belg. (112) 18

Mentha spicata longifolia — Fl. Palaest. (70) 22

Mentha spicata viridis — Prodr. fl. Dan. (82) 20

Mentha sylvestris — Menthae (153) [2], 4

Mentha viridis — Demonstr. pl. (49) 16; Menthae (153) [2]

Mentha zeylanica aquatica inodora latifolia — Nova pl. gen. 1747 (14) 8

Menthastrum amboinicum — Herb. Amboin. (57) 28

Mentula cylindrica striis annularibus, glande striis longitudinalibus elevatis — Chin. Lagerstr. (64) 30

Mentula marina — Chin. Lagerstr. (64) 30

Mentzelia aspera — Pl. Jam. (102) 14; Fl. Jam. (105) 17

Menyanthes — Peloria (3) 10; Fl. oecon. (17) 5; Pl. hybr. (33) 7

Menyanthes foliis orbiculatis, corollis margine laceris — Pl. hybr. (33) 27

Menyanthes foliis ternatis — Pl. hybr. (33) 27

Menyanthes indica — Herb. Amboin. (57) 28; Fl. Jam. (105) 13, 25

Menyanthes nymphoides — Fl. Angl. (56) 12; Fl. Monsp. (74) 11; Fl. Belg. (112) 8, 14

Menyanthes trifoliata — Pan Svec. (26) 17; Herbat. Upsal. (50) 7; Pl. officin. (52) 19; Stat. pl. (55) 13; Fl. Angl. (56) 12; Fl. Monsp. (74) 11; Prodr. fl. Dan. (82) 15; Fl. Belg. (112) 14; Fl. Åker. (162) 8[as trifolia]; Pand. fl. Ryb. (165) 17; Febr. interm. (167) 38; Esca avium (174) 11

Mercurialis — Peloria (3) 16; Spons. pl. (12) [2], 32; Vir. pl. (13) 27; Fl. oecon. (17) 27; Pan Svec. (26) 9; Pl. hybr. (33) 6; Pand. insect. (93) 22; Fl. Cap. (99) 9; Nom. bot. (107) 19

Mercurialis annua — Demonstr. pl. (49) 26; Pl. officin. (52) 13; Fl. Angl. (56) 24; Fl. Palaest. (70) 31; Calend. fl. (72) [22]; Fl. Monsp. (74) 28; Fl. Belg. (112) 23

Mercurialis caule brachiato, foliis glabris — Peloria (3) 16

Mercurialis foliis capillaceis — Peloria (3) 16

Mercurialis foliis in varias et inaequales lacinias quasi dilaceratis — Peloria (3) 16

Mercurialis perennis — Spons. pl. (12) 41; Pan Svec. (26) [37, as 39]; Hosp. insect. fl. (43) 38; Demonstr. pl. (49) 26; Stat. pl. (55) 17; Fl. Angl. (56) 24; Oves (61) 17; Calend. fl. (72) [9]; Fl. Monsp. (74) 28; Prodr. fl. Dan. (82) 25; Pl. tinct. (97) 10

Mercurialis procumbens — Fl. Cap. (99) 19

Mercurialis tomentosa — Fl. Monsp. (74) 28

Merda papaveris seu lignum stercoris — Nova pl. gen. 1747 (14) 29

Mergulus lutorlska — Hist. nat. Rossia (144) 16

138

Mergus — Oecon. nat. (20) [37, as 7]; Migr. avium (79) 25; Polit. nat. (109) 13; Fund. ornith. (137) 18, 26; Usum hist. nat. (145) 25

Mesembryanthemum — Ficus (2) 9; Passifl. (8) 30; Oecon. nat. (20) 19; Pl. hybr. (33) 29; Metam. pl. (67) 14; Fl. Cap. (99) 6, 7, 8, 9; Pl. rar. Afr. (115) 4, 5; Pl. Alstr. (121) 5; Fund. fr. (123) 16, 17, 21, 22; Aphyteia (185) 6

Mesembryanthemum acaule, foliis linguiformibus altero margine crassioribus — Hort. Upsal. (7) 40

Mesembryanthemum acinaciforme — Fl. Cap. (99) 15

Mesembryanthemum aureum — Fl. Cap. (99) 15

Mesembryanthemum barbatum — Demonstr. pl. (49) 14; Fl. Cap. (99) 9, 15; Prol. pl. 1760 (114) 12

Mesembryanthemum bellidiflorum — Fl. Cap. (99) 15

Mesembryanthemum bicolorum — Fl. Cap. (99) 15

Mesembryanthemum calamiforme — Fl. Cap. (99) 15

Mesembryanthemum caulescens, foliis glabris subulatis semicylindraceis recurvis connatis longissimis — Hort. Upsal. (7) 40

Mesembryanthemum crassifolium — Fl. Cap. (99) 15

Mesembryanthemum crystallinum — Demonstr. pl. (49) 13; Fl. Cap. (99) 15

Mesembryanthemum deltoides — Fl. Cap. (99) 15

Mesembryanthemum difforme — Fl. Cap. (99) 15

Mesembryanthemum dolabriforme — Fl. Cap. (99) 15

Mesembryanthemum edule — Fl. Cap. (99) 15

Mesembryanthemum expansum — Fl. Cap. (99) 15

Mesembryanthemum falcatum — Fl. Cap. (99) 15

Mesembryanthemum filamentosum — Fl. Cap. (99) 15

Mesembryanthemum foliis alternis ovatis obtusis undulatis — Hort. Upsal. (7) 40

Mesembryanthemum foliis apice barbatis — Hort. Upsal. (7) 40

Mesembryanthemum foliis lanceolatis glabris crenulatis — Hort. Upsal. (7) 40

Mesembryanthemum foliis semicylindraceis acutis connatis arcuatis laevibus — Hort. Upsal. (7) 40

Mesembryanthemum foliis subulatis semiteretibus glabris internodio longioribus — Hort. Upsal. (7) 40

Mesembryanthemum foliis subulatis subtus undique scabris — Hort. Upsal. (7) 40

Mesembryanthemum foliis teretibus alternis obtusis — Hort. Upsal. (7) 40

Mesembryanthemum forficatum — Fl. Cap. (99) 15

Mesembryanthemum geniculiflorum — Fl. Cap. (99) 15

Mesembryanthemum glaucum — Fl. Cap. (99) 15

Mesembryanthemum glomeratum — Fl. Cap. (99) 15

Mesembryanthemum hispidum — Fl. Cap. (99) 15

Mesembryanthemum linguiforme — Fl. Cap. (99) 9, 15

Mesembryanthemum loreum — Demonstr. pl. (49) 14; Fl. Cap. (99) 15

Mesembryanthemum micans — Fl. Cap. (99) 15

Mesembryanthemum noctiflorum — Fl. Cap. (99) 15

Mesembryanthemum nodiflorum — Demonstr. pl. (49) 13; Fl. Palaest. (70) 21

Mesembryanthemum pugioniforme — Fl. Cap. (99) 15

Mesembryanthemum ringens — Fl. Cap. (99) 9, 15

Mesembryanthemum rostratum — Fl. Cap. (99) 15

Mesembryanthemum scabrum — Demonstr. pl. (49) 14; Fl. Cap. (99) 15

Mesembryanthemum serratum — Fl. Cap. (99) 15

Mesembryanthemum spinosum — Fl. Cap. (99) 15

Mesembryanthemum splendens — Fl. Cap. (99) 15

Mesembryanthemum stipulaceum — Fl. Cap. (99) 15

Mesembryanthemum tenuifolium — Fl. Cap. (99) 15

Mesembryanthemum tortuosum — Fl. Cap. (99) 15

Mesembryanthemum tripolium — Demonstr. pl. (49) 14; Fl. Cap. (99) 15

Mesembryanthemum tuberosum — Fl. Cap. (99) 15

Mesembryanthemum umbellatum — Fl. Cap. (99) 15

Mesembryanthemum uncinatum — Fl. Cap. (99) 15

Mesembryanthemum veruculatum — Fl. Cap. (99) 15

Mesembryanthemum villosum — Fl. Cap. (99) 15

Mesosphaerum — Pl. Jam. (102) 15; Fl. Jam. (105) 26

Mespilus — Vir. pl. (13) 21, 33; Sapor. med. (31) 15; Chin. Lagerstr. (64) 6; Fr. Svec. (91) [ii]; Nom. bot. (107) 13; Prol. pl. 1760 (114) 11

Mespilus amelanchier — Fl. alp. (71) 18; Fl. Monsp. (74) 17

Mespilus chamaemespilus — Fl. alp. (71) 18

Mespilus cotoneaster — Gem. arb. (24) 25; Pan Svec. (26) 24; Demonstr. pl. (49) 13; Herbat. Upsal. (50) 7[as cotonaster]; Stat. pl. (55) 23; Fl. Angl. (56) 6; Calend. fl. (72) [10]; Fl. Monsp. (74) 17; Prodr. fl. Dan. (82) 18; Fr. Svec. (91) 4, 19, 24; Fl. Åker. (162) 13

Mespilus germanica — Gem. arb. (24) 24; Demonstr. pl. (49) 13; Pl. officin. (52) 13; Fl. Angl. (56) 17; Fr. escul. (127) 8

Metopium — Fl. Jam. (105) 26[as Methopium]

Metrosideros — Herb. Amboin. (57) 11

Metrosideros amboinensis — Herb. Amboin. (57) 11

Metrosideros macassarensis — Herb. Amboin. (57) 11

Metrosideros molucca — Herb. Amboin. (57) 11

Metrosideros spuria — Herb. Amboin. (57) 11

Metrosideros vera — Herb. Amboin. (57) 11

Michelia champaca — Herb. Amboin. (57) 10

Microcos — Nova pl. gen. 1747 (14) [vi], 20

Microcos foliis alternis oblongis acuminatis — Nova pl. gen. 1747 (14) 20

Microcos paniculis terminatricibus — Nova pl. gen. 1747 (14) 20

Microcos pedunculis axillaribus confertis dichotomis — Nova pl. gen. 1747 (14) 20

Micronymphaea — Fl. Belg. (112) 9

Micropus — Hort. Upsal. (7) 34

Micropus caule erecto, calycibus edentatis — Demonstr. pl. (49) 24

Micropus erectus — Demonstr. pl. (49) 24; Cent. I. pl. (65) 2

Micropus supinus — Demonstr. pl. (49) 24

Milium — Vir. pl. (13) 31, 32; Fl. oecon. (17) 3; Odor. med. (40) 12; Vern. arb. (47) 9; Nom. bot. (107) 9; Fund. agrost. (152) 15, 16, 21, 27, 31, 37

Milium effusum — Demonstr. pl. (49) 3; Herbat. Upsal. (50) 8; Stat. pl. (55) 17; Fl. Angl. (56) 10; Fl. Belg. (112) 13; Fund. agrost. (152) 7; Fl. Åker. (162) 6; Esca avium (174) 10

Milium lendigerum — Colon. pl. (158) 13

Milium punctatum — Pl. Jam. (102) 6; Fl. Jam. (105) 13

Milium suaveolens — Pan Svec. (26) 13

Millefolium — Vir. pl. (13) 23; Inebr. (117) 13

Millefolium aquaticum — Herb. Amboin. (57) 28

Millena [error for Milleria?] — Hort. Upsal. (7) 37

Millepeda africana — Mus. Ad.-Frid. (11) 46

Millepeda orientalis omnium maxima — Mus. Ad.-Frid. (11) 46

Millepora — Corallia Balt. (4) 2, 4; Nat. pelagi (84) 8

Millepora arenosa anglica — Corallia Balt. (4) 9

Millepora dichotoma, repens, teres, poris axillaribus solitariis eminentibus — Corallia Balt. (4) 37

Millepora membranacea, plana, punctis contiguis, quincuncialibus — Corallia Balt. (4) 38

Millepora plana simplicissima superficie alteri adnata — Corallia Balt. (4) 38

Millepora poris contiguis, angulatis; diaphragmatibus transversalibus plurimis — Corallia Balt. (4) 32

Millepora poris contiguis, subrotundis; diaphragmatibus transversalibus plurimis — Corallia Balt. (4) 33

Millepora ramis cylindraceis, dichotomis, seriebus longitudinalibus punctatis — Corallia Balt. (4) 28

Millepora ramis vagis, punctis imbricatis — Corallia Balt. (4) 28

Millepora ramis vagis, punctis sparsis — Corallia Balt. (4) 27

Millepora repens, ramis dichotomis, lineolis subulatis, imbricatis poros distinguentibus — Corallia Balt. (4) 29

Millepora rubra, striis obsoletis flexuosis — Mat. med. anim. (29) 20

Millepora subrotunda, poris contiguis, angulatis, farctis, subtus sulcata — Corallia Balt. (4) 31

Millepora subrotunda, poris minimis confertis, majoribusque crenatis remotis — Corallia Balt. (4) 30

Millepora tubis ovatis, longitudinaliter reticulatimque concatenatis — Corallia Balt. (4) 34

Millepora tubulis cylindraceo-flexuosis, distantibus, congestis plurimis — Corallia Balt. (4) 37

Milleria — Fund. fr. (123) 17; see also Millena

Milleria quinqueflora — Calend. fl. (72) [21]

Milvus — Migr. avium (79) 20

Mimosa — Hort. Upsal. (7) 37; Spons. pl. (12) 12; Gem. arb. (24) 6, 9; Herb. Amboin. (57) 11, 17; Somn. pl. (68) 21; Anim. comp. (98) 5; Generat. ambig. (104) 10; Fl. Jam. (105) 26; Nom. bot. (107) 14; Nect. fl. (122) 4; Fund. fr. (123) 21; Prol. pl. 1763 (130) 8

Mimosa arborea — Fl. Jam. (105) 22

Mimosa cinerea — Fl. Jam. (105) 22

Mimosa entada — Pl. Surin. (177) 16

Mimosa farnesiana — Demonstr. pl. (49) 14; Fl. Palaest. (70) 21

Mimosa foliis bipinnatis opposite aculeatis: spina erecta longiore inter singula partialia — Cent. I. pl. (65) 13

Mimosa gigas — Fl. Jam. (105) 22

Mimosa inga — Pl. Surin. (177) 16

Mimosa lebbeck — Fl. Palaest. (70) 21[as lebbek]

Mimosa nilotica — Demonstr. pl. (49) 14; Fl. Palaest. (70) 21

Mimosa pernambucana — Demonstr. pl. (49) 14

Mimosa pigra — Cent. I. pl. (65) 13

Mimosa pudica — Demonstr. pl. (49) 14; Fl. Jam. (105) 22

Mimosa punctata — Fl. Jam. (105) 22

Mimosa scandens — Rar. Norv. (157) 12; Colon. pl. (158) 5

Mimosa senegal — Demonstr. pl. (49) 14; Pl. officin. (52) 3, 5; Fl. Palaest. (70) 21

Mimosa sensitiva — Somn. pl. (68) 7

Mimosa tortuosa — Pl. Jam. (102) 29; Fl. Jam. (105) 22

Mimosa unguis cati — Fl. Jam. (105) 22

Mimosa virgata — Somn. pl. (68) 21

Mimosa viva — Fl. Jam. (105) 22

Mimosa zygia — Fl. Jam. (105) 22

Mimulus — Hort. Upsal. (7) 35; Nova pl. gen. 1747 (14) [iv]; Nova pl. gen. 1751 (32) 9, 12; Specif. Canad. (76) 22

Mimusops — Nova pl. gen. 1747 (14) [vi], 14

Mimusops elengi — Herb. Amboin. (57) 10

Mimusops foliis alternis — Nova pl. gen. 1747 (14) 14

Mimusops foliis confertis — Nova pl. gen. 1747 (14) 14

Mimusops kauki — Herb. Amboin. (57) 11

Minuartia campestris — Demonstr. pl. (49) 4; Fung. melit. (69) 2

Minuartia dichotoma — Demonstr. pl. (49) 4; Fung. melit. (69) 2

Minuartia montana — Demonstr. pl. (49) 4; Fung. melit. (69) 2

Mirabilis — Vir. pl. (13) 19; Vern. arb. (47) 9; Stat. pl. (55) 5; Herb. Amboin. (57) 21; Calend. fl. (72) [17]; Generat. ambig. (104) 6; Prol. pl. 1760 (114) 16; Nect. fl. (122) 10; Mund. invis. (149) 17; Med. purg. (181) 16

Mirabilis caule dichotomo, corollis limbo patentibus, staminibus pistillo brevioribus — Cent. I. pl. (65) 7

Mirabilis caule foliisque villosis et glutinosis, tubo floris pedali — Cent. I. pl. (65) 7

Mirabilis dichotoma — Fl. Jam. (105) 14; Med. purg. (181) 16, 17

Mirabilis floribus solitariis axillaribus erectis sessilibus — Med. purg. (181) 16

Mirabilis foliis villosis, corollis folio longioribus — Cent. I. pl. (65) 7

Mirabilis jalapa — Demonstr. pl. (49) 6[as jalappa]; Pl. officin. (52) 11; Herb. Amboin. (57) 21[as jalappa]; Cent. I. pl. (65) 7[as jalappa], 8[as jalappa]; Hort. cul. (132) 25

Mirabilis longiflora — Cent. I. pl. (65) 7; Purg. indig. (143) 15; Med. purg. (181) 17

Mirabilis odorata — Cent. I. pl. (65) 7

Mirabilis planta, foliis amplexicaulibus et fulcimentis adnascentibus — Herb. Amboin. (57) 25

Mitchella — Nova pl. gen. 1751 (32) 8, 12, 24, 25, 48

Mitella — Nova pl. gen. 1751 (32) 9, 29[as Mittella]

Mitella foliis ternatis — Pl. rar. Camsch. (30) 18; Nova pl. gen. 1751 (32) 29

Mitella petalis multifidis scapo nudo — Pl. rar. Camsch. (30) 19

Mitella scapo diphyllo — Pl. rar. Camsch. (30) 19; Nova pl. gen. 1751 (32) 29

Mitella scapo nudo — Pl. rar. Camsch. (30) 19; Nova pl. gen. 1751 (32) 29

Mitra — Fund. test. (166) 10

Mitreola americana — Cui bono? (42) 23

Mnium — Nova pl. gen. 1747 (14) [iv]; Fl. oecon. (17) 29; Splachnum (27) 5; Sem. musc. (28) 6, 7, 14, 15, 17; Cui bono? (42) 14; Buxbaumia (85) 11; Usum musc. (148) 2

Mnium caule procumbente simplici, foliis imbricatis integerrimis alternis antice appendiculatis — Pl. Mart.-Burs. (6) 28

Mnium fontanum — Herbat. Upsal. (50) 11; Usum musc. (148) 11[as fontale], 12[as fontale]

Mnium hygrometricum — Herbat. Upsal. (50) 8; Fl. Palaest. (70) 32; Usum musc. (148) 14

Mnium jungermannia — Herbat. Upsal. (50) 9

Mnium palustre — Herbat. Upsal. (50) 11; Usum musc. (148) 11

Mnium pellucidum — Herbat. Upsal. (50) 9

Mnium pyriforme — Herbat. Upsal. (50) 9

Mnium serpyllifolium — Herbat. Upsal. (50) 9

Mnium serpyllifolium cuspidatum — Prodr. fl. Dan. (82) 25

Mnium serpyllifolium punctatum — Prodr. fl. Dan. (82) 25

Mnium triquetrum — Usum musc. (148) 5[as Minum]

Modecca — Passifl. (8) 30

Moehringia — Hort. Upsal. (7) 34; Splachnum (27) 2; Nom. bot. (107) 8

Moehringia lapponica — Pan Svec. (26) 21

Moehringia muscosa — Fl. Angl. (56) 15; Fl. alp. (71) 16; Fl. Monsp. (74) 15

Moldavica — Anandria (9) 4

Mollugo — Hort. Upsal. (7) 37

Mollugo tetraphylla — Demonstr. pl. (49) 4

Mollugo verticillata — Fl. Jam. (105) 13

Molucca laevis — Pl. hybr. (33) 26

Molucca spinosa — Pl. hybr. (33) 26

Moluccella — Hort. Upsal. (7) 34; Pl. hybr. (33) 7

Moluccella frutescens — Colon. pl. (158) 11

Moluccella spinosa — Demonstr. pl. (49) 16; Fl. Palaest. (70) 23

Momordica — Hort. Upsal. (7) 37; Herb. Amboin. (57) 24; Pl. Surin. (177) 16

Momordica balsamina — Demonstr. pl. (49) 25; Herb. Amboin. (57) 24; Somn. pl. (68) 6[as balsamita]; Fl. Palaest. (70) 30; Fl. Jam. (105) 21

Momordica charantia — Demonstr. pl. (49) 25; Fl. Jam. (105) 21[as charanthia]

Momordica elaterium — Demonstr. pl. (49) 25; Pl. officin. (52) 9; Fl. Palaest. (70) 30; Fl. Monsp. (74) 28; Fl. Belg. (112) 22; Purg. indig. (143) 16; Med. purg. (181) 11

Momordica indica — Herb. Amboin. (57) 24

Momordica luffa — Herb. Amboin. (57) 23; Fl. Palaest. (70) 30

Momordica pomis hispidis, cirrhis nullis — Med. purg. (181) 11

Momordica trifolia — Cent. I. pl. (65) 2

Momordica trifolia, foliis ternatis dentatis — Herb. Amboin. (57) 24

Monarda — Hort. Upsal. (7) 35; Nova pl. gen. 1751 (32) 7; Cui bono? (42) 21

Monarda clinopodifolia — Demonstr. pl. (49) 2

Monarda fistulosa — Demonstr. pl. (49) 2; Febr. interm. (167) 39

Monarda mollis — Demonstr. pl. (49) 2; Cent. I. pl. (65) 2; Calend. fl. (72) [17]; Specif. Canad. (76) 26

Monarda rubra — Calend. fl. (72) [18]

Monedula — Migr. avium (79) 31

Monedula pyrrhocorax — Migr. avium (79) 19

Monieria — Fl. Jam. (105) 26

Monitor — Migr. avium (79) 21

141

Monnieria — Nect. fl. (122) 7

Monoculus — Oecon. nat. (20) 29, 41; Mirac. insect. (45) 9

Monoculus pulex — Pand. fl. Ryb. (165) 16

Monodon — Mat. med. anim. (29) 12

Monorchis — Betula (1) 12

Monotropa — Vir. pl. (13) 25; Somn. pl. (68) 6; Pl. tinct. (97) 10; Nect. fl. (122) 13; Aphyteia (185) 9

Monotropa hypopitys — Herbat. Upsal. (50) 18[as hypopithys]; Stat. pl. (55) 18[as hypopithys]; Fl. Angl. (56) 15; Fung. melit. (69) 3[as hypopithys]; Prodr. fl. Dan. (82) 17[as hypopithys]; Pand. fl. Ryb. (165) 18[as hypopithys]

Monotropa parasitica — Pan Svec. (26) 22

Monotropa uniflora — Fung. melit. (69) 3

Monsonia — Aphyteia (185) 6

Montia — Morb. hyeme (38) 8; Fund. fr. (123) 21

Montia fontana — Herbat. Upsal. (50) 18; Stat. pl. (55) 13; Fl. Angl. (56) 11; Fung. melit. (69) 2; Fl. Monsp. (74) 10; Prodr. fl. Dan. (82) 14

Montia palustris — Pan Svec. (26) 15

Moraea — Pl. Alstr. (121) 6

Mordella — Hosp. insect. fl. (43) 9, 16, 21, 28; Noxa insect. (46) 13, 19, 22

Mordella brassicae — Hosp. insect. fl. (43) 28

Mordella flava — Pand. fl. Ryb. (165) 9

Mordella frontalis — Pand. fl. Ryb. (165) 9

Mordella thoracica — Pand. fl. Ryb. (165) 9

Morfalla — Herb. Amboin. (57) 11

Morinda — Vir. pl. (13) 28

Morinda citrifolia — Herb. Amboin. (57) 13; Fl. Jam. (105) 14

Morinda royoc — Fl. Jam. (105) 14

Moringa — Fr. escul. (127) 14

Morisonia — Nect. fl. (122) 5

Morisonia americana — Pl. Jam. (102) 14; Fl. Jam. (105) 17[as Morisona]

Morisonia flexuosa — Pl. Jam. (102) 14

Moroficus — Ficus (2) 3

Morunga — Herb. Amboin. (57) 8

Morus — Ficus (2) 9, 11, 18, 27; Hort. Upsal. (7) 36; Spons. pl. (12) 41, 48; Vir. pl. (13) 33; Sapor. med. (31) 14; Hosp. insect. fl. (43) 12, 32; Vern. arb. (47) 9; Phalaena (78) 4ff.; Pand. insect. (93) 19; Nom. bot. (107) 18; Polit. nat. (109) 8; Inebr. (117) 13; Var. cib. (156) 4; Fraga (170) 7

Morus alba — Fl. Palaest. (70) 30; Fl. Monsp. (74) 27; Phalaena (78) 6, 7, 12; Fl. Jam. (105) 21; Fr. escul. (127) 8

Morus indica — Phalaena (78) 6, 8

Morus nigra — Gem. arb. (24) 31; Pl. officin. (52) 13; Calend. fl. (72) [19]; Fl. Monsp. (74) 27; Phalaena (78) 6, 7; Fr. escul. (127) 8; Hort. cul. (132) 21

Morus papyrifera — Phalaena (78) 6; Fl. Jam. (105) 21

Morus rubra — Phalaena (78) 6, 7; Fl. Jam. (105) 21; Fr. escul. (127) 8

Morus tatarica — Phalaena (78) 6[as tartarica], 8[as tartarica]; Hist. nat. Rossia (144) 24; Usum hist. nat. (145) 12[as tartarica]

Morus tinctoria — Phalaena (78) 6; Pl. tinct. (97) 25; Fl. Jam. (105) 8, 21

Moschetus — Migr. avium (79) 19

Moschus — Mat. med. anim. (29) 6

Moschus moschifer — Ambros. (100) 9

Moschus orientalis — Oves (61) 20

Motacilla — Oecon. nat. (20) 33; Morb. hyeme (38) 3; Calend. fl. (72) [19]; Migr. avium (79) 13, 16, 21, 34; Polit. nat. (109) 12, 22

Motacilla alba — Calend. fl. (72) [9]; Migr. avium (79) 20, 30, 34

Motacilla capite et ventre flavo — Hist. nat. Rossia (144) 16

Motacilla flava — Migr. avium (79) 34

Motacilla luscinia — Calend. fl. (72) [10]; Migr. avium (79) 34; Fund. ornith. (137) 27[as lucinia]

Motacilla oenanthe — Calend. fl. (72) [9]; Migr. avium (79) 34, 35; Fund. ornith. (137) 26

Motacilla phoenicurus — Migr. avium (79) 35

Motacilla regulus — Migr. avium (79) 35

Motacilla rubecula — Migr. avium (79) 35

Motacilla suecica — Migr. avium (79) 35

Mucor — Spons. pl. (12) 19; Fl. oecon. (17) 30; Mund. invis. (149) 12, 14, 16, 21, 22

Mucor erysiphe — Arb. Svec. (101) 17; Pand. fl. Ryb. (165) 23

Mucor mucedo — Pand. fl. Ryb. (165) 23

Mucor septicus — Mund. invis. (149) 16, 21, 23

Mugil — Fund. ornith. (137) 10

Mugil alatus — Mus. Ad.-Frid. (11) 42

Mullus — Cul. mut. (88) 9

Mulus — Peloria (3) 15; Pl. hybr. (33) 3; Fund. fr. (123) 14

Mungos — Lign. colubr. (21) 9ff.

Muntingia calabura — Fl. Jam. (105) 17

Muraena — Mus. Ad.-Frid. (11) 40; Oecon. nat. (20) 45[as Murena]; Cul. mut. (88) 9; Mund. invis. (149) 15

Muraena pinnis pectoralibus carens — Mus. Ad.-Frid. (11) 40

Muraena sive conger brasiliensibus — Mus. Ad.-Frid. (11) 40

Muraena tartesia — Var. cib. (156) 8

Murex — Fund. test. (166) 17, 23, 27, 37

Murex erinaceus — Iter Chin. (161) 8

Murex ramosus — Iter Chin. (161) 8

Murex reticularis — Fund. test. (166) 38

Murex ricinus — Fund. test. (166) 38

Murex saxatilis — Fund. test. (166) 39

142

Murex tribulus — Iter Chin. (161) 8; Fund. test. (166) 37

Murex turbinellus — Iter Chin. (161) 8

Murex vertagus — Fund. test. (166) 39

Murucuja — Passifl. (8) 4ff.

Murucuja 2 maliformis — Passifl. (8) 28

Murucuja 3 maliformis — Passifl. (8) 21

Murucuja 4 pyriformis 1, quae murucuja guacu — Passifl. (8) 25

Murucuja 4, seu pyriformis altera — Passifl. (8) 8

Murucuja brasiliensis 5, seu murucuja miri — Passifl. (8) 8

Murucuja folio lunato — Passifl. (8) 13

Murucuja guacu — Passifl. (8) 25

Murucuja miri — Passifl. (8) 8

Murucuja pyriformis altera — Passifl. (8) 8

Murucujae species, foliis hederae scandentis — Passifl. (8) 16

Mus — Oecon. nat. (20) 39, 44; Pan Svec. (26) 6; Morb. hyeme (38) 3, 13; Mus ind. (62) 6ff.; Polit. nat. (109) 14, 15, 18

Mus aegyptius — Mus ind. (62) 8, 9

Mus africanus hayopolin dictus — Mus. Ad.-Frid. (11) 2

Mus alpinus — Morb. hyeme (38) [2]

Mus americanus guineensis porcelli pilis et voce — Mus ind. (62) 10

Mus cauda carens — Hist. nat. Rossia (144) 16

Mus cauda longa nudiuscula, corpore cinereo fusco, abdomine subalbescente — Mat. med. anim. (29) 5

Mus cauda nulla, palmis tetradactylis, plantis tridactylis — Mus ind. (62) 10

Mus domesticus vulgaris seu minor — Mat. med. anim. (29) 5

Mus indicus — Mus ind. (62) 5ff.

Mus javanensis — Mus ind. (62) 9

Mus musculus — Mors. serp. (119) 5

Mus norvegicus — Cervus (60) 10; Mus ind. (62) 4, 8, 9

Mus seu sorex sylvaticus americanus — Mus. Ad.-Frid. (11) 2

Musa — Ficus (2) 9; Spons. pl. (12) 39, 40, 55, 58; Vir. pl. (13) 26; Pl. escul. (35) 4; Herb. Amboin. (57) 20; Pand. insect. (93) 22; Nom. bot. (107) 19; Prol. pl. 1760 (114) 18; Nect. fl. (122) 10; Fund. fr. (123) 15

Musa bihai — Fl. Jam. (105) 22

Musa paradisiaca — Demonstr. pl. (49) 26; Herb. Amboin. (57) 20; Fl. Palaest. (70) 31; Calend. fl. (72) [19]; Fl. Jam. (105) 22; Fund. fr. (123) 15; Fr. escul. (127) 9; Iter Chin. (161) 7; Pl. Surin. (177) 16

Musa sapientum — Fl. Jam. (105) 22

Musa simiarum — Herb. Amboin. (57) 20

Musa uranoscopos — Herb. Amboin. (57) 20

Musca — Ficus (2) 17; Spons. pl. (12) 15, 16, 50; Oecon. nat. (20) 16, 29, 41, 44; Cui bono? (42) 9, 24; Hosp. insect. fl. (43) 9, 17, 22, 24, 30, 32; Mirac. insect. (45) 7, 18; Noxa insect. (46) 11, 12, 27; Metam. pl. (67) 11, 12; Pand. insect. (93) 4, 5, 7, 8, 10; Polit. nat. (109) 12, 21; Hort. cul. (132) 11; Fund. entom. (154) 5, 13, 16, 17, 18, 27; Pand. fl. Ryb. (165) 13; Esca avium (174) 2; Bigas insect. (184) 2

Musca alba villosa — Hosp. insect. fl. (43) 27

Musca albifrons — Pand. fl. Ryb. (165) 14

Musca alis albis, fasciis fuscis repandis, oculis viridibus — Hosp. insect. fl. (43) 18

Musca amica — Pand. fl. Ryb. (165) 15

Musca anilis — Pand. fl. Ryb. (165) 14

Musca arbustorum — Pand. fl. Ryb. (165) 14

Musca arnicae — Pand. fl. Ryb. (165) 15

Musca aurata — Hosp. insect. fl. (43) 37

Musca bicincta — Pand. fl. Ryb. (165) 14

Musca bombylans — Pand. fl. Ryb. (165) 14; Esca avium (174) [9, as 17]

Musca caesar — Polit. nat. (109) 11; Pand. fl. Ryb. (165) 14; Esca avium (174) [9, as 17]

Musca cardui — Pand. insect. (93) 18

Musca carnaria — Exanth. viva (86) 14; Polit. nat. (109) 11; Fund. entom. (154) 24

Musca carnivora — Spons. pl. (12) 17; Oecon. nat. (20) 29; Noxa insect. (46) 12

Musca cerasi — Pand. insect. (93) 15

Musca cinerea — Hosp. insect. fl. (43) 30

Musca clavipes — Pand. fl. Ryb. (165) 14

Musca cupraria — Pand. fl. Ryb. (165) 15

Musca devia — Pand. fl. Ryb. (165) 14

Musca diophthalma — Pand. fl. Ryb. (165) 14[as diophtalma]

Musca domestica — Polit. nat. (109) 11; Esca avium (174) [9, as 17]

Musca femorata — Esca avium (174) [9, as 17]

Musca fenestralis — Pand. fl. Ryb. (165) 14

Musca fera — Pand. fl. Ryb. (165) 15

Musca festiva — Pand. fl. Ryb. (165) 14

Musca filamentaria — Cervus (60) 15

Musca flava — Pand. fl. Ryb. (165) 15

Musca florea — Pand. fl. Ryb. (165) 14

Musca florescentiae — Esca avium (174) [9, as 17]

Musca frit — Pand. insect. (93) 11; Usum hist. nat. (145) 11

Musca fusca, segmentis abdominalibus tribus margine albidis, primo latere flavo, thorace vix maculato — Taenia (19) 10

Musca glaucia — Pand. fl. Ryb. (165) 14

Musca grossa — Pand. fl. Ryb. (165) 15

Musca heraclii — Pand. insect. (93) 13

Musca hordei — Noxa insect. (46) 23

Musca hortulana — Pand. insect. (93) 13

Musca hyoscyami — Pand. insect. (93) 12; Pand. fl. Ryb. (165) 15

Musca lappona — Pand. fl. Ryb. (165) 14

Musca larvarum — Pand. fl. Ryb. (165) 15

Musca lucorum — Pand. fl. Ryb. (165) 14

Musca maura — Pand. fl. Ryb. (165) 14

Musca mellina — Polit. nat. (109) 10[as melina]; Pand. fl. Ryb. (165) 14

Musca menthastri — Polit. nat. (109) 10

Musca meridiana — Pand. fl. Ryb. (165) 14

Musca meteorica — Pand. fl. Ryb. (165) 15

Musca morio — Pand. fl. Ryb. (165) 14

Musca mortuorum — Pand. fl. Ryb. (165) 14

Musca mystacea — Pand. fl. Ryb. (165) 14; Esca avium (174) [9, as 17]

Musca nemorum — Pand. fl. Ryb. (165) 14

Musca parietina — Pand. fl. Ryb. (165) 15

Musca pellucens — Pand. fl. Ryb. (165) 14

Musca penaula — Pand. fl. Ryb. (165) 14

Musca petronella — Pand. fl. Ryb. (165) 15

Musca pipiens — Pand. fl. Ryb. (165) 14

Musca plebeja — Pand. fl. Ryb. (165) 14

Musca pluvialis — Polit. nat. (109) 21; Pand. fl. Ryb. (165) 15

Musca putris — Polit. nat. (109) 11; Pand. fl. Ryb. (165) 15

Musca pyrastri — Pand. insect. (93) 15; Polit. nat. (109) 10

Musca radicum — Pand. insect. (93) [17, as 38]; Pand. fl. Ryb. (165) 15

Musca ribesii — Polit. nat. (109) 10; Pand. fl. Ryb. (165) 14

Musca roralis — Pand. fl. Ryb. (165) 15

Musca scolopacea — Pand. fl. Ryb. (165) 14

Musca scripta — Polit. nat. (109) 10; Pand. fl. Ryb. (165) 14

Musca scyballaria — Esca avium (174) [9, as 17]

Musca segnis — Pand. fl. Ryb. (165) 14

Musca solstitialis — Pand. insect. (93) 18

Musca stercoraria — Pand. fl. Ryb. (165) 15

Musca subcutanea — Hosp. insect. fl. (43) 17, 26, 30

Musca ungulata — Pand. fl. Ryb. (165) 15

Musca urticae — Pand. insect. (93) 19

Musca vibrans — Pand. fl. Ryb. (165) 15

Musca viduata — Pand. fl. Ryb. (165) 15

Musca vomitoria — Polit. nat. (109) 11; Pand. fl. Ryb. (165) 14

Muscus — Nom. bot. (107) 19

Muscus aureus capillaris minor norvegicus, summo caule ad capitulum scutigerus — Splachnum (27) 8, 10

Muscus capillaceus aphyllos, capitulo crasso bivalvi — Buxbaumia (85) 7, 10[as aphyllus]

Muscus capillaris — Herb. Amboin. (57) 27

Muscus coralloides, squamis loricatus — Mat. med. anim. (29) 20

Muscus coronatus norvegicus, pediculo longissimo, umbraculo amplo — Splachnum (27) 8, 10

Muscus cumatilis — Taenia (19) 10; Usum musc. (148) 14

Muscus fruticescens — Herb. Amboin. (57) 27

Muscus nanus, tuberosa radice, foliis juniperinis tenuissime serratis, capitulo magno ovato ventricoso, calyptra tomentosa — Buxbaumia (85) 8, 10

Muscus norvegicus, umbraculo ruberrimo insignitus — Splachnum (27) 8, 9, 11

Muscus rupestris repens virginianus, clavis foliosis erectis quadratis — Pl. rar. Camsch. (30) 6

Muscus zeylanicus arboreus clavatus, foliis crassis rotundis, lycopodii fructu compresso — Acrostichum (10) 9

Mussaenda — Nova pl. gen. 1747 (14) [vi][as Mussenda], 10

Mussaenda arbor indica, floribus in summis ramulis velut in fasciculos dispositis, e quorum medio folium latum singulare flavicans — Nova pl. gen. 1747 (14) 11[as Mussenda]

Mussaenda formosa — Pl. Surin. (177) 6

Mussaenda frondosa — Herb. Amboin. (57) 17

Mussaenda zeylanica, flore rubro, fructu oblongo polyspermo, folio ex florum thyrso prodeunte albo — Nova pl. gen. 1747 (14) 10

Mustela — Lign. colubr. (21) 9ff.; Morb. hyeme (38) 13; Usum hist. nat. (145) 23

Mustela daurica cauda carens — Hist. nat. Rossia (144) 16

Mustela ermina — Ambros. (100) 8

Mustela glauca — Lign. colubr. (21) 9

Mustela seu viverra indis mungutia, lusitanis mungo, batavis muncus — Lign. colubr. (21) 9

Mustela zibellina — Fl. alp. (71) 25

Mutilla acarorum — Pand. fl. Ryb. (165) 14

Mya — Fund. test. (166) 18, 41

Mya pictorum — Fund. test. (166) 41; Esca avium (174) 10

Myagrum — Fl. oecon. (17) 17; Hort. acad. (63) 2; Nom. bot. (107) 15

Myagrum hispanicum — Demonstr. pl. (49) 17

Myagrum holmense — Pan Svec. (26) 28

Myagrum monospermum minor — Fl. Monsp. (74) 30

Myagrum paniculatum — Demonstr. pl. (49) 17; Fl. Monsp. (74) 20; Prodr. fl. Dan. (82) 20

Myagrum perenne — Demonstr. pl. (49) 17; Fl. Monsp. (74) 20; Fl. Belg. (112) 19

Myagrum perfoliatum — Demonstr. pl. (49) 17

Myagrum rugosum — Demonstr. pl. (49) 17

Myagrum sativum — Pan Svec. (26) 28; Herbat. Upsal. (50) 12; Stat. pl. (55) 19; Fl. Angl. (56) 19;

Fl. Monsp. (74) 20; Prodr. fl. Dan. (82) 20; Fl. Belg. (112) 19; Pand. fl. Ryb. (165) 20

Mydas — Amphib. Gyll. (5) 31

Mylabris — Fund. entom. (154) 29, 30, [31, as 30]

Myosotis — Vir. pl. (13) 18; Fl. oecon. (17) 5; Pan Svec. (26) 9

Myosotis apula — Fl. Palaest. (70) 14; Fl. Monsp. (74) 11

Myosotis aquatica — Usum hist. nat. (145) 22

Myosotis arvensis — Pl. rar. Afr. (115) 6

Myosotis caule hirsuto, foliis perangustis glabris, flore calycem excedente — Pl. Mart.-Burs. (6) 17

Myosotis foliis glabris — Pl. Mart.-Burs. (6) 21

Myosotis foliis hirsutis — Pl. Mart.-Burs. (6) 21

Myosotis lappula — Pan Svec. (26) 16; Herbat. Upsal. (50) 20; Stat. pl. (55) 20; Fl. Monsp. (74) 11; Prodr. fl. Dan. (82) 14

Myosotis nana — Fl. alp. (71) 13

Myosotis palustris — Pan Svec. (26) 16; Herbat. Upsal. (50) 18; Fl. Monsp. (74) 11

Myosotis pratensis — Pan Svec. (26) 16

Myosotis scorpioides — Herbat. Upsal. (50) 7; Stat. pl. (55) 21; Fl. Angl. (56) 12; Fl. Monsp. (74) 11; Prodr. fl. Dan. (82) 14; Fl. Jam. (105) 13[as scorpiodes], 25[as scirpioides]; Fl. Belg. (112) 14; Hist. nat. Rossia (144) 28; Fl. Åker. (162) 8; Pand. fl. Ryb. (165) 17

Myosotis scorpioides arvensis — Oves (61) 17

Myosotis scorpioides palustris — Oves (61) 17

Myosotis virginiana — Demonstr. pl. (49) 5

Myosurus — Nect. fl. (122) 11; Fund. fr. (123) 23

Myosurus campestris — Pan Svec. (26) 19

Myosurus minimus — Herbat. Upsal. (50) 10; Stat. pl. (55) 22; Fl. Angl. (56) 14[as Myosuros]; Fl. Monsp. (74) 14; Prodr. fl. Dan. (82) 16; Fl. Belg. (112) 15[as Myosuros]; Fl. Åker. (162) 10; Pand. fl. Ryb. (165) 18

Myrica — Hort. Upsal. (7) 33; Spons. pl. (12) 41; Fl. oecon. (17) 26; Gem. arb. (24) 12; Pl. escul. (35) 25; Fr. Svec. (91) [ii]; Nom. bot. (107) 18; Cimicifuga (173) 8; Ledum (178) 3

Myrica asplenifolia — Specif. Canad. (76) 16

Myrica brabantica — Pan Svec. (26) [37, as 39]

Myrica cerifera — Specif. Canad. (76) 26; Ledum (178) 12

Myrica cordifolia — Fl. Cap. (99) 19

Myrica foliis ternatis dentatis — Pl. rar. Afr. (115) 28

Myrica gale — Gem. arb. (24) 18; Demonstr. pl. (49) 26; Pl. officin. (52) 14; Stat. pl. (55) 14; Fl. Angl. (56) 24; Cervus (60) 8; Prodr. fl. Dan. (82) 25; Fr. Svec. (91) 4, 20; Pl. tinct. (97) 26; Fl. Belg. (112) 23; Pot. theae (142) 7; Rar. Norv. (157) 14; Fl. Åker. (162) 20; Pand. fl. Ryb. (165) 22; Ledum (178) 2

Myrica quercifolia — Fl. Cap. (99) 19

Myrica trifoliata — Pl. rar. Afr. (115) 28

Myriophyllum — Hort. Upsal. (7) 41; Spons. pl. (12) 39, 44; Fl. Belg. (112) 8

Myriophyllum minus — Fl. Angl. (56) 26

Myriophyllum spicatum — Stat. pl. (55) 12; Fl. Angl. (56) 24; Fl. Monsp. (74) 27; Prodr. fl. Dan. (82) 24; Fl. Belg. (112) 22

Myriophyllum verticillatum — Pan Svec. (26) 35; Herbat. Upsal. (50) 10; Fl. Angl. (56) 24; Fl. Monsp. (74) 27; Prodr. fl. Dan. (82) 24; Fl. Belg. (112) 22; Pand. fl. Ryb. (165) 22

Myriophyllum vulgare — Pan Svec. (26) 35

Myrisma — Pl. Surin. (177) 5

Myristica — Vir. pl. (13) 7; Curios. nat. (18) 12; Odor. med. (40) 14; Pl. officin. (52) 12, 13; Herb. Amboin. (57) 8; Inebr. (117) 9; Opobals. (135) 2; Usum hist. nat. (145) 15

Myrmecophaga — Polit. nat. (109) 16

Myrmeleon — Fund. entom. (154) 29, 30

Myrmeleon formicarium — Pand. fl. Ryb. (165) 12

Myrrha — Sapor. med. (31) 18; Nova pl. gen. 1751 (32) 12

Myrsine — Vir. pl. (13) 20; Fl. Cap. (99) 6; Erica (163) 3

Myrsine africana — Fl. Cap. (99) 12

Myrsinites — Euphorbia (36) 3

Myrstiphyllum — Fl. Jam. (105) 27

Myrtillus — Cervus (60) 12, 16

Myrtus — Hort. Upsal. (7) 36; Sapor. med. (31) 15; Herb. Amboin. (57) 11, 12; Fung. melit. (69) 10; Fl. Jam. (105) 9, 26; Nom. bot. (107) 13; Inebr. (117) 13; Obs. mat. med. (171) 6

Myrtus biflora — Pl. Jam. (102) 13; Fl. Jam. (105) 17[as Myrthus]

Myrtus brasiliana — Fl. Jam. (105) 17[as Myrthus]

Myrtus caryophyllata — Pl. officin. (52) 7

Myrtus chytraculia — Pl. Jam. (102) 13; Fl. Jam. (105) 17[as Myrthus]

Myrtus communis — Demonstr. pl. (49) 13; Pl. officin. (52) 13; Fl. Palaest. (70) 20

Myrtus leucadendra — Cent. I. pl. (65) 2

Myrtus leucadendra, baccis sessilibus urceolatis, foliis lanceolatis — Herb. Amboin. (57) 9

Myrtus pimenta — Pl. officin. (52) 15; Fl. Jam. (105) 17[as Myrthus pimento]

Myrtus vulgaris — Gem. arb. (24) 20

Myrtus zuzygium — Pl. Jam. (102) 13; Fl. Jam. (105) 17[as Myrthus]

Mystus altus — Chin. Lagerstr. (64) 26

Mystus corpore ensiformi — Chin. Lagerstr. (64) 26

Mystus corpore ovato — Chin. Lagerstr. (64) 26

Mystus ensiformis — Chin. Lagerstr. (64) 26, 36

Mytilus — Var. cib. (156) 5[as Mutylis]; Fund. test. (166) 10, 18

Myxine — Polit. nat. (109) 12; Hirudo (136) 2

Nabca paliurus athenaei — Demonstr. pl. (49) 6

Naghawalli colubrina zeylanica, periclymeni species, foliis maculatis — Lign. colubr. (21) 14ff.

Naja — Lign. colubr. (21) 6ff.; Rad. senega (23) 5; Fl. Cap. (99) [1]

Naja altera — Mus. Ad.-Frid. (11) 27

Najas marina — Pan Svec. (26) 36; Stat. pl. (55) 12

Nama — Nova pl. gen. 1747 (14) [vi], 11

Nama jamaicensis — Fl. Jam. (105) 14

Napaea — Nova pl. gen. 1751 (32) 10, 30, 48; Pl. hybr. (33) 7

Napaea dioica — Pl. hybr. (33) 27[as Napoea]; Demonstr. pl. (49) 18

Napaea dioica mas — Calend. fl. (72) [17][as diocia]

Napaea dioica scabra — Nova pl. gen. 1751 (32) 30

Napaea hermaphrodita — Demonstr. pl. (49) 18[as hermaphroditica]; Calend. fl. (72) [17][as hermaphrodiaca]

Napaea hermaphrodita glabra — Nova pl. gen. 1751 (32) 30

Napaea monoica — Pl. hybr. (33) 27[as Napoea]

Napus — Vir. pl. (13) 22; Usum hist. nat. (145) 16

Narcissus — Hort. Upsal. (7) 33; Spons. pl. (12) 33, 43, 46, 59; Vir. pl. (13) 20, 24, 31; Gem. arb. (24) 11; Calend. fl. (72) [11]; Fl. Monsp. (74) 7; Nom. bot. (107) 12; Prol. pl. 1760 (114) 13; Nect. fl. (122) 9; Fund. fr. (123) 16

Narcissus albus, magno odoro flore, circulo pallido — Cent. II. pl. (66) 14

Narcissus albus min. — Fl. Monsp. (74) 30

Narcissus jonquilla — Demonstr. pl. (49) 9; Fl. Monsp. (74) 14

Narcissus latifolius 7 — Cent. II. pl. (66) 14

Narcissus latifolius, calyce amplo et aureo, caule striato — Cent. II. pl. (66) 14

Narcissus latifolius maximus, albo flore, calyce brevi tubo — Cent. II. pl. (66) 14

Narcissus latifolius pallidus, calyce amplo, alter — Cent. II. pl. (66) 14

Narcissus latifolius sulphureus, brevi calyce — Cent. II. pl. (66) 14

Narcissus odorus — Cent. II. pl. (66) 14; Fl. Monsp. (74) 14

Narcissus poeticus — Demonstr. pl. (49) 9; Fl. Angl. (56) 14; Calend. fl. (72) [11], [12]; Fl. Monsp. (74) 14; Pl. Alstr. (121) [4]; Hort. cul. (132) 23, 25

Narcissus pseudonarcissus — Demonstr. pl. (49) 9; Fl. Angl. (56) 14; Fl. alp. (71) 15; Calend. fl. (72) [10], [11]; Fl. Monsp. (74) 14; Prodr. fl. Dan. (82) 16; Pl. Alstr. (121) [4]; Hort. cul. (132) 23, 25; Colon. pl. (158) 9

Narcissus spatha uniflora, nectario campanulato petalis dimidio breviore — Cent. II. pl. (66) 14

Narcissus tazetta — Demonstr. pl. (49) 9; Fl. Palaest. (70) 17; Fl. Monsp. (74) 14; Pl. Alstr. (121) [4]

Nardus — Fl. oecon. (17) 2; Fund. agrost. (152) 15, 26, 35

Nardus articulata — Fl. Angl. (56) 10; Fl. Monsp. (74) 9[as articulatus]

Nardus gangitis — Fl. Monsp. (74) 9[as gangeticus]

Nardus pratensis — Pan Svec. (26) 13

Nardus stricta — Herbat. Upsal. (50) 13; Stat. pl. (55) 15; Fl. Angl. (56) 10; Prodr. fl. Dan. (82) 13; Fl. Belg. (112) 12; Fund. agrost. (152) 7; Fl. Åker. (162) 6; Hypericum (186) 14

Nasturtium — Peloria (3) 10; Sapor. med. (31) 19; Odor. med. (40) 15; Cul. mut. (88) 6; Nom. bot. (107) 15; Raphania (126) 14

Nasturtium alpinum tenuissime divisum — Cent. II. pl. (66) 23

Nasturtium aquaticum — Vir. pl. (13) 22, 29; Stat. pl. (55) 13; Var. cib. (156) 18

Nasturtium aquaticum praecox — Fl. Angl. (56) 27[as praecoius]

Nasturtium flore parvissimo — Fl. Monsp. (74) 30

Nasturtium hortense — Scorb. (180) 16

Nasturtium sylvestre — Metam. pl. (67) 15

Nasua — Polit. nat. (109) 15, 17

Natrix — Oecon. nat. (20) 28

Natrix torquata — Amphib. Gyll. (5) 8; Mat. med. anim. (29) 12

Naucoseris — Fund. entom. (154) 30

Nautilus — Chin. Lagerstr. (64) 6; Fund. test. (166) 17, 24, 29, 37

Nautilus beccarii — Fund. test. (166) 37

Nautilus papyraceus — Corallia Balt. (4) 10

Nautilus pompilius — Iter Chin. (161) 8

Neanthe — Fl. Jam. (105) 27

Necydalis — Fund. entom. (154) [31, as 30]

Necydalis minor — Fund. entom. (154) 30; Pand. fl. Ryb. (165) 9

Nelumbo — Chin. Lagerstr. (64) 6

Neottia — Vir. pl. (13) 24

Neottia corallorrhiza — Pan Svec. (26) 34

Neottia nectarii labio bifido lineari — Pl. rar. Camsch. (30) 28

Neottia nidus avis — Pan Svec. (26) 34

Nepa — Fund. entom. (154) 18, 21, 30

Nepenthes — Oecon. nat. (20) 20; Nect. fl. (122) 5

Nepenthes distillatoria — Herb. Amboin. (57) 20

Nepeta — Vir. pl. (13) 29, 35[as Nepetha]; Fl. oecon. (17) 16; Cui bono? (42) 20; Nom. bot. (107) 14; Usum hist. nat. (145) 23; Menthae (153) 5; Marum (175) 10[as Nepetha]

Nepeta cataria — Demonstr. pl. (49) 15; Pl. officin. (52) 14; Stat. pl. (55) 20; Fl. Angl. (56) 18; Fl. Monsp. (74) 19; Prodr. fl. Dan. (82) 20; Fl. Belg. (112) 18; Fl. Åker. (162) 14

Nepeta corymbis geminis pedunculatis axillaribus, foliis cordato-oblongis acuminatis serratis — Pl. hybr. (33) 14

Nepeta floribus obliquis — Anandria (9) 5

Nepeta foliis cordatis obtusis, floribus verticillatis — Cent. II. pl. (66) 20

Nepeta indica — Herb. Amboin. (57) 22

Nepeta italica — Demonstr. pl. (49) 16

Nepeta lophanthus — Hort. Upsal. (7) 34[as lophantus]

Nepeta pannonica — Demonstr. pl. (49) 15; Fl. Palaest. (70) 22

Nepeta pectinata — Fl. Jam. (105) 18

Nepeta scordotis — Cent. II. pl. (66) 20

Nepeta sibirica — Demonstr. pl. (49) 16; Calend. fl. (72) [13]; Hist. nat. Rossia (144) 30

Nepeta tuberosa — Demonstr. pl. (49) 16

Nepeta violacea — Demonstr. pl. (49) 16

Nepeta vulgaris — Pan Svec. (26) 26

Nepetoides — Fund. fr. (123) 22

Nereis — Noctiluca (39) 4, 5; Chin. Lagerstr. (64) 29; Metam. pl. (67) 9

Nereis caerulea — Chin. Lagerstr. (64) 29[as coerulaea]

Nereis noctiluca — Nat. pelagi (84) 9, 15

Nereis phosphorans — Noctiluca (39) 8

Nereis sacculo induta — Chin. Lagerstr. (64) 29, 36

Nerita — Fund. test. (166) 17, 39

Nerita canrena — Fund. test. (166) 39

Nerita histrio — Iter Chin. (161) 8

Nerium — Hort. Upsal. (7) 37; Vir. pl. (13) 31, 34; Gem. arb. (24) 6; Hort. acad. (63) 2; Pand. insect. (93) 12; Aer habit. (106) 20; Nom. bot. (107) 11; Nect. fl. (122) 9

Nerium antidysentericum — Pl. officin. (52) 16

Nerium foliis lanceolatis oppositis, ramis rectis — Cent. II. pl. (66) 12

Nerium oleander — Demonstr. pl. (49) 7; Fl. Palaest. (70) 15

Nerium zeylonicum — Cent. II. pl. (66) 12

Nessatus — Herb. Amboin. (57) 11

Neurada procumbens — Fl. Palaest. (70) 20

Nicotiana — Passifl. (8) [iii]; Vir. pl. (13) 8, 19, 31; Odor. med. (40) 13; Hosp. insect. fl. (43) 12; Vern. arb. (47) 9; Herb. Amboin. (57) 21; Oves (61) 24; Nom. bot. (107) 10; Esca avium (174) 2

Nicotiana fruticosa — Pl. rar. Afr. (115) 6

Nicotiana glutinosa — Demonstr. pl. (49) 6

Nicotiana paniculata — Demonstr. pl. (49) 6

Nicotiana rustica — Demonstr. pl. (49) 6; Fl. Jam. (105) 14

Nicotiana tabacum — Hosp. insect. fl. (43) 16; Demonstr. pl. (49) 6; Pl. officin. (52) 19; Calend. fl. (72) [20]; Hort. cul. (132) 10

Nigella — Hort. Upsal. (7) 34; Spons. pl. (12) 30, 59; Vir. pl. (13) 21, 24; Hort. acad. (63) 3; Metam. pl. (67) 17; Nom. bot. (107) 14; Mors. serp. (119) 2; Nect. fl. (122) 13, 15; Fund. fr. (123) 16, 23

Nigella annua — Demonstr. pl. (49) 15

Nigella arvensis — Fl. Monsp. (74) 18; Opobals. (135) 15

Nigella arvensis cornuta — Spons. pl. (12) 38

Nigella damascena — Fl. Palaest. (70) 22; Calend. fl. (72) [22]; Hort. cul. (132) 23, 25

Nigella flore foliis nudo, pistillis corollam aequantibus — Pl. Mart.-Burs. (6) 10

Nigella sativa — Pl. officin. (52) 14; Fl. Palaest. (70) 21; Opobals. (135) 15

Nintipolonga — Amphib. Gyll. (5) 3

Nintipolonga zeylanica — Mors. serp. (119) 14

Nitraria schoberi — Metam. pl. (67) 13; Hist. nat. Rossia (144) 23

Noctilio — Fund. ornith. (137) 10

Noctiluca — Morb. hyeme (38) 15

Noctiluca marina — Mund. invis. (149) 9

Noctua daurica — Hist. nat. Rossia (144) 16

Notaxis — Fund. entom. (154) 30

Notonecta — Fund. entom. (154) 18, 21, 30

Novella — Herb. Amboin. (57) 10

Novella litorea — Herb. Amboin. (57) 10

Novella nigra — Herb. Amboin. (57) 10

Nugae sylvarum — Herb. Amboin. (57) 19

Numenius — Oecon. nat. (20) 40

Nummularia — Nova pl. gen. 1751 (32) 35, 48; Nom. bot. (107) 10

Nummularia foliis ellipticis carnosis — Nova pl. gen. 1751 (32) 36[as Numularia]

Nummularia foliis orbiculatis hirsutis — Nova pl. gen. 1751 (32) 36[as Numularia]

Nummularia foliis subcordatis — Nova pl. gen. 1751 (32) 36[as Numularia]

Nummularia major — Herb. Amboin. (57) 24

Nummularia minor — Herb. Amboin. (57) 25

Nux americana, foliis alatis bifidis — Lign. Qvas. (128) 7

Nux juglans zeylanica magna bifida, flore puniceo stercus humanum redolente, nucleis ovalibus triplici cortice vestitis oleosis — Nova pl. gen. 1747 (14) 29

Nux juglans zeylanica minor bifida, flore puniceo — Nova pl. gen. 1747 (14) 29

Nux malabarica sulcata mucilaginosa fabacea — Nova pl. gen. 1747 (14) 30

Nux myristica — Herb. Amboin. (57) 8

Nux myristica mas — Herb. Amboin. (57) 8

Nux tacia — Var. cib. (156) 8

Nux zeylanica; folio multifido digitato, flore merdam olente — Nova pl. gen. 1747 (14) 29

Nyctanthes — Hort. Upsal. (7) 37; Passifl. (8) 30; Pl. hybr. (33) 29; Odor. med. (40) 12; Herb. Amboin. (57) 16

Nyctanthes sambac — Herb. Amboin. (57) 19

Nyctanthes scandens — Gem. arb. (24) 15

Nyctanthes undulata — Fl. Palaest. (70) 11

Nymphaea — Spons. pl. (12) 44; Vir. pl. (13) 21, 29; Fl. oecon. (17) 14; Oecon. nat. (20) 19; Pl. escul. (35) 3; Morb. hyeme (38) 8; Cui bono? (42) 18[as Nymphea]; Hosp. insect. fl. (43) 40; Mirac. insect. (45) 11; Noxa insect. (46) 24; Cul. mut. (88) 6; Pand. insect. (93) 16; Nom. bot. (107) 14; Fl. Belg. (112) 8; Siren. lacert. (146) 7

Nymphaea alba — Hort. Upsal. (7) [42]; Pan Svec. (26) 25; Hosp. insect. fl. (43) 26; Stat. pl. (55) 12; Fl. Angl. (56) 17; Calend. fl. (72) [12]; Fl. Monsp. (74) 18; Prodr. fl. Dan. (82) 19; Fl. Belg. (112) 18; Fl. Åker. (162) 13

Nymphaea calyce magno quinquefido — Pl. hybr. (33) 27

Nymphaea lotus — Fl. Palaest. (70) 21; Fl. Jam. (105) 17, 25

Nymphaea lutea — Hort. Upsal. (7) [42]; Pan Svec. (26) 25; Hosp. insect. fl. (43) 26; Herbat. Upsal. (50) 14; Pl. officin. (52) 14; Stat. pl. (55) 12; Fl. Angl. (56) 17; Calend. fl. (72) [9], [12][as Nymhaea]; Fl. Monsp. (74) 18; Prodr. fl. Dan. (82) 19; Fl. Belg. (112) 18; Fl. Åker. (162) 13; Esca avium (174) 4

Nymphaea major — Herb. Amboin. (57) 28

Nymphaea minor — Herb. Amboin. (57) 28

Nymphaea nelumbo — Herb. Amboin. (57) 28; Transm. frum. (87) 11; Fl. Jam. (105) 17, 25; Fr. escul. (127) 22; Prol. pl. 1763 (130) 16

Nypa — Herb. Amboin. (57) 6

Nyssa — Nova pl. gen. 1751 (32) 10

Obolaria — Nova pl. gen. 1751 (32) 10; Aphyteia (185) 9

Ochna — Pl. escul. (35) 4; Lign. Qvas. (128) 7

Ochna jabotapita — Herb. Amboin. (57) 11; Fl. Cap. (99) 15[as japotapita]; Fr. escul. (127) 11

Ocimum — Vir. pl. (13) 12, 34; Sapor. med. (31) 12; Herb. Amboin. (57) 21; Acetaria (77) 10; Nom. bot. (107) 15; Menthae (153) 7

Ocimum americanum — Demonstr. pl. (49) 16; Cent. I. pl. (65) 15

Ocimum basilicum — Demonstr. pl. (49) 16; Pl. officin. (52) 5[as basilica]; Fl. Palaest. (70) 23; Fl. Jam. (105) 24; Hort. cul. (132) 15

Ocimum foliis sublanceolatis acuminatis serratis, racemis rotundis, caule subherbaceo — Cent. I. pl. (65) 15

Ocimum frutescens — Demonstr. pl. (49) 16; Herb. Amboin. (57) 22; Hort. acad. (63) 19[as fruticosum]; Somn. pl. (68) 10[as fruticosum]

Ocimum gratissimum — Demonstr. pl. (49) 16; Herb. Amboin. (57) 21

Ocimum minimum — Demonstr. pl. (49) 16

Ocimum tenuiflorum — Herb. Amboin. (57) 21

Oculus astaci — Herb. Amboin. (57) 25

Ocymastrum flore viridi — Pl. Mart.-Burs. (6) 16

Oenanthe — Hort. Upsal. (7) 36; Fl. oecon. (17) 7[as Oenante]

Oenanthe aquatica — Pan Svec. (26) 19

Oenanthe crocata — Stat. pl. (55) 13[as Oenante]; Fl. Angl. (56) 13[as Oenante]; Prodr. fl. Dan. (82) 16

Oenanthe fistulosa — Stat. pl. (55) 13[as Oenante]; Fl. Angl. (56) 13[as Oenante]; Fl. Monsp. (74) 13; Prodr. fl. Dan. (82) 16; Fl. Belg. (112) 15

Oenanthe foliis omnibus multifidis obtusis subaequalibus — Pl. Mart.-Burs. (6) 11[as Oenante]

Oenanthe globulosa — Fl. Monsp. (74) 13

Oenanthe pimpinelloides — Fl. Angl. (56) 13[as Oenante]; Fl. Monsp. (74) 13

Oenanthe semine atriplicis — Fl. Monsp. (74) 30

Oenanthe succo crocante — Pan Svec. (26) 19

Oenothera — Hort. Upsal. (7) 34; Nova pl. gen. 1751 (32) 9, 47; Vern. arb. (47) 9; Nect. fl. (122) 6

Oenothera biennis — Demonstr. pl. (49) 11; Calend. fl. (72) [15], [22]; Fl. Monsp. (74) 15; Fl. Belg. (112) 16; Pl. Alstr. (121) 5; Colon. pl. (158) 10

Oenothera hirta — Fl. Jam. (105) 15

Oenothera mollissima — Demonstr. pl. (49) 11[as molissima]; Somn. pl. (68) 15[as mollis]; Calend. fl. (72) [16][as mollis]

Oenothera parviflora — Fl. Jam. (105) 15

Oestrus — Oecon. nat. (20) 29; Mirac. insect. (45) 11, 20; Noxa insect. (46) 27, 28, 29; Cervus (60) 5ff.; Oves (61) 22; Pand. insect. (93) 7, 8; Polit. nat. (109) 12, 21; Usum hist. nat. (145) 21

Oestrus bovis — Pand. fl. Ryb. (165) 14

Oestrus nasalis — Usum hist. nat. (145) 23

Oestrus ovis — Usum hist. nat. (145) 22

Oestrus rangiferinus — Cervus (60) 13; Usum hist. nat. (145) 22

Olax — Nova pl. gen. 1747 (14) [vi], 3; Nect. fl. (122) 9

Oldenlandia — Pl. Jam. (102) 8

Oldenlandia corymbosa — Fl. Jam. (105) 13

Olea — Vir. pl. (13) 32; Fl. Monsp. (74) 7; Acetaria (77) 8; Nom. bot. (107) 9; Usum hist. nat. (145) 29

Olea cajeput — Obs. mat. med. (171) 5

Olea capensis — Fl. Cap. (99) 11

Olea europaea — Pl. officin. (52) 14; Fl. Palaest. (70) 11; Fl. Monsp. (74) 8; Fl. Jam. (105) 24; Fr. escul. (127) 13

Olea sylvestris malabarica, fructu dulci — Nova pl. gen. 1747 (14) 19

Oliva — Vir. pl. (13) 33; Sapor. med. (31) 15

Olus album — Herb. Amboin. (57) 8

Olus album insulare — Herb. Amboin. (57) 8

Olus calappoides — Herb. Amboin. (57) 6

Olus catappanicum — Herb. Amboin. (57) 14

Olus crepitans — Herb. Amboin. (57) 24

Olus crepitans mas — Herb. Amboin. (57) 25

Olus crudum — Herb. Amboin. (57) 19

Olus palustre — Herb. Amboin. (57) 28

Olus sanguinis — Herb. Amboin. (57) 25

Olus squillarum — Herb. Amboin. (57) 26

Olus vagum — Herb. Amboin. (57) 24

Olus vespertilionis — Herb. Amboin. (57) 24

Olyra — Fund. agrost. (152) 28, 37

Olyra latifolia — Pl. Jam. (102) 26; Fl. Jam. (105) 21

Omphalea — Fl. Jam. (105) 26

Omphalea diandra — Fl. Jam. (105) 21

Omphalea triandra — Pl. Jam. (102) 26; Fl. Jam.
   (105) 21

Onagra — Nova pl. gen. 1751 (32) 9

Oniscus — Noxa insect. (46) 21, 30; Migr. avium
   (79) 32; Nat. pelagi (84) 10; Meloe (124) 10; Lepra
   (140) 10; Fund. entom. (154) 19, 24

Oniscus asellus — Pand. fl. Ryb. (165) 16

Oniscus asilus — Iter Chin. (161) 12, 13

Oniscus cauda obtusa bifurca — Mat. med. anim.
   (29) 18

Oniscus cauda quadridentata — Cent. insect. (129) 32

Oniscus linearis — Cent. insect. (129) 32

Onobrychis — Usum hist. nat. (145) 18

Onobrychis minor — Fl. Monsp. (74) 30

Onobrychis tertia purpurea — Rad. senega (23) 14

Onoclea — Nova pl. gen. 1751 (32) 10, [13, as 15],
   34, 48

Ononis — Fl. oecon. (17) 19; Pl. Jam. (102) 20;
   Nom. bot. (107) 16

Ononis alopecuroides — Demonstr. pl. (49) 19

Ononis capensis — Pl. rar. Afr. (115) 16

Ononis cernua — Pl. rar. Afr. (115) 16

Ononis fruticosa — Pl. rar. Afr. (115) 6

Ononis inermis — Pan Svec. (26) 31

Ononis minutissima — Demonstr. pl. (49) 19; Fl.
   Palaest. (70) 25; Fl. Monsp. (74) 22

Ononis mitis — Fl. Belg. (112) 20

Ononis natrix — Fl. Palaest. (70) 25; Fl. Monsp. (74)
   22

Ononis ornithopodioides — Demonstr. pl. (49) 19

Ononis pedunculis unifloris seta terminatis — Pl.
   Mart.-Burs. (6) 27

Ononis pumila — Fl. alp. (71) 20

Ononis racemis pedunculatis longis, foliis ternatis
   suborbiculatis — Pl. rar. Afr. (115) 16

Ononis repens — Fl. Angl. (56) 20

Ononis spicis sessilibus, leguminibus nutantibus
   pilosis linearibus — Pl. rar. Afr. (115) 16

Ononis spinosa — Pan Svec. (26) 31; Demonstr. pl.
   (49) 19; Pl. officin. (52) 14; Stat. pl. (55) 18; Fl.
   Angl. (56) 20; Calend. fl. (72) [15]; Fl. Monsp.
   (74) 22; Prodr. fl. Dan. (82) 21; Fl. Belg. (112) 20;
   Usum hist. nat. (145) 10; Fl. Åker. (162) 16

Ononis viscosa — Demonstr. pl. (49) 19; Fl. Palaest.
   (70) 25; Fl. Monsp. (74) 22

Onopordum — Fl. oecon. (17) 19; Oecon. nat. (20)
   22[as Onopordon]; Pan Svec. (26) 32[as
   Onopordon]; Pl. escul. (35) 23

Onopordum acanthium — Demonstr. pl. (49) 22[as
   Onopordon]; Herbat. Upsal. (50) 17; Stat. pl. (55)
   20; Fl. Angl. (56) 22; Fl. Monsp. (74) 25; Prodr. fl.
   Dan. (82) 23[as Onopordon]; Fl. Belg. (112) 21[as
   Onopordon]; Mac. olit. (113) 16[as Onopordon]

Onopordum illyricum — Fl. Monsp. (74) 25

Ophioglossum — Acrostichum (10) 3, 7[as
   Ophiglossum and Opioglossum], 8

Ophioglossum flexuosum — Herb. Amboin. (57) 26

Ophioglossum laciniatum — Herb. Amboin. (57) 28

Ophioglossum palmatum — Fl. Jam. (105) 22

Ophioglossum pendulum — Cent. I. pl. (65) 2

Ophioglossum pendulum, foliis linearibus longissimis
   subindivisis — Herb. Amboin. (57) 27

Ophioglossum reticulatum — Fl. Jam. (105) 22

Ophioglossum sarmentosum — Fl. Jam. (105) 22

Ophioglossum scandens — Herb. Amboin. (57) 26;
   Pl. Surin. (177) 17

Ophioglossum simplex — Herb. Amboin. (57) 28

Ophioglossum sylvaticum — Pan Svec. (26) [37, as
   39]

Ophioglossum vulgatum — Herbat. Upsal. (50) 13;
   Stat. pl. (55) 23; Fl. Angl. (56) 25; Herb. Amboin.
   (57) 28; Fl. Monsp. (74) 29; Prodr. fl. Dan. (82) 25;
   Fl. Belg. (112) 23; Fl. Åker. (162) 20

Ophiorrhiza — Lign. colubr. (21) 16ff.[as
   Ophiorhiza]; Mors. serp. (119) 18

Ophiorrhiza asiatica — Cui bono? (42) 23

Ophiorrhiza mungos — Pl. officin. (52) 8[as
   Ophioriza], 18[as Ophioriza]; Mors. serp. (119) 17

Ophioxylon — Lign. colubr. (21) 16; Nova pl. gen.
   1751 (32) 45, 48

Ophioxylon foliis quaternis — Lign. colubr. (21) 22

Ophioxylon serpentinum — Herb. Amboin. (57) 9;
   Febr. interm. (167) 36

Ophrys — Vir. pl. (13) 24; Fl. Angl. (56) 6

Ophrys alpina — Stat. pl. (55) 16; Fl. alp. (71) 23

Ophrys anthropophora — Fl. Angl. (56) 23[as
   antropophora]; Fl. Monsp. (74) 27

Ophrys arachnites — Fl. Angl. (56) 23

Ophrys bulbis ---, nectarii labio reniformi latissimo
   emarginato — Pl. rar. Afr. (115) 28

Ophrys bulbis fibrosis, caule folioso, floribus
   tripetalis: galea ventricosa magna, labello cruciato
   — Pl. rar. Afr. (115) 27

Ophrys bulbis indivisis, corollis tripetalis: alis
   emarginatis, labello trifido: lateralibus circumflexis
   — Pl. rar. Afr. (115) 27

Ophrys caffra — Pl. rar. Afr. (115) 28

Ophrys camtschatea — Hist. nat. Rossia (144) 33[as
   camtschataea]

Ophrys catholica — Pl. rar. Afr. (115) 27

Ophrys circumflexa — Pl. rar. Afr. (115) 27

Ophrys corallorhiza — Herbat. Upsal. (50) 20; Stat. pl. (55) 15

Ophrys cordata — Fl. Angl. (56) 23; Fl. Belg. (112) 22; Hist. nat. Rossia (144) 33

Ophrys insectifera — Fl. Angl. (56) 23; Fl. Monsp. (74) 27

Ophrys insectifera myodes — Calend. fl. (72) [13]

Ophrys lilifolia — Fl. Angl. (56) 23

Ophrys loeselii — Stat. pl. (55) 15

Ophrys major — Pan Svec. (26) 34

Ophrys minima — Betula (1) 12

Ophrys minor — Pan Svec. (26) 34; Fl. Angl. (56) 28

Ophrys monorchis — Herbat. Upsal. (50) 18; Stat. pl. (55) 14[as monochris]; Fl. Angl. (56) 23; Prodr. fl. Dan. (82) 24

Ophrys myoides — Demonstr. pl. (49) 24

Ophrys nidus — Herbat. Upsal. (50) 9

Ophrys nidus avis — Stat. pl. (55) 17; Fl. Angl. (56) 23; Fl. Monsp. (74) 27; Prodr. fl. Dan. (82) 24

Ophrys ovata — Demonstr. pl. (49) 24; Fl. Angl. (56) 23; Prodr. fl. Dan. (82) 24; Fl. Belg. (112) 22; Hist. nat. Rossia (144) 33; Pand. fl. Ryb. (165) 22

Ophrys paludosa — Demonstr. pl. (49) 24; Herbat. Upsal. (50) 20; Stat. pl. (55) 15

Ophrys spiralis — Fl. Angl. (56) 23; Fl. Monsp. (74) 27

Ophrys zeelandica — Fl. Belg. (112) 22

Opobalsamum — Opobals. (135) 2ff.

Opossum — Mus. Ad.-Frid. (11) 2

Opulus — Spons. pl. (12) 59; Vir. pl. (13) 27; Vern. arb. (47) 10; Nom. bot. (107) 11; Nect. fl. (122) 5

Opulus palustris — Gem. arb. (24) 20; Pan Svec. (26) 19

Opuntia — Spons. pl. (12) 56; Vir. pl. (13) 8

Opuntia americana minima flagelliformis — Hort. Upsal. (7) 38

Orbis cauda productiore, dorso levi, ventre spinoso — Mus. Ad.-Frid. (11) 32

Orbis echinatus — Hort. Upsal. (7) 43

Orbis lagocephalus — Mus. Ad.-Frid. (11) 32

Orbis levis oblongus, cinereis et fuscis maculis notatus — Mus. Ad.-Frid. (11) 31

Orbis oblongus testudinis capite — Mus. Ad.-Frid. (11) 31

Orchidi affinis aquatica verna exigua — Nova pl. gen. 1751 (32) 23

Orchidi affinis flore luteo — Pl. rar. Afr. (115) 27

Orchidion — Nova pl. gen. 1751 (32) 12, 23

Orchis — Peloria (3) 10; Spons. pl. (12) 32; Vir. pl. (13) 24, 35; Odor. med. (40) 13; Herb. Amboin. (57) 27; Specif. Canad. (76) 11; Nom. bot. (107) 17; Nect. fl. (122) 12

Orchis abortiva — Fl. Angl. (56) 23; Fl. Monsp. (74) 26

Orchis barba carens, flore luteo viridi — Pl. rar. Afr. (115) 28

Orchis bicornis — Pl. rar. Afr. (115) 26

Orchis bifolia — Pan Svec. (26) 34; Herbat. Upsal. (50) 6; Pl. officin. (52) 14, 17; Stat. pl. (55) 18; Fl. Angl. (56) 23; Fl. Monsp. (74) 26; Prodr. fl. Dan. (82) 24; Fl. Belg. (112) 21; Fl. Åker. (162) 18; Pand. fl. Ryb. (165) 22

Orchis bulbis indivisis, corollae galea bicalcarata, labello quinquepartito — Pl. rar. Afr. (115) 26[as palea]

Orchis bulbis indivisis, corollae galea unicalcarata alis patentibus, labello minimo subovato — Pl. rar. Afr. (115) 27

Orchis bulbis indivisis, nectarii labello imbricato, petalis occultatis filiformibus, scapo flexuoso — Pl. rar. Afr. (115) 26

Orchis bulbis indivisis, nectarii labello multipartito-lineari, folio amplexicauli cordato — Pl. rar. Afr. (115) 26

Orchis burmanniana — Pl. rar. Afr. (115) 26

Orchis calcaribus oblongis — Pan Svec. (26) 34

Orchis conopsea — Fl. Angl. (56) 23; Fl. Monsp. (74) 26; Prodr. fl. Dan. (82) 24; Fl. Belg. (112) 21; Fl. Åker. (162) 18

Orchis coriophora — Fl. Monsp. (74) 26

Orchis cornuta — Pl. rar. Afr. (115) 27

Orchis cubitalis — Herb. Amboin. (57) 27

Orchis cucullata — Hist. nat. Rossia (144) 33

Orchis flexuosa — Pl. rar. Afr. (115) 26

Orchis fuscescens — Hist. nat. Rossia (144) 33

Orchis habenaria — Pl. Jam. (102) 25; Fl. Jam. (105) 20

Orchis hians — Pan Svec. (26) 34

Orchis latifolia — Herbat. Upsal. (50) 18; Fl. Angl. (56) 23; Calend. fl. (72) [11]; Prodr. fl. Dan. (82) 24; Fl. Belg. (112) 21

Orchis lutea, caule geniculato — Pl. rar. Afr. (115) 26

Orchis maculata — Pan Svec. (26) 34; Fl. Angl. (56) 23; Calend. fl. (72) [12]; Fl. Monsp. (74) 26; Prodr. fl. Dan. (82) 24; Fl. Belg. (112) 22; Fl. Åker. (162) 18; Pand. fl. Ryb. (165) 22

Orchis major — Herb. Amboin. (57) 27

Orchis mascula — Prodr. fl. Dan. (82) 24; Fl. Belg. (112) 21

Orchis militaris — Demonstr. pl. (49) 24; Fl. Angl. (56) 23; Fl. Monsp. (74) 26; Prodr. fl. Dan. (82) 24; Fl. Belg. (112) 21

Orchis minor — Herb. Amboin. (57) 27

Orchis morio — Pan Svec. (26) 34; Fl. Angl. (56) 23; Fl. Monsp. (74) 26; Prodr. fl. Dan. (82) 24; Fl. Belg. (112) 21

Orchis obscure purpurea — Fl. Angl. (56) 28

Orchis odoratissima — Fl. Monsp. (74) 26

Orchis pusilla alba — Fl. Angl. (56) 28

Orchis pyramidalis — Fl. Angl. (56) 23; Fl. Monsp. (74) 26[as pyramidata]

Orchis rubra — Fl. Angl. (56) 28

Orchis sambucina — Pan Svec. (26) 34; Pand. fl. Ryb. (165) 22

Orchis sancta — Fl. Palaest. (70) 29

Orchis speciosa — Fl. Angl. (56) 28

Orchis spicornis — Nect. fl. (122) 12

Orchis strateumatica — Herb. Amboin. (57) 27

Orchis susannae — Herb. Amboin. (57) 22

Orchis ustulata — Pan Svec. (26) 34; Demonstr. pl. (49) 24; Fl. Angl. (56) 23; Fl. Monsp. (74) 26; Rar. Norv. (157) 11

Origanum — Vir. pl. (13) 29, 34; Fl. oecon. (17) 16; Pl. escul. (35) 19, 29; Nom. bot. (107) 15

Origanum aegyptiacum — Fl. Palaest. (70) 23

Origanum creticum — Pl. officin. (52) 14; Fl. Palaest. (70) 23; Fl. Monsp. (74) 19

Origanum dictamnus — Pl. officin. (52) 9

Origanum foliis ovatis obtusis scabris integerrimis, spicis confertis compactis glabris — Pl. Mart.-Burs. (6) 19

Origanum indicum — Fl. Palaest. (70) 23

Origanum majorana — Demonstr. pl. (49) 16; Pl. officin. (52) 12; Fl. Palaest. (70) 23; Fl. Jam. (105) 24; Hort. cul. (132) 15

Origanum maru — Fl. Palaest. (70) 23

Origanum monspeliense pulchrum — Pl. Mart.-Burs. (6) 19

Origanum onites — Fl. Angl. (56) 18

Origanum vulgare — Pan Svec. (26) 26; Demonstr. pl. (49) 16; Herbat. Upsal. (50) 8; Pl. officin. (52) 14; Stat. pl. (55) 23; Fl. Angl. (56) 18; Calend. fl. (72) [16]; Fl. Monsp. (74) 19; Prodr. fl. Dan. (82) 20; Pl. tinct. (97) 20; Fl. Belg. (112) 18; Pot. theae (142) 8; Pand. fl. Ryb. (165) 20

Ornithogali lactei species major — Cent. II. pl. (66) 15

Ornithogalum — Hort. Upsal. (7) 33; Fl. oecon. (17) 8; Gem. arb. (24) 5; Fl. Monsp. (74) 7; Pl. Jam. (102) 11; Nom. bot. (107) 12; Prol. pl. 1760 (114) 8, 10, 14; Pl. rar. Afr. (115) 4[as Ornitogalum]

Ornithogalum bifolium germanicum, flore exalbido — Pl. Mart.-Burs. (6) 5

Ornithogalum canadense — Fl. Cap. (99) 9, 13

Ornithogalum capense — Fl. Cap. (99) 13

Ornithogalum comosum — Cent. II. pl. (66) 15

Ornithogalum luteum — Herbat. Upsal. (50) 10; Stat. pl. (55) 17; Fl. Angl. (56) 14; Calend. fl. (72) [9]; Prodr. fl. Dan. (82) 16; Fl. Belg. (112) 15; Fl. Åker. (162) 10; Pand. fl. Ryb. (165) 18; Esca avium (174) 11

Ornithogalum majus — Pan Svec. (26) 20

Ornithogalum majus spicatum, flore albo — Cent. II. pl. (66) 15

Ornithogalum minimum — Herbat. Upsal. (50) 10; Stat. pl. (55) 17; Fl. Monsp. (74) 14; Prodr. fl. Dan. (82) 16; Fl. Belg. (112) 15; Pand. fl. Ryb. (165) 18

Ornithogalum minus — Pan Svec. (26) 20

Ornithogalum narbonense — Cent. II. pl. (66) 15; Fl. Monsp. (74) 14

Ornithogalum nutans — Demonstr. pl. (49) 10; Hort. cul. (132) 24

Ornithogalum pyrenaicum — Demonstr. pl. (49) 10; Fl. Angl. (56) 14; Fl. alp. (71) 15; Calend. fl. (72) [14][as Ornitogalum]; Fl. Monsp. (74) 14

Ornithogalum racemo brevissimo, bracteis lanceolatis longitudine florum, petalis obtusis, filamentis subulatis — Cent. II. pl. (66) 15

Ornithogalum racemo oblongo, filamentis lanceolatis membranaceis, pedunculis floribusque patentibus — Cent. II. pl. (66) 15

Ornithogalum spicatum seu comosum, flore lacteo — Cent. II. pl. (66) 15

Ornithogalum spicis florum longissimis ramosis — Pl. rar. Camsch. (30) 16

Ornithogalum umbellatum — Demonstr. pl. (49) 10; Fl. Angl. (56) 14; Fl. Palaest. (70) 17; Calend. fl. (72) [12]; Fl. Monsp. (74) 14; Fl. Belg. (112) 9[as Ornitogalum], 15; Hort. cul. (132) 24

Ornithopus — Hort. Upsal. (7) 34

Ornithopus compressus — Fl. Monsp. (74) 23

Ornithopus perpusillus — Fl. Angl. (56) 21[as pusillus]; Fl. Monsp. (74) 23; Prodr. fl. Dan. (82) 22; Fl. Belg. (112) 9[as pusillus], 20[as pusillus]; Pl. rar. Afr. (115) 6

Ornithopus scorpioides — Fl. Monsp. (74) 23

Ornithopus tetraphyllus — Pl. Jam. (102) 19; Fl. Jam. (105) 19

Orobanche — Fl. oecon. (17) 16; Nova pl. gen. 1751 (32) 12; Fung. melit. (69) 3, 4, 6; Nom. bot. (107) 15; Aphyteia (185) 9

Orobanche alandica — Pan Svec. (26) 27

Orobanche laevis — Fl. Palaest. (70) 23; Fl. Monsp. (74) 20

Orobanche major — Fl. Angl. (56) 19; Fl. Monsp. (74) 20; Fl. Belg. (112) 19

Orobanche ramosa — Fl. Angl. (56) 19; Fl. Monsp. (74) 20; Fl. Cap. (99) 16; Fl. Belg. (112) 19

Orobus — Fl. oecon. (17) 18; Pl. escul. (35) 27, 28; Cui bono? (42) 20

Orobus angustifolius — Hist. nat. Rossia (144) 31

Orobus caulibus decumbentibus hirsutis ramosis — Cent. I. pl. (65) 23

Orobus lathyroides — Demonstr. pl. (49) 20; Hist. nat. Rossia (144) 23[as latyroides], 31

Orobus luteus — Fl. alp. (71) 21; Hist. nat. Rossia (144) 31

Orobus niger — Pan Svec. (26) 30; Pl. escul. (35) 21; Demonstr. pl. (49) 20; Herbat. Upsal. (50) 9; Stat. pl. (55) 22; Fl. Angl. (56) 6; Calend. fl. (72) [16]; Fl. Monsp. (74) 22; Pl. tinct. (97) 10; Fl. Åker. (162) 16; Esca avium (174) 13

Orobus pyrenaicus — Fl. alp. (71) 20; Fl. Monsp. (74) 22

Orobus sibiricus — Calend. fl. (72) [13]

Orobus sylvaticus — Fl. Angl. (56) 21; Cent. I. pl. (65) 23; Fl. Monsp. (74) 22

Orobus sylvaticus nostras — Pl. Mart.-Burs. (6) 26; Cent. I. pl. (65) 23

Orobus tuberosus — Pan Svec. (26) 30; Pl. escul. (35) 20; Herbat. Upsal. (50) 7; Stat. pl. (55) 18; Fl. Angl. (56) 21; Fl. Monsp. (74) 22; Fl. Åker. (162) 16; Pand. fl. Ryb. (165) 21; Esca avium (174) 13

Orobus varius — Demonstr. pl. (49) 20

Orobus vernus — Pan Svec. (26) 30; Vern. arb. (47) 8; Herbat. Upsal. (50) 7; Stat. pl. (55) 17; Fl. Angl. (56) 6; Fl. Monsp. (74) 22; Prodr. fl. Dan. (82) 21; Fl. Åker. (162) 16

Orobus virginianus, foliis fulva lanugine incanis foliorum nervo in spinam abeunte — Nova pl. gen. 1751 (32) 32

Orontium — Nova pl. gen. 1751 (32) 12, 26, 27, 48; Metam. pl. (67) 14

Orphus — Mus. Ad.-Frid. (11) 36

Ortega hispanica — Demonstr. pl. (49) 2

Orthocera — Nat. pelagi (84) 8

Orthoceros — Corallia Balt. (4) 10

Orvala garganica — Fl. alp. (71) 19

Oryza — Oecon. nat. (20) 40; Pl. escul. (35) 5; Herb. Amboin. (57) 20; Hort. acad. (63) 2; Migr. avium (79) 15, 16; Pane diaet. (83) 19; Instr. peregr. (96) 10; Nom. bot. (107) 12; Cent. insect. (129) 12; Fund. agrost. (152) 5, 15, 16, 27, 36; Colon. pl. (158) 12

Oryza sativa — Demonstr. pl. (49) 10; Pl. officin. (52) 14; Fl. Cap. (99) 13; Fl. Jam. (105) 15; Fr. escul. (127) 19; Iter Chin. (161) 9

Osmerus eperlanus — Calend. fl. (72) [9]

Osmites asteriscoides — Pl. rar. Afr. (115) 24

Osmites bellidiastrum — Pl. rar. Afr. (115) 24

Osmites camphorina — Pl. rar. Afr. (115) 24

Osmites foliis lanceolatis punctatis, calycibus foliosis — Pl. rar. Afr. (115) 24

Osmites foliis lanceolatis subserratis — Pl. rar. Afr. (115) 24

Osmites foliis linearibus tomentosis, calycibus scariosis — Pl. rar. Afr. (115) 24

Osmunda — Acrostichum (10) 3, 7, 8; Herb. Amboin. (57) 26

Osmunda crispa — Fl. Monsp. (74) 29

Osmunda florida — Pan Svec. (26) [37, as 39]

Osmunda fronde pinnatifida caulina, fructificationibus spicatis — Rad. senega (23) 12

Osmunda frondibus pinnatis, foliolis superioribus basi coadunatis, omnibus lanceolatis pinnato subulatis — Nova pl. gen. 1751 (32) 34

Osmunda hirsuta — Fl. Jam. (105) 22

Osmunda lunaria — Pan Svec. (26) [37, as 39]; Herbat. Upsal. (50) 10; Stat. pl. (55) 18; Fl. Angl. (56) 25; Fl. Palaest. (70) 32; Fl. Monsp. (74) 29; Prodr. fl. Dan. (82) 25; Fl. Belg. (112) 23; Prol. pl.

1763 (130) 18; Fl. Åker. (162) 20; Pand. fl. Ryb. (165) 23

Osmunda regalis — Stat. pl. (55) 13; Fl. Angl. (56) 25; Fl. Monsp. (74) 29; Prodr. fl. Dan. (82) 25; Fl. Belg. (112) 23

Osmunda spicant — Fl. Angl. (56) 25; Fl. Monsp. (74) 29; Prodr. fl. Dan. (82) 25; Fl. Belg. (112) 23; Rar. Norv. (157) 11

Osmunda struthiopteris — Pan Svec. (26) [37, as 39]; Stat. pl. (55) 17[as struthioptheris]; Prodr. fl. Dan. (82) 25; Rar. Norv. (157) 11; Pand. fl. Ryb. (165) 22, 23

Osmunda zeylanica — Herb. Amboin. (57) 28

Osteospermum — Hort. Upsal. (7) 36; Fl. Cap. (99) 6; Pl. rar. Afr. (115) 5; Fund. fr. (123) 17

Osteospermum ilicifolium — Fl. Cap. (99) 18

Osteospermum moniliferum — Demonstr. pl. (49) 24; Fl. Cap. (99) 18

Osteospermum pisiferum — Fl. Cap. (99) 18

Osteospermum polygaloides — Fl. Cap. (99) 18

Osteospermum spinosum — Fl. Cap. (99) 18

Osteospermum uvedalia — Demonstr. pl. (49) 24

Ostracion — Pand. insect. (93) 3

Ostracion cathetoplateo-oblongus, ventre tantum aculeato et subrotundo — Mus. Ad.-Frid. (11) 31

Ostracion conico-oblongus; aculeis undique longis tereti formibus imprimis in lateribus — Mus. Ad.-Frid. (11) 32

Ostracion hispidus — Chin. Lagerstr. (64) 22

Ostracion oblongus glaber, capite longo, corpore figuris variis ornato — Mus. Ad.-Frid. (11) 31

Ostracion tetraodon, ventricosus, corpore toto muricato — Chin. Lagerstr. (64) 22

Ostracion ventricosus — Chin. Lagerstr. (64) 22

Ostrea — Mat. med. anim. (29) 19; Instr. peregr. (96) 11; Var. cib. (156) 5; Fund. test. (166) 9, 10, 18, 30, 33, 40

Ostrea fornicata — Iter Chin. (161) 8

Ostrea nodosa — Iter Chin. (161) 8

Ostrea pallium — Iter Chin. (161) 8; Fund. test. (166) 40

Ostrea tarentina — Var. cib. (156) 8

Ostrea valvata — Iter Chin. (161) 8

Osyris — Peloria (3) 7; Fl. Monsp. (74) 7

Osyris alba — Fl. Palaest. (70) 31; Fl. Monsp. (74) 28

Osyris linaria — Peloria (3) 7

Osyris linaria seu urinaria — Peloria (3) 7

Osyris major — Peloria (3) 7

Osyris urinaria — Peloria (3) 7

Othonna — Anandria (9) 5; Cui bono? (42) 20; Fl. Cap. (99) 7; Fund. fr. (123) 17, 18

Othonna abrotanifolia — Fl. Cap. (99) 18

Othonna bulbosa — Fl. Cap. (99) 18; Pl. rar. Afr. (115) 5

Othonna caule fruticoso, foliis linearibus confertis, pedunculis unifloris — Pl. rar. Afr. (115) 25

Othonna cheirifolia — Fl. Cap. (99) 18

Othonna cineraria — Demonstr. pl. (49) 24

Othonna coronopifolia — Fl. Cap. (99) 18

Othonna cymbalarifolia — Pl. rar. Afr. (115) 24

Othonna dentata — Fl. Cap. (99) 18

Othonna foliis lyratis: impari reniformi dentato; caulinis summis amplexicaulibus lobatis integris — Pl. rar. Afr. (115) 24

Othonna geifolia — Fl. Cap. (99) 18

Othonna helenitis — Fl. Monsp. (74) 26[as Othenna helenites]; Hist. nat. Rossia (144) 33[as Otthonna]

Othonna integrifolia — Fl. Angl. (56) 23; Fl. alp. (71) 22; Hist. nat. Rossia (144) 33[as Otthonna]

Othonna linifolia — Pl. rar. Afr. (115) 25

Othonna maritima — Fl. Monsp. (74) 26[as Othenna]

Othonna palustris — Stat. pl. (55) 13; Fl. Angl. (56) 23; Prodr. fl. Dan. (82) 23; Fl. Belg. (112) 21; Hist. nat. Rossia (144) 33[as Otthonna]

Othonna pectinata — Fl. Cap. (99) 18

Othonna rigens — Pl. rar. Afr. (115) 24; see also O. rigida

Othonna rigida [error for rigens?] — Pl. rar. Afr. (115) 5

Othonna scapis unifloris, foliis pinnatifidis — Pl. rar. Afr. (115) 24

Othonna sibirica — Demonstr. pl. (49) 24; Calend. fl. (72) [17]; Hist. nat. Rossia (144) 23, 33[as Otthonna]

Othonna sonchifolia — Fl. Cap. (99) 18

Othonna tagetis — Fl. Cap. (99) 18

Otis — Fund. ornith. (137) 27

Otis tetrax — Migr. avium (79) 27

Ouragoga — Viola ipecac. (176) 5, 8

Ova piscium — Herb. Amboin. (57) 20

Ovis — Vir. pl. (13) 16, 17; Oecon. nat. (20) 32, 35; Generat. calc. (22) 17; Pan Svec. (26) 3, 6, 8ff.; Mat. med. anim. (29) 8; Noxa insect. (46) 28, 29; Oves (61) [3]ff.; Instr. peregr. (96) 11

Ovis africana — Oves (61) 8

Ovis anglicana — Oves (61) 8, 18, 19

Ovis auribus pendulis, palearibus laxis, occipite prominente — Oves (61) 7

Ovis communis — Oves (61) 7, 8

Ovis cornibus compressis lunatis — Mat. med. anim. (29) 8; Oves (61) 7

Ovis cornibus erectis spiralibus — Oves (61) 7

Ovis domestica — Oves (61) 7

Ovis guineensis — Oves (61) 7[as guinensis]

Ovis hispanica — Oves (61) 8, 18, 19

Ovis laticauda — Oves (61) 8

Ovis polycerata — Oves (61) 9

Ovis rustica — Oves (61) 8, 9, 12, 18, 19

Ovis strepsiceros — Oves (61) 7

Ovis strepsiceros cretica — Oves (61) 7

Oxalis — Spons. pl. (12) 11, 35; Vir. pl. (13) 33; Fl. oecon. (17) 11; Oecon. nat. (20) 17; Pl. escul. (35) 29; Anim. comp. (98) 5; Fl. Cap. (99) 4, 7, 8; Generat. ambig. (104) 10

Oxalis acetosella — Pl. escul. (35) 15[as acetocella]; Herbat. Upsal. (50) 11; Pl. officin. (52) 3; Stat. pl. (55) 18; Fl. Angl. (56) 16; Calend. fl. (72) [10]; Fl. Monsp. (74) 16; Prodr. fl. Dan. (82) 18; Fl. Belg. (112) 17; Fl. Åker. (162) 12; Pand. fl. Ryb. (165) 19

Oxalis corniculata — Fl. Palaest. (70) 19; Fl. Monsp. (74) 16; Prodr. fl. Dan. (82) 18; Fl. Belg. (112) 17

Oxalis flava — Fl. Cap. (99) 14

Oxalis foliis pinnatis — Spons. pl. (12) 12

Oxalis hirta — Fl. Cap. (99) 14

Oxalis incarnata — Fl. Cap. (99) 14

Oxalis pes caprae — Fl. Cap. (99) 14

Oxalis purpurea — Fl. Cap. (99) 14

Oxalis sensitiva — Herb. Amboin. (57) 22; Somn. pl. (68) 7

Oxalis stricta — Fl. Jam. (105) 16

Oxalis sylvatica — Pan Svec. (26) 23

Oxalis versicolor — Fl. Cap. (99) 14

Oxyacantha — Nom. bot. (107) 13; Inebr. (117) 13; Usum hist. nat. (145) 17

Oxycoccus — Vir. pl. (13) 36

Oxys lutea indica — Herb. Amboin. (57) 21

Ozimum citratum — Herb. Amboin. (57) 21

Padus — Ficus (2) 22; Hort. Upsal. (7) 36; Vir. pl. (13) 21; Fl. oecon. (17) 12; Pl. escul. (35) 15, 28; Hosp. insect. fl. (43) 40; Noxa insect. (46) 26; Vern. arb. (47) 10, table; Calend. fl. (72) 5, [10], [20]; Prol. pl. 1760 (114) 9, 10, 19

Padus folio deciduo — Gem. arb. (24) 26; Pan Svec. (26) 24

Padus laurocerasus — Gem. arb. (24) 26; Pl. officin. (52) 12

Padus vulgaris — Hosp. insect. fl. (43) 22

Paeonia — Spons. pl. (12) 59; Vir. pl. (13) 21[as Poeonia]; Hort. acad. (63) 3; Metam. pl. (67) 17; Fl. Monsp. (74) 7; Nom. bot. (107) 14

Paeonia multifida — Pl. Alstr. (121) 6

Paeonia officinalis — Demonstr. pl. (49) 14[as Poeonia]; Pl. officin. (52) 14[as Poeonia]; Fl. Monsp. (74) 18; Pl. Alstr. (121) 5; Hort. cul. (132) 24, 25

Paeonia plena — Calend. fl. (72) [12], [14]; Fund. fr. (123) 13

Paeonia simplex — Calend. fl. (72) [11], [12]

Paeonia tenuifolia — Hort. cul. (132) 24; Hist. nat. Rossia (144) 23

Palacca — Herb. Amboin. (57) 14

Palala secunda — Herb. Amboin. (57) 8

Palala tertia — Herb. Amboin. (57) 8

Palamedea — Fund. ornith. (137) 20

Palamedea satyra — Fund. ornith. (137) 20

Palasia — Aphyteia (185) 9

Paliurus — Gem. arb. (24) 6; Fl. Monsp. (74) 7

Palma — Spons. pl. (12) 42

Palma aegyptiaca — Var. cib. (156) 8

Palmifilix — Herb. Amboin. (57) 26

Palmijuncus albus — Herb. Amboin. (57) 19

Palmijuncus calapparius — Herb. Amboin. (57) 19

Palmijuncus draco — Herb. Amboin. (57) 20

Palmijuncus equestris — Herb. Amboin. (57) 20

Palmijuncus laevis — Herb. Amboin. (57) 20

Palmijuncus niger — Herb. Amboin. (57) 19

Palmijuncus verus — Herb. Amboin. (57) 19

Palmijuncus viminalis — Herb. Amboin. (57) 20

Palmijuncus zalacca — Herb. Amboin. (57) 20

Panacea — Nova pl. gen. 1751 (32) 10, 12

Panax — Nova pl. gen. 1751 (32) 10, 12; Fund. fr. (123) 23

Panax pastinacae folio — Pl. Mart.-Burs. (6) 10

Panax quinquefolium — Demonstr. pl. (49) 27[as quinquefolia]; Pl. officin. (52) 10

Pancratium — Vir. pl. (13) 20; Nect. fl. (122) 9

Pancratium caribaeum — Fl. Jam. (105) 15

Pancratium illyricum — Fl. Palaest. (70) 17[as Pancratum]

Pancratium maritimum — Fl. Monsp. (74) 14

Pancratium narbonense — Herb. Amboin. (57) 28

Pancratium zeylanicum — Herb. Amboin. (57) 28

Pandanus — Herb. Amboin. (57) 5

Pandanus caricosus — Herb. Amboin. (57) 18

Pandanus ceramicus — Herb. Amboin. (57) 18

Pandanus funicularis — Herb. Amboin. (57) 18

Pandanus humilis — Herb. Amboin. (57) 17

Pandanus latifolius — Herb. Amboin. (57) 17

Pandanus moschatus — Herb. Amboin. (57) 17

Pandanus repens — Herb. Amboin. (57) 18

Pandanus spurius — Herb. Amboin. (57) 17

Pandanus sylvestris — Herb. Amboin. (57) 17

Pandanus verus — Herb. Amboin. (57) 17

Panel — Opobals. (135) 2; Obs. mat. med. (171) 7

Pangium — Herb. Amboin. (57) 10

Panicum — Hort. Upsal. (7) 34; Vir. pl. (13) 32; Fl. oecon. (17) 2; Herb. Amboin. (57) 20; Pl. Jam. (102) 6; Nom. bot. (107) 9; Fund. agrost. (152) 15, 16, 20, 26, 31, 33, 35

Panicum adhaerens — Pan Svec. (26) 13

Panicum alopecuroides — Fl. Palaest. (70) 12; Fl. Jam. (105) 12

Panicum clandestinum — Demonstr. pl. (49) 3

Panicum colonum — Fl. Jam. (105) 12

Panicum compositum — Fund. agrost. (152) 33

Panicum crus-corvi — Fl. Jam. (105) 12

Panicum crus-galli — Demonstr. pl. (49) 3; Stat. pl. (55) 19; Fl. Angl. (56) 10; Fl. Monsp. (74) 9; Prodr. fl. Dan. (82) 13; Fl. Belg. (112) 12

Panicum dactylon — Demonstr. pl. (49) 3; Fl. Angl. (56) 10; Fl. Monsp. (74) 9; Obs. mat. med. (171) 6

Panicum dimidiatum — Fl. Jam. (105) 13

Panicum divaricatum — Pl. Jam. (102) 6; Fl. Jam. (105) 13; Iter Chin. (161) 7

Panicum glaucum — Fl. Angl. (56) 10; Fl. Monsp. (74) 9; Prodr. fl. Dan. (82) 13; Fl. Jam. (105) 12; Fl. Belg. (112) 12; Fund. agrost. (152) 33; Iter Chin. (161) 7

Panicum grossarium — Pl. Jam. (102) 6; Fl. Jam. (105) 13; Fund. agrost. (152) 33

Panicum hirtellum — Pl. Jam. (102) 6; Fl. Jam. (105) 13; Colon. pl. (158) 12

Panicum indicum — Demonstr. pl. (49) 3

Panicum italicum — Demonstr. pl. (49) 3; Herb. Amboin. (57) 20; Fl. Palaest. (70) 12; Fl. Jam. (105) 13; Fr. escul. (127) 20; Hort. cul. (132) 9

Panicum latifolium — Fl. Jam. (105) 13

Panicum miliaceum — Demonstr. pl. (49) 3; Fl. Palaest. (70) 12; Fr. escul. (127) 20; Hort. cul. (132) 9

Panicum panicula minore — Fl. Monsp. (74) 30

Panicum patens — Fl. Palaest. (70) 12; Fund. agrost. (152) 33

Panicum reptans — Fl. Jam. (105) 13

Panicum sanguinale — Demonstr. pl. (49) 3; Fl. Angl. (56) 10; Fl. Monsp. (74) 9; Fl. Belg. (112) 12; Fund. agrost. (152) 7

Panicum viride — Fl. Jam. (105) 12; Fund. agrost. (152) 33

Panorpa — Pand. insect. (93) 4; Fund. entom. (154) 22

Panorpa communis — Pand. fl. Ryb. (165) 12; Esca avium (174) 8

Papa — Polit. nat. (109) 14

Papaver — Hort. Upsal. (7) 34, 35; Anandria (9) 4; Spons. pl. (12) 35, 59; Vir. pl. (13) 21, 25; Sem. musc. (28) 13; Pl. hybr. (33) 13; Cui bono? (42) 20; Fl. Angl. (56) 5; Metam. pl. (67) 17; Nom. bot. (107) 14; Prol. pl. 1760 (114) 16; Fund. fr. (123) 11, 12; Cimicifuga (173) 9; Esca avium (174) 2; Opium (179) 2ff.

Papaver alpinum — Fl. alp. (71) 18

Papaver argemone — Demonstr. pl. (49) 14; Fl. Angl. (56) 17; Fl. Monsp. (74) 18; Prodr. fl. Dan. (82) 19; Fl. Belg. (112) 18

Papaver cambricum — Demonstr. pl. (49) 14; Fl. Angl. (56) 17; Fl. alp. (71) 18[as chambricum]; Opium (179) 4

Papaver corniculatum violaceum — Pl. hybr. (33) 13

Papaver dubium — Stat. pl. (55) 19; Fl. Monsp. (74) 18; Prodr. fl. Dan. (82) 19; Pand. fl. Ryb. (165) 19

Papaver glabrum — Pan Svec. (26) 25

Papaver hispidum — Pan Svec. (26) 25

154

Papaver hybridum — Demonstr. pl. (49) 14; Fl. Angl. (56) 17; Fl. Monsp. (74) 18

Papaver medium — Demonstr. pl. (49) 14; Fl. Angl. (56) 17

Papaver nigrum — Vir. pl. (13) 37

Papaver nudicaule — Demonstr. pl. (49) 14; Hist. nat. Rossia (144) 23, 30; Rar. Norv. (157) 9

Papaver orientale — Calend. fl. (72) [15]; Opium (179) 4

Papaver orientale hirsutissimum, flore magno — Spons. pl. (12) 51

Papaver rhoeas — Demonstr. pl. (49) 14; Herbat. Upsal. (50) 13; Pl. officin. (52) 16[as rhaeas]; Fl. Angl. (56) 17[as rhaeas]; Fl. Palaest. (70) 21[as rhaeas]; Fl. Monsp. (74) 18[as rhaeas]; Prodr. fl. Dan. (82) 19; Fl. Belg. (112) 18; Hort. cul. (132) 25

Papaver somniferum — Demonstr. pl. (49) 14; Pl. officin. (52) 14; Fl. Angl. (56) 17; Calend. fl. (72) [15]; Fl. Monsp. (74) 18; Inebr. (117) 10; Hort. cul. (132) 23, 25; Opium (179) 3

Papaya — Ficus (2) 9; Herb. Amboin. (57) 7

Papilio — Spons. pl. (12) 50, 55; Curios. nat. (18) 8, 11; Oecon. nat. (20) 28, 30; Cui bono? (42) 10; Noxa insect. (46) 20; Metam. pl. (67) 11, 12; Polit. nat. (109) 8; Prol. pl. 1760 (114) 3; Fund. fr. (123) 20; Fund. agrost. (152) 10; Fund. entom. (154) 13, 17, 19, 20, 25, 27, 32; Esca avium (174) 8; Bigas insect. (184) 2

Papilio achilles — Pand. insect. (93) 14

Papilio actorion — Cent. insect. (129) 26

Papilio aedea — Cent. insect. (129) 20

Papilio aegira — Pand. insect. (93) 11

Papilio aegistus — Cent. insect. (129) 18[as aegisthus]

Papilio agamemnon — Fund. entom. (154) 32

Papilio aglaja — Pand. insect. (93) 18

Papilio alis caudatis nigris: fasciis duabus hyalinis, caudis caeruleis — Cent. insect. (129) 26

Papilio almana — Iter Chin. (161) 10

Papilio alpicola — Hosp. insect. fl. (43) 21

Papilio ammiralis — Hosp. insect. fl. (43) 31

Papilio anacardii — Pand. insect. (93) 14

Papilio anchises — Pand. insect. (93) [17, as 38]

Papilio antiopa — Pand. insect. (93) 18, 21; Pand. fl. Ryb. (165) 10

Papilio apollo — Pand. insect. (93) 14; Pand. fl. Ryb. (165) 10

Papilio arcanius — Pand. fl. Ryb. (165) 11

Papilio arcius — Cent. insect. (129) 26

Papilio argiolus — Pand. fl. Ryb. (165) 10

Papilio argus — Pand. insect. (93) 12; Pand. fl. Ryb. (165) 10

Papilio argus caecus — Hosp. insect. fl. (43) 25

Papilio argus oculatus — Hosp. insect. fl. (43) 17

Papilio argyrius — Iter Chin. (161) 10

Papilio ariadne — Cent. insect. (129) 24

Papilio arion — Pand. fl. Ryb. (165) 10

Papilio ascanius — Iter Chin. (161) 7

Papilio atalanta — Pand. insect. (93) 19

Papilio atlites — Cent. insect. (129) 24

Papilio augias — Cent. insect. (129) 27

Papilio aurora — Hosp. insect. fl. (43) 12, 27, 28

Papilio bella donna — Hosp. insect. fl. (43) 30, 32

Papilio betulae — Pand. insect. (93) 14, 18

Papilio bombyx — Phalaena (78) 11

Papilio brassicae — Pand. insect. (93) 16, [17, as 38]; Polit. nat. (109) 8; Hort. cul. (132) 11; Fund. entom. (154) 24, 25; Var. cib. (156) 4; Pand. fl. Ryb. (165) 10

Papilio brassicaria — Hosp. insect. fl. (43) 28; Noxa insect. (46) 18

Papilio brassicaria latis venis — Hosp. insect. fl. (43) 28

Papilio brassicaria minor — Hosp. insect. fl. (43) 20, 28

Papilio brassicaria vulgaris — Hosp. insect. fl. (43) 28

Papilio c album — Pand. insect. (93) 12, 19, 22; Pand. fl. Ryb. (165) 10; Esca avium (174) 8

Papilio c duplex — Hosp. insect. fl. (43) 17, 18, 32, 38

Papilio calliope — Fund. entom. (154) 33

Papilio canace — Cent. insect. (129) 23

Papilio canicularis — Hosp. insect. fl. (43) 17

Papilio canidia — Iter Chin. (161) 12, 13

Papilio cardamines — Pand. insect. (93) 16

Papilio cardui — Pand. insect. (93) 18; Esca avium (174) 7

Papilio caricae — Pand. insect. (93) 22

Papilio cassiae — Pand. insect. (93) 14

Papilio caudatus — Hosp. insect. fl. (43) 12, 18, 19, 21

Papilio cinxia — Pand. insect. (93) 11, [17, as 38]

Papilio clio — Pand. insect. (93) 14

Papilio comes — Hosp. insect. fl. (43) 16

Papilio comma — Pand. fl. Ryb. (165) 11

Papilio crataegi — Pand. insect. (93) 14, 15; Pand. fl. Ryb. (165) 10

Papilio cupido — Pand. insect. (93) [17, as 38]

Papilio cydippe — Cent. insect. (129) 26; Pand. fl. Ryb. (165) 10

Papilio danaus — Fund. entom. (154) 32, 33

Papilio danaus alis albidis fasciis duabus margineque fuscis; posticis subtus subincarnatis — Cent. insect. (129) 23

Papilio danaus alis flavis: primoribus supra albis margine nigris, posticis margine nigro-punctatis — Cent. insect. (129) 20

Papilio danaus alis fuscis: subtus primoribus ocellis quatuor, posticis sex — Cent. insect. (129) 23

Papilio danaus alis integerrimis angulatis flavis; primoribus macula; posticis limbo luteis — Cent. insect. (129) 21

Papilio danaus alis integerrimis angulatis flavis: primoribus punctis duobus maculaque nigris, posticis ocello caeruleo — Cent. insect. (129) 23

Papilio danaus alis integerrimis concoloribus luteis limbo nigro punctis septem albis — Cent. insect. (129) 22

Papilio danaus alis integerrimis fuscis; primoribus ocello unico, posticis ter duabus — Cent. insect. (129) 21

Papilio danaus alis integerrimis nigris: primoribus albo maculatis; posticis basis subtusque albis — Cent. insect. (129) 22

Papilio danaus alis integerrimis: posticis dentatis: supra fusco virentibus, subtus viridi sericeis venis atris — Cent. insect. (129) 21

Papilio danaus alis integerrimis rotundatis albis venis maculisque nigris: primoribus margine nigro albo punctato — Cent. insect. (129) 22

Papilio danaus alis integerrimis rotundatis luteis margine nigris; posticis subtus ocello sesquialtero albo — Cent. insect. (129) 21

Papilio danaus alis rotundatis fuscis: primoribus maculis albis basique sanguineis; posticis area alba — Cent. insect. (129) 24

Papilio demoleus — Iter Chin. (161) 10

Papilio demophile — Cent. insect. (129) 23

Papilio dido — Cent. insect. (129) 25

Papilio ecclipsis — Cent. insect. (129) 7, 23

Papilio electo — Cent. insect. (129) 21

Papilio eques — Fund. entom. (154) 32

Papilio eques alis caudatis nigris albido-virescente fasciatis, caudis albis — Cent. insect. (129) 19

Papilio eques alis fuscis viridescente maculatus; subtus subincarnatus maculis virescentibus rarioribus — Cent. insect. (129) 18

Papilio eques alis subcaudatis fuscis, subtus fasciis albidis, ocellis duabus caudaque ocellis geminis — Cent. insect. (129) 19

Papilio eques alis subcaudatis nigris concoloribus; posticis macula alba suturis sexfida lunulisque septem rubris — Cent. insect. (129) 18

Papilio eques alis supra nigris: primoribus fascia lutea apiceque albo, posticis disco caerulescentibus — Cent. insect. (129) 19

Papilio euphrosyne — Pand. fl. Ryb. (165) 10

Papilio eurydice — Cent. insect. (129) 23

Papilio flammeus — Hosp. insect. fl. (43) 33

Papilio galathea — Pand. insect. (93) 11

Papilio hecabe — Iter Chin. (161) 10

Papilio helcita — Cent. insect. (129) 22

Papilio helena — Pand. insect. (93) [23, as 31]; Fund. entom. (154) 5

Papilio heliconius — Fund. entom. (154) 32, 33

Papilio heliconius alis flavis: superioribus supra nigris, lineis duabus fasciaque flavis — Cent. insect. (129) 20

Papilio heliconius alis oblongis integerrimis albo maculatis: superioribus virescentibus; inferioribus fascia flava — Cent. insect. (129) 20

Papilio heliconius alis oblongis integerrimis nigris basi fulvis: primoribus fascia maculisque tribus flavis — Cent. insect. (129) 20

Papilio hexapus; alis secundariis angulo acuto: subtus cinereis, linea alba, punctis duobus fulvis — Hosp. insect. fl. (43) 34

Papilio hiemalis — Hosp. insect. fl. (43) 22, 23

Papilio hippothoe — Pand. fl. Ryb. (165) 11

Papilio hyperanthus — Pand. fl. Ryb. (165) 10 [as hyperantus]

Papilio hyperbius — Cent. insect. (129) 25

Papilio hypermnestra — Cent. insect. (129) 24

Papilio idas — Pand. fl. Ryb. (165) 10

Papilio idea — Cent. insect. (129) 22

Papilio io — Pand. insect. (93) 19, 22; Pand. fl. Ryb. (165) 10

Papilio iris — Pand. insect. (93) 19

Papilio janira — Pand. fl. Ryb. (165) 10

Papilio jatrophae — Cent. insect. (129) 25

Papilio java — Iter Chin. (161) 12

Papilio jurtina — Pand. insect. (93) 11; Pand. fl. Ryb. (165) 10

Papilio leilus — Pand. insect. (93) [17, as 38]

Papilio lemonias — Iter Chin. (161) 10

Papilio leucothoe — Iter Chin. (161) 10

Papilio levana — Pand. insect. (93) 19

Papilio ligaea — Pand. fl. Ryb. (165) 10

Papilio linea nigra — Hosp. insect. fl. (43) 28

Papilio lucina — Pand. fl. Ryb. (165) 10

Papilio machaon — Pand. insect. (93) 12, 13, 14

Papilio maera — Pand. insect. (93) 11; Pand. fl. Ryb. (165) 10

Papilio malvae — Pand. insect. (93) [17, as 38]; Pand. fl. Ryb. (165) 11; Esca avium (174) 8

Papilio maturna — Pand. insect. (93) 11, 13, 20; Erica (163) 15

Papilio medon — Cent. insect. (129) 19

Papilio melite — Cent. insect. (129) 20

Papilio menelaus — Fund. entom. (154) 5

Papilio midamus — Iter Chin. (161) 10

Papilio mneme — Cent. insect. (129) 20

Papilio morio — Hosp. insect. fl. (43) 33, 36

Papilio napi — Pand. insect. (93) [17, as 38]; Pand. fl. Ryb. (165) 10

Papilio nereus — Fund. entom. (154) 33

Papilio nestor — Pand. insect. (93) 14

Papilio niobe — Pand. fl. Ryb. (165) 10

Papilio nymphalis — Fund. entom. (154) 32, 33

Papilio nymphalis alis angulatis pallidis lineis undatis maculisque: primoribus puncto unico: posticisque duobus nigricantibus — Cent. insect. (129) 25

Papilio nymphalis alis angulatis supra caeruleis fascia dilutiori, subtus luteo virideque marmoratis — Cent. insect. (129) 23

Papilio nymphalis alis cinerascentibus; supra primoribus ocellis senis, posticis quinis: quibusdam caecis — Cent. insect. (129) 24

Papilio nymphalis alis dentatis luteis; primoribus extimo nigris: fascia alba; posticis subtus argentatis quinque ocellatis — Cent. insect. (129) 25

Papilio nymphalis alis dentatis supra nigro-caerulescentibus albo maculatis; area communi rubra; subtus marmoratis — Cent. insect. (129) 26

Papilio nymphalis alis nigricantibus: subtus ferrugineo nebulosis; posticae postice ferrugineis puncto albo — Cent. insect. (129) 24

Papilio nymphalis alis oblongis dentatis subconcoloribus nigris viridi maculatis; posticis fascia maculisque septem transversis — Cent. insect. (129) 25

Papilio nymphalis alis supra subferrugineis strigis nigris undulatis; primoribus antice puncto niveo — Cent. insect. (129) 24

Papilio oculus pavonis — Hosp. insect. fl. (43) 32, 38

Papilio oculus pavonis dictus — Curios. nat. (18) 8

Papilio orithya — Iter Chin. (161) 10

Papilio orontes — Cent. insect. (129) 19

Papilio pammon — Iter Chin. (161) 10

Papilio pamphilus — Pand. fl. Ryb. (165) 10

Papilio paphia — Pand. insect. (93) 19

Papilio paris — Fund. entom. (154) 32; Iter Chin. (161) 10

Papilio peleus — Cent. insect. (129) 26

Papilio phidippus — Cent. insect. (129) 19

Papilio philea — Cent. insect. (129) 21

Papilio philomela — Cent. insect. (129) 21

Papilio phlaeus — Pand. fl. Ryb. (165) 11[as phlaeas]

Papilio plebejus — Fund. entom. (154) 32[as Pebejus], 33

Papilio plebejus alis integerrimis divaricatis fulvis; fascia obliqua margineque postico nigris — Cent. insect. (129) 27

Papilio plebejus alis integerrimis utrinque atris primoribus fascia lineari rubra, exteriusque luteo maculatis — Cent. insect. (129) 26

Papilio plebejus alis subcaudatis fuscis superioribus fascia lutescente exteriore maculaque caerulea postica; subtus ocello — Cent. insect. (129) 26

Papilio polybe — Cent. insect. (129) 21

Papilio polychloros — Hosp. insect. fl. (43) 18, 21, 23, 36; Pand. insect. (93) 12, 14, 15, 21[as polychlorus]; Esca avium (174) 8

Papilio polydamas — Pand. insect. (93) [17, as 38]

Papilio polydorus — Cent. insect. (129) 18

Papilio populi — Pand. insect. (93) 22

Papilio priamus — Fund. entom. (154) 5, 32

Papilio prorsa — Pand. insect. (93) 19

Papilio proteus — Pand. insect. (93) 11

Papilio pruni — Pand. insect. (93) 14

Papilio psidii — Pand. insect. (93) 14

Papilio pyrene — Iter Chin. (161) 10

Papilio quercus — Pand. insect. (93) 19

Papilio rapae — Pand. insect. (93) 13, [17, as 38]; Pand. fl. Ryb. (165) 10

Papilio rex — Hosp. insect. fl. (43) 31

Papilio rhamni — Pand. insect. (93) 12; Pand. fl. Ryb. (165) 10; Esca avium (174) 7

Papilio ricini — Pand. insect. (93) 20

Papilio rubi — Pand. insect. (93) 15; Pand. fl. Ryb. (165) 10

Papilio scylla — Cent. insect. (129) 20

Papilio semele — Pand. fl. Ryb. (165) 10

Papilio sennae — Pand. insect. (93) 14

Papilio sinapis — Pand. insect. (93) [17, as 38]; Pand. fl. Ryb. (165) 10

Papilio sophorae — Pand. insect. (93) 14

Papilio strilidore — Cent. insect. (129) 22

Papilio talaus — Cent. insect. (129) 24

Papilio terpsicore — Fund. entom. (154) 33

Papilio teucer — Pand. insect. (93) 22

Papilio urania — Fund. entom. (154) 33

Papilio urticae — Pand. insect. (93) 6, 19; Var. cib. (156) 4; Pand. fl. Ryb. (165) 10; Esca avium (174) 15

Papilio urticaria — Hosp. insect. fl. (43) 32; Mirac. insect. (45) 6; Calend. fl. (72) [8][as urticarius]

Papilio vanillae — Pand. insect. (93) 18

Papilio virgaureae — Pand. insect. (93) 18; Pand. fl. Ryb. (165) 11; Esca avium (174) 8

Papio — Anthrop. (111) 5

Parietaria — Ficus (2) 11; Spons. pl. (12) 47, 58; Sapor. med. (31) 12; Stat. pl. (55) 6; Pl. Jam. (102) 28; Nom. bot. (107) 19

Parietaria judaica — Fl. Palaest. (70) 32

Parietaria lusitanica — Fl. Palaest. (70) 32

Parietaria microphylla — Pl. Jam. (102) 30; Fl. Jam. (105) 22

Parietaria officinalis — Demonstr. pl. (49) 27; Pl. officin. (52) 14; Fl. Angl. (56) 25[as officinarum]; Fl. Palaest. (70) 32; Fl. Monsp. (74) 28[as Parictaria]; Prodr. fl. Dan. (82) 25; Fl. Belg. (112) 10[as offinalis], 23

Paris — Pl. Mart.-Burs. (6) [vi]; Nom. bot. (107) 12; Viola ipecac. (176) 5

Paris foliis ternis, flore pedunculato erecto — Pl. Mart.-Burs. (6) 12; Pl. rar. Camsch. (30) 5

Paris nemorum — Pan Svec. (26) 22

Paris quadrifolia — Herbat. Upsal. (50) 8; Stat. pl. (55) 17; Fl. Angl. (56) 15; Cervus (60) 7; Fl.

Monsp. (74) 15; Prodr. fl. Dan. (82) 17; Med. grav. (92) 9; Fl. Åker. (162) 11; Pand. fl. Ryb. (165) 18; Obs. mat. med. (171) 3; Esca avium (174) 12

Parkinsonia — Hort. Upsal. (7) 37; Spons. pl. (12) 12

Parkinsonia aculeata — Demonstr. pl. (49) 11[as acculeata, corr. p. 27]; Fl. Jam. (105) 16

Parnassia — Spons. pl. (12) 29, 35, 46; Vir. pl. (13) 25; Fl. oecon. (17) 8; Sem. musc. (28) 13; Vern. arb. (47) 19; Nect. fl. (122) 13; Fund. fr. (123) 21; Erica (163) 2

Parnassia palustris — Herbat. Upsal. (50) 14; Pl. officin. (52) 11; Stat. pl. (55) 14; Fl. Angl. (56) 14; Cervus (60) 7; Calend. fl. (72) [12]; Fl. Monsp. (74) 13; Prodr. fl. Dan. (82) 16; Fl. Belg. (112) 15; Fl. Åker. (162) 10; Pand. fl. Ryb. (165) 18

Parnassia vulgaris — Pan Svec. (26) 19

Parra — Fund. ornith. (137) 20; Siren. lacert. (146) 8

Parsonsia — Fl. Jam. (105) 26

Parthenium foliis lanceolatis serratis — Nova pl. gen. 1751 (32) 45

Parthenium hysterophorus — Fl. Jam. (105) 21

Parthenium partheniastrum — Somn. pl. (68) 16

Parus — Migr. avium (79) 35; Polit. nat. (109) 12

Parus major — Migr. avium (79) 35

Paspalum — Fund. agrost. (152) 21, 28, 37

Paspalum dissectum — Iter Chin. (161) 12

Paspalum distichum — Pl. Jam. (102) [5]; Fl. Jam. (105) 12

Paspalum paniculatum — Fl. Jam. (105) 12

Paspalum virgatum — Fl. Jam. (105) 12, 25[as Paspatum]

Passer — Curios. nat. (18) 11; Oecon. nat. (20) 26, 31, 32, 41

Passer caeruleo-fuscus — Surin. Grill. (16) 10

Passer canariensis — Vir. pl. (13) 17; Pl. hybr. (33) 3

Passer nivalis — Oecon. nat. (20) 40; Cervus (60) 10

Passer stultus — Chin. Lagerstr. (64) 13

Passerina — Fl. Cap. (99) 8; Fund. fr. (123) 18

Passerina capitata — Pl. rar. Afr. (115) 11

Passerina ciliata — Fl. Cap. (99) 14

Passerina dodecandra — Cent. I. pl. (65) 10

Passerina filiformis — Fl. Cap. (99) 14

Passerina foliis lanceolatis, glabris, acuminatis; floribus lateralibus; staminibus quatuor inclusis — Cent. I. pl. (65) 10

Passerina foliis lanceolato-linearibus glabris, floribus capitatis: receptaculis incrassatis — Pl. rar. Afr. (115) 11

Passerina foliis ovatis glabris acutis, floribus obtusis — Cent. II. pl. (66) 15

Passerina foliis ovatis tomentosis, caule hirsuto, floribus coronatis — Cent. II. pl. (66) 15

Passerina fragi — Nova pl. gen. 1747 (14) 17

Passerina hirsuta — Fl. Palaest. (70) 18

Passerina laevigata — Cent. II. pl. (66) 15[as levigata]; Fl. Cap. (99) 14

Passerina sericea — Cent. II. pl. (66) 15; Fl. Cap. (99) 14

Passerina uniflora — Fl. Cap. (99) 14

Passiflora — Hort. Upsal. (7) 37; Passifl. (8) 3ff.; Spons. pl. (12) 30, 38; Pl. hybr. (33) 29; Nect. fl. (122) 4, 10; Fund. fr. (123) 16, 18, 22; Pl. Surin. (177) 14

Passiflora americana brevi folio, et flore minore — Passifl. (8) 7

Passiflora americana flore suave rubente, folio bicorni — Passifl. (8) 12

Passiflora americana folio bisuco, fructu minimo per maturitatem nigricante — Passifl. (8) 26

Passiflora arborea, laurinis foliis, americana — Passifl. (8) 10

Passiflora caerulea — Demonstr. pl. (49) 24; Fl. Jam. (105) 20[as coerulea]

Passiflora eadem foliis latioribus citius florens — Passifl. (8) 23

Passiflora florum involucris triphyllis multifido-capillaribus — Passifl. (8) 19

Passiflora foetida — Demonstr. pl. (49) 24; Pl. Surin. (177) 14

Passiflora foliis bilobis basi emarginatis petiolatis — Passifl. (8) 12

Passiflora foliis bilobis cuneiformibus, basi biglandulosis, lobis acutis divaricatis — Passifl. (8) 14

Passiflora foliis bilobis oblongis transversis amplexicaulibus — Passifl. (8) 12

Passiflora foliis bilobis obtusis basi indivisis, nectariis monophyllis — Passifl. (8) 13

Passiflora foliis bilobis obtusis, nectariis … — Passifl. (8) 13

Passiflora foliis bilobis obtusis, nectario multifido — Passifl. (8) 15

Passiflora foliis cordatis trilobis integerrimis glabris, lateribus angulatis — Passifl. (8) 15

Passiflora foliis cordato-oblongis integerrimis, floribus solitariis, involucro tripartito integerrimo — Passifl. (8) 10

Passiflora foliis cordato-trilobis integerrimis, basi utrinque denticulo reflexo — Passifl. (8) 17

Passiflora foliis crenatis tripartito-divisis — Passifl. (8) 21

Passiflora foliis indivisis cordatis integerrimis, petiolis aequalibus — Passifl. (8) 9

Passiflora foliis indivisis cordato-oblongis integerrimis, petiolis biglandulosis, involucris integerrimis — Passifl. (8) 10

Passiflora foliis indivisis integerrimis, involucris dentatis — Passifl. (8) 10

Passiflora foliis indivisis oblongis integerrimis, floribus confertis — Passifl. (8) 11

Passiflora foliis indivisis ovatis integerrimis, petiolis aequalibus — Passifl. (8) 8

Passiflora foliis indivisis ovatis integerrimis, petiolis biglandulosis — Passifl. (8) 7

Passiflora foliis indivisis serratis — Passifl. (8) 7

Passiflora foliis naviformibus umbilicatis, americana — Passifl. (8) 26

Passiflora foliis ovato-lanceolatis integris, serratis — Passifl. (8) 7

Passiflora foliis palmatis integerrimis — Passifl. (8) 22

Passiflora foliis palmatis quinque partitis integerrimis, involucris cordatis triphyllis — Passifl. (8) 22

Passiflora foliis palmatis serratis — Passifl. (8) 23

Passiflora foliis pedatis serratis — Passifl. (8) 24

Passiflora foliis semitrifidis serratis: basi duabus glandulis convexis: lobis ovatis — Passifl. (8) 21

Passiflora foliis solitariis oblongis integerrimis, floribus solitariis, involucro tripartito dentato — Passifl. (8) 10

Passiflora foliis trilobis, basi utrinque denticulo reflexo — Passifl. (8) 17

Passiflora foliis trilobis cordatis aequalibus obtusis glabris integerrimis — Passifl. (8) 15

Passiflora foliis trilobis cordatis pilosis, involucris multifido-capillaribus — Passifl. (8) 19

Passiflora foliis trilobis integerrimis, laciniis semiovatis obtuse acutis integerrimis glabris — Passifl. (8) 15

Passiflora foliis trilobis integerrimis, lobis sublanceolatis: intermedio productiore — Passifl. (8) 20

Passiflora foliis trilobis oblongis subtus punctatis: intermedio minore — Passifl. (8) 15

Passiflora foliis trilobis peltatis — Passifl. (8) 16

Passiflora foliis trilobis peltatis integris, glandulis duabus sub basi convexis — Passifl. (8) 16

Passiflora foliis trilobis serratis — Passifl. (8) 21

Passiflora foliis trilobis villosis, floribus oppositis — Passifl. (8) 18

Passiflora folio angusto tricuspidi, fructu olivaeforma — Passifl. (8) 17

Passiflora hepaticae nobilis folio parvo non crenato, flore ex luteo viridante — Passifl. (8) 15

Passiflora incarnata — Fl. Jam. (105) 20; Pl. Alstr. (121) 5

Passiflora laurifolia — Fl. Jam. (105) 20

Passiflora laurinis foliis, polyanthos americana — Passifl. (8) 11

Passiflora lutea — Demonstr. pl. (49) 24; Fl. Jam. (105) 20

Passiflora maliformis — Fl. Jam. (105) 20

Passiflora naviformibus foliis, americana — Passifl. (8) 26

Passiflora normalis — Pl. Jam. (102) 26; Fl. Jam. (105) 20

Passiflora obverse lunulatis, punctis duobus melliferis sub basi — Passifl. (8) 14

Passiflora perfoliata — Fl. Jam. (105) 20

Passiflora quadrangularis — Fl. Jam. (105) 20; Pl. Surin. (177) 14

Passiflora rubra — Fl. Jam. (105) 20

Passiflora scaphoides, seu foliis naviformibus umbilicatis, americana — Passifl. (8) 26

Passiflora seu flos passionis curassavicus, folio glabro trilobato et angusto, flore flavescente omnium minimo — Passifl. (8) 20

Passiflora spuria bryonioides — Passifl. (8) 28

Passiflora suberosa — Fl. Jam. (105) 20

Passiflora tuberosa — Demonstr. pl. (49) 24

Passiflora vesicaria — Fl. Jam. (105) 20

Passiflora vesicaria hederacea, foliis lanuginosis, odore tetro, filamentis florum ex albo et purpureo-variegatis — Passifl. (8) 19

Passiflora vesicaria, lanuginoso longiore folio, flore candido — Passifl. (8) 18

Passiflora vespertilio — Pl. Surin. (177) 14

Passiflorae affinis, hederae folio, americana; nandiroba brasiliensium — Passifl. (8) 17

Passula — Vir. pl. (13) 32; Sapor. med. (31) 16

Pastinaca — Vir. pl. (13) 12, 19; Pl. escul. (35) 22; Cul. mut. (88) 2[as Pastinacia]; Pand. insect. (93) 13; Generat. ambig. (104) 8; Nom. bot. (107) 11; Obs. mat. med. (171) 8[as Pastinacia]

Pastinaca opopanax — Pl. officin. (52) 14

Pastinaca orientalis, foliis eleganter incisis — Cent. I. pl. (65) 9

Pastinaca sativa — Hosp. insect. fl. (43) 19; Demonstr. pl. (49) 8; Pl. officin. (52) 14; Fl. Angl. (56) 13; Fl. Monsp. (74) 13; Prodr. fl. Dan. (82) 16; Cul. mut. (88) 5; Fl. Jam. (105) 24; Fl. Belg. (112) 15; Mac. olit. (113) 10; Hort. cul. (132) 12

Patella — Curios. nat. (18) 5; Generat. calc. (22) 2; Fund. test. (166) 17, 25, 26

Patella equestris — Fund. test. (166) 36

Patella nubecula — Iter Chin. (161) 8

Patella saccharina — Fund. test. (166) 36

Paullinia — Hort. Upsal. (7) 37

Paullinia curassavica — Fl. Jam. (105) 15

Paullinia pinnata — Fl. Jam. (105) 15; Pl. Surin. (177) 7

Paussus — Bigas insect. (184) 6ff.

Paussus microcephalus — Bigas insect. (184) 6ff.

Pavate — Nova pl. gen. 1747 (14) 5

Pavate, arbor foliis mali aureae — Nova pl. gen. 1747 (14) 5

Pavetta — Nova pl. gen. 1747 (14) [vi], 4, 5

Pavetta foliis oblongo-ovatis oppositis, stipulis setaceis petiolis interpositis — Pot. coff. (118) 7

Pavetta indica — Herb. Amboin. (57) 16

Pavetta seu malleomothe — Nova pl. gen. 1747 (14) 5

Pavo — Curios. nat. (18) 3, 17; Oecon. nat. (20) 26; Mat. med. anim. (29) 9; Noxa insect. (46) 29; Metam. pl. (67) [5]; Calend. fl. (72) [14]; Migr. avium (79) [5]; Pl. tinct. (97) 5; Polit. nat. (109) 13; Fund. ornith. (137) 18, 27; Usum hist. nat. (145) 24

Pavo cauda longa — Mat. med. anim. (29) 9

Pavo samius — Var. cib. (156) 8

Pawatha — Nova pl. gen. 1747 (14) 5

Pecten — Fund. test. (166) 31

Pectis ciliaris — Pl. Jam. (102) 24; Fl. Jam. (105) 20

Pectis linifolia — Pl. Jam. (102) 24; Fl. Jam. (105) 20

Pectunculus chius — Var. cib. (156) 8

Pedicularis — Fl. oecon. (17) 16; Gem. arb. (24) 5; Fl. Angl. (56) 6; Nom. bot. (107) 15; Prol. pl. 1763 (130) 18

Pedicularis aethiopica, rutae caninae aspero et fragili folio — Pl. rar. Afr. (115) 12

Pedicularis alpina, foliis alternis pinnatis pinnulis pinnatis, floribus ochroleucis rostratis in spicam congestis — Pl. Mart.-Burs. (6) 11

Pedicularis alpina lutea — Pan Svec. (26) 27

Pedicularis calyce angulato — Pan Svec. (26) 27

Pedicularis calyce tuberculoso — Pan Svec. (26) 27

Pedicularis caule simplici, foliis lanceolatis semipinnatis serratis acutis — Pl. Mart.-Burs. (6) 11

Pedicularis comosa — Fl. alp. (71) 20

Pedicularis flammea — Pan Svec. (26) 27; Stat. pl. (55) 16; Fl. alp. (71) 19

Pedicularis hirsuta — Stat. pl. (55) 16; Fl. alp. (71) 19; Rar. Norv. (157) 11

Pedicularis incarnata — Hist. nat. Rossia (144) 31

Pedicularis lapponica — Stat. pl. (55) 16; Fl. alp. (71) 19; Rar. Norv. (157) 11

Pedicularis palustris — Pl. officin. (52) 15; Stat. pl. (55) 15; Fl. Angl. (56) 19; Cervus (60) 8; Prodr. fl. Dan. (82) 20; Fl. Belg. (112) 19; Fl. Åker. (162) 15; Pand. fl. Ryb. (165) 20

Pedicularis palustris rubra elatior — Pl. Mart.-Burs. (6) 11

Pedicularis pratensis lutea erectior, calyce floris hirsuto — Pl. hybr. (33) 26

Pedicularis recutita — Fl. alp. (71) 19

Pedicularis resupinata — Hist. nat. Rossia (144) 31

Pedicularis rostrata — Fl. alp. (71) 19

Pedicularis sceptrum — Hist. nat. Rossia (144) 31; Rar. Norv. (157) 10; Ledum (178) [1]

Pedicularis sceptrum carolinum — Pan Svec. (26) 27; Herbat. Upsal. (50) 16, 20; Stat. pl. (55) 16; Cervus (60) 8; Fl. alp. (71) 19; Colon. pl. (158) 6

Pedicularis sylvatica — Herbat. Upsal. (50) 18; Stat. pl. (55) 15; Fl. Angl. (56) 19; Prodr. fl. Dan. (82) 20; Fl. Belg. (112) 19

Pedicularis tristis — Hist. nat. Rossia (144) 31

Pedicularis tuberosa — Fl. alp. (71) 20; Fl. Monsp. (74) 20

Pedicularis verticillata — Hist. nat. Rossia (144) 31

Pedicularis villosa — Pan Svec. (26) 27

Pediculus — Oecon. nat. (20) 46; Noxa insect. (46) 8, 9, 11, 14, 16, 21, 28, 29; Instr. peregr. (96) 12; Usum hist. nat. (145) 24, 29; Usum musc. (148) 12; Ledum (178) 12

Pediculus ovinus — Oves (61) 22

Pediculus pulsatorius — Mirac. insect. (45) 12

Peganum — Hort. Upsal. (7) 36; Odor. med. (40) 16; Nect. fl. (122) 14

Peganum dauricum — Hist. nat. Rossia (144) 29

Peganum harmala — Demonstr. pl. (49) 12; Fl. Palaest. (70) 20; Inebr. (117) 10

Pegasus — Pand. insect. (93) 3; Fund. ornith. (137) 10

Pelamis chalcedonica — Var. cib. (156) 8

Pelecanus — Oecon. nat. (20) 35[as Pelicanus]; Polit. nat. (109) 13

Pelecanus aquilus — Nat. pelagi (84) 13[as Pelicanus]; Iter Chin. (161) 6[as Pelicanus]

Pelecanus bassanus — Nat. pelagi (84) 13[as basanus]

Pelecanus carbo — Migr. avium (79) 25; Usum hist. nat. (145) 24

Pelecanus cauda forcipata — Chin. Lagerstr. (64) 11

Pelecanus niger, capite abdomineque albis — Chin. Lagerstr. (64) 11

Pelecanus occidentalis — Iter Chin. (161) 15[as Pelicanus]

Pelecanus onocrotalus — Migr. avium (79) 19[as onocratalus]

Pelecanus piscator — Chin. Lagerstr. (64) 11; Nat. pelagi (84) 13; Fund. ornith. (137) 25; Usum hist. nat. (145) 24

Pelecanus rostro serrato, cauda cuneiformi — Chin. Lagerstr. (64) 11

Peloria — Peloria (3) [2]ff.; Pl. hybr. (33) 6

Peltis — Fund. entom. (154) 29

Penaea — Rad. senega (23) [13, as 14]; Fl. Cap. (99) 6; Fund. fr. (123) 18

Penaea arborescens, buxi folio aspero — Rad. senega (23) 17

Penaea mucronata — Fl. Cap. (99) 11

Penaea sarcocolla — Pl. officin. (52) 17; Fl. Cap. (99) 11

Penaea squarrosa — Fl. Cap. (99) 11

Pendulinus — Oecon. nat. (20) 32

Penicillus — Corallia Balt. (4) 8

Penna marina — Taenia (19) 2; Nat. pelagi (84) 9, 15

Pennula phosphorea — Chin. Lagerstr. (64) 32

Pennula rachi apice nuda — Chin. Lagerstr. (64) 33

Pennula rachi summitate undique pinnata — Chin. Lagerstr. (64) 32

Pennula sagittata — Chin. Lagerstr. (64) 33, 36

Penstemon — Nova pl. gen. 1751 (32) 10, 12; Pl. Surin. (177) 4

Penstemon chelonoides — Pl. Surin. (177) 6

Pentagonia — Sem. musc. (28) 3

Pentapetes — Nova pl. gen. 1747 (14) [vi], 23; Chin. Lagerstr. (64) 5

Pentapetes foliis cordatis repandis — Nova pl. gen. 1747 (14) 24

Pentapetes foliis ovatis repandis — Nova pl. gen. 1747 (14) 23

Pentapetes phoenicea — Demonstr. pl. (49) 19; Herb. Amboin. (57) 22

Pentaphylloides — Anandria (9) 4

Penthorum — Nova pl. gen. 1751 (32) 9

Peplis — Euphorbia (36) 16; Nom. bot. (107) 8

Peplis annua, foliis acutis, flore muscoso — Euphorbia (36) 22

Peplis major brasiliensibus — Euphorbia (36) 14

Peplis maritima, folio obtuso — Euphorbia (36) 16

Peplis minor — Fl. Monsp. (74) 30[as Peplus]

Peplis palustris — Pan Svec. (26) 20

Peplis portula — Stat. pl. (55) 14; Fl. Angl. (56) 14; Prodr. fl. Dan. (82) 17; Fl. Åker. (162) 10

Peplis seu esula rotunda — Euphorbia (36) 19

Peplum — Euphorbia (36) 3

Peplus — Euphorbia (36) 3, 19

Pepo — Hort. Upsal. (7) 35; Spons. pl. (12) 47

Peponaster — Herb. Amboin. (57) 25

Perca — Usum hist. nat. (145) 26

Perca fluviatilis — Mat. med. anim. (29) 13; Cul. mut. (88) 9

Perca pinnis dorsalibus distinctis: secuna radiis sedecim — Mat. med. anim. (29) 13

Percnopterus — Oecon. nat. (20) 44

Perdicium — Fund. fr. (123) 22

Perdicium capense — Pl. rar. Afr. (115) 22

Perdix — Instr. peregr. (96) 11; Usum hist. nat. (145) 25

Perdix cinerea — Mat. med. anim. (29) 10

Perenopterus — Polit. nat. (109) 14[as Perinopterus]

Pereskia — Gem. arb. (24) 6

Periclymeni perfoliati folio — Passifl. (8) 12

Periclymenum parvum — Viola ipecac. (176) 5

Periclymenum zeylanicum herbaceum, foliis variegatis diversicoloribus maculis ornatis — Lign. colubr. (21) 18

Periploca — Vir. pl. (13) 25; Nect. fl. (122) 13

Periploca africana — Fl. Cap. (99) 12

Periploca graeca — Fl. Palaest. (70) 15

Periploca tenuifolia — Fl. Cap. (99) 12

Perla — Fund. entom. (154) 30

Perlarius alter — Herb. Amboin. (57) 17

Perlarius primus — Herb. Amboin. (57) 17

Perola — Herb. Amboin. (57) 23

Perrana rubra — Herb. Amboin. (57) 18

Persica — Hort. Upsal. (7) 36; Vir. pl. (13) 10; Pl. escul. (35) 4; Chin. Lagerstr. (64) 6; Metam. pl. (67) 17; Nom. bot. (107) 13

Persicaria — Peloria (3) 10; Anandria (9) 5; Vir. pl. (13) 29; Fl. oecon. (17) 10; Sapor. med. (31) 19; Rhabarbarum (41) 5, 6; Raphania (126) 14; Febr. interm. (167) 51

Persicaria amphibia — Spons. pl. (12) 44; Pan Svec. (26) 21

Persicaria angustifolia — Fl. Angl. (56) 26

Persicaria ferrea — see Perticaria f.

Persicaria minor — Fl. Angl. (56) 26

Persicaria mitis — Pan Svec. (26) 21

Persicaria orientalis — Vern. arb. (47) 9

Persicaria subtus incana — Fl. Angl. (56) 26

Persicaria tertia — see Perticaria t.

Persicaria urens — Pan Svec. (26) 21; Specif. Canad. (76) 22

Perticaria ferrea [error for Persicaria?] — Herb. Amboin. (57) 12

Perticaria tertia [error for Persicaria?] — Herb. Amboin. (57) 14

Pes equinus — Herb. Amboin. (57) 24

Petasites — Anandria (9) 13, 14; Vir. pl. (13) 23; Nom. bot. (107) 17; Rar. Norv. (157) 19

Petasites agrestis — Herb. Amboin. (57) 17

Petasites amboinensis — Herb. Amboin. (57) 17

Petesia — Fl. Jam. (105) 26

Petesia lygistum — Fl. Jam. (105) 13

Petesia stipularis — Fl. Jam. (105) 13

Petiveria — Hort. Upsal. (7) 37; Vir. pl. (13) 7; Gem. arb. (24) 6; Odor. med. (40) 12

Petiveria alliacea — Demonstr. pl. (49) 11; Fl. Jam. (105) 15

Petola — Amphib. Gyll. (5) 13

Petola americana — Hort. Upsal. (7) 43

Petola anguina — Herb. Amboin. (57) 24

Petola bengalensis — Herb. Amboin. (57) 24

Petola sylvestris — Herb. Amboin. (57) 24

Petromyzon — Usum hist. nat. (145) 26

Petroselinum — Pan Svec. (26) 7; Nom. bot. (107) 11; Usum hist. nat. (145) 24

Peucedanum — Vir. pl. (13) 19

Peucedanum germanicum — Calend. fl. (72) [15]

Peucedanum minus — Fl. Angl. (56) 27

Peucedanum officinale — Demonstr. pl. (49) 8; Pl. officin. (52) 15; Fl. Angl. (56) 13; Fl. Monsp. (74) 13

Peucedanum silaus — Fl. Monsp. (74) 13

Peziza lentifera — Herbat. Upsal. (50) 10; Prodr. fl. Dan. (82) 26; Mund. invis. (149) 15

Phaca — Fl. Angl. (56) 6

Phaca alpina — Stat. pl. (55) 16; Fl. alp. (71) 21; Hist. nat. Rossia (144) 31

Phaca sibirica — Hist. nat. Rossia (144) 31

Phaelypea — Pl. Jam. (102) 15

Phaeton — Polit. nat. (109) 14[as Phaethon]

Phaeton aethereus — Nat. pelagi (84) 13; Fund. ornith. (137) 26; Iter Chin. (161) 6, 7[as Phaethon]

Phaeton demersus — Nat. pelagi (84) 13; Fund. ornith. (137) 10, 16

Phalaena — Spons. pl. (12) 50, 55; Oecon. nat. (20) 23, 28, 36[as Phalena], 41; Pan Svec. (26) 7; Cui bono? (42) 10; Hosp. insect. fl. (43) 9, 16, 17, 18, 19, 20, 22, 23, 24, 27, 28, 29, 31, 32, 33, 34, 35, 36, 37, 38, 39; Mirac. insect. (45) 7, 9, 13, 20; Noxa insect. (46) 13, 18, 19, 20, 22, 23, 31; Instr. mus. (51) 8[as Phalena]; Metam. pl. (67) 12; Phalaena (78) 4ff.; Pand. insect. (93) 8, 11, [17, as 38]; Polit. nat. (109) 8, 11, 12, 14; Fund. fr. (123) 20[as Phalena]; Meloe (124) 10; Lepra (140) 10; Usum hist. nat. (145) 23; Mund. invis. (149) 10; Fund. agrost. (152) 10; Fund. entom. (154) 6, 20, 21, 22, 24, 30, [31, as 30]; Esca avium (174) 3; Bigas insect. (184) 2

Phalaena aceris — Pand. insect. (93) 13, 20, 22

Phalaena alchemillata — Pand. insect. (93) 11

Phalaena alis ramosis — Hosp. insect. fl. (43) 16, 17

Phalaena alis superioribus subincarnatis litura longitudinali nigra postice abrupta, abdomine supra sanguineo — Cent. insect. (129) 27

Phalaena alniaria — Pand. insect. (93) 19

Phalaena altica — Iter Chin. (161) 10, 11

Phalaena alucita — Fund. entom. (154) 19, 32

Phalaena amata — Pand. insect. (93) 20

Phalaena ameriana — Pand. insect. (93) 21

Phalaena anastomosis — Pand. insect. (93) 21

Phalaena annularia — Hosp. insect. fl. (43) 22, 24

Phalaena ano flavo — Hosp. insect. fl. (43) 21, 23, 24, 32; Noxa insect. (46) 17

Phalaena antennulata — Hosp. insect. fl. (43) 17, 22, 24, 25, 29

Phalaena antiqua — Hosp. insect. fl. (43) 22[as antiquata], 25[as antiquata], 36[as antiquatae]; Noxa insect. (46) 17[as antiquata]; Pand. insect. (93) 14[as antiquata], 16, 19; Fund. fr. (123) 8[as antiquata]; Fund. entom. (154) 22[as Phalana]

Phalaena aptera — Noxa insect. (46) 17

Phalaena arbutella — Pand. insect. (93) 14

Phalaena argentella — Pand. fl. Ryb. (165) 11

Phalaena atlas — Phalaena (78) 4; Pand. insect. (93) [17, as 38]; Fund. entom. (154) 5; Iter Chin. (161) 10

Phalaena atomaria — Pand. insect. (93) 16; Pand. fl. Ryb. (165) 11

Phalaena atriplicis — Pand. insect. (93) 13, 22

Phalaena aurata — Hosp. insect. fl. (43) 27

Phalaena avellana — Pand. insect. (93) 15, 20

Phalaena batis — Pand. insect. (93) 15

Phalaena betularia — Pand. insect. (93) 12, 15, 18

Phalaena bicincta — Iter Chin. (161) 11

Phalaena bilineata — Pand. fl. Ryb. (165) 11

Phalaena bombyx — Hosp. insect. fl. (43) 32; Phalaena (78) 5, 11; Pand. insect. (93) 7; Fund. entom. (154) 7, 10, 32; Var. cib. (156) 4

Phalaena brassicae — Pand. insect. (93) [17, as 38]

Phalaena brumata — Pand. insect. (93) 14, 15, 20; Fund. fr. (123) 8; Fund. entom. (154) 22[as Phalana]

Phalaena brunnichana — Pand. fl. Ryb. (165) 11

Phalaena bucephala — Pand. insect. (93) 16, 19, 21

Phalaena caeruleocephala — Hosp. insect. fl. (43) 21, 22, 23, 24; Noxa insect. (46) 17; Pand. insect. (93) 14[as caerulocephala], 15[as caerulocephala]; Arb. Svec. (101) 20

Phalaena caja — Pand. insect. (93) 18; Pand. fl. Ryb. (165) 11

Phalaena calamitosa — Noxa insect. (46) 24; Usum hist. nat. (145) 17

Phalaena camelina — Pand. insect. (93) 16

Phalaena castrensis — Pand. insect. (93) 11, 14, [17, as 38], 18, 21

Phalaena chaerophyllata — Fund. entom. (154) [31, as 30]; Pand. fl. Ryb. (165) 11

Phalaena chenopodiata — Pand. insect. (93) 12; Pand. fl. Ryb. (165) 11

Phalaena chi — Pand. insect. (93) 16, [17, as 38]

Phalaena chrysitis — Pand. insect. (93) 16

Phalaena chrysorrhoea — Pand. insect. (93) 19[as chrysorrhaea]

Phalaena cingulata — Pand. fl. Ryb. (165) 11

Phalaena citrago — Pand. insect. (93) 14, 21

Phalaena clathrata — Pand. fl. Ryb. (165) 11

Phalaena colonella — Pand. fl. Ryb. (165) 11

Phalaena complanata — Pand. insect. (93) 19

Phalaena contortuplicata — Hosp. insect. fl. (43) 34

Phalaena corticosa — Hosp. insect. fl. (43) 34

Phalaena coryli — Pand. insect. (93) 20

Phalaena cossus — Hosp. insect. fl. (43) 32, 36; Fund. entom. (154) 7; Pand. fl. Ryb. (165) 11

Phalaena crataegi — Pand. insect. (93) 15

Phalaena crepuscularis — Iter Chin. (161) 12

Phalaena cucullata [error for cucullatella?] — Hosp. insect. fl. (43) 34, 35

Phalaena cucullatella — Pand. insect. (93) 15[as cuccullatella]; see also P. cucullata

Phalaena culmella — Pand. insect. (93) 11; Pand. fl. Ryb. (165) 11

Phalaena curtula — Pand. insect. (93) 19, 21, 22

Phalaena cynosbatella — Pand. insect. (93) 15

Phalaena delphinii — Pand. insect. (93) 16

Phalaena didactyla — Pand. insect. (93) 12

Phalaena dispar — Pand. insect. (93) 16, 19

Phalaena dodecella — Pand. insect. (93) 21

Phalaena dominula — Pand. insect. (93) 11, 21, [23, as 31][as Phalena]

Phalaena elinguaria — Pand. insect. (93) 15

Phalaena erucae tithymali — Hosp. insect. fl. (43) 26

Phalaena euonymella — Hosp. insect. fl. (43) 16[as euonymaria], 22[as euonymaria], 23[as euonymaria], 24[as euonymaria]; Noxa insect. (46) 26[as euonymaria]; Pand. insect. (93) 12

Phalaena exclamationis — Pand. fl. Ryb. (165) 11

Phalaena exsoleta — Pand. insect. (93) 12, [17, as 38], 22

Phalaena fagi — Pand. insect. (93) 18, 20

Phalaena falcatoria — Pand. insect. (93) 18, 19

Phalaena farinalis — Pand. fl. Ryb. (165) 11

Phalaena fascelina — Pand. insect. (93) 15, 16, [17, as 38], 18, 22

Phalaena festucae — Pand. insect. (93) 11

Phalaena fluctuata — Pand. insect. (93) 13; Pand. fl. Ryb. (165) 11

Phalaena follicularis — Hosp. insect. fl. (43) 31

Phalaena forficalis — Pand. insect. (93) [17, as 38]

Phalaena fraxini — Pand. insect. (93) [23, as 31][as Phalena]

Phalaena fuliginosa — Pand. insect. (93) 13, [17, as 38]

Phalaena fullonica — Iter Chin. (161) 7

Phalaena gallae resinosae — Hosp. insect. fl. (43) 36

Phalaena gamma — Hosp. insect. fl. (43) 22[as littera gamma], 23[as littera gamma], 24[as littera gamma], 26[as littera gamma], 34[as littera gamma]; Pand. insect. (93) 12, 18

Phalaena gamma aureum — Hosp. insect. fl. (43) 16, 29, 30, 31

Phalaena gangis — Cent. insect. (129) 27

Phalaena gemella — Pand. insect. (93) 20

Phalaena geometra — Hosp. insect. fl. (43) 16, 20, 21, 23, 26, 27, 33, 34, 35, 39; Hirudo (136) 2; Fund. entom. (154) 20, 32

Phalaena glabra aptera — Pand. insect. (93) [23, as 31]

Phalaena glyphica — Pand. insect. (93) 12

Phalaena goedartella — Pand. insect. (93) 19

Phalaena graminis — Pand. insect. (93) 11; Polit. nat. (109) 9; Fund. agrost. (152) 11; Fund. entom. (154) 7, [31, as 30]; Pand. fl. Ryb. (165) 11

Phalaena granella — Pand. insect. (93) 11

Phalaena gregaria — Hosp. insect. fl. (43) 29

Phalaena grossulariata — Pand. insect. (93) 12, 14; Pand. fl. Ryb. (165) 11

Phalaena hastiana — Pand. insect. (93) 21

Phalaena heracliana — Hosp. insect. fl. (43) 18[as heraclei]; Pand. insect. (93) 13[as heraclina]

Phalaena hesperus — Pand. insect. (93) [17, as 38]

Phalaena heteroclita — Cent. insect. (129) 28

Phalaena holmiana — Pand. insect. (93) 15

Phalaena hortulata — Pand. insect. (93) 19

Phalaena humuli — Hosp. insect. fl. (43) 38[as humularia]; Pand. insect. (93) 22; Hort. cul. (132) 9; Usum hist. nat. (145) 14; Fund. entom. (154) 22

Phalaena ilicifolia — Pand. insect. (93) 21

Phalaena jacobaeae — Hosp. insect. fl. (43) 31[as jacobaea]; Pand. insect. (93) 18; Pand. fl. Ryb. (165) 11

Phalaena jatropharia — Pand. insect. (93) 20

Phalaena juniperata — Pand. insect. (93) 22

Phalaena lacertinaria — Pand. insect. (93) 20

Phalaena lanestris — Pand. insect. (93) 14, 16, 21

Phalaena lapella — Pand. insect. (93) 18

Phalaena larva — Hosp. insect. fl. (43) 17

Phalaena larva grisea — Hosp. insect. fl. (43) 24

Phalaena larva speciosa — Hosp. insect. fl. (43) 28

Phalaena lecheana — Pand. insect. (93) 14

Phalaena lediana — Pand. insect. (93) 14; Ledum (178) 10

Phalaena lemnata — Pand. insect. (93) 22

Phalaena leopardus — Hosp. insect. fl. (43) 24

Phalaena leporina — Pand. insect. (93) 19, 21

Phalaena libatrix — Hosp. insect. fl. (43) 27; Pand. insect. (93) 15, 16, 21

Phalaena lubricipeda — Hosp. insect. fl. (43) 18, 21, 22, 23, 32, 34; Pand. insect. (93) 12, 13, 15, 19, 22; Pand. fl. Ryb. (165) 11

Phalaena luteolata — Pand. insect. (93) 15

Phalaena macrops — Iter Chin. (161) 11

Phalaena marginata — Pand. insect. (93) 20

Phalaena mesomella — Pand. insect. (93) 11

Phalaena meticulosa — Hosp. insect. fl. (43) 26, 28, 32, 38; Pand. insect. (93) 16, [17, as 38], 19, 22[as meliculosa]

Phalaena militaris — Iter Chin. (161) 7

Phalaena mirabilis — Hosp. insect. fl. (43) 23

Phalaena monacha — Pand. insect. (93) 15, 19, 21

Phalaena mori — Pand. insect. (93) 19; Fund. entom. (154) 22, [31, as 30]

Phalaena nasuta — Hosp. insect. fl. (43) 17, 22, 24, 34, 35, 36

Phalaena nasuta aurata — Hosp. insect. fl. (43) 37

Phalaena nasuta viridis — Hosp. insect. fl. (43) 37

Phalaena nemorella — Pand. insect. (93) 12

Phalaena neustria — Pand. insect. (93) 14; Fund. entom. (154) 25

Phalaena nigrella — Iter Chin. (161) 10

Phalaena nigromaculata — Hosp. insect. fl. (43) 17, 18, 22, 37

Phalaena noctua — Hosp. insect. fl. (43) 16, 20, 27, 29, 31; Fund. entom. (154) 32

Phalaena noctua spirilinguis, alis flavis: posticis concoloribus disco flavis lunula ambituque nigro — Cent. insect. (129) 28

Phalaena noctua spirilinguis, alis superioribus angustioribus fuscis maculis 3 flavis, posticis flavis extimo fuscis — Cent. insect. (129) 28

Phalaena nymphaeata — Pand. insect. (93) 16, 22; Pand. fl. Ryb. (165) 11

Phalaena occultella — Mund. invis. (149) 10; Fund. entom. (154) 5

Phalaena ocellata — Hosp. insect. fl. (43) 18, 22, 25, 33, 36

Phalaena oleracea — Pand. insect. (93) 18

Phalaena omicron-upsilon — Hosp. insect. fl. (43) 20

Phalaena oo — Pand. insect. (93) 19

Phalaena ophthalmoidea — Hosp. insect. fl. (43) 24

Phalaena oporana — Pand. insect. (93) 15

Phalaena oxyacanthae — Pand. insect. (93) 14, 15, 22[as oxyacantha]

Phalaena pacta — Pand. insect. (93) 19, 21

Phalaena padella — Pand. insect. (93) 14, 15

Phalaena papilionaria — Pand. insect. (93) 16[as papilionac.]

Phalaena pavonia — Pand. insect. (93) 12, 14, 15, 18, 20, 21

Phalaena pectinicornis — Hosp. insect. fl. (43) 24[as pecticornis], 25

Phalaena pectinicornis elinguis — Hosp. insect. fl. (43) 20, 23, 24, 28, 34, 37

Phalaena pectinicornis elinguis, alis cinereis, fasciis quinque dimidiatis — Hosp. insect. fl. (43) 25

Phalaena pectinicornis elinguis, alis deflexis griseis, fascia pallidiore pone punctum album: inferioribus prominulis — Hosp. insect. fl. (43) 33

Phalaena pectinicornis elinguis, alis reversis albidis: fasciis obsoletis fuscis; macula lunari — Phalaena (78) 11

Phalaena pectinicornis elinguis, bombyx dicta — Mat. med. anim. (29) 15

Phalaena pectinicornis spirilinguis — Hosp. insect. fl. (43) 16, 25, 32, 36, 37

Phalaena petulca — Iter Chin. (161) 7

Phalaena phalonia — Cent. insect. (129) 28

Phalaena picearia — Pand. insect. (93) 20

Phalaena pinella — Pand. insect. (93) 20

Phalaena pinetella — Pand. fl. Ryb. (165) 11

Phalaena pinguinalis — Pand. fl. Ryb. (165) 11

Phalaena pini — Pand. insect. (93) 20; Pand. fl. Ryb. (165) 11

Phalaena piniaria — Pand. insect. (93) 20; Fund. entom. (154) 22

Phalaena pisi — Pand. insect. (93) [17, as 38]; Pand. fl. Ryb. (165) 11

Phalaena plantaginis — Pand. insect. (93) 11, 13, 19

Phalaena pomonella — Pand. insect. (93) 15; Polit. nat. (109) 8; Pand. fl. Ryb. (165) 11

Phalaena popularia — Pand. insect. (93) 22

Phalaena populi — Pand. insect. (93) 15, 20, 22

Phalaena porcellus — Hosp. insect. fl. (43) 20, 31

Phalaena potamogeton — Pand. insect. (93) 11

Phalaena potatoria — Pand. insect. (93) 11

Phalaena praecox — Pand. insect. (93) [17, as 38]

Phalaena prasinaria — Pand. insect. (93) 20

Phalaena pratella — Pand. insect. (93) 11; Pand. fl. Ryb. (165) 11

Phalaena processionaria — Hosp. insect. fl. (43) 34; Pand. insect. (93) 19

Phalaena proletella — Pand. insect. (93) 16, [17, as 38]; Esca avium (174) 2

Phalaena pronuba — Pand. insect. (93) 12, 16, [17, as 38], 18; Pand. fl. Ryb. (165) 11

Phalaena prunaria — Pand. insect. (93) 14

Phalaena prunata — Pand. insect. (93) 14

Phalaena pruni — Pand. insect. (93) 14

Phalaena psi — Pand. insect. (93) 15, 16, 19, 20

Phalaena pudibunda — Pand. insect. (93) 15, 19, 20

Phalaena purpuralis — Pand. fl. Ryb. (165) 11

Phalaena purpuraria — Pand. insect. (93) 14, 20; see also P. purpurata

Phalaena purpurata [error for purpuraria?] — Pand. insect. (93) 12; Pand. fl. Ryb. (165) 11

Phalaena pusaria — Pand. fl. Ryb. (165) 11

Phalaena pyralis — Fund. entom. (154) 32

Phalaena pyramidea — Pand. insect. (93) 14, 20

Phalaena quadra — Pand. insect. (93) 19, 20

Phalaena quercifolia — Pand. insect. (93) 11, 14, 15[as quircifolia], 21

Phalaena quercus — Pand. insect. (93) 14, 18, 19; Erica (163) 15

Phalaena rajella — Pand. insect. (93) 19

Phalaena ramella — Pand. insect. (93) 20

Phalaena resinella — Pand. insect. (93) 21

Phalaena roesella — Pand. insect. (93) 15; Pand. fl. Ryb. (165) 11

Phalaena rosaria — Pand. insect. (93) 13, 15

Phalaena rostralis — Pand. insect. (93) 20, 22

Phalaena rubi — Pand. insect. (93) 15, 21

Phalaena rubicunda — Hosp. insect. fl. (43) 34

Phalaena rumicis — Pand. insect. (93) 13, [17, as 38]

Phalaena russula — Fund. entom. (154) 22

Phalaena salicella — Pand. insect. (93) 21

Phalaena salicis — Hosp. insect. fl. (43) 36[as salicina], 38[as salicina]; Noxa insect. (46) 26[as salicina]; Pand. insect. (93) 21; Arb. Svec. (101) 26, 27; Pand. fl. Ryb. (165) 11

Phalaena sambucaria — Pand. insect. (93) 13

Phalaena schaeferella — Pand. insect. (93) 20

Phalaena secalis — Pand. insect. (93) 11

Phalaena seticornis — Hosp. insect. fl. (43) 16, 18, 19, 25, 26, 32, 33, 34, 36, 37; Noxa insect. (46) 25

Phalaena seticornis, alis patentibus cinereis: media extremitate postica fusco nebulosis, fascia fusca — Hosp. insect. fl. (43) 29

Phalaena seticornis elinguis cinerea: fascia transversa saturatiore — Hosp. insect. fl. (43) 20

Phalaena seticornis spirilinguis — Hosp. insect. fl. (43) 29, 32, 33, 35, 38

Phalaena seticornis spirilinguis, alis incumbentibus: superioribus cinereo-griseis, puncto atro; inferioribus atris, omnibus margine postico interiore barbatis — Hosp. insect. fl. (43) 30

Phalaena seticornis spirilinguis, alis reflexis pone divaricatis cruce testacea — Hosp. insect. fl. (43) 17

Phalaena seticornis spirilinguis fasciculata, alis depressis griseo-fuscis — Noxa insect. (46) 22

Phalaena seticornis spirilinguis fusca: dorso vitta alba: alarum apicibus acuminatis recurvatis — Hosp. insect. fl. (43) 17

Phalaena seticornis spirilinguis nasuta, cinereo fuscoque nebulosa — Hosp. insect. fl. (43) 36

Phalaena seticornis spirilinguis nasuta, fasciis argenteis variis — Hosp. insect. fl. (43) 21

Phalaena sociella — Pand. fl. Ryb. (165) 11

Phalaena solandriana — Pand. insect. (93) 18

Phalaena sphinx — Hosp. insect. fl. (43) 17, 24, 26, 36, 38, 39

Phalaena spirilinguis cucullata — Hosp. insect. fl. (43) 34

Phalaena stratiotata — Hosp. insect. fl. (43) 26[as stratiotis]; Pand. insect. (93) 16[as statiotata]

Phalaena strigilata — Pand. fl. Ryb. (165) 11

Phalaena strobilella — Pand. insect. (93) 21; Polit. nat. (109) 8, 10

Phalaena strobili abietis — Hosp. insect. fl. (43) 36

Phalaena subcutanea — Hosp. insect. fl. (43) 24, 25, 32, 34

Phalaena syringana — Pand. insect. (93) 11

Phalaena tau — Pand. insect. (93) 18

Phalaena terribilis — Hosp. insect. fl. (43) 32, 33

Phalaena tetradactyla — Pand. fl. Ryb. (165) 11

Phalaena tiliaria — Pand. insect. (93) 16

Phalaena tinea — Pand. insect. (93) 7[as tinaea]; Fund. entom. (154) 5, 32

Phalaena tortrix — Pand. insect. (93) 7; Fund. entom. (154) 32

Phalaena trax — Iter Chin. (161) 7

Phalaena triplasia — Pand. insect. (93) [17, as 38][as triplaria], 22; Pand. fl. Ryb. (165) 11[as triplacia]

Phalaena turionella — Pand. insect. (93) 21

Phalaena typica — Pand. insect. (93) 21

Phalaena umbratica — Pand. insect. (93) [17, as 38]

Phalaena undulata — Pand. insect. (93) 21

Phalaena ursus — Hosp. insect. fl. (43) 16; Noxa insect. (46) 18

Phalaena ursus flavus — Hosp. insect. fl. (43) 18, 32

Phalaena urticata — Pand. fl. Ryb. (165) 11

Phalaena uxor nuda — Hosp. insect. fl. (43) 23, 24, 31, 35

Phalaena verbasci — Pand. insect. (93) 12, 16[as verbasei]

Phalaena verticalis — Pand. insect. (93) 19

Phalaena villica — Pand. insect. (93) 13, 19

Phalaena vinula — Hosp. insect. fl. (43) 32, 34, 36, 38; Pand. insect. (93) 19, 21, 22

Phalaena vinula minor — Hosp. insect. fl. (43) 23

Phalaena viridana — Pand. insect. (93) 20; Pand. fl. Ryb. (165) 11; see also P. viridaria

Phalaena viridaria [error for viridana or viridata?] — Pand. insect. (93) 21

Phalaena viridata — Pand. insect. (93) 20; see also P. viridaria

Phalaena viridis — Hosp. insect. fl. (43) 34

Phalaena vulpinaria — Pand. insect. (93) 11

Phalaena w littera — Hosp. insect. fl. (43) 17, 18, 27

Phalaena wauaria — Pand. insect. (93) 12[as wauvaria], 16[as wauvaria]

Phalaena xylosteana — Pand. insect. (93) 12

Phalaena xylostella — Pand. insect. (93) 12

Phalaena ziczac — Hosp. insect. fl. (43) 37; Pand. insect. (93) 21

Phalangium — Fund. entom. (154) 19, 21

Phalangium americanum — Mus. Ad.-Frid. (11) 44

Phalangium monstrosum — Mus. Ad.-Frid. (11) 44

Phalangium opilio — Esca avium (174) 3

Phalaris — Hort. Upsal. (7) 34; Vir. pl. (13) 17; Fl. oecon. (17) 2; Cui bono? (42) 17; Pand. insect. (93) 11; Nom. bot. (107) 9; Fund. agrost. (152) 16, 22, 27, 31, 36

Phalaris aquatica — Cent. I. pl. (65) 4; Fl. Palaest. (70) 12

Phalaris arundinacea — Pan Svec. (26) 13; Herbat. Upsal. (50) 12; Stat. pl. (55) 13; Fl. Angl. (56) 10; Fl. Monsp. (74) 9; Prodr. fl. Dan. (82) 13; Fl. Belg. (112) 12; Fund. agrost. (152) 7; Fl. Åker. (162) 6

Phalaris bulbosa — Cent. I. pl. (65) 4; Fl. Palaest. (70) 12; Fund. agrost. (152) 17

Phalaris bulbosa, albo semine — Cent. I. pl. (65) 4

Phalaris canariensis — Demonstr. pl. (49) 3; Pl. officin. (52) 6; Fl. Monsp. (74) 9; Fl. Belg. (112) 12; Hort. cul. (132) 9

Phalaris erucaeformis — Hist. nat. Rossia (144) 27

Phalaris oryzoides — Cent. II. pl. (66) 6; Fl. Jam. (105) 12; Colon. pl. (158) 13

Phalaris panicula oblonga — Pl. Mart.-Burs. (6) 3

Phalaris panicula spiciformi ovato-oblonga, glumis carinatis lanceolatis — Cent. I. pl. (65) 4

Phalaris phleiformis — Pan Svec. (26) 13

Phalaris phleoides — Demonstr. pl. (49) 3; Fl. Angl. (56) 10; Fl. Monsp. (74) 9; Prodr. fl. Dan. (82) 13[as phleodis]; Fl. Belg. (112) 12; Fund. agrost. (152) 7

Phalaris spica cylindrica — Pl. Mart.-Burs. (6) [1]

Phalaris spica cylindrica, glumis carinatis — Cent. I. pl. (65) 4

Phalaris utriculata — Fl. Monsp. (74) 9

Phallus — Fl. oecon. (17) 30; Cui bono? (42) 16

Phallus esculentus — Pand. fl. Ryb. (165) 23

Phallus impudicus — Prodr. fl. Dan. (82) 26

Pharmacum magnum — Herb. Amboin. (57) 19

Pharmacum papetarium — Herb. Amboin. (57) 17

Pharmacum sagueri — Herb. Amboin. (57) 9

Pharnaceum cerviana — Demonstr. pl. (49) 9

Pharnaceum cordifolium — Pl. rar. Afr. (115) 9

Pharnaceum foliis obcordatis — Pl. rar. Afr. (115) 9

Pharnaceum mollugo — Fl. Cap. (99) 13[as Pharnacium]

Pharus — Fl. Jam. (105) 26; Fund. agrost. (152) 18, 28, 37

Pharus latifolius — Pl. Jam. (102) 27

Pharus resupinatus — Fl. Jam. (105) 21

Phascum — Sem. musc. (28) 17; Buxbaumia (85) 14

Phaseoloides — Hort. Upsal. (7) 36

Phaseolus — Vir. pl. (13) 23, 32; Pl. hybr. (33) 29; Vern. arb. (47) 9; Demonstr. pl. (49) [vii]; Stat. pl. (55) 5; Cul. mut. (88) 2, 6; Nom. bot. (107) 16

Phaseolus arborescens zeylanicus monocarpos hermanni — Nova pl. gen. 1747 (14) 23

Phaseolus balicus — Herb. Amboin. (57) 23

Phaseolus caule erectiusculo laevi, leguminibus pendulis compressis rugosis — Cent. I. pl. (65) 23

Phaseolus coccineus — Demonstr. pl. (49) 19

Phaseolus cylindraceus — Herb. Amboin. (57) 23

Phaseolus farinosus — Demonstr. pl. (49) 19

Phaseolus inamoenus — Fl. Cap. (99) 17

Phaseolus lunatus — Demonstr. pl. (49) 20

Phaseolus maritimus — Herb. Amboin. (57) 23

Phaseolus max — Herb. Amboin. (57) 23

Phaseolus minimus — Herb. Amboin. (57) 23

Phaseolus minor — Herb. Amboin. (57) 23

Phaseolus montanus — Herb. Amboin. (57) 28

Phaseolus nanus — Cent. I. pl. (65) 23; Hort. cul. (132) 16

Phaseolus parvus italicus — Cent. I. pl. (65) 23

Phaseolus radiatus — Herb. Amboin. (57) 23

Phaseolus strumosa radice, flore purpureo, siliqua angustissima — Somn. pl. (68) 19

Phaseolus unguiculatus — Herb. Amboin. (57) 23

Phaseolus vulgaris — Demonstr. pl. (49) 19; Pl. officin. (52) 15; Fr. escul. (127) 17; Hort. cul. (132) 16

Phaseolus vulgaris italicus humilis seu minor, albus cum orbita nigricante — Cent. I. pl. (65) 23

Phasianus — Mus. Ad.-Frid. (11) [viii], 5

Phasianus crista flava, pectore coccineo, remigibus secundariis coeruleis — Mus. Ad.-Frid. (11) 5

Phasianus gallus — Fund. ornith. (137) 20; Iter Chin. (161) 10; Esca avium (174) 6ff.

Phasianus lanatus — Iter Chin. (161) 10

Phasianus pusillus — Iter Chin. (161) 10

Phellandrium — Hort. Upsal. (7) 41; Vir. pl. (13) 28, 29; Fl. oecon. (17) 7; Oecon. nat. (20) 36; Pan Svec. (26) 19; Noxa insect. (46) 27; Usum hist. nat. (145) 23

Phellandrium aquaticum — Hosp. insect. fl. (43) 19; Herbat. Upsal. (50) 14; Stat. pl. (55) 13; Fl. Angl. (56) 13; Fl. Monsp. (74) 13; Prodr. fl. Dan. (82) 16; Fl. Belg. (112) 15; Fl. Åker. (162) 9; Pand. fl. Ryb. (165) 18

Phellandrium mutellina — Fl. alp. (71) 15

Philadelphus — Hort. Upsal. (7) 21; Vir. pl. (13) 10, 31; Calend. fl. (72) 5; Fr. Svec. (91) [ii], 24

Philadelphus coronarius — Demonstr. pl. (49) 13; Calend. fl. (72) [10], [13], [16]; Fr. Svec. (91) 5, 22; Hort. cul. (132) 25

Philander — Mus. Ad.-Frid. (11) 2

Philander americanus — Mus. Ad.-Frid. (11) 2

Philander maximus orientalis — Mus. Ad.-Frid. (11) 2

Phillyrea — Hort. Upsal. (7) 36; Gem. arb. (24) 9; Fl. Monsp. (74) 7; Nom. bot. (107) 9

Phillyrea angustifolia — Demonstr. pl. (49) [1]; Fl. Palaest. (70) 11; Fl. Monsp. (74) 8

Phillyrea foliis lanceolatis integerrimis — Pl. Mart.-Burs. (6) 30

Phillyrea latifolia — Fl. Monsp. (74) 8

Phillyrea ligustrifolia — Gem. arb. (24) 15[as ligustri folio]; Fl. Monsp. (74) 8

Phlegmaria — Usum musc. (148) 4

Phleum — Fl. oecon. (17) 2; Fund. agrost. (152) 22, 25, 36

Phleum alpinum — Pan Svec. (26) 13; Fl. alp. (71) 12

Phleum arenarium — Stat. pl. (55) 22; Fl. Angl. (56) 10; Prodr. fl. Dan. (82) 13; Fl. Belg. (112) 13

Phleum bulbosum — Fund. agrost. (152) 17

Phleum nodosum — Prodr. fl. Dan. (82) 13; Fl. Belg. (112) 13

Phleum pratense — Demonstr. pl. (49) 3; Herbat. Upsal. (50) 6; Stat. pl. (55) 21; Fl. Angl. (56) 10; Fl. Monsp. (74) 9; Prodr. fl. Dan. (82) 13; Fl. Belg. (112) 13; Fund. agrost. (152) 7; Fl. Åker. (162) 6; Pand. fl. Ryb. (165) 16; Esca avium (174) 10[as Pheum]

Phleum reclinatum — Fl. Belg. (112) 13

Phleum spica ovali cylindracea — Pl. Mart.-Burs. (6) 2

Phleum vulgare — Pan Svec. (26) 13

Phlomis — Hort. Upsal. (7) 36; Anandria (9) 4; Cui bono? (42) 20; Fl. Cap. (99) 6

Phlomis fruticosa — Demonstr. pl. (49) 16; Fl. Palaest. (70) 23

Phlomis herba venti — Demonstr. pl. (49) 16; Fl. Palaest. (70) 23; Fl. Monsp. (74) 19

Phlomis leonurus — Fl. Cap. (99) 8, 15; Hort. cul. (132) 24; Aphyteia (185) [5]

Phlomis lychnitis — Fl. Monsp. (74) 19

Phlomis nepetifolia — Fl. Cap. (99) 15; Pl. Surin. (177) 11

Phlomis sibirica — Calend. fl. (72) [13]

Phlomis tuberosa — Demonstr. pl. (49) 16; Hist. nat. Rossia (144) 31

Phlox — Hort. Upsal. (7) 36; Nova pl. gen. 1751 (32) 8; Pl. hybr. (33) 29; Fund. fr. (123) 18, 23

Phlox foliis lanceolatis margine scabris, corymbis compositis — Pl. rar. Camsch. (30) 10

Phlox foliis linearibus villosis, pedunculis ternis — Pl. rar. Camsch. (30) 9

Phlox foliis lineari-lanceolatis glabris, caule erecto, corymbo terminali — Pl. rar. Camsch. (30) 10

Phlox foliis lineari-lanceolatis villosis, caule erecto, corymbo terminali — Pl. rar. Camsch. (30) 10

Phlox foliis ovatis, floribus solitariis — Pl. rar. Camsch. (30) 10

Phlox foliis setaceis glabris, floribus solitariis — Pl. rar. Camsch. (30) 11

Phlox foliis subulatis hirsutis, floribus oppositis — Pl. rar. Camsch. (30) 10

Phlox sibirica — Hist. nat. Rossia (144) 28

Phoca — Oecon. nat. (20) 36, 41; Instr. peregr. (96) 11; Polit. nat. (109) 15; Lepra (140) 6; Usum hist. nat. (145) 23

Phoca ursina — Hist. nat. Rossia (144) 12

Phoenicopterus — Fund. ornith. (137) 24

Phoenix — Hort. Upsal. (7) 37; Spons. pl. (12) [1][as Phaenix]; Vir. pl. (13) 26; Chin. Lagerstr. (64) 5; Fund. agrost. (152) 16

Phoenix dactylifera — Demonstr. pl. (49) 27; Pl. officin. (52) 9; Fl. Palaest. (70) 32; Fl. Jam. (105) 23; Fr. escul. (127) 13

Phoenix montana — Herb. Amboin. (57) 25

Phoenix seu palma — Spons. pl. (12) 42

Pholas — Var. cib. (156) 5; Fund. test. (166) 7, 18, 31, 32, 34, 40

Pholas dactylus — Fund. test. (166) 40

Phryganea — Metam. pl. (67) 6; Pand. insect. (93) 7[as Phryganaea]

Phryganea bimaculata — Pand. fl. Ryb. (165) 11

Phryganea flava — Pand. fl. Ryb. (165) 12

Phryganea nigra — Pand. fl. Ryb. (165) 11

Phryganea phalaenoides — Esca avium (174) 8

Phryma — Nova pl. gen. 1751 (32) 12, 33, 34, 48

Phryma leptostachya — Demonstr. pl. (49) 16[as Phyma, corr. p. 27]; Calend. fl. (72) [15]

Phylica — Fl. Cap. (99) 6, 9, 10; Fund. fr. (123) 18

Phylica buxifolia — Fl. Cap. (99) 12

Phylica dioica — Fl. Cap. (99) 12

Phylica ericoides — Fl. Cap. (99) 12

Phylica foliis linearibus triquetris, sparsis caule piloso, bracteis apice coloratis glabrisque — Cent. I. pl. (65) 8

Phylica plumosa — Fl. Cap. (99) 12

Phylica radiata — Cent. I. pl. (65) 8; Fl. Cap. (99) 12

Phyllanthus — Hort. Upsal. (7) 37; Vir. pl. (13) 12, 27; Oecon. nat. (20) 17

Phyllanthus emblica — Pl. officin. (52) 13

Phyllanthus epiphyllanthus — Fl. Jam. (105) 21

Phyllanthus niruri — Herb. Amboin. (57) 26

Phyllanthus urinaria — Demonstr. pl. (49) 25; Herb. Amboin. (57) 26

Phyllis — Hort. Upsal. (7) 37

Phyllitis — Acrostichum (10) 6, 8, 14

Phyllitis amboinica — Herb. Amboin. (57) 26

Phyllitis non sinuata minor, apice folii radices agente — Pl. rar. Camsch. (30) 5

Phyllitis ramosa jamaicensis maxima, aversa parte ferruginea lanugine circumquaque obducta — Acrostichum (10) 14[as serruginea]

Phyllitis ramosa trifida — Acrostichum (10) 15

Phyllitis repens scandensve, foliis duplicibus, aliis latis et subrotundis, aliis longis et angustis — Acrostichum (10) 9

Phyllitis saxatilis virginiana, per summitates foliorum prolifera — Pl. rar. Camsch. (30) 5

Physalis — Hort. Upsal. (7) 37; Vir. pl. (13) 19; Pl. hybr. (33) 29; Nom. bot. (107) 10

Physalis alkekengi — Demonstr. pl. (49) 6; Pl. officin. (52) 4; Calend. fl. (72) [13]; Fl. Monsp. (74) 12; Hort. cul. (132) 24

Physalis angulata — Calend. fl. (72) [18]; Fl. Jam. (105) 14

Physalis annua — Vern. arb. (47) 9

Physalis pruinosa — Demonstr. pl. (49) 6; Fl. Jam. (105) 14

Physalis pubescens — Demonstr. pl. (49) 6; Herb. Amboin. (57) 26

Physalis somnifera — Demonstr. pl. (49) 6

Physalis viscosa — Calend. fl. (72) [19]

Physeter — Nat. pelagi (84) 14[as Physecter]

Physis pelagica — Chin. Lagerstr. (64) 29, 36[as palagica]

Phyteuma — Gem. arb. (24) 13

Phyteuma comosa — Fl. alp. (71) 14; Fl. Monsp. (74) 11

Phyteuma hemisphaerica — Fl. alp. (71) 13[as hemispherica]; Fl. Monsp. (74) 11

Phyteuma orbicularis — Fl. Angl. (56) 12; Fl. alp. (71) 14

Phyteuma pauciflora — Fl. alp. (71) 13; Fl. Monsp. (74) 11

Phyteuma spica oblonga nuda, foliis caulinis lanceolatis serratis — Pl. Mart.-Burs. (6) 6

Phyteuma spicata — Fl. alp. (71) 14; Fl. Monsp. (74) 11; Prodr. fl. Dan. (82) 15

Phytolacca — Pl. Mart.-Burs. (6) [vi]; Hort. Upsal. (7) 36; Spons. pl. (12) 35; Nova pl. gen. 1751 (32) 9; Prol. pl. 1760 (114) 10[as Phytalacca]; Pot. theae (142) 10

Phytolacca americana — Demonstr. pl. (49) 12; Pl. officin. (52) 15; Calend. fl. (72) [17]; Specif. Canad. (76) 16, 28; Pl. tinct. (97) 18; Fl. Jam. (105) 16; Mac. olit. (113) 20; Fr. escul. (127) 11; Cimicifuga (173) 9

Phytolacca asiatica — Fl. Palaest. (70) 19

Phytolacca decandra — Obs. mat. med. (171) 4

Phytolacca foliis integerrimis — Pl. Mart.-Burs. (6) 7[as Phytolaica]

Phytolacca icosandra — Fl. Jam. (105) 16

Phytolacca octandra — Pl. Surin. (177) 9

Pica — Migr. avium (79) 22, 23

Pica caudata varia — Mat. med. anim. (29) 8

Pica daurica — Hist. nat. Rossia (144) 16

Picris — Vir. pl. (13) 25

Picris echioides — Demonstr. pl. (49) 22; Fl. Angl. (56) 21[as echiodes]; Calend. fl. (72) [16], [22]

Picris foliis lanceolatis subdentatis, caule nudiusculo — Pl. Mart.-Burs. (6) 10

Picris hieracioides — Fl. Angl. (56) 21; Fl. Palaest. (70) 27; Prodr. fl. Dan. (82) 22; Fl. Belg. (112) 20

Picris scanica — Pan Svec. (26) 31

Picus — Oecon. nat. (20) 25, 41; Migr. avium (79) 8; Polit. nat. (109) 14

Picus viridis — Esca avium (174) 3

Pigmentaria — Herb. Amboin. (57) 9

Pigritia — Surin. Grill. (16) 7

Pigrus — Surin. Grill. (16) 9

Pilosella — Hosp. insect. fl. (43) 12; Oves (61) 14

Pilosella amboinica — Herb. Amboin. (57) 28

Pilularia — Acrostichum (10) 6

Pilularia globulifera — Stat. pl. (55) 13; Fl. Angl. (56) 25; Rar. Norv. (157) 11

Pimenta — Fl. Jam. (105) 9[as Pimento]

Pimpinella — Peloria (3) 16; Vir. pl. (13) 19; Sapor. med. (31) 19; Metam. pl. (67) 16; Pand. insect. (93) 13; Nom. bot. (107) 11; Menthae (153) 6

Pimpinella anisum — Demonstr. pl. (49) 9; Pl. officin. (52) 4; Fl. Palaest. (70) 16; Pl. rar. Afr. (115) 6; Hort. cul. (132) 16

Pimpinella foliolis subrotundis — Pl. Mart.-Burs. (6) 11

Pimpinella glauca — Fl. Monsp. (74) 13

Pimpinella officinarum — Pan Svec. (26) 19; Hosp. insect. fl. (43) 19

Pimpinella saxifraga — Pl. officin. (52) 15; Stat. pl. (55) 21; Fl. Angl. (56) 13; Fl. Palaest. (70) 16; Fl. Monsp. (74) 13; Prodr. fl. Dan. (82) 16; Fl. Belg. (112) 15; Fl. Åker. (162) 9; Pand. fl. Ryb. (165) 18

Pinanga — Herb. Amboin. (57) 6

Pinanga sylvestris — Herb. Amboin. (57) 6

Pinguicula — Fl. oecon. (17) [1]; Pan Svec. (26) 9; Cervus (60) 21; Nom. bot. (107) 9; Usum hist. nat. (145) 29

Pinguicula alba — Pan Svec. (26) 12

Pinguicula alpina — Stat. pl. (55) 16; Fl. alp. (71) 12

Pinguicula flore amplo purpureo cum calcari longissimo — Pl. Mart.-Burs. (6) 20

Pinguicula minima — Pan Svec. (26) 12

Pinguicula nectario cylindraceo, longitudine petali — Pl. Mart.-Burs. (6) 20

Pinguicula villosa — Stat. pl. (55) 16; Fl. Angl. (56) 9; Fl. alp. (71) 12; Hist. nat. Rossia (144) 27

Pinguicula vulgaris — Pan Svec. (26) 12; Pl. escul. (35) 6; Herbat. Upsal. (50) 6; Stat. pl. (55) 15; Fl. Angl. (56) 9; Fl. Monsp. (74) 8; Prodr. fl. Dan. (82) 13; Fl. Belg. (112) 12

Pinna — Fund. test. (166) 18

Pinus — Spons. pl. (12) [2], 13, 21, 29, 39; Vir. pl. (13) 24; Fl. oecon. (17) 25; Oecon. nat. (20) 15, 18; Pl. escul. (35) 25, 27, 28; Morb. hyeme (38) 12; Hosp. insect. fl. (43) 40; Noxa insect. (46) 25; Mus ind. (62) 14; Fung. melit. (69) 3; Fl. alp. (71) 24; Calend. fl. (72) [11]; Pand. insect. (93) 20; Arb. Svec. (101) [3], 4, 11, 12; Nom. bot. (107) 18; Prol. pl. 1760 (114) 2, 19; Prol. pl. 1763 (130) 5; Usum musc. (148) 7

Pinus abies — Herbat. Upsal. (50) 11; Pl. officin. (52) 3; Stat. pl. (55) 18; Fl. Angl. (56) 24; Cervus (60) 8; Metam. pl. (67) 22, 23; Fl. Monsp. (74) 28; Fl. Cap. (99) 2; Arb. Svec. (101) 8, 12; Prol. pl. 1760 (114) 9; Hist. nat. Rossia (144) 34; Rar. Norv. (157) 16; Fl. Åker. (162) 19; Pand. fl. Ryb. (165) 22; Esca avium (174) 14

Pinus arbor — Pan Svec. (26) 36

Pinus cedrus — Fl. Palaest. (70) 30; Fl. alp. (71) 23, 24, 26; Hist. nat. Rossia (144) 34

Pinus cembra — Fl. alp. (71) 23, 25; Fr. escul. (127) 21; Hist. nat. Rossia (144) 22, 34; Usum hist. nat. (145) 12

Pinus foliis quinis scabris — Gem. arb. (24) 32

Pinus larix — Pl. officin. (52) 19; Fl. alp. (71) 23, 25; Hist. nat. Rossia (144) 34

Pinus maritima — Fl. Monsp. (74) 30

Pinus mugo — Metam. pl. (67) 22

Pinus picea — Fl. Angl. (56) 24; Fl. alp. (71) 23, 24; Hist. nat. Rossia (144) 34

Pinus pinea — Demonstr. pl. (49) 25; Pl. officin. (52) 15; Fl. Monsp. (74) 28; Fr. escul. (127) 21

Pinus sativa — Pl. escul. (35) 4

Pinus sylvestris — Gem. arb. (24) 32; Hosp. insect. fl. (43) 36; Herbat. Upsal. (50) 11; Pl. officin. (52) 15, 19; Stat. pl. (55) 17; Fl. Angl. (56) 24; Cervus (60) 8; Metam. pl. (67) 22; Fl. Palaest. (70) 30; Fl. Monsp. (74) 28; Pane diaet. (83) 20; Arb. Svec. (101) 8, 11, 13, 15, 30; Fl. Belg. (112) 22; Prol. pl. 1760 (114) 2; Hist. nat. Rossia (144) 34; Fl. Åker. (162) 19; Erica (163) 11; Pand. fl. Ryb. (165) 22

Piper — Vir. pl. (13) 25; Pan Svec. (26) 7; Sapor. med. (31) 19; Pl. escul. (35) 13; Odor. med. (40) 15; Herb. Amboin. (57) 19, 22; Nom. bot. (107) 9; Inebr. (117) 12; Prol. pl. 1763 (130) 13; Usum hist. nat. (145) 24; Obs. mat. med. (171) 8

Piper acuminatum — Fl. Jam. (105) 12

Piper aduncum — Fl. Jam. (105) 12

Piper amalago — Herb. Amboin. (57) 22; Fl. Jam. (105) 12

Piper betle — Fl. Jam. (105) 12

Piper caninum — Herb. Amboin. (57) 19

Piper decumanum — Cent. I. pl. (65) 2

Piper decumanum, foliis cordatis novemnerviis reticulatis — Herb. Amboin. (57) 19

Piper indicum — Ambros. (100) 14

Piper longum — Pl. officin. (52) 15; Herb. Amboin. (57) 22

Piper malamiris — Herb. Amboin. (57) 19, 22

Piper nigrum — Pl. officin. (52) 15

Piper obtusifolium — Fl. Jam. (105) 12

Piper pellucidum — Fl. Jam. (105) 12

Piper peltatum — Herb. Amboin. (57) 27; Fl. Jam. (105) 12

Piper rotundifolium — Fl. Jam. (105) 12

Piper siriboa — Herb. Amboin. (57) 22

Piper trifoliatum — Fl. Jam. (105) 12

Piper umbellatum — Fl. Jam. (105) 12

Piper verticillatum — Pl. Jam. (102) [5]

Piscidia erythrina — Fl. Jam. (105) 19

Piscis trigonus — Hort. Upsal. (7) 43

Pisonia aculeata — Fl. Jam. (105) 22

Pistacia — Betula (1) 5; Ficus (2) 17; Spons. pl. (12) [2], 43; Vir. pl. (13) 32; Pl. escul. (35) 4; Mirac. insect. (45) 15; Metam. pl. (67) 24; Fl. Monsp. (74) 7; Opobals. (135) 6

Pistacia balsamus — Fl. Palaest. (70) 31

Pistacia lentiscus — Pl. officin. (52) 12; Fl. Palaest. (70) 31; Fl. Monsp. (74) 28; Pl. tinct. (97) 28

Pistacia narbonensis — Fl. Monsp. (74) 28

Pistacia simaruba — Pl. officin. (52) 18; Fl. Jam. (105) 22

Pistacia terebinthus — Gem. arb. (24) 23; Pl. officin. (52) 19; Fl. Palaest. (70) 31; Fl. Monsp. (74) 28; Opobals. (135) 10

Pistacia vera — Pl. officin. (52) 15; Fl. Palaest. (70) 31; Fr. escul. (127) 21[as Pitstacia]

Pistia stratiotes — Herb. Amboin. (57) 28; Fl. Palaest. (70) 29; Fl. Jam. (105) 20

Pisum — Vir. pl. (13) 23, 32; Fl. oecon. (17) 18; Curios. nat. (18) 6; Pl. escul. (35) 27; Oves (61) 18, 23; Hort. acad. (63) 2; Metam. pl. (67) 13; Fung. melit. (69) 3; Calend. fl. (72) [15]; Pane diaet. (83) 14; Pand. insect. (93) [17, as 38]; Instr. peregr. (96) 10; Nom. bot. (107) 16; Usum hist. nat. (145) 24

Pisum arvense — Stat. pl. (55) 19

Pisum hortense — Fl. Cap. (99) 2

Pisum maritimum — Pan Svec. (26) 30; Pl. escul. (35) 21; Demonstr. pl. (49) 20; Stat. pl. (55) 12; Fl. Angl. (56) 20; Prodr. fl. Dan. (82) 21; Fr. escul. (127) 18[as maritima]

Pisum ochrus — Demonstr. pl. (49) 20; Fl. Monsp. (74) 22

Pisum sativum — Hosp. insect. fl. (43) 28; Demonstr. pl. (49) 20; Pl. officin. (52) 15; Fl. Angl. (56) 20; Fl. Jam. (105) 24; Fr. escul. (127) 18; Hort. cul. (132) 16

Pisum sativum nanum — Hort. cul. (132) 16

Pisum sativum quadratum — Hort. cul. (132) 16

Pisum westrogothicum — Pan Svec. (26) 30

Pithyusa — Euphorbia (36) 3, 23

Pithyusa seu esula minor altera, floribus rubris — Euphorbia (36) 23[as Pityusa]

Planta anatis — Herb. Amboin. (57) 21

Planta folia habens oblongo rotunda — Nova pl. gen. 1747 (14) 31

Planta lactaria africana — Euphorbia (36) 10

Planta pluribus foliis triquetris, instar graminis cyprini, summitate foliorum in plurima folia biuncialia divisis — Acrostichum (10) 10

Planta zeylanica menthae aquaticae in insula zeylana nascentis species — Nova pl. gen. 1747 (14) 8

Plantago — Peloria (3) 10; Pand. insect. (93) 11; Nom. bot. (107) 10

Plantago albicans — Fl. Monsp. (74) 10

Plantago alpina — Fl. alp. (71) 13

Plantago aquatica — Herb. Amboin. (57) 28

Plantago asiatica — Hist. nat. Rossia (144) 28

Plantago coronopus — Pan Svec. (26) 15; Stat. pl. (55) 12; Fl. Angl. (56) 11; Fl. Monsp. (74) 10; Prodr. fl. Dan. (82) 14; Fl. Belg. (112) 13

Plantago cynops — Demonstr. pl. (49) 4; Pl. officin. (52) 16; Fl. Palaest. (70) 14; Fl. Monsp. (74) 10

Plantago dubia — Prodr. fl. Dan. (82) 14

Plantago foliis lanceolato-linearibus, scapo longitudine foliorum, spica oblonga — Pl. Mart.-Burs. (6) 14

Plantago foliis linearibus pinnato-dentatis — Pl. Mart.-Burs. (6) 15

Plantago incana — Pan Svec. (26) 15

Plantago lagopus — Demonstr. pl. (49) 4; Fl. Palaest. (70) 14; Fl. Monsp. (74) 10

Plantago lanceolata — Pan Svec. (26) 15; Herbat. Upsal. (50) 13; Fl. Angl. (56) 11; Fl. Monsp. (74) 10; Prodr. fl. Dan. (82) 14; Fl. Belg. (112) 13; Fl. Åker. (162) 7; Pand. fl. Ryb. (165) 17

Plantago latifolia — Fl. Jam. (105) 13, 25

Plantago linearis maculatis — Pan Svec. (26) 15

Plantago loeflingii — Demonstr. pl. (49) 4; Fl. Angl. (56) 11

Plantago major — Herbat. Upsal. (50) 7; Pl. officin. (52) 15; Stat. pl. (55) 20; Fl. Angl. (56) 11; Fl. Palaest. (70) 14; Fl. Monsp. (74) 10; Prodr. fl. Dan. (82) 14; Fl. Belg. (112) 13; Fl. Åker. (162) 7; Pand. fl. Ryb. (165) 17

Plantago major rosea — Demonstr. pl. (49) 4

Plantago maritima — Demonstr. pl. (49) 4; Stat. pl. (55) 12; Fl. Angl. (56) 11; Fl. Monsp. (74) 10;

Prodr. fl. Dan. (82) 14; Fl. Belg. (112) 13; Pand. fl. Ryb. (165) 17, 21

Plantago media — Hosp. insect. fl. (43) 16; Herbat. Upsal. (50) 7; Fl. Angl. (56) 11; Fl. Monsp. (74) 10; Prodr. fl. Dan. (82) 14; Fl. Belg. (112) 13; Fl. Åker. (162) 7; Pand. fl. Ryb. (165) 17; Esca avium (174) 11

Plantago monanthos — Pan Svec. (26) 15; Stat. pl. (55) 13

Plantago psyllium — Calend. fl. (72) [22]; Fl. Monsp. (74) 10

Plantago radice lanata — Pan Svec. (26) 15

Plantago scapo unifloro — Pl. Mart.-Burs. (6) 17

Plantago strictissima — Fl. Monsp. (74) 10

Plantago uniflora — Fl. Angl. (56) 11; Prodr. fl. Dan. (82) 14

Plantago vulgaris — Pan Svec. (26) 15

Plantula marilandica, caule non ramoso, spica in fastigio singulari, e flosculis albis composita — Rad. senega (23) 17

Platanus orientalis — Fl. Palaest. (70) 30

Platyceros — Fund. entom. (154) 29

Plinia petiolata — Pl. Surin. (177) 10

Plukenetia — Demonstr. pl. (49) 27[as Pluknetia]; Nect. fl. (122) 11[as Plukenutia]

Plukenetia volubilis — Herb. Amboin. (57) 8; Pl. Surin. (177) 15

Plumbago — Hort. Upsal. (7) 37; Nect. fl. (122) 9

Plumbago americana — Fl. Jam. (105) 14

Plumbago europaea — Demonstr. pl. (49) 5; Pl. officin. (52) 9; Fl. Monsp. (74) 11; Usum hist. nat. (145) 27

Plumbago indica — Gem. arb. (24) 23; Herb. Amboin. (57) 24

Plumbago zeylanica — Demonstr. pl. (49) 5[as zeylonica]; Fl. Jam. (105) 25

Plumeria — Vir. pl. (13) 25

Plumeria alba — Herb. Amboin. (57) 16; Obs. mat. med. (171) 3; Pl. Surin. (177) 6[as Plumieria]

Plumeria rubra — Fl. Jam. (105) 14[as Plumieria]

Poa — Fl. oecon. (17) 3; Splachnum (27) 2; Cui bono? (42) 17; Fl. alp. (71) 8; Anim. comp. (98) 6; Fund. agrost. (152) 28, 31, 37

Poa alpina — Stat. pl. (55) 16; Fund. agrost. (152) 6, 7

Poa alpina variegata — Pan Svec. (26) 14

Poa alpina vivipara — Demonstr. pl. (49) 3; Fl. alp. (71) 12

Poa angustifolia — Pan Svec. (26) 14; Herbat. Upsal. (50) 14; Fl. Angl. (56) 10; Fl. Palaest. (70) 12; Fl. Belg. (112) 13; Fund. agrost. (152) 7; Fl. Åker. (162) 6

Poa angustifolia media — Stat. pl. (55) 21

Poa annua — Pan Svec. (26) 14; Herbat. Upsal. (50) 14; Stat. pl. (55) 14; Fl. Angl. (56) 10; Fl. Palaest. (70) 12; Fl. Monsp. (74) 9; Prodr. fl. Dan. (82) 13;

Fl. Belg. (112) 13; Fl. Åker. (162) 6; Esca avium (174) 10

Poa aquatica — Stat. pl. (55) 13; Fl. Angl. (56) 10; Prodr. fl. Dan. (82) 13; Fl. Belg. (112) 13; Fund. agrost. (152) 7; Fl. Åker. (162) 6

Poa bulbosa — Fl. Palaest. (70) 12; Fl. Monsp. (74) 9

Poa chinensis — Fl. Jam. (105) 13

Poa ciliaris — Pl. Jam. (102) 7; Fl. Jam. (105) 13

Poa compressa — Demonstr. pl. (49) 3; Herbat. Upsal. (50) 7; Stat. pl. (55) 23; Fl. Monsp. (74) 9; Prodr. fl. Dan. (82) 13; Fl. Belg. (112) 13; Fund. agrost. (152) 7; Fl. Åker. (162) 6; Pand. fl. Ryb. (165) 16

Poa compressa repens — Pan Svec. (26) 14

Poa gigantea — Pan Svec. (26) 14

Poa media — Pan Svec. (26) 14

Poa nemoralis — Demonstr. pl. (49) 3; Stat. pl. (55) 17; Fund. agrost. (152) 7; Fl. Åker. (162) 6

Poa panicula diffusa, spiculis trifloris glabris, culmo erecto tereti — Pl. Mart.-Burs. (6) [1]

Poa panicula lanceolata subramosa, floribus alternis secundis — Cent. I. pl. (65) 5

Poa pilosa — Fl. Palaest. (70) 12

Poa pratensis — Herbat. Upsal. (50) 6; Fl. Angl. (56) 10; Fl. Monsp. (74) 9; Prodr. fl. Dan. (82) 13; Fl. Belg. (112) 13; Fund. agrost. (152) 7; Fl. Åker. (162) 6

Poa rigida — Fl. Angl. (56) 10; Cent. I. pl. (65) 5; Fl. Palaest. (70) 12

Poa trivialis — Herbat. Upsal. (50) 6[as trivialis]; Fl. Angl. (56) 10; Fl. Monsp. (74) 9; Prodr. fl. Dan. (82) 13; Fl. Belg. (112) 13; Fl. Åker. (162) 6; Pand. fl. Ryb. (165) 16; Esca avium (174) 10

Poa vivipara — Fl. Palaest. (70) 12

Poa vulgaris magna — Pan Svec. (26) 14

Podophyllum — Hort. Upsal. (7) 41; Nova pl. gen. 1751 (32) 9

Podophyllum peltatum — Demonstr. pl. (49) 14

Podura — Mirac. insect. (45) 10, 13; Pand. insect. (93) 6; Mund. invis. (149) 10; Fund. entom. (154) 21

Podura fimetaria — Pand. fl. Ryb. (165) 16

Podura minuta — Pand. fl. Ryb. (165) 16

Poinciana caule inermi — Cent. II. pl. (66) 16

Poinciana elata — Cent. II. pl. (66) 16

Poinciana pulcherrima — Demonstr. pl. (49) 11; Herb. Amboin. (57) 15; Fl. Jam. (105) 16, 25[as Poinicana]; Pl. Surin. (177) 8

Polemonium — Anandria (9) 4; Nect. fl. (122) 9

Polemonium caeruleum — Demonstr. pl. (49) 5[as coeruleum]; Fl. Angl. (56) 12; Calend. fl. (72) [12], [22]; Fl. Monsp. (74) 11; Hort. cul. (132) 24; Hist. nat. Rossia (144) 21; Fl. Åker. (162) 8

Polemonium glabrum — Pan Svec. (26) 17

Polianthes — Vir. pl. (13) 31, 34; Odor. med. (40) 12

Polianthes tuberosa — Demonstr. pl. (49) 10; Herb. Amboin. (57) 22; Hort. cul. (132) 25

Polium hispanicum montanum pumilum, rosmarini folio, flore rubro — Cent. I. pl. (65) 15[as rorismarini]

Polium montanum pumilum rubrum, viridi stoechadis folio, caule tomentoso — Cent. I. pl. (65) 15

Polycarpon tetraphyllum — Fl. Palaest. (70) 13; Fl. Monsp. (74) 10

Polycarpum — Cent. II. pl. (66) 16

Polycnemum arvense — Fl. Monsp. (74) 8

Polydactylon — Fund. agrost. (152) 16

Polygala — Amphib. Gyll. (5) 3; Vir. pl. (13) 15; Rad. senega (23) 12ff.; Cui bono? (42) 21, 23; Fl. Monsp. (74) 7; Nom. bot. (107) 16; Fund. fr. (123) 18

Polygala acutioribus foliis, monspeliaca — Rad. senega (23) 14

Polygala aethiopica, angustis hirsutis foliis, flore obsolete purpureo — Rad. senega (23) 15

Polygala aethiopica, strictissimis glabris foliis, flore phoeniceo — Rad. senega (23) 15

Polygala africana frutescens angustifolia major — Rad. senega (23) 15

Polygala africana glabra, florum galea binis cristis fimbriatis ornata ex involucro … — Rad. senega (23) 14

Polygala africana, lini folio, magno flore — Rad. senega (23) 14

Polygala arborea myrtifolia, capitis bonae spei, floribus albis intus purpureis — Rad. senega (23) 15

Polygala arborea, myrtilli subrotundis foliis, fructu magno tordylii — Rad. senega (23) 15

Polygala bracteolata — Fl. Cap. (99) 16

Polygala capensis, folio angustissimo, flore minore — Rad. senega (23) 15

Polygala caule simplici erecto, foliis ovato-lanceolatis alternis integerrimis, racemo terminatrice erecto — Hort. Upsal. (7) 3; Mus. Ad.-Frid. (11) 21; Rad. senega (23) 16

Polygala caulibus filiformibus, foliis linearibus alternis, pedunculis spicatis — Rad. senega (23) 16

Polygala chamaebuxus — Fl. alp. (71) 20

Polygala chinensis — Fl. Jam. (105) 19, 26

Polygala cortusi — Cent. II. pl. (66) 28

Polygala cruciata, floribus ex viridi rubentibus in globum compactis — Rad. senega (23) 16

Polygala diversifolia — Fl. Jam. (105) 19

Polygala floribus cristatis alternis, caule erecto suffruticoso ramoso, foliis linearibus obtusis scabris — Rad. senega (23) 15

Polygala floribus cristatis racemosis: carina cristis breviore, caule suffruticoso, foliis lineari-subulatis — Rad. senega (23) 14

Polygala floribus cristatis racemosis: carina cristis longiore, caule suffruticoso, foliis lineari-lanceolatis — Rad. senega (23) 14

Polygala floribus cristatis racemosis, caule erecto suffruticoso simplisissimo, foliis subulatis — Rad. senega (23) 15

Polygala floribus cristatis racemosis, caulibus herbaceis simplicibus procumbentibus, foliis lineari-lanceolatis — Rad. senega (23) [13, as 14]

Polygala floribus cristatis racemoso-sparsis: carina lunulata, caule fruticoso, foliis lanceolatis obtusis — Rad. senega (23) 15

Polygala floribus imberbibus, capsulis ciliatis, caule herbaceo erecto — Rad. senega (23) 16

Polygala floribus imberbibus, caule herbaceo erecto, foliis linearibus alternis, pedunculis subtrifloris — Rad. senega (23) 18

Polygala floribus imberbibus, foliis quaternis — Rad. senega (23) 16

Polygala floribus imberbibus globoso-capitatis, caule erecto herbaceo simplicissimo, foliis lanceolatis obtusiusculis — Rad. senega (23) 17

Polygala floribus imberbibus lateralibus, caule arboreo spinoso, foliis ovalibus mucronatis — Rad. senega (23) 18

Polygala floribus imberbibus lateralibus solitariis, caule arboreo, foliis obtusis petiolatis — Rad. senega (23) 17

Polygala floribus imberbibus oblongo-capitatis, caule erecto herbaceo, foliis lanceolatis acutis — Rad. senega (23) 17

Polygala floribus imberbibus, pedunculis multifloris lateralibus, caule diffuso herbaceo ramosissimo, foliis acuminatis — Rad. senega (23) 16

Polygala floribus imberbibus racemosis, caule arboreo, foliis senioribus oblongo-ovatis, recentibus subovatis — Rad. senega (23) 18

Polygala floribus imberbibus sparsis; carinae apice subrotundo, caule fruticoso, foliis lanceolatis — Rad. senega (23) 18

Polygala floribus imberbibus spicatis, caule erecto herbaceo filiformi ramoso, foliis linearibus — Rad. senega (23) 16

Polygala floribus imberbibus spicatis, caule erecto herbaceo simplicissimo, foliis lato lanceolatis — Rad. senega (23) 16

Polygala foliis imis subrotundis, superioribus angustis acutis — Rad. senega (23) 14

Polygala foliis lanceolatis alternis, caule simplicissimo, corymbo terminali capitato — Rad. senega (23) 17

Polygala foliis lanceolatis obtusis, caule frutescente — Rad. senega (23) 15

Polygala foliis linearibus acutis, flore purpureo minore — Rad. senega (23) 15

Polygala foliis lineari-lanceolatis, caulibus diffusis herbaceis — Hort. Upsal. (7) 3; Rad. senega (23) [13, as 14]

Polygala foliis lineari-subulatis — Rad. senega (23) 14

Polygala foliis oblongo acutis, flore purpureo latiori — Rad. senega (23) 14

Polygala foliis omnibus acutis — Rad. senega (23) [13, as 14]

Polygala foliis quaternis — Rad. senega (23) 16

Polygala foliis ramorum provectiorum oblongo-ovatis, tenellorum subovatis, caule arboreo — Rad. senega (23) 18

Polygala folio lineari obtuso, flore albente minimo — Rad. senega (23) 15

Polygala frutescens angustifolia ramosa, floribus in summitate velut umbellatis — Rad. senega (23) 14

Polygala frutescens, foliis linearibus, flore majore purpureo — Rad. senega (23) 14

Polygala frutescens, foliis oblongis glabris, flore purpureo — Rad. senega (23) 15

Polygala fruticosa buxifolia, flore ex purpura rubente — Rad. senega (23) 18

Polygala heisteria — Fl. Cap. (99) 8, 16

Polygala major — Rad. senega (23) [13, as 14]

Polygala mariana, floribus rubris spicatis — Rad. senega (23) 17

Polygala mariana quadrifolia minor, spica parva albicante — Rad. senega (23) 16

Polygala minor, foliis circa radicem rotundiusculis — Rad. senega (23) 14

Polygala monspeliaca — Fl. Monsp. (74) 22

Polygala myrtifolia — Fl. Cap. (99) 16

Polygala paniculata — Pl. Jam. (102) 18; Fl. Jam. (105) 19

Polygala quadrifolia minima marilandica, spicis florum parvis albentibus — Rad. senega (23) 16

Polygala quadrifolia seu cruciata, floribus ex viridi rubentibus in globum compactis — Rad. senega (23) 16

Polygala rubra virginiana, spica parva compacta — Rad. senega (23) 17

Polygala scabra — Fl. Cap. (99) 16

Polygala senega — Rad. senega (23) plate [1]; Pl. officin. (52) 18; Specif. Canad. (76) 17, 28; Mors. serp. (119) 17

Polygala seu flos ambervalis, floribus luteis in capitulum oblongum congestis — Rad. senega (23) 17

Polygala sibirica — Hist. nat. Rossia (144) 31

Polygala spinosa — Fl. Cap. (99) 16

Polygala virginiana, flore luteocapitato — Rad. senega (23) 17

Polygala virginiana, foliis oblongis, floribus in thyrso candidis, radice alexipharmaca — Rad. senega (23) 16

Polygala vulgaris — Rad. senega (23) 14; Pan Svec. (26) 29; Herbat. Upsal. (50) 19; Fl. Angl. (56) 20; Fl. Monsp. (74) 22; Prodr. fl. Dan. (82) 21; Fl. Belg. (112) 20; Fl. Åker. (162) 16; Pand. fl. Ryb. (165) 21

Polygaloides — Rad. senega (23) 18

Polygonum — Pl. escul. (35) 15, 27; Rhabarbarum (41) 5, 6; Fl. alp. (71) 8; Pand. insect. (93) 13; Nom. bot. (107) 12; Prol. pl. 1760 (114) 14; Nect. fl. (122) 7

Polygonum amphibium — Herbat. Upsal. (50) 10; Stat. pl. (55) 13; Fl. Angl. (56) 15; Metam. pl. (67) 16; Fl. Monsp. (74) 15; Prodr. fl. Dan. (82) 17; Fl. Belg. (112) 8, 16; Fund. fr. (123) 13; Usum hist. nat. (145) 10; Fl. Åker. (162) 11; Pand. fl. Ryb. (165) 18

Polygonum amphibium beta — Herbat. Upsal. (50) 13

Polygonum angustissimo gramineo folio, erectum — Nova pl. gen. 1747 (14) 3

Polygonum aviculare — Pl. officin. (52) 7[as ariculare]; Cynogr. (54) 11; Stat. pl. (55) 20; Fl. Angl. (56) 15; Fl. Palaest. (70) 18; Fl. Monsp. (74) 15; Prodr. fl. Dan. (82) 17; Fl. Belg. (112) 16; Fl. Åker. (162) 11; Pand. fl. Ryb. (165) 18; Esca avium (174) 12

Polygonum barbarum — Fl. Jam. (105) 15

Polygonum bistorta — Demonstr. pl. (49) 11; Pl. officin. (52) 6; Fl. Angl. (56) 15; Fl. alp. (71) 16; Calend. fl. (72) [22]; Fl. Monsp. (74) 15; Prodr. fl. Dan. (82) 17; Fl. Belg. (112) 16

Polygonum chinense — Iter Chin. (161) 9

Polygonum convolvulus — Stat. pl. (55) 19[as convolvolus]; Fl. Angl. (56) 15; Fl. Monsp. (74) 15; Prodr. fl. Dan. (82) 17; Fl. Belg. (112) 16; Usum hist. nat. (145) 10; Fl. Åker. (162) 11

Polygonum divaricatum — Demonstr. pl. (49) 11; Calend. fl. (72) [15]; Hist. nat. Rossia (144) 23, 29

Polygonum fagopyrum — Demonstr. pl. (49) 11; Pl. officin. (52) 10; Fr. escul. (127) 20[as fagogyrum]; Hort. cul. (132) 9; Erica (163) [14, as 10]

Polygonum frutescens — Hist. nat. Rossia (144) 29

Polygonum hydropiper — Herbat. Upsal. (50) 17; Pl. officin. (52) 15; Stat. pl. (55) 20; Fl. Angl. (56) 15; Fl. Monsp. (74) 15; Prodr. fl. Dan. (82) 17; Fl. Jam. (105) 15, 25; Fl. Belg. (112) 16; Fl. Åker. (162) 11; Pand. fl. Ryb. (165) 18

Polygonum incanum rotundifolium halimoides fruticans hispanicum — Cent. I. pl. (65) 34

Polygonum maritimum — Fl. Angl. (56) 6, 15; Fl. Monsp. (74) 15

Polygonum montanum, vermiculatae foliis — Cent. II. pl. (66) 16

Polygonum ocreatum — Hist. nat. Rossia (144) 29

Polygonum pensylvanicum — Demonstr. pl. (49) 11; Fl. Angl. (56) 15

Polygonum persicaria — Herbat. Upsal. (50) 13; Stat. pl. (55) 20; Fl. Angl. (56) 15; Fl. Monsp. (74) 15; Prodr. fl. Dan. (82) 17; Pl. tinct. (97) 16; Fl. Belg. (112) 16; Fl. Åker. (162) 11; Pand. fl. Ryb. (165) 18

Polygonum scandens — Demonstr. pl. (49) 11; Calend. fl. (72) [18]; Nect. fl. (122) 5

Polygonum tataricum — Demonstr. pl. (49) 11; Fr. escul. (127) 20[as tartaricum]; Hort. cul. (132) 9; Hist. nat. Rossia (144) 23

Polygonum uvifera — Demonstr. pl. (49) 11

Polygonum viviparum — Demonstr. pl. (49) 11; Stat. pl. (55) 22; Fl. Angl. (56) 15[as vivipara]; Fl. alp. (71) 16; Pand. fl. Ryb. (165) 18

Polygonum vulgare — Pan Svec. (26) 21; Hosp. insect. fl. (43) 21

Polymnia — Nova pl. gen. 1751 (32) [13, as 15], 22, 48; Fund. fr. (123) 17

Polype a panache — Taenia (19) 5

Polypodium — Acrostichum (10) 3, 6, 7, 8, 12, 13; Sapor. med. (31) 16

Polypodium aculeatum — Fl. Angl. (56) 25; Fl. Monsp. (74) 29

Polypodium angustata — Pan Svec. (26) [37, as 39]

Polypodium arboreum — Fl. Jam. (105) 23

Polypodium aureum — Fl. Jam. (105) 23

Polypodium cambricum — Fl. Angl. (56) 25

Polypodium cicutarium — Fl. Jam. (105) 23

Polypodium coadunata — Pan Svec. (26) 38

Polypodium deflexa — Pan Svec. (26) 38

Polypodium dissimile — Fl. Jam. (105) 23

Polypodium dryopteris — Herbat. Upsal. (50) 11; Stat. pl. (55) 17; Fl. Angl. (56) 25; Fl. Monsp. (74) 29[as drypteris]; Prodr. fl. Dan. (82) 25; Fl. Åker. (162) 20; Pand. fl. Ryb. (165) 23

Polypodium exaltatum — Fl. Jam. (105) 23

Polypodium filix femina — Fl. Monsp. (74) 29; Fl. Åker. (162) 20

Polypodium filix mas — Pan Svec. (26) [37, as 39]; Pl. escul. (35) 26; Pl. officin. (52) 10; Stat. pl. (55) 18; Fl. Angl. (56) 25; Fl. Monsp. (74) 29; Prodr. fl. Dan. (82) 25; Fl. Belg. (112) 23; Fl. Åker. (162) 20; Esca avium (174) 15

Polypodium fontanum — Hist. nat. Rossia (144) 34

Polypodium fragile — Herbat. Upsal. (50) 9; Stat. pl. (55) 23; Fl. Angl. (56) 25; Fl. Åker. (162) 20

Polypodium fragrans — Hist. nat. Rossia (144) 34

Polypodium frondibus pinnatis: pinnis oblongis subserratis obtusis; radice squamata — Med. purg. (181) 23

Polypodium horridum — Fl. Jam. (105) 23

Polypodium ilvensis — Pan Svec. (26) 38

Polypodium indicum — Herb. Amboin. (57) 26

Polypodium lonchitis — Fl. Angl. (56) 25; Fl. alp. (71) 23; Fl. Monsp. (74) 29

Polypodium lycopodioides — Fl. Jam. (105) 23

Polypodium minus virginianum, foliis brevibus subtus argenteis — Acrostichum (10) 12, 14

Polypodium officinarum — Pan Svec. (26) [37, as 39]

Polypodium pectinatum — Fl. Jam. (105) 23

Polypodium phegopteris — Herbat. Upsal. (50) 8; Stat. pl. (55) 17; Fl. Angl. (56) 25; Fl. Åker. (162) 20; Pand. fl. Ryb. (165) 23

Polypodium phyllitidis — Fl. Jam. (105) 23

Polypodium piloselloides — Fl. Jam. (105) 23

Polypodium pubescens — Fl. Jam. (105) 23

Polypodium quercifolium — Herb. Amboin. (57) 26

Polypodium ramosa — Pan Svec. (26) 38

Polypodium reticulatum — Fl. Jam. (105) 23

Polypodium rhaeticum — Fl. Monsp. (74) 29

Polypodium saxatilis — Pan Svec. (26) 38

Polypodium scolopendroides — Fl. Jam. (105) 23

Polypodium simile — Fl. Jam. (105) 23

Polypodium spinosum — Fl. Jam. (105) 23

Polypodium tornatile — Fl. Jam. (105) 23

Polypodium trifoliatum — Fl. Jam. (105) 23

Polypodium unitum — Fl. Jam. (105) 23

Polypodium virginianum majus, osmundae facie, tenerius — Nova pl. gen. 1751 (32) 34

Polypodium vulgare — Herbat. Upsal. (50) 8; Pl. officin. (52) 15; Stat. pl. (55) 23; Fl. Angl. (56) 25; Fl. Monsp. (74) 29; Prodr. fl. Dan. (82) 25; Fl. Belg. (112) 23; Purg. indig. (143) 12; Fl. Åker. (162) 20; Pand. fl. Ryb. (165) 23; Med. purg. (181) 23

Polyporus — Taenia (19) 5

Polypremum — Nova pl. gen. 1747 (14) [iv]; Nova pl. gen. 1751 (32) 8, 12

Polypus — Corallia Balt. (4) 7; Spons. pl. (12) 17, 18, 56; Taenia (19) 3ff.; Oecon. nat. (20) 30; Noctiluca (39) 2; Chin. Lagerstr. (64) [1], 34; Metam. pl. (67) 9; Lepra (140) 9; Mund. invis. (149) 6ff.

Polypus anastaticam referens — Taenia (19) 5

Polypus campanulatus integerrimus prolifer subcylindricus, ore setis obvallato — Taenia (19) 5

Polypus collinsonii — Taenia (19) 5

Polypus conglomeratus — Chin. Lagerstr. (64) 33

Polypus corpore oblongo cylindraceo, tentaculis ad circumferentiam capitis — Corallia Balt. (4) 9

Polypus dichotomus, apicibus campanulatis — Taenia (19) 5

Polypus glomeratus — Chin. Lagerstr. (64) 36

Polypus mirabilis — Chin. Lagerstr. (64) 33

Polypus stellis cordato-campanulatis radiatis — Taenia (19) 5

Polypus subcylindricus, ore setis circiter denis radiato — Taenia (19) 4

Polystachia — Pl. Surin. (177) 16

Polytrichum — Spons. pl. (12) 27; Fl. oecon. (17) 28[as Polytricum]; Oecon. nat. (20) [5, as 7], 25; Splachnum (27) 5, 6; Sem. musc. (28) 6, 7, 15, 16, 17; Cui bono? (42) 14; Buxbaumia (85) 6, 8; Arb. Svec. (101) 15; Usum musc. (148) 7, 9, 10, 13

Polytrichum alpinum — Fl. alp. (71) 24

Polytrichum aureum — Usum musc. (148) 13

Polytrichum commune — Herbat. Upsal. (50) 9[as
Polytricum]; Pl. officin. (52) 4; Stat. pl. (55) 18[as
Polytricum]; Prodr. fl. Dan. (82) 25; Buxbaumia
(85) 10; Pand. fl. Ryb. (165) 23[as Polyctricum]

Polytrichum vulgare — Sem. musc. (28) 14

Pombalia — Viola ipecac. (176) 8

Pombalia ipecacuanha — Viola ipecac. (176) 7

Pomum amoris — Herb. Amboin. (57) 24

Pomum draconum — Herb. Amboin. (57) 7

Pomum draconum sylvestre — Herb. Amboin. (57) 7

Pontederia — Herb. Amboin. (57) 28; Nect. fl. (122)
6[as Pontedera]

Pontederia ovata — Fl. Jam. (105) 15

Pontederia rotundifolia — Pl. Surin. (177) 7

Poppya — Herb. Amboin. (57) 24

Populus — Pl. Mart.-Burs. (6) 28; Spons. pl. (12) 41,
49; Fl. oecon. (17) 27; Oecon. nat. (20) 29; Gem.
arb. (24) 5, 9, 12; Hosp. insect. fl. (43) 40; Noxa
insect. (46) 25; Vern. arb. (47) 10, table; Pl. officin.
(52) 19; Oves (61) 18; Metam. pl. (67) 24; Pand.
insect. (93) 22; Pl. tinct. (97) 10; Arb. Svec. (101)
25; Nom. bot. (107) 19; Nect. fl. (122) 14, 15;
Usum hist. nat. (145) 27

Populus alba — Gem. arb. (24) 29; Pan Svec. (26)
[37, as 39]; Hosp. insect. fl. (43) 38; Demonstr. pl.
(49) 26; Fl. Angl. (56) 24; Calend. fl. (72) [10],
[20]; Fl. Monsp. (74) 28; Prodr. fl. Dan. (82) 25;
Arb. Svec. (101) 8, 9, 26, 30; Nom. bot. (107) 19;
Fl. Belg. (112) 23; Meloe (124) 4; Hist. nat. Rossia
(144) 34; Pand. fl. Ryb. (165) 22

Populus alnus — Febr. interm. (167) 42

Populus balsamifera — Hist. nat. Rossia (144) 34;
Obs. mat. med. (171) 7

Populus nigra — Ficus (2) 17; Oecon. nat. (20) 29;
Gem. arb. (24) 29; Pan Svec. (26) [37, as 39];
Hosp. insect. fl. (43) 38; Mirac. insect. (45) 13, 14;
Demonstr. pl. (49) 26; Pl. officin. (52) 15; Fl. Angl.
(56) 24; Calend. fl. (72) [10], [20]; Fl. Monsp. (74)
28; Prodr. fl. Dan. (82) 25; Arb. Svec. (101) 8, 9,
25, 30; Fl. Belg. (112) 8, 23; Meloe (124) 4; Hist.
nat. Rossia (144) 34

Populus tremula — Gem. arb. (24) 29; Pan Svec. (26)
[37, as 39]; Hosp. insect. fl. (43) 38; Mirac. insect.
(45) 14; Herbat. Upsal. (50) 7; Stat. pl. (55) 18; Fl.
Angl. (56) 24; Calend. fl. (72) [9], [10], [20];
Prodr. fl. Dan. (82) 25; Arb. Svec. (101) 8, 9, 25,
26, 30; Fl. Belg. (112) 23; Hist. nat. Rossia (144)
34; Fl. Åker. (162) 20; Pand. fl. Ryb. (165) 22

Porcellus guineensis — Mus ind. (62) 23[as
Porculus]

Porcellus indicus — Mus ind. (62) 10, 23[as
Porculus]

Porcus — Rad. senega (23) 9

Porcus maritimus — Mus ind. (62) 6

Porella — Nova pl. gen. 1747 (14) [iv]; Splachnum
(27) 5, 6; Sem. musc. (28) 6, 17; Nova pl. gen.
1751 (32) 10

Porophyllum foliis deltoidibus angulatis — Pl. rar.
Camsch. (30) 5

Porpita minor nummularis — Corallia Balt. (4) 19[as
numularis]

Porpites — Corallia Balt. (4) 2; Chin. Lagerstr. (64)
31

Porpites lapia — Chin. Lagerstr. (64) 36

Porrum — Hort. Upsal. (7) 35; Vir. pl. (13) 7, 20; Fl.
oecon. (17) 8; Sapor. med. (31) 19; Pl. escul. (35)
29; Nom. bot. (107) 12

Porrum amphicarpon — Pl. escul. (35) 12

Porrum anceps — Pan Svec. (26) 20

Porrum scapo nudo ancipiti ante florescentiam
nutante — Anandria (9) 5

Portlandia — Fl. Jam. (105) 26

Portlandia grandiflora — Fl. Jam. (105) 14

Portulaca — Fl. oecon. (17) [1]; Vern. arb. (47) 9;
Demonstr. pl. (49) [vii]; Metam. pl. (67) 14;
Acetaria (77) 15; Fl. Cap. (99) 7; Fl. Jam. (105) 26;
Nom. bot. (107) 13; Fraga (170) [1]; Scorb. (180)
21

Portulaca anacampseros — Demonstr. pl. (49) 13; Fl.
Cap. (99) 14

Portulaca arborea — Metam. pl. (67) 14[as Porutlaca]

Portulaca arborescens — Demonstr. pl. (49) 13

Portulaca marina — Fung. melit. (69) 10

Portulaca oleracea — Demonstr. pl. (49) 12; Pl.
officin. (52) 15; Fl. Palaest. (70) 20; Fl. Monsp.
(74) 17; Acetaria (77) 15; Fl. Jam. (105) 17, 25; Fl.
Belg. (112) 17; Mac. olit. (113) 15; Hort. cul. (132)
14; Iter Chin. (161) 14, 15

Portulaca pilosa — Demonstr. pl. (49) 12; Fl. Jam.
(105) 17

Portulaca portulacastrum — Herb. Amboin. (57) 28

Porus — Corallia Balt. (4) 2

Porus tuberiformis, figura sua ac magnitudine tubera
terrestria referens — Corallia Balt. (4) 30

Poryphyllon — Hort. Upsal. (7) 37

Potamogeton — Hort. Upsal. (7) 41; Spons. pl. (12)
44; Fl. oecon. (17) 5; Oecon. nat. (20) 19; Cui
bono? (42) 18; Hosp. insect. fl. (43) 40; Noxa
insect. (46) 24; Pand. insect. (93) 11; Nom. bot.
(107) 10; Fl. Belg. (112) 8; Erica (163) 2

Potamogeton capillaceum — Pan Svec. (26) 16

Potamogeton caule compresso — Pan Svec. (26) 16

Potamogeton compressum — Fl. Angl. (56) 11[as
Potamogeten]; Prodr. fl. Dan. (82) 14; Fl. Belg.
(112) 14

Potamogeton crispum — Pan Svec. (26) 16; Stat. pl.
(55) 13; Fl. Angl. (56) 11[as Potamogeten]; Fl.
Monsp. (74) 10; Prodr. fl. Dan. (82) 14; Fl. Belg.
(112) 14

Potamogeton densum — Fl. Monsp. (74) 10

Potamogeton fluitans — Pan Svec. (26) 16

Potamogeton foliis oblongo-ovatis petiolatis —
Spons. pl. (12) 44

Potamogeton folio longissimo — Fl. Angl. (56) 26

Potamogeton folio pellucido gramineo — Fl. Angl. (56) 26

Potamogeton gramineum — Fl. Angl. (56) 12[as Potamogeten]; Fl. Åker. (162) 8; Pand. fl. Ryb. (165) 17

Potamogeton gramineum tenuifolium — Pl. Mart.-Burs. (6) 16

Potamogeton lineare — Pan Svec. (26) 16

Potamogeton lucens — Stat. pl. (55) 13; Fl. Angl. (56) 11[as Potamogeten]; Prodr. fl. Dan. (82) 14; Fl. Jam. (105) 13, 25; Fl. Belg. (112) 13; Fl. Åker. (162) 8; Pand. fl. Ryb. (165) 17

Potamogeton marinum — Stat. pl. (55) 12; Prodr. fl. Dan. (82) 14

Potamogeton marinum, in utriculis epiphyllo spermon, minus — Nova pl. gen. 1747 (14) 27

Potamogeton maritimum — Fl. Angl. (56) 26

Potamogeton natans — Pan Svec. (26) 16; Hosp. insect. fl. (43) 16; Herbat. Upsal. (50) 13; Stat. pl. (55) 12; Fl. Angl. (56) 11[as Potamogeten]; Prodr. fl. Dan. (82) 14; Fl. Belg. (112) 13; Fl. Åker. (162) 8; Pand. fl. Ryb. (165) 17; Esca avium (174) 11

Potamogeton pectinatum — Prodr. fl. Dan. (82) 14

Potamogeton pectiniforme — Pan Svec. (26) 16

Potamogeton perfoliatum — Pan Svec. (26) 16; Herbat. Upsal. (50) 14; Stat. pl. (55) 13; Fl. Angl. (56) 11[as Potamogeten]; Prodr. fl. Dan. (82) 14; Fl. Åker. (162) 8; Pand. fl. Ryb. (165) 17; Esca avium (174) 11

Potamogeton plantaginis — Pan Svec. (26) 16

Potamogeton pusillum — Herbat. Upsal. (50) 14; Fl. Angl. (56) 12[as Potamogeten]; Fl. Monsp. (74) 10; Prodr. fl. Dan. (82) 14; Fl. Åker. (162) 8

Potamogeton serratum — Fl. Angl. (56) 11[as Potamogeten]; Fl. Belg. (112) 14

Potamogeton setaceum — Fl. Monsp. (74) 10

Potamogeton tenuifolium — Fl. Angl. (56) 26

Potentilla — Ficus (2) 12; Anandria (9) 4; Vir. pl. (13) 27; Fl. oecon. (17) 14; Fr. Svec. (91) [ii]; Pand. insect. (93) 16; Nom. bot. (107) 14; Nect. fl. (122) 6; Fund. fr. (123) 20, 23; Fraga (170) [1]

Potentilla acaulis — Demonstr. pl. (49) 14; Hist. nat. Rossia (144) 30

Potentilla adscendens — Pan Svec. (26) 24

Potentilla alba — Fl. alp. (71) 18

Potentilla anserina — Pan Svec. (26) 24; Pl. officin. (52) 4; Fl. Angl. (56) 17; Cervus (60) 7; Prodr. fl. Dan. (82) 19; Fl. Belg. (112) 17; Usum hist. nat. (145) 10; Fl. Åker. (162) 13; Pand. fl. Ryb. (165) 19; Esca avium (174) 13

Potentilla anserina alba — Stat. pl. (55) 22

Potentilla argentea — Pan Svec. (26) 24; Herbat. Upsal. (50) 7; Stat. pl. (55) 20; Fl. Angl. (56) 17; Fl. Monsp. (74) 18; Prodr. fl. Dan. (82) 19; Fl. Belg. (112) 17; Fl. Åker. (162) 13; Pand. fl. Ryb. (165) 19

Potentilla aurea — Cent. II. pl. (66) 18; Fl. alp. (71) 18; Rar. Norv. (157) 9, 10; Pand. fl. Ryb. (165) 19

Potentilla bifurca — Hist. nat. Rossia (144) 30

Potentilla caulescens — Cent. II. pl. (66) 19; Fl. alp. (71) 18

Potentilla erecta — Cervus (60) 7

Potentilla foliis digitatis apice conniventi-serratis, caulibus filiformibus procumbentibus — Pl. Mart.-Burs. (6) 24

Potentilla foliis digitatis apice conniventi-serratis, caulibus multifloris; receptaculis hirsutis — Cent. II. pl. (66) 19

Potentilla foliis digitatis tomentosis apice conniventi-tridentatis, caulibus unifloris, receptaculis lanatis — Cent. II. pl. (66) 18

Potentilla foliis quinatis acute serratis ora sericea, petalis maculatis — Cent. II. pl. (66) 18

Potentilla foliis radicalibus quinatis serratis acuminatis, caulinis ternatis, caule declinato — Cent. II. pl. (66) 18

Potentilla foliis radicalibus septenatis cuneiformibus serratis; caulinis ternatis, ramis filiformibus decumbentibus — Cent. I. pl. (65) 13

Potentilla fragarioides — Hist. nat. Rossia (144) 30

Potentilla fragifera — Pan Svec. (26) 24

Potentilla fruticosa — Gem. arb. (24) 27; Pan Svec. (26) 24; Hosp. insect. fl. (43) 26; Demonstr. pl. (49) 14; Stat. pl. (55) 14; Fl. Angl. (56) 5, 17; Calend. fl. (72) [12]; Fr. Svec. (91) 4, 20; Hort. cul. (132) 26; Hist. nat. Rossia (144) 30; Colon. pl. (158) 6

Potentilla grandiflora — Fl. alp. (71) 18; Hist. nat. Rossia (144) 30

Potentilla heptaphylla — Cent. I. pl. (65) 13; Fl. alp. (71) 18

Potentilla hirta — Fl. Monsp. (74) 18

Potentilla minus repens aureum — Fl. Angl. (56) 27

Potentilla monspeliensis — Demonstr. pl. (49) 14; Calend. fl. (72) [14][as monspeliaca]

Potentilla multifida — Demonstr. pl. (49) 14; Hist. nat. Rossia (144) 30

Potentilla nitida — Cent. II. pl. (66) 18

Potentilla nivea — Stat. pl. (55) 16; Fl. alp. (71) 18; Hist. nat. Rossia (144) 30

Potentilla norvegica — Pan Svec. (26) 24; Demonstr. pl. (49) 14; Calend. fl. (72) [22]; Prodr. fl. Dan. (82) 19; Pl. rar. Afr. (115) 6; Fl. Åker. (162) 13

Potentilla opaca — Prodr. fl. Dan. (82) 19

Potentilla recta — Demonstr. pl. (49) 14

Potentilla repens — Herbat. Upsal. (50) 13; Pl. officin. (52) 15; Stat. pl. (55) 22; Fl. Monsp. (74) 18; Febr. interm. (167) 43

Potentilla repens aureum — Fl. Angl. (56) 27

Potentilla reptans — Pan Svec. (26) 24; Fl. Angl. (56) 17; Hort. acad. (63) 10; Prodr. fl. Dan. (82) 19; Fl. Belg. (112) 17; Fl. Åker. (162) 13; Pand. fl. Ryb. (165) 19

Potentilla rupestris — Demonstr. pl. (49) 14; Fl. Angl. (56) 17; Calend. fl. (72) [14]; Prodr. fl. Dan. (82) 19; Hist. nat. Rossia (144) 30

Potentilla sericea — Hist. nat. Rossia (144) 30

Potentilla stipularis — Hist. nat. Rossia (144) 30

Potentilla supina — Demonstr. pl. (49) 14; Fl. Palaest. (70) 21; Fl. Belg. (112) 17; Hist. nat. Rossia (144) 30

Potentilla verna — Demonstr. pl. (49) 14; Stat. pl. (55) 21; Cervus (60) 7; Calend. fl. (72) [10], [14]; Prodr. fl. Dan. (82) 19; Fl. Åker. (162) 13; Pand. fl. Ryb. (165) 19

Potentilla vernalis — Herbat. Upsal. (50) 11

Poterium — Pl. hybr. (33) 6; Nom. bot. (107) 18

Poterium agrimonioides — Pl. hybr. (33) 10[as agrimonoides]

Poterium hybridum — Demonstr. pl. (49) 25; Fl. Monsp. (74) 27[as hybrida]

Poterium inerme — Pl. Mart.-Burs. (6) 11

Poterium inerme, filamentis longissimis — Pl. hybr. (33) 10

Poterium pimpinella — Mac. olit. (113) 23

Poterium sanguisorba — Demonstr. pl. (49) 25; Pl. officin. (52) 15; Fl. Angl. (56) 24; Fl. Palaest. (70) 30; Fl. Monsp. (74) 27; Acetaria (77) 10; Prodr. fl. Dan. (82) 24; Fl. Belg. (112) 22; Pl. rar. Afr. (115) 7[as sauguisorba]; Hort. cul. (132) 18

Poterium spinosum — Fl. Palaest. (70) 30

Pothos — Nova pl. gen. 1747 (14) [vi], 26; Herb. Amboin. (57) 25; Chin. Lagerstr. (64) 6[as Potos]

Pothos latifolius, foliis ovatis, petiolo latioribus — Herb. Amboin. (57) 25

Pothos scandens — Fung. melit. (69) 2

Pothos scandens, petiolis foliorum latitudine — Herb. Amboin. (57) 25

Pothos zeylanica — Nova pl. gen. 1747 (14) 27

Prasium — Hort. Upsal. (7) 36

Prasium majus — Demonstr. pl. (49) 16; Fl. Palaest. (70) 23

Prenanthes — Mus. Ad.-Frid. (11) 21; Vir. pl. (13) 25; Fl. alp. (71) 24

Prenanthes altissima — Hist. nat. Rossia (144) 32

Prenanthes autumnalis, flore dilute purpureo deorsum nutante, spicatim ad caulem disposito, foliis scabris incisis, caule singulari — Rad. senega (23) 12

Prenanthes flosculis plurimis, foliis hastatis angulatis — Rad. senega (23) 12

Prenanthes muralis — Herbat. Upsal. (50) 8; Stat. pl. (55) 18; Fl. Angl. (56) 21; Calend. fl. (72) [16]; Fl. Monsp. (74) 24; Prodr. fl. Dan. (82) 22; Fl. Belg. (112) 20; Fl. Åker. (162) 17; Pand. fl. Ryb. (165) 21

Prenanthes repens, foliis trilobis — Pl. rar. Camsch. (30) 27

Prenanthes tenuifolia — Fl. alp. (71) 21

Prenanthes umbrosa — Pan Svec. (26) 31

Prenanthes viminea — Fl. Monsp. (74) 24

Primula — Peloria (3) 9; Hort. Upsal. (7) 33; Fl. oecon. (17) 5; Oecon. nat. (20) 15; Pl. hybr. (33) 6, 12; Pl. escul. (35) 28, 29; Hort. acad. (63) 3; Calend. fl. (72) [11]; Acetaria (77) 10; Pand. insect. (93) 12; Nom. bot. (107) 10; Fund. fr. (123) 11

Primula acaulis — Fl. Angl. (56) 12

Primula auricula — Demonstr. pl. (49) 5; Fl. alp. (71) 13; Calend. fl. (72) [10]; Pl. Alstr. (121) [4]; Hort. cul. (132) 24, 25

Primula cortusoides — Hist. nat. Rossia (144) 28

Primula elatior — Fl. Angl. (56) 12; Fl. Belg. (112) 8

Primula farinosa — Herbat. Upsal. (50) 14; Stat. pl. (55) 14; Fl. Angl. (56) 12; Fl. alp. (71) 13; Calend. fl. (72) [11]; Fl. Monsp. (74) 11; Prodr. fl. Dan. (82) 15; Pand. fl. Ryb. (165) 17

Primula flore subsessili, foliis linearibus — Pl. Mart.-Burs. (6) 20

Primula foliis glabris carnosis integerrimis — Pl. hybr. (33) 12

Primula foliis petiolatis, sublobatis crenatis — Pl. hybr. (33) 12

Primula integrifolia — Fl. alp. (71) 13; Rar. Norv. (157) 9, 10

Primula minima — Fl. alp. (71) 13

Primula officinalis — Demonstr. pl. (49) 5

Primula purpurea — Pan Svec. (26) 17

Primula veris — Herbat. Upsal. (50) 10; Stat. pl. (55) 22; Mac. olit. (113) 19; Hort. cul. (132) 24, 25; Hist. nat. Rossia (144) 28; Fl. Åker. (162) 8; Pand. fl. Ryb. (165) 17; Esca avium (174) 11

Primula veris acaulis — Prodr. fl. Dan. (82) 14

Primula veris elatior — Fl. Monsp. (74) 11; Prodr. fl. Dan. (82) 14; Fl. Belg. (112) 14

Primula veris hortensis — Calend. fl. (72) [9]

Primula veris odorata, flore luteo simplici — Pl. hybr. (33) 12

Primula veris officinalis — Pl. officin. (52) 15; Fl. Angl. (56) 12; Prodr. fl. Dan. (82) 14

Primula vitaliana — Fl. alp. (71) 13

Primula vulgaris — Pan Svec. (26) 16; Pl. escul. (35) 10; Hosp. insect. fl. (43) 16

Prinos — Nova pl. gen. 1751 (32) 9

Prionus — Fund. entom. (154) 30

Procellaria — Chin. Lagerstr. (64) 14

Procellaria aequinoctialis — Nat. pelagi (84) 12

Procellaria albo fuscoque varia — Chin. Lagerstr. (64) 13

Procellaria capensis — Chin. Lagerstr. (64) 13; Nat. pelagi (84) 12; Fl. Cap. (99) 3; Fund. ornith. (137) 26; Iter Chin. (161) 6

Procellaria pelagica — Migr. avium (79) 26; Nat. pelagi (84) 12; Fund. ornith. (137) 26; Iter Chin. (161) 6

Proserpinaca — Nova pl. gen. 1747 (14) [iv]; Nova pl. gen. 1751 (32) 7, 12

Protea — Pl. hybr. (33) 29; Incr. bot. (48) 11; Fl. Cap. (99) 6, 9; Fund. fr. (123) 18; Aphyteia (185) 6

Protea argentea — Fl. Cap. (99) 11

Protea fusca — Fl. Cap. (99) 11

Pruna sylvestria praecocia — Cent. I. pl. (65) 12

Prunella — Sapor. med. (31) 15; Metam. pl. (67) 21; Nom. bot. (107) 15

Prunella hortensis — Herb. Amboin. (57) 26

Prunella hyssopifolia — Fl. Monsp. (74) 20

Prunella laciniata — Fl. Monsp. (74) 20

Prunella vulgaris — Pan Svec. (26) 27[as Brunella]; Herbat. Upsal. (50) 6; Pl. officin. (52) 16; Stat. pl. (55) 18; Fl. Angl. (56) 19; Fl. Monsp. (74) 20; Prodr. fl. Dan. (82) 20; Fl. Belg. (112) 18; Fl. Åker. (162) 14; Pand. fl. Ryb. (165) 20

Prunum stellatum — Herb. Amboin. (57) 7

Prunus — Vir. pl. (13) 33, 36; Fl. oecon. (17) 12; Oecon. nat. (20) 22; Pl. escul. (35) 29; Hosp. insect. fl. (43) 40; Vern. arb. (47) 10, table; Hort. acad. (63) 2; Calend. fl. (72) [11]; Fr. Svec. (91) [ii]; Pand. insect. (93) 14; Nom. bot. (107) 13; Inebr. (117) 13; Nect. fl. (122) 6; Pot. theae (142) 16; Usum hist. nat. (145) 17; Usum musc. (148) 12

Prunus armeniaca — Gem. arb. (24) 24; Hosp. insect. fl. (43) 22; Demonstr. pl. (49) 13; Fr. escul. (127) 12; Hort. cul. (132) 21

Prunus avium — Arb. Svec. (101) 7, 9, 18

Prunus cerasus — Demonstr. pl. (49) 13; Pl. officin. (52) 7; Fl. Angl. (56) 17; Calend. fl. (72) [10], [11]; Fl. Monsp. (74) 17; Arb. Svec. (101) 7, 9; Fr. escul. (127) 12; Hort. cul. (132) 21

Prunus cerasus avium — Hort. cul. (132) 21

Prunus cerasus bigarella — Hort. cul. (132) 21

Prunus cerasus sativa — Arb. Svec. (101) 28

Prunus domestica — Demonstr. pl. (49) 13; Pl. officin. (52) 16; Fl. Monsp. (74) 17; Pl. tinct. (97) 19; Arb. Svec. (101) 7, 9, 28; Fr. escul. (127) 11; Hort. cul. (132) 20; Colon. pl. (158) 8

Prunus domestica cerea — Hort. cul. (132) 20

Prunus gallica — Hosp. insect. fl. (43) 22

Prunus hortensis — Calend. fl. (72) [11]

Prunus indica fructu nigro — Nova pl. gen. 1747 (14) 15

Prunus inermis — Noxa insect. (46) 17, 20

Prunus insititia — Cent. I. pl. (65) 12; Fr. escul. (127) 11

Prunus laurocerasus — Demonstr. pl. (49) 13

Prunus mahaleb — Demonstr. pl. (49) 13; Fl. Monsp. (74) 17

Prunus padus — Stat. pl. (55) 17; Fl. Angl. (56) 17; Calend. fl. (72) [10], [11]; Prodr. fl. Dan. (82) 18; Arb. Svec. (101) 7, 9, 19; Fl. Belg. (112) 17; Fr. escul. (127) 12; Usum hist. nat. (145) 23; Fl. Åker. (162) 12; Pand. fl. Ryb. (165) 19; Esca avium (174) 4

Prunus pentaphyllos malabarica, fructus calyce insidente — Nova pl. gen. 1747 (14) 29

Prunus racemosa, celastrifolio — Nova pl. gen. 1747 (14) 19

Prunus sativa — Gem. arb. (24) 24

Prunus sibirica — Hist. nat. Rossia (144) 30; Usum hist. nat. (145) 12

Prunus spinosa — Pan Svec. (26) 24; Cui bono? (42) 20; Hosp. insect. fl. (43) 22, 40; Demonstr. pl. (49) 13; Herbat. Upsal. (50) 7; Pl. officin. (52) 3; Stat. pl. (55) 22; Fl. Angl. (56) 17; Oves (61) 18; Calend. fl. (72) [11]; Fl. Monsp. (74) 17; Prodr. fl. Dan. (82) 18; Fr. Svec. (91) 3, 14, 17, 23, 24, 26; Nom. bot. (107) 13; Fl. Belg. (112) 17; Fr. escul. (127) 11; Pot. theae (142) 8; Purg. indig. (143) 9; Fl. Åker. (162) 12; Pand. fl. Ryb. (165) 19; Febr. interm. (167) 41

Prunus spinosa, foliis ovatis subtus villosis, pedunculis geminis — Cent. I. pl. (65) 12

Prunus sylvestris — Pl. escul. (35) 16

Prunus sylvestris major — Cent. I. pl. (65) 12

Prunus virginiana — Demonstr. pl. (49) 13; Fr. escul. (127) 12

Prunus zeylanica, laurifolio, veralu zeylanensibus — Nova pl. gen. 1747 (14) 19

Pseudo-acacia — Nova pl. gen. 1751 (32) 10

Pseudochina amboinensis — Herb. Amboin. (57) 24

Pseudocytisus — Metam. pl. (67) 15

Pseudorchis — Betula (1) 12[as Pseudoorchis]

Pseudosandalum amboinense — Herb. Amboin. (57) 9

Pseudo-sycomorus — Ficus (2) 3

Pseudo-triticum — Fund. agrost. (152) 16

Pseudo-valeriana annua, semine coronato, major lusitanica — Demonstr. pl. (49) 2

Psidium — Hort. Upsal. (7) 37; Vir. pl. (13) 21; Pl. escul. (35) 4; Herb. Amboin. (57) 7; Pand. insect. (93) 14

Psidium cujavus — Cent. I. pl. (65) 2

Psidium cujavus pedunculis trifloris — Herb. Amboin. (57) 7

Psidium guajacana — Gem. arb. (24) 20; Fr. escul. (127) 10

Psidium guajana pedunculis unifloris — Herb. Amboin. (57) 7

Psidium guajava — Fl. Jam. (105) 17, 25

Psidium pyriforme — Pl. Surin. (177) 10

Psittacus — Fund. ornith. (137) 19

Psittacus brachiurus, viridis, pectore urrhopygioque coccineis, vertice caeruleo — Chin. Lagerstr. (64) 8[as caerulaeo]

Psittacus caroliniensis — Migr. avium (79) 14

Psittacus macrourus — Chin. Lagerstr. (64) 8

Psittacus minutissimus — Chin. Lagerstr. (64) 8

Psittacus pendulinus — Somn. pl. (68) 7[as pendulus]; Siren. lacert. (146) 8

Psittacus viridis, pectore sanguineo, gula nigra — Chin. Lagerstr. (64) 8[as sanguinaeo]

Psophia — Siren. lacert. (146) 8[as Psophaa]

Psoralea — Hort. Upsal. (7) 37[as Psoralia]

Psoralea aculeata — Fl. Cap. (99) 17

Psoralea aphylla — Pl. rar. Afr. (115) 15

Psoralea bituminosa — Demonstr. pl. (49) 21; Fl. Monsp. (74) 23

Psoralea bituminosa angustifolia — Fl. Palaest. (70) 26[as Psoralia]

Psoralea bituminosa latifolia — Fl. Palaest. (70) 26[as Psoralia]

Psoralea corylifolia — Demonstr. pl. (49) 21

Psoralea foliis ovatis sessilibus adpressis acutis — Pl. rar. Afr. (115) 15

Psoralea foliis supradecompositis digitatis linearibus — Pl. rar. Afr. (115) 15

Psoralea foliis ternatis, floribus ternatis sessilibus — Pl. rar. Afr. (115) 15[as Psoralfa]

Psoralea glandulosa — Viola ipecac. (176) [4]

Psoralea hirta — Pl. rar. Afr. (115) 15[as Psoralfa]

Psoralea pinnata — Somn. pl. (68) 17[as Psoralia]; Fl. Cap. (99) 17

Psoralea prostrata — Pl. rar. Afr. (115) 15

Psoralea tenuifolia — Fl. Cap. (99) 17

Psychotria — Fl. Jam. (105) 26[as Psycotthia]

Psychotria asiatica — Pl. Jam. (102) 9[as Psycothria]; Fl. Jam. (105) 14[as Psychothria], 25[as Psycothria ascatica]

Psychotria repens — Fl. Jam. (105) 14[as Psychothria], 25[as Psycothria]

Psychotrophum — Fl. Jam. (105) 26

Psyllium — Sapor. med. (31) 12

Ptarmica — Vir. pl. (13) 23

Ptelea — Nova pl. gen. 1751 (32) 8; Prol. pl. 1760 (114) 4

Ptelea trifoliata — Demonstr. pl. (49) 4

Ptelea viscosa — Demonstr. pl. (49) 4; Herb. Amboin. (57) 17; Fl. Jam. (105) 13

Pteridium aquilinum — Erica (163) 12

Pteris — Acrostichum (10) 3, 8, 17; Fl. oecon. (17) 28

Pteris aquilina — Hosp. insect. fl. (43) 39; Herbat. Upsal. (50) 11; Stat. pl. (55) 18; Fl. Angl. (56) 25; Calend. fl. (72) [19]; Fl. Monsp. (74) 29; Prodr. fl. Dan. (82) 25; Fl. Belg. (112) 23; Usum hist. nat. (145) 10; Fl. Åker. (162) 20; Pand. fl. Ryb. (165) 23

Pteris biauriculata — Fl. Jam. (105) 23

Pteris caudata — Fl. Jam. (105) 23

Pteris filix femina — Pan Svec. (26) [37, as 39]

Pteris grandifolia — Fl. Jam. (105) 23

Pteris heterophylla — Fl. Jam. (105) 23

Pteris lineata — Fl. Jam. (105) 23

Pteris lonchitis — Pan Svec. (26) [37, as 39]

Pteris longifolia — Fl. Jam. (105) 23

Pteris mutilata — Fl. Jam. (105) 23

Pteris pedata — Hist. nat. Rossia (144) 34

Pteris stipularis — Fl. Jam. (105) 23

Pteris trichomanes — Fl. Jam. (105) 23

Pteris vittata — Fl. Jam. (105) 23

Pterocarpus — Pl. officin. (52) 9, 17; Herb. Amboin. (57) 10

Pterocarpus lunatus — Pl. Surin. (177) 13

Pterocarpus ovalis — Pl. Surin. (177) 12

Pterophora camphorata — Pl. rar. Afr. (115) 17

Pterophora camphorata, foliis ad margines pilosis — Pl. rar. Afr. (115) 18

Pterophorus — Fund. entom. (154) 30

Pterospermadendron — Nova pl. gen. 1747 (14) 23

Pterospermadendron foliis accretis, flore fructuque majore — Nova pl. gen. 1747 (14) 24

Pterospermadendron suberis folio anguloso subtus incano, floribus albis — Nova pl. gen. 1747 (14) 24

Pterota — Fl. Jam. (105) 26

Ptinus — Fund. entom. (154) 29

Ptinus fur — Fund. entom. (154) 30; Pand. fl. Ryb. (165) 7

Ptinus mollis — Pand. fl. Ryb. (165) 7

Ptinus pectinicornis — Pand. fl. Ryb. (165) 7

Ptinus pertinax — Pand. fl. Ryb. (165) 7

Pubeta — Pl. Surin. (177) 4, 16

Pugnax — Fund. ornith. (137) 18

Pulassarium — Herb. Amboin. (57) 18

Pulassarius — Herb. Amboin. (57) 12

Pulegium — Fl. Monsp. (74) 7; Nom. bot. (107) 14

Pulex — Spons. pl. (12) 15, 16; Mirac. insect. (45) 10; Noxa insect. (46) 9, 29; Cynogr. (54) 21; Instr. peregr. (96) 12; Usum hist. nat. (145) 29; Fund. entom. (154) 7, 19, 23, 26

Pulex subcutaneus — Exanth. viva (86) 14

Pulmonaria — Vir. pl. (13) 18; Sapor. med. (31) 12; Pand. insect. (93) 12

Pulmonaria angustifolia — Fl. Angl. (56) 12; Prodr. fl. Dan. (82) 14

Pulmonaria immaculata — Pan Svec. (26) 16; Hosp. insect. fl. (43) 16

Pulmonaria maculata — Fl. Belg. (112) 14

Pulmonaria maritima — Fl. Angl. (56) 12; Rar. Norv. (157) 9; Colon. pl. (158) 8

Pulmonaria officinalis — Demonstr. pl. (49) 5; Herbat. Upsal. (50) 7; Pl. officin. (52) 16; Stat. pl. (55) 17[as officinarum]; Fl. Angl. (56) 6; Calend. fl. (72) [9]; Fl. Monsp. (74) 11; Prodr. fl. Dan. (82) 14; Fl. Åker. (162) 8; Pand. fl. Ryb. (165) 17; Esca avium (174) 11

Pulmonaria sibirica — Demonstr. pl. (49) 5; Hist. nat. Rossia (144) 28

Pulmonaria virginica — Hist. nat. Rossia (144) 12

Pulsatilla — Hort. Upsal. (7) 33; Vir. pl. (13) 21, 30; Vern. arb. (47) 8; Nom. bot. (107) 14

Pulsatilla dalekarlica — Pan Svec. (26) 25

Pulsatilla reflexa — Pan Svec. (26) 25

Pulsatilla vulgaris — Pan Svec. (26) 25

Pumilea — Pl. Jam. (102) 10; Fl. Jam. (105) 26

Punica — Spons. pl. (12) 59; Vir. pl. (13) 21, 33; Fl. Monsp. (74) 7; Pand. insect. (93) 14; Nom. bot. (107) 13; Inebr. (117) 13

Punica granatum — Demonstr. pl. (49) 13; Pl. officin. (52) 5, 11, 12; Herb. Amboin. (57) 9; Fl. Palaest. (70) 20; Fl. Monsp. (74) 17[as granatus]; Fl. Jam. (105) 17; Fr. escul. (127) 15

Pustula arborum — Herb. Amboin. (57) 25

Putorius — Usum hist. nat. (145) 24

Pyrethrum — Hort. Upsal. (7) 36[as Pyretrum]; Vir. pl. (13) 23[as Pyretrum]; Sapor. med. (31) 19

Pyrola — Spons. pl. (12) 33, 35; Vir. pl. (13) 20; Oecon. nat. (20) 19; Pl. hybr. (33) 7; Fr. Svec. (91) [ii]; Nom. bot. (107) 13; Erica (163) 3; Ledum (178) 7

Pyrola alsines flore brasiliana major — Pl. Mart.-Burs. (6) 15[as brasillana]

Pyrola alsines flore brasiliana minor — Pl. Mart.-Burs. (6) 15

Pyrola arbuti folio — Pl. hybr. (33) 21

Pyrola floribus racemosis dispersis, staminibus pistillisque rectis — Pl. hybr. (33) 21

Pyrola halleri — Pan Svec. (26) 22

Pyrola irregularis — Pan Svec. (26) 22

Pyrola minor — Fl. Angl. (56) 15; Prodr. fl. Dan. (82) 17; Rar. Norv. (157) 11; Pand. fl. Ryb. (165) 18

Pyrola pedunculis apice bifloris triflorisve — Pl. hybr. (33) 21

Pyrola racemis unilateralibus — Pl. hybr. (33) 21

Pyrola repens, foliis scabris, flore pentapetaloide fistuloso — Nova pl. gen. 1751 (32) 28

Pyrola rotundifolia — Herbat. Upsal. (50) 6; Pl. officin. (52) 16; Stat. pl. (55) 18; Fl. Angl. (56) 15; Prodr. fl. Dan. (82) 17; Fl. Belg. (112) 16; Fl. Åker. (162) 11; Pand. fl. Ryb. (165) 18

Pyrola secunda — Pan Svec. (26) 22; Herbat. Upsal. (50) 11; Stat. pl. (55) 18; Fl. Angl. (56) 15; Prodr. fl. Dan. (82) 17; Fl. Åker. (162) 11; Pand. fl. Ryb. (165) 18

Pyrola staminibus adscendentibus, pistillis declinatis — Pl. Mart.-Burs. (6) 15[as ascendentibus, pistillo declinato]; Spons. pl. (12) 32; Pl. hybr. (33) 21

Pyrola umbellata — Pan Svec. (26) 22; Stat. pl. (55) 18; Fr. Svec. (91) 5, 21; Obs. mat. med. (171) 4

Pyrola uniflora — Pan Svec. (26) 22; Herbat. Upsal. (50) 11; Stat. pl. (55) 18; Fl. Monsp. (74) 15; Fl. Belg. (112) 16; Rar. Norv. (157) 15; Pand. fl. Ryb. (165) 18; Obs. mat. med. (171) 4

Pyrolae affinis virginiana repens fruticosa, foliis rigidis scabritie exasperatis, flore pentapetaloide fistuloso — Nova pl. gen. 1751 (32) 28

Pyrus — Spons. pl. (12) 42; Vir. pl. (13) 21; Fl. oecon. (17) 12, 13; Pan Svec. (26) 6; Pl. escul. (35) 3; Hosp. insect. fl. (43) 40; Noxa insect. (46) 18, 20; Vern. arb. (47) 10, table; Hort. acad. (63) 2; Calend. fl. (72) [11]; Arb. Svec. (101) 30; Nom. bot. (107) 13; Polit. nat. (109) 8; Prol. pl. 1760 (114) 11; Inebr. (117) 13; Nect. fl. (122) 6

Pyrus communis — Demonstr. pl. (49) 13; Pl. officin. (52) 9; Stat. pl. (55) 20; Fl. Angl. (56) 17; Fl. Palaest. (70) 20; Calend. fl. (72) [11]; Fl. Monsp. (74) 17; Pand. insect. (93) 15; Arb. Svec. (101) 7, 9, 20; Fl. Belg. (112) 17; Fr. escul. (127) 14; Hort. cul. (132) 20

Pyrus communis falerna — Hort. cul. (132) 20

Pyrus communis pompejana — Hort. cul. (132) 20

Pyrus communis pyraster — Hort. cul. (132) 20

Pyrus coronaria — Demonstr. pl. (49) 13

Pyrus cydonia — Demonstr. pl. (49) 13; Fl. Palaest. (70) 21; Fl. Monsp. (74) 17; Fr. escul. (127) 15

Pyrus malus — Gem. arb. (24) 25; Pan Svec. (26) 24; Hosp. insect. fl. (43) 24; Demonstr. pl. (49) 13; Pl. officin. (52) 15; Stat. pl. (55) 20; Fl. Angl. (56) 17; Fl. Palaest. (70) 21; Calend. fl. (72) [10], [11]; Prodr. fl. Dan. (82) 18; Pand. insect. (93) 15; Pl. tinct. (97) 19; Arb. Svec. (101) 7, 9, 20; Fl. Jam. (105) 24; Fl. Belg. (112) 17; Fr. escul. (127) 14; Hort. cul. (132) 19; Fl. Åker. (162) 13; Pand. fl. Ryb. (165) 19; Esca avium (174) 12

Pyrus malus diaphana — Hort. cul. (132) 20

Pyrus malus paradisiaca — Hort. cul. (132) 20

Pyrus malus prasomila — Hort. cul. (132) 20

Pyrus malus sylvestris — Herbat. Upsal. (50) 7; Hort. cul. (132) 20

Pyrus narcissos — Peloria (3) 8

Pyrus pyraster — Gem. arb. (24) 25; Pan Svec. (26) 24; Hosp. insect. fl. (43) 23; Fl. Monsp. (74) 17

Pyrus sylvestris — Anthrop. (111) 3; Fund. fr. (123) 13

Pyxidaria montia — Colon. pl. (158) 11

Quamoclit minima humifusa palustris, herniariae folio — Nova pl. gen. 1747 (14) 12

Quassia — Lign. Qvas. (128) 4ff.

Quassia amara — Lign. Qvas. (128) 7, plate [1]; Obs. mat. med. (171) 4; Pl. Surin. (177) 8

Quercus — Ficus (2) 17; Spons. pl. (12) [2], 41; Vir. pl. (13) 7; Fl. oecon. (17) 23; Curios. nat. (18) 6; Pan Svec. (26) 6; Sapor. med. (31) 15; Pl. hybr. (33) 29; Pl. escul. (35) 24, 27; Hosp. insect. fl. (43) 40; Mirac. insect. (45) 14; Noxa insect. (46) 26; Vern. arb. (47) 10, 11, table; Hort. acad. (63) 14; Metam. pl. (67) 24; Calend. fl. (72) [20]; Cul. mut. (88) 2; Pand. insect. (93) 19; Pl. tinct. (97) 10; Arb. Svec. (101) [3], 4, 30; Nom. bot. (107) 18; Ping. anim. (108) 16; Fl. Belg. (112) 8; Prol. pl. 1760

(114) 2; Fund. fr. (123) 18; Usum musc. (148) 7; Pl. Surin. (177) 15

Quercus aegilops — Pl. tinct. (97) 26

Quercus coccifera — Fl. Palaest. (70) 30; Fl. Monsp. (74) 4, 27; Pl. tinct. (97) 29

Quercus cupula crinata — Fl. Palaest. (70) 30

Quercus glande recondita — Fl. Palaest. (70) 30

Quercus gramuntia — Fl. Palaest. (70) 30; Fl. Monsp. (74) 27

Quercus ilex — Fl. Monsp. (74) 27

Quercus longo pedunculo — Gem. arb. (24) 30; Pan Svec. (26) 36; Hosp. insect. fl. (43) 33

Quercus molucca — Herb. Amboin. (57) 12[incl. as moluccam]

Quercus nigra — Demonstr. pl. (49) 25

Quercus robur — Herbat. Upsal. (50) 7; Pl. officin. (52) 16; Stat. pl. (55) 22; Fl. Angl. (56) 24; Calend. fl. (72) [10]; Fl. Monsp. (74) 27; Prodr. fl. Dan. (82) 24; Pl. tinct. (97) 25, 28; Arb. Svec. (101) 7, 9, 22, 23; Fl. Belg. (112) 22; Fl. Åker. (162) 19; Pand. fl. Ryb. (165) 22; Febr. interm. (167) 42

Quercus smilax — Fl. Monsp. (74) 27

Quercus suber — Pl. officin. (52) 19; Fl. Monsp. (74) 27

Queria hispanica — Demonstr. pl. (49) 4; Fung. melit. (69) 2

Quinquefolio similis enneaphyllos hirsuta — Cent. I. pl. (65) 13

Quinquefolium 2 minus, albo flore — Cent. II. pl. (66) 19

Quinquefolium album majus — Cent. II. pl. (66) 19

Quinquefolium album majus caulescens — Cent. II. pl. (66) 19

Quinquefolium album minus alterum — Cent. II. pl. (66) 19

Quinquefolium minus repens alpinum aureum — Cent. II. pl. (66) 18

Quis qualis — Herb. Amboin. (57) 19

Quiscula — Polit. nat. (109) 18

Radix deiparae — Herb. Amboin. (57) 9

Radix deiparae spuria — Herb. Amboin. (57) 9

Radix pucoronila — Herb. Amboin. (57) 25

Radix serpentum ekawerya dicta — Lign. colubr. (21) 13ff.

Radix toxicaria — Herb. Amboin. (57) 28

Radix vesicatoria — Herb. Amboin. (57) 24

Raja — Oecon. nat. (20) 45; Polit. nat. (109) 12

Raja torpedo — Ambros. (100) 8

Rallus aquaticus — Migr. avium (79) 27

Rallus crex — Migr. avium (79) 17, 27; Usum hist. nat. (145) 25

Rallus lariformis — Migr. avium (79) 28

Ramium majus — Herb. Amboin. (57) 21

Ramphastos — Fund. ornith. (137) 14

Ramphastos cornutus — Chin. Lagerstr. (64) 9

Ramphastos fronte ossea, plana, antice bicorni — Chin. Lagerstr. (64) 9

Rana — Amphib. Gyll. (5) [1], 28; Mus. Ad.-Frid. (11) 6; Spons. pl. (12) 23; Oecon. nat. (20) 28, 41, 44; Metam. pl. (67) 6; Migr. avium (79) 27; Arb. Svec. (101) 25; Polit. nat. (109) 12, 13; Lepra (140) 10; Var. cib. (156) 5

Rana aquatica seu innoxia — Mat. med. anim. (29) 11

Rana arborea — Siren. lacert. (146) 13

Rana brasiliensis gracilis — Amphib. Gyll. (5) 29

Rana bufo — Arb. Svec. (101) 25; Esca avium (174) 3

Rana innoxia — Mat. med. anim. (29) 11

Rana manibus tetradactylis fissis, plantis hexadactylis palmatis, pollice breviore — Mat. med. anim. (29) 11

Rana manibus tetradactylis fissis, plantis hexadactylis palmatis, pollice longiore — Mat. med. anim. (29) 11

Rana maxima, virginiana, eximia, rara — Mus. Ad.-Frid. (11) 9

Rana palmis tetradactylis fissis, plantis hexadactylis, subpalmatis: pollice latiusculo brevissimo — Mus. Ad.-Frid. (11) 9

Rana palmis tetradactylis fissis, plantis pentadactylis palmatis, apicibus digitorum subrotundis — Mus. Ad.-Frid. (11) 7

Rana palmis tetradactylis fissis, plantis pentadactylis palmatis, femoribus postice oblique striatis — Metam. pl. (67) 7

Rana pedibus fissis, palmis tetradactylis, plantis pentadactylis; geniculis subtus tuberosis — Mus. Ad.-Frid. (11) 8[as Bana]

Rana pedibus fissis, unguibus subrotundis, corpore laevi, pone angustato — Amphib. Gyll. (5) 29

Rana piscis — Metam. pl. (67) 6

Rana surinamensis — Mus. Ad.-Frid. (11) 8

Rana surinamensis, prone coerulescentis, supine albi coloris, ad latera utrinque maculis nigris notata — Amphib. Gyll. (5) 29

Rana temporaria — Calend. fl. (72) [8], [9]; Fund. fr. (123) 8; Esca avium (174) 3

Randia — Demonstr. pl. (49) 27

Randia aculeata — Fl. Jam. (105) 14

Rangifer — Oecon. nat. (20) 34; Pan Svec. (26) 5, 38; Mat. med. anim. (29) 7; Morb. hyeme (38) 3; Cervus (60) 3ff.[incl. as Rhangifer]; Usum musc. (148) 9

Ranula americana rubra — Amphib. Gyll. (5) 29

Ranunculus — Peloria (3) 10; Hort. Upsal. (7) 33; Spons. pl. (12) 59, 60; Vir. pl. (13) 21, 29; Fl. oecon. (17) 15; Pl. escul. (35) 28; Fl. Angl. (56) 6; Oves (61) 16; Metam. pl. (67) 17; Calend. fl. (72) [12]; Fl. Monsp. (74) 7; Pand. insect. (93) 16; Nom. bot. (107) 14; Prol. pl. 1760 (114) 18; Nect.

fl. (122) 11; Fund. fr. (123) 23; Pand. fl. Ryb. (165) 19; Febr. interm. (167) 51

Ranunculus abortivus — Specif. Canad. (76) 13

Ranunculus aconitifolius — Demonstr. pl. (49) 15; Metam. pl. (67) 15; Fl. alp. (71) 19; Calend. fl. (72) [11]; Rar. Norv. (157) 9

Ranunculus acris — Pan Svec. (26) 26; Hosp. insect. fl. (43) 26; Herbat. Upsal. (50) 7; Stat. pl. (55) 21; Fl. Angl. (56) 18; Cervus (60) 8[as Rannunculus]; Metam. pl. (67) 15; Fl. Monsp. (74) 19; Prodr. fl. Dan. (82) 19; Fl. Belg. (112) 18; Pl. rar. Afr. (115) 6; Rar. Norv. (157) 16; Fl. Åker. (162) 14; Esca avium (174) 13

Ranunculus alpestris — Fl. alp. (71) 19

Ranunculus ammania lapponica — Pan Svec. (26) 26

Ranunculus amplexicaulis — Fl. alp. (71) 19; Fl. Monsp. (74) 19; Prodr. fl. Dan. (82) 19

Ranunculus aquaticus — Herbat. Upsal. (50) 11; Esca avium (174) 13

Ranunculus aquatilis — Pan Svec. (26) 26; Stat. pl. (55) 13; Fl. Angl. (56) 18; Metam. pl. (67) 15, 16; Fl. Monsp. (74) 19; Prodr. fl. Dan. (82) 19; Fl. Belg. (112) 8, 18; Fl. Åker. (162) 14; Pand. fl. Ryb. (165) 20

Ranunculus arvensis — Hosp. insect. fl. (43) 26; Demonstr. pl. (49) 15; Stat. pl. (55) 19; Fl. Monsp. (74) 19; Prodr. fl. Dan. (82) 19; Fl. Belg. (112) 18; Usum hist. nat. (145) 10

Ranunculus asiaticus — Demonstr. pl. (49) 15; Hort. cul. (132) 25

Ranunculus auricomus — Herbat. Upsal. (50) 8[as auricormus]; Stat. pl. (55) 14; Fl. Angl. (56) 18; Prodr. fl. Dan. (82) 19; Fl. Åker. (162) 14

Ranunculus bulbosus — Pan Svec. (26) 26; Fl. Angl. (56) 18; Metam. pl. (67) 16; Fl. Monsp. (74) 19; Prodr. fl. Dan. (82) 19; Fl. Belg. (112) 18; Fl. Åker. (162) 14; Pand. fl. Ryb. (165) 20

Ranunculus bullata — Metam. pl. (67) 15

Ranunculus calycibus hirsutis, caule unifloro, foliis radicalibus palmatis, caulinis multipartitis sessilibus — Pl. Mart.-Burs. (6) 13

Ranunculus cassubicus — Hist. nat. Rossia (144) 30

Ranunculus chaerophyllos — Fl. Monsp. (74) 19[as chaerophyllus]

Ranunculus chelidonium minus — Pan Svec. (26) 26

Ranunculus dannemorensis — Pan Svec. (26) 26

Ranunculus echinatus — Pan Svec. (26) 26

Ranunculus ficaria — Pl. escul. (35) 19; Vern. arb. (47) 8; Herbat. Upsal. (50) 8; Pl. officin. (52) 8; Stat. pl. (55) 17; Fl. Angl. (56) 18; Metam. pl. (67) 15; Calend. fl. (72) [9]; Fl. Monsp. (74) 19; Prodr. fl. Dan. (82) 19; Polit. nat. (109) 5; Fl. Belg. (112) 18; Mac. olit. (113) 19; Fl. Åker. (162) 14; Pand. fl. Ryb. (165) 19

Ranunculus flammula — Pan Svec. (26) 26; Herbat. Upsal. (50) 6[as flamula]; Stat. pl. (55) 15; Fl. Angl. (56) 18; Metam. pl. (67) 15; Fl. Monsp. (74) 19; Prodr. fl. Dan. (82) 19; Fl. Belg. (112) 18;

Usum hist. nat. (145) 22; Fl. Åker. (162) 14; Pand. fl. Ryb. (165) 19

Ranunculus foliatus — Fl. Monsp. (74) 19

Ranunculus foliis linearibus, caule repente — Pl. Mart.-Burs. (6) 13

Ranunculus foliis radicalibus reniformibus crenatis, caulinis digitatis, petiolatis — Specif. Canad. (76) 23

Ranunculus glacialis — Stat. pl. (55) 16; Fl. alp. (71) 19; Rar. Norv. (157) 10

Ranunculus gramineus — Metam. pl. (67) 15; Fl. alp. (71) 19; Fl. Monsp. (74) 19

Ranunculus hederaceus — Fl. Angl. (56) 18; Prodr. fl. Dan. (82) 19; Fl. Belg. (112) 8, 18

Ranunculus illyricus — Fl. Monsp. (74) 19; Colon. pl. (158) 6

Ranunculus lanuginosus — Fl. Monsp. (74) 19

Ranunculus lapponicus — Stat. pl. (55) 16; Fl. alp. (71) 19

Ranunculus lingua — Herbat. Upsal. (50) 19; Stat. pl. (55) 13; Fl. Angl. (56) 18; Prodr. fl. Dan. (82) 19; Fl. Belg. (112) 8, 18

Ranunculus luteus alpinus — Pan Svec. (26) 26

Ranunculus monspeliacus — Fl. Monsp. (74) 19

Ranunculus montanus, folio gramineo — Pl. Mart.-Burs. (6) 13

Ranunculus muricatus — Fl. Angl. (56) 18; Fl. Monsp. (74) 19

Ranunculus nivalis — Stat. pl. (55) 16; Fl. alp. (71) 19

Ranunculus orientalis — Fl. Palaest. (70) 22

Ranunculus orientalis palustris — Fl. Palaest. (70) 22

Ranunculus orientalis palustris, apii folio, caule subhirsuto — Fl. Palaest. (70) 22

Ranunculus pallidus — Fl. Monsp. (74) 30

Ranunculus parviflorus — Fl. Belg. (112) 18

Ranunculus platanifolius — Rar. Norv. (157) 9

Ranunculus polyanthemos — Herbat. Upsal. (50) 19[as polyanthemus]; Stat. pl. (55) 21; Somn. pl. (68) 22[as polyanthemus]; Prodr. fl. Dan. (82) 19; Fl. Åker. (162) 14

Ranunculus polyanthes — Pan Svec. (26) 26

Ranunculus pratensis, radice verticilli modo rotunda — Pl. Mart.-Burs. (6) 13

Ranunculus purpureus alpinus — Pan Svec. (26) 26

Ranunculus repens — Pan Svec. (26) 26; Herbat. Upsal. (50) 15; Stat. pl. (55) 19; Fl. Angl. (56) 18; Metam. pl. (67) 16; Fl. Monsp. (74) 19; Prodr. fl. Dan. (82) 19; Fl. Belg. (112) 18; Pl. rar. Afr. (115) 6; Fl. Åker. (162) 14; Pand. fl. Ryb. (165) 20; Esca avium (174) 13

Ranunculus reptans — Pan Svec. (26) 26; Herbat. Upsal. (50) 18; Stat. pl. (55) 13; Prodr. fl. Dan. (82) 19; Rar. Norv. (157) 11; Fl. Åker. (162) 14; Esca avium (174) 13

Ranunculus rutifolius — Fl. alp. (71) 19

Ranunculus saxatilis — Fl. Monsp. (74) 30

Ranunculus sceleratus — Pan Svec. (26) 26[as scelerata]; Herbat. Upsal. (50) 18; Stat. pl. (55) 14; Fl. Angl. (56) 18; Fl. Palaest. (70) 22; Fl. Monsp. (74) 19; Prodr. fl. Dan. (82) 19; Fl. Belg. (112) 18; Raphania (126) 14; Fl. Åker. (162) 14; Pand. fl. Ryb. (165) 20

Ranunculus sulcatus — Demonstr. pl. (49) 15

Ranunculus thora — Fl. alp. (71) 19

Ranunculus trifolius — Pan Svec. (26) 26

Ranunculus vernus — Pan Svec. (26) 26

Ranunculus villosus — Fl. Monsp. (74) 30

Rapa — Vir. pl. (13) 7; Sapor. med. (31) 11; Pl. escul. (35) 19; Oves (61) 16, 23; Hort. acad. (63) 2; Generat. ambig. (104) 8; Nom. bot. (107) 15

Raphanistrum arvense, flore albo — Raphania (126) 19

Raphanistrum flore albo striato, siliqua articulata striata minore — Raphania (126) 19

Raphanistrum segetum, flore luteo vel pallido — Raphania (126) 19

Raphanistrum segetum, flore purpureo seu dilute violaceo — Raphania (126) 19

Raphanistrum siliqua articulata glabra majore et minore — Raphania (126) 18

Raphanus — Vir. pl. (13) 22; Fl. oecon. (17) 17; Pl. escul. (35) 22; Pand. insect. (93) [17, as 38]; Nom. bot. (107) 15; Raphania (126) 13ff.

Raphanus cakile — Pan Svec. (26) 29

Raphanus raphanistrum — Pan Svec. (26) 29; Stat. pl. (55) 19; Fl. Angl. (56) 20[as Rhaphanus]; Fl. Monsp. (74) 21; Prodr. fl. Dan. (82) 21; Raphania (126) 13ff., plate [1]; Usum hist. nat. (145) 10; Fl. Åker. (162) 15; Pand. fl. Ryb. (165) 20

Raphanus sativus — Demonstr. pl. (49) 18; Pl. officin. (52) 16; Fl. Jam. (105) 24; Hort. cul. (132) 13

Raphanus sativus aestivus — Hort. cul. (132) 13

Raphanus sativus hiemalis — Hort. cul. (132) 13

Raphanus sativus radicula — Hort. cul. (132) 13

Raphanus sibiricus — Hist. nat. Rossia (144) 31

Raphanus siliquis teretibus articulatis laevibus unilocularibus — Raphania (126) 18[as unilolocularibus]

Raphanus sylvestris — Raphania (126) 18

Raphidia — Pand. insect. (93) 6; Fund. entom. (154) 21

Rapistrum album articulatum — Raphania (126) 19

Rapistrum flore albo — Raphania (126) 19

Rapistrum flore albo, erucae foliis — Raphania (126) 19

Rapistrum flore albo lineis nigris depicto — Raphania (126) 19

Rapistrum flore albo, siliqua articulata — Raphania (126) 19

Rapistrum flore albo striato, sinapi album agreste trago — Raphania (126) 19

Rapistrum flore luteo, siliqua glabra articulata — Raphania (126) 19

Rapistrum maximum rotundifolium monospermum — Metam. pl. (67) 15[as rotundi foliam]

Rapistrum montanum, irionis folio, macroleptoceraton — Cent. I. pl. (65) 18

Rapoza lusitanis — Mus. Ad.-Frid. (11) 2

Rapum sylvestre — Fl. Monsp. (74) 30

Rapunculus — Nom. bot. (107) 10

Rapunculus foliis angustissimis dentatis, floribus umbellatis — Cent. II. pl. (66) 22; Pl. rar. Afr. (115) 12

Rapunculus foliis imis cordatis, superioribus angustis, spica cylindracea longissima — Pl. Mart.-Burs. (6) 6

Rauvolfia — Vir. pl. (13) 25

Reaumuria — Nect. fl. (122) 5[as Reaumaria], 12

Reaumuria vermiculata — Fl. Palaest. (70) 21

Recurvirostra — Oecon. nat. (20) 40

Recurvirostra avocetta — Migr. avium (79) 28[as avosetta]

Remora — Mus. Ad.-Frid. (11) 41

Renealmia — Fung. melit. (69) 3

Renealmia disticha — Fl. Jam. (105) 15[as distica]

Renealmia polystachia — Fl. Jam. (105) 15

Renealmia recurva — Fl. Jam. (105) 15

Renealmia usneoides — Herb. Amboin. (57) 27; Fl. Jam. (105) 15

Reseda — Hort. Upsal. (7) 34; Mus. Ad.-Frid. (11) 21; Fl. oecon. (17) 15; Pl. hybr. (33) 7; Fl. Angl. (56) 5; Metam. pl. (67) 19; Nom. bot. (107) 13; Nect. fl. (122) 8

Reseda aegyptiaca — Fl. Palaest. (70) 20

Reseda alba — Demonstr. pl. (49) 13; Fl. Monsp. (74) 17

Reseda alba minor — Pl. Mart.-Burs. (6) 7

Reseda foliis integris trilobisque, calycibus corollam aequantibus — Pl. hybr. (33) 25

Reseda foliis integris trilobisque, calycibus maximis — Pl. hybr. (33) 25

Reseda foliis lanceolatis, caule simplicissimo — Rad. senega (23) 12

Reseda glauca — Fl. alp. (71) 17

Reseda lutea — Fl. Angl. (56) 16; Hort. acad. (63) 11; Fl. Palaest. (70) 20; Fl. Monsp. (74) 17

Reseda luteola — Pan Svec. (26) 25; Demonstr. pl. (49) 13; Stat. pl. (55) 20; Fl. Angl. (56) 16; Calend. fl. (72) [22]; Fl. Monsp. (74) 17; Prodr. fl. Dan. (82) 18; Pl. tinct. (97) 18; Fl. Belg. (112) 17; Colon. pl. (158) 9

Reseda phyteuma — Demonstr. pl. (49) 13; Calend. fl. (72) [22]; Fl. Monsp. (74) 17

Reseda polygalae folio — Fl. Angl. (56) 28

Reseda purpurascens — Fl. Monsp. (74) 17

Reseda sesamoides — Fl. Monsp. (74) 17

Reseda vulgaris — Fl. Belg. (112) 17

Restiaria alba — Herb. Amboin. (57) 14

Restiaria nigra — Herb. Amboin. (57) 14

Retepora — Corallia Balt. (4) 39

Retepora sive eschara marina imperati lapidea gothlandica — Corallia Balt. (4) 38

Reticularia — Corallia Balt. (4) 2

Rex amaroris — Herb. Amboin. (57) 9

Rhabarbarum — Vir. pl. (13) 4, 8, 30, 36; Odor. med. (40) 14, 15; Rhabarbarum (41) 2ff.

Rhabarbarum folio longiori hirsuto crispo, florum thyrso longiori et tenuiori — Rhabarbarum (41) 6

Rhabarbarum rheum — Calend. fl. (72) [11]

Rhabarbarum sinense, folio crispo, flagellis rarioribus et minoribus — Rhabarbarum (41) 6

Rhacoma — Fl. Jam. (105) 26

Rhacoma crossopetalum — Pl. Jam. (102) 8; Fl. Jam. (105) 13

Rhamnus — Vir. pl. (13) 27; Fl. oecon. (17) 6; Oecon. nat. (20) 22; Cui bono? (42) 20; Vern. arb. (47) 10; Fr. Svec. (91) [ii], 23, 25; Pand. insect. (93) 12; Nom. bot. (107) 11; Polit. nat. (109) 5; Inebr. (117) 13

Rhamnus alaternus — Demonstr. pl. (49) 6; Fl. Monsp. (74) 12

Rhamnus alpinus — Fl. alp. (71) 14[as Ramnus]

Rhamnus catharticus — Vir. pl. (13) 7; Gem. arb. (24) 21; Pan Svec. (26) 17; Demonstr. pl. (49) 6; Herbat. Upsal. (50) 7[as catarthicus]; Pl. officin. (52) 18; Fl. Angl. (56) 12[as Ramnus]; Fl. Monsp. (74) 12; Prodr. fl. Dan. (82) 15; Fr. Svec. (91) 3, 13, 26; Pl. tinct. (97) 14; Purg. indig. (143) 7[as chatharticus]; Med. purg. (181) 12

Rhamnus cervispina — Calend. fl. (72) [10]

Rhamnus creticus amygdali folio — Fl. Palaest. (70) 15

Rhamnus frangula — Pan Svec. (26) 17; Hosp. insect. fl. (43) 17; Pl. officin. (52) 10; Stat. pl. (55) 6, 17; Fl. Angl. (56) 12[as Ramnus]; Fl. Monsp. (74) 12; Prodr. fl. Dan. (82) 15; Fr. Svec. (91) 3, 10, 24[as Frangula only]; Pl. tinct. (97) 14; Fl. Belg. (112) 14; Purg. indig. (143) 7; Fl. Åker. (162) 9; Pand. fl. Ryb. (165) 17; Esca avium (174) 11; Med. purg. (181) 13

Rhamnus inermis, floribus hermaphroditis, foliis ovatis lineatis repandis subtus reticulatis — Cent. II. pl. (66) 11

Rhamnus inermis, floribus monogynis hermaphroditis, foliis integerrimis — Med. purg. (181) 13

Rhamnus jujuba — Herb. Amboin. (57) 9; Fr. escul. (127) 14

Rhamnus lineatus — Cent. II. pl. (66) 11[as lineata]; Iter Chin. (161) 9

Rhamnus lotus — Demonstr. pl. (49) 6; Fl. Palaest. (70) 15; Fr. escul. (127) 14

Rhamnus micranthus — Pl. Jam. (102) 10; Fl. Jam. (105) 14

Rhamnus minor — Pl. tinct. (97) 14

Rhamnus napeca — Herb. Amboin. (57) 9

Rhamnus paliurus — Fl. Palaest. (70) 15; Fl. Monsp. (74) 12

Rhamnus sarcomphalus — Pl. Jam. (102) 9; Fl. Jam. (105) 14

Rhamnus spina christi — Demonstr. pl. (49) 6; Fl. Palaest. (70) 15; Fl. Cap. (99) 12

Rhamnus spinis terminalibus, floribus quadrifidis dioicis, foliis ovatis, caule erecto — Med. purg. (181) 12

Rhamnus zizyphus — Demonstr. pl. (49) 6; Pl. officin. (52) 11; Fl. Monsp. (74) 12; Fr. escul. (127) 14

Rhaponticum — Vir. pl. (13) 30; Rhabarbarum (41) 9, 10, 15, 23

Rhaponticum folio lapathi majoris glabro — Rhabarbarum (41) 10

Rheno — Generat. calc. (22) 5; Cervus (60) 3ff.; Usum musc. (148) 9

Rheum — Hort. Upsal. (7) 33; Sapor. med. (31) 18; Rhabarbarum (41) 4ff.

Rheum compactum — Hist. nat. Rossia (144) 29; Med. purg. (181) 20

Rheum foliis glabris — Rhabarbarum (41) 10

Rheum foliis palmatis acuminatis — Med. purg. (181) 20

Rheum foliis subvillosis — Rhabarbarum (41) 6

Rheum palmatum — Purg. indig. (143) 15; Hist. nat. Rossia (144) 29; Med. purg. (181) 20

Rheum rhabarbarum — Demonstr. pl. (49) 11; Pl. officin. (52) 16; Calend. fl. (72) [12]; Hist. nat. Rossia (144) 29

Rheum rhaponticum — Demonstr. pl. (49) 11; Pl. officin. (52) 16; Calend. fl. (72) [12][as raponticum]; Med. purg. (181) 20

Rheum ribes — Fl. Palaest. (70) 18

Rhexia — Nova pl. gen. 1751 (32) 9; Fl. Jam. (105) 27

Rhexia acisanthera — Pl. Jam. (102) 11; Fl. Jam. (105) 15

Rhexia virginica — Pl. Jam. (102) 12

Rhinanthus — Fl. oecon. (17) 16; Pan Svec. (26) 27; Pl. hybr. (33) 7, 26; Vern. arb. (47) 19

Rhinanthus corollarum labio superiore breviore — Pl. Mart.-Burs. (6) 12

Rhinanthus crista — Pl. tinct. (97) 10; Fl. Belg. (112) 19

Rhinanthus crista galli — Herbat. Upsal. (50) 6; Stat. pl. (55) 21; Fl. Angl. (56) 19; Calend. fl. (72) [16]; Fl. Monsp. (74) 20; Prodr. fl. Dan. (82) 20; Fl. Åker. (162) 15; Pand. fl. Ryb. (165) 20

Rhinanthus crista galli gamma — Stat. pl. (55) 19

Rhinoceros — Oecon. nat. (20) 34; Mus ind. (62) 7; Chin. Lagerstr. (64) 6; Fl. Cap. (99) [1]

Rhinomacer — Fund. entom. (154) 30

Rhizophora — Herb. Amboin. (57) 13; Febr. interm. (167) 42

Rhizophora caseolaris — Cent. I. pl. (65) 2

Rhizophora caseolaris, foliis ovatis obtusis, floribus solitariis, fructibus orbiculatis depressis mucronatis — Herb. Amboin. (57) 13

Rhizophora corniculata — Cent. I. pl. (65) 2

Rhizophora corniculata, foliis ovatis, floribus confertis, pedunculis bifloris, fructibus arcuatis acuminatis — Herb. Amboin. (57) 13

Rhizophora cylindrica — Herb. Amboin. (57) 12

Rhizophora gymnorhiza — Herb. Amboin. (57) 12

Rhizophora mangle — Herb. Amboin. (57) 13; Fl. Jam. (105) 16[as Rizophora]; Pl. Surin. (177) 9

Rhodia — Sapor. med. (31) 15

Rhodiola — Hort. Upsal. (7) 33; Spons. pl. (12) 49; Pl. rar. Camsch. (30) 19; Fl. Angl. (56) 5; Nect. fl. (122) 13

Rhodiola lapponica — Pan Svec. (26) [37, as 39]

Rhodiola rosea — Demonstr. pl. (49) 26; Pl. officin. (52) 16; Stat. pl. (55) 16; Fl. Angl. (56) 24; Fl. alp. (71) 23; Rar. Norv. (157) 11, 14, 17

Rhodium — Opobals. (135) 2

Rhododendron — Erica (163) 3; Ledum (178) 4

Rhododendron chamaecistus — Fl. alp. (71) 16

Rhododendron ferrugineum — Fl. alp. (71) 16

Rhododendron hirsutum — Fl. alp. (71) 16

Rhoe — Vir. pl. (13) 37; Fund. fr. (123) 18

Rhus — Ficus (2) 22; Vir. pl. (13) 25, 27; Gem. arb. (24) 6; Sapor. med. (31) 15; Pl. hybr. (33) 7; Calend. fl. (72) [20]; Fl. Monsp. (74) 7; Fl. Jam. (105) 26; Nom. bot. (107) 11; Fund. fr. (123) 18; Obs. mat. med. (171) 7

Rhus africana — Hort. Upsal. (7) 37

Rhus angustifolium — Fl. Cap. (99) 12

Rhus cominia — Pl. Jam. (102) 10; Fl. Jam. (105) 15

Rhus copalinum — Pl. officin. (52) 8

Rhus coriaria — Pl. officin. (52) 19; Fl. Palaest. (70) 16; Fl. Monsp. (74) 13; Pl. tinct. (97) 15

Rhus cotinus — Pl. tinct. (97) 15

Rhus elatior, foliis cum impari pinnatis petiolis membranaceis articulatis — Pl. hybr. (33) 19

Rhus foliis pinnatis argute serratis lanceolatis; subtus tomentosis — Cent. II. pl. (66) 14

Rhus foliis pinnatis integerrimis — Pl. hybr. (33) 19

Rhus foliis ternatis angulatis — Pl. hybr. (33) 28

Rhus foliis ternatis, caule repente — Pl. hybr. (33) 28

Rhus foliis ternatis: foliolis petiolatis ovatis acutis pubescentibus: integris sinuatisque — Pl. hybr. (33) 19

Rhus glabra — Demonstr. pl. (49) 9

Rhus lucidum — Demonstr. pl. (49) 9; Fl. Cap. (99) 12

Rhus metopium — Pl. Jam. (102) 10; Fl. Jam. (105) 15

Rhus obsoniorum — Cul. mut. (88) 2, 7

Rhus radicans — Demonstr. pl. (49) 9; Fung. melit. (69) 2

Rhus tomentosum — Fl. Cap. (99) 12

Rhus toxicodendron — Demonstr. pl. (49) 9

Rhus trifoliatum virginicum — Pl. hybr. (33) 16

Rhus typhinum — Cent. II. pl. (66) 14

Rhus vernix — Demonstr. pl. (49) 9; Pl. officin. (52) 20

Rhus virginianum — Cent. II. pl. (66) 14

Rhus zeylanicus trifoliatus, phaseoli facie, floribus copiosis spicatis — Nova pl. gen. 1747 (14) 23

Ribes — Spons. pl. (12) 17; Vir. pl. (13) 33, 36, 37; Fl. oecon. (17) 6; Sapor. med. (31) 14; Pl. escul. (35) 10, 28; Cui bono? (42) 20; Mirac. insect. (45) 15; Vern. arb. (47) 10, table; Hort. acad. (63) 2; Fr. Svec. (91) [ii], 15, 24, 25; Pand. insect. (93) 12; Nom. bot. (107) 11; Prol. pl. 1760 (114) 10; Nect. fl. (122) 6

Ribes album — Hort. cul. (132) 21

Ribes alpinum — Gem. arb. (24) 23[as alpina]; Pan Svec. (26) 18[as alpina]; Demonstr. pl. (49) 6; Herbat. Upsal. (50) 7; Stat. pl. (55) 17; Fl. Angl. (56) 12; Fl. Monsp. (74) 12; Fr. Svec. (91) 3, 9, 24; Fr. escul. (127) 5; Pand. fl. Ryb. (165) 17; Esca avium (174) 11

Ribes cynosbati — Fr. escul. (127) 6

Ribes grossularia — Gem. arb. (24) 23; Pan Svec. (26) 18; Pl. escul. (35) 10; Hosp. insect. fl. (43) 17; Demonstr. pl. (49) 7; Hort. cul. (132) 21

Ribes inerme floribus planiusculis caulinis erectis — Pl. Mart.-Burs. (6) 30

Ribes montana oxyacanthae sapore — Pl. Mart.-Burs. (6) 30

Ribes nigrum — Gem. arb. (24) 22[as nigra]; Pan Svec. (26) 18[as nigra]; Demonstr. pl. (49) 7; Pl. officin. (52) 16; Fl. Angl. (56) 12; Calend. fl. (72) [11]; Fl. Monsp. (74) 12; Prodr. fl. Dan. (82) 15; Fr. Svec. (91) 3, 9, 23; Fl. Belg. (112) 14; Fr. escul. (127) 5; Hort. cul. (132) 21; Fl. Åker. (162) 9

Ribes oxyacanthoides — Demonstr. pl. (49) 7[as oxyacanthadis]

Ribes reclinatum — Demonstr. pl. (49) 7; Fr. Svec. (91) 5, 22

Ribes rubrum — Pan Svec. (26) 18[as rubra]; Hosp. insect. fl. (43) 18[as rubra]; Demonstr. pl. (49) 6; Pl. officin. (52) 16; Fl. Angl. (56) 12; Prodr. fl. Dan. (82) 15; Fr. Svec. (91) 3, 9, 22, 23; Fl. Cap. (99) 2; Fl. Belg. (112) 14; Fr. escul. (127) 5; Hort. cul. (132) 21; Fl. Åker. (162) 9

Ribes uva crispa — Demonstr. pl. (49) 7; Herbat. Upsal. (50) 10; Fl. Monsp. (74) 12; Fr. Svec. (91) 4[as crispsa], 15, 23; Fl. Belg. (112) 14; Fr. escul. (127) 6; Fl. Åker. (162) 9

Riccia crystallina — Herbat. Upsal. (50) 18

Ricino affinis odorifera — Pl. Jam. (102) 29

Ricinus — Hort. Upsal. (7) 36; Spons. pl. (12) 33, 39; Vir. pl. (13) 27; Pl. hybr. (33) 27; Pand. insect. (93) 20; Nom. bot. (107) 18; Nect. fl. (122) 4

Ricinus albus — Herb. Amboin. (57) 16

Ricinus communis — Demonstr. pl. (49) 25; Pl. officin. (52) 7, 16; Herb. Amboin. (57) 16; Fl. Palaest. (70) 30; Fl. Jam. (105) 21; Pl. Surin. (177) 15

Ricinus mappa — Cent. I. pl. (65) 2

Ricinus mappa, foliis peltatis integris — Herb. Amboin. (57) 14

Ricinus ruber — Herb. Amboin. (57) 16

Ricinus tanarius — Cent. I. pl. (65) 2

Ricinus tanarius, foliis peltatis repandis — Herb. Amboin. (57) 14

Rilla — Acrostichum (10) 12

Rivina — Hort. Upsal. (7) 37[as Rivinna]

Rivina floribus octandris — Cent. II. pl. (66) 9

Rivina humilis — Demonstr. pl. (49) 4; Fl. Jam. (105) 13

Rivina humilis racemosa, baccis puniceis — Cent. II. pl. (66) 9

Rivina octandra — Cent. II. pl. (66) 9; Fl. Jam. (105) 13

Rivina paniculata — Cent. II. pl. (66) 9

Rivina paniculata racemis compositis — Cent. II. pl. (66) 9

Rivina scandens racemosa, amplis solani foliis, baccis violaceis — Cent. II. pl. (66) 9

Robinia — Anandria (9) 5; Nova pl. gen. 1751 (32) 10; Cui bono? (42) 20; Calend. fl. (72) [10]; Fr. Svec. (91) [ii]

Robinia caragana — Gem. arb. (24) 27; Demonstr. pl. (49) 19; Calend. fl. (72) [11][as Robina], [12][as Robina], [20]; Fr. Svec. (91) 22; Pl. Alstr. (121) 6; Hort. cul. (132) 26; Hist. nat. Rossia (144) 22, 31; Usum hist. nat. (145) 12

Robinia frutex — Demonstr. pl. (49) 19; Fr. Svec. (91) 5, 22; Pl. Alstr. (121) 6; Hort. cul. (132) 26; Hist. nat. Rossia (144) 22, 31

Robinia grandiflora — Herb. Amboin. (57) 8[as Robina]

Robinia pseudo-acacia — Demonstr. pl. (49) 19[as pseud-acacia]; Somn. pl. (68) 20

Robinia pygmaea — Hist. nat. Rossia (144) 31

Robinia tetraphylla — Gem. arb. (24) 27

Roccella — Usum musc. (148) 13

Roella — Fl. Cap. (99) 6; Nect. fl. (122) 9

Roella ciliaris — Fl. Cap. (99) 12

Roella reticulata — Fl. Cap. (99) 12

Rondeletia — Vir. pl. (13) 27

Ros solis folio angusto, flore albo, caule folioso — Pl. rar. Afr. (115) 9

Rosa — Ficus (2) 12, 17; Peloria (3) 10; Spons. pl. (12) 59, 60; Vir. pl. (13) 21, 27, 33; Fl. oecon. (17) 13; Sapor. med. (31) 15; Pl. escul. (35) 18, 27, 28,

29; Hosp. insect. fl. (43) 40; Mirac. insect. (45) 15; Vern. arb. (47) 10; Pl. officin. (52) 16; Calend. fl. (72) [10], [17]; Fr. Svec. (91) [ii], 23; Pand. insect. (93) 15; Pl. tinct. (97) 10; Nom. bot. (107) 13; Prol. pl. 1760 (114) 9, 11, 12, 14, 18; Fund. fr. (123) 20, 23; Fr. escul. (127) 5; Hort. cul. (132) 25; Iter Chin. (161) 7; Fraga (170) [1], 2, 3, 7

Rosa alba — Demonstr. pl. (49) 14; Fl. Palaest. (70) 21; Calend. fl. (72) [15]; Fl. Monsp. (74) 17; Pl. Alstr. (121) 5; Hort. cul. (132) 26

Rosa canina — Herbat. Upsal. (50) 7; Stat. pl. (55) 22; Fl. Angl. (56) 17; Calend. fl. (72) [15]; Fl. Monsp. (74) 17; Prodr. fl. Dan. (82) 19; Fr. Svec. (91) 4, 15, 16; Fl. Åker. (162) 13; Pand. fl. Ryb. (165) 19

Rosa carmina — Hosp. insect. fl. (43) 24

Rosa carolina — Demonstr. pl. (49) 14

Rosa centifolia — Demonstr. pl. (49) 14; Fl. Palaest. (70) 21; Hort. cul. (132) 26

Rosa cinnamomea — Demonstr. pl. (49) 14; Calend. fl. (72) [12]; Pl. Alstr. (121) 5

Rosa eglanteria — Demonstr. pl. (49) 14; Fl. Angl. (56) 17; Calend. fl. (72) [12]; Fl. Monsp. (74) 17; Prodr. fl. Dan. (82) 19; Fr. Svec. (91) 4[as eleganteria], 16; Fl. Belg. (112) 17; Pl. Alstr. (121) 5; Hort. cul. (132) 26

Rosa gallica — Calend. fl. (72) [15], [18]; Fl. Jam. (105) 24; Hort. cul. (132) 25

Rosa gallica variegata — Demonstr. pl. (49) 14

Rosa lutea — Fl. Palaest. (70) 21

Rosa major — Gem. arb. (24) 26; Pan Svec. (26) 24

Rosa millesia — Fl. Monsp. (74) 18

Rosa minor — Pan Svec. (26) 24

Rosa moschata — Fl. Monsp. (74) 18

Rosa pomifera, fructu spinoso — Fl. Angl. (56) 29

Rosa praecox — Calend. fl. (72) [12]

Rosa rubus — Metam. pl. (67) 17

Rosa sempervirens — Fl. Palaest. (70) 21

Rosa serotina — Calend. fl. (72) 5, [15]

Rosa spinosissima — Fl. Angl. (56) 17; Calend. fl. (72) [12]; Fl. Monsp. (74) 18; Prodr. fl. Dan. (82) 19; Fr. Svec. (91) 4, 15; Fl. Belg. (112) 17; Fl. Åker. (162) 13

Rosa sylvestris — Fl. Belg. (112) 17

Rosa villosa — Calend. fl. (72) [12]; Fl. Monsp. (74) 17; Fr. Svec. (91) 4, 16; Fl. Åker. (162) 13

Rosmarinum sylvestre — Ledum (178) 5

Rosmarinus — Hort. Upsal. (7) 36; Vir. pl. (13) 7, 29; Oves (61) 16; Fl. Monsp. (74) 7; Nom. bot. (107) 9; Marum (175) 13[as Rorismarinus]

Rosmarinus officinalis — Demonstr. pl. (49) 2; Pl. officin. (52) 16; Fl. Palaest. (70) 11; Fl. Monsp. (74) 8; Fl. Jam. (105) 24; Hort. cul. (132) 15; Febr. interm. (167) 27

Rosmarinus spontaneus latiore folio — Pl. Mart.-Burs. (6) 19

Rosmarinus sylvestris — Ledum (178) 5

Rosmarinus sylvestris minor — Ledum (178) 5

Royena — Vir. pl. (13) 20[incl. as Rojenia]; Erica (163) 3

Royena glabra — Fl. Cap. (99) 14

Royena hirsuta — Fl. Cap. (99) 14

Royena lucida — Fl. Cap. (99) 14

Rubia — Hort. Upsal. (7) 36; Vir. pl. (13) 8, 17; Nom. bot. (107) 10; Pot. coff. (118) 7

Rubia angustifolia — Fl. Monsp. (74) 30

Rubia aspera — Fl. Monsp. (74) 30

Rubia cynanchica — Fl. Angl. (56) 5

Rubia linifolia aspera — Nova pl. gen. 1747 (14) 32

Rubia tinctorum — Demonstr. pl. (49) 4; Pl. officin. (52) 16; Fl. Angl. (56) 11; Fl. Palaest. (70) 13; Fl. Monsp. (74) 10; Pl. tinct. (97) 13; Fl. Belg. (112) 13; Usum hist. nat. (145) 15

Rubus — Vir. pl. (13) 21, 27, 33, 36, 37; Fl. oecon. (17) 13, 14; Oecon. nat. (20) 19; Sapor. med. (31) 14; Pl. escul. (35) 18, 28, 29; Hosp. insect. fl. (43) 40; Fl. Angl. (56) 6; Fr. Svec. (91) [ii], 23; Pand. insect. (93) 15; Nom. bot. (107) 13; Nect. fl. (122) 6; Fund. fr. (123) 20, 23; Usum hist. nat. (145) 17; Fraga (170) [1], 2, 3

Rubus arcticus — Demonstr. pl. (49) 14; Pl. officin. (52) 14; Fung. melit. (69) [1]; Calend. fl. (72) [11], [16]; Fr. escul. (127) 4; Hort. cul. (132) 19; Pot. theae (142) 8; Hist. nat. Rossia (144) 30; Usum hist. nat. (145) 12; Usum musc. (148) 11; Fraga (170) 3; Ledum (178) [1]

Rubus caesius — Gem. arb. (24) 27; Pan Svec. (26) 24; Hosp. insect. fl. (43) 25; Herbat. Upsal. (50) 19; Stat. pl. (55) 18; Fl. Angl. (56) 17[as Rubes]; Calend. fl. (72) [14]; Fl. Monsp. (74) 18; Prodr. fl. Dan. (82) 19; Fr. Svec. (91) 4, 16, 17; Fl. Belg. (112) 17; Fr. escul. (127) 4; Usum hist. nat. (145) 10; Fl. Åker. (162) 13; Pand. fl. Ryb. (165) 19

Rubus canadensis — Calend. fl. (72) [15]

Rubus caule aculeato, foliis ternatis — Specif. Canad. (76) 24

Rubus chamaemorus — Pan Svec. (26) 24; Pl. escul. (35) 18; Herbat. Upsal. (50) 6; Pl. officin. (52) 7; Stat. pl. (55) 15; Fl. Angl. (56) 17[as Rubes]; Fung. melit. (69) [1]; Fl. alp. (71) 18; Calend. fl. (72) [11], [16]; Prodr. fl. Dan. (82) 19; Fr. escul. (127) 5; Usum musc. (148) 11; Rar. Norv. (157) 5, 11, 13; Fl. Åker. (162) 13; Pand. fl. Ryb. (165) 19; Esca avium (174) 12; Ledum (178) [1]

Rubus creticus — Fl. Palaest. (70) 21

Rubus fruticosus — Demonstr. pl. (49) 14; Fl. Angl. (56) 17[as Rubes]; Fl. Palaest. (70) 21; Calend. fl. (72) [9]; Fl. Monsp. (74) 18; Prodr. fl. Dan. (82) 19; Fr. Svec. (91) 4, 16; Fl. Cap. (99) 15; Fl. Belg. (112) 17; Fr. escul. (127) 4; Fl. Åker. (162) 13

Rubus idaeus — Gem. arb. (24) 27; Pan Svec. (26) 24; Pl. escul. (35) 18; Hosp. insect. fl. (43) 25; Herbat. Upsal. (50) 9; Pl. officin. (52) 16; Stat. pl. (55) 23; Fl. Angl. (56) 17[as Rubes]; Prodr. fl. Dan. (82) 19; Fr. Svec. (91) 4, 17; Fl. Belg. (112) 17; Fr. escul. (127) 4; Fl. Åker. (162) 13; Pand. fl. Ryb. (165) 19; Esca avium (174) 12

Rubus maritimus — Pan Svec. (26) 24

Rubus moluccanus — Herb. Amboin. (57) 19

Rubus moluccus — Herb. Amboin. (57) 19

Rubus niger — Gem. arb. (24) 27

Rubus norlandicus — Pan Svec. (26) 24; Pl. escul. (35) 18

Rubus occidentalis — Demonstr. pl. (49) 14; Fl. Jam. (105) 17; Fr. escul. (127) 4; Hort. cul. (132) 22

Rubus odoratus — Demonstr. pl. (49) 14

Rubus parvifolius — Herb. Amboin. (57) 19

Rubus saxatilis — Pan Svec. (26) 24; Pl. escul. (35) 18; Hosp. insect. fl. (43) 25; Herbat. Upsal. (50) 7; Fl. Angl. (56) 17[as Rubes]; Fl. Monsp. (74) 18; Prodr. fl. Dan. (82) 19; Fr. escul. (127) 4; Fl. Åker. (162) 13; Pand. fl. Ryb. (165) 19; Esca avium (174) 12

Rudbeckia — Hort. Upsal. (7) 35; Nova pl. gen. 1751 (32) 10; Fund. fr. (123) 17

Rudbeckia hirta — Demonstr. pl. (49) 24; Calend. fl. (72) [16]

Rudbeckia laciniata — Demonstr. pl. (49) 24; Calend. fl. (72) [17]; Hort. cul. (132) 24

Rudens sylvaticus — Herb. Amboin. (57) 19

Ruellia — Hort. Upsal. (7) 37; Sem. musc. (28) 3; Fl. Jam. (105) 26

Ruellia antipoda — Herb. Amboin. (57) 24

Ruellia biflora — Fl. Jam. (105) 18[as Ruelia]

Ruellia blechnum — Pl. Jam. (102) 16; Fl. Jam. (105) 18[as Ruelia]; Fund. fr. (123) 12

Ruellia clandestina — Demonstr. pl. (49) [vii], 17; Fl. Jam. (105) 18[as Ruelia]; Fund. fr. (123) 12; Siren. lacert. (146) 7

Ruellia foliis obovatis, verticillis obvallatis: spinis longis inermibus bifurcatis — Cent. II. pl. (66) 22

Ruellia foliis petiolatis, pedunculis longis subdivisis nudis — Sem. musc. (28) 3

Ruellia paniculata — Fl. Jam. (105) 18[as Ruelia]

Ruellia tentaculata — Cent. II. pl. (66) 22

Rumex — Vir. pl. (13) 33; Fl. oecon. (17) 9; Gem. arb. (24) 5; Pl. escul. (35) 27, 28, 29; Rhabarbarum (41) 5, 6, 8, 17, 18; Hosp. insect. fl. (43) 13, 40; Noxa insect. (46) 21; Pl. officin. (52) 16; Pand. insect. (93) 13; Nom. bot. (107) 12

Rumex acetosa — Pl. escul. (35) 13; Hosp. insect. fl. (43) 20; Herbat. Upsal. (50) 6; Pl. officin. (52) 3; Stat. pl. (55) 16, 21; Fl. Angl. (56) 14; Cervus (60) 16; Fl. alp. (71) 15; Prodr. fl. Dan. (82) 17; Cul. mut. (88) 4; Pl. tinct. (97) 16; Fl. Belg. (112) 16; Hort. cul. (132) 18; Fl. Åker. (162) 10; Pand. fl. Ryb. (165) 18; Esca avium (174) 12

Rumex acetosa maxima — Mac. olit. (113) 18

Rumex acetosa pratensis — Pan Svec. (26) 21

Rumex acetosella — Herbat. Upsal. (50) 7; Stat. pl. (55) 21; Fl. Angl. (56) 14; Fl. Monsp. (74) 15; Prodr. fl. Dan. (82) 17; Fl. Belg. (112) 16; Fl. Åker. (162) 10

Rumex acutus — Hosp. insect. fl. (43) 20[as acuta]; Herbat. Upsal. (50) 14; Pl. officin. (52) 12; Fl. Angl. (56) 14; Fl. Palaest. (70) 18; Fl. Monsp. (74) 15; Prodr. fl. Dan. (82) 17; Fl. Åker. (162) 10; Pand. fl. Ryb. (165) 18

Rumex alpinus — Fl. alp. (71) 15; Fl. Monsp. (74) 15; Cul. mut. (88) 4[as alpina]

Rumex aquatica, calycis foliolis omnibus aequalibus et similibus, radice exterius et interius flava — Nova pl. gen. 1747 (14) [33]

Rumex aquatica, calycis foliolis omnibus similibus, radice exterius nigra, interius aurantii vel crocci coloris — Nova pl. gen. 1747 (14) [33]

Rumex aquaticus — Herbat. Upsal. (50) 10; Pl. officin. (52) 6; Stat. pl. (55) 13; Fl. Angl. (56) 14; Fl. Monsp. (74) 15; Specif. Canad. (76) 27; Prodr. fl. Dan. (82) 17; Fl. Belg. (112) 16; Pand. fl. Ryb. (165) 18

Rumex britannica — Pan Svec. (26) 20; Hosp. insect. fl. (43) 20; Specif. Canad. (76) 15, 27

Rumex bucephalophorus — Fl. Palaest. (70) 18

Rumex crispus — Pan Svec. (26) 20[as crispa]; Stat. pl. (55) 20; Fl. Angl. (56) 14; Prodr. fl. Dan. (82) 17; Fl. Belg. (112) 16; Rar. Norv. (157) 15; Fl. Åker. (162) 10; Pand. fl. Ryb. (165) 18; Esca avium (174) 12

Rumex digynus — Stat. pl. (55) 16; Fl. Angl. (56) 15; Fl. alp. (71) 15; Rar. Norv. (157) 10

Rumex emarginata — Pan Svec. (26) 21

Rumex floribus hermaphroditis: valvulis integerrimis, nudis, foliis cordato-lanceolatis — Nova pl. gen. 1747 (14) [33]

Rumex granulata — Pan Svec. (26) 20

Rumex lanceolata — Pan Svec. (26) 21

Rumex lapathum — Pl. escul. (35) 13

Rumex maritimus — Stat. pl. (55) 12; Prodr. fl. Dan. (82) 17; Pl. tinct. (97) 16

Rumex obtusifolius — Fl. Angl. (56) 14; Fl. Belg. (112) 16

Rumex patientia — Demonstr. pl. (49) 10; Calend. fl. (72) [16]; Scorb. (180) 21

Rumex persicarioides — Demonstr. pl. (49) 10

Rumex pulcher — Demonstr. pl. (49) 10; Fl. Angl. (56) 14; Fl. Monsp. (74) 15

Rumex roseus — Fl. Palaest. (70) 18

Rumex sanguineus — Demonstr. pl. (49) 10; Pl. officin. (52) 12; Fl. Angl. (56) 14; Fung. melit. (69) 12; Fl. Belg. (112) 16

Rumex scutatus — Pl. officin. (52) 3; Fl. alp. (71) 15; Fl. Monsp. (74) 15; Mac. olit. (113) 18

Rumex scutatus beta — Demonstr. pl. (49) 11

Rumex sinuatus — Fl. Monsp. (74) 15

Rumex vesicarius — Demonstr. pl. (49) 11; Fl. Cap. (99) 7[as vesicaria], 13

Rupicapra — Generat. calc. (22) 2, 5

Ruppia maritima — Stat. pl. (55) 12[as marina]; Fl. Angl. (56) 12; Fl. Monsp. (74) 10; Prodr. fl. Dan. (82) 14

Ruscus — Hort. Upsal. (7) 36; Gem. arb. (24) 11; Pand. insect. (93) 22; Nom. bot. (107) 19; Nect. fl. (122) 10

Ruscus aculeatus — Demonstr. pl. (49) 26; Pl. officin. (52) 16; Fl. Angl. (56) 25; Fl. Monsp. (74) 28

Ruscus hypoglossum — Demonstr. pl. (49) 26; Pl. officin. (52) 20[as hippoglossum]

Ruscus hypophyllum — Demonstr. pl. (49) 26; Fl. Palaest. (70) 31

Ruta — Vir. pl. (13) 31, 36; Gem. arb. (24) 6; Sapor. med. (31) 19; Odor. med. (40) 14, 15; Metam. pl. (67) 20; Fl. Monsp. (74) 7; Pand. insect. (93) 14; Nom. bot. (107) 12; Mors. serp. (119) 18; Nect. fl. (122) 14; Usum hist. nat. (145) 29; Menthae (153) 6

Ruta dictamnus — Lign. Qvas. (128) 7

Ruta graveolens — Hosp. insect. fl. (43) 21; Pl. officin. (52) 16; Metam. pl. (67) 20; Fl. Monsp. (74) 15; Fl. Cap. (99) 7, 14; Fl. Jam. (105) 24; Pl. rar. Afr. (115) 6; Hort. cul. (132) 18

Ruta graveolens minor — Fl. Palaest. (70) 19

Ruta graveolens montana — Demonstr. pl. (49) 11

Ruta montana — Fl. Monsp. (74) 15

Ruta muraria — Acrostichum (10) 7

Ruta tenuifolia — Metam. pl. (67) 20[as tenuefolia]

Rutilus — Usum hist. nat. (145) 26

Ruyschiana — Hort. Upsal. (7) 35; Anandria (9) 5

Sabella — Fund. test. (166) 17, 22

Sabina — Gem. arb. (24) 6; Fr. Svec. (91) [ii], 23, 24; Nom. bot. (107) 19; Menthae (153) 6

Sabina folio aculeato — Fl. Palaest. (70) 31[under Juniperus]

Saccharum — Generat. calc. (22) 14; Cui bono? (42) 4; Chin. Lagerstr. (64) 5; Fl. Cap. (99) 2; Fl. Jam. (105) 9; Nom. bot. (107) 9; Ping. anim. (108) 17; Fund. agrost. (152) 10, 26, 30, 35

Saccharum officinarum — Pl. officin. (52) 17; Herb. Amboin. (57) 20; Fl. Palaest. (70) 12[as officinale]; Fl. Jam. (105) 12

Saccharum spicatum — Herb. Amboin. (57) 25

Sagina — Splachnum (27) 2; Nom. bot. (107) 8

Sagina erecta — Fl. Angl. (56) 12; Fl. Monsp. (74) 10

Sagina mimima — Pan Svec. (26) 16

Sagina procumbens — Herbat. Upsal. (50) 10; Stat. pl. (55) 14; Fl. Angl. (56) 12; Prodr. fl. Dan. (82) 14; Fl. Belg. (112) 14; Fl. Åker. (162) 8; Pand. fl. Ryb. (165) 17

Sagittaria — Hort. Upsal. (7) 41; Spons. pl. (12) 39; Mirac. insect. (45) 11; Chin. Lagerstr. (64) 6; Fl. Belg. (112) 8

Sagittaria aquatica — Pan Svec. (26) 35

Sagittaria lancifolia — Pl. Jam. (102) 27; Fl. Jam. (105) 21

Sagittaria pugioniformis — Pl. Surin. (177) 15

Sagittaria sagittifolia — Herbat. Upsal. (50) 14; Stat. pl. (55) 13; Fl. Angl. (56) 24; Fl. Monsp. (74) 27; Prodr. fl. Dan. (82) 24; Fl. Belg. (112) 22; Colon. pl. (158) 6; Fl. Åker. (162) 19

Saguaster major — Herb. Amboin. (57) 6

Saguaster minor — Herb. Amboin. (57) 6

Saguerus — Herb. Amboin. (57) 6

Sagus — Herb. Amboin. (57) 6

Sagus filtaris — Herb. Amboin. (57) 6

Salamandra — Amphib. Gyll. (5) 15, 25; Hort. Upsal. (7) 43

Salamandra americana amphibia — Mus. Ad.-Frid. (11) 11

Salamandra americana lacertae aemula altera — Mus. Ad.-Frid. (11) 11

Salamandra bufonis capite, grisea, tuberculis albis notata — Amphib. Gyll. (5) 27

Salamandra maculosa nostras — Amphib. Gyll. (5) 25

Salamandra terrestris — Amphib. Gyll. (5) 25

Salamandra terrestris maculis luteis distincta — Amphib. Gyll. (5) 25[as lutaeis]

Salamandra vera — Amphib. Gyll. (5) 27

Salicaria — Peloria (3) 10

Salicornia — Vir. pl. (13) 32; Fl. oecon. (17) [1]; Sapor. med. (31) 13; Pl. escul. (35) 28; Nom. bot. (107) 9; Aphyteia (185) 9

Salicornia cupressiformis erecta — Fl. Angl. (56) 26

Salicornia europaea — Pl. officin. (52) 18; Stat. pl. (55) 12

Salicornia europaea fruticosa — Fl. Palaest. (70) 11; Fl. Monsp. (74) 8; Fl. Belg. (112) 12

Salicornia europaea herbacea — Fl. Angl. (56) 9[as europea]; Fl. Monsp. (74) 8; Prodr. fl. Dan. (82) 12; Fl. Belg. (112) 12

Salicornia fruticosa — Fl. Angl. (56) 9

Salicornia herbacea — Pl. escul. (35) 6

Salicornia maritima — Pan Svec. (26) 12

Salicornia myosuroides procumbens — Fl. Angl. (56) 26

Salicornia ramosior procumbens — Fl. Angl. (56) 26

Salicornia virginea — Fl. Jam. (105) 12

Salix — Hort. Upsal. (7) 21; Spons. pl. (12) 41, 49; Fl. oecon. (17) 26; Gem. arb. (24) 5, 9, 12; Pan Svec. (26) 6; Sapor. med. (31) 15; Pl. hybr. (33) 29; Cui bono? (42) 20; Hosp. insect. fl. (43) 36, 40; Mirac. insect. (45) 14; Noxa insect. (46) 26; Vern. arb. (47) 10, table; Oves (61) 18; Hort. acad. (63) 14; Metam. pl. (67) 23, 24; Fl. alp. (71) 8, 24;

Calend. fl. (72) [20]; Fr. Svec. (91) [ii], 15; Pand. insect. (93) 21; Pl. tinct. (97) 10, 28; Arb. Svec. (101) 26, 27; Nom. bot. (107) 18; Prol. pl. 1760 (114) 2, 8, 9, 19; Prol. pl. 1763 (130) 10

Salix aegyptiaca — Cent. I. pl. (65) 33; Fl. Palaest. (70) 31

Salix alba — Noxa insect. (46) 26; Pl. officin. (52) 17; Fl. Angl. (56) 24; Fl. Monsp. (74) 28; Prodr. fl. Dan. (82) 25; Arb. Svec. (101) 8, 9, 27; Fl. Belg. (112) 22; Febr. interm. (167) 42

Salix amygdalina — Fl. Monsp. (74) 28; Fr. Svec. (91) 3, 12; see also S. amygdaloides

Salix amygdaloides [error for amygdalina?] — Fl. Angl. (56) 24

Salix arbuscula — Fr. Svec. (91) 4, 21; Hist. nat. Rossia (144) 34

Salix arenaria — Fl. Angl. (56) 24; Prodr. fl. Dan. (82) 25; Fr. Svec. (91) 4, 21; Fl. Belg. (112) 22; Hist. nat. Rossia (144) 34

Salix aurita — Stat. pl. (55) 14; Fr. Svec. (91) 3, 12

Salix babylonica — Fl. Palaest. (70) 31

Salix caprea — Demonstr. pl. (49) 26; Herbat. Upsal. (50) 8[as capraea]; Stat. pl. (55) 22; Fl. Angl. (56) 24; Calend. fl. (72) [9][as capraea], [10]; Fl. Monsp. (74) 28; Prodr. fl. Dan. (82) 25; Fr. Svec. (91) 23; Arb. Svec. (101) 8, 9[as capraea], 27[as capraea], 30[as capraea]; Fl. Belg. (112) 22; Hist. nat. Rossia (144) 34[as capraea]; Fl. Åker. (162) 19; Pand. fl. Ryb. (165) 22

Salix caprea pumila — Fl. Angl. (56) 29

Salix cinerea — Prodr. fl. Dan. (82) 25; Fr. Svec. (91) 3, 12, 24; Fl. Åker. (162) 20; Pand. fl. Ryb. (165) 22

Salix depressa — Fr. Svec. (91) 4

Salix flore caeruleo — Pan Svec. (26) 36

Salix foenimessorum — Pan Svec. (26) 36

Salix foliis auritis — Pan Svec. (26) 36

Salix foliis betulae nanae — Pan Svec. (26) 36

Salix foliis citri — Pan Svec. (26) 36

Salix foliis integris subtus villosis nitidis ovatis — Pl. Mart.-Burs. (6) 30

Salix foliis lanceolatis diaphanis — Pan Svec. (26) 36

Salix foliis longissimis viridibus — Fl. Angl. (56) 29

Salix foliis myrti tarentini — Pan Svec. (26) 36

Salix foliis phylicae — Pan Svec. (26) 36

Salix foliis salviae auritis — Pan Svec. (26) 36

Salix foliis subcaeruleis — Fl. Angl. (56) 29

Salix foliis subserratis, lanceolato-ovalibus, nudis, venosis; petiolis simplicibus exstipulatis — Cent. I. pl. (65) 33

Salix foliis subtus reticulatis — Pan Svec. (26) 36

Salix foliis vaccini maximi — Pan Svec. (26) 36

Salix foliis vitis idaeae — Pan Svec. (26) 36

Salix folio rotundo minore — Pan Svec. (26) 36; Fl. Angl. (56) 29

Salix fragilis — Stat. pl. (55) 14; Fl. Angl. (56) 24; Fl. Monsp. (74) 28; Prodr. fl. Dan. (82) 24; Fr. Svec. (91) 24; Arb. Svec. (101) 8, 9, 26; Fl. Belg. (112) 22; Fl. Åker. (162) 19; Pand. fl. Ryb. (165) 22

Salix fusca — Fr. Svec. (91) 4

Salix glabra arborea — Gem. arb. (24) 28; Pan Svec. (26) 36

Salix glauca — Stat. pl. (55) 15; Fl. alp. (71) 23; Fr. Svec. (91) 5, 21

Salix hastata — Fr. Svec. (91) 3, 12

Salix herbacea — Stat. pl. (55) 15; Fl. Angl. (56) 24; Fl. alp. (71) 23; Rar. Norv. (157) 11

Salix hermaphroditica — Demonstr. pl. (49) 26; Fr. Svec. (91) 3, 12

Salix hirsuta — Nom. bot. (107) 18

Salix incubacea — Stat. pl. (55) 14; Prodr. fl. Dan. (82) 25; Fr. Svec. (91) 4, 20, 21

Salix inferne cinerea — Fl. Angl. (56) 29

Salix inferne lanuginosa — Fl. Angl. (56) 29

Salix lanata — Fl. alp. (71) 23; Fr. Svec. (91) 4

Salix lapponum — Stat. pl. (55) 15; Fl. alp. (71) 23; Fr. Svec. (91) 3, 12

Salix latifolia erecta — Pan Svec. (26) 36

Salix latifolia rotunda — Gem. arb. (24) 28; Pan Svec. (26) 36

Salix minima turfacea — Pan Svec. (26) 36

Salix myrsinites — Stat. pl. (55) 15; Fl. alp. (71) 23; Fr. Svec. (91) 5

Salix myrtilloides — Herbat. Upsal. (50) 6; Fr. Svec. (91) 4; Fl. Åker. (162) 19

Salix pentandra — Pan Svec. (26) 36; Demonstr. pl. (49) 26; Herbat. Upsal. (50) 6; Stat. pl. (55) 14; Fl. Angl. (56) 24; Transm. frum. (87) 3; Fr. Svec. (91) 3, 12, 25; Pl. tinct. (97) 26; Fl. Belg. (112) 22; Hist. nat. Rossia (144) 34

Salix phylicifolia — Fr. Svec. (91) 3, 12

Salix pratensis argentea — Pan Svec. (26) 36

Salix pratensis repens — Pan Svec. (26) 36

Salix purpurea — Demonstr. pl. (49) 26; Fl. Angl. (56) 24; Prodr. fl. Dan. (82) 25; Fr. Svec. (91) 3, 11, 24, 25; Fl. Belg. (112) 22

Salix repens — Stat. pl. (55) 14; Fl. Angl. (56) 24; Fr. Svec. (91) 4, 21

Salix reticulata — Demonstr. pl. (49) 26; Stat. pl. (55) 15; Fl. Angl. (56) 24; Fl. alp. (71) 23; Rar. Norv. (157) 11

Salix retusa — Fl. alp. (71) 23

Salix rosmarinifolia — Fl. Angl. (56) 24; Fr. Svec. (91) 4, 20; Fl. Belg. (112) 22

Salix rubra — Fr. Svec. (91) 23

Salix stipulis latissimis — Pan Svec. (26) 36

Salix stipulis trapeziformibus — Pan Svec. (26) 36[as trapetziformibus]

Salix syriaca, folio oleagineo argenteo — Cent. I. pl. (65) 33

Salix triandra — Hist. nat. Rossia (144) 34

Salix viminalis — Gem. arb. (24) 28; Pan Svec. (26) 36; Demonstr. pl. (49) 26; Fl. Angl. (56) 24; Calend. fl. (72) [9], [10]; Fl. Monsp. (74) 28; Prodr. fl. Dan. (82) 25; Fr. Svec. (91) 3, 10, 23; Fl. Belg. (112) 22; Hist. nat. Rossia (144) 34; Fl. Åker. (162) 19

Salix vitellina — Fl. Monsp. (74) 28; Fl. Belg. (112) 22

Salmo — Oecon. nat. (20) 27; Calend. fl. (72) [11]; Usum hist. nat. (145) 26; Var. cib. (156) 17

Salsola — Vir. pl. (13) 32; Sapor. med. (31) 13

Salsola frutescens, foliis pilosis inermibus — Pl. rar. Camsch. (30) 14

Salsola herbacea erecta, foliis subulatis spinosis laevibus, calycibus ovatis — Cent. II. pl. (66) 13

Salsola kali — Demonstr. pl. (49) 7; Stat. pl. (55) 12; Fl. Angl. (56) 13[as Sasola]; Prodr. fl. Dan. (82) 15; Fl. Belg. (112) 14

Salsola prostrata — Demonstr. pl. (49) 7[as prostata]

Salsola pungens — Pan Svec. (26) 18

Salsola sediformis [error for sedoides?] — Fl. Monsp. (74) 12

Salsola sedoides — Fl. Belg. (112) 14; see also S. sediformis

Salsola soda — Fl. Monsp. (74) 12

Salsola tragus — Cent. II. pl. (66) 13; Fl. Monsp. (74) 12; Prodr. fl. Dan. (82) 15

Salsola vermiculata — Demonstr. pl. (49) 7

Salvadora — Nova pl. gen. 1751 (32) 36, 48

Salvia — Hort. Upsal. (7) 36; Vir. pl. (13) 29; Fl. Monsp. (74) 7; Nom. bot. (107) 9; Fund. fr. (123) 16

Salvia aethiopis — Fl. Cap. (99) 11

Salvia africana caerulea — Fl. Cap. (99) 11

Salvia africana frutescens, flore violaceo, folio scorodoniae — Pl. hybr. (33) 28

Salvia africana frutescente, flore magno aureo — Pl. hybr. (33) 28

Salvia africana lutea — Fl. Cap. (99) 11

Salvia agrestis — Demonstr. pl. (49) 2; Cent. I. pl. (65) 2; Calend. fl. (72) [17]

Salvia canariensis — Demonstr. pl. (49) 2; Oves (61) 14; Calend. fl. (72) [17]

Salvia ceratophylla — Demonstr. pl. (49) 2

Salvia foliis cordatis, summis amplexicaulibus, corollarum galea labium aequante — Demonstr. pl. (49) 2

Salvia glutinosa — Hort. acad. (63) 10; Fl. Monsp. (74) 8

Salvia hispanica — Demonstr. pl. (49) 2; Calend. fl. (72) [18]

Salvia horminum — Pan Svec. (26) 12[as hominem]; Pl. officin. (52) 11[as horminium]; Fl. Palaest. (70) 11

Salvia nutans — Demonstr. pl. (49) 2; Calend. fl. (72) [17]; Hist. nat. Rossia (144) 27

Salvia officinalis — Demonstr. pl. (49) 2; Pl. officin. (52) 17; Fl. Monsp. (74) 8; Fl. Jam. (105) 24; Hort. cul. (132) 15

Salvia pomifera — Fl. Palaest. (70) 11

Salvia pratensis — Demonstr. pl. (49) 2; Fl. Angl. (56) 9; Fl. Monsp. (74) 8; Fl. Belg. (112) 12

Salvia pyrenaica — Fl. alp. (71) 12

Salvia samia frutescens — Fl. Palaest. (70) 11

Salvia samia verbascifolia — Fl. Palaest. (70) 11

Salvia sclarea — Demonstr. pl. (49) 2; Pl. officin. (52) 10, 17; Fl. Monsp. (74) 8

Salvia sylvestris — Calend. fl. (72) [12]

Salvia syriaca — Fl. Palaest. (70) 11

Salvia verbenaca — Demonstr. pl. (49) [vii], 2; Fl. Angl. (56) 9; Fl. Palaest. (70) 11; Fl. Monsp. (74) 8; Fl. Belg. (112) 8, 12; Fund. fr. (123) 12

Salvia verticillata — Demonstr. pl. (49) 2; Fl. Palaest. (70) 11[as verticillatum]

Salvia viridis — Demonstr. pl. (49) 2

Samama — Herb. Amboin. (57) 11

Sambucus — Vir. pl. (13) 27, 31, 35, 36; Fl. oecon. (17) 8; Sapor. med. (31) 20; Odor. med. (40) 13; Vern. arb. (47) 10, table; Fr. Svec. (91) [ii], 23, 24; Pand. insect. (93) 13; Aer habit. (106) 20; Nom. bot. (107) 11; Purg. indig. (143) 17; Usum hist. nat. (145) 25; Cimicifuga (173) 9

Sambucus arborea — Gem. arb. (24) 20; Pan Svec. (26) 19

Sambucus canadensis — Demonstr. pl. (49) 9

Sambucus ebulus — Demonstr. pl. (49) 9; Pl. officin. (52) 9; Stat. pl. (55) 19; Fl. Angl. (56) 14; Calend. fl. (72) [17]; Fl. Monsp. (74) 13; Prodr. fl. Dan. (82) 16; Fl. Belg. (112) 15; Purg. indig. (143) 11

Sambucus herbacea — Pan Svec. (26) 19

Sambucus humilis zeylanica, pawatha zeylonensibus — Nova pl. gen. 1747 (14) 5

Sambucus laciniata — Fl. Angl. (56) 14

Sambucus nigra — Hosp. insect. fl. (43) 19; Pl. officin. (52) 17; Stat. pl. (55) 19; Fl. Angl. (56) 14; Calend. fl. (72) [14]; Fl. Monsp. (74) 13; Prodr. fl. Dan. (82) 16; Fr. Svec. (91) 3, 5; Fl. Belg. (112) 15; Meloe (124) 4; Fr. escul. (127) 7; Purg. indig. (143) 11; Fl. Åker. (162) 10

Sambucus nigra laciniata — Demonstr. pl. (49) 9

Sambucus racemosa — Demonstr. pl. (49) 9; Calend. fl. (72) [9], [11]; Fl. Monsp. (74) 13

Samolus — Erica (163) 2

Samolus africanus — Demonstr. pl. (49) 5

Samolus maritima — Pan Svec. (26) 17

Samolus valerandi — Stat. pl. (55) 12; Fl. Angl. (56) 12; Fl. Monsp. (74) 11; Prodr. fl. Dan. (82) 15; Fl. Belg. (112) 14; Colon. pl. (158) 7

Sampacca — Herb. Amboin. (57) 10

Sampacca sylvestris — Herb. Amboin. (57) 10

Samyda — Nova pl. gen. 1747 (14) [vi], 17, 18

Samyda guidonia — Fl. Jam. (105) 16

Samyda nitida — Fl. Jam. (105) 16

Samyda parviflora — Fl. Jam. (105) 16

Sandalum — Herb. Amboin. (57) 8

Sandalum rubrum — Herb. Amboin. (57) 8

Sandoricum — Herb. Amboin. (57) 8

Sanguinaria — Vir. pl. (13) 25; Nova pl. gen. 1751 (32) 9

Sanguinaria canadensis — Specif. Canad. (76) 8

Sanguis draconis — Sapor. med. (31) 15; Chin. Lagerstr. (64) 5

Sanguisorba — Hort. Upsal. (7) 33; Fl. Belg. (112) 8[as Sanguiasorba]

Sanguisorba gotlandica — Pan Svec. (26) 16

Sanguisorba officinalis — Demonstr. pl. (49) 4; Pl. officin. (52) 15; Fl. Angl. (56) 11[as officinar:]; Calend. fl. (72) [15]; Fl. Monsp. (74) 10; Fl. Belg. (112) 13; Colon. pl. (158) 7

Sanicula aizoides serpyllifolia minor — Pl. rar. Afr. (115) 10

Sanicula canadensis — Mors. serp. (119) 17

Sanicula europaea — Pl. officin. (52) 17; Stat. pl. (55) 17; Fl. Angl. (56) 13; Fl. Monsp. (74) 12; Prodr. fl. Dan. (82) 15; Fl. Belg. (112) 15; Pl. rar. Afr. (115) 6

Sanicula sylvatica — Pan Svec. (26) 18

Santalum — Aer habit. (106) 20[as Satalum]

Santalum album — Pl. officin. (52) 17; Herb. Amboin. (57) 8; Pl. tinct. (97) 16

Santolina — Hort. Upsal. (7) 36; Vir. pl. (13) 23, 33; Fl. Monsp. (74) 7; Fl. Cap. (99) 8

Santolina amellus — Pl. Jam. (102) 21; Fl. Jam. (105) 19

Santolina annua — Fl. Cap. (99) 17

Santolina capitata — Pl. rar. Afr. (115) 18

Santolina chamaecyparissus — Demonstr. pl. (49) 22; Pl. officin. (52) 17; see also S. cyparissus

Santolina corymbis simplicibus fastigiatis, foliis lanceolatis indivisis villosis — Cent. II. pl. (66) 31

Santolina corymbo composito, foliis ovatis amplexicaulibus subdentatis recurvis — Pl. rar. Afr. (115) 18

Santolina crenata — Fl. Cap. (99) 17

Santolina crithmifolia — Fl. Cap. (99) 17

Santolina cyparissus [error for chamaecyparissus?] — Fl. Monsp. (74) 25

Santolina dentata — Fl. Cap. (99) 17

Santolina floribus terminalibus sessilibus, foliis lanceolatis hirsutis — Pl. rar. Afr. (115) 18

Santolina foliis ovalibus mucronatis recurvatis — Pl. rar. Afr. (115) 18

Santolina jamaicensis — Pl. Jam. (102) 21; Fl. Jam. (105) 19

Santolina laevigata — Pl. rar. Afr. (115) 18

Santolina oppositifolia — Pl. Jam. (102) 21; Fl. Jam. (105) 19

Santolina pedunculis unifloris lateralibus, foliis ovalibus mucronatis recurvatis — Cent. II. pl. (66) 30

Santolina pubescens — Cent. II. pl. (66) 31

Santolina squarrosa — Cent. II. pl. (66) 30; Pl. rar. Afr. (115) 18

Santolina trifurcata — Fl. Cap. (99) 17

Sapindus — Lign. Qvas. (128) 7

Sapindus melicoccus — Fl. Jam. (105) 15

Sapindus saponaria — Pl. officin. (52) 17; Fl. Jam. (105) 15

Sapium — Fl. Jam. (105) 26

Saponaria — Hort. Upsal. (7) 33; Spons. pl. (12) 46; Pl. hybr. (33) 6; Herb. Amboin. (57) 9

Saponaria calycibus monophyllis cylindraceis ovato lanceolatis — Pl. hybr. (33) 11

Saponaria calycibus pentaphyllis, corollis crenato emarginatis, foliis subulatis planis — Nova pl. gen. 1751 (32) 42

Saponaria calycibus pentaphyllis, corymbis fastigiatis, foliis lanceolatis, caule adscendente — Nova pl. gen. 1751 (32) 41

Saponaria calycibus pentaphyllis, corymbis fastigiatis, foliis linearibus, caule adscendente — Nova pl. gen. 1751 (32) 42

Saponaria caule dichotomo, foliis subulatis planis — Nova pl. gen. 1751 (32) 42

Saponaria caule simplici, foliis subulatis planis ex alis ramulosa — Betula (1) 12

Saponaria concava anglica — Peloria (3) 9; Pl. hybr. (33) 11

Saponaria foliis knawel — Pan Svec. (26) 22

Saponaria gypsophyton — Pan Svec. (26) 22

Saponaria ocymoides — Fl. Monsp. (74) 16

Saponaria officinalis — Demonstr. pl. (49) 12; Pl. officin. (52) 17; Fl. Angl. (56) 16; Calend. fl. (72) [17]; Fl. Monsp. (74) 16; Prodr. fl. Dan. (82) 18; Fl. Belg. (112) 16

Saponaria orientalis — Demonstr. pl. (49) 12; Fl. Palaest. (70) 19

Saponaria vaccaria — Fl. Palaest. (70) 19; Fl. Monsp. (74) 16

Sargassum pelagium — Herb. Amboin. (57) 28

Sargazo — Oecon. nat. (20) 27; Nat. pelagi (84) 7

Sargus — Mus. Ad.-Frid. (11) 36

Saribus — Herb. Amboin. (57) 6

Sarothra — Nova pl. gen. 1751 (32) 8, [13, as 15], 14, 15, 48

Sarothra gentianoides — Specif. Canad. (76) 11[as gentionoides]

Sarracenia — Nova pl. gen. 1751 (32) 9[as Sarracena]; Fung. melit. (69) 2[as Sarracena]; Nect. fl. (122) 5; Fund. fr. (123) 18; Siren. lacert. (146) 7[as Sarracena]; Usum musc. (148) 11

Satureja — Vir. pl. (13) 29, 34; Fl. Monsp. (74) 7; Nom. bot. (107) 14; Marum (175) 13

Satureja capitata — Pl. officin. (52) 19; Fl. Palaest. (70) 22

Satureja cretica — Pl. Mart.-Burs. (6) 19

Satureja cretica frutescens spinosa — Pl. Mart.-Burs. (6) 19; Cent. II. pl. (66) 19

Satureja cretica spinosa — Cent. II. pl. (66) 19

Satureja hortensis — Demonstr. pl. (49) 15; Pl. officin. (52) 17; Fl. Monsp. (74) 19; Hort. cul. (132) 15

Satureja mastichina — Fl. Palaest. (70) 22

Satureja montana — Fl. Monsp. (74) 19

Satureja ramis spinosis, foliis hispidis — Cent. II. pl. (66) 19

Satureja spinosa — Cent. II. pl. (66) 19

Satureja viminea — Pl. Jam. (102) 14; Fl. Jam. (105) 18

Satureja virginiana — Demonstr. pl. (49) 15; Calend. fl. (72) [18]

Satyrium — Betula (1) 12; Peloria (3) 10; Vir. pl. (13) 24; Nect. fl. (122) 12

Satyrium albidum — Prodr. fl. Dan. (82) 24

Satyrium bulbis ---, corollis pedunculatis, labello emarginato utrinque dentato — Pl. rar. Afr. (115) 27

Satyrium bulbis indivisis, foliis lanceolatis, nectarii labio trifido: lacinia intermedia lineari obliqua praemorsa — Pl. rar. Camsch. (30) 28

Satyrium bulbo indiviso, corolla galea unicalcarata, labello indiviso apice lanceolato — Pl. rar. Afr. (115) 27

Satyrium capense — Pl. rar. Afr. (115) 27

Satyrium cornutum — Pl. rar. Afr. (115) 27

Satyrium epipogium — Hist. nat. Rossia (144) 33[as epigogium]

Satyrium hircinum — Fl. Angl. (56) 23; Fl. Monsp. (74) 26; Menthae (153) 6

Satyrium jemtium — Pan Svec. (26) 34

Satyrium latifolium — Fl. Jam. (105) 20

Satyrium nigrum — Stat. pl. (55) 16; Cervus (60) 8; Fl. alp. (71) 23; Pl. tinct. (97) 24

Satyrium plantagineum — Pl. Jam. (102) 25; Fl. Jam. (105) 20

Satyrium pyrolaeforme — Pan Svec. (26) 34

Satyrium repens — Hist. nat. Rossia (144) 33; Fl. Åker. (162) 18

Satyrium scanense — Pan Svec. (26) 34

Satyrium viride — Fl. Angl. (56) 23; Cervus (60) 8; Prodr. fl. Dan. (82) 24

Satyrium viridi flore — Pan Svec. (26) 34

Satyrus — Fl. Cap. (99) [1]

Saururus — Hort. Upsal. (7) 37; Vir. pl. (13) 25; Gem. arb. (24) 8; Pl. Jam. (102) [5]

Saururus cernuus — Demonstr. pl. (49) 11; Specif. Canad. (76) 8

Saururus frutescens foliis plantagineis — Herb. Amboin. (57) 19

Sauvagesia — Fl. Jam. (105) 27; Nect. fl. (122) 8; Fund. fr. (123) 21

Sauvagesia erecta — Fl. Jam. (105) 14

Saxifraga — Hort. Upsal. (7) 33; Spons. pl. (12) 45; Gem. arb. (24) 5; Splachnum (27) 2; Pl. hybr. (33) 29; Fl. Angl. (56) 5, 6; Fl. alp. (71) 8; Pand. insect. (93) 14; Nom. bot. (107) 13[as Saxafragia]; Erica (163) 2

Saxifraga adscendens — Fl. alp. (71) 17

Saxifraga aizoides — Stat. pl. (55) 16; Fl. Angl. (56) 15; Fl. alp. (71) 16; Fl. Monsp. (74) 7, 16; Rar. Norv. (157) 10

Saxifraga ajugaefolia — Cent. I. pl. (65) 11

Saxifraga androsacea — Fl. alp. (71) 16; Hist. nat. Rossia (144) 29

Saxifraga autumnalis — Fl. Angl. (56) 15

Saxifraga bavarica — Cent. II. pl. (66) 17

Saxifraga bronchialis — Hist. nat. Rossia (144) 29

Saxifraga bryoides — Fl. alp. (71) 16

Saxifraga bulbifera — Pan Svec. (26) 22; Pl. hybr. (33) 28

Saxifraga burseriana — Fl. alp. (71) 16

Saxifraga caerulea — Pan Svec. (26) 23

Saxifraga caesia — Fl. alp. (71) 16

Saxifraga capitata — Pan Svec. (26) 22

Saxifraga caule nudo simplici, foliis dentatis, coma foliosa — Pl. hybr. (33) 28

Saxifraga cernua — Stat. pl. (55) 16; Fl. alp. (71) 16; Rar. Norv. (157) 10

Saxifraga cespitosa — Fl. alp. (71) 17; Fl. Monsp. (74) 7, 16; Rar. Norv. (157) 10

Saxifraga cornubiae — Cent. II. pl. (66) 13

Saxifraga cotyledon — Demonstr. pl. (49) 11; Stat. pl. (55) 16; Fl. alp. (71) 16; Fl. Monsp. (74) 7, 16; Rar. Norv. (157) 10, 15

Saxifraga crassifolia — Fl. alp. (71) 16; Hist. nat. Rossia (144) 29

Saxifraga foliis palmatis — Pan Svec. (26) 22

Saxifraga foliis radicalibus palmato-quinquepartitis, caulinis linearibus indivisis, caulibus adscendentibus multifloris — Cent. I. pl. (65) 11

Saxifraga foliis radicalibus reniformibus quinquelobis multifidis, caulinis linearibus; caule subnudo ramoso — Cent. I. pl. (65) 10

Saxifraga foliorum limbo cartilagineo integro, spica longa, floribus purpureo croceis — Pl. Mart.-Burs. (6) 24

Saxifraga geranioides — Cent. I. pl. (65) 10; Fl. alp. (71) 17

Saxifraga geum — Demonstr. pl. (49) 11; Fl. alp. (71) 16

Saxifraga granulata — Herbat. Upsal. (50) 7; Pl. officin. (52) 17; Stat. pl. (55) 22; Fl. Angl. (56) 15; Calend. fl. (72) [11]; Fl. Monsp. (74) 16; Prodr. fl.

Dan. (82) 17; Fl. Åker. (162) 11; Pand. fl. Ryb. (165) 19; Esca avium (174) 12

Saxifraga granulata plena — Demonstr. pl. (49) 12

Saxifraga groenlandica — Fl. alp. (71) 17; Rar. Norv. (157) 5

Saxifraga hirculus — Hist. nat. Rossia (144) 29; Rar. Norv. (157) 10; Colon. pl. (158) 6

Saxifraga hybrida — Fl. alp. (71) 16

Saxifraga hypnoides — Fl. Angl. (56) 15; Fl. alp. (71) 17; Fl. Monsp. (74) 16; Fl. Belg. (112) 9, 16

Saxifraga lingulata — Pan Svec. (26) 22

Saxifraga nivalis — Stat. pl. (55) 16; Fl. Angl. (56) 15; Fl. alp. (71) 16; Rar. Norv. (157) 10

Saxifraga officinarum — Pan Svec. (26) 22

Saxifraga oppositifolia — Stat. pl. (55) 16; Fl. Angl. (56) 16; Fl. alp. (71) 16; Rar. Norv. (157) 10

Saxifraga pallida — Pan Svec. (26) 23

Saxifraga punctata — Hist. nat. Rossia (144) 29

Saxifraga pyrenaica tridactylites latifolia — Pl. Mart.-Burs. (6) 24

Saxifraga quae sedum serratum minus album, longissimis foliis, marginibus serratis — Pl. Mart.-Burs. (6) 23

Saxifraga rivularis — Stat. pl. (55) 16; Fl. alp. (71) 16; Rar. Norv. (157) 10

Saxifraga rotundifolia — Demonstr. pl. (49) 12; Fl. alp. (71) 16; Fl. Monsp. (74) 7, 16; Hist. nat. Rossia (144) 29

Saxifraga sedoides — Hist. nat. Rossia (144) 29

Saxifraga smolandica — Pan Svec. (26) 23

Saxifraga stellaris — Stat. pl. (55) 16; Fl. Angl. (56) 15; Fl. alp. (71) 16; Rar. Norv. (157) 10

Saxifraga stellata — Pan Svec. (26) 22; Pl. hybr. (33) 28

Saxifraga tridactylites — Pan Svec. (26) 22[as tradactylites]; Herbat. Upsal. (50) 13[as tridactyloides]; Stat. pl. (55) 21; Fl. Angl. (56) 15; Fl. alp. (71) 17; Fl. Monsp. (74) 16; Prodr. fl. Dan. (82) 18; Fl. Belg. (112) 16; Fl. Åker. (162) 11

Saxifraga uniflora bulbifera — Splachnum (27) 2

Scabiosa — Hort. Upsal. (7) 34; Fl. oecon. (17) 4; Gem. arb. (24) 13; Pand. insect. (93) 11; Fl. Cap. (99) 6; Nom. bot. (107) 10

Scabiosa africana — Fl. Cap. (99) 11; Febr. interm. (167) 38

Scabiosa africana frutescens, foliis rigidis splendentibus et serratis, flore albicante — Pl. rar. Afr. (115) 8

Scabiosa alpina — Demonstr. pl. (49) 4; Fl. alp. (71) 12; Calend. fl. (72) [16]

Scabiosa argentea angustifolia — Cent. I. pl. (65) 6

Scabiosa arvensis — Demonstr. pl. (49) 4; Herbat. Upsal. (50) 17; Pl. officin. (52) 17; Stat. pl. (55) 19; Fl. Angl. (56) 11; Calend. fl. (72) [14], [22]; Fl. Monsp. (74) 10; Prodr. fl. Dan. (82) 14; Fl. Belg. (112) 13; Fl. Åker. (162) 7; Pand. fl. Ryb. (165) 17; Febr. interm. (167) 38

Scabiosa atropurpurea — Calend. fl. (72) [17]; Hort. cul. (132) 23

Scabiosa columbaria — Fl. Angl. (56) 11; Fl. Monsp. (74) 10; Prodr. fl. Dan. (82) 14; see also S. columbina

Scabiosa columbina [error for columbaria?] — Stat. pl. (55) 22

Scabiosa corollis quadrifidis subradiantibus: squamis calycinis obtusis, foliis lanceolatis serratis — Pl. rar. Afr. (115) 8

Scabiosa corollulis quinquefidis; foliis lineari-lanceolatis integerrimis, caule herbaceo — Cent. I. pl. (65) 6

Scabiosa corollulis quinquefidis radiantibus calyce brevioribus, foliis pinnatis: summis linearibus integerrimis — Cent. II. pl. (66) 8

Scabiosa gotlandica — Pan Svec. (26) 15

Scabiosa graminea argentea — Cent. I. pl. (65) 6

Scabiosa graminifolia — Cent. I. pl. (65) 6; Fl. Monsp. (74) 10

Scabiosa integrifolia — Fl. Monsp. (74) 10

Scabiosa leucantha — Fl. Monsp. (74) 10[as leucanthem.]

Scabiosa maritima — Cent. II. pl. (66) 8; Calend. fl. (72) [18]; Fl. Monsp. (74) 10

Scabiosa maritima parva — Cent. II. pl. (66) 8

Scabiosa maritima, rutae caninae folio — Cent. II. pl. (66) 8

Scabiosa ochroleuca — Fl. Monsp. (74) 10

Scabiosa papposa — Fl. Palaest. (70) 13

Scabiosa perennis glabra laciniata, flore albo minore — Pl. Mart.-Burs. (6) 23

Scabiosa rigida — Pl. rar. Afr. (115) 8

Scabiosa stellata — Fl. Palaest. (70) 13

Scabiosa succisa — Pan Svec. (26) 15; Vern. arb. (47) 19; Herbat. Upsal. (50) 17; Pl. officin. (52) 13; Fl. Angl. (56) 11; Calend. fl. (72) [18]; Fl. Monsp. (74) 10; Prodr. fl. Dan. (82) 14; Pl. tinct. (97) 12; Fl. Belg. (112) 13; Fl. Åker. (162) 7; Pand. fl. Ryb. (165) 16

Scabiosa syriaca — Fl. Palaest. (70) 13

Scabiosa tatarica — Demonstr. pl. (49) 4; Calend. fl. (72) [15]

Scabiosa transsylvanica — Pl. rar. Afr. (115) 6[as transylvanica]

Scabiosa triandra — Fl. Monsp. (74) 10

Scabiosa vulgaris — Pan Svec. (26) 15

Scammonia — Vir. pl. (13) 7

Scandix — Hort. Upsal. (7) 34; Fl. oecon. (17) 7; Pl. escul. (35) 28, 29

Scandix anthriscus — Demonstr. pl. (49) 8; Stat. pl. (55) 20; Fl. Angl. (56) 13; Prodr. fl. Dan. (82) 16; Fl. Belg. (112) 15

Scandix australis — Fl. Monsp. (74) 13

Scandix cerefolium — Pl. escul. (35) 11; Demonstr. pl. (49) 8; Pl. officin. (52) 7; Prodr. fl. Dan. (82)

16; Fl. Cap. (99) 2; Mac. olit. (113) 18; Hort. cul. (132) 14

Scandix hispida — Pan Svec. (26) 19

Scandix nodosa — Demonstr. pl. (49) 8

Scandix odorata — Demonstr. pl. (49) 8; Fl. alp. (71) 15; Cul. mut. (88) 4; Mac. olit. (113) 18; Hort. cul. (132) 18

Scandix pecten veneris — Demonstr. pl. (49) 8; Fl. Angl. (56) 13; Fl. Palaest. (70) 16; Fl. Monsp. (74) 13; Prodr. fl. Dan. (82) 16; Fl. Belg. (112) 15

Scandix sativa — Pan Svec. (26) 19

Scarabaeus — Oecon. nat. (20) 29, 46; Hosp. insect. fl. (43) 22, 24, 35; Noxa insect. (46) 18, 22, 30; Metam. pl. (67) 6; Migr. avium (79) 8; Pand. insect. (93) 4, 7; Polit. nat. (109) 21; Fund. entom. (154) 13, 17, 18, 29[as Scararabaeus]; Esca avium (174) 3; Bigas insect. (184) 2

Scarabaeus acteon — Fund. entom. (154) 5

Scarabaeus auratus — Pand. fl. Ryb. (165) 7; Esca avium (174) 6

Scarabaeus brunneus — Pand. fl. Ryb. (165) 7

Scarabaeus capreolus — Cent. insect. (129) 8

Scarabaeus carnifex — Fund. entom. (154) 24[as carnisex]

Scarabaeus ceratoniae — Pand. insect. (93) 22

Scarabaeus cervus — Pand. insect. (93) 20

Scarabaeus conspurcatus — Pand. fl. Ryb. (165) 7

Scarabaeus cornibus duobus mobilibus aequalibus, apice bifurcis, introrsum ramo denticulisque instructis — Mat. med. anim. (29) 14

Scarabaeus cylindricus — Pand. fl. Ryb. (165) 7

Scarabaeus erraticus — Pand. fl. Ryb. (165) 7

Scarabaeus fasciatus — Pand. fl. Ryb. (165) 7

Scarabaeus fimetarius — Pand. fl. Ryb. (165) 7

Scarabaeus fossor — Pand. fl. Ryb. (165) 7

Scarabaeus haemisphaericus cochineelifer — Mat. med. anim. (29) 15

Scarabaeus horticola — Pand. insect. (93) 14, 15

Scarabaeus maxillosus: maxillis exsertis apice tantum furcatis — Cent. insect. (129) 8

Scarabaeus melolontha — Noxa insect. (46) 25; Pand. insect. (93) 20; Pand. fl. Ryb. (165) 7

Scarabaeus molossus — Cent. insect. (129) 8

Scarabaeus muticus niger, thoracis incisurarumque marginibus flavis, sterno porrecto — Cent. insect. (129) 8

Scarabaeus nigricans alarum alis rubicundis limbis — Mat. med. anim. (29) 15

Scarabaeus nuchicornis — Pand. fl. Ryb. (165) 7

Scarabaeus orichalcus — Iter Chin. (161) 12, 13

Scarabaeus pilularius — Fund. entom. (154) 24

Scarabaeus sabulosus — Pand. fl. Ryb. (165) 7

Scarabaeus solstitialis — Pand. fl. Ryb. (165) 7

Scarabaeus stercorarius — Pand. fl. Ryb. (165) 7; Esca avium (174) 3, 6

Scarabaeus surinamus — Cent. insect. (129) 8

Scarabaeus thorace bicorni, capitis clypeo integerrimo: cornu erecto, elytris laevibus — Cent. insect. (129) 8

Scarabaeus thorace tricorni: intermedio maximo simplicissimo, capitis cornu recurvato simplicissimo — Cent. insect. (129) 8

Scarabaeus tityus — Cent. insect. (129) 8

Scarabaeus variabilis — Pand. insect. (93) 20

Scarabaeus vernalis — Pand. fl. Ryb. (165) 7; Esca avium (174) 6

Scarus — Cul. mut. (88) 9

Scarus cilliceus — Var. cib. (156) 8

Sceptrum carolinum — Betula (1) 12; Hort. Upsal. (7) 34

Scheuchzeria — Hort. Upsal. (7) 41

Scheuchzeria alpina — Rar. Norv. (157) 11

Scheuchzeria palustris — Pan Svec. (26) 21; Herbat. Upsal. (50) 16, 20; Stat. pl. (55) 15; Fl. alp. (71) 16; Hist. nat. Rossia (144) 29; Fl. Åker. (162) 10; Ledum (178) [1]

Schinus — Fl. Jam. (105) 26

Schinus limonia — Herb. Amboin. (57) 9

Schoenanthum — Fund. agrost. (152) 16[as Schaenanthum]

Schoenanthum amboinicum — Herb. Amboin. (57) 20[as Schaenanthum]

Schoenanthus — Fund. agrost. (152) 14

Schoenanthus avenaceus procumbens maderaspatanus, bupleuri folio — Cent. II. pl. (66) 7

Schoenus — Hort. Upsal. (7) 41; Fl. oecon. (17) 2; Fl. Cap. (99) 6; Fund. agrost. (152) 4, 29, 38

Schoenus aculeatus — Fl. Monsp. (74) 8

Schoenus albus — Herbat. Upsal. (50) 20; Stat. pl. (55) 15; Fl. Angl. (56) 10; Fl. alp. (71) 12; Fund. agrost. (152) 7; Fl. Åker. (162) 6

Schoenus capensis — Cent. I. pl. (65) 4; Fl. Cap. (99) 9, 11

Schoenus coloratus — Fl. Jam. (105) 12

Schoenus culmo subtriquetro folioso, floribus fasciculatis, foliis setaceis — Pl. Mart.-Burs. (6) 4

Schoenus culmo tereti, foliis margine dorsoque aculeatis — Pl. Mart.-Burs. (6) 4

Schoenus culmo tereti ramosissimo vaginato, spicis ovatis nudis — Cent. I. pl. (65) 4

Schoenus fagara — Pl. Jam. (102) 8

Schoenus lithospermus — Fl. Jam. (105) 12, 25

Schoenus mariscus — Pan Svec. (26) 13; Demonstr. pl. (49) 3; Stat. pl. (55) 15; Fl. Angl. (56) 10; Fl. Belg. (112) 12; Fund. agrost. (152) 8; Colon. pl. (158) 7

Schoenus minimus — Pan Svec. (26) 13

Schoenus mucronatus — Fl. Monsp. (74) 8; Prodr. fl. Dan. (82) 13

Schoenus nigricans — Pan Svec. (26) 13; Stat. pl. (55) 15; Fl. Angl. (56) 10; Fl. Monsp. (74) 9; Fl. Belg. (112) 12

Schoenus secans — Pl. Jam. (102) [5]

Schoenus vulgaris — Pan Svec. (26) 13

Schwalbea — Nova pl. gen. 1751 (32) 9

Sciaena fasciata — Chin. Lagerstr. (64) 22

Sciaena fasciis decem, maculaque operculorum fuscis — Chin. Lagerstr. (64) 22

Scilla — Vir. pl. (13) 20; Sapor. med. (31) 19; Pl. rar. Afr. (115) 4

Scilla amoena — Demonstr. pl. (49) 10; Fl. Palaest. (70) 17; Pl. Alstr. (121) 5; Hort. cul. (132) 24

Scilla autumnalis — Fl. Angl. (56) 14; Fl. Monsp. (74) 14

Scilla bifolia — Fl. Angl. (56) 14; Fl. Palaest. (70) 17

Scilla maritima — Demonstr. pl. (49) 10; Pl. officin. (52) 18

Scinum — Passifl. (8) [iii]

Sciodaphyllum — Fl. Jam. (105) 26

Scirpus — Hort. Upsal. (7) 41; Vir. pl. (13) 17; Fl. oecon. (17) 2; Oecon. nat. (20) [5, as 7]; Pan Svec. (26) 11; Pl. escul. (35) 27; Morb. hyeme (38) 8; Cui bono? (42) 18; Mirac. insect. (45) 11; Fund. agrost. (152) 4, 14, 15, 29, 31, 38

Scirpus acicularis — Herbat. Upsal. (50) 14; Stat. pl. (55) 12; Fl. Angl. (56) 10; Prodr. fl. Dan. (82) 13; Fund. agrost. (152) 7; Fl. Åker. (162) 6

Scirpus articulatus — Pl. Jam. (102) 6; Fl. Jam. (105) 12

Scirpus capillaris — Fl. Cap. (99) 11

Scirpus capitatus — Fl. Jam. (105) 12

Scirpus cespitosus — Pan Svec. (26) 13; Herbat. Upsal. (50) 14; Stat. pl. (55) 15; Fl. Angl. (56) 10; Fl. Jam. (105) 12[as caespitosus]; Fl. Belg. (112) 12[as caespitosus]; Fund. agrost. (152) 7[as caespitosus], 9[as caespitosus]

Scirpus corymbosus — Cent. II. pl. (66) 7

Scirpus culmo tereti nudo, spica subovata imbricata terminatrice — Pl. Mart.-Burs. (6) 3

Scirpus culmo triquetro folioso, corymbis lateralibus simplicibus; terminali prolifero, spicis subulatis — Cent. II. pl. (66) 7

Scirpus fluitans — Fl. Angl. (56) 10; Prodr. fl. Dan. (82) 13

Scirpus geniculatus — Fl. Jam. (105) 12

Scirpus glomeratus — Herb. Amboin. (57) 25

Scirpus holoschoenus — Fl. Angl. (56) 10[as holoscoenus]; Fl. Monsp. (74) 9

Scirpus lacustris — Pan Svec. (26) 13; Herbat. Upsal. (50) 14; Stat. pl. (55) 12; Fl. Angl. (56) 10; Fl. Monsp. (74) 9; Prodr. fl. Dan. (82) 13; Fl. Jam. (105) 12, 25; Fl. Belg. (112) 12; Fund. agrost. (152) 7; Fl. Åker. (162) 6

Scirpus maderaspatanus, capitulo squamoso, subrotundo — Nova pl. gen. 1747 (14) 4

Scirpus maritimus — Pan Svec. (26) 13; Pl. escul.
(35) 7; Stat. pl. (55) 12; Fl. Angl. (56) 10; Fl.
Monsp. (74) 9; Prodr. fl. Dan. (82) 13; Pane diaet.
(83) 20; Fl. Belg. (112) 12; Fund. agrost. (152) 7;
Pand. fl. Ryb. (165) 16

Scirpus minimus — Pan Svec. (26) 13

Scirpus mucronatus — Fl. Angl. (56) 10; Fl. Monsp.
(74) 9

Scirpus mutatus — Pl. Jam. (102) 6; Fl. Jam. (105)
12

Scirpus palustris — Pan Svec. (26) 13; Herbat. Upsal.
(50) 13; Stat. pl. (55) 13; Fl. Angl. (56) 10; Fl.
Monsp. (74) 9; Prodr. fl. Dan. (82) 13; Transm.
frum. (87) 3; Fl. Belg. (112) 12; Fl. Åker. (162) 6;
Pand. fl. Ryb. (165) 16

Scirpus romanus — Demonstr. pl. (49) 3

Scirpus setaceus — Fl. Angl. (56) 10

Scirpus sylvaticus — Pan Svec. (26) 13; Demonstr.
pl. (49) 3; Herbat. Upsal. (50) 19; Fl. Angl. (56)
10; Fl. Monsp. (74) 9; Prodr. fl. Dan. (82) 13; Fl.
Belg. (112) 12

Sciurus — Oecon. nat. (20) 36, 39; Rad. senega (23)
10; Morb. hyeme (38) 12, 13; Mus ind. (62) 6ff.;
Polit. nat. (109) 15; Usum hist. nat. (145) 23; Usum
musc. (148) 9

Sciurus cauda tereti: pilis brevibus, auribus
subrotundis — Mus. Ad.-Frid. (11) 4

Sclarea — Nom. bot. (107) 9; Inebr. (117) 13

Scleranthus — Fl. oecon. (17) 11; Hosp. insect. fl.
(43) 12[as Schleranthus]; Pand. insect. (93) 14

Scleranthus annuus — Pan Svec. (26) 22[as annus];
Herbat. Upsal. (50) 10; Stat. pl. (55) 22; Fl. Angl.
(56) 16; Fl. Monsp. (74) 16; Prodr. fl. Dan. (82) 18;
Fl. Belg. (112) 16; Fl. Åker. (162) 12; Pand. fl.
Ryb. (165) 19

Scleranthus calycibus fructus patentissimis spinosis,
caule subvilloso — Cent. II. pl. (66) 16

Scleranthus perennis — Pan Svec. (26) 22; Hosp.
insect. fl. (43) 21; Stat. pl. (55) 21; Fl. Angl. (56)
16; Prodr. fl. Dan. (82) 18; Pl. tinct. (97) 29

Scleranthus polycarpos — Cent. II. pl. (66) 16; Fl.
Monsp. (74) 7[as polycarpus], 16[as polycarpus]

Scolopax — Migr. avium (79) 18, 36

Scolopendra — Corallia Balt. (4) 8; Mus. Ad.-Frid.
(11) [v]; Lign. colubr. (21) 5; Noctiluca (39) 5;
Metam. pl. (67) 9; Polit. nat. (109) 19; Fund.
entom. (154) 19, 26

Scolopendra capensis major lutescens, cauda longiore
— Mus. Ad.-Frid. (11) 46

Scolopendra forficata — Pand. fl. Ryb. (165) 16

Scolopendra lagura — Esca avium (174) 3, [9, as 17]

Scolopendra magna peregrina — Surin. Grill. (16) 31

Scolopendra marina corallina multipes — Mus. Ad.-
Frid. (11) 47

Scolopendra marina lucens — Noctiluca (39) 4

Scolopendra phosphorea — Nat. pelagi (84) 10; Iter
Chin. (161) 5

Scolopendra plana, pedibus utrinque viginti — Mus.
Ad.-Frid. (11) 46; Surin. Grill. (16) 31

Scolopendra teres, pedibus utrinque 96 — Mus. Ad.-
Frid. (11) 46

Scolopendria — Acrostichum (10) 8; Herb. Amboin.
(57) 27

Scolopendrium — see Scopendrium

Scolymus hispanicus — Fl. Monsp. (74) 24

Scolymus maculatus — Fl. Palaest. (70) 27; Fl.
Monsp. (74) 24

Scomber — Noctiluca (39) 5; Nat. pelagi (84) 11;
Cul. mut. (88) 8

Scomber ductor — Nat. pelagi (84) 11

Scomber glaucus — Nat. pelagi (84) 11

Scomber linaea laterali curva, tabellis osseis
muricata, corpore lato et tenui — Chin. Lagerstr.
(64) 24

Scomber linaea laterali squamis latis pinnata — Chin.
Lagerstr. (64) 24

Scomber pelamis — Nat. pelagi (84) 11; Iter Chin.
(161) 14

Scomber tabellatus — Chin. Lagerstr. (64) 24

Scomber thynnus — Nat. pelagi (84) 11; Iter Chin.
(161) 14

Scoparia — Nova pl. gen. 1751 (32) 37, 48

Scoparia dulcis — Fl. Jam. (105) 13; Pl. rar. Afr.
(115) 6; Pl. Surin. (177) 5

Scoparia foliis tenuissimis in plurimos et tenuissimos
ramulos divisa et subdivisa, floribus et fructu in
summis ramulis prae parvitate vix discernendis —
Nova pl. gen. 1751 (32) 14

Scopendrium [error for Scolopendrium?] — Fl. Belg.
(112) 9

Scopiarium marilandium novum — Nova pl. gen.
1751 (32) 15

Scordium — Vir. pl. (13) 7; Sapor. med. (31) 18;
Odor. med. (40) 12, 14, 15; Marum (175) 9

Scordium alterum lanuginosius verticillatum — Cent.
II. pl. (66) 20

Scordotis — Cent. II. pl. (66) 20

Scorpio — Lign. colubr. (21) 5; Mat. med. anim. (29)
17; Pand. insect. (93) 2, 6; Mors. serp. (119) 2;
Fund. entom. (154) 19, 21, 22

Scorpio ceilonicus — Mus. Ad.-Frid. (11) 45

Scorpio ceilonicus niger maximus — Mus. Ad.-Frid.
(11) 45

Scorpio indicus niger magnitudine cancrum
fluviatilem aequans — Mus. Ad.-Frid. (11) 45

Scorpio javanicus major pilosus e nigro coerulescente
splendens — Mus. Ad.-Frid. (11) 45

Scorpio majore ex india orientali — Mus. Ad.-Frid.
(11) 46

Scorpio pectinum denticulis 13 — Mus. Ad.-Frid.
(11) 45

Scorpio pectinum denticulis 30 — Mat. med. anim.
(29) 17

Scorpiurus — Hort. Upsal. (7) 34

Scorpiurus subvillosus — Fl. Monsp. (74) 23

Scorpiurus sulcata — Fl. Palaest. (70) 25; Fl. Monsp. (74) 23[as sulcatus]

Scorzonera — Vir. pl. (13) 23; Fl. oecon. (17) 19; Pan Svec. (26) 11; Sapor. med. (31) 11; Pl. escul. (35) 22, 27, 28; Nom. bot. (107) 16; Ping. anim. (108) 15; Mund. invis. (149) 14

Scorzonera graminifolia — Hist. nat. Rossia (144) 32

Scorzonera hispanica — Demonstr. pl. (49) 22; Stat. pl. (55) 7; Fl. Palaest. (70) 27; Calend. fl. (72) [13]; Fl. Monsp. (74) 24; Mac. olit. (113) 10; Hort. cul. (132) 13; Hist. nat. Rossia (144) 32

Scorzonera humilis — Demonstr. pl. (49) 22; Pl. officin. (52) 17; Stat. pl. (55) 7, 21; Fl. Monsp. (74) 24; Prodr. fl. Dan. (82) 22; Fl. Åker. (162) 17; Pand. fl. Ryb. (165) 21

Scorzonera laciniata — Demonstr. pl. (49) 22

Scorzonera laciniatis foliis — Pl. Mart.-Burs. (6) 23

Scorzonera lusitanica, gramineo folio, flore pallido luteo — Pl. Mart.-Burs. (6) 23

Scorzonera pannonica — Pan Svec. (26) 31

Scorzonera picroides — Calend. fl. (72) [22][as Sorzonera]; Fl. Monsp. (74) 24; Mac. olit. (113) 21

Scorzonera purpurea — Prodr. fl. Dan. (82) 22; Hist. nat. Rossia (144) 32

Scorzonera sylvestris — Vir. pl. (13) 30

Scorzonera veslingii — Fl. Palaest. (70) 27

Scrofa dorso antice setoso, cauda pilosa — Ping. anim. (108) 11

Scrophularia — Hosp. insect. fl. (43) 12, 40; Noxa insect. (46) 21; Pand. insect. (93) 16; Nom. bot. (107) 15; Polit. nat. (109) 8, 9

Scrophularia aquatica — Demonstr. pl. (49) 16[as Schrophularia, corr. p. 27]; Pl. officin. (52) 17; Fl. Angl. (56) 19; Calend. fl. (72) [16]; Fl. Monsp. (74) 20; Prodr. fl. Dan. (82) 20; Fl. Belg. (112) 19

Scrophularia canina — Fl. Monsp. (74) 20

Scrophularia foetida — Pan Svec. (26) 27; Hosp. insect. fl. (43) 27

Scrophularia marilandica — Hosp. insect. fl. (43) 12; Demonstr. pl. (49) 16[as Schrophularia, corr. p. 27]; Fund. fr. (123) 19

Scrophularia nodosa — Herbat. Upsal. (50) 9; Pl. officin. (52) 17; Stat. pl. (55) 20; Fl. Angl. (56) 19; Fl. Monsp. (74) 20; Prodr. fl. Dan. (82) 20; Fl. Belg. (112) 19; Fund. fr. (123) 19; Fl. Åker. (162) 15; Pand. fl. Ryb. (165) 20

Scrophularia peregrina — Fl. Monsp. (74) 20; Pl. rar. Afr. (115) 6

Scrophularia sambucifolia — Fl. Palaest. (70) 23

Scrophularia scorodonia — Fl. Angl. (56) 19

Scrophularia vernalis — Demonstr. pl. (49) 16[as Schrophularia, corr. p. 27]

Scurrula — Pl. Jam. (102) 11; Polit. nat. (109) 5

Scutellaria — Hort. Upsal. (7) 35; Vir. pl. (13) 29; Cui bono? (42) 20; Nom. bot. (107) 15

Scutellaria alpina — Demonstr. pl. (49) 16; Fl. alp. (71) 19

Scutellaria flore purpurascente — Fl. Angl. (56) 27

Scutellaria galericulata — Herbat. Upsal. (50) 6; Stat. pl. (55) 13; Fl. Angl. (56) 18; Calend. fl. (72) [13]; Prodr. fl. Dan. (82) 20; Fl. Belg. (112) 18; Fl. Åker. (162) 14; Pand. fl. Ryb. (165) 20

Scutellaria indica — Herb. Amboin. (57) 24

Scutellaria integrifolia — Pan Svec. (26) 27

Scutellaria lateriflora — Demonstr. pl. (49) 16; Calend. fl. (72) [17]

Scutellaria orientalis — Demonstr. pl. (49) 16

Scutellaria prima — Herb. Amboin. (57) 16

Scutellaria secunda — Herb. Amboin. (57) 16

Scutellaria supina — Demonstr. pl. (49) 16; Hist. nat. Rossia (144) 31

Scutellaria tertia — Herb. Amboin. (57) 16

Scutellaria vulgaris — Pan Svec. (26) 27

Scyllaea pelagica — Iter Chin. (161) 15

Scytale americanum amphisbaena et caecilia vocata — Mus. Ad.-Frid. (11) 19[as Schytale]

Scytale ex nova hispania — Mus. Ad.-Frid. (11) 19

Sebesten — Sapor. med. (31) 12

Secale — Peloria (3) 15; Spons. pl. (12) 41; Vir. pl. (13) 32; Fl. oecon. (17) 4; Oecon. nat. (20) 17; Pl. escul. (35) 5; Cui bono? (42) 26; Hosp. insect. fl. (43) 12; Noxa insect. (46) 23; Fl. Angl. (56) 4; Mus ind. (62) 14; Hort. acad. (63) 2; Calend. fl. (72) [11]; Pane diaet. (83) 11; Transm. frum. (87) 12ff.; Pand. insect. (93) 11; Instr. peregr. (96) 10; Nom. bot. (107) 9; Polit. nat. (109) 13; Raphania (126) 10ff.; Usum hist. nat. (145) 9; Fund. agrost. (152) 5, 15, 22, 25, 32, 34

Secale cereale — Fr. escul. (127) 19; Hort. cul. (132) 8; Hist. nat. Rossia (144) 20; Esca avium (174) 5, 11

Secale cereale annuum — Hort. cul. (132) 8

Secale cereale hybernum — Hort. cul. (132) 8

Secale hybernum — Calend. fl. (72) [12], [13], [18]

Secale spiculis geminatis — Nova pl. gen. 1751 (32) 35; Pl. hybr. (33) 15

Secale vernum — Vern. arb. (47) 13

Sechium — Fl. Jam. (105) 27

Securidaca — Hort. Upsal. (7) 34

Securidaca volubilis — Herb. Amboin. (57) 18; Fl. Jam. (105) 19; Pl. Surin. (177) 12

Sedoides africana annua centauroides — Pl. rar. Afr. (115) 9[as Sedroides]

Sedum — Hort. Upsal. (7) 35; Anandria (9) 4; Fl. oecon. (17) 11; Sapor. med. (31) 19; Pl. escul. (35) 29; Metam. pl. (67) 14; Pand. insect. (93) 14; Nom. bot. (107) 13; Nect. fl. (122) 13, 15

Sedum acre — Vir. pl. (13) 30; Pan Svec. (26) 23; Herbat. Upsal. (50) 12; Pl. officin. (52) 18; Stat. pl. (55) 23; Fl. Angl. (56) 16; Calend. fl. (72) [11], [13], [16]; Fl. Monsp. (74) 16; Prodr. fl. Dan. (82) 18; Fl. Belg. (112) 17; Rar. Norv. (157) 15; Fl.

Åker. (162) 12; Pand. fl. Ryb. (165) 19; Febr. interm. (167) 19, 29

Sedum africanum annuum, centaurii minoris folio, flore aureo — Pl. rar. Afr. (115) 10

Sedum aizoon — Calend. fl. (72) [13]; Hist. nat. Rossia (144) 29

Sedum album — Pan Svec. (26) 23; Herbat. Upsal. (50) 19; Stat. pl. (55) 23; Fl. Angl. (56) 16; Calend. fl. (72) [16]; Fl. Monsp. (74) 16; Prodr. fl. Dan. (82) 18; Fl. Belg. (112) 17; Pand. fl. Ryb. (165) 19

Sedum alpinum, saxifragae albae flore vel grandiflorum — Pl. Mart.-Burs. (6) 23

Sedum anacampseros — Calend. fl. (72) [16]; Fl. Monsp. (74) 16

Sedum annuum — Pan Svec. (26) 23[as annum]; Herbat. Upsal. (50) 19; Stat. pl. (55) 22; Fl. Åker. (162) 12

Sedum cepaea — Fl. Monsp. (74) 16; Fl. Belg. (112) 8, 17

Sedum dasyphyllum — Fl. Angl. (56) 16; Fl. Monsp. (74) 16

Sedum foliis quaternis — Pl. rar. Camsch. (30) 19

Sedum foliis teretiusculis acutis: radicalibus fasciculatis; cyma pubescente — Cent. I. pl. (65) 12

Sedum fruticosum minus, alterum — Fl. Angl. (56) 26

Sedum hispanicum — Cent. I. pl. (65) 12

Sedum hispanicum, folio glauco acuto, flore albido — Cent. I. pl. (65) 12

Sedum hybridum — Hist. nat. Rossia (144) 29

Sedum libanoticum — Fl. Palaest. (70) 19

Sedum majus montanum, foliis dentatis — Cent. I. pl. (65) 12

Sedum non acre album — Fl. Angl. (56) 27

Sedum reflexum — Fl. Palaest. (70) 19; Calend. fl. (72) [15]; Mac. olit. (113) 21

Sedum rupestre — Pan Svec. (26) 23; Pl. escul. (35) 15; Stat. pl. (55) 23; Fl. Angl. (56) 16; Calend. fl. (72) [15]; Fl. Monsp. (74) 16; Fl. Belg. (112) 17; Mac. olit. (113) 21

Sedum saxatilis variegato flore — Pl. Mart.-Burs. (6) 24

Sedum sexangulare — Pan Svec. (26) 23; Herbat. Upsal. (50) 19; Stat. pl. (55) 22; Fl. Monsp. (74) 16; Prodr. fl. Dan. (82) 18

Sedum telephium — Pan Svec. (26) 23; Hosp. insect. fl. (43) 21; Herbat. Upsal. (50) 12; Pl. officin. (52) 19; Stat. pl. (55) 23; Fl. Angl. (56) 16; Metam. pl. (67) 21; Calend. fl. (72) [17]; Fl. Monsp. (74) 16; Prodr. fl. Dan. (82) 18; Fl. Belg. (112) 17; Fl. Åker. (162) 12; Pand. fl. Ryb. (165) 19; Esca avium (174) 12

Sedum verticillatum — Hist. nat. Rossia (144) 29

Sedum villosum — Fl. Angl. (56) 16; Rar. Norv. (157) 9

Selaginoides — Sem. musc. (28) 16

Selago — Fl. Cap. (99) 6; Fund. fr. (123) 18

Selago coccinea — Pl. rar. Afr. (115) 12[as cocinea]

Selago corymbosa — Fl. Cap. (99) 15

Selago dubia — Fl. Cap. (99) 15

Selago foliis obovatis crenatis, caule prostrato, racemis ramosis — Pl. rar. Afr. (115) 13

Selago lychnidea — Pl. rar. Afr. (115) 12

Selago prunastri — Fl. Cap. (99) 15

Selago rapunculoides — Cent. II. pl. (66) 22; Pl. rar. Afr. (115) 12

Selago spica terminali, foliis lanceolatis subpetiolatis serratis obtusiusculis subtomentosis — Pl. rar. Afr. (115) 12

Selago spicis corymbosis, foliis dentatis — Cent. II. pl. (66) 22

Selago spicis corymbosis, foliis inferioribus lineatibus integerrimis; superioribus lanceolatis subdentatis — Pl. rar. Afr. (115) 12

Selago spicis corymbosis, foliis omnibus dentatis — Pl. rar. Afr. (115) 12

Selago spuria — Fl. Cap. (99) 15

Selago tomentosa — Pl. rar. Afr. (115) 13

Selinum — Pl. Mart.-Burs. (6) 11; Fl. oecon. (17) 7; Pand. insect. (93) 12

Selinum cervaria — Fl. Monsp. (74) 13

Selinum monnieri — Cent. I. pl. (65) 9

Selinum oreoselinum — Pan Svec. (26) 18

Selinum palustre — Pan Svec. (26) 18; Hosp. insect. fl. (43) 18; Herbat. Upsal. (50) 16; Stat. pl. (55) 15; Prodr. fl. Dan. (82) 16; Fl. Belg. (112) 15; Fl. Åker. (162) 9

Selinum pinnis pinnatis, pinnulis appendiculato circumserratis triangularibus — Pl. Mart.-Burs. (6) 10

Selinum sylvestre — Demonstr. pl. (49) 8; Fl. Belg. (112) 15

Selinum umbella conferta, involucro universali reflexo, seminibus quinque costis membranaceis — Cent. I. pl. (65) 9

Sempervivum — Vir. pl. (13) 33; Fl. oecon. (17) 12; Sapor. med. (31) 14; Pl. escul. (35) 15, 29; Nom. bot. (107) 13

Sempervivum arachnoideum — Fl. alp. (71) 17; Fl. Monsp. (74) 17

Sempervivum arboreum — Demonstr. pl. (49) 13

Sempervivum canariense — Hort. Upsal. (7) 37

Sempervivum caule inferne nudo laevi ramoso — Hort. Upsal. (7) 41[as Sempervivam]

Sempervivum foliis caule petalorumque apicibus hirtis — Cent. I. pl. (65) 12

Sempervivum globiferum — Hist. nat. Rossia (144) 30

Sempervivum hirtum — Cent. I. pl. (65) 12; Fl. alp. (71) 17

Sempervivum majus — Herb. Amboin. (57) 21

Sempervivum montanum — Fl. alp. (71) 17; Fl. Monsp. (74) 17

Sempervivum tectorum — Pan Svec. (26) 24; Demonstr. pl. (49) 13; Pl. officin. (52) 18; Stat. pl. (55) 23; Fl. Angl. (56) 17; Fl. Monsp. (74) 17; Prodr. fl. Dan. (82) 18; Fl. Belg. (112) 17; Fl. Åker. (162) 12

Seneca — Rad. senega (23) 17

Senecio — Hort. Upsal. (7) 35; Anandria (9) 12; Pl. hybr. (33) 29; Pand. insect. (93) 18; Fl. Cap. (99) 7; Pl. Jam. (102) 23; Nom. bot. (107) 17; Fund. fr. (123) 17

Senecio abrotanifolius — Fl. alp. (71) 22

Senecio aegyptius — Fl. Palaest. (70) 28[as aegygtius]

Senecio amboinicus sylvestris — Herb. Amboin. (57) 26

Senecio corollis nudis, foliis lanceolatis integerrimis basi subdentatis — Pl. rar. Afr. (115) 20

Senecio corollis nudis, foliis lyratis subtus tomentosis, pedunculis unifloris squamis subulatis — Pl. rar. Afr. (115) 20

Senecio corollis radiantibus calyce longioribus, foliis pinnato-dentatis denticulatis: laciniis distantibus — Pl. rar. Afr. (115) 21

Senecio corollis radiantibus, petiolis radicalibus lanatis, foliis pinnatifidis, caulibus simplicissimis, floribus lateralibus sessilibus — Pl. rar. Afr. (115) 21

Senecio doria — Fl. Monsp. (74) 25

Senecio elegans — Fl. Cap. (99) 18; Hort. cul. (132) 23

Senecio erigeron — Calend. fl. (72) [22]

Senecio erucifolius — Colon. pl. (158) 8

Senecio glaucus — Fl. Palaest. (70) 28

Senecio gothoburgensis — Pan Svec. (26) 33

Senecio halimifolius — Fl. Cap. (99) 18

Senecio halleri — Pan Svec. (26) 33

Senecio hastatus — Fl. Cap. (99) 18

Senecio hieracifolius — Fl. Jam. (105) 20

Senecio ilicifolius — Fl. Cap. (99) 18

Senecio incanus — Fl. alp. (71) 22

Senecio jacobaea — Pan Svec. (26) 33; Hosp. insect. fl. (43) 31; Demonstr. pl. (49) 23; Herbat. Upsal. (50) 9; Stat. pl. (55) 14; Fl. Angl. (56) 22; Metam. pl. (67) 21; Fl. Monsp. (74) 25; Prodr. fl. Dan. (82) 23; Pl. tinct. (97) 23[as Senesio]; Fl. Belg. (112) 8, 9, 21; Fl. Åker. (162) 18

Senecio jacobaeae folio — Pl. Mart.-Burs. (6) 10

Senecio lanatus — Fl. Cap. (99) 18

Senecio linifolius — Fl. Cap. (99) 18

Senecio lividus — Demonstr. pl. (49) 23

Senecio montanus — Fl. Angl. (56) 22

Senecio nemorensis — Demonstr. pl. (49) 23; Hist. nat. Rossia (144) 33

Senecio paludosus — Stat. pl. (55) 13; Prodr. fl. Dan. (82) 23; Fl. Belg. (112) 21; Hist. nat. Rossia (144) 33

Senecio palustris — Fl. Angl. (56) 22

Senecio persicifolius — Pl. rar. Afr. (115) 20

Senecio pubigerus — Pl. rar. Afr. (115) 21

Senecio rigidus — Fl. Cap. (99) 18

Senecio saracenicus — Demonstr. pl. (49) 23[as sarracenica]; Fl. Angl. (56) 22[as sarracenus]; Calend. fl. (72) [17][as sarracenicus]; Polit. nat. (109) 5; Fl. Belg. (112) 21[as sarracenicus]

Senecio sylvaticus — Fl. Angl. (56) 22

Senecio triflorus — Demonstr. pl. (49) 23; Fl. Palaest. (70) 28

Senecio umbellatus — Pl. rar. Afr. (115) 21

Senecio virgatus — Pl. rar. Afr. (115) 20

Senecio viscosus — Demonstr. pl. (49) 23; Fl. Angl. (56) 22; Calend. fl. (72) [22]; Fl. Monsp. (74) 25[as viscosa]; Prodr. fl. Dan. (82) 23; Fl. Belg. (112) 21

Senecio vulgaris — Pan Svec. (26) 33; Hosp. insect. fl. (43) 31; Herbat. Upsal. (50) 20; Stat. pl. (55) 20; Fl. Angl. (56) 22; Calend. fl. (72) [12]; Fl. Monsp. (74) 25; Prodr. fl. Dan. (82) 23; Fl. Belg. (112) 21; Fl. Åker. (162) 18; Pand. fl. Ryb. (165) 21; Esca avium (174) 14

Senega — Rad. senega (23) 17ff.; Menthae (153) 5

Seneka — Rad. senega (23) 17

Seneka officinarum — Rad. senega (23) 17

Senembi seu iguana — Amphib. Gyll. (5) 18

Senna — Vir. pl. (13) 31; Odor. med. (40) 14

Sepia — Mus. Ad.-Frid. (11) 47; Mat. med. anim. (29) 18; Noctiluca (39) 5

Sepia corpore oblongo depresso, tentaculis 6 brevioribus: 2 longioribus, os inclusum corpori, oculi 2 magni infra tentacula — Corallia Balt. (4) 10

Sepia loligo — Nat. pelagi (84) 10; Iter Chin. (161) 14

Sepia octopodia — Nat. pelagi (84) 10

Sepia officinalis — Nat. pelagi (84) 10

Seps — Amphib. Gyll. (5) 3

Seps sive lacerta chalcidica — Mus. Ad.-Frid. (11) 16

Septas capensis — Pl. rar. Afr. (115) 10

Serapias — Vir. pl. (13) 24

Serapias bulbis subrotundis, caule unifloro — Nova pl. gen. 1751 (32) 23

Serapias helleborine — Cervus (60) 8; Metam. pl. (67) 21[as Serapies]; Prodr. fl. Dan. (82) 24

Serapias helleborine latifolia — Fl. Angl. (56) 23; Fl. Monsp. (74) 27

Serapias helleborine longifolia — Fl. Monsp. (74) 27

Serapias helleborine palustris — Calend. fl. (72) [14]; Fl. Monsp. (74) 27

Serapias latifolia — Demonstr. pl. (49) 24; Fl. Belg. (112) 22

Serapias lingua — Fl. Monsp. (74) 27

Serapias longifolia — Fl. Angl. (56) 23; Fl. Belg. (112) 22

Serapias palustris — Fl. Angl. (56) 23; Fl. Belg. (112) 22

Serapias sylvatica — Pan Svec. (26) 34

Seriphium — Fl. Cap. (99) 6, 9; Fund. fr. (123) 18

Seriphium cinereum — Fl. Cap. (99) 18

Seriphium floribus spicatis unifloris — Cent. I. pl. (65) 30

Seriphium fuscum — Fl. Cap. (99) 18

Seriphium gnaphaloides — Cent. I. pl. (65) 30

Seriphium plumosum — Fl. Cap. (99) 18

Serotinum album — Fl. Monsp. (74) 12

Serotinum botrys — Fl. Monsp. (74) 12

Serotinum hirsutum — Fl. Monsp. (74) 12

Serotinum hybridum — Fl. Monsp. (74) 12

Serotinum maritimum — Fl. Monsp. (74) 12

Serotinum polyspermum — Fl. Monsp. (74) 12

Serotinum vulvaria — Fl. Monsp. (74) 12

Serpens — Amphib. Gyll. (5) [1]

Serpens africana ab hottentottis sibon dicta — Mus. Ad.-Frid. (11) 26

Serpens africana hippo dicta — Mus. Ad.-Frid. (11) 24

Serpens amboinensis niger et albus, apachykoatl dicta — Mus. Ad.-Frid. (11) 22

Serpens americana — Amphib. Gyll. (5) 13

Serpens americana annulata — Amphib. Gyll. (5) 14

Serpens americana arborea, singulari artificio picta, magni aestimata — Surin. Grill. (16) 21

Serpens americana caecilia dicta — Mus. Ad.-Frid. (11) 17

Serpens americana grossa versicolor — Mus. Ad.-Frid. (11) 17

Serpens americana lemniscata — Surin. Grill. (16) 16

Serpens americana niger, annulis latis albis, ac inter ipsos singulos duo annuli albi tenuiores, ore squamularum albarum nigricante — Amphib. Gyll. (5) 11[as americanus]

Serpens americana rarior, lemniscis rubris et albis longitudinalibus notata — Mus. Ad.-Frid. (11) 24

Serpens americana viperae aemula — Amphib. Gyll. (5) 12

Serpens amphisbaena — Mus. Ad.-Frid. (11) 19

Serpens amphisbaena orientalis — Mus. Ad.-Frid. (11) 19

Serpens anguis — Amphib. Gyll. (5) 8

Serpens apamea syriaca biceps — Mus. Ad.-Frid. (11) 17[as cyriaca]

Serpens brasiliensis cum conspicillo cordis oculati formam habente — Lign. colubr. (21) 7

Serpens caecilia americana — Mus. Ad.-Frid. (11) 17

Serpens ceylanica caecilia dicta — Mus. Ad.-Frid. (11) 17

Serpens ceylanica conspicillo notata seu cobra de capello — Lign. colubr. (21) 7

Serpens ceylanica lemniscis latis — Amphib. Gyll. (5) 11[as ceilonica]

Serpens ceylanica lineis subfuscis — Amphib. Gyll. (5) 7[as ceylonica]

Serpens ceylanica maxima, pimberah dicta — Surin. Grill. (16) 21[as ceylonica]

Serpens ceylanica sibilans, pulchre lemniscata — Mus. Ad.-Frid. (11) 24[as ceilonica]

Serpens cobella dicta americana — Amphib. Gyll. (5) 9

Serpens conspicillo ornata ex nova hispania — Lign. colubr. (21) 7

Serpens crotalophora seu vipera caudisona americana — Mus. Ad.-Frid. (11) 20

Serpens cum conspicillo minor — Lign. colubr. (21) 7

Serpens ex regno peru conspicillo insignita — Lign. colubr. (21) 6

Serpens excellens ac speciosa brasiliensis e regione guaira, regina serpentum habita — Surin. Grill. (16) 21

Serpens exquisitissima zeylanica, malpolon dicta — Mus. Ad.-Frid. (11) 24

Serpens ibiboboca brasiliensibus — Mus. Ad.-Frid. (11) 24

Serpens indicus bubalinus, anacandia ceylonensibus — Surin. Grill. (16) 20

Serpens indicus coronatus diademate seu conspicillo insignitus — Lign. colubr. (21) 6

Serpens indicus cum conspicillo lepide circulatus — Lign. colubr. (21) 7

Serpens indicus gracilis viridis in arboretis et fruticetis degens, ahaetulla ceilonensibus, i. e. oculis infestus — Amphib. Gyll. (5) 7

Serpens indicus naja seu lusitanis cobra de capello dictus maximus conspicillo notatus, mas — Lign. colubr. (21) 7

Serpens indicus seu cobra de capello femina sine perspicillo — Lign. colubr. (21) 7

Serpens ludicus coronatus diademate seu conspicillo insignitus, lusitanis cobras de capello dictus — Lign. colubr. (21) 6

Serpens malabarica diademate coronata sive conspicillo insignita, cobra de capello dicta — Lign. colubr. (21) 6

Serpens naja siamensis cum conspicillo seu cobra de capello, vel cabelo dictus — Lign. colubr. (21) 7

Serpens oculea mexicana foemina — Surin. Grill. (16) 21

Serpens peregrinus — Surin. Grill. (16) 21

Serpens venenosus maximus virginianus cum ratulis — Surin. Grill. (16) 23

Serpentaria — Menthae (153) 5

Serpentaria virginiana officinarum — Rad. senega (23) 11

Serpentis aesculapii species — Surin. Grill. (16) 19

Serpentula ceilonica seu naja altera — Mus. Ad.-Frid. (11) 27

Serpentula ex insula ceylon — Amphib. Gyll. (5) 11

Serpula — Anim. comp. (98) 2; Fund. test. (166) 17

Serpyllum — Nom. bot. (107) 15

Serratula — Fl. oecon. (17) 20; Cui bono? (42) 20; Fl. Angl. (56) 5; Pand. insect. (93) 18; Nom. bot. (107) 17

Serratula alpina — Demonstr. pl. (49) 22; Stat. pl. (55) 16; Fl. Angl. (56) 22; Fl. alp. (71) 21; Calend. fl. (72) [13]; Hist. nat. Rossia (144) 32; Rar. Norv. (157) 11

Serratula alpina lapatifolia — Calend. fl. (72) [17]

Serratula amara — Herb. Amboin. (57) 24; Hist. nat. Rossia (144) 32

Serratula arvensis — Hosp. insect. fl. (43) 30; Herbat. Upsal. (50) 13; Stat. pl. (55) 18; Fl. Angl. (56) 22; Cervus (60) 8; Oves (61) 15; Fl. Monsp. (74) 24; Prodr. fl. Dan. (82) 22; Fl. Belg. (112) 20; Usum hist. nat. (145) 10; Fl. Åker. (162) 17; Pand. fl. Ryb. (165) 21

Serratula babylonica — Fl. Palaest. (70) 27

Serratula carduus avenae — Pan Svec. (26) 32

Serratula centauroides — Demonstr. pl. (49) 22; Calend. fl. (72) [17]; Hist. nat. Rossia (144) 32

Serratula coronata — Hist. nat. Rossia (144) 32

Serratula lanceolatus — Fl. Monsp. (74) 24

Serratula lapponica — Pan Svec. (26) 32

Serratula latifolia — Demonstr. pl. (49) 22

Serratula multiflora — Hist. nat. Rossia (144) 32

Serratula praealta — Demonstr. pl. (49) 22

Serratula salicifolia — Hist. nat. Rossia (144) 32

Serratula spicata — Specif. Canad. (76) 9

Serratula tinctoria — Pan Svec. (26) 32; Hosp. insect. fl. (43) 30; Herbat. Upsal. (50) 16; Stat. pl. (55) 17[as tinctorum]; Fl. Angl. (56) 22; Fl. Monsp. (74) 24; Prodr. fl. Dan. (82) 22; Pl. tinct. (97) 23; Fl. Åker. (162) 17; Pand. fl. Ryb. (165) 21

Serratula tinctoria praealta — Calend. fl. (72) [16]

Sertularia — Noctiluca (39) 5; Metam. pl. (67) 9; Somn. pl. (68) 5; Nat. pelagi (84) 8; Transm. frum. (87) 9; Anim. comp. (98) 2; Hist. nat. Rossia (144) 12; Mund. invis. (149) 8, 20

Sertularia quae corollina fistulosa fragilis, internodiis prolongis laevibus albis — Pl. Mart.-Burs. (6) 28

Sertularia ramis teretibus, articulis cylindraceis, lapideis aequalibus — Mat. med. anim. (29) 20

Seruneum aquatile — Herb. Amboin. (57) 24

Sesamum — Nect. fl. (122) 8

Sesamum indicum — Herb. Amboin. (57) 20; Fl. Jam. (105) 18

Sesamum orientale — Pl. officin. (52) 18; Fl. Palaest. (70) 23

Sesban — Hort. Upsal. (7) 37; Somn. pl. (68) 9

Seseli annuum — Fl. Monsp. (74) 13[as annnum]

Seseli glaucum — Fl. Monsp. (74) 13

Seseli involucro universali monophyllo, seminibus striatis villosis stylatis — Cent. II. pl. (66) 14

Seseli longifolium — Fl. Monsp. (74) 13

Seseli montano, cicutae folio glabro — Pl. Mart.-Burs. (6) 11

Seseli pyrenaicum — Fl. alp. (71) 15

Seseli tertium — Cent. II. pl. (66) 14

Seseli tortuosum — Fl. Monsp. (74) 13

Seseli turbith — Cent. II. pl. (66) 14

Sherardia — Hort. Upsal. (7) 34

Sherardia arvensis — Demonstr. pl. (49) 4; Stat. pl. (55) 19; Fl. Angl. (56) 11; Fl. Monsp. (74) 10; Prodr. fl. Dan. (82) 14; Pl. rar. Afr. (115) 6

Sherardia muralis — Demonstr. pl. (49) 4

Sherardia scanica — Pan Svec. (26) 15

Sibbaldia — Vir. pl. (13) 27[as Sibaldia]; Fl. Angl. (56) 5; Fund. fr. (123) 23; Fraga (170) [1], 3

Sibbaldia erecta — Hist. nat. Rossia (144) 28

Sibbaldia lapponica — Pan Svec. (26) 19

Sibbaldia procumbens — Stat. pl. (55) 15; Fl. Angl. (56) 14; Fl. alp. (71) 15; Rar. Norv. (157) 10

Sibthorpia — Nova pl. gen. 1751 (32) 38, 48[as Sibtorpia]; Pl. hybr. (33) 7, 28[as Sibtorpia]; Fl. Angl. (56) 5

Sibthorpia africana — Fl. Cap. (99) 16

Sibthorpia europaea — Fl. Angl. (56) 19

Sibthorpia foliis orbiculatis integris crenatis, pedunculis solitariis — Nova pl. gen. 1751 (32) 39

Sibthorpia foliis reniformibus crenatis, pedunculis binis — Nova pl. gen. 1751 (32) 39

Sibthorpia foliis reniformi-subpeltato crenatis — Nova pl. gen. 1751 (32) 38

Sicchius — Herb. Amboin. (57) 11

Sicelium — Fl. Jam. (105) 27

Sicyoides — Nova pl. gen. 1751 (32) 10

Sicyos — Nova pl. gen. 1751 (32) 10; Vern. arb. (47) 9

Sicyos angulata — Demonstr. pl. (49) 26

Sida — Hort. Upsal. (7) 37; Nova pl. gen. 1751 (32) 30; Pl. hybr. (33) 29; Pl. Jam. (102) 17, 18

Sida abutilon — Demonstr. pl. (49) 18; Somn. pl. (68) 15

Sida abutilon alpha — Herb. Amboin. (57) 15

Sida abutilon beta — Herb. Amboin. (57) 15

Sida alba — Fl. Jam. (105) 18

Sida alnifolia — Herb. Amboin. (57) 26

Sida asiatica — Cent. II. pl. (66) 26; Fl. Palaest. (70) 24; Fl. Jam. (105) 18

Sida capitata — Demonstr. pl. (49) 18; Fl. Jam. (105) 18

Sida ciliaris — Pl. Jam. (102) 17; Fl. Jam. (105) 18

Sida cordifolia — Fl. Jam. (105) 18

Sida crispa — Fl. Jam. (105) 18

Sida cristata — Demonstr. pl. (49) 18

Sida foliis cordatis indivisis, stipulis reflexis, pedunculis petiolo longioribus, capsulis hirsutis, calyce brevioribus — Cent. II. pl. (66) 26

Sida foliis cordatis sublobatis, stipulis patentibus, pedunculis petiolo brevioribus, capsulis pendulis obtusis — Cent. II. pl. (66) 26

Sida foliis cordatis sublobatis, stipulis reflexis, pedunculis petiolo longioribus, capsulis scabris calyce longioribus — Cent. II. pl. (66) 26

Sida foliis palmatis: laciniis laciniato-attenuatis — Nova pl. gen. 1751 (32) 30

Sida indica — Cent. II. pl. (66) 26

Sida jamaicensis — Pl. Jam. (102) 17; Fl. Jam. (105) 18

Sida occidentalis — Cent. II. pl. (66) 26

Sida paniculata — Pl. Jam. (102) 17; Fl. Jam. (105) 18

Sida periplocifolia — Fl. Jam. (105) 18

Sida rhombifolia — Fl. Jam. (105) 18

Sida spinosa — Demonstr. pl. (49) 18; Herb. Amboin. (57) 26; Fl. Jam. (105) 18; Pl. rar. Afr. (115) 6

Sida umbellata — Pl. Jam. (102) 17; Fl. Jam. (105) 18

Sida urens — Pl. Jam. (102) 18; Fl. Jam. (105) 18

Sida viscosa — Pl. Jam. (102) 18; Fl. Jam. (105) 18

Sideritis — Oves (61) 14; Nom. bot. (107) 15

Sideritis cretica — Demonstr. pl. (49) 16

Sideritis foliis ovatis lanceolatis inciso serratis — Pl. Mart.-Burs. (6) 19

Sideritis heraclea 3 — Cent. II. pl. (66) 20

Sideritis hirsuta — Fl. Monsp. (74) 19

Sideritis hirsuta lutea — Fl. Angl. (56) 27

Sideritis hirsuta procumbens — Cent. II. pl. (66) 20

Sideritis hyssopifolia — Fl. alp. (71) 19

Sideritis lanata — Fl. Palaest. (70) 22

Sideritis lanata foliis tomentosis, calycibus inermis, verticillis lanatis — Fl. Palaest. (70) 22

Sideritis marrubiastrum — Pan Svec. (26) 26

Sideritis minima — Fl. alp. (71) 19

Sideritis montana — Demonstr. pl. (49) 16; Fl. Palaest. (70) 22

Sideritis romana — Calend. fl. (72) [14], [22]; Fl. Monsp. (74) 19

Sideritis viminea — Pl. Jam. (102) 14

Sideroxylon inerme — Fl. Cap. (99) 12

Sigesbeckia — Hort. Upsal. (7) 37[as Siegesbeckia]; Acrostichum (10) 5

Sigesbeckia orientalis — Demonstr. pl. (49) 23

Silagurium angustifolium — Herb. Amboin. (57) 26

Silagurium vulgare — Herb. Amboin. (57) 26

Silene — Pl. Mart.-Burs. (6) 16, 17; Anandria (9) 5; Fl. oecon. (17) 11; Cui bono? (42) 20; Nom. bot. (107) 13

Silene acaulis — Pan Svec. (26) 23

Silene alpina — Pan Svec. (26) 23

Silene amoena — Demonstr. pl. (49) 12

Silene anglica — Fl. Angl. (56) 16

Silene armeria — Demonstr. pl. (49) 12; Fl. Angl. (56) 16; Fl. Palaest. (70) 19; Calend. fl. (72) [13], [22]; Fl. Monsp. (74) 16; Prodr. fl. Dan. (82) 18; Hort. cul. (132) 23

Silene behen — Fl. Palaest. (70) 19

Silene caule subdichotomo, floribus erectis subsessilibus, foliis lanceolatis piloso-viscidis — Pl. Mart.-Burs. (6) 17; Cent. II. pl. (66) 17

Silene conica — Fl. Angl. (56) 16; Fl. Monsp. (74) 16

Silene conoidea — Demonstr. pl. (49) 12

Silene cretica — Fl. Palaest. (70) 19

Silene fruticosa — Demonstr. pl. (49) 12

Silene gallica — Fl. Monsp. (74) 16

Silene inaperta — Demonstr. pl. (49) 12; Fl. Monsp. (74) 16

Silene lusitanica — Demonstr. pl. (49) 12

Silene muscipula — Fl. Monsp. (74) 16

Silene mutabilis — Cent. II. pl. (66) 16

Silene noctiflora — Demonstr. pl. (49) 12; Fl. Angl. (56) 16

Silene nocturna — Demonstr. pl. (49) 12

Silene nutans — Pan Svec. (26) 23; Herbat. Upsal. (50) 17; Stat. pl. (55) 22; Calend. fl. (72) [12]; Fl. Monsp. (74) 16; Prodr. fl. Dan. (82) 18; Fl. Åker. (162) 12; Pand. fl. Ryb. (165) 19

Silene petalis bifidis, calycibus angulatis pedunculatis, foliis lanceolato-linearibus — Cent. II. pl. (66) 16[as patalis]

Silene petalis bipartitis, fructificationibus erectis subsessilibus; calycibus subpilosis — Cent. II. pl. (66) 16

Silene petalis emarginatis, calycibus glabris reticulato-venosis acuminatis, pedunculo longioribus, caule dichotomo stricto — Cent. II. pl. (66) 17

Silene portensis — Demonstr. pl. (49) [vii], 12; Fund. fr. (123) 12

Silene quinquevulnera — Demonstr. pl. (49) 12; Fl. Monsp. (74) 16

Silene rigidula — Cent. II. pl. (66) 16

Silene rupestris — Herbat. Upsal. (50) 18; Stat. pl. (55) 23; Fl. Monsp. (74) 16

Silene saxifraga — Fl. Monsp. (74) 16

Silene stricta — Cent. II. pl. (66) 17

Silene viscaria — Pan Svec. (26) 23; Herbat. Upsal. (50) 7

Silene westrogothica — Pan Svec. (26) 23

Silpha — Polit. nat. (109) 21; Fund. entom. (154) 18, 29, 30

Silpha aquatica — Pand. fl. Ryb. (165) 7

Silpha atrata — Pand. fl. Ryb. (165) 7

Silpha ferruginea — Pand. fl. Ryb. (165) 7

Silpha opaca — Pand. fl. Ryb. (165) 7

Silpha quadripustulata — Pand. fl. Ryb. (165) 7

Silpha rugosa — Esca avium (174) 6

Silpha sabulosa — Pand. fl. Ryb. (165) 7

Silpha vespillo — Fund. entom. (154) 34; Pand. fl. Ryb. (165) 7

Silphium — Hort. Upsal. (7) 35; Nova pl. gen. 1751 (32) 10; Cul. mut. (88) 2, 8; Fund. fr. (123) 17

Silphium laciniatum — Demonstr. pl. (49) 24

Silphium trilobatum — Pl. Jam. (102) 25; Fl. Jam. (105) 20

Simia — Oecon. nat. (20) 34, 43; Pan Svec. (26) 3; Mus ind. (62) 7; Polit. nat. (109) 16, 20; Anthrop. (111) 2ff.

Simia acauda, digitorum indicum ungue subulato — Mus. Ad.-Frid. (11) [1]

Simia capucina — Ambros. (100) 8

Simia cauda abrupta, unguibus compressis obtusiusculis, pollice palmarum digitis adhaerentc — Mus. Ad.-Frid. (11) [1]

Simia charletoni a robino visa — Mus. Ad.-Frid. (11) [1]

Simia cynocephalos parva, quae caudam non habet — Mus. Ad.-Frid. (11) [1]

Simia ecaudata ferruginea, capite lacertisque pilis reversis — Anthrop. (111) 7

Simia ecaudata subtus nuda abdomine gibboso — Anthrop. (111) 8

Simia parva ex cinereo-fusca, naso productiore, brachiis manibus pedibusque longis tenuibus — Mus. Ad.-Frid. (11) 2

Sinapi erucae folio — Cent. I. pl. (65) 18

Sinapi hispanicum pumilum album — Cent. II. pl. (66) 24

Sinapi orientale maximum, rapi folio — Cent. I. pl. (65) 19

Sinapi quartum candidis floribus — Raphania (126) 19

Sinapi sinense — Herb. Amboin. (57) 22[as Senapi]

Sinapis — Vir. pl. (13) 22; Fl. oecon. (17) 17; Pan Svec. (26) 28; Sapor. med. (31) 19; Pl. escul. (35) 20, 28, 29; Odor. med. (40) 15; Pand. insect. (93) [17, as 38]; Nom. bot. (107) 15; Raphania (126) 13ff.; Var. cib. (156) 18

Sinapis alba — Demonstr. pl. (49) 18; Fl. Angl. (56) 20; Fl. Jam. (105) 24; Hort. cul. (132) 17

Sinapis anguria — Fl. Jam. (105) 24

Sinapis arvensis — Pan Svec. (26) 28; Pl. escul. (35) 20; Herbat. Upsal. (50) 12; Stat. pl. (55) 19; Fl. Angl. (56) 20; Fl. Monsp. (74) 21; Prodr. fl. Dan. (82) 21; Mac. olit. (113) 19; Usum hist. nat. (145) 10; Fl. Åker. (162) 15; Pand. fl. Ryb. (165) 20

Sinapis brassicata — Iter Chin. (161) 9

Sinapis erucoides — Cent. II. pl. (66) 24; Fl. Palaest. (70) 24

Sinapis hispanica — Fl. Palaest. (70) 24

Sinapis incana — Cent. I. pl. (65) 19

Sinapis indica — Calend. fl. (72) [22]

Sinapis juncea — Demonstr. pl. (49) 18

Sinapis laevigata — Cent. I. pl. (65) 20

Sinapis nigra — Demonstr. pl. (49) 18; Pl. officin. (52) 18; Fl. Angl. (56) 20; Fl. Monsp. (74) 21; Prodr. fl. Dan. (82) 21; Hort. cul. (132) 17; Fl. Åker. (162) 15

Sinapis orientalis — Cent. I. pl. (65) 19

Sinapis rapistrum — Fl. Belg. (112) 19

Sinapis siliquis hispidis, rostro obliquo longissimo — Pl. hybr. (33) 15

Sinapis siliquis laevibus aequalibus, foliis lyratis oblongis glabris, caule scabro — Cent. II. pl. (66) 24

Sinapis siliquis laevibus patulis, foliis lyratis glabris: summis lanceolatis, caule laevi — Cent. I. pl. (65) 20

Sinapis siliquis racemo appressis laevibus, foliis inferioribus lyratis scabris: summis lanceolatis, caule scabro — Cent. I. pl. (65) 19

Sinapis siliquis retrorsum hispidis, apice subtetragonis, compressis — Cent. I. pl. (65) 19

Sinapis sylvestris — Cent. I. pl. (65) 18

Sinapister — Herb. Amboin. (57) 19

Sindoc — Herb. Amboin. (57) 9

Siren — Siren. lacert. (146) 13ff.

Siren bartholini — Siren. lacert. (146) plate [1]

Siren lacertina — Siren. lacert. (146) 15, plate [1]

Sirex — Fund. entom. (154) 28, 29

Sirex abdomine mucronato nigro fasciis testaceis — Cent. insect. (129) 29

Sirex camelus — Pand. fl. Ryb. (165) 12

Sirex columba — Cent. insect. (129) 29

Sirex gigas — Pand. fl. Ryb. (165) 12

Siriboa — Herb. Amboin. (57) 22

Sirioides — Herb. Amboin. (57) 19

Sirium — Herb. Amboin. (57) 22

Sirium arborescens — Herb. Amboin. (57) 19

Sirium decumanum — Herb. Amboin. (57) 19

Sirium frigidum — Herb. Amboin. (57) 22

Sirium sylvestre — Herb. Amboin. (57) 22

Sirium terrestre — Herb. Amboin. (57) 22

Sisarum — Vir. pl. (13) 30; Hort. acad. (63) 3; Cul. mut. (88) 2; Nom. bot. (107) 11; Usum hist. nat. (145) 12

Sison — Vir. pl. (13) 19

Sison amomum — Demonstr. pl. (49) 8; Pl. officin. (52) 4; Fl. Angl. (56) 13

Sison aromaticum — Fl. Monsp. (74) 13

Sison canadense — Demonstr. pl. (49) 8

Sison inundatum — Stat. pl. (55) 13; Fl. Angl. (56) 13; Prodr. fl. Dan. (82) 16; Fl. Belg. (112) 15; Colon. pl. (158) 7

Sison segetum — Fl. Angl. (56) 13

Sison verticillatum — Fl. Monsp. (74) 13

Sisymbrium — Hort. Upsal. (7) 41; Vir. pl. (13) 22; Fl. oecon. (17) 17; Pl. escul. (35) 28; Fund. entom. (154) 25

Sisymbrium altissimum — Cent. I. pl. (65) 18; Fl. Monsp. (74) 21; Hist. nat. Rossia (144) 31

Sisymbrium amphibium — Stat. pl. (55) 14; Fl. Angl. (56) 19[as Sisymbrum]; Metam. pl. (67) 16; Fl. Monsp. (74) 21; Prodr. fl. Dan. (82) 21; Fl. Belg. (112) 19; Fl. Åker. (162) 15; Pand. fl. Ryb. (165) 20

Sisymbrium aquaticum — Herbat. Upsal. (50) 12

Sisymbrium arenosum — Prodr. fl. Dan. (82) 21

Sisymbrium asperum — Fl. Monsp. (74) 21

Sisymbrium bursifolium — Cent. II. pl. (66) 24

Sisymbrium caule erecto folioso, racemo flexuoso, foliis lyratis — Cent. II. pl. (66) 24

Sisymbrium foliis infimis capillaceis, summis pinnatifidis — Pl. Mart.-Burs. (6) 7

Sisymbrium foliis integerrimis: infimis tripinnatifidis, supremis integris — Cent. I. pl. (65) 18

Sisymbrium foliis pinnato-hastatis acutis hirtis, caule retrorsum hispido — Cent. I. pl. (65) 18

Sisymbrium foliis pinnato-hastatis tomentosis, caule laevi — Cent. II. pl. (66) 24

Sisymbrium integrifolium — Hist. nat. Rossia (144) 31

Sisymbrium irio — Fl. Angl. (56) 19[as Sisymbrum]; Fl. Palaest. (70) 24; Fl. Monsp. (74) 21; Colon. pl. (158) 5; Esca avium (174) 13

Sisymbrium loeselii — Cent. I. pl. (65) 18; Calend. fl. (72) [22]

Sisymbrium monense — Fl. Angl. (56) 5, 19[as Sisymbrum]

Sisymbrium murale — Fl. Palaest. (70) 24; Fl. Monsp. (74) 21

Sisymbrium nasturtium aquaticum — Pan Svec. (26) 28; Pl. escul. (35) 20; Demonstr. pl. (49) 17; Pl. officin. (52) 14; Fl. Angl. (56) 19[as Sisymbrum]; Fl. Palaest. (70) 24; Fl. Monsp. (74) 21; Prodr. fl. Dan. (82) 21; Fl. Jam. (105) 18, 25; Fl. Belg. (112) 19; Mac. olit. (113) 22

Sisymbrium orientale — Cent. II. pl. (66) 24; Calend. fl. (72) [22]

Sisymbrium pinnatifidum — Pan Svec. (26) 28[as pinatifidum]

Sisymbrium polyceratium — Demonstr. pl. (49) 17; Fl. Monsp. (74) 21

Sisymbrium serratum — Pan Svec. (26) 28

Sisymbrium sophia — Pan Svec. (26) 28; Herbat. Upsal. (50) 12; Pl. officin. (52) 18; Cynogr. (54) 11; Stat. pl. (55) 20; Fl. Angl. (56) 19[as Sisymbrum]; Prodr. fl. Dan. (82) 21; Fl. Belg. (112) 19; Fl. Åker. (162) 15; Pand. fl. Ryb. (165) 20; Esca avium (174) 13

Sisymbrium strictissimum — Demonstr. pl. (49) 17; Fl. alp. (71) 20

Sisymbrium sylvestre — Fl. Angl. (56) 19[as Sisymbrum]; Prodr. fl. Dan. (82) 21; Fl. Belg. (112) 19

Sisymbrium tenuifolium — Cent. I. pl. (65) 18; Fl. Belg. (112) 19

Sisymbrium vimineum — Calend. fl. (72) [22]; Fl. Monsp. (74) 21

Sisyrinchium — Hort. Upsal. (7) 36; Vir. pl. (13) 26; Pl. rar. Afr. (115) 10[as Sisyrrhinchium]

Sisyrinchium bermudiana — Demonstr. pl. (49) 24; Calend. fl. (72) [15][as Sisyrrinchium]; Fl. Jam. (105) 20[as Sichyrinchium]

Sisyrinchium ramosum aethiopicum, foliis plicatis nervosis et incanis, radice tuberosa phoenicea — Cent. II. pl. (66) 4[as Sisyrrhinchium]

Sisyrinchium viperarum — Pl. rar. Afr. (115) 8

Sitta ano sanguineo — Chin. Lagerstr. (64) 10[as sanguinaeo]

Sitta europaea — Migr. avium (79) 23

Sitta palpebra inferiori purpurea — Chin. Lagerstr. (64) 10[as purpuraea]

Sium — Hort. Upsal. (7) 41; Vir. pl. (13) 29; Noxa insect. (46) 27; Pand. insect. (93) 13; Mors. serp. (119) 2

Sium falcaria — Fl. Monsp. (74) 13

Sium latifolium — Herbat. Upsal. (50) 14; Stat. pl. (55) 13; Fl. Angl. (56) 13; Fl. Monsp. (74) 13; Prodr. fl. Dan. (82) 16; Fl. Belg. (112) 15; Fl. Åker. (162) 9

Sium majus — Pan Svec. (26) 19; Hosp. insect. fl. (43) 19

Sium ninsi — Pl. officin. (52) 14

Sium nodiflorum — Stat. pl. (55) 13; Fl. Angl. (56) 13; Fl. Monsp. (74) 13; Prodr. fl. Dan. (82) 16; Fl. Belg. (112) 15

Sium sisarum — Demonstr. pl. (49) 8; Calend. fl. (72) [17]; Cul. mut. (88) 5; Mac. olit. (113) 11; Hort. cul. (132) 17

Sloanea emarginata — Fl. Jam. (105) 17

Smilax — Fl. Monsp. (74) 7

Smilax aspera — Demonstr. pl. (49) 26; Fl. Palaest. (70) 31; Fl. Monsp. (74) 28; Mac. olit. (113) 13

Smilax china — Pl. officin. (52) 8; Herb. Amboin. (57) 24; Fl. Jam. (105) 22

Smilax excelsa — Fl. Palaest. (70) 31

Smilax pseudo-china — Fl. Jam. (105) 22

Smilax sarsaparilla — Pl. officin. (52) 17

Smilax siliqua sursum rigente — Cent. I. pl. (65) 23

Smyrnium — Hort. Upsal. (7) 36; Nom. bot. (107) 11

Smyrnium aegyptiacum — Cent. I. pl. (65) 10; Fl. Palaest. (70) 16

Smyrnium aureum — Pl. rar. Afr. (115) 6

Smyrnium foliis floralibus, binis, cordatis, integerrimis — Cent. I. pl. (65) 10

Smyrnium integerrimum — Demonstr. pl. (49) 8

Smyrnium olusatrum — Demonstr. pl. (49) 8; Fl.
Angl. (56) 13; Fl. Monsp. (74) 13; Fl. Belg. (112)
9, 15

Smyrnium perfoliatum — Fl. Palaest. (70) 16

Smyrnium tenuifolium — Fl. Angl. (56) 27; Cent. II.
pl. (66) 13

Soccus arbor major — Herb. Amboin. (57) 7

Soccus arbor minor — Herb. Amboin. (57) 7

Soccus granosus — Herb. Amboin. (57) 7

Soccus sylvestris — Herb. Amboin. (57) 7

Sojar volubilis — Herb. Amboin. (57) 8

Solanum — Ficus (2) 22; Hort. Upsal. (7) 37; Vir. pl.
(13) 18, 19, 31; Fl. oecon. (17) 5; Gem. arb. (24) 6;
Pl. hybr. (33) 29; Odor. med. (40) 13, 16; Fr. Svec.
(91) [ii]; Nom. bot. (107) 11; Dulcamara (164) 5, 7

Solanum aethiopicum — Cent. II. pl. (66) 10

Solanum arborescens indicum, foliis napecae
majoribus magis mucronatis — Lign. colubr. (21)
17

Solanum bahamense — Somn. pl. (68) 10; Fl. Jam.
(105) 14

Solanum bonariense — Demonstr. pl. (49) 6

Solanum caule inermi herbaceo, foliis ovatis dentato-
angulatis, pedunculis fertilibus unifloris — Cent.
II. pl. (66) 10

Solanum caule inermi herbaceo, foliis pinnatis
integerrimis, racemis simplicibus — Cent. I. pl.
(65) 8

Solanum dulcamara — Gem. arb. (24) 22; Pan Svec.
(26) 17; Herbat. Upsal. (50) 17; Pl. officin. (52) 9;
Stat. pl. (55) 14; Fl. Angl. (56) 12; Fl. Monsp. (74)
12; Prodr. fl. Dan. (82) 15; Fr. Svec. (91) 4, 18; Fl.
Belg. (112) 14; Fl. Åker. (162) 9; Dulcamara (164)
5ff.; Pand. fl. Ryb. (165) 17; Esca avium (174) 11

Solanum guineense — Fl. Cap. (99) 12

Solanum incanum — Fl. Palaest. (70) 15; Fr. escul.
(127) 9

Solanum indicum — Herb. Amboin. (57) 21; Iter
Chin. (161) 7

Solanum lignosum — Dulcamara (164) 6

Solanum lycopersicum — Demonstr. pl. (49) 6[as
lycopersicon]; Herb. Amboin. (57) 24[as
lycopersicon]; Fl. Jam. (105) 14; Fr. escul. (127) 9;
Dulcamara (164) 7

Solanum mammosum — Demonstr. pl. (49) 6; Fl.
Jam. (105) 14; Pl. Surin. (177) 6

Solanum melongena — Demonstr. pl. (49) 6; Herb.
Amboin. (57) 21; Fl. Palaest. (70) 15; Fl. Cap. (99)
12; Fl. Jam. (105) 14; Fr. escul. (127) 9; Dulcamara
(164) 7[as mellangena]

Solanum nigrum — Pl. officin. (52) 18; Stat. pl. (55)
20; Fl. Angl. (56) 12; Herb. Amboin. (57) 26; Fl.
Palaest. (70) 15; Fl. Monsp. (74) 12; Prodr. fl. Dan.
(82) 15; Fl. Jam. (105) 14, 25; Fl. Belg. (112) 14;
Hist. nat. Rossia (144) 28; Fl. Åker. (162) 9;
Dulcamara (164) 5; Pand. fl. Ryb. (165) 17

Solanum nigrum guineense — Demonstr. pl. (49) 6

Solanum nigrum judaicum — Demonstr. pl. (49) 6

Solanum nigrum villosum — Demonstr. pl. (49) 6

Solanum officinarum — Pl. Mart.-Burs. (6) 12

Solanum peruvianum — Demonstr. pl. (49) 6; Fl.
Jam. (105) 14

Solanum pimpinellifolium — Demonstr. pl. (49) 6;
Cent. I. pl. (65) 8

Solanum pomiferum, fructu rotundo striato duro —
Cent. II. pl. (66) 11

Solanum pomiferum herbariorum — Cent. II. pl. (66)
11

Solanum pseudocapsicum — Demonstr. pl. (49) 6

Solanum quercifolium — Demonstr. pl. (49) 6; Pl.
Alstr. (121) 11; Dulcamara (164) 7

Solanum racemosum — Pl. Surin. (177) 6

Solanum radicans — Pl. Alstr. (121) 11

Solanum scandens — Dulcamara (164) 6; Pl. Surin.
(177) 6

Solanum sodomeum — Demonstr. pl. (49) 6; Fl. Cap.
(99) 12

Solanum subinerme — Pl. Surin. (177) 6

Solanum tomentosum — Fl. Cap. (99) 12

Solanum triphyllum brasilianum — Pl. Mart.-Burs.
(6) 12

Solanum triphyllum canadense — Pl. Mart.-Burs. (6)
12

Solanum tuberosum — Demonstr. pl. (49) 6; Pane
diaet. (83) 20; Transm. frum. (87) 3; Fl. Jam. (105)
14; Mac. olit. (113) 12; Hort. cul. (132) 17;
Dulcamara (164) 7; Aphyteia (185) 12

Solanum vulgare — Pan Svec. (26) 17

Soldanella — Fl. Belg. (112) 10

Soldanella alpina — Fl. alp. (71) 13

Solen — Fund. test. (166) 18, 31, 41

Solen strigilatum — Fund. test. (166) 41

Solidago — Anandria (9) 12; Vir. pl. (13) 23; Pand.
insect. (93) 18; Nom. bot. (107) 17

Solidago alpina — Fl. alp. (71) 22; Fl. Monsp. (74) 7,
25

Solidago altissima — Specif. Canad. (76) 9

Solidago canadensis — Demonstr. pl. (49) 23;
Calend. fl. (72) [17]

Solidago doronicum — Fl. alp. (71) 22; Fl. Monsp.
(74) 25

Solidago lateriflora — Demonstr. pl. (49) 23

Solidago maritima — Pan Svec. (26) 33

Solidago scanica — Pan Svec. (26) 33

Solidago sempervirens — Demonstr. pl. (49) 23;
Calend. fl. (72) [21]

Solidago serotina — Calend. fl. (72) [19]

Solidago virgaurea — Pan Svec. (26) 33[as virga
aurea]; Pl. officin. (52) 20[as virga aurea]; Stat. pl.
(55) 18[as virga aurea]; Fl. Angl. (56) 22; Fl.
Palaest. (70) 28; Fl. Monsp. (74) 25; Prodr. fl. Dan.
(82) 23[as virga aurea]; Fl. Belg. (112) 21; Fl.

Åker. (162) 18[as virga auraea]; Pand. fl. Ryb. (165) 21

Solidago virginiana — Calend. fl. (72) [15]

Solium — Taenia (19) 13; Hypericum (186) 11

Solulus arbor — Herb. Amboin. (57) 14

Sonchus — Fl. oecon. (17) 19; Pl. escul. (35) 28; Cui bono? (42) 20; Fl. Angl. (56) 6; Pand. insect. (93) [17, as 38]; Nom. bot. (107) 17

Sonchus alpinus — Pl. escul. (35) 22; Vern. arb. (47) 8, 9; Demonstr. pl. (49) [vii], 22; Stat. pl. (55) 6, 16; Fl. alp. (71) 21, 24; Calend. fl. (72) [17]; Fl. Monsp. (74) 24; Mac. olit. (113) 14; Rar. Norv. (157) 11

Sonchus amboinicus — Herb. Amboin. (57) 22

Sonchus annuus — Pl. escul. (35) 22

Sonchus aphyllocaulis — Fl. Angl. (56) 26

Sonchus arvensis — Hosp. insect. fl. (43) 30; Herbat. Upsal. (50) 13; Stat. pl. (55) 18; Fl. Angl. (56) 21; Calend. fl. (72) [16]; Fl. Monsp. (74) 24; Prodr. fl. Dan. (82) 22; Fl. Belg. (112) 20; Fl. Åker. (162) 17; Pand. fl. Ryb. (165) 21

Sonchus laevis — Pan Svec. (26) 31

Sonchus laevis in plurimas et tenuissimas lacinias divisi — Pl. Mart.-Burs. (6) 7

Sonchus lapponicus — Pan Svec. (26) 31

Sonchus maritimus — Pand. fl. Ryb. (165) 21

Sonchus oleraceus — Stat. pl. (55) 19; Fl. Angl. (56) 21; Fl. Palaest. (70) 27; Fl. Monsp. (74) 24; Prodr. fl. Dan. (82) 22; Fl. Jam. (105) 19, 25; Fl. Belg. (112) 20; Pl. rar. Afr. (115) 6; Fl. Åker. (162) 17; Pand. fl. Ryb. (165) 21; Esca avium (174) 14[as oleraccus]

Sonchus oleraceus asper — Herbat. Upsal. (50) 15

Sonchus oleraceus laevis — Herbat. Upsal. (50) 15

Sonchus palustris — Demonstr. pl. (49) 22; Fl. Angl. (56) 21; Calend. fl. (72) [17]; Fl. Belg. (112) 8, 20

Sonchus pedunculis tomentosis — Pl. Mart.-Burs. (6) 7

Sonchus repens — Pan Svec. (26) 31

Sonchus rotundo folio — Fl. Angl. (56) 26

Sonchus sibiricus — Demonstr. pl. (49) 22; Calend. fl. (72) [13]; Hist. nat. Rossia (144) 32

Sonchus tenerrimus — Demonstr. pl. (49) 22; Fl. Monsp. (74) 24

Sonchus volubilis — Herb. Amboin. (57) 22

Soncorus — Herb. Amboin. (57) 20

Songium — Herb. Amboin. (57) 9

Sophia — Migr. avium (79) 32, 34; Nom. bot. (107) 15; Pl. Surin. (177) 4

Sophia carolina — Pl. Surin. (177) 11

Sophora — Pand. insect. (93) 14

Sophora biflora — Fl. Cap. (99) 14

Sophora foliis ternatis, spica verticillata — Pl. rar. Camsch. (30) 17

Sophora genistoides — Fl. Cap. (99) 14

Sophora heptaphylla — Demonstr. pl. (49) 11; Pl. officin. (52) 18[as leptaphylla]; Herb. Amboin. (57) 5, 16; Obs. mat. med. (171) 4

Sophora lupinoides — Hist. nat. Rossia (144) 29

Sophora tomentosa — Fl. Jam. (105) 16; Iter Chin. (161) 7

Sorbus — Vir. pl. (13) 21, 36; Fl. oecon. (17) 12; Pl. escul. (35) 16, 27; Noxa insect. (46) 26; Vern. arb. (47) 10, table; Calend. fl. (72) [20]; Migr. avium (79) 32; Pand. insect. (93) 15; Nom. bot. (107) 13; Inebr. (117) 13; Nect. fl. (122) 6

Sorbus aucuparia — Gem. arb. (24) 23; Pan Svec. (26) 24; Hosp. insect. fl. (43) 23; Herbat. Upsal. (50) 7; Pl. officin. (52) 18; Fl. Angl. (56) 17; Fl. Palaest. (70) 20; Calend. fl. (72) [10]; Fl. Monsp. (74) 17; Prodr. fl. Dan. (82) 18; Arb. Svec. (101) 7, 9, 19, 30; Fl. Belg. (112) 17; Fl. Åker. (162) 12; Pand. fl. Ryb. (165) 19; Esca avium (174) 12

Sorbus domestica — Fl. Angl. (56) 17; Fl. Monsp. (74) 17

Sorbus hybrida — Fund. fr. (123) 15, 21; Rar. Norv. (157) 9

Sorbus sativa — Fr. escul. (127) 8

Sorex — Vir. pl. (13) 16; Oecon. nat. (20) 44; Polit. nat. (109) 15; Mors. serp. (119) 2

Sorex minutus — Siren. lacert. (146) 8

Sorex sylvaticus americanus — Mus. Ad.-Frid. (11) 2

Sorgum — Herb. Amboin. (57) 20; Fund. agrost. (152) 16

Sparganium — Hort. Upsal. (7) 41; Spons. pl. (12) 29, 39; Fl. oecon. (17) 21; Nom. bot. (107) 18; Fund. agrost. (152) 4, 15

Sparganium erectum — Pan Svec. (26) 35; Herbat. Upsal. (50) 14[as Sperganium]; Fl. Angl. (56) 24; Fl. Monsp. (74) 27; Prodr. fl. Dan. (82) 24; Fl. Belg. (112) 22; Fl. Åker. (162) 19; Pand. fl. Ryb. (165) 22

Sparganium natans — Pan Svec. (26) 35; Stat. pl. (55) 12; Fl. Angl. (56) 24; Prodr. fl. Dan. (82) 24; Fl. Åker. (162) 19; Pand. fl. Ryb. (165) 22

Spartium — Hort. Upsal. (7) 36; Fl. oecon. (17) 18; Pl. escul. (35) 20, 29; Fr. Svec. (91) [ii]; Fund. agrost. (152) 16

Spartium arenosum — Fl. Palaest. (70) 25

Spartium capense — Pl. rar. Afr. (115) 14[as Spatium]

Spartium complicatum — Fl. Monsp. (74) 22[as Sparteum]

Spartium foliis superioribus sparsis filiformibus — Pl. rar. Afr. (115) 13

Spartium junceum — Demonstr. pl. (49) 19; Fl. Palaest. (70) 25; Fl. Monsp. (74) 22[as Sparteum]

Spartium monospermum — Fl. Palaest. (70) 25

Spartium procumbens — Pan Svec. (26) 30

Spartium ramis lateralibus alternis, foliis alternis lanceolatis — Pl. rar. Afr. (115) 14[as Spatium ... lateraribus]

Spartium scoparium — Demonstr. pl. (49) 19; Stat. pl. (55) 21; Fl. Angl. (56) 20; Hort. acad. (63) 10; Fl. Monsp. (74) 22[as Sparteum]; Prodr. fl. Dan. (82) 21; Fr. Svec. (91) 4[as scoparicum], 20; Fl. Belg. (112) 8, 20; Pl. rar. Afr. (115) 13; Colon. pl. (158) 7

Spartium scorpius — Fl. Monsp. (74) 22[as Sparteum]

Spartium spinosum — Fl. Palaest. (70) 25; Fl. Monsp. (74) 22[as Sparteum]

Spartum herba alterum — Cent. I. pl. (65) 4

Spartum herba plinii — Cent. I. pl. (65) 6

Sparus — Mus. Ad.-Frid. (11) 36

Sparus fasciis quinque transversis, subfuscis — Mus. Ad.-Frid. (11) 34

Spathe — Fl. Jam. (105) 27

Spergula — Pl. Mart.-Burs. (6) 18; Fl. oecon. (17) 11; Pl. escul. (35) 15, 27; Nom. bot. (107) 13

Spergula arvensis — Herbat. Upsal. (50) 12; Stat. pl. (55) 19; Fl. Angl. (56) 16; Prodr. fl. Dan. (82) 18; Pane diaet. (83) 20; Fl. Belg. (112) 17; Usum hist. nat. (145) 10; Fl. Åker. (162) 12; Pand. fl. Ryb. (165) 19

Spergula germanica — Pan Svec. (26) 23

Spergula laricina — Hist. nat. Rossia (144) 29

Spergula nodosa — Herbat. Upsal. (50) 13; Stat. pl. (55) 14; Fl. Angl. (56) 16; Prodr. fl. Dan. (82) 18; Fl. Belg. (112) 17; Pand. fl. Ryb. (165) 19

Spergula pentandra — Fl. Angl. (56) 16; Fl. Monsp. (74) 16

Spergula saginoides — Hist. nat. Rossia (144) 29

Spergula verticillata — Pan Svec. (26) 23

Spermacoce — Vir. pl. (13) 18; Herb. Amboin. (57) 26

Spermacoce hispida — Fl. Jam. (105) 13

Spermacoce tenuior — Fl. Jam. (105) 13

Spermacoce verticillata — Fl. Cap. (99) 11; Fl. Jam. (105) 13

Sphaeranthus — Gem. arb. (24) 13

Sphagnum — Fl. oecon. (17) 28; Oecon. nat. (20) [5, as 7], 19; Splachnum (27) 5, 6; Sem. musc. (28) 6, 17; Cui bono? (42) 13; Buxbaumia (85) 14; Fund. agrost. (152) 9; Ledum (178) 6, 7

Sphagnum palustre — Herbat. Upsal. (50) 6; Stat. pl. (55) 15; Prodr. fl. Dan. (82) 25; Usum musc. (148) 5, 9, 11; Pand. fl. Ryb. (165) 23

Sphex — Mors. serp. (119) 2; Fund. entom. (154) 22, 24

Sphex abdomine plicato atro, alis subviolaceis — Cent. insect. (129) 29

Sphex arenaria — Pand. fl. Ryb. (165) 13

Sphex caerulea — Cent. insect. (129) 29

Sphex caerulea, alis fuscis — Cent. insect. (129) 29

Sphex cribraria — Pand. fl. Ryb. (165) 13

Sphex fossoria — Pand. fl. Ryb. (165) 13

Sphex leucostoma — Pand. fl. Ryb. (165) 13

Sphex ligustri — Pand. insect. (93) 13

Sphex pectinipes — Pand. fl. Ryb. (165) 12

Sphex pensylvanica — Cent. insect. (129) 29

Sphex rufipes — Pand. fl. Ryb. (165) 13

Sphex rybyensis — Pand. fl. Ryb. (165) 13

Sphex sabulosa — Pand. fl. Ryb. (165) 12, 13

Sphex tropica — Iter Chin. (161) 7

Sphex vaga — Pand. fl. Ryb. (165) 13

Sphex viatica — Pand. fl. Ryb. (165) 12

Sphinx — Fl. Cap. (99) [1]; Fund. fr. (123) 20; Iter Chin. (161) 7

Sphinx alecto — Iter Chin. (161) 7

Sphinx alis integris omnibus margine postico albo punctis, abdomine ocellis duodecim fulvis — Cent. insect. (129) 27

Sphinx apiformis — Pand. fl. Ryb. (165) 11

Sphinx atropos — Pand. insect. (93) 11

Sphinx caricae — Pand. insect. (93) 22

Sphinx celerio — Pand. insect. (93) 12

Sphinx convolvuli — Pand. insect. (93) 12

Sphinx elpenor — Pand. insect. (93) 12, 13, 18

Sphinx euphorbiae — Pand. insect. (93) 11, 14[as Spinx]

Sphinx ficus — Pand. insect. (93) [23, as 31]

Sphinx filipendulae — Pand. insect. (93) 15; Pand. fl. Ryb. (165) 11

Sphinx labruscae — Pand. insect. (93) 12

Sphinx ligustri — Pand. insect. (93) 11, 12, [23, as 31]

Sphinx nerii — Pand. insect. (93) 12

Sphinx ocellata — Pand. insect. (93) 15, 21

Sphinx pinastri — Pand. insect. (93) 20

Sphinx polymita — Iter Chin. (161) 13

Sphinx populi — Pand. insect. (93) 21, 22

Sphinx porcellus — Pand. insect. (93) 13, 18; Iter Chin. (161) 10[as Spinx]

Sphinx salicis — Pand. insect. (93) 21, 22

Sphinx sexta — Cent. insect. (129) 27

Sphinx statices — Pand. fl. Ryb. (165) 11

Sphinx stellatarum — Pand. insect. (93) 11

Sphinx tiliae — Pand. insect. (93) 16

Sphinx vitis — Pand. insect. (93) 12

Spica trifolia — Cent. I. pl. (65) 24

Spigelia anthelmia — Spigelia (89) 10ff.; Fl. Jam. (105) 9, 14; Obs. mat. med. (171) 2

Spigelia anthelmintica — Specif. Canad. (76) 16, 27

Spigelia ramis indivisis, foliis terminalibus, verticillatis — Spigelia (89) 12

Spina vaccarum — Herb. Amboin. (57) 18

Spinacia — Sapor. med. (31) 11; Rhabarbarum (41) 23; Hort. acad. (63) 3; Cul. mut. (88) 2; Nom. bot. (107) 18; Scorb. (180) 21

Spinacia oleracea — Demonstr. pl. (49) 26; Pl. officin. (52) 18; Cul. mut. (88) 3; Mac. olit. (113) 17; Hort. cul. (132) 14; Hist. nat. Rossia (144) 18

Spiraea — Hort. Upsal. (7) 21; Fr. Svec. (91) [ii], 24; Pand. insect. (93) 15; Nect. fl. (122) 6

Spiraea aruncus — Fl. Monsp. (74) 17

Spiraea chamaedrifolia — Hist. nat. Rossia (144) 30

Spiraea crenata — Hist. nat. Rossia (144) 23, 24[as Spirea], 30

Spiraea filipendula — Herbat. Upsal. (50) 6; Pl. officin. (52) 17; Stat. pl. (55) 20; Fl. Angl. (56) 17; Fl. Monsp. (74) 17; Prodr. fl. Dan. (82) 18; Pane diaet. (83) 20; Fl. Belg. (112) 17; Fl. Åker. (162) 13; Pand. fl. Ryb. (165) 19

Spiraea foliis integerrimis, umbellis sessilibus — Pl. rar. Camsch. (30) 5

Spiraea foliis pinnatis — Pl. rar. Camsch. (30) 19

Spiraea hypericifolia — Gem. arb. (24) 21; Hist. nat. Rossia (144) 12, 23, 24[as Spirea]

Spiraea salicifolia — Demonstr. pl. (49) 14; Calend. fl. (72) [10], [13]; Fr. Svec. (91) 5, 22; Hist. nat. Rossia (144) 22, 30

Spiraea sorbifolia — Hist. nat. Rossia (144) 24, 30; Usum hist. nat. (145) 12

Spiraea sorbifolio tenuiter crenato, floribus in thyrso albis — Pl. rar. Camsch. (30) 19

Spiraea theophrasti — Gem. arb. (24) 21; Hosp. insect. fl. (43) 24

Spiraea trifoliata — Specif. Canad. (76) 16; Viola ipecac. (176) [4]

Spiraea ulmaria — Herbat. Upsal. (50) 7; Pl. officin. (52) 20; Stat. pl. (55) 14; Fl. Angl. (56) 17; Calend. fl. (72) [15]; Fl. Monsp. (74) 17; Prodr. fl. Dan. (82) 18; Fl. Belg. (112) 17; Fl. Åker. (162) 13; Pand. fl. Ryb. (165) 19

Spiranthes — Hosp. insect. fl. (43) 13

Splachnum — Splachnum (27) 7ff.; Sem. musc. (28) 6, 17; Nova pl. gen. 1751 (32) 46, 48; Buxbaumia (85) 6

Splachnum ampullaceum — Herbat. Upsal. (50) 20; Stat. pl. (55) 15; Usum musc. (148) 12; Rar. Norv. (157) 5

Splachnum luteum — Stat. pl. (55) 15; Fl. alp. (71) 24; Usum musc. (148) 12

Splachnum rubrum — Stat. pl. (55) 15; Fl. alp. (71) 23; Hist. nat. Rossia (144) 34; Usum musc. (148) 12

Splachnum umbraculo convexo — Splachnum (27) 8

Splachnum umbraculo inflato turbinato — Nova pl. gen. 1751 (32) 47

Splachnum umbraculo membranaceo convexo — Nova pl. gen. 1751 (32) 47

Splachnum umbraculo membranaceo plano — Nova pl. gen. 1751 (32) 47[as Splacnum]

Splachnum umbraculo plano — Splachnum (27) 9

Splachnum vasculosum — Usum musc. (148) 12

Spondias — Pl. escul. (35) 4

Spondias mombin — Fl. Jam. (105) 16; Fr. escul. (127) 13

Spondias myrobalanus — Fl. Jam. (105) 16

Spondylococcus — Nova pl. gen. 1751 (32) 8, 12

Spondylus — Fund. test. (166) 18

Spondylus gaederopus — Fund. test. (166) 42

Spongia — Anim. comp. (98) 2

Spongia fluviatilis — Herbat. Upsal. (50) 14

Spongia lacustris — Stat. pl. (55) 12

Spongia officinalis — Pl. officin. (52) 18

Squalus — Oecon. nat. (20) 45; Noctiluca (39) [1]; Nat. pelagi (84) 11, 12; Fl. Cap. (99) [1]; Polit. nat. (109) 12; Iter Chin. (161) 6

Squamaria — Betula (1) 12; Hort. Upsal. (7) 33; Fung. melit. (69) 3

Stachys — Vir. pl. (13) 29, 31, 35; Fl. oecon. (17) 16; Pan Svec. (26) 11; Pl. escul. (35) 27, 28; Odor. med. (40) 13

Stachys alpina — Demonstr. pl. (49) 16; Calend. fl. (72) [14]

Stachys arvensis — Pan Svec. (26) 27

Stachys cretica — Demonstr. pl. (49) 16; Calend. fl. (72) [16]

Stachys foetida — Pan Svec. (26) 27; Stat. pl. (55) 8[as Stachy]

Stachys germanica — Demonstr. pl. (49) 16; Fl. Angl. (56) 18; Calend. fl. (72) [16]; Fl. Monsp. (74) 19

Stachys palustris — Pl. escul. (35) 19; Stat. pl. (55) 18; Fl. Angl. (56) 18; Fl. Monsp. (74) 19; Prodr. fl. Dan. (82) 20; Pane diaet. (83) 20; Ping. anim. (108) 15; Fl. Belg. (112) 18; Usum hist. nat. (145) 10; Fl. Åker. (162) 14

Stachys spinosa — Fl. Palaest. (70) 23

Stachys sylvatica — Herbat. Upsal. (50) 8; Stat. pl. (55) 17; Fl. Angl. (56) 18; Cervus (60) 8; Calend. fl. (72) [13][as Sachys]; Fl. Monsp. (74) 19; Prodr. fl. Dan. (82) 20; Med. grav. (92) 9; Pl. tinct. (97) 20; Fl. Belg. (112) 18; Fl. Åker. (162) 14; Pand. fl. Ryb. (165) 20

Staehelina centauroides — Fl. Cap. (99) 17

Staehelina dubia — Fl. Monsp. (74) 25

Staehelina gnaphalodes — Fl. Cap. (99) 17

Stapelia — Spons. pl. (12) 56; Vir. pl. (13) 24, 31; Odor. med. (40) 13; Fl. Cap. (99) 6, 8; Pl. rar. Afr. (115) 4; Pl. Alstr. (121) 5; Nect. fl. (122) 13

Stapelia denticulis ramorum erectis — Spons. pl. (12) 17

Stapelia hirsuta — Fl. Cap. (99) 12

Stapelia variegata — Demonstr. pl. (49) 7; Fl. Cap. (99) 4, 12

Staphisagria — Vir. pl. (13) 21; Usum hist. nat. (145) 29

Staphylea — Nom. bot. (107) 11[as Staphylaea]

Staphylea pinnata — Fl. Angl. (56) 14[as Staphyllaea]

Staphylea pinnatifolia — Gem. arb. (24) 28[as Staphylaea]

Staphylea trifolia — Demonstr. pl. (49) 9[as Staphyllea]

Staphylinus biguttatus — Pand. fl. Ryb. (165) 10

Staphylinus boleti — Pand. insect. (93) [23, as 31]

Staphylinus chrysomelinus — Pand. fl. Ryb. (165) 10

Staphylinus erythropterus — Pand. fl. Ryb. (165) 10

Staphylinus lignorum — Pand. fl. Ryb. (165) 10

Staphylinus maxillosus — Pand. fl. Ryb. (165) 10

Staphylinus murinus — Pand. fl. Ryb. (165) 9

Staphylinus piceus — Pand. fl. Ryb. (165) 10

Staphylinus politus — Pand. fl. Ryb. (165) 10; Esca avium (174) 7

Statice — Hort. Upsal. (7) 35; Gem. arb. (24) 13; Pl. hybr. (33) 29; Pl. tinct. (97) 10; Nom. bot. (107) 11; Fund. fr. (123) 16

Statice armeria — Herbat. Upsal. (50) 12; Stat. pl. (55) 21; Fl. Angl. (56) 14; Fl. Monsp. (74) 14; Prodr. fl. Dan. (82) 16; Fl. Belg. (112) 15; Pand. fl. Ryb. (165) 18, 21

Statice capitata — Pan Svec. (26) 19

Statice caule nudo simplicissimo capitato — Pl. Mart.-Burs. (6) 17

Statice echioides — Fl. Monsp. (74) 14

Statice flava — Fl. Palaest. (70) 17

Statice flexuosa — Hist. nat. Rossia (144) 28

Statice limonium — Pan Svec. (26) 19; Demonstr. pl. (49) 9; Pl. officin. (52) 5; Fl. Angl. (56) 14; Fl. Monsp. (74) 14; Prodr. fl. Dan. (82) 16; Fl. Belg. (112) 15; Fl. Åker. (162) 10

Statice monopetala — Fl. Palaest. (70) 17; Fl. Monsp. (74) 14

Statice reticulata — Fl. Monsp. (74) 14

Statice sinuata — Fl. Palaest. (70) 17; Fl. Cap. (99) 13

Statice speciosa — Hist. nat. Rossia (144) 28

Statice tatarica — Hist. nat. Rossia (144) 28

Stella chinensis pereleganz, dupliciter radiata — Chin. Lagerstr. (64) 32

Stella marina decacnemos fimbriata — Chin. Lagerstr. (64) 32

Stellaria — Nova pl. gen. 1751 (32) 42; Nom. bot. (107) 13

Stellaria aquatica — Cent. I. pl. (65) 31

Stellaria biflora — Stat. pl. (55) 16; Fl. alp. (71) 17; Rar. Norv. (157) 10

Stellaria cerastoides — Fl. alp. (71) 17

Stellaria dichotoma — Fl. alp. (71) 17; Hist. nat. Rossia (144) 29

Stellaria foliis omnibus angustis, apice resecto — Cent. I. pl. (65) 31

Stellaria foliis omnibus subrotundis — Cent. I. pl. (65) 31

Stellaria graminea — Herbat. Upsal. (50) 14; Prodr. fl. Dan. (82) 18; Fl. Belg. (112) 16; Fl. Åker. (162) 12; Pand. fl. Ryb. (165) 19; Esca avium (174) 12

Stellaria graminea aquatica — Prodr. fl. Dan. (82) 18

Stellaria holostea — Stat. pl. (55) 17; Fl. Monsp. (74) 16; Prodr. fl. Dan. (82) 18; Fl. Belg. (112) 16

Stellaria nemorum — Stat. pl. (55) 17; Fl. Monsp. (74) 16; Prodr. fl. Dan. (82) 18; Fl. Belg. (112) 16

Stellera — Nova pl. gen. 1747 (14) [vi], 16

Stellera chamaejasme — Hist. nat. Rossia (144) 29

Stellera foliis lanceolatis, corollis quinquefidis — Nova pl. gen. 1747 (14) 16

Stellera foliis linearibus, corollis quadrifidis — Nova pl. gen. 1747 (14) 17

Stellera passerina — Fl. Monsp. (74) 15

Stemodia — Fl. Jam. (105) 26

Stemodia maritima — Pl. Jam. (102) 15; Fl. Jam. (105) 18

Stenocoris — Fund. entom. (154) 30

Sterculia — Nova pl. gen. 1747 (14) [vi], 29

Sterculia balanghas — Herb. Amboin. (57) 14

Sterculia foetida — Herb. Amboin. (57) 14

Sterculia foliis digitatis — Nova pl. gen. 1747 (14) 29

Sterculia foliis ovalibus integerrimis, alternis petiolatis, floribus paniculatis — Nova pl. gen. 1747 (14) 29

Sterna — Oecon. nat. (20) [37, as 7]; Migr. avium (79) 26; Polit. nat. (109) 13

Sterna hirundo — Migr. avium (79) 16

Sterna nigra, fronte albicante, cauda cuneiformi — Chin. Lagerstr. (64) 12

Sterna stolida — Chin. Lagerstr. (64) 12

Sterna stulta — Nat. pelagi (84) 13

Stewartia — Nova pl. gen. 1747 (14) [iv][as Stewertia]; Nova pl. gen. 1751 (32) 10, 12; Pot. theae (142) 9[as Steuartia], 10[as Steuartia]

Stillingia sylvatica — Obs. mat. med. (171) 6

Stincus — Mat. med. anim. (29) 11

Stipa — Fund. agrost. (152) 27, 30, 36

Stipa aristis basi pilosis, panicula spicata, foliis filiformibus — Cent. I. pl. (65) 6

Stipa juncea — Fl. Monsp. (74) 9

Stipa pennata — Fl. Angl. (56) 11; Fl. Monsp. (74) 9; Fund. agrost. (152) 21

Stipa tenacissima — Cent. I. pl. (65) 6

Stisseria — Vir. pl. (13) 10

Stoebe aethiopica — Fl. Cap. (99) 17

Stoebe cauliculis argenteis minor — Pl. Mart.-Burs. (6) 23[as Staebe]

Stoechas — Hort. Upsal. (7) 36; Vir. pl. (13) 23; Sapor. med. (31) 9; Fl. Monsp. (74) 7

Stoechas purpurea — Pl. Mart.-Burs. (6) 19[as Staechas]

Stomoxoides — Fund. entom. (154) 30

Stramonia indica — Herb. Amboin. (57) 21

Stramonium ferox — Demonstr. pl. (49) 6

Stramonium longioribus aculeis — Demonstr. pl. (49) 6

Stratiotes — Spons. pl. (12) 44; Fl. oecon. (17) 15; Morb. hyeme (38) 8; Noxa insect. (46) 24; Pand. insect. (93) 16

Stratiotes aloides — Hosp. insect. fl. (43) 26; Herbat. Upsal. (50) 11; Stat. pl. (55) 13; Fl. Angl. (56) 18; Prodr. fl. Dan. (82) 19; Fl. Belg. (112) 18

Stratiotes aquatica — Pan Svec. (26) 25

Strepsiceros cretensis — Oves (61) 7

Strix — Migr. avium (79) 21; Polit. nat. (109) 14, 16; Fund. ornith. (137) 19

Strix albida — Migr. avium (79) 21

Strix bubo — Oecon. nat. (20) 33

Strizolobium — Fl. Jam. (105) 26

Strombus — Fund. test. (166) 17, 27, 38

Strombus auris dianae — Metam. pl. (67) [5]

Strombus fissurella — Fund. test. (166) 40

Strombus lambis — Metam. pl. (67) [5]

Strombus millepeda — Metam. pl. (67) [5]; Iter Chin. (161) 8[as millepida]

Strombus pes pelicani — Fund. test. (166) 38

Strombus podagra — Metam. pl. (67) [5]

Strombus scorpius — Metam. pl. (67) [5]; Fund. test. (166) 39[as scorpio]

Struthio — Oecon. nat. (20) 27[as Strutio]; Mat. med. anim. (29) 9; Fl. Cap. (99) [1][as Strutio]; Fund. ornith. (137) 10, 11, 12, 16, 24; Bigas insect. (184) 2

Struthio camelus — Mat. med. anim. (29) 9; Fund. ornith. (137) 20, 25

Struthiopteris — Hort. Upsal. (7) 33[as Strutiopteris]; Acrostichum (10) 4

Strychnos — Lign. colubr. (21) 17; Herb. Amboin. (57) 8, 9; Febr. interm. (167) 35, 39

Strychnos colubrina — Mors. serp. (119) 18

Strychnos foliis ovatis, cirrhis simplicibus — Lign. colubr. (21) 17[as cirris]

Strychnos nux vomica — Pl. officin. (52) 20[as Strychnus]

Sturnus — Oecon. nat. (20) 40; Migr. avium (79) 13, 17, 18, 22; Polit. nat. (109) 12

Sturnus vulgaris — Migr. avium (79) 31

Styrax — Hort. Upsal. (7) 37; Vir. pl. (13) 20

Styrax officinale — Pl. officin. (52) 18; Fl. Palaest. (70) 20; Fl. Monsp. (74) 17

Suber — Vir. pl. (13) 7; Nom. bot. (107) 18

Subularia aquatica — Pan Svec. (26) 28; Stat. pl. (55) 13; Fl. Angl. (56) 19; Rar. Norv. (157) 11; Fl. Åker. (162) 15

Subularia repens — Fl. Angl. (56) 27

Surenus — Herb. Amboin. (57) 12

Suriana maritima — Fl. Jam. (105) 15

Sus — Vir. pl. (13) 16, 17; Curios. nat. (18) 14; Oecon. nat. (20) 18, 36, 42; Generat. calc. (22) 2;

Pan Svec. (26) 3, 7, 11ff.; Mat. med. anim. (29) 6; Instr. peregr. (96) 11; Ping. anim. (108) 11ff.; Polit. nat. (109) 15, 17, 18, 21; Usum hist. nat. (145) 25

Sus aper — Ping. anim. (108) 11; Usum hist. nat. (145) 23

Sus babyrussa — Ping. anim. (108) 11

Sus chinensis — Ping. anim. (108) 11

Sus dorso antice setoso, cauda pilosa — Mat. med. anim. (29) 6

Sus porcus — Ping. anim. (108) 11

Sus scrofa — Ping. anim. (108) 11

Sus tajacu — Ping. anim. (108) 11

Sussuela esculenta — Herb. Amboin. (57) 24

Suzygium — see Zuzygium

Swertia corniculata — Nect. fl. (122) 13; Hist. nat. Rossia (144) 12[as Swertzia], 28

Swertia corollis quadricornibus — Pl. rar. Camsch. (30) 6

Swertia corollis quadrifidis ecornibus — Pl. rar. Camsch. (30) 13

Swertia corollis quadrifidis quadricornibus — Pl. rar. Camsch. (30) 12

Swertia dichotoma — Hist. nat. Rossia (144) 28

Swertia perennis — Fl. alp. (71) 14

Swertia rotata — Hist. nat. Rossia (144) 28

Swietenia — Nect. fl. (122) 9; Opobals. (135) 2

Swietenia mahagoni — Obs. mat. med. (171) 4[as Switenia]

Sycomorus — Ficus (2) 3, 4, 9

Sylvanus — Fl. Cap. (99) [1]

Symphonia — Pl. Surin. (177) 4, 11

Symphoranthus — Nova pl. gen. 1751 (32) 8, 12

Symphytum — Spons. pl. (12) 33; Vir. pl. (13) 18; Nom. bot. (107) 10

Symphytum majus — Pan Svec. (26) 16

Symphytum officinale — Demonstr. pl. (49) 5; Pl. officin. (52) 8; Fl. Angl. (56) 12; Fl. Monsp. (74) 11; Prodr. fl. Dan. (82) 14; Fl. Belg. (112) 14; Fl. Åker. (162) 8

Symphytum orientale — Fl. Palaest. (70) 14

Symphytum orientale, echii folio minori — Cent. I. pl. (65) 7

Symphytum tuberosum — Fl. Monsp. (74) 11

Synanchia — Nova pl. gen. 1747 (14) 32

Syngnathus — Pand. insect. (93) 3

Syngnathus argentea — Nat. pelagi (84) 11[as Sygnathus]

Syngnathus corpore quadrangulo, pinna caudae carens — Mus. Ad.-Frid. (11) 43[as Syngnatus]

Syngnathus pelagicus — Nat. pelagi (84) 11[as Sygnathus]

Syringa — Hort. Upsal. (7) 21; Gem. arb. (24) 9; Pl. hybr. (33) 7; Calend. fl. (72) 5, [10]; Fr. Svec. (91) [ii], 24; Nom. bot. (107) 9

Syringa foliis lanceolatis integris — Pl. hybr. (33) 16

Syringa foliis lanceolatis integris laciniatisque — Pl. hybr. (33) 16

Syringa foliis ovato-cordatis — Pl. hybr. (33) 16

Syringa ligustrina — Gem. arb. (24) 15

Syringa persica — Demonstr. pl. (49) [1]

Syringa vulgaris — Gem. arb. (24) 15; Demonstr. pl. (49) [1]; Calend. fl. (72) [12], [13]; Fr. Svec. (91) 5, 21; Meloe (124) 4; Hort. cul. (132) 25; Pot. theae (142) 16

Tabacum — Aer habit. (106) 18; Polit. nat. (109) 6; Mors. serp. (119) 2; Usum hist. nat. (145) 29; Cimicifuga (173) 8

Tabacus — Herb. Amboin. (57) 21

Tabanus — Noxa insect. (46) 10, 27, 29; Cervus (60) 5, 13

Tabanus arcticus — Esca avium (174) [9, as 17]

Tabanus autumnalis — Pand. fl. Ryb. (165) 15

Tabanus bovinus — Pand. fl. Ryb. (165) 15

Tabanus bromius — Pand. fl. Ryb. (165) 15

Tabanus caecutiens — Pand. fl. Ryb. (165) 15

Tabanus pluvialis — Pand. fl. Ryb. (165) 15

Tabanus rusticus — Pand. fl. Ryb. (165) 15

Tabanus tropicus — Pand. fl. Ryb. (165) 15

Tabernaemontana — Fl. Jam. (105) 26[as Tabernamontana]

Tabernaemontana echites — Pl. Jam. (102) 10

Tacca litorea — Herb. Amboin. (57) 22

Tacca montana — Herb. Amboin. (57) 22

Tacca phallifera — Herb. Amboin. (57) 22

Tacca sativa — Herb. Amboin. (57) 22

Taenia — Taenia (19) [iii]ff.; Splachnum (27) 2; Cynogr. (54) 20; Metam. pl. (67) 9; Transm. frum. (87) 8, 9; Spigelia (89) 5, 6; Anim. comp. (98) 3, 9; Prol. pl. 1763 (130) 17; Lepra (140) 10; Mund. invis. (149) 8, 9; Morb. naut. (160) 3; Hypericum (186) 11

Taenia articulata plana — Taenia (19) 17

Taenia articulata teres — Taenia (19) 13

Taenia continua plana, sulcis longitudinalibus — Taenia (19) 11

Taenia intestinorum — Taenia (19) 17

Taenia osculis lateralibus geminis — Taenia (19) 17, 36

Taenia osculis lateralibus solitariis — Taenia (19) 19, 36

Taenia osculis marginalibus alternis — Taenia (19) 36

Taenia osculis marginalibus oppositis — Taenia (19) 20, 36

Taenia osculis marginalibus solitariis — Taenia (19) 13

Taenia vulgaris — Taenia (19) 17

Tagetes — Peloria (3) 9; Anandria (9) 12; Spons. pl. (12) 59; Vir. pl. (13) 31, 36; Odor. med. (40) 13; Vern. arb. (47) 9; Demonstr. pl. (49) [vii]; Stat. pl.

(55) 5; Hort. acad. (63) 3; Pl. Jam. (102) 24; Nom. bot. (107) 17; Pl. Alstr. (121) 11

Tagetes erecta — Demonstr. pl. (49) 23; Hort. cul. (132) 23, 25

Tagetes patula — Demonstr. pl. (49) 23; Calend. fl. (72) [13]; Hort. cul. (132) 23, 25

Talpa — Oecon. nat. (20) 18, 38, 41; Sem. musc. (28) 2; Morb. hyeme (38) [2]; Polit. nat. (109) 15, 17; Usum hist. nat. (145) 24

Talpa aurea — Hist. nat. Rossia (144) 16

Tamarindus — Spons. pl. (12) 12, 38; Vir. pl. (13) 33; Sapor. med. (31) 14; Herb. Amboin. (57) 9; Somn. pl. (68) 9; Nom. bot. (107) 9; Nect. fl. (122) 8

Tamarindus indica — Pl. officin. (52) 19; Herb. Amboin. (57) 9; Somn. pl. (68) 20; Fl. Palaest. (70) 11; Fl. Jam. (105) 12[as indicus], 25; Fr. escul. (127) 17; Iter Chin. (161) 9; Pl. Surin. (177) 5[as indicus]; Med. purg. (181) 22

Tamariscus — Sapor. med. (31) 15

Tamarix — Vir. pl. (13) 33; Gem. arb. (24) 6; Nect. fl. (122) 5

Tamarix gallica — Demonstr. pl. (49) 9; Pl. officin. (52) 19; Fl. Palaest. (70) 16; Fl. Monsp. (74) 13

Tamarix germanica — Rar. Norv. (157) 9, 14; Colon. pl. (158) 8

Tamarix orientalis — Fl. Palaest. (70) 16

Tamoata brasiliensibus, lusitanis soldigo — Mus. Ad.-Frid. (11) 38

Tamus — Nect. fl. (122) 14

Tamus communis — Demonstr. pl. (49) 26; Fl. Angl. (56) 24; Fl. Monsp. (74) 28; Mac. olit. (113) 13

Tanacetum — Vir. pl. (13) 23, 33; Fl. oecon. (17) 20; Sapor. med. (31) 18; Pl. hybr. (33) 7; Pl. escul. (35) 23, 29; Metam. pl. (67) 19; Pand. insect. (93) 18; Fl. Cap. (99) 6; Pl. Jam. (102) 24; Nom. bot. (107) 17; Febr. interm. (167) 39

Tanacetum annuum — Demonstr. pl. (49) 22

Tanacetum balsamita — Demonstr. pl. (49) 22; Pl. officin. (52) 5; Calend. fl. (72) [21]; Hort. cul. (132) 24

Tanacetum crispum — Demonstr. pl. (49) 22

Tanacetum crithmifolium — Fl. Cap. (99) 17

Tanacetum foliis crispis — Pl. hybr. (33) 24

Tanacetum fruticosum — Fl. Cap. (99) 17

Tanacetum sibiricum — Hist. nat. Rossia (144) 32

Tanacetum suffruticosum — Fl. Cap. (99) 17

Tanacetum vulgare — Pan Svec. (26) 32; Pl. hybr. (33) 24; Hosp. insect. fl. (43) 31; Herbat. Upsal. (50) 18; Pl. officin. (52) 19; Stat. pl. (55) 22; Fl. Angl. (56) 22; Cervus (60) 8; Calend. fl. (72) [16]; Prodr. fl. Dan. (82) 23; Fl. Jam. (105) 24; Fl. Belg. (112) 21; Hist. nat. Rossia (144) 21; Pand. fl. Ryb. (165) 21

Tanacetum vulgare crispum — Hort. cul. (132) 24

Tanarius major — Herb. Amboin. (57) 14

Tanarius minor — Herb. Amboin. (57) 14

Tanionus litorea — Herb. Amboin. (57) 10

Tantalus loculator — Migr. avium (79) 14

Tarandus — Cervus (60) 3, 4

Tarantula — Rad. senega (23) 10

Taraxacum — Vir. pl. (13) 23; Sapor. med. (31) 11; Acetaria (77) 13

Tarchonanthus — Nova pl. gen. 1751 (32) 44[as Tharchonanthus]; Fl. Cap. (99) 6

Tarchonanthus camphoratus — Fl. Cap. (99) 17

Tardigradus — Surin. Grill. (16) 9

Tardigradus major — Mus. Ad.-Frid. (11) 2

Tatou juvenis seu armodillus minor americanus — Mus. Ad.-Frid. (11) 3

Tatou seu armodillo americanus — Mus. Ad.-Frid. (11) 3

Tatue brasiliensicus — Mus. Ad.-Frid. (11) 3

Taurus — Oecon. nat. (20) 26

Taurus volans — Mat. med. anim. (29) 14

Taxus — Fl. oecon. (17) 27; Oecon. nat. (20) 15; Gem. arb. (24) 9, 32; Mat. med. anim. (29) 4; Arb. Svec. (101) 30; Aer habit. (106) 20; Nom. bot. (107) 19

Taxus arborea — Pan Svec. (26) [37, as 39]

Taxus baccata — Demonstr. pl. (49) 26; Stat. pl. (55) 18; Fl. Angl. (56) 25; Prodr. fl. Dan. (82) 25; Arb. Svec. (101) 8, 13

Tejuguacu — Hort. Upsal. (7) 43

Tejuguacu altera — Amphib. Gyll. (5) 22

Telephium imperati — Demonstr. pl. (49) 9; Calend. fl. (72) [15]

Tellina — Fund. test. (166) 18, 31, 41

Tellina remies — Fund. test. (166) 41

Temapara — Amphib. Gyll. (5) 23; Hort. Upsal. (7) 43

Tenebrio — Pane diaet. (83) 17; Fund. entom. (154) 22

Tenebrio alatus ater elytris striatis thorace laevi — Cent. insect. (129) 13

Tenebrio gigas — Cent. insect. (129) 13

Tenebrio molitor — Pand. fl. Ryb. (165) 9

Tenebrio mortisagus — Pand. fl. Ryb. (165) 9

Tenebrio quisquilius — Pand. fl. Ryb. (165) 9

Tenthredo — Ficus (2) 17, 20; Oecon. nat. (20) 29[as Tentredo]; Hosp. insect. fl. (43) 11, 17, 18, 19, 20, 22, 33, 34, 35; Mirac. insect. (45) 13; Noxa insect. (46) 20, 26; Polit. nat. (109) 8; Fund. fr. (123) 19; Fund. entom. (154) 28, 30, [31, as 30], 33

Tenthredo abietis — Pand. insect. (93) 21; Pand. fl. Ryb. (165) 12

Tenthredo alni — Pand. insect. (93) 19

Tenthredo amerinae — Pand. insect. (93) 21

Tenthredo antennis clavatis — Hosp. insect. fl. (43) 33, 37

Tenthredo antennis duodecim-nodiis nigris, abdomine subtus ferrugineo, pedibus flavis, alis immaculatis — Mat. med. anim. (29) 16

Tenthredo antennis pectinatis — Hosp. insect. fl. (43) 38

Tenthredo atra — Pand. fl. Ryb. (165) 12

Tenthredo atra, ore tibiisque anticis luteis — Hosp. insect. fl. (43) 36; Noxa insect. (46) 25

Tenthredo betulae — Pand. insect. (93) 18

Tenthredo campestris — Pand. fl. Ryb. (165) 12

Tenthredo caprea — Pand. insect. (93) 21

Tenthredo carbonaria — Pand. fl. Ryb. (165) 12

Tenthredo cerasi — Pand. insect. (93) 14; Pand. fl. Ryb. (165) 12

Tenthredo cincta — Pand. insect. (93) 15; Pand. fl. Ryb. (165) 12

Tenthredo cynosbati — Pand. insect. (93) 15

Tenthredo erythrocephala — Pand. insect. (93) 21[as erytrocephala]

Tenthredo flava — Hosp. insect. fl. (43) 37

Tenthredo gallae glabrae foliorum querci — Mat. med. anim. (29) 15

Tenthredo intercus — Pand. insect. (93) 18

Tenthredo juniperi — Pand. insect. (93) 22

Tenthredo livida — Pand. fl. Ryb. (165) 12

Tenthredo lonicerae — Pand. insect. (93) 12

Tenthredo lucorum — Pand. insect. (93) 19

Tenthredo lutea — Pand. insect. (93) 18, 19, 21

Tenthredo mesomela — Pand. fl. Ryb. (165) 12

Tenthredo ovata — Pand. fl. Ryb. (165) 12

Tenthredo populnea — Hosp. insect. fl. (43) 38; Pand. insect. (93) 22

Tenthredo pruni — Pand. insect. (93) 14

Tenthredo pyri — Hosp. insect. fl. (43) 23; Pand. insect. (93) 15

Tenthredo rapae — Pand. fl. Ryb. (165) 12

Tenthredo rosae — Hosp. insect. fl. (43) 25; Pand. insect. (93) 15; Pand. fl. Ryb. (165) 12

Tenthredo rufipes — Pand. fl. Ryb. (165) 12

Tenthredo rumicis — Pand. insect. (93) 13

Tenthredo salicis — Hosp. insect. fl. (43) 37[as salicina]; Pand. insect. (93) 21

Tenthredo scrophulariae — Hosp. insect. fl. (43) 27; Pand. insect. (93) 16[as scophulariae]; Polit. nat. (109) 8

Tenthredo ulmi — Pand. insect. (93) 12

Tenthredo viridis — Pand. fl. Ryb. (165) 12; Esca avium (174) 8

Tenthredo vitellinae — Pand. fl. Ryb. (165) 12

Teramnus — Fl. Jam. (105) 27

Terebinthina — Spons. pl. (12) 52; Vir. pl. (13) 7[as Therebintina]; Herb. Amboin. (57) 28

Terebinthus — Pl. escul. (35) 3[as Therebintus]; Mirac. insect. (45) 15[as Terebintus]; Fl. alp. (71) 25; Fl. Monsp. (74) 7; Pl. tinct. (97) 10, 28; Opobals. (135) 6

Terebinthus major, betulae cortice, fructu triangulare — Betula (1) 5

Terebinthus maxima — Pl. Jam. (102) 10

Teredo — Instr. peregr. (96) 12; Hirudo (136) 2; Fund. test. (166) 17

Teredo navalis — Oecon. nat. (20) 25

Terminalis alba — Herb. Amboin. (57) 16

Terminalis angustifolia — Herb. Amboin. (57) 16

Testudo — Amphib. Gyll. (5) [1], 30, 32; Mus. Ad.-Frid. (11) 6

Testudo major terrestris americana — Amphib. Gyll. (5) 31

Testudo marina — Amphib. Gyll. (5) 32; Oecon. nat. (20) 28

Testudo marina americana — Amphib. Gyll. (5) 32; Mus. Ad.-Frid. (11) 7

Testudo marina major — Taenia (19) 27

Testudo midas — Nat. pelagi (84) 12; Iter Chin. (161) 15

Testudo minor amboinensis — Amphib. Gyll. (5) 34

Testudo nigricantibus et flavescentibus figuris geometricis — Amphib. Gyll. (5) 34

Testudo picta vel stellata — Amphib. Gyll. (5) 34

Testudo stellata — Amphib. Gyll. (5) 34

Testudo terrestris pusilla ex india orientali — Amphib. Gyll. (5) 33

Testudo tessellata minor — Amphib. Gyll. (5) 34

Testudo testa tessellata major, e madagascar — Amphib. Gyll. (5) 34

Testudo unguibus acuminatis, palmarum duobus, plantarum unico — Amphib. Gyll. (5) 32

Testudo unguibus acuminatis, palmarum plantarumque quaternis — Amphib. Gyll. (5) 33

Testudo unguibus acuminatis, palmarum plantarumque solitariis — Mus. Ad.-Frid. (11) 7

Testudo virginica — Amphib. Gyll. (5) 33

Tethys mentula — Chin. Lagerstr. (64) 30

Tetracera volubilis — Fl. Jam. (105) 17

Tetragonia — Hort. Upsal. (7) 40; Fl. Cap. (99) 7; Pl. rar. Afr. (115) 4

Tetragonia foliis linearibus — Demonstr. pl. (49) 13

Tetragonia fruticosa — Fl. Cap. (99) 15

Tetragonia herbacea — Fl. Cap. (99) 15

Tetragonotheca — Fund. fr. (123) 17

Tetrao — Oecon. nat. (20) 31, 39; Morb. hyeme (38) 3, 5, 13; Cervus (60) 12; Migr. avium (79) 29; Instr. peregr. (96) 11; Polit. nat. (109) 13; Fund. ornith. (137) 18, 19, 20; Esca avium (174) 4

Tetrao bonasia — Betula (1) 18; Migr. avium (79) 29

Tetrao coturnix — Migr. avium (79) 17, 19, 29, 30

Tetrao lagopus — Betula (1) 18; Erica (163) 15[as lapopus]

Tetrao lagopus alpinus — Cervus (60) 10

Tetrao macula nuda coccinea pone oculos, rectricibus ferrugineis — Mat. med. anim. (29) 10

Tetrao perdix — Migr. avium (79) 29

Tetrao tetrix — Calend. fl. (72) [8]; Migr. avium (79) 22, 29

Tetrao urogallus — Migr. avium (79) 22, 29; Erica (163) 15

Tettigonia — Fund. entom. (154) 30

Teucrii facie bisnagarica tetracoccos rostrata — Nova pl. gen. 1747 (14) 10

Teucrium — Hort. Upsal. (7) 36; Fl. oecon. (17) 16; Nom. bot. (107) 14; Marum (175) 8ff.

Teucrium botrys — Demonstr. pl. (49) 15; Fl. Monsp. (74) 19

Teucrium canadense — Demonstr. pl. (49) 15

Teucrium capitatum — Fl. Monsp. (74) 19

Teucrium chamaedrys — Pl. officin. (52) 7; Fl. Palaest. (70) 22; Fl. Monsp. (74) 19; Fl. Belg. (112) 18; Febr. interm. (167) 38

Teucrium chamaepitys — Demonstr. pl. (49) 15[as chamaepithys]; Pl. officin. (52) 7[as camaepithys]; Fl. Angl. (56) 18; Fl. Palaest. (70) 22[as chamaepithys]; Calend. fl. (72) [16][as chamaepythis]; Fl. Monsp. (74) 19[as chamaepithys]; Fl. Belg. (112) 18[as chamaepithys]; Febr. interm. (167) 38[as chamaepithys]

Teucrium creticum — Pl. officin. (52) 15; Fl. Palaest. (70) 22

Teucrium flavum — Demonstr. pl. (49) 15; Fl. Monsp. (74) 19

Teucrium floribus capitatis, foliis linearibus planis quadrifariis confertis, caule procumbente tomentoso — Cent. I. pl. (65) 15

Teucrium foliis integerrimis, ovatis, acutis petiolatis, subtus tomentosis, floribus racemosis secundis — Marum (175) 6, 10

Teucrium fruticans — Demonstr. pl. (49) 15

Teucrium hircanicum — Hist. nat. Rossia (144) 23

Teucrium iva — Fl. Monsp. (74) 19; Fund. fr. (123) 12

Teucrium marum — Demonstr. pl. (49) 15; Pl. officin. (52) 12; Marum (175) 6, 10

Teucrium montanum — Fl. Monsp. (74) 19

Teucrium polium album — Fl. Palaest. (70) 22

Teucrium polium gnaphalodes — Fl. Palaest. (70) 22

Teucrium polium luteum — Fl. Palaest. (70) 22

Teucrium polium smyrnaeum — Fl. Palaest. (70) 22[as smyrneum]

Teucrium pumilum — Cent. I. pl. (65) 15

Teucrium pyrenaicum — Fl. alp. (71) 19

Teucrium scordium — Pan Svec. (26) 26; Demonstr. pl. (49) 15; Pl. officin. (52) 17; Fl. Angl. (56) 18; Fl. Monsp. (74) 19; Prodr. fl. Dan. (82) 20; Fl. Belg. (112) 18

Teucrium scordium minor — Fl. Palaest. (70) 22

Teucrium scorodonia — Fl. Angl. (56) 18; Fl. Monsp. (74) 19; Fl. Belg. (112) 10, 18

Teucrium sibiricum — Hist. nat. Rossia (144) 30

Thalia — Vir. pl. (13) 26

Thalia geniculata — Fl. Jam. (105) 12

Thalictroides — Cimicifuga (173) [1], 5

Thalictroides foetidissimum christophorianae facie — Pl. rar. Camsch. (30) 21; Usum hist. nat. (145) 27; Cimicifuga (173) 3, 6

Thalictroides glutinosum foetidissimum amplissimis foliis — Cimicifuga (173) 6

Thalictrum — Hort. Upsal. (7) 33; Pl. rar. Camsch. (30) 22; Pl. hybr. (33) 7; Cimicifuga (173) 2

Thalictrum alpinum — Demonstr. pl. (49) 15; Stat. pl. (55) 16; Fl. Angl. (56) 18; Fl. alp. (71) 19; Rar. Norv. (157) 10

Thalictrum angustifolium — Demonstr. pl. (49) 15; Fl. Monsp. (74) 18

Thalictrum aquilegifolium — Demonstr. pl. (49) 15; Stat. pl. (55) 17; Calend. fl. (72) [12]; Fl. Monsp. (74) 18; Prodr. fl. Dan. (82) 19; Purg. indig. (143) 13

Thalictrum arvense — Pan Svec. (26) 25

Thalictrum canadense — Pan Svec. (26) 25

Thalictrum contortum — Demonstr. pl. (49) 15; Hist. nat. Rossia (144) 23[as Talictrum], 30

Thalictrum dioicum — Demonstr. pl. (49) 15; Calend. fl. (72) [14][as diocium]

Thalictrum flavum — Herbat. Upsal. (50) 7; Stat. pl. (55) 14; Fl. Angl. (56) 18; Calend. fl. (72) [14]; Prodr. fl. Dan. (82) 19; Pl. tinct. (97) 20; Fl. Belg. (112) 18; Fl. Åker. (162) 14; Pand. fl. Ryb. (165) 19

Thalictrum foetidum — Fl. alp. (71) 19; Fl. Monsp. (74) 18

Thalictrum foliis lanceolato-linearibus integerrimis — Pl. hybr. (33) 22

Thalictrum hybridum, seminibus contortis — Pl. hybr. (33) 21

Thalictrum lapponicum — Pan Svec. (26) 25

Thalictrum majus — Pl. hybr. (33) 21

Thalictrum minus — Pl. hybr. (33) 21, 22; Demonstr. pl. (49) 15; Fl. Angl. (56) 18; Fl. Monsp. (74) 18; Prodr. fl. Dan. (82) 19; Fl. Belg. (112) 18

Thalictrum pratense — Pl. hybr. (33) 22

Thalictrum sibiricum — Demonstr. pl. (49) 15; Calend. fl. (72) [14]; Hist. nat. Rossia (144) 30

Thalictrum simplex — Prodr. fl. Dan. (82) 19; Rar. Norv. (157) 11

Thalictrum striatum — Pan Svec. (26) 25

Thamnia — Fl. Jam. (105) 27

Thapsia alpina lucida — Fl. alp. (71) 15

Thapsia foeniculi folio — Cent. II. pl. (66) 14

Thapsia villosa — Fl. Monsp. (74) 13; Pl. tinct. (97) 15

Thea — Vir. pl. (13) 21; Pl. escul. (35) 19, 29; Migr. avium (79) 33; Pot. theae (142) [1]ff.; Usum hist. nat. (145) 15; Iter Chin. (161) 5

Thea bohea — Pot. theae (142) 2, plate [1]; Iter Chin. (161) 9

Thea chinensis — Pl. officin. (52) 19

Thea viridis — Pot. theae (142) 2

Thèe — Pot. theae (142) 3

Thèe frutex — Pot. theae (142) 3

Thèe sinensium — Pot. theae (142) 3

Theligonum cynocrambe — Fl. Monsp. (74) 27

Theobroma — Passifl. (8) [iii]; Nom. bot. (107) 16; Nect. fl. (122) 8

Theobroma cacao — Pl. officin. (52) 6; Fl. Jam. (105) 19; Fr. escul. (127) 21; Pot. choc. (141) 3; Pl. Surin. (177) 13

Theobroma foliis integerrimis — Pot. choc. (141) 3

Theobroma guazuma — Fl. Jam. (105) 19

Thesium alpinum — Fl. alp. (71) 14; Colon. pl. (158) 7

Thesium capitatum — Fl. Cap. (99) 12

Thesium junceum — Fl. Cap. (99) 12

Thesium linophyllum — Stat. pl. (55) 23; Fl. Angl. (56) 12; Fl. Monsp. (74) 12

Thevetia — Vir. pl. (13) 25

Thlaspi — Fl. oecon. (17) 16, 17; Pand. insect. (93) 16

Thlaspi alliaceum — Odor. med. (40) 12; Med. grav. (92) 13

Thlaspi alpinum, bellidis caeruleae folio — Cent. I. pl. (65) 17

Thlaspi alterum minus umbellatum, nasturtii hortensis folio, narbonense — Cent. I. pl. (65) 18

Thlaspi arvense — Pan Svec. (26) 28; Herbat. Upsal. (50) 12; Pl. officin. (52) 19; Stat. pl. (55) 19; Fl. Angl. (56) 19; Cervus (60) 8; Oves (61) 15; Hort. acad. (63) 10; Prodr. fl. Dan. (82) 20[as Thlapsi]; Fl. Belg. (112) 19; Usum hist. nat. (145) 10; Fl. Åker. (162) 15; Pand. fl. Ryb. (165) 20

Thlaspi bursa-pastoris — Pan Svec. (26) 28; Hosp. insect. fl. (43) 27; Herbat. Upsal. (50) 12; Pl. officin. (52) 6; Stat. pl. (55) 20; Fl. Angl. (56) 19; Fl. Palaest. (70) 23; Fl. Monsp. (74) 20; Prodr. fl. Dan. (82) 20[as Thlapsi]; Fl. Belg. (112) 19; Usum hist. nat. (145) 21; Rar. Norv. (157) 16; Fl. Åker. (162) 15; Pand. fl. Ryb. (165) 20; Esca avium (174) 13

Thlaspi campestre — Pan Svec. (26) 28; Hosp. insect. fl. (43) 12, 27; Herbat. Upsal. (50) 13; Stat. pl. (55) 22[as Tlaspi and as campenstre]; Fl. Angl. (56) 19; Cervus (60) 8; Fl. Monsp. (74) 20; Prodr. fl. Dan. (82) 20[as Thlaspi]; Fl. Belg. (112) 19; Pand. fl. Ryb. (165) 20

Thlaspi hirtum — Fl. Angl. (56) 19[as hirsutum]; Fl. Monsp. (74) 20

Thlaspi humile, spica purpurea — Cent. I. pl. (65) 17

Thlaspi incanum minus — Fl. Monsp. (74) 30

Thlaspi montanum — Fl. Angl. (56) 19; Fl. alp. (71) 20; Fl. Monsp. (74) 20

Thlaspi montanum 2 — Cent. I. pl. (65) 17

Thlaspi montanum, bursae pastoris fructu — Cent. I. pl. (65) 17

Thlaspi montanum minimum — Cent. II. pl. (66) 23

Thlaspi perfoliatum — Fl. Angl. (56) 19; Fl. Monsp. (74) 20

Thlaspi saxatile — Fl. alp. (71) 20; Fl. Monsp. (74) 20

Thlaspi saxatile, vermiculato folio — Cent. II. pl. (66) 24

Thlaspi umbellatum, nasturtii folio, monspeliacum — Cent. I. pl. (65) 18

Thrips — Hosp. insect. fl. (43) 29; Mund. invis. (149) 10[as Trips]; Fund. entom. (154) 5[as Trips]

Thrips fusca, elytris abbreviatis, antennis pectinatis fissilibus aliformibus — Cent. insect. (129) 18[as Trips]

Thrips juniperina — Hosp. insect. fl. (43) 38[as juniperi]; Pand. insect. (93) 22[as Trips]

Thrips paradoxa — Cent. insect. (129) 7[as Trips], 18[as Trips]

Thrips physapus — Pand. insect. (93) 11[as Trips], [17, as 38][as physopus]; Pand. fl. Ryb. (165) 10

Thuja — Hort. Upsal. (7) 36; Vir. pl. (13) 24; Gem. arb. (24) 6; Nom. bot. (107) 18

Thuja aphylla — Cent. I. pl. (65) 32; Fl. Palaest. (70) 30

Thuja occidentalis — Hist. nat. Rossia (144) 34

Thuja orientalis — Demonstr. pl. (49) 25

Thuja strobilis quadrivalvibus: foliis turbinatis vaginantibus, hinc mucronatis, frondibus imbricatis — Cent. I. pl. (65) 32

Thymbra juliana — Fl. Palaest. (70) 22

Thymbra spicata — Fl. Palaest. (70) 22

Thymbra verticillata — Fund. fr. (123) 12

Thymelaea buxifolia villosa — Fl. Palaest. (70) 18[under Daphne]

Thymelaea floribus albis primo vere erumpentibus, foliis oblongis acuminatis, viminibus et cortice valde tenacibus — Nova pl. gen. 1751 (32) 18

Thymelaea foliis linearibus alternis, ex uno petiolo copioso — Pl. rar. Afr. (115) 11[as Thymeleae]

Thymelaea foliis planis acutis, coma et floribus purpureis — Cent. II. pl. (66) 15

Thymelaea folio oleae villoso — Fl. Palaest. (70) 18[under Daphne]

Thymelaea linariae folio, germanica — Nova pl. gen. 1747 (14) 17

Thymelaea sericea, foliis oblongis, floribus tubulosis angustissimis — Cent. II. pl. (66) 15

Thymus — Vir. pl. (13) 29, 30, 34; Fl. oecon. (17) 16; Oves (61) 16; Fl. Monsp. (74) 7; Pand. insect. (93) 16; Nom. bot. (107) 15; Menthae (153) 7; Marum (175) 13

Thymus acinos — Pan Svec. (26) 26; Herbat. Upsal. (50) 9; Stat. pl. (55) 22; Fl. Angl. (56) 18; Fl. Monsp. (74) 19; Prodr. fl. Dan. (82) 20; Fl. Belg. (112) 18; Fl. Åker. (162) 14

Thymus alpinus — Demonstr. pl. (49) 16; Fl. alp. (71) 19

Thymus floribus verticillatis, calycibus lanuginosis, dentibus setaceis villosis — Marum (175) 6

Thymus mastichina — Marum (175) 6, 13

Thymus pulegioides — Fl. Monsp. (74) 19

Thymus serpyllum — Vir. pl. (13) 30; Pan Svec. (26) 26; Hosp. insect. fl. (43) 27; Pl. officin. (52) 18[as serphyllum]; Stat. pl. (55) 21; Fl. Angl. (56) 18; Hort. acad. (63) 10; Fl. Monsp. (74) 19; Prodr. fl. Dan. (82) 20; Fl. Belg. (112) 18; Rar. Norv. (157) 16; Fl. Åker. (162) 14; Pand. fl. Ryb. (165) 20

Thymus vulgaris — Demonstr. pl. (49) 16; Pl. officin. (52) 19; Fl. Monsp. (74) 19; Fl. Jam. (105) 24; Hort. cul. (132) 15

Tiarella — Nova pl. gen. 1751 (32) 29, 48

Tiarella foliis cordatis — Nova pl. gen. 1751 (32) 29

Tiarella foliis ternatis — Nova pl. gen. 1751 (32) 29

Tiarella trifoliata — Hist. nat. Rossia (144) 29

Tigris — Curios. nat. (18) 9, 17; Oecon. nat. (20) 35, 42, 43; Fl. Cap. (99) [1]; Polit. nat. (109) 20

Tilia — Ficus (2) 7; Spons. pl. (12) [2], 17; Vir. pl. (13) 31; Fl. oecon. (17) 14; Oecon. nat. (20) 14; Odor. med. (40) 12; Hosp. insect. fl. (43) 40; Noxa insect. (46) 26; Vern. arb. (47) 10, table; Oves (61) 18; Metam. pl. (67) 24; Calend. fl. (72) [20]; Transm. frum. (87) 9; Fr. Svec. (91) 24; Pand. insect. (93) 16; Arb. Svec. (101) 30; Nom. bot. (107) 14; Prol. pl. 1763 (130) 9

Tilia communis — Gem. arb. (24) 29; Pan Svec. (26) 25

Tilia europaea — Hosp. insect. fl. (43) 26[as europea]; Herbat. Upsal. (50) 8; Pl. officin. (52) 19; Stat. pl. (55) 17; Fl. Angl. (56) 17; Calend. fl. (72) [10], [16]; Fl. Monsp. (74) 18; Prodr. fl. Dan. (82) 19; Arb. Svec. (101) 7, 8, 16; Fl. Belg. (112) 18; Fl. Åker. (162) 13; Pand. fl. Ryb. (165) 19

Tillaea aquatica — Herbat. Upsal. (50) 17[as Tillea]; Stat. pl. (55) 14; Fung. melit. (69) 2; Fl. Åker. (162) 8

Tillaea muscosa — Fung. melit. (69) 2; Fl. Monsp. (74) 10[as Tillea]

Tillaea rubra — Fl. Monsp. (74) 10[as Tillea]

Tillandsia — Cryst. gen. (15) 6[as Tillantia]; Oecon. nat. (20) 20; Fung. melit. (69) 3; Polit. nat. (109) 5

Tillandsia lingulata — Fl. Jam. (105) 15; Pl. Surin. (177) 7

Tillandsia serrata — Fl. Jam. (105) 15

Tillandsia usneoides — Aphyteia (185) 9

Tillandsia utriculata — Fl. Jam. (105) 15

Timonius — Herb. Amboin. (57) 15

Tinea — Hosp. insect. fl. (43) 9; Ledum (178) 11

Tinnunculus — Migr. avium (79) 13, 20

Tinnunculus fuliginosus — Hist. nat. Rossia (144) 16

Tinus — Hort. Upsal. (7) 36; Vir. pl. (13) 27; Herb. Amboin. (57) 14; Hort. acad. (63) 2; Fl. Monsp. (74) 7; Nect. fl. (122) 10

Tinus occidentalis — Fl. Jam. (105) 15

Tipula — Oecon. nat. (20) 29; Hosp. insect. fl. (43) 9, 19; Mirac. insect. (45) 14; Noxa insect. (46) 18, 19, 24; Pand. insect. (93) 7; Polit. nat. (109) 12, 14; Fund. entom. (154) 22, 30; Pand. fl. Ryb. (165) 13; Esca avium (174) 2

Tipula bimaculata — Pand. fl. Ryb. (165) 14

Tipula crocata — Pand. fl. Ryb. (165) 14; Esca avium (174) 8

Tipula febrilis — Pand. fl. Ryb. (165) 14; Esca avium (174) 8

Tipula juniperina — Pand. insect. (93) 22

Tipula longicornis — Pand. insect. (93) 18

Tipula lunata — Pand. fl. Ryb. (165) 14

Tipula oleracea — Pand. fl. Ryb. (165) 14

Tipula plumosa — Pand. fl. Ryb. (165) 14

Tipula putris — Pand. fl. Ryb. (165) 14

Tipula rivosa — Pand. fl. Ryb. (165) 14; Esca avium (174) 8

Tipula triglochidis — Hosp. insect. fl. (43) 38

Tipula ultima — Hosp. insect. fl. (43) 30

Tithymaloides — Euphorbia (36) 5

Tithymaloides lauro-cerasifolio, non serrato — Euphorbia (36) 12

Tithymalus — Vir. pl. (13) 7; Euphorbia (36) [2], 5

Tithymalus africanus humilis, foliis latioribus oblongis, tuberosa radice — Euphorbia (36) 18

Tithymalus africanus seu peplis major brasiliensibus — Euphorbia (36) 14

Tithymalus africanus spinosus, cerei effigie — Euphorbia (36) 9

Tithymalus aizoides africanus, simplici squamato caule, chamenerii folio — Euphorbia (36) 10

Tithymalus aizoides africanus, validissimis spinis ex tuberculorum internodiis provenientibus — Euphorbia (36) 9

Tithymalus aizoides arborescens spinosus, caudice angulari, nerii folio — Euphorbia (36) 10

Tithymalus aizoides fruticosus canariensis aphyllus quadrangularis et quinquangularis, spinis geminis aduncis atronitentibus armatus — Euphorbia (36) 7

Tithymalus aizoides lactifluus sive euphorbia canariensis quadrilatera et quinquelatera, cerei effigie, ad angulos per crebra intervalla spinis rectis atronitentibus gazellae cornua referentibus armata — Euphorbia (36) 7

Tithymalus aizoides triangularis et quadrangularis articulosus et spinosus, ramis compressis — Euphorbia (36) 6

Tithymalus americanus erectus, floribus in capitulum, longo pedunculo congestis — Euphorbia (36) 14

Tithymalus amygdaloides angustifolius — Euphorbia (36) 29

Tithymalus annuus erectus, folio oblongo acuminato — Euphorbia (36) 22

Tithymalus annuus, lunato flore, linariae folio longiore — Euphorbia (36) 22

Tithymalus aphyllus mauritaniae — Euphorbia (36) 8

Tithymalus arborescens, caule aphyllo — Euphorbia (36) 11

Tithymalus arboreus americanus, cotini folio — Euphorbia (36) 13

Tithymalus arboreus, caule corallino, folio hyperici, pericarpio barbato — Euphorbia (36) 24

Tithymalus arboreus curassavicus, cotini folio — Euphorbia (36) 13

Tithymalus arvensis latifolius germanicus — Euphorbia (36) 25

Tithymalus botryoides erectus, florum capitulis conjugatis et longiori pedunculo insidentibus — Euphorbia (36) 15

Tithymalus botryoides major zeylanicus procumbens, foliis et cauliculis villosis — Euphorbia (36) 15

Tithymalus botryoides zeylanicus, cauliculis villosis — Euphorbia (36) 15

Tithymalus botryoides zeylanicus hirsutus — Euphorbia (36) 15

Tithymalus characias — Euphorbia (36) 26, 27

Tithymalus characias amygdaloides — Euphorbia (36) 27

Tithymalus characias, folio serrato — Euphorbia (36) 26

Tithymalus characias rubens peregrinus — Euphorbia (36) 27

Tithymalus creticus characias — Fl. Palaest. (70) 20[under Euphorbia]

Tithymalus cupressinus — Euphorbia (36) 29

Tithymalus curassavicus, folio cotini, triphyllos, petalis florum serratis — Euphorbia (36) 13

Tithymalus curassavicus myrtifolius, flore coccineo, mellifluo — Euphorbia (36) 12[as curassaricus]

Tithymalus curassavicus myrtifolius, flore papilionaceo coccineo parvo — Euphorbia (36) 12[as curassaricus]

Tithymalus curassavicus, salicis et atriplicis foliis hirsutis, caulibus subrubentibus — Euphorbia (36) 12

Tithymalus cyparissias — Euphorbia (36) 23, 29

Tithymalus dendroides — Euphorbia (36) 30

Tithymalus erectus acris, parietariae foliis glabris, floribus ad caulium nodos conglomeratis — Euphorbia (36) 14

Tithymalus erectus, floribus rarioribus, foliis oblongis glabris integris — Euphorbia (36) 13

Tithymalus exiguus glaber, nummulariae folio — Euphorbia (36) 16[as numulariae]

Tithymalus exiguus procumbens, chamaesyce dictus — Euphorbia (36) 16

Tithymalus exiguus saxatilis — Euphorbia (36) 20

Tithymalus exiguus villosus, nummulariae folio — Euphorbia (36) 16[as numulariae]

Tithymalus flore cristato — Fl. Palaest. (70) 20[under Euphorbia]

Tithymalus flore exiguo viridi, apicibus flavis, antequam folia emittit florens — Euphorbia (36) 17

Tithymalus foliis brevibus, aculeatis — Euphorbia (36) 23

Tithymalus foliis inferioribus capillareis, superioribus myrto similibus — Euphorbia (36) 23

Tithymalus foliis pini — Euphorbia (36) 29

Tithymalus foliis subhirsutis ad caulem ellipticis, sub floribus binis subrotundis — Euphorbia (36) 21

Tithymalus helioscopius — Euphorbia (36) 26

Tithymalus hibernicus vasculis muricatis erectis — Euphorbia (36) 29

Tithymalus humilis, flore lapathi — Euphorbia (36) 18

Tithymalus humilis ramosissimus hirsutus, foliis thymi serratis — Euphorbia (36) 16, 17

Tithymalus incanus — Fl. Monsp. (74) 30

Tithymalus indicus annuus dulcis, botryoides, geniculatus — Euphorbia (36) 15

Tithymalus indicus annuus dulcis, floribus albis, caulibus viridantibus et rubentibus — Euphorbia (36) 15

Tithymalus indicus annuus dulcis, floribus albis, cauliculis viridantibus — Euphorbia (36) 13

Tithymalus indicus frutescens — Euphorbia (36) 11

Tithymalus indicus spinosus, nerii folio — Euphorbia (36) 10

Tithymalus indicus vimineus, penitus aphyllos — Euphorbia (36) 11

Tithymalus latifolius hispanicus — Euphorbia (36) 29[as hisponicus]

Tithymalus leptophyllos — Euphorbia (36) 22

Tithymalus lunato flore — Euphorbia (36) 27

Tithymalus maritimo affinis — Euphorbia (36) 29

Tithymalus maritimo affinis, linariae folio — Euphorbia (36) 22[as adfinis]

Tithymalus maritimus — Euphorbia (36) 31

Tithymalus maritimus, spinosus — Euphorbia (36) 21

Tithymalus maximus oelandicus — Euphorbia (36) 28

Tithymalus minimus ruber rotundifolius procumbens — Euphorbia (36) 16

Tithymalus montanus, non acris — Euphorbia (36) 23

Tithymalus myrsinites — Euphorbia (36) 30

Tithymalus myrsinites angustifolius — Euphorbia (36) 30

Tithymalus myrsinites latifolius — Euphorbia (36) 30

Tithymalus myrsinites legitimus — Euphorbia (36) 30

Tithymalus myrtifolius arboreus — Euphorbia (36) 30

Tithymalus myrtites valentinus — Euphorbia (36) 26

Tithymalus orientalis articulatus, junceus aphyllos — Euphorbia (36) 12

Tithymalus orientalis, salicis folio, caule purpureo, flore magno — Euphorbia (36) 25

Tithymalus palustris fruticosus — Euphorbia (36) 28

Tithymalus paralios — Euphorbia (36) 31

Tithymalus parvus annuus, foliis subrotundis non crenatis, peplis dictus — Euphorbia (36) 19

Tithymalus perennis, portulacae folio — Euphorbia (36) 18

Tithymalus platyphyllos — Euphorbia (36) 25

Tithymalus ragusinus, flore luteo pentapetalo — Euphorbia (36) 22

Tithymalus ramosissimus frutescens pene aphyllos — Euphorbia (36) 11

Tithymalus ramosissimus non frutescens pene aphyllus — Euphorbia (36) 11

Tithymalus segetum longifolius — Euphorbia (36) 22

Tithymalus seu esula exigua — Euphorbia (36) 20

Tithymalus seu esula exigua, foliis obtusis — Euphorbia (36) 20

Tithymalus sive chamaesyce villosa major, cauliculis viridibus — Euphorbia (36) 16

Tithymalus sylvaticus, lunato flore — Euphorbia (36) 27

Tithymalus tuberosa, pyriformi radice — Euphorbia (36) 21

Tithymalus tuberosa radice — Euphorbia (36) 21

Tithymalus tuberosus acaulos, foliis oblongis cucullatis et planis — Euphorbia (36) 18

Tithymalus zeylanicus spinosus arborescens — Euphorbia (36) 10

Tittius — Herb. Amboin. (57) 11

Tittius litorea — Herb. Amboin. (57) 11

Toluifera — Passifl. (8) [iii]

Toluifera balsamum — Pl. officin. (52) 19

Tomex — Nova pl. gen. 1747 (14) [vi], 5; Oves (61) 14

Tomex tomentosa — Nova pl. gen. 1747 (14) 5

Tordylium — Hort. Upsal. (7) 34; Vir. pl. (13) 19

Tordylium anthriscus — Herbat. Upsal. (50) 13; Fl. Angl. (56) 13; Fl. Monsp. (74) 13; Prodr. fl. Dan. (82) 15; Fl. Belg. (112) 15; Fl. Åker. (162) 9

Tordylium latifolium — Fl. Angl. (56) 13; Calend. fl. (72) [13]; Fl. Monsp. (74) 13; Fl. Belg. (112) 15

Tordylium maximum — Demonstr. pl. (49) 8; Fl. Angl. (56) 13; Pl. rar. Afr. (115) 6

Tordylium nodosum — Fl. Angl. (56) 13; Fl. Palaest. (70) 16; Fl. Monsp. (74) 13; Pl. rar. Afr. (115) 6

Tordylium officinale — Demonstr. pl. (49) 8; Pl. officin. (52) 18; Fl. Angl. (56) 13; Fl. Monsp. (74) 12

Tordylium rubrum — Pan Svec. (26) 18

Tordylium syriacum — Demonstr. pl. (49) 8

Torenia — Nova pl. gen. 1751 (32) 45, 48; Pl. hybr. (33) 7

216

Torenia asiatica — Iter Chin. (161) 9

Torenia kakapu — Pl. hybr. (33) 28

Tormentilla — Vir. pl. (13) 27; Fl. oecon. (17) 14; Sapor. med. (31) 15; Nom. bot. (107) 14; Fund. fr. (123) 20, 23; Fraga (170) [1], 2, 3

Tormentilla erecta — Demonstr. pl. (49) 14; Herbat. Upsal. (50) 6; Pl. officin. (52) 19; Fl. Angl. (56) 17; Prodr. fl. Dan. (82) 19; Pl. tinct. (97) 19; Fl. Belg. (112) 17; Fl. Åker. (162) 13; Pand. fl. Ryb. (165) 19; Esca avium (174) 13

Tormentilla officinarum — Pan Svec. (26) 24

Tormentilla reptans — Fl. Angl. (56) 17

Torpedo — Hort. Upsal. (7) 43; Mus. Ad.-Frid. (11) 29; Fl. Cap. (99) [1]; Usum hist. nat. (145) 26

Tournefortia — Vir. pl. (13) 18

Tournefortia foetida [error for foetidissima?] — Fl. Jam. (105) 13

Tournefortia foetidissima — Herb. Amboin. (57) 17; see also T. foetida

Tournefortia glabra — Fl. Jam. (105) 13

Tournefortia volubilis — Demonstr. pl. (49) 5; Fl. Jam. (105) 13

Tournesol — Hort. Upsal. (7) 37

Toxicodendron — Hort. Upsal. (7) 36; Vern. arb. (47) 9; Aer habit. (106) 17, 20

Tozzia alpina — Fl. alp. (71) 19

Trachelium — Hort. Upsal. (7) 36

Trachelium caeruleum — Demonstr. pl. (49) 5[as coeruleum]

Trachinus — Mus. Ad.-Frid. (11) 33

Trachinus capite inermi nudo, pinnis pectoralibus coadunatis — Mus. Ad.-Frid. (11) 32

Trachinus draco — Mors. serp. (119) 2

Tradescantia — Hort. Upsal. (7) 33; Nova pl. gen. 1751 (32) 9

Tradescantia virginiana — Demonstr. pl. (49) 9; Hort. cul. (132) 24[as virginica]

Tragacantha — Sapor. med. (31) 12; Nom. bot. (107) 16

Tragelaphus — Cervus (60) 4

Tragia — Vir. pl. (13) 27

Tragia mercurialis — Herb. Amboin. (57) 26; Pl. Jam. (102) 26; Fl. Jam. (105) 25

Tragia scandens — Herb. Amboin. (57) 18

Tragopogon — Vir. pl. (13) 25; Fl. oecon. (17) 19; Sapor. med. (31) 11; Pl. hybr. (33) 7; Pl. escul. (35) 22, 28; Nom. bot. (107) 16; Ping. anim. (108) 15; Fund. fr. (123) 15

Tragopogon alterum — Fl. Monsp. (74) 30

Tragopogon angustifolium — Fl. Monsp. (74) 30

Tragopogon asperum — Fl. Palaest. (70) 27; Fl. Monsp. (74) 24

Tragopogon calycibus corollae radio longioribus, foliis integris, seminibus laevibus: disci papposis, radii calyculatis — Pl. hybr. (33) 13

Tragopogon crocifolium — Fl. Monsp. (74) 24

Tragopogon dalechampii — Fl. Monsp. (74) 24[as dalechampi]

Tragopogon foliis crassioribus — Fl. Monsp. (74) 30

Tragopogon hirsutum — Fl. Monsp. (74) 30

Tragopogon hybridum — Demonstr. pl. (49) 21; Fl. Palaest. (70) 27; Fund. fr. (123) 15

Tragopogon luteum — Pan Svec. (26) 31

Tragopogon orientale — Demonstr. pl. (49) 21

Tragopogon picroides — Fl. Palaest. (70) 27; Fl. Monsp. (74) 24; Pl. rar. Afr. (115) 6

Tragopogon porrifolium — Demonstr. pl. (49) 21; Fl. Monsp. (74) 24; Generat. ambig. (104) 13

Tragopogon pratense — Herbat. Upsal. (50) 10; Stat. pl. (55) 22; Fl. Angl. (56) 21; Calend. fl. (72) [22]; Fl. Monsp. (74) 24; Prodr. fl. Dan. (82) 22; Generat. ambig. (104) 12, 13; Fl. Belg. (112) 20; Mac. olit. (113) 10; Hort. cul. (132) 12; Mund. invis. (149) 14; Fl. Åker. (162) 17; Pand. fl. Ryb. (165) 21

Tragopogon purpureo caeruleum — Pl. hybr. (33) 13

Tragopogon tenuissime dentatum — Fl. Monsp. (74) 30

Tragoriganum 2 — Fl. Palaest. (70) 22[under Sideritis]

Tragoriganum latifolium — Marum (175) 6

Trapa — Fl. oecon. (17) 5; Pl. escul. (35) 9, 28; Cui bono? (42) 18; Nom. bot. (107) 10; Fl. Belg. (112) 8

Trapa aquatica — Pan Svec. (26) 16

Trapa natans — Pl. officin. (52) 14; Fl. Belg. (112) 13; Fr. escul. (127) 22; Colon. pl. (158) 6

Tremella — Pl. Mart.-Burs. (6) 28[as Tremilla]; Taenia (19) 3; Obst. med. (34) 9; Usum musc. (148) 14

Tremella auricula — Pl. officin. (52) 5; Prodr. fl. Dan. (82) 26

Tremella nostoc — Prodr. fl. Dan. (82) 26

Tremella verrucosa — Herbat. Upsal. (50) 13

Trianthema portulacastrum — Fl. Jam. (105) 14[as Thrianthema]

Tribulus — Hort. Upsal. (7) 34; Cryst. gen. (15) 20

Tribulus cistoides — Fl. Jam. (105) 16

Tribulus maximus — Fl. Jam. (105) 16

Tribulus terrestris — Fl. Monsp. (74) 15; Pl. rar. Afr. (115) 6

Trichechus — Nat. pelagi (84) 14

Trichilia — Fl. Jam. (105) 26[as Thrichilia]; Nect. fl. (122) 9

Trichilia glabra — Fl. Jam. (105) 16

Trichilia hirta — Fl. Jam. (105) 16

Trichiurus lepturus — Iter Chin. (161) 10

Trichogamila — Fl. Jam. (105) 27

Trichomanes — Acrostichum (10) 3, 6, 7, 9, 17; Spons. pl. (12) 27

Trichomanes aculeatum — Fl. Jam. (105) 23

Trichomanes adiantoides — Fl. Cap. (99) 19[as
   adianthoides]

Trichomanes aethiopicus — Fl. Cap. (99) 19

Trichomanes capillare — Fl. Jam. (105) 23

Trichomanes membranaceum — see T.
   membranoides

Trichomanes membranoides [error for
   membranaceum?] — Fl. Jam. (105) 23

Trichomanes pyxidiferum — Colon. pl. (158) 10

Trichomanes scandens — Fl. Jam. (105) 23

Trichomanes tunbrigense — Fl. Angl. (56) 25[as
   tunbrigensis]; Fl. Jam. (105) 23, 25; Colon. pl.
   (158) 11[as tunbrigensis]

Trichosanthes — Nect. fl. (122) 4

Trichostema — Nova pl. gen. 1751 (32) 9

Trientalis — Pl. Mart.-Burs. (6) [vi]

Trientalis capensis — Fl. Cap. (99) 13

Trientalis europaea — Pl. Mart.-Burs. (6) 15; Herbat.
   Upsal. (50) 6; Stat. pl. (55) 18; Fl. Angl. (56) 15;
   Calend. fl. (72) [11]; Prodr. fl. Dan. (82) 17; Fl.
   Åker. (162) 11; Pand. fl. Ryb. (165) 18; Ledum
   (178) [1], 8

Trientalis thalii — Pan Svec. (26) 21

Trifoliastrum supinum corymbiferum annuum album
   majus, folio longiore obtuso — Pl. hybr. (33) 17

Trifolium — Peloria (3) 10; Anandria (9) 4; Spons.
   pl. (12) 11; Vir. pl. (13) 23; Fl. oecon. (17) 18; Pl.
   hybr. (33) 7; Pl. escul. (35) 27; Oves (61) 18; Fl.
   Monsp. (74) 7; Pand. insect. (93) [17, as 38]; Fl.
   Cap. (99) 6; Pl. Jam. (102) 20; Nom. bot. (107) 16;
   Usum hist. nat. (145) 18

Trifolium agrarium — Herbat. Upsal. (50) 8; Stat. pl.
   (55) 22; Fl. Angl. (56) 21; Fl. Monsp. (74) 23;
   Prodr. fl. Dan. (82) 22; Fl. Belg. (112) 20; Fl. Åker.
   (162) 16; Pand. fl. Ryb. (165) 21

Trifolium album — Pan Svec. (26) 30

Trifolium alexandrinum — Cent. I. pl. (65) 25; Fl.
   Palaest. (70) 26

Trifolium alpinum — Fl. Monsp. (74) 23

Trifolium alpinum argenteum, persici flore — Cent.
   II. pl. (66) 19

Trifolium anglicum — Pan Svec. (26) 31

Trifolium angustifolium — Fl. Palaest. (70) 26; Fl.
   Monsp. (74) 23

Trifolium arvense — Herbat. Upsal. (50) 17; Stat. pl.
   (55) 21; Fl. Angl. (56) 21; Fl. Monsp. (74) 23;
   Prodr. fl. Dan. (82) 22; Fl. Belg. (112) 20; Pand. fl.
   Ryb. (165) 21

Trifolium capitulis dipsaci — Fl. Angl. (56) 28

Trifolium capitulis fructus imbricatis, calycibus
   reflexis patulis corolla longioribus — Demonstr.
   pl. (49) 21

Trifolium capitulis globosis, leguminibus dispermis,
   caule erecto, foliis lanceolatis serrulatis, stipulis
   rhombeis — Cent. I. pl. (65) 24

Trifolium capitulis pedunculatis, foliis infimis
   oppositis — Cent. I. pl. (65) 25

Trifolium capitulis villosis globosis terminalibus
   bractea orbiculata terminatis — Cent. I. pl. (65) 25

Trifolium capitulis villosis globosis terminalibus,
   calycibus omnius fertilibus — Demonstr. pl. (49)
   21

Trifolium capitulis villosis hemisphaericis
   terminalibus solitariis, calycibus omnibus fertilibus
   — Cent. I. pl. (65) 24

Trifolium capitulis villosis, involucro terminatrice
   reflexo rigido capitulum involvente — Pl. Mart.-
   Burs. (6) 25

Trifolium cherleri — Demonstr. pl. (49) 21; Cent. I.
   pl. (65) 24; Fl. Monsp. (74) 23

Trifolium echinatum arvense — Pl. Mart.-Burs. (6)
   25

Trifolium filiforme — Fl. Angl. (56) 21

Trifolium fragiferum — Demonstr. pl. (49) 21; Fl.
   Angl. (56) 21; Fl. Monsp. (74) 23; Prodr. fl. Dan.
   (82) 22; Fl. Belg. (112) 20

Trifolium fruticans — Fl. Cap. (99) 17

Trifolium globosum — Cent. I. pl. (65) 25; Fl.
   Palaest. (70) 26

Trifolium glomeratum — Pan Svec. (26) 30;
   Demonstr. pl. (49) 21; Fl. Angl. (56) 21

Trifolium glomerulis mollioribus — Fl. Angl. (56) 28

Trifolium hybridum — Pl. hybr. (33) 17; Demonstr.
   pl. (49) 21; Prodr. fl. Dan. (82) 22

Trifolium incarnatum — Demonstr. pl. (49) 21;
   Somn. pl. (68) 18; Fl. Palaest. (70) 26

Trifolium lagopus — Pan Svec. (26) 30

Trifolium lappaceum — Fl. Monsp. (74) 23

Trifolium lupinaster — Demonstr. pl. (49) 21;
   Calend. fl. (72) [14]; Hist. nat. Rossia (144) 32

Trifolium lupulinum — Pan Svec. (26) 30

Trifolium maritimum — Demonstr. pl. (49) 21

Trifolium medium — Prodr. fl. Dan. (82) 22

Trifolium melilotus — Pan Svec. (26) 31; Calend. fl.
   (72) [14]

Trifolium melilotus alba — Calend. fl. (72) [15][as
   album], [22][as melitotus album]; Fl. Belg. (112)
   20

Trifolium melilotus caerulea — Demonstr. pl. (49)
   21[as melit. coeruleum]; Fl. Belg. (112) 20

Trifolium melilotus indica — Demonstr. pl. (49)
   21[as melit. indicum]; Fl. Palaest. (70) 26[as
   melitot.]; Fl. Monsp. (74) 23; Fl. Cap. (99) 17

Trifolium melilotus italica — Demonstr. pl. (49)
   21[as melit. italicum]; Somn. pl. (68) 19

Trifolium melilotus lutea — Fl. Belg. (112) 20

Trifolium melilotus officinalis — Pl. officin. (52) 13;
   Fl. Angl. (56) 21; Fl. Monsp. (74) 23; Prodr. fl.
   Dan. (82) 22

Trifolium melilotus polonica — Demonstr. pl. (49)
   21[as melit. polonicum]

Trifolium melilotus polonica officinalis et caerulea
   — Somn. pl. (68) 18

Trifolium melilotus repens — Fl. Monsp. (74) 23

Trifolium montanum — Pan Svec. (26) 30; Herbat. Upsal. (50) 17; Stat. pl. (55) 22; Fl. Angl. (56) 6; Calend. fl. (72) [15]; Prodr. fl. Dan. (82) 22; Fl. Åker. (162) 16; Pand. fl. Ryb. (165) 21

Trifolium ochroleucum — Fl. Angl. (56) 28[as ochroleucon]

Trifolium orientale capite lanuginoso — Cent. I. pl. (65) 25

Trifolium ornithopodioides — Fl. Angl. (56) 21

Trifolium pedunculis communibus subtrifloris, stipulis foliorum brevioribus — Cent. I. pl. (65) 24

Trifolium pratense — Hosp. insect. fl. (43) 29; Vern. arb. (47) 19; Demonstr. pl. (49) 21; Herbat. Upsal. (50) 7; Stat. pl. (55) 20; Fl. Angl. (56) 21; Calend. fl. (72) [16]; Fl. Monsp. (74) 23; Prodr. fl. Dan. (82) 22; Pl. tinct. (97) 22; Fl. Belg. (112) 20; Fl. Åker. (162) 16; Pand. fl. Ryb. (165) 21; Esca avium (174) 14

Trifolium pratense album — Pl. hybr. (33) 17

Trifolium pratense annuum erectum minimum, foliis longis angustis pulchre venatis et tenuissime serratis, floribus albis in capitulum congestis, siliquis minoribus dispermis — Cent. I. pl. (65) 24

Trifolium procumbens — Fl. Angl. (56) 21; Fl. Palaest. (70) 26

Trifolium purpureum — Pan Svec. (26) 30; Pl. escul. (35) 21

Trifolium reflexum — Demonstr. pl. (49) 21

Trifolium repens — Pl. escul. (35) 21; Demonstr. pl. (49) 21; Herbat. Upsal. (50) 7; Pl. officin. (52) 19; Stat. pl. (55) 22; Fl. Angl. (56) 21; Prodr. fl. Dan. (82) 22; Fl. Belg. (112) 20; Fl. Åker. (162) 16; Pand. fl. Ryb. (165) 21

Trifolium resupinatum — Demonstr. pl. (49) 21; Somn. pl. (68) 18; Fl. Palaest. (70) 26; Fl. Monsp. (74) 23; Fl. Belg. (112) 20

Trifolium retusum — Demonstr. pl. (49) 21; Cent. I. pl. (65) 2

Trifolium rubens — Fl. Monsp. (74) 23

Trifolium scabrum — Fl. Angl. (56) 21; Hort. acad. (63) 11; Fl. Monsp. (74) 23

Trifolium spicis villosis, caule diffuso, foliolis integerrimis — Pl. hybr. (33) 18

Trifolium spinosum — Demonstr. pl. (49) 21

Trifolium spumosum — Fl. Monsp. (74) 30; Prodr. fl. Dan. (82) 22

Trifolium stellatum — Pl. Mart.-Burs. (6) 25; Demonstr. pl. (49) 21; Fl. Palaest. (70) 26; Fl. Monsp. (74) 23

Trifolium strictum — Cent. I. pl. (65) 24

Trifolium subterraneum — Demonstr. pl. (49) 21; Fl. Angl. (56) 21; Somn. pl. (68) 7; Fl. Monsp. (74) 23

Trifolium tomentosum — Fl. Palaest. (70) 26; Fl. Monsp. (74) 23

Trifolium uniflorum — Cent. I. pl. (65) 24; Fl. Palaest. (70) 26

Trifolium vernum repens, flore albo exiguo — Cent. I. pl. (65) 24

Trifolium vernum repens purpureum — Cent. I. pl. (65) 24

Trifolium vesicarium — Pan Svec. (26) 30

Trigla — Polit. nat. (109) 14; Fund. ornith. (137) 10

Triglochin — Hort. Upsal. (7) 41; Vir. pl. (13) 16, 32; Fl. oecon. (17) 9; Usum hist. nat. (145) 21

Triglochin capsulis sexlocularibus ovatatis — Pl. Mart.-Burs. (6) [vii]

Triglochin maritimum — Herbat. Upsal. (50) 14; Stat. pl. (55) 12; Fl. Angl. (56) 15; Fl. Monsp. (74) 15; Prodr. fl. Dan. (82) 17; Fl. Belg. (112) 16[as Triglochia]; Pand. fl. Ryb. (165) 18, 21

Triglochin palustre — Herbat. Upsal. (50) 14; Stat. pl. (55) 14; Fl. Angl. (56) 15; Fl. Palaest. (70) 18; Fl. Monsp. (74) 15; Prodr. fl. Dan. (82) 17; Fl. Belg. (112) 16[as Triglochia]; Fl. Åker. (162) 10; Pand. fl. Ryb. (165) 18

Triglochin sexlocularis — Pan Svec. (26) 21

Triglochin tricapsularis — Pan Svec. (26) 21

Trigonella — Hort. Upsal. (7) 34; Anandria (9) 4; Vir. pl. (13) 23

Trigonella foenum graecum — Demonstr. pl. (49) 21; Pl. officin. (52) 10[as foenu-graecum]; Fr. escul. (127) 19

Trigonella foenum graecum sylvestre — Fl. Monsp. (74) 23

Trigonella hamosa — Fl. Palaest. (70) 26

Trigonella monspeliaca — Demonstr. pl. (49) 21; Fl. Palaest. (70) 26

Trigonella platycarpos — Demonstr. pl. (49) 21; Hist. nat. Rossia (144) 23[as platycarpa], 32[as platycarpa]

Trigonella polyceratia — Demonstr. pl. (49) 21; Fl. Monsp. (74) 23

Trigonella ruthenica — Hist. nat. Rossia (144) 32

Trigonella spinosa — Fl. Palaest. (70) 26

Trilopus — Nova pl. gen. 1751 (32) 8, 12

Tringa — Migr. avium (79) 17, 28

Tringa alba — Migr. avium (79) 14

Tringa arquata — Migr. avium (79) 17

Tringa charadrius — Migr. avium (79) 18

Tringa fusca — Migr. avium (79) 15

Tringa interpres — Migr. avium (79) 28

Tringa lobata — Migr. avium (79) 28

Tringa pugnax — Migr. avium (79) 28

Tringa rusticola — Migr. avium (79) 29

Tringa samoedica — Hist. nat. Rossia (144) 16

Tringa vanellus — Migr. avium (79) 18, 28; Fund. ornith. (137) 25

Trionum — Hort. Upsal. (7) 34

Triopteris jamaicensis — Pl. Surin. (177) 9

Triosteum perfoliatum — Specif. Canad. (76) 9; Febr. interm. (167) 19

Trips — see Thrips

Tripsacum — Fund. agrost. (152) 26, 35

Tripsacum dactyloides — Fund. agrost. (152) 32

Tripsacum hermaphroditum — Fl. Jam. (105) 21; Fund. agrost. (152) 32

Triticum — Peloria (3) 15; Spons. pl. (12) 17; Vir. pl. (13) 32; Fl. oecon. (17) 4; Pan Svec. (26) 11; Pl. escul. (35) 5, 27; Hosp. insect. fl. (43) 12; Fl. Angl. (56) 4; Hort. acad. (63) 2; Pane diaet. (83) 11; Transm. frum. (87) 12; Instr. peregr. (96) 10; Nom. bot. (107) 9; Inebr. (117) 13; Fr. escul. (127) 19; Usum hist. nat. (145) 9; Mund. invis. (149) 13, 14, 19; Fund. agrost. (152) 5, 15, 16, 18, 25, 32, 34

Triticum aestivum — Hort. cul. (132) 8; Hist. nat. Rossia (144) 20[as aestinum]

Triticum calycibus truncatis quinquefloris, foliis involutis — Cent. I. pl. (65) 6

Triticum caninum — Fl. Angl. (56) 11

Triticum hybernum — Fl. Palaest. (70) 13; Hort. cul. (132) 8

Triticum junceum — Cent. I. pl. (65) 6; Fl. Palaest. (70) 13

Triticum manecoccum [error for monococcum?] — Fl. Monsp. (74) 9

Triticum monococcum — see T. manecoccum

Triticum perenne — Fl. Palaest. (70) 13

Triticum radice officinarum — Pan Svec. (26) 15

Triticum radice repente, foliis viridibus — Pl. Mart.-Burs. (6) 4

Triticum repens — Pl. escul. (35) 8; Herbat. Upsal. (50) 12; Pl. officin. (52) 11; Cynogr. (54) 10; Stat. pl. (55) 18; Fl. Angl. (56) 11; Metam. pl. (67) 9; Fl. Monsp. (74) 9; Prodr. fl. Dan. (82) 14; Ping. anim. (108) 15; Fl. Belg. (112) 13; Usum hist. nat. (145) 10[as reptans]; Mund. invis. (149) 8[as reptans]; Fund. agrost. (152) 7, 9; Fl. Åker. (162) 7; Pand. fl. Ryb. (165) 16; Obs. mat. med. (171) 6; Esca avium (174) 11

Triticum spelta — Fl. Palaest. (70) 13; Hort. cul. (132) 8

Triticum turgidum — Hort. cul. (132) 8

Triumfetta — Hort. Upsal. (7) 37; Nova pl. gen. 1747 (14) 17

Triumfetta bartramia — Iter Chin. (161) 9[as barthramia]

Triumfetta decima tertia — Nova pl. gen. 1747 (14) 17

Triumfetta lappula — Fl. Jam. (105) 16

Trixis — Nova pl. gen. 1751 (32) 7, 12; Fl. Jam. (105) 26; Fund. fr. (123) 22

Trochilus — Oecon. nat. (20) 16; Migr. avium (79) [5]; Fl. Cap. (99) [1]; Fund. ornith. (137) 27; Siren. lacert. (146) 8

Trochilus colubris — Migr. avium (79) 14

Trochus — Fund. test. (166) 17, 38

Trochus maculatus — Fund. test. (166) 38

Trochus niloticus — Iter Chin. (161) 8

Trochus perdix — Iter Chin. (161) 13

Trochus perspectivus — Iter Chin. (161) 13

Trochus telescopium — Fund. test. (166) 39

Troglodytes — Fl. Cap. (99) [1]

Trollius — Nect. fl. (122) 13; Fund. fr. (123) 23

Trollius asiaticus — Hist. nat. Rossia (144) 30

Trollius europaeus — Demonstr. pl. (49) 15; Stat. pl. (55) 16, 20; Fl. Angl. (56) 18; Cervus (60) 8; Fl. alp. (71) 19; Calend. fl. (72) [11]; Fl. Monsp. (74) 19; Prodr. fl. Dan. (82) 19; Hort. cul. (132) 24[as europeus]; Fl. Åker. (162) 14; Esca avium (174) 13

Trongum agreste — Herb. Amboin. (57) 21

Trongum album — Herb. Amboin. (57) 21

Trongum hortense — Herb. Amboin. (57) 21

Tropaeolum — Hort. Upsal. (7) 34; Passifl. (8) [iii]; Spons. pl. (12) 59; Vern. arb. (47) 9[as Tropeolum]; Demonstr. pl. (49) [vii]; Stat. pl. (55) 5; Acetaria (77) 10; Pand. insect. (93) 13; Nom. bot. (107) 12; Pl. Alstr. (121) 11; Nect. fl. (122) 14[as Tropeolum]; Fund. fr. (123) 16; Scorb. (180) 16

Tropaeolum majus — Hosp. insect. fl. (43) 20; Demonstr. pl. (49) 11; Pl. officin. (52) 14; Fl. Jam. (105) 15[as Tropeolum]; Mac. olit. (113) 23; Hort. cul. (132) 15

Tropaeolum minus — Demonstr. pl. (49) 11; Pl. Alstr. (121) 5

Trophis — Fl. Jam. (105) 26[as Throphis]

Trophis americana — Pl. Jam. (102) 28; Fl. Jam. (105) 21

Tschiptirra tungusica messerschmidii — Hist. nat. Rossia (144) 16

Tuba baccifera — Herb. Amboin. (57) 18

Tuba flava — Herb. Amboin. (57) 18

Tuba radicum — Herb. Amboin. (57) 18

Tuba siliquosa — Herb. Amboin. (57) 18

Tubera — Cui bono? (42) 16; Nom. bot. (107) 19; Ping. anim. (108) 16, 25

Tubipora musica — Iter Chin. (161) 13; see also Tubularia m.

Tubularia — Corallia Balt. (4) 8, 32, 34, 35; Mund. invis. (149) 8

Tubularia fossilis albicans calcaria, ex tubulis exiguis innumeris concreta, lignum faginum petrificatum utcunque referens — Corallia Balt. (4) 32

Tubularia fossilis candida, ex tubulis brevioribus angustis teretibus constans, et tribus ordinibus fistulosis distincta — Corallia Balt. (4) 32

Tubularia fossilis catenulata silicea scanica … — Corallia Balt. (4) 35

Tubularia fossilis fistulosa, candida, undata et catenulata — Corallia Balt. (4) 34

Tubularia musica [error for Tubipora?] — Anim. comp. (98) 8

Tubularia pentagona, in qua tenuissimi tubuli intersepimentis albidis segregantur — Corallia Balt. (4) 31

Tubulus — Corallia Balt. (4) 8

Tulipa — Peloria (3) 16; Spons. pl. (12) 29, 48; Vir. pl. (13) 20; Pl. escul. (35) 12, 28; Hort. acad. (63) 3; Calend. fl. (72) [10], [11]; Fl. Monsp. (74) 7; Arb. Svec. (101) 19; Nom. bot. (107) 12; Prol. pl. 1760 (114) 4, 13; Fund. fr. (123) 11; Prol. pl. 1763 (130) 9, 10, 16

Tulipa breyniana — Fl. Cap. (99) 13

Tulipa gesneriana — Demonstr. pl. (49) 10; Fl. Palaest. (70) 17; Calend. fl. (72) [11]; Pl. Alstr. (121) 5; Hort. cul. (132) 23, 25

Tulipa javana — Herb. Amboin. (57) 22

Tulipa scanensis — Pan Svec. (26) 20

Tulipa sylvestris — Demonstr. pl. (49) 10; Fl. Monsp. (74) 14; Prodr. fl. Dan. (82) 16; Prol. pl. 1763 (130) 9; Colon. pl. (158) 9

Tuna major, spinis validis flavicantibus, flore sulphureo — Hort. Upsal. (7) 38

Tuna mitior, flore sanguineo, cochenillifera — Hort. Upsal. (7) 38

Turbo — Fund. test. (166) 17, 36

Turbo bidens — Fund. test. (166) 36

Turbo clathrus — Pl. tinct. (97) 30

Turbo scalaris — Instr. mus. (51) 11; Fund. test. (166) 36

Turbo striatulus — Iter Chin. (161) 8

Turdus — Spons. pl. (12) 19; Vir. pl. (13) 7; Oecon. nat. (20) 17, 18, 40; Migr. avium (79) 17, 31; Polit. nat. (109) 13

Turdus ampelis — Migr. avium (79) 32

Turdus aquaticus — Migr. avium (79) 32

Turdus ater, pectore coccineo — Chin. Lagerstr. (64) 14[as cocinaeo]

Turdus chinensis — Chin. Lagerstr. (64) 14

Turdus griseus, subtus ferrugineus, linaea alba ad cutem capitis — Chin. Lagerstr. (64) 14[as grisaeus … ferruginaeus]

Turdus hoematodos — Chin. Lagerstr. (64) 14

Turdus iliacus — Migr. avium (79) 17

Turdus musicus — Migr. avium (79) 17; Fund. ornith. (137) 27

Turdus orpheus — Fund. ornith. (137) 27

Turdus pilaris — Migr. avium (79) 17

Turdus polyglottos — Fund. ornith. (137) 27

Turdus roseus — Migr. avium (79) 31

Turia — Herb. Amboin. (57) 8

Turnera — Cui bono? (42) 22; Fl. Jam. (105) 26; Nect. fl. (122) 5

Turnera pumilea — Pl. Jam. (102) 10; Fl. Jam. (105) 15

Turnera ulmifolia — Demonstr. pl. (49) 9; Fl. Jam. (105) 15

Turrita — Fund. test. (166) 29

Turritis exilis — Fl. Angl. (56) 27

Turritis foliis omnibus dentatis hispidis, caulinis amplexicaulibus — Pl. Mart.-Burs. (6) 7

Turritis glabra — Pan Svec. (26) 28; Herbat. Upsal. (50) 7; Stat. pl. (55) 21; Fl. Angl. (56) 20; Prodr. fl. Dan. (82) 21; Fl. Belg. (112) 19; Fl. Åker. (162) 15; Pand. fl. Ryb. (165) 20

Turritis hirsuta — Herbat. Upsal. (50) 7; Stat. pl. (55) 21; Fl. Angl. (56) 20; Fl. Monsp. (74) 21; Prodr. fl. Dan. (82) 21; Fl. Belg. (112) 19; Pand. fl. Ryb. (165) 20

Tussilago — Anandria (9) 12ff.; Vir. pl. (13) 23; Sem. musc. (28) 3; Sapor. med. (31) 12; Pl. hybr. (33) 7; Vern. arb. (47) 8; Fl. Angl. (56) 6; Metam. pl. (67) 14; Nom. bot. (107) 17

Tussilago albo flore — Pan Svec. (26) 32

Tussilago alpina — Fl. alp. (71) 22

Tussilago anandria — Hort. Upsal. (7) 35; Demonstr. pl. (49) [vii], 23; Pl. Jam. (102) 23; Fund. fr. (123) 12; Hist. nat. Rossia (144) 23, 33

Tussilago farfara — Pan Svec. (26) 32; Herbat. Upsal. (50) 11; Pl. officin. (52) 10, 19; Stat. pl. (55) 22; Fl. Angl. (56) 22; Hort. acad. (63) 10; Calend. fl. (72) [9]; Fl. Monsp. (74) 25; Migr. avium (79) 20; Prodr. fl. Dan. (82) 23; Fl. Belg. (112) 21; Fl. Åker. (162) 17; Pand. fl. Ryb. (165) 21

Tussilago frigida — Stat. pl. (55) 16; Cervus (60) 8; Fl. alp. (71) 22; Hist. nat. Rossia (144) 33; Rar. Norv. (157) 11

Tussilago hybrida — Fl. Angl. (56) 22; Fl. Belg. (112) 9, 21

Tussilago lapponica — Pan Svec. (26) 32

Tussilago nutans — Pl. Jam. (102) 23; Fl. Jam. (105) 20

Tussilago petasites — Pan Svec. (26) 32; Demonstr. pl. (49) 23; Pl. officin. (52) 15; Fl. Angl. (56) 22; Calend. fl. (72) [9], [10]; Prodr. fl. Dan. (82) 23; Fl. Belg. (112) 21; Fl. Åker. (162) 17

Tussilago scapo imbricato, thyrsifloro, flosculis omnibus hermaphroditis — Pl. hybr. (33) 19

Tussilago scapo imbricato, thyrso fastigiato, flosculis foemineis nudis paucis, centralibus hermaphroditis — Pl. hybr. (33) 19

Tussilago scapo imbricato, thyrso oblongo, flosculis foemineis nudis; paucissimis centralibus hermaphroditis — Pl. hybr. (33) 19

Tussilago scapo unifloro calyce clauso — Anandria (9) 14

Typha — Spons. pl. (12) 29, 39; Fl. oecon. (17) 21; Nom. bot. (107) 18; Fund. agrost. (152) 4, 15

Typha angustifolia — Stat. pl. (55) 13; Fl. Angl. (56) 24; Fl. Monsp. (74) 27; Prodr. fl. Dan. (82) 24; Fl. Belg. (112) 22

Typha latifolia — Stat. pl. (55) 13; Fl. Angl. (56) 24; Fl. Monsp. (74) 27; Prodr. fl. Dan. (82) 24; Fl. Jam. (105) 21, 25; Fl. Belg. (112) 22

Typha palustris — Pan Svec. (26) 35

Ubium anguinum — Herb. Amboin. (57) 23

Ubium anniversarium — Herb. Amboin. (57) 23

Ubium digitatum — Herb. Amboin. (57) 23

Ubium nummularium — Herb. Amboin. (57) 24

Ubium ovale — Herb. Amboin. (57) 23

Ubium polypoides — Herb. Amboin. (57) 23

Ubium pomiferum — Herb. Amboin. (57) 23

Ubium quinquefolium — Herb. Amboin. (57) 23

Ubium sylvestre — Herb. Amboin. (57) 23

Ubium vulgare — Herb. Amboin. (57) 22

Ulassium — Herb. Amboin. (57) 11

Ulet — Herb. Amboin. (57) 12

Ulex — Nom. bot. (107) 16; Polit. nat. (109) 5

Ulex capensis — Fl. Cap. (99) 17

Ulex europaeus — Demonstr. pl. (49) 20; Fl. Angl. (56) 20; Fr. Svec. (91) 26

Ulex folio sub spina singula subulato plano acuto — Pl. Mart.-Burs. (6) 29

Ulmaria — Pan Svec. (26) 8; Sapor. med. (31) 15; Usum hist. nat. (145) 19, 21; Fraga (170) 2

Ulmus — Ficus (2) 17; Fl. oecon. (17) 7; Hosp. insect. fl. (43) 40; Mirac. insect. (45) 15; Noxa insect. (46) 26; Vern. arb. (47) 10, table; Oves (61) 18; Calend. fl. (72) [20]; Phalaena (78) 5; Fr. Svec. (91) 24; Pand. insect. (93) 12; Arb. Svec. (101) 16, 30; Nom. bot. (107) 11; Fl. Belg. (112) 8; Prol. pl. 1760 (114) 13

Ulmus campestris — Gem. arb. (24) 29; Pan Svec. (26) 18; Hosp. insect. fl. (43) 18; Herbat. Upsal. (50) 8; Pl. officin. (52) 20; Stat. pl. (55) 19; Fl. Angl. (56) 13; Fl. Palaest. (70) 16; Calend. fl. (72) [9], [10]; Fl. Monsp. (74) 12; Prodr. fl. Dan. (82) 15; Pl. tinct. (97) 29; Arb. Svec. (101) 7, 8, 15; Fl. Belg. (112) 14; Fl. Åker. (162) 9; Pand. fl. Ryb. (165) 17

Ulmus pumila — Hist. nat. Rossia (144) 28; Usum hist. nat. (145) 12

Ulula — Migr. avium (79) 21

Ulva — Vir. pl. (13) 12; Hort. acad. (63) 11

Ulva bucciniformis — Iter Chin. (161) 14

Ulva compressa — Stat. pl. (55) 12; Fl. Palaest. (70) 32

Ulva intestinalis — Herbat. Upsal. (50) 10; Stat. pl. (55) 12

Ulva lactuca — Stat. pl. (55) 12; Prodr. fl. Dan. (82) 26

Ulva latissima — Stat. pl. (55) 12

Ulva linza — Stat. pl. (55) 12

Ulvaria — Vir. pl. (13) 35

Umbellata — Herb. Amboin. (57) 9, 21

Umbraculum maris — Herb. Amboin. (57) 13

Unau — Surin. Grill. (16) 7

Uniola — Nova pl. gen. 1751 (32) 7; Fund. agrost. (152) 20, 28, 31, 37

Unxia — Pl. Surin. (177) 4

Unxia camphorata — Pl. Surin. (177) 14

Upupa epops — Migr. avium (79) 23

Urena — Hort. Upsal. (7) 37; Nova pl. gen. 1747 (14) 17; Nect. fl. (122) 4

Urena americana — Pl. Surin. (177) 11

Urena lobata — Demonstr. pl. (49) 19; Iter Chin. (161) 12

Urena procumbens — Iter Chin. (161) 9

Urena sinuata — Fl. Jam. (105) 19; Pl. Surin. (177) 11

Uroceros — Fund. entom. (154) 29

Ursus — Oecon. nat. (20) 38, 45; Mat. med. anim. (29) [2]; Morb. hyeme (38) [2]; Noxa insect. (46) 30; Cervus (60) 18; Polit. nat. (109) 20; Usum hist. nat. (145) 23; Usum musc. (148) 9

Ursus cauda abrupta — Mat. med. anim. (29) [2]

Ursus cauda elongata — Mus ind. (62) 4

Ursus meles — Esca avium (174) 3

Urtica — Ficus (2) 11; Peloria (3) 10; Hort. Upsal. (7) 35; Anandria (9) 5; Fl. oecon. (17) 21; Curios. nat. (18) 8; Pan Svec. (26) 4; Pl. hybr. (33) 7, 20; Pl. escul. (35) 28; Cui bono? (42) 9, 20; Hosp. insect. fl. (43) 13, 40; Herb. Amboin. (57) 27; Phalaena (78) 5, 6; Pand. insect. (93) 19; Pl. Jam. (102) 28, 30; Nom. bot. (107) 18; Polit. nat. (109) 9; Usum hist. nat. (145) 25; Esca avium (174) 4

Urtica aestuans — Fl. Jam. (105) 21

Urtica altera pilulifera, parietariae foliis — Pl. hybr. (33) 20

Urtica annua — Pan Svec. (26) 35

Urtica canadensis — Demonstr. pl. (49) 25; Calend. fl. (72) [18]; Hist. nat. Rossia (144) 34

Urtica cannabina — Demonstr. pl. (49) 25; Calend. fl. (72) [16]; Hist. nat. Rossia (144) 23, 34

Urtica cylindrica — Fl. Jam. (105) 21

Urtica decumana — Herb. Amboin. (57) 26

Urtica dioica — Hosp. insect. fl. (43) 32; Herbat. Upsal. (50) 20; Pl. officin. (52) 20; Stat. pl. (55) 19; Fl. Angl. (56) 24; Fl. Monsp. (74) 27; Prodr. fl. Dan. (82) 24; Transm. frum. (87) 3; Pl. tinct. (97) 25; Fl. Belg. (112) 22; Mac. olit. (113) 19; Pot. theae (142) 10; Var. cib. (156) 4; Fl. Åker. (162) 19; Pand. fl. Ryb. (165) 22

Urtica dioica, foliis oblongo-cordatis — Pl. hybr. (33) 20

Urtica dioica maxima — Fl. Palaest. (70) 30

Urtica foliis oblonge cordatis — Pl. Mart.-Burs. (6) 19

Urtica grandifolia — Pl. Jam. (102) 26; Fl. Jam. (105) 21

Urtica interrupta — Herb. Amboin. (57) 26

Urtica marina — Taenia (19) 2

Urtica mortua — Herb. Amboin. (57) 26

Urtica nivea — Herb. Amboin. (57) 21

Urtica perennis — Pan Svec. (26) 35; Pl. escul. (35) 24

Urtica pilulifera — Demonstr. pl. (49) 25; Pl. officin. (52) 20; Fl. Angl. (56) 24; Fl. Monsp. (74) 27

Urtica pilulifera, folio profundius urticae majoris in modum serrato, semine magno lini — Pl. hybr. (33) 20

Urtica romana — Fl. Palaest. (70) 30; Calend. fl. (72) [22]

Urtica urens — Herbat. Upsal. (50) 20; Stat. pl. (55) 19; Fl. Angl. (56) 24; Fl. Monsp. (74) 27; Prodr. fl. Dan. (82) 24; Fl. Belg. (112) 22; Fl. Åker. (162) 19; Pand. fl. Ryb. (165) 22; see also U. urentissima

Urtica urentissima [error for urens?] — Hosp. insect. fl. (43) 31

Ustilago — Lepra (140) 10; Mund. invis. (149) 13, 14

Ustilago hordei — Siren. lacert. (146) 8; Mund. invis. (149) 12

Ustilago tritici — Mund. invis. (149) 12

Utricularia — Hort. Upsal. (7) 41; Nect. fl. (122) 5; Erica (163) 2

Utricularia foliosa — Fl. Jam. (105) 12

Utricularia major — Pan Svec. (26) 12

Utricularia minor — Pan Svec. (26) 12; Herbat. Upsal. (50) 16; Stat. pl. (55) 13; Fl. Angl. (56) 9

Utricularia vulgaris — Herbat. Upsal. (50) 16; Stat. pl. (55) 13; Fl. Angl. (56) 9; Fl. Monsp. (74) 8; Prodr. fl. Dan. (82) 13; Esca avium (174) 10

Utricularia vulgaris minor — Herbat. Upsal. (50) 20

Uva ursi — Sapor. med. (31) 15; Erica (163) 12

Uva zeylanica sylvestris, mali aurantiae sapore — Nova pl. gen. 1747 (14) 21

Uvaria — Nova pl. gen. 1747 (14) [vi], 21; Herb. Amboin. (57) 10, 19; Opobals. (135) 2; Obs. mat. med. (171) 7

Uvaria zeylanica — Herb. Amboin. (57) 10, 11

Uvifera arbor americana per funiculos e summis ramis ad terram usque demissis prolifera — Ficus (2) 5

Uvularia — Pl. Mart.-Burs. (6) [vi]; Nova pl. gen. 1751 (32) 9; Nect. fl. (122) 11

Uvularia caule perfoliato — Pl. rar. Camsch. (30) 5

Uvularia foliis perfoliatis — Pl. rar. Camsch. (30) 5

Uvularia folio integerrimo — Pl. rar. Camsch. (30) 5

Uvularia perfoliata — Specif. Canad. (76) 9, 15; Mors. serp. (119) 17; Hist. nat. Rossia (144) 12

Vacca — Curios. nat. (18) 9; Oecon. nat. (20) 36; Pan Svec. (26) 7

Vaccinium — Spons. pl. (12) 33; Vir. pl. (13) 20, 36, 37; Fl. oecon. (17) 10; Pl. escul. (35) 28; Morb. hyeme (38) 12; Cervus (60) 12; Migr. avium (79) 29; Fr. Svec. (91) [ii]; Nom. bot. (107) 12; Fund. fr. (123) 18; Erica (163) 3

Vaccinium arctostaphylos — Usum musc. (148) 11

Vaccinium hispidulum — Fr. escul. (127) 6

Vaccinium maximum — Gem. arb. (24) 16; Pan Svec. (26) 21; Pl. escul. (35) 14

Vaccinium minus — Gem. arb. (24) 16

Vaccinium myrtillus — Herbat. Upsal. (50) 6; Pl. officin. (52) 14; Stat. pl. (55) 18; Fl. Angl. (56) 15; Cervus (60) 7; Calend. fl. (72) [16]; Fl. Monsp. (74) 15; Prodr. fl. Dan. (82) 17; Fr. Svec. (91) 5, 21; Fl. Belg. (112) 16; Fr. escul. (127) 6; Fl. Åker. (162) 11; Erica (163) 12; Pand. fl. Ryb. (165) 18[as Vaxinium]; Esca avium (174) 12

Vaccinium nigrum — Pan Svec. (26) 21; Pl. escul. (35) 14

Vaccinium oxycoccos — Gem. arb. (24) 16; Pan Svec. (26) 21[as oxycoccus]; Pl. escul. (35) 14[as oxycoccus]; Herbat. Upsal. (50) 6; Stat. pl. (55) 15; Fl. Angl. (56) 15[as oxycoccus]; Prodr. fl. Dan. (82) 17; Fl. Belg. (112) 16[as oxycoccus]; Fr. escul. (127) 6[as oxycoccus]; Fl. Åker. (162) 11[as oxycoccus]; Pand. fl. Ryb. (165) 18[as Vaxinium oxycoccus]; Esca avium (174) 12

Vaccinium rubrum — Hosp. insect. fl. (43) 20

Vaccinium uliginosum — Herbat. Upsal. (50) 6; Stat. pl. (55) 14; Fl. Angl. (56) 15; Cervus (60) 7; Prodr. fl. Dan. (82) 17; Fr. Svec. (91) 4, 20; Fr. escul. (127) 6; Pand. fl. Ryb. (165) 18[as Vaxinium]; Esca avium (174) 12

Vaccinium vitis idaea — Gem. arb. (24) 16; Pan Svec. (26) 21; Pl. escul. (35) 14[as idea]; Herbat. Upsal. (50) 6; Pl. officin. (52) 20; Stat. pl. (55) 18; Fl. Angl. (56) 15; Cervus (60) 7; Prodr. fl. Dan. (82) 17; Fr. Svec. (91) 5, 21; Fl. Belg. (112) 16; Fr. escul. (127) 6; Fl. Åker. (162) 11; Esca avium (174) 12

Vaccinium vitis idaeae — Pand. fl. Ryb. (165) 18[as Vaxinium … idaeae]

Valantia — Hort. Upsal. (7) 34; Spons. pl. (12) 58[as Vaillantia]; Somn. pl. (68) 7

Valantia aparine — Demonstr. pl. (49) 26; Fl. Angl. (56) 25; Fl. Monsp. (74) 28

Valantia articulata — Fl. Palaest. (70) 32

Valantia cruciata — Spons. pl. (12) 46; Demonstr. pl. (49) 27; Fl. Angl. (56) 25; Calend. fl. (72) [22]; Fl. Monsp. (74) 28; Pl. Jam. (102) 30; Fl. Belg. (112) 23; Pl. rar. Afr. (115) 7

Valantia cucullaria — Cent. I. pl. (65) 33[as cucullaris]; Fl. Palaest. (70) 32[as cucullata]

Valantia floribus masculis binis trifidis pedunculo hermaphroditi insidentibus — Pl. Mart.-Burs. (6) 25

Valantia fructificationibus singulis bractea ovata deflexa tectis — Cent. I. pl. (65) 33

Valantia hypocarpa — Pl. Jam. (102) 30; Fl. Jam. (105) 22

Valantia muralis — Fl. Palaest. (70) 32; Fl. Monsp. (74) 28

Valeriana — Hort. Upsal. (7) 35; Vir. pl. (13) 31, 35; Fl. oecon. (17) 2; Pan Svec. (26) 2; Sapor. med. (31) 20; Pl. escul. (35) 28; Nom. bot. (107) 9; Nect. fl. (122) 12; Menthae (153) 5; Erica (163) 2; Marum (175) 10

Valeriana calcitrapa — Demonstr. pl. (49) 2; Calend. fl. (72) [22]; Fl. Monsp. (74) 8

Valeriana celtica — Pl. officin. (52) 18; Fl. alp. (71) 12

Valeriana cornucopiae — Demonstr. pl. (49) 2; Fl. Monsp. (74) 8

Valeriana cretica filipendulae radice — Pl. Mart.-Burs. (6) 12

Valeriana dioica — Pan Svec. (26) 13; Stat. pl. (55) 14; Fl. Angl. (56) 10; Fl. Palaest. (70) 11; Fl. Monsp. (74) 8; Prodr. fl. Dan. (82) 13; Fl. Belg. (112) 12

Valeriana floribus tetrandris — Anandria (9) 4[as tetrandis]

Valeriana foliis cordatis serratis petiolatis — Pl. Mart.-Burs. (6) 12

Valeriana foliis pinnato-laciniatis, floribus diandris — Pl. Mart.-Burs. (6) 12

Valeriana locusta — Pan Svec. (26) 13; Pl. hybr. (33) 29; Pl. escul. (35) 7; Stat. pl. (55) 22; Fl. Angl. (56) 10; Fl. Monsp. (74) 8; Acetaria (77) 13; Prodr. fl. Dan. (82) 13; Fl. Belg. (112) 12; Mac. olit. (113) 21

Valeriana locusta coronata — Demonstr. pl. (49) 2

Valeriana locusta discoidea — Demonstr. pl. (49) 2

Valeriana locusta sibirica — Demonstr. pl. (49) 2

Valeriana montana — Fl. alp. (71) 12

Valeriana officinalis — Herbat. Upsal. (50) 14; Pl. officin. (52) 19; Stat. pl. (55) 14; Fl. Angl. (56) 10; Calend. fl. (72) [12]; Fl. Monsp. (74) 8; Prodr. fl. Dan. (82) 13; Fl. Belg. (112) 12; Pl. rar. Afr. (115) 6[as Valleriana]; Purg. indig. (143) 10; Fl. Åker. (162) 5; Pand. fl. Ryb. (165) 16

Valeriana phu — Demonstr. pl. (49) 2; Pl. officin. (52) 15[as Valeariana]; Calend. fl. (72) [12]

Valeriana pyrenaica — Fl. Monsp. (74) 8

Valeriana rubra — Demonstr. pl. (49) 2; Calend. fl. (72) [22]; Fl. Monsp. (74) 8

Valeriana saxatilis — Fl. alp. (71) 12

Valeriana sibirica — Hist. nat. Rossia (144) 23, 27

Valeriana tripteris — Fl. alp. (71) 12; Fl. Monsp. (74) 8

Valeriana tuberosa — Fl. Monsp. (74) 8

Valeriana vulgaris — Pan Svec. (26) 13

Valerianella foliis nervosis acutis, flosculis in caulium summo quasi involucratis — Nova pl. gen. 1747 (14) 8

Valerianella foliis nervosis oblongis, flosculis ad caulium nodos inter foliorum sinus collectis — Vir. pl. (13) 18

Valerianella palustris, foliis nervosis oblongis, flosculis ad caulium nodos inter foliorum sinus collectis — Nova pl. gen. 1747 (14) 8

Vallisneria — Spons. pl. (12) 44; Nect. fl. (122) 8; Siren. lacert. (146) 8

Vallisnerioides — Spons. pl. (12) 44

Vanutscha sibirica, cimicifuga foetida, christophorianae foliis, floribus in thyrso stamineis

luteolis, semine in corniculis villoso rufo — Cimicifuga (173) 5

Vanutscha trava russorum foetidissima, radice perenni, christophorianae foliis, procerior, flore in racemis luteo staminoso, capitulo seminali quadrivaginato, semine villis foliaceis hispido plurimo — Cimicifuga (173) 5

Varinga latifolia — Herb. Amboin. (57) 13

Varinga parvifolia — Herb. Amboin. (57) 13

Varinga repens — Herb. Amboin. (57) 13

Varronia — Fl. Jam. (105) 26

Varronia bullata — Pl. Jam. (102) 9; Fl. Jam. (105) 13

Varronia lineata — Pl. Jam. (102) 9; Fl. Jam. (105) 13

Velezia rigida — Demonstr. pl. (49) 10; Fl. Palaest. (70) 18; Fl. Monsp. (74) 15

Vella annua — Demonstr. pl. (49) 17; Fl. Angl. (56) 19

Vena medinensis — Exanth. viva (86) 14; Lepra (140) 10

Venus — Fund. test. (166) 18, 42

Venus dione — Fund. test. (166) 42, 43

Venus mercenaria — Iter Chin. (161) 8

Veratrum — Spons. pl. (12) 39, 58; Vir. pl. (13) 31; Odor. med. (40) 13, 14; Pand. insect. (93) 22; Usum hist. nat. (145) 24, 29

Veratrum album — Demonstr. pl. (49) 26; Pl. officin. (52) 11; Fl. Monsp. (74) 28; Hort. cul. (132) 24; Hist. nat. Rossia (144) 34; Med. purg. (181) 18

Veratrum caule simplicissimo — Rad. senega (23) 12; Nova pl. gen. 1751 (32) 16

Veratrum luteum — Specif. Canad. (76) 15; Mors. serp. (119) 17

Veratrum nigrum — Hist. nat. Rossia (144) 34; Med. purg. (181) 18

Veratrum racemo composito, corollis patentibus — Med. purg. (181) 18

Veratrum racemo supradecomposito, corollis erectis — Med. purg. (181) 18

Verbasculum pratense vel sylvaticum inodorum — Pl. hybr. (33) 12

Verbasculum sylvaticum inodorum — Pl. hybr. (33) 12

Verbascum — Vir. pl. (13) 19; Fl. oecon. (17) 5; Pand. insect. (93) 12; Nom. bot. (107) 10; Esca avium (174) 2

Verbascum angustifolium ramosum, flore aureo, folio crassiori — Fund. fr. (123) 14

Verbascum blattaria — Demonstr. pl. (49) 6; Fl. Angl. (56) 12; Somn. pl. (68) 22; Fl. Palaest. (70) 15; Fl. Monsp. (74) 12, 30[as blattariae]; Prodr. fl. Dan. (82) 15; Fl. Belg. (112) 14

Verbascum caule fruticoso spinoso — Cent. II. pl. (66) 10

Verbascum creticum spinosum frutescens — Cent. II. pl. (66) 10

Verbascum hirsutum — Pan Svec. (26) 17; Hosp. insect. fl. (43) 17

Verbascum lychnitis — Demonstr. pl. (49) 6; Fl. Angl. (56) 12; Fl. Monsp. (74) 11; Prodr. fl. Dan. (82) 15; Fund. fr. (123) 14

Verbascum lychnitis album — Calend. fl. (72) [14]

Verbascum myconi — Fl. alp. (71) 14

Verbascum nigrum — Pan Svec. (26) 17; Demonstr. pl. (49) 6; Herbat. Upsal. (50) 8; Pl. officin. (52) 19; Stat. pl. (55) 20; Fl. Angl. (56) 12; Calend. fl. (72) [14]; Fl. Monsp. (74) 12; Prodr. fl. Dan. (82) 15; Fl. Belg. (112) 14; Rar. Norv. (157) 14; Fl. Åker. (162) 8; Pand. fl. Ryb. (165) 17

Verbascum phlomoides — Demonstr. pl. (49) 6[as phlomidis]

Verbascum pulverulentum — Fl. Angl. (56) 27

Verbascum scanicum — Pan Svec. (26) 17

Verbascum sinuatum — Fl. Palaest. (70) 15; Fl. Monsp. (74) 11

Verbascum spinosum — Cent. II. pl. (66) 10

Verbascum thapsus — Herbat. Upsal. (50) 9; Pl. officin. (52) 19; Stat. pl. (55) 18[as tapsus]; Fl. Angl. (56) 12; Oves (61) 14; Hort. acad. (63) 10; Fl. Monsp. (74) 11; Prodr. fl. Dan. (82) 15; Fl. Belg. (112) 14; Fund. fr. (123) 14, 15, 16, 17; Fl. Åker. (162) 8; Pand. fl. Ryb. (165) 17

Verbena — Hort. Upsal. (7) 35; Pl. hybr. (33) 7; Fl. Angl. (56) 5; Nom. bot. (107) 9

Verbena americana altissima, spica multiplici, urticae foliis angustis — Pl. hybr. (33) 16

Verbena bonariensis — Demonstr. pl. (49) [1]

Verbena hastata — Demonstr. pl. (49) [1]; Calend. fl. (72) [17]; Pl. rar. Afr. (115) 6

Verbena indica — Fl. Jam. (105) 12

Verbena jamaicensis — Demonstr. pl. (49) [1]; Fl. Jam. (105) 12

Verbena lappulacea — Fl. Jam. (105) 12

Verbena nodiflora — Demonstr. pl. (49) [1]; Fl. Jam. (105) 12

Verbena officinalis — Pl. hybr. (33) 7[as officinarum]; Demonstr. pl. (49) [1]; Pl. officin. (52) 19; Stat. pl. (55) 20; Fl. Angl. (56) 9; Fl. Palaest. (70) 11; Fl. Monsp. (74) 8; Prodr. fl. Dan. (82) 13; Generat. ambig. (104) 12; Fl. Belg. (112) 12

Verbena prismatica — Fl. Jam. (105) 12

Verbena racemo simplicissimo, floribus sessilibus, calycibus fructus reflexis racemoque appressis — Nova pl. gen. 1751 (32) 34

Verbena stoechadifolia — Fl. Jam. (105) 12

Verbena supina — Fl. Palaest. (70) 11

Verbena tetrandra, spicis filiformibus, foliis multifidis laciniatis, caulibus numerosis — Pl. hybr. (33) 16

Verbena tetrandra, spicis longis acuminatis, foliis multifido-laciniatis — Pl. hybr. (33) 16[as tetranda]

Verbena urticifolia — Demonstr. pl. (49) [1]; Calend. fl. (72) [17]; Fl. Jam. (105) 12

Verbena vulgaris — Pan Svec. (26) 12

Verbesina — Vir. pl. (13) 23; Herb. Amboin. (57) 24, 26; Pl. Jam. (102) 25

Verbesina acmella — Pl. officin. (52) 3; Herb. Amboin. (57) 28

Verbesina alata — Demonstr. pl. (49) 23; Fl. Jam. (105) 20

Verbesina alba — Fl. Jam. (105) 20

Verbesina calendulacea — Iter Chin. (161) 9

Verbesina foliis oppositis; calycibus oblongis, sessilibus, confertis; caule laterali — Cent. I. pl. (65) 28

Verbesina nodiflora — Cent. I. pl. (65) 28; Fl. Jam. (105) 20

Verbesina prostrata — Fl. Jam. (105) 20

Vermis — Cui bono? (42) 10

Vermis casei — Taenia (19) 12

Vermis cucurbitinus — Taenia (19) 13ff.

Veronica — Fl. oecon. (17) [1]; Oecon. nat. (20) 29; Pl. hybr. (33) 6, 7; Cui bono? (42) 20; Mirac. insect. (45) 16; Fl. Angl. (56) 6; Pand. insect. (93) 11; Nom. bot. (107) 9; Fund. fr. (123) 21; Pot. theae (142) 8; Erica (163) 2

Veronica africana, floribus ad genicula pedicellis biuncialibus — Pl. rar. Afr. (115) 8

Veronica agrestis — Herbat. Upsal. (50) 12; Stat. pl. (55) 19; Fl. Angl. (56) 9; Fl. Palaest. (70) 11; Fl. Monsp. (74) 8; Prodr. fl. Dan. (82) 12; Fl. Belg. (112) 12; Fl. Åker. (162) 5; Esca avium (174) 10

Veronica alpina — Pan Svec. (26) 12; Stat. pl. (55) 15; Fl. alp. (71) 12

Veronica anagallis — Herbat. Upsal. (50) 14; Fl. Belg. (112) 12; Pand. fl. Ryb. (165) 16

Veronica anagallis aquatica — Fl. Angl. (56) 9; Fl. Palaest. (70) 11; Fl. Monsp. (74) 8; Prodr. fl. Dan. (82) 12

Veronica aphylla — Fl. alp. (71) 12

Veronica arvensis — Demonstr. pl. (49) [1]; Herbat. Upsal. (50) 12; Stat. pl. (55) 19; Fl. Angl. (56) 9; Fl. Monsp. (74) 8; Prodr. fl. Dan. (82) 12; Fl. Belg. (112) 12; Fl. Åker. (162) 5

Veronica beccabunga — Herbat. Upsal. (50) 11; Pl. officin. (52) 5; Stat. pl. (55) 13; Fl. Angl. (56) 9; Fl. Monsp. (74) 8; Prodr. fl. Dan. (82) 12; Fl. Belg. (112) 12; Mac. olit. (113) 21[as deccabunga]; Fl. Åker. (162) 5; Pand. fl. Ryb. (165) 16

Veronica beccabunga oblongifolia — Pan Svec. (26) 12

Veronica beccabunga rotundifolia — Pan Svec. (26) 12

Veronica bellidioides — Fl. alp. (71) 12[as bellidoides]

Veronica bonarota — Fl. alp. (71) 12

Veronica caule non ramoso, floribus congestis terminato, foliis ovatis pene glabris — Pl. Mart.-Burs. (6) 20

Veronica cauliculis adhaerentibus — Pan Svec. (26) 12

Veronica chamaedryoides [error for chamaedrys?] — Fl. Angl. (56) 27

Veronica chamaedrys — Demonstr. pl. (49) [1]; Herbat. Upsal. (50) 6; Stat. pl. (55) 20; Fl. Angl. (56) 9; Calend. fl. (72) [11]; Fl. Monsp. (74) 8; Prodr. fl. Dan. (82) 12; Fl. Belg. (112) 12; Pot. theae (142) 8; Fl. Åker. (162) 5; Pand. fl. Ryb. (165) 16; see also V. chamaedryoides

Veronica clinopodifolia — Pan Svec. (26) 12

Veronica cymbalariae folio — Pl. hybr. (33) 28

Veronica cymbalarifolia — Pan Svec. (26) 12

Veronica femina — Pan Svec. (26) 12

Veronica floribus spicatis, foliis ternis — Pl. Mart.-Burs. (6) 20; Pl. hybr. (33) 7

Veronica foliis ovatis raro crenatis, fructu ovali minori, floribus in summo caule coeruleis — Pl. Mart.-Burs. (6) 20

Veronica hederaefolia — Demonstr. pl. (49) [1]; Fl. Angl. (56) 9[as hederifolia]; Fl. Palaest. (70) 11[as hederifolia]; Fl. Monsp. (74) 8[as hederifolia]; Prodr. fl. Dan. (82) 12; Fl. Belg. (112) 12[as hederifolia]

Veronica hybrida — Pl. hybr. (33) 7; Fl. Angl. (56) 9

Veronica incana — Demonstr. pl. (49) [1]

Veronica latifolia — Demonstr. pl. (49) [1]; Fl. Monsp. (74) 8; Colon. pl. (158) 7

Veronica longifolia — Demonstr. pl. (49) [1]; Calend. fl. (72) [13]; Fl. Belg. (112) 12; Fl. Åker. (162) 5

Veronica maritima — Demonstr. pl. (49) [1]; Stat. pl. (55) 12; Calend. fl. (72) [13]; Prodr. fl. Dan. (82) 12; Generat. ambig. (104) 12

Veronica mas — Pan Svec. (26) 12; Pl. hybr. (33) 23

Veronica minima — Pan Svec. (26) 12

Veronica minima, clinopodii minoris folio, romana, flore purpuro-coerulea — Pl. Mart.-Burs. (6) 21

Veronica montana — Cent. I. pl. (65) 3

Veronica oblongis cauliculis — Pan Svec. (26) 12

Veronica officinalis — Demonstr. pl. (49) [1][as officinarum]; Pl. officin. (52) 20; Stat. pl. (55) 18[as officinarum]; Fl. Angl. (56) 9; Fl. Monsp. (74) 8; Prodr. fl. Dan. (82) 12; Fl. Belg. (112) 12; Pot. theae (142) 8; Fl. Åker. (162) 5; Pand. fl. Ryb. (165) 16

Veronica peregrina — Demonstr. pl. (49) [1]; Prodr. fl. Dan. (82) 12

Veronica procumbens — Cent. I. pl. (65) 3

Veronica prostrata — Pot. theae (142) 8

Veronica pseudo chamaedrys — Pan Svec. (26) 12

Veronica racemis lateralibus paucifloris, calycibus hirsutis, foliis ovatis rugosis crenatis petiolatis, caule debili — Cent. I. pl. (65) 3

Veronica rutaefolia — Pan Svec. (26) 12

Veronica scutellata — Pan Svec. (26) 12; Demonstr. pl. (49) [1]; Herbat. Upsal. (50) 16; Stat. pl. (55) 14; Fl. Angl. (56) 9; Prodr. fl. Dan. (82) 12; Fl. Belg. (112) 12; Fl. Åker. (162) 5

Veronica serpyllifolia — Herbat. Upsal. (50) 7; Stat. pl. (55) 14; Fl. Angl. (56) 9; Fl. Monsp. (74) 8; Prodr. fl. Dan. (82) 12; Fl. Belg. (112) 12; Pl. rar. Afr. (115) 6; Fl. Åker. (162) 5; Pand. fl. Ryb. (165) 16

Veronica sibirica — Hist. nat. Rossia (144) 23

Veronica spicata — Pan Svec. (26) 12; Demonstr. pl. (49) [1]; Herbat. Upsal. (50) 7; Stat. pl. (55) 21; Fl. Angl. (56) 9; Calend. fl. (72) [15]; Prodr. fl. Dan. (82) 12; Fl. Belg. (112) 12; Fl. Åker. (162) 5

Veronica spicata cambrobritannica — Pl. hybr. (33) 23

Veronica spicata minor — Pl. hybr. (33) 23

Veronica spuria — Demonstr. pl. (49) [1]; Calend. fl. (72) [17]; Hist. nat. Rossia (144) 27

Veronica ternifolia — Pan Svec. (26) 12

Veronica tomentosa — Calend. fl. (72) [16]

Veronica triphyllos — Stat. pl. (55) 19; Fl. Angl. (56) 9; Fl. Monsp. (74) 8; Prodr. fl. Dan. (82) 12; Fl. Belg. (112) 12[as triphylla]

Veronica verbena — Fund. fr. (123) 15

Veronica verna — Stat. pl. (55) 21; Fl. Åker. (162) 5

Veronica virginiana [error for virginica?] — Specif. Canad. (76) 13

Veronica virginica — Specif. Canad. (76) 14; see also V. virginiana

Verruca — Corallia Balt. (4) 10

Vertifolia — Herb. Amboin. (57) 12

Vespa — Noxa insect. (46) 31; Fund. entom. (154) 20, 22, 23

Vespa annularis — Cent. insect. (129) 30

Vespa arvensis — Pand. fl. Ryb. (165) 13

Vespa atra, thorace quadridentato, scutello primoque segmento abdominis niveo — Cent. insect. (129) 30

Vespa bidens — Pand. fl. Ryb. (165) 13

Vespa bifasciata — Pand. fl. Ryb. (165) 13

Vespa campestris — Pand. fl. Ryb. (165) 13

Vespa crabro — Esca avium (174) 8

Vespa fusca, genubus antennarum apicibus margineque primi segmenti abdominis flavis — Cent. insect. (129) 30

Vespa ichneumon, antennis reflexis, pedibus anterioribus velut clypeatis — Mirac. insect. (45) 16

Vespa maculata — Cent. insect. (129) 29

Vespa muraria — Pand. fl. Ryb. (165) 13

Vespa nigra, thorace albo maculato, scutelloque quadrimaculata, abdomine postice albo maculato — Cent. insect. (129) 29

Vespa parietum — Pand. fl. Ryb. (165) 13

Vespa quadridens — Cent. insect. (129) 30

Vespa rufa — Pand. fl. Ryb. (165) 13

Vespa spinipes — Pand. fl. Ryb. (165) 13

Vespa vulgaris — Pand. fl. Ryb. (165) 13; Esca avium (174) 3, 4, 8

Vespertilio — Oecon. nat. (20) 38, 41; Morb. hyeme (38) [2]; Polit. nat. (109) 14, 16; Mors. serp. (119) 2; Fund. ornith. (137) 10; Usum hist. nat. (145) 23

Viburnum — Vir. pl. (13) 27; Gem. arb. (24) 6; Fl. Monsp. (74) 7; Fr. Svec. (91) [ii]; Nom. bot. (107) 11; Erica (163) 2

Viburnum americanum odoratum, folio parvo orbiculato, floribus et baccis folio interceptis — Cent. II. pl. (66) 22

Viburnum lantana — Fl. Angl. (56) 13; Fl. Monsp. (74) 13

Viburnum nudum — Demonstr. pl. (49) 9

Viburnum opulus — Herbat. Upsal. (50) 7; Stat. pl. (55) 14; Fl. Angl. (56) 14; Calend. fl. (72) [10]; Prodr. fl. Dan. (82) 16; Fr. Svec. (91) 3, 9, 24, 25; Fl. Belg. (112) 15; Hort. cul. (132) 25; Fl. Åker. (162) 9; Pand. fl. Ryb. (165) 18; Esca avium (174) 11

Viburnum opulus flore pleno — Hort. cul. (132) 25

Viburnum opulus rosea — Demonstr. pl. (49) 9

Viburnum tinus — Fl. Monsp. (74) 13

Vicia — Hort. Upsal. (7) 34, 35; Anandria (9) 4; Vir. pl. (13) 23; Fl. oecon. (17) 18; Pl. escul. (35) 21; Hort. acad. (63) 2; Pand. insect. (93) [17, as 38]; Nom. bot. (107) 16

Vicia benghalensis — Demonstr. pl. (49) 20

Vicia biennis — Demonstr. pl. (49) 20; Calend. fl. (72) [16], [22]; Fl. Monsp. (74) 22; Hist. nat. Rossia (144) 31

Vicia cassubica — Rar. Norv. (157) 9; Fl. Åker. (162) 16

Vicia cracca — Pan Svec. (26) 30; Hosp. insect. fl. (43) 29; Herbat. Upsal. (50) 12; Stat. pl. (55) 18; Fl. Angl. (56) 21; Fl. Monsp. (74) 22; Prodr. fl. Dan. (82) 21; Fl. Belg. (112) 20; Fr. escul. (127) 18; Usum hist. nat. (145) 10; Fl. Åker. (162) 16; Pand. fl. Ryb. (165) 21; Esca avium (174) 14

Vicia dumetorum — Fl. Angl. (56) 20; Fl. Monsp. (74) 22; Prodr. fl. Dan. (82) 21; Esca avium (174) 14

Vicia faba — Hosp. insect. fl. (43) 29; Demonstr. pl. (49) 20; Pl. officin. (52) 10; Fl. Angl. (56) 21; Somn. pl. (68) 17; Fl. Palaest. (70) 25; Fl. Cap. (99) 2; Fl. Jam. (105) 24; Fr. escul. (127) 18; Hort. cul. (132) 16

Vicia foetida — Pan Svec. (26) 30

Vicia frugum — Fl. Monsp. (74) 30

Vicia hybrida — Fl. Palaest. (70) 25; Fl. Monsp. (74) 22

Vicia incana — Fl. Monsp. (74) 30

Vicia lathyroides — Prodr. fl. Dan. (82) 22

Vicia leguminibus adscendentibus, petiolis polyphyllis, foliolis ovatis acutis integerrimis — Pl. Mart.-Burs. (6) 26

Vicia leguminibus erectis, petiolis polyphyllis, foliolis acumine emarginatis, stipulis dentatis — Pl. Mart.-Burs. (6) 27

Vicia lutea — Demonstr. pl. (49) 20; Fl. Angl. (56) 21; Fl. Monsp. (74) 22

Vicia minima — Cent. II. pl. (66) 28

Vicia minima praecox parisiensium — Cent. II. pl. (66) 28

Vicia narbonensis — Demonstr. pl. (49) 20; Fl. Monsp. (74) 22

Vicia nissolia angustifolia — Fl. Palaest. (70) 25

Vicia onobrychidis — Fl. Monsp. (74) 22

Vicia pedunculis multifloris, stipulis utrinque acutis integris — Pl. Mart.-Burs. (6) 26

Vicia pedunculis uni-biflorisve, petiolis diphyllis, brevissime cirrhosis — Cent. II. pl. (66) 28

Vicia peregrina — Fl. Monsp. (74) 22

Vicia praecox verna minima soloniensis, semine hexaedro — Cent. II. pl. (66) 28

Vicia sativa — Pan Svec. (26) 30; Demonstr. pl. (49) 20; Herbat. Upsal. (50) 18; Stat. pl. (55) 19; Fl. Angl. (56) 20; Fl. Monsp. (74) 22; Prodr. fl. Dan. (82) 22; Pane diaet. (83) 14; Fl. Belg. (112) 20; Pl. rar. Afr. (115) 6; Fr. escul. (127) 18; Fl. Åker. (162) 16; Pand. fl. Ryb. (165) 21

Vicia scanica maxima — Pan Svec. (26) 30

Vicia semine rotundo nigro — Fl. Angl. (56) 28

Vicia sepium — Pan Svec. (26) 30; Herbat. Upsal. (50) 18; Stat. pl. (55) 17; Prodr. fl. Dan. (82) 22; Fl. Belg. (112) 20; Fl. Åker. (162) 16

Vicia siliquis latis — Fl. Monsp. (74) 30

Vicia siliquis longioribus — Fl. Monsp. (74) 30

Vicia sylvatica — Herbat. Upsal. (50) 8; Stat. pl. (55) 17; Fl. Angl. (56) 21; Prodr. fl. Dan. (82) 21; Pand. fl. Ryb. (165) 21; Esca avium (174) 14

Vidara litorea — Herb. Amboin. (57) 9

Vidoricum — Herb. Amboin. (57) 8, 14

Vinca — Hort. Upsal. (7) 33; Hort. acad. (63) 17; Nom. bot. (107) 11

Vinca caule volubili, foliis oblongis — Cent. II. pl. (66) 12

Vinca lutea — Cent. II. pl. (66) 12

Vinca major — Demonstr. pl. (49) 7; Fl. Angl. (56) 12; Fl. Monsp. (74) 12

Vinca minor — Demonstr. pl. (49) 7; Pl. officin. (52) 20; Fl. Angl. (56) 12; Fl. Belg. (112) 14; Hort. cul. (132) 24

Vinca rosea — Hort. cul. (132) 26

Viola — Pl. Mart.-Burs. (6) [vi]; Spons. pl. (12) 46, 59; Vir. pl. (13) 31; Sem. musc. (28) 3; Hosp. insect. fl. (43) 13; Vern. arb. (47) 8; Fl. Angl. (56) 6; Pand. insect. (93) 18; Nom. bot. (107) 17; Nect. fl. (122) 12; Purg. indig. (143) 17; Erica (163) 2; Viola ipecac. (176) 6ff.; Med. purg. (181) 17

Viola acaulis, foliis reniformibus — Pl. Mart.-Burs. (6) 16

Viola alba — Calend. fl. (72) [9]

Viola apetala — Pan Svec. (26) 34

Viola bicolor — Herbat. Upsal. (50) 12

Viola biflora — Stat. pl. (55) 16; Fl. alp. (71) 23; Rar. Norv. (157) 11

Viola calcarata — Fl. alp. (71) 22; Nect. fl. (122) 12

Viola canina — Pan Svec. (26) 33; Herbat. Upsal. (50) 7; Stat. pl. (55) 18; Fl. Angl. (56) 23; Fl. Monsp. (74) 26; Prodr. fl. Dan. (82) 24; Fl. Belg. (112) 21; Fl. Åker. (162) 18; Pand. fl. Ryb. (165) 22

Viola caulescens, foliis cordatis oblongis acuminatis — Pl. Mart.-Burs. (6) 16

Viola diandra — Viola ipecac. (176) 8

Viola enneasperma — Nect. fl. (122) 12[as enneosperma]

Viola floribus radicalibus corollatis abortientibus, caulinis apetalis seminiferis — Pl. Mart.-Burs. (6) 16; Sem. musc. (28) 4

Viola foliis ovalibus margine subtusque pilosis — Med. purg. (181) 17

Viola grandiflora, veronicae folio villoso — Viola ipecac. (176) 6

Viola hirta — Herbat. Upsal. (50) 7; Stat. pl. (55) 17; Fl. Angl. (56) 23; Calend. fl. (72) [9]; Prodr. fl. Dan. (82) 23; Fl. Åker. (162) 18; Pand. fl. Ryb. (165) 22

Viola ipecacuanha — Viola ipecac. (176) 7; Med. purg. (181) 17

Viola lanceolata — Hist. nat. Rossia (144) 33

Viola lutea — Pan Svec. (26) 34

Viola martia — Vir. pl. (13) 30

Viola mirabilis — Herbat. Upsal. (50) 8; Stat. pl. (55) 17; Prodr. fl. Dan. (82) 24; Pand. fl. Ryb. (165) 22; Esca avium (174) 14

Viola montana — Demonstr. pl. (49) 24; Stat. pl. (55) 16; Fl. alp. (71) 22

Viola montana, laciniato folio — Sem. musc. (28) 4

Viola odorata — Demonstr. pl. (49) 24; Pl. officin. (52) 20; Fl. Angl. (56) 23; Fl. Palaest. (70) 29; Calend. fl. (72) [9], [10]; Fl. Monsp. (74) 26; Prodr. fl. Dan. (82) 23; Pl. tinct. (97) 24; Arb. Svec. (101) 16; Fl. Belg. (112) 21; Hort. cul. (132) 24, 25; Purg. indig. (143) 13

Viola officinarum — Pan Svec. (26) 33

Viola palustris — Pan Svec. (26) 33; Herbat. Upsal. (50) 8; Fl. Angl. (56) 23; Prodr. fl. Dan. (82) 23; Fl. Åker. (162) 18; Pand. fl. Ryb. (165) 22

Viola pinnata — Fl. alp. (71) 22; Hist. nat. Rossia (144) 33

Viola primulifolia — Hist. nat. Rossia (144) 33

Viola trachelifolia — Pan Svec. (26) 34

Viola tricolor — Spons. pl. (12) 33, 37; Vir. pl. (13) 30; Pan Svec. (26) 34; Stat. pl. (55) 21; Fl. Angl. (56) 23; Fl. Monsp. (74) 26; Prodr. fl. Dan. (82) 24;

Nom. bot. (107) 17; Fl. Belg. (112) 21; Fl. Åker. (162) 18; Pand. fl. Ryb. (165) 22

Viola tricolor beta — Hosp. insect. fl. (43) 31

Viola uniflora — Hist. nat. Rossia (144) 33

Vipera — Amphib. Gyll. (5) 3, 5, 6; Surin. Grill. (16) 32; Oecon. nat. (20) 28; Rad. senega (23) 5; Mat. med. anim. (29) 12

Vipera americana caudisona, longitudine 4 pedes exaequans, coloris leucophaei, hinc inde in dorso fusco colore adspersa, tintinabulum seu crepitaculum in cauda extrema a multis squamis compositum, habens — Surin. Grill. (16) 23

Vipera anglica fusca, dorso linea undata nigricante conspicua — Amphib. Gyll. (5) 6

Vipera anglica nigricans — Amphib. Gyll. (5) 5

Vipera caudisona — Amphib. Gyll. (5) 3, 6; Hort. Upsal. (7) 3, 43; Spons. pl. (12) 23; Vir. pl. (13) 15

Vipera caudisona americana — Mus. Ad.-Frid. (11) 20

Vipera caudisona americana minor — Rad. senega (23) 7

Vipera cobras de cabelos, naja dicta — Lign. colubr. (21) 6

Vipera orientalis, maxima caudisona — Mus. Ad.-Frid. (11) 20

Vipera vera indiae orientalis — Amphib. Gyll. (5) 6

Virecta — Pl. Surin. (177) 4

Virecta virens — Pl. Surin. (177) 7

Virga aurea — Vir. pl. (13) 23

Virga aurea americana hirsuta, radice odorata — Specif. Canad. (76) 9

Virga aurea minor, foliis glutinosis et graveolentibus — Cent. I. pl. (65) 28

Viscago — Pl. Mart.-Burs. (6) 17

Viscago cerastii foliis, vasculis erectis sessilibus — Pl. Mart.-Burs. (6) 17; Cent. II. pl. (66) 16

Viscum — Spons. pl. (12) 19, 41; Vir. pl. (13) 12; Cryst. gen. (15) 37; Fl. oecon. (17) 26; Oecon. nat. (20) 17; Sapor. med. (31) 12; Stat. pl. (55) 23; Fr. Svec. (91) [ii]; Nom. bot. (107) 18; Polit. nat. (109) 5; Erica (163) 2; Aphyteia (185) 9, 10

Viscum album — Pl. officin. (52) 20; Fl. Angl. (56) 24; Fung. melit. (69) 2; Fl. Palaest. (70) 31; Fl. Monsp. (74) 28; Prodr. fl. Dan. (82) 25; Fr. Svec. (91) 5, 21; Fl. Belg. (112) 23

Viscum amboinicum — Herb. Amboin. (57) 19

Viscum arboreum — Pan Svec. (26) 36

Viscum opuntioides — Fung. melit. (69) 2; Fl. Jam. (105) 21

Viscum purpureum — Fung. melit. (69) 2

Viscum rubrum — Fung. melit. (69) 2

Viscum verticillatum — Fung. melit. (69) 2; Fl. Jam. (105) 21

Vitex — Herb. Amboin. (57) 18

Vitex agnus — Fl. Palaest. (70) 23

Vitex agnus castus — Pl. officin. (52) 4

Vitex negundo — Herb. Amboin. (57) 15; Fl. Jam. (105) 18

Vitex pinnata — Herb. Amboin. (57) 18

Vitex trifolia — Herb. Amboin. (57) 15; see also V. trifoliata

Vitex trifoliata [error for trifolia?] — Iter Chin. (161) 12

Viticella — Nova pl. gen. 1751 (32) 11

Vitis — Hort. Upsal. (7) 36; Vir. pl. (13) 33; Nova pl. gen. 1747 (14) 6; Vern. arb. (47) 9; Pand. insect. (93) 12; Nom. bot. (107) 11; Inebr. (117) 13; Fraga (170) [1]

Vitis alba — Herb. Amboin. (57) 24

Vitis foliis quinatis — Pl. hybr. (33) 28

Vitis idaea — Cervus (60) 12[as idaeae]

Vitis indica — Herb. Amboin. (57) 24

Vitis labrusca — Demonstr. pl. (49) 7; Fl. Jam. (105) 14

Vitis maderaspatana, fructu azureo, folio subrotundo et anguloso — Nova pl. gen. 1747 (14) 6

Vitis trifolia — Herb. Amboin. (57) 24

Vitis vinifera — Gem. arb. (24) 27; Demonstr. pl. (49) 7; Pl. officin. (52) 14, 20; Fl. Palaest. (70) 15; Fl. Monsp. (74) 12; Fl. Jam. (105) 24; Fr. escul. (127) 8; Hort. cul. (132) 21

Vitis vulpina — Demonstr. pl. (49) 7

Viverra — Lign. colubr. (21) 9; Mors. serp. (119) 18

Viverra indica ex griseo rufescens — Lign. colubr. (21) 9

Viverra indica, qwil et qwirpele dicta — Lign. colubr. (21) 9

Viverra memphitis — Ambros. (100) 8

Viverra putorius — Ambros. (100) 8

Volkameria — Hort. Upsal. (7) 37[as Volchameria]

Volkameria inermis — Herb. Amboin. (57) 19

Volubilis — Sem. musc. (28) 3, 4

Voluta — Fund. test. (166) 17

Voluta turbinellus — Iter Chin. (161) 8

Volvox — Anim. comp. (98) 3, 9; Prol. pl. 1760 (114) 21; Siren. lacert. (146) 8; Mund. invis. (149) 15

Volvox globator — Prol. pl. 1760 (114) 4

Vorticella — Mund. invis. (149) 5

Vulpes — Oecon. nat. (20) 26, 45; Mat. med. anim. (29) 3; Morb. hyeme (38) 12, 13

Vulpes alba — Oecon. nat. (20) 44; Morb. hyeme (38) 3; Cynogr. (54) 3; Cervus (60) 10

Vulpes campestris — Cynogr. (54) 3

Vulpes vulgaris — Cynogr. (54) 3

Vultur gryphus — Fund. ornith. (137) 11

Vulvaria — Hort. Upsal. (7) 34; Odor. med. (40) 13

Wachendorfia — Pl. rar. Afr. (115) 4; Pl. Alstr. (121) 6[as Wachendorffia]; Nect. fl. (122) 8; Fund. fr. (123) 18

Wachendorfia paniculata — Fl. Cap. (99) 11

Wachendorfia thyrsiflora — Fl. Cap. (99) 11

Wachendorfia villosa — Fl. Cap. (99) 11

Waeranya — Nova pl. gen. 1747 (14) 8

Walikaha seu waelikaha — Nova pl. gen. 1747 (14) 16

Waltheria angustifolia — Fl. Jam. (105) 18

Waltheria indica — Fl. Jam. (105) 18, 26

Weimannia — Fl. Jam. (105) 26

Weimannia pinnata — Fl. Jam. (105) 15

Winterana — Fl. Jam. (105) 26; Nect. fl. (122) 10

Winterana canella — Fl. Jam. (105) 17, 26

Xanthium — Spons. pl. (12) 39; Gem. arb. (24) 13; Vern. arb. (47) 9[as Xantium]; Stat. pl. (55) 6; Fund. agrost. (152) 18, 22

Xanthium inerme — Pan Svec. (26) 35

Xanthium spinosum — Fl. Monsp. (74) 27; Colon. pl. (158) 10

Xanthium strumarium — Demonstr. pl. (49) 25; Pl. officin. (52) 20; Fl. Angl. (56) 24[as strumosum]; Fl. Monsp. (74) 27; Prodr. fl. Dan. (82) 24; Pl. tinct. (97) 25; Fl. Belg. (112) 22

Xeranthemum — Hort. Upsal. (7) 34; Fund. fr. (123) 17, 18

Xeranthemum annuum — Demonstr. pl. (49) 23; Fl. Palaest. (70) 28; Fl. Monsp. (74) 25

Xeranthemum canescens — Pl. rar. Afr. (115) 20

Xeranthemum caulibus fruticosis, foliis ovatis nudis, pedunculis squamosis — Pl. rar. Afr. (115) 20

Xeranthemum erucifolium — Hist. nat. Rossia (144) 33

Xeranthemum foliis imbricatis, ovato-subulatis glabris — Pl. rar. Afr. (115) 20

Xeranthemum imbricatum — Pl. rar. Afr. (115) 20

Xeranthemum incanum, foliis subrotundis, flore purpureo — Pl. rar. Afr. (115) 20

Xeranthemum paniculatum — Fl. Cap. (99) 18

Xeranthemum proliferum — Fl. Cap. (99) 17; Aphyteia (185) [5]

Xeranthemum retortum — Fl. Cap. (99) 18

Xeranthemum sesamoides — Fl. Cap. (99) 18

Xeranthemum spinosum — Fl. Cap. (99) 18

Xeranthemum vestitum — Fl. Cap. (99) 17

Ximenia aegyptiaca — Fl. Palaest. (70) 32

Xylobalsamum — Opobals. (135) 6ff.

Xylopia — Fl. Jam. (105) 26

Xylopia strigilata — Fl. Jam. (105) 20

Xylopicrum — Fl. Jam. (105) 26

Xyris — Nova pl. gen. 1751 (32) 7

Yucca — Hort. Upsal. (7) 37

Yucca draconis — Demonstr. pl. (49) 10

Yucca gloriosa — Demonstr. pl. (49) 10

Yucca sanguis draconis — Demonstr. pl. (49) 10

Yvana — Amphib. Gyll. (5) 18

Yvana seu iguana — Amphib. Gyll. (5) 18

Zannichellia — Pl. Mart.-Burs. (6) [1]; Pan Svec. (26) 34

Zannichellia palustris — Herbat. Upsal. (50) 10; Stat. pl. (55) 13[as Zanichellia]; Fl. Angl. (56) 23[as Zanichellia]; Fl. Monsp. (74) 27[as Zannichella]; Prodr. fl. Dan. (82) 24[as Zanichellia]; Fl. Belg. (112) 22[as _anichellia]

Zanthoxylum — Nova pl. gen. 1751 (32) 25, 48

Zanthoxylum clava herculis — Fl. Jam. (105) 22[as Zantoxylon]

Zanthoxylum spinosum, lentisci longioribus foliis, euonymi fructu capsulari — Nova pl. gen. 1751 (32) 25

Zea — Spons. pl. (12) 33, 39, 50; Vir. pl. (13) 32; Nova pl. gen. 1751 (32) 10; Nom. bot. (107) 18; Fund. agrost. (152) 16, 25, 32, 34

Zea mays — Demonstr. pl. (49) 25; Fl. Palaest. (70) 29; Pane diaet. (83) 20; Fl. Cap. (99) 2; Fl. Jam. (105) 21; Pl. Alstr. (121) 11; Fr. escul. (127) 20

Zebra — Fl. Cap. (99) [1]

Zedoaria — Sapor. med. (31) 19; Odor. med. (40) 15; Herb. Amboin. (57) 5

Zerumbed — Herb. Amboin. (57) 20

Zerumbet — Herb. Amboin. (57) 5

Zerumbet claviculatum — Herb. Amboin. (57) 20

Zeugites — Fl. Jam. (105) 26

Zibetha — Fl. Cap. (99) [1]; Ambros. (100) 8

Zingiber — Hort. Upsal. (7) 37; Sapor. med. (31) 19; Pl. escul. (35) 13[as Zingebra]; Herb. Amboin. (57) 5

Zingiber majus — Herb. Amboin. (57) 20

Zingiber minus — Herb. Amboin. (57) 20

Zizania — Vir. pl. (13) 16; Nova pl. gen. 1751 (32) 10, 12; Fund. agrost. (152) 5, 26, 35

Zizania aquatica — Fl. Jam. (105) 21; Fr. escul. (127) 20; Usum hist. nat. (145) 10

Zizania canadensis — Cui bono? (42) 18

Ziziphora — Hort. Upsal. (7) 35; Pl. hybr. (33) 28; Marum (175) 13

Ziziphora acinoides — Hist. nat. Rossia (144) 27

Ziziphora foliis ovatis, floribus racemoso-spicatis, bracteis obovatis nervosis acutis — Cent. I. pl. (65) 3

Ziziphora hispanica — Cent. I. pl. (65) 3

Ziziphora tenuior — Demonstr. pl. (49) 2; Hist. nat. Rossia (144) 23

Zizyphus — Pl. escul. (35) 4; Fl. Monsp. (74) 7

Zoophthalmum — Fl. Jam. (105) 26[as Zoophtalmum]

Zoopterygius — Nat. pelagi (84) 9, 12

Zostera — Nova pl. gen. 1747 (14) [vi], 27; Fl. oecon. (17) 30; Nom. bot. (107) 17

Zostera marina — Pan Svec. (26) 34[as maritima]; Stat. pl. (55) 12; Fl. Angl. (56) 23; Fl. Monsp. (74) 27; Prodr. fl. Dan. (82) 24; Fl. Belg. (112) 22

Zuzygium — Fl. Jam. (105) 26[as Suzygium]

Zygia — Fl. Jam. (105) 26

Zygophyllum — Hort. Upsal. (7) 36; Metam. pl. (67) 13; Fl. Cap. (99) 6, 8; Nect. fl. (122) 9; Fund. fr. (123) 16; Lign. Qvas. (128) 7

Zygophyllum aestuans — Lign. Qvas. (128) 5

Zygophyllum coccineum — Fl. Cap. (99) 14

Zygophyllum fabago — Demonstr. pl. (49) 11; Fl. Palaest. (70) 19

Zygophyllum fulvum — Fl. Cap. (99) 14

Zygophyllum morgsana — Fl. Cap. (99) 14

Zygophyllum nitraria — Demonstr. pl. (49) 11

Zygophyllum sessilifolium — Fl. Cap. (99) 14

Zygophyllum spinosum — Fl. Cap. (99) 14

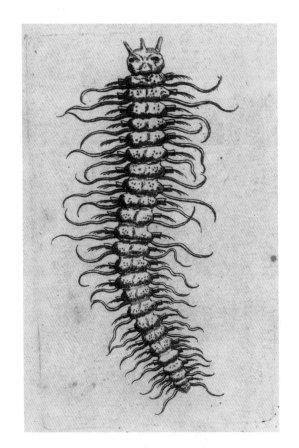

Plate from Noctiluca marina ... *(1752), a dissertation defended by C. F. Adler with Linnaeus as praeses.*

Synoptic Bibliography

Introduction

The 186 original Linnaean dissertations, published between 1743 and 1776, were the joint products of Carl Linnaeus and his students. Their subject matter includes such diverse topics as Baltic coral, the flora of England, insects, medical botany, the botanical garden at Uppsala, dogs, and chocolate. In accordance with the standard practice of the time, although the studies were the 18th-century equivalent of today's doctoral dissertations, the ideas defended therein were those of the Praeses rather than of the Respondent. Thus the dissertations are often attributed to Linnaeus, rather than to the students who published and defended them.

Conventions Used

This bibliography lists the dissertations chronologically and includes in each entry the respondent, title, date of defense and original pagination. The dates are based on those in Soulsby's *A catalogue of the works of Linnaeus* …, ed. 2. Notes have been added to reflect those instances in which information on copies in the Strandell Collection at the Hunt Institute ("Strandell copies" hereafter) differs from that reported by Soulsby et al.

Curly brackets { } indicate date information that has been supplied in manuscript on our copies of the dissertations, whether to fill a blank or to alter printed information. Regarding pagination, any references to unnumbered or misnumbered pages refer to all Strandell copies of a given dissertation unless our copies are at variance with one other, in which case a note is supplied. Square brackets [] indicate unnumbered preliminary, beginning or ending pages. In a few cases where there are page numbering errors on a beginning or ending page, notes in parentheses () are added to clarify these irregularities.

Initial dedicatory phrases and further qualifying phrases have been omitted from the titles as we have reproduced them here. The additional short title is that by which the dissertation is cited in the Index to Scientific Names. The number and title used by Lidén to cite each dissertation are given, as are the titles by which the dissertations are cited in the standard reference works by Soulsby and Drake.

Original Dissertations

Lidén Number	1
Respondent	Klase, L. M.
Title	... de Betula nana,...
Date of Defense	{30} June 1743
Pagination	[iv], 1–20, 1 plate
Short Title	Betula
Lidén title	Betula Nana.
Soulsby title	Betula.
Drake title	Betula nana.

Lidén Number	2
Respondent	Hegardt, C.
Title	... Ficus, ...
Date of Defense	15 September 1744
Pagination	[iv], 1–28, 1 plate
Short Title	Ficus
Lidén title	Ficus, ejusque historia naturalis & medica.
Soulsby title	Ficus.
Drake title	Ficus.

Lidén Number	3
Respondent	Rudberg, D.
Title	... de Peloria, ...
Date of Defense	19 December 1744
Pagination	[x], 3–18, [4], 1 plate
Short Title	Peloria
Lidén title	Peloria.
Soulsby title	Peloria.
Drake title	Peloria.

Lidén Number	4
Respondent	Fougt, H.
Title	... Corallia Baltica adumbrans, ...
Date of Defense	8 June 1745
Pagination	[viii], [1], 2–40, 1 plate
Short Title	Corallia Balt.
Lidén title	Corallia Baltica.
Soulsby title	Corallia.
Drake title	Corallia baltica.

Lidén Number	5
Respondent	Hast, B. R.
Title	Amphibia Gyllenborgiana, ...
Date of Defense	18 June 1745
Pagination	[viii], [1], 2–34, [2]
Short Title	Amphib. Gyll.
Lidén title	Amphibia Gyllenborgiana.
Soulsby title	Amphib. Gyll.
Drake title	Amphibia Gyllenborgiana.

Lidén Number	6
Respondent	Martin, R.
Title	... Plantae Martino-Burserianae explicantur ...
Date of Defense	12 December 1745
Pagination	[viii], [1], 2–31, [1]
Short Title	Pl. Mart.-Burs.
Lidén title	Plantae Martino-Burserianae explicatae.

Soulsby title	Plant. Mart.-Burser.
Drake title	Plantae Martino-Burserianae.
Note	P. 19 unnumbered in two of three Strandell copies.

Lidén Number	7
Respondent	Nauclér, S.
Title	Hortus Upsaliensis, …
Date of Defense	16 December 1745
Pagination	[iv], [1], 2–45, [3], 4 plates
Short Title	Hort. Upsal.
Lidén title	Hortus Upsaliensis.
Soulsby title	Hort. Upsal.
Drake title	Hortus Upsaliensis.
Note	P. 42 unnumbered in one of two Strandell copies.

Lidén Number	8
Respondent	Hallman, J. G.
Title	… de Passiflora …
Date of Defense	18 December 1745
Pagination	[iv], [1], 2–37, [1], 1 plate
Short Title	Passifl.
Lidén title	Passiflora.
Soulsby title	Passiflora.
Drake title	Passiflora.

Lidén Number	9
Respondent	Tursén, E. Z.
Title	… de Anandria, …
Date of Defense	20 December 1745
Pagination	[iv], [1], 2–15, [1], 1 plate
Short Title	Anandria
Lidén title	Anandria.
Soulsby title	Anandria.
Drake title	Anandria.

Lidén Number	10
Respondent	Heiligtag, J. B.
Title	… Acrostichum …
Date of Defense	23 December 1745
Pagination	[iv], [1], 2–17
Short Title	Acrostichum
Lidén title	Acrostichum.
Soulsby title	Acrostichum.
Drake title	Acrostichum.
Note	Soulsby notes a plate cited in the text, but he hadn't seen one, and the Strandell copy also has no plate.

Lidén Number	11
Respondent	Balk, L.
Title	Museum Adolpho-Fridericianum, …
Date of Defense	31 May 1746
Pagination	[viii], [1], 2–48, [2], 2 plates
Short Title	Mus. Ad.-Frid.
Lidén title	Museum Adolpho-Fridericianum.
Soulsby title	Mus. Ad.-Frid.
Drake title	Museum Adolpho-Fridericianum.

Lidén Number	12
Respondent	Wahlbom, J. G.
Title	Sponsalia Plantarum, …
Date of Defense	{11} June 1746
Pagination	[xii], [1], 8–60, [2], 1 plate

Short Title	Spons. pl.
Lidén title	Sponsalia Plantarum.
Soulsby title	Spons. Plant.
Drake title	Sponsalia plantarum.
Lidén Number	13
Respondent	Hasselquist, F.
Title	Vires Plantarum, …
Date of Defense	{20} June 1747
Pagination	[ii], [1], 4–37, [3]
Short Title	Vir. pl.
Lidén title	Vires Plantarum.
Soulsby title	Vires Plant.
Drake title	Vires plantarum.
Note	Two Strandell copies have day left blank; one Strandell copy has day supplied in ms. as {25} or {29}, partly illegible.
Lidén Number	14
Respondent	Dassow, C. M.
Title	Nova Plantarum Genera, …
Date of Defense	{15} June 1747
Pagination	[vi], 1–32, [2]
Short Title	Nova pl. gen. 1747
Lidén title	Nova Plantarum Genera.
Soulsby title	Nova Plant. Gen.
Drake title	Nova plantarum genera 1747.
Lidén Number	15
Respondent	Kähler, M.
Title	… de Crystallorum generatione …
Date of Defense	22 December 1747
Pagination	[viii], [1], 2–30, [2], 1 plate
Short Title	Cryst. gen.
Lidén title	Crystallorum Generatione.
Soulsby title	Crystall. Gen.
Drake title	Crystallorum generatio.
Note	P. 3 unnumbered; p. 26 misnumbered 29.
Lidén Number	16
Respondent	Sundius, P.
Title	Surinamensia Grilliana …
Date of Defense	18 June 1748
Pagination	[vi], 1–34, 1 plate
Short Title	Surin. Grill.
Lidén title	Surinamensia Grilliana.
Soulsby title	Surin. Grill.
Drake title	Surinamensa [sic] Grilliana.
Note	P. 24 misnumbered 42.
Lidén Number	17
Respondent	Aspelin, E.
Title	Flora oeconomica, …
Date of Defense	25 June 1748
Pagination	[viii], [1], 2–30
Short Title	Fl. oecon.
Lidén title	Flora Oeconomica.
Soulsby title	Flora oecon.
Drake title	Flora oeconomica.
Note	P. 19 misnumbered 11.
Lidén Number	18
Respondent	Söderberg, O.

Title	… de Curiositate Naturali, …
Date of Defense	{30} June 1748
Pagination	[vi], [1], 2–25, [1]
Short Title	Curios. nat.
Lidén title	Curiositate Naturali.
Soulsby title	Curios. Nat.
Drake title	Curiositas naturalis.

Lidén Number	19
Respondent	Dubois, G.
Title	… de Taenia, …
Date of Defense	{9} December 1748
Pagination	[iv], [1], 2–36, 1 plate, title page figure
Short Title	Taenia
Lidén title	Taenia.
Soulsby title	Taenia.
Drake title	Taenia.
Note	Two Strandell copies agree on this date; one Strandell copy has day left blank.

Lidén Number	20
Respondent	Biberg, I. I.
Title	… de OEconomia Naturae, …
Date of Defense	4 March 1749
Pagination	[viii], [1], 2–48
Short Title	Oecon. nat.
Lidén title	OEconomia Naturae.
Soulsby title	OEcon. Nat.
Drake title	Oeconomia naturae.
Note	P. 5 misnumbered 7; p. 37 misnumbered 7.

Lidén Number	21
Respondent	Darelli, J. A. af.
Title	Lignum colubrinum leviter delineatum …
Date of Defense	11 March 1749
Pagination	[i], [1], 3–22
Short Title	Lign. colubr.
Lidén title	Lignum Colubrinum.
Soulsby title	Lignum col.
Drake title	Lignum colubrinum.
Note	P. 17 misnumbered 13 in one of three Strandell copies.

Lidén Number	22
Respondent	Hagström, J. O.
Title	… de Generatione Calculi, …
Date of Defense	5 April 1749
Pagination	[iv], [1], 2–17 (i.e., 27), [1]
Short Title	Generat. calc.
Lidén title	Generatione Calculi.
Soulsby title	Gener. Calc.
Drake title	Generatio calculi.
Note	P. 27 misnumbered 17.

Lidén Number	23
Respondent	Kiernander, J. A.
Title	Radix Senega, …
Date of Defense	{8} April 1749
Pagination	[ii], [1], 4–32, 1 plate
Short Title	Rad. Senega
Lidén title	Radix Senega.
Soulsby title	Radix.
Drake title	Radix Senega.
Note	P. 13 misnumbered 14.

Lidén Number	24
Respondent	Löfling, P.
Title	Gemmae Arborum, …
Date of Defense	18 November 1749
Pagination	[iv], [1], 2–32
Short Title	Gem. arb.
Lidén title	Gemmae Arborum.
Soulsby title	Gemmae.
Drake title	Gemmae arborum.
Note	P. 31 misnumbered 13.

Lidén Number	25
Respondent	Elff, E. E.
Title	… de Haemorrhagiis uteri sub statu graviditatis, …
Date of Defense	6 December 1749
Pagination	[i], [1], 3–23, [1]
Short Title	Haemor. uteri
Lidén title	Haemorrhagiis uteri sub statu graviditatis.
Soulsby title	Haemorrh.
Drake title	Haemorrhagiae uteri sub statu graviditatis.
Note	P. 12 misnumbered 2.

Lidén Number	26
Respondent	Hesselgren, N. L.
Title	Pan Svecicus, …
Date of Defense	9 December 1749
Pagination	[iv], [1], 2–38
Short Title	Pan Svec.
Lidén title	Pan Svecicus.
Soulsby title	Pan Svec.
Drake title	Pan svecicus.
Note	P. 37 misnumbered 39.

Lidén Number	27
Respondent	Montin, L. J.
Title	… sistens Splachnum, …
Date of Defense	{28} March 1750
Pagination	[iv], [1], 2–15, [1], 1 plate
Short Title	Splachnum
Lidén title	Splachnum.
Soulsby title	Splachn.
Drake title	Splachnum.
Note	Two Strandell copies agree on this date; one Strandell copy has day left blank.

Lidén Number	28
Respondent	Bergius, P. J.
Title	Semina Muscorum detecta …
Date of Defense	25 April {1750}
Pagination	[vi], [1], 2–18, title page figure
Short Title	Sem. musc.
Lidén title	Semina Muscorum detecta.
Soulsby title	Semin. Musc.
Drake title	Semina muscorum detecta.
Note	Two Strandell copies have year printed 1750.

Lidén Number	29
Respondent	Sidrén, J.
Title	… de Materia Medica in Regno Animali, …
Date of Defense	25 June 1750
Pagination	[i], [1], 3–20
Short Title	Mat. med. anim.
Lidén title	Materia Medica in Regno Animali.

Soulsby title	Mater. Med.
Drake title	Materia medica in regno animali.

Lidén Number	30
Respondent	Halenius, J. P.
Title	Plantae rariores Camschatcenses, ...
Date of Defense	22 December 1750
Pagination	[iv], [1], 2–30, 1 plate
Short Title	Pl. rar. Camsch.
Lidén title	Plantae rariores Camschatcenses.
Soulsby title	Plant. Camsch.
Drake title	Plantae rariores camschatcenses.
Note	P. 26 misnumbered 62 in one of three Strandell copies.

Lidén Number	31
Respondent	Rudberg, J.
Title	... sistens Saporem Medicamentorum, ...
Date of Defense	23 February 1751
Pagination	[ii], [1], 4–20
Short Title	Sapor. med.
Lidén title	Sapor Medicamentorum.
Soulsby title	Sapor. Med.
Drake title	Sapor. medicamentorum.
Note	One Strandell copy agrees on this date; two Strandell copies altered in ms. to {20} February 1751.

Lidén Number	32
Respondent	Chenon, L. J.
Title	..., qua Nova Plantarum Genera ...
Date of Defense	19 October 1751
Pagination	[viii], [2], 3–47, [1], 1 plate
Short Title	Nova pl. gen. 1751
Lidén title	Nova Plantarum Genera.
Soulsby title	Nova Plant. Gener.
Drake title	Nova plantarum genera [1751].
Note	P. 13 misnumbered 15.

Lidén Number	33
Respondent	Haartman, J. J.
Title	Plantae Hybridae, ...
Date of Defense	23 November 1751
Pagination	[iv], [1], 2–30, 1 plate
Short Title	Pl. hybr.
Lidén title	Plantae Hybridae.
Soulsby title	Plant. Hybrid.
Drake title	Plantae hybridae.

Lidén Number	34
Respondent	Beyersten, J. G.
Title	Obstacula Medicinae ...
Date of Defense	{19} February 1752
Pagination	[ii], [1], 4–12
Short Title	Obst. med.
Lidén title	Obstacula Medicinae.
Soulsby title	Obstac. Med.
Drake title	Obstacula medicinae.

Lidén Number	35
Respondent	Hiorth, J.
Title	Plantae Esculentae Patriae, ...
Date of Defense	22 February 1752
Pagination	[iv], [1], 2–28, [2]

Short Title	Pl. escul.
Lidén title	Plantae esculentae Patriae.
Soulsby title	Plant. Escul.
Drake title	Plantae esculentae patriae.

Lidén Number	36
Respondent	Wiman, J. J. F.
Title	... quo Euphorbia ejusque historia naturalis et medica exhibetur ...
Date of Defense	6 May 1752
Pagination	[ii], [2], 3–33, [1]
Short Title	Euphorbia
Lidén title	Euphorbia, ejusque Historia naturalis & medica.
Soulsby title	Euphorbia.
Drake title	Euphorbia.

Lidén Number	37
Respondent	Lindhult, J.
Title	... de Materia medica in Regno Lapideo ...
Date of Defense	15 May 1752
Pagination	[i], [1], 3–28
Short Title	Mat. med. lapid.
Lidén title	Materia Medica in Regno Lapideo.
Soulsby title	Mater. Med.
Drake title	Materia medica in regno lapideo.
Note	All three Strandell copies dated 18 May 1752, not 15 May.

Lidén Number	38
Respondent	Brodd, S.
Title	... de Morbis ex Hyeme, ...
Date of Defense	2 June 1752
Pagination	[iii], [1], 3–23
Short Title	Morb. Hyeme
Lidén title	De Morbis ex Hyeme.
Soulsby title	Morb. ex Hyem.
Drake title	Morbi ex hyeme.

Lidén Number	39
Respondent	Adler, C. F.
Title	Noctiluca marina, ...
Date of Defense	{9} June 1752
Pagination	[iv], [1], 2–8, 1 plate
Short Title	Noctiluca
Lidén title	Noctiluca Marina.
Soulsby title	Noctiluca.
Drake title	Noctiluca marina.
Note	Three Strandell copies altered in ms. to {9 July} 1752.

Lidén Number	40
Respondent	Wåhlin, A. M.
Title	... Odores Medicamentorum exhibens, ...
Date of Defense	{30} June 1752
Pagination	[iv], [1], 2–16
Short Title	Odor. med.
Lidén title	Odores Medicamentorum.
Soulsby title	Odor. Med.
Drake title	Odores medicamentorum.

Lidén Number	41
Respondent	Ziervogel, S.
Title	... sistens Rhabarbarum, ...
Date of Defense	17 July 1752
Pagination	[vi], [2], 3–24, 1 plate

Short Title	Rhabarbarum
Lidén title	Rhabarbarum.
Soulsby title	Rhabarb.
Drake title	Rhabarbarum.

Lidén Number	42
Respondent	Gedner, C. E.
Title	Quaestio historico naturalis: Cui Bono? Quam breviter solutam …
Date of Defense	21 October 1752
Pagination	[viii], [1], 2–29, [1]
Short Title	Cui bono?
Lidén title	Quaestio Historico-naturalis: Cui bono? soluta.
Soulsby title	Cui Bono?
Drake title	Cui bono.

Lidén Number	43
Respondent	Forsskåhl, J. G.
Title	Hospita Insectorum Flora, …
Date of Defense	4 November 1752
Pagination	[iv], [1], 2–40
Short Title	Hosp. insect. fl.
Lidén title	Hospita Insectorum Flora.
Soulsby title	Hospita.
Drake title	Hospita insectorum flora.

Lidén Number	44
Respondent	Lindberg, F.
Title	Nutrix Noverca, …
Date of Defense	7 November 1752
Pagination	[ii], [1], 4–20, [2]
Short Title	Nutr. noverca
Lidén title	Nutrix Noverca.
Soulsby title	Nutrix Nov.
Drake title	Nutrix noverca.

Lidén Number	45
Respondent	Avelin, G. E.
Title	… sistens Miracula Insectorum, …
Date of Defense	11 November 1752
Pagination	[iv], [1], 2–22, [2]
Short Title	Mirac. insect.
Lidén title	Miracula Insectorum.
Soulsby title	Mirac. Insect.
Drake title	Miracula insectorum.

Lidén Number	46
Respondent	Baeckner, M. A.
Title	Noxa Insectorum. …
Date of Defense	{18} December 1752
Pagination	[iv], [1], 2–32, [4]
Short Title	Noxa insect.
Lidén title	Noxa Insectorum.
Soulsby title	Noxa Ins.
Drake title	Noxa insectorum.

Lidén Number	47
Respondent	Barck, H.
Title	Vernatio Arborum, …
Date of Defense	5 May 1753
Pagination	[iv], [1], 6–20, 1 chart
Short Title	Vern. arb.
Lidén title	Vernatio Arborum.

Soulsby title	Vern. Arb.
Drake title	Vernatio arborum.

Lidén Number	48
Respondent	Bjuur, J.
Title	Incrementa Botanices proximae praeterlapsi semiseculi, …
Date of Defense	2 June 1753
Pagination	[iv], [1], 2–20
Short Title	Incr. bot.
Lidén title	Incrementa Botanices proxime praeterlapsi Semiseculi.
Soulsby title	Increm. Bot.
Drake title	Incrementa botanices.

Lidén Number	49
Respondent	Höjer, J. C.
Title	Demonstrationes Plantarum in Horto Upsaliense 1753, …
Date of Defense	3 October 1753
Pagination	[viii], [1], 2–27, [1]
Short Title	Demonstr. pl.
Lidén title	Demonstrationes Plantarum in Horto Upsaliensi MDCCLIII.
Soulsby title	Demonstr. Plant.
Drake title	Demonstrationes plantarum in horto upsaliensi 1753.

Lidén Number	50
Respondent	Fornander, A. N.
Title	Herbationes Upsalienses, …
Date of Defense	13 October 1753
Pagination	[ii], [1], 4–20
Short Title	Herbat. Upsal.
Lidén title	Herbationes Upsalienses.
Soulsby title	Herbat. Upsal.
Drake title	Herbationes upsalienses.
Note	Three Strandell copies agree on this date; one Strandell copy has day {13} supplied in ms.

Lidén Number	51
Respondent	Hultman, D.
Title	Instructio Musei Rerum Naturalium, …
Date of Defense	14 November 1753
Pagination	[iv], [1], 2–19, [1]
Short Title	Instr. mus.
Lidén title	Instructio Musei Rerum Naturalium.
Soulsby title	Instruct. Mus.
Drake title	Instructio musei rerum naturalium.

Lidén Number	52
Respondent	Gahn, N.
Title	… exhibens Plantas Officinales, …
Date of Defense	15 December 1753
Pagination	[iv], [1], 2–31, [1]
Short Title	Pl. officin.
Lidén title	Plantae Officinales.
Soulsby title	Plant. Officin.
Drake title	Plantae officinales.

Lidén Number	53
Respondent	Carlbohm, G. J.
Title	Censura Medicamentorum simplicium Vegetabilium, …
Date of Defense	{19} December 1753
Pagination	[iv], [1], 2–24
Short Title	Cens. med.
Lidén title	Censura Medicamentorum Simplicium Vegetabilium.

| Soulsby title | Censura. |
| Drake title | Censura medicamentorum simplicium vegetabilium. |

Lidén Number	54
Respondent	Lindecrantz, E. M.
Title	Cynographia, …
Date of Defense	21 December 1753
Pagination	[vi], [1], 2–23, [1], 1 plate
Short Title	Cynogr.
Lidén title	Cynographia.
Soulsby title	Cynogr.
Drake title	Cynographia.

Lidén Number	55
Respondent	Hedenberg, A.
Title	… sistens Stationes Plantarum, …
Date of Defense	3 April 1754
Pagination	[vi], [1], 2–23, [1]
Short Title	Stat. pl.
Lidén title	Stationes Plantarum.
Soulsby title	Stat. Plant.
Drake title	Stationes plantarum.

Lidén Number	56
Respondent	Grufberg, I. O.
Title	Flora Anglica, …
Date of Defense	3 April 1754
Pagination	[viii], [1], 2–29, [3]
Short Title	Fl. Angl.
Lidén title	Flora Anglica.
Soulsby title	Flora Angl.
Drake title	Flora anglica.

Lidén Number	57
Respondent	Stickman, O.
Title	Herbarium Amboinense, …
Date of Defense	11 May 1754
Pagination	[iv], [1], 2–28
Short Title	Herb. Amboin.
Lidén title	Herbarium Amboinense.
Soulsby title	Herbar. Amboin.
Drake title	Herbarium amboinense.

Lidén Number	58
Respondent	Hiortzberg, L.
Title	… de Methodo investigandi Vires Medicamentorum chemica, …
Date of Defense	2 October 1754
Pagination	[iii], [1], 5–16
Short Title	Vir. med.
Lidén title	Methodo Investigandi Vires Medicamentorum Chemica.
Soulsby title	Vires Medic.
Drake title	Methodus investigandi vires medicamentorum chemica.

Lidén Number	59
Respondent	Zetzell, P.
Title	Consectaria electrico-medica …
Date of Defense	12 October 1754
Pagination	[i], [1], 3–8
Short Title	Cons. elec.-med.
Lidén title	Consectaria Electrico-Medica.
Soulsby title	Consect. electr.
Drake title	Consectaria electrico-medica.

Lidén Number	60
Respondent	Hoffberg, C. F.
Title	Cervus Rheno, …
Date of Defense	23 October 1754
Pagination	[iv], [1], 2–24, 1 plate (plate is on p. [iv])
Short Title	Cervus
Lidén title	Cervus Rheno.
Soulsby title	Cervus.
Drake title	Cervus Rheno.

Lidén Number	61
Respondent	Palmér, I. N.
Title	… Oves breviter adumbrans, …
Date of Defense	30 October 1754
Pagination	[ii], [1], 4–24
Short Title	Oves
Lidén title	Oves.
Soulsby title	Oves.
Drake title	Ovis.
Note	P. 12 misnumbered 13.

Lidén Number	62
Respondent	Nauman, J. J.
Title	… de Mure Indico …
Date of Defense	20 {18} November {December} 1754
Pagination	[ii], [1], 2–23, [1], 1 plate
Short Title	Mus ind.
Lidén title	Mure Indico.
Soulsby title	Mus ind.
Drake title	Mus indicus.
Note	Two Strandell copies dated 20 November 1754; one Strandell copy altered in ms. to {19 December} 1754.

Lidén Number	63
Respondent	Wollrath, J. G.
Title	… de Horticultura academica, …
Date of Defense	18 December 1754
Pagination	[viii], [1], 2–21, [3]
Short Title	Hort. acad.
Lidén title	Horticultura Academica.
Soulsby title	Hortic. acad.
Drake title	Horticultura academica.

Lidén Number	64
Respondent	Odhelius, J. L.
Title	… s[i]stens Chinensia Lagerströmiana, …
Date of Defense	{23} December 1754
Pagination	[iv], [1], 2–36, 1 plate
Short Title	Chin. Lagerstr.
Lidén title	Chinensia Lagerströmiana.
Soulsby title	Chin. Lagers.
Drake title	Chinensia Lagerströmiana.

Lidén Number	65
Respondent	Juslenius, A. D.
Title	Centuria I. Plantarum, …
Date of Defense	19 February 1755
Pagination	[iv], [1], 2–35, [1]
Short Title	Cent. I. pl.
Lidén title	Centuria I. Plantarum.
Soulsby title	Cent. I. Plant.
Drake title	Centuria plantarum I.

Lidén Number	66
Respondent	Torner, E.
Title	Centuria II. Plantarum, ...
Date of Defense	2 June 1756 {1755}
Pagination	[iv], [1], 2–33, [1]
Short Title	Cent. II. pl.
Lidén title	Centuria II. Plantarum.
Soulsby title	Cent. II. Plant.
Drake title	Centuria plantarum II.
Note	Two Strandell copies dated 1756.

Lidén Number	67
Respondent	Dahlberg, N. E.
Title	... Metamorphoses Plantarum sistens ...
Date of Defense	{3} June {July} 1755
Pagination	[iv], [1], 6–26
Short Title	Metam. pl.
Lidén title	Metamorphoses Plantarum.
Soulsby title	Metam. Plant.
Drake title	Metamorphis [sic] plantarum.
Note	Two Strandell copies agree on this date; one Strandell copy altered in ms. to {3} June 1755.

Lidén Number	68
Respondent	Bremer, P. P.
Title	Somnus Plantarum ...
Date of Defense	10 December 1755
Pagination	[iii], [1], 5–22, 1 plate
Short Title	Somn. pl.
Lidén title	Somnus Plantarum.
Soulsby title	Somn. Plant.
Drake title	Somnus plantarum.

Lidén Number	69
Respondent	Pfeiffer, J.
Title	... Fungus melitensis ...
Date of Defense	20 December 1755
Pagination	[iv], [1], 2–16, 1 plate
Short Title	Fung. melit.
Lidén title	Fungus Melitensis.
Soulsby title	Fungus melit.
Drake title	Fungus melitensis.

Lidén Number	70
Respondent	Strand, B. J.
Title	Flora Palaestina, ...
Date of Defense	{10} March 1756
Pagination	[v], [1], 7–32, [2]
Short Title	Fl. Palaest.
Lidén title	Flora Palaestina.
Soulsby title	Flora Palaest.
Drake title	Flora palaestina.
Note	Three Strandell copies agree on this date; one Strandell copy has day left blank.

Lidén Number	71
Respondent	Åmman, N. N.
Title	Flora Alpina, ...
Date of Defense	24 March 1756
Pagination	[iv], [1], 2–27, [1]
Short Title	Fl. alp.
Lidén title	Flora Alpina.

Soulsby title	Flora Alp.
Drake title	Flora alpina.

Lidén Number	72
Respondent	Berger, A. M.
Title	Calendarium Florae, …
Date of Defense	31 March 1756
Pagination	[iv], [1], 2–5, [19]
Short Title	Calend. fl.
Lidén title	Calendarium Florae.
Soulsby title	Calend. Florae.
Drake title	Calendarium florae.

Lidén Number	73
Respondent	Wåhlin, A. M.
Title	… de Pulsu intermittente, …
Date of Defense	5 May 1756
Pagination	[iv], [1], 2–18
Short Title	Puls. interm.
Lidén title	Pulsu Intermittente.
Soulsby title	Pulsus intermitt.
Drake title	Pulsus intermittens.

Lidén Number	74
Respondent	Nathorst, T. E.
Title	Flora Monspeliensis, …
Date of Defense	15 June 1756
Pagination	[ii], [1], 2–30
Short Title	Fl. Monsp.
Lidén title	Flora Monspeliensis.
Soulsby title	Flora Monspel.
Drake title	Flora monspeliensis.

Lidén Number	75
Respondent	Engström, P.
Title	… Fundamenta Valetudinis sistens, …
Date of Defense	17 June 1756
Pagination	[iv], [1], 2–13, [1]
Short Title	Fund. valet.
Lidén title	Fundamenta Valetudinis.
Soulsby title	Fund. Valet.
Drake title	Fundamenta valetudines.

Lidén Number	76
Respondent	Coelln, J. von.
Title	… sistens Specifica Canadensium …
Date of Defense	{19 June} 1756
Pagination	[iv], [1], 2–28
Short Title	Specif. Canad.
Lidén title	Specifica Canadensium.
Soulsby title	Specif. Canad.
Drake title	Specifica canadensium.
Note	Two Strandell copies agree on this date; one Strandell copy has day and month left blank.

Lidén Number	77
Respondent	Burg, H. von der
Title	… de Acetariis, …
Date of Defense	29 June 1756
Pagination	[iv], [1], 2–16
Short Title	Acetaria
Lidén title	Acetariis.

Soulsby title	Acetaria.
Drake title	Acetaria.

Lidén Number	78
Respondent	Lyman, J.
Title	… de Phalaena Bombyce, …
Date of Defense	4 December 1756
Pagination	[i], [1], 3–12
Short Title	Phalaena
Lidén title	Phalaena Bombyce.
Soulsby title	Phalaena Bomb.
Drake title	Phalaena bombyx.

Lidén Number	79
Respondent	Ekmarck, C. D.
Title	… Migrationes Avium sistens, …
Date of Defense	2 March 1757
Pagination	[iv], [1], 6–38
Short Title	Migr. avium
Lidén title	Migrationes Avium.
Soulsby title	Migrat. Av.
Drake title	Migrationes avium.

Lidén Number	80
Respondent	Bjerkén, P. af.
Title	Morbi Expeditionis Classicae 1756, …
Date of Defense	18 May 1757
Pagination	[ii], [1], 4–22
Short Title	Morb. exped.
Lidén title	Morbi Expeditionis Classicae.
Soulsby title	Morbi Exped.
Drake title	Morbi expeditiones classicae 1756.

Lidén Number	81
Respondent	Boström, A.
Title	Febris Upsaliensis, …
Date of Defense	21 May 1757
Pagination	[ii], [1], 2–12
Short Title	Febr. Upsal.
Lidén title	Febris Upsaliensis.
Soulsby title	Febris Upsal.
Drake title	Febris upsaliensis.

Lidén Number	82
Respondent	Holm, J. T.
Title	Prodromus Florae Danicae, …
Date of Defense	2 June 1757
Pagination	[iii], [1], 5–26, [2]
Short Title	Prodr. fl. Dan.
Lidén title	Prodromus Florae Danicae.
Soulsby title	Flora Dan.
Drake title	Flora danica.

Lidén Number	83
Respondent	Svensson, I.
Title	… de Pane Diaetetico, …
Date of Defense	8 June 1757
Pagination	[iv], [1], 6–20
Short Title	Pane diaet.
Lidén title	Pane Diaetetico.
Soulsby title	Panis Diaet.
Drake title	Panis diaeteticus.

Lidén Number	84
Respondent	Hager, J. H.
Title	Natura Pelagi, …
Date of Defense	18 June 1757
Pagination	[iv], [1], 6–15, [1]
Short Title	Nat. pelagi
Lidén title	Natura Pelagi.
Soulsby title	Nat. Pelag.
Drake title	Natura pelagi.

Lidén Number	85
Respondent	Martin, A. R.
Title	Buxbaumia, …
Date of Defense	22 June 1757
Pagination	[iv], [1], 6–16, title page figure
Short Title	Buxbaumia
Lidén title	Buxbaumia.
Soulsby title	Buxbaumia.
Drake title	Buxbaumia.

Lidén Number	86
Respondent	Nyander, J. C.
Title	Exanthemata Viva, …
Date of Defense	23 June 1757
Pagination	[iii], [1], 5–16
Short Title	Exanth. viva
Lidén title	Exanthemata Viva.
Soulsby title	Exanth. Viva.
Drake title	Exanthemata viva.

Lidén Number	87
Respondent	Hornborg, B.
Title	… de Transmutatione Frumentorum, …
Date of Defense	28 September 1757
Pagination	[vi], [1], 2–16, [2]
Short Title	Transm. frum.
Lidén title	Transmutatione Frumentorum.
Soulsby title	Transmut. Frument.
Drake title	Transmutatio frumentorum.

Lidén Number	88
Respondent	Österman, M. G.
Title	Culina mutata, …
Date of Defense	16 November 1757
Pagination	[iv], [1], 2–12
Short Title	Cul. mut.
Lidén title	Culina Mutata.
Soulsby title	Culina.
Drake title	Culina mutata.

Lidén Number	89
Respondent	Colliander, J. G.
Title	… de Spigelia anthelmia, …
Date of Defense	22 {30} March 1758
Pagination	[iii], [1], 5–16, 1 plate
Short Title	Spigelia
Lidén title	Spigelia Anthelmia.
Soulsby title	Spigelia anth.
Drake title	Spigelia anthelmia.
Note	Three Strandell copies have date as 22 March 1758.

Lidén Number	90	
Respondent	Petersen, J. C. P.	
Title	... de Cortice Peruviano, ...	
Date of Defense	{10} May 1758	
Pagination	[ii], [1], 2–38	
Short Title	Cort. peruv.	
Lidén title	Cortice Peruviano.	
Soulsby title	Cortex Peruv.	
Drake title	Cortex peruvianus.	
Note	Two Strandell copies agree on this date; two Strandell copies have day left blank.	

Lidén Number	91
Respondent	Virgander, D. M.
Title	Frutetum Svecicum, ...
Date of Defense	23 May 1758
Pagination	[ii], [1], 2–26
Short Title	Fr. Svec.
Lidén title	Frutetum Svecicum.
Soulsby title	Frut. Svec.
Drake title	Frutetum svecicum.

Lidén Number	92
Respondent	Fagraeus, J. T.
Title	... sistens Medicamenta graveolentia ...
Date of Defense	13 June 1758
Pagination	[vi], [1], 2–24
Short Title	Med. grav.
Lidén title	Medicamenta Graveolentia.
Soulsby title	Medic. grav.
Drake title	Medicamenta graveolentia.

Lidén Number	93
Respondent	Rydbeck, E. O.
Title	Pandora Insectorum, ...
Date of Defense	15 July 1758
Pagination	[ii], [1], 2–31 (i.e., 23), 1 plate
Short Title	Pand. insect.
Lidén title	Pandora Insectorum.
Soulsby title	Pandora.
Drake title	Pandora insectorum.
Note	P. 17 misnumbered 38; p. 23 misnumbered 31.

Lidén Number	94
Respondent	Pilgren, J.
Title	Senium Salomoneum, ...
Date of Defense	{21} February 1759
Pagination	[ii], [1], 4–24
Short Title	Senium
Lidén title	Senium Salomoneum.
Soulsby title	Senium Salom.
Drake title	Senium Salomoneum.
Note	Two Strandell copies agree on this date; one Strandell copy has day left blank.

Lidén Number	95
Respondent	Loo, A.
Title	Auctores Botanici ...
Date of Defense	14 March 1759
Pagination	[iii], [1], 3–20
Short Title	Auct. bot.
Lidén title	Auctores Botanici.
Soulsby title	Auct. Bot.
Drake title	Auctores botanici.

Lidén Number	96
Respondent	Nordblad, E. A.
Title	Instructio Peregrinatoris, …
Date of Defense	9 May 1759
Pagination	[iv], [1], 2–15
Short Title	Instr. peregr.
Lidén title	Instructio Peregrinatoris.
Soulsby title	Instruct. Peregrin.
Drake title	Instructio peregrinatoris.

Lidén Number	97
Respondent	Jörlin, E.
Title	Plantae Tinctoriae, …
Date of Defense	16 May 1759
Pagination	[iii], [1], 5–30
Short Title	Pl. tinct.
Lidén title	Plantae Tinctoriae.
Soulsby title	Plant. Tinct.
Drake title	Plantae tinctoriae.

Lidén Number	98
Respondent	Bäck, A.
Title	Animalia composita, …
Date of Defense	23 May 1759
Pagination	[iv], [1], 2–9, [1]
Short Title	Anim. comp.
Lidén title	Animalia Composita.
Soulsby title	Animal. compos.
Drake title	Animalia composita.

Lidén Number	99
Respondent	Wännman, C. H.
Title	Flora Capensis, …
Date of Defense	30 May 1759
Pagination	[iv], [1], 2–19, [1]
Short Title	Fl. Cap.
Lidén title	Flora Capensis.
Soulsby title	Flora Cap.
Drake title	Flora capensis.

Lidén Number	100
Respondent	Hidén, J.
Title	Ambrosiaca, …
Date of Defense	20 June 1759
Pagination	[i], [1], 3–14
Short Title	Ambros.
Lidén title	Ambrosiaca.
Soulsby title	Ambrosiaca.
Drake title	Ambrosiaca.

Lidén Number	101
Respondent	Pontin, D. D.
Title	Arboretum Svecicum, …
Date of Defense	{30} June 1759
Pagination	[ii], [1], 4–30
Short Title	Arb. Svec.
Lidén title	Arboretum Svecicum.
Soulsby title	Arb. Svec.
Drake title	Arboretum svecicum.
Note	P. 28 misnumbered 23.

Lidén Number	102
Respondent	Elmgren, G.
Title	Plantarum Jamaicensium Pugillus, …
Date of Defense	28 November 1759
Pagination	[ii], [1], 4–31, [1]
Short Title	Pl. Jam.
Lidén title	Plantarum Jamaicensium Pugillus.
Soulsby title	Plant. Jam. Pug.
Drake title	Plantarum jamaicensium pugillus.
Note	P. 5 unnumbered.

Lidén Number	103
Respondent	Schröder, J.
Title	Genera morborum, …
Date of Defense	5 December 1759
Pagination	[iii], [1], 5–32
Short Title	Gen. morb.
Lidén title	Genera Morborum.
Soulsby title	Gen. Morb.
Drake title	Genera morborum.
Note	P. 6 unnumbered.

Lidén Number	104
Respondent	Ramström, C. L.
Title	Generatio Ambigena, …
Date of Defense	12 December 1759
Pagination	[ii], [1], 2–17, [1]
Short Title	Generat. ambig.
Lidén title	Generatio Ambigena.
Soulsby title	Gen. Ambig.
Drake title	Generatio ambigena.

Lidén Number	105
Respondent	Sandmark, C. G.
Title	Flora Jamaicensis, …
Date of Defense	{22} December 1759
Pagination	[vi], [1], 8–27, [1]
Short Title	Fl. Jam.
Lidén title	Flora Jamaicensis.
Soulsby title	Flor. Jam.
Drake title	Flora jamaicensis.
Note	One Strandell copy agrees on this date; two Strandell copies have day left blank.

Lidén Number	106
Respondent	Siefvert, J. V.
Title	Aer habitabilis, …
Date of Defense	22 December 1759
Pagination	[ii], [1], 4–25, [1]
Short Title	Aer habit.
Lidén title	Aër Habitabilis.
Soulsby title	Aer habit.
Drake title	Aer habitabilis.

Lidén Number	107
Respondent	Berzelius, B.
Title	… sistens Nomenclatorem Botanicum, …
Date of Defense	{24} December 1759
Pagination	[iii], [1], 7–19, [1]
Short Title	Nom. bot.
Lidén title	Nomenclator Botanicus.
Soulsby title	Nomencl. Bot.
Drake title	Nomenclator botanicus.

Lidén Number	108
Respondent	Lindh, J.
Title	… de Pingvedine Animali, …
Date of Defense	24 December 1759
Pagination	[vi], [1], 8–32
Short Title	Ping. anim.
Lidén title	Pingvedine Animali.
Soulsby title	Ping. Anim.
Drake title	Pingvedo animalis.

Lidén Number	109
Respondent	Wilcke, H. C. D.
Title	… de Politia naturae, …
Date of Defense	29 March 1760
Pagination	[ii], [1], 2–22
Short Title	Polit. nat.
Lidén title	Politia Naturae.
Soulsby title	Polit. Nat.
Drake title	Politia naturae.

Lidén Number	110
Respondent	Schreber, J. C. D. von
Title	Theses medicae, …
Date of Defense	14 June 1760
Pagination	[i], [1], 3–4
Short Title	Th. med.
Lidén title	Theses Medicae.
Soulsby title	Thes. med.
Drake title	Theses medicae.

Lidén Number	111
Respondent	Hoppius, C. E.
Title	… in qua Anthropomorpha …
Date of Defense	6 September 1760
Pagination	[vi], [1], 2–16, 1 plate
Short Title	Anthrop.
Lidén title	Anthropomorpha.
Soulsby title	Anthrop.
Drake title	Anthropomorpha.

Lidén Number	112
Respondent	Rosenthal, C. F.
Title	Flora Belgica, …
Date of Defense	15 October 1760
Pagination	[iv], [1], 2–23
Short Title	Fl. Belg.
Lidén title	Flora Belgica.
Soulsby title	Flor. Belg.
Drake title	Flora belgica.

Lidén Number	113
Respondent	Jerlin, P.
Title	Macellum olitorium, …
Date of Defense	{20} December 1760
Pagination	[v], [1], 7–23, [1]
Short Title	Mac. olit.
Lidén title	Macellum Olitorium.
Soulsby title	Mac. olit.
Drake title	Macellum olitorium.
Note	Three Strandell copies agree on this date; one Strandell copy has day left blank. Also, p. 8 misnumbered 6 in all four copies.

Lidén Number	114
Respondent	Ullmark, H.
Title	Prolepsis Plantarum, …
Date of Defense	22 December 1760
Pagination	[iv], [1], 2–22
Short Title	Prol. pl. 1760
Lidén title	Prolepsis Plantarum.
Soulsby title	Prol. Plant.
Drake title	Prolepsis plantarum.

Lidén Number	115
Respondent	Printz, J.
Title	Plantae rariores Africanae, …
Date of Defense	{22} December 1760
Pagination	[ii], [1], 4–28
Short Title	Pl. rar. Afr.
Lidén title	Plantae Rariores Africanae.
Soulsby title	Plant. rar. Afr.
Drake title	Plantae rariores africanae.
Note	One Strandell copy has day {20} supplied in ms.; two Strandell copies have day left blank.

Lidén Number	116
Respondent	Vigelius, E.
Title	Diaeta acidularis, …
Date of Defense	18 February 1761
Pagination	[iv], [1], 2–12
Short Title	Diaet. acid.
Lidén title	Diaeta Acidularis.
Soulsby title	Diaet. acid.
Drake title	Diaeta acidularis.

Lidén Number	117
Respondent	Alander, O. R.
Title	… sistens Inebriantia, …
Date of Defense	{7 April} 1761 {1762}
Pagination	[vi], [1], 8–26
Short Title	Inebr.
Lidén title	Inebriantia.
Soulsby title	Inebr.
Drake title	Inebriantia.
Note	Two Strandell copies agree on this date; one Strandell copy has year as 1761.

Lidén Number	118
Respondent	Sparschuch, H.
Title	… in qua Potus Coffee leviter adumbratur, …
Date of Defense	16 December 1761
Pagination	[ii], [1], 2–18, 1 plate
Short Title	Pot. coff.
Lidén title	Potus Coffeae.
Soulsby title	Pot. Coff.
Drake title	Potus coffeae.

Lidén Number	119
Respondent	Acrel, J. G.
Title	… de Morsura Serpentum, …
Date of Defense	16 June 1762
Pagination	[iv], [1], 2–19, [1] (1 figure)
Short Title	Mors. serp.
Lidén title	Morsura Serpentum.
Soulsby title	Mors. Serp.
Drake title	Morsura serpentum.

Lidén Number	120
Respondent	Elmgren, J.
Title	Termini Botanici, …
Date of Defense	22 June 1762
Pagination	[iii], [1], 5–32
Short Title	Term. bot.
Lidén title	Termini Botanici.
Soulsby title	Term. Bot.
Drake title	Termini botanici.

Lidén Number	121
Respondent	Falck, J. P.
Title	Planta Alströmeria, …
Date of Defense	23 June 1762
Pagination	[iii], [1], 5–16, 1 plate
Short Title	Pl. Alstr.
Lidén title	Planta Alströmeria.
Soulsby title	Plant. Alstr.
Drake title	Planta Alströmeria.

Lidén Number	122
Respondent	Hall, B. M.
Title	… sistens Nectaria Florum, …
Date of Defense	25 June 1762
Pagination	[ii], [1], 2–16
Short Title	Nect. fl.
Lidén title	Nectaria Florum.
Soulsby title	Nect. Flor.
Drake title	Nectaria florum.

Lidén Number	123
Respondent	Gråberg, J. M.
Title	Fundamentum Fructificationis, …
Date of Defense	16 October 1762
Pagination	[iv], [1], 2–24
Short Title	Fund. fr.
Lidén title	Fundamentum Fructificationis.
Soulsby title	Fund. Fruct.
Drake title	Fundamentum fructificationis.

Lidén Number	124
Respondent	Lenaeus, K. A.
Title	… de Meloë vesicatorio, …
Date of Defense	20 {22?} December 1762
Pagination	[iv], [1], 2–15, [1]
Short Title	Meloë
Lidén title	Meloë Vesicatorio.
Soulsby title	Mel. vesic.
Drake title	Meloe vesicatoria.
Note	Two Strandell copies have a title page dated 20 December 1762; one of these copies also has an additional title page dated 22 December 1762.

Lidén Number	125
Respondent	Reftelius, J. M.
Title	Reformatio Botanices, …
Date of Defense	18 December 1762
Pagination	[iv], [1], 2–21, [2]
Short Title	Reform. bot.
Lidén title	Reformatio Botanices.
Soulsby title	Reform. Bot.
Drake title	Reformatio botanices.
Note	P. 20 misnumbered 22 in two of four Strandell copies.

Lidén Number	126
Respondent	Rothman, G.
Title	De Raphania …
Date of Defense	27 May 1763
Pagination	[iii], [1], 2–21, 1 plate
Short Title	Raphania
Lidén title	Raphania.
Soulsby title	Raph.
Drake title	Raphania.

Lidén Number	127
Respondent	Salberg, J.
Title	Fructus esculenti, …
Date of Defense	11 June 1763
Pagination	[ii], [1], 2–22
Short Title	Fr. escul.
Lidén title	Fructus Esculenti.
Soulsby title	Fruct. escul.
Drake title	Fructus esculenti.

Lidén Number	128
Respondent	Blom, C. M.
Title	… sistens Lignum Qvassiae, …
Date of Defense	28 May 1763
Pagination	[ii], [1], 2–13, [1], 1 plate
Short Title	Lign. Qvas.
Lidén title	Lignum Qvassiae.
Soulsby title	Lign. Quass.
Drake title	Lignum Quassiae.

Lidén Number	129
Respondent	Johansson, B.
Title	Centuria Insectorum Rariorum, …
Date of Defense	23 June 1763
Pagination	[vi], [1], 2–32
Short Title	Cent. insect.
Lidén title	Centuria Insectorum Rariorum.
Soulsby title	Cent. Ins. Rar.
Drake title	Centuria insectorum rariorum.

Lidén Number	130
Respondent	Ferber, J. J.
Title	… de Prolepsi Plantarum, …
Date of Defense	22 June 1763
Pagination	[ii], [1], 2–18
Short Title	Prol. pl. 1763
Lidén title	De Prolepsi Plantarum.
Soulsby title	Prol. Plant.
Drake title	Disquisitio de prolepsi plantarum.

Lidén Number	131
Respondent	Lado, C.
Title	… in qua Motus polychrestus delineatur, …
Date of Defense	23 December 1763
Pagination	[iii], [1], 2–20
Short Title	Mot. polychr.
Lidén title	Motus Polychrestus.
Soulsby title	Mot. poly.
Drake title	Motus polychrestus.

Lidén Number	132
Respondent	Tengborg, J. C.

Title	Hortus Culinaris, …
Date of Defense	20 {21} June 1764
Pagination	[v], [1], 7–26
Short Title	Hort. cul.
Lidén title	Hortus Culinaris.
Soulsby title	Hort. Cul.
Drake title	Hortus culinaris.
Lidén Number	133
Respondent	Bergius, P.
Title	… in qua Spiritus Frumenti proponitur, …
Date of Defense	19 December 1764
Pagination	[ii], [1], 4–20
Short Title	Spir. frum.
Lidén title	Spiritus Frumenti.
Soulsby title	Spir. Frum.
Drake title	Spiritus frumenti.
Lidén Number	134
Respondent	Öhrqvist, D. J.
Title	… de Diaeta per scalam aetatis humanae observanda, …
Date of Defense	{20 December} 1764
Pagination	[iii], [1], 5–12
Short Title	Diaet. scal.
Lidén title	Diaeta per Scalam Aetatis Humanae observanda.
Soulsby title	Diaet. per scal.
Drake title	Diaeta aetatum.
Lidén Number	135
Respondent	Le Moine, W.
Title	Opobalsamum declaratum …
Date of Defense	22 December 1764
Pagination	[iv], [1], 2–19 (i.e., 18)
Short Title	Opobals.
Lidén title	Opobalsamum Declaratum in Dissertat. Medica.
Soulsby title	Opobals.
Drake title	Opobalsamum declaratum.
Note	P. 16 misnumbered 19, p. 18 misnumbered 19.
Lidén Number	136
Respondent	Weser, D. L.
Title	… de Hirudine, …
Date of Defense	{6} May {March} 1764 {1765}
Pagination	[iv], [1], 2–15, [1]
Short Title	Hirudo
Lidén title	De Hirudine.
Soulsby title	Hirud.
Drake title	Hirudo.
Lidén Number	137
Respondent	Bäckman, A. P.
Title	… Fundamenta Ornithologica exhibituram, …
Date of Defense	4 May 1765
Pagination	[v], [1], 6 (i.e., 7)–28, 1 plate
Short Title	Fund. ornith.
Lidén title	Fundamenta Ornithologica.
Soulsby title	Fund. Ornith.
Drake title	Fundamenta ornithologica.
Note	P. 7 misnumbered 6, p. 8 misnumbered 7.
Lidén Number	138
Respondent	Ribben, C.

Title	Circa Fervidorum et Gelidorum Usum Paraenesis, ...
Date of Defense	12 June 1765
Pagination	[ii], [1], 4–23
Short Title	Ferv. gel.
Lidén title	Circa Fervidorum & Gelidorum Usum Paraenesis.
Soulsby title	Ferv. Gel.
Drake title	Fervidorum et gelidorum usus.

Lidén Number	139
Respondent	Skragge, N.
Title	... qua Morbi Artificum leviter adumbrantur ...
Date of Defense	15 June 1765
Pagination	[i], [1], 2 (i.e., 3)–12
Short Title	Morb. artif.
Lidén title	Morbi Artificum.
Soulsby title	Morb. Artif.
Drake title	Morbi artificum.
Note	P. 3 misnumbered 2; p. 4 misnumbered 3.

Lidén Number	140
Respondent	Uddman, I.
Title	Lepra, ...
Date of Defense	17 June 1765
Pagination	[ii], [1], 2–14
Short Title	Lepra
Lidén title	Lepra.
Soulsby title	Lepra.
Drake title	Lepra.

Lidén Number	141
Respondent	Hoffman, A.
Title	... de Potu Chocolatae, ...
Date of Defense	18 June 1765
Pagination	[ii], [1], 2–10
Short Title	Pot. choc.
Lidén title	De Potu Chocolate.
Soulsby title	Pot. Choc.
Drake title	Potus chocolatae.

Lidén Number	142
Respondent	Tillaeus, P. C.
Title	Potus theae, ...
Date of Defense	7 December 1765
Pagination	[iv], [1], 2–16, 1 plate
Short Title	Pot. theae
Lidén title	Potus Theae.
Soulsby title	Pot. Theae.
Drake title	Potus thaeae.

Lidén Number	143
Respondent	Strandman, P.
Title	... sistens Purgantia Indigena, ...
Date of Defense	26 February 1766
Pagination	[iv], [1], 2–17, [1]
Short Title	Purg. indig.
Lidén title	Purgantia Indigena.
Soulsby title	Purg. Indig.
Drake title	Purgantia indigena.

Lidén Number	144
Respondent	Karamyschew, A. von.
Title	... demonstrans Necessitatem promovendae Historiae Naturalis in Rossia, ...

Date of Defense	{ } May 1764
Pagination	[ii], [1], 2–34, [10], 1 plate
Short Title	Hist. nat. Rossia
Lidén title	Diss. demonstrans Necessitatem Promovendae Historiae Naturalis in Rossia.
Soulsby title	Nec. Prom. Hist. Nat.
Drake title	Necessitas promovendae historia naturalis in Rossia.
Note	Originally issued in 1764 , this dissertation was not publicly submitted until 1766; Strandell copy of original issue altered in ms. to {16} May {1766}.

Lidén Number	144.1
Respondent	Karamyschew, A. von.
Title	… demonstrans Necessitatem promovendae Historiae Naturalis in Rossia, …
Date of Defense	16 May 1766
Pagination	[vi], [1], 2–34, [10], 1 plate
Short Title	Hist. nat. Rossia
Lidén title	Diss. demonstrans Necessitatem Promovendae Historiae Naturalis in Rossia.
Soulsby title	Nec. Prom. Hist. Nat.
Drake title	Necessitas promovendae historia naturalis in Rossia.
Note	This is the reissued version for public submission.

Lidén Number	145
Respondent	Aphonin, M.
Title	… demonstrans Usum Historiae Naturalis in vita communi, …
Date of Defense	17 May 1766
Pagination	[vii], [1], 3–30, [2], 1 plate
Short Title	Usum hist. nat.
Lidén title	Usus Historiae Naturalis in Vita Communi.
Soulsby title	Usus Hist. Nat.
Drake title	Usus historiae naturalis in vita communi.

Lidén Number	146
Respondent	Österdam, A.
Title	Siren lacertina …
Date of Defense	21 June 1766
Pagination	[iv], [1], 2–15, [1], 1 plate
Short Title	Siren lacert.
Lidén title	Siren Lacertina.
Soulsby title	Siren lacert.
Drake title	Siren lacertina.

Lidén Number	147
Respondent	Bergman, J. G.
Title	… de Effectu et Cura Vitiorum Diaeteticorum Generali, …
Date of Defense	10 December 1766
Pagination	[ii], [1], 4–24
Short Title	Eff. cura vit.
Lidén title	Effectu & Cura Vitiorum Diaeteticorum Generali.
Soulsby title	Cura Gen.
Drake title	Cura generalis.

Lidén Number	148
Respondent	Berlin, A. H.
Title	… Usum Muscorum breviter delineatura, …
Date of Defense	17 December 1766
Pagination	[iv], [1], 2–14, [2]
Short Title	Usum musc.
Lidén title	Usus Muscorum.
Soulsby title	Usus Musc.
Drake title	Usus muscorum.

Lidén Number	149
Respondent	Roos, J. C.

Title	… Mundum invisibilem breviter delineatura, …
Date of Defense	6 {7} March 1767
Pagination	[i], [1], 3–23
Short Title	Mund. invis.
Lidén title	Mundus Invisibilis.
Soulsby title	Mund. invis.
Drake title	Mundus invisibilis.

Lidén Number	150
Respondent	Gråberg, J. M.
Title	… de Haemoptysi, …
Date of Defense	13 May 1767
Pagination	[iii], [1], 5–14
Short Title	Haemopt.
Lidén title	De Haemoptysi.
Soulsby title	Haemopt.
Drake title	Haemoptysis.

Lidén Number	151
Respondent	Thunberg, C. P.
Title	… de Venis resorbentibus …
Date of Defense	2 June 1767
Pagination	[iv], [1], 2–10
Short Title	Ven. resorb.
Lidén title	Venis Resorbentibus.
Soulsby title	Venae res.
Drake title	Venae resorbentes.

Lidén Number	152
Respondent	Gahn, H.
Title	Fundamenta Agrostographiae …
Date of Defense	27 June 1767
Pagination	[ii], [1], 4–38, tabs. 1–2
Short Title	Fund. agrost.
Lidén title	Fundamenta Agrostographiae.
Soulsby title	Fund. Agrost.
Drake title	Fundamenta agrostographiae.

Lidén Number	153
Respondent	Laurin, C. G.
Title	… de Menthae usu, …
Date of Defense	30 June 1767
Pagination	[v], [1], 3–11, [1]
Short Title	Menthae
Lidén title	Menthae Usus.
Soulsby title	Menth. usus.
Drake title	Menthae usus.

Lidén Number	154
Respondent	Blad, A. J.
Title	Fundamenta Entomologiae, …
Date of Defense	{14} June 1767
Pagination	[ii], [1], 4–34
Short Title	Fund. entom.
Lidén title	Fundamenta Entomologiae.
Soulsby title	Fund. Entom.
Drake title	Fundamenta entomologiae.
Note	Two Strandell copies have day left blank.

Lidén Number	155
Respondent	Wadström, J. A.
Title	… sistens Metamorphosin Humanam, …

Date of Defense	16 December 1767
Pagination	[iv], [1], 2–18, 1 table
Short Title	Metam. hum.
Lidén title	Metamorphosis Humana.
Soulsby title	Metam. Hum.
Drake title	Metamorphis [sic] humana.

Lidén Number	156
Respondent	Wedenberg, A. F.
Title	… de Varietate Ciborum …
Date of Defense	19 December 1767
Pagination	[iii], 4–19, [1]
Short Title	Var. cib.
Lidén title	De Varietate Ciborum.
Soulsby title	Variet. Cib.
Drake title	Varietas ciborum.
Note	One Strandell copy agrees on this date; one Strandell copy has day altered in ms. to {18} (i.e., changed from XIX to XIIX).

Lidén Number	157
Respondent	Tonning, H.
Title	… sistens Rariora Norvegiae …
Date of Defense	27 February 1768
Pagination	[vi], [1], 2–19, [1] (1 text figure)
Short Title	Rar. Norv.
Lidén title	Rariora Norvegiae.
Soulsby title	Rari. Norv.
Drake title	Rariora norvegiae.

Lidén Number	158
Respondent	Flygare, J.
Title	… de Coloniis Plantarum, …
Date of Defense	15 June 1768
Pagination	[ii], [1], 4–13
Short Title	Colon. pl.
Lidén title	Coloniis Plantarum.
Soulsby title	Colon. Plant.
Drake title	Coloniae plantarum.

Lidén Number	159
Respondent	Grysselius, J.
Title	… de Medico sui ipsius, …
Date of Defense	{11} January 1768
Pagination	[i], [1], 3–12
Short Title	Medicus
Lidén title	Medico Sui Ipsius.
Soulsby title	Medicus.
Drake title	Medicus sui ipsius.
Note	Strandell copy has date as {11} June 1768, not January.

Lidén Number	160
Respondent	Wänman, C. H.
Title	… de Morbis Nautorum Indiae, …
Date of Defense	5 November 1768
Pagination	[i], [1], 3–4
Short Title	Morb. naut.
Lidén title	Morbis Nautarum Indiae.
Soulsby title	Morb. Naut.
Drake title	Morbi nautarum Indiae.

Lidén Number	161
Respondent	Sparrman, A.

Title	... sistens iter in Chinam ...
Date of Defense	30 November 1768
Pagination	[iii], [1], 5–16
Short Title	Iter Chin.
Lidén title	Iter in Chinam.
Soulsby title	Iter. Chin.
Drake title	Iter in Chinam.

Lidén Number	162
Respondent	Luut, C. J.
Title	Flora Åkeroensis, ...
Date of Defense	23 December 1769
Pagination	[ii], [1], 4–20
Short Title	Fl. Åker.
Lidén title	Flora Åkeröensis.
Soulsby title	Flor. åkerö.
Drake title	Flora åkeröensis.

Lidén Number	163
Respondent	Dahlgren, J. A.
Title	... de Erica ...
Date of Defense	19 December 1770
Pagination	[iv], [1], 2–15, [1], 1 plate
Short Title	Erica
Lidén title	Erica.
Soulsby title	Erica.
Drake title	Erica.
Note	P. 14 misnumbered 10.

Lidén Number	164
Respondent	Hallenberg, G.
Title	... de Dulcamara ...
Date of Defense	29 May 1771
Pagination	[i], [1], 3–14
Short Title	Dulcamara
Lidén title	Dulcamara.
Soulsby title	Dulcam.
Drake title	Dulcamara.

Lidén Number	165
Respondent	Söderberg, D. H.
Title	Pandora et Flora Rybyensis, ...
Date of Defense	26 June 1771
Pagination	[iv], [1], 6–23, [1]
Short Title	Pand. fl. Ryb.
Lidén title	Pandora & Flora Rybyensis.
Soulsby title	Pand. Ryb.
Drake title	Pandora et flora rybyensis.

Lidén Number	166
Respondent	Murray, A.
Title	Fundamenta Testaceologiae ...
Date of Defense	29 June 1771
Pagination	[iv], [1], 2–43, tabs. I, II
Short Title	Fund. test.
Lidén title	Fundamenta Testaceologiae.
Soulsby title	Fund. Testac.
Drake title	Fundamenta testaceologiae.

Lidén Number	167
Respondent	Tillaeus, P. C.
Title	... de varia Febrium intermittentium curatione, ...

Date of Defense	11 December 1771
Pagination	[ii], [1], 4–56, [2]
Short Title	Febr. interm.
Lidén title	Varia Febrium Intermittentium Curatione.
Soulsby title	Febr. interm.
Drake title	Febrium intermittentium curatio varia.

Lidén Number	168
Respondent	Ullholm, J.
Title	Respiratio Diaetetica, …
Date of Defense	29 April 1772
Pagination	[ii], [1], 2–26
Short Title	Resp. diaet.
Lidén title	Respiratio Diaetetica.
Soulsby title	Resp. Diaet.
Drake title	Respiratio diaetetica.

Lidén Number	169
Respondent	Heidenstam, E. J. M. ab.
Title	… de Haemorrhagiis ex Plethora, …
Date of Defense	23 May 1772
Pagination	[iv], [1], 2–32
Short Title	Haemor. pleth.
Lidén title	Haemorrhagiis ex Plethora.
Soulsby title	Haemorr.
Drake title	Haemorrhagia ex plethora.

Lidén Number	170
Respondent	Hedin, S. A.
Title	Fraga vesca …
Date of Defense	26 May 1772
Pagination	[iv], [1], 2–13, [1]
Short Title	Fraga
Lidén title	Fraga Vesca.
Soulsby title	Fraga vesca.
Drake title	Fraga vesca.

Lidén Number	171
Respondent	Lindwall, J.
Title	Observationes in Materiam medicam, …
Date of Defense	5 June 1772
Pagination	[ii], [1], 2–8
Short Title	Obs. mat. med.
Lidén title	Observationes in Materiam Medicam.
Soulsby title	Mater. Med.
Drake title	Observationes in materiam medicam.

Lidén Number	172
Respondent	Boecler, C. E.
Title	De Suturis Vulnerum in genere …
Date of Defense	27 June 1772
Pagination	[ii], [1], 4–21, [1]
Short Title	Sutur. vuln.
Lidén title	Suturis Vulnerum in Genere.
Soulsby title	Sutur. Vuln.
Drake title	Suturae vulnerum.
Note	One Strandell copy has [iv] preliminary pages, not [ii].

Lidén Number	173
Respondent	Hornborg, J.
Title	Planta cimicifuga, …
Date of Defense	{ } September 1774

Pagination	[ii], [1], 2–10, 1 plate
Short Title	Cimicifuga
Lidén title	Planta Cimicifuga.
Soulsby title	Plant. cimici.
Drake title	Planta cimicifuga.

Lidén Number	174
Respondent	Holmberger, P.
Title	… de Esca Avium Domesticarum, …
Date of Defense	{26} November 1774
Pagination	[ii], [1], 2–15
Short Title	Esca avium
Lidén title	Esca Avium Domesticarum.
Soulsby title	Esca Avium.
Drake title	Esca avium domesticarum.
Note	One Strandell copy agrees on this date; one Strandell copy has day left blank; also, p. 9 misnumbered 17.

Lidén Number	175
Respondent	Dahlgren, J. A.
Title	… de Maro …
Date of Defense	3 December 1774
Pagination	[ii], [1], 4–18
Short Title	Marum
Lidén title	De Maro.
Soulsby title	Marum.
Drake title	Marum.

Lidén Number	176
Respondent	Wickman, D.
Title	… de Viola Ipecacuanha, …
Date of Defense	16 December 1774
Pagination	[iii], [1], 5–12
Short Title	Viola ipecac.
Lidén title	Viola Ipecacuanha.
Soulsby title	Viola Ipec.
Drake title	Viola Ipecacuanhae.

Lidén Number	177
Respondent	Alm, J.
Title	Plantae Surinamenses, …
Date of Defense	23 June 1775
Pagination	[ii], [1], 4–18, 1 plate
Short Title	Pl. Surin.
Lidén title	Plantae Surinamenses.
Soulsby title	Plant. Surin.
Drake title	Plantae surinamenses.

Lidén Number	178
Respondent	Westring, J. P.
Title	… de Ledo palustri, …
Date of Defense	25 October 1775
Pagination	[ii], [1], 2–18
Short Title	Ledum
Lidén title	De Ledo Palustri.
Soulsby title	Led. palustr.
Drake title	Ledum palustre.

Lidén Number	179
Respondent	Georgii, G. E.
Title	Opium, …
Date of Defense	15 November 1775

Pagination	[ii], [1], 2–17, [1]
Short Title	Opium
Lidén title	Opium.
Soulsby title	Opium.
Drake title	Opium.

Lidén Number	180
Respondent	Salomon, E. D.
Title	... de Scorbuto, ...
Date of Defense	{22} November 1775
Pagination	[ii], [1], 4–23
Short Title	Scorb.
Lidén title	De Scorbuto.
Soulsby title	Scorbutus.
Drake title	Scorbutus.

Lidén Number	181
Respondent	Rotheram, J.
Title	Medicamenta Purgantia ...
Date of Defense	22 November 1775
Pagination	[ii], [1], 2–24
Short Title	Med. purg.
Lidén title	Medicamenta Purgantia.
Soulsby title	Medic. Purg.
Drake title	Medicamenta purgantia.

Lidén Number	182
Respondent	Avellan, N.
Title	... de Perspiratione insensibili, ...
Date of Defense	{25} November 1775
Pagination	[ii], [1], 4–11
Short Title	Persp. insen.
Lidén title	Perspiratione Insensibili.
Soulsby title	Perspir. insens.
Drake title	Perspiratio insensibilis.

Lidén Number	183
Respondent	Hedin, S. A.
Title	Canones Medici, ...
Date of Defense	29 November 1775
Pagination	[ii], [1], 2–12
Short Title	Canones med.
Lidén title	Canones Medici.
Soulsby title	Can. Med.
Drake title	Canones medicae.

Lidén Number	184
Respondent	Dahl, A.
Title	... Bigas Insectorum sistens, ...
Date of Defense	18 December 1775
Pagination	[iv], [1], 2–7, [1], 1 plate
Short Title	Bigas insect.
Lidén title	Diss. Entomol. Bigas Insectorum sistens.
Soulsby title	Bigae Insect.
Drake title	Bigae insectorum.

Lidén Number	185
Respondent	Acharius, E.
Title	Planta Aphyteia, ...
Date of Defense	22 June 1776
Pagination	[iv], [1], 6–12, [1], 1 plate
Short Title	Aphyteia

Lidén title	Planta Aphyteia.
Soulsby title	Aphyteia.
Drake title	Planta Aphyteia.

Lidén Number	186
Respondent	Hellens, C. N. von
Title	Hypericum, ...
Date of Defense	20 November 1776
Pagination	[iv], [2], 3-14, 1 plate
Short Title	Hypericum
Lidén title	Hypericum.
Soulsby title	Hypericum.
Drake title	Hypericum.

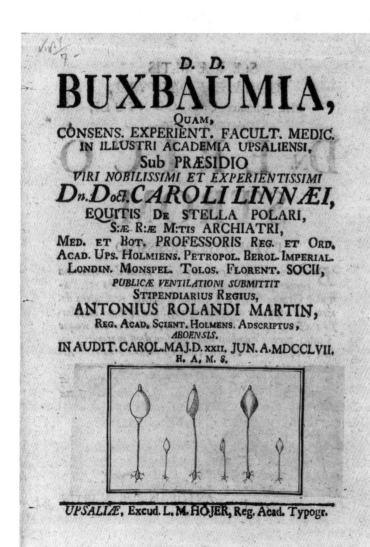

Title page with figure from Buxbaumia ... *(1757), a dissertation defended by A. R. Martin with Linnaeus as praeses.*

Historical Overview of Collected Editions

These notes and the citations in the following section have been adapted from the draft catalogue of the Strandell Collection of Linnaeana at the Hunt Institute for Botanical Documentation, with the purpose of providing a historical overview of the various collected editions of the dissertations, along with bibliographic citations.

Following their original publication as individual items, the Linnaean dissertations were collected and reprinted, often along with selected orations and programmata, in several editions, generally known as the *Amoenitates academicae*. The first edition of these *Amoenitates,* edited by Petrus Camper, appeared in 1749 and reprinted a selection of 19 dissertations with no editorial changes. Included were Linnaeus' own doctoral dissertation and 18 other dissertations that were chosen by Camper and were not the first 18 to have been originally published. Only the first of several projected volumes was published, and later that year Linnaeus, dissatisfied with Camper's work, persuaded Godofred Kieswetter of Stockholm to print the first volume of a new and revised collection of the dissertations, arranged chronologically. Volumes 2–7 of this edition were printed by Lars Salvius of Stockholm. This "Linnaeus edition" (1749–1769), edited and revised by Linnaeus himself, comprises 150 dissertations and three orations in seven volumes and contains many substantive and some nomenclatural changes from the original works.

A re-issue of volumes 2–7 of the Linnaeus edition, without revision, was published in Leiden (1752–1769) by Jacob de Wetstein, a printer at Leiden. (He did not re-issue volume 1, as it had been published earlier by Haak — the so-called Camper edition.) Soulsby referred to this edition as having been pirated, while Günther Buchheim has noted that the only distinction between this and the Linnaeus edition is the cancelled title pages in the former, concluding that this edition might more accurately be considered the Wetstenius issue.

Volumes 2 and 3 of the Linnaeus edition were revised by Linnaeus and published by Salvius in 1762 and 1764, and are often referred to as the Linnaeus revised edition. The revised volume 3 bears no indication of revision on the title page and, as the pagination and layout of the 1756 edition are closely followed, this edition is frequently cited as a reprint. However, while the revisions are not extensive, several of the dissertations included in this volume, in particular *Demonstrationes plantarum*, are important nomenclaturally. The revisions that involve nomenclature tend to reflect additions or changes recorded in the second edition of *Species plantarum* (1762–1763).

Wetstenius also re-issued volume 2 of this Linnaeus revised edition in 1764.

Linnaeus' son, also named Carl von Linné, projected a continuation of the Linnaeus edition series, to include all of the dissertations from *Coloniae plantarum* to the final one, *Hypericum*. This plan ended with his death in 1783, and his father's pupil J. C. D. von Schreber produced the continuation as volumes 8–10 of the *Amoenitates* (1785–1790), simultaneously reissuing, with some editorial changes, volumes 1–7 (1787–1789), which were by that time out of print. This is known as the Schreber edition, and it contains 186 dissertations, along with 12 orations by Linnaeus and four dissertations by his son. It incorporated the Linnaean revisions of volume 2 but not of volume 3, the revision of the latter apparently being unknown to Schreber at the time.

As an aside, those who consult the Schreber edition will notice that Schreber refers to his volumes 1 and 2 as being of the third edition, while volumes 3–7 are designated the second edition. This might be explained as follows. For volume 1, the Camper edition might be considered the first edition (i.e., of the *Amoenitates*, not counting the original dissertations themselves), and the Linnaeus edition would be the second edition. For volume 2, the Linnaeus edition would be seen as the first edition, and the Linnaeus revised edition as the second. This line of reasoning would also follow for volume 3, except that, as noted above, Schreber seems not to have acknowledged or incorporated Linnaeus' revisions to volume 3. By contrast, Hulth refers to Schreber's volumes 1–3 as being the third edition, and volumes 4–7 as being the second edition.

Apart from the editions noted above, several other translations or collections of material from the *Amoenitates* were published.

The Biwald edition, *Selectae ex Amaenitatibus* [*sic*] *academicis* (1764), contains six dissertations and one oration, previously published in the Camper edition and in volume 2 of the Linnaeus edition, with notes by Leopold Gottlieb von Biwald. This collection is continued by his *Continvatio selectarvm ex Amoenitatibvs academicis* (1766) and *Continvatio altera selectarvm ex Amoenitatibvs academicis* (1769). The former is an edition of ten dissertations, published earlier in volumes 3 and 4 of the Linnaeus edition, with notes by Biwald, plus an original contribution by Nikolaus Poda von Neuhaus and Giovanni Antonio Scopolie. The *Continvatio altera* contains nine dissertations from volumes 5 and 6 of the Linnaeus edition, with notes by Biwald plus two original mineralogical contributions by Nikolaus Poda von Neuhaus. While these collections were largely based on the Linnaeus edition of the *Amoenitates academicae*, Biwald deleted the passages relating to the sexes of plants and animals.

Ernst Justus Höpfner produced a German edition (1776–1778) of the *Amoenitates academicae*, that includes translations of 35 dissertations and of two papers by Linnaeus. *Auserlesene Abhandlungen aus der Naturgeschichte, Physik und Arzneywissenschaft* appeared in three volumes and is sometimes referred to as the Hoepfner edition.

In 1759, Benjamin Stillingfleet published the first edition of his *Miscellaneous tracts*, providing English translations of a travel account by Linnaeus and five Linnaean dissertations, together with his own account of grasses pertaining to English agriculture (with a flora of 21 genera). Stillingfleet reviewed Linnaeus' major works, the importance of explorations and collections in foreign lands by his pupils, and a defense of Linnaeus' systems of plant and animal classification. This was the first major introduction to Linnaeus and his principles published in England, and its appearance initiated the era of Linnaean botany there. While the individual translations are all of Linnaeus' writings, the work as a whole is attributed to Stillingfleet.

In 1781, F. J. Brand published *Select dissertations from the Amoenitates academicae, a supplement to Mr. Stillingfleet's Tracts relating to natural history,* a collection of ten dissertations, an oration and an essay by Linnaeus. British names of plants and animals were supplied in footnotes. Although often catalogued either as a work by Stillingfleet or as an English translation of Linnaeus' works, a comparison of these "translations" with the originals reveals that Brand made extensive and unnoted changes of various kinds. A projected second volume was never published.

English summaries of selected Linnaean dissertations appeared in Richard Pulteney's *A general view of the writings of Linnaeus* (first edition, 1781), which was also translated into French in 1789. The work includes biographical accounts of Linnaeus and Pulteney, synopses of selected Linnaean dissertations, an account of the medals awarded to Linnaeus, and a translation of Linnaeus' paper on pearl culture.

J. E. Gilibert's seven-volume *Systema plantarum Europae* (1785–1787) is a compilation of abridged versions of the works of Linnaeus, with additions and alterations to the Linnaean text, along with Latin translations of five papers that originally appeared in Swedish. Volumes 5 and 6 were also issued separately as *Amoenitates academicae* (1786). While bearing half-titles of *Systema plantarum Europae,* they are separately entitled *Fundamentorum botanicorum,* pars prima and pars secunda, and are frequently cited as such. Gilibert made few revisions to these *Amoenitates* and therefore his volumes 5 and 6, which contain over 50 Linnaean dissertations and orations, are commonly attributed to Linnaeus, although Gilibert is credited with the *Systema plantarum Europae* as a whole, reflecting the extent of his revisions in the other volumes.

In recent decades a series of Swedish translations of a number of Linnaeus' dissertations, essays, and addresses, with commentaries, has been published under the title of *Valda avhandlingar.*

Collected Editions

Camper edition:

Linnaeus, Carl. Amoenitates academicae, seu dissertationes variae physicae, medicae, botanicae antehac seorsim editae nunc collectae et auctae cum tabulis aeneis, accedit hypothesis nova de febrium intermittentium causa. Volumen primum. Lugduni Batavorum; Apud Cornelium Haak; 1749. [vi], 610, [9] pp., 15 plates.

> References: Hulth: p. 65; Krok: p. 458, no. 168a; Lindell: 343; Pritzel (ed. 1): 5996; Pritzel (ed. 2): 5425; Soulsby: 1279; Rudolph & Williams: 111.

Linnaeus edition:

Linnaeus, Carl. Amoenitates academicae seu dissertationes variae physicae, medicae botanicae antehac seorsim editae nunc collectae et auctae cum tabulis aeneis. Holmiae & Lipsiae, Apud Godofredum Keisewetter, 1749–1769. 7 vols.

> References: Hulth: pp. 65–70; Krok: pp. 458–459, no. 168a; Lindell: 344–349; Pritzel (ed. 1): 5996; Pritzel (ed. 2): 5425; Soulsby: 1280; Rudolph & Williams: 112, 143, 222, 267, 292, 331, 426.

Volume 1:

Linnaeus, Carl. Amoenitates academicae seu dissertationes variae physicae, medicae botanicae antehac seorsim editae nunc collectae et auctae cum tabulis aeneis. [Volumen primum.] Holmiae et Lipsiae, apud Godofredum Kiesewetter, 1749. [iv], 565 pp., 16 plates.

> References: Hulth: p. 66; Krok: p. 458, no. 168a; Lindell: 5425; Pritzel (ed. 1): 5996; Pritzel (ed. 2): 5425; Soulsby: 1282; Rudolph & Williams: 112.

Volume 2:

Linnaeus, Carl. Amoenitates academicae; seu dissertationes variae, physicae, medicae botanicae, antehac seorsim editae nunc collectae et auctae cum tabulis aenaeis. Volumen secundum. Holmiae, apud Laurentium Salvium, 1751. [iv], 478 pp., 4 plates.

> References: Hulth: pp. 66–67; Krok: p. 458, no. 168a; Pritzel (ed. 1): 5996; Pritzel (ed. 2): 5425; Soulsby: 1285; Rudolph & Williams: 143.

Volume 3:

Linnaeus, Carl. Amoenitates academicae; seu dissertationes variae physicae, medicae, botanicae, antehac seorsim editae, nunc collectae et auctae cum tabulis aenaeis. Volumen tertium. Holmiae, Sumtu & literis Laurentii Salvii, 1756. [iv], 464 pp., 4 plates, 1 table.

References: Hulth: p. 67; Krok: p. 458, no. 168a; Pritzel (ed. 1): 5996; Pritzel (ed. 2): 5425; Soulsby: 1291; Rudolph & Williams: 222.

Volume 4:

Linnaeus, Carl. Amoenitates academicae; seu dissertationes variae physicae, medicae, botanicae, antehac seorsim editae, nunc collectae et auctae, cum tabulis aeneis. Volumen qvartum. Holmiae, Sumtu & literis direct. Laurentii Salvii, 1759. [iv], 600 pp., 4 plates.

References: Hulth: p. 68; Krok: p. 458, no. 168a; Lindell: 346; Pritzel (ed. 1): 5996; Pritzel (ed. 2): 5425; Soulsby: 1296; Rudolph & Williams: 267.

Volume 5:

Linnaeus, Carl. Amoenitates academicae; seu dissertationes variae physicae, medicae, botanicae, antehac seorsim editae, nunc collectae et auctae, cum tabulis aeneis. Volumen quintum. Holmiae, Sumtu & literis direct. Laurentii Salvii, 1760. [iv], 483, [8] pp., 3 plates.

References: Hulth: pp. 68–69; Krok: p. 458, no. 168a; Lindell: 347; Pritzel (ed. 1): 5996; Pritzel (ed. 2): 5425; Soulsby: 1300; Rudolph & Williams: 292.

Volume 6:

Linnaeus, Carl. Amoenitates academicae; seu dissertationes variae physicae, medicae, botanicae, antehac seorsim editae, nunc collectae et auctae cum tabulis aeneis. Volumen sextum. Holmiae, Sumtu & literis direct. Laurentii Salvii, 1763. [iv], 486 pp., 5 plates.

References: Hulth: p. 69; Krok: p. 458, no. 168a; Lindell: 348; Pritzel (ed. 1): 5996; Pritzel (ed. 2): 5425; Soulsby: 1304; Rudolph & Williams: 331.

Volume 7:

Linnaeus, Carl. Amoenitates academicae; seu dissertationes variae physicae, medicae, botanicae, antehac seorsim editae, nunc collectae et auctae, cum tabulis aeneis. Volumen septimum. Holmiae, Sumtu & literis direct. Laurentii Salvii, 1769. [iv], 606, [2] pp., 7 plates, 1 table.

References: Hulth: pp. 69–70; Krok: pp. 458–459, no. 168a; Lindell: 349; Pritzel (ed. 1): 5996; Pritzel (ed. 2): 5425; Soulsby: 1308; Rudolph & Williams: 426.

Linnaeus revised edition:

Volume 2:

Linnaeus, Carl. Amoenitates academicae; seu dissertationes variae, physicae, medicae, botanicae, antehac seorsim editae, nunc collectae et auctae, cum tabulis aenaeis. Volumen secundum. Editio secunda revisa & aucta. Holmiae, Impensis direct. Laurentii Salvii, 1762. [ii], 444 pp., 4 plates.

References: Hulth: pp. 66–67; Krok: p. 458, no. 168a; Lindell: 344; Pritzel (ed. 1): 5996; Pritzel (ed. 2): 5425; Soulsby: 1287; Rudolph & Williams: 315.

Volume 3:

Linnaeus, Carl. Amoenitates academicae; seu dissertationes variae physicae, medicae, botanicae, antehac seorsim editae, nunc collectae et auctae, cum tabulis aeneis. Volumen tertium. Holmiae, Sumtu & literis direct. Laurentii Salvii, 1764. [iv], 464 pp., 4 plates, 1 table.

References: Hulth: p. 67; Krok: p. 458, no. 168a; Lindell: 345; Soulsby: 1293; Rudolph & Williams: 347.

Wetstenius edition / issue:

Linnaeus, Carl. Amoenitates academicae; seu dissertationes variae, physicae, medicae, botanicae, antehac seorsim editae, nunc collectae & auctae, cum tabulis aenaeis. [Wetstenius issue.] Amstelaedami, Amstelaed. et Lugd. Bat., Lugduni Batavorum, Apud J. Wetstenium; 1752–1769. 6 vols.

References: Hulth: pp. 66–69; Krok: pp. 458–459, no. 168a; Pritzel (ed. 1): 5996; Pritzel (ed. 2): 5425; Soulsby: 1286, 1292, 1297, 1301, 1305, 1309.

Volume 2:

Linnaeus, Carl. Amoenitates academicae; seu dissertationes variae, physicae, medicae, botanicae, antehac seorsim editae, nunc collectae & auctae cum tabulis aenaeis. Volumen secundum. Amstelaedami, apud J. Wetstenium, 1752. [iv], 478 pp., 4 plates.

References: Hulth: p. 66; Krok: p. 458, no. 168a; Soulsby: 1286; Rudolph & Williams: 154.

Volume 2, Linnaeus revised edition:

Linnaeus, Carl. Amoenitates academicae; seu dissertationes variae, physicae, medicae, botanicae, antehac seorsim editae, nunc collectae & auctae, cum tabulis aeneis. Volumen secundum. Editio secunda revisa & aucta. Lugduni Batavorum, apud Wetstenium, 1764. [iv], 444 pp., 4 plates.

Reference: Soulsby: 1288.

Volume 3:

Linnaeus, Carl. Amoenitates academicae, seu dissertationes variae, physicae, medicae, botanicae, antehac seorsim editae, nunc collectae & auctae, cum tabulis aenaeis. Volumen tertium. Amstelaed. & Lugd. Bat., Apud Wetstenium, 1756. [iv], 464 pp., 4 plates, 1 table.

References: Hulth: p. 67; Krok: p. 458, no. 168a; Soulsby: 1292; Rudolph & Williams: 223.

Volume 4:

Linnaeus, Carl. Amoenitates academicae; seu dissertationes variae, physicae, medicae, botanicae, antehac seorsim editae, nunc collectae & auctae, cum tabulis aeneis. Volumen quartum. Lugduni Batavorum apud Wetstenium, 1760. [iv], 600 pp., 4 plates.

References: Hulth: p. 68; Krok: p. 458, no. 168a; Pritzel (ed. 1): 5996; Pritzel (ed. 2): 5425; Soulsby: 1297; Rudolph & Williams: 293.

Volume 5:

Linnaeus, Carl. Amoenitates academicae; seu dissertationes variae, physicae, medicae, botanicae, antehac seorsim editae, nunc collectae & auctae, cum tabulis aeneis. Volumen quintum. Lugduni Batavorum, apud Wetstenium, 1760. [iv], 483, [8] pp., 3 plates.

References: Hulth: p. 68; Krok: p. 458, no. 168a; Pritzel (ed. 1): 5996; Pritzel (ed. 2): 5425; Soulsby: 1301; Rudolph & Williams: 294.

Volume 6:

Linnaeus, Carl. Amoenitates academicae; seu dissertationes variae, physicae, medicae, botanicae, antehac seorsim editae, nunc collectae & auctae, cum tabulis aeneis. Volumen sextum. Lugduni Batavorum, apud Wetstenium, 1764. [iv], 486 pp., 5 plates.

References: Hulth: p. 69; Krok: p. 458, no. 168a; Pritzel (ed. 1): 5996; Pritzel (ed. 2): 5425; Soulsby: 1305.

Volume 7:

Linnaeus, Carl. Amoenitates academicae; seu dissertationes variae, physicae, medicae, botanicae, antehac seorsim editae, nunc collectae & auctae, cum tabulis aeneis. Volumen septimum. Lugduni Batavorum, apud Wetstenium, 1769. [iv], 506, [2] pp., 7 plates, 1 table.

References: Hulth: p. 69; Krok: p. 459, no. 168a; Pritzel (ed. 1): 5996; Pritzel (ed. 2): 5425; Soulsby: 1309.

Schreber edition:

Linnaeus, Carl. Amoenitates academicae seu dissertationes variae physicae, medicae, botanicae antehac seorsim editae nunc collectae et auctae, cum tabulis aeneis. Editio tertia [Editio secunda]. Curante D. Jo. Christiano Daniele Schrebero. [Schreber edition.] Erlangae, sumtu Jo. Jacobi Palm, 1785–1790. 10 vols.

References: Hulth: pp. 66–71; Krok: p. 458, no. 168a; Lindell: 350–359; Pritzel (ed. 1): 5996; Pritzel (ed. 2): 5425; Soulsby: 1281; Rudolph & Williams: 601, 602, 630, 631, 632, 644, 645, 654, 655, 680.

Volume 1:

Linnaeus, Carl. Amoenitates academicae seu dissertationes variae physicae, medicae botanicae antehac seorsim editae nunc collectae et auctae cum tabulis aeneis. Volumen primum. Editio tertia curante Jo. Christiano Daniele Schrebero. Erlangae, sumtu Jo. Jacobi Palm, 1787. [vi], 1–571 pp., 17 (i.e., 14) plates.

References: Hulth: p. 66; Krok: p. 458, no. 168a; Lindell: 350; Pritzel (ed. 1): 5996; Pritzel (ed. 2): 5425; Soulsby: 1283; Rudolph & Williams: 630.

Volume 2:

Linnaeus, Carl. Amoenitates academicae, seu dissertationes variae physicae, medicae botanicae antehac seorsim editae nunc collectae et auctae cum tabulis aeneis. Volumen secundum. Editio tertia curante Jo. Christiano Daniele Schrebero. Erlangae, sumtu Jo. Jacobi Palm, 1787. [iv], 472, [2] pp., 4 plates.

References: Hulth: p. 67; Krok: p. 458, no. 168a; Lindell: 351; Pritzel (ed. 1): 5996; Pritzel (ed. 2): 5425; Soulsby: 1289; Rudolph & Williams: 631.

Volume 3:

Linnaeus, Carl. Amoenitates academicae seu dissertationes variae physicae, medicae botanicae antehac seorsim editae nunc collectae et auctae cum tabulis aeneis. Volumen tertium. Editio secunda curante D. Io. Christiano Daniele Schrebero. Erlangae, sumtu Io. Iacobi Palm, 1787. [iv], 464, [2] pp., 4 plates, 1 table.

References: Hulth: p. 67; Krok: p. 458, no. 168a; Lindell: 352; Pritzel (ed. 1): 5996; Pritzel (ed. 2): 5425; Soulsby: 1294; Rudolph & Williams: 632.

Volume 4:

Linnaeus, Carl. Amoenitates academicae seu dissertationes variae physicae, medicae botanicae antehac seorsim editae nunc collectae et auctae cum tabulis aeneis. Volumen quartum. Editio secunda curante D. Io. Christiano Daniele Schrebero. Erlangae, sumtu Io. Iacobi Palm, 1788. [iv], 600, [3] pp., 4 plates.

References: Hulth: p. 69; Krok: p. 458, no. 168a; Lindell: 353; Pritzel (ed. 1): 5996; Pritzel (ed. 2): 5425; Soulsby: 1298; Rudolph & Williams: 644.

Volume 5:

Linnaeus, Carl. Amoenitates academicae seu dissertationes variae physicae, medicae botanicae antehac seorsim editae nunc collectae et auctae cum tabulis aeneis. Volumen quintum. Editio secunda curante D. Io. Christiano Daniele Schrebero. Erlangae, sumtu Io. Iacobi Palm, 1788. [iv], 483, [7] pp., 3 (i.e., 4) plates. Includes Index dissertationum tom. I–V and Explicatio iconum voluminis V.

References: Hulth: pp. 68–69; Krok: p. 458, no. 168a; Lindell: 354; Pritzel (ed. 1): 5996; Pritzel (ed. 2): 5425; Soulsby: 1302; Rudolph & Williams: 645.

Volume 6:

Linnaeus, Carl. Amoenitates academicae seu dissertationes variae physicae, medicae botanicae antehac seorsim editae nunc collectae et auctae cum tabulis aeneis. Volumen sextum. Editio secunda curante D. Io. Christiano Daniele Schrebero. Erlangae, sumtu Io. Iacobi Palm, 1789. [iv], 486, [3] pp., 5 plates.

> References: Hulth: p. 69; Krok: p. 458, no. 168a; Lindell: 355; Pritzel (ed. 1): 5996; Pritzel (ed. 2): 5425; Soulsby: 1306; Rudolph & Williams: 654.

Volume 7:

Linnaeus, Carl. Amoenitates academicae seu dissertationes variae physicae, medicae botanicae antehac seorsim editae nunc collectae et auctae cum tabulis aeneis. Volumen septimum. Editio secunda curante D. Io. Christiano Daniele Schrebero. Erlangae, sumtu Io. Iacobi Palm, 1789. [iv], 506, [4] pp., 7 plates, 1 table. Includes Index tabularum aenearum voluminis septim and Editiones operum auctoris, quae ad manus nostras pervenere. [1736–1752.]

> References: Hulth: pp. 69–70; Krok: p. 458, no. 168a; Lindell: 356; Pritzel (ed. 1): 5996; Pritzel (ed. 2): 5425; Soulsby: 1310; Rudolph & Williams: 655.

Volume 8:

Linnaeus, Carl. Amoenitates academicae seu dissertationes variae physicae, medicae botanicae antehac seorsim editae nunc collectae et auctae cum tabulis aeneis. Volumen octavum. Edidit Jo. Christianus Daniel Schreberus. Erlangae, sumtu Jo. Jacobi Palm, 1785. [iv], 332, [1] pp., 8 plates.

> References: Hulth: p. 70; Krok: p. 458, no. 168a; Lindell: 357; Pritzel (ed. 1): 5996; Pritzel (ed. 2): 5425; Soulsby: 1312; Rudolph & Williams: 601.

Volume 9:

Linnaeus, Carl. Amoenitates academicae seu dissertationes variae physicae, medicae botanicae antehac seorsim editae nunc collectae et auctae. Volumen nonum. Edidit Jo. Christianus Daniel Schreberus. Erlangae, sumtu Jo. Jacobi Palm, 1785. [vi], 331 pp.

> References: Hulth: pp. 70–71; Krok: p. 458, no. 168a; Lindell: 358; Pritzel (ed. 1): 5996; Pritzel (ed. 2): 5425; Soulsby: 1314; Rudolph & Williams: 602.

Volume 10:

Linnaeus, Carl. Amoenitates academicae. Volumen decimum accedunt Caroli a Linné fil. Dissertationes botanicae collectae cum tabulis aeneis curante D. Io. Christiano Daniele Schrebero. Erlangae, sumtu Io. Iacobi Palm, 1790. [vi], 148 (i.e. 172), [2]; [iv], 131 pp., 6 plates.

> References: Hulth: p. 71; Krok: p. 458, no. 168a; Lindell: 359; Soulsby: 1316; Rudolph & Williams: 680.

Hoepfner edition:

Linnaeus, Carl. Auserlesene Abhandlungen aus der Naturgeschichte, Physik und Arzneywissenschaft. Mit Kupfern. Leipzig, Verlegts Adam Friedrich Böhme, 1776–1778. 3 vols. in 1. [vi], 330, [ii] pp.; [iv], 387, [vii] pp.; [ii], 366 pp.

> References: Hulth: pp. 72–73; Lindell: 362, 363, 364; Pritzel (ed. 1): 6001; Pritzel (ed. 2): 5435; Soulsby: 1329; Rudolph & Williams: 521, 529, 537.

Biwald edition:

Linnaeus, Carl. Selectae ex Amaenitatibvs [*sic*] academicis Caroli Linnaei, dissertationes ad vniversam natvralem historiam pertinentes, qvas edidit, et additamentis avxit L.B. E S.I. [Biwald edition.] Graecii, Sumptibvs Iosephi Mavritii Lechner, Typis Haeredvm VVidmanstadii, 1764. [viii], 316 pp., 3 plates.

> References: Hulth: p. 71; Krok: p. 459, no. 168b; Lindell: 360; Pritzel (ed. 1): 5997; Pritzel (ed. 2): 5425; Soulsby: 1324; Rudolph & Williams: 362.

Linnaeus, Carl. Continvatio selectarvm ex Amoenitatibvs academicis Caroli Linnaei Dissertationvm ad vniversam natvralem historiam pertinentivm, qvas, edidit, et additamentis avxit L.B. E S.I. [Biwald edition.] Graecii, svmtibvs Iosephi Mavritii Lechner, Typis Haeredvm VVismanstadii, 1766. [vi], 297 pp., 2 plates.

> References: Hulth: p. 72; Krok: p. 459, no. 168b; Lindell: 361; Pritzel (ed. 1): 5997; Pritzel (ed. 2): 5425; Soulsby: 1326; Rudolph & Williams: 381.

Linnaeus, Carl. Continvatio altera selectarvm ex Amoenitatibvs academicis Caroli Linnaei dissertationvm. Qvas edidit, et additamentis avxit L.B. E S.I. [Biwald edition.] Graecii, Svmtibvs Iosephi Mavritii Lechner, Typis Haeredvm Widmanstadii, 1769. [xvi], 277 pp., 3 plates.

> References: Hulth: p. 72; Krok: p. 459, no. 168b; Pritzel (ed. 1): 5997; Pritzel (ed. 2): 5425; Soulsby: 1328; Rudolph & Williams: 428.

Stillingfleet translations:

Stillingfleet, Benjamin. Miscellaneous tracts relating to natural history, husbandry, and physick. Translated from the Latin, with notes, by Benj. Stillingfleet. London, R. and J. Dodsley & S. Baker, & M. Cooper, 1759. xxx, [i], 230 pp.

> References: Hulth: pp. 73–74; Pritzel (ed. 1): 5998, 9934; Pritzel (ed. 2): 5435, 8978; Soulsby: 1319; Rudolph & Williams: 280.

Stillingfleet, Benjamin. Miscellaneous tracts relating to natural history, husbandry, and physick. To which is added the Calendar of flora. [Translated] By Benj. Stillingfleet. The second edition. Corrected and augmented with additional notes throughout, particularly on some of the English grasses, which are illustrated by copper plates. London, R. and J. Dodsley & S. Baker, & T. Payne, 1762. xxx, [i], 391 pp., 11 plates.

References: Hulth: pp. 73–74; Lindell: 365; Pritzel (ed. 1): 9934; Pritzel (ed. 2): 8978; Soulsby: 1320; Rudolph & Williams: 320.

Stillingfleet, Benjamin. Miscellaneous tracts relating to natural history, husbandry, and physick. To which is added the Calendar of flora …. The third edition. London, Printed for J. Dodsley, Baker and Leigh, & T. Payne, 1775. xxxi, 391 pp., 11 plates.

References: Hulth: p. 74; Lindell: 366; Pritzel (ed. 1): 9934; Pritzel (ed. 2): 8978; Soulsby: 1321; Rudolph & Williams: 511.

Stillingfleet, Benjamin. Miscellaneous tracts relating to natural history, husbandry, and physick. To which is added the Calendar of flora …. The fourth edition. London, J. Dodsley, Leigh & Sotheby, & T. Payne, 1791. xxxi, [i], 391 pp., 11 plates.

References: Hulth: p. 74; Lindell: 367; Pritzel (ed. 1): 9934; Pritzel (ed. 2): 8978; Soulsby: 1322; Rudolph & Williams: 693.

Brand edition:

Linnaeus, Carl. Select dissertations from the Amoenitates academicae, a supplement to Mr. Stillingfleet's Tracts relating to natural history. Translated by the Rev. F. J. Brand …. In two volumes. Volume I. London, Sold by G. Robinson … and J. Robson, 1781. xiv, 480 pp. [Projected second volume never published.]

References: Hulth: p. 153; Soulsby: 1323.

Pulteney:

Pulteney, Richard. A general view of the writings of Linnaeus …. London, Printed for T. Payne and B. White, 1781 [iv], 425, [1] pp.

References: Lindell: 1752; Pritzel (ed. 1): 6143, 8253; Soulsby: 33a, 2607; Rudolph & Williams: 566.

Pulteney, Richard. A general view of the writings of Linnaeus ….The second edition; with corrections, considerable additions, and memoirs of the author, by William George Maton … To which is annexed the diary of Linnaeus, written by himself, and now translated into English [by

Carl Troilius], from the Swedish manuscript in the possession of the editor. London, Printed for J. Mawman, by R. Taylor and Co., 1805. xv, 595, [1] pp., portrait frontispiece, 4 plates, 1 table.

References: Lindell: 1753; Soulsby: 33b, 2608; Tullberg: 131, 439, 447, 461; Rudolph & Williams: 765.

Pulteney, Richard. Revue générale des écrits de Linné; Ouvrage dans lequel on trouve les anecdotes les plus intéressantes de sa vie privée, un abrégé de ses systêmes et de ses ouvrages, un extrait de ses Aménités académiques, &c. &c. &c. Par … traduit de l'Anglois, par L. A. Millin de Grandmaison; avec des notes et des additions du traducteur. 2 vols. Londres & Paris, Chez Buisson, 1789. Vol. 1: [iv], vi, 386 pp.; vol. 2: [iv], 400 pp., 1 table.

References: Lindell: 1754–1755; Pritzel (ed. 1): 6143, 8254; Soulsby: 33c, 2609; Rudolph & Williams: 667. 668.

Gilibert's *Systema plantarum Europae*:

Gilibert, J. E. Caroli Linnaei botanicorum principis Systema plantarum Europae, exhibens characteres naturales generum, characteres essentiales generum & specierum, synonima antiquorum, phrases specificas recentiorum Halleri, Scopoli, &c. Descriptiones rariorum, necnon floras tres novas, Lugdunaeam, Delphinalem, Lithuanicam, non omissis plantis exoticis in hortis Europae vulgo obviis. Curante …. 7 volumes. Coloniae-Allobrogum, Sumptibus Piestre & Delamolliere, 1785–1787.

References: Hulth: p. 154–156; Krok: p. 459, no. 168b; Lindell: 612–617; Pritzel (ed. 1): 3633; Pritzel (ed. 2): 3327; Soulsby: 20, 21; Rudolph & Williams: 618, 619.

Gilibert edition:

Linnaeus, Carl. Amoenitates academicae seu dissertationes botanicae antehac seorsim editae, nunc primum methodice dispositae & auctae, cum tabulis aeneis. Curante Joan. Emman. Gilibert. [Gilibert edition.] Coloniae-Allobrogum, Sumptibus Piestre & Delamolliere, 1786. Vol. 1: [viii], lxxv, lxxvj, 604 pp., 4 plates, 1 table; vol. 2: [iii], 732, 52 pp., 2 plates.

References: Krok: p. 459, no. 168b; Soulsby: 1330.

Valda avhandlingar:

Valda avhandlingar av Carl von Linné i översättning utgivna av Svenska Linné-Sällskapet. [Selected dissertations by Carl Linnaeus in translation published by Svenska Linné-Sällskapet.] Uppsala & Ekenäs, Svenska Linné-Sällskapet, 1921–1973.

Reference: Soulsby: 1331.

Concordance for Selected Editions

Introduction

This concordance has been compiled to facilitate access to particular references as they appear in selected editions of the collected dissertations, for which page numbering is continuous within each volume and so will not match that of the original dissertations. To augment the references to original pagination that are given in the Index, the Concordance provides the corresponding paginations in the collected editions which have become known as the following: the Camper edition, the Linnaeus edition, the Linnaean revised edition, the Wetstenius edition (including the Wetstenius issue of vol. 2 of the Linnaeus revised edition), and vols. 1–9 of the Schreber edition, as well as in the more recent translations provided in the *Valda avhandlingar* series. The Camper edition is included because it was the first reprinting of some of the dissertations; the Linnaeus editions, edited by the author, are included for their authoritativeness; the Wetstenius edition is included because it repeats the content of the Linnaeus edition and was relatively widely distributed; the Schreber edition includes the later dissertations (151–186) not found in earlier editions; and the *Valda avhandlingar* translations, an incomplete set of modern Swedish translations made in the light of two centuries of Linnaean scholarship, are included because of their recentness and availability (only 63 have been published, and most are still in print).

The Index to Scientific Names lists references as they appear in the original dissertations. Because page numbering is continuous within each volume in subsequent collected editions, pagination does not match that of the originals. The accompanying bibliographic concordance provides the pagination for dissertations as they appear in selected collected editions, providing a tool for locating references from an original dissertation in one of these subsequent editions. Using the Index to find the page on which a given scientific name occurs in a dissertation, the reader can then approximate the corresponding page number in any of the subsequent editions listed above by adding the original page number to the beginning page number of the later version in question, and then checking backward a page or two from the resulting page number.

Conventions Used

Square brackets [] indicate unnumbered preliminary or ending pages or, in a few cases, page numbering errors on initial or ending pages. They are also used in the Concordance to indicate the sequence numbers for dissertations in the Camper edition. Notes in parentheses () are added as needed to clarify irregularities in pagination to assist those trying to match an Index reference to a given page in one of the collected editions covered here.

276

Concordance

Lidén Number	1
Short Title	Betula
Camper Ed.	no. [12], pp. 333–351, 1 plate, 1749
Linnaeus Ed.	Vol. 1, no. 1, pp. 1–22, tab. I, 1749
Schreber Ed.	Vol. 1, no. 1, pp. 1–22, tab. I, 1787

Lidén Number	2
Short Title	Ficus
Camper Ed.	no. [8], pp. 213–243 (p. 235 misnumbered 135, p. 236 misnumbered 136, p. 237 misnumbered 137), 1 plate, 1749
Linnaeus Ed.	Vol. 1, no. 2, pp. 23–54, tab. II, 1749
Schreber Ed.	Vol. 1, no. 2, pp. 23–54, tab. II, 1787

Lidén Number	3
Short Title	Peloria
Camper Ed.	no. [10], pp. 280–298, 1 plate, 1749
Linnaeus Ed.	Vol. 1, no. 3, pp. 55–73, tab. III, 1749
Schreber Ed.	Vol. 1, no. 3, pp. 55–73, tab. III, 1787

Lidén Number	4
Short Title	Corallia Balt.
Camper Ed.	no. [7], pp. 177–212, 1 plate, 1749
Linnaeus Ed.	Vol. 1, no. 4, pp. 74–106, tab. IV, 1749
Schreber Ed.	Vol. 1, no. 4, pp. 74–106 (p. 100 misnumbered 110, p. 103 misnumbered 109), tab. IV, 1787

Lidén Number	5
Short Title	Amphib. Gyll.
Camper Ed.	no. [18], pp. 520–555, 1749
Linnaeus Ed.	Vol. 1, no. 5, pp. 107–140, 1749
Schreber Ed.	Vol. 1, no. 5, pp. 107–140, 1787

Lidén Number	6
Short Title	Pl. Mart.-Burs.
Camper Ed.	no. [11], pp. 299–332 (p. 314 misnumbered 214, p. 316 misnumbered 216), 1749
Linnaeus Ed.	Vol. 1, no. 6, pp. 141–171, 1749
Schreber Ed.	Vol. 1, no. 6, pp. 141–171, 1787

Lidén Number	7
Short Title	Hort. Upsal.
Camper Ed.	no. [2], pp. 20–60 (p. 53 unnumbered), tabs. I–III, 1 unnumbered plate, 1749
Linnaeus Ed.	Vol. 1, no. 7, pp. 172–210, tabs. V, VII–IX, 1749
Schreber Ed.	Vol. 1, no. 7, pp. 172–210, tabs. V–IX, 1787

Lidén Number	8
Short Title	Passifl.
Camper Ed.	no. [9], pp. 244–279, 1 plate, 1749
Linnaeus Ed.	Vol. 1, no. 8, pp. 211–242, tab. X, 1749
Schreber Ed.	Vol. 1, no. 8, pp. 211–242, tab. X, 1787

Lidén Number	9
Short Title	Anandria

Camper Ed.	no. [6], pp. 161–176 (p. 176 misnumbered 174), 1749
Linnaeus Ed.	Vol. 1, no. 9, pp. 243–259, tab. XI, 1749
Schreber Ed.	Vol. 1, no. 9, pp. 243–259, tab. XI, 1787

Lidén Number	10
Short Title	Acrostichum
Camper Ed.	no. [5], pp. 144–160 (p. 148 misnumbered 152, p. 152 misnumbered 148, p. 153 misnumbered 157, p. 157 misnumbered 153), 1 plate, 1749
Linnaeus Ed.	Vol. 1, no. 10, pp. 260–276, tab. XII, 1749
Schreber Ed.	Vol. 1, no. 10, pp. 260–276, tab. XII, 1787

Lidén Number	11
Short Title	Mus. Ad.-Frid.
Camper Ed.	no. [19], pp. 556–610 (p. 569 misnumbered 566), tabs. I, II, 1749
Linnaeus Ed.	Vol. 1, no. 11, pp. 277–326, tabs. XIII, XIV, 1749
Schreber Ed.	Vol. 1, no. 11, pp. 277–327, tabs. XIII, XIV, 1787

Lidén Number	12
Short Title	Spons. pl.
Camper Ed.	no. [3], pp. 61–109, 1 plate, 1749
Linnaeus Ed.	Vol. 1, no. 12, pp. 327–380, tab. XV, 1749
Schreber Ed.	Vol. 1, no. 12, pp. 328–380 (p. 370 misnumbered 362), tab. XV, 1787

Lidén Number	13
Short Title	Vir. pl.
Camper Ed.	no. [14], pp. 389–428, 1749
Linnaeus Ed.	Vol. 1, no. 14, pp. 418–453, 1749
Schreber Ed.	Vol. 1, no. 14, pp. 418–453, 1787
Valda Avhandlingar	No. 57, pp. 3–36, 1970
Valda Avhandlingar Title	Växternas krafter (Vires plantarum)

Lidén Number	14
Short Title	Nova pl. gen. 1747
Camper Ed.	no. [4], pp. 110–143, 1749
Linnaeus Ed.	Vol. 1, no. 13, pp. 381–417, 1749
Schreber Ed.	Vol. 1, no. 13, pp. 381–417, 1787

Lidén Number	15
Short Title	Cryst. gen.
Camper Ed.	no. [16], pp. 454–488, 1 plate, text fig., 1749
Linnaeus Ed.	Vol. 1, no. 15, pp. 454–482, tab. XVI, text fig., 1749
Schreber Ed.	Vol. 1, no. 15, pp. 454–482, tab. XVI, text fig., 1787

Lidén Number	16
Short Title	Surin. Grill.
Camper Ed.	no. [17], pp. 489–519, 1 plate, 1749
Linnaeus Ed.	Vol. 1, no. 16, pp. 483–508, tab. XVII, 1749
Schreber Ed.	Vol. 1, no. 16, pp. 483–508, tab. XVII, 1787

Lidén Number	17
Short Title	Fl. oecon.
Camper Ed.	no. [13], pp. 352–388, 1749
Linnaeus Ed.	Vol. 1, no. 17, pp. 509–539, 1749
Schreber Ed.	Vol. 1, no. 17, pp. 509–540 (p. 512 misnumbered 516), 1787

Lidén Number	18
Short Title	Curios. nat.
Camper Ed.	no. [15], pp. 429–453, 1749
Linnaeus Ed.	Vol. 1, no. 18, pp. 540–563, 1749
Schreber Ed.	Vol. 1, no. 16 (i.e., no. 18, misnumbered 16), pp. [540]–563 (last page of dissertation no. 17 is p. 540; first page of dissertation no. 18 is unnumbered, followed by p. 541), 1787

Lidén Number	19
Short Title	Taenia
Linnaeus Ed.	Vol. 2, no. 20, pp. 59–99, tab. I, illus., 1751
Linnaeus Rev. Ed.	Vol. 2, no. 20, pp. 53–88, tab. I, illus., 1762
Wetstenius Linnaeus Ed.	Vol. 2, no. 20, pp. 59–99, tab. I, illus., 1752
Wetstenius Linn. Rev. Ed.	Vol. 2, no. 20, pp. 53–88, tab. I, illus., 1764
Schreber Ed.	Vol. 2, no. 20, pp. 59–99, tab. I, illus., 1787

Lidén Number	20
Short Title	Oecon. nat.
Linnaeus Ed.	Vol. 2, no. 19, pp. 1–58, 1751
Linnaeus Rev. Ed.	Vol. 2, no. 19, pp. 1–52, 1762
Wetstenius Linnaeus Ed.	Vol. 2, no. 19, pp. 1–58, 1752
Wetstenius Linn. Rev. Ed.	Vol. 2, no. 19, pp. 1–52, 1764
Schreber Ed.	Vol. 2, no. 19, pp. 1–58, 1787

Lidén Number	21
Short Title	Lign. colubr.
Linnaeus Ed.	Vol. 2, no. 21, pp. 100–125, 1751
Linnaeus Rev. Ed.	Vol. 2, no. 21, pp. 89–111, 1762
Wetstenius Linnaeus Ed.	Vol. 2, no. 21, pp. 100–125, 1752
Wetstenius Linn. Rev. Ed.	Vol. 2, no. 21, pp. 89–111, 1764
Schreber Ed.	Vol. 2, no. 21, pp. 100–125, 1787

Lidén Number	22
Short Title	Generat. calc.
Linnaeus Ed.	Vol. 2, no. 23, pp. 154–181, 1751
Linnaeus Rev. Ed.	Vol. 2, no. 23, pp. 137–162 (p. 140 misnumbered 130), 1762
Wetstenius Linnaeus Ed.	Vol. 2, no. 23, pp. 154–181, 1752
Wetstenius Linn. Rev. Ed.	Vol. 2, no. 23, pp. 137–162 (p. 140 misnumbered 130), 1764
Schreber Ed.	Vol. 2, no. 23, pp. 154–181, 1787

Lidén Number	23
Short Title	Rad. Senega
Linnaeus Ed.	Vol. 2, no. 22, pp. 126–153, tab. II, 1751
Linnaeus Rev. Ed.	Vol. 2, no. 22, pp. 112–136, tab. II, 1762
Wetstenius Linnaeus Ed.	Vol. 2, no. 22, pp. 126–153, tab. II, 1752
Wetstenius Linn. Rev. Ed.	Vol. 2, no. 22, pp. 112–136, tab. II, 1764
Schreber Ed.	Vol. 2, no. 22, pp. 126–153, tab. II, 1787

Lidén Number	24
Short Title	Gem. arb.
Linnaeus Ed.	Vol. 2, no. 24, pp. 182–224 (p. 208 misnumbered 108), 1751
Linnaeus Rev. Ed.	Vol. 2, no. 24, pp. 163–202, 1762
Wetstenius Linnaeus Ed.	Vol. 2, no. 24, pp. 182–224 (p. 208 misnumbered 108), 1752
Wetstenius Linn. Rev. Ed.	Vol. 2, no. 24, pp. 163–202, 1764
Schreber Ed.	Vol. 2, no. 24, pp. 182–224, 1787

Lidén Number	25
Short Title	Haemor. uteri
Schreber Ed.	vol. 9, no. 172, pp. 1–22, 1785

Lidén Number	26
Short Title	Pan Svec.
Linnaeus Ed.	Vol. 2, no. 25, pp. 225–262 (p. 242 misnumbered 142), 1751
Linnaeus Rev. Ed.	Vol. 2, no. 25, pp. 203–241, 1762
Wetstenius Linnaeus Ed.	Vol. 2, no. 25, pp. 225–262 (p. 242 misnumbered 142), 1752
Wetstenius Linn. Rev. Ed.	Vol. 2, no. 25, pp. 203–241, 1764
Schreber Ed.	Vol. 2, no. 25, pp. 225–262 (p. 226 misnumbered 204), 1787

Lidén Number	27
Short Title	Splachnum
Linnaeus Ed.	Vol. 2, no. 26, pp. 263–283, tab. III (figs. I–III), 1751
Linnaeus Rev. Ed.	Vol. 2, no. 26, pp. 242–260, tab. III (figs. I–III), 1762
Wetstenius Linnaeus Ed.	Vol. 2, no. 26, pp. 263–283, tab. III (figs. I–III), 1752
Wetstenius Linn. Rev. Ed.	Vol. 2, no. 26, pp. 242–260, tab. III (figs. I–III), 1764
Schreber Ed.	Vol. 2, no. 26, pp. 263–283, tab. III (figs. I–III), 1787

Lidén Number	28
Short Title	Sem. musc.
Linnaeus Ed.	Vol. 2, no. 27, pp. 284–306, tab. III (fig. IV), 1751
Linnaeus Rev. Ed.	Vol. 2, no. 27, pp. 261–280, tab. III (fig. IV), 1762
Wetstenius Linnaeus Ed.	Vol. 2, no. 27, pp. 284–306, tab. III (fig. IV), 1752
Wetstenius Linn. Rev. Ed.	Vol. 2, no. 27, pp. 261–280, tab. III (fig. IV), 1764
Schreber Ed.	Vol. 2, no. 27, pp. 284–306, tab. III (fig. IV), 1787

Lidén Number	29
Short Title	Mat. med. anim.
Linnaeus Ed.	Vol. 2, no. 28, pp. 307–331, 1751
Linnaeus Rev. Ed.	Vol. 2, no. 28, pp. 281–305, 1762
Wetstenius Linnaeus Ed.	Vol. 2, no. 28, pp. 307–331, 1752
Wetstenius Linn. Rev. Ed.	Vol. 2, no. 28, pp. 281–305, 1764
Schreber Ed.	Vol. 2, no. 28, pp. 307–331, 1787

Lidén Number	30
Short Title	Pl. rar. Camsch.
Linnaeus Ed.	Vol. 2, no. 29, pp. 332–364, tab. IV, 1751
Linnaeus Rev. Ed.	Vol. 2, no. 29, pp. 306–334, tab. IV, 1762
Wetstenius Linnaeus Ed.	Vol. 2, no. 29, pp. 332–364, tab. IV, 1752
Wetstenius Linn. Rev. Ed.	Vol. 2, no. 29, pp. 306–334, tab. IV, 1764
Schreber Ed.	Vol. 2, no. 29, pp. 332–364, tab. IV, 1787

Lidén Number	31
Short Title	Sapor. med.
Linnaeus Ed.	Vol. 2, no. 30, pp. 365–387 (p. 384 misnumbered 284), 1751
Linnaeus Rev. Ed.	Vol. 2, no. 30, pp. 335–355, 1762
Wetstenius Linnaeus Ed.	Vol. 2, no. 30, pp. 365–387 (p. 384 misnumbered 284), 1752
Wetstenius Linn. Rev. Ed.	Vol. 2, no. 30, pp. 335–355, 1764
Schreber Ed.	Vol. 2, no. 30, pp. 365–387 (p. 384 misnumbered 284), 1787
Valda Avhandlingar	No. 31, pp. 3–24, 1958
Valda Avhandlingar Title	Läkemedlens smak (Sapor medicamentorum)

Lidén Number	32
Short Title	Nova pl. gen. 1751
Linnaeus Ed.	Vol. 3, no. 31, pp. 1–27, tab. I, 1756

Linnaeus Rev. Ed.	Vol. 3, no. 31, pp. 1–27, tab. I, 1764
Wetstenius Linnaeus Ed.	Vol. 3, no. 31, pp. 1–27, tab. I, 1756
Schreber Ed.	Vol. 3, no. 31, pp. 1–27, tab. I, 1787

Lidén Number	33
Short Title	Pl. hybr.
Linnaeus Ed.	Vol. 3, no. 32, pp. 28–62, tab. II, 1756
Linnaeus Rev. Ed.	Vol. 3, no. 32, pp. 28–62, tab. II, 1764
Wetstenius Linnaeus Ed.	Vol. 3, no. 32, pp. 28–62, tab. II, 1756
Schreber Ed.	Vol. 3, no. 32, pp. 28–62, tab. II, 1787

Lidén Number	34
Short Title	Obst. med.
Linnaeus Ed.	Vol. 3, no. 33, pp. 63–73, 1756
Linnaeus Rev. Ed.	Vol. 3, no. 33, pp. 63–73, 1764
Wetstenius Linnaeus Ed.	Vol. 3, no. 33, pp. 63–73, 1756
Schreber Ed.	Vol. 3, no. 33, pp. 63–73, 1787
Valda Avhandlingar	No. 5, pp. 3–24, 1948
Valda Avhandlingar Title	Hinder för läkekonsten (Obstacula medicinae)

Lidén Number	35
Short Title	Pl. escul.
Linnaeus Ed.	Vol. 3, no. 34, pp. 74–99, 1756
Linnaeus Rev. Ed.	Vol. 3, no. 34, pp. 74–99, 1764
Wetstenius Linnaeus Ed.	Vol. 3, no. 34, pp. 74–99, 1756
Schreber Ed.	Vol. 3, no. 34, pp. 74–99, 1787

Lidén Number	36
Short Title	Euphorbia
Linnaeus Ed.	Vol. 3, no. 35, pp. 100–131, 1756
Linnaeus Rev. Ed.	Vol. 3, no. 35, pp. 100–131 (p. 110 misnumbered 200), 1764
Wetstenius Linnaeus Ed.	Vol. 3, no. 35, pp. 100–131, 1756
Schreber Ed.	Vol. 3, no. 35, pp. 100–131, 1787

Lidén Number	37
Short Title	Mat. med. lapid.
Linnaeus Ed.	Vol. 3, no. 36, pp. 132–157, 1756
Linnaeus Rev. Ed.	Vol. 3, no. 36, pp. 132–157, 1764
Wetstenius Linnaeus Ed.	Vol. 3, no. 36, pp. 132–157, 1756
Schreber Ed.	Vol. 3, no. 36, pp. 132–157, 1787

Lidén Number	38
Short Title	Morb. Hyeme
Linnaeus Ed.	Vol. 3, no. 37, pp. 158–182, 1756
Linnaeus Rev. Ed.	Vol. 3, no. 37, pp. 158–182, 1764
Wetstenius Linnaeus Ed.	Vol. 3, no. 37, pp. 158–182, 1756
Schreber Ed.	Vol. 3, no. 37, pp. 158–182, 1787
Valda Avhandlingar	No. 14, pp. 3–28, 1953
Valda Avhandlingar Title	Om vintersjukdomar (De morbis ex hyeme)

Lidén Number	39
Short Title	Noctiluca
Linnaeus Ed.	Vol. 3, no. 39, pp. 202–210, tab. III, 1756
Linnaeus Rev. Ed.	Vol. 3, no. 39, pp. 202–210, tab. III, 1764
Wetstenius Linnaeus Ed.	Vol. 3, no. 39, pp. 202–210, tab. III, 1756
Schreber Ed.	Vol. 3, no. 39, pp. 202–210, tab. III, 1787

Lidén Number	40
Short Title	Odor. med.
Linnaeus Ed.	Vol. 3, no. 38, pp. 183–201, 1756
Linnaeus Rev. Ed.	Vol. 3, no. 38, pp. 183–201, 1764
Wetstenius Linnaeus Ed.	Vol. 3, no. 38, pp. 183–201, 1756
Schreber Ed.	Vol. 3, no. 38, pp. 183–201, 1787
Valda Avhandlingar	No. 15, pp. 3–21, 1954
Valda Avhandlingar Title	Läkemedlens lukt (Odores medicamentorum)

Lidén Number	41
Short Title	Rhabarbarum
Linnaeus Ed.	Vol. 3, no. 40, pp. 211–230 (p. 211 misnumbered 112, p. 224 misnumbered 214), tab. IV, 1756
Linnaeus Rev. Ed.	Vol. 3, no. 40, pp. 211–230, tab. IV, 1764
Wetstenius Linnaeus Ed.	Vol. 3, no. 40, pp. 211–230 (p. 211 misnumbered 112, p. 224 misnumbered 214), tab. IV, 1756
Schreber Ed.	Vol. 3, no. 40, pp. 211–230, tab. IV, 1787

Lidén Number	42
Short Title	Cui bono?
Linnaeus Ed.	Vol. 3, no. 41, pp. 231–255, 1756
Linnaeus Rev. Ed.	Vol. 3, no. 41, pp. 231–255, 1764
Wetstenius Linnaeus Ed.	Vol. 3, no. 41, pp. 231–255, 1756
Schreber Ed.	Vol. 3, no. 41, pp. 231–255, 1787

Lidén Number	43
Short Title	Hosp. insect. fl.
Linnaeus Ed.	Vol. 3, no. 43, pp. 271–312, 1756
Linnaeus Rev. Ed.	Vol. 3, no. 43, pp. 271–312, 1764
Wetstenius Linnaeus Ed.	Vol. 3, no. 43, pp. 271–312, 1756
Schreber Ed.	Vol. 3, no. 43, pp. 271–312 (p. 289 misnumbered 298), 1787

Lidén Number	44
Short Title	Nutr. noverca
Linnaeus Ed.	Vol. 3, no. 42, pp. 256–270, 1756
Linnaeus Rev. Ed.	Vol. 3, no. 42, pp. 256–270, 1764
Wetstenius Linnaeus Ed.	Vol. 3, no. 42, pp. 256–270, 1756
Schreber Ed.	Vol. 3, no. 42, pp. 256–270, 1787
Valda Avhandlingar	No. 4, pp. 3–24, 1947
Valda Avhandlingar Title	Amman såsom styvmoder (Nutrix noverca)

Lidén Number	45
Short Title	Mirac. insect.
Linnaeus Ed.	Vol. 3, no. 44, pp. 313–334 (p. 314 misnumbered 214), 1756
Linnaeus Rev. Ed.	Vol. 3, no. 44, pp. 313–334, 1764
Wetstenius Linnaeus Ed.	Vol. 3, no. 44, pp. 313–334 (p. 314 misnumbered 214), 1756
Schreber Ed.	Vol. 3, no. 44, pp. 313–334 (p. 314 misnumbered 214), 1787

Lidén Number	46
Short Title	Noxa insect.
Linnaeus Ed.	Vol. 3, no. 45, pp. 335–362, 1756
Linnaeus Rev. Ed.	Vol. 3, no. 45, pp. 335–362 (p. 339 misnumbered 393, p. 355 misnumbered 535), 1764
Wetstenius Linnaeus Ed.	Vol. 3, no. 45, pp. 335–362, 1756
Schreber Ed.	Vol. 3, no. 45, pp. 335–362, 1787

Lidén Number	47
Short Title	Vern. arb.
Linnaeus Ed.	Vol. 3, no. 46, pp. 363–376, 1 chart, 1756
Linnaeus Rev. Ed.	Vol. 3, no. 46, pp. 363–376, 1 chart, 1764
Wetstenius Linnaeus Ed.	Vol. 3, no. 46, pp. 363–376, 1 chart, 1756
Schreber Ed.	Vol. 3, no. 46, pp. 363–376, 1 chart, 1787

Lidén Number	48
Short Title	Incr. bot.
Linnaeus Ed.	Vol. 3, no. 47, pp. 377–393, 1756
Linnaeus Rev. Ed.	Vol. 3, no. 47, pp. 377–393, 1764
Wetstenius Linnaeus Ed.	Vol. 3, no. 47, pp. 377–393, 1756
Schreber Ed.	Vol. 3, no. 47, pp. 377–393, 1787

Lidén Number	49
Short Title	Demonstr. pl.
Linnaeus Ed.	Vol. 3, no. 48, pp. 394–424, 1756
Linnaeus Rev. Ed.	Vol. 3, no. 48, pp. 394–424 (p. 404 misnumbered 04), 1764
Wetstenius Linnaeus Ed.	Vol. 3, no. 48, pp. 394–424, 1756
Schreber Ed.	Vol. 3, no. 48, pp. 394–424, 1787

Lidén Number	50
Short Title	Herbat. Upsal.
Linnaeus Ed.	Vol. 3, no. 49, pp. 425–445, 1756
Linnaeus Rev. Ed.	Vol. 3, no. 49, pp. 425–445, 1764
Wetstenius Linnaeus Ed.	Vol. 3, no. 49, pp. 425–445, 1756
Schreber Ed.	Vol. 3, no. 49, pp. 425–445, 1787
Valda Avhandlingar	No. 1, pp. 5–39, 1921
Valda Avhandlingar Title	Botaniska exkursioner i trakten av Uppsala (Herbationes Upsalienses)

Lidén Number	51
Short Title	Instr. mus.
Linnaeus Ed.	Vol. 3, no. 50, pp. 446–464 (p. 460 misnumbered 560), 1756
Linnaeus Rev. Ed.	Vol. 3, no. 50, pp. 446–464, 1764
Wetstenius Linnaeus Ed.	Vol. 3, no. 50, pp. 446–464 (p. 460 misnumbered 560), 1756
Schreber Ed.	Vol. 3, no. 50, pp. 446–464, 1787

Lidén Number	52
Short Title	Pl. officin.
Linnaeus Ed.	Vol. 4, no. 51, pp. 1–25, 1759
Wetstenius Linnaeus Ed.	Vol. 4, no. 51, pp. 1–25, 1760
Schreber Ed.	Vol. 4, no. 51, pp. 1–25, 1788
Valda Avhandlingar	No. 10, pp. 3–26, 1950
Valda Avhandlingar Title	Officinella växter (Plantae officinales)

Lidén Number	53
Short Title	Cens. med.
Linnaeus Ed.	Vol. 4, no. 52, pp. 26–42, 1759
Wetstenius Linnaeus Ed.	Vol. 4, no. 52, pp. 26–42, 1760
Schreber Ed.	Vol. 4, no. 52, pp. 26–42, 1788
Valda Avhandlingar	No. 8, pp. 3–16, 1950
Valda Avhandlingar Title	Granskning av de enkla läkemedlen ur växtriket (Censura medicamentorum simplicium vegetabilium)

Lidén Number	54
Short Title	Cynogr.
Linnaeus Ed.	Vol. 4, no. 53, pp. 43–63, tab. I, 1759

Lidén Number	72
Short Title	Calend. fl.
Linnaeus Ed.	Vol. 4, no. 67, pp. 387–414 (pp. 396 and 399 unnumbered), 1759
Wetstenius Linnaeus Ed.	Vol. 4, no. 67, pp. 387–414 (pp. 396 and 399 unnumbered), 1760
Schreber Ed.	Vol. 4, no. 67, pp. 387–414, 1788

Lidén Number	73
Short Title	Puls. interm.
Schreber Ed.	vol. 9, no. 175, pp. 43–63, 1785

Lidén Number	74
Short Title	Fl. Monsp.
Linnaeus Ed.	Vol. 4, no. 70, pp. 468–495, 1759
Wetstenius Linnaeus Ed.	Vol. 4, no. 70, pp. 468–495, 1760
Schreber Ed.	Vol. 4, no. 70, pp. 468–495 (p. 487 misnumbered 453), 1788

Lidén Number	75
Short Title	Fund. valet.
Linnaeus Ed.	Vol. 4, no. 71, pp. 496–506, 1759
Wetstenius Linnaeus Ed.	Vol. 4, no. 71, pp. 496–506, 1760
Schreber Ed.	Vol. 4, no. 71, pp. 496–506, 1788
Valda Avhandlingar	No. 28, pp. 3–15, 1958
Valda Avhandlingar Title	Grunderna till hälsan (Fundamenta valetudinis)

Lidén Number	76
Short Title	Specif. Canad.
Linnaeus Ed.	Vol. 4, no. 72, pp. 507–535, 1759
Wetstenius Linnaeus Ed.	Vol. 4, no. 72, pp. 507–535, 1760
Schreber Ed.	Vol. 4, no. 72, pp. 507–535, 1788

Lidén Number	77
Short Title	Acetaria
Linnaeus Ed.	Vol. 4, no. 73, pp. 536–552, 1759
Wetstenius Linnaeus Ed.	Vol. 4, no. 73, pp. 536–552, 1760
Schreber Ed.	Vol. 4, no. 73, pp. 536–552, 1788
Valda Avhandlingar	No. 29, pp. 3–18, 1958
Valda Avhandlingar Title	Om salladsväxter (De acetariis)

Lidén Number	78
Short Title	Phalaena
Linnaeus Ed.	Vol. 4, no. 74, pp. 553–564, 1759
Wetstenius Linnaeus Ed.	Vol. 4, no. 74, pp. 553–564, 1760
Schreber Ed.	Vol. 4, no. 74, pp. 553–564, 1788

Lidén Number	79
Short Title	Migr. avium
Linnaeus Ed.	Vol. 4, no. 75, pp. 565–600, 1759
Wetstenius Linnaeus Ed.	Vol. 4, no. 75, pp. 565–600, 1760
Schreber Ed.	Vol. 4, no. 75, pp. 565–600, 1788

Lidén Number	80
Short Title	Morb. exped.
Linnaeus Ed.	Vol. 5, no. 76, pp. 1–17, 1760
Wetstenius Linnaeus Ed.	Vol. 5, no. 76, pp. 1–17, 1760
Schreber Ed.	Vol. 5, no. 76, pp. 1–17, 1788

Lidén Number	81
Short Title	Febr. Upsal.
Linnaeus Ed.	Vol. 5, no. 77, pp. 18–29, 1760
Wetstenius Linnaeus Ed.	Vol. 5, no. 77, pp. 18–29, 1760
Schreber Ed.	Vol. 5, no. 77, pp. 18–29, 1788
Valda Avhandlingar	No. 32, pp. 3–19, 1959
Valda Avhandlingar Title	Uppsalafebern (Febris Upsaliensis)

Lidén Number	82
Short Title	Prodr. fl. Dan.
Linnaeus Ed.	Vol. 5, no. 78, pp. 30–49, 1760
Wetstenius Linnaeus Ed.	Vol. 5, no. 78, pp. 30–49, 1760
Schreber Ed.	Vol. 5, no. 78, pp. 30–49, 1788

Lidén Number	83
Short Title	Pane diaet.
Linnaeus Ed.	Vol. 5, no. 79, pp. 50–67, 1760
Wetstenius Linnaeus Ed.	Vol. 5, no. 79, pp. 50–67, 1760
Schreber Ed.	Vol. 5, no. 79, pp. 50–67, 1788
Valda Avhandlingar	No. 44, pp. 3–20, 1964
Valda Avhandlingar Title	Om brödet som födoämne (De pane diaetetico)

Lidén Number	84
Short Title	Nat. pelagi
Linnaeus Ed.	Vol. 5, no. 80, pp. 68–77, 1760
Wetstenius Linnaeus Ed.	Vol. 5, no. 80, pp. 68–77, 1760
Schreber Ed.	Vol. 5, no. 80, pp. 68–77, 1788

Lidén Number	85
Short Title	Buxbaumia
Linnaeus Ed.	Vol. 5, no. 81, pp. 78–91, tab. I, 1760
Wetstenius Linnaeus Ed.	Vol. 5, no. 81, pp. 78–91, tab. I, 1760
Schreber Ed.	Vol. 5, no. 81, pp. 78–91, tab. I, 1788

Lidén Number	86
Short Title	Exanth. viva
Linnaeus Ed.	Vol. 5, no. 82, pp. 92–105, 1760
Wetstenius Linnaeus Ed.	Vol. 5, no. 82, pp. 92–105, 1760
Schreber Ed.	Vol. 5, no. 82, pp. 92–105, 1788

Lidén Number	87
Short Title	Transm. frum.
Linnaeus Ed.	Vol. 5, no. 83, pp. 106–119, 1760
Wetstenius Linnaeus Ed.	Vol. 5, no. 83, pp. 106–119, 1760
Schreber Ed.	Vol. 5, no. 83, pp. 106–119, 1788
Valda Avhandlingar	No. 61, pp. 3–17, 1971
Valda Avhandlingar Title	Sädesslagens förvandling (Transmutatio frumentorum)

Lidén Number	88
Short Title	Cul. mut.
Linnaeus Ed.	Vol. 5, no. 84, pp. 120–132, 1760
Wetstenius Linnaeus Ed.	Vol. 5, no. 84, pp. 120–132, 1760
Schreber Ed.	Vol. 5, no. 84, pp. 120–132, 1788
Valda Avhandlingar	No. 24, pp. 3–17, 1956
Valda Avhandlingar Title	Det förändrade köket (Culina mutata)

Lidén Number	89
Short Title	Spigelia
Linnaeus Ed.	Vol. 5, no. 85, pp. 133–147, tab. II, 1760
Wetstenius Linnaeus Ed.	Vol. 5, no. 85, pp. 133–147, tab. II, 1760
Schreber Ed.	Vol. 5, no. 85, pp. 133–147, tabs. II, VI, 1788

Lidén Number	90
Short Title	Cort. peruv.
Schreber Ed.	vol. 9, no. 176, pp. 64–105, 1785

Lidén Number	91
Short Title	Fr. Svec.
Linnaeus Ed.	Vol. 5, no. 88, pp. 204–231, 1760
Wetstenius Linnaeus Ed.	Vol. 5, no. 88, pp. 204–231, 1760
Schreber Ed.	Vol. 5, no. 88, pp. 204–231, 1788

Lidén Number	92
Short Title	Med. grav.
Linnaeus Ed.	Vol. 5, no. 86, pp. 148–173, 1760
Wetstenius Linnaeus Ed.	Vol. 5, no. 86, pp. 148–173, 1760
Schreber Ed.	Vol. 5, no. 86, pp. 148–173, 1788
Valda Avhandlingar	No. 54, pp. 3–24, 1968
Valda Avhandlingar Title	Starkt luktande läkemedel (Medicamenta graveolentia)

Lidén Number	93
Short Title	Pand. insect.
Linnaeus Ed.	Vol. 5, no. 89, pp. 232–252, tab. III, 1760
Wetstenius Linnaeus Ed.	Vol. 5, no. 89, pp. 232–252, tab. III, 1760
Schreber Ed.	Vol. 5, no. 89, pp. 232–252 (p. 236 misnumbered 136), tab. III, 1788

Lidén Number	94
Short Title	Senium
Linnaeus Ed.	Vol. 5, no. 90, pp. 253–272, 1760
Wetstenius Linnaeus Ed.	Vol. 5, no. 90, pp. 253–272, 1760
Schreber Ed.	Vol. 5, no. 90, pp. 253–272, 1788
Valda Avhandlingar	No. 27, pp. 3–23, 1958
Valda Avhandlingar Title	Ålderdomen enligt Salomo (Senium Salomoneum)

Lidén Number	95
Short Title	Auct. bot.
Linnaeus Ed.	Vol. 5, no. 91, pp. 273–297, 1760
Wetstenius Linnaeus Ed.	Vol. 5, no. 91, pp. 273–297, 1760
Schreber Ed.	Vol. 5, no. 91, pp. 273–297, 1788
Valda Avhandlingar	No. 63, pp. 3–17, 1973
Valda Avhandlingar Title	Botaniska författare (Auctores botanici)

Lidén Number	96
Short Title	Instr. peregr.
Linnaeus Ed.	Vol. 5, no. 92, pp. 298–313, 1760
Wetstenius Linnaeus Ed.	Vol. 5, no. 92, pp. 298–313, 1760
Schreber Ed.	Vol. 5, no. 92, pp. 298–313, 1788

Lidén Number	97
Short Title	Pl. tinct.
Linnaeus Ed.	Vol. 5, no. 93, pp. 314–342, 1760
Wetstenius Linnaeus Ed.	Vol. 5, no. 93, pp. 314–342, 1760
Schreber Ed.	Vol. 5, no. 93, pp. 314–342, 1788

Lidén Number	98
Short Title	Anim. comp.
Linnaeus Ed.	Vol. 5, no. 94, pp. 343–352, 1760
Wetstenius Linnaeus Ed.	Vol. 5, no. 94, pp. 343–352, 1760
Schreber Ed.	Vol. 5, no. 94, pp. 343–352, 1788

Lidén Number	99
Short Title	Fl. Cap.
Linnaeus Ed.	Vol. 5, no. 95, pp. 353–370, 1760
Wetstenius Linnaeus Ed.	Vol. 5, no. 95, pp. 353–370, 1760
Schreber Ed.	Vol. 5, no. 95, pp. 353–370 (p. 367 misnumbered 736), 1788

Lidén Number	100
Short Title	Ambros.
Schreber Ed.	vol. 9, no. 177, pp. 106–117, 1785
Valda Avhandlingar	No. 58, pp. 3–14, 1970
Valda Avhandlingar Title	Ambrosiska läkemedel (Ambrosiaca)

Lidén Number	101
Short Title	Arb. Svec.
Linnaeus Ed.	Vol. 5, no. 87, pp. 174–203, 1760
Wetstenius Linnaeus Ed.	Vol. 5, no. 87, pp. 174–203, 1760
Schreber Ed.	Vol. 5, no. 87, pp. 174–203, 1788

Lidén Number	102
Short Title	Pl. Jam.
Linnaeus Ed.	Vol. 5, no. 97, pp. 389–413, 1760
Wetstenius Linnaeus Ed.	Vol. 5, no. 97, pp. 389–413, 1760
Schreber Ed.	Vol. 5, no. 97, pp. 389–413, 1788

Lidén Number	103
Short Title	Gen. morb.
Linnaeus Ed.	Vol. 6, no. 124, pp. 452–486 (p. 467 misnumbered 67), 1763
Wetstenius Linnaeus Ed.	Vol. 6, no. 124, pp. 452–486 (p. 477 misnumbered 4747), 1764
Schreber Ed.	Vol. 6, no. 124, pp. 452–486, 1789
Valda Avhandlingar	No. 7, pp. 3–40, 1949
Valda Avhandlingar Title	Genera morborum (Sjukdomsgrupperna)

Lidén Number	104
Short Title	Generat. ambig.
Linnaeus Ed.	Vol. 6, no. 101, pp. 1–16, 1763
Wetstenius Linnaeus Ed.	Vol. 6, no. 101, pp. 1–16, 1764
Schreber Ed.	Vol. 6, no. 101, pp. 1–16, 1789
Valda Avhandlingar	No. 39, pp. 3–19, 1962
Valda Avhandlingar Title	Tvåkönad alstring (Generatio ambigena)

Lidén Number	105
Short Title	Fl. Jam.
Linnaeus Ed.	Vol. 5, no. 96, pp. 371–388, 1760
Wetstenius Linnaeus Ed.	Vol. 5, no. 96, pp. 371–388, 1760
Schreber Ed.	Vol. 5, no. 96, pp. 371–388, 1788

Lidén Number	106
Short Title	Aer habit.
Linnaeus Ed.	Vol. 5, no. 99, pp. 442–460, 1760
Wetstenius Linnaeus Ed.	Vol. 5, no. 99, pp. 442–460, 1760
Schreber Ed.	Vol. 5, no. 99, pp. 442–460, 1788

Valda Avhandlingar	No. 43, pp. 3–21, 1964
Valda Avhandlingar Title	Den beboeliga luften (Aer habitabilis)

Lidén Number	107
Short Title	Nom. bot.
Linnaeus Ed.	Vol. 5, no. 98, pp. 414–441, 1760
Wetstenius Linnaeus Ed.	Vol. 5, no. 98, pp. 414–441, 1760
Schreber Ed.	Vol. 5, no. 98, pp. 414–441, 1788

Lidén Number	108
Short Title	Ping. anim.
Linnaeus Ed.	Vol. 5, no. 100, pp. 461–483, 1760
Wetstenius Linnaeus Ed.	Vol. 5, no. 100, pp. 461–483, 1760
Schreber Ed.	Vol. 5, no. 100, pp. 461–483, 1788

Lidén Number	109
Short Title	Polit. nat.
Linnaeus Ed.	Vol. 6, no. 102, pp. 17–39, 1763
Wetstenius Linnaeus Ed.	Vol. 6, no. 102, pp. 17–39, 1764
Schreber Ed.	Vol. 6, no. 102, pp. 17–39, 1789

Lidén Number	110
Short Title	Th. med.
Linnaeus Ed.	Vol. 6, no. 103, pp. 40–43, 1763
Wetstenius Linnaeus Ed.	Vol. 6, no. 103, pp. 40–43, 1764
Schreber Ed.	Vol. 6, no. 103, pp. 40–43, 1789

Lidén Number	111
Short Title	Anthrop.
Linnaeus Ed.	Vol. 6, no. 105, pp. 63–76, 1 plate, 1763
Wetstenius Linnaeus Ed.	Vol. 6, no. 105, pp. 63–76, tab. I, 1764
Schreber Ed.	Vol. 6, no. 105, pp. 63–76, tab. I, 1789
Valda Avhandlingar	No. 21, pp. 3–22, 1955
Valda Avhandlingar Title	Menniskans cousiner (Antropomorpha)

Lidén Number	112
Short Title	Fl. Belg.
Linnaeus Ed.	Vol. 6, no. 104, pp. 44–62, 1763
Wetstenius Linnaeus Ed.	Vol. 6, no. 104, pp. 44–62, 1764
Schreber Ed.	Vol. 6, no. 104, pp. 44–62, 1789

Lidén Number	113
Short Title	Mac. olit.
Linnaeus Ed.	Vol. 6, no. 107, pp. 116–131, 1763
Wetstenius Linnaeus Ed.	Vol. 6, no. 107, pp. 116–131, 1764
Schreber Ed.	Vol. 6, no. 107, pp. 116–131, 1789
Valda Avhandlingar	No. 25, pp. 3–21, 1956
Valda Avhandlingar Title	Grönsakstorget (Macellum olitorium)

Lidén Number	114
Short Title	Prol. pl. 1760
Linnaeus Ed.	Vol. 6, no. 118, pp. 324–341, 1763
Wetstenius Linnaeus Ed.	Vol. 6, no. 118, pp. 324–341, 1764
Schreber Ed.	Vol. 6, no. 118, pp. 324–341, 1789

Lidén Number	115
Short Title	Pl. rar. Afr.

Linnaeus Ed.	Vol. 6, no. 106, pp. 77–115 (p. 115 misnumbered 11), 1763
Wetstenius Linnaeus Ed.	Vol. 6, no. 106, pp. 77–115 (p. 115 misnumbered 11), 1764
Schreber Ed.	Vol. 6, no. 106, pp. 77–115, 1789

Lidén Number	116
Short Title	Diaet. acid.
Linnaeus Ed.	Vol. 6, no. 109, pp. 148–159, 1763
Wetstenius Linnaeus Ed.	Vol. 6, no. 109, pp. 148–159, 1764
Schreber Ed.	Vol. 6, no. 109, pp. 148–159, 1789
Valda Avhandlingar	No. 13, pp. 3–14, 1953
Valda Avhandlingar Title	Levnadsordning vid en surbrunn (Diaeta acidularis)

Lidén Number	117
Short Title	Inebr.
Linnaeus Ed.	Vol. 6, no. 111, pp. 180–196, 1763
Wetstenius Linnaeus Ed.	Vol. 6, no. 111, pp. 180–196, 1764
Schreber Ed.	Vol. 6, no. 111, pp. 180–196, 1789
Valda Avhandlingar	No. 40, pp. 3–20, 1963
Valda Avhandlingar Title	Berusningsmedel (Inebriantia)

Lidén Number	118
Short Title	Pot. coff.
Linnaeus Ed.	Vol. 6, no. 110, pp. 160–179, 1 plate, 1763
Wetstenius Linnaeus Ed.	Vol. 6, no. 110, pp. 160–179, 1 plate, 1764
Schreber Ed.	Vol. 6, no. 110, pp. 160–179, tab. II, 1789
Valda Avhandlingar	No. 49, pp. 3–20, 1966
Valda Avhandlingar Title	Kaffeedrycken (Potus coffeae)

Lidén Number	119
Short Title	Mors. serp.
Linnaeus Ed.	Vol. 6, no. 112, pp. 197–216, fig. on plate at p. 247, 1763
Wetstenius Linnaeus Ed.	Vol. 6, no. 112, pp. 197–216, fig. on plate at p. 247, 1764
Schreber Ed.	Vol. 6, no. 112, pp. 197–216, fig. on tab. III, 1789
Valda Avhandlingar	No. 47, pp. 3–24, 1965
Valda Avhandlingar Title	Om ormbett (De morsura serpentum)

Lidén Number	120
Short Title	Term. bot.
Linnaeus Ed.	Vol. 6, no. 113, pp. 217–246, 1763
Wetstenius Linnaeus Ed.	Vol. 6, no. 113, pp. 217–246, 1764
Schreber Ed.	Vol. 6, no. 113, pp. 217–246, 1789

Lidén Number	121
Short Title	Pl. Alstr.
Linnaeus Ed.	Vol. 6, no. 114, pp. 247–262, 1 plate, 1763
Wetstenius Linnaeus Ed.	Vol. 6, no. 114, pp. 247–262, 1 plate, 1764
Schreber Ed.	Vol. 6, no. 114, pp. 247–262, tab. III, 1789

Lidén Number	122
Short Title	Nect. fl.
Linnaeus Ed.	Vol. 6, no. 115, pp. 263–278 (p. 263 misnumbered 26), 1763
Wetstenius Linnaeus Ed.	Vol. 6, no. 115, pp. 263–278 (p. 263 misnumbered 26), 1764
Schreber Ed.	Vol. 6, no. 115, pp. 263–278, 1789

Lidén Number	123
Short Title	Fund. fr.
Linnaeus Ed.	Vol. 6, no. 116, pp. 279–304, 1763

Wetstenius Linnaeus Ed.	Vol. 6, no. 116, pp. 279–304, 1764
Schreber Ed.	Vol. 6, no. 116, pp. 279–304, 1789

Lidén Number	124
Short Title	Meloë
Linnaeus Ed.	Vol. 6, no. 108, pp. 132–147, 1763
Wetstenius Linnaeus Ed.	Vol. 6, no. 108, pp. 132–147, 1764
Schreber Ed.	Vol. 6, no. 108, pp. 132–147, 1789

Lidén Number	125
Short Title	Reform. bot.
Linnaeus Ed.	Vol. 6, no. 117, pp. 305–323, 1763
Wetstenius Linnaeus Ed.	Vol. 6, no. 117, pp. 305–323, 1764
Schreber Ed.	Vol. 6, no. 117, pp. 305–323, 1789

Lidén Number	126
Short Title	Raphania
Linnaeus Ed.	Vol. 6, no. 123, pp. 430–451, 1 plate, 1763
Wetstenius Linnaeus Ed.	Vol. 6, no. 123, pp. 430–451, 1 plate, 1764
Schreber Ed.	Vol. 6, no. 123, pp. 430–451, tab. V, 1789
Valda Avhandlingar	No. 36, pp. 3–28, 1960
Valda Avhandlingar Title	Om dragsjukan (De raphania)

Lidén Number	127
Short Title	Fr. escul.
Linnaeus Ed.	Vol. 6, no. 119, pp. 342–364, 1763
Wetstenius Linnaeus Ed.	Vol. 6, no. 119, pp. 342–364, 1764
Schreber Ed.	Vol. 6, no. 119, pp. 342–364, 1789
Valda Avhandlingar	No. 48, pp. 3–24, 1965
Valda Avhandlingar Title	Åtliga frukter (Fructus esculenti)

Lidén Number	128
Short Title	Lign. Qvas.
Linnaeus Ed.	Vol. 6, no. 122, pp. 416–429, 1 plate, 1763
Wetstenius Linnaeus Ed.	Vol. 6, no. 122, pp. 416–429, 1 plate, 1764
Schreber Ed.	Vol. 6, no. 122, pp. 416–429, tab. IV, 1789
Valda Avhandlingar	No. 62, pp. 3–12, 1971
Valda Avhandlingar Title	Kvassiaveden (Lignum Qvassiae)

Lidén Number	129
Short Title	Cent. insect.
Linnaeus Ed.	Vol. 6, no. 121, pp. 384–415, 1763
Wetstenius Linnaeus Ed.	Vol. 6, no. 121, pp. 384–415, 1764
Schreber Ed.	Vol. 6, no. 121, pp. 384–415, 1789

Lidén Number	130
Short Title	Prol. pl. 1763
Linnaeus Ed.	Vol. 6, no. 120, pp. 365–383, 1763
Wetstenius Linnaeus Ed.	Vol. 6, no. 120, pp. 365–383, 1764
Schreber Ed.	Vol. 6, no. 120, pp. 365–383 (p. 368 misnumbered 468), 1789

Lidén Number	131
Short Title	Mot. polychr.
Linnaeus Ed.	Vol. 7, no. 125, pp. 1–17, 1769
Wetstenius Linnaeus Ed.	Vol. 7, no. 125, pp. 1–17, 1769
Schreber Ed.	Vol. 7, no. 125, pp. 1–17, 1789

Valda Avhandlingar	No. 42, pp. 3–19, 1963
Valda Avhandlingar Title	Nyttan av rörelse (Motus polychrestus)

Lidén Number	132
Short Title	Hort. cul.
Linnaeus Ed.	Vol. 7, no. 126, pp. 18–41, 1769
Wetstenius Linnaeus Ed.	Vol. 7, no. 126, pp. 18–41, 1769
Schreber Ed.	Vol. 7, no. 126, pp. 18–41, 1789

Lidén Number	133
Short Title	Spir. frum.
Linnaeus Ed.	Vol. 7, no. 139, pp. 264–281, 1769
Wetstenius Linnaeus Ed.	Vol. 7, no. 139, pp. 264–281, 1769
Schreber Ed.	Vol. 7, no. 139, pp. 264–281, 1789

Lidén Number	134
Short Title	Diaet. scal.
Linnaeus Ed.	Vol. 7, no. 129, pp. 74–83, 1769
Wetstenius Linnaeus Ed.	Vol. 7, no. 129, pp. 74–83, 1769
Schreber Ed.	Vol. 7, no. 129, pp. 74–83, 1789
Valda Avhandlingar	No. 16, pp. 3–18, 1954
Valda Avhandlingar Title	Levnadsordning under människans olika åldrar (Diaeta per scalam aetatis humanae)

Lidén Number	135
Short Title	Opobals.
Linnaeus Ed.	Vol. 7, no. 128, pp. 55–73, 1769
Wetstenius Linnaeus Ed.	Vol. 7, no. 128, pp. 55–73, 1769
Schreber Ed.	Vol. 7, no. 128, pp. 55–73, 1789

Lidén Number	136
Short Title	Hirudo
Linnaeus Ed.	Vol. 7, no. 127, pp. 42–54, 1769
Wetstenius Linnaeus Ed.	Vol. 7, no. 127, pp. 42–54, 1769
Schreber Ed.	Vol. 7, no. 127, pp. 42–54, 1789

Lidén Number	137
Short Title	Fund. ornith.
Linnaeus Ed.	Vol. 7, no. 132, pp. 109–128, tab. I, 1769
Wetstenius Linnaeus Ed.	Vol. 7, no. 132, pp. 109–128, tab. I, 1769
Schreber Ed.	Vol. 7, no. 132, pp. 109–128, tab. I, 1789

Lidén Number	138
Short Title	Ferv. gel.
Linnaeus Ed.	Vol. 7, no. 136, pp. 214–235, 1769
Wetstenius Linnaeus Ed.	Vol. 7, no. 136, pp. 214–235, 1769
Schreber Ed.	Vol. 7, no. 136, pp. 214–235, 1789
Valda Avhandlingar	No. 55, pp. 3–24, 1968
Valda Avhandlingar Title	Om bruket av varm och kall mat och dryck (Circa fervidorum et gelidorum usum)

Lidén Number	139
Short Title	Morb. artif.
Linnaeus Ed.	Vol. 7, no. 130, pp. 84–93, 1769
Wetstenius Linnaeus Ed.	Vol. 7, no. 130, pp. 84–93, 1769
Schreber Ed.	Vol. 7, no. 130, pp. 84–93, 1789

Valda Avhandlingar	No. 20, pp. 3–18, 1955
Valda Avhandlingar Title	Hantverkarnas sjukdomar (Morbi artificum)

Lidén Number	140
Short Title	Lepra
Linnaeus Ed.	Vol. 7, no. 131, pp. 94–108, 1769
Wetstenius Linnaeus Ed.	Vol. 7, no. 131, pp. 94–108, 1769
Schreber Ed.	Vol. 7, no. 131, pp. 94–108, 1789
Valda Avhandlingar	No. 26, pp. 3–19, 1957
Valda Avhandlingar Title	Spetälska (Lepra)

Lidén Number	141
Short Title	Pot. choc.
Linnaeus Ed.	Vol. 7, no. 138, pp. 254–263, 1769
Wetstenius Linnaeus Ed.	Vol. 7, no. 138, pp. 254–263, 1769
Schreber Ed.	Vol. 7, no. 138, pp. 254–263, 1789
Valda Avhandlingar	No. 34, pp. 3–15, 1959
Valda Avhandlingar Title	Om chokladdrycken (De potu chocolatae)

Lidén Number	142
Short Title	Pot. theae
Linnaeus Ed.	Vol. 7, no. 137, pp. 236–253, tab. IV, 1769
Wetstenius Linnaeus Ed.	Vol. 7, no. 137, pp. 236–253, tab. IV, 1769
Schreber Ed.	Vol. 7, no. 137, pp. 236–253, tab. IV, 1789

Lidén Number	143
Short Title	Purg. indig.
Linnaeus Ed.	Vol. 7, no. 141, pp. 293–310, 1769
Wetstenius Linnaeus Ed.	Vol. 7, no. 141, pp. 293–310, 1769
Schreber Ed.	Vol. 7, no. 141, pp. 293–310, 1789

Lidén Number	144
Short Title	Hist. nat. Rossia
Linnaeus Ed.	Vol. 7, no. 148, pp. 438–465, tab. VII, 1769
Wetstenius Linnaeus Ed.	Vol. 7, no. 148, pp. 438–465, tab. VII, 1769
Schreber Ed.	Vol. 7, no. 148, pp. 438–465, tab. VII, 1789

Lidén Number	145
Short Title	Usum hist. nat.
Linnaeus Ed.	Vol. 7, no. 147, pp. 409–437, tab. VI, 1769
Wetstenius Linnaeus Ed.	Vol. 7, no. 147, pp. 409–437, tab. VI, 1769
Schreber Ed.	Vol. 7, no. 147, pp. 409–437, tab. VI, 1789

Lidén Number	146
Short Title	Siren lacert.
Linnaeus Ed.	Vol. 7, no. 142, pp. 311–325, tab. V, 1769
Wetstenius Linnaeus Ed.	Vol. 7, no. 142, pp. 311–325, tab. V, 1769
Schreber Ed.	Vol. 7, no. 142, pp. 311–325, tab. V, 1789

Lidén Number	147
Short Title	Eff. cura vit.
Linnaeus Ed.	Vol. 7, no. 144, pp. 345–369, 1769
Wetstenius Linnaeus Ed.	Vol. 7, no. 144, pp. 345–369, 1769
Schreber Ed.	Vol. 7, no. 144, pp. 345–369, 1789
Valda Avhandlingar	No. 53, pp. 3–27, 1967
Valda Avhandlingar Title	Om följderna av dietetiska fel och deras behandling (De effectu et cura vitiorum diaeteticorum generali)

Lidén Number	148
Short Title	Usum musc.
Linnaeus Ed.	Vol. 7, no. 145, pp. 370–384, 1769
Wetstenius Linnaeus Ed.	Vol. 7, no. 145, pp. 370–384, 1769
Schreber Ed.	Vol. 7, no. 145, pp. 370–384, 1789

Lidén Number	149
Short Title	Mund. invis.
Linnaeus Ed.	Vol. 7, no. 146, pp. 385–408 (p. 406 misnumbered 496), 1769
Wetstenius Linnaeus Ed.	Vol. 7, no. 146, pp. 385–408 (p. 406 misnumbered 496), 1769
Schreber Ed.	Vol. 7, no. 146, pp. 385–408, 1789

Lidén Number	150
Short Title	Haemopt.
Schreber Ed.	vol. 9, no. 178, pp. 118–130, 1785

Lidén Number	151
Short Title	Ven. resorb.
Schreber Ed.	vol. 9, no. 179, pp. 131–142, 1785
Valda Avhandlingar	No. 33, pp. 3–13, 1959
Valda Avhandlingar Title	Om lymfkärlen (De venis resorbentibus)

Lidén Number	152
Short Title	Fund. agrost.
Linnaeus Ed.	Vol. 7, no. 134, pp. 160–196, tabs. II, III, 1769
Wetstenius Linnaeus Ed.	Vol. 7, no. 134, pp. 160–196, tabs. II, III, 1769
Schreber Ed.	Vol. 7, no. 134, pp. 160–196, tabs. II, III, 1789

Lidén Number	153
Short Title	Menthae
Linnaeus Ed.	Vol. 7, no. 140, pp. 282–292, 1769
Wetstenius Linnaeus Ed.	Vol. 7, no. 140, pp. 282–292, 1769
Schreber Ed.	Vol. 7, no. 140, pp. 282–292, 1789
Valda Avhandlingar	No. 59, pp. 3–13, 1971
Valda Avhandlingar Title	Om bruket av Mentha (De Menthae usu)

Lidén Number	154
Short Title	Fund. entom.
Linnaeus Ed.	Vol. 7, no. 133, pp. 129–159, 1769
Wetstenius Linnaeus Ed.	Vol. 7, no. 133, pp. 129–159, 1769
Schreber Ed.	Vol. 7, no. 133, pp. 129–159, 1789

Lidén Number	155
Short Title	Metam. hum.
Linnaeus Ed.	Vol. 7, no. 143, pp. 326–344, 1 table, 1769
Wetstenius Linnaeus Ed.	Vol. 7, no. 143, pp. 326–344, 1 table, 1769
Schreber Ed.	Vol. 7, no. 143, pp. 326–344, 1 table, 1789
Valda Avhandlingar	No. 22, pp. [ii], 3–22, 1956
Valda Avhandlingar Title	Människans förvandling (Metamorphosis humana)

Lidén Number	156
Short Title	Var. cib.
Linnaeus Ed.	Vol. 7, no. 135, pp. 197–213, 1769
Wetstenius Linnaeus Ed.	Vol. 7, no. 135, pp. 197–213, 1769
Schreber Ed.	Vol. 7, no. 135, pp. 197–213, 1789
Valda Avhandlingar	No. 50, pp. 3–20, 1966
Valda Avhandlingar Title	Om omväxling i födan (De varietate ciborum)

Lidén Number	157
Short Title	Rar. Norv.
Linnaeus Ed.	Vol. 7, no. 149, pp. 466–496 (p. 496 misnumbered 486), text fig., 1769
Wetstenius Linnaeus Ed.	Vol. 7, no. 149, pp. 466–496 (p. 496 misnumbered 486), text fig., 1769
Schreber Ed.	Vol. 7, no. 149, pp. 466–496, text fig., 1789

Lidén Number	158
Short Title	Colon. pl.
Schreber Ed.	vol. 8, no. 151, pp. 1–12, 1785

Lidén Number	159
Short Title	Medicus
Schreber Ed.	vol. 8, no. 152, pp. 13–25, 1785

Lidén Number	160
Short Title	Morb. naut.
Schreber Ed.	vol. 8, no. 153, pp. 26–28, 1785

Lidén Number	161
Short Title	Iter Chin.
Linnaeus Ed.	Vol. 7, no. 150, pp. 497–506, 1769
Wetstenius Linnaeus Ed.	Vol. 7, no. 150, pp. 497–506, 1769
Schreber Ed.	Vol. 7, no. 150, pp. 497–506, 1789

Lidén Number	162
Short Title	Fl. Åker.
Schreber Ed.	vol. 8, no. 154, pp. 29–45 (p. 32 misnumbered 23), 1785
Valda Avhandlingar	No. 9, pp. 5–18, 1950
Valda Avhandlingar Title	Två sörmlandsflorer (Flora åkeröensis) (Pandora et flora rybyensis)

Lidén Number	163
Short Title	Erica
Schreber Ed.	vol. 8, no. 155, pp. 46–62 (pp. 55–56 on double-size folded leaf), tab. I, 1785

Lidén Number	164
Short Title	Dulcamara
Schreber Ed.	vol. 8, no. 156, pp. 63–74, 1785

Lidén Number	165
Short Title	Pand. fl. Ryb.
Schreber Ed.	vol. 8, no. 157, pp. 75–106, 1785
Valda Avhandlingar	No. 9, pp. 21–40, 1950
Valda Avhandlingar Title	Två sörmlandsflorer (Flora Åkeröensis) (Pandora et Flora Rybyensis)

Lidén Number	166
Short Title	Fund. test.
Schreber Ed.	vol. 8, no. 158, pp. 107–150, tabs. II, III, 1785

Lidén Number	167
Short Title	Febr. interm.
Schreber Ed.	vol. 9, no. 180, pp. 143–194 (p. 170 misnumbered 154), 1785

Lidén Number	168
Short Title	Resp. diaet.
Schreber Ed.	vol. 8, no. 159, pp. 151–168, 1785

Valda Avhandlingar	No. 46, pp. 3–19, 1965
Valda Avhandlingar Title	Andningens dietetik (Respiratio diaetetica)

Lidén Number	169
Short Title	Haemor. pleth.
Schreber Ed.	vol. 9, no. 181, pp. 195–222, 1785

Lidén Number	170
Short Title	Fraga
Schreber Ed.	vol. 8, no. 160, pp. 169–181, 1785
Valda Avhandlingar	No. 37, pp. 3–15, 1961
Valda Avhandlingar Title	Om smultron (Fraga vesca)

Lidén Number	171
Short Title	Obs. mat. med.
Schreber Ed.	vol. 8, no. 161, pp. 182–192, 1785
Valda Avhandlingar	No. 6, pp. 3–19, 1949
Valda Avhandlingar Title	Observationer i materia medica (Observationes in materiam medicam)

Lidén Number	172
Short Title	Sutur. vuln.
Schreber Ed.	vol. 9, no. 182, pp. 223–244, 1785

Lidén Number	173
Short Title	Cimicifuga
Schreber Ed.	vol. 8, no. 162, pp. 193–204, tab. IV, 1785

Lidén Number	174
Short Title	Esca avium
Schreber Ed.	vol. 8, no. 163, pp. 205–220, 1785

Lidén Number	175
Short Title	Marum
Schreber Ed.	vol. 8, no. 164, pp. 221–237, 1785

Lidén Number	176
Short Title	Viola ipecac.
Schreber Ed.	vol. 8, no. 165, pp. 238–248, 1785

Lidén Number	177
Short Title	Pl. Surin.
Schreber Ed.	vol. 8, no. 166, pp. 249–267, tab. V, 1785

Lidén Number	178
Short Title	Ledum
Schreber Ed.	vol. 8, no. 167, pp. 268–288, 1785

Lidén Number	179
Short Title	Opium
Schreber Ed.	vol. 8, no. 168, pp. 289–302, 1785

Lidén Number	180
Short Title	Scorb.
Schreber Ed.	vol. 9, no. 186, pp. 291–314, 1785

Lidén Number	181
Short Title	Med. purg.
Schreber Ed.	vol. 9, no. 183, pp. 245–267 (p. 255 misnumbered 552), 1785

Lidén Number	182
Short Title	Persp. insen.
Schreber Ed.	vol. 9, no. 184, pp. 268–277, 1785

Lidén Number	183
Short Title	Canones med.
Schreber Ed.	vol. 9, no. 185, pp. 278–290, 1785

Lidén Number	184
Short Title	Bigas insect.
Schreber Ed.	vol. 8, no. 169, pp. 303–309, tab. VI, 1785

Lidén Number	185
Short Title	Aphyteia
Schreber Ed.	vol. 8, no. 170, pp. 310–317, tab. VII, 1785

Lidén Number	186
Short Title	Hypericum
Schreber Ed.	vol. 8, no. 171, pp. 318–332, tab. VIII, 1785

Plate from Sponsalia plantarum *... (1746), a dissertation defended by J. G. Wahlbom with Linnaeus as praeses.*

Sources

Drake, G. Linnés disputationer. En översikt utgiven med anslag från längmanska kulturfonden.... Nässjö, Nässjö-Tryckeriet, 1939.

Hulth, J. M. Bibliographia Linnaeana: Matériaux pour servir a une bibliographie Linnéenne. Partie I — Livraison I. Uppsala, Almqvist & Wiksell, 1907.

Krok, T. O. B. N. Bibliotheca botanica suecana ab antiquissimis temporibus ad finem anni MCMXVIII.... Uppsala och Stockholm, Almqvist & Wiksell, 1925.

Lindell, E. Bibliotheca Linnaeana — Works by or relating to Carolus Linnaeus, his predecessors, contemporaries and pupils with sequels — from the library of Emil Lindell.... Växjö, Smålandspostens, 1932.

Pritzel, G. A. Thesaurus literaturae botanicae omnium gentium, inde a rerum botanicarum initiis ad nostra usque tempora, quindecim millia operum recensens. Lipsiae, F. A. Brockhaus, 1851.

Pritzel, G. A. Thesaurus literaturae botanicae omnium gentium, inde a rerum botanicarum initiis ad nostra usque tempora, quindecim millia operum recensens. Editionem novam reformatam. Lipsiae, F. A. Brockhaus, 1872.

Rudolph, G. A. and E. Williams. Linnaeana. Manhattan, Kansas, Kansas State University Library, 1970. (Kansas State University Library bibliography series, no. 7.)

[Soulsby, B. H.] A catalogue of the works of Linnaeus (and publications more immediately relating thereto) preserved in the libraries of the British Museum (Bloomsbury) and the British Museum (Natural History) (South Kensington). Ed. 2. London, printed by order of the Trustees of the British Museum, 1933.

Tullberg, T. Linnéporträtt vid Uppsala Universitets minnesfest på tvåhundraårsdagen af Carl von Linnés födelse. Stockholm, Aktiebolaget Ljus, 1907.

Figure from p. 19 of Disputatio medica, de Morsura serpentum ... *(1762), a dissertation defended by J. G. Acrell with Linnaeus as praeses.*